DISCARDED

DATE DUE 12/9

GAYLORD			PRINTED IN U.S.A.

The New York Times
PRACTICAL GUIDE
TO PRACTICALLY
EVERYTHING

The Essential Companion for Everyday Life

AMY D. BERNSTEIN & PETER W. BERNSTEIN, EDITORS

ANNA G. ISGRO, MANAGING EDITOR

JANICE OLSON, DESIGN DIRECTOR

St. Martin's Press

New York

THE NEW YORK TIMES PRACTICAL GUIDE TO PRACTICALLY EVERYTHING: SECOND EDITION
Copyright © 2009, 2006 by The New York Times and Amberstone Publishing.
All rights reserved. Printed in the United States of America. For information, address
St. Martin's Press, 175 Fifth Avenue, New York, N.Y. 10010.
www.stmartins.com

Library of Congress Cataloging-in-Publication Data

The New York Times practical guide to practically everything : the essential companion
for everyday life / edited by Amy D. Bernstein and Peter W. Bernstein. – 2nd ed.
     p. cm.
   Includes index.
   ISBN 978-0-312-55169-8
   1. Life skills—Handbooks, manuals, etc.
   2. Life skills—United States—Handbooks, manuals, etc.
  I. Bernstein, Amy D. II. Bernstein, Peter W. III. New York Times.
  HQ2037.N48 2009
  646.700973—dc22

                                2009032199

First Edition: October 2006
Second Edition: December 2009

10 9 8 7 6 5 4 3 2 1

CONTENTS

Having Children

First Aid & Survival

CHAPTER 2:

FOOD & DRINK
Diet & Nutrition

CHAPTER 3:

MONEY
Personal Finance

Investing

Real Estate

Insurance & Taxes

CHAPTER 4:

SPENDING & SAVING
Consumer Advice

CHAPTER 6:

CAREERS
Getting Hired

CHAPTER 7:

HOUSE & GARDEN

Around the House

In the Garden

Chapter 8:

TRAVEL
Getting There

Great Destinations

Natural Treasures

Adventures

CHAPTER 9:

SPORTS & GAMES
A Fan's Guide

An Athlete's Guide

Games & Puzzles

CHAPTER 10:

ARTS & ENTERTAINMENT
Movies & TV

Music

Museums & Books

CHAPTER 11:

SCIENCE & SYMBOLS

Weather & Geology

Stars & Tides

Figures & Formulas

CHAPTER 12:

MORES & MANNERS
Legal Guide

Calendars & Customs

Manners & Miscellany

Index

INTRODUCTION

These days, when a Google search takes a nanosecond and gigabytes of data are a click away, who needs a practical guide to everyday life? The answer is practically everyone. Despite the abundance of information at every turn, sorting the salient from the silly, the sensible from the useless and the reliable from the reckless is still a time-consuming and often dissatisfying chore.

That's why we created *The New York Times Practical Guide to Practically Everything*. It's designed to be an all-in-one, do-it-yourself resource, packed with all the information necessary to help you live a rich and well-considered life. Think of it as life's big instruction book, a user's manual for everyday living.

Some books tell you a lot—often too much—about just one thing, like how to play the harmonica, strengthen your abs or plant perfect peas. But for most of us there aren't enough hours in the day to read at length about all the things that interest us. The goal of this book is to offer concise, authoritative—and sometimes entertaining—tips and strategies to serve as reassuring signposts as you navigate the twists and turns of modern life.

How did we go about it? First of all, we chose key areas—Health, Food & Drink, Money, Spending & Saving, Education, Careers, House & Garden, Travel, Sports & Games, Arts & Entertainment, Science & Symbols and Mores & Manners. Then we zeroed in on important topics, researching and selecting the most useful advice and strategies. We wanted readers to be able to reach for this book with complete confidence, knowing that they will find high-quality information that will stand the test of time.

To meet those high standards, we relied on *New York Times* writers, reporters and critics who are respected voices in their own fields, from money to health, gardening to home tech, art to music.

They, in turn, sought out the opinions and expertise of doctors, lawyers, academicians, scientists, cooks and musicians, to name a few. The result is hundreds of expert opinions from *Times* writers and the people they interviewed.

One of the most interesting lessons we learned as editors was that as fast as the world seems to be moving, some of the chief delights of living well remain enduring and unchanged—from getting the best rate on a mortgage to planting a scented garden, dancing the fox trot, stocking a wine cellar or finding a puppy. This is as true in the world of manners as it is in dealing with your money and your health. Handwritten thank-you notes may be losing out to e-mail, but the gesture still rewards both writer and recipient. Stocks go up and down every day and fortunes are made and lost, but the most successful long-term investors, like Warren Buffett, still swear by value investing. Weight-loss fads come and go, but a balanced diet and regular exercise still are the linchpins for enduring health.

There is a world of difference between doing something and doing it well, of course, which is the moral to be drawn from all that you will read here. In that respect, we are emulating Benjamin Franklin—a practical philosopher if ever there was one—who claimed, "He that lives well is learned enough."

—Amy and Peter Bernstein

The New York Times

PRACTICAL GUIDE TO PRACTICALLY EVERYTHING

Editors: Amy D. Bernstein and Peter W. Bernstein
Managing Editor: Anna G. Isgro
Design Director: Janice Olson
Copy Editor: Robin Bellinger
Illustrations: Steve Noble, Steve McCracken
Indexing: Doric Wilson

FOR THE NEW YORK TIMES
Administration: Cristian L. Edwards, *President, News Services;*
Nancy Lee, *Editor and Vice President of Licensing, the* New York Times *Syndicate;*
Alex Ward, *Editorial Director*

ACKNOWLEDGMENTS

This book could not have been written without the relentless collective effort of the reporters, writers, critics and editors of the New York Times, *who every day search out practical, useful and reliable information. More than 300 of them contributed pieces to this edition. In addition, numerous outside experts and authorities added their special expertise and knowledge. Some were kind enough to be interviewed; others generously contributed pieces. Our thanks to them all.*

Thanks to Anna Isgro, a creative and meticulous editor, and Janice Olson, a talented designer and production wizard, both of whom made invaluable contributions and were indispensable. Robin Bellinger gamely and expertly took on copy-checking, fact-checking and other editorial chores. Paul Berger and Alex Ulam updated and added fresh information to several chapters. Sam Bernstein helped verify information about golf. Once again, Doric Wilson did a yeoman's job creating a comprehensive index for the book.

Alex Ward at the New York Times *smoothed our way at every turn. Phyllis Collazo tracked down many graphics and illustrations. Lisa Senz at St. Martin's Press once again put all the pieces together to make this book possible, and Daniela Rapp, also at St. Martin's Press and our editor for this edition, guided us through the publishing process.*

And finally, a very special thanks to Christopher Ma, co-creator of the original Practical Guides and trusted friend and adviser.

HEALTH & FITNESS

CHAPTER **1. HEALTH & FITNESS**

Fitness

Getting Fit and Staying Trim

It's a combination of diet and exercise

For many Americans, the battle of the bulge is a way of life, and for some it begins as early as childhood. According to the U.S.D.A., the percentage of children who are overweight has doubled since 1980, and the percentage of adolescents who are overweight has nearly tripled. About nine million young Americans, or more than 15 percent of all children, are overweight. This is particularly troubling, since many of the behaviors that lead to adult obesity are established during childhood.

And even those who manage to stay trim during their youth and into adulthood have difficulty staying trim as they age. A recent study published in the *Annals of Internal Medicine* says that 9 out of 10 men and 7 out of 10 women, and half of those who had reached adulthood without a weight problem, ultimately became overweight. A third of those women and quarter of the men became obese.

Obesity is reaching epidemic proportions in the United States, bringing with it a host of related diseases. Diagnosed cases of Type-2 diabetes, a major consequence of obesity, have risen dramatically. It is therefore never too early to start paying attention to fitness, which, any expert will tell you, must be a combination of diet and daily exercise, because neither is effective without the other. And it is not a short-lived endeavor. Fitness is for life, a long-term commitment to healthy eating, which necessitates the avoidance of overly protein-rich, fat-laden foods and carving out enough time for daily, vigorous activity.

The reason most people fail to lose weight permanently when they turn to weight-loss programs, liquid diets, or diet pills is that they are seeking rapid, short-term results and abandon the regime once they have achieved their goal. In some cases, it is in fact inadvisable to stay on a particular diet or diet pill for more than a short time. In many cases, the diets and pills do not help shed more than a limited number of pounds, can cost quite a lot and cannot guarantee that you will be able to keep the weight off. The result is that Americans spend billions on weight-loss programs and products, and they are fatter than ever.

Here, then, are some ideas on how to get fit without spending a lot of money. This advice comes from fitness and diet experts, writers at the *New York Times* and U.S. government sources, such as the U.S.D.A. and the National Institutes of Health.

Forget quick fixes. Gimmicks don't work. Losing weight and keeping it off requires changing your lifestyle and your mindset—not an easy undertaking. Before throwing away money on programs that don't match your lifestyle, do some research. There are many inexpensive ways to gather information: sign up for free educational classes, nutritional counseling or introductory weight-loss programs given by a local hospital or H.M.O.; buy a good nutrition or exercise book or borrow one from the library.

Customize your diet plan. Many dieters pay top dollar for commercial weight-loss programs and either don't complete the program or soon regain the weight they lost. The key to permanent weight loss is finding a program that fits your food preferences and lifestyle, says Anne Fletcher, a registered dietitian and diet book author. "Instead of saying I blew it with Weight Watchers or Jenny Craig, go back and look at what worked in those programs,"

ⓘ INSIDE INFO

Weight and Height Guidelines

○ The latest guidelines, which apply to both men and women regardless of age, prescribe acceptable ranges rather than specific weights, because people of the same height may have different amounts of muscle and bone.

○ The further you are above the healthy weight range for your height, the higher are your risks of developing weight-related health problems.

GENERAL HEIGHT AND WEIGHT CHART FOR MEN AND WOMEN

HEIGHT	WEIGHT (lbz.) Ages 19 to 34	WEIGHT (lbs.) Ages 35 and up
5'0	97-128	108-138
5'1"	101-132	111-143
5'2"	104-137	115-148
5'3"	107-141	119-152
5'4"	111-146	122-157
5'5"	114-150	126-162
5'6"	118-155	130-167
5'7"	121-160	134-172
5'8"	125-164	138-178
5'9"	129-169	142-183
5'10"	132-174	146-188
5'11"	136-179	151-194
6'0	140-184	155-199
6'1"	144-189	159-205
6'2"	148-195	164-210
6'3"	152-200	168-216
6'4"	156-205	173-222
6'5"	160-211	177-228

SOURCES: U.S.D.A.; U.S. Department of Health and Human Services

---

suggests Fletcher. If eating four grapefruits or bowls of cabbage soup a day didn't work, but packing your lunch every day did, then incorporate that lesson into your weight-reduction plan.

Get to work in the kitchen. Many weight-loss programs involve using prepackaged foods, prepared by a diet center or purchased at the supermarket. Prepared foods can help in teaching how to control portions, but they cost two to three times as much as the raw ingredients required to make the meal from scratch. "Some of the foods labeled diet are automatically marked up, but if you buy regular products and eat less of them, you save money," advises Dr. Denise Bruner, a weight-loss specialist in Arlington, Va. "If you spend a few extra minutes in the kitchen putting a piece of chicken in the microwave and steaming vegetables, for example, you'd have a less expensive and more nutritious meal," she says.

Find cost-effective workouts. Exercise is the other major component of weight loss. But high-priced spa memberships and fancy training equipment aren't needed to reap the benefits of exercise. Invest in a good pair of walking shoes. For results, it's the best and cheapest thing you can do. Other inexpensive and effective exercise tools include elastic bands, an exercise ball, and aerobic and yoga videotapes. More sophisticated home exercise equipment can be worth the cost—if it's not lying idle.

Make a schedule of exercise times and develop a realistic goal of how many hours you can devote each week, and push yourself to meet those goals. Team up with a compatible family member or friend who shares your motivation, and work out together, or at least keep track of each other's hours. If you find exercise boring, do it in front of a TV or with music. If you have children, get them to participate as well.

If you need the motivation of a health club, shop for one that gives you punch for your dollar. Staff

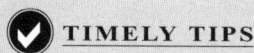 **TIMELY TIPS**

Helping You Stick to Your Diet

Each year millions of us resolve to lose weight or at least eat more healthfully. Several Web sites offer tips and tools for getting there.

✔ **A better food pyramid:** Harvard nutritionists advise starting with exercise and then adding more plant-based foods and less red meat, refined grains and sugary drinks to your diet.
www.hsph.harvard.edu/nutritionsource/ what-should-you-eat/pyramid/

✔ **Calorie-counting sites:** Counts for various foods are found at *CalorieKing.com* and *TheCalorieCounter.com*. Find calories burned in various activities at *CaloriesPerHour.com* and *NutriStrategy.com*.

✔ **Cooking Light:** A great site for finding healthy and delicious foods that won't make you feel like you're on a diet. *cookinglight.com*

✔ **Dr. Gourmet:** Free diet software by New Orleans physician Timothy S. Harlan ("Dr. Gourmet") helps you plan healthy meals. You also get food and exercise diaries and a place to analyze your own recipes. *drgourmet.com*

✔ **3FatChicks.com:** Begun as a personal source of diet support for sisters Suzanne, Jennifer and Amy, the site has 70,000 members. Aside from resources and tools, it features access to a support group.

✔ **Food Blog Search:** It's not a diet site, but if you've resolved to cook at home more, this is a great resource for finding new recipes. This custom-built search engine uses Google technology to search for recipes in more than 2,600 food blogs. *foodblogsearch.com*

✔ **Live Strong:** Biker Lance Armstrong's site on fitness, diet, nutrition and health. Track daily calories, measure your body mass index, share your story, and more. *livestrong.com*

✔ **National Body Challenge:** Free fitness and weight loss program by Discovery Health. Register online, set your goals and create an eating and exercise plan. You also get weight and fitness trackers and a 30-day free health club membership.
health.discovery.com/ national-body-challenge/about.html

✔ **Weight Watchers:** Often offers a one-week free trial to its online plan. Normal price: around $65 for three months. Much of what Weight Watchers claims is backed by science; 80 percent of dieters retain at least 5 percent of their weight loss one year later. *weightwatchers.com*
—Tara Parker-Pope

credentials are important. Before joining a club, have a staff member perform a fitness evaluation and draw up an exercise plan for you. Consistent use of the club will help justify the cost. Engaging a personal trainer can be expensive but can also make workouts more effective. To defray the cost, meet with the trainer less frequently or train with a partner.

Be focused. Losing weight on your own is, of course, the best money saver. Half of the dieters in Fletcher's books lose weight by using no-cost strategies, such as accepting weight loss as a permanent lifestyle change and devising ways to nip small weight gains in the bud.

But the most important lesson they learned is that money can't buy motivation and commitment—the real secret to weight loss.

To give your motivation a boost, take advantage of the free advice available on the Web. Or, test out an online dieting site, many of which offer free trial periods. For some ideas, see the list above.

Are You Overweight? Check Your Body Mass Index

Your body mass index (BMI) is an important calculation for judging fitness, though it is not a 100 percent accurate indicator, since muscle weighs more than fat. Very muscled bodies will have a higher body mass index, and older people with little muscle will usually have less. The Centers for Disease Control and Prevention suggest that you use it as just one of many factors in judging whether you are in good shape. The formula:

$$\text{BMI} = \frac{(\textit{Weight in pounds})}{(\textit{Height in inches}) \times (\textit{Height in inches})} \times 703$$

BODY MASS INDEX (BMI) TABLE

Use this table to estimate your BMI. Find height in inches in the first column. Then move across to the right and choose the weight in pounds nearest to yours. Your BMI can be found at the bottom of that column.

HEIGHT	WEIGHT (in pounds)																	
4'10" (58")	91	96	100	105	110	115	119	124	129	134	138	143	148	153	158	162	167
4'11" (59")	94	99	104	109	114	119	124	128	133	138	143	148	153	158	163	168	173
5'0" (60")	97	102	107	112	118	123	128	133	138	143	148	153	158	163	168	174	179
5'1" (61")	100	106	111	116	122	127	132	137	143	148	153	158	164	169	174	180	185
5'2" (62")	104	109	115	120	126	131	136	142	147	153	158	164	169	175	180	186	191
5'3" (63")	107	113	118	124	130	135	141	146	152	158	163	169	175	180	186	191	197
5'4" (64")	110	116	122	128	134	140	145	151	157	163	169	174	180	186	192	197	204
5'5" (65")	114	120	126	132	138	144	150	156	162	168	174	180	186	192	198	204	210
5'6" (66")	118	124	130	136	142	148	155	161	167	173	179	186	192	198	204	210	216
5'7" (67")	121	127	134	140	146	153	159	166	172	178	185	191	198	204	211	217	223
5'8" (68")	125	131	138	144	151	158	164	171	177	184	190	197	203	210	216	223	230
5'9" (69")	128	135	142	149	155	162	169	176	182	189	196	203	209	216	223	230	236
5'10" (70")	132	139	146	153	160	167	174	181	188	195	202	209	216	222	229	236	243
5'11" (71")	136	143	150	157	165	172	179	186	193	200	208	215	222	229	236	243	250
6'0 (72")	140	147	154	162	169	177	184	191	199	206	213	221	228	235	242	250	258
6'1" (73")	144	151	159	166	174	182	189	197	204	212	219	227	235	242	250	257	265
6'2" (74")	148	155	163	171	179	186	194	202	210	218	225	233	241	249	256	264	272
6'3" (75")	152	160	168	176	184	192	200	208	216	224	232	240	248	256	264	272	279
BMI	19	20	21	22	23	24	25	26	27	28	29	30	31	32	33	34	35

RISK OF ASSOCIATED DISEASE ACCORDING TO BMI AND WAIST SIZE

BMI values between 18.5 and 24.9 are considered "normal" or "healthy" weight. BMIs above 25 are unhealthy and have been shown to increase the risk of certain chronic diseases. BMIs under 18.5 are considered "underweight."

BMI		Waist less than or equal to 40 in. (men) or 35 in. (women)	Waist greater than 40 in. (men) or 35 in. (women)
18.5 or less	UNDERWEIGHT	—	N/A
18.5–24.9	NORMAL	–	N/A
25.0–29.9	OVERWEIGHT	Increased	High
30.0–34.9	OBESE	High	Very High
35.0–39.9	OBESE	Very High	Very High
40 or greater	EXTREMELY OBESE	Extremely High	Extremely High

SOURCE: National Institutes of Health

Where Do You Carry the Weight?

It's more dangerous around the belly than the hips

How your weight is distributed may be even more important than how much weight you have in the first place, at least when it comes to determining risks to your health. If you are carrying too much weight around your waist, your health is at far greater risk than if you are carrying extra weight around your hips, buttocks and thighs. All of that excessive fat around the belly has been found by researchers to be associated with an increased risk of breast and uterine cancer, heart disease and diabetes, as well as a host of other ailments.

To assess whether your weight distribution puts you at higher risk for disease, ask yourself whether your body more closely resembles the shape of an apple or of a pear. "Apples" are often bigger at the waist than in the hips—traits found more often in men than in women. "Pears," on the other hand, carry their weight low. Their waists are smaller than their hips, and they are usually women.

Researchers at the University of Glasgow have suggested an easy way to gauge your health risks from carrying too much weight in the wrong places. Their study found significantly higher health risks among women whose waists measure more than 34.5 inches, and for men whose waists exceed 40 inches. Their advice: to ward off health problems, keep your waist size to 31.5 inches if you are a woman, and to 37 inches for a man.

Another study has found that waist-to-hip ratio is a better predictor of heart attack than body mass index (BMI), the most common way of determining who is obese. A waist-to-hip ratio (waist measurement divided by hip measurement) below 0.85 in women or 0.9 in men is average. Anything above that is a risk for heart disease.

A body mass index greater than 28.2 in women

TIMELY TIPS

A No-Frills, Low-Cost Home Gym

A mat, weights, a resistance band and a stability ball may be all you need to work out at home

Not a fan of the crowded, expensive local gym? Who needs it, when you can make your own version of a home gym with a few modular, easily stashable pieces of equipment. More than nine million Americans have decided, for reasons of convenience, flexibility, privacy or cost, to exercise at home. With just a few simple, inexpensive pieces—a set of weights, a mat, a stability ball and a resistance band—anybody can get toned as well at home as at the gym. Here are some low-tech ways of strength-training at home.

✔ **Use an exercise band to work shoulders**, as follows: Step on the center of a band with one or both feet. Then, with your palms facing forward and elbows bent, grasp the ends of the band and extend your arms above your head. Different bands provide more or less resistance, just as a machine would.

✔ **Create circuits within your house.** Though some trainers recommend investing in an aerobic workout tape or a treadmill, stationary bike or elliptical machine for cardiovascular exercise, ingenuity can often take the place of technology; doing squats and marching in place and then going up and down the stairs, for example. Running up a flight of stairs is the low-tech version of the treadmill.

✔ **Use a stability ball to work abdominals.** Pull it between your legs during sit-ups, and it works as a resistance device. An old tie can substitute for a yoga strap. Chairs can stand in for weight benches. Use them for tricep dips, seated bicep curls or step-ups.

—Melena Ryzik

WORKOUT BENEFITS AT A GLANCE

From puttering around to Olympic skiing, the estimated calories burned during 30 minutes of activity depends on body weight and intensity of effort.

ACTIVITY		105	120	135	WEIGHT 150	165	180	195
DAILY ACTIVITY	Work, sedentary office	36	41	46	51	56	61	66
	Cooking	60	68	77	85	94	102	111
	Cleaning (heavy)	107	123	138	153	169	184	199
AEROBICS	Low-impact dance	119	136	153	170	188	205	222
	High-impact dance	167	191	215	239	263	286	310
	Water	95	109	122	136	150	163	177
ALPINE SKIING	Moderate (recreational)	119	136	153	170	188	205	222
	Vigorous (steep slope)	167	191	215	239	263	286	310
BASEBALL		119	136	153	170	188	205	222
BASKETBALL	Half-court	143	164	184	205	225	245	266
	Full-court (slow)	191	218	245	273	300	327	355
	Full-court (fast break)	315	360	405	450	495	540	585
BICYCLING	10–12 m.p.h.	143	164	184	205	225	245	266
	12–14 m.p.h.	191	218	245	273	300	327	355
	14–16 m.p.h.	239	273	307	341	375	409	443
BOWLING		72	82	92	102	113	123	133
CALISTHENICS	Light	107	123	138	153	169	184	199
	Heavy	191	218	245	273	300	327	355
CROSS-COUNTRY SKIING	2.5 m.p.h.	167	191	215	239	263	286	310
	4–5 m.p.h.	191	218	245	273	300	327	355
FISHING	Sitting	60	68	77	85	94	102	111
	Standing	84	95	107	119	131	143	155
FOOTBALL	Playing catch	60	68	77	85	94	102	111
	Touch or flag	191	218	245	273	300	327	355
GARDENING		95	109	123	136	150	164	177
GOLF	Pulling cart	119	136	153	170	188	205	222
	Carrying clubs	131	150	169	187	206	225	244
HIKING AND CLIMBING	Cross-country hiking	143	164	184	205	225	245	266
	Mountain trek	191	218	245	273	300	327	355
	Rock climb (vigorous)	253	289	325	361	398	434	470
HORSEBACK RIDING	Leisure riding	95	109	123	136	150	164	177
	Posting to trot	143	164	184	205	225	245	266
	Galloping	188	215	242	269	296	323	350

ACTIVITY		WEIGHT						
----------	--	105	120	135	150	165	180	195
ICE OR ROLLER SKATING/BLADING	Sustained moderate	167	191	215	239	263	286	310
	Vigorous (9+ m.p.h.)	215	245	276	307	338	368	399
JOGGING AND RUNNING	12 min./mile pace	191	218	245	273	300	327	355
	10 min./mile pace	239	273	307	341	375	409	443
	8 min./mile pace	298	341	384	426	469	511	554
	6 min./mile pace	382	436	491	545	600	655	709
JUMPING ROPE	Slow	191	218	245	273	300	327	355
	Moderate	239	273	307	341	375	409	443
	Fast	286	327	368	409	450	491	532
MARTIAL ARTS	Tae kwon do, karate, judo	239	273	307	341	375	409	443
	Tai chi	95	109	123	136	150	164	177
RACKET AND COURT GAMES	Racquetball (social)	167	191	215	239	263	286	310
	Racquetball (competitive)	239	273	307	341	375	409	443
	Handball and squash	286	327	368	409	450	491	532
ROWING AND CANOEING	Leisurely	84	95	107	119	131	143	155
	Vigorous sustained	167	191	215	239	263	286	310
	Very vigorous	286	327	368	409	450	491	532
SAILING	Leisurely	72	82	92	102	113	123	133
	Racing	109	136	153	170	188	205	222
SOCCER	Casual	167	191	215	239	263	286	310
	Competitive	239	273	307	341	375	409	443
SWIMMING	Laps freestyle (moderate)	191	218	245	273	300	327	355
	Laps freestyle (fast)	239	273	307	341	375	409	443
TENNIS	Social doubles	119	136	153	170	188	205	222
	Social singles	157	180	202	225	248	270	293
	Competitive doubles	172	196	221	245	270	295	319
	Competitive singles	227	259	291	324	356	389	421
VOLLEYBALL	Leisurely	74	85	96	106	117	128	138
	Competitve	167	191	215	239	263	286	310
WALKING	24 min./mile pace	72	82	92	102	113	123	133
	20 min./mile pace	84	95	107	119	131	143	155
	17min./mile pace	95	109	123	136	150	164	177
	15 min./mile pace	107	123	138	153	169	184	194
	12 min./mile pace	119	136	153	170	188	205	222
WEIGHT TRAINING	Free weights or machines	143	164	184	205	225	245	266
	Circuit weight training	191	218	245	273	300	327	355

SOURCE: Dr. David R. Stutz, *Forty-Plus Guide to Fitness: A Physicians's Exercise and Sports Program*, Consumer Reports.

or 28.6 in men did indicate an increased risk of heart attack, but the relationship disappeared after adjusting for age, sex, geographic region and tobacco use. Waist-to-hip ratio, on the other hand, showed a continuous relationship to heart attack risk even after adjusting for other risk factors. Those in the highest fifth were 2.52 times as likely to have a heart attack as those in the lowest fifth. Waist-to-hip ratio was a predictor of heart attack even in people regarded as very lean, those with body mass indexes under 20. Also, there was no evidence of a threshold where the risk would level off: the higher the waist-to-hip ratio, the higher the risk of a heart attack.

—Nicholas Bakalar

Exercises for the Time-Crunched
Workouts that fit your own schedule

Swim, bike, run, rake leaves. Climb monkey bars if you're a child, do water aerobics if you're older. Do whatever you like. Just keep moving.

That's the essence of the Surgeon General's recent guidelines for physical activity. The core recommendation: Americans should get about 150 minutes of moderately intense activity per week,

---

INSIDE INFO

The Top Fitness Activity in the U.S.

○ Walking is the top fitness activity in the U.S. with more than 89 million Americans taking part.

○ While many people walk in running shoes, experts say they shouldn't. Shoes designed for fitness walking have lower heels than running shoes, which are better for preventing shin splints.

— Dana Sullivan

---

with an emphasis on a variety of activities, including daily chores that can reap the health benefits of exercise. The recommendations advise 30 minutes of exercise five times a week. But there are ways for the time-crunched to stay fit without such an onerous schedule.

If you can't find five days a week to exercise, train three days instead but pick up the pace. Try a Wednesday-Saturday-Sunday routine. That way you are only interrupting one of your workdays, but you don't have any more than two days off at a time.

Training for 30 minutes three times a week may fall short of the 150-minute goal, but the guidelines allow for as little as 75 minutes of exercise a week, provided the activities are higher in intensity.

Interval training is one way to achieve a high intensity workout. After a 5-minute warm-up (on a treadmill or stationary bike, in a pool or even walking or jogging around a park), pick up the pace for five minutes, then go a little easier for three minutes. Repeat that pattern for the rest of the 30 minutes, making sure to end with an easy-effort, 3- to 4-minute cool-down. On an intensity scale of 1 to 10 (with 1 being the easiest effort, and 10 being all-out), your hardest intervals should be at 7 to 8, and recoveries at 5 to 6.

The same is true with strength training. Work the major muscles groups during at least two sessions a week. You can begin to meet that goal through a 10-minute workout using just three bodyweight exercises—abdominal crunches, back extensions and push-ups. For details on this program, visit www. myexerciseplan.com/assessment. Look for the Basic Bodyweight Strength Plan under "Keep It Simple."

If you want to increase the duration or intensity of your regimen, consider these combinations.

• Riding a stationary bicycle for 45 minutes two days a week; playing basketball for 60 minutes on two days; doing calisthenics on three days.

TIMELY TIPS

A Basic Formula for Fitness

The amount and range of exercise you fit in each week may be governed by a personal goal or simply by a lack of time. Here is a basic formula for physical health devised by the President's Council on Physical Fitness and Sports.

✔ **Daily: 10 to 12 minutes**

STRETCHING. Stretching exercises should be performed slowly, without any bouncing motion.

✔ **Twice weekly: 20-minute sessions**

MUSCULAR STRENGTH. Exercise all of the major muscle groups. Lifting weights is the most effective means of doing so.

✔ **Threetimes or more per week: 30-minute workouts**

MUSCULAR ENDURANCE. Exercise all of the major muscle groups. Calisthenics, push-ups, sit-ups, pull-ups and weight training are most effective.

20-minuteprograms

CARDI-RESPIRATORY ENDURANCE. Engage in continuous aerobic activity that puts your heart and lungs through the paces. Brisk walking, jogging, swimming, cycling, jumping rope, cross-country skiing and continuous-action games like racquetball and handball fit the bill.

✔ **Everyworkout: 5 to 10 minutes**

WARM UP. Exercises such as walking, slow jogging, knee lifts, arm circles or trunk rotations are effective.
COOL DOWN. Slow walking, or other low-level exercise, and stretching keep muscles loose.

• Running for 45 minutes three or four days a week; doing circuit weight training in the gym (without stopping from exercise to exercise and getting both an aerobic and strengthening workout) two or three days a week.

• Playing soccer for 90 minutes one day; walking briskly for 15 minutes, three days a week; lifting weights on two days.

As you increase your exercise time beyond 150 minutes, remember the 10 percent rule: to reduce the risk of injury, increase your training by no more than 10 percent a week.

—John Hanc

Exercises for Older Adults
The older you are, the more you need to keep fit

Regular participation in aerobics, strength training and balance and flexibility exercises can delay and may even prevent a life-limiting loss of physical abilities into one's 90s and beyond.

Even if you have a chronic health problem or physical limitation, there are safe ways to improve fitness and well-being. Any delay can increase the risk of injury and make it harder to recoup your losses.

The key is to start slowly and build gradually as ability and strength improve. Most important is simply to start—now—perhaps under the guidance of a fitness professional or by creating a program based on the guidelines outlined here.

Although medical clearance may not be necessary for everyone for the moderate level of activity suggested, those with a known or possible problem would be wise to consult a doctor. And a few sessions with a trainer can help assure that the exercises are being done correctly and not likely to cause injury.

Until recently, physical activity recommendations for all ages have emphasized aerobics, or cardiovascular conditioning, through moderate to vigorous activities like brisk walking, cycling, lap swimming or jogging for half an hour a day five or more days a week. For those unable to do 30 minutes at a time, the activities can be broken up into three 10-minute intervals a day. If you have long been sedentary, start with even shorter intervals.

For people who prefer indoor workouts, a treadmill, cross-trainer, step machine or exercise bike can provide excellent aerobic training for the heart, lungs and circulation. Those unable to do weight-bearing exercise might try swimming or water aerobics. Keep in mind that 30 minutes a day of aerobic activity five days a week is the minimum recommendation. More is better and can reduce the risk of chronic disease related to inactivity.

Contrary to what many active adults seem to believe, physical fitness does not end with aerobics. Strength training has long been advocated by the National Institute on Aging, and the American Heart Association has recognized the added value of muscle strength to reduce stress on joints, bones and soft tissues; enhance stability and reduce the risk of falls; and increase the ability to meet the demands of daily life, like rising from a chair, climbing stairs and opening jars.

Strength training can be done in a gym on a series of machines, each working a different set of major

muscle groups: hips, legs, chest, back, shoulders, arms and abdomen. Or it can be done at home with resistance bands or tubes, hand-held barbells or dumbbells or even body weight. One program, the Key 3 program (see diagram), was devised by Michael J. Hewitt, research director for exercise science at the Canyon Ranch Health Resort in Tucson. It can be completed in 10 minutes with practice.

As Dr. Hewitt explains, skeletal muscles can only contract and thus are always arranged in pairs. "One muscle of the pair pulls to bend the joint (flexion), and its antagonist pulls to straighten the joint (extension)." Thus, a strengthening program must be balanced, he writes, "pairing every pulling lift with an opposite pushing action."

To reduce the risk of injury and premature muscle fatigue, the large muscles should be exercised first, followed by the smaller muscles, with the postural muscles exercised last. For example, one would start with chest and upper back muscles, then the arms and shoulders and finally the lower back and abdomen.

Muscles have to be overworked to grow stronger. The goal for each exercise is three sets of 8 to 12 repetitions to muscle fatigue. Muscles also need time to recover. So strength training should be done two or three times a week on nonconsecutive days.

The new recommendations add flexibility and balance to the mix. Improving balance and reducing the risk of falls is critical as you age—if you fall, break your hip and die of pneumonia, aerobic capacity will not save you. Ten minutes a day stretching legs, arms, shoulders, hips and trunk can help assure continued mobility, and daily exercises like standing on one foot and then the other, walking heel to toe or practicing tai chi can improve balance.

One balancing exercise to try involves a body movement resembling a stork. Stand with your feet slightly apart. Raise one knee, while keeping your arms to the sides or your hands on your hips.

THE "KEY 3" EXERCISE PROGRAM

■ Slowly slide down wall to a sitting position, then up until legs are nearly straight.

■ Press hands toward ceiling. Keep forearms straight and bring weights together.

■ Slowly raise weight to just under shoulder, then slowly lower.

SOURCE: Michael J. Hewitt

✔ TIMELY TIPS

Keeping Your Kids Fit

Getting kids started on fitness

Starting from when they are very little, make time for an exercise period every day with your children. Turn on music in the family room and have them pick favorite songs. Walk briskly in place or dance to the music, moving your arms up and down, for 5 or 10 minutes so you get your heart pumping for a good cardiovascular workout.

✔ **Make it fun.** After you cool down, do some stretching for about 10 minutes. Get the children to touch their toes and reach their arms over their heads while bending sideways. Incorporate some yoga moves, such as standing on one leg, to improve balance. Show them how good it feels.

✔ **Choose exercises that your children like,** such as jumping rope and doing sit-ups on a bouncy exercise ball. All the things your children like to do naturally, like leapfrog and cartwheels and handstands, are part of a good gymnastic workout. Make the exercise a game and build up the repetitions slowly, so they can feel a sense of accomplishment when they have increased their endurance.

✔ **Begin slowly, with three sets of five or ten reps.** If they start doing five push-ups and get tired, rest, come back and do it again. If you have a pull-up bar, get them to start with one pull-up and slowly help them increase the number they can do. Don't push them and make them too sore. Let them suggest the exercise.

And Keeping Fitness Up

✔ Aim for at least 60 minutes of moderate to vigorous activity a day.

✔ A younger child could walk to school (20 min.), kick a ball around (20 min.), climb monkey bars (10 min.) and ride a bike (10 min.).

✔ Older kids can accumulate 60 minutes a day of aerobic and bone- and muscle-strengthening activities by walking the dog (10 min.), shooting basketballs (30 min.) and stretching or doing push-ups or sit-ups while watching TV (20 min.).

Hold for 30 seconds, then switch legs. Repeat. If you have trouble at first, place your fingertips on a hard surface until you can balance.

The recommendations, are geared to healthy adults 18 to 64, with a companion set for those 65 and older or those 50 to 64 who have chronic health problems or physical limitations. —Jane E. Brody

The Value of a Simple Push-Up

It's the ultimate barometer of fitness

"It takes strength to do them, and it takes endurance to do a lot of them," says Jack LaLanne, the fitness pioneer who astounded television viewers in the 1950s with his fingertip push-ups. "It's a good indication of what kind of physical condition you're in."

The push-up is the ultimate barometer of fitness. It tests the whole body, engaging muscle groups in the arms, chest, abdomen, hips and legs. It requires the body to be taut like a plank with toes and palms on the floor. The act of lifting and lowering one's entire weight is taxing even for the very fit.

"You are just using your own body and your body's weight," says Steven G. Estes, a physical education professor and dean of the college of professional studies at Missouri Western State University. "If you're going to demonstrate any kind of physical strength and power, that's the easiest, simplest, fastest way to do it."

But many people simply can't do push-ups. Health

Checking Your Pulse Rate

○ Checking your pulse rate is one of the best ways to gauge whether you're exercising hard enough to improve your heart and lungs. The American Heart Association advises that you push your heartbeat during exercise to between 50 percent and 70 percent of your maximum heart rate (calculated by subtracting your age from 220).

○ Anything lower than 50 percent does little for your heart's conditioning; anything higher than 75 percent can cause problems unless you're in superb shape. When you're just starting an exercise program, cardiologists recommend aiming for the lower part of the target heart zone and gradually stepping up your pace.

AGE	TARGET HEART RATE (beats per minute)	MAXIMUM HEART RATE
20	100–150	200
25	98–146	195
30	95–142	190
35	93–138	185
40	90–135	180
45	88–131	175
50	85–127	170
55	83–123	165
60	80–120	160
65	78–116	155
70	75–113	150

○ IMPORTANT NOTE: A few high blood pressure medicines lower the maximum heart rate and thus the target rate zone. If you are taking high blood pressure medications, call your physician to find out if your exercise program needs to be adjusted.

and fitness experts, including the American College of Sports Medicine, have urged more focus on upper-body fitness. But, in a recent study, researchers at East Carolina University administered push-up tests to about 70 students ages 10 to 13. Almost half the boys and three-quarters of the girls didn't pass.

Push-ups are important for older people, too. The ability to do them more than once and with proper form is an important indicator of the capacity to withstand the rigors of aging.

Researchers who study the biomechanics of aging, for instance, note that push-ups can provide the strength and muscle memory to reach out and break a fall. When people fall forward, they typically reach out to catch themselves, ending in a move that mimics the push-up. The hands hit the ground, the wrists and arms absorb much of the impact, and the elbows bend slightly to reduce the force.

"What so many people really need to do is develop enough strength so they can break a fall safely without hitting their head on the ground," says Dr. Ashton-Miller, director of the biomechanics research laboratory at the University of Michigan. "If you can't do a single push-up, it's going to be difficult to resist that kind of loading on your wrists in a fall." And people who can't do a push-up may not be able to help themselves up if they do fall.

Natural aging causes nerves to die off and muscles to weaken. People lose as much as 30 percent of their strength between 20 and 70. But regular exercise enlarges muscle fibers and can stave off the decline by increasing the strength of the muscle you have left.

Women are at a particular disadvantage because they start off with about 20 percent less muscle than men. Many women bend their knees to lower the amount of weight they must support.

Based on national averages, a 40-year-old woman should be able to do 16 push-ups, and a man the same age should be able to do 27. By the age of 60, those numbers drop to 17 for men and six for women. Those numbers are just slightly less than what is required of Army soldiers who are subjected to regular push-up tests.

If the floor-based push-up is too difficult, start by leaning against a countertop at a 45-degree angle and pressing up and down. Eventually move to stairs and then the floor.

As for nonagenarian LaLanne, who once set a world record by doing 1,000 push-ups in 23 minutes, he still does push-ups as part of his daily workout.

—Tara Parker-Pope

The Best Cardio Machines

Which workouts do the most for you?

Take a peek into most gyms, and it is obvious which cardio machines are the favorites. Quite often rows of treadmills are parked on prime real estate in front of the televisions. Close by, stationary bikes also crowd the floor. And rightly so; these have been the two most popular machines for a cardiovascular workout at health clubs. But, their dominance has been challenged by the elliptical motion trainer, a machine that aims to replicate running without the stress on joints.

But of all the machines at health clubs, which one is really the best, the latest fads aside? To help gym-goers make an informed choice, the *New York Times* asked 10 experts—physiologists, researchers, doctors and personal trainers—to rate the five most popular cardio machines according to overall muscle conditioning, and how enjoyable it is to use each one.

The winner, by a solid margin, is the elliptical trainer. Our 10 experts thought it had many virtues, chiefly that it allows a low-impact, high-energy workout that is fun. Used correctly, an elliptical trainer works the muscles of the central core as well as the lower body, although some experts think research is needed to determine how hard a workout its users really get.

"These devices are not always effective in providing much resistance to movement," says Edward F. Coyle, the director of the Human Performance Laboratory at the University of Texas at Austin. "People seem to be able to move effortlessly." But for the most part the panel of experts felt that the elliptical was the best all-around choice.

The rowing machine, which has plummeted in popularity, ranked a surprising second, tied with the treadmill. Several panelists argue that rowing machines are highly underrated; when used properly they offer a thorough workout of the major muscle groups, including the back, hips, arms and legs. But despite their advantages, rowing machines demand an intensity of effort that many exercisers find too challenging.

The experts caution that no one machine is right for everyone at all times. Instead, gym-goers should rotate among machines at least once a week. Cross-training, as this is called, addresses a variety of muscles and will help to avoid injuries from

---

ⓘ INSIDE INFO

Joggers Live Longer

○ Various studies have found that jogging adds years to life. Over all, each hour spent exercising (up to 30 hours a week) adds about two hours to a person's life expectancy, according to the Harvard Alumni Study, which has tracked deaths among 17,000 men for more than two decades.

○ Even those who did not start exercising until midlife had a 23 percent lower risk of death over the next 20-odd years. Endurance activities like running, cycling, lap swimming, brisk walking and cross-country skiing conferred the greatest benefit, adding six years of life expectancy over that of a couch potato.

○ Outdoor running burns about 5 percent more calories than treadmills do, in part because there is greater wind resistance and no assistance from the treadmill belt. However, treadmill exercisers suffer fewer stress injuries in the leg. —Jane E. Brody and Anahad O'Connor

WHICH FITNESS MACHINES DO YOU PREFER?

The New York Times *asked 10 fitness experts to give five gym machines ratings of 1 to 10 in five catego-ries, with 10 being the highest score. The highest overall score went to the machine with the least wear and tear on the joints and the highest enjoyment factor.*

	CARDIO BENEFIT	CALORIES BURNED	MUSCLES USED	WEAR AND TEAR	MONOTONY FACTOR	GRAND TOTALS
ELLIPTICAL MACHINE	80	76	78	76	59	369
TREADMILL	88	86	68	49	49	340
ROWING MACHINE	78	71	83	68	40	340
STAIR CLIMBER	79	77	69	59	50	334
STATIONARY BIKE	75	69	61	59	49	313

overuse. "People are always asking me, 'What is the best exercise?'" says Dr. Paul D. Thompson, a cardiologist at Hartford Hospital. "My answer always is, 'What do you enjoy doing?'"

The best exercise machine, the experts agree, is the one that gets you moving each day. Here are the pros and cons of each machine.

Elliptical trainer. Joggers, especially those with knee and back problems, use elliptical machines to limit wear and tear on their bodies. Because standing tall on an elliptical requires balance, users could potentially work their core muscles and their heart, and have just as rigorous a workout as when jogging or biking.

CONS: It is easier to coast on an elliptical machine than on a treadmill. The jury is still out on the machine's overall physiological effects, so users should progress slowly. Anyone with balance problems should be especially careful.

Stair climber. Stair climbers get high marks in terms of cardiovascular benefit and calories burned. And they aren't hard for beginners to figure out.

CONS: It's hard work. Climbing stairs leaves one wiped out and not anxious to jump back on. And even when a participant uses the full range of motion, it still only targets a limited amount of muscles.

Stationary bike. People with knee or ankle problems may be more comfortable using a bike than running. Stationary bikes come in three styles: upright, recum-bent and those for spinning classes led by an instruc-tor. Some models offer a ton of feedback. Spinning

EXPERT ANSWER

To Stretch or Not to Stretch

Q. Does stretching before a workout help?

After dozens of studies and years of debate, it is still not clear whether stretching helps, harms, or does anything in particular for per-formance or injury rates.

One fact seems certain: if your goal is to prevent injury, stretching does not seem to be enough. But warming up can help. And if you start out by moving through a range of motions that you'll use during the activity, you are less likely to be injured.

Some athletes, such as gymnasts, hurdlers and swimmers, may need to stretch to gain the flex-ibility they need for their sport. But distance run-ners do not benefit from being flexible. Indeed, one recent study found that the most efficient runners, those who exerted the least effort to maintain a pace, were the stiffest. —Gina Kolata

bikes are mostly used in a class setting, so the intensity tends to be higher and monotony lower.

Cons: Indoor bikes that offer little pedal resistance are far removed from the outdoor experience and can be boring. Cycling, because of its constant identical motion, can lead to tendonitis.

Rowing machine. Unlike the other machines, a rowing machine works the upper body and is an excellent all-around calorie-burning device.

Cons: Most people struggle to figure out how to use a rowing machine correctly, so it tends to appeal only to a small but avid following of rowers and self-taught exercisers who want a full-body cardio workout. Another disadvantage: rowing machines tend to place the exerciser low to the ground, where it's more difficult to watch TV.

Treadmill. The treadmill retains its popularity, because running is one of the best ways to get into shape and burn calories. Running surfaces of treadmills have improved in recent years to better absorb impact. Jogging while watching TV is easy

TIMELY TIPS

8 Glasses of Water a Day?

The advice to drink eight glasses of water or caffeine-free beverages a day to keep hydrated and prevent constipation, it turns out, is not supported by science.

✔ Researchers find that you can meet your body's needs for liquids in many ways, including drinking caffeinated coffee and tea, and eating fruits and vegetables.

✔ If you are very active, especially in hot weather, sip cold water repeatedly. But beyond two quarts, you may also need to replace the salts lost in sweat by drinking a sports drink or eating foods high in salt and potassium.   —Jane E. Brody

to do, so workouts pass more quickly.

Cons: Running puts quite a lot of stress on joints. Also keep in mind that treadmill running does not burn as many calories as running outdoors.

—Christian DeBenedetti

TIMELY TIPS

Exercises That Relieve Stress

Techniques that improve mental and physical health

✔ **Tai Chi.** An active exercise, sometimes called moving meditation, involving extremely slow, continuous movement and extreme concentration. The movements are to balance the vital energy of the body. BENEFIT: Some studies find it can reduce blood pressure in patients. There is some evidence that it can help elderly people improve balance.

✔ **Transcendental Meditation.** Meditators sit comfortably, eyes closed, and breathe naturally. They repeat and concentrate on the mantra, a word or sound chosen by the instructor, to achieve state of

deep, transcendent absorption. BENEFIT: Studies suggest it can reduce blood pressure in some patients.

✔ **Mindfulness Meditation.** Practitioners find a comfortable position, close the eyes and focus first on breathing, passively observing it. The aim is to achieve focused awareness on what is happening moment to moment. BENEFIT: Studies find that it can help manage chronic pain. Two trials suggest that it can cut the rate of relapse in people who have had several bouts of depression.

✔ **Yoga.** Enhanced awareness through breathing techniques and specific postures. Schools vary widely, aiming to achieve total absorption in the present and a release from ordinary thoughts. BENEFIT: Studies are mixed, but evidence shows it can reduce stress.   —Benedict Carey

Sculpting a Trophy Body

A program to give muscles tone and definition

Aerobic exercises improve cardiovascular fitness and endurance and can help you lose weight, but they don't necessarily tone or sculpt your muscles. Even if you're an avid jogger, swimmer or cyclist and can run, paddle or pedal forever, your muscles still may not be as toned as you'd like them to be. The only way to achieve muscle definition is to lift weights or do strength training, or anaerobic, exercises that use the body's weight as resistance.

The American College of Sports Medicine recommends including aerobic and anaerobic exercise in any balanced physical fitness program—as does the President's Council on Physical Fitness and Sports. Women, in particular, may reap benefits from a program of weight training: strength training improves the muscle and bone strength of women in their 40s, and boosts body image and self-esteem.

Designing a training regimen starts by taking into account your current physique. A rule of thumb: how much weight you lift depends on whether you want to build muscle mass or merely tone and shape your muscles. If you carry more weight and body fat than you are happy with in a certain area, you'll want to go with lighter weights and higher repetitions, 25 to 30, to help burn fat. Don't use too much weight in areas you want to slim down, because you'll end up building up that area. If you're trying to put on weight in specific areas, go with heavier weights and do fewer reps, about 8 to 10.

The key to achieving maximum results is proper form. For starters, don't just lift up and down. Rather, contract your muscles from the moment you start an exercise until you're finished. It's not so much about how much weight you lift, but how

hard you squeeze. Also, be sure to extend your muscle entirely with each repetition; that is, use the full range of motion.

Even if you don't have access to a gym, you can invest in inexpensive equipment, such as small free weights, that will help you slim down or build up specific muscle groups. Here are some exercises to help you tone and shape common trouble spots.

Dumbbell flies: *Tone the pectoral chest muscles without making you look like a bodybuilder.* Lie on your back on a bench with a small dumbbell in each hand. Hold your arms out to the side with your arms bent and your wrists turned toward each other. Lift up toward the ceiling, then bring both arms back down to the side. If you raise the bench so it's on an incline, you'll work muscles higher in your chest. If you lower the bench so your head is below your torso, you'll work the lower chest muscles.

Bicep curls: *Tone and shape the biceps; build muscles if more weight is used.* Hold a dumbbell in each hand and stand with your arms at your side and your palms facing forward. Curl the dumbbell up toward your chest and turn your wrist out when you are at the end of the curl. Lower the weight slowly, because you're resisting weight and strengthening your muscles as you go down, too. Do 15 to 20 repetitions, alternating arms or lifting both at the same time.

Lunges: *Trim and tone the quadriceps in the legs and gluteal muscles in the buttocks. Using dumbbells adds resistance and helps build muscle rather than slimming you down.*

With a dumbbell in each hand, stand with your hands on your hips and take a big step forward with your right foot, bending your knee to form a 90-degree angle. Keep your body straight and be sure your right knee doesn't extend beyond your right toe. Step forward with your left foot, and continue lunging across the room. Repeat 20 to 25 times.

Leg raises: *The best way to tone the lower abdomen.*

To begin, hang from a bar and lift your legs straight in front of you as high as possible, at least at a 90-degree angle. Eventually, work up to 15 to 20 leg raises, but try not to swing. It's a difficult maneuver, so beginners should start by lifting their knees up while someone helps balance them.

Step-ups: *A simple exercise, yet far more effective at trimming and toning the buttocks than the step machine.* Step up onto a bench or high step, then step down, squeezing your muscles with each step. Do 15 to 20 repetitions on each leg. The higher the bench, the harder the workout.

Don't Lift Weights to Lose Weight
Strength training helps build muscle, but not shed pounds

Personal trainers, fitness instructors, magazines and books have sold a double-barreled promise that any strength training builds muscle and that having more muscle dramatically speeds metabolism, increasing the calories a person burns while at rest. With all that calorie burning, the story goes, excess weight comes off effortlessly.

The story is wrong in two ways, researchers say. First, muscle is not such an amazing calorie burner. "Even if weight training increases muscle and metabolism, there is little evidence showing that it is enough to cause weight loss," says Joseph Donnelly, the director of the Energy Balance Laboratory at the University of Kansas, who has extensively reviewed studies on the link between resistance training and weight loss.

And, second, many who try weight training—especially women—fail to do what it actually takes to build more muscle. They lift too light a weight, or they neglect to progress to heavier weights as they grow stronger. And often, women who take up weight lifting also diet. In fact, it is nearly impossible to increase muscle while cutting calories.

Regular resistance training, done correctly, has many benefits. It can prevent some of the muscle loss that occurs with weight loss. It can also lower body fat levels and even help preserve bone mass. But the idea that it can magically increase calorie burning is "a very big stretch," says Edward Melanson, an assistant professor in the division of endocrinology, diabetes and metabolism at the University of Colorado Health Sciences Center in Denver.

Proponents of the theory that weight lifting leads to weight loss argue that it is the long-term effect of gaining more muscle, which burns more calories at rest, that causes weight loss. Still, that has never been proven in studies, which show, rather, that even women who do what it takes to get stronger develop only 2 to 4 pounds of muscle after six months of progressive lifting. Given that 1 pound of muscle burns between 7 to 13 calories a day (as determined by studies that measured oxygen and blood flow to tissues), that means the average boost in metabolism is only 14 to 52 calories a day.

The effect of weight lifting "on metabolism is minor and certainly not the savior of dieters," says William Kraemer, a professor of physiology and neurobiology at the University of Connecticut. When people lift light weights and fail to progressively increase the load, they only increase endurance, he noted.

Genetics may also help determine the impact that weight lifting can have on muscle development and metabolism. Researchers at the University of Massachusetts at Amherst looked at almost 600 men and women who did a strenuous, progressive resistance routine for three months, according to a recent study published in *Medicine & Science in Sports & Exercise.* Three percent were "high responders," some of whom doubled their strength. One percent were "low responders," who became only 1 percent stronger than they were when they started. The majority of men and women increased muscle size 15 to 25 percent; most men improved their muscle strength 40 percent, while women increased theirs 65 percent.

—Martica Heaner

Exercising When You Are Ill

Whatever your ailment—from heart disease to depression—exercise can help

Exercise can lower the risk of heart attack, stroke, hypertension, diabetes, obesity, depression, dementia, osteoporosis, gallstones, diverticulitis, falls, erectile dysfunction, periph-

eral vascular disease and 12 kinds of cancer.

But what if you already have one of these conditions? Or an ailment like rheumatoid arthritis, multiple sclerosis, Parkinson's disease, congestive heart failure or osteoarthritis? How can you exercise if you're always tired or in pain or have trouble breathing? Can exercise really help?

Yes. "The data show that regular moderate exercise increases your ability to battle the effects of disease," says Dr. Marilyn Moffat, a professor of physical therapy at New York University and co-author with Carole B. Lewis of *Age-Defying Fitness.* "It has a positive effect on both physical and mental well-being. The goal is to do as much physical activity as your body lets you do, and rest when you need to rest."

In years past, doctors were afraid to let heart patients exercise. Now, heart attack patients are in bed barely half a day before they are up and moving.The core of cardiac rehab is a progressive exercise program to increase the ability of the heart to pump oxygen- and nutrient-rich blood more effectively throughout the body. The outcome is better endurance, greater ability to enjoy life and decreased mortality.

Aerobic exercise lowers blood pressure in people with hypertension, and it improves peripheral circulation in people who develop cramping leg pains when they walk—a condition called intermittent claudication. The treatment for it, in fact, is to walk a little farther each day.

In people who have had transient ischemic attacks, or ministrokes, "gradually increasing exercise improves blood flow to the brain and may diminish the risk of a full-blown stroke," Dr. Moffat says. And aerobic and strength exercises have been shown to improve endurance, walking speed and the ability to perform tasks of daily living up to 6 years after a stroke.

For those with diabetes, exercise improves

glucose tolerance—less medication is needed to control blood sugar—and reduces the risk of life-threatening complications.

Perhaps the most immediate benefits are reaped by people with joint and neuromuscular disorders. Without exercise, those at risk of osteoarthritis become crippled by stiff, deteriorated joints. But exercise that increases strength and aerobic capacity can reduce pain, depression and anxiety and improve function, balance and quality of life.

Likewise for people with rheumatoid arthritis. "The less they do, the worse things get," Dr. Moffat says. "The more their joints move, the better." Exercise that builds gradually and protects inflamed joints can diminish pain, fatigue, morning stiffness, depression and anxiety, and improve strength, walking speed and activity. Exercise is crucial to improving function of total hip or knee replacements.

Water exercises are particularly helpful for people with multiple sclerosis, who must avoid overheating. And for those with Parkinson's, resistance training and aerobic exercise can increase their ability to function independently and improve their balance, stride length, walking speed and mood.

Resistance training, along with aerobic exercise, is especially helpful for people with chronic obstructive pulmonary disease; it helps counter the loss of muscle mass and strength from lack of oxygen.

Writing in the journal *ACE Certified News*, Natalie Digate Muth, a registered dietitian and personal trainer, emphasized the value of a good workout for people suffering from depression. Mastering a new skill increases their sense of worth, social contact improves mood, and the endorphins released during exercise improve well-being.

"Exercise is an important adjunct to pharmacological therapy, and it does not matter how severe the depression—exercise works equally well for people with moderate or severe depression," writes Muth.

As for the question of whether to exercise when you have a cold, studies show that subjects who had cold symptoms and exercised showed the same lung function and exercise capacity as their healthy counterparts. Researchers also found that exercising had no effect on cold symptoms or recovery time.

—Jane E. Brody

How to Avoid Sports Injuries
The New York Knicks' doc on avoiding injuries

There's little difference between the injuries sustained by recreational and professional athletes, says Dr. W. Norman Scott, director of the Insall Scott Kelly Institute for Orthopaedics and Sports Medicine, as well as a professor at Einstein College of Medicine and team physician for the New York Knicks basketball team for almost 30 years. The only dissimilarity is that pros are more likely to suffer serious injuries, because they play with more force. Below, Scott helps explain what causes some common athletic injuries, how to avoid them and what to do if you get laid up.

NECK: Serious neck injuries are rare among athletes other than those who participate in contact sports like football and rugby. However, weight lifting, wrestling and even racket sports like tennis can cause chronic aches and pains, especially flare-ups along the nerve route.

CAUSES: Neck injuries in older amateur athletes are usually a sign of arthritic changes (joint inflammation), which are often totally asymptomatic. Strenuous neck movements often result in an inflammation that is associated with pain

Signs That You Are Overdoing It

Excessive exercise can damage tendons, ligaments, bones, cartilage, joints and muscles and not give minor injuries a chance to heal. Instead of building muscle, too much exercise can lead to muscle breakdown. Girls and young women may stop menstruating and start losing bone, as if they were in menopause.

Excessive exercise can also release loads of free radicals, which can cause mutations and may increase cancer risk.

But it is not so much the amount of activity that defines the obligatory exerciser as it is its effects. Some people's bodies can handle more physical stress than others. While there is no clear definition of obligatory exercise, there are telltale signs that exercise is becoming too important to a person and creating undue physical and psychological stress.

✔ Continuing to train even when ill or injured.

✔ Experiencing anxiety when a workout is missed.

✔ Constantly talking about their sport, training schedule and diet.

✔ Neglecting other important areas of life.

✔ Justifying excessive exercise as necessary to their sport.

✔ Having friends and family notice a loss of perspective.

—Jane E. Brody

running down the arm into the fingers.

PREVENTION: Better overall conditioning is the best way to prevent neck injuries.

TREATMENT: If discomfort is acute, avoid exercise, and don't stretch the muscle. Apply ice immediately, and don't apply heat until 48 to 72 hours after the injury occurs. If necessary, take nonsteroidal anti-inflammatory medications like Motrin, Advil or Aleve (the same is true of all minor injuries).

BACK: Almost any sport that requires trunk rotations, as in golf or racket sports like tennis.

CAUSES: Most back injuries are muscular in origin, but, depending on your age, back pain can also be due to arthritic changes like osteoarthritis.

PREVENTION: The best way to prevent back pain is through good overall conditioning and following a good stretching program to increase flexibility.

TREATMENT: Apply ice early on, then apply heat after 72 hours. Water therapy like swimming helps decrease spasms. Try gentle stretching exercises, including an abdominal-strengthening workout.

SHOULDER: Pitching, racket sports, golf, lifting weights and other activities where you put your arm in an overhead position.

CAUSES: The most common cause is bursitis, an inflammation of a normal structure called the bursa. Shoulder injuries are much more common as a person gets older due to muscle atrophy. Damage to the rotator cuff, a group of tendons that allows you to raise your arm up and down, is usually caused by repetitive motions like pitching a baseball.

PREVENTION: A program for stretching and strengthening muscles can reduce your chances of getting a shoulder injury.

TREATMENT: Continue to move the shoulder; if you don't, it can freeze up very quickly. Rotate your arms and shoulder, moving your hand in front of your body, then backwards, and up and down; also, try to stretch from side to side, bringing your right hand over to touch your left shoulder.

KNEE: Any sport that requires a pivoting motion, like tennis and basketball; runners are also prone to knee injuries.

CAUSES: The knee is a joint that's especially susceptible to injuries, usually caused by sudden rotational movements.

PREVENTION: Develop very strong leg muscles by biking, lifting weights and using step machines.

TREATMENT: Follow the RICE principle: Rest (but don't completely immobilize it), Ice, Compression (wrap the knee to reduce swelling) and Elevation. Apply ice for 48 hours, then progress to strengthening exercises. Sprained ligaments will need 3 to 12 weeks of rehabilitative exercise, but a torn ligament or cartilage may need surgery.

ANKLE: Ankle injuries are common in any sport that requires a lot of running, such as jogging, racket sports, baseball and football.

CAUSES: Sprains and strains are common injuries that occur when the joint or ligaments connecting bones are overstretched or twisted.

PREVENTION: Make sure you warm up—and your sneakers aren't untied.

TREATMENT: Again, follow the RICE principle, applying ice immediately. If the swelling is slight, you can exercise the following day, but keep your ankle wrapped or wear high-top sneakers. Try strengthening exercises a couple of days after swelling and pain subside.

ELBOW: Besides tennis, you can develop tennis elbow from any sport that requires you to rotate your hand up and down repeatedly, as when you swing a golf club incorrectly.

CAUSES: Tennis elbow (pain in the forearm and wrist) is a common injury caused by too much tension on the tendons around the elbow.

PREVENTION: Strengthening exercises, like squeezing a rubber ball, build muscles in your forearm.

TREATMENT: Apply ice. If necessary, take anti-inflammatory medications.

The Right Exercise Shoes
Fact vs. fiction in the shoe department

The adage "if the shoe fits, wear it" may be good advice in most situations, but it's no guarantee that your next pair of exercise shoes will fit properly when you get them home from the store. That's because foot sizes vary depending on the time of day, the temperature of your feet and what you've been doing with them. A long jog in warm weather, for example, can expand a runner's feet as much as half a size. Foot specialists advise that the best time of day to shop for shoes is at the end of the day, when your foot is largest. Beyond that, forget fancy designs and high-tech gizmos. Here's what you really need to consider, according to Dr. Stephen Pribut, a podiatrist in Washington, D.C.

The running shoe: This shoe is not only a suitable choice for running, but also good for casual walking and other lower-impact activities that do not involve repetitive lateral motion. But if you are looking for a shoe to participate in fitness walking or an activity that involves a lot of repetitive lateral motion, like basketball, tennis and squash, or activities with excessive jumping, such as aerobics—watch out. Wearing running shoes for any of these activities practically invites injury, because they lack adequate support around the ankles.

Basketball and tennis shoes: They should be judged on whether they offer good traction, good ankle support and firm cushioning. The extra money you spend for shoes that fit these criteria will pay off in the medical bills good shoes help you avoid. Some models that boast flared soles to enhance ankle support also help to prevent the kind of ankle rollovers that result in painful torn ligaments and sprained or broken ankles.

TIMELY TIPS

Protecting Your Feet

Runners and joggers can keep their feet happy by using a little common sense

1. Buy new running shoes every 250 to 450 miles. Buy new walking shoes after every 400 hours of use. That translates into 10 hours of walking weekly for 40 weeks.

2. Remember that your feet aren't identical. Fit the larger one when buying shoes.

3. Always test new shoes before you buy them. Ask the salesperson if you can jog around the block first. Good shoes should feel comfortable right away, not after they've been "broken in."

4. Wear clean, dry socks. You can get blisters otherwise.

5. Avoid running on sidewalks and sand. When your foot hits sand, it keeps going because the sand gives. This can stretch the achilles tendon painfully. Concrete doesn't give at all. It transmits shock through your legs, knees and back.

6. Never begin a workout without first stretching. Gentle, regular stretching can reduce the risk of injury.

7. Follow the 10 percent rule. Runners should increase their mileage by 10 percent a week, but level off every third week.

Working out in excess of 3 to 5 days a week strains limbs and joints and can cause heel problems, shin splints, ankle twists and stress fractures.

8. Don't be a weekend warrior. Busy weeks leave little time, but it is dangerous to cram a week's worth of exercise into a weekend.

9. Stop exercising at the first signs of pain. Follow the mnemonic RICE—which stands for Rest, Ice, Compression and Elevation—to ease the discomfort.

10. See a doctor if the pain persists. It is difficult to tell if a foot bone is broken.

SOURCE: Dr. Stephen Pribut,
podiatrist, Washington, D.C.

The cross-trainer: Designed for maximum versatility, cross-trainers can be worn for running, walking, racket sports and aerobics, as well as some indoor-court sports, such as basketball and volleyball. Though cross-trainers are versatile, serious runners are best off wearing real running shoes, because cross-trainers lack the sufficient amount of cushioning and ankle support required for regular jogging.

The walking shoe: These are designed for the serious race-walker. They are a needless and expensive investment for those who jog as well as walk for exercise, though. The majority of running shoes are better for your feet than most walking shoes anyway, because running shoes provide more wiggle room for your toes.

Shoes with air-cushioned soles: Air-cushioning sounds high-tech and therefore helpful, but it can cause more problems than it can prevent. Although air-cushioned athletic shoes provide helpful shock absorption, they lack a firm shank below the back of the foot. A firm shank and a slight heel lift prevent the arch of the foot from dropping down too far when the foot moves. If the foot drops too far, it can cause a shift of bones and the development of a variety of podiatric deformities.

Beauty

Taking Care of Your Skin

You can't erase your genetic makeup, but you can avoid damage from the sun

Nearly everyone wants to look like Halle Berry at 40, Michelle Pfeiffer at 50 or Meryl Streep at 60, yet few people take the preventive measures necessary to maintain youthful-looking skin.

Two factors are critical in determining how your skin ages: genetics and sun exposure. To some extent, your skin's appearance is predetermined by genetic traits inherited from your parents. In addition, fair-skinned people are more likely than the darker-complexioned to age prematurely or to develop skin cancer from sun exposure. That's because the fairer-skinned have less pigment to protect them from the sun's rays and are more susceptible to the process known as photoaging, which comes from a person's cumulative exposure to the sun.

Photoaging actually plays a bigger role in your skin's appearance than your chronological age. Skin can age as a result of getting too much sun over a short period of time as well as from the gradual damage of long-term exposure. But most damage occurs by the time you reach age 18. If you were dealt a bad hand genetically, and you want to make sure you don't get advanced signs of aging, the best thing you can do is avoid the sun.

Below is a guide to what you can expect of your skin from your 20s through your 50s, and what you can do to combat the toll of time.

Two factors are critical in determining how your skin ages: genetics and sun exposure.

• • •

The 20s. "No one is as gorgeous as a woman in her early 20s. This is the best you're ever going to look," says Dr. Wilma Bergfeld, head of clinical research for the department of dermatology at the Cleveland Clinic Foundation and past president of the American Academy of Dermatology. By the time you reach the late 20s, fine lines will probably develop around the mouth and eyes and be noticeable when you wear makeup. If you become pregnant, you may develop brown spots on your face, either now or later; sun exposure exacerbates the problem.

But how fast your skin ages depends on whether you stay out of the sun and use sunscreen religiously. Other skin-saving strategies include not smoking, controlling your weight and maintaining good health. "It's like anything else—if you wait until the damage is done, it's pretty hard to turn it around," says Bergfeld.

The 30s. The first real signs of aging usually become apparent after age 30. That's when you'll start to notice more fine wrinkles, see the skin on your eyelids begin to droop, and find the circles under your eyes becoming darker and maybe even puffy. Smokers will develop even more lines around their eyes and mouth.

For many women, the discovery of those first few wrinkles is enough to send them directly to the cosmetics counter. Happily, some products show promise in counteracting the damaging effects of the sun. There's no doubt, says Bergfeld, that

Checking for Melanoma

Why moles need to be watched carefully

Everyone has moles, an average of 10 to 40 a person, and new ones can develop at any time. Most are smaller than a pencil eraser. If they stay that way, without changing shape, color, size or surface, there is nothing to worry about. But in some cases an overdose of sun can transform innocent moles into potentially deadly cancers.

Most serious cases of melanoma and most melanoma deaths, however, can be prevented. All it takes is vigilance and a respect for the damage that the sun can cause on unprotected skin. A person with a history of severe sunburns (even one or two) as a child or teen is at a higher risk for melanoma later in life.

Dermatologists have long relied on an ABCD criteria: A for asymmetry, B for border irregularity, C for color variations, and D for diameter greater than 6 millimeters (about a quarter of an inch). Dermatologists at New York University School of Medicine and Royal Prince Albert Hospital in Sydney, Australia, have recently suggested a revised mnemonic device for helping people recognize trouble signs in a mole. In the *Journal of the American Medical Association,* the physicians suggested adding an E, for evolving, signifying changes in size; shape; symptoms, like itching or tenderness; surface, especially bleeding; and shades of color.

But you won't know if a mole has changed unless you know where all of them are and what they look like. Dr. Howard L. Kaufman, co-director of the Columbia University Melanoma Center and author of *The Melanoma Book,* suggests making a map of all your moles and noting what each looks like while standing naked in front of a full-length mirror and using a hand-held mirror to see your back.

Be sure to also examine your scalp (part your hair in sections), ears, under your breasts and armpits, under your fingernails and toenails, the palms of your hands and the soles of your feet. As you go, record what you find on a front and rear map of your body. Repeat this examination once a month. If you cannot do this on your own, have a close relative or friend help you, and perhaps return the favor.

If anything unusual is found, either in a new mole or old one, see a dermatologist without delay. If melanoma is caught and treated while it's still a flat lesion, the cure rate is 100 percent. Usually the treatment is simple outpatient surgery. But the cure rate drops to 70 percent once the cancer has invaded underlying tissue or reached a nearby lymph node, and survival is less than 15 percent once the disease has spread elsewhere in the body.

—Jane E. Brody

simply moisturizing can reduce fine wrinkling up to about 16 percent.

If you're looking for something more potent, moisturizers containing alpha hydroxy acids (AHAs) derived from fruit, sugar cane or lactic acid exfoliant can shed the upper layer of skin, exposing newer skin. Research has demonstrated that using AHAs can even reverse some of the signs of photoaging. In a study of 17 adults with severely sun-damaged skin, a lotion with a 25 percent concentration of AHA thickened the outer layers of the skin, increased its elasticity and lightened age spots. There is no evidence, however, that you can prevent wrinkles or turn back the aging clock with AHAs, even in the higher concentrations found in prescription-only formulas. AHAs, says Dr. Cherie Ditre, a Philadelphia dermatologist and researcher, are "not a facelift in a jar."

The 40s. Between ages 40 and 50, your skin loses its collagen and elastin (tissues that keep skin firm and plump), which means wrinkles get bigger and deeper and your skin begins to sag. In addition, your skin gets drier and appears more sallow, pores get larger, eyelids droop more, frown lines show themselves and flat brown spots called liver or age spots appear.

At this stage, says Bergfeld, you should routinely inspect your face and body for potentially cancerous lesions and investigate any suspicious moles or growths, because you're more susceptible to developing skin cancer.

If you already have extensive wrinkling, you may be a candidate for Retin-A at this age. Renova, the acne cream derived from Vitamin A, has long been prescribed to fight wrinkles, and can be used to treat sun-damaged skin and lighten and smooth skin that has turned brown or rough. Renova cannot increase elasticity, eliminate deep wrinkles, or rejuvenate dull or sallow skin, however. But it can bring about noticeable improvements.

Drawbacks shouldn't be ignored, however. Most people who use it experience temporary redness, dryness, itching, peeling and a slight burning sensation. For pregnant women and nursing mothers, the medication is entirely off-limits. Moreover, the cream has no lasting benefits if you stop using it.

The 50s. The changes that began two decades ago evolve still more—deeper wrinkles, especially around the eyes and mouth; sagging, dry skin; and age spots. By now, your wrinkles are clearly noticeable if you've spent a lot of time tanning yourself over the years, or if you smoke. You're also more likely to see wrinkles if your weight has fluctuated significantly. "It's like stretching a balloon," says Bergfeld. "If it collapses after a while, the skin is really wrinkled and the wrinkles are exaggerated." Aesthetically, it's better to keep on a few extra pounds because they act as a filler, giving you a better-looking face.

Protecting Your Skin from the Sun
Sunscreen is essential but only the beginning in the battle against skin cancer

Everyone in the family should be using sunscreen with a sun protection factor (SPF) of at least 15 on exposed skin all year long. Babies should always be kept out of the sun, and toddlers, older children and adults should be well protected with hats and clothing or sunscreen. Be sure to protect your skin on cloudy days, too, since clouds do not filter out UVA radiation.

It should take an ounce of lotion to cover an adult in a bathing suit. Sunscreen should be applied about 20 to 30 minutes before going out and reapplied on dry skin after swimming ("waterproof" screens are helpful, but not enough once you're out of the water).

Look for sunscreens that protect against both UVA and UVB rays. Ultraviolet rays from the sun travel in different wavelengths classified as A and B. UVA rays, which make skin tan, are the most abundant; they also cause skin cancer and aging. UVB rays burn. All sunscreens contain substances that block the UVB rays (the SPF rating refers only to these agents). The most effective protection against skin-damaging, cancer-causing UVA rays comes from zinc oxide, Parsol 1789 (avobenzone) and Eusolex 8020. Some UVA protection is afforded by titanium oxide, oxybenzone and dioxybenzone.

Melanomas can also develop on the scalp and in the eyes, so don't forget a hat and sunglasses, and on the lips, which should be protected by sunblocking lip balm or lipstick. Too much sun can also increase the risk of developing premature cataracts or degeneration of the retina. Now there are contact lenses that can absorb the sun's harmful rays. A study by Dr. Nadia-Marie Quesnel of the University of Montreal College of Optometry found that contact lenses with a built-in UV filter provide

Treating Sunburn

Sunburn occurs when overexposure to the sun's ultraviolet rays kills cells in the top layer of skin and triggers reactions like inflammation, redness, pain and blistering. About one third of American adults have at least one sunburn a year, according to surveys by the Centers for Disease Control and Prevention.

✔ For mild discomfort, doctors recommend ibuprofen or naproxen to bring down inflammation. For more acute sunburns, try corticosteroid creams. Also recommended are cold water compresses or cool, but not icy, baths to relieve inflamed skin and fragrance-free moisturizers for dryness and flakiness.

But there is no consensus among doctors on how to treat acute sunburn, which can include symptoms like severe skin inflammation, peeling and fever. Indeed, there is no definitive proof that common therapies like corticosteroids, antihistamines and antioxidants are effective treatments for acute sunburn, according to an article published in the *American Journal of Clinical Dermatology.* The authors wrote that studies showed that such treatments are actually ineffective at decreasing recovery time. Still, even if such treatments can't accelerate sunburn recovery or repair skin damage, they may help with problems like pain, swelling, itching and flaking.

✔ There is, however, a simpler way to reduce sunburn damage. "No matter what is used to alleviate the discomfort of sunburn, there is no better way, at this time, to treat sunburn than prevention with physical protection and sunscreens," the report said.   —Natasha Singer

better protection against UV rays than regular contacts. However, warns Quesnel, UV-blocking lenses don't eliminate the need for sunglasses. For more information, a helpful book is *Sun Protection for Life* by Mary Mills Barrow and John F. Barrow.

Beyond sunscreens. At online sites like Solumbra.com, Coolibar.com and Sungrubbies.com, you can buy clothing designed to block ultraviolet rays. Features to look for are an opaque fabric and a dense weave. Hold clothing up to the light; any pinpricks of light you see are evidence that the sun can penetrate. The effectiveness of clothing is measured by an ultraviolet protective factor (UPF) scale that calculates how well ultraviolet rays are blocked.

A light-colored fabric, like a white cotton T-shirt, only has a UPF factor of 7; a dark T-shirt has a factor of 10 to 12. But a dark, tightly woven fabric, like a denim shirt, can give you a sun protective factor as high as 1,700. Look for sites that publish ratings, like Coolibar.com, which guarantees a UPF higher than 50 for the clothing they sell.

Another option is a laundry additive called Sun Guard from Rit. The product, available from Sunguardsunprotection.com, provides washable clothes with temporary sun protection without damaging fabrics.   —Jane E. Brody and Michelle Slatalla

Do Night Creams Really Work?
Cheaper creams sometimes yield bigger benefits

Considering the benefits that many night creams claim to offer, it's easy to see their appeal. They promise not only to moisturize skin during sleep, but to neutralize damaging free radicals, improve skin tone and texture, firm up sagginess, minimize wrinkles and lines, or wipe out mottling and sun spots.

But dermatologists say that many night creams do not offer much value, especially given the substantial investment required for so many of them. Is glop-ping something onto your face really any better than allowing your skin to breathe while you rest? And how do you sift through the many products, when so little sound and unbiased information is available?

Nighttime treatments may represent more of a marketing triumph than a skin care essential. Though some products may be helpful, they are largely expensive, nicely packaged moisturizers.

For the most part, there's no magic in the night that warrants using a special cream. Companies say that your skin rejuvenates itself at night, or that it does special processes that it doesn't do in the day. But, there's no proof that such is the case.

Yet some anti-aging ingredients, like retinol, are inactivated by the sun, so it makes good sense to wear them while you sleep. Conversely, there's little point in applying a sunscreen-laden product in the evening, when a visit from Mr. Sandman is the closest you'll get to a beach.

According to dermatologists, there can be ben-efits to moisturizing and treating the skin at night. Many night creams contain compounds known to improve the skin's appearance in measurable ways. Peptides—found in Rodan and Fields Anti-Age P.M. Cream—are known to rev up the production of collagen, boosting firmness and smoothing wrinkles. Vitamin C—contained in Neutrogena Healthy Skin Visibly Even Night Concentrate—has been identified as an essential factor needed by the skin to make collagen.

By halting damage caused by the sun, antioxi-dants like idebenone, vitamin E, coenzyme Q and green tea may help prevent new wrinkles from forming. Ingredients like ceramides, fatty acids and cholesterol help trap in moisture and repair the skin's protective barrier, while salicylic acid, feverfew, chamomile and aloe vera can help soothe an irritated or inflamed complexion.

Hydroquinone (which the Food and Drug Admin-

Protecting Your Skin Against Winter
January is the cruelest month

Simple moisturizing products are best at keeping skin from getting dry, flaky and irritated, because they are denser and more durable than expensive creams and therefore can provide greater and longer-lasting protection. It is not the cold itself, but the dryness it brings to the air, that parches the skin, breaking down its natural protective layer of dead cells. Made of both proteins and fats, this layer, called the stra-tum corneum, forms an oily coating that usually helps to keep moisture in the skin. When it dries out, the skin is more vulnerable to the elements, slower to heal from injuries, and more prone to flaking and cracking.

To help retain moisture, dermatologists also recommend avoiding scalding showers and harsh soaps, which can strip away the oily layer. It may also be beneficial to add a little fragrance-free oil to bath water for increased hydration. And after a bath or shower it is pref-erable to gently pat yourself dry rather than rub and buff the skin with a towel. Also, while your skin is still wet, consider coating yourself with a humectant to seal the moisture in. Basic mois-turizers like Aveeno or Purpose work well, but you can also use a little olive oil or Crisco.

Lips, too, are vulnerable to dry air. Windburn and cold winter air cause the corners of the lips to crack and split. Dermatologists often recom-mend covering them with A+D Original Oint-ment, a diaper rash cream made with lanolin that helps treat irritated skin. —Natasha Singer

istration has said may not be safe in over-the-counter products), kojic acid and the extracts of cucumber, licorice or mulberry alleviate blotching and spot-ting, as does a new glucosamine compound in Olay Definity Intense Hydrating Cream, a formula many women use at night because it is creamy.

First, Apply a Foundation Primer
You'll move, but your makeup will stay in place

It seems logical enough: in order to keep your makeup from disappearing, you need to give it something to hold on to. That's the premise behind products known as foundation primers.

Primers have been a staple in makeup artists' lines—including those of Laura Mercier, Sue Devitt, Vincent Longo and Nars—for several years. But now specialty lines like Tarte and E.I. Solutions have introduced primers; Estée Lauder has Prime FX; and the products have reached the mass market with the introduction of Cover-Girl Outlast, a two-compartment tube that holds a primer in one side and foundation in the other. But is this something women need? Why take the time or spend the money on these products, which generally cost $25 to $40?

Where once there was only a foundation layer for the face, now there are anti-aging serums, day moisturizers and sunscreens meant to go on first. Primers are the newest layer, made necessary, makeup experts say, by ever lighter and sheerer foundations. "Back when we used super-matte, opaque foundation that just covered everything, you didn't need primer," says Jose Parron, the director of the Image Studio at Barneys New York. It is no coincidence that these products share a name with what is put on the walls—or that an artist puts on the canvas—before starting to paint. "Walls and canvas, like the skin, have texture to them," Parron says. Using primer smoothes out that texture so that it doesn't interfere with what the artist wants to create. On the face that means filling in oversize pores, creases and fine lines that can make even the best foundation look less than smooth.

Yet not all women will bother with primer, nor does everyone need to. An oil-free sunscreen can double as primer for problem skin, as can a rich moisturizer for very dry skin. —Sally Wadyka

Retinol, found in L'Oréal's Advanced RevitaLift Night Cream and several other products, is perhaps the most highly regarded ingredient available without a prescription. Dermatologists say it does work to treat existing wrinkles.

To work, a cream must contain active ingredients in a sufficient concentration. Ingredients must also penetrate the skin and stay there long enough to have an effect. Inexpensive brands backed by large companies, like Neutrogena, L'Oréal, Revlon, Olay, Dove, Pond's and Aveeno, often have the resources to perform scientific studies to identify an effective formula and prove that it works. Therefore, some of the less expensive products backed by large companies may be more effective than the pricier smaller brands.

Wearing any night cream requires patience. Eight weeks is not an unreasonable amount of time to expect to wait to see an improvement—but women tend to lose interest quickly.

—Laurel Naversen Geraghty

Tips from a Top Makeup Artist
What makes a woman beautiful

Are you unhappy with your looks? Plagued by freckles or a prominent nose? Do you think your lips are too small or too big? Well, take heart in the fact that even supermodels like Kate Moss struggle with beauty crises and skin care woes, according to Bobbi Brown, who has been makeup artist to Moss and a bevy of other beauties. Brown believes the problem lies not with women, but with conventional notions of beauty.

The key to being perceived as pretty, says Brown, author of a handful of beauty guides, is to exude self-confidence, by being satisfied with your looks and developing an individual beauty style. "My crusade is to make women comfortable

HEALTH

 **TIMELY TIPS**

Adding That Youthful Glow

Is it new love, yoga or skin luminizers?

Famous women glow, don't they? Celebrity interviews suggest that their radiance comes from within via Kabbalah, Scientology, new motherhood, new love, yoga, fasting or a humanitarian trip to Africa. But their makeup artists say the radiance comes from skin luminizers, mica and other minerals ground into fine particles to form a veil of delicate sparkle.

By reflecting light, luminizers can balance the appearance of uneven skin tone. "When it's used strategically, it makes everyone look a lot younger, and it adds vibrancy to dull skin," says Patti Dubroff, a makeup artist whose clients include the actresses Jennifer Connelly and Naomi Watts.

To avoid spreading glitter over the entire face, some makeup artists recommend adding only a touch of shine to the cheeks with a creamy blush or a powder. Apply it to the apples of the cheeks and blend it across the cheekbones, says April Greaves, a makeup artist in Los Angeles. Then put a touch only over the brow bones. "On the forehead and nose it can look like oil," Greaves says. "Don't apply it around the eyes, to avoid the wrinkles." She also recommends avoiding pearly white or light gold colors. "Rosy, bronze or fleshy color pigment makes it more realistic."

When applied with a sparing hand, shimmering makeup should merely illuminate the face a little. "Without it, people look noticeably less vibrant," Dubroff says. "It can make anyone look brighter and happier, cleaner and well rested. What could be wrong with that?"

—Christine Lennon

in their own skin," says Brown, founder of Bobbi Brown Essentials, a line of cosmetic and skin care products. We asked Brown how cosmetics can help you achieve a face you can love.

Don't fix it, enhance it. First of all, things like a small mouth and big nose are traits, not flaws. Sadly, women who have these features have been taught not to like them. The challenge is to reverse this way of thinking. For me, the question is not "how do you fix it?" It's taking the features that make you who you are and making the most of them. Accept the features you have, learn to feel good about them and start playing them up.

Use the right foundation. Flaws like uneven skin colorations and dark circles under the eyes should be concealed. But it has to be done naturally. A bad concealer looks worse than dark circles. It's important to use a yellow-toned concealer. Using the right foundation for your skin is key. I only

apply oil-free foundation on oily skin because most women need some moisture. The trick to finding the right foundation is to apply it on the side of your face. If it disappears, then it's the right one.

Don't cover up wrinkles. The closest thing I've found to a miracle in skin care is alpha hydroxy acid, which gives the skin a smoother look. Don't try to cover up wrinkles. Instead, apply a brighter blush on the cheeks or line the eyes to make them more prominent.

Diet and exercise to rescue lackluster skin. I've found that the more you exercise and feel healthy, the younger and fresher you look. If I eat well, I look good. Drinking a lot of water also works for me, both by staving off my appetite and giving my skin a clearer, plumped-up appearance.

Don't take trends too far. Makeup that works for the runway isn't necessarily meant to be worn on the streets. Don't take trends too literally. For example, if a model is wearing black lipstick on the runway, you might want to go for a darker tone than you normally wear. If the look is lots of shine, use shimmer on select spots, not everywhere. It's what works on you that matters.

Make makeup last. The trick to having makeup last for hours is to layer creamy and dry textures. A concealer, for example, is moist and will stay on only if you layer it with a dry powder. Also, lipstick will stay on longer if you apply color with a lip pencil over it. And using moistened eyeshadow to line your eyes instead of a pencil will result in longer-wearing eye liner.

Expect bad beauty days. Most women tend to put more makeup on when they're having a bad day, but that only makes matters worse. If you're not looking your best, skip the foundation that day. Use a tinted moisturizer and blush instead. And drink lots of water. On a bad day, I wear a baseball cap and sunglasses.

How to Prevent Aging

Some simple and inexpensive tips

When $89 anti-aging creams promise to lift saggy faces in just minutes, and some sunscreens claim to offer all-day protection, truth can be scarce. But dermatologists say there are simple and inexpensive ways to stave off premature aging and its attendant wrinkles and loss of collagen. Some of the following advice is backed by independent clinical research, while other practical tips come from board-certified dermatologists.

Cleanse, treat, prevent. "I'm big on simplifying everything," says Dr. Jeffrey S. Dover, an associate clinical professor of dermatology at Yale Universi-

ty School of Medicine. So he counsels his patients to "cleanse, treat, prevent" daily. Wash your face with your scrub, gel or foam of choice; slather on a sunscreen every morning to forestall further sun damage; and reverse the signs of photoaging nightly by applying a prescription retinoid like Renova or Retin-A, which is available generically as tretinoin.

Boost your skin's thickness. Despite the fact that it has been proved for more than a decade that alpha-hydroxy acids (like glycolic acid) in topical forms can increase skin thickness and improve wrinkled and sun-damaged skin, most consumers hunting for an anti-aging cream on drugstore shelves don't realize it. One potential downside is that alpha-hydroxy acids "thin out the epidermis, making it a little more sensitive to being sunburned," says Dr. Bruce Katz, clinical professor of dermatology at the Mount Sinai School of Medicine. But not nearly as sensitive as it is to Retin-A. Dr Katz recommends that people who wear either product be sure to keep sunscreen on during the day as well.

Choose an invisible mask. No need to go white-faced wearing zinc oxide anymore just to protect against short UVB rays and longer UVA rays, says Dr. Amy Derick, a board-certified dermatologist in Barrington, Ill. The Food and Drug Administration has approved more broad-spectrum sunscreen products with Mexoryl SX, a European formula that is now widely available here and much less visible on the skin. Dr. Derick also recommends Neutrogena sunscreens with Helioplex, which has a form of stabilized avobenzone for prolonged UVB/UVA effectiveness that won't leave consumers feeling as if they're "wearing a white mask."

Take your vitamins. Several studies have shown that antioxidants also protect the skin from light, scavenging free radicals, says Dr. Derick, explaining, "antioxidants hook onto the free radicals generated by UV light and basically negate them." She recommends applying vitamins C and E in the form of a serum.

Protect your head. Finally, don't neglect your noggin. A recent epidemiological study of 51,704 melanoma cases nationwide showed that melanomas of the scalp and neck are disproportionately fatal. So dermatologists should inspect scalps for melanomas, and beachgoers should wear wide-brimmed hats.

—Catherine Saint Louis

How to Remove Wrinkles

Proven treatments for aging skin

A review in *The Archives of Dermatology* concludes that three anti-aging treatments are proven clinically effective: the topical application of retinol; carbon dioxide laser resurfacing; and injection of hyaluronic acid, a moisture-retaining acid that occurs naturally in the skin. Each depends on the same mechanism, the interaction of skin cells called fibroblasts with the collagen they produce.

Skin deteriorates as it ages, and its exposure to sunlight inhibits the ability of fibroblasts to produce collagen. The hands, face, neck and upper chest all suffer more than unexposed skin, and light-pigmented people wrinkle more readily than others. This damage, the authors write, is essentially an accelerated version of chronological aging. Ultraviolet radiation induces production of the same enzymes that degrade collagen with age.

Collagen fibers last as long as 30 years. But with age and ultraviolet exposure, they deteriorate and fragment, and fragmented collagen impairs the collagen-producing function of the fibroblasts that created it. As the fragmented collagen accumulates, new collagen production declines, the connections

between the fibroblasts and the collagen weaken, and the skin, now lacking support, begins to wrinkle.

But there are treatments that counter this process. Topical application of retinol, a form of vitamin A, was the first to be proved useful. Although the molecular pathways are not well understood, retinol causes new collagen to form in chronologically aged skin and in skin damaged by ultraviolet light.

Skin creams with retinol are available over the counter, but many do not indicate the concentration of the active ingredient. Concentrations of 0.2 to 0.6 percent are enough, but preparations strong enough to have an effect can also have a side effect, a rash called retinoid dermatitis. If a rash occurs you should stop using the cream. The rash can sometimes be avoided if the concentration is increased gradually. Retinol also makes the skin more sensitive to damage from ultraviolet light, so protection from the sun while using it is essential.

Carbon dioxide laser resurfacing is another well-tested treatment for wrinkles. The laser removes thin layers of skin without damaging surrounding tissue. As the wound heals, new collagen is produced. The treatment works first by inducing high levels of matrix metalloproteinase, or MMP, an enzyme that destroys fragmented collagen. Then it reduces MMP and increases the production of new and undamaged replacement material. The procedure is also used for removing scars, warts and birthmarks.

Healing takes 2 to 3 weeks, and the wound has to be cleaned with saline or diluted vinegar and treated with ointments to prevent scarring. In most cases, the procedure is done only once, and lasts many years. There are now some less invasive laser procedures, but their effectiveness is doubtful.

The third effective treatment is injecting a form of hyaluronic acid, similar to a substance the skin normally produces, into the dermis that underlies the wrinkles. This was originally designed as a space filler, with no intended physiological effect.

TIMELY TIPS

Six Injections and What They Do

All of the following have been approved as safe by the Food and Drug Administration, though not necessarily for treating wrinkles.

✔ **Fat,** harvested via liposuction, can be purified and safely injected into cheeks, lips or temples, because patients are never allergic to their own fat. Treatments last from six months to several years.

✔ **Botox** smoothes frown lines (those vertical furrows between the eyebrows) by paralyzing the muscles that cause them. The F.D.A. has approved its cosmetic use for this part of the face only, but some doctors also use it on horizontal forehead wrinkles, crow's-feet, neck bands (vertical cords than run below the chin) and the area under the nose to stretch out lines above the lip. If injected incorrectly, Botox can temporarily make the eyelids or lips droop. Treatments last up to four months.

✔ **Collagen** is a fibrous protein that is used to fill wrinkles and acne scars as well as plump lips. Zyderm and Zyplast, made of bovine collagen, can cause itching, swelling and other allergic reactions, so doctors test potential patients to see if they are sensitive. CosmoDerm and CosmoPlast, made of human collagen, usually do not cause such reactions. Treatments last three to six months.

✔ **Radiesse** is approved by the F.D.A. to fill in cheeks, chins and deep wrinkles. Made of microscopic calcium particles suspended in a gel, it may cause tiny lumps or bumps, doctors say. The effects are expected to last 1 to 3 years.

✔ **Restylane and Juvéderm,** spongy gels made of hyaluronic acid, are used to fill moderate to deep facial folds or, off label, to plump lips. Side effects include swelling, bruising and lumpiness for a few days. Treatments last up to six months. Hylaform and Captique, other hyaluronic acids, cause less swelling, but last only four to five months, doctors say.

✔ **Sculptra** is a synthetic compound that has been approved by the F.D.A. to treat facial wasting in AIDS patients. Some doctors use Sculptra off label to fill hollow cheeks associated with ordinary weight loss or aging, but others question whether it might cause inflammation in people with healthy immune systems. Treatments last up to 2 years.

—Natasha Singer

But as the injection stretches the dermis, the fibroblasts respond by producing more collagen and less MMP. Studies have demonstrated that increased collagen production is visible within a month after the injection. The benefit lasts about six months.

This type of hyaluronic acid should not be confused with hyaluronic acid in some topical cosmetic products. Rubbing such products on the skin will not stimulate collagen production.

Do the benefits of these treatments outweigh the risks? Dr. Gary J. Fisher, the lead author of the review and a professor of dermatology at the University of Michigan, thinks so. Says Dr. Fisher, "For these treatments, which have sound research behind them, and for people who want to improve their appearance, the benefits far outweigh any problems." —Nicholas Bakalar

Do-It-Yourself Facial Peels

They are cheaper and safe

The facial peel is hardly a new idea. Cleopatra, before 30 B.C., soaked her face in sour milk, which is high in lactic acid, to remove the top layer of dead cells gently, revealing the smoother skin beneath. Over the next 2,000 years, women tried remedies as varied as old wine and sandpaper to do the same thing.

But there is a new level of do-it-yourself exfoliation: the at-home peel kit, a personal chemistry set meant to mimic the professional peels performed by doctors and spa technicians, but with less irritation. Beauty brands in every price range have some version of it, from L'Oréal to Chanel. All these kits are supposed to diminish wrinkles, spots and blemishes. Kits for microdermabrasion, another form of exfoliation done at doctors' offices and spas, are also available: the Classic Personal MicroDermabrasion System from Dermanew, for example, and Neutrogena's At Home MicroDermabrasion System.

At-home microdermabrasion is gentler, but less effective than the office kind. In professional microdermabrasion, tiny aluminum oxide crystals are sprayed onto the skin at high pressure and quickly vacuumed away. The do-it-yourself method involves using a battery-operated scrubber to apply thick, gritty creams. The abrasion is effective, but what is missing, doctors say, is the vacuum component, which clears pores and is thought to stimulate the production of collagen in the skin. But some users say they're willing to settle for a milder peel in exchange for being able to do it themselves.

The steps involved in chemical peel kits typically include cleaning the face to remove oils, applying an acid solution (with a wide flat brush), removing the product after 5 to 10 minutes and applying a moisturizer. Chemical peel kits come with a warning, recommended by the Food and Drug Administration, that the chemicals make the skin more sensitive to sunlight, so users should wear sunscreen. Some mild redness or stinging is to be expected, but unless the products are left on too long or used too often, nothing worse should result.

—Christine Lennon

Should You Get a Facelift?

Or a tummy tuck or breast enlargement?

The facelift was traditionally the most-elected cosmetic surgical procedure to combat the effects of aging skin. Now, however, multi-injection procedures, or filler facelifts, represent a kinder, gentler alternative to surgical facelifts, a way of plumping up rather than cutting away and hoisting sagging tissue. The rising popularity of these techniques is part of a marked national trend. Indeed, since 2005 surgical facelifts have not made the list of the top five surgical procedures reported by the American Society of Plastic Surgeons. Between 2000 and 2008, the ASPS recorded 16 percent fewer facelift procedures. In that same time period Botox procedures increased by 537 percent.

As opposed to the 5- to 10-year effect of a surgical facelift, injections offer only temporary results—lasting 6 months to 2 years, depending on which materials are used—but they are far cheaper and less invasive. They also require less recovery time. And though their results are not as dramatic as a facelift, injection cocktails, say doctors who offer them, are sufficient for patients in their 30s, 40s and 50s who do not have a lot of loose skin to cut away.

Side effects like bruising and skin irritation can occur even when only one filler is used. Cosmetic treatments sometimes have adverse aesthetic side effects, which is why potential patients are often advised to take care that the doctor they choose shares their sense of how much work is too much.

Beyond injections, there are other minimally invasive procedures that are currently very popular: chemical peels and microdermabrasion for the skin surface, to smooth and even it out and remove fine wrinkles; laser hair removal for the entire body; and

ⓘ INSIDE INFO

Contemplating Facial Surgery?

O   More than 241,000 eyelid surgeries, 43,000 forehead lifts and 118,400 face-lifts were performed in 2007, according to the American Society of Plastic Surgeons.

O   But a recent study by Yale University researchers shows that people contemplating facial surgery should ask how a procedure might affect their facial expressions. Drooping of the upper eyelid, for instance, is often seen as an indicator of tiredness. But when shown a picture that simulated a type of eyelid surgery involving the removal of excess skin from the upper eyelid, study participants reported that the woman looked even more tired and sad than before.

O   And some people might want to think twice about eliminating some sets of wrinkles. Researchers found that a digitally-altered picture that added crow's-feet—tiny wrinkles around the eyes—received high ratings by study participants for "happiness."   —Tara Parker-Pope

schlerotherapy (injection of blood vessels to remove varicose veins), primarily for the face and legs.

But when it comes to some aspects of the beauty quotient, there is no better choice than to go under the knife to achieve optimum results. Here are a few of the most-elected surgical procedures.

Liposuction. Exercise-resistant fat deposits are removed by a vacuum device. Areas commonly addressed are the abdomen, buttocks, calves, chin, cheeks, neck, thighs and upper arms. Typically an outpatient procedure, liposuction can improve body shape. Permanent if a sensible diet is followed, combined with exercise.

Nose reshaping. A procedure to change the shape of the bridge or tip of the nose or narrow the width of the nostrils, or some or all of the above.

Sometimes the reshaping is necessary to alleviate a breathing problem. The procedure is usually outpatient. Recovery time is 1 to 2 weeks, but it may take as much as a year before the nose's permanent appearance is fully determined.

Breast enlargement. Implants filled with saline solution are inserted between the breast tissue and the muscles of the chest wall. It is usually outpatient, with general or local (with sedation) anesthesia. Recovery may take a few days, and healing a year or more. The results are variable; for some people, replacement or removal is sometimes necessary.

Eyelid surgery. Removes excess fat or drooping flesh from the upper eyelid or under the eyes to reverse the signs of aging, as well as for aesthetic improvement at any time. Usually outpatient, with general anesthesia. Healing takes several weeks.

Tummy tuck. Involves a surgical tightening of the abdominal wall and removing excess fat and skin to obtain a flatter stomach and more waist definition. A general or local (with sedation) anesthetic is used. Two to 4 weeks' recovery is necessary, and healing takes 2 to 4 weeks.

All of these procedures have their own risks and side effects. For more information, visit the American Society of Plastic Surgeons site at www. plasticsurgery.org.   —Natasha Singer

Keeping Your Hands Young
A few ways to battle the appearance of aging

In the battle against aging, the hands matter, too. You can spend all the time you want getting your face treatments and facelifts and creams, but your hands will betray your age every time. The most common problem is dryness. Because hands do not have as many oil glands as other areas of the body, and because they so often are washed in soap (or worse, detergents) and exposed to air and sun, the protective top layer of skin cells is easily stripped away. Here are a few ways to counteract dryness.

Moisturizing creams and lotions contain humectants—like glycerin or hyaluronic acid—which attract moisture from the air and from the deeper layers of skin, and emollients—like petroleum jelly, mineral oil, lanolin or shea butter—which soften the skin and provide a protective coating. Prices vary wildly, from a few dollars for drugstore brands to close to $100 for some creams. Is there a difference? Many dermatologists say no.

Three inexpensive drugstore moisturizers doctors often recommend are Aquaphor, Vaseline Intensive Care lotion and Cutemol cream. Doctors advise applying moisturizer when the hands are still damp from washing, so that it can trap the water in. Another trick is to apply moisturizer to the hands before bedtime and then wear a pair of cotton gloves overnight to increase penetration.

In addition to dryness, hands suffer from overexposure to sunlight and from aging. Symptoms include wrinkles, brown spots and an increasingly leathery texture. To address this damage, hand creams include a variety of special ingredients— alpha hydroxy acids (to exfoliate), vitamins A, C and E (to reduce oxidative damage), amino acids and fatty acids (to block moisture loss), retinoids (to stimulate the production of collagen, which makes skin firm) and skin lighteners (to fade brown spots).

Microdermabrasion, chemical peels and laser resurfacing can make skin smoother, even out its color, promote the growth of collagen and get rid of rough patches, dark spots and shallow wrinkles. Wrinkle fillers used on the face, including Restylane and Sculptra, can also plump up the skin on the backs of the hands.

By far the best way to have beautiful hands is to prevent damage in the first place. Keep them out of hot water whenever possible. And remember that nothing short of gloves beats the daily use of a high-SPF sunscreen.

–Elizabeth Hayt

The Bald Truth About Baldness
And what men—and women—can do about it

When it comes to hair loss, men are often as vain as women. As many as one in two men lose their hair by the age of 50. Women are not immune from balding, either, and are just as anxious about it. An estimated 30 million women—about one in five—suffer from female pattern hair loss, though for them it is rarely as obvious as men's bald crowns; women's hair thins noticeably over the entire head. However, female pattern hair loss is usually permanent.

Balding men today have a number of treatment options. They can choose hair-loss therapies to strengthen remaining follicles and prevent further loss. This is somewhat easier in men than in women, because in men the hormone that triggers hair loss—dihydrotestosterone—is known. Doctors can counteract its effect by prescribing Propecia for men. Rogaine (the brand name of the drug minoxidil) is the only medicine known to slow hair loss in both men and women. Women's Rogaine is less potent than men's—a 2 percent strength, rather than 5 percent as in men's—but many dermatologists recommend the 5 percent solution for women, too. It is meant to be dripped onto the scalp twice daily. Because it has not been studied in pregnant women, patients are advised to talk to

✔ TIMELY TIPS

Tender Loving Care for Delicate Hair

Suffering from fragile or thinning hair? Here's a list of things to avoid to help preserve your "crowning glory."

✔ **DO NOT ignore the problem.** Early treatment offers the best chance to preserve and thicken the hair that remains. "Like brain cells, once hair cells are destroyed or programmed to destroy, they cannot be regenerated," says Dr. Susan C. Taylor, a Philadelphia dermatologist.

✔ **DO NOT treat hair with heat or harsh chemicals.** Relaxers, peroxide, hot combs, flat irons and even blow-dryers can leave hair brittle and prone to break. "Probably blow-drying with a hot hair dryer is the most damaging thing that women do on a daily basis," says Dr. Janet L. Roberts, a clinical professor of dermatology at Oregon Health &

Science University, in Portland.

✔ **DO NOT crash diet.** Sudden weight fluctuations are a prime culprit for hair loss among young women. Gradual losses of one to two pounds a week may help avoid it.

✔ **DO NOT skimp on protein or iron.** The body needs both to grow healthy hair. "Get some form of protein for breakfast, lunch and dinner," Dr. Roberts says.

✔ **DO NOT style too tightly.** Over time tight braids, cornrows and ponytails may place stress on the hair and the follicle, leading to temporary breakage or even permanent hair loss, Dr. Taylor says.

✔ **DO NOT wash with drying or clarifying shampoos.** Gentle formulas or those labeled "body building" that don't strip the hair of moisture are best for thin, delicate strands.

✔ **DO NOT skip conditioner.** This helps prevent damage to thin or delicate hair by "minimizing

friction between the strands," Dr. Roberts says.

✔ **DO NOT handle hair roughly.** Vigorous towel drying, teasing and scratching may be damaging to the hair and scalp.

✔ **DO NOT brush frequently.** The old adage about brushing 100 strokes a day for healthy hair is actually a recipe for breakage, according to Dr. Roberts. A wide-tooth comb is least damaging of all.

—Laurel Naversen Geraghty

...And How Not to Pick a Hairpiece

✔ **Don't** choose one with too much hair.

✔ **Don't** pick an unrealistic hairline. A 40-year-old, for example, shouldn't have bangs.

✔ **Don't** try to cover up gray hair with a hairpiece. If you have some gray, match the piece with it.

SOURCE: American Hair Loss Council

their doctors if they are expecting or thinking of becoming pregnant. Also, Rogaine is not suitable for people with some medical conditions, such as high blood pressure.

Other drugs target specific causes of hair loss. Those who have abnormally high levels of male hormones, for instance, may be prescribed birth-control pills containing estrogen or may take spironolactone, a drug that blocks the metabolism of male hormones. Those who have

alopecia areata, which results from an autoimmune disorder, may be given cortisone shots in the scalp or a topical cream. Some doctors give patients a series of treatments with low-intensity laser light.

For those who are really determined to regain a head of natural hair, there is hair transplantation micrograft surgery, which implants hair follicles taken from the back of the head two or three at a time. The best candidates for transplants are men with typical male pattern baldness and most women, who tend to lose hair all over. Men and women should consider undergoing transplant surgery as soon as they start to lose hair, doctors advise. When you have enough hair, it looks imperceptible.

—Laurel Naversen Geraghty

The Perils of Tooth Whitening

Bleaching can sometimes go too far

A fondness for pearly white teeth is ancient. In the Bible, Jacob hopes that his son Judah will have "teeth white with milk." But never in history have paper-white teeth been as popular or easy to obtain as they are now.

Whitening treatments in which teeth are coated in a high-strength bleaching gel and then put under an ultraviolet or visible light for three 15- to 20-minute sessions are said to be the fastest method of tooth whitening. Three treatments can lighten teeth as much as using a dentist-dispensed bleaching tray for 10 nights or wearing over-the-counter whitening strips for 16 days, according to a study published this year in the journal *Operative Dentistry*. But many people have found that the initial brilliance begins to fade in a matter of weeks.

"If my daughter were getting married tomorrow and needed quick bleaching, I would recommend an in-office light treatment," says Dr. Bruce A. Matis of the Indiana University School of Dentistry. "But for those who have time and prefer longer-lasting whitening, I recommend using a dentist-dispensed bleaching tray." But some dentists say that when people routinely use high-strength bleaches or use whitening products in every step of their oral-care routine, it may add up to a level of exposure to bleaching agents that

goes beyond what has been studied.

American products are much more powerful and getting stronger all the time, raising the risk of overexposure to bleach. Fifteen years ago the first trays dispensed by dentists used gels that were 10 percent carbamide peroxide, equivalent to about $3^1/_3$ percent hydrogen peroxide. Today some products contain as much as 22 percent carbamide peroxide whitener. And the strongest bleaching strips sold by dentists now contain 14 percent hydrogen peroxide gels. "Once you get above 15 percent carbamide, you are pushing the envelope," says Dr. Van B. Haywood, a professor at the School of Dentistry at the Medical College of Georgia. Because of the unknown risks of high peroxide exposure, some dentists advise pregnant women as well as cancer patients and smokers (who are at risk of developing cancer) to avoid tooth whitening altogether.

—Natasha Singer

INSIDE INFO

Finding Beauty Abroad

○ For at least two decades, medical tourism has been an increasingly popular alternative for the uninsured desperate for care, and for middle-class Americans willing to travel to secure affordable health care.

○ Roughly half a million Americans sought medical care abroad in 2006, of which 40 percent were dental tourists, according to the National Coalition on Health Care. That's up from an estimated 150,000 in 2004.

○ Dental bridges and bonding ranked No. 1 and 2 on a list of most sought-after procedures for Americans traveling abroad for medical care, according to a report published by HealthCare Tourism International, a nonprofit group that tracks health care.

—Camille Sweeney

Sexuality

Hormones and Sex

When it comes to sex drive, hormones rule

In the the nearly 60 years since Masters and Johnson began groundbreaking research on the sex lives of Americans, it has become increasingly clear that the relationship between hormones and sex drive is complex and intimate. Hormones regulate every aspect of our sex lives and, to a large degree, our behaviors as well.

According to Dr. Theresa Crenshaw, a sexual medicine specialist and author of *The Alchemy of Love and Lust*, the difference between men and women lies in how their hormones behave. She calls the mix of hormones and their interactions a "sex soup." As the ingredients interact, so do

 **INSIDE INFO**

Fertility by the Numbers

Ever since the researcher Alfred Kinsey published his famous statistical portrait of male sexual behavior in 1948, Americans have sought to quantify information about sexual and reproductive activity. Here are a few facts.

○ **Sperm Story:** The average male produces sperm at the rate of 500 million per day. Between 120 million and 600 million sperm are released during one ejaculation.

○ **Eggs Aplenty:** A woman is born with 200,000 to 400,000 eggs in her ovaries, all that will ever be available to her. But she will only experience about 500 menstrual cycles during her lifetime, so her egg supply is more than ample for any reproductive needs.

predominant human sexual patterns and many other attitude-related behaviors. Testosterone, the principal male sex hormone, has circadian rhythms that change during the course of the day, influencing male behavior, chiefly in a man's desire for orgasm. The production of testosterone, like that of estrogen, is governed by the brain's pituitary gland, which secretes hormones that in women stimulate the ovaries to produce estrogen and in men prompt the testes to generate testosterone.

Women have many more hormones (including testosterone), which have a more complex rhythm and interaction, which in turn makes their sex drive more complicated and subject to variability. Testosterone provokes an interest in sexual fantasies and genital sex in both sexes. "Lust is associated primarily with testosterone in both men and women," says Helen Fisher, an anthropologist and author of *Why We Love*. Although the neuroanatomical path of testosterone can be mapped, its underlying behavioral mechanism is not known. German researchers, writing in the *Journal of Endocrinology* a few years back, posited the following: "Testosterone might have direct effects on cognitive behavior, e.g., influence the awareness of sexual cues, but it is also suggested that testosterone may act peripherally to enhance sexual pleasure and thereby increase sexual desire and even sexual activity, circumstances and partner permitting." In other words, a tincture of testosterone for a woman having sex could mean the difference between making a mental grocery list or hearing Beethoven's Ninth.

Romantic love is linked with the natural stimulant dopamine and perhaps norepinethrine and serotonin. Feelings of attachment are produced primarily by the hormones oxytocin and vaso-pressin, which at elevated levels can actually suppress the circuits for lust, says Fisher. Just as male hormones are subject to daily, even hourly fluctuations, female hormone levels rise and fall, though they follow the rhythm of the monthly cycle. When estrogen is predominant, Crenshaw says, "It's the Marilyn Monroe in us." It makes a woman ready and receptive for a man. It may also impair a woman's judgment slightly, and cause her to be less selective. Once she has ovulated, a woman "enters the proceptive or seductive nature of her sex drive."

It is normal, Crenshaw adds, for people to have different sex drives and different rhythms. One partner could be a morning person and the other could be an afternoon person, or they might feel desire on different days of the week. Unless a couple learns to handle, negotiate and make the best of different sex drives early on in their relationship, they're destined for problems. Sexual incompatibility is cited as a top reason for divorce in the United States.

Hormones and aging: Endocrinologists, who study the delicate balance of hormones, emphasize that there is no true male equivalent of menopause. While women's levels of the female hormone estro-gen plunge sharply over a relatively short period of time, falling to vestigial amounts, men almost never undergo as precipitous a change in concentrations of the male hormone testosterone.

Nevertheless, a number of recent studies have suggested that male testosterone levels do slump gradually with age, perhaps by as much as 30 to 40 percent between the ages of 48 and 70.

Most studies indicate that the testes, rather than the brain, are to blame for any testosterone decline with age, and that for unknown reasons the testicu-

---

ⓘ INSIDE INFO

The Effects of Sex

○ **Morning High:** Testosterone levels are highest in the early morning and lowest in the late afternoon and evening. October is the high point of the year for testosterone levels. February is the nadir.

○ **BiggerBreasts:** During intercourse, a woman's breast size may increase as much as 25 percent, and the nipples by 1 centimeter.

○ **Night Moves:** Average erections per night by age:

Young men:	4
Age 30-39:	3
Age 40-69:	2+
Age 70+:	1.7

○ **Peak Time:** Men reach their sexual peak at age 17 and slowly decline from there. Women are at their most receptive around age 40.

---

lar tissue becomes gradually less responsive to the tweak of pituitary hormones. As a result, sex drive diminishes and all the hormones and mechanisms that make erections predictably available become unpredictably available. The frequency of sex goes down, and some men are not able to have sex at all. For those for whom this becomes a problem, testosterone has been used to treat hypogonadism, low testosterone levels in men; but, as with the research on female hormones, the benefits and potential risks of male hormone therapy have yet to be thoroughly studied.

Almost all women can begin menopause as early as 40 and finish in their late 50s. The average age of women at menopause today is 51.4 years. Estrogen levels decrease and almost disappear after menopause. But testosterone, still present in small amounts in the female hormonal mix, may

The Ins and Outs of Birth Control

Better safe than dismayed

Birth control techniques don't work unless they're practiced consistently and correctly. The following efficacy rates are published by the Guttmacher Institute, a nonprofit corporation for reproductive health research, policy analysis and public education.

Understandably, when it comes to sexual intercourse, the stakes are high, because pregnancy is always a risk. Without contraception, some 85 percent of sexually active women would most likely become pregnant within a year. Here's a list of the most popular contraceptives, listed in descending order. (STD is an acronym for sexually transmitted disease.)

ORAL CONTRACEPTIVES:

91.3 to 99.7 percent effective

USE: Pill must be taken on daily schedule, regardless of the frequency of intercourse. Prescription.

RISKS: Water retention, weight gain, bleeding, breast tenderness, hypertension, mood change and nausea. In rare cases, blood clots, heart attacks, strokes. Not usually recommended for women who smoke, especially over age 35.

STD PROTECTION: Confers some protection against pelvic inflammatory disease.

TUBAL LIGATION (women):

99.5 percent effective

USE: A one-time procedure performed in an operating room. It requires the use of general anesthesia. Procedure is considered permanent but can sometimes be reversed.

RISKS: Pain, infection and, for tubal ligation, possible surgical complications and bleeding.

STD PROTECTION: None.

MALE CONDOM:

82.6 to 98 percent effective

USE: Applied immediately before intercourse; used only once and discarded. Effectiveness largely depends on proper, consistent use. Nonprescription.

RISKS: Rare irritation and allergic reactions.

---

become a more dominant presence than it was before, relative to the ratio of other hormones that previously dominated. That's why some women, as they age, develop mustaches and lower voices. The good aspect of the continued presence of female testosterone, however, is that it allows a woman to retain her sex drive, "I'm not so sure that sex drive diminishes when most people believe it does," says Fisher. "Show me a middle-aged woman who says she's lost her sex drive, and I'll bet if she got a new partner, who excited her, her neurochemical levels for lust and romantic love would shoot back up." For women who complain of low or no libido, prescriptions for testosterone creams, gels and other transdermal treatments have become the means of treatment.

—Camille Sweeney and Natalie Angier

Sex After Menopause

A variety of treatments for low libido

Many women report a gradual decline in sexual desire as they age. In a survey of 580 menopausal women conducted by SIECUS, the Sexuality Information and Education Council of the United States, 45 percent reported a decrease in sexual desire after menopause, 37 percent reported no change and 10 percent reported an increase.

Although individual experiences certainly vary, "Changes in arousal clearly are associated with menopause," according to a recent article in *The Journal of the American Medical Association*. The author, Dr. Jennifer E. Potter of Harvard Medical School and Beth Israel Deaconess Medical Center in Boston, said physical factors include less blood

STD PROTECTION: Latex condoms help protect against all sexually transmitted diseases, including herpes and HIV.

VASECTOMY (men):
99.8 to 99.9 percent effective

USE: A one-time procedure usually performed in a doctor's office under local anesthesia. Procedure is considered permanent but can sometimes be reversed.

RISKS: Pain, infection and, as with tubal ligation, possible surgical complications and bleeding.

STD PROTECTION: None.

INJECTION (women):
93.3 to 99.7 percent effective

USE: One injection every three months. Prescription.

RISKS: Amenorrhea, headache, nausea, weight gain.

STD PROTECTION: None.

WITHDRAWAL:
81.6 to 96 percent effective

USE: Withdrawal of penis before ejaculation.

STD PROTECTION: None.

COPPER T IUD:
99.4 to 99 percent effective;
MIRENA IUD:
99.9 percent effective

USE: After insertion, stays in until physician removes it. Can remain in place for 1 to 10 years, depending on the type. The IUD should only be used by women in monogamous relationships, because multiple partners may increase the risk of developing or aggravating pelvic inflammatory disease. Prescription.

RISKS: Cramps, bleeding, pelvic inflammatory disease.

STD PROTECTION: None.

PERIODIC ABSTINENCE:
25.3 percent effective or higher, depending on method

USE: Requires the woman to frequently monitor her body's functions and periods of abstinence; effectiveness depends on accurately predicting when ovulation will occur. Can be used in conjunction with barrier methods to increase effectiveness.

RISKS: None.

STD PROTECTION: None.

---

flow to genital organs, a decrease in vaginal lubrication and a decreased response to touch.

Women can achieve orgasm throughout their lives, but they typically need more direct, more intense and longer stimulation of the clitoris to reach a climax, Dr. Potter noted.

Another common experience is a diminished intensity of orgasm and painful uterine contractions after orgasm, although the women surveyed by SIECUS said overall that they remained satisfied with sex. Yet as Dr. Potter put it, "What might be a satisfying sexual life for one woman may seem woefully inadequate to another," adding that what a woman expects from her sex life can make a difference. She cited the findings of various large surveys: "Only one-third to one-half of women who report decreased desire or response believe they have a problem or feel distress for which they would like help."

So what happens to a woman's body when levels of sex hormones fall?

Although estrogen is a woman's predominant hormone before menopause, testosterone, produced in women primarily by the ovaries and adrenal glands, is considered the libido hormone for both men and women.

Testosterone levels in women decline by about 50 percent between the ages of 20 and 45, and the amount of testosterone produced continues to decline gradually as women age. While menopause itself has no direct effect on testosterone production, surgical removal of the ovaries can cause an abrupt drop in this hormone and accompanying sexual desire, especially for women who have not gone through natural menopause.

For some women, the increased ratio of testosterone to estrogen that occurs after menopause gives their sex drive a boost.

But for most women, the menopausal effects of low levels of estrogen are the primary deterrents to sexual pleasure. In addition to the infamous hot flashes, changes in the vagina and vulva can have serious effects on the sexual experience.

- With little or no estrogen, vaginal walls become dry, thin and less elastic, causing pain during penetration.
- Diminished blood flow to the genital area means it can take much longer for a woman to feel aroused.
- The anticipation of painful uterine contractions with orgasm can be a turnoff.
- A leakage of urine some women experience during sex can prompt them to avoid it.

Treatments: A prescription of the drug Estratest, which combines estrogen and testosterone, can solve some problems. But taking estrogen orally is not recommended for women who have had breast cancer or are at high risk for developing it. Also, to protect the uterus against cancer, estrogen should be combined with a progestin.

An alternative that works for some is vaginal application of a little estrogen via a cream, ring or tablet, which keeps the hormone from passing through the liver and diminishes the amount that enters the bloodstream.

Gynecologists concerned about safety are more likely to recommend a non-oil-based lubricant. Besides such popular products as K-Y jelly, doctors suggest several longer-lasting products that have an adhesive quality, including Replens, K-Y Long-Lasting Vaginal Moisturizer and Astroglide Silken Secret. Generally, women who have intercourse regularly seem to generate more lubrication than those who do it less frequently.

Infrequent intercourse or prolonged periods without it can result in a narrowing of the vagina that can be countered by the use of lubricated vaginal dilators. For women whose sex lives are disrupted by lack of a partner, some sex experts recommend self-stimulation. Dr. Potter suggested that even for women with partners, a vibrator or small battery-powered vacuum pump can aid in arousal.

While a Viagra-like drug is not yet an option for women, use of the antidepressant bupropion (Wellbutrin at 300 mg a day) may improve sexual arousal and satisfaction in women who are not depressed. Remaining physically fit can also help.

—Jane E Brody

Help for Sexual Dysfunction

What causes erectile dysfunction and how to treat it

In the past decades, there has been a revolution in the treatment of erectile dysfunction, the inability of the penis to develop and maintain an erection for satisfactory sexual intercourse or activity. Estimates of the prevalence of this dysfunction vary, ranging from about 5 percent of men in their 40s to over 50 percent in their 70s, depending in part on how the disorder is defined. An estimated 15 million to 30 million Americans have erectile problems. But a majority of men afflicted by them have never received a medical diagnosis of erectile dysfunction, and only a small fraction are being treated, experts report. Many men are too embarrassed to mention the problem to their doctors, and many doctors are equally reluctant to ask patients about it.

A man's ability to perform sexually can be impaired by a host of usually interrelated factors, including disorders that affect nerves, blood vessels or hormonal output; certain medications (both prescription and over the counter); diseases like diabetes, stroke, multiple sclerosis or epilepsy; aging; psychological problems like depression and performance anxiety; pelvic trauma, radiation or certain operations; and, of course, a loss of interest in one's sexual partner.

Risk factors for cardiovascular disease—hypertension, abnormal blood lipids, smoking and diabetes—are associated with an increased prevalence of erectile dysfunction, strongly suggesting that men seeking treatment first be evaluated for heart and blood vessel disease. This is best done with a full medical history,

measurement of blood pressure, blood sugar and blood lipids, and possibly a treadmill test. A cardiovascular assessment is especially important for men of middle age and older, since resumption of sexual activity after treatment can result in a heart attack in those unaccustomed to the exertion.

Insufficient testosterone is an uncommon cause of erectile dysfunction, affecting about 6 percent of men with this problem. Although giving testosterone to someone with a deficiency may not in itself correct the erectile problem, testosterone is the libido hormone for both men and women, and is an important stimulant of sexual desire.

To appreciate the value of the new drugs, it helps to understand how a normal erection occurs. It is important for men and their partners to understand that these drugs by themselves do not cause an erection or affect libido. They work only as a

---

ⓘ **INSIDE INFO**

How Sex Life Changes

A widely cited study by Edward O. Laumann, a University of Chicago sociology professor, and others, found that:

○ **By age 30** three-quarters of Americans are either married or living with someone, but they are starting to have "partnered sex" less often than people in their 20s.

○ **During their 30s** more people are having sex with a partner a few times a month, and fewer are having sex a few times a week.

○ **By their 40s** this disparity more than doubles for both men and women.

○ **All ages:** Forty-three percent of women reported some sexual dysfunction, the most prevalent being loss of libido.

—Camille Sweeney

IF YOU GET A SEXUALLY TRANSMITTED DISEASE: A QUICK PRIMER

Every year, approximately 15 million people contract a bacterial sexually transmitted disease (STD), such as syphilis or gonorrhea, or a viral sexually transmitted disease, like herpes. Following are descriptions of the most common STDs, along with some possible symptoms and treatments.

DISEASE HOW SPREAD	SYMPTOMS	TREATMENT
BACTERIAL VAGINOSIS Sexual intercourse, multiple partners, douching, using an IUD	Grayish vaginal discharge	Metronidazole, clindamycin
CHLAMYDIA Vaginal, oral, anal sex; mother to child during birth	Vaginal discharge, vaginal bleeding; burning during urination, discharge in men	Azithromycin, doxycycline, erythromycin (for pregnant women), chlortetracycline (for eyes)
CRABS Contact with infected person, using his/her clothes, towels or bedding	Intolerable itching in genital or other areas	Kwell lotion; clean clothes, towels and bedding
HUMAN PAPILLOMA VIRUS (HPV) Sexual intercourse, oral sex	Women: small, painless warts in labia, vulva, cervix or anus Men: warts on penis or scrotum	Laser beam; podophyllin, trichloracetic acid
GONORRHEA Sexual intercourse, oral sex; mother to child during birth; hand-to-eye contact	Thick, milky discharge; burning, painful urination; pain in lower abdomen, vomiting, rash, chills; fever, pain in wrists and extremities; almost all men show symptoms; women may be asymptomatic	Ceftriaxone, Ciprofloxacin

result of sexual stimulation. With sexual arousal, the penis must fill with blood, causing it to enlarge and become rigid. For as long as arousal persists, fibrous tissue in the penis preserves the erection by creating a cinch to prevent blood from leaving.

In addition to a receptive state of mind, adequate levels of testosterone and healthy blood vessels and nerves, an erection requires the chemical messenger nitric oxide. It plays two critical roles, transmitting arousal impulses between nerves, and relaxing the smooth muscles in arteries, allowing them to expand and fill with blood.

Nitric oxide signals production within artery cells of a chemical called cyclic guanosine mono-phosphate (cGMP), which increases blood flow to the penis. This chemical is broken down by another, phosphodiesterase-5 (PDE-5), to end the erection. The new drugs all work by inhibiting PDE-5, allowing cGMP to produce and sustain an erection. The erectile drugs come in various dosages, and if a low dose is not effective, a higher can often be tried. In men over 65, however, only the lowest dosages are recommended.

A MAN'S CHOICES

The new drugs for erectile dysfunction are revolutionary, because earlier treatments were more complicated. Here are some options.

DISEASE		
HOW SPREAD	SYMPTOMS	TREATMENT
GENITAL HERPES		
Sexual intercourse, oral sex	Tingling, itching in genital area, legs, buttocks; painful genital sores	Keep sores clean and dry; xylocaine, ethyl chloride may ease pain
HIV/AIDS		
Sexual intercourse, anal sex, blood transfusions, infected needles	Fatigue, weight loss, swollen glands, fever, night sweats, bronchial infections, sores, loss of appetite, trouble swallowing, recurrent yeast infections (women)	Protease inhibitors in combination with AZT and other drugs
NONGONOCOCCAL URETHRITIS		
Sexual intercourse	Often none; discharge from penis and inflamed urethra	Doxycycline, erythromycin
PELVIC INFLAMMATORY DISEASE (PID)		
Generalized infection of uterus from an STD	Fever, vaginal discharge, painful intercourse, painful urination	Antibiotics to treat specific infection
SCABIES		
Sexual contact, towels	Intense itching, red bumps on torso or hands	Permethrin, eurax
SYPHILIS		
Sexual or skin contact, mother to child at birth	Painless genital sore, rash, sore throat, swollen joints, aching bones, hair loss	Penicillin; tetracycline doxycycline
TRICHOMONIASIS		
Sexual contact	Women: yellow-green frothy discharge with strong odor, discomfort during intercourse, irritation and itching of genitals Men: mild discharge or slight burning after urination or ejaculation	One dose of metronidazole

Alprostadil. Must be administered directly into the urethra or injected into the penis. The injections, which are more effective, can help men with a variety of underlying causes, both psychological and physical. In one study, more than 80 percent of men and their partners reported satisfactory results.

Vacuum constrictor devices. Use vacuum pressure to promote blood flow into the penis and a constricting ring to keep the blood from escaping. Though it works in about two-thirds of cases, it does prevent ejaculation.

Prosthesis implantation. One kind is a semirigid rod that, in effect, creates a permanent erection, and the other is an inflatable device that can readily pump up the penis when sexual activity is desired.

Drugs such as Viagra, Cialis and Levitra. The three drugs are about equally effective, but there are differences in their actions. In general, the drugs should be taken about an hour before expected sexual activity, and none should be used more than once a day. Viagra is best taken on an empty stomach (dietary fat delays its effect by about an hour). Levitra and Cialis are not affected by food, but the blood level of Levitra is reduced by high-fat meals. None of the drugs should be taken with alcohol, though only Cialis is said to cause dizziness when combined with normal amounts of alcohol.

Viagra and Levitra are effective for about four hours; Cialis, for up to 36 hours. Viagra is most effective after an hour. Levitra may work within 20 minutes and Cialis within 45.

Side effects from these drugs are as follows: headache in 10 to 30 percent of patients; flushing in 10 to 20 percent; heartburn in 3 to 16 percent; runny nose in 1 to 11 percent; changes in color perception in 2 to 10 percent; muscle aches and back pain in up to 10 percent; and dizziness in up to 5 percent. There have also been more than three dozen cases of blindness reported in men taking Viagra and four cases in men taking Cialis. Likewise, deaths and nonfatal heart attacks have been reported in users, but no cause-and-effect evidence in either case has been shown. There are also possible serious interactions with other medications, like nitrates (including nitroglycerin pills, patches and pastes); alpha blockers for hypertension; protease inhibitors used in AIDS treatment; the antifungals ketoconazole and itraconazole; and the acid reducer cimetidine.

Several other drugs, including rifampin, carbamazepine and phenytoin, may decrease the effectiveness of the erectile drugs. In addition, patients should not take Levitra if they have a heart problem called prolonged QT syndrome.   —Jane E. Brody

---

Protecting Yourself from AIDS

There's still no cure for the disease, but much can be done to avoid contracting it

Acquired immune deficiency disease (AIDS) is caused by human immunodeficiency virus (HIV). It is spread through contact with infected body fluids such as blood and semen. Infected people may harbor the virus within their bodies for several years or even longer before develop-ing symptoms of AIDS. Though symptomless, they can still infect others. Worldwide, most HIV transmission occurs during sexual relations between heterosexual partners. In the United States, the majority of transmission has been between homosexual partners. Transmission among drug addicts who share infected needles is another significant route of transmission in many countries.

The surest way to avoid any risk of getting HIV/AIDS is to eschew sexual intercourse and never take intravenous drugs. HIV is spread primarily by sexual contact with an infected person, by sharing needles and/or syringes with someone who is infected or through transfusions of infected blood or blood clotting factors. Babies born to HIV-infected women may also become infected in the womb or through breastfeeding. The Centers for Disease Control provides some guidelines to prevent exposure.

How It Is–and Isn't–Transmitted

Kissing. Casual contact through closed-mouth or "social" kissing is not a risk for transmission of HIV. Because of the potential for contact with blood during "French" or open-mouth kissing, the C.D.C. recommends against engaging in this activity with a person known to be infected. However, the risk of acquiring HIV during open-mouth kissing is believed to be very low.

Biting. In 1997, the C.D.C. published findings from a state health department investigation of an incident that suggested blood-to-blood transmission of HIV by a human bite. There have been other reports in the medical literature in which HIV appeared to have been transmitted by a bite. Severe trauma with extensive tissue tearing and damage and presence of blood were reported in each of these instances. Biting is not a common way of transmitting HIV.

ⓘ **INSIDE INFO**

The AIDS Toll in the U.S.

○ Despite the significant medical advances in the treatments available, people are still getting sick with HIV/AIDS, and too many are still dying.

○ Listed below are the cumulative estimated numbers of diagnosed AIDS cases since the beginning of the epidemic in 1981, as well as the estimated number of diagnosed cases in the U.S. in 2007. The numbers are distributed according to the person's age at time of diagnosis.

AGE	Estimated # of AIDS Cases in 2007	Cumulative estimated # of AIDS Cases, through 2007*
Under 13:	28	9,209
Ages 13 to 14:	80	1,169
Ages 15 to 19:	455	6,089
Ages 20 to 24:	1,927	38,175
Ages 25 to 29:	3,380	120,464
Ages 30 to 34:	4,187	201,906
Ages 35 to 39:	5,888	219,601
Ages 40 to 44:	6,813	177,250
Ages 45 to 49:	5,749	112,896
Ages 50 to 54:	3,636	63,408
Ages 55 to 59:	2,040	34,160
Ages 60 to 64:	980	18,249
Ages 65 or older:	800	15,853

*Includes persons with a diagnosis of AIDS from the beginning of the epidemic through 2007.

SOURCE: Centers for Disease Control and Prevention

In fact, there are numerous reports of bites that did not result in HIV infection.

Saliva, tears and sweat. HIV has been found in saliva and tears in very low quantities from some AIDS patients. Finding a small amount of HIV in a body fluid, however, does not necessarily mean that HIV can be transmitted by that body fluid. HIV has not been recovered from the sweat of HIV-infected persons. Contact with saliva, tears or sweat has never been shown to result in transmission of HIV.

Insects. From the onset of the HIV epidemic, there has been concern about transmission of the virus by biting and bloodsucking insects. However, studies conducted by researchers at C.D.C. and elsewhere have shown no evidence of HIV transmission through insects—even in areas where there are many cases of AIDS and large populations of insects such as mosquitoes.

WHAT YOU CAN DO

Condoms. The proper and consistent use of latex or polyurethane (a type of plastic) condoms when engaging in sexual intercourse—vaginal, anal or oral—can greatly reduce a person's risk of acquiring or transmitting sexually transmitted diseases, including HIV infection.

There are many different types and brands of condoms available—however, only latex or polyurethane condoms provide a highly effective mechanical barrier to HIV. When condoms are used reliably, they have been shown to prevent pregnancy up to 98 percent of the time among couples using them as their only method of contraception. Similarly, numerous studies among sexually active people have demonstrated that a properly used latex condom provides a high degree of protection against a variety of sexually transmitted diseases, including HIV infection.

Skin penetration. Instruments that are intended to penetrate the skin (such as tattooing and acupuncture needles and ear-piercing devices) should be used once and disposed of or thoroughly cleaned and sterilized. Instruments not intended to penetrate the skin but which may become contaminated with blood (for example, razors) should be used for only one person and disposed of, or thoroughly cleaned and disinfected after each use.

The Search for an AIDS Vaccine

Most vaccines work by mimicking infection, which stimulates the body to make antibodies that kill the disease. But HIV infection generally does not produce those kinds of antibodies. HIV also mutates constantly and comes in many different varieties, factors that further complicate the search for a vaccine.

Many vaccines provide nearly 100 percent protection. But that's not on the horizon for AIDS, where 50 to 60 percent efficacy is still dreamed of. The best candidates in the vaccine pipeline right now—which won't be ready until 2013 at the earliest—wouldn't keep you from getting HIV They instead would seek to change your body's response to the virus so that if you did get infected, the disease would progress more slowly—or not at all—and you would be less infectious to others.

An efficacy rate of 50 to 60 percent is actually a lot better than it sounds, because of herd immunity. We get AIDS from one another. Every time a person is rendered less infectious, the chance of an uninfected person catching HIV from each sexual contact drops, and in a virtuous circle, the whole community becomes progressively safer. A vaccine of 50 to 60 percent efficacy might come close to wiping out the epidemic in places with low AIDS rates. In high-prevalence areas, it could reduce the epidemic and save millions of lives.

CIRCUMCISION AND AIDS. In 2006, a vaccine—of sorts—finally arrived when scientists announced that circumcision helps protect men from AIDS infection. For years, AIDS researchers had observed that many African tribes that circumcise boys or young men had lower AIDS rates than those that don't, and that Africa's Muslim nations, where circumcision is near universal, had far fewer AIDS cases than predominantly Christian ones. The first research proof came in 2005, when a study in South Africa was stopped early in the face of evidence that the men who had been randomly assigned to be circumcised were getting 60 percent fewer HIV infections than the men assigned to the control group. In 2006, ethics boards halted two similar studies, in Uganda and Kenya, when they found similar results. In both, the circumcised men caught the AIDS virus half as often as the uncircumcised control group.

In contrast to a vaccine, circumcision's origins are about as far from the laboratory as you can get. But the effects may be very similar to those of a vaccine. So far, we have proof only that circumcision protects the circumcised men. But there are strong indications that it also protects their sexual partners.

—Tina Rosenberg

If there is someone with an HIV infection in your house. Gloves should be worn during contact with blood or other body fluids that could possibly contain visible blood, such as urine, feces or vomit.

Cuts, sores or breaks on both the caregiver's and patient's exposed skin should be covered with bandages. Hands and other parts of the body should be washed immediately after contact with blood or other body fluids, and surfaces soiled with blood should be disinfected appropriately.

Practices that increase the likelihood of blood contact, such as sharing of razors and toothbrushes, should be avoided.

Needles and other sharp instruments should be used only when medically necessary and handled according to recommendations for health care settings. Do not put caps back on needles by hand or remove needles from syringes. Dispose of needles in puncture-proof containers.

SOURCE: Centers for Disease Control and Prevention

Abortion: Facts and Figures

Despite restrictions, they are easy to obtain

More than 45 million Americans have had abortions since the Supreme Court handed down Roe v. Wade, the 1973 decision that made abortion legal, according to the Guttmacher Institute, which provides statistics on reproductive matters. Abortion cuts across all income levels, religions, races, lifestyles, political parties and marital circumstances and remains one of the most common surgical procedures for women in America. More than one in five pregnancies ends in abortion.

As of 2008, states have enacted 581 laws restricting patients or providers, in many cases calling for mandatory counseling, waiting periods and parental consent for minors, according to Naral Pro-Choice America. The result is a patchwork of laws and regulations that vary from state to state. In surveys, Americans largely support these restrictions, even if they say abortion should be legal.

As laws have become more restrictive, technology has gone the other way, making abortions possible both earlier and later in pregnancy, and by pill or surgery. Doctors can perform abortions as early as 8 days after conception, and 59 percent of women having abortions do so within 8 weeks, according to government data.

Through the first 56 days of pregnancy, there are two options for ending a pregnancy: medication abortion or abortion by vacuum aspiration. After 56 days, vacuum aspiration is the only abortion option through the end of the first trimester.

Fewer than 1 percent of women have abortions after 20 weeks. A late-term procedure called intact dilation and extraction, sometimes known as "partial-birth" abortion, accounted for less than two-tenths of 1 percent of all abortions in 2000.

The early-abortion drug mifepristone, sold as Mifeprex and sometimes called RU-486, is another option. Mifepristone is given in conjunction with a second pill, misoprostol, usually over 2 or 3 days, and requires a follow-up exam with a doctor.

There has been concern, however, because a number of women who took Mifepex subsequently died of a systemic infection from a virulent form of bacteria that infect the bloodstream.

—John Leland

Options for the Morning After

How to avoid pregnancy after unprotected sex

To err is very human, especially when it comes to sexual intercourse. There are currently two types of emergency contraception for unprotected sex: pills and an emergency IUD. These are for emergencies only, and are not recommended as an alternative form of birth control.

PILLS, OR ECPs: *75 to 89 percent effective if started within 72 hours after unprotected vaginal intercourse.*

USE: Some ECPs are combination pills, with estrogen and progestin; others are progestin only. Taken by mouth in one or two doses after unprotected sex, these drugs stop the release of an egg from an ovary, may prevent the union of sperm and egg and may prevent a fertilized egg from attaching to the womb. In 2009, Plan B, a combination pill, was made available over the counter to anyone 17 or older. The pill's manufacturer claims that it is effective at stopping seven out of eight pregnancies.

RISKS: Nausea, vomiting and cramping.

EMERGENCY IUD INSERTION: *99.9 percent effective within 5 days of unprotected intercourse.*

USE: Insertion of IUD by a clinician to prevent implantation of any egg that may have been fertilized.

RISKS: Same as those from using IUDs for ongoing contraception.

SOURCE: Planned Parenthood Federation of America, Inc.

Doctors & Medicine

Where to Find a Good Doctor

The best place to search may be online

Consumers commonly turn to the Internet to research their own medical symptoms, but many are now taking the next step: comparisonshopping online for hospitals and doctors.

So far the various consumer databases, many available only to individuals enrolled in insurance plans, have some gaps. At this point there is much more quality-of-care information available about hospitals than about individual doctors, except in states, including Florida, Pennsylvania and Wisconsin, that make statistics available on the

---

✔ TIMELY TIPS

Docs Who Make House Calls

If you are willing to pay the money, you can procure the services of a new breed, the "concierge" or "boutique" doctors, who lavish time, phone calls and attention on patients, using the latest in electronic communications to streamline their care.

✔ These doctors charge fees as high as $10,000 a year, depending on the services promised. The majority charge $1,500 to $2,000.

✔ Basic services consist of same-day or next-day appointments and 24-hour telephone access to the doctor. The most expensive may also promise the doctor will make home visits, deliver medications and accompany patients on visits to other doctors.

—Abigail Zuger

---

numbers of procedures that surgeons perform. And pricing information still tends to be scarce. But the databases can grow only more robust, now that the full weight of the health insurance industry is behind the trend and the federal government is beginning to wield its influence.

Anyone, insured or not, can log on to a federal Department of Health and Human Services Web site called Hospital Compare (hospitalcompare. hhs.gov), which uses Medicare and Medicaid data to assess the track records of more than 4,000 hospitals around the country. Want to know which hospitals in your city to go to for treating heart attacks or pneumonia? Log on to Hospital Compare, plug in the step-by-step particulars and judge for yourself, based on criteria that include whether the hospitals provide appropriate medicines when patients are admitted and discharged.

Private health plans typically provide more comparative data than the federal Web site. Wellpoint, the nation's largest commercial health insurer, allows its millions of members to log on to an expanded list of health care information services, which includes software to help members compare their own potential costs under various health plans. Besides Wellpoint, most of the big insurance companies—including United Healthcare, Aetna and Cigna, as well as many state and regional Blue Cross and Blue Shield insurers—provide this type of information.

The raw material for the information on the Web systems is typically assembled from data that include medical payment claims, hospitals' reports to Medicare and health care information from employers.

—Milt Freudenheim

The Doctor Is Online

Here's a selective list of some of the best health and medical information Web sites. In addition, you can find links organized by diseases at www.nytimes.com/library/national/science/health/health-navigator.html.

Agency for Healthcare Research and Quality. Compare the quality of health plans: *www.talkingquality.gov/compendium/index.html*

American Board of Medical Specialties. Find a doctor's certification: *www.abms.org*

American Medical Association. Search for data on a doctor's training and any disciplinary action; go to "About AMA" and click on "Physician Data": *www.ama-assn.org*

Association of Online Cancer Resources. Tracks cancer developments: *www.acor.org*

C.D.C. National Prevention Information Network. HIV, STD and TB info from the Centers for Disease Control: *www.cdcnpin.org*

Columbia University's Complete Home Medical Guide. *www.cumc.columbia.edu/health/index.html*

Foundation for Informed Medical Decision Making. Get involved in the decision-making process: *informedmedicaldecisions.org.*

Go Ask Alice. Health Q and A's from Columbia University: *www.goaskalice.columbia.edu*

Hardin Meta Directory of Internet Health Sources. From the University of Iowa: *www.lib.uiowa.edu/hardin/md/index.html*

Hospital Compare. Pick three local hospitals and compare quality factors: *www.hospitalcompare.hhs.gov*

Innerbody.com. Interactive guide to human anatomy: *www.innerbody.com*

Intelihealth. Features health info from Harvard Medical School: *www.intelihealth.com*

Martindale's Health Science Guide. Links to scientific and medical sources: *www.martindalecenter.com/HSguide*

Mayo Clinic. A wealth of medical data: *www.mayoclinic.com*

Medem. Info from numerous medical societies: *www.medem.com*

Medical Library Association. A guide to the Web's offerings: *www.mlanet.org/resources/userguide.html*

Medical Matrix. Medical search engine: *www.medmatrix.org*

Medicine.net. Info provided by doctors: *www.medicinenet.com*

Medline Plus. The latest on health, drugs and news: *www.medlineplus.gov*

Medscape. Up-to-date medical news for doctors and patients: *www.medscape.com*

National Alliance of Breast Cancer Organizations: *www.nabco.org*

National Library of Medicine. From the National Institutes of Health: *www.nlm.nih.gov*

Nutrient database from the U.S.D.A.: *www.nal.usda.gov/fnic/foodcomp/search*

Oncolink. Cancer information from the University of Pennsylvania Cancer Center: *www.oncolink.com*

Pregnancy and Parenting iVillage. Articles and advice for parents and those who want to be: *www.parenting.ivillage.com*

Pubmed. Medline and other journal searches: *www.ncbi.nlm.nih.gov/pubmed/*

Rate MDs. Allows patients to rate and review their doctors: *www.ratemds.com*

RxList: The Internet Drug Index. Pharmaceutical data: *www.rxlist.com*

University of Wisconsin Comprehensive Cancer Center. *www.uwhealth.org*

WebMD. Reliable and timely medical news: *www.webmd.com*

Yahoo Health. Info on diet, fitness, diseases, etc.: *www.health.yahoo.com*

Talking with Your Doctor

How to get the best care from your physician

During the years he served as surgeon general, C. Everett Koop became a household name and something of a media star as he made health issues a national topic. After leaving Washington, he founded the C. Everett Koop Institute at Dartmouth College, which develops programs to teach young people about health issues. In this conversation, held in the late 1990s, he offers timeless advice about how to go about finding a good doctor.

Q How should patients choose a doctor?

With a large percentage of the country now in managed care, most people don't have much choice. But if you do have a choice of doctors, one of the things people find most helpful is getting referrals from patients who are satisfied with their doctor. If a doctor doesn't listen to you or doesn't communicate, that's not a doctor to seek out unless there's something very special about him and his knowledge.

ⓘ INSIDE INFO

The Doctor Is In–for a Moment

○ Patients, on average, have 18 seconds to talk to a doctor before they are interrupted. Women doctors interrupt at the same rate as men.

○ Dr. Richard Frankel, a professor of medicine and geriatrics at Indiana University, recommends that patients decide ahead of time what they want to convey and deflect interruptions to say it. He also suggests that patients take a list of their complaints and ask the doctor to staple it to their chart. That way, Dr. Frankel says, the doctor almost always addresses them.

—Gina Kolata

Q How can patients determine whether their doctor is qualified to treat their condition, or whether they need to see a specialist?

It depends on your confidence in your doctor. You don't have to know everything to be able to do the right thing. It's those tricky situations where a difference of opinion can make a real difference in the patient's quality of life, or even life itself. Sometimes people understand by attitude, innuendo and body language what their doctor's comfort level is with what he's telling them and whether he is qualified to treat them in that instance.

Q What if you do need a specialist?

If your primary care physician thinks you should see a specialist, ask whether this person has board certification—which means he has passed an exam recognizing his expertise in a particular field of medicine. If you visit the doctor you've been referred to and he says, "You ought to have X, Y and Z done," you say, "Are there other options?" When he answers, ask, "How often have you done X, Y and Z, and what are the results?" The more that patients ask, the more honesty they're going to get from physicians.

Q Is there any statistically reliable way to gauge a physician's skill?

In many places now, the batting average of doctors and hospitals in the management of certain problems is being made available. In several states, doctors who do open heart surgery are not only listed with their mortality rate overall, but also their mortality rate in different hospitals where they work. You have pretty good objective evidence, all based on the same kind of statistics. Say your cardiologist says that there are three surgeons to consider in your town, and you can see that one has a 95 percent success rate, one a 92 percent rate and one 89 percent. That gives you a place to go. You then can talk to the doctor with the lowest rating, and he may say, "I'm different from the other two because I take every patient that comes my way, and sometimes I take very high-risk patients, and of course they tend to have more problems than the others, while my competitor only takes patients that he knows he's going to succeed with." There are ways you can ferret out the answers you want, but it takes digging.

💬 When do you advise getting a second opinion?

Second opinions are very important for surgical procedures, especially those that even the laity knows are not always successful, like operations for lower back pain. Then there are the situations where one doctor says you need your gallbladder out and "I can do that through three little incisions with a laparoscope and you'll be out the next day." Another doctor says, "You need an old-fashioned surgical procedure." Then another opinion is necessary. Insurance companies are willing to pay for second opinions, because if the second opinion is not to have surgery and the patient believes it, they save money.

💬 What questions should patients ask before undergoing surgery?

Ask about your particular situation and why it's absolutely necessary to have surgery. Then ask about the risk versus the benefit, and whether you have something that is premalignant or just a nuisance. If you ask questions like this, you can weigh whether the surgery's risk is relatively small and is worth the benefit. I don't think patients should think about the economics of it if it's at all possible to do so.

💬 Should patients in an H.M.O. question a decision not to treat their condition?

They have every right to. One of the sad things about managed care is that in some systems the physician gets docked for doing too

---

ⓘ INSIDE INFO

Who's at Risk for Disease

○ The more education and income people have, the less likely they are to have and die of heart disease, strokes, diabetes and many types of cancer.

○ Upper-middle-class Americans live longer and in better health than middle-class Americans, who live longer and better than those at the bottom. And the gaps are widening, say people who have researched social factors in health.

○ Smoking has dropped sharply among the better educated, but not among the less.

○ Physical inactivity is more than twice as common among high school dropouts as among college graduates. Lower-income women are more likely than other women to be overweight, though the pattern among men may be the opposite.

○ The risk factors for a heart attack—smoking, poor diet, inactivity, obesity, hypertension, high cholesterol and stress—are all more common among the less educated and less affluent, the same group that is less likely to receive cardiopulmonary resuscitation, to get emergency room care or to adhere to lifestyle changes after heart attacks.

—Janny Scott

---

much—if he has too many referrals, if his prescriptions are too expensive, if he is seeing too many patients for 20 minutes instead of 15. It's the same thing for a test. If a doctor says, "You ought to have a stress test," you should say, "Doctor, talk to me about why you think it's important that I should have the test." But that demands a frankness with doctors that patients are frequently loath to show.

HEALTH

Men, Women and Heart Disease

The symptoms are different for men and women

Heart disease, strokes and other cardiovascular diseases are the leading causes of death in the United States and other developed countries. They kill about one million people in the United States every year; more than half the deaths are among women. But scientists have only recently started to explore the differences in heart disease in men and women. Among them:

- Women with heart disease tend to be sicker than men by the time it is diagnosed.

- Women tend to benefit less from bypass surgery and to have more severe symptoms when they develop heart failure. Some of the difference is because women are older and frailer when they develop heart disease.

- Symptoms of heart attack tend to differ between men and women. Men report crushing pain in the chest, while women are more likely to feel dizzy, sick, short of breath and sweaty.

- Women are more likely than men to have a hidden type of coronary disease in which their heart muscle is starved for oxygen, even though their coronary arteries look clear and free of blockages on X-rays. The condition, which may affect three million American women, greatly increases the risk of a heart attack. Its main symptom is chest pain or discomfort. In many women, the pain occurs but nothing shows up on an angiogram, a test in which dye is injected into the coronary arteries and they are X-rayed in a search for blockages, so doctors conclude that no treatment is needed.

- Overall death rates from coronary disease have declined in the past few decades, but most of the improvements have been in men's rates.

—Denise Grady

● **TIMELY TIPS**

When Seconds Count

✔ Heart attack victims are less likely to die in hospitals where angioplasty is the usual emergency treatment rather than clot-destroying drugs, according to a large study, reported in *Circulation*.

✔ Dr. Harlan M. Krumholz, the senior author of the report and a professor of medicine at Yale, says that if he lived 10 minutes from a hospital that provided angioplasty and 10 minutes from one that provided only the drug treatment, he would "choose the one that did the invasive procedure every time." Still, Dr. Krumholz emphasizes that practical limits must be considered.

Why Every Stroke Matters

Paying attention to early warning signs could save your life

If you have a T.I.A.—a transient ischemic attack, commonly called a mini-stroke, a brief episode when blood is cut off to your brain—you should take it seriously. Although the blockage is brief and no detectable brain damage or symptoms persist, such attacks are often the warning sign for a major stroke. Most of these attacks occur in people over 60, and some of them may incorrectly dismiss the short-lived symptoms as merely another sign of age. As a result, it is critically important for someone with such an attack to get prompt medical attention and treatment to prevent a far more serious blockage to the brain.

✓ TIMELY TIPS

Handicapping Your Mini-Stroke

Oxford and Edinburgh university researchers reporting in the journal *The Lancet* recommend this scoring system—called ABCD—that can help predict the risk of a stroke within a week of a transient ischemic attack (T.I.A.):

✓ **A for age 60 or older,** 1 point.

✓ **B for blood pressure,** systolic (the top number) greater than 140 millimeters of mercury, diastolic equal to or greater than 90 millimeters or both, 1 point.

✓ **C for clinical features,** weakness on one side, 2 points; speech disturbance without weakness, 1 point.

✓ **D for duration of symptoms** in minutes, 60 or more, 2 points; 10 to 59, 1 point.

✓ The risk of suffering a stroke within 7 days of a T.I.A. was 0.4 percent among patients scoring fewer than 5 points; 12.1 percent for those who scored 5 points; and 31.4 percent for those who scored 6 points.

✓ The early risk of stroke of about 30 percent in T.I.A. patients with an ABCD score of 6 necessitates not only emergency investigation and treatment but also admission to a hospital.

Symptoms. Stroke symptoms occur suddenly, without warning or any precipitating event, and they can vary widely from patient to patient. The symptoms usually last from only minutes to an hour or two, and the patient generally recovers as if nothing happened.

- Confusion, slurred or garbled speech or difficulty understanding
- Numbness, weakness or paralysis in the face, arm or leg, especially on one side of the body
- Blindness in one or both eyes or double vision
- Trouble walking, dizziness, loss of balance or coordination
- Severe headache with no known cause

Diagnosis. Among the tests that can help in diagnosis are a sonogram of the carotid arteries to look for narrowing or clogging of these crucial blood vessels; C.T. scan or M.R.I. of the brain; C.T. angiogram or M.R.I. angiogram to evaluate the arteries in the neck and brain; and possibly a transesophageal echocardiogram to obtain detailed images of the heart to look for things like blood clots.

Treatment. Most commonly, patients are prescribed one of two types of medication—anti-platelet drugs or anti-coagulants—to prevent excessive clotting of the blood.

The most common anti-platelet medication is aspirin, usually one 325 mg tablet a day. Another is clopidogrel (trade name Plavix), which may be used in combination with aspirin.

Anti-coagulants are trickier and require careful monitoring to be sure that the clotting potential is not excessively reduced—a reaction that can cause hemorrhaging. The two anti-coagulants commonly used are warfarin (Coumadin) and heparin.

If one or both carotid arteries are found to be seriously narrowed, surgical removal of the plaque or insertion of a stent to expand the arterial opening may be the recommended therapy.

Researchers point out that even if preventive measures fail to head off a stroke in such patients, the fact that they are in the hospital means that immediate treatment can dissolve the blood clot in the brain and stem the extent and the residual effects of a stroke.   —Jane E. Brody

How to Avoid a Heart Attack

Statins can help, but can they prolong lives?

Statins are among the most prescribed drugs in the world, and there is no doubt that they work as advertised—they not only lower cholesterol but also the risk for heart attack.

But many people are asking a more fundamental question about statins in general: do they prolong your life? For many users, the surprising answer appears to be no.

Some patients do receive significant benefits from statins, like Lipitor (from Pfizer), Crestor (AstraZeneca) and Pravachol (Bristol-Myers Squibb). In studies of middle-aged men with cardiovascular disease, statin users were less likely to die than those who were given a placebo. But many statin users don't have established heart disease; they simply have high cholesterol. For healthy men, for women with or without heart disease and for people over 70, there is little evidence, if any, that taking a statin will make a meaningful difference in how long they live. "High-risk groups have a lot to gain," says Dr. Mark H. Ebell, a professor at the University of Georgia who is deputy editor of the journal *American Family Physician.* "But patients at low risk benefit little if at all. We end up over-treating a lot of patients."

How is this possible, if statins lower the risk of heart attack? Because preventing a heart attack is not the same thing as saving a life. In many statin studies that show lower heart attack risk, the same number of patients end up dying, whether they are taking statins or not. "You may have helped the heart, but you haven't helped the patient,"

> ❝
>
> **High-risk groups have a lot to gain, but patients at low risk benefit very little if at all. We end up over-treating a lot of patients.**
>
> • • •

says Dr. Beatrice Golomb, an associate professor of medicine at the University of California, San Diego and co-author of an editorial in *The Journal of the American College of Cardiology* questioning the data on statins. "You still have to look at the impact on the patient overall."

A 2006 study in *The Archives of Internal Medicine* looked at seven trials of statin use in nearly 43,000 patients, mostly middle-aged men without heart disease. In that review, statins didn't lower mortality. Nor did they in a study called Prosper, published in *The Lancet* in 2002, which studied statin use in people 70 and older. Nor did they in a 2004 review in *The Journal of the American Medical Association*, which looked at 13 studies of nearly 20,000 women, both healthy and with established heart disease.

A pharmaceutical company official notes that a decline in heart disease death rates, reported recently by the American Heart Association suggests that medications like statins are having an impact. But to consistently show a mortality benefit from statins in a research setting would take years of study. "We've concentrated on whether Lipitor reduces the risk of heart attacks and strokes," says Halit Bander, medical team leader for Lipitor. "We've proven that again and again."

In 2008, *The Journal of the American College of Cardiology* published a report combining data from several studies of people 65 and older who had a prior heart attack or established heart disease. This "meta-analysis" showed that 18.7 percent of the placebo users died during the studies, compared with 15.6 percent of the statin users. This translates into a 22 percent lower mortality risk for high-risk patients over 65. A co-author of the

Attention Acetaminophen Users

A popular pain killer can damage your liver

The drug acetaminophen is best known under the brand name Tylenol. But many consumers don't realize that it is also found in widely varying doses in several hundred common cold remedies and combination pain relievers. These compounds include Excedrin, Midol Teen Formula, Theraflu, Alka-Seltzer Plus Cold Medicine, and NyQuil Cold and Flu, as well as other over-the-counter drugs and many prescription narcotics, like Vicodin and Percocet.

The combination of acetaminophen's quiet ubiquity in over-the-counter remedies and its pairing with narcotics in potentially addictive drugs can make it too easy for some patients to swallow much more than the maximum recommended dose inadvertently, according to a study appearing in *Hepatology*. "It's extremely frustrating to see people come into the hospital who felt fine several days ago, but now need a new liver," says Dr. Tim Davern, one of the authors and a gastroenterologist with the liver transplant program of the University of California at San Francisco. The numbers of poisonings, however, are still tiny in comparison with the millions of people who use over-the-counter and prescription drugs with acetaminophen.

—Deborah Franklin

study, Dr. Jonathan Afilalo, a cardiology fellow at McGill University in Montreal, says that for every 28 patients over 65 with heart disease who take statins, one life will be saved. "If a patient has had a heart attack," Dr. Afilalo says, "they generally should be on a statin."

Of course, prolonging life is not the only measure that matters. If preventing a heart attack improves the quality of life, that would be an argument for taking statins even if it didn't reduce

mortality. But critics say there's no evidence that statin users have a better quality of life than other people. "If you can show me one study that people who have a disability from their heart are worse off than people who have a disability from other causes, I would find that a compelling argument," Dr. Golomb says. "There's not a shred of evidence that you've mitigated suffering in the groups where there is not a mortality benefit."

One big concern is that the side effects of statins haven't been well studied. Reported side effects include muscle pain, cognitive problems and impotence. "Statins have side effects that are underrated," says Dr. Uffe Ravnskov, a retired Swedish physician and a vocal critic of statins. "It's much more frequent and serious than has been reported." Dr. Ebell acknowledges that there are probably patients with heart disease who could benefit from a statin but who aren't taking it. But he added, "There are probably more of the opposite—patients who are taking a statin when they probably don't need one."

—Tara Parker-Pope

Dealing with Diabetes

It's incurable, but there are ways to prevent and control it

Nearly 24 million Americans are believed to be diabetic, according to the Centers for Disease Control, and at least 57 million are at risk of developing diabetes. Here are some facts and figures.

What diabetes is. Type-1 and Type-2 diabetes are diseases in which the amount of sugar in the blood rises to dangerous levels. Neither is truly curable. Type-2 is more prevalent, representing more than 90 percent of all cases. In Type-1, a gland, the pancreas, no longer produces insulin because the

INSIDE INFO

Let the Patient Beware

○ The authors of the guidelines widely used to establish standards for prescribing medicines are often paid by the drug companies whose products they discuss.

○ A study by the journal *Nature* found that more than one-third of the guideline authors acknowledged some financial interest in the drugs they recommended.

○ In half of the more than 200 guidelines examined, at least one author had received research financing from a relevant company, and 43 percent had at least one author who had been a paid speaker for the company.

○ Thirty-four percent of guidelines explicitly stated that their authors had no conflicts of interest at all. Almost half the published guidelines included no information about potential conflicts.

—Nicholas Bakalar

immune system has destroyed the cells that make it. Thus sugar builds up in the blood, causing internal damage, while cells starve. In Type-2, the body can generally produce insulin, but the diabetic's cells cannot properly use it. In some Type-2 cases, insulin production is insufficient. (A third type, gestational diabetes, afflicts a small number of pregnant women. It usually vanishes after the birth, though it increases the woman's risk of developing Type-2.)

How people get it and how it's treated. The cause of diabetes remains unclear. Type-1 typically surfaces in childhood and is believed to stem from genetic factors activated by an environmental trigger, like a virus. Type-1 diabetics require daily insulin injections to live. Traditionally, Type-2 appears in people over 40. Its onset is also tied to genetics, but is linked to obesity and inactivity as well. Researchers agree that in many cases the disease can be delayed, and possibly prevented, through exercise and weight loss. However, people typically have Type-2 for 7 to 10 years before it is diagnosed, by which time its untreated presence will often have led to complications. Type-2 diabetics typically take medicines that improve responsiveness to insulin and stimulate the pancreas to make more of it.

Who gets diabetes. African-Americans and Latinos, particularly Mexican-Americans and Puerto Ricans, incur diabetes at close to twice the rate of whites. Some Asian-Americans and Pacific Islanders also appear more prone, and they can develop the disease at much lower weights. The velocity of new cases among all races has accelerated significantly from just a few decades ago. Genetics cannot explain this surge, because the human gene pool does not change that fast. Instead, the culprit is thought to be behavior: faulty diet and inactivity.

Why doctors are worried. So-called Type-2 diabetes, the predominant form, is becoming a childhood disease, almost unheard of two decades ago.

• One in three children born in the United States 5 years ago is expected to become diabetic in his/her lifetime, according to a projection by the Centers for Disease Control and Prevention. The forecast is even bleaker for Latinos: one in every two.

• The American Diabetes Association says the disease could actually lower the average life expectancy of Americans for the first time in more than a century.

• Even among Americans who know they have the disease, about two-thirds are not doing enough to treat it.

• Diabetics are two to four times more likely than

others to develop heart disease or have a stroke, and three times more likely to die of complications from flu or pneumonia, according to the Centers for Disease Control.

- Most diabetics suffer nervous-system damage and poor circulation, which can lead to amputations of toes, feet and entire legs. According to the federal Agency for Healthcare Research and Quality, some 70 percent of lower-limb amputations in 2003 were performed on diabetics. Studies suggest that as many as 70 percent of amputees die within 5 years.

- Women with diabetes are at higher risk for complications in pregnancy, including miscarriages and birth defects. Men with diabetes run a higher risk of impotence. Diabetes is the principal reason adults go blind. Young adults with diabetes have twice the chance of getting gum disease and losing teeth.

—N. R. Kleinfield

The ABCs of Breast Cancer

Knowing the risk factors will cut your risk

After lung cancer, breast cancer is the second largest cause of cancer death in women aged 40 to 55, and the disease also afflicts a small number of men. Marilyn Leitch, professor of surgical oncology and medical director of the Southwestern Center for Breast Care, explains the risks, the precautions that should be followed and the treatment options that are available.

● What are the symptoms of the disease?

The most common symptom is a painless mass found during a breast self-exam. Less common signs are nipple discharge, a change in the appearance of the skin on the breast, such as redness or nipple dimpling, or a lump or swelling under the arm.

● Who is most at risk of breast cancer?

All women are at risk of breast cancer. Breast cancer only rarely occurs in men. Advancing age is the most important risk factor—the older a woman gets, the more likely she is to get breast cancer. Roughly 77 percent of women diagnosed with breast cancer in a given year are over age 50.

● Are there other factors that predispose a woman to developing breast cancer?

They include a prior personal diagnosis of breast cancer or a family history of breast cancer (the closer

---

ⓘ INSIDE INFO

Foods to Fight Cancer

○ A decade after the American Institute for Cancer Research issued its first major report on diet and cancer, a recent major study in concert with the World Cancer Research Fund based on 7,000 studies of 17 kinds of cancer, concluded that being overweight now ranks second only to smoking as a preventable cause of cancer.

○ "Convincing evidence" of an increased risk resulting from body fatness was found for cancers of the kidney, endometrium, breast, colon and rectum, pancreas and esophagus.

○ Other major findings of increased risk included red and processed meats for colon and rectal cancer and alcoholic drinks for cancers of the mouth, throat, larynx, esophagus, breast and colon and rectum.

○ "Convincing evidence" for cancer protection was found for physical activity against colon and rectal cancers and against breast cancer. "Probable" protection against various cancers was also found for dietary fiber; nonstarchy vegetables; fruits; foods rich in folates, beta-carotene, vitamin C and selenium; milk; and calcium supplements. —Jane E. Brody

the relative is, the greater the risk). Having a breast biopsy in the past which shows abnormal changes in the breast's fibrocystic tissue (such as atypia), menstruating at an early age or having a late menopause, never having a baby and getting pregnant for the first time after age 30 are also risk factors.

What can one do to detect breast cancer early?

Detecting breast cancer involves a three-pronged approach. The most important emphasis is placed on having mammograms, since a mammogram can find the smallest of breast cancers. However, women often find the cancer by self-exam. All women—with or without risk factors—should be aware of their breasts so that they can recognize a lump. Performing breast self-exams every month beginning at age 20 is a good way to become familiar with what is normal for you.

It's ideal to do the exam about 5 to 7 days after the menstrual period starts, when breasts are the least tender or full. Postmenopausal women should perform self-exams at the same time each month. Statistically, most women aren't going to detect any abnormalities, but if something seems out of the ordinary, you'll be able to detect it because you'll be familiar with how the breast tissue feels. Examination by a health care professional can also help detect breast cancer. An exam should be performed at least every 3 years starting at age 20 and every year starting at age 40. A clinical breast exam may be recommended more frequently if you have a strong family history of breast cancer.

What is a mammogram? Is the procedure safe?

A mammogram is an X-ray of the breast that can detect smaller tumors before they can be felt in physical exams. The theoretic risk of radiation is extremely low compared to the risk of getting breast cancer. Today, the technical aspects of doing mammograms have become very rigorous, and women are only exposed to very low doses of radiation. In addition, the Mammography Qual-

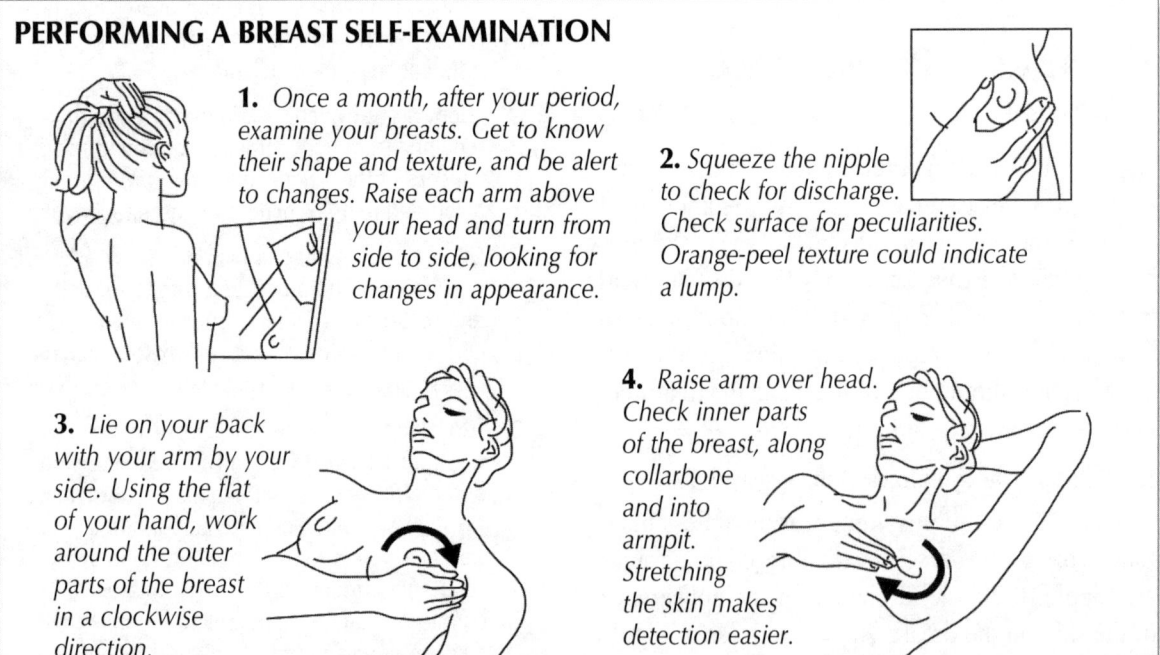

PERFORMING A BREAST SELF-EXAMINATION

1. *Once a month, after your period, examine your breasts. Get to know their shape and texture, and be alert to changes. Raise each arm above your head and turn from side to side, looking for changes in appearance.*

2. *Squeeze the nipple to check for discharge. Check surface for peculiarities. Orange-peel texture could indicate a lump.*

3. *Lie on your back with your arm by your side. Using the flat of your hand, work around the outer parts of the breast in a clockwise direction.*

4. *Raise arm over head. Check inner parts of the breast, along collarbone and into armpit. Stretching the skin makes detection easier.*

ity Standards Act, which requires mammography facilities to be certified by the Food and Drug Administration, ensures that high-quality equipment and technicians are used.

How much do mammograms cost?

A diagnostic mammogram costs more than a screening mammogram, because it requires more work on the part of the technician and the radiologist. Costs of mammograms vary by the technique, whether it is digital or analog and whether computer-aided detection (CAD) is added to the radiologist's reading. A screening digital mammogram with CAD costs around $300, and a diagnostic digital mammogram may cost around $350, although the price varies, depending on where you are in the country. Mammograms performed on analog machines with standard X-ray films and without CAD are significantly less expensive, $125 to $150.

What does it mean if a woman finds a lump during a self-exam?

Sometimes a lump is just a thickening in the breast tissue that does not need further treatment. But all women who find a lump should have it checked by their primary care doctor to determine whether it's a dominant mass. If it is, women should have a mammogram and/or an ultrasound to evaluate the lump. If it is a fluid-filled cyst, the fluid can be removed with a needle, and the lump goes away. If it is a solid lump, a needle biopsy can be done and the cells examined under a microscope to determine if the lump is benign or malignant.

What are the treatment options once you're diagnosed with breast cancer?

Most women with breast cancer are candidates for a breast-saving surgery called lumpectomy, which involves removing the cancerous tumor in the breast, then getting radiation treatment to the breast.

HEALTH

ⓘ INSIDE INFO

Mammograms

○ Film mammography, a filmed image produced by very low dosage X-rays, is not perfect. A recent study showed that 10 to 20 percent of breast cancers detected by a physical exam were missed by a film mammogram. Yet none of the alternatives have yet been as thoroughly vetted in terms of lives saved.

○ In a study by the National Cancer Institute, digital mammograms were found to be better than film mammograms at detecting cancer among three groups of women: those with very dense breasts, as determined by their doctors; women under 50, whatever their breast density; and women of any age who were premenopausal or who had had at least one menstrual period within 12 months of the last mammogram.

—Deborah Franklin

The other option for treatment is a mastectomy, which involves removing the entire breast. Breast reconstruction can often be performed immediately, if the woman chooses. With both procedures, the lymph nodes under the arm must be checked to see if cancer has spread. In recent years, this is being done with a minimally invasive technique called sentinel node biopsy. This more limited surgery has fewer long-term side effects than complete removal of the lymph nodes under the arm.

What are the chances of beating the disease through various treatments?

It depends on the stage of disease when patients are treated. When the breast cancer is confined to the breast, the survival at 5 years is 98 percent. If it has spread to the lymph nodes, the 5-year survival is about 80 percent. The good news is that breast cancer death rates have been declining at a rate of 2.3 percent for more than a decade. This is due to early detection with mammograms and better chemotherapy and anti-hormonal treatments.

❓ Can a low-fat diet or exercise reduce your risk of breast cancer?

It seems there is some relationship between obesity, a high-fat diet and the development of breast cancer. Breast cancer is more common in countries where there's a high fat content in the diet, like the U.S., and is quite low in countries that have a lower fat content, like Japan. The decreased risk may be related to reducing the level of estrogen in the body.

Younger women who are very athletic and women who have multiple pregnancies have fewer menstrual periods, which may have a protective effect because fewer hormones are produced than in women who are overweight and tend to produce more estrogen. One study suggests that women who exercise when they're first menstruating and who continue through their reproductive years can greatly reduce their risk of premenopausal cancer, possibly because it can reduce the number of menstrual cycles. A couple of studies have suggested that reduction of weight and fat in the diet improves outcome even after a woman develops breast cancer.

Agonizing Over Prostate Cancer

Diagnosis is tricky, and there's a huge debate about how it should be treated

Prostate cancer is the second biggest cancer killer among men, after lung cancer. Each year there are about 30,000 deaths from the disease and over 230,000 diagnoses. Fortunately, this form of cancer doesn't have to be fatal and, especially if caught early, can be treated effectively. Nevertheless, prostate cancer is a tricky disease.

ⓘ INSIDE INFO

A Tomato a Day

○ A study by Harvard University researchers suggests that tomatoes in the diet can help ward off prostate cancer.

○ Men who ate at least 10 servings a week of tomato-based products had a 45 percent less chance of getting prostate cancer; men who ate at least four servings lowered their risk by 20 percent. The reduced risk may be derived from the antioxidant lycopene, abundant in tomatoes.

There are two tests used to detect the presence of prostate cancer. The prostate-specific antigen test measures proteins that are produced by the prostate. The P.S.A. test does have limitations: it will yield positive results in two-thirds of the men who take it, but only 30 to 40 percent of those with high P.S.A. levels will actually have prostate cancer. P.S.A. levels are also elevated in men with an enlarged prostate, a noncancerous condition known as benign prostatic hyperplasia, or B.P.H. The second test is the digital rectal exam, where the doctor probes the rectum to check the size of the prostate gland.

Both of these tests have been shown to have limited effectiveness in reducing mortality. The reason? Prostate cancer can progress slowly or very quickly and is unpredictable in its behavior. Unfortunately, it's difficult to determine accurately which cancers will advance quickly and spread and which might not progress for as long as a decade or more. There are no symptoms in the disease's early stages, but there can be urinary difficulties and some pain as it progresses.

Most doctors agree that not all prostate cancers need to be treated, but it remains unclear which patients with localized prostate cancer will benefit from treatment and which should be left alone.

Prostate cancer is typically found in men 50 years and older, and more often than not, it grows slowly. Some doctors adopt a "surveillance" approach, examining the patient periodically to determine if the disease is spreading. Other doctors treat most cases by either removing the prostate with a procedure called radical prostatectomy, often done robotically now, or administering radiation therapy that kills the cancer cells.

To help clarify the treatment options, the American Urological Association offers guidelines for both doctors and patients that spell out factors to consider when choosing a treatment.

Consider the stage and grade of a tumor. That means estimating the size of the tumor and the extent to which it has spread to other parts of the body. A grade is assigned to a tumor based on the results of an ultrasound test and biopsy, procedures that help determine how aggressive the tumor is, or how quickly it's expected to grow. Patients with small, low-grade tumors fare better than patients with high-grade tumors, regardless of the type of treatment. Some patients with low-grade tumors diagnosed at an early stage may choose surveillance as a treatment option.

Take into account a patient's age, health and life expectancy. Because it's difficult to accurately determine the grade and stage of the cancer, doctors also rely on a patient's age, health and life expectancy at the time of diagnosis to determine whether he's a good candidate for treatment. According to the guidelines, a man's life expectancy should be at least 10 years to be considered a candidate for treatment, because that's how long it usually takes prostate cancer to spread and become fatal.

The younger a man is the more likely he will benefit from treatment, because the disease will probably progress during his lifetime if left untreated. Regardless of the size and grade of the tumor, prostate cancer needs to be treated in someone age 50 or younger.

Understand the side effects of treatment. Some patients are reluctant to undergo prostate surgery because it may result in impotence and pain. But removal of the entire prostate greatly reduces the likelihood, though does not guarantee, that the cancer will recur. With radiation therapy the risk of impotence and incontinence is somewhat less, but the cancer may recur because the prostate remains in place. Because the best treatment for prostate cancer remains unclear, patients need to be involved in making decisions, particularly if their case is borderline.

Finally, the American Cancer Society and the American Urological Association recommend that all men age 50 and older who have at least a 10-year life expectancy have both an annual digital rectal exam and a P.S.A. test. African-American men and those with a family history of early prostate cancer should have an annual

---

TIMELY TIPS

Watch Your Waist—and Prostate
A correlation between fitness and prostate cancer

✔ Men who gain weight rapidly from age 25 to 40 are twice as likely to have a recurrence of prostate cancer even after surgery as those who do not, according to a report that appeared in *Clinical Cancer Research*. Being overweight at the time of the surgery also appears to increase the risk of recurrence, the study found.

✔ The men at greatest risk had gained an average of 3 ½ pounds a year from age 25 to 40. Weight gain remained a significant risk factor, even when controlling for clinical characteristics, family history, physical activity, smoking and other factors.   —Nicholas Bakalar

? EXPERT ANSWERS

Should You Be Tested or Not?

New questions about prostate cancer screening

As soon as the P.S.A. blood test, used to screen for prostate cancer, was introduced in 1987, it became a routine part of preventive health care for many men age 40 and older. Experts debated its value, but their views were largely based on less compelling data that often involved statistical modeling and inferences. But, after the release of two studies in 2009, one American and one European, cancer experts say men should carefully consider the possible risks and benefits of treatment before deciding to be screened. Some may decide not to be screened at all.

According to the two studies, the P.S.A. blood test saves few lives and leads to risky and unnecessary treatments for large numbers of men. The findings, the first based on rigorous, randomized studies, confirm some longstanding concerns about the wisdom of widespread prostate cancer screening. Although the studies are continuing, results so far are considered significant and the most definitive to date. Here are some answers to frequently asked questions about prostate cancer screening and treatment.

Q What did the studies really show?

The bottom line of both studies is that P.S.A. screening does find more prostate cancers—but finding those cancers early doesn't do much to reduce the risk of dying from the disease.

The American study showed no statistical difference in prostate cancer death rates between a group of men who had the screening and a control group who did not. The European researchers found that P.S.A. screening does reduce the risk of dying from prostate cancer by about 20 percent.

But in terms of individual risk, even that is not a huge benefit. It means that a man who isn't screened has about a 3 percent average risk of dying from prostate cancer. If that man undergoes annual P.S.A. screenings, his risk drops to about 2.4 percent.

And there is an important tradeoff. P.S.A. testing increases a man's risk of being treated for a cancer that would never have harmed him in the first place. The European study found that for every man who was helped by P.S.A. screening, at least 48 received unnecessary treatment that increased risk for impotency and incontinence. Dr. Otis Brawley, chief medical officer of the American Cancer Society, sums up the European data this way: "The test is about 50 times more likely to ruin your life than it is to save your life."

Q So do these studies settle the debate about the value of P.S.A. screening?

Not necessarily. Both have problems that make it difficult to interpret the data. The American study found no benefit in P.S.A. screening over a period of 7 to 10 years. But so far, only about 170 men out of 77,000 studied have died of prostate cancer. Prostate cancer is slow-growing, so it's possible that in the next few years, meaningful differences in mortality rates between the two groups will emerge.

A larger concern is what statisticians call "contamination" in the unscreened control group. Because it would have been unethical to tell men in the control group that they could not be screened, many either sought the test or were offered it by their doctors.

Investigators initially estimated that 20 percent of the control group would fit in this category, but the numbers ended up being far higher—38 to 52 percent. As a result, the study doesn't really compare the risks and benefits of screening and no screening. It compares aggressive screening and some screening.

The European research has its own set of problems. Although the finding that P.S.A. screening reduces cancer deaths by 20 percent is statistically significant, experts say it's on the borderline, and a few more years of data could weaken the result.

● **Does this mean men should not receive prostate cancer screening?**

No. Before the studies were released, most major medical groups said P.S.A. testing was a personal decision that a man should discuss with his doctor. The two new studies are unlikely to change that advice, experts say; instead, they give men and their doctors more information with which to make the decision.

For older men, the screening decision should be easier. P.S.A. screening is already not advised for those 75 and older. And the American research confirms that P.S.A. testing is not helpful for men with 10 years or less of life expectancy. In the European study, among men 70 or older, there were more deaths in the P.S.A. screening group, although the trend could be caused by chance.

The advice is murkier for middle-aged men. In the European study, 50- to 54-year-olds didn't benefit from screening. But men ages 55 to 69 were 20 percent less likely to die from prostate cancer than those who weren't screened. (Still, men in that age group must decide whether the high risks of unnecessary treatment are worth it.)

● **What if I'm in a high-risk group, like African-Americans or men with a strong family history of prostate cancer?**

The studies don't include enough data to make definitive recommendations for either group. Men at higher risk who receive a diagnosis of prostate cancer as a result of screening should be reas-

sured by the data that they don't have to rush into aggressive treatment. Bear in mind that prostate cancer is usually not fatal.

● **Should men still undergo a digital rectal exam?**

Neither study offers insights into the value of this traditional test, in which a doctor feels the prostate for hardness or bumps that may signal risk for prostate cancer. The American study looked at a combination of P.S.A. and rectal screening and found no benefit. The European study provides no specific evidence about the exam.

● **Do the new studies mean I should cancel surgery or radiation?**

The study data speak only to the risks and benefits of P.S.A. screening in healthy men without symptoms. If your cancer was detected as a result of symptoms, nothing in the study should change the medical advice you have already received. Early signs of prostate cancer may include difficulty urinating or blood in the semen or urine.

And even if the cancer was detected as a result of P.S.A. screening, the data have limited applicability to one's personal situation. The two studies look at the average risk and benefits across a large group of men, but they don't take into account the specific factors that influence a man's individual risk.

What is your Gleason score—a measure of the cancer's aggressiveness? What is your family history? How much cancer was in each biopsy? Did you do a repeat biopsy to confirm your case? The answers to those questions will give a man better information about how to proceed. At the same time, even those answers can't reliably predict a man's risk for having a serious cancer.

—Tara Parker-Pope

Because the best treatment for prostate cancer remains unclear, patients need to be involved in making decisions.

• • •

P.S.A. and D.R.E. test beginning at age 45. Men at even higher risk (because they have several first-degree relatives who had prostate cancer at an early age) should begin testing at age 40.

Why You Need a Colonoscopy
Still essential, although not perfect

Cancer of the colon should be one of the easiest tumors to prevent. Just submit yourself to a colonoscopy—recommended for everyone over 50 every 5 years—and the odds are good that a vigilant doctor will find and eliminate any suspicious growth that might become lethal. But a study in Canada has come up with disheartening evidence that colonoscopies may be less reliable than previously thought. What is a patient to do?

In a colonoscopy, a doctor inserts a long tube with a camera through the rectum and up to the top of the colon, then withdraws it slowly while looking for precancerous polyps or malignant tumors on the colon walls. If a polyp is there, the doctor snips it out and the danger is likely gone. Some doctors estimate that colonoscopy reduces the risk of dying from colon cancer by 90 percent.

There have been occasional disquieting reports that doctors may miss polyps or cancers that they should have seen. The large Canadian study, published in the *Annals of Internal Medicine,* makes that conclusion hard to escape. The study found that colonoscopies missed almost all of the cancers on the right side of the colon and a third of the cancers on the left side of the colon. An editorial

---

● **TIMELY TIPS**

Red Flags for Hereditary Cancers

Sometimes, a single potent cancer-causing mutation is inherited and can be passed from one generation to the next. An estimated 5 to 10 percent of cancers are strongly hereditary, and 20 to 30 percent are more weakly hereditary.

In hereditary cancer, the mutated gene can be transmitted through the egg or sperm to children, with each child facing a 50 percent chance of inheriting the gene if one parent carries it and a 75 percent chance if both parents carry the same defect.

✔ The following are red flags that suggest a cancer might be hereditary:

- Diagnosis of cancer at a significantly younger age than it ordinarily occurs.
- Occurrence of the same cancer in more than one generation of a family.
- Occurrence of two or more cancers in the same patient or blood relatives.

✔ Knowing that you have a high-risk cancer gene mutation offers the chance to take preventive actions like scheduling frequent screenings starting at a young age or removing the organ at risk. While surgery is clearly a drastic form of cancer prevention, in the future drugs may be able to thwart cancers in people at high risk.

✔ A third possibility, when a cancer gene runs in a family, is in vitro fertilization and genetic analysis to identify affected embryos and implant those lacking the defective gene.

✔ Before choosing surgery to reduce risk in an otherwise healthy person, the following factors should be carefully considered:

- Possible nonsurgical alternatives.
- Actual cancer risk from the inherited gene and how much surgery can reduce it.
- Timing of any operation.
- Effects of surgery on quality of life.

—Nicholas Bakalar

✔ TIMELY TIPS

Tough Questions to Ask Your Doctor

Patients armed with clear-cut facts are often able to make wiser choices about their care. Yet doctors are sometimes reluctant to broach these matters. Here are some questions you should ask.

✔ BEFORE MAJOR SURGERY:

If a doctor recommends major surgery requiring an overnight hospital stay, here are some of the questions patients should ask about the hospital. If the answers are not satisfactory, the patient might want to consider having the procedure done elsewhere.

- Does the doctor have any financial interest in the hospital where the surgery will be performed?

- Is there a doctor at the hospital at all times during a patient's recovery? If not, what is the medical training of the staff who will be on site? How quickly can a physician be summoned?

- Does the hospital have an emergency room? How is it staffed and equipped?

- In the event of a serious complication, is it the hospital's policy to transfer a patient to another hospital? Does it have a formal agreement with another hospital to take those patients?

- What kind of access to specialists does the hospital have if a patient has other existing medical conditions, like diabetes, that might complicate the recovery?

✔ ABOUT CHEMOTHERAPY:

In their review in *The Journal of the American Medical Association* of the role of chemotherapy at the end of life, Dr. Thomas J. Smith and Dr. Sarah Elizabeth Harrington listed these questions to ask—of professionals and of yourself—when considering chemotherapy that is unlikely to cure the cancer but may extend the length and quality of life.

✔ Treatment and Prognosis:

What is my chance of cure?

- What is the chance that this chemotherapy will make my cancer shrink? Stay stable? Grow?

- If I cannot be cured, will I live longer with chemotherapy? How much longer?

- What are the main side effects of the chemotherapy?

- Will I feel better or worse?

- Are there other options, like hospice or palliative care?

- How do other people make these decisions?

- Are there clinical trials available? What are the benefits? Am I eligible? What is needed to enroll?

- What are the likely things that will happen to me?

- How long will I live? (Ask for a range, the most likely scenario for the period ahead and when death might be expected.)

✔ Planning:

Are there other things I should be doing?

- Should I prepare a will?

- Do I have an advance directive?

- Have I assigned a durable power of attorney for health care?

- Are there financial or family legal issues that should be addressed?

- Do I need a durable power of attorney for financial affairs?

- Should I be setting up a trust?

✔ Family issues:

Will you help me talk with my children?

✔ Spiritual and psychological issues:

Who can help me cope?

✔ Legacy and life review:

What do I want to pass on to my family to tell them about my life?

—Reed Abelson and Jane E. Brody

● **TIMELY TIPS**

What to Ask About Depression

Confronting a new diagnosis can be frightening—and because research changes so often, confusing. Here are some questions to ask your doctor, along with notes on why they're important.

✔ **What type of depression do I have? Is it mild, moderate or severe?** There are several forms of this mood disorder, including major depression, dysthymia, cyclothymia and seasonal affective disorder. Criteria for determining disease severity vary, depending on the specific diagnosis.

✔ **Could my depression be caused by an underlying medical condition?** Depression often arises in patients coping with cancer, heart disease, stroke, Parkinson's disease and other long-term chronic illnesses. Management of the illness should be addressed in conjunction with treatment of the depression.

✔ **Should I see a psychiatrist? A psychologist?** Many patients rely on their family physicians for diagnosis and treatment, but several studies have found that the most effective treatment includes both medication and some form of talk therapy provided by a mental health professional.

✔ **What if I don't want to take a drug?** Talk therapy alone can be effective in many cases, particularly in treating moderate depression, and exercise is clearly a mood elevator. St. John's wort is a widely used alternative remedy; however, rigorous studies generally have failed to find it helpful in depression, and the herb interacts with a wide range of other drugs. Light therapy is effective in seasonal affective disorder.

✔ **I am already taking other medications. Would an antidepressant be safe for me?** Antidepressants interact with a variety of other drugs, though newer ones are less likely to do so. Patients should give their doctors a list of medications and supplements they are taking. Use of a single pharmacy can help reduce potential interactions.

✔ **If medication needs to be prescribed, how soon will I feel better?** Eight weeks at the full dose usually is adequate for an antidepressant to take effect. Oddly, mood may be the last symptom to improve. Many patients first experience improved energy and concentration, deeper sleep and improved appetite.

✔ **How long do I need to take an antidepressant?** Use of antidepressants usually is long term. To treat a first episode of depression, the medication is typically taken for 1 year; for a second episode, 2 years. Many chronically depressed patients never stop taking antidepressants.

✔ **If the antidepressant is not working, what do I do?** It is impossible for doctors to know which medication will be most effective for a particular patient in advance. Transitions from one drug to another are common and should be overseen by a doctor, as many patients suffer withdrawal symptoms.

— Gerald Secor Couzens

in the publication concluded that colonoscopies probably reduce the risk of death from colorectal cancer by 60 percent to 70 percent.

Nobody is quite sure why the tests fell short of expectations. Among theories, many Canadian doctors may have lacked enough experience to perform the test well, many patients may not have cleansed their bowels sufficiently and some polyps on the right side of the colon often have shapes that are difficult to detect.

Patients who want the best results should pick an outstanding colonoscopist, cleanse their bowels scrupulously and probably take the final laxative dose shortly before the procedure. Colonoscopies have helped reduce the death rate from colorectal cancer. The main problem with colonoscopies is that too few people bother to get them.

— *New York Times* editorial

Coping with Depression

The first step is to recognize that it's treatable

Depression and anxiety are closely related mental illnesses that are among the most common psychiatric problems suffered by Americans. In recent years, there have been a number of advances in treating mental disorders with psychoactive drugs, but each medication has its drawbacks. Following is a guide to help you understand depression and anxiety and the medications available to treat the disorders.

DEPRESSION. Almost 15 million American adults will suffer a bout of depression each year, according to the National Institute of Mental Health. Women are more likely to be afflicted than men. The telltale symptoms include persistent feelings of sadness or irritability, changes in weight or appetite, impaired sleep or concentration, fatigue, restlessness, thoughts of death or suicide and loss of interest in sex.

Even though the disorder is very common, nearly two-thirds of depressed people don't get treatment because they don't seek it or their symptoms aren't recognized, according to N.I.M.H. Primary care physicians are the health care providers most likely to see depressed patients, and they should do a thorough physical examination to discover underlying causes. Untreated, prolonged depression is associated with higher rates of heart attack and stroke, especially in older people. Further, it's estimated that at least half of all people who commit suicide are severely depressed.

Yet depression is a very treatable illness. According to N.I.M.H., 80 to 90 percent of those with serious depression can improve significantly, restoring normal function. The most common treatments for depression are psychotherapy and antidepressant medications, often used in combination.

ANXIETY. Experiencing anxiety at some point in life is normal, but for people who suffer anxiety disorders, it becomes overwhelming and completely disrupts their existence. Anxiety disorders encompass several distinct disorders:

- Panic disorders occur when a person experiences recurrent panic attacks, which are overwhelming, immobilizing fears with no apparent cause.

- Generalized anxiety disorders are characterized by unrealistic, persistent fears or concerns that

HEALTH

ⓘ **INSIDE INFO**

Foods for the Brain

As the population ages and the prevalence of dementia rises, the focus is on how diet may help keep cognitive decline at bay. Here are the latest findings.

O A heart-healthy diet that keeps clogged arteries from limiting the brain's supply of oxygen and nutrients has been linked to a lower risk of dementia.

O Omega-3 fatty acids in fish and fish oil, which counter inflammation, appear to protect the brain as well as the heart and joints.

O But the new kid on the block may be vitamin B12. A recent British study found an increased risk of cognitive decline in older adults who had low blood levels of vitamin B12. This vitamin is found only in foods from animals, yet it is common for older people, especially those on limited budgets, to cut back on foods like meats and fish. A serving of cooked meat, fish or poultry is only 3 to 4 ounces.

—Jane E. Brody

something bad is going to happen.

- Phobias occur when people dread a situation or object and go to great lengths to avoid it. Examples include fear of heights (acrophobia) and agoraphobia (fear of going out in public).

- Obsessive-compulsive disorders result in persistent irrational thoughts, such as fear of contamination, that are relieved by repeating routine acts, like washing your hands.

- Post-traumatic stress disorder afflicts survivors of extraordinary trauma, such as war or violent crime.

Although anxiety disorders are more common than depression, people who suffer depression are more likely to seek treatment than those with anxiety disorders. According to the Anxiety Disorders Association of America, only 23 percent of those who suffer an anxiety disorder undergo treatment. Untreated, anxiety disorders can lead to depression, suicide, substance abuse and an increased risk of heart attack.

Both anti-anxiety medications and cognitive behavioral therapy, which teaches patients how to allay their fears and modify anxiety-producing behaviors, can relieve the symptoms of all types of anxiety disorders. Receiving both treatments simultaneously appears more effective than either one alone, doctors say.

It is also common to be afflicted with two distinct anxiety disorders or to experience symptoms of both depression and anxiety at the same time. Dr. Jack Gorman, psychiatry professor at the Columbia University College of Physicians and Surgeons, estimates that 50 percent of people with anxiety disorders will ultimately develop depression: "Anxiety disorders are frequently complicated by depression, and when they are, it's a good idea to use medications."

ⓘ INSIDE INFO

Holiday Depression

Psychiatrists have long argued that the holiday season can be fraught with stress, expectations that go unfulfilled, depression and, for some, loneliness.

- O Studies over the years have found little evidence that depression rates actually climb around Christmas, Hanukkah and New Year's Eve.

- O Most studies, including one by the Mayo Clinic that looked at a 35-year period, have found virtually no relationship between the holidays and suicides. If anything, studies have found, suicide rates are at their lowest in December, possibly because those with depression have more family and friends around to help them cope.

- O One form of depression, seasonal affective disorder, is tightly linked with winter. But the treatable condition has more to do with the short, dark winter days than with holiday stress.

—Anahad O'Connor

New Ways of Healing

Biofeedback, visual imagery and yoga, among others, are entering the mainstream

Homeopathy? Acupuncture? Massage therapy? Alternative and complementary approaches to medicine are now being recognized as potentially beneficial and valuable by the mainstream medical profession. Complementary medicine, an alternative therapy used as a complement to conventional medicine, is now practiced by many doctors. An example of this would be the use of aromatherapy to help mitigate a patient's pain after surgery.

Dr. James Gordon, founder and director of the Washington, D.C.-based Center for Mind-Body Medicine and a former chair of the White House Commission on Complementary and Alternative Medicine Policy, discusses the use of some alternative therapies.

Q **What is alternative medicine and how does it differ from holistic or mind-body medicine?**

Alternative medicine uses the techniques of other healing systems, cultures and approaches as an integral part of medical care. Holistic medicine, which comes from the Greek word *holos*, meaning whole, was developed in the 1970s to describe medicine that understood the whole person in his or her total environment and appreciated that a human being was different from and greater than the sum of his or her parts. Mind-body medicine refers to the effects of the mind on the body and the reciprocal effects of the body on the mind. It emphasizes the largely untapped power we all have to affect our health simply by using our minds through biofeedback, visual imagery, meditation and relaxation. Some physical exercises, like yoga and tai chi, can also profoundly affect mental and emotional function.

Q **How does alternative medicine differ from conventional medicine in its approach to treating illness?**

The understanding that dominates our health care is that if somebody has a disease, we have to go in and find out what the biological basis is and develop something to solve the biological problem. When you focus on a specific biological reaction and develop a drug for that, like antibiotics, you destroy the bacteria you want to destroy. But in the process you may wipe out all the other bacteria and affect the immune system negatively. A more holistic approach might be to ask, "What can people do for themselves to strengthen their immune system so they don't

---

ⓘ INSIDE INFO

Bright Lights, Brighter Mood

○ Exposure to bright artificial light can relieve some cases of depression as effectively as psychotherapy or antidepressant medication, new research suggests.

○ Strong evidence that exposure to artificial broad-spectrum light was a good treatment not only for seasonal affective disorder, in which people become more depressed in the darker days of winter, but also for the more common nonseasonal depression was found in a statistical review of 20 rigorously designed studies.

○ Light therapy usually involves sitting in front of white fluorescent lights with eyes open but not looking directly at the light source.

○ Treatment time varies from 15 minutes to 90 minutes a day. Symptoms can start to diminish within weeks.

—Nicholas Bakalar

---

get infections?" Instead of attacking the disease process as if it were the offender, you strengthen the whole human being, so the disease process no longer has a place.

Q **Which alternative treatments are best-established?**

The best evidence shows that we can use our minds to change in a positive direction many physiological functions that were believed to be beyond our voluntary control 30 years ago. For example, you can lower blood pressure, relieve pain and improve functioning in asthma patients. There's a good deal of evidence that relaxation therapies like biofeedback, hypnosis and guided imagery are effective for treating insomnia and pain. There are also very good studies on acupuncture and herbal therapies; many of them have been done in Asia and Europe.

Other research focuses on the use of chiropractic

Five Alternative Approaches

Alternative and complementary approaches to medicine (CAM) are being recognized as potentially beneficial and valuable by the mainstream medical profession. They come in five types:

1. ALTERNATIVE MEDICAL SYSTEMS are built upon complete systems of theory and practice. Some have developed in Western cultures, such as homeopathic and naturopathic medicine. Non-Western medical systems are those such as traditional Chinese medicine and Ayurveda.

2. MIND-BODY INTERVENTIONS. Mind-body medicine uses a variety of techniques designed to enhance the mind's capacity to affect bodily function and symptoms:
- patient support groups
- cognitive behavioral therapy
- meditation, prayer, mental healing
- art, music or dance used as therapy

3. BIOLOGICALLY BASED THERAPIES include dietary supplements, herbal products and the use of other so-called natural, but as yet scientifically unproven, therapies.

4. MANIPULATIVE AND BODY-BASED METHODS such as chiropractic or osteopathic manipulation, and massage.

5. ENERGY THERAPIES
- Qi gong, Reiki and Therapeutic Touch; these all claim to affect the energy fields surrounding the body.
- Bioelectromagnetic-based therapies; use of electromagnetic fields, such as pulsed fields, magnetic fields or alternating-current or direct-current fields.

SOURCE: National Center for Complementary and Alternative Medicine, National Institutes of Health

techniques to treat lower back pain, and on the effectiveness of homeopathic remedies for a variety of conditions, including hay fever in children and arthritis. Studies of therapeutic touch show that when people trained as healers bring their hands close to other people, it relaxes them and improves their physiological functioning.

❓ How do nutrition and exercise fit in?

They are sometimes considered alternative therapies, because they're not ordinarily a part of physicians' practices, although there is an increasing understanding of how nutrition, particularly the Mediterranean diet, can help prevent cardiovascular disease. The same with exercise. Most doctors know a bit about the benefits of aerobic exercise, but most know little about yoga or tai chi, which are enormously helpful in treating many chronic conditions. For example, there are many studies done in India where people have used yoga as part of the treatment for asthma, arthritis, hypertension, anxiety and depression—with good results.

❓ What should patients look for in a physician who practices alternative medicine?

At a minimum, every physician using alternative approaches should know about relaxation therapies, self-awareness, meditation, nutrition and exercise. Beyond that, it's hard to know which system will be most effective. Sometimes you'll have a sense of which techniques are most important to you. For example, if you have a bad back or musculoskeletal problems, it's best to go to someone who knows manipulation (an M.D. or osteopathic physician) in addition to conventional medicine. If you have food allergies, clearly you want somebody who knows about nutrition. If you have chronic pain, acupuncture is a good bet. It's important to work with someone who knows at least one approach well but won't beat you over the head with it whether it works or not.

AHH, A FOOT MASSAGE

The lure of the foot massage isn't difficult to understand. What else confers so much pleasure? What's more, there's evidence that a therapeutic foot massage technique known as reflexology not only relieves stress and tension, but improves circulation, alleviates minor aches and pains brought on by stress, and promotes healing.

Step 1: *Warm the foot and knead it a little to get the circulation going. Rub a little lotion or aromatic oil on your hands to make it easier to massage.*

Step 2: *Start at the top of the foot with the big toe and work down to the heel, using your thumb or knuckle to gently push each point. If you push gently and hold a reflex point, it will send a message to sedate the corresponding body part, but if you "pulse" the point by pushing in and out, it will stimulate the connecting part. Never*

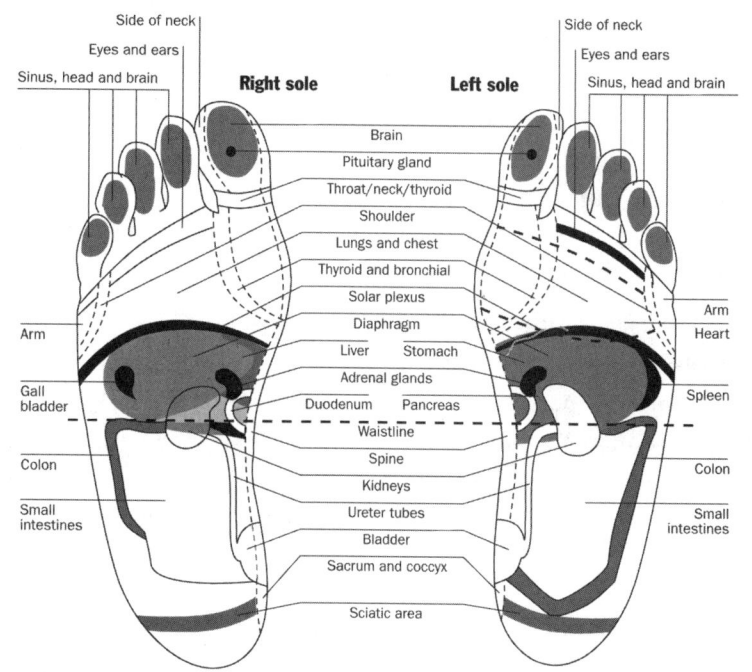

Right sole / Left sole

Side of neck · Eyes and ears · Sinus, head and brain · Brain · Pituitary gland · Throat/neck/thyroid · Shoulder · Lungs and chest · Thyroid and bronchial · Solar plexus · Arm · Diaphragm · Heart · Liver · Stomach · Adrenal glands · Duodenum · Pancreas · Spleen · Waistline · Spine · Colon · Kidneys · Ureter tubes · Small intestines · Bladder · Sacrum and coccyx · Sciatic area · Gall bladder · Small intestines

pump or pulse the adrenal points or the intestine (see graphic), just push in and hold them.

Step 3: *Gently rub the sensitive areas and hard spots to help break up calcium deposits. If you hit a*

point that hurts, you've found a trouble spot. For example, if someone has a stomachache, when you massage the corresponding reflex point, it's going to hurt. When that happens push gently and hold the points, but don't pump them.

Q How does the relationship between alternative practitioners and their patients differ from the typical doctor-patient relationship?

It involves a teaching relationship—which is not primarily the kind of relationship conventional doctors have with patients. What you want are people who are going to help you learn how to take care of yourself, not people who are going to make you dependent on them. Alternative medicine practitioners sometime use groups as a way of maximizing therapeutic work because we've found that people can help each other make real changes not only in psychology but also in

basic biological processes, simply by sharing their experiences.

A striking study was done at Stanford University, where one group of women with breast cancer received the conventional medical treatment—surgery, chemotherapy and sometimes radiation—and another group, in addition, met together with a psychiatrist once a week for an hour and a half for a year. Women in the support group lived on average 18 months longer than women not in the support group. This increased life span has not been found in several other studies, but they are consistent in showing significant improvements in quality of life.

Q Does insurance cover alternative therapies?

A lot of things are considered part of general medical treatment—so if I'm a doctor and I do homeopathy or nutritional counseling, that's covered. Most plans also cover chiropractic, and in some states acupuncture. But that's not the case for many of the services by practitioners who are not medical doctors.

Q What should a patient do if his doctor is reluctant to discuss alternative therapies?

Roughly 70 percent of patients receiving alternative therapies don't discuss it with their doctors because they fear their doctors will not only be unsympathetic, they will be angry.

If a doctor reacts negatively, say, "I need you to help me and to not make uninformed judgments."

How to Ease Back Pain
Finding a cure for back pain isn't easy

Back pain is one of the most common physical complaints, so it's no surprise that treatments for it have multiplied over the years. That ought to be good; instead, many patients find that sudden back pain opens the door to a world of medical confusion.

Indeed, the effectiveness of virtually every pharmaceutical or surgical remedy, however, has been questioned. And for all the money sufferers spend on doctor visits, hospital stays, procedures and drugs, backs are not improving. *The Journal of the American Medical Association* reported that spending on back treatments jumped 65 percent to nearly $86 billion from 1997 to 2005, after adjusting for inflation. But during the same period, the proportion of people with reduced function because of spine problems increased, even after controlling for an aging population.

The mystery begins with the first doctor's visit. The exact cause of back pain is never found in 85 percent of patients. Even magnetic resonance imaging seldom sheds light; in many studies the scans have picked up spinal abnormalities in many people who have never reported back pain.

So what's a sufferer to do? Narcotic pain relievers like OxyContin, used regularly by more than eight million Americans, can help, but doctors remain deeply divided over when to prescribe them. The painkillers can also be highly addictive and lead to mood changes. Alternatives to narcotics have proved problematic, too. Two

---

✔ TIMELY TIPS

You're Ill, Who Needs to Know?

One of the first decisions you make in the emotional hours after a scary diagnosis is whether to tell others. Most of us share the news with our loved ones, but what of the circles beyond, particularly those at work? Your boss?

✔ The Americans with Disabilities Act prohibits an employer from dismissing or failing to hire a chronically ill employee on the basis of that disability "if they are able to do the job with reasonable accommodation." But in many cases, "reasonable" and "able" and even "job" all become open to interpretation, said Gayle Backstrom, the author of *I'd Rather Be Working*.

✔ An excellent resource for workers facing this choice is the Job Accommodation Network, a service of the federal Department of Labor. Most questions on its site come from workers, not management, and many users are looking for suggestions on how to adjust their work without bringing it to the attention of their bosses.

—Lisa Belkin

anti-inflammatory drugs, Vioxx and Bextra, were taken off the market after being linked to heart attacks. And ibuprofen and aspirin can cause gastrointestinal bleeding or organ damage at high doses.

Spinal injections of steroids and anesthetics increased by nearly a third during the 1990s, but several scientific reviews found scant evidence that these provided more than short-term relief. Some doctors have begun prescribing drugs like Lyrica, an anticonvulsant, and Cymbalta, an anti-depressant, to treat chronic back pain. But the data on antidepressants is also mixed.

While the quest for a safe and effective pain pill continues, Americans undergo more than 300,000 spinal fusion surgeries a year, at an average cost of $59,000 each, according to the National Center for Health Statistics. Almost as many undergo laminectomies or diskectomies to remove damaged vertebrae and disks.

For some, back surgery can be life-changing, eliminating pain and disability. But for others, it can have serious consequences. One study found that 11.6 percent of patients in the 78 spinal surgeries that were analyzed developed infections and other complications.

Newer procedures, like implants of medication pumps and stimulators, have received mixed reviews, too. The jury is still out on kyphoplasty, an outpatient procedure for patients with vertebrae fracture from osteoporosis. The doctor inserts a needle into the spine and inflates a balloon, then injects a cement, gluing the bones together. The procedure works only for some patients.

With such uncertainties, it is little wonder that many doctors have fallen back on more traditional approaches to easing the pain, like exercise or counseling. The reality is that most people with back pain heal on their own, slowly, without major intervention.   —Leslie Berger

HEALTH

TIMELY TIPS

Exercising Away Back Pain

Pilates, water aerobics and elliptical machines may provide some benefits

The question of whether to exercise during back pain has confused doctors and patients for years. Research has shown that movement can help heal backs, and within the last several years the medical consensus has shifted away from bed rest and toward exercise, even for people who are not used to daily workouts. Many back specialists now write prescriptions for Pilates, elliptical machines and water aerobics.

✔ In an age of M.R.I. scans and spinal fusion surgery, a treatment as low-tech as exercise can seem to some patients rudimentary or even dangerously illogical. But cardiovascular exercise can increase mobility and help circulation, while strengthening the core muscles closest to the spine can protect against future pain.

✔ Which types of exercise are best for back pain? That depends a little on which doctor you ask. The consensus is that if you do not have shooting leg pain or problems with bowel function, any type of activity—like gardening or dog walking—can speed recovery.

✔ Some doctors strongly advocate aerobic activity, urging patients to continue cycling or jogging to increase blood flow to the back. But other doctors consider running iffy, because they say it puts a lot of stress on the spine. Almost all encourage walking.

✔ Exercises to strengthen the core—the deep muscles of the abdomen—are generally considered beneficial.

—Melena Z. Ryzik

How to Stop Snoring

A little night music that you'd rather not hear

Snoring is rampant, with some statistics showing that as much as 20 percent of the population snores. And there is no question that men snore a lot more than women; some experts say they are eight times more likely to than women.

In large part that has to do with men's thicker neck muscles, since snoring results when air passes over relaxed tissue in the throat, causing a full-throttle vibration. Indulging in too many cocktails makes snoring worse for the simple reason that it overrelaxes the body. Growing older and less toned exacerbates the problem. Sometimes genes are to blame; some people are just born with a flabby or narrow airway. Weight gain, too, worsens snoring, because the neck grows thicker. As America has gotten fatter, it also appears to have gotten louder, at least during sleep hours.

Beyond the sleeplessness it inevitably brings for those who must bed down with snorers, snoring can cause serious health problems. More than 12 million Americans suffer from sleep apnea—in which the soft tissue at the back of the throat repeatedly collapses during sleep and blocks off air—and a large number of these people find themselves sleepy at work or behind the wheel, irritable and unable to concentrate. In the most serious cases, apnea can lead to high blood pressure and, less commonly, to stroke or heart attack as the body struggles for oxygen.

In response to a need for treatment of snoring and sleep apnea, sleep centers are found in just about every city and major hospital. Patients at sleep centers are asked to stay overnight so their snoring can be monitored and the cause pinpointed. One company, SleepQuest, sells a sleep-monitoring kit that people can use at home.

Depending on the diagnosis, doctors (typically ear, nose and throat specialists) recommend weight loss or some form of mechanical treatment. Patients may be given air pressure machines, which continuously pump air through a mask while the patient sleeps. Or the patient's adenoids, tonsils or uvula (that bell at the back of the throat) can be removed to minimize vibration.

—Lizette Alvarez

Trouble Sleeping? Try This

Cognitive behavior therapy can help insomnia

A form of talk therapy has been shown to be more effective than sleeping pills at reducing insomnia, and its effects are longer lasting, a recent study has found.

Published in the *Archives of Internal Medicine,* the study compared zolpidem tartrate, sold as Ambien, the most widely used sleeping pill, with cognitive behavior therapy. In cognitive behavior therapy, a patient is taught to recognize and change patterns of thought and behavior that contribute to problems.

The patients in the therapy group received five 30-minute sessions over 6 weeks. The patients were given daily exercises to "recognize, challenge and change stress-inducing" thoughts, and they were taught techniques like delaying bedtime or getting up to read if they were unable to fall asleep within 20 minutes.

The patients who were given Ambien took a full dose for a month and then were weaned off the drug over the course of another month. Long-term use of sleeping pills is not recommended because dependence can result, the study said.

Two weeks after all treatment had ended, the gap had widened. The patients receiving the therapy fell asleep in half the time it had taken before the study, while the decrease for patients taking sleeping pills was only 17 percent.

—John O'Neil

Having Children

Before You're Pregnant

The right time to take care of your baby is before you conceive

Once a woman learns she's pregnant, she's likely to revamp her lifestyle by eating balanced meals and avoiding cigarettes and alcohol. What many women may not realize is that fetal development begins soon after conception, and well before a woman is aware that she is pregnant. Since more than half of all pregnancies are unplanned, many women miss a critical period of time during which they could maximize their chances of delivering a healthy baby.

"We have to change the outdated paradigm that the time to take care of yourself is when you look pregnant," says Merry-K. Moos, a research professor in the Department of Obstetrics and Gynecology at the University of North Carolina at Chapel Hill. Any woman with the potential of becoming pregnant should consider preconceptional counseling. In reality, most women consult a doctor about 6 to 8 weeks after conceiving.

A preconceptional visit involves a series of tests, including screening for existing medical conditions and for any family history of genetic defects. The visit can prevent a lot of potential problems for mother and child. Studies suggest that adopting a healthy lifestyle before conceiving can increase the chances of having a healthy baby. While nothing can guarantee a perfect birth every time, the following advice can raise the odds.

Take folic acid and eat a well-balanced diet. Studies show that a daily dose of folic acid in the very early stages of pregnancy reduces by 50 to 70 percent the likelihood of having a baby with a neural tube defect, such as spina bifida and anencephaly (the absence of a brain). The F.D.A. recommends that all women of childbearing age consume at least 400 micrograms of folic acid each day in addition to the recommended daily amount they should take in from food sources. Folic acid is found in some foods, such as dark leafy greens like spinach and whole wheat or enriched bread. The surest way for a woman to get enough folic acid is to take a daily vitamin.

Avoid all undercooked or raw fish, shellfish, egg dishes, red meats and poultry and sausages. Raw, unpasteurized milk, yogurt and cheeses should not

 INSIDE INFO

The Best Day to Try Your Luck

A study conducted by researchers at the National Institute of Environmental Health Sciences, and published in the *New England Journal of Medicine*, concluded that:

○ A woman's chances of becoming pregnant are greatest if she has sexual intercourse on the day of ovulation (when the egg is released from the ovary) or in the 5 days before she ovulates.

○ The finding challenges the conventional wisdom that a woman is fertile from about 3 days prior to ovulation to about 3 days afterward.

○ Most surprising was the finding that a woman's chances of conceiving after ovulation are virtually nil.

be consumed, nor any unpasteurized juices. Carefully wash all vegetables. Raw vegetable sprouts should be avoided.

Put on just enough weight. Many women gain 40 to 50 pounds while pregnant, putting them at an increased risk for complications, including diabetes and high blood pressure, and increasing their likelihood of birth by cesarean section. On the other hand, being underweight can lead to low-birth-weight babies. The ideal weight gain for a woman of normal weight, according to the Institute of Medicine, is 25 to 35 pounds. Women should not try to lose

weight during pregnancy; those who are overweight beforehand should try to get within a normal weight range before becoming pregnant.

Exercise. There's ample evidence that moderate to vigorous exercise can be good for both the mother and her fetus. Exercise can boost energy and ease discomforts associated with pregnancy, such as backache, constipation and varicose veins. A study published in the *American Journal of Public Health* claims that women who exercise throughout their pregnancy have more full-term pregnancies than those who do not. Of course, some sports, like downhill skiing, rock climbing and horseback riding, which can harm the fetus, are off-limits. Research also suggests that exercise may prevent gestational diabetes, especially in women with a body mass index greater than 33.

Consult your doctor. Before you become pregnant, you should ask about any prescription drugs you are taking. If possible, you should avoid all drugs during pregnancy, including over-the-counter drugs and herbal medicines and teas. Make sure your immunizations are up to date well before you become pregnant. Ask your doctor before you take any vitamins. Vitamin A, for instance, if taken in large doses can cause birth defects.

Don't smoke or drink. After drug abuse, smoking cigarettes has the most harmful effect on a developing fetus. Studies show that smoking doubles a woman's risk of having an ectopic pregnancy (a pregnancy outside the uterus). It also increases the chances of miscarriage and of delivering a low-birth-weight baby, as well as a baby with a higher risk of having an attention deficit hyperactivity disorder.

Excessive alcohol consumption during pregnancy is a leading cause of preventable mental retardation, learning disabilities and fetal alcohol syndrome. As it is unclear how much alcohol

---

 INSIDE INFO

Fertility Facts

O Each woman is born with millions of immature eggs.

O Normally only one egg is released at each ovulation.

O A menstrual period can occur even if ovulation has not occurred.

O Ovulation can occur even if a menstrual period has not occurred.

O Ovulation can be affected by stress, illness or disruption of normal routines.

O Some women may experience some light blood spotting during ovulation.

O Some women can feel a bit of pain or aching near the ovaries during ovulation; it is called mittelschmerz, which means "middle pain" in German.

O An egg lives 12 to 24 hours after leaving the ovary.

O Implantation of a fertilized egg normally takes place 6 to 12 days after ovulation.

O If an egg is not fertilized, it disintegrates and is absorbed into the uterine lining.

SOURCE: American Pregnancy Association

causes harm, the only way to be entirely safe is to refrain from drinking alcohol while pregnant.

Avoid exposure to all toxic substances. These include such things as paints and other solvents, pesticides, mercury and lead.

Avoid dyeing your hair. This should be avoided, particularly during the first trimester of pregnancy.

Leave cat litter care to others. There is a danger of exposure to parasites from animal feces, which might cause toxoplasmosis. Rodents and their droppings carry lymphocytic choriomeningitis virus, which can cause severe abnormalities or loss of the pregnancy.

Limit your intake of caffeine.

Do not take hot baths or use saunas or hot tubs. Hyperthermia can put severe stress on the fetus.

Medical Checks in the Womb

Today's tests for genetic defects make far more information available

About 150,000 babies are born with birth defects each year in the United States, according to the March of Dimes. The American College of Obstetricians and Gynecologists says that out of every 100 babies born, three have some kind of major birth defect. The shortlist of the most common birth defects includes:

• Congenital heart defects (approximately 1 out of every 125 births)

• Down syndrome (approximately 1 in 1,250 children born to women in their 20s; 1 in 400 by age 35; and 1 in 100 at age 40)

• Cleft lip and palate (approximately 1 in every 1,000 births)

 INSIDE INFO

The Odds of Having a Boy

○ A study of 5,283 Dutch women, which appeared in the *British Medical Journal,* revealed that 57.6 percent of those who took longer than 12 months to become pregnant had boys, compared with 51.1 percent boys among those who became pregnant in less than a year.

○ Maternal age, body mass index and smoking or alcohol use made no difference in the findings.

○ The authors calculated that for each additional year of trying to get pregnant, a couple had a 4 percent increased probability of having a boy.

—Nicholas Bakalar

• Neural tube defects such as spina bifida (a damaged spinal cord) and anencephaly (the absence of a part of the brain) (1 in every 2000 live births)

These days, however, there is an increasing number of genetic tests that offer women a chance to learn before, or very early in pregnancy, the likelihood of whether their baby will have a serious birth defect caused by genetic abnormalities. These tests are being administered more frequently, as childbearing couples are now better screened prenatally and, when necessary, counseled to seek more information through diagnostic testing.

At the same time, scientific breakthroughs are providing an increasing number of ways to ensure the development of a healthy fetus. Here is a description of some of the tests that have been used to date and are commonly available.

Carrier screening tests. When the family of a couple has been identified as having inherited disorders, a carrier screen is done to search for the presence of the defective gene, since such disorders

SOME DRUGS THAT CAN CAUSE PROBLEMS DURING PREGNANCY

Drugs should not be used during pregnancy. However, they are sometimes essential for the health of the pregnant woman and the fetus. A woman should always discuss the risks and benefits of taking any drug with her doctor.

TYPE	EXAMPLES	PROBLEM
Antianxiety drug	**Diazepam**	• When the drug is taken late in pregnancy, depression, irritability, shaking and exaggerated reflexes in the newborn
Antibiotics	**Chloramphenicol**	• Gray baby syndrome • In women or fetuses with glucose-6-phosphate dehydrogenase (G6PD) deficiency, the breakdown of red blood cells
	Fluoroquinolones	• Possibility of joint abnormalities (seen only in animals)
	Kanamycin	• Damage to the fetus's ear, resulting in deafness
	Nitrofurantoin	• In women or fetuses with G6PD deficiency, the breakdown of red blood cells
	Streptomycin	• Damage to the fetus's ear, resulting in deafness
	Sulfonamides	• Jaundice, possibly brain damage in the newborn (much less likely with sulfasalazine) • In women or fetuses with G6PD deficiency, the breakdown of red blood cells
	Tetracycline	• Slowed bone growth, permanent yellowing of teeth and increased susceptibility to dental cavities in the baby • Occasionally, liver failure in the pregnant woman
Anticoagulants	**Heparin**	• When the drug is taken for a long time, osteoporosis and a decrease in the number of platelets (which help blood clot) in the pregnant woman
	Warfarin	• Birth defects; bleeding problems in the fetus and the pregnant woman
Anticonvulsants	**Carbamazepine Phenobarbital Phenytoin**	• Some risk of birth defects • Bleeding problems in the newborn, which can be prevented if the pregnant woman takes vitamin K by mouth every day for a month before delivery or if the newborn is given an injection of vitamin K soon after birth
	Trimethadione	• Increased risk of miscarriage; high (70%) risk of birth defects, including a cleft palate and defects of the heart, face, skull, hands or abdominal organs
	Valproate	• Some (1%) risk of birth defects, including a cleft palate and defects of the heart, face, skull, spine or limbs
Antihypertensives	**Angiotensin-converting enzyme (ACE) inhibitors**	• When the drugs are taken late in pregnancy, kidney damage in the fetus, a reduction in the amount of fluid around the developing fetus (amniotic fluid) and deformities of the face, limbs and lungs
	Beta-blockers	• A slowed heart rate and low blood sugar level in the fetus and possibly slowed growth
	Thiazide diuretics	• A decrease in the levels of oxygen, sodium, and potassium and in the number of platelets in the fetus's blood; slowed growth

may recur in their baby. The test involves taking a sample of saliva or blood to screen for diseases such as cystic fibrosis, Tay-Sachs, sickle cell anemia, and a number of others. This test is done ideally before a woman becomes pregnant but may be done before, during and after pregnancy.

Screening once you're pregnant. It's important to understand the difference between screening tests

like AFP, a blood test that measures a chemical called alpha-fetoprotein and helps detect spina bifida and anencephaly, and ultrasound and diagnostic tests, like amniocentesis or chorionic villus sampling (CVS). A screening test doesn't give you a yes or no answer; it just tells you if your risk is average or above or below average. A normal result on a screening test doesn't guarantee you a

TYPE	EXAMPLES	PROBLEM
Chemotherapy drugs	**Busulfan Chlorambucil Cyclophosphamide Mercaptopurine Methotrexate**	• Birth defects such as less than expected growth before birth, underdevelopment of the lower jaw, cleft palate, abnormal development of the skull bones, spinal defects, ear defects and clubfoot
Mood-stabilizing drug	**Lithium**	• Birth defects (mainly of the heart), lethargy, reduced muscle tone, poor feeding, underactivity of the thyroid gland and nephrogenic diabetes insipidus in the newborn
Nonsteroidal anti-inflammatory drugs (NSAIDs)	**Aspirin and other salicylates Ibuprofen Naproxen**	• When the drugs are taken in large doses, a delay in the start of labor, premature closing of the connection between the aorta and artery to the lungs (ductus arteriosus), jaundice, (occasionally) brain damage in the fetus and bleeding problems in the woman and in the newborn during and after delivery • When the drugs are taken late in pregnancy, a reduction in the amount of fluid around the developing fetus
Oral hypo-glycemic drugs	**Chlorpropamide Tolbutamide**	• A very low level of sugar in the blood of the newborn • Inadequate control of diabetes in the pregnant woman
Sex hormones	**Danazol Synthetic progestins** *(but not the low doses used in oral contraceptives)*	• Masculinization of a female fetus's genitals, sometimes requiring surgery to correct
	Diethylstilbestrol (DES)	• Abnormalities of the uterus, menstrual problems, and an increased risk of vaginal cancer and complications during pregnancy in daughters • Abnormalities of the penis in sons
Skin treatments	**Etretinate Isotretinoin**	• Birth defects, such as heart defects, small ears and hydrocephalus (sometimes called water on the brain); mental retardation; risk of miscarriage
Thyroid drugs	**Methimazole Propylthiouracil Radioactive iodine Triiodothyronine**	• An underactive or enlarged thyroid gland in the fetus • Scalp defects in the newborn • Destruction of the thyroid gland in the fetus • An overactive and enlarged thyroid gland in the fetus
Vaccines (live virus)	**Vaccine for German measles (rubella), chickenpox (varicella)** **For measles, mumps, polio, or yellow fever**	• Potential infection of the placenta and developing fetus; • Potential but unknown risks

SOURCE: Merck.com; revised by Dr. Michael R. Foley, 2007

healthy pregnancy, but your chances of developing certain problems are lower than most. Conversely, if you have an abnormal result from a screening test, you may still have a healthy pregnancy, but you should have a diagnostic test.

The AFP and associated blood tests. The AFP Plus, or triple test, was developed in the 1980's, when researchers established that certain blood tests in the second trimester could predict the risk of Down syndrome in the fetus and thus enable many women to avoid having amniocentesis. These tests measure a chemical called alpha-feto-protein (AFP), which is produced by the fetus; a hormone called unconjugated estriol, produced by both the fetus and the placenta; and HCG, human chorionic gonadotropin, a hormone produced within the placenta, in a woman's blood. Later, a fourth blood test for inhibin A improved the ability to predict the presence of the syndrome. Taken together, the results of these tests provide a risk estimate that could be higher or lower, often much lower, than that based solely on a woman's age.

The test, which is normally offered to all pregnant women, is most accurate at detecting spina bifida and anencephaly, which are suspected when there's an elevated AFP level, but it can also help detect Down syndrome. The AFP Plus test detects 80 to 85 percent of cases of spina bifida and about 65 percent of Down syndrome, which still means that almost one in three cases would not show up.

Ultrasound. An ultrasound test is usually offered only when there's another risk factor for a genetic

disorder or birth defect, like the mother's age, family history or an abnormal AFP test. Ultrasound uses sound waves that emit from a transducer (a reverse microphone) and bounce off structures. It allows doctors to look at the physical development of the baby and get a general picture of the legs, arms and body. The denser the structure, such as bone, the brighter the image.

For example, a birth defect like anencephaly is very accurately picked up on ultrasound, because you can see the part of the skull that's not formed. When ultrasound is done after 18 weeks, it will detect most serious heart defects and more than 50 percent of neural tube defects, and it's even more likely to detect major physical problems.

Diagnostic tests. These tests are usually offered only to women age 35 or older at the time their baby is due, unless there's another indication, such as if a woman has already had a baby with a chromosomal abnormality, there's another hereditary risk or a screening test indicates a problem. Diagnostic tests almost always give you a yes or no answer. Both amniocentesis and CVS have greater than 99 percent accuracy in detecting chromosomal abnormalities. Amniocentesis may also be offered to women at least 14 weeks pregnant because of an AFP or ultrasound finding, but by that time the window of opportunity has closed to perform CVS, which is done between 10 and 13 weeks of pregnancy.

What factors should a couple consider in deciding whether to have a diagnostic test? Couples should consider whether the information the test provides has a real benefit, such as peace of mind or being able to make a decision about the pregnancy. Some decide to have the test because they feel that any risk of an abnormality would justify finding out. Others decide to have the test not based on the statistics but on fear of the unknown.

● **TIMELY TIPS**

Help for a Safe Pregnancy

✔ **Center for the Evaluation of Risks to Human Reproduction** *cerhr.niehs.nih.gov/*

✔ The **March of Dimes** Web site offers a bounty of advice on pregnancy (before, during and after) and features an interactive tool for your questions: *www.marchofdimes.com*

✔ **Merck.com** The drug company's pregnancy pages list drugs that can cause health problems during a pregnancy. *www.merck.com*

✔ **Motherisk Program.** *www.motherisk.org*

✔ **National Center on Birth Defects and Developmental Disabilities** *www.cdc.gov/ncbddd/*

✔ **National Women's Health Information Center** *www.4woman.gov/*

✔ **Organization of Teratology Information Services** *www.otispregnancy.org*

Amniocentesis. Amniocentesis is a procedure done from 14 to 18 weeks of gestation in which a small sample of the amniotic fluid surrounding the fetus is removed by a thin needle inserted through the woman's abdomen. Fetal cells in the fluid are then analyzed for a possible chromosomal abnormality, a process that takes up to 2 weeks. Amniocentesis can also detect neural tube defects. The risk of miscarriage associated with amniocentesis is one in 200 to 400. If an abnormality is found, the woman can choose to have a second-trimester abortion, which can be physically and emotionally more traumatic than one performed earlier in pregnancy.

Chorionic Villus Sampling (CVS). CVS involves removing a small amount of the cells called the chorionic villi that form the placenta by inserting either a catheter into the cervix or a needle into the mother's abdomen. Then genetic tests are performed on the cells. CVS is performed most often in order to identify chromosomal abnormalities. It is usually performed if a woman desires results early in her pregnancy, if a woman has had a previous pregnancy with chromosomal abnormalities or if the couple is at risk of having a child with a genetic disease. The risk of miscarriage associated with CVS is one in 100 to 200.

SOURCE: National Institutes of Health; March of Dimes

Understanding Miscarriages

The odds of a pregnancy after a miscarriage are very high

If you know or read about all the things that can go wrong in achieving and maintaining a successful pregnancy, you will no doubt wonder how so many healthy babies manage to be born. More than half of pregnancies are spontaneously lost even before the woman has missed a menstrual

---

ⓘ INSIDE INFO

For Expectant Mothers Over 35

○ For women over 35, noninvasive and more reliable screening is fast becoming standard care in gynecological practices.

○ It now appears that such screening can be completed with great accuracy in the first trimester, according to a recent study published in the *New England Journal of Medicine*. The report found that a combination of three noninvasive tests conducted at 11 to 13 weeks of gestation was 87 percent accurate in predicting the presence of Down syndrome.

○ The screening tests used were an ultrasound evaluation of the thickness of the fetal neck, called nuchal translucency, and two blood tests, pregnancy-associated plasma protein A, or PAPP-A, and beta human chorionic gonadotropin, or HCG. Adding a second ultrasound of the fetal nasal bone may push the accuracy of these tests even higher.

—Jane E. Brody

---

period and knows that she is pregnant, and about 15 to 20 percent of recognized pregnancies are miscarried in the next few months. For couples who want a baby, these are daunting numbers.

Quick on their heels, however, are very reassuring numbers. For 80 to 90 percent of women who lose one pregnancy, the next one, even with no treatment, results in a successful birth. But the devastation is compounded and the statistics slightly less hopeful when a woman has lost two or more pregnancies. After two consecutive miscarriages, there is a 75 percent chance that the next pregnancy will be maintained. After three miscarriages, there is a 65 percent chance.

Myths abound as to why women experience recurrent miscarriages. The uninformed tend to blame factors like undue stress, too much exercise, being too thin or too fat, exposure to occupational or environmental toxins, excessive use of computers or cellphones and bad habits like smoking or drinking too much coffee. Affected couples, often desperate for a solution, sometimes grasp at unproven or useless remedies. What they need instead is factual information, emotional support and, if possible, treatment based on a medically established cause.

In 2008, the American College of Obstetricians and Gynecologists issued a report on what is known and not known about the causes of repeated miscarriage and its proper treatment.

Perhaps most telling is the bottom line. Approximately one woman of reproductive age in 100 will experience recurrent pregnancy loss, and in no more than half of couples will a definite cause be established. Furthermore, several reported causes are controversial, as are their treatments.

"Although a common concern of patients," the report says, "environmental factors rarely have been linked to sporadic pregnancy loss, and no associations between environmental factors and recurrent pregnancy loss have been established." It adds, "No association between occupational exposure or working itself and recurrent pregnancy loss have been established." Neither have any infectious agents been proved to cause recurrent miscarriage, the report adds.

One of the report's authors, Dr. Sandra A. Carson of Brown University, notes that "the

---

When Morning Sickness Strikes

It isn't only early in the day

Most women experience morning sickness early in their pregnancies. But it does not necessarily strike only in the morning, nor does it always end after the first trimester.

Nausea and vomiting affect 70 to 85 percent of pregnant women, various studies show. Half experience both, and a quarter have nausea only. Some people can be sick through the full nine months. The problem can be so severe that women have to be hospitalized to prevent dehydration and other complications. In fact, severe nausea accompanied by vomiting is the second most common reason, after premature labor, for hospitalization in pregnancy.

Some women suffer such serious psychological and social disturbances as a result of persistent vomiting that they choose to terminate their pregnancies, according to a report from the American College of Obstetricians and Gynecologists. Severe nausea and vomiting, called hyperemesis gravidarum, occurs in up to 2 percent of pregnancies, the association reported in issuing new guidelines for diagnosing and treating the problem.

What can you do to alleviate morning sickness? There are many safe ways to relieve and possibly eliminate the problem. Some suggestions:

✔ **Eat frequent small meals,** avoiding spicy or fatty foods, eliminating pills with iron, eating bland or dry foods or high-protein snacks and eating dry crackers in the morning before rising.

✔ **Eat ginger, in capsule form** (it can also curb motion sickness).

✔ **Electrical stimulation of an acupressure point on the inside of the wrists,** and round-the-clock use of vitamin B6, particularly when taken with the over-the-counter drug doxylamine, an antihistamine often used as a sleep aid.

✔ **Other medications listed as safe** and effective are two kinds of prescription antiemetics, phenothiazines and benzamides.

—Jane E. Brody

How to Figure Your Due Date

This simple mathematical equation was devised by a 19th-century German obstetrician named Franz Karl Naegele, based on the idea that a woman's pregnancy normally lasts 280 days.

✔ Subtract three months from the first day of your last menstrual period and add 7 days to that date, or 280 days from your last menstrual period. If you know your date of conception, you can add 38 weeks or 266 days and come up with the same date.

overwhelming majority of recurrent miscarriages occur because something is wrong with the baby, most often a chromosomal abnormality." This risk increases with the mother's age and, some studies suggest, with the father's age, because of genetic errors in the egg or sperm that result in embryos with too many or too few chromosomes.

In 2 to 4 percent of couples with recurrent loss, one partner is found to have a problem, a genetically balanced rearrangement of chromosomes. He or she is normal, but when the egg or sperm is formed, it can end up with an extra chromosome piece or a missing segment, resulting in an embryo that cannot survive. In such cases, a couple may choose in vitro fertilization, with genetic analysis of the resulting embryos performed to select a chromosomally normal one for implantation.

Structural abnormalities of the uterus are found in 10 to 15 percent of women who have recurrent miscarriages, though experts disagree over whether these problems impede a successful pregnancy. Likewise, the role of fibroids and endometriosis is controversial, and surgery to remove such extra tissue may not prevent another miscarriage.

One popular notion to explain recurrent miscar- riage is inadequate production of progesterone, the hormone released after ovulation that prepares the uterus for pregnancy. This idea has resulted in many efforts to support an incipient pregnancy by administering progesterone, a treatment that Dr. Carson described as harmless but not likely to be effective. Some researchers suggest that if a hormonal problem exists it may begin before the egg is released and that drugs to stimulate ovula- tion may be more helpful.

Even after the most thorough work-up, half to three-fourths of couples with recurrent pregnancy loss "will have no certain diagnosis," the report states. For such couples, the best medicine is good information and sympathetic counseling. combined with optimistic statistics. Live birth rates between 35 and 85 percent are commonly reported in couples with unexplained recurrent pregnancy loss.

—Jane E. Brody

Quick Delivery? Try Exercise

Pelvic exercises help women get better control

Finally, there may be a way for pregnant women to try to shorten their labor and delivery: by building up their pelvic floor muscles in advance.

Women in Norway who took 12 weekly one-hour classes in exercising those muscles between the 20th week of pregnancy and the 36th were less likely than others to spend more than an hour in the pushing stage of labor.

The women who received the training were also encouraged to practice 8 to 12 intensive contrac- tions of the pelvic floor twice a day at home.

The results of the study contradict the assump- tion that strong pelvic floor muscles—like those developed in women who ride horses or practice gymnastics, for example—make it more difficult to deliver a baby. "This is a myth, because actually

GROWTH OF THE FETUS FROM 8 TO 40 WEEKS

Fetal development has already begun 17 days after conception. While the average pregnancy lasts 280 days from the last menstrual period, it is normal to give birth anywhere from 37 to 42 weeks after the last period.

Week	8	12	16	20	24	28	32	36	40
Length	1 in.	3 in.	6.5 in.	10 in.	13 in.	14.5 in.	16 in.	18 in.	20 in.
Weight	0.07 oz	0.6 oz	5 oz	12 oz.	1.3 lbs	2 lbs	3.5 lbs	5.5 lbs	7.5 lbs

SOURCES: *The American Medical Association Encyclopedia of Medicine* © 1989 by Dorling Kindersley; American Medical Association

quite the opposite thing happens," says Dr. Kjell A. Salvesen, a co-author of the study and a professor of obstetrics and gynecology at Trondheim University Hospital in Saint Olav. "With strong pelvic floor muscles, women maybe get better control in delivery," he says.

The training also seemed to make a difference in the number of women who needed an episiotomy, an incision to enlarge the birth canal. Fifty-six women in the exercise group had them, and 72 in the comparison group.

The study was originally intended to find out whether pelvic floor strengthening could prevent urinary incontinence during and after pregnancy. The researchers found that it did in some women.

–Mary Duenwald

Do You Need a Doula?

Adding a helping hand during labor and after

In an era of nurse shortages and high Caesarean rates, doulas—the word means "servant" in Greek—and lactation consultants can be godsends for many women. Indeed, multiple studies show that a doula's presence during childbirth leads to shorter labor, less medical intervention and a happier experience.

Similarly, lactation consultants are often necessary for mothers having difficulty breast-feeding. Overwhelmed nurses don't always have the time for one-on-one instruction, and because formula use peaked in the 1970s, a mom's own mother may be ill-equipped to offer advice.

But the increased popularity of doulas and lactation consultants has also led to more conflict—not only with parents but doctors and nurses as well.

There are no national statistics on the phenomenon, and few women readily admit to doula discord. But according to a recent study of women who used doulas in Alabama, 44 percent of women described the relationship between their hospital nurses and doulas as hostile, resentful and confrontational.

The American College of Obstetricians and Gynecologists has issued no official statement on doulas. Dr. Sarah Kilpatrick, chairwoman of the academy's committee on obstetric practice, says that doulas can be helpful, but "occasionally you have someone who attempts to interfere with the medical aspect of delivery."

Doulas contend that doctors and nurses aren't

always cooperative. One major source of conflict is an absence of standardization and oversight. Between 1994 and 2005, the number of doulas certified by Doulas of North America grew to 5,842, up from 750. But a doula requires no certification—anyone can be a doula, regardless of training.

Similarly, since 2003, the number of lactation consultants certified by the International Board of Lactation Consultant Examiners, which requires 2,500 hours of practice and 45 hours of course work, has increased 15 percent to nearly 9,000. But most consultants are not that well trained. Dozens of groups offer certification after completion of 1- to 5-day courses, and there are at least six different acronyms signifying lactation credentials. How can a sleep-deprived mother differentiate among a C.L.E., a C.B.E. and a C.L.C.?

Though childbirth and breast-feeding seem like the most natural of acts, the complexities that arise—from emergency C-sections to inverted nipples—demand a great deal of training and experience.

—Pamela Paul

 **TIMELY TIPS**

Cutting Toxins in Your Breast Milk

✔ Don't drink much alcohol or caffeine.

✔ Avoid spicy foods, strawberries and cruciferous vegetables, which are believed to cause gas in babies.

✔ Don't smoke.

✔ Be aware of concerns about pesticides and heavy metals and take precautions. If possible, buy mostly organic food to avoid pesticides. A three-stage reverse-osmosis filter for tap water and ice maker will filter out heavy metals and contaminants.   —Florence Williams

Ways to Treat Infertility
Options for couples having trouble conceiving

What causes infertility? Late marriages and biological clocks are frequent factors. Environmental toxins, scarring from infections or previous surgery, and declining sperm counts may also play a role. The age of the mother is one of the biggest factors that influences the ability to conceive, because as women age, they are less likely to ovulate.

The procedures used to correct these problems vary. Sometimes couples just need to adjust their schedules, undergo minor surgery to correct problems in their reproductive organs or take prescription medications to conceive. Certain women who don't release enough eggs can be treated with a fertility drug such as Clomid or Serophene. But others must subject themselves to demanding and costly tests and treatments like hormone injections, egg retrieval and embryo transfers.

So-called assisted reproductive technologies have increased dramatically in the last decade. Technologies such as gamete intrafallopian transfer (GIFT) and zygote intrafallopian transfer (ZIFT) have also become more widespread, and their live birth rates are steadily improving. With GIFT, the sperm and egg are inserted into the fallopian tubes, where fertilization occurs naturally. For in vitro fertilization (IVF) and ZIFT, fertilization of the eggs by the sperm takes place in the laboratory, and the fertilized egg is placed directly into the woman's uterus (for IVF) or her fallopian tubes (for ZIFT).

Another option is to treat male infertility, which accounts for as much as 40 percent of all cases. For example, intracytoplasmic sperm injection, which involves injecting a single sperm into an egg, then returning the egg to the uterus, is a technique designed to overcome infertility caused by weak or abnormal sperm. The aggressive procedure has made it possible for men with extremely low sperm counts or defective sperm to become fathers. However, the technique may lead to what is known as inherited infertility, a condition in which newborns develop the same genetic problem that caused their fathers' infertility.

But these high-tech treatments have their limits. There's little evidence that repeating the same procedure more than four to six times increases the likelihood of pregnancy.

Adopting a Baby or Child

To avoid pitfalls, examine your motivation

Though the joys of welcoming an adoptive child into your home can be worth any amount of effort, there are considerable challenges involved in meshing the child's needs with those of your existing household. There is also the small but significant risk that your child's birth parents might change their minds during the window of time before the adoption becomes final, and decide to keep their child or baby.

Most adoptive parents, however don't experience that kind of trauma. And though they routinely have to contend with what can seem like long waits and lots of paperwork, particularly in the case of international adoptions, in some ways, that is a useful test of their commitment to completing an adoption. Deb Harder, adoption information supervisor at Children's Home Society & Family Services, has the following advice on how to have a successful adoption.

Examine what's motivating you to adopt. The first step for anyone considering adoption is to make sure you're firmly committed to rearing and nurturing a child. Look very carefully at your skills and strengths as a person, and how they translate to being an effective parent. If you're dealing with infertility, it's important to acknowledge that you're unlikely to bear children. You should see adoption not as a second-best option, but as an alternative way to become a parent and create a family.

Decide what kind of child you can effectively parent. Many families only consider adopting a healthy, same-race infant, and don't think of a child born in another country or a child who has special needs. Some folks are prepared to parent a child with special needs, but not all—assess your strengths and decide what you can manage. In the same way, you must consider whether you can understand the needs of children from other cultural backgrounds. You have to value your child's heritage and have a plan for incorporating that heritage into your family's day-to-day life.

First, learn as much as you can about adoption and how it meets a child's need for a family. Learn about the children who need to be adopted in the

U.S. and other countries so that when you consider the types of adoption programs available, you understand how your desire to be a parent matches a child's need for a family, as well as how your hopes for a particular type of child affect your program options and wait times. Take advantage of educational opportunities that prepare you for adoptive parenting as well as set the stage for you to begin the process of adoption with good information and confidence.

Learn what your state law requires of agencies and families to complete an adoption and what is required by U.S. Citizenship and Immigration for international adoption. Among the first things a family should do is contact their state department of social services and talk to an adoption supervisor to find out what they are legally required to do to complete an adoption in their state.

Choose the type of adoption you're interested in. One of the first decisions is whether you'd like to adopt an older child, in which case you can adopt through a public agency, which primarily works with kids in foster care and group home settings. If you want to adopt an infant or a child from another country, you will work with a private agency. You can also opt for an independent, or private, adoption (if state law allows), in which adoptive parents work with a lawyer or other non-agency adoption provider to find a birth parent or child. There are certain risks with private adoptions and more of a safety net with an agency.

Assess the costs. The cost of adopting a child ranges from several thousand dollars to more than $40,000, particularly for an adoption done with a private agency and/or an attorney. However, parents adopting a U.S. Waiting Child through their state's public system do not pay for adoption expenses and actually receive adoption assistance after placement, in which case there is no cost apart from certain out-of-pocket expenses that are often reimbursed by the state.

International adoptions tend to be more expensive, because there are costs for additional documents and travel.

Private adoption has the reputation of being more expensive, because the costs usually aren't set up front, while some agencies may charge on a sliding scale basis. Different agencies have different fee structures, services and missions. Try to get details about the services they provide, and insist that they assign a service to each fee.

Expect to feel like you're being scrutinized during the adoption process. Most agencies now do open adoptions, meaning that the birth parent(s) choose(s) which prospective adopter(s) they want to adopt their child, and the two families make an adoption plan together. The agency staff can and does compile a book of dossiers with biographical information about prospective families for birth parents to review. Some prospective adopters choose international adoption because they feel uncomfortable with openness and/or the feeling of "marketing" themselves.

Be honest during the adoption study, also known as a home study. All prospective adoptive parents must undergo an adoption study, a process that helps agency personnel to assess your readiness for adoptive parenting. It's not unlike applying for a mortgage—lots of personal questions to answer that require verification. For example, they assess what's motivating you to adopt, how you were parented and how you plan to discipline the child. They'll also ask for references and look at your finances and psychological stability. If you have a criminal history or a history of psychiatric illnesses, you need to fully disclose these details—don't lie about the situation—or it will cause greater problems than if you're upfront and explain what's what.

Resources for Adoptive Parents

Adopting.org: Resource for birth parents and adoptive parents. *www.adopting.org*

Adoption.com: For all types of adoption. Lots and lots of information about all types of adoption and lots of links to additional resources for families. *www.adoption.com*

Adoptive Families Magazine: For all adoptive families and prospective adopters. Excellent Web site with articles and searchable databases. *www.adoptivefamilies.com*

American Academy of Adoption Attorneys: Primarily for domestic adoption. An advocacy organization for legal professionals working in adoption; these attorneys dedicate a certain percentage of their practice to adoption and custody work for families and children.

They publish a national directory of adoption attorneys. *www.adoptionattorneys.org*

Comeunity: Provides information, resources and links to additional resources for families that are just beginning the adoption process and those who are actively parenting. *www.comeunity.com*

Joint Council for International Children's Services: For international adoption. An advocacy/education organization made up of international adoption agencies. *www.JCICS.org*

Karen's Adoption Links: For international adoption. A Web site that links families to adoption resources: parent support groups, listservs, books/cultural products and much more. *www.karensadoptionlinks.com*

The National Adoption Center: For domestic adoption. 800-TO-ADOPT or *www.adopt.org*

North American Council on Adoption Children: An advocacy/education organization focusing primarily on older children and their families, who wait for adoption while in U.S. and Canadian foster care; provides excellent resources for families with children who have special needs. *www.nacac.org*

Perspective Press: Books and articles on adoption. *www.perspectivespress.com*

Rainbow Kids: Comprehensive adoption resource. *www.rainbowkids.com*

U.S. Citizenship and Immigration Services and the **U.S. Department of State** : Both sites offer families information and guidance about the processes that they must go through in order to adopt a child from another country. *www.uscis.gov* *www.adoption.state.gov*

Think about the type of child you want to adopt and which program helps you meet that goal. If you want to adopt a domestic newborn, then you need to consider your comfort with an open adoption, because you will likely be working directly with a birth family in making an adoption plan and a plan for ongoing communication after the baby's placement with you. Think not only about your feelings now, but also about how your relationship with your child's birth family might evolve.

Find out how quickly adopted children join their adoptive families. In the case of open adoption, agencies have a difficult time estimating how long

you will wait. The agency should be able to give you a time line as to what to expect at their agency—how long the adoption study process will take and what are their average wait times. Be flexible, and remember that agencies really act as a family's advocate in the process. Because they work on a child's behalf, they are seeking families that are good matches for the children.

Make sure the people you're working with are reputable. Unless the people you are working with are competent, qualified and ethical, the whole process is jeopardized. If you opt for a private adoption, don't go to a family lawyer unless he or she has experience in adoption. And bear in mind that just because a lawyer knows how to complete an adoption according to the letter of the law, it doesn't mean he or she has a background in or understanding of the sociological and psychological aspects of adoption.

If you are trying to arrange an international adoption, be aware that what is culturally acceptable in other countries may be counter to our experience or what we may deem acceptable. For example, families report that when they adopted they were asked for gifts that they thought were possibly bribes; a reputable, ethical U.S. agency won't allow gifts other than the small customary presents you would take to a host.

The Answer to Colic

Imitate the womb, and the crying will stop

Regard the colicky baby at full throttle. Tiny arms and legs stiffen. Tummy goes hard. Face resembles a beet emitting paroxysmal shrieks. Unbelievably, the crying goes on for one, two, even three hours without pause.

No, nothing is wrong. Studies of infants around the world show that unsoothable colic is a natural phase of early infant development. Babies typically begin crying at 2 weeks of age. Colicky crying peaks at 6 weeks and ends by three to four months. It is not related to weak parental skills, being a single parent, postpartum depression or anything done by adults. Infants in primitive tribes who are held 24 hours a day and breast-feed constantly show the same pattern in peak inconsolable crying.

Dr. Harvey Karp, who has a private practice in Santa Monica, Calif., claims that he has devised a method for calming screaming babies—in minutes. In his book and DVD called *The Happiest Baby on the Block*, Karp shows parents five steps

that, performed together, set off what he calls an infant's innate calming instinct. He says the method can also help infants who do not have colic to sleep an extra hour or two a night.

His solution: recreate for infants sensations in the womb to help them stay calm. In the womb, the soon-to-be-born infant is packed tightly, head down, in fetal position, with lots of jiggling and a whooshing sound—blood flowing through the placenta—that is louder than a vacuum cleaner. According to Karp, these conditions put the fetus into a trance.

To calm a baby, Karp sets out five maneuvers that he says will touch off a calming reflex and put the infant to sleep. They must be carried out progressively, as a kind of dance, to work their magic.

• The first is swaddling or snug wrapping that imitates the restrictiveness of the womb for the last two months of pregnancy. But this will not by itself stop the crying.

• The second step is to hold the swaddled infant in one's arms or on one's lap and roll the baby onto its side or stomach.

ⓘ **INSIDE INFO**

Starting Babies Off Right

○ To get babies to eat fruits and vegetables, a recent study published in *Pediatrics* found that what breast-feeding mothers regularly eat influences their babies' initial acceptance of foods like peaches and green beans.

○ Nonetheless, repeated exposure to green beans, which initially provoked a grimace on babies' faces, increased their consumption of this vegetable, whether they were breast-fed or formula-fed.

○ The researchers suggest that mothers ignore their babies' facial expressions and keep offering foods that are good for them.

—Jane E. Brody

- Third is a very loud shushing noise delivered directly into the baby's ear. The sound imitates what the fetus hears inside the womb as blood pulses through the placenta. The shushing must be as loud as or louder than the infant's cries.

- Next comes the jiggling. A fetus is accustomed to certain motions that can be replicated for the crying infant. Karp recommends supporting the baby's head and neck while delivering tiny energetic movements, like shivering. The movements must be gentle to avoid shaking the baby's vulnerable head.

- The last step is non-nutritive sucking. A baby will calm itself if it can suck on a finger.

—Sandra Blakeslee

✔ TIMELY TIPS

Body Mass Index for Children

✔ Body mass is a means of judging the fitness of an individual. To calculate your body mass, divide your weight by your height squared, and multiply that number by 703.

✔ You can find a childhood BMI calculator on the Centers for Disease Control Web site at www.cdc.org. Type "children BMI calculator" in the search box at top of the main page.

✔ The chart below shows the body mass index percentiles for children.

BMI-FOR-AGE	
UNDERWEIGHT	< 5th percentile
NORMAL	5th percentile to < 85th percentile
AT RISK OF OVERWEIGHT	85th percentile to < 95th percentile
OVERWEIGHT	> 95th percentile

SOURCE: Centers for Disease Control and Prevention

As They Grow...and Grow

Here's how to tell if their weight and height are in the normal range

Few processes can be as engrossing to parents as watching their child grow and trying to divine how tall or thin their precious offspring might eventually be. While no one has yet figured out how to predict a child's full adult weight and height, there are plenty of tools, such as the growth charts on the facing page, to help you determine if your child's growth is in the normal range.

Infants grow at an incredible pace—doubling their weight in the first four to five months and tripling it by the time they are one. By the end of their first year, their height increases by 50 percent. By age three, a child's head is almost 90 percent of its adult size. Heredity greatly determines a child's ultimate height and weight.

As a rule of thumb, children are considered obese if their weight is 20 percent or more above the expected weight for their height. In between regular pediatric visits, parents can keep tabs on their child's growth rate by using these charts, which are similar to the ones used in a pediatrician's office.

To plot the child's height, find the vertical line for his or her age at the bottom of the height chart. Locate the horizontal line for the child's stature on the sides of the chart, and mark the point at which the two lines cross. Do the same for the weight chart, using the child's weight and age.

The numbers on the curved lines represent percentiles. For example, if your daughter weighs 125 pounds at age 12, she is at about the 90th percentile. This means that about 90 percent of normal girls weigh less than she does, and about 10 percent weigh more.

BOYS

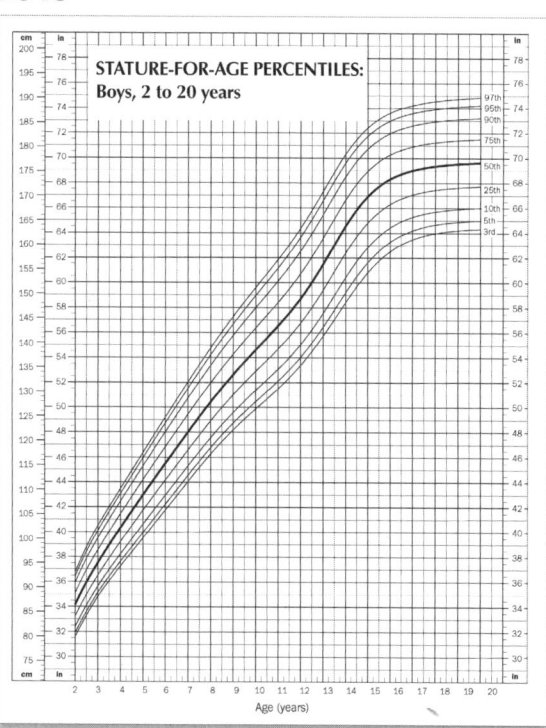

STATURE-FOR-AGE PERCENTILES:
Boys, 2 to 20 years

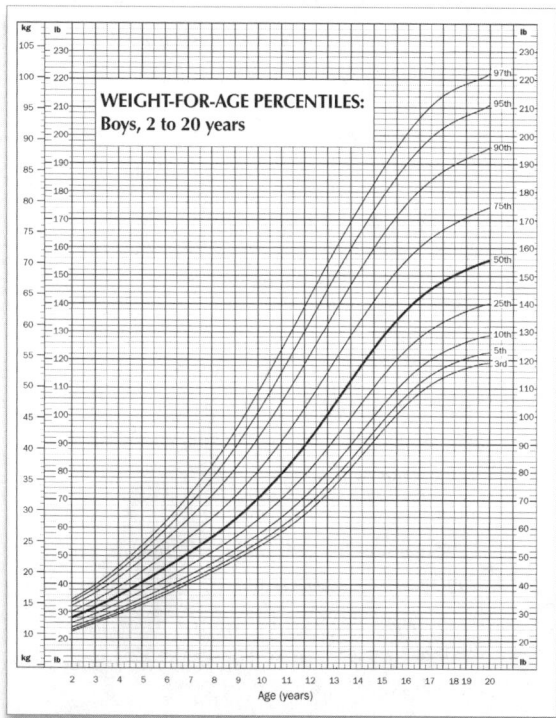

WEIGHT-FOR-AGE PERCENTILES:
Boys, 2 to 20 years

GIRLS

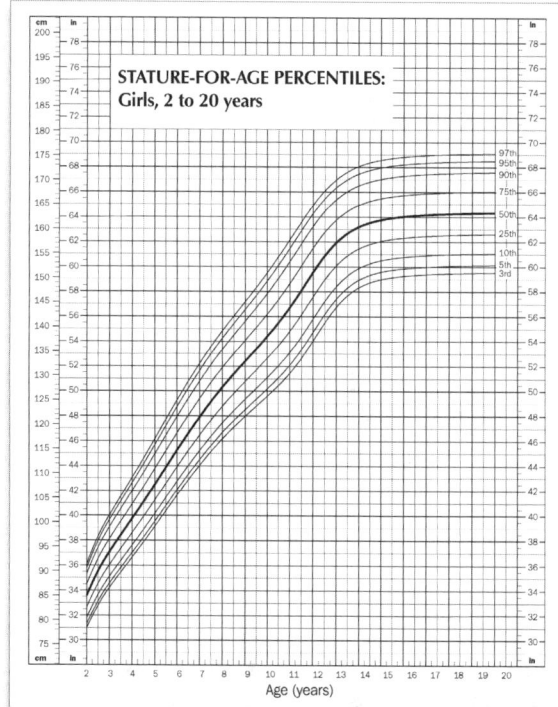

STATURE-FOR-AGE PERCENTILES:
Girls, 2 to 20 years

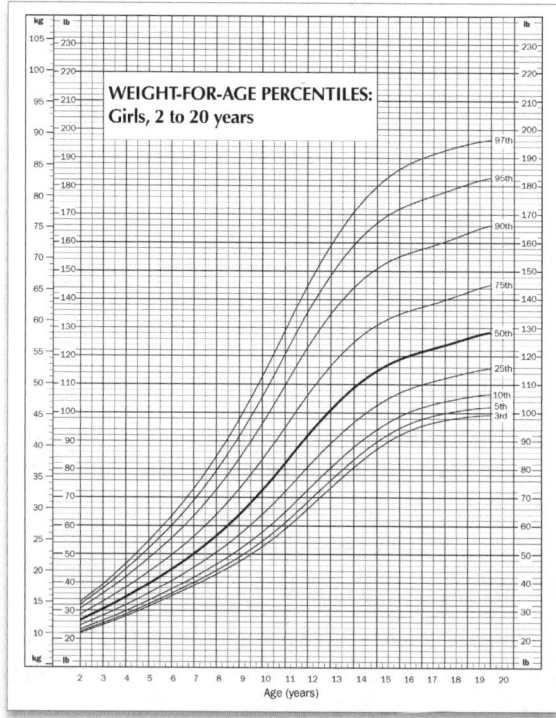

WEIGHT-FOR-AGE PERCENTILES:
Girls, 2 to 20 years

What to Ask About Vaccines

Be sure to find out about new protocols

At every doctor visit, ask about any new recommended immunizations. Most pediatricians follow the recommended schedule for childhood vaccinations, making a parent's job easier. Or, go to the Centers for Disease Control and Prevention website at www.cdc.gov/vaccines for the latest recommended vaccines.

With all the new vaccines that have been rolled out in recent years, it's a good idea to have a vaccine conversation with your doctor, especially when it comes to older children. Here are some questions to ask, along with notes on why they're important.

Q What new vaccines does my child need?

There are two new recommendations, one for hepatitis A and another for flu.

The flu vaccine is recommended for children six months to 5 years old. A new intranasal form, approved for 2- to 5-year-olds, can be given instead of a shot. Ask about the cost difference between the two if you're paying out of pocket, as the nasal spray is more expensive. A flu shot is also recommended for older children with chronic conditions like asthma.

The hepatitis A vaccine was initially recommended only in certain states where the incidence of the disease was high but is now recommended for all children beginning at 1 year old.

Q Should I get my child a thimerosal-free flu shot?

The evidence is very strong that there is no connection between autism and thimerosal, a mercury-containing vaccine preservative. But a thimerosal-free influenza vaccine for children is available.

Q What vaccines does my teenager need?

Three vaccines have recently become available for teenagers: one that guards against meningitis;

another that includes protection against pertussis, or whooping cough; and a third for cervical cancer. The meningococcal vaccine protects teenagers against potentially deadly meningitis and bloodstream infections.

It used to be recommended only for those entering college, but the new form has longer-lasting protection and is now recommended starting at age 11, as the protection will now carry teenagers through college, when risk is highest. Children 8 to 12 may also be at risk at overnight camps and on sports teams.

The Tdap vaccine, for tetanus, diphtheria and pertussis, is now routinely recommended for teenagers as well as adults. In the past, teenagers would get just tetanus and diphtheria boosters because of safety concerns surrounding the pertussis vaccine, but the new vaccine is considered safe. Pertussis boosters are necessary because the immunization

---

HAVE YOUR KIDS HAD ALL THEIR SHOTS?

Children receive their first vaccination, for Hepatitis B, shortly after birth. During the next 18 years, they are immunized against a range of diseases, many requiring booster shots. Here are recommended childhood vaccines, according to the Centers for Disease Control and Prevention. To get the dosage schedule, ask your pediatrician or go to www.cdc.gov/vaccines.

Hepatitis B
Rotavirus
Diphtheria, Tetanus, Pertussis (DTaP)
H. influenza (type B)
Pneumococcal
Inactivated Poliovirus
Influenza
Measles, Mumps and Rubella (MMR)
Varicella
Meningococcal
Hepatitis A
Human Papillomavirus (girls only)

effects of the single shot fade. Whooping cough is one of the few vaccine-preventable diseases that are still not under control.

The third vaccine, Gardasil, protects teenage girls against cervical cancer by taking aim at the human papillomavirus, or HPV. It is recommended at age 11 to 12 and requires three injections over a six-month period, or up to age 26 for those who did not get it when younger.

Q Does my teenager need a chickenpox booster?

The initial recommendation for the chickenpox vaccine was one shot for children 12 to 18 months old. In 2005, because of evidence that the vaccine wears off, it was recommended that all children get a booster dose between ages 4 and 6. Children 8 to 12 and teenagers who received one dose as infants but haven't gotten the booster need to get one, research shows, because the effects can wear off, and getting chickenpox later in life can have serious complications.

Q Do you send out reminders about boosters or other vaccinations?

Most doctors don't. But if they did, there would be more compliance.

Q What vaccine side effects should I look out for?

Vaccine Information Statements, produced by the Centers for Disease Control (cdc.gov), explain the benefits, risks and potential side effects of various vaccines, from anthrax to yellow fever. Federal law requires that these or similar informational statements be handed out before certain vaccinations are given. It's good practice to review this material to become aware of possible side effects and what symptoms to look for.

Q What if a bad reaction occurs?

Most reactions are not serious, but federal health officials urge vaccine recipients to help them monitor reactions by reporting to their doctors unusual symptoms (like high fever, behavior changes or allergic reactions like difficulty breathing, rapid heart beat, dizziness, hives or wheezing) and asking the doctors to file a Vaccine Adverse Event Report. Patients can file reports themselves through www. vaers.hhs.gov or by calling 800-822-7967.

Serious Face Time with Baby
Talking to infants makes them smarter

Some researchers say the number of words an infant hears each day is the single most important predictor of later intelligence, school success and social competence. There is one catch—the words have to come from an attentive, engaged human being. As far as anyone has been able to determine, radio and television do not work.

Dr. William Staso, a school psychologist from Orcutt, Calif., and an expert in neurological development, has written a book called *What Stimulation Your Baby Needs to Become Smart.* Some people think that any interaction with very young children that involves their intelligence must also involve pushing them to excel, he says, but the "curriculum" that most benefits young babies is simply common sense. It does not involve teaching several languages or numerical concepts, but rather carrying out an ongoing dialogue with adult speech. Vocabulary words are a magnet for a child's thinking and reasoning skills. Different kinds of stimulation should be emphasized at different ages, but at all stages, parental interaction and a conversational dialogue with the child are important. Here are some examples.

First month. A low level of stimulation reduces stress and increases the infant's wakefulness and alertness. The brain essentially shuts down the system when there is overstimulation from competing sources. When talking to an infant, for example, filter out distracting noises, like a radio.

Months 1 to 3. Light/dark contours, like high-contrast pictures or objects, foster development in neural networks that encode vision. The brain also starts to discriminate among acoustic patterns of language, like intonation, lilt and pitch. Speaking to the infant, especially in an animated voice, aids this process.

Months 3 to 5. The infant relies primarily on vision to acquire information about the world. Make available increasingly complex designs that correspond to real objects in the baby's environment; motion also attracts attention. A large-scale picture of a fork, moved across the field of vision, would offer more stimulation than just an actual fork.

Months 6 to 7. The infant becomes alert to relationships like cause and effect, the location of objects and the functions of objects. Demonstrate and talk about situations, like how the turning of a doorknob leads to the opening of a door.

Months 7 to 8. The brain is oriented to make associations between sounds and some meaningful activity or object. For example, parents can deliberately emphasize in conversation that the sound of water running in the bathroom signals an impending bath, or that a doorbell means a visitor.

Months 9 to 12. Learning adds up to a new level of awareness of the environment and increased interest in exploration; sensory and motor skills coordinate in a more mature fashion. This is the time to let the child turn on a faucet or a light switch, under supervision.

Months 13 to 18. The brain establishes accelerated and more complex associations, especially if the toddler experiments directly with objects. A rich environment will help the toddler make such associations, understand sequences, differentiate between objects and reason about them.   —Sandra Blakeslee

Toddler Talk
When should your child begin speaking?

If your 18-month-old speaks fewer than 10 words, your 2-year-old uses no two-word combinations, or your 3-year-old's speech is unintelligible to anyone but the immediate family, should you worry? Is the child merely a slow talker who will eventually catch up to his or her peers, or does the child have a speech or language disorder in need of evaluation and therapy?

Every parent knows that children develop at different rates. There is a very wide range of normal. When children's ability to communicate lags way behind that of their peers, however, there may be reason for concern and a need to attend to the matter. Studies have shown that without any intervention, half of children with delays in the ability to express language at age 2 catch up to their peers by 3, and that another 25 percent have normal speech when they start school. But this leaves 25 percent of late-talking children who do not grow out of their problem before starting school. In such seriously speech-delayed children, intelligible speech may not appear on its own; these children often require professional help if they are to develop with normal social and academic skills.

Speech and language difficulties can have many causes, including an undetected hearing impairment, poor oral muscle tone or coordination, or a neurological disorder like apraxia, a breakdown in the transmission of messages from the brain to the muscles in the jaw, cheeks, lips, tongue and palate.

Too often, when parents express concern to the pediatrician or preschool teacher about what they believe are a child's speech and language problems, they are told to "wait and see." That can result in the loss of precious time during which the child might be receiving therapy. Uncorrected, these problems can lead to learning difficulties and

The Pros and Cons of Day Care

It's not who provides the care, but the quality

Preschool programs and day care centers have been studied extensively by researchers, and the reports are usually a mixed bag of risks and benefits.

The consensus of most child development specialists is that participation in day care and preschool programs is associated with improving children's pre-academic skills, language and memory; preparing them for kindergarten; and giving them an edge that persists through elementary school. A study of public school prekindergartens in Tulsa, Okla., for example, found that children experienced gains of nine months in prereading skills and five months in premath skills compared with other children their age.

The downside of day care—an increase in aggressiveness noted in several studies—persists through elementary school, and the more hours a child spends in day care, the worse it is. But many researchers dismiss the problem, saying the increases are so small as to be insignificant.

However, researchers agree it is critical that child care programs be of high quality and staffed by well-trained teachers who are responsive to children's developmental needs.

When parents are choosing a child care center, experts say they should seek out a program that is certified and licensed, meaning it meets basic requirements, and that is accredited by a professional organization like the National Association for Education of Young Children. They should ask about the qualifications of teachers and the staff turnover rates, and inquire about the caregiver-to-child ratio, which should be 1 caregiver for every 4 infants or toddlers, and 1 to 10 for prekindergarteners. Parents should always be free to drop in at a center unannounced.

It may be reassuring to parents to hear that ultimately, according to psychologists, it is family characteristics—including income, parents' education level and the mother's sensitivity—that are more strongly linked to child development than any element of child care.   —Roni Caryn Rabin

---

school failure, social ostracism, poor self-image, anxiety disorders and behavioral problems.

The authors of *The Late Talker: What to Do If Your Child Isn't Talking Yet,* Dr. Marilyn C. Agin, Lisa F. Geng and Malcolm J. Nicholl, point out that "speech and language disorders are the No. 1 developmental impairment in children under the age of 5." They offer age-appropriate guidelines to help parents detect early warning signs of serious communication gaps and urge parents to act if they find reason for concern. Here, briefly is what they say to look for.

What's Normal

• Typically, by age 2 children use a variety of two-word combinations (more cookie, Mommy work), know at least 50 words and mostly use words to communicate.

• At the age of 4, difficulties pronouncing "l" and "th" and frequent failure to string two consonants together ("geen" for "green") is also within the range of normal.

• It is not unusual for a child of 4 or 5 to mispronounce l, s, r, v, z, j, ch, sh and th. A 5- or 6-year-old who says "tiziz" for "scissors" does not have a speech or language disorder.

• All children misarticulate sounds in the course of normal speech development. They may use sound substitutions, like "wady" for "lady." They may omit sounds, saying "baw" instead of "ball." Or they may distort a sound, so that "spaghetti" comes out as "psketti."

One should be concerned, however, when these errors continue beyond the time when a child normally outgrows them—usually by 7 or 8.

Real Problems

- Toddlers who have little sound play as infants, who produce a limited number of consonants and make vowel errors

- Toddlers who do not try to imitate word combinations when prompted or fail to use gestures to complement their communicative efforts

- Children who do not show a vocabulary spurt by 30 months

- Children who at 33 months use a limited number of all-purpose verbs—want, go, get, do, make—as in "Me make water down"

- Three-year-olds who often omit consonants at the beginning and end of words, or who substitute consonants most often found at the end of words for front ones, as in "gun" for "done"

- Four-year-olds with weak grammar, as in "Her goed home"

- Children who are unable to repeat nonsense words of two or more syllables

For referrals to qualified professionals, contact the American Speech-Language-Hearing Association (asha.org) at 10801 Rockville Pike, Rockville, Md. 20852; 301-897-5700 or 800-638-8255.

—Jane E. Brody

If Your Child Has A.D.H.D

To medicate or not, that is the question

About 2.5 million children in the United States take stimulant drugs for attention and hyperactivity problems. But concerns about side effects have prompted many parents to look elsewhere: as many as two-thirds of children with attention deficit hyperactivity disorder, or A.D.H.D., have used some form of alternative treatment.

The most common strategy involves diet changes, like giving up processed foods, sugars and food additives. About 20 percent of children with the disorder have been given some form of herbal therapy; others have tried supplements like vitamins and fish oil or have used biofeedback, massage and yoga. While some studies of alternative treatments show promise, there is little solid research to guide parents. That is unfortunate, because for some children, prescription drugs aren't an option.

The drugs have been life-changing for many children. But nearly one-third experience worrisome side effects, and a 2001 report in *The Canadian Medical Association Journal* found that for more than 10 percent, the effects could be severe—including decreased appetite and weight loss, insomnia, abdominal pain and personality changes.

Although the drugs are widely viewed as safe, many parents were alarmed when the Food and Drug Administration ordered in 2006 that stimulants like Adderall, Ritalin and Concerta carry warnings of risk for sudden death, heart attacks and hallucinations in some patients.

What about the alternatives? *The Journal of the American Medical Association* reported that the first study of the herb St. John's wort worked no better than a placebo to counter A.D.H.D. But the trial, of 54 children, lasted only 8 weeks, and even prescription drugs can take up to three months to show a measurable effect. The larger issue may be that in complementary medicine, one treatment is rarely used alone, making the range of alternative remedies difficult to study.

Other herbal treatments for the disorder include echinacea, ginkgo biloba and ginseng. There are no reliable data on echinacea; a 2001 study showed improvement after 4 weeks in children using ginkgo and ginseng, but there was no control group for comparison.

HEALTH

If You Suspect a Child Has A.D.H.D.

💬 **When and where should parents seek help if they suspect that their child may have A.D.H.D?**

All children are inattentive, hyperactive, and impulsive to some extent, but the severity has to be great enough to cause impairment. Treatment should be sought when there is notable dysfunctionality, usually a significant disruption at home or school. Schools are often the first to recognize it. After that, parents typically go to their pediatrician, a child psychiatrist or maybe a pediatric neurologist. If there's no interest in treating A.D.H.D. with medication, a child psychiatrist might be able to deal with the problem through behavior modification.

Some online resources:

- **ADD Resources:** *www.addresources.org*

- **Centers for Disease Control and Prevention:** *www.cdc.gov*

- **CHADD (Children and Adults with Hyperactivity Disorder):** *www.chadd.org*

- **PediatricNeurology.Com:** *www.pediatricneurology.com*

There is more hope for omega-3 fatty acids, found in fish and fish-oil supplements. A review in the journal *Pediatric Clinics of North America* concluded that a "growing body of evidence" supported the use of such supplements for children with A.D.H.D.

As for dietary changes, a recent study in *The Lancet* examined the effect of artificial coloring and preservatives on hyperactive behavior in children. The study found that hyperactivity increased in the group of children given foods and drinks with additives. The results caused many pediatricians to rethink their skepticism about a link between diet and A.D.H.D.

Data on sugar avoidance are less persuasive. Several studies suggest that any link between sugar and hyperactivity is one of parental perception, rather than reality. In one study, mothers who were told the child received sugar reported more hyperactive behavior, even when the food was in fact artificially sweetened. Mothers who were told the child received a low-sugar snack were less likely to report worse behavior.

One interesting option is a form of biofeedback therapy in which children wear electrodes on their head and learn to control video games by exercising the parts of the brain related to attention and focus. Research has suggested that the method works just as well as medication, and many children report that they enjoy it.

The challenge is finding a doctor who will help explore the range of options. For instance, the best way to tell whether dietary changes may help is to eliminate the foods and then reintroduce them, monitoring the child's behavior all the while. The best evidence may come from a teacher who is unaware of any change in diet.

The Integrative Pediatrics Council, at www.integrativepeds.org, offers a list of pediatricians who offer alternative treatments. Its chairman, Dr. Lawrence D. Rosen, chief of pediatric integrative medicine at Hackensack University Medical Center in New Jersey, says parents should seek a holistic approach. But he notes that that may well include prescription drugs.

"I do prescribe medications in my practice, and there are kids whose lives have been saved by that," he says. "But it's a holistic approach that is very different than one pill, one symptom. We're addressing not just the physical, chemical needs of kids, but their total emotional and mental health."

—Tara Parker-Pope

How to Protect Your Children from Harm

Here's what should be high on your list of worries

Many parents worry that their children may be harmed by exposure to environmental factors they cannot avoid or control. But, a recent report in the journal *Pediatrics* discusses what are unquestionably the leading risks to infants, children and adolescents.

Accidents are the leading cause of death in children under 15. Most accidents involving children could be prevented by vigilance. Here are the most important hazards.

Sudden Infant Death Syndrome. Risk is reduced by putting infants to sleep on their backs and providing a nonsmoking environment.

Falls. Infants can suffer head injuries by falling from strollers, down stairs, off beds or against sharp-pointed furniture. Toddlers and children aged 5 to 9 fall from windows, stairs, trees, roofs and ladders.

Vehicular accidents. Infants and children under 10 should never ride in the front seat, and those under 80 pounds should always ride in a properly installed car seat or booster seat appropriate to the child's age and size.

Outside the car, children under 10 are at risk of death from pedestrian accidents, including being run over by the family car in their own driveway and ignoring safety rules when crossing the street.

For teenagers, reckless driving, impulsive behavior and drunken driving make auto accidents a leading cause of death.

Burns. Infants can suffer burns from kitchen equipment or hot items pulled off the table, as well as hot water in a tub and uncovered radiators. Toddlers should never have access to matches, cigarette lighters, or fuel-filled or flint igniters.

Every home should be equipped with one or more working smoke alarms.

Poisoning. As soon as children can crawl, they are at risk of poisoning from medications, household chemicals (including drain and oven cleaners, alcohol and paint thinner), pesticides and rodent killers. Such items should be stored out of children's reach, in cupboards with childproof locks.

Lead poisoning, though much reduced, is still a risk for millions of children who live in old homes with lead-based paint, plaster or putty, as well as those with old toys, cribs and imported pottery. A child's blood lead level should be checked and elevated levels treated to prevent cognitive deficits.

Drowning. Pools, hot tubs and wading pools must have supervision and be fenced in, locked or covered. Drowning is also a problem in bathtubs, bathinettes and kiddie wading pools. An infant or young child in or around water should never be left unattended, not even for a minute. Children relying on flotation devices and those under 4 who can swim are not safe in the water. Children should always swim with another swimmer. When boating, every infant and child—even good swimmers—should wear an approved life jacket.

Choking. Any item that can block a child's airway is a choking hazard. An infant or toddler can aspirate toys with small parts, deflated balloons, and foods like peanuts, raisins, raw carrots and popcorn. In addition to preventing exposure, every caretaker should know how to perform the Heimlich maneuver on infants and small children.

Guns. There are firearms in 40 million American homes. Guns in the home, including the homes of law enforcement officers, are dangers even to infants if there are older children around. Firearms should be stored in locked cabinets separate from their ammunition.

...And How to Raise a Moral Child

Empathy is the key to developing morality

"Children are going to learn morality not from what you tell them, but from how you treat them," says child psychiatrist Stanley Greenspan, whose book, *The Growth of the Mind and Its Endangered Future*, discusses how children develop their sense of morality. The way a child is treated is crucial, says Greenspan, whose research has shown that morality depends on a person's ability to feel empathy for someone else.

That sense of shared humanity, or "buying into the human race," comes from a child experiencing intimacy and warmth in a relationship with another person, whether that figure is the child's parents, relative or other close contact. It's impossible to develop a concern for others, Greenspan argues, unless someone in your life has shown concern for you.

That sense of shared humanity is only the starting point, however, for encouraging morality in children. "You can't empathize with someone else unless you can picture what the other person wants and desires and are able to put yourself in the other's shoes," says Greenspan. "If you can't put yourself in another's shoes, you can't really contemplate how your actions are going to affect them."

Empathy is essential, Greenspan says, because it helps guide children's judgments in cases where there may not be a clear-cut rule to follow, and a child may have to decide how to handle a moral dilemma on his own. If you simply tell a child, "You don't do this, you don't do that," says Greenspan, some children will obey out of a fear of being "a bad person," without really understanding what that means. Such children have what Greenspan calls "a concrete sense of morality, and can just as soon be immoral as moral" if a new authority figure with less savory rules appears. To make moral judgments, stresses Greenspan, "the kind we want in our Supreme Court justices, comes from a sense of empathy."

Electrocution. As soon as children can crawl, they are at risk of electrocution from uncovered outlets and frayed or brittle lamp or appliance cords. Older children should be taught what to do when a thunderstorm approaches—get out of the water immediately, and never stand under a tall tree.

Secondhand smoke. Parents or caretakers who smoke in the house or car in the presence of infants or children increase their risk of sudden death, asthma and pneumonia. They also set a terrible example.

Sports injuries. Riding a bicycle with an infant, even one in a child carrier and wearing a helmet, is dangerous. A child riding a tricycle, bicycle, scooter or skateboard should always wear a properly fitted helmet, which can reduce the risk of head injury and brain damage by 85 percent in a fall or crash. Cycling by children should be restricted to safe locations in daylight hours only. Children who play football, baseball, soccer, hockey and lacrosse should always wear protective equipment and be properly supervised.

Power tools. Each year nearly 10,000 children 15 and younger are injured by lawn mowers. A young child should not be nearby when a power mower is in use; children under 12 should not be allowed to operate a walk-behind mower; and children under 14 should not operate a riding mower.

Obesity. Children are getting fatter today, thanks to excessive amounts of snacks and fast foods, and the lack of exercise. Obesity that begins in childhood becomes a lifelong problem, greatly increasing the risk of a host of health and social problems, including premature death.
—Jane E. Brody

First Aid & Survival

The ABCs of CPR

Every adult should know how to perform CPR

Each year in the United States, emergency medical services treat more than 300,000 cardiac arrest victims. The American Heart Association estimates that almost 95 percent of them die before they get to the hospital. According to the A.H.A., about 75 to 80 percent of all cardiac arrests outside a hospital happen at home, and effective emergency CPR (cardiopulmonary resuscitation), can double or triple a victim's chance of survival.

"The most common reason many people die from cardiac arrest is that no one nearby knows CPR," says Dr. Michael Sayre, a professor of emergency medicine at Ohio State University who helped develop the updated 2008 guidelines on cardiopulmonary resuscitation for the American Heart Association. For the sake of their families and communities, all adults should learn to properly administer CPR.

ⓘ INSIDE INFO

CPR to the Rescue

○ For every minute that passes without immediate CPR and defibrillation, the chance of survival from cardiac arrest decreases by 10 percent.

○ CPR is used not only in the case of cardiac arrest from heart attacks, but also for victims of drowning, electrocution and other respiratory causes.

SOURCE: American Heart Association

Updating the way everyday people do CPR, the American Heart Association now recommends that rescuers give twice as many chest compressions—30 instead of 15—for every two rescue breaths. Indeed, the A.H.A. believes that chest compressions alone are as effective as CPR with breaths for adult victims of cardiac arrest.

Studies show that the increased number of chest compressions create more blood flow through the heart to the rest of the body, buying time until a defibrillator can be used to shock the heart, or the heart can pump blood on its own. Studies have also shown that blood circulation increases with each chest compression and must be built back up after an interruption, the Association says in its online journal, *Circulation*.

"When you stop compressions, blood flow stops," says Mary Fran Hazinski, a clinical nurse specialist at Vanderbilt University Medical Center. "You have to make up for that lost ground. We think that the fewer the interruptions, the better for blood flow. The bottom line is, we think more people need to learn CPR."

The guidelines also include these points:

• Comatose patients should have their body temperature cooled to about 90 degrees Fahrenheit for 12 to 24 hours after resuscitation. Two significant studies have shown that the practice can improve survival and brain function in such patients.

• After giving two rescue breaths, rescuers should not stop to check for signs of circulation before starting compressions.

- Instead of applying defibrillator pads up to three times before beginning CPR, rescuers should give one shock and then do two minutes of CPR, beginning with chest compressions, before trying the defibrillator again.

For more information on how to learn CPR, go to the American Heart Association's Web site: www.americanheart.org.

FOR ADULTS AND CHILDREN: CPR should be given where there is no breathing and no pulse. Tilt the victim's head backward and give two rescue breaths.

Step 1: Place the heel of your hand on the notch where the ribs meet the lower breastbone.

Step 2: Place your other hand on top of the first. Using the heel of your bottom hand, apply pressure on the breastbone. Your shoulders should be directly over your hands, and your elbows should be locked. Press the victim's chest down about 2 inches and then release. Repeat 30 times, keeping a smooth rhythm.

Step 3: Tilt the victim's head back slightly, lift his chin, place your mouth over his and give two slow breaths.

Step 4: Do three more sets of 30 compressions and two breaths (Steps 2 and 3). Each set should take about 15 seconds.

Step 5: Recheck the victim's pulse and breathing. If there is no pulse,

Step 6: Continue repeating Steps 2 and 3, pausing every couple of minutes to check the victim's pulse.

FOR INFANTS: Babies require lighter chest pressure delivered in shorter, more frequent cycles. If the infant is not breathing, give one rescue breath and begin the compressions.

A PRIMER ON RESCUE BREATHING

The timing intervals for administering mouth-to-mouth respiration to adults and children are somewhat different, but the mechanics are the same. If the victim is unable to breathe,

Step 1: The victim should be on his or her back. You begin by tilting the head slightly back and lifting the chin to move the tongue away from the back of the throat. You should also pinch the victim's nose shut.

Step 2: Make a tight seal with your mouth around the victim's mouth, breathing slowly into the victim until his chest gently rises. You should give two breaths, each lasting about two seconds. Pause between breaths to let the air flow out.

Step 3: Check the victim's pulse after the two initial breaths. If pulse is present, but the person is still not breathing,

Step 4: For adults, continue giving one breath about every 5 seconds, or 12 breaths per minute.

For infants and children, continue giving one breath about every 3 seconds, or 20 breaths per minute.

Step 5: Recheck the victim's pulse every minute. Continue rescue breathing as long as the pulse is present but the victim is not breathing.

Reminder: Call the local emergency number as soon as possible.

Step 1: Place two fingers on the breastbone just below an imaginary line between the nipples.

Step 2: Using the two fingers, apply pressure on the infant's breastbone. Press the infant's chest

HEALTH

down and then release. Give 5 to 10 compressions of about 3 seconds each, keeping a smooth rhythm.

Step 3: Tilt the infant's head back slightly, place your mouth over his nose and mouth and give one slow breath.

Step 4: Do 12 cycles of 5 compressions and one breath. This should take about one minute.

If you haven't yet called the local emergency number, do. Be sure to carry the infant with you so you can continue giving CPR.

Step 5: Recheck the victim's pulse and breathing. If there is no pulse,

Step 6: Continue repeating Steps 2 and 3, pausing every few minutes to check the infant's pulse.

Dealing with Shock

When the body shuts down because of injury, immediate care is critical

Shock is the body's way of trying to deal with a bad situation. When a body experiences trauma from a serious injury, it often finds itself unable to maintain proper blood flow to all its organs. Shock is the mechanism that allows the body to ration blood flow so that the most important organs, such as the brain, heart, lungs and kidneys, get the blood they need, even when that means that less vital parts, such as arms, legs and skin, have to make do with less. This natural triage cannot be sustained for very long, however, without causing potentially life-threatening damage to the brain and heart.

CONTROLLING BLEEDING FROM AN OPEN WOUND

Pressure is the key to stopping blood from a serious injury. Bearing down on arterial pressure points may be necessary.

Step 1: Cover the wound with a sterile dressing or clean cloth and press firmly against the wound with your hand. Don't waste time washing the wound.

Step 2: Elevate the wound, if possible, above the level of the heart.

Step 3: Apply a roller bandage over the dressing to keep pressure on the wound. Tie or tape the bandage in place. After applying the bandage, check fingers or toes for warmth, color and feeling. If they are pale and cold, the bandage is too tight and needs to be loosened.

Step 4: If the bleeding doesn't stop, apply additional dressings. Also find a pressure point where you can squeeze the artery against the bone.

When the emergency that requires your assistance involves heavy bleeding, it's important to protect yourself against the risk of infection—especially if you have a cut, scrape or sore that could allow the victim's blood to mix with yours. One of the easiest ways for an infectious disease, such as the AIDS virus or hepatitis B, to be transmitted is through direct blood-to-blood exchange. To reduce risk, the American Red Cross advises the following:

- Avoid blood splashes.

- Use disposable latex gloves in emergencies involving bleeding.

- If gloves are unavailable, cover the wound with a dressing or other available barrier, such as plastic wrap.

- Avoid any contact in which the victim's blood touches any cuts, scrapes or skin irritations you may have.

- Always wash your hands as soon as possible, whether or not you wore gloves.

Shock, says the Red Cross, "can't be managed effectively by first aid alone. A victim of shock requires advanced medical care as soon as possible."

Early signs of shock include:

- Restlessness or irritability
- Altered or confused consciousness
- Pale, cool, moist skin
- Rapid breathing and rapid pulse

The proper response to shock is to:

- Stretch the victim out on his or her back.
- Treat any open bleeding.
- Help the injured restore normal body temperature, covering him or her if there is chilling.
- Talk to the victim reassuringly.
- Prop the legs up about a foot unless there are possible head, neck or back injuries, or broken bones in the hips or legs.
- Withhold food or drink, even though the victim probably feels thirsty.
- Call the rescue service immediately.

Saving a Choking Victim

Dr. Heimlich's maneuver has saved thousands

Since Dr. Henry Heimlich first published his findings on a technique to rescue choking victims in 1974, many thousands of lives have been saved through its use.

FOR ADULTS: If you see someone who is unable to speak and is choking and turning blue, you need to act immediately. Step behind the person and wrap your arms around them. Make a fist and place the thumb of that hand high up against

---

WHEN A CHILD IS CHOKING

Dr. Henry Heimlich of Cincinnati recommends:

Seat the infant on the rescuer's lap and use the pads of the index and middle fingers of both hands to press upward—abruptly but gently—just under the diaphragm where the central chest bone (sternum) ends.

Or place the baby faceup on a flat surface and press upward under the diaphragm using the same fingers.

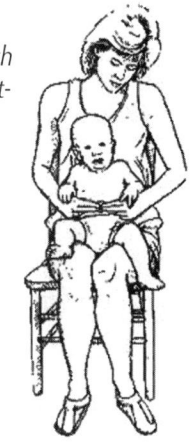

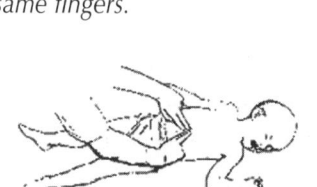

SOURCE: Heimlich Institute

---

the person's abdomen, though below the ribcage. Grasp your fist with your other hand and quickly push your fist into the abdomen with an upward thrust. Continue to repeat this motion until the obstruction has been expelled.

FOR INFANTS AND CHILDREN: First, it is important to distinguish between choking that is life-threatening and what people commonly call choking. The time to act immediately to try to dislodge an object obstructing the windpipe is when the child cannot make a sound, cough or cry, or the child's face turns from red to blue.

If a child can cough, then the windpipe is not obstructed, because coughing requires breathing. The situation is unlikely to become dangerous unless you start slapping the child on the back. The slaps can push the object farther down and perhaps obstruct the trachea.

When it comes to treating choking in infants, Heimlich's advice remains at odds with the American Heart Association, which says a repeated sequence of thrusts using your index and middle fingers should be used. But he maintains that could be challenging for a panicked caretaker to execute. Furthermore, Heimlich recommends seating the infant on the rescuer's lap or placing the baby faceup on a flat surface and, using the pads of the index and middle fingers of both hands, pressing upward—abruptly but gently—just under the diaphragm where the central chest bone (the sternum) ends. That compresses the lungs evenly, producing a forceful flow of air that can expel the choking object.

The American Heart Association says this method can damage organs. Instead, it recommends chest thrusts, which Heimlich says do not produce the air pressure needed to push out an obstructing object.

For toddlers and older children, Heimlich and the A.H.A. agree that the Heimlich maneuver is the method of choice. It can be done with the child lying faceup or standing or sitting with the rescuer kneeling behind the child.

For a toddler or small child, the rescuer should use the heel of one hand to exert an upward thrust just under the diaphragm. For a larger child, a standard Heimlich can be done, using the fist of one hand with the other hand clasped over it.

Heimlich says the Heimlich maneuver can also dislodge an object like a chicken bone that is stuck in the throat but not completely obstructing the windpipe, because the resulting force of air produces a hurricanelike effect in the airway that can blow out the object.

—Jane E. Brody

Treating a Burn

Dos and don'ts for treating a slight singe and much worse

Burns are classified by the amount of damage done to the skin and other body tissue. Every family member should be able to identify the severity of burns and know how to treat them.

First-degree burns are minor and heal quickly. SYMPTOMS: *reddened skin; tender and sore*

TIMELY TIPS

What's Dangerous for Babies

Anything bite-size or larger, or any food or object that does not melt or break down easily, can obstruct a baby's windpipe if it is accidentally inhaled instead of swallowed. Thus, Cheerios are safe for babies starting to feed themselves, but raisins are not.

The foods that are hazards for young children include:

✔ **grapes:** remove the skin and quarter the grape for children 4 and under

✔ **apples and pears:** peel and cook to soften for children under 4, peel and cut small for those 4 to 6

✔ **raisins:** not for children under 3

✔ **nuts:** not for children under 6

✔ **popcorn:** not for those under 4

✔ **carrots:** purée for children 2 and younger; cook to soften for those 3 and up

✔ **celery:** never raw for children 4 and under; bite-size for 5- and 6-year-olds

✔ **hotdogs:** never for children under 3; remove skin and cut into small pieces for older children

✔ **peanut butter:** not for children under 4; spread thinly on bread for those 4 to 6

✔ **hardcandy:** never for children 4 and under.

—Jane E. Brody

Second-degree burns are serious injuries and require immediate first aid and professional medical treatment. SYMPTOMS: *blistered skin; very painful*

Third-degree burns are severe injuries and require immediate professional medical treatment. SYMPTOMS: *white, brown or charred tissue, often surrounded by blisters; little or no pain at first*

If a person has been burned badly by fire, fast action on your part is very important. Have someone call 911. Meanwhile, you must act to begin the cooling process, prevent shock, prevent contamination and control pain.

- **DO** Wet, cover and cool the burn: gently pour water over the burns. Place the cleanest available cloth material over all burned areas, such as sterile gauze, clean sheets or a T-shirt, and gently pour water over them, keeping the material wet. Ensure that the cooling process does not become excessive and cause shivering.

- **DO** Remove smoldering clothing only if it is NOT stuck to the skin.

- **DO** Carefully remove clothing or jewelry that may constrict during swelling.

- **DO** Have the victim lie down. Make certain his head and chest are a little lower than the rest of his body. Raise his legs if possible.

- **DO** Treat for shock: to reduce the risk of shock, keep the victim's body temperature normal. Cover unburned areas with a dry blanket.

- **DO** Get immediate medical help. Call 911.

- **DO NOT** Put ice, burn ointments, butter, grease or anything else besides water on a burn.

- **DO NOT** Remove clothing that is stuck to a burn.

- **DO NOT** Break blisters.

SOURCE: Virginia Department of Fire Programs

When Someone Is Poisoned

How to deal with a variety of toxins

Poison can be inhaled, ingested, injected, or the result of a bite or sting. The more information you have on the cause of the poisoning, the better. Here is what to do.

1. Remain calm.

2. If you have a poison emergency and the victim has collapsed or is not breathing, call 911. If you have a poison exposure and the victim is alert, call 800-222-1222. Try to have the following information ready if possible:

- the person's age and estimated weight
- the container or bottle of the poisonous product, if available
- time that the poison exposure occurred
- your name and phone number

3. Follow the instructions from the emergency operator or the poison control center.

SOURCE: Centers for Disease Control and Prevention

TREATING INSECT BITES

When it comes to emergency treatment for insect bites, unless you do not have one essential ingredient in your first-aid kit, you may be out of luck.

Everyone who has ever had even a mild systemic reaction to an insect bite, or who is suspected of having severe allergies to insect bites should always carry self-injectable epinephrine whenever they venture outside. Guidelines on emergency room treatment call for patients who manifest symptoms of less severe systemic reactions—for example, a sting in one place and a rash or hives in another—to be given immediate treatment with epinephrine, a prescription for self-injectable epinephrine for future prevention and a referral to an allergist. Dr. Carlos A.

Camargo, associate professor of medicine and epidemiology at Harvard, says that self-injectable epinephrine is essential equipment for anyone with a history of systemic allergic reactions.

—Nicholas Bakalar

IF A SNAKE STRIKES AND BITES

Follow these three steps:

1. Calm the victim and wash the bite with soap and water.

2. Keep the bitten area lower than the heart and restrict movement. Remove anything constrictive, as the area may swell.

3. If a victim is unable to reach medical care within 30 minutes, wrap an Ace bandage 2 to 4 inches above the bite to help slow the venom's progress toward the heart. Do not use ice. Place a pump suction device over the wound and remove as much of the venom as possible. Get anti-venom medicine as soon as possible, preferably administered by a doctor.

SOURCE: John Henkel, *FDA Consumer Magazine*

HEROIN OVERDOSES

The sad thing about heroin overdoses is that they are preventable with a simple injection. Heroin is an opioid, just like methadone, OxyContin and Vicodin, to name a few. Because overdosing kills by slowly stopping a person's breathing, there is a short time in which a person can be injected with an antidote called naloxone, quickly reversing an opioid overdose.

If given early enough, naloxone can prevent damage to the brain caused by lack of oxygen and leave the victim unharmed. According to research by Dr. Sandro Galea of the Center for Urban Epidemiological Studies at the New York Academy of Medicine, at least 75 percent of overdose deaths involve multiple drugs, usually mixtures of heroin and other depressants like alcohol. Removing the opioid from the mix with naloxone is often enough to revive victims.

Naloxone itself is virtually harmless. Its most common side effects are withdrawal symptoms like nausea, shakiness and agitation in those who are

---

THE FIRST STEP: A FIRST-AID KIT

Assemble a first-aid kit for your home and one for each car. A first-aid kit should include the following items:

- Sterile adhesive bandages in assorted sizes
- Two-inch and 4-inch sterile gauze pads (four to six of each)
- Hypoallergenic adhesive tape

- Triangular bandages (three)
- Two-inch and 3-inch sterile roller bandages (three rolls of each)
- Splints:$1/4$ inch thick x 3 inches wide x 12 to 15 inches long
- Scissors, tweezers, needle
- Moistened towelettes
- Antiseptic
- Sterile saline solution
- Thermometer
- Tongue blades (two)

- Tube of petroleum jelly or other lubricant
- Assorted sizes of safety pins
- Cleansing agent/soap
- Latex gloves (two pairs)
- Eye goggles
- Sunscreen

NONPRESCRIPTION DRUGS SUCH AS:

- Aspirin or nonaspirin pain reliever (Remember: no aspirin for children!)

- Anti-diarrhea medication
- Antacid (for stomach upset)
- Laxative
- Syrup of Ipecac (use to induce vomiting if advised by the Poison Control Center)
- Activated charcoal (use if advised by the Poison Control Center)
- Self-injectable epinephrine

SOURCE: Centers for Disease Control and Prevention

physically dependent on opioids. While uncomfortable, these symptoms are not dangerous. Rarely, seizures can occur, but this risk is far lower than the risk to those who are not treated. The drug has no effect on those who haven't taken opioids.

—Maia Szalavitz

How to Alleviate Heatstroke
Cooling the body from the inside out

The thinking used to be that when you were suffering from heatstroke you should cool the outside of the body as quickly as possible. But recently it has been found that these methods are not only an inefficient way for the body to cool down, they can actually be quite dangerous.

Stanford professors Craig Heller and Dennis Grahn conducted a series of experiments on "exertional hyperthermia" and the methods for combating it. What they found was surprising. Bringing someone suffering from hyperthermia into a cool environment, it turns out, is precisely the wrong thing to do. When warm skin encounters coldness, the blood vessels near the surface of the skin constrict. Heat becomes trapped inside the body and is redirected to the core, which causes a spike in temperature. The better thing to do is to cool the palms of the hand. This thinking is premised on the little-known fact that our palms, along with the soles of our feet and our cheeks, are "natural mammalian radiators," as Heller puts it. When the body is overheated, it naturally increases blood flow to the palms.

Heller and Grahn invented a machine called The Glove. It consists of an airtight, transparent chamber shaped like a giant Dustbuster, inside of which is a metal plate resting on top of a pool of circulating cool water. A heatstroke victim puts his or her hand into the chamber and places it on

---

ⓘ INSIDE INFO

If You Get Hypothermia

○ Do not use a stove, electric blankets or a hot tub to warm someone up. Doing so can cause dangerous physiological changes.

○ Do get the victim out of the cold and to the hospital quickly. At the hospital, a victim can be warmed using special hypothermia blankets, warmed IVs, and humidified oxygen.

○ In severe cases cardiopulmonary bypass or dialysis can be used to warm the patient from the inside out, according to cold weather care specialists.

—Aimée Berg

---

the plate, which is usually about 70 degrees Fahrenheit. A mild vacuum pressure further increases blood flow to the hand. After the blood has been cooled in the person's palm, it returns through the veins directly to the heart, and is then circulated to overheated muscles and organs, cooling the body, according to trials, by more than 3 degrees in 10 minutes. For those who do not have access to a machine, the next best thing is to submerge a heatstroke victim's hand in cool, not icy, water until medical help can be summoned.

—Joel Lovell

Dealing with Flu Pandemics
Ways to prevent and treat influenza

The Centers for Disease Control and Prevention offers these responses to frequently asked questions about flu prevention and treatment.

ⓠ How can I protect myself from getting sick?

There are everyday actions that can help prevent the spread of germs that cause respiratory illnesses like influenza.

SOURCE: pandemicflu.gov

ⓘ INSIDE INFO

Flu Terms to Know

○ **Avian(or Bird) flu** is caused by influenza viruses that occur naturally among wild birds. Some are common and cause few problems in birds. But the H5N1 is deadly to birds, chickens, and other fowl. There is no human immunity against the virus; vaccine availability is limited. As a result, the bird flu is deadly to humans.

○ **H1N1 influenza** is a respiratory disease of pigs caused by type A influenza viruses; the outbreaks are fairly common in swine. Infections can be transmitted to humans, as was the case in 2009, when H1N1, commonly called the swine flu, spread to many parts of the world.

- Cover your nose and mouth with a tissue when you cough or sneeze. Throw the tissue in the trash after you use it.
- Wash your hands often with soap and water, especially after you cough or sneeze. Alcohol-based hand cleaners are also effective.
- Avoid touching your eyes, nose or mouth. Germs spread this way.
- Try to avoid close contact with sick people. Stay home if you are sick for 7 days after your symptoms begin or until you have been symptom-free for 24 hours, whichever is longer. This means avoiding normal activities, including work, school, travel, shopping, social events, and public gatherings to keep from infecting others and spreading the virus.

ⓠ What is the best technique for washing my hands to avoid getting the flu?

Wash your hands often with soap and water for 15 to 20 seconds. When soap and water are not available, use alcohol-based disposable hand wipes or gel sanitizers. If using gel, rub your hands until the gel is dry. The gel doesn't need water to work; the alcohol in it kills the germs.

ⓠ What are influenza symptoms?

Symptoms include fever, body aches, runny or stuffy nose, sore throat, nausea, or vomiting or diarrhea.

ⓠ What should I do if I get sick?

If you have a severe illness or are at high risk for flu complications, contact your doctor, who will determine whether flu testing or treatment is needed.

Children experiencing any of these symptoms need urgent medical care:

- Fast or troubled breathing
- Bluish or gray skin color
- Not drinking enough fluids
- Severe or persistent vomiting
- Not waking up or not interacting
- Being so irritable that the child does not want to be held
- Flu-like symptoms improve but then return with fever and worse cough

For adults, warning signs that require urgent medical care include:

- Difficulty breathing or shortness of breath
- Pain or pressure in the chest or abdomen
- Sudden dizziness
- Confusion
- Severe or persistent vomiting
- Flu-like symptoms improve but then return with fever and worse cough

ⓠ What other things can I do during a flu outbreak?

Other important actions you can take are:

- Follow public health advice regarding school closures and avoiding crowds.
- Be prepared in case you get sick and need to stay home for a week or so. Have supplies on hand of over-the-counter medicines and other items you need to avoid making trips outdoors while you are sick and contagious.

Q Are there medicines to treat influenza infections?

That depends on the strain of influenza. Antiviral drugs, such as oseltamivir or zanamivir, are recommended for the treatment and prevention of infection with the H1N1 flu virus. Antiviral drugs are prescription medicines (pills, liquid or an inhaler) that keep flu viruses from reproducing in your body.

If you get sick, antiviral drugs can make your illness milder and may also prevent serious flu complications.

What to Do in an Earthquake

Ways to prepare for a temblor and a tsunami

The sheer force of the earth's shifting tectonic plates is tough to imagine. Most people don't realize that 39 states are at risk from earthquakes, and the threat isn't confined to towns on fault lines. (For further information about why earthquakes happen, see page 761, Weather and Geology section.)

Here are some frequently asked questions, and answers about what to do if an earthquake strikes in your area, from the geophysicists at the U.S. Geological Survey in Menlo Park, California.

Q What should be done to prepare for an earthquake?

The collapse of a house isn't very likely, unless the house is located near a ledge where a landslide is possible. Fire as a result of ripping a gas line or shaking water heaters is much more likely. So the first step you should take if you live

in an earthquake-prone area is to find and repair faulty electrical wiring, leaky gas and inflexible utility connections. Bolt down water heaters and gas appliances, and put heavy objects on lower shelves, then fasten the shelves to the walls. Store bottled foods, glass and china on low shelves that can be fastened shut.

If you live in an apartment built before the 1980s, there are engineering retrofits that can fix "soft" first floors—buildings with garages on the first floor, where the foundation would be most likely to collapse. You may want to check to see if your building has had that done. If you live in a house, make sure you have it anchored to the foundation.

Q Where are the most dangerous places to be in a quake?

In your home, it's a bad idea to be near anything that can topple over, like tall bookcases and light fixtures. You should also stay away from windows where the glass can shatter, and from fireplaces—the brick or stone could crumble.

If you're inside, get under a sturdy desk, table or bench, or hold on to an inside wall. In crowded public places, don't rush for a doorway, since other people will be doing the same thing.

TIMELY TIPS

Disaster Info

Some useful Web sites for disaster information:

✔ **American Medical Association:** *www.ama-assn.org*

✔ **Centers for Disease Control and Prevention:** *www.cdc.gov*

✔ **Federal Emergency Management Agency (FEMA):** *www.fema.gov*

✔ **National Weather Service:** *www.nws.noaa.gov*

✔ **Red Cross:** *www.redcross.org*

Take cover and move away from display shelves and anything else that could fall on you. Stay on the same floor, and don't use elevators. If you're outside, stay there. Move away from buildings, street lights and utility poles and wires.

SOURCES: U.S. Geological Survey; reporting by Kenneth Chang

Riding Out a Thunderstorm
Keep away from metal, water and tall structures

All thunderstorms are dangerous because they produce lightning, an electrical discharge that results from the buildup of positive and negative charges within a thunderstorm. When the buildup becomes strong enough, lightning appears as a "bolt." This flash of light usually occurs within the clouds or between the clouds and the ground. A bolt of lightning reaches a temperature approaching 50,000 degrees Fahrenheit in a split second. It is the rapid heating and cooling of the air near the lightning that causes thunder.

In the United States, an average of 300 people are injured and 80 people are killed each year by lightning. Although most victims survive, people struck by lightning often report a variety of long-term, debilitating symptoms.

Other associated dangers of thunderstorms include tornadoes, strong winds, hail and flash flooding. Flash flooding is responsible for more fatalities—more than 140 annually—than any

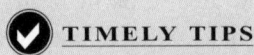 **TIMELY TIPS**

Surviving a Flood
You can't build an ark, but you can take some precautions

Floods cause more damage nationwide than any other natural disaster. Often the result of hurricanes, floods occur most frequently during the hurricane season, which runs roughly from July through November. To estimate your own flood risk, go to floodsmart.gov and plug in your address in the Risk Profile box. Here are some tips from the Federal Emergency Management Agency (FEMA) to help you survive rising waters.

BEFORE THE FLOOD

✔ **Make an itemized list** of your furnishings, clothing and valuables. Photos can help insurance adjusters settle your claims and help you verify uninsured losses, which are tax-deductible.

✔ **Keep your insurance policies** and the inventory of your personal property in a secure place, such as a safe-deposit box.

DURING THE FLOOD

✔ **Have a battery-operated radio on hand** and keep it tuned to a local station for announcements regarding evacuation plans.

✔ **Turn off all utilities at the main switch.** Do not touch electrical equipment unless it is dry or you are standing on a piece of dry wood and are wearing rubber gloves and rubber footwear.

✔ **Open basement windows** to equalize the water pressure on the foundation and walls.

✔ If you are caught in the house and flood waters are suddenly rising around your house, move to the second floor and, if necessary, to the roof. Take warm clothing, a flashlight and the radio with you. Do not try to swim to safety.

✔ **If you evacuate your home,** do not attempt to cross any stretch of flood waters on foot if the water is above your knees.

✔ **Do not drive through flooded roads.** Rapidly rising water could carry your car away, possibly trapping you inside. Be careful if you must evacuate at night, when flooded areas are harder to see. If your car stalls, get out and climb to higher ground.

other thunderstorm-associated hazard. Here is some advice for what to do in a thunderstorm.

If indoors: Do not handle any electrical equipment or telephones, because lightning could follow the wire. Television sets are particularly dangerous at this time.

- Avoid bathtubs, water faucets and sinks, because metal pipes can transmit electricity.
- Close all windows.

If outdoors: Attempt to get into a building or car. If no structure is available, get to an open space and squat low to the ground as quickly as possible. (If in the woods, find an area protected by a low clump of trees—never stand underneath a single large tree in the open.) Be aware of the potential for flooding in low-lying areas.

- Crouch with hands on knees.
- Avoid tall structures such as towers, tall trees, fences, telephone lines or power lines.
- Stay away from natural lightning rods such as golf clubs, tractors, fishing rods, bicycles or camping equipment.
- Stay away from rivers, lakes or other bodies of water. If on the water, get to land if possible.
- If you are isolated in a level field or prairie and you feel your hair stand on end (which indicates that lightning is about to strike), bend forward, putting your hands on your knees. A crouching position with feet together while removing all metal objects is recommended. Do not lie flat on the ground.

If in a car: Pull safely onto the shoulder of the road away from any trees that could fall on the vehicle.

- Stay in the car and turn on the emergency flashers until the heavy rains subside.
- Avoid flooded roadways.

SOURCE: FEMA

When a Twister Is Approaching
Go to the lowest, innermost room in the building, and crawl under a table away from windows

Tornadoes are nature's most violent and erratic storms. In an average year, around 1,000 tornadoes are reported nationwide, according to the Storm Prediction Center in Norman, Okla.; 60 people die and 1,500 are injured as a result of twisters. The most violent of these storms are capable of reaching wind speeds of 250 m.p.h. or more, creating damage paths that can be over a mile wide and 50 miles long. Meteorologists for the National Weather Service in Topeka, Kan. offer some tips on surviving a tornado.

Plan ahead, no matter where you live. You are at greatest risk for tornadoes if you live in the Midwest, particularly in the plains and the Mississippi Valley, but during the spring and summer, tornadoes have been spotted across the United States. The Northeast is least likely to be hit by tornadoes—Connecticut had 35 over a 30 year period ending in 2008, compared to Texas's 4,581, according to the National Oceanic and Atmospheric Administration's Storm Prediction Center. Tornadoes do hit major cities: several have occurred in large population centers such as Jacksonville, Fla.; Brooklyn, N.Y.; Nashville, Tenn.; Fort Worth, Tex.; Oklahoma City, Okla.; and Topeka, Kan. Tornadoes can occur in the mountains, in cities and over bodies of water.

Know the warning signs. Regardless of where you are, tornadoes rarely arrive unannounced. Before a tornado can develop, first there have to be thunderstorms in the area. There will be thunder, lightning and dark skies. Figure out ahead of time where you would seek shelter if a tornado occurs, and practice this emergency maneuver with your family on a sunny day.

Preparing for a Hurricane

Trying to ride out a tropical storm is a huge risk

As hurricanes approach the coast, a huge dome of water called a storm surge crashes into the coastline—9 out of 10 people killed in hurricanes are victims of these storm surges. And as any survivor of Hurricane Katrina, the powerful storm that hit the Gulf Coast in 2005, all too painfully knows, if you live in a coastal area near the ocean, you cannot take the risk of riding out the storm at home.

To be considered a hurricane, a tropical storm must have winds that reach speeds of at least 74 m.p.h. and blow counterclockwise around a center eye. Hurricane winds have been clocked at 175 m.p.h., and the combination of the winds and torrential rains can spawn torna-does and cause severe flooding, affecting areas hundreds of miles inland. Some tips from the National Hurricane Center:

✔ **Know how little time a hurricane watch or warning gives you.** If a hurricane watch is issued, you have 24 to 36 hours before the hurricane hits land. A hurricane warning means that hurricane winds and storm tides are expected in a specific coastal area within 24 hours. A NOAA (National Oceanic and Atmospheric Administration) Weather Radio with a warning alarm and battery backup is useful in case the power goes out.

✔ **Ask your local emergency management office about community evacuation plans.** Learn your evacuation routes and plan a place for your family to meet in case you are separated. As part of this plan, choose an out-of-state contact for everyone to call and say they're O.K.

✔ **Cover your windows.** People who live in Florida, Texas and along the Gulf Coast should have shutters in their homes. If you don't have them, you should cover your windows with 5/8-inch marine plywood, cut to fit and ready to install. Put some sort of slugs in the wall, or lag-bolts, to secure the wood.

✔ **If you live right on the ocean, go far inland.** Fill up your car's gas tank ahead of time if there's a chance you might need to evacuate. Once the storm has arrived, service stations may be closed.

✔ **Know how to shut off your utilities.** It's important that you know where the shut-off devices are for the gas, plumbing and electrical lines in the house. Before leaving your home, turn these systems off.

✔ **Make arrangements for housing your pets.** Many emergency shelters don't allow pets. Call your local humane society for more information.

Keep a NOAA Weather Radio plugged in or with fresh batteries. Take it with you if you are outdoors or traveling. This special receiver will be activated when severe weather watches or warnings are issued by the National Weather Service. You'll find stations between 162.400 and 162.550 on the dial. Since this band isn't available on most radios, know where the closest transmitter is, and tune in—this is particularly helpful if you are in a car, or have already sought shelter in a room where television is unavailable and you need a tornado update.

Understand the difference between tornado watches and tornado warnings. The Storm Prediction Center issues tornado watches when the weather is favorable for the formation of severe thunderstorms that will be capable of producing deadly tornadoes. Tornado warnings are issued by the National Weather Service when forecasters have detected a tornado using Doppler radar or when a report of a tornado has been received. Tornadoes can occur without a watch or warning in effect.

Don't open your windows to equalize pressure in the house. This is one of the biggest myths of tornado preparation. Use that time to seek appropriate shelter in a sturdy building, on the lowest floor or innermost room, away from windows. Although houses cannot explode from pressure, the strong winds that accompany severe thunderstorms and tornadoes cause damage to buildings.

Get to the lowest floor of the building you're in. But don't get caught in an elevator trying to do it. If the building has no basement, find an interior room like a bathroom or closet. The pipes in the walls usually reinforce the building structure. Be sure to avoid windows—flying glass is a major cause of tornado injury.

Find a heavy table or workbench to get under. If you have no basement, go to an inside room on the lowest floor, like a closet, hallway or bathroom with no windows. If possible, cover your body with a blanket, sleeping bag or pillows to protect yourself from falling debris. Again, stay away from windows.

Escape to the east if you're in a car and have time. Tornadoes generally move from west to east. If the storm is over a mile away, and you know the area, drive away from it, heading east or south. As it nears, however, do not stay in your car, and do not seek shelter in highway underpasses. High-force winds can easily lift cars—even 18-wheelers. The most dangerous place to be during a tornado is in a car. You could be injured by flying debris funneled beneath the bridge.

Find a gully, ditch or low spot on the ground if you are caught outside. Lie flat and put your arms over your head. If possible, cover yourself with a blanket or sweater. Culverts, the drainage pipes that run under roads, are good places to be if you're caught outside. If you are abandoning your vehicle, move a safe distance away from it. Boards and stones lofted at high speeds become quite dangerous. Flying pieces of glass and metal are like razors when they're caught by tornado winds. The winds are unimaginably strong, and there are many stories of people who were picked up by tornadoes and carried several miles from where they were.

Walking Away from a Plane Crash
A crash survivor shares what she learned

Robin Fech was the only flight attendant aboard a 30-seat twin-engine Atlantic Southeast Airlines turboprop on August 21, 1995. That was the day it careened to the ground, crashed and burst into flames on a Georgia hayfield, killing eight of the 27 people on board. The surviving passengers praised Fech's remarkable composure, crediting her ability to maintain calm and order as the reason they came out of the crash alive. Fech has thought a lot about her ordeal, and here she offers advice on safety measures to take before flying, during a troubled flight and in the aftermath of a crash.

Wear loose-fitting cotton clothing. Jogging pants may not be fashionable, but they allow you ease of movement and removal. And opt for natural fibers. "Synthetic materials are often highly flammable. People who are really concerned about crashing don't wear nail polish, hair spray or perfume, which are also flammable," Fech explains. Fech would add tennis shoes to that list. In the crash, she spotted a man whose jeans were on fire, but she couldn't remove them because the soles of his shoes had melted and stuck to his feet. She herself was wearing panty hose, which melted on her legs.

Fech recommends comfortable, flat shoes that are easy to slip off yet offer support to your feet if you need to climb, for example.

As you board a plane, look around. Touch the seats and count them until you reach yours. This helps you to feel your way out in case of darkness or smoke. Locate not only the exit nearest you but alternates as well. "Our passenger door wouldn't open," Fech recalls, "but in our case, we didn't really need the exit, because the plane had split in half."

Pay close attention during the safety demonstration. "Frequent-flyers are the worst offenders," says Fech. "Some of the survivors on our flight later remembered that they were reading their books instead of paying attention to the safety demonstration." Fortunately, Fech had time to demonstrate the crash position before the plane hit the ground: lean forward, cross your arms on the seat in front of you and place your head on your arms. If there's room in front of you, grab your ankles and put your chest on your thighs and your head between your knees. The intent is to lean forward as much as possible. Seat belts should be low and tight. Legs should be uncrossed and both feet should be flat on the floor.

Fech also asked passengers to empty their pockets; items there could cause injury upon impact. "Anything in your lap, like a computer, becomes a flying javelin," says Fech. Things like eyeglasses, pens and pencils, should be removed and put in the seat pocket.

When Your Home Catches Fire

Simple precautions can prevent a major bonfire

Recent figures from the U.S. Fire Administration show that residential fires kill more than 3,000 Americans a year. Here are some tips from the U.S.F.A. and Federal Emergency Management Agency to make sure you're never trapped in a burning house, or if you are, how to cope.

Put smoke detectors on every floor of your house. Smoke detectors double your chances of living through a fire. They should be near bedrooms and away from air vents. To ensure that they're not shielded from smoke, keep them at least 4 to 6 inches away from walls and corners. Replace batteries at least once a year, at the same time, perhaps, as you're changing clocks for daylight saving time.

Ask your local fire department to inspect your house for fire safety. Often local fire houses provide this service. They could help you identify faulty furnaces or stoves, chimneys with buildup and places where home insulation is touching electrical wiring—all potential fire-starters. They can also give you advice on choosing and using fire extinguishers.

Don't overlook basic fire hazards. Be wary of frayed or cracked wiring, and don't put wiring under rugs, over nails or in high traffic areas. Avoid overloading outlets—if you're not sure, check to make certain they're staying cool to the touch. Never fill kerosene heaters with gasoline or camp stove fuel. Plug electric space heaters directly into the wall socket, not into extension cords. For wood-stoves and fireplaces, use only seasoned wood and always use a protective screen. Don't let old newspapers and magazines accumulate in storage areas.

Plan your escape before the emergency. If you have children, teach them two escape routes from every room. Keep emergency numbers, a whistle and a flashlight near the phone. Sleeping with doors closed helps delay the spread of fire. If you hear the alarm, feel your door. If it's cool, open it to exit, but crawl to avoid the smoke that rises. Cover your nose and mouth with a moist cloth. Stop, drop and roll if your clothes are on fire—teach it to your kids. Use the stairs, never an elevator, during a fire.

If you are trapped. Call the fire department for assistance. If you cannot get to a phone, yell out the window for help. Wave or hang a sheet or other large object to attract attention. Close as many doors as possible between yourself and the fire. Seal your door with rags. Open windows slightly at the top and bottom, but close them if smoke comes in.

What to Do If You're Mugged

How to up the odds of fending off an attacker

One out of three women in America will be attacked in her lifetime, according to government estimates. It's no wonder that women—and men, too—are anxious about walking to their cars in parking lots, going somewhere by themselves at night or even opening their front door at the end of the day. But no one wants to go through life being paranoid, and learning self-defense is a viable way to reach a balanced awareness.

The first step in self-defense is to figure out a plan, whether it is running to safety or delivering a crippling blow. Just as you have a fire escape plan in your house, you should have a plan for physical safety.

Women should be conscious of their body language when they are walking in public places. A confident stride, with eyes up and shoulders down, is preferable. Avoid carrying numerous bags or otherwise showing that you could not immediately fight back.

If a person stops you to ask for directions while you are walking, make sure you can see his feet in your peripheral vision. That means he's a safe distance away. If he asks you for help, volunteer to call the police rather than going anywhere with him.

Carrying Mace or pepper spray can be an effective defense tool, but only if you are both

TIMELY TIPS

Basic Moves in Your Own Defense

There are two times when experts say you should immediately fight back physically. One is if the attacker has rope, duct tape or some other means of tying your hands and feet, which will probably make it impossible for you to escape. The other is if someone wants to take you somewhere else; chances of surviving are lower if you are moved to a second location. Rosalind Wiseman, author of *Defending Ourselves,* describes what moves to make to repel an attacker.

✔ **A FRONTAL ATTACK.** The palm strike has the power of a punch but reduces injury to your hand and fingers. The primary target is the nose, but you can hit the mouth, chin, throat, ear or Adam's apple. The proper hand position is shown at far left and the follow-through in the next two figures.

✔ **CLOSE QUARTERS.** You can use your knee if you are at a close distance to the attacker. The two main targets with the knee are the attacker's groin and his head.

✔ **ATTACKS FROM BEHIND.** If you are attacked from behind or the side, you need to break the attacker's hold and create space between you. When you are touched, immediately yell and round your shoulders to protect your lungs and sternum. Then, look for his closest foot and stomp on it.

Surviving a Wild Animal Attack

If you face a wild beast someday, here's some advice

LION: Lions will usually not attack people unless they do not have anything else to eat. Nevertheless, make sure that you are not alone in an area inhabited by lions.

TIGER: Tigers will usually not attack unless they are able to sneak up on you or you have your back turned. In Nepal, for instance, natives wear a mask with eyes in the back to scare them off. If you do encounter a tiger, act aggressively. Hopefully, this is enough to make the largest predator in the world flee.

RHINO: Rhinos have bad eyesight and only attack if panicked. If you encounter a rhino, make sure that you give it plenty of distance.

GORILLA: When a gorilla attacks you, kneel down and don't look it in the eye.

prepared to use it and have practiced using it. A can of Mace in your purse with a safety latch you've never tried isn't going to do you much good in an emergency.

If someone with a weapon demands your wallet, you should comply—throwing the wallet away from you at a 45-degree angle. When the attacker goes after it, run to safety. Go where other people are—to a neighbor, a store, a gas station, but be sure to think about your destination instead of running blindly. Without a plan, a woman robbed in a parking garage, for example, might run into a stairwell, setting herself up for a second attack.

If you are being followed, use verbal self-defense. State loudly and clearly what you want the person to do, such as, "Go away! Leave me alone!" Fighting back should only be used as a last resort, but it can be a very powerful tool because it greatly reduces your chances of being raped or otherwise harmed.

If you are a woman fighting back, remember that your lower body is five times stronger than your upper body. When using self-defense techniques, aim for the attacker's eyes, nose, throat, groin, knees or feet. If it seems you can't defend yourself—if the attacker has a knife to your throat, for example—try to lull the assailant into thinking he has control. Convince him he's got you but needs to put down the knife. When he does, strike.

Dealing with Toxic Threats
In case of a biological or chemical attack

One lesson of the 2001 terrorist attacks on U.S. soil is that potential future disasters, perhaps involving biological and chemical agents, are not beyond the realm of the possible. Here are some sensible survival guidelines from the Centers for Disease Control and Prevention and the Federal Emergency Management Agency.

Preparing for a biological attack. Biological agents are organisms or toxins that can kill or incapacitate people, livestock and crops. The three groups of biological agents that would likely be used as weapons are bacteria, viruses and toxins. Most biological agents are difficult to grow and maintain. Many break down quickly when exposed to sunlight and other environmental factors, while others, such as anthrax spores, are very long lived. Biological agents can be dispersed by spraying them into the air, by infecting animals that carry the disease to humans and by contaminating food and water. You can find more information at the Centers for Disease Control Web site at bt.cdc.gov.

Before a biological attack. Check with your doctor to ensure all required or suggested immunizations are up to date. Children and older adults are particularly vulnerable to biological agents.

Consider installing a High Efficiency Particulate Air (HEPA) filter in your furnace return duct. These filters remove particles in the 0.3-to-10-micron range and will filter out most biological agents that may enter your house. HEPA filters will not filter chemical agents. If you do not have a central heating or cooling system, a stand-alone portable HEPA filter can be used.

During a biological attack. Public health officials may not immediately be able to provide information on what you should do. Watch television, listen to radio or check the Internet for official news on areas in danger, symptoms of the disease and where to get medical attention.

The first evidence of an attack may be when you notice symptoms of the disease caused by exposure to an agent. Be suspicious of unusual symptoms but do not assume that they are related to the attack. If you are exposed to a biological agent:

- Remove and bag your clothes and personal items. Follow official instructions for disposal of contaminated items.
- Wash yourself with soap and water and put on clean clothes.
- Seek medical assistance. You may be advised to stay away from others or even quarantined.

Facing a chemical attack. Be sure your supplies kit includes duct tape, scissors and plastic for doors, windows and ducts in the room where you will

If Confronted by a Bear

First decide if he's predatory or defensive

Common wisdom holds that the way to react to a bear, when all else fails, is simple: curl up in a ball and play dead. But that is not always the best idea. Attacks can generally be divided into two groups: predatory and defensive. Each calls for a different strategy.

Black and grizzly bears are capable of both types of attack. Those involving grizzlies tend to be defensive, when the animal feels threatened, according to Stephen Herrero, a bear expert at the University of Calgary and the author of *Bear Attacks: Their Causes and Avoidance.* Playing dead then lets the bear know you're not a threat and can cause it to back off.

Black bears usually flee from humans, but when they do attack, the motive tends to be predatory, and playing dead doesn't work. Neither does running away, since bears are much faster than humans.

If the bear is after food, it is best to drop it and back away, Herrero says. If the animal presses, he adds, be aggressive: shout, bang on objects or use pepper spray to scare it off. The National Parks Service and the National Wildlife Federation recommend similar measures.

—Anahad O'Connor

seek shelter. Premeasure and cut plastic sheeting for each opening.

Choose an internal room as a shelter, preferably without windows and on the highest level. Turn off all ventilation, including furnaces, air conditioners, vents and fans. Seal the room with duct tape and plastic sheeting.

- Listen to a radio for instructions from authorities.
- If you are caught in or near a contaminated

Preparing Your Mind for Disaster

Most discussions of disaster preparedness focus on community resources, but the most important variable in a disaster is your own behavior. Here is advice from experts on training yourself to become your own best defence in an emergency.

✔ **Rehearse.** Amanda Ripley, author of *The Unthinkable: Who Survives When Disaster Strikes—and Why*, says that although panic, denial and fear may be inevitable during a disaster, your brain will perform best in a stressful situation if you have already put it through a few rehearsals. Go through a fire drill, count seats to the nearest exit in an airplane. Your brain stores the data and responds to it more quickly and fully than words.

✔ **Resist your first impulse.** Whether it's a building fire or a plane emergency, people often move surprisingly slowly and find reasons to delay evacuation. Even on burning planes, passengers routinely open overhead bins to retrieve bags. Fight the "gathering instinct," even though it won't be your first impulse.

✔ **Shed the herd mentality.** Crowd behavior in a disaster is surprisingly predictable. Although there are cases of panic and stampedes during emergencies, "group think" is a more common reaction. People stick together, follow one another and are painfully slow during evacuations. A person who takes a leadership role will invariably be followed.

✔ **Be proactive.** Small steps can improve survival odds. Change smoke-detector batteries on schedule. And get to know your neighbors, who can be a valuable resource in emergencies.

—Tara Parker-Pope

area, you should move away immediately in a direction upwind of the source. Find shelter as quickly as possible.

After a chemical attack. Decontamination is needed within minutes of exposure to minimize health consequences. Do not leave to help others until authorities announce it is safe to do so.

A person affected by a chemical agent requires immediate medical attention from a professional. If medical help is not immediately available, decontaminate yourself and assist in decontaminating others. Decontamination guidelines are as follows:

- Use extreme caution when helping others who have been exposed to chemical agents.
- Remove all clothing and other items in contact with the body. Contaminated clothing normally removed over the head should be cut off to avoid contact with the eyes, nose and mouth. Put contaminated clothing and items into a plastic bag and seal it. Remove eyeglasses or contact lenses. Put glasses in a pan of household bleach to decontaminate them, and then rinse and dry.
- Flush eyes with water. Gently wash face and hair with soap and water before thoroughly rinsing.
- Decontaminate other body areas. Blot (do not swab or scrape) with a cloth soaked in soapy water and rinse with clear water, then change into uncontaminated clothes. Clothing stored in drawers or closets is likely to be uncontaminated.
- Proceed to a medical facility for screening and professional treatment.

FOOD & DRINK

FOOD

Diet & Nutrition

How to Eat Your Way to a Healthy Heart

The bottom line on healthy eating

Most people think heart-healthy living involves sacrifice. Give up your favorite foods. Break a sweat. Lose weight. But some of the best things you can do for your heart do not involve deprivation or medication. Simple and even pleasurable changes in the foods you eat can rival medication in terms of the benefit to your heart.

Just a few small changes—eating more fish, vegetables, nuts and fiber—can have a major impact on your risk for heart problems. For some people, drinking moderate amounts of wine may offer additional benefits. Even a 55-year-old man who is about 20 pounds overweight and does not exercise regularly will have a heart-disease risk far below average if he regularly consumes fish, nuts, fiber and vegetables and drinks moderate amounts of wine.

It's hard to believe that such simple food changes can make a meaningful difference, but data from hundreds of studies show they can.

For instance, a recent review of nearly 100 studies evaluating various cholesterol-lowering agents and diets showed just how potent fish can be as a heart protector. In studies of people who consume diets rich in omega-3 fatty acids like those found in fish, heart risk was 23 percent lower compared with a control group.

The same report, in *The Archives of Internal Medicine,* also reviewed studies of statin use and showed a 13 percent lower heart risk. Because it was not a head-to-head comparison, it cannot be concluded that eating fish is better than using statins. But the results clearly show the powerful effect of fish in the diet.

Many studies of fish consumption and heart health are based on observation of Eskimos and people in Mediterranean regions. And random clinical trials have shown that consuming omega-3 fatty acids can reduce heart attacks and cardiovascular death. These fatty acids can also slow the progress of atherosclerosis in coronary patients, according to the American Heart Association.

Several studies now show that regular consumption of omega-3s from a variety of sources, including fish, nuts and soybean oil, can lower cardiovascular risk as much as 60 percent, according to a review in *The American Journal of Cardiology.*

It doesn't take much fish. Doctors recommend eating it, particularly fatty kinds like mackerel, lake trout, herring, sardines, albacore tuna and salmon, just twice a week.

People worry about exposure to mercury and toxins from fish, but experts say that for middle-age and older men and postmenopausal women, the benefits of fish far outweigh the risks of exposure to environmental pollutants.

The data on increasing consumption of fiber-rich foods, vegetables and nuts is also compelling. A report in *Nutrition Reviews* concluded that eating just

**Eat food.
Not too much.
Mostly plants.**

Michael Pollan, author of
*In Defense of Food:
An Eater's Manifesto*

U.S.D.A. FOOD GUIDE

Below are U.S. government guidelines for recommended daily food intake. But Harvard's School of Public Health has its own "independent" version of a healthy eating pyramid, which places vegetables and fruits at the broad end and less-healthful foods like red meat and refined grains at the narrow end. You can find it at: www.hsph.harvard.edu/ nutritionsource/what-should-you-eat/pyramid/

MyPyramid.gov
STEPS TO A HEALTHIER YOU

FRUITS

***2 cups
(4 servings)***

1 SERVING IS:

½ *cup fresh, frozen or canned fruit*

1 medium fruit

¼ *cup dried fruit, ½ cup fruit juice*

OILS

27 grams (6 tsp)

1 TSP EQUIVALENT IS:

1 tbsp low-fat mayo

2 tbsp light salad dressing

1 tsp vegetable oil

VEGETABLES

***2.5 cups
(5 servings)***

Dark green vegetables
   3 cups/week

Orange vegetables
   2 cups/week

Legumes (dry beans)
   3 cups/week

Starchy vegetables
   3 cups/week

Other vegetables
   6.5 cups/week

1 SERVING IS:

½ *cup cut-up raw or cooked vegetable*

1 cup raw leafy vegetable

½ *cup vegetable juice*

GRAINS

6 servings

Whole grains
   3 servings/ day

Other grains
   3 servings/ day

1 SERVING IS:

1 slice bread, 1 cup dry cereal

½ *cup cooked rice, pasta, cereal*

MEAT AND BEANS

5.5 servings

1 SERVING IS:

1 oz cooked lean meats, poultry, fish

1 egg

¼ *cup cooked dry beans or tofu*

1 tbsp peanut butter, ½ oz nuts or seeds

MILK AND DAIRY

3 servings

1 SERVING IS:

1 cup low-fat/ fat-free milk or yogurt

1½ oz low-fat or fat-free natural cheese

2 oz low-fat or fat-free processed cheese

DISCRETIONARY CALORIC ALLOWANCE

267 calories

Example of distribution:	SOLID FAT [c]	18 GRAMS;
	ADDED SUGARS	8 TSP
1 TSP ADDED SUGAR EQUIVALENT IS:		½ oz jelly beans
		8 oz lemonade

a All servings are per day unless otherwise noted. U.S.D.A. vegetable subgroup amounts are per week.

b The 2,000-calorie U.S.D.A. Food Guide is appropriate for many sedentary males 51 to 70 years of age, sedentary females 19 to 30 years of age, and for some other gender/age groups who are more physically active. See "Caloric Requirements" table on the next page for information about gender/age/activity levels and appropriate calorie intakes.

c The oils listed in this table are not considered to be part of discretionary calories because they are a major source of the vitamin E and polyunsaturated fatty acids, including the essential fatty acids, in the food pattern. In contrast, solid fats (i.e., saturated and trans fats) are listed separately as a source of discretionary calories.

CALORIE REQUIREMENTS

These are estimated amounts of calories needed to maintain energy balance for various gender and age groups at three different levels of physical activity. If you exercise more, you are able to consume more calories. [a]

Age (years)	ACTIVITY LEVEL		
	SEDENTARY [b]	MODERATELY ACTIVE [c]	ACTIVE [d]
CHILD			
2-3	1,000	1,000-1,400[e]	1,000-1,400[e]
FEMALE			
4-8	1,200	1,400-1,600	1,400-1,800
9-13	1,600	1,600-2,000	1,800-2,200
14-18	1,800	2,000	2,400
19-30	2,000	2,000-2,200	2,400
31-50	1,800	2,000	2,200
51+	1,600	1,800	2,000-2,200
MALE			
4-8	1,400	1,400-1,600	1,600-2,000
9-13	1,800	1,800-2,200	2,000-2,600
14-18	2,200	2,400-2,800	2,800-3,200
19-30	2,400	2,600-2,800	3,000
31-50	2,200	2,400-2,600	2,800-3,000
51+	2,000	2,200-2,400	2,400-2,800

a These levels are based on Estimated Energy Requirements from the Institute of Medicine (I.O.M.) Dietary Reference Intakes macronutrients report, 2002, calculated by gender, age and activity level for reference-sized individuals. "Reference size," as determined by I.O.M., is based on median height and weight for ages up to age 18 years of age and median height and weight for that height to give a body mass index (BMI) of 21.5 for adult females and 22.5 for adult males.

b Sedentary means a lifestyle that includes only the light physical activity associated with typical day-to-day life.

c Moderately active means a lifestyle that includes physical activity equivalent to walking about 1.5 to 3 miles per day at 3 to 4 miles per hour, in addition to the light physical activity associated with typical day-to-day life.

d Active means a lifestyle that includes physical activity equivalent to walking more than 3 miles per day at 3 to 4 miles per hour, in addition to the light physical activity associated with typical day-to-day life.

e The calorie ranges shown are to accommodate needs of different ages within the group. For children and adolescents, more calories are needed at older ages. For adults, fewer calories are needed at older ages.

SOURCE: U.S.D.A.

a handful of nuts (about three to four tablespoons) five times a week can reduce risk of coronary artery disease between 25 and 40 percent.

And while everyone knows it is good to eat your vegetables, many people do not realize how easy it really is to consume five to nine servings of fruits and vegetables a day. Just having a salad of leafy greens (two cups) with tomatoes and half a cup of broccoli, for instance, totals four servings. If you had juice with breakfast, you're already up to five by lunchtime.

Whether to add alcohol to your daily diet is more controversial. Increasingly, studies support the idea that drinking a small amount each day—no more than one to two servings—is better for you than not drinking. Large observational studies show that drinking moderate amounts of alcohol can lower the risk of dying in a given year by about 25 percent, compared with those who rarely drink. But it's not true for everyone. Excessive use of alcohol can lead to addiction, traffic accidents and potentially fatal medical problems.

Even small amounts of alcohol can increase risk for certain health worries, like breast and colon cancer. Although those risks are generally offset by the extra heart benefits, some people may decide it is not worth it. Much of the research on alcohol's benefits comes from studies that observe people over time rather than from controlled clinical trials, which are more reliable. So while there is a strong association with moderate alcohol consumption and better health, the results are not conclusive.

Making better food choices won't always produce obvious results, like weight loss. But substituting fish for red meat, high-fiber foods for processed pastries and eating more vegetables may push more fattening foods off your plate and, at the least, prevent weight gain. Add a half-hour walk after dinner and you have gone a long way toward lowering heart risk.

—Tara Parker-Pope

The Skinny on Fat

A primer on fats and trans fats

How much and what kind of fats should you eat? The U.S.D.A. recommends that you limit excess calories, saturated fat, trans fat and dietary cholesterol.

- **Saturated fat** intake should be 7 to 10 percent of calories (or even less).

- **Polyunsaturated fat** intake should be up to 10 percent of calories.

- **Monounsaturated fat** can make up up to 15 percent of total calories.

- **Cholesterol** intake should be less than 300 milligrams per day. Dietary cholesterol raises LDL cholesterol levels in the blood.

- **Total fat** intake should be adjusted to caloric needs. Overweight people should consume no more than 30 percent of total calories from fat.

SATURATED FAT INTAKE

The U.S.D.A.'s chart shows you the maximum gram amounts of saturated fat that you should consume to keep your saturated fat intake below 10 percent of total calorie intake at selected recommended calorie levels. A 2,000-calorie example is included so that you can compare it with the amounts shown on food labels, which are based on a 2,000-calorie diet.

1,600	18 g or less
2,000	20 g or less
2,200	24 g or less
2,500	25 g or less
2,800	31 g or less

TRANS FATTY ACIDS

Trans fatty acids are formed by the process of hydrogenating vegetable fats. They can be found in shortenings, stick (or hard) margarine, cookies, crackers, snack foods, fried foods, doughnuts, pastries, baked goods and other processed foods made with or fried in partially hydrogenated oils. Consumption of trans fat raises LDL cholesterol levels and lowers HDL cholesterol levels, increasing the risk of heart disease and stroke. The U.S.D.A. lists these foods in order of highest to lowest in trans fats.

Cake, cookies, pie, bread, etc.	40
Animal products	21
Margarine	17
Fried potatoes	8
Potato, corn chips, popcorn	5
Household shortening	4
Breakfast cereal, candy, etc.	5

FOOD

The Lowdown on Low-Fat Diets

A large study says that fat intake does not affect your risk of getting cancer or heart disease

After years of being admonished to cut down on fat intake by nearly every medical professional, the confusion is growing for all of us who are trying to eat well. A recent study by the Women's Health Initiative, published in the *Journal of the American Medical Association* in, has provided rigorous evidence that a low-fat diet is not protective against breast cancer or colorectal cancer. The study found that women who were randomly assigned to follow a low-fat diet ate significantly less fat over the next 8 years. But they had just as much breast and colon

cancer and just as much heart disease. The women were not trying to lose weight, and their weights remained fairly steady. But their experiences with the diets allowed researchers to question some popular notions about diet and obesity.

There is a common belief that Americans get fat because they eat too many carbohydrates. The idea is that a high-carbohydrate, low-fat diet leads to weight gain, higher insulin and blood glucose levels, and more diabetes, even if the calories are the same as in a higher-fat diet. Others have said the opposite: that low-fat diets enable people to lose weight naturally. But that belief was not supported by this study. As for heart disease risk factors, the only one affected was LDL cholesterol, which increases heart disease risk. The levels were slightly higher in women eating the higher-fat diet, but not high enough to make a noticeable difference in their risk of heart disease.

Although all the study participants were women, the colon cancer and heart disease results should also apply to men. Critics of the study now say that it was flawed because it focused on total fat in the diet, rather than on saturated fat, which raises cholesterol levels. Others say the study made a mistake in aiming for a diet allowing 20 percent of calories to come from fat. Dietary fat should be even lower, they say, as low as 10 percent. Many medical researchers say that the best dietary advice for now is to follow federal guidelines for healthy eating, with less saturated and trans fats, more grains and more fruits and vegetables.

Some, like Dr. Dean Ornish, a longtime promoter of low-fat diets, said that the women did not reduce their fat to low enough levels or eat enough fruits and vegetables, and that the study, even at 8 years, did not give the diets enough time. Others said that diet could still make a difference, at least with heart disease, if people were to eat the so-called Mediterranean diet, low in saturated fats like butter and high in oils like olive oil. The women in the study reduced all kinds of fat. But the Mediterranean diet has not been subjected to a study of this scope, researchers say.

—Gina Kolata

FAT ATTACK

Saturated fat slows down the elimination of cholesterol in your bloodstream, and that can lead to heart disease. Here are some household oils listed by saturated fat content per single tablespoon serving.

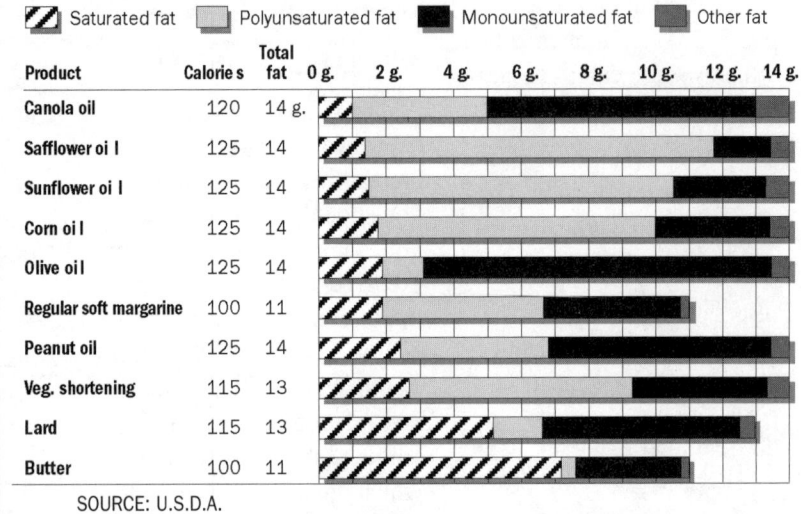

SOURCE: U.S.D.A.

The Home Vitamin Shelf
Where to find the most needed vitamins

Your body needs vitamins to form blood cells, build strong bones and regulate the nervous system, but it can't generate most of them on its own. Ideally, all vitamins should be derived from food, not supplements, though that is not always possible. Some limited supplementation is recommended for particular populations, as noted below.

VITAMIN A

DAILY VALUE:	*700 micrograms RAE (retinol activity equivalents)*
1 scrambled egg:	118 mcg
1 cup nonfat milk:	149 mcg
1 nectarine:	50 mcg
1 piece of watermelon:	27 mcg

WHAT IT DOES: Aids in good vision; helps build and maintain skin, teeth, bones and mucous membranes. Promotes growth and helps keep lining of mouth, nose, throat and digestive tract healthy and resistant to infection. Deficiency can increase susceptibility to infectious disease.

What it may do: May increase resistance to infection. Excessive supplementation may also cause osteoporosis and increase risk of cancer.

Food sources: Milk, eggs, liver, cheese, fish oil. Plus fruits and vegetables that contain beta carotene. You need not consume preformed vitamin A if you eat foods rich in beta carotene.

Supplementation: Not recommended, since toxic in high doses.

VITAMIN B₁ (THIAMIN)

DAILY VALUE:	1.1 milligrams
1 slice enriched white bread:	0.10 mg
3 oz fried liver:	0.17 mg
1 cup black beans:	0.42 mg
1/2 cup dry-hull sunflower seeds:	1.65 mg

What it does: Helps convert carbohydrates into energy. Necessary for healthy brain, nerve cells and heart function. Promotes good appetite and digestion.

Food sources: Whole grains, enriched grain products, beans, meats, liver, wheat germ, nuts, fish, brewer's yeast.

Supplementation: Not necessary, not recommended.

VITAMIN B₂ (RIBOFLAVIN)

DAILY VALUE:	1.1 milligrams
3 oz chicken:	0.10 mg
1 bagel:	0.33 mg
1 cup whole milk:	0.4 mg
1 cup cooked spinach:	0.42 mg

What it does: Helps cells use oxygen to release energy from food. Essential for growth, production of red blood cells, and health of skin and eyes.

Food sources: Dairy products, liver, meat, chicken, fish, enriched grain products, leafy greens, beans, nuts, eggs and almonds.

Supplementation: Not necessary, not recommended.

VITAMIN B₃ (NIACIN)

DAILY VALUE:	14 milligrams
1 slice bread:	1.0 mg
3 oz wild Atlantic salmon:	8.6 mg
1 oz dry roasted peanuts:	3.8 mg
1/2 chicken breast, roasted:	12.5 mg

What it does: Aids in release of energy from foods. Maintains health of skin, tongue, digestive tract and nervous system.

What it may do: Helps lower blood cholesterol.

Food sources: Nuts, meat, fish, chicken, liver, enriched grain products, dairy products, peanut butter, brewer's yeast.

Supplementation: Large doses may be prescribed by doctor to lower blood cholesterol. May cause flushing and gastrointestinal distress.

VITAMIN B₅ (PANTOTHENIC ACID)

DAILY VALUE:	5 milligrams
8 oz nonfat milk:	0.81 mg
1 large egg:	0.63 mg
8 oz low-fat fruit-flavored yoghurt:	1.23 mg
3 oz liver:	3.88 mg

What it does: Necessary for metabolism of fat and helps in the formation of cholesterol and hormones.

Food Sources: Whole grains, egg yolk, milk, liver.

Supplementation: Not necessary, not recommended. May cause diarrhea.

VITAMIN B₆ (PYROXIDINE)

DAILY VALUE:	1.3 milligrams
1 oat bran muffin:	0.22 mg
1 cup lima beans:	0.14 mg
3 oz cooked bluefin tuna:	0.45 mg
1 banana:	0.68 mg

What it does: Assists in the metabolism of proteins, carbohydrates and fats. Helps to maintain the health of the skin and red blood cells.

What it may do: May help to boost immunity in the elderly.

FOOD

The 11 Best Foods You Aren't Eating

Nutritionist and author Jonny Bowden has created several lists of healthful foods people should be eating but aren't. Sadly, some of his favorites, like purslane, guava and goji berries, aren't always available at regular grocery stores. Here, Dr. Bowden, author of The 150 Healthiest Foods on Earth, *updates his list with some favorite foods that are easily available but don't always find their way into our shopping carts.*

Beets: Think of beets as red spinach, Dr. Bowden said, because they are a rich source of folate as well as natural red pigments that may be cancer fighters.

How to eat it: Fresh, raw and grated to make a salad. Heating decreases the antioxidant power.

Cabbage: Loaded with nutrients like sulforaphane, a chemical said to boost cancer-fighting enzymes.

How to eat: Asian-style slaw or as a crunchy topping on burgers and sandwiches.

Pomegranate juice: Appears to lower blood pressure and loaded with antioxidants.

How to eat: Just drink it.

Dried plums: Okay, so they are really prunes, but they are packed with antioxidants.

How to eat: Wrapped in prosciutto and baked.

Swiss chard: A leafy green vegetable packed with carotenoids that protect aging eyes.

How to eat: Chop and sauté in olive oil.

Cinnamon: May help control blood sugar and cholesterol.

How to eat it: Sprinkle on coffee or oatmeal.

Pumpkin seeds: The most nutritious part of the pumpkin, packed with magnesium; high levels of the mineral are associated with lower risk for early death.

How to eat: Roasted as a snack, or sprinkled on salad.

Sardines: Dr. Bowden calls them "health food in a can." They are high in omega-3s, contain virtually no mercury and are loaded with calcium. They also contain iron, magnesium, phosphorus, potassium, zinc, copper and manganese as well as a full complement of B vitamins.

How to eat: Choose sardines packed in olive or sardine oil. Eat plain, mixed with salad, on toast, or mashed with dijon mustard and onions as a spread.

Turmeric: The "superstar of spices" was used in ancient times to treat everything from rheumatism to skin diseases to colic. It may have anti-inflammatory and anti-cancer properties.

How to eat: Mix with scrambled eggs or in any vegetable dish.

Canned pumpkin: A low-calorie vegetable that is high in fiber and immune-stimulating vitamin A; fills you up on very few calories.

How to eat: Mix with a little butter, cinnamon and nutmeg.

Frozen blueberries: Even though freezing can degrade some of the nutrients in fruits and vegetables, frozen blueberries are available year-round and don't spoil; associated with better memory in animal studies.

How to eat: Blended with yogurt or chocolate soy milk and sprinkled with crushed almonds.

—Tara Parker-Pope

FOOD SOURCES: Whole grains, bananas, lean meats, beans, nuts, wheat germ, brewer's yeast, chicken, fish, liver.

SUPPLEMENTATION: Large doses can cause numbness and other neurological disorders.

VITAMIN B₁₂

DAILY VALUE:	2.4 micrograms
¹/₂ chicken breast:	0.29 mcg
1 large egg:	0.50 mcg
1 cup nonfat milk:	0.93 mcg
3 oz lean braised beef flank:	2.81 mcg

WHAT IT DOES: Necessary in the development of normal growth and helps body produce normal red blood cells. Protects against pernicious anemia.

FOOD SOURCES: Liver, beef, pork, poultry, eggs, milk, cheese, yogurt, shellfish, fortified cereals and fortified soy products.

SUPPLEMENTATION: Not usually necessary, but people who are on strict vegetarian diets may need supplementation. Also, some elderly people may be deficient in the vitamin because they lose their ability to absorb it from foods.

VITAMIN C (ASCORBIC ACID)

DAILY VALUE:	75 milligrams
1 orange:	70 mg
1 green pepper (¹/₂ cup):	56 mg
1 cup raw broccoli:	82 mg
8 oz tomato juice:	44 mg

WHAT IT DOES: Strengthens blood vessels and hastens healing of wounds and bones. Increases resistance to infections and helps body absorb iron in the diet.

WHAT IT MAY DO: May reduce the risk of lung, esophagus, stomach and bladder cancers, as well as coronary artery disease; may prevent or delay cataracts and slow the aging process.

FOOD SOURCES: Citrus fruits and juices, strawberries, tomatoes, peppers, broccoli, potatoes, kale, cabbage, cauliflower, cantaloupe, brussels sprouts.

SUPPLEMENTATION: 250 to 500 mgs a day for smokers. Larger doses may cause diarrhea.

VITAMIN D

DAILY VALUE:	.005 milligrams or 5 micrograms
1 oz Cheddar cheese:	.000075 mg or 0.75 mcg
1 large egg:	.000675 mg or .675 mcg
1 cup nonfat milk:	.0025 mg or 2.5 mcg

WHAT IT DOES: Strengthens bones and teeth by aiding the absorption of calcium. Helps maintain phosphorus in the blood.

WHAT IT MAY DO: May reduce risk of osteoporosis, forestall breast and colon cancers.

FOOD SOURCES: Milk, fish oil, fortified margarine; also produced by exposure to sunlight.

SUPPLEMENTATION: May be necessary for vegetarians, the elderly, those who don't drink milk or get sun exposure. Toxic in high doses.

VITAMIN E

DAILY VALUE:	15 mg ATE (alpha tocopherol equivalent)
¹/₂ cup boiled brussel sprouts:	0.7 mg
1 cup boiled spinach:	1.7 mg
1 oz almonds:	7.5 mg

WHAT IT DOES: Active in maintaining the involuntary nervous system, vascular system and involuntary muscles.

WHAT IT MAY DO: May reduce the risk of esophageal or stomach cancers; may prevent or delay cataracts; may boost immunity in the elderly.

FOOD SOURCES: Vegetable oil, nuts, margarine, wheat germ, leafy greens, seeds, almonds, olives and asparagus.

SUPPLEMENTATION: Not recommended.

BIOTIN (VITAMIN B)

DAILY VALUE: *30 micrograms*

1 cup cooked enriched noodles:	4 mcg
1 large egg:	11 mcg
1 oz almonds:	24 mcg

WHAT IT DOES: Important in breakdown of protein, carbohydrates and fats in the body.

FOOD SOURCES: Egg yolk, milk, liver, kidneys, vegetables and fruits (especially bananas, grapefruits, watermelon and strawberries).

SUPPLEMENTATION: Not recommended.

FOLATE (VITAMIN B)
(Also called folacin or folic acid)

DAILY VALUE: *400 micrograms*

1 navel orange:	47.6 mcg
1 cup raw spinach:	102.6 mcg
1 cup homemade baked beans:	121.4 mcg
1/2 cup asparagus, boiled:	131.4 mcg

WHAT IT DOES: Aids in the biochemical reactions of cells in the production of energy. Helps body produce normal red blood cells and reduces the risk of neural tube birth defects in newborns.

WHAT IT MAY DO: May reduce the risk of breast, colon and pancreatic cancer. May be of help to those with high levels of homocysteine in their blood, which may be associated with increased risks of heart disease.

FOOD SOURCES: Leafy greens, wheat germ, liver, beans, whole grains, broccoli, asparagus, citrus fruit juices and enriched flour.

SUPPLEMENTATION: 400 mcg, for all women who may become pregnant, to help prevent birth defects, in addition to the recommended amount that they should normally consume in a balanced diet. Pregnant women should take a 600 mg supplement.

SOURCES: U.S.D.A.—Food and Nutrition; Institute of Medicine; *Bowes and Church's Food Values of Portions Commonly Used,* eighteenth edition, by Jean A. T. Pennington and Judith Spungen Douglass.

Do You Take Too Many Vitamins?
There is usually danger in too many, not too few

As much as 70 percent of the population in America is taking supplements, mostly vitamins, convinced that the pills will make them healthier. But, in fact, some of the vitamins, especially in high doses, may cause serious harm.

"There has been a transition from focusing on minimum needs to the reality that today our problem is excess—excess calories and, yes, excesses of vitamins and minerals as well," says Dr. Benjamin Caballero, director of the Center for Human Nutrition at Johns Hopkins University.

The beneficial aspects of supplements such

? EXPERT ANSWER

When to Take Your Vitamins

Q. What's the best time: morning, noon or night? With meals or without?

The time of day isn't as important as ensuring that they are taken consistently. Most vitamins should be taken with food. Water-soluble vitamins B and C can be absorbed when taken with food or on an empty stomach. But, the fat-soluble vitamins A, D, E and K are most efficiently absorbed when taken with fatty foods. Beta carotene, and other carotenoids, such as lycopene and lutein, are also best absorbed with some fat.

Minerals should also generally be taken with food. Absorption efficiency of calcium carbonate on an empty stomach is poor; it increases significantly when taken with food. Calcium citrate can be taken on an empty stomach. Iron is absorbed best on an empty stomach, but it can upset the stomach and is usually taken with a small amount of food.

Dr. Sheldon S. Hendler, co-editor, The Physicians' Desk Reference for Nutritional Supplements

as vitamins A, C and E, which in earlier studies had shown promise of having a preventive effect against cancer and heart disease, have since been discounted; warnings about excess consumption through supplementation and an overenriched diet are now being issued.

With vitamin A in particular, it is easy to step over the edge into a danger zone, says Dr. Joan McGowan, chief of the musculoskeletal diseases branch at the National Institute of Arthritis and Musculoskeletal and Skin Diseases. If you are eating Total cereal, drinking fortified milk and taking a multivitamin, you might be getting more than you need. Now, she adds, "we may have to rethink the issues." Several recent large studies indicate that people with high levels of vitamin A in their blood have a greater risk for osteoporosis. Two large randomized trials of vitamin A and beta carotene that researchers hoped would show a protective value against cancer found no benefit, and one found that participants who took the supplements had more cancer. Another study, of women with heart disease, found that antioxidant vitamins might actually increase the rate of atherosclerosis.

Similar questions are being raised about other vitamins and minerals, notably iron and vitamins E and C, which are the most popular individual supplements, says Dr. Robert M. Russell, director the Human Nutrition Research Center on Aging at Tufts University and head of the Food and Nutrition Board at the National Academy of Sciences. Scientists once thought those vitamins could help prevent ailments like cancer and heart disease, but rigorous studies found no such effects. Vitamin E supplements can increase the risk of heart attacks and strokes, and studies of vitamin C supplements consistently failed to show that they had any beneficial effects. A large study of vitamin E and heart disease found that it did not prevent heart attacks and that people taking it had more strokes.

Excess vitamin C is excreted in the urine, but excesses of some other vitamins are stored in fat, where they can build up. Others warn about overdosing on vitamins and minerals. Dr. Richard J. Wood, director of the mineral bioavailability laboratory at Tufts, also worries about iron overload, which can increase the risk of heart disease. In a large federal research effort, the Framingham study, Wood found that 12 percent of the elderly participants had worrisome levels. "Hardly anyone had iron deficiency anemia," he says. "But 16 percent were taking iron-containing supplements."

—Gina Kolata

Why Minerals Matter

These important nutrients should not be overlooked; here's where to find them

Minerals help your body form bones, regulate the heart and synthesize enzymes, but experts say too many, or too few, can lead to heart disease, diabetes or even cancer. Here are the F.D.A.'s daily values and where to get them.

CALCIUM

DAILY VALUE:	*1,000 milligrams*
Sardines, Atlantic, 3 oz.	325 mg
1 cup nonfat milk:	301 mg
1 oz cheddar cheese:	204 mg
8 oz nonfat yogurt:	452 mg

WHAT IT DOES: Helps form strong bones and teeth. Helps regulate heartbeat, muscle contractions, nerve function and blood clotting.

FOOD SOURCES: Milk, cheese, butter and margarine, green vegetables, legumes, nuts, soybean products, hard water.

SUPPLEMENTATION: High intakes may cause constipation and increase risk of kidney stones and renal insufficiency.

A Daily Dose of Calcium

Taking calcium and vitamin D supplement can reduce the risk of bone fractures

Calcium supplements, or calcium and vitamin D taken in combination, may reduce the risk for bone fracture and bone density loss in older people, provided the supplements are taken regularly and in large enough doses.

A review of 29 randomized trials including more than 63,000 men and women older than 50 found that the risk for fracture could be reduced 12 percent with calcium and vitamin D supplements. The rate of bone loss was reduced by about 0.5 of 1 percent at the hip and 1.9 percent at the spine. Fracture risk was reduced by nearly one-quarter in studies in which people took their supplements conscientiously.

The review, published in *The Lancet,* found that the effect was best with doses of 1,200 milligrams of calcium and 800 international units of vitamin D. The recommended dietary allowance for calcium in people over 50 is 1,200 milligrams, but the recommendation for vitamin D is 400 international units for people 50 to 70 and 600 for those 71 and older.

Adding vitamin D to calcium did not appear to offer increased protection. But the studies lacked enough figures on high doses of the vitamin. Still, the authors recommend that if vitamin D is to be used as an adjunct, it should be in doses that exceed 800 international units.

"For anyone over 50, especially postmenopausal women, you should see your family doctor and address with him the issue of taking calcium supplementation," says Dr. Benjamin M. P. Tang, the lead author and a researcher at the University of Western Sydney in Australia. "It's always better to have overall health assessed before undertaking supplements."

—Nicholas Bakalar

COPPER

DAILY VALUE:	900 micrograms
2/3 cup seedless raisins:	310 mg
1 oz dry roasted pistachios:	340 mg
1/2 cup boiled mushrooms:	390 mg

WHAT IT DOES: Helps in formation of red blood cells. Helps keep bones, blood vessels, nerves and immune system healthy.

FOOD SOURCES: Red meat, poultry, liver, fish, seafood, whole-grain cereals and breads, green vegetables, legumes, nuts, raisins, mushrooms.

SUPPLEMENTATION: Not recommended. A balanced diet includes enough copper.

IODINE

DAILY VALUE:	150 micrograms
1 oz cheddar cheese:	12 mcg
1 tsp iodized salt:	400 mcg

WHAT IT DOES: Necessary for proper thyroid gland function and thus normal cell metabolism. Prevents goiter (enlargement of thyroid).

FOOD SOURCES: Milk, cheese, butter and margarine, fish, whole-grain cereals and breads, iodized table salt.

SUPPLEMENTATION: Not recommended. Widely dispersed in the food supply, so even if you eat little iodized salt, you probably get enough iodine.

IRON

DAILY VALUE:	18 milligrams
1 slice whole wheat bread:	1 mg
3 scrambled eggs:	2.19 mg
3 oz lean sirloin steak, broiled:	2.6 mg
3 oz fried liver:	5.3 mg
1 packet instant oatmeal:	6.7 mg

WHAT IT DOES: Vital in forming hemoglobin (which carries oxygen in blood) and myoglobin (in muscle).

FOOD SOURCES: Red meat, poultry, liver, eggs, fish, whole-grain cereals and breads.

SUPPLEMENTATION: Often (but not always) advised for dieters, strict vegetarians. Large doses may damage the heart, liver and pancreas.

MAGNESIUM

DAILY VALUE:	*310 milligrams*
1 tbsp peanut butter:	28 mg
1 baked potato:	55 mg
1/2 cup cooked spinach:	79 mg

WHAT IT DOES: Aids in bone growth, basic metabolic functions and the functioning of nerves and muscles, including the regulation of normal heart rhythm.

FOOD SOURCES: Milk, fish, whole-grain cereals and breads, green vegetables, legumes, nuts and hard water.

SUPPLEMENTATION: Not usually recommended, unless there is a dietary deficiency.

PHOSPHORUS

DAILY VALUE:	*700 milligrams*
6 scallops:	200 mg
1 cup nonfat milk:	250 mg
3 oz broiled trout:	260 mg
1 cup tuna salad:	280 mg
1 cup low-fat cottage cheese:	340 mg

WHAT IT DOES: Helps form bones, teeth, cell membranes and genetic material. Essential for energy production.

FOOD SOURCES: Nearly all foods, including red meat, poultry, liver, milk, cheese, butter and margarine, eggs, fish, whole-grain cereals and breads, green and root vegetables, legumes, nuts and fruit.

SUPPLEMENTATION: Not recommended. Deficiencies in Americans are virtually unknown. Excessive intake may lower blood calcium level.

POTASSIUM

DAILY VALUE:	*4700 milligrams*
1 cup nonfat milk:	406 mg
1 banana:	422 mg
1 baked potato, with skin:	610 mg
1 cup cooked spinach:	838 mg

WHAT IT DOES: Needed for muscle contraction, nerve impulses, and function of heart and kidneys. Aids in regulation of water balance in cells and blood.

WHAT IT MAY DO: May fight osteoporosis and help lower blood pressure.

FOOD SOURCES: Unprocessed foods such as fruits, vegetables and fresh meats.

SUPPLEMENTATION: Not usually recommended. Take only under a doctor's advice and supervision.

ZINC

DAILY VALUE:	*8 milligrams*
8 oz low-fat fruit yogurt:	1.52 mg
1 cup boiled lentils:	2.5 mg
3.5 oz roast turkey, dark:	4.4 mg

WHAT IT DOES: Stimulates enzymes needed for cell division, growth and repair (wound healing). Helps immune system function properly. Also plays a role in acuity of taste and smell.

FOOD SOURCES: Red meat, fish, seafood, eggs, milk, whole-grain cereals and breads, legumes.

SUPPLEMENTATION: Not recommended, except by a doctor for the few Americans who have low zinc levels.

SOURCES: U.S.D.A.; Institute of Medicine; and *Bowes and Church's Food Values of Portions Commonly Used,* eighteenth edition, by Jean A. T. Pennington and Judith Spungen Douglass.

How to Read a Food Label

Finding out what is in those cookies

The F.D.A.'s food label contains an up-to-date, easy-to-use nutrition information guide, and is required on almost all packaged foods. It serves as an aid in planning a healthy diet for you and your family.

Serving sizes are standardized to make it easier to compare similar foods; they are provided in familiar units, such as cups or pieces, followed by the metric amount, e.g., the number of grams. Pay attention to the serving size, especially how many servings there are in the food package. For every serving you eat, count the additional number of calories and nutrients per serving.

Calories provide a measure of how much energy you get from a serving of this food. Many Americans consume more calories than they need without meeting recommended intakes for a number of nutrients. Here are simple guidelines for calorie intake:

— 40 calories is low

—100 calories is moderate

—400 calories or more is high

Fat calories are shown on the label to help you meet diet guidelines that recommend you get no more than 30 percent of your calories from fat.

Fat, saturated fat, trans fat, cholesterol or sodium. Americans generally eat these nutrients in adequate amounts, or even too much. Health experts recommend that you keep your percentage intake of them as low as possible as part of a nutritionally balanced diet.

Dietary fiber, vitamin A, vitamin C, calcium and iron. Most Americans need to get enough, but not too much, of these in their diets. You can use the Nutrition Facts label not only to help limit those nutrients you want to cut back on, but also to increase those nutrients you need to consume in greater amounts.

The percent daily value. The % DV helps you determine if a serving of food is high or low in a nutrient, and is a frame of reference for how many of your total calories you are consuming in that serving. The % daily values are based on the daily value recommendations for key nutrients, but only for a 2,000-calorie daily diet—not 2,500 calories.

Nutrients without a % DV. Note that trans fat, sugars and protein do not list a % DV on the Nutrition Facts label. Experts could not provide a reference value for trans fat nor any other information that the F.D.A. believes is sufficient to establish a Daily Value or % DV. A % DV is required to be listed if a claim is made for protein, such as "high in protein." Otherwise, unless the food is meant for use by infants and children under 4 years old, none is needed.

Current scientific evidence indicates that protein intake is not a public health concern for adults and children over 4 years of age. No daily reference value has been established for sugars because no recommendations have been made for the total amount to eat in a day. Remember, the sugars listed on the Nutrition Facts label also include naturally occurring sugars (like those in fruit and milk).

Footnote to % DV. The recommended daily values for each nutrient listed in the footnote at the bottom of the label are based on public health experts' advice for recommended levels of intakes.

Nutrition Facts

Serving Size 1 cup
Servings Per Container 9

Amount Per Serving

Calories 110	Calories from Fat 15

	% Daily Value*
Total Fat 2g	**3%**
Saturated Fat 0g	**0%**
Polyunsaturated Fat 0.5g	
Monounsaturated Fat 0.5g	
Cholesterol 0 mg	**0%**
Potassium 95mg	**3%**
Sodium 280 mg	**12%**
Total Carbohydrate 22g	**7%**
Dietary Fiber 3g	**11%**
Soluble Fiber 1g	
Insoluble Fiber 2g	
Sugars 1g	
Protein 3g	

Vitamin A 10%	•	Vitamin C 10%
Calcium 4%	•	Iron 45%

* Percent Daily Values are based on a 2,000 calorie diet. Your values may be higher or lower, depending on your calorie needs:

	Calories:	2,000	2,500
Total Fat	Less than	65g	80g
Sat Fat	Less than	20g	25g
Cholesterol	Less than	300mg	300mg
Sodium	Less than	2,400mg	2,400mg
Total Carbohydrate		300g	375g
Dietary Fiber		25g	30g

Calories per gram:
Fat 9 • Carbohydrate 4 • Protein 4

Recommended DVs in the footnote are based on a 2,000- or 2,500-calorie diet.

Upper daily limits. The nutrients that have "upper daily limits" are listed first on the footnote of larger labels. Upper limits means it is recommended that you stay below—eat "less than"—the Daily Value nutrient amounts listed per day. For example, the DV for Saturated Fat is 20g or less. This amount is 100% DV for this nutrient. What is the goal or dietary advice? To eat "less than" 20 g or 100% DV for the day.

Lower limits—eat "at least"...
The DV for Total Carbohydrate is 300g or 375g, both 100% DV respectively for either a 2,000- or 2,500-calorie diet. This is the minimum amount recommended for a balanced daily diet, but healthy actual amounts can vary, depending on your daily intake of fat and protein.

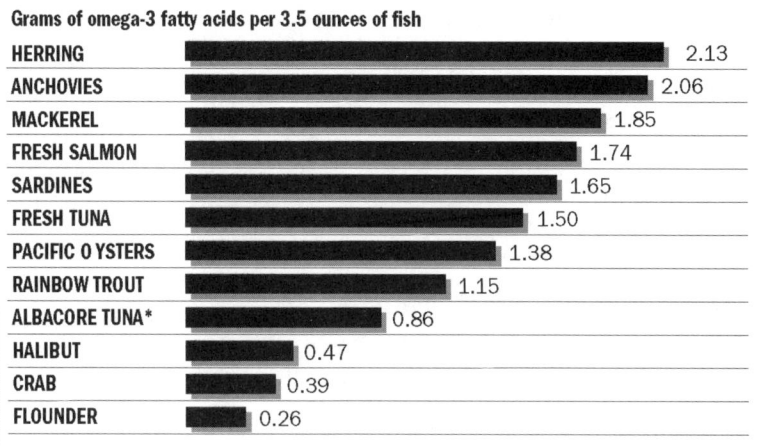

FISH OIL: FROM ANCHOVIES TO TROUT

Here's a lineup of the fish and shellfish with the highest concentrations of omega-3 fish oil. Fish caught in the wild generally contain more omega-3 than farm-raised fish.

Grams of omega-3 fatty acids per 3.5 ounces of fish

Fish	Grams
HERRING	2.13
ANCHOVIES	2.06
MACKEREL	1.85
FRESH SALMON	1.74
SARDINES	1.65
FRESH TUNA	1.50
PACIFIC OYSTERS	1.38
RAINBOW TROUT	1.15
ALBACORE TUNA*	0.86
HALIBUT	0.47
CRAB	0.39
FLOUNDER	0.26

* Canned in water; it has more omega-3 than tuna canned in oil.
SOURCE: University of Washington Cardiovascular Health Research Unit

How Fish Can Help Your Heart

Two servings a week can make a difference

Evidence suggests that eating just two fish meals a week—two 3-ounce servings—can make a significant difference in the risk of developing ills like heart attacks and strokes.

Part of the benefit may come simply from eating fish in place of red meat, a supposed culprit in cardiovascular disease. But another more important part, the evidence suggests, involves the fats found in fish, namely omega-3 fatty acids, which may have a physiological role in preventing cardiovascular disease.

But as with most worthwhile things in life, with fish and shellfish, there's no free lunch. Risks as well as benefits attend eating seafood, although a wise and well-informed consumer can certainly tip the balance in favor of the benefits.

The Benefits

For fish to maintain fluidity in cold water, their fats have to remain liquid, and liquid fats (really oils) are polyunsaturated. But fish oils, rich in omega-3 fatty acids, are chemically different from the polyunsaturated oils in plants like corn and soybeans, and it is that difference that has given fish star billing.

The two omega-3s in fish are eicosapentaenoic acid, or EPA, and docosahexaenoic acid, or DHA. They are considered essential fatty acids, although they can be formed in the body from another

☑ **TIMELY TIPS**

The Many Benefits of Olive Oil

As Greeks say, olives are a gift from the gods

Researchers may have pinned down one important reason for the positive effect olive oil appears to have on cardiovascular health: it contains a naturally occurring anti-inflammatory chemical. The substance, which the researchers call oleocanthal, has the same anti-inflammatory effect as drugs like ibuprofen and aspirin, which can inhibit the sometimes harmful effects of enzymes called cox-1 and cox-2.

✔ Scientists have long known that low doses of the cox inhibitors confer various benefits on the people who use them. "There is ample evidence that chronic low-dose anti-inflammatories have multiple health benefits that may range from reducing the risk of heart disease, stroke and certain cancers—breast, lung, colon—to reducing the risk of terminal dementias such as Alzheimer's," says Paul A. S. Breslin, who is a co-author of the report that appeared in *Nature* and a researcher at the Monell Chemical Senses Center in Philadelphia. "Olive oil contains an ibuprofen-like anti-inflammatory that may turn out to convey similar benefits," he continues.

✔ Extra-virgin olive oil has the most benefit, but consumers do not necessarily need to buy the most expensive brands. "What matters is that it is an extra-virgin olive oil that has a good throat sting, indicating it has high levels of oleocanthal," Dr. Breslin says. He suggests that the Mediterranean diet—with extra-virgin olive oil used liberally on bread and vegetables and in salad dressing—may be the best way to consume it, "particularly if it substitutes for butter, margarine and creamy dressings."

—Nicholas Bakalar

omega-3, alpha-linolenic acid, or ALA. It is found in plants like flaxseed, spinach, mustard greens, soybeans, canola oil, wheat germ and walnuts, as well as in marine animals that eat plants containing ALA. The conversion rate is poor, however, and you will have to consume large amounts of ALA to obtain a meaningful amount of EPA and DHA. Eating fish is far more efficient.

DHA is a natural ingredient in breast milk, and it is critical to the normal development of the brain and retina. It has been approved as an additive to infant formula. In addition, the omega-3 acids perform many biochemical functions that can benefit the heart and blood vessels. They can inhibit the synthesis of substances that promote inflammation, reduce the tendency of the blood to form clots, stabilize the electrical activity of the heart, lower triglyceride levels, reduce blood pressure moderately and improve the functioning of artery linings.

Most, but not all, studies have found that people who eat fish regularly experience significant reductions in the risk of heart attacks, strokes and deaths from all causes. The benefit has been most clear-cut among people who already have cardiovascular disease, but it has also been found among those who are initially healthy. In one study of 334 people who had suffered first heart attacks and 493 healthy people matched for age, sex and location, eating just 5.5 grams of omega-3 fatty acids a month was associated with a 50 percent reduction in the risk of cardiac arrest. That amount of omega-3s can come from just four 3-ounce servings of Atlantic salmon a month.

The omega-3s have proved especially beneficial for people with Type-2 diabetes, who have a greatly increased risk of developing heart disease. Other suggested benefits include an anti-inflammatory effect that can help people with autoimmune diseases like rheumatoid arthritis, psoriasis and ulcerative colitis.

The various findings prompted the American Heart Association to recommend that everyone strive to consume at least two fish servings a week, especially fatty fish like salmon, sardines, mackerel, herring, lake trout, tuna and anchovies.

The Risks

Some fish are contaminated with mercury and other toxic substances introduced as industrial pollutants into their waters. An international research team reporting in the *New England Journal of Medicine* noted that the mercury content of some fish might diminish their cardioprotective effects. Again, not every study has shown this. Mercury at levels experienced by Americans may also cause problems with fine motor control and memory in adults, a study by Dr. Edna M. Yokoo and colleagues at Johns Hopkins says.

Mercury is a well-known neurologic and kidney toxin that is best not ingested. The fish most likely to be contaminated are large deep-sea species like swordfish, king mackerel, shark and tilefish; they are best avoided, especially by pregnant women. Fish, especially shellfish, can become contaminated by harmful micro-organisms that occur naturally and those that result from sewage pollution.

Raw fish and shellfish are the most common sources of food poisoning. Only ocean-dwelling fish should be used in sushi, sashimi and ceviche, and only from reliable sources that know how to spot contamination by parasites. The filter-feeders—clams, oysters and other mollusks like mussels and scallops—can accumulate waterborne bacteria, viruses or toxins that can cause severe gastrointestinal problems when the shellfish is eaten uncooked. Local health departments periodically issue advisories about contaminated species.

Finally, about 1 percent of adults have clinically proven food allergies, and shellfish are among the most common culprits, so it would be wise for them to avoid all sources. Even kissing someone who just ate shrimp, for example, can cause a reaction in someone allergic to it.

—Jane E. Brody

 **TIMELY TIPS**

A Yogurt a Day

Why bacteria can be good for you

The elderly people in those yogurt ads some years ago who said, "I'm 110 years old, and I eat yogurt every day," may have been on to something.

✔ Yogurt has been receiving an increasing amount of attention these days from health-oriented consumers and nutrition scientists because it has been linked to a variety of potential health benefits, from protection against intestinal and vaginal infections and bowel cancer to increased calcium absorption and overall enhancement of the immune system.

✔ Yogurt is made by adding bacteria to cow's or soy milk, which causes fermentation and creates its distinctive creamy texture and tart taste. The bacteria most often used to prepare yogurts sold in the United States are *Lactobacillus bulgaricus* and *Streptococcus thermophilus*.

Some manufacturers add as many as four others to the two basic bacteria: *Lactobacillus acidophilus, casei* and *reuteri,* and *Bifidobacterium bifidum.*

✔ All of these organisms are known as probiotics because, when consumed live and in sufficient quantities, they benefit the consumer through their effects on the intestinal tract. They help to keep illness-causing organisms under control. The best kind of yogurt is low-fat and without sugar.

—Jane E. Brody

In the Kitchen

Getting to Know a Recipe

Read it through carefully, then make it your own

Looking at a new recipe in a cookbook, a magazine or a newspaper is a little like meeting someone for the first time. Will this be the start of a lovely new relationship, or is it best not to become involved? Like people, recipes can be judged on their physical and sensory qualities.

The first step with any recipe is to read it through. There are a number of parts that all bear scrutiny:

• Does the title suggest an appealing dish?

• Are the ingredients on the list palatable to you, and are they familiar and accessible? Does the recipe include suggestions of sources or substitutions for exotic components?

• Do the techniques required in the directions seem simple and straightforward, and if not, are they clearly explained?

• Do you have the proper equipment?

• And is the yield, or the number of servings, satisfactory for the occasion; if not, does the recipe seem easy to cut in half or to double, or would leftovers be welcome?

A vote of no for any of these elements should be enough to keep you from lighting the stove. There are a million recipes out there, so it makes no sense to take a chance.

But if all these basics appear to be acceptable, then it's time to give the recipe a closer look. Read through the list of ingredients carefully and check each against the directions to make sure that every ounce, cup or spoonful is accounted for in the preparation. Then ask yourself whether the quantities make sense.

As a rule of thumb, a portion of soup should be one to one and one-half cups. Is the quantity of ingredients enough to supply the servings you will need? Main course servings for stews or casseroles are about two cups. For meat, fish or poultry on the bone, figure a pound of the raw ingredient per person; off the bone, around 6 ounces should do.

When it comes to dessert, depending on the richness, half a cup to a cup per person is a good average. But for cakes, pies, puddings and the like, you can also measure the capacity of a baking dish and make sure the recipe calls for the correct amount of ingredients for the size of the pan. And do not forget to allow for expansion, especially for cakes.

Finally, before lighting the stove, read through the directions once more, mentally completing each step to see that you understand all the details. And then, as much as a recipe may be a formula, keep your wits about you and your tastebuds on line. Be prepared to vary the timing, depending on how your pots and stove conduct heat. Do not hesitate to make other adjustments, as you go, to the amount of liquid in a sauce, perhaps, or to the seasonings.

Then, when you serve the dish, you will have increased the chances of success, and regardless of who wrote the recipe, you can add it to your repertory and call it your own.

—Florence Fabricant

TIMELY TIPS

Basic Needs for a Modern Cook

The following lists will help anyone start a kitchen and help the more serious cook improve one.

Basics:
- 8-inch chef's knife
- Bread knife
- Three or more small knives with 3- to 5-inch blades
- Cutting boards, one large and one small, preferably dishwasher-safe
- Set of lightweight mixing bowls—pottery ones look beautiful but are too hard to wash
- Large grater, dishwasher-safe
- Skillets, one 8 inches, one 12
- Lightweight pot, about 6 quarts, with a pasta/steamer insert
- Heavyweight Dutch oven, at least 4 quarts

- 2-quart saucepan with lid
- Hand blender (also called an immersion blender); some also serve as miniature food processors
- Large toaster oven
- Food processor
- Two rimmed cookie sheets and nonstick baking liners to fit them
- Two cooling racks
- Two 9-inch cake pans
- A 9-inch glass pie dish
- A 9-by-13-inch baking pan
- Adjustable pepper mill and large salt shaker for the kitchen
- Large salad bowl, preferably wood
- Dishwasher-safe china for 12
- Dishwasher-safe flatware for 12
- Three serving platters
- Two serving bowls
- Serving spoons
- 24 wineglasses

The Next Steps:
- 6-inch chef's knife
- Carving knife
- Tall, narrow stockpot
- Miniature food processor
- Standing mixer
- Ice cream machine
- Waffle iron
- Cast-iron griddle
- Microplane graters
- Storage canisters for rice, grains, etc.
- A large (10- to 12-cup) Bundt pan
- Nonstick tart pan, removable sides
- Thanksgiving gear: large roasting pan with rack, meat thermometer, turkey baster, potato masher
- Table linens: placemats, tablecloths
- Silver flatware
- 12 globe-shaped glasses for red wine
- A serving fork and a cake server

—Julia Moskin

FOOD

Outfitting a No-Frills Kitchen

How to start a kitchen for $200 or less

The question I'm asked more often than any other is, "What kitchen equipment should I buy?" Like cookbooks, kitchen equipment is a talisman; people believe that buying the right kind will make them good cooks. Yet, I contend that with a bit of savvy, patience and a willingness to forgo steel-handle knives, copper pots and other extravagant items, $200 can equip a basic kitchen that will be adequate for just about any task, and

$300 can equip one quite well.

To prove my point I put together a list of everything needed for almost any cooking task. I bought most of the equipment at Bowery Restaurant Supply in New York City, where the bill came to just about $200. Throw in a few items the store didn't have and a few extras, and the total would be about $300. (New York happens to have scores of restaurant supply shops, but every metropolitan area has at least one.)

I started with an 8-inch, plastic-handle stainless alloy chef's knife for $10. This is probably the most essential tool in the kitchen. People obsess about knives, and it's true that you can easily spend over $100 on just one. Yet go into any restaurant kitchen and you will see most of the cooks using this same plastic-handle Dexter-Russell tool. (Go to the wrong store and you'll spend $20 or even $30 on the same knife.)

I found an instant-read thermometer, a necessity for beginning cooks and obsessive-compulsives, for $5. Three stainless steel bowls—not gorgeous and maybe a little thin—set me back about $5. Sturdy tongs, an underappreciated tool: $3.50 (don't buy them too long, make sure the spring is nice and tight and don't shop for them at a "culinary" store, where they'll cost four times as much).

For less than $6, I picked up a sturdy sheet pan. It's not an ideal cookie sheet, but it's useful for

There is no point at all in anything that does only one job.

Laurie Colwin,
food writer, on kitchen
utensils and machines

• • •

roasting and baking (not a bad tray, either, and one of the more common items in restaurant kitchens). A plastic cutting board was about the same price. For aesthetic purposes I'd rather have wood, but plastic can go into the dishwasher.

At $3, a paring knife was so cheap I could replace it every year or two. I splurged on a Japanese mandoline for $25.

You, or the college graduate you are thinking of, might own some of the things I bought: a $4 can opener; a vegetable peeler (I like the U-shaped type, which cost me $3); a colander ($7).

You are thinking to yourself: "Humph. He's ignoring pots and pans, the most expensive items of all." Au contraire, my friend; I bought five, and I could live with four: a small, medium and large cast-aluminum saucepan (total: about $30); a medium nonstick cast-aluminum pan

---

✔ **TIMELY TIPS**

10 Gadgets You Can Live Without

Most people don't really need the following kitchen items:

✔ **Bread machine.** You can make the real thing without much practice.

✔ **Microwave.** If you do a lot of reheating or fast (and damaging) defrosting, you may want one. But essential? No. And think about that counter space!

✔ **Stand mixer.** Unless you're a baking fanatic, it takes up too much room to justify it. A good whisk or a crummy handheld mixer will do fine.

✔ **Boning/filleting knives.** Really? You're a butcher now? Or a fishmonger? I haven't used my boning knife in years.

✔ **Wok.** Counterproductive without a good wok station equipped with a high-B.T.U. burner.

✔ **Stockpot.** The pot you use for boiling pasta will suffice,

until you start making gallons of stock at a time.

✔ **Pressure cooker.** It's useful, but do you need one? No.

✔ **Anything made of copper.** More trouble than it's worth, unless you have a pine-paneled wall you want to decorate.

✔ **Rice cooker.** Yes, if you eat rice twice daily. Otherwise, no.

✔ **Countertop convection oven, rotisserie, or "roaster."** Only if you're a sucker for late-night cooking infomercials.

—Mark Bittman

(10-inch; $13); and a large, steep-sided, heavier duty steel pan (14-inch; $25). I bought a single lid ($5; I often use plates or whatever's handy for lids because I can never find the right one anyway).

I like cast iron, and I have used it in some kitchens for nearly everything; but it can be more expensive than this quite decent cheap stuff, and it's very heavy. What you don't want is the awful wafer thin (and relatively more expensive) sets of stainless or aluminum pots and pans sold in big-box stores.

You should also have a food processor (you want 12-cup capacity, and Amazon.com, for example, has an adequate 14-cup Hamilton Beach for $60); a salad spinner (you will find one for $15 somewhere); a Microplane grater (the old box graters have been largely replaced by the food processor, but you'll need something for cheese, nutmeg and your oft-used asafetida; it'll set you back less than $10). A coffee and spice grinder is another $10 item.

A blender is a bit more optional. An immersion one is nice, but standard ones are more useful, and you can find them for as little as $15.

And, finally, something with which to keep those knives sharp. A whetstone costs about $6, and if you use it, it will work fine; a decent steel blade is expensive enough that you may as well graduate to an electric sharpener. Though sharpeners take up counter space and cost at least $30, they work well.

The point is not so much that you can equip a real kitchen without much money, but that the fear of buying the wrong kind of equipment is unfounded. It needs only to be functional, not prestigious, lavish or expensive. Keep that in mind, stay out of the fancy places and find a good restaurant supply house.

—Mark Bittman

Cook's Choice: Cast-Iron Pans

Forget Teflon, stainless steel or copper

My recommendation for cookware? Old-fashioned cast iron. As most experienced cooks know, you can't brown food unless you preheat your skillet, and if you often transfer food from stove top to oven, cast iron is the logical choice. Plus, it distributes heat far better than stainless steel or aluminum.

Seasoning a cast-iron pan is simple, and maintaining it is even simpler. To season a new pan wash it well and dry it. Preheat the oven to 350 degrees while you warm the pan gently over low heat on top of the stove. Using a brush or a paper towel, spread a tablespoon or so of a neutral oil like corn or grape seed in the pan; the surface should be evenly covered, with no excess. Put the pan in the oven, bake it for about an hour and let it cool in the oven.

Once the pan is seasoned, routine washing can be done with a scouring pad (not steel wool or anything else that will damage the seasoning, although the worst that can happen is that the pan will have to be reseasoned) and even a little mild soap. If rust does appear, scour it off with steel wool or sandpaper and reseason.

For "grilling" a steak indoors, cast iron can't be beat. Ridged cast-iron "grill pans" are good for two reasons: they raise the meat slightly above the surface, which promotes browning by preventing escaping liquids from contacting the meat, and they leave grill marks, which are attractive if nothing else.

Cast iron is good at browning, and its mass lets it hold a steady temperature so well that it is perfect for deep- or shallow-frying. But braising in cast iron, especially with acidic ingredients like tomato or wine, may degrade the seasoning slightly. In extreme cases, you may have to reseason the pan.

—Mark Bittman

FOOD

The Case for Eating Locally

Who's coming to dinner? A factory farm chicken or a local bird?

Louella Hill is a former executive director of Farm Fresh Rhode Island (www.farmfreshri.org), an online organization that links farmers with local eaters and businesses, and one of the leaders of the local food movement that is sweeping the country. Here she offers the arguments for eating locally.

Every time you eat, you are making a choice. For example, consider that chicken you plan to roast for tomorrow night's dinner. When you buy that chicken, you usually have two options. You can buy a chicken that comes from a factory farm 2,000 miles away. The factory farm may house over 20,000 birds. Hormones and antibiotics must be used to help the birds gain weight and fight disease. Tomorrow night's dinner will probably never see sunlight or blue sky, or even have room to move around in its cage. Or you can buy a chicken from a local family-owned poultry farm. The farm where the chicken was raised is probably less than 40 minutes from your house. The chicken spent its life in sunlight and open air. It is an heirloom breed and was raised without the use of hormones or antibotics.

 INSIDE INFO

Where the Pesticides Are

○ The lowest pesticide levels are found in asparagus, avocados, bananas, broccoli, cauliflower, sweet corn, kiwi, mangoes, onions, papaya, pineapples and sweet peas.

○ The highest pesticide levels are found in apples, bell peppers, celery, cherries, imported grapes, nectarines, peaches, pears, potatoes, red raspberries, spinach and strawberries.

SOURCE: The Environmental Working Group. See www.foodnews.org for a more complete guide.

Eating locally means waiting until July for tomatoes or not expecting berries to always be at the grocery store. But the payoff is an enhanced flavor and freshness to all that you eat. There are many ways to get involved in building a more sustainable food system. Here are a few suggestions:

• Eat with the seasons.

• Shop at farmers' markets and farm stands or at pick-your-own orchards.

• Find groceries that carry locally produced foods.

• Join a C.S.A. (Community Supported Agriculture) program in which you prepay for weekly shares of a farm's harvest.

• Ask your waiter which dishes feature locally produced foods the next time you eat out.

• Tell your neighbors, family and friends why that home-grown tomato tasted so good.

• Host a "local flavors" dinner party and highlight as many local ingredients as you can.

• Help a local school district develop their "farm to school" program

More information about farms, farmers' markets and businesses that support local farmers in your area can be found at www.localharvest.com. The Community Food Security Coalition's Web page (www.foodsecurity.org) covers food system policy issues, from community gardens to local foods in hospital cafeterias.

How Green Is Your Kitchen?

It's not only the food you eat, but how you buy it and what you throw away

The shift toward local, seasonal and sustainable agriculture makes sense for the taste buds, the body and the planet. But there's a next step: making home kitchens just as environmentally sound as those pastoral organic farms.

"Once you make the leap into understanding it's better to shop organically and locally, it's a natural step to think about how you store and prepare the food," says Mindy Pennybacker, a former editor-in-chief of *The Green Guide*, an online newsletter devoted to environmentally friendly options for the home (thegreenguide.com).

"It's a matter of pleasure," says Annie Berthold-Bond, known as the "Green Heloise" for books like *The Green Kitchen Handbook* and *Better Basics for the Home.* "Your enjoyment of life is exponentially improved when the food you eat is wonderful and you don't have a headache from cleaning with chemicals. In the end, it's a much richer, better living experience."

Make Wise Choices. Washing fruit and vegetables reduces pesticide residue but does not eliminate it. Peeling works better, but then valuable nutrients in the skin are lost. Lab tests conducted by the scientists and engineers at the Environmental Working Group have determined some unsettling results, such as nine different pesticides on a single sample.

Cut down on packaging waste by buying in bulk at health food stores. Bring your favorite display bottles and mason jars into your local health food store, have the cashier weigh and mark them, then turn on the spigots for high-quality olive and canola oil priced by the ounce. The cashier will deduct the weight of the container before totaling the bill.

Starve the Garbage. "Remember our rule," Mario Batali, the well-known chef, once told an apprentice while retrieving a handful of greens from the garbage, "we do not make money by buying food and then throwing it away." Find your inner Mario. After you trim the greens off celery, carrots and beets (you want them off because they drain the moisture from the root), freeze them. Over time, add the trimmings of other stock vegetables,

---

ⓘ INSIDE INFO

Creating Your Own Compost

○ The average household discards—daily—roughly 2 pounds of naturally recyclable waste, the raw material for black gold, otherwise known as compost, which could be spread around home gardens or community parks or near street trees, according to the New York City Compost Project.

○ You can compost these items: fruits, vegetables, flowers, dead plants, coffee grounds, egg shells, nut shells, stale bread, flour, cereal, spices, beans, spoiled juice, food-soiled paper towels, napkins, cardboard, coffee filters, tea bags (staple removed), shredded paper and cornstarch packing peanuts.

○ It takes three to four months for organic material to decompose sufficiently to become compost. Worms speed along the composting process but are not necessary unless your compost pile is in an indoor container. Finished compost resembles dark, crumbly topsoil and should bear no resemblance to the original materials. Compost should have a pleasant earthy smell to it.

---

including onion and garlic skins and tomato. Parmesan rinds add a wonderful flavor.

If you make roast chicken for a dinner party, clean the bird after the main course and toss it in a stockpot, adding water and the contents of a couple of freezer bags of trimmings, some salt and a bay leaf. During dessert, a fresh batch of broth will have made itself. It's ready for the freezer by the time the dishes are done.

Pouring out perfectly good, undrunk wine after a party is a sin. Nigella Lawson, the food writer, says that it can be frozen in Ziploc bags and thawed for stews, ragus and deglazing.

A household of one or two can also freeze sliced bread, which preserves the quality better than refrigerating it. Pull out a few slices at a time for toast; no thawing necessary. A leftover baguette can be split and cut into 4- to-6-inch lengths and frozen, to be reheated quickly in the oven for a French breakfast with butter and jam. Stale bread, whirred in the food processor, makes perfect, freezable breadcrumbs.

—Julie Besonen and Andrea Kannapell

Picking Produce at Its Prime

A guide to picking fresh fruits and vegetables

There are a few universal truths about choosing the freshest and most flavorful fruits and vegetables: buy seasonally and as close to the source as possible. If you are buying organic or from a local farmer, don't worry about imperfections, including a few insect holes. Perfection and flavor are not necessarily related.

What you don't want are soft, bruised or brown spots, all signs of immediate or impending decay. And you don't want to cause them yourself by

---

 INSIDE INFO

Nudging a Fruit to Ripen

○ To speed the ripening of soft fruits such as avocados, bananas, kiwis, nectarines, peaches, pears, plums and tomatoes, store them in a paper bag with an apple. The apple will boost the partly ripe fruit's exposure to ethylene, a gas required for ripening.

Fruits That Don't Ripen After Harvest:

○ Apples	○ Cherries	○ Grapefruit
○ Grapes	○ Lemons	○ Limes
○ Oranges	○ Pineapples	○ Strawberries
○ Tangerines	○ Tangelos	○ Watermelons

SOURCE: The Produce Marketing Association

---

squeezing tender fruits, like peaches. Keep all fruits at room temperature as long as possible, and don't wash them until just before eating. Refrigerate only to prevent overripening or decay. Contrary to popular belief, watermelon thumping, cantaloupe shaking and pineapple leaf plucking are not valid tests for determining ripeness.

Whether melons ripen a little bit at room temperature appears controversial: some authorities say they do; others say no. It may depend more on how much time has elapsed between the time they were picked and the time they reach the customer. Out of season, you should purchase melons cut up to see the color.

CHOOSING FRUITS

Apples: Firm, smooth, shiny skin, good color with no shrivelling; overlarge usually means mealy.

Apricots: Sweetest the moment before they turn from slightly firm to almost soft.

Avocados: Feel heavy for size, yield to pressure when gently pressed; no bruises.

Bing cherries: Darker are the ripest and sweetest.

Bananas: Yellow, with a little browning; no green tinge.

Cantaloupes: Heavy for size; should smell sweet; yield to pressure at indentation.

Grapefruits: Large, firm, fine-grained, heavy for their size.

Grapes: Plump and juicy, firmly attached to stem; no shriveling, soft spots, dried stems.

Honeydews: Heavy for size; characteristic aroma; blossom end should yield to slight pressure.

Kiwis: Plump and fresh, yielding to gentle palm pressure. No bruises, soft spots or shriveling.

Lemons and limes: Heavy for their size; firm with thin skin; bright yellow lemons are more acid than darker yellow; limes should be bright green.

Mangoes: Flesh gives slightly when ripe and is starting to wrinkle; avoid any with black spots.

Oranges: Firm, heavy for size; don't worry about green on skin.

Papayas: Between green and yellow in color, slightly soft, no bruising or shriveling; no aroma.

Peaches, nectarines and plums: Yield to slight pressure and have a delicate fragrance.

Pears: Yield slightly to finger pressure at stem end; better to ripen fully at home.

Pineapples: Deep green leaves; fresh tropical smell; no skin discoloration or soft spots.

Red raspberries: Lighter berries have more flavor than darker ones.

Strawberries: All red, bright and shiny.

Watermelons: Rind is dull green, side that was on the ground should be creamy yellow, not white.

CHOOSING VEGETABLES

Artichokes: Firm without brown tips, with leaves curling inward.

Arugula: Bright green, no yellowing or limpness; the smaller the leaves the better.

Asparagus: No ridges; the diameter is immaterial. The best are standing in water and are firm, the outcroppings close to the spear.

Carrots: Medium to dark orange with no white spots.

Corn: Silky tassels, no dryness in the husk. Pull down a little of husk and stick a fingernail into a kernel. If it bursts easily, corn is fresh; never buy shucked corn.

Cucumbers and summer squashes: Firm, no soft spots or wrinkling (smaller are tastier).

Eggplant: Rich purple color with shiny skin, no wrinkles; the smaller the sweeter.

Fennel: No sign of browning or drying on cut edges; bulb compact, not spread out.

Garlic: Firm and plump.

Green beans: No lumps; when bent should snap.

Lettuces: No wilting, brown or rust spots.

Onion: Firm, no wet spots, no sign of dust.

Peas (all kinds): Pods should be bright green with no dryness.
> **Snow peas:** small and flat.
> **Green peas:** pods ready to burst.
> **Sugar snaps:** plump.

Peppers: Shiny, unblemished skins, without wrinkles or soft spots.

Potatoes: Firm without growth around the eyes and no green spots.

Sweet potatoes: Smooth skin.

Zucchini, yellow summer squash: Firm, not overly large, no soft spots. —Marian Burros

What to Stock in Your Pantry
Items to keep on the shelf or in the fridge

If your goal is to cook and cook quickly, to get a satisfying and enjoyable variety of real food on the table as often as possible, a well-stocked pantry and fridge can sustain you. Replenished weekly or even less frequently, with an occasional stop for fresh vegetables, meat, fish and dairy, they are the core supply houses for the home cook.

While you're stocking up, you might clear out a bit of the detritus that's cluttering your shelves. Some of these things take up more space than they're worth, while others are so much better in their real forms that the difference is laughable. My

The Children's Menu

Don't be afraid to feed your kids good food

To test out the theory that children could be educated to eat better, the *New York Times* polled several chefs with young children to see what they fed them and found serious challenges to the notion that small people simply will not brook fresh vegetables, texture or spice.

The fact that chefs' kids eat better than yours or mine isn't surprising. They often bring the little ones to work, where they eat tiny plates of duck confit or buckwheat pasta. Here are some of their rules for getting kids to eat well.

✔ **Have your children eat at the table from a very young age.** A chef in Cambridge, Mass., says her children never had highchairs. "It was really hard, because 2-year-olds throw food. But I saw the benefit in treating the dinner table as something that everyone had to participate in."

✔ **Make them eat what you do, even if you have to purée it.** "If we ate butternut squash and carrots, so did they," a chef in Boulder, Colo., says, "and sometimes fish." A Chicago chef treated his 4-year-old to a 10-course dinner. "He didn't finish everything, but he tried every course, which included white truffles, crab, bison," he says.

✔ **Pack lunches fashioned from leftovers.** "If we order Thai food," says a chef in Portland, Ore., her daughter "takes pad Thai the next day."

✔ **Eschew Bugles.** "If kids are hungry, they're going to eat," another chef in Portland, Ore. reports. "If you fill them up on Bugles, they won't."

—Jennifer Steinhauer (Adapted from *In the Hands of a Chef* by Jody Adams and Ken Rivard)

point here is not to criminalize their use, but to point out how easily and successfully we can substitute for them, in every case with better results.

Here, then, is my little list of items you might spurn, along with some essential pantry and long-keeping refrigerator items you might consider.

OUT *Packaged bread crumbs or croutons.*

IN Take crumbs, cubes or slices of bread, and either toast evenly in a low oven until dry and lightly browned, tossing occasionally; or cook in olive oil until brown and crisp, stirring frequently. The first keep a long time, and are multipurpose; the second are best used quickly, and are incomparably delicious.

OUT *Bouillon cubes or powder, or canned stock.*

IN Simmer a carrot, a celery stalk and half an onion in a couple of cups of water for 10 minutes and you're better off; if you have any chicken scraps, even a half-hour of cooking with those same vegetables will give you something 10 times better than any canned stock.

OUT *Aerosol oil. At about $12 a pint, twice as expensive as halfway decent extra virgin olive oil, which spray oil is not; and it contains additives.*

IN Get good olive oil and a hand-pumped sprayer or, even simpler, a brush. Simplest: your fingers.

OUT *Bottled salad dressing and marinades. The biggest rip-offs imaginable.*

IN Take good oil and vinegar or lemon juice, and combine them with salt, pepper, maybe a little Dijon, in a proportion of about three parts oil to one of vinegar. Customize from there, because you may like more vinegar or less, and you undoubtedly will want a little shallot, or balsamic vinegar, or honey, or garlic, or tarragon, or soy sauce...

OUT *Bottled lemon juice.*

IN **Lemons**. Try buying six at a time, then experiment; I never put lemon on something and

 **TIMELY TIPS**

Home Cooking Tricks

Some money-saving—and time-saving—ideas for the family cook

When times are tougher and reconfigured budgets force a cutback on eating out, taking out and buying expensive processed foods, a growing number of American families rely more on home cooking. Before you despair at the prospect of spending many more hours in the kitchen, realize that there are time-honored tricks to making budget-conscious meals efficiently. There are also some very real benefits to home cooking for you and your loved ones. Not the least of them is the improvement in nutrition and health that comes from cooking for a few instead of many and from being in control of the ingredients and portion sizes.

✔ **Cook in batches.** Time is a valuable commodity, not to be squandered. But when you prepare only one meal at a time, you do just that. Who made a rule that you can't eat the same meal two or three nights in a row? I cook in batches, making enough of a recipe for two, three, even four meals and often enough to freeze a portion or two.

✔ **Back to basics.** Beans can be combined with many other foods, including rice or pasta (very cheap) and couscous or bulgur (more expensive but also more nutritious).

Pasta or potatoes can be mixed with simple sauces containing vegetables and small amounts of meat, fish, poultry or beans to create a one-dish family meal.

For desserts, try seasonal fruits, fresh or cooked, either alone or as a topping on low-fat or nonfat vanilla yogurt.

For breakfast, try a hot cereal like oatmeal—regular or quick-cooking—or French toast made with whole wheat bread.

✔ **Other money savers.** While relatively few Americans have the space and climate to grow their own food year-round, nearly everyone can grow herbs in pots on a windowsill and add flavor to foods without overdoing salt, sugar and fat.

As for beverages, forget bottled water and soda. Tap water is fine. Consider buying milk by the gallon for a family.

And for meals that must be eaten out, I've been a brown-bagger my whole life, both at work and on family excursions. It saves time and lots of money.

—Jane E. Brody

FOOD

regret it. Don't forget the zest: you can grate it and add it to many pan sauces, or hummus and other purées. And don't worry about reamers, squeezers or any of that junk; squeeze from one hand into the other and let your fingers filter out the pits.

***OUT** Spices older than a year.*

IN Fresh spices. Almost all spices are worth having. But some that you might think about using more frequently include cardamom, ground cumin, fennel seeds, an assortment of dried chilies, fresh—or at least dried—ginger, pimentón, the smoked Spanish red pepper that is insanely popular in restaurants but still barely

making inroads among home cooks, and good curry powder.

***OUT** Dried parsley and basil. They're worthless.*

IN Fresh parsley, which keeps at least a week in the refrigerator. And dried tarragon, rosemary and dill, all of which I use all winter.

***OUT** Canned beans (except in emergencies).*

IN Dried beans. More economical, better tasting, space saving and available in far more varieties. Cook a pound once a week and you'll always have them around (you can freeze small amounts in their cooking liquid, or water, indefinitely).

Eat More Nuts, But Not Too Many

Some fats, mostly polyunsaturated and mono-unsaturated fatty acids from plant sources, do not have an adverse effect on health if consumed judiciously—just the contrary.

✔ Nuts are high in good fats, as well as excellent sources of vegetable protein, fiber, magnesium, calcium, and vitamins K, B6, E and folate. A diet high in nuts may protect against both heart disease and diabetes.

✔ If you simply snack on nuts, it's easy to eat too many, and pack on the calories. A more sensible way to work them into your diet is to make some of the delicious Mediterranean and Mexican nut-based sauces and dips, which can be served with fish or vegetables, or as a topping for crostini.

OUT *Imitation vanilla.*
  IN Vanilla beans. They're costly, but they keep.

OUT *Grated imitation "Parmesan."*
  IN • Real Parmigiano-Reggiano. Save the rinds to throw in pots of sauce, soup, stew or risotto.

OUT *Canned peas (and most other canned vegetables, come to think of it).*
  IN Frozen peas. Especially if you have little kids and make pasta or rice with peas (and Parmesan!).

OUT *Tomato paste in a can.*
  IN Tomato paste in a tube. You rarely need more than two tablespoons, so you feel guilty opening a can; this solves that problem.

OUT *Premade pie crusts.*
  IN Graham crackers. Crumble with melted butter and press into a pan.

OUT *Cheap balsamic or flavored vinegars.*

  IN Sherry vinegar. More acidic and more genuine than all but the most expensive balsamic.

OUT *Minute Rice or boil-in-a-bag grains.*
  IN Genuine grains. Critical; as many different types as you have space for. Short grain rice, of course. Barley, pearled or not; a super rice alternative, with any kind of gravy, reduction sauce or pan drippings. Ground corn for polenta, grits, cornbread or thickener. Quinoa—people can't believe how flavorful this is until they try it. Bulgur, which is ready in maybe 10 minutes (it requires only steeping), and everyone likes. If you're in doubt about how to cook any of these, combine them with abundant salted water and cook as you would pasta, then drain when tender; you can't go far wrong.

OUT *"Pancake" syrup, which is more akin to Coke than to the real thing.*
  IN Real maple syrup, an indigenous gift from nature and the north country.

YOU SHOULD ALSO STOCK: Real bacon, prosciutto or other traditionally smoked or cured meat of some kind; fish sauce; canned coconut milk; miso paste; capers, good olives, (buy in bulk, not cans) and good anchovies (in olive oil, please); walnuts and/or other nuts; pignoli; dried fruit; dried mushrooms; frozen shrimp; winter squash and sweet potatoes.
                                              —Mark Bittman

How to Boil an Egg
So simple, but not so easy

Cooking hard-boiled eggs can be bewildering. Confused cooks fall victim to conflicting advice on avoiding rubbery whites, stuck-on shells and what Elizabeth David, the food writer, called "the unhealthy greenish hue" of overcooked yolks.

Julia Child's recipe in *The Way to Cook* prescribes a cooking time of exactly 17 minutes, followed by a 2-minute ice bath, a 10-second return to boiling water, and then yet another ice bath. The recipe provided by *The Joy of Cooking* goes to the other extreme, simply directing cooks to put eggs into boiling water and leave them there for anywhere from 10 to 17 minutes. Chefs and food scientists do agree on a few points, however.

Salted water should be used (so that if the eggs crack, the escaping whites will coagulate more quickly and seal off the hole).

Cooked eggs should be immersed in cold water immediately (some say this is to stop the cooking; others say it makes the eggs easier to peel).

Rubbery egg whites and green-ringed yolks are both caused by cooking eggs too long or at a temperature that is too high, or both.

There is a longstanding tradition among Sephardic Jews of boiling eggs for hours—even overnight. "They are quite different from 15-minute eggs," says Claudia Roden, author of *The Book of Jewish Food*, who simmers hers for at least four hours. "But they are not rubbery at all. The whites turn beige and the yolks are buttery and sweet."

My mother's method, adapted from one published in *Cook's Illustrated* magazine, gives consistently excellent results.

Place the eggs in a single layer in a heavy saucepan and cover with cold water by at least one inch. Add a teaspoon of salt. Leaving the pot uncovered, turn the heat to high. As soon as the water comes to a boil, turn off the heat and cover. After 10 minutes, remove the cover and run cold water over eggs for 1 minute. (For firmer yolks, leave the eggs to cool in the water for up to two hours.) Refrigerate up to 1 week.

To peel, gently tap each egg against the counter, turning to make a crackle pattern. Start peeling at the broad end, where there is an air pocket. For the best flavor, eggs, once peeled, should be used within a few hours.

—Julia Moskin

Soufflés for Beginners

Even some of the most experienced home cooks are afraid of soufflés. The fears: they'll never rise, they'll immediately fall, they're difficult to make, they're temperamental.

Try this, which is not only not scary, it's also easy. It can be made ahead of time, it's rich and light, it will dazzle your significant other (or anyone else) and it requires no more effort than it takes to beat a few eggs.

> About 1 tablespoon butter for dish
> 1/3 cup sugar, plus some for dish
> 3 eggs, separated
> 2 oz good-quality bittersweet chocolate, melted
> Pinch salt
> 1/4 teaspoon cream of tartar.
> 4 large egg yolks

1. Preheat oven to 350 degrees. Butter two 2-cup or one 4-cup soufflé or other deep baking dish(es). Sprinkle each with sugar, invert it and tap to remove excess sugar.

2. Beat egg yolks with all but 1 tablespoon sugar until very light and very thick; mixture will fall in a ribbon from beaters when it is ready. Mix in the melted chocolate until well combined; set aside.

3. Wash beaters well, then beat egg whites with salt and cream of tartar until whites hold soft peaks; continue to beat, gradually adding remaining tablespoon sugar, until they are very stiff and glossy. Stir a good spoonful of whites thoroughly into egg yolk mixture to lighten it; then fold in remaining whites, using a rubber spatula. Transfer to prepared soufflé dish(es); at this point you can cover and refrigerate until you are ready to bake.

4. Bake until center is nearly set, 20 minutes for individual soufflés and 25 to 35 minutes for a single large soufflé. Serve immediately.
SERVES 2.

—Mark Bittman

FOOD

GERM WARFARE

The right temperatures to keep bacteria at bay

240°	Canning temperatures for low-acid vegetables, meat and poultry in pressure canner.
212°	Canning temperature for fruits, tomatoes and pickles in water-bath canner. Cooking temperatures destroy most bacteria. Time required to kill bacteria is decreased as temperature is increased.
165°	Warming temperatures prevent growth but allow survival of some bacteria.
140°	Some bacterial growth may occur. Many bacteria survive. **DANGER ZONE. Temperatures in this zone allow rapid growth of bacteria and production of toxins by some bacteria.**
60°	Some growth of food-poisoning bacteria may occur. (Do not store meats, poultry or seafoods for more than one week in the refrigerator.)
40°	Cold temperatures permit slow growth of some bacteria that cause spoilage.
32°	Freezing temperatures stop growth of bacteria, but may allow bacteria to survive. (Do not store food above 10° F for more than a few weeks.)

SOURCE: U.S.D.A.

The Perfect Roast Beef and...

Intimidated by that rack of lamb? Look no further

Specific cuts and types of meat have optimum methods and temperatures for cooking. Some meats, such as turkey, require more care (such as basting with broth and olive oil or melted butter) as they cook. Others require simply that the temperature and timing be carefully observed.

For all boneless meat, allow 1/3 to 1/2 pound per serving; if the meat contains bone, estimate 1/2 to 3/4 pound per serving.

TO BROIL STEAK *l-inch thick, 2-4 inches from preheated oven broiler.*
If grilling steak, grill 3 inches from fire and cook 1 minute less per side.

• **Sirloin, Porterhouse, T-bone or Rib**
rare – 5 minutes each side	
medium – 7 minutes each side	
well-done – 10 minutes each side	

• **Filet mignon**, cook 1 minute less per side.

TO ROAST BEEF *(350° F)*

Cut / Weight – Minutes per pound (m/lb)	Internal temp (F)
• **Standing rib** (4 to 8 lbs.)	
rare – 20 to 25 m/lb	140°
medium – 25 to 30 m/lb	160°
well-done – 30 to 35 m/lb	170°
• **Rolled rib** (5 to 7 lbs.)	
rare – 30 to 35 m/lb	140°
medium – 35 to 40 m/lb	160°
well-done – 40 to 45 m/lb	170°
• **Rib eye** (4 to 6 lbs.)	
rare – 20 m/lb	140°
medium – 22 m/lb	160°
well-done – 24 m/lb	170°
• **Tenderloin** *(425° F)*	
whole / 4 to 6 lbs.– 45-60 min. total	140°
half / 2 to 3 lbs.– 35-45 min. total	140°
• **Sirloin tip** – 30 to 40 m/lb	160°

TO ROAST VEAL *(325° F)*

	INTERNAL TEMP (F)
• **Leg** / 5 to 8 lbs. – 25 to 30 m/lb	170°
• **Loin** / 4 to 6 lbs. – 30 to 35 m/lb	170°
• **Rib (rack)** (3 to 5 lbs.) – 35 to 40 m/lb	170°

TO ROAST LAMB (325° F)

• **Leg** / 5 to 8 lbs. – 20 to 25 m/lb	145° to 170°
• **Shoulder** / 4 to 6 lbs. – 30 to 35 m/lb	140° to 155°
• **Rib** (6 chops) *(400°F)* – 25 min. total	145°
• **Crown** *(375°F)* / 3 to 4 lbs. – 20 to 30 m/lb	145° to 170°

TO ROAST PORK *(325° F)*

• **Loin**, center / 3 to 5 lbs. – 40 m/lb	185°
half / 5 to 7 lbs. – 45 m/lb	185°
rolled / 3 to 5 lbs. – 50 m/lb	185°
• **Sirloin** / 3 to 4 lbs. – 50 m/lb	185°
• **Crown** / 4 to 6 lbs. – 45 m/lb	185°
• **Picnic shoulder** / 5 to 8 lbs. – 40 m/lb	185°
• **Rolled shoulder** / 3 to 5 lbs. – 45 m/lb	185°
• **Spareribs** / 3 lbs. – 40 m/lb	185°
• **Fresh ham (leg)** / 10 to 14 lbs. – 30 m/lb	185°
half / 5 to 7 lbs. – 40 m/lb	185°

TO ROAST HAM, OTHER CURED PORK *(325° F)*

	INTERNAL TEMP (F)
• **Whole ham** / 10 to 14 lbs.	
uncooked – 20 m/lb	160°
fully cooked – 15 m/lb	130°
• **Picnic shoulder** / 5 to 8 lbs. – 30 m/lb	170°
• **Rolled shoulder** / 2 to 4 lbs. – 40 m/lb	170°

TO BROIL PORK

Chops *(¾- to 1-inch thick)*, **Shoulder steaks** *(½- to 1-inch thick)*, and **Patties** *(1-inch thick) should be broiled about 11 minutes on each side.*

TO ROAST TURKEY *(325° F)*   165°

READY TO COOK WEIGHT	HOURS
4 to 8 lbs.	3 to 4
8 to 12 lbs.	4 to 4 ½
12 to 16 lbs.	4 ½ to 5
16 to 20 lbs.	6 to 7 ½
20 to 24 lbs.	7 ½ to 9

TO ROAST DUCK OR GOOSE *(350° F)*   165°

Preheat oven to 450°; cook at reduced temperature 20 min./lb. unstuffed.

HOW TO CARVE A TURKEY

Show off at the table next Thanksgiving dinner. Here's what to do.

1. *Move drumstick and thigh by pulling leg away from body. Joint connecting leg to bone will often snap free or may be severed easily with knife point. Cut dark meat from body by following body* contour carefully with a knife.

2. *Place drumstick and thigh on cutting surface and cut through connecting joint.*

3. *Hold turkey breast firmly on carving surface with fork. Place knife parallel and as close to wing as possible. Make deep cut into breast, cutting toward ribs. This makes a base cut.*

4. *Slice breast by carving downward, ending at the base cut. Keep slices thin and even.*

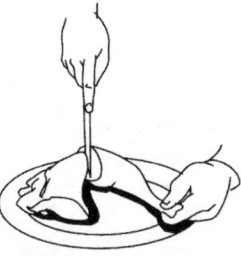

Source: National Turkey Federation

TO ROAST CHICKEN *(350° F)*   165°

Chicken weighing between 2 and 4 pounds should be roasted about 30 minutes per pound to an internal temperature of 165 degrees. Add 15 minutes to the total roasting time if the chicken is stuffed. With bones, estimate about ¹/₂ pound per serving.

TO COOK FISH

Cook fish thoroughly or to an internal temperature of 140 degrees.

• **Fin fish** *– allow 8 to 10 minutes of cooking time for each inch of thickness. Turn the fish over halfway through the cooking time, unless it is less than a half-inch thick. Add 5 minutes to the total cooking time if the fish is wrapped in foil or cooked in sauce.*

Method	Cooking temp. (F)	Time
Baked	350°	10 minutes
Broiled	500°	15 minutes
Deep-fried	370°	2 minutes
Pan-fried		10 minutes
Poached or steamed		10 m/lb

TO COOK SHELLFISH

Cooking shellfish thoroughly or to an internal temperature of 140 degrees F is required to help avoid the threat of food poisoning. Boil for three to five minutes after the shells have opened.

Steam shellfish 4 to 9 minutes from the start of steaming. Use small pots for boiling or steaming. If too many shells are cooking in the same pot, it's possible that the ones in the middle won't be thoroughly cooked. Discard any clams, mussels or oysters that do not open during cooking. If the shells remain closed, it may mean they have not received adequate heat.

	Simmer in boiling water
• **Shrimp**	5 minutes
• **Crab**	20 minutes
• **Lobster**	10 to 15 minutes per lobster

Shrimp, scallops, clams and oysters *can be deep-fried at 370 degrees F for about 3 minutes.*

Shrimp and scallops *can also be sautéed. Other shellfish are best boiled or steamed.*

HOW TO CLEAN A FISH

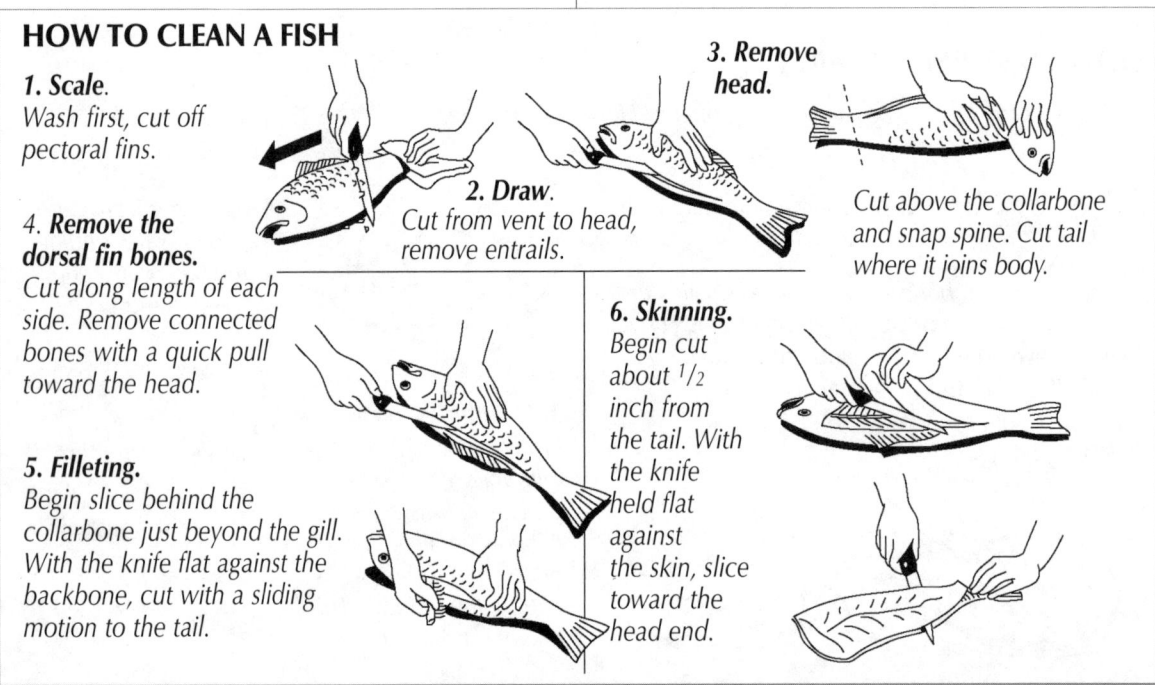

1. Scale.
Wash first, cut off pectoral fins.

4. Remove the dorsal fin bones.
Cut along length of each side. Remove connected bones with a quick pull toward the head.

5. Filleting.
Begin slice behind the collarbone just beyond the gill. With the knife flat against the backbone, cut with a sliding motion to the tail.

2. Draw.
Cut from vent to head, remove entrails.

3. Remove head.
Cut above the collarbone and snap spine. Cut tail where it joins body.

6. Skinning.
Begin cut about ¹/₂ inch from the tail. With the knife held flat against the skin, slice toward the head end.

BEYOND CANNED TUNA: HOW TO PICK YOUR FISH

These days, in local supermarkets and restaurants, Americans can get fish caught in waters the world over. But according to the National Fisheries Institute's study of data collected by the National Marine Fisheries Service, most Americans' idea of fish is still the old standby: canned tuna. If you want to expand your taste horizons, the guide below will help you decide between bluefish and mahi mahi the next time you're in the grocery store or scanning the restaurant menu.

FISH	⇌ Source	🐟 Type of meat	⇌ Flavor
SEA BASS	Northeast Atlantic coast	***Dark***	Light to moderate
STRIPED BASS	Atlantic and Pacific coastal waters; also farm-raised	***Light***	Light to moderate
BLUEFISH	Atlantic coastal waters	***Dark***	Light to moderate
CARP	Freshwater lakes, ponds worldwide	***Light***	Wild carp may taste muddy
FARMED CARP	Farms worldwide	***Light***	Farmed carp is light to moderate
CATFISH	Lakes, ponds and rivers	***White***	Wild catfish may taste muddy
FARMED CATFISH	Farms worldwide	***White***	Farmed catfish is light to moderate
COBIA	Mid-Atlantic from U.S. to Argentina	***White***	Light to moderate
COD	North to mid-Atlantic or North to mid-Pacific	***Light***	Very light, delicate
FLOUNDER	Atlantic, Pacific coasts, Asian Pacific coast and Bering Sea	***White***	Very light, delicate
GROUPER	Tropical and subtropical coastal waters and Atlantic coast	***Light***	Very light, delicate
HALIBUT	North Atlantic or Pacific coast, depending on species	***Light***	Very light, delicate
LAKE HERRING	Lakes and rivers in Canada and northern U.S.	***Light***	Light to moderate
MACKEREL	Atlantic or Gulf coast, Pacific, Eur. Atl. coast, Indian O.	***Light***	Pronounced flavor
MAHI MAHI	Off Hawaii and Florida, Gulf Stream, Pacific Calif. to S. America	***White***	Light to moderate
MONKFISH	North to mid-Atlantic	***Light***	Light to moderate
ORANGE ROUGHY	Deep waters off New Zealand and Australia	***White***	Very light, delicate
PIKE	Rivers and streams worldwide	***Light***	Light to moderate
POLLOCK	North Pacific or North Atlantic and the North Sea	***Light***	Light to moderate
RED SNAPPER	Gulf coast, Atlantic coast from N. Car. to Fla.	***Light***	Light to moderate
SALMON	North Atlantic or Pacific, rivers when spawning; also farmed	***Light***	Light to moderate
SAND SHARK	Western Atlantic	***Light***	Light to moderate
SMELT	Lakes, rivers and North Atlantic and Pacific coasts	***Light***	Very light, delicate
SWORDFISH	Off Calif., New Eng., Hawaii, Spain, Japan, Greece, S. America	***Light***	Light to moderate
RAINBOW TROUT	North American rivers and streams; farmed	***Light***	Very light, delicate
TUNA	Tropical to temperate waters worldwide	***Dark***	Light to moderate
WALLEYE	Northern North American lakes and rivers	***Light***	Very light, delicate
WHITEFISH	Northern U.S. and Canadian lakes	***White***	Light to moderate

SOURCE: National Fisheries Institute

FOOD

How to Grill a Fish

The secret is not to overcook it

Grilling fish intimidates many people, and not without reason: fish is slippery. More fish has been lost through grill grates than probably any other food. The key is not so much to remember to keep the grill clean, or to oil it—though these are not bad ideas and definitely help—but to choose fish that is most suitable for grilling.

Attempting to grill delicate, ultra-lean fillets—like flounder or sole, or even cod, which is thicker but falls apart almost as soon as you look at it—is an exercise in futility. You can use a grill basket, and this will keep you from losing the fish through the grates, but it will fall apart as you take it out of the basket, ruining your presentation. For these kinds of fish, stick to the broiler (which is really an upside-down grill, anyway) and you'll get good results.

For grilling, it pays to stick to heartier fish. The safest cut is steak: think swordfish, salmon, tuna, even steaks of halibut and cod (in this instance, the bones will hold it together). Small, firm, whole fish like mackerel, pompano, and red snapper (and, of course, many shellfish) are also practical. Grilling fillets is possible, too, as long as you choose the right ones: salmon, red snapper, catfish, monkfish, striped bass, sea bass, rockfish, tilefish and blackfish are all sturdy enough to grill, as are several others.

Once you have the right cut (and a clean, oiled grill), start with a fairly hot fire. Grill the fish with the skin side down. If you let the skin—or the first side you grill—firm up for a couple of minutes before you turn the fish, it will be easier. Once you turn it, remember not to overcook: overcooked fish is dry, and the lack of moisture makes it more likely that the fish will fall apart. Use a sharp knife to peek inside the thickest part of the fish to judge doneness.

Most fish are cooked to well-done at a rate of about 8 to 10 minutes per inch of thickness. So that's a decent rule of thumb for timing; if you prefer it less well-done, remove it from the grill sooner. When done to your liking, about 3 to 5 minutes after you turn, remove it to a platter or serving plates.

—Mark Bittman

Now, the Perfect Sauce for Fish

Any white-fleshed fish— roasted, poached or pan-cooked—will take beautifully to beurre blanc. If you prefer, you can make the sauce first and keep it warm over minimum heat, stirring now and then, for the brief time it takes to cook the fish.

This sauce is easy, foolproof, silken-smooth, impressive, fast and delicious. Start by reducing wine, vinegar and shallots; experienced cooks will recognize that as the first step in making béarnaise sauce. When this is syrupy, stir in butter a bit at a time so that it emulsifies, or combines smoothly with the wine syrup. As long as you take your time and do not stir all the butter in at once, you will succeed on the first try.

2 tablespoons minced shallots

2 cups white wine

2 tablespoons white wine vinegar

1 stick butter, cut into 6 or 8 pieces

Chopped fresh parsley or chervil for garnish.

1. Combine shallots, wine and vinegar in a small saucepan and turn heat to high. Cook until it is reduced to about ¼ cup, 10 minutes or so.

2. When white wine mixture has reduced, turn heat to very low. Add butter a piece at a time, stirring after each addition until it is incorporated. When all butter has been added, taste and adjust seasoning. Spoon sauce over fish, garnish if you like and serve. Serves 2.

—Mark Bittman

White House Spinach

One of Michelle Obama's favorite healthful foods is creamed spinach—without the cream. The dish is a hit with the president, but not with their youngest daughter, Sasha.

Here is a recipe for the dish from White House executive chef Cristeta Comerford.

NO-CREAM CREAMED SPINACH
2 pounds baby spinach, washed and cleaned
2 tablespoons olive oil
4 shallots, minced
2 garlic cloves, minced
Salt and freshly ground pepper

1. Blanch half a pound of spinach in salted, boiling water. Immediately "shock" the blanched spinach in a bowl of ice water. Drain and squeeze out the excess water. Purée in a blender. Set aside.

2. In a large skillet, sweat the shallots and garlic until translucent. Add the rest of the spinach leaves. Toss and sauté until wilted. Fold in the spinach purée. Season with salt and pepper.
Serves 6.

Cooking With a Foreign Accent
For those who'd like a little on-vacation training

Culinary instruction is available in France and Italy for every type of student, from seasoned chefs to casual cooks. One resource for cooking school vacations is *The Guide to Cooking Schools,* an index of programs throughout the world that ShawGuides publishes annually. The Web site, www.cookforfun.shawguides.com, offers a directory searchable by location and month.

The International Kitchen (800-945-8606; www.theinternationalkitchen.com) organizes cooking school vacations to France, Italy and Spain. Options include the Amalfi Coast, Tuscany,

Sicily, the Loire Valley, Provence and the French Riviera. All lessons are in English.

A trip to the Walnut Cooking School in Mayenne, Loire, includes a five-night stay at a country farmhouse, five hands-on cooking classes and all meals and excursions, including visits to an 18th-century windmill, a medieval city and a local fromagerie.

An alternative in Italy could be a six-night trip to Chianciano in southern Tuscany, with four cooking lessons and excursions to Siena, Montepulciano, Montalcino, Pienza and Montefollonico.

In addition to vacations exclusively devoted to cooking lessons, Jo-Ann Gaidosz, the owner of Active Gourmet Holidays, (203-732-0771; www.activegourmetholidays.com), offers holidays for those who want variety or have traveling companions with different interests. For example, a six-night vacation to Sorrento includes five Italian-language lessons, four cooking lessons, all breakfasts and dinners, excursions to Pompeii and Positano and transfers to and from the Naples airport. In France, a vacation could include cooking instruction, wine tasting and bicycle rides in Bordeaux, six nights at a bed and breakfast, all meals and wine, four cooking lessons in private homes and all excursions.   —Marjorie Connelly

Tips for Chocoholics
How to hold a chocolate tasting

Sitting in a room with piles of the world's best chocolate might seem like a dream, but you can have too much of a good thing. A successful chocolate-tasting event requires some preparation. For starters, keep the tasting small.

Be sure the chocolate is at room temperature. A temperature of 60° F is perfect for storing chocolate,

FOOD

 **TIMELY TIPS**

Why French Women Don't Get Fat

Eat soup, breath in fresh herbs and know that love is slimming

While close to two-thirds of American adults are either obese or overweight, French women really don't get fat. The reason behind that most enviable difference, says Mireille Guiliano, is that "French women take pleasure in staying thin by eating well, while American women see it as a conflict and obsess over it." Put another way, "French women typically think about good things to eat. American women typically worry about bad things to eat."

✔ Guiliano, the author of the best seller *French Women Don't Get Fat*, urges us to relax. Walk to the market, breathe in the fresh herbs, cook a good dinner, have a glass of wine or champagne. Just sip it slowly (she makes hers last through a meal). She rejects the "American rule" of "no pain, no gain" and describes exercise machines as a "vestige of Puritanism: instruments of public self-flagellation to make up for private sins of couch riding and overeating." French women make a ritual out of every meal.

✔ She knows we eat portions that are too big and food that is too bland. (Bland food and too much of one kind, a big bowl of pasta, for example, breeds boredom, which leads you to alleviate it by eating more.) French women, on the other hand, stress flavor and variety over quantity and, therefore, are more satisfied with less. She knows our tendency to gorge ourselves on Snickers bars rather than savor a single piece of fine, dark chocolate. French women eat slowly and "with all five senses."

✔ She offers no scientific "food plan," just suggestions and seemingly indulgent recipes, including one for fingerling potatoes and caviar. Guiliano reminds us that a half-dozen oysters contain only 60 or 70 calories, that soups fill you up and supply much-needed water to your body. ("The theory goes that the French, who eat soup up to five times a week for dinner, eat better and less.")

✔ Guiliano ends her book with a list of more observations about French women. They don't weigh themselves, they don't snack all the time, they eat more fruit but would never give up their bread or other carbs. They dress to take out the garbage, they understand the importance of a good haircut and expensive perfume, they know love is slimming. At the very least, we would all do ourselves a favor to make like Colette, for whom the table was "a date with love and friendship" instead of the root of all evil.

—Julia Reed, a senior writer for *Vogue* and author of *Queen of the Turtle Derby and Other Southern Phenomena*

but you can keep it well wrapped in plastic or a zip-top bag in the refrigerator until an hour or so before you taste. Still water is about all you need, but a few palate-cleaning tortilla chips nearby help.

First consider appearance. It should be smooth and shiny. Color can vary from copperish to nearly black.

Then break off a piece and smell it. Good chocolate should snap cleanly. Rub a finger over the surface to release some aroma. Overfermented beans can make chocolate smell like rotting fruit. Badly dried beans can be unpleasantly smoky. Cheap chocolate might smell overwhelmingly of vanilla. Good chocolate can smell like caramel, flowers, dried fruit, licorice—even mushrooms or dirt.

Next let it melt in your mouth for 15 to 20 seconds. Some cacao beans, especially of the forastero variety, contribute an earthy note. Rare criollos or the hybrid trinitario variety offer brighter flavors. Some chocolates taste like dairy, others like fruit. Some produce an astringent feeling in the mouth that comes from tannins like those found in wine or tea. Your preferred flavors will become clear pretty quickly.

—Kim Severson

Preparing the Perfect Picnic

Fresh ideas for a tasty take-out

With a little shopping, a little effort, and 20 minutes or less for assembly, you can create the kind of carry-out food that will put the local prepared food shops to shame while saving you a small fortune.

Beet salad. Peel beets and grate them (a food processor will keep the juice contained). Add pistachios or hazelnuts; dress with orange zest and juice, and olive oil. Add bits of goat cheese and chopped parsley.

Curried egg salad. Make egg salad with hard-cooked eggs, mayo, curry powder, Dijon mustard, fresh lime juice, salt, pepper, cilantro, red onion and, if you like, diced apple.

Gazpacho. Combine a couple of pounds of ripe tomatoes, one of cucumbers, a slice or two of bread, olive oil, vinegar, garlic, salt and pepper in a blender. Chill and pour into a thermos. Additionally, combine tomatoes and cucumber in a blender with lemongrass (only the most tender part), cilantro, fish sauce and lime. Voilà: Thai gazpacho.

Lentils. Cook lentils with garlic, onion and thyme. Toss with salt, pepper and fresh chopped herbs: marjoram, tarragon, chervil or basil. Dress with vinaigrette made with oil, vinegar and mustard.

Pesto chicken rolls. Season and grill chicken cutlets. Brush lavash or any other wrap-type bread with pesto; layer with the chicken, sun-dried tomatoes and arugula; roll up and cut on the bias.

Potato salad. Make potato salad with mustard vinaigrette. Add chopped cooked asparagus, peas, green beans, etc. Or steamed mussels. Alternatively, make potato salad with mayo and crumbled bacon, and add grated cheddar, celery, onion and chopped egg.

Roast beef and blue. Start with whole-grain rolls. Smear blue cheese on one side and prepared horseradish on the other. Add red onion and thin-sliced roast beef, pork or lamb. Pack lettuce and tomato on the side. Potato chips are mandatory.

Tomatoes and peaches. Toss together sliced, seeded tomatoes and peaches along with thinly sliced red onion and chopped cilantro or rosemary. Dress at the last minute with olive oil, lemon juice, salt and pepper.

—Mark Bittman

FOOD

Super Simple Sorbet

How to make sorbet (in seconds) without an ice cream machine

> **1 pound frozen strawberries or other fruit**
> **1/2 cup yogurt, crème fraîche or silken tofu**
> **1/4 cup sugar, more or less.**

1. Put all the ingredients in a food processor container along with a couple of tablespoons of water. Process until just puréed and creamy, stopping to scrape down the sides of the bowl as needed. If the fruit does not break down completely, add a little more water through the feed tube, a tablespoon or two at a time, being careful not to over-process or the sorbet will liquefy.

2. Serve immediately or freeze it for later; if serving later, allow 10 to 15 minutes for sorbet to soften at room temperature.

SERVES 4.

—Mark Bittman

Wine, etc.

Starting a Wine Collection

A Times' wine critic stocks a $1,000 cellar

Recent years have not been kind to the novice wine collector. What with poor exchange rates and the general economic decline, wine prices are up and disposable income is down. Back in 2006, when the first edition of *The New York Times Practical Guide to Practically Everything* was published, I felt $1,500 might be a minimum investment for beginning a wine cellar. For that price one could put together a collection of fine bottles for everyday drinking and classics for long-term aging.

But $1,500 won't buy you in 2010 what it would back then, and who's even got that much to spend on wine? Today, we have to take an entirely different approach: here is a starter wine cellar for a modest $1,000. Even for less money, the structure of the cellar remains the same: Six bottles of sparkling wine,

two cases for everyday drinking—one white and one red—and two cases of more ambitious bottles for aging. Instead of gravitating to the best-known regions, though, we're going to search for values in some of the less-renowned areas of the wine-producing world, where top-quality bottles can still be had for less. We'll also look at some of the less-popular grapes—it's hard to find a good everyday chardonnay, for example, for under $18 or so.

Nowadays, with decent Champagnes starting at about $30, California is an excellent alternative. One of my favorite producers, Roederer Estate in Mendocino County, is also one of the most reasonably priced at $18 a bottle. Six bottles of Roederer Estate Brut will run about $110. Don't reserve sparkling wine solely for celebrations. It's great with sushi, Chinese food and fried chicken.

For the everyday table wines, we'll divide each case into three groups of four bottles, for variety's sake. The world is full of crisp, dry white wines, but if they offer a little character as well, you're in luck. Rueda is an up-and-coming district in Spain, producing delicious, mineral-y wines largely of the verdejo grape. The 2008 Cuevas de Castilla Con Class from Sitios de Bodega is a steal at $9 a bottle.

Muscadet is a famous name from the Loire Valley of France. It is the world's greatest wine with oysters, and goes with many other seafood and light-bodied dishes. What many people don't realize is that a Muscadet from a good producer can age and evolve for up to 20 years. The 2007 Pierre de la Grange from Luneau-Papin is a great value at $12 a bottle.

 INSIDE INFO

Wines Have Temperatures, Too

The best temperature for serving a wine varies according to its individual characteristics. Here is a rough guideline.

○ **Sparkling wines and Champagnes**: 40 to 45° F

○ **White wines:** 45 to 50° F

○ **Rosé and light reds:** 50 to 55° F

○ **Medium-bodied reds:** 55 to 60° F

○ **Full-bodied reds:** 60 to 65° F

Finally, for a different sort of wine, gruner velt-liner from Austria offers peppery citrus flavors and has become surprisingly popular in recent years. The 2007 Niederosterreich Veltliner #1 from Hirsch is $15 a bottle. Total for everyday whites: $144.

For the reds, a good raspy, fruity barbera is a necessity for pizza and pasta. The 2006 Barbera d'Asti from Michele Chiarlo is $10 a bottle. For times when you need a richer, juicier wine, it would be hard to find a better $9 bottle than the 2007 Les Hérétiques, made by Chateau d'Oupia in the Languedoc. And, because I love gamay, not only in its classic Beaujolais guise but in its earthy Loire variant, I would spend $16 a bottle for the 2007 Touraine gamay from Clos Roche Blanche, peren-nially one of the world's best wine values. That's a total of $140 for our everyday reds.

That leaves us about $300 each for our two cases of fancier wines. It's not enough cap room for Burgundy and Bordeaux. In fact, it doesn't offer much flexibility at all, but we can be creative. For instance, one of the great white wines of the world is the white Rioja of López de Heredia, the arch-traditionalist Spanish producer, which ages wines for years in its cellars before releasing them. Its 1998 Viña Gravonia is $28 a bottle. Six bottles of that and six bottles of a dry 2006 Vouvray, Le Haut Lieu, from the greatest Vouvray producer, Huet, ($32 each), comes to about $360.

For the reds, we reach to the Loire for Bernard Baudry's superb 2006 Chinon Clos Guillot, made from the cabernet franc grape, which could age potentially another 5 to 10 years. It costs $30 a bottle. And finally, back to López de Heredia for its 2000 Viña Bosconia Reserva, a lovely wine, for $34 a bottle. Six of each puts us at $384.

All right, so we've gone slightly over our bud-get, spending $1,138. Believe me, it's good prac-tice for the future. No wine-lover at any level has ever stuck to a budget. —Eric Asimov

How to Savor a Good Wine
Mind the texture as well as the aroma and flavor

When evaluating a wine, efforts generally focus on aromas and flavors. But another important feature is not detectable by eyes, nose or taste buds. That is texture, the tactile sense of wine on the mouth, tongue and throat.

The idea of texture in a liquid is difficult to describe. You won't find the word "texture" in the encyclopedic *Oxford Companion to Wine*, for example. Instead, you'll find the unwieldy term "mouthfeel" and its constituents: body, density, weight and, for the truly geeky, viscosity.

Whatever you call it, great texture demands that you take another sip because it feels so good. One way to think of texture is to keep in mind its components—acidity and, especially in red wines, tannins. Most wine drinkers are familiar with tannins. They are the astringent compounds that in a young, tannic red wine—a Barolo, say, or a Bordeaux—can seem to suck all the moisture out of your mouth. Ideally, the tannins soften over time.

Acidity is the juicy, zingy quality. Too much acidity, and a wine can feel harsh and aggres-sive. Too little, and it feels flabby and shapeless. When you taste a wine, treat it gently. "On first sip, I just let it sit there," says Joshua Wesson, chairman of Best Cellars, "then I push it around with my tongue slowly ...and get a much better sense of texture." —Eric Asimov

A Worldwide Wine Sampler
Global reports from our expert tasters

Eric Asimov, wine critic for the *New York Times,* and Frank J. Prial, a former critic at the paper, have long scoured the world for the best bottles—often with the help of tasting panels consisting of other wine and food reporters at the *Times,* as

FOOD

well as outside experts. What follows are some of their wine selections and comments—on vintages ranging from the elegant and serious to the casual and affordable.

FRANCE

BORDEAUX

Premier wines at every price point

Bordeaux is a magic name. It's a city, a region and a source of fine wines. It's also a powerful, unassailable brand. The millionaire chateau owner in Margaux and the debt-ridden little winemaker from some distant corner of the appellation can both proudly say, "My wine is a Bordeaux."

But consistently great Bordeaux wines are a relatively recent phenomenon. There have been many memorable vintages, but until recently, excellence was not routine. The 1929 vintage was superb, but most of the wines of the 1930s were dreadful. Except for 1945, so were most of the vintages in the 1940s. Old-timers still shudder at the mention of 1951, 1954 and 1956. The 1961 vintage was a triumph, but 1963, 1965 and 1968 were barely drinkable.

Deceived by their self-image, Bordeaux winemakers were slow to profit from research and new techniques that had revolutionized winemaking elsewhere. But adapt they did, and by the 1970s their wines began to excel. The 1980s and 1990s were truly golden years in Bordeaux wine country, and the great 2000 vintage was, many Bordelais were convinced, a harbinger of lots of good vintages.

A succession of good vintages makes specific vintages less important. Starting with 1990, and except for 1991 and 1992, Bordeaux has had an amazing streak of good years, with 1990, 2000 and 2005 ranking among the best ever. Cabernet sauvignon may be the most important grape in Bordeaux, but Americans have often been partial to the softer, fruitier, merlot-based wines of St.-Émilion and Pomerol. These days, though, it's

✅ **TIMELY TIPS**

Wine by the Numbers

There are effectively two mega-validators for wines these days. Both use a 100-point scale to rate wines, both report on thousands of wines each year and both have extraordinary influence on what people drink.

✔ **The Wine Spectator,** a magazine and Web site (www.winespectator.com).

✔ **The Wine Advocate,** Robert M. Parker Jr.'s newsletter (www.eRobertParker.com). Also available on the site is the indispensable *The Wine Advocate*'s **Vintage Chart,** ranking hundreds of wines.

...And Wine by the Book

Frank J. Prial, the former *New York Times* wine writer, recommends three classic books with staying power:

✔ Hugh Johnson and Jancis Robinson's *World Atlas of Wine*

✔ Kevin Zraly's *Windows on the World Complete Wine Course*

✔ Matt Kramer's *Making Sense of Wine*

hard to go wrong with wines from anywhere in Bordeaux in almost any price range.

BURGUNDY (WHITE)

Renowned for its reds, this region also produces several of the world's finest white wines

From the inexpensive but appealing wines of Mâcon and Pouilly, produced in the southernmost part of the Burgundy appellation, or region, to the elegant, flinty whites of Chablis in the far north, Burgundy produces a wealth of distinctive white wines, all but a few made from the chardonnay grape.

Once considered the best-known white wine, Chablis is out of fashion. But its wines, especially its grands crus (the top Burgundy classification), like Vaudésir, Les Clos, Grenouilles and Valmur, can hold their own with most of the finest whites from the Côte d'Or region, the heart of Burgundy, 50 miles to the south. These grands crus sell in the $100 range, but lesser Chablis can be found at prices beginning around $20.

The lower part of the Côte d'Or is the Côte de Beaune, the traditional home of Burgundy's white wines. From Aloxe-Corton, just outside the city of Beaune, comes the grand cru Corton-Charlemagne, which, its fans contend, rivals Montrachet. Perhaps, but because so much is made, 25,000 cases in some years, quality can vary. A fine Corton-Charlemagne will cost as much as $250 a bottle, while a Le Montrachet, when one can be found, can cost $500 a bottle or more.

Meursault is probably the best known of the white wine villages in Burgundy's Côte d'Or. It has no grands crus, but its top wines, Les Perrières, Genevrières and Les Charmes, are exceptionally fine. Simple Meursaults are often good bargains at around $30, but they rarely show the depth and finesse of the top wines. A Meursault Genevrières from a year like 2005 will sell for $70 to $90.

BEAUJOLAIS
Finding the good stuff gets harder

Over the last 25 years or so the identity of Beaujolais has become muddied, with any number of mediocre, pallid wines giving themselves the name. Once it was clearly an inexpensive, exuberant wine, served by the barrelful in French bistros. Then came the Beaujolais nouveau explosion a few decades back, which turned a quaint local custom of celebrating the new vintage into a worldwide

marketing phenomenon. But soon enough the world got over the hype and yawned at yet another proclamation that the Beaujolais "est arrivé."

Nevertheless, there are still terrific Beaujolais wines to be had. Although Beaujolais can sometimes age well it is best enjoyed fairly young. It will never be profound the way Burgundy, Barolo or Bordeaux can be, and notwithstanding young Morgons, which can be tough on tender mouths, Beaujolais tends more toward elegance than power.

Just consider, for example, the purity of those whispering Lapierre Morgons, surprisingly light-bodied and elegant, or the density and balance of a Fleurie from Clos de la Roilette. To taste the fresh yet complex Moulin-à-Vent and Fleurie

FOOD

ℹ **INSIDE INFO**

Ranking Elite French Wines

○ Few hierarchies of wine producers have had so long and influential a run as classification of the wines of the Médoc (the peninsula north of the city of Bordeaux), where most of the famous wine estates, like Latour and Lafite-Rothschild, are located.

○ Wine properties are divided into five classes, called growths. For 150 years, this ranking has largely determined how much money the châteaux that are in the classes can charge for their wines. Since then, the rankings have barely changed at all.

○ The five chateaux in the *premier cru*, or first growth, are:
  • Château Lafite-Rothschild, Pauillac
  • Château Latour, Pauillac
  • Château Margaux, Margaux
  • Château Haut-Brion, Pessac, Graves
  • Château Mouton-Rothschild, Pauillac (since 1973)
  (The names Pauillac, Margaux, Pessac and Graves refer to the particular area of the Médoc where the châteaux are located.)

of Domaine du Vissoux, the pretty, floral Côte de Brouilly of Jean-Paul Brun or the powerful, structured Morgons of Louis-Claude Desvignes is to realize that there is a world of Beaujolais beyond the fatiguingly sappy, candied wines that by comparison taste like tutti-frutti gamay juice.

RHÔNE WINES
Syrah and Grenache from as little as $8

The Rhone's main grapes are, for red wines, syrah in the north and grenache in the south. Little white wine is made in the northern Rhone, but what there is comes mostly from viognier, marsanne and roussanne grapes. In the south, the main white wine grapes are viognier and muscat.

The Rhone's best-known, or at least the most popular, wine is Côtes-du-Rhône, a simple, inexpensive cousin to the greatest wines of the region. Decent Côtes-du-Rhône can sell for $8, Côtes-du-Rhône Villages for a few dollars more. One of the best, the Coudoulet de Beaucastel, may go as high as $25.

The best wine of the northern Rhone is Hermitage, a deep, powerful, long-lived red wine made entirely from syrah. Quantities are always small, and a Hermitage from a producer like Jaboulet can cost up to $200 a bottle.

Côte-Rôtie, also made from syrah, often with a touch of viognier, is a profound, elegant red wine that, coming from a producer like Guigal, can cost $80 to $100 a bottle.

In the south, the most important wine by far is Châteauneuf-du-Pape (the pope's new castle). There are red and white Châteauneuf-du-Papes. One of the best red Châteauneufs comes from the Château de Beaucastel and will cost around $100.

THE LOIRE
Where chenin blanc and sauvignon dominate

There are five distinct wine regions, and more than 40 *appellations contrôlées* (legally defined wine-growing regions) along the Loire river, producing 25 million cases of wine a year, two-thirds of it white.

Beginning at the Atlantic, the first is the *Pays* (region) Nantais, best known for Muscadet, the quintessential wine for fish. A tasty Muscadet called "La Nobleraie" sells for about $10 a bottle.

Then comes Anjou-Saumur, famous for its rosé and a variety of white wines made from chenin blanc. Good Savennières sells for upward of $25.

The Touraine region includes the town of Vouvray, another chenin blanc community. If Savennières is said to be the best of the chenin blanc wines, then Vouvray is a close second. A pleasant Vouvray can be bought for around $12.

Then comes the Central Region, dominated by Sancerre and Pouilly-Fumé, quality sauvignon blanc wines. Sharp, pungent Sancerre is immensely popular but is in danger of pricing itself out of the market, something its neighbor Pouilly-Fumé seems already to have accomplished. Good Sancerres will sell for up to $35 a bottle. A neighbor, the less assertive Quincy, is an attractive substitute at around $12.

Finally there is the Massif Central region, where the best wines, Côte Roannaise and the Côtes du Forez, are both made from gamay grapes.

ALSACE
A taste of France and Germany

Tucked away in the northeast corner of France, Alsace is a fascinating amalgam of the German and the French. The principal grapes are gewürztraminer riesling, pinot gris and muscat.

Alsace is similar to California in that wines are named after the grape type predominantly used in vinification, rather than the locale where the grapes were harvested, as is the usual French practice. The best bottles carry the words "Alsace Grand Cru" and the name of the particular vineyard on the label, as well as the grape type.

Some of the most famous grape-growing areas in Alsace are called "clos." They are special vineyards, usually enclosed by a wall (a clos) and owned by one or two proprietors.

If an Alsatian wine is also labeled "VT," it was made from late harvested *(vendange tardive)* grapes, which can be sweet. The designation "SGN," for *sélection de grains nobles,* means the wine was made from individually chosen, supersweet grapes harvested by successive passes through the vineyard. The wines require considerable effort to make, and sell for high prices.

Gewürztraminer, with its pungent, spicy flavors, is the best introduction to Alsace. Producers like Zind-Humbrecht can make sublime gewürztraminers—rich, complex and endlessly nuanced—but for a newcomer, the lighter, uncomplicated wines of Trimbach and Hugel are the way to go. Both houses put out simple gewürztraminers that start at around $15.

A gewürztraminer Wintzenheim, from Zind-Humbrecht, will cost around $35. A pinot gris vendange tardive from Trimbach sells for about $65. For a memorable Alsatian riesling, Trimbach's famous Cuvée Frédéric Émile sells for about $35.

ITALY

THE PIEDMONT
From the majestic to the easygoing

The Piedmont is a 230,000-acre wine region in Italy's northwest that stands between the Alps and the Mediterranean Sea. Up to 50 million cases of wine are produced annually in Piedmont from, among others, barbera, dolcetto, muscat and nebbiolo—which is the noblest of all the region's

FOOD

The Best Organic Wines
The vin naturel movement is rapidly growing.

While no official definition of "natural" wine exists, the term mostly addresses wine with no added ingredients such as yeasts, enzymes, tannins, acid, sugar, bacteria, gum arabic or oak chips. So what's inside the bottle? Grape. And perhaps a splash of the preservative sulfur dioxide. Hard core naturalists even leave out the SO2. Soft or hard, the vin naturel movement is rapidly growing thanks to passionate drinkers and winemakers who believe wines can only truly be expressive with no flavor-, aroma- or texture-changing adjunct. The results are mostly delicious, if sometimes a little erratic, but the bottom line is adventure.

The highest concentration of these radical winemakers is in France but their numbers are spreading in Spain, Italy and even in America. Unfortunately there's no labeling to indicate a natural process. Looking for organic or biodynamic wine (not grapes, but wine) is a step in the right direction. Morethanorganic.com has some good information.

Some of the producers and labels to seek out.

- Silver Thread *(Finger Lakes)*
- Coturri Winery *(California)*
- Sky Vineyards *(California)*
- Claude Courtois *(Loire, France)*
- Coulée de Serrant *(Loire, France)*
- Theirry Puzelat *(Loire, France)*
- Cascina Degli Ulivi *(Gavi, Italy)*
- Nikolaihoff *(Wachau, Austria)*
- Chandon Des Brialles *(Burgundy, France)*
- Château Le Puy *(Bordeaux, France)*
- Domaine Frick *(Alsace, France)*
- Emmanuel Houillon *(Jura, France)*
- Eric Texier *(Rhone, France)*
- Bodegas López de Heredia *(Rioja, Spain)*
- Château Musar *(Bekka Valley, Lebanon)*

—Alice Feiring, a freelance wine critic
(www.alicefeiring.com) and author of
*The Battle for Wine and Love or How I
Saved the World From Parkerization.*

grapes and the grape of Piedmont's greatest wines, Barolo, Barbaresco and Gattinara.

Barolo is one of the great wines of the world. Choosing a favorite can be hard work. An attractive Barolo from Michele Chiarlo might sell for around $40; a great one from Bruno Giacosa might cost $150 or more.

Most of the local barbera is sold as simple Barbera di Piemonte; the rest, better quality wine, is sold as Barbera d'Alba and Barbera d'Asti. A Barbera d'Asti might sell for $17; Giacosa's 2005 is around $30.

The Piedmont's most popular wine happens to be none of the above. It's Asti, formerly Asti Spumante, Italy's foremost sparkling wine, made entirely from the Moscato di Canelli grape.

TUSCANY
Chianti country is well known for its reds

Tuscany is home to Chianti, the country's best-known wine. In some years Tuscany produces more than 60 million cases, of which some 8 million are Chianti. Sangiovese, which is ubiquitous in Tuscany, is Chianti's principal grape. It is also the main grape in Vino Nobile di Montepulciano, Carmignano and the legendary Brunello di Montalcino, a powerful, tannic red made entirely from the Brunello grape. The wine must be aged 4 years to be bottled as Brunello. With less aging it is known as Rosso di Montalcino. An Altesino Brunello, one of the best, sells for around $100.

Tuscan whites are largely indifferent. Most are made from the lackluster trebbiano grape, used in cheap table wine and as part of the traditional Chianti blend.

SPAIN
RIOJA AND PRIORAT
Ripe for rediscovery

Rioja, the best-known Spanish region, is ripe for rediscovery. A simple bottle of Conde de Valde-

Picking a Fine Rosé
Well-chilled rosé is a perfect summer wine

Rosés range in color from pale salmon to shades that border on red. There are generally two ways to make them. The first is to make a pink wine from red grapes. The depth of shade depends on the strength of pigmentation in the grapes and how long the juice is kept in contact with the skins. A less elegant method is to blend a small amount of finished red wine with a finished white.

Classic rosés come from the South of France, particularly Provence, where dry wines provide relief from the extreme heat of summer. French rosés include cabernet d'Anjou from the western Loire Valley, Tavel and Gigondas from the southern Rhone, and pink wines from Bordeaux. Spain, Italy, Australia, Germany and South Africa can also produce marvelous rosés. An outstanding American example is the iconic Vin Gris de Cigare from Randall Grahm of Bonny Doon Winery in California.

Most rosés aren't built to last and are best drunk within a year of their release. Wine shops generally take delivery on rosés in the mid- to late spring, so that is when you should stock up. If you want to splurge, there is nothing better than a delicious rosy Champagne from Nicholas Feuillatte with sweet-tart notes of cranberry.

Spain has delicious rosés, or rosados, as they are called there. Artazuri Navarra, pale red, dry and refreshing, has light berry aromas and a slight effervescence that leave you wanting more. From Napa, try a Saintsbury Vin Gris of Pinot Noir, a clear red with generous aromas of fruit and flowers, a wine of body and substance. Or try a Domaine de Nizas Languedoc from France; a dark salmon color, dry, with balanced, persistent fruit and mineral flavors, it is lively and energizing.

—Eric Asimov

mar from Bodegas Valdemar, compared alongside a bottle like the Grandes Añadas from Bodegas Artadi will show you why Riojas are among the best red wine values in the world, offering juicy, balanced pleasures.

White Riojas come in two styles: one crisp and modern, made to be consumed young, and a more traditional version, rich and oaky, with flavors of vanilla, coconut, almond and hazelnut shining through. They are great values. Excellent examples can easily be found for less than $15; even a well-aged version, like a 1981 Gran Reserva, is only $80; not much, considering the cost of other age-worthy whites of similar vintage.

One of the best tales of late-20th-century winemaking is the rebirth of the Priorat region in northeastern Spain. The area makes intense, concentrated, expensive wines that appeal to globalized tastes without sacrificing their distinctive character. In the Ribera del Duero, Peter Sissek at the Dominio de Pingus has produced intense red wines that go for $400 a bottle and more. At the other end of the price scale, Marques de Caceres Rioja is under $10; Torres Gran Coronas Reserva is under $20.

ARGENTINA AND CHILE
MERLOTS AND MALBECS
Have the Argentinians finally arrived?

Every decade, it seems, Argentina's and Chile's wine industry announces that it has arrived. Maybe this time, it has. After sampling 28 red wines, almost all made from Bordeaux grapes, a *Times* tasting panel was surprised and pleased by the quality of the wines. The wines included cabernet sauvignons, merlots, malbecs, blends and even one pinot noir. The panel's favorite was a 1999 Montes Alpha "M" from La Finca Estate in Chile; a 2000 Navarro Correas, a cabernet sauvignon from Argentina also was admired.

In a separate examination of malbecs under $25, a *Times* tasting panel was pleased by the quality of the winemaking it found—and the price. Four of the top five wines were $12 or less. The favorite, a 2004 Zagal from Hacienda del Plata ($12) was dense and fruity yet well balanced and structured. And the second place, a 2005 Trapiche Broquel ($12), offered winning aromas of violets, lavender, licorice and berries.

AUSTRALIA
SHIRAZ-CABERNET
Young wines from $5 to $500

Until the 1970s, Australia was dismissed as a major source of serious wine. But things changed, and today Australia is the world's fourth largest wine exporter.

Grange, first released in 1952, is probably Australia's greatest wine, but very little is made and it's very expensive. Today Grange is made from various grape varieties, including cabernet sauvignon, from different wine regions. The blend is secret, but shiraz is still a major player.

Yellowtail, a simple, modest wine that's even younger than Grange, was first imported to America in 2001 when a New York importer reluctantly agreed to bring in 112,000 cases. By 2005, Yellowtail's sales in the States were 7.5 million cases—and it remains strong. Grange, when you can find it, costs $500 a bottle or more. Yellowtail is about $5.

In the 1970s, the production of quality wines increased, and today, along with Grange, Australian winemakers produce a panoply of world class cabernets, merlots and blends. Chardonnays rival anything made in California, while cabernet sauvignons from Coonawarra and Margaret River can be ravishing. Penfolds Bin 128 Shiraz, Fireblock Old Vines Grenache and D'Arenberg's Galvo Garage Red, all around $25, are a few worth seeking out.

GRÜNER VELTLINERS AND RIESLINGS

An adventure for the jaded palette

On those rare occasions when people give any thought to Austrian wines, they most likely think of grüner veltliner. And why not? Austria is the only place on earth that produces these peppery, lively wines. As they have become more popular, grüner veltliner has solidified its place as the semi-pronounceable headliner of Austrian wines.

Total exports of quality Austrian wines amount to fewer than a few million cases per year, less than some of California's larger wineries. Yet the wines are often well made and a pleasure to drink. Austrian rieslings are almost always bone dry and are characterized by power and richness. They have great texture, presence and weight, yet are rarely heavy, with wonderful mineral aromas and gentle flavors of peaches and apricots. They resemble rieslings from Alsace, but while the best Alsatian rieslings tend toward austerity, the Austrians are more generous, without losing focus.

CALIFORNIA

Quantity and quality in America's premier wine-producing region

At the beginning of 2008, there were an astonishing 2,687 bonded wineries in California, producing 650 million gallons a year. Some California wineries are huge. The E. & J. Gallo winery, for example, the largest in the world, produces 75 million cases a year, or one in every four bottles sold in America.

The 25 largest California wineries produce 90 percent of the state's wine, but half the wineries produce fewer than 5,000 cases each annually.

Some small wineries produce extraordinary wines in sufficient quantities for distribution throughout the country. Most make 20,000 cases and up. They frequently offer two or three price ranges, with a top of $100 to $200 a bottle. Stag's Leap Wine Cellars SLV lists in New York for around $130. Its Hawk Crest cabernet sells for about $12.95.

Cabernet sauvignon is California's most prestigious grape, but chardonnay, spurred by America's preference for white wine, is the most popular. It accounts for 25 to 30 percent of the state's table-wine volume. Merlot shot to prominence in the 1990s because it was thought to have the elegance but not the harsher tannins of cabernet sauvignon. Syrah, the signature grape of France's Rhone Valley, has grown steadily in stature in California's vineyards. But the biggest star recently has been Burgundy's fickle grape, the pinot noir. Pinot noir was extolled in the movie *Sideways* and supermarket sales throughout the United States jumped.

WASHINGTON

Home to some of the finest cabernet sauvignons in the U.S.

Fine wine has become a $3 billion industry in Washington, the second largest wine-producing state, after California.

For almost a decade, eastern Washington has produced some of the finest cabernet sauvignons in the country. Top Washington cabernets like L'Ecole No. 41, Leonetti Cellars and Quilceda Creek are hard to find. Since production is relatively small and demand high, much of the best wine is sold at the wineries or through the mail. However, L'Ecole No. 41's top-of-the-line, cabernet-based Apogee, about $45 at the winery, may appear in some shops. Woodward Canyon's 2004 Artists Series cabernet is a bargain at about

$30. Sageland Vineyards 2005 cabernet is a good value at about $12.

If California chardonnays are rich and powerful, Washington's are crisp and delicate. Here are a few good examples, with early 2008 prices: Woodward Canyon's 2005 Washington appellation at $36 is highly recommended. Then there are Andrew Will's Cuvee Lucia 2005 and Dusted Valley Vintners 2004 Old Vine Yakima Valley, both at around $22. On the chardonnay bargain shelf are a Chateau Ste. Michelle 2006 at about $10 and Hogue Cellars, Columbia Crest and Covey Run for about $8 each.

OREGON

The courage to bottle some of its moderately priced wines under screw caps

Oregon has become one of the country's top three wine states, with 350 wineries producing an average of 5,000 cases each a year. Most of it is pinot noir, but there's also pinot gris, chardonnay and modest amounts of riesling and merlot. In fact, 70 varieties of wine grapes are grown and vinified in Oregon.

Oregon wines are not promoted as heavily as California wines, but they are not hard to come by. A distinctive Oregon pinot noir comes from Yamhill Valley Vineyards, one of the better Willamette wineries. Like most Oregon wineries, Yamhill Valley has a regular line and a reserve wine. Other popular Oregon pinots include Domaine Drouhin, Argyle, Ponzi Vineyards, Rex Hill, Erath and Adelsheim.

Many of these wines are in the $25 to $45 a bottle range. Beaux Frères, which is partly owned by the well-known wine critic Robert Parker, concentrates on elegant, higher priced wines (up to $90). Benton Lane is one of the few wineries, in Oregon or anywhere, that has the courage to bottle some of its moderately priced wines (around $20) under screw caps.

—Howard G. Goldberg and Alice Gabriel
contributed to these reports

Prosecco: A Cheery—and Cheaper—Fizz

Millions of Italians can't be wrong

It's hard to think of another wine with the lightness and easygoing grace of a prosecco—maybe a rosé. Aside from enlivening garden parties, proseccos, like rosés, make excellent aperitifs. One glass, two at most, and you are ready to move on. Unless, of course, you are making Bellinis, the cocktails of sparkling wine and peach purée, for which prosecco is the ideal ingredient.

Prosecco is made in almost every Italian wine region, and among all the Italian sparkling wines it is rising rapidly in popularity, trailing in the United States only that old standby, Asti spumante.

A *Times* tasting panel sampled 25 wines, all of which were made predominantly of prosecco, the grape, sometimes mixed with a small percentage of pinot bianco, pinot grigio or chardonnay. Some, but not all, of these proseccos were Prosecco di Conegliano-Valdobbiadene, the *denominazione di origine controllata*, or D.O.C., a designation earned if wines meet certain standards, such as which grapes are used, where they are grown and how the wines are aged.

For example, Zardetto, one of the leading prosecco producers, made two wines that cracked the panel's top 10 list. The Zeta was a prosecco D.O.C. made from grapes grown in a single vineyard. It was also the most expensive bottle, at $22. But Zardetto also makes a non-D.O.C. prosecco, which the panel liked practically as much. It sells for $10 a bottle, and was the best value. Other favorites included Drusian D.O.C. Brut NV ($17) and Nino Franco Rustico D.O.C. NV ($15).   —Eric Asimov

CHAMPAGNES OF BIBLICAL PROPORTIONS

Many of the largest bottles are named after legendary Biblical kings. Sizes are in liters.

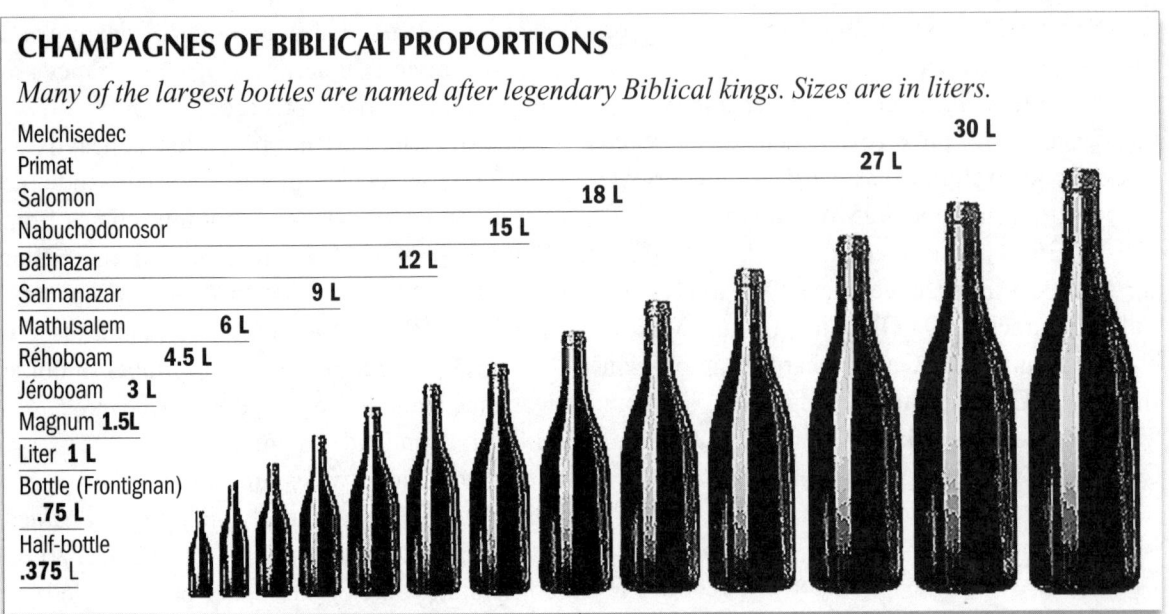

Melchisedec	30 L
Primat	27 L
Salomon	18 L
Nabuchodonosor	15 L
Balthazar	12 L
Salmanazar	9 L
Mathusalem	6 L
Réhoboam	4.5 L
Jéroboam	3 L
Magnum	1.5L
Liter	1 L
Bottle (Frontignan)	.75 L
Half-bottle	.375 L

Champagne on the Cheap

Some sage advice on buying your bubbly for $30 and under

Genuine Champagne must be made in the strictly delimited Champagne region of France in a complicated succession of steps known collectively as the *méthode champenoise.*

Producers tend to baby their more expensive vintage Champagnes. Grapes from the best plots—those designated premier cru and grand cru—are generally reserved for the better and more expensive Champagnes.

Basic Champagnes typically receive far less consideration. None of the best wine goes into the blend that will result in the final nonvintage product, which can differ from year to year depending on which wines are available.

Of course, some Champagne houses, like Bollinger, Louis Roederer and Billecart-Salmon, are among those who still make superb nonvintage Champagnes, and smaller houses like Gosset, Alfred Gratien and Bruno Paillard also make excel-

lent nonvintage Champagnes. But you are not likely to find any of these bottles for less than $30, certainly not anymore.

Included on the list of champagnes below are a couple of blanc de blancs, which are wines made entirely of chardonnay, rather than of the usual Champagne blend of chardonnay, pinot noir and pinot meunier. These blanc de blancs are not necessarily lighter than conventional Champagnes and often have a creamy texture, surprising complexity and precise mineral flavors. Each bottle typically sells for $30 or less.

Lanson Black Label Brut. *Dry and refreshing, with snappy acidity, mineral and citrus flavors.*

Louis de Sacy Brut Grand Cru. *Toasty and full bodied, with a creamy texture and lasting flavors.*

Paul Goerg Blanc de Blancs. *Yeasty, toasty aromas, with complex floral and fruit flavors.*

Pierre Gimmonet & Fils Brut Blanc de Blancs. *Unusually complex and persistent flavors of apples, minerals and anise.*

Nicolas Feuillatte Brut NV. *Bright, substantial, with citrus and floral flavors; not quite bone dry.*

—Eric Asimov

Beyond the Basic Six-Pack
Our picks of the best beers and ales

As anyone who has peered into the fridge of a liquor store, supermarket or convenience store lately knows, there are plenty of choices besides Budweiser. For those ready to venture beyond the familiar, here are some picks, along with expert observations, from the *New York Times* tasting panels.

PILSNER
The prince of summer is not small beer

Pilsners are a subset of lagers, one of the two main types of beer. Ale, the other main type, is the older style, dating back to ancient Mesopotamia. Lager beers were developed around the 15th century when, before refrigeration, beer could only be brewed in cold weather. To have beer for summer drinking, Bavarian brewers began storing it in frigid alpine caves. Pilsner, a golden lager, is named after the town of Pilsen in Czech Bohemia. It is now the most popular style of beer in the world.

OUR PICKS: Victory Prima Pils, Downingtown, Pa.; Stoudt Pils, Adamstown, Pa.; Dortmunder Gold, Great Lakes Brewing Company, Cleveland, Ohio; Würzburger Hofbräu, Radeberger Pilsner, Germany.

PALE ALES
When they're good, they're complex and stimulating

Pale ale is more complex than a lager. You can discover a host of aromas and flavors in every paradoxically dry, bitter, brisk and refreshing sip. In the 1970's and 1980's, American brewers started using American hops in their pale ales instead of English hops. Far from the restrained aromas and flavors of English hops, American hops are a regular brass band, giving American pale ales their signature raucous aromas of grapefruit, flowers and pine.

OUR PICKS: Petrus Aged Pale, Bavik, Belgium; La Roja Amber Ale, Jolly Pumpkin, Dale's, Oskar Blues Brewery, Lyons, Colo.; Otter Creek, Middlebury, Vt.; Flying Dog Classic, Denver, Colo.; Southampton Publick House, Southampton, N.Y.

INDIA PALE ALE
A refreshing soldier's brew

This style of beer was developed in Britain in the 18th century, as a way to provide the empire's colonial troops in steamy India with rations of their beloved brew. A brewer named George Hodgson realized that a higher alcohol content would inhibit spoilage, and that bacterial action could be slowed by adding extra doses of hops, which impart bitterness, liveliness and aromatic complexity. The strong ale that resulted had a distinctive backbone of aggressive bitterness that could withstand the journey and still refresh the troops.

✔ **TIMELY TIPS**

The Dos and Don'ts of Drinking

✔ Drinking on an empty stomach gets you intoxicated faster. As soon as alcohol is consumed, the body starts to break it down, but some gets absorbed directly into the bloodstream.

✔ Having food in the stomach—particularly proteins, fats and dense carbohydrates—slows the absorption process.

✔ Carbonated mixers, soda and warm drinks speed up absorption.

—Anahad O'Connor

FOOD

TIMELY TIPS

How to Cure a Hangover

✔ Doctors recommend drinking orange juice or sports drinks that replenish electrolytes, and taking pain relievers like aspirin or ibuprofen.

✔ Tylenol is inadvisable because, like alcohol, it is metabolized by the already-overworked liver. No one advises more alcohol, the "hair of the dog that bit you."

✔ Many experts agree that the best cure for a hangover is to avoid drinking too much in the first place. Dr. Marc K. Siegel, an internist at New York University Medical School, says the best bet is a cup of coffee, a dash of Mylanta and a lot of water. "It's not sexy," Siegel says. "But those things work."

—Alex Williams and Jonathan Glater

OUR PICKS: Smutty Nose Big A, Porstmouth, N.H.; Stone, San Diego, Calif.; Dogfish Head 90 Minute Imperial, Milton, Del.; Weyerbacher Double Simcoe, Easton, Pa.; Lagunitas Maximus, Petaluma, Calif.; Harpoon, Boston, Mass.

STOUT

Robust, complex brews are a meal in themselves

What makes an ale a stout? Primarily it's the dark, almost black color achieved by brewing with barley that has been roasted to the point of charring. This gives stout its characteristic chocolate-coffee flavor as well as a fuller body than other dark beers. Hops lend stout a floral aroma and a little bitterness.

OUR PICKS: Pozharnik Espresso Russian Imperial Stout, Pennichuck, N.H.; Samuel Smith's Imperial Stout, England; Samuel Smith Oatmeal Stout, England; Rogue Shakespeare Stout, Ore.; Brooklyn Brewery Black Chocolate, N.Y.; Young's Oatmeal Stout, England; Rogue Chocolate Stout, Ore.

TRAPPIST ALES

Heavenly brews with lots of character

The term "Trappist" describes the source of the ales rather than a brewing style. In fact, the beers vary considerably, but they are always strong, ranging in alcohol from about 7 percent to 12 percent. Only six breweries in the world, all affiliated with Trappist monasteries in Belgium, are permitted to use the hexagonal seal designating each bottle an "Authentic Trappist Product," which guarantees that the beer is brewed in an abbey under the supervision of the religious order, and that most of the income will be used for charitable work.

Dozens of Belgian breweries make excellent versions of Trappist ales. Some of them are even commissioned by monasteries to brew ales or are licensed to use a monastery name. These are known as abbey beers. North American craft brewers, likewise inspired by these beers, have made their own distinctive versions.

OUR PICKS: Abbaye de Saint Bon-Chien (2006 vintage), Brasserie des Franches-Montagnes, Switzerland (caution: a 25.4-ounce bottle costs $35); Westmalle Abbey Triple, Belgium; Unibroue La Fin du Monde, Chambly, Quebec; Affligem Abbey Triple, Belgium; Weyerbacher Quad, Easton, Pa.; Achel Trappist Extra, Belgium.

—Eric Asimov and the Tasting Panel

Stocking the Liquor Cabinet
Our picks for some good basic bottles

Need help choosing bottles for the bar? Here are some recommendations from the tasting panels at the *New York Times*.

VODKA. Most spirits can be made only from certain prescribed ingredients, but vodka can be distilled from just about anything that can be fermented into alcohol: grains, vegetables, even fruits. What sets vodkas apart from one another are essentially the base ingredients used in the distillation and the water. Recommendations:

- Smirnoff (United States) Grain. Pure, clean and ultrasmooth, with pleasing texture and classic vodka aroma.

- Wyborowa (Poland) Single Estate Rye. Elegant and intriguing, with mild flavors and great persistence.

- Belvedere (Poland) Rye. Great smoothness and purity, with good texture and body.

GIN. High-end gins start off as vodka and then are infused with any number of botanicals, mostly juniper berries, but also coriander, anise, lemon and grapefruit zest, cinnamon and many others. While the classic flavor of gin is dominated by juniper, these high-end gins each have their own flavor signatures. Recommendations:

- Boodles and Beefeater make excellent gins, classic yet completely different from each other.

- Bombay Sapphire London Dry, 94 Proof. Elegant; lemon, lavender, coriander and juniper blend deliciously.

BOURBON. Deluxe bourbons, with their complex perfumes and amalgams of fruit, sugar and spice flavors, are meant to be drunk slowly. In their rustic quality, they resemble Armagnac, but with the flavor of corn, not grapes. By law, bourbon must be distilled at not more than 80 percent alcohol (160 proof) and must contain at least 51 percent corn.

- Pappy Van Winkle's Family Reserve 20-Year-Old is a sipping whiskey of wonderful complexity. The Vintage 17-Year-Old is fruity and chocolate-and-caramel-flavored.

- W.L. Weller Centennial 10-Year-Old shows lingering, complex flavors of citrus, spice, butterscotch and mint.

- As a mixer, try the brisk, spicy Knob Creek

RUM. Rum can vary greatly, depending on where it is produced and by what method. Like gin and vodka, rum can be made anywhere in the world.

TIMELY TIPS

How to Drink Whiskey

✔ According to Richard Paterson, a master blender, don't make the mistake of serving whiskey on the rocks: ice bruises the flavor. Instead, before drinking, swirl a little whiskey around the glass to clean out lingering odors, then discard. Pour a small amount and dilute with room-temperature water. Even a teardrop will be enough to activate the chemical reaction that releases whiskey's flavors. If in doubt, add water until the vapors don't sting your eyes when you raise the glass to drink.

✔ Then, follow the years-as-seconds rule: a 12-year-old whiskey, for instance, reveals its complexity after 12 seconds in the mouth.

✔ Pairing a cigar with whiskey is a scam. This affectation simply grew from the tradition of serving them at the end of a meal and helped to provide an excuse for a lingering male-bonding session. Instead, try a morsel of dark chocolate chewed as a chaser to each sip.

✔ Some recommendations: The Balvenie Signature Batch 001 12 Years Old; Glen Grant bottled by Gordon & MacPhail 12 Years Old; Tamdhu 10 Years Old.

—Mark Ellwood , Eric Asimov and the Tasting Panel

FOOD

A Proper Mojito

The technique is simple; the results are heavenly

2 sprigs fresh mint
2 oz fresh lime juice
1¹/₂ oz white rum
1 teaspoon superfine sugar
Crushed ice
4 oz club soda

In a mixing glass, muddle the mint leaves with the lime juice in the bottom of a tall cocktail glass. (To muddle, you mash or crush the mint leaves, using the back of a spoon, or a special muddling tool. Muddling releases the oils of the mint into the lime juice.)

Add the rum, sugar, crushed ice and soda. Cover and shake, and uncover, serving with a lime wedge.

YIELD: 1 cocktail.

—Dale DeGroff

Most rums use molasses as their base, but many use sugar cane juice instead, especially rums made in French-speaking areas, which are labeled *rhum agricole*, or agricultural rum. By contrast, molasses-based rums are sometimes referred to as industrial rum, often an unfairly pejorative term. Here are recommendations for white and amber rums:

- 10 Cane Trinidad Light. Neither white nor amber, but pure, smooth and elegant, with luscious sugar-cane flavor and enticing texture.

- Demerara El Dorado. Rich amber color, with aromas of banana and vanilla; pure and subtle.

- St. James Royal Amber. Smooth, rich, floral; lingering flavors, with great personality.

- Cane Louisiana White. Vanilla aroma; smooth, with a thick texture and long, lingering flavors.

- Mount Gay Eclipse. Mellow, pure and smooth, with vanilla and butter aromas.

TEQUILA. Tequila can be called tequila only if it is made in Mexico, from the blue agave plant. The least expensive tequilas need only be distilled from 51 percent blue agave juice. The more expensive, and many say the best, are made from 100 percent blue agave juice, and those words must appear on the label.

After the tequila is produced, it is further classified by how long it has aged. Silver tequila, also called blanco or plata, is bottled immediately after distillation. Reposado is "rested" in wood for at least two months. Añejo tequila is aged in barrels for at least a year. There is also gold tequila, which is unaged but treated with additives to give it an aged effect. Recommendations:

- Chinaco Blanco. Classic agave character and complex mineral and herbal flavors.

- Hacienda del Cristero. Smooth, pure and complex, with a great finish, nutty, peppery and vanilla flavors.

- El Tesoro de Don Felipe Silver. Intense mineral and roasted, spicy flavors and a long finish.

—Eric Asimov and Frank J. Prial with R. W. Apple Jr. and the Tasting Panel on bourbon.

Mixing the Classic Cocktails

From the Bloody Mary to the gimlet

The cocktail's golden age in America lasted from 1870 to 1912, when barmen in white coats were master craftsmen who spent years in apprenticeships and concocted their own bitters, syrups and cordials. Now, a hundred years later, the art of the cocktail is receiving renewed interest. Enterprising bartenders are reaching for off-label brands and adding homemade touches for new old-fashioned drinks. They are resurrecting such forgotten spirits as pisco, Madeira,

Chartreuse herbal liqueur, maraschino liqueur and sloe gin.

In that spirit, here are recipes from some of the finest mixologists in the business:

BLOODY MARY (or the Red Snapper)

Adapted from the St. Regis

The queen of the hangover drinks is the Bloody Mary. But the concoction is notoriously difficult to get right, demanding a balance of strength and flavor, as any cocktail does, plus a degree of spice suited to the drinker, then the real trick, texture.

Dale DeGroff, former head bartender at the Rainbow Room in New York City and an authority on mixology, cautions that too many bartenders overdo the Tabasco and Worcestershire. "They want something that will fry your tonsils, when the beauty of it is the sweetness of the tomato juice," he says. Small ice cubes melt too fast, so large square cubes only, please.

1 oz vodka
2 oz tomato juice
1 dash lemon juice
2 dashes salt
2 dashes black pepper
2 dashes cayenne pepper
3 dashes of Worcestershire sauce

Mix all ingredients but vodka. Pour vodka over ice. Add mix. Stir. Do not garnish.

THE CLASSIC MARTINI

John Conti's version

Theories about the origins of the martini are as varied as those concerning the proportion of gin to vermouth. Most people agree, though, that the standard martini is a gin-based drink with a five-to-one ratio of gin to vermouth. A recipe for a dry martini cocktail from 1907 calls for orange bitters, half a jigger of dry vermouth and half a jigger of dry gin. Although vodka has become a frequent substitute

Not Just Any Old Mint Julep

How to make the orginal Kentucky Derby recipe—complete with silver cup

The classic julep—first served to Kentucky Derby guests in 1875 by Col. Meriwether Lewis Clark Jr., the founder of Churchill Downs—is made with just four ingredients: finely crushed ice, a little sugar water, fresh spearmint and fine, aged, 90-proof straight Kentucky bourbon. And, of course, the essential silver julep cup.

KENTUCKY DERBY MINT JULEPS
1 cup spring or bottled water
1 cup granulated sugar
1/2 cup small spearmint leaves, no stems
Finely crushed or shaved ice, enough to fill the cups completely
High-quality Kentucky bourbon, like Maker's Mark or Woodford Reserve
Sprigs of spearmint

1. The day before serving, or even earlier, put the julep cups in the freezer. Put the water and sugar in a small saucepan, bring to a boil without stirring, and boil for 2 minutes, or until sugar is completely dissolved.

2. Put the mint leaves in a glass jar or cup, pour the slightly cooled syrup over them, let cool, then cover and refrigerate for 12 hours or longer. When ready to use, strain out the mint leaves.

3. Half an hour before serving, pack the julep cups tightly up to the rim with crushed ice and return them to the freezer.

4. For each julep pour 3 ounces of bourbon over the ice, followed by two teaspoons of mint syrup. Do not stir or agitate. Use a cloth to hold each cup by the rim, so as not to disturb the frost. Use a short straw or a chopstick to make a hole in the ice on the side of the cup and insert a sprig of mint. Serve immediately, on a silver tray.
YIELD: Up to 20 juleps.

—Suzanne Hamlin

for gin in martinis, it is a modern invention.

John Conti, a pupil of master bartender Dale DeGroff, concocted a version that uses a regular premium gin, like Boodles or Tanqueray, not one of the super-premiums like Ten or Wet, which he considers too aromatic for the drink. He uses a long-necked spoon, bent slightly so that it follows the sides of the glass. "You slide the spoon down and twirl, as opposed to agitating," he says.

> **3 oz gin**
> **½ oz dry vermouth**
> **Green olive**

Chill a 7-ounce martini glass by filling it with ice and water. Fill a professional bartender's glass, or a tall 16-ounce glass, two-thirds full with ice. Add gin and vermouth to the bartender's glass and stir with a long-necked spoon, keeping the spoon close to the side of the glass as you swirl the ice. Stir until the glass frosts, about 20 seconds. Empty the martini glass and strain the contents of the bartender's glass into it. Garnish with the olive.

THE MANHATTAN

Adapted from Morgan's Bar at Morgan's Hotel

The Manhattan was created in 1874, using rye whiskey, at the Manhattan Club in New York at the behest of Jenny Jerome, a socialite better known in later years as the mother of Winston Churchill. The occasion was an elaborate party celebrating the election of Samuel J. Tilden as governor. Popular tastes have changed the standard Manhattan into a bourbon drink with sweet vermouth, and a cherry or twist of lemon.

> **One or two dashes Angostura bitters**
> **Maraschino cherry or lemon twist**
> **2 ½ oz Maker's Mark bourbon (or a rye whiskey, if you prefer)**
> **1 oz sweet vermouth**

Shake one or two dashes of bitters into a cocktail glass, gently twisting the glass from side to side. Shake out the excess, leaving only the residue. Mix bourbon or rye with sweet vermouth in a mixing glass. Add ice. Shake well. Strain the contents into the cocktail glass. Garnish with cherry or lemon.

THE GIMLET

From Fifty Seven Fifty Seven Bar at the Four Seasons Hotel

The gimlet's logic seems clear: gin or vodka, with Rose's Lime Juice and fresh lime juice in equal parts, shaken or stirred until ice cold and served straight up in a stemmed cocktail glass. The garnish—and a gimlet should have it—is a thin crescent moon of lime, floated in the drink invitingly, not perched on the side like a timid swimmer looking at a cold lake. Making a gimlet icy gives it smoothness when sipped. For that reason, it is an excellent summer drink.

Some prefer vodka, for its understatement. Gin talks too much, with its juniper bush-berry accent. And what you want, as everyone knows, is a drinking companion who listens.

> **4 oz vodka (or gin if you insist)**
> **$^1/_2$ oz fresh lime juice**
> **$^1/_2$ oz Rose's Lime Juice**
> **1 thin lime wedge**

Combine liquid ingredients in a cocktail shaker with ice. Shake, and then strain into a martini glass. Garnish with lime wedge.

THE MARGARITA

Adapted from Dale DeGroff, former head bartender at the Rainbow Room

The margarita is an American staple, whether in its frozen-slush frat-party style or as a straight-up cocktail that can rival a martini for elegance. It first appeared in the days after the repeal of Prohibition when everyone was creating new cocktails. One widely circulated creation myth credits a bartender who some versions say worked outside Los Angeles and others place near Tijuana. He reportedly concocted the drink for a starlet who could only drink tequila, but didn't like its taste. Her name was Marjorie—Margarita in Spanish.

> **Lime slice, 1/2-inch thick, for salting glass**
> **Kosher salt**
> **2 oz silver tequila**
> **1 oz Cointreau**
> **3/4 oz fresh lime juice**

Rub lime slice around outer rim of cocktail glass. Place salt in a dish. Holding glass parallel to dish, coat only the outside with salt. Place glass in refrigerator.

Fill a cocktail shaker with ice and add tequila, Cointreau and lime juice. Shake well. Strain into chilled cocktail glass.

> —Frank Prial and William L. Hamilton, with contributions from R. W. Apple Jr., Michael Brick and Christine Muhlke

How to Make a Perfect Espresso
An insider's tricks for brewing a great cup

A good cup of espresso can be as close as your kitchen counter. Gerald Baldwin, director of Peet's Tea & Coffee in Berkeley, Calif., a premier coffee company, shares some secrets on preparing a perfect cup.

To enjoy espresso at home, you need a machine that uses steam, says Baldwin. That's because stovetop moka pots and some cheaper espresso machines do not generate enough pressure to produce the intense flavor of espresso. Start with fresh cold water—never use water from the hot tap, or water that has already boiled. Bottled or filtered water is recommended when old plumbing imparts an unpleasant flavor, or in areas with heavily chlorinated or hard water.

Home grinding is essential, because finely

What You'll Find in a Tea Box
A sipper's guide to various blends

From a single evergreen plant, *camillia sinensis,* come the thousands of nonherbal teas consumed around the world. The variety depends on where the tea is grown and how it is gathered and processed. Some variables that determine the type of tea are whether the tea is made from long leaves or short leaves, early buds or later pickings; whether the leaves are whole, broken or rolled and, most important, whether they are allowed to oxidize.

Because tea readily picks up foreign aromas and fades in contact with light, teas should be sold and stored in containers that are airtight and opaque. It should never be stored in the refrigerator or freezer.

Black teas. Black teas are dark, tannic teas made by allowing the fresh green leaves to wither and darken through oxidation. The process takes about a day, after which the leaves are dried by warm air. Black teas include winy Keemun and smoky Lapsang Souchong from China, Ceylon teas from Sri Lanka and India, Assam, and Darjeeling, the exquisitely delicate tea grown in the Himalayan foothills. Traditional blends like English breakfast are made of black teas.

Green teas. All Japanese and many Chinese teas are green teas, prized for aroma and finesse. They are processed by lightly drying the leaves. Some are whole-leaf while others are made from leaves rolled into little balls. Japanese matcha is powdered green tea. Green teas should be sipped plain, without sweeteners, lemon or milk. One exception is Moroccan mint tea, made by pouring sweetened green tea over lightly crushed fresh mint leaves.

Herbal teas. Verbena, chamomile, lemon grass, peppermint and linden are some of the more popular herbal teas, or infusions. Herbal teas are often believed to have curative properties.

FOOD

ground coffee goes stale in just a few hours. Precise grinding is crucial in the formation of golden-brown crema, the true sign of a well-made espresso. Crema will not form if the coffee is improperly ground; if it is too coarse, the espresso will come through in less than 15 seconds and there will be too much fluid; if it is too fine, longer than 20 seconds will be required, and there will be only a small amount of bitter fluid. (White crema is another indication that the infusion was too slow.)

If the coffee is fresh, making the appropriate adjustments to the grind should produce the result you're aiming for—1½ to 2 oz. of rich, brown ambrosia with the desired crema—though you might also try tamping the coffee into the portafilter more or less firmly to slow down or speed up the process.

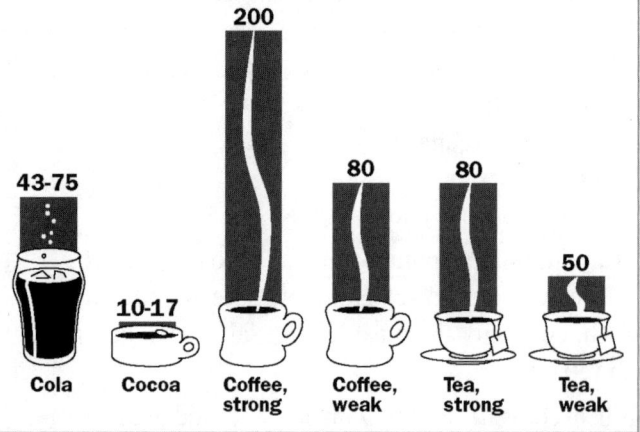

HOW LARGE A JOLT ARE YOU GETTING?

Shown here are the drinks that contain caffeine—and the number of milligrams in each serving.

- Cola: 43-75
- Cocoa: 10-17
- Coffee, strong: 200
- Coffee, weak: 80
- Tea, strong: 80
- Tea, weak: 50

A Good Cup of Tea

Different approaches to an ancient brew

Tea is one of the world's most popular beverages, and there's seemingly no limit to the various ways to prepare it.

The Simple Approach. Making a good cup of tea is simple. First, heat the teapot by filling it with water that has just come to a boil. Discard this water, and place 1 teaspoon of loose tea per cup in the teapot (the amount may vary according to taste). Pour in fresh water that has just come to a boil, 6 ounces for each cup. Allow the tea to steep for 3 to 5 minutes; then, pour it through a strainer into a cup or mug. Some types of green tea should be made with water that has cooled down a bit. Using a tea bag eliminates the strainer, but it is still best to make the tea in a teapot so the water stays sufficiently hot.

When tea is made, the leaves release their caffeine first, so the amount of caffeine can be reduced by pouring off all the tea after 30 seconds, then adding fresh boiling water to the leaves or the tea bag.

The British Cuppa. British writer George Orwell devoted an entire essay, "A Nice Cup of Tea," to the art of making tea, with Indian or Ceylon leaves (no tea bags, please). He said the pot should be warmed beforehand, and the water should be poured boiling onto the leaves. Tea should be drunk strong, with milk and no sugar, with many additional cups of tea produced by merely adding more hot water to the pot. Tea should have a bitter taste, like beer, Orwell claimed.

A Purist's Approach. Roy Fong, owner of The Imperial Tea Court in San Francisco, recommends preparing loose, whole-leaf teas fresh by the cup, steeping them in water for only a minute or two at temperatures not greater than 185 degrees Fahrenheit. The delicate, decidedly nonbitter liquor is then drained from the leaves using a small utility strainer or the lid of a Chinese covered teacup (*gai-wan*) to retain the leaves in the cup. The leaves may be used again for additional infusions with slightly increased water temperature and steeping time, as desired. White, green and yellow teas are prepared this way. For loose red (black), oolong and puerh teas, use a higher water temperature, but for the gourmet palate, never at the boiling point.

The European Way. Europeans generally drink their tea with lemon and sugar or honey, and some Russians drink their tea sweetened with fruit jam. Many of them drink tea out of glasses. They tend to favor scented teas as well, but very often add sugar.

Moroccan Tea: Garden Mint. There is nothing more refreshing to drink than fresh-cut spearmint, steeped in hot water for 2 minutes. For Moroccan-style mint tea, add several teaspoons of sugar per cup.

You Are What You Drink

The health benefits—and hazards—of various beverages

Many health problems—decaying teeth, thinning bones, heart disease, stroke, diabetes, dementia, cancer and obesity, to name a few—are linked to the beverages you drink—or don't drink.

A few years ago, with the support of the Unilever Health Institute in the Netherlands (Unilever owns Lipton Tea), a panel of experts on nutrition and health published a "Beverage Guidance System" in the hopes of getting people to stop drinking calories that contribute little or nothing to their health and may detract from it.

The panel was distressed by the contribution that popular beverages make to weight problems.

The experts reviewed nearly 150 reports to find the best evidence of the effects of various beverages on health problems. Here is a summary of the findings.

At the head of the list of preferred drinks: water. No calories, no hazards, only benefits. But the panel expressed concern about bottled water fortified with nutrients, saying that consumers may think they don't need to eat certain nutritious foods, which contain fiber and phytochemicals lacking in these waters.

Sweet Liquid Calories. There has been a huge increase in sugar-sweetened drinks in recent decades, primarily at the expense of milk, which has clear nutritional benefits. The calories from these sugary drinks account for half the rise in caloric intake by Americans since the late 1970s.

Not only has the number of servings of these drinks risen, but serving size has ballooned, as well, with some retail outlets offering 32 ounces and free refills.

Add the current passion for smoothies and sweetened coffee drinks (there are 240 calories in a 16-ounce Starbucks Caffé Mocha without the whipped cream), and you can see why people are drinking themselves into XXXL sizes.

But calories from sweet drinks are not the only problem. The other concern is that these beverages do little or nothing to curb your appetite, and people do not compensate for the calories they drink by eating less.

Furthermore, some soft drinks contribute to other health problems. The American Academy of General Dentistry says that noncola carbonated beverages and canned (sweetened) iced tea harm tooth enamel, especially when consumed apart from meals. And a study of 2,500 adults in Framingham, Mass., linked cola consumption (regular and diet) to the thinning of hip bones in women.

FOOD

If you must drink something sweet, the panel suggested a no-calorie beverage like diet soda prepared with an approved sweetener, though the experts recognized a lack of long-term safety data and the possibility that these drinks "condition" people to prefer sweetness.

Fruit juices are also a sweet alternative, although not nearly as good as whole fruits, which are better at satisfying hunger.

Coffee, tea and caffeine. Here the news is better. Several good studies have linked regular coffee consumption to a reduced risk of developing Type-2 diabetes, colorectal cancer and, in men and in women who have not taken postmenopausal hormones, Parkinson's disease.

Most studies have not linked a high intake of either coffee or caffeine to heart disease, even though caffeinated coffee raises blood pressure somewhat and boiled unfiltered coffee (French-pressed and espresso) raises harmful LDL and total cholesterol levels.

Caffeine itself is not thought to be a problem for health or water balance in the body, up to 400 milligrams a day (the amount in about 30 ounces of brewed coffee). But pregnant women should limit their intake because more than 300 milligrams a day might increase the risk of miscarriage and low birth weight, the panel said.

Mice prone to an Alzheimer's-like disease were protected by drinking water spiked with caffeine equivalent to what people get from five cups of coffee a day. And a study of more than 600 men suggested that drinking three cups of coffee a day protects against age-related memory and thinking deficits.

For tea, the evidence on health benefits is mixed and sometimes conflicting. Tea lowers cancer risk in experimental animals, but the effects in people are unknown. It may benefit bone density and help prevent kidney stones and tooth decay. And four or five cups of black tea daily helps arteries expand and thus may improve blood flow to the heart.

Alcohol. Alcohol is a classic case of "a little may be better than none, but a lot is worse than a little." Moderate consumption—one drink a day for women and two for men—has been linked in many large, long-term studies to lower mortality rates, especially from heart attacks and strokes, and may also lower the risk of Type-2 diabetes and gallstones. The panel found no convincing evidence that one form of alcohol, including red wine, was better than another.

But alcohol even at moderate intakes raises the risk of birth defects and breast cancer, possibly because it interferes with folate, an essential B vitamin. And heavy alcohol consumption is associated with several lethal cancers, cirrhosis of the liver, hemorrhagic stroke, hypertension, dementia and some forms of heart disease.

Dairy and Soy Drinks. The panel acknowledged the benefits of milk for bone density, while noting that unless people continue to drink it, the benefit to bones of the calcium and vitamin D in milk is not maintained.

Other essential nutrients in milk include magnesium, potassium, zinc, iron, vitamin A, riboflavin, folate and protein—about 8 grams in an 8-ounce glass. A 10-year study of overweight individuals found that milk drinkers were less likely to develop a constellation of coronary risk factors that includes hypertension and low levels of protective HDLs. That suggests that you may never outgrow your need for milk.

"Fortified soy milk is a good alternative for individuals who prefer not to consume cow milk," the panel said, but it cautioned that soy milk provides only 75 percent of the calcium the body obtains from cow's milk.

—Jane E. Brody

MONEY

Personal Finance

How to Balance Your Budget
Keeping yourself on track and in the black

Most of us don't think of ourselves as economic units, small business enterprises with inflows and outflows. But, in some sense, of course, we are. Money comes in, hopefully, and we spend it on food, shelter, clothing and various and sundry other things. Not all of us have a clear picture of the relationship between our inflows and outlays, although understanding it is vital to our financial health. Here are a few essential calculations to help keep track of You, Inc.

 INSIDE INFO

Just How Rich Are You?

That depends on where you live. The average household income of America's top 5 percent of earners is $311,000. But that includes households—from widows to families of ten—living in places where the cost of living differs widely. To get a more accurate picture, researchers at *U.S. News & World Report* recently crunched Census Bureau numbers. They determined figures on what it takes to be rich in 40 cities, for both a couple with no children and for a family of four. Here are some of their findings:

	HOUSEHOLD INCOME	
	COUPLE, NO KIDS	FAMILY OF FOUR
New York	$359,494	$718,989
San Francisco	$359,061	$718,123
Washington, D.C.	$347,917	$695,833
Boston	$316,613	$633,227
Omaha	$207,019	$414,038
Albuquerque	$193,483	$386,965
El Paso	$175,161	$350,321

SOURCE: *U.S. News & World Report*

Figuring your budget. A budget is the ultimate reality check. It reveals exactly what you're bringing in and what you're shelling out, no delusions, no fantasies, just the steel-knife economic reality. Start making a budget by tallying up your income and then itemizing your expenses. (See chart on next page.) At the end of the exercise, if your expenses exceed your income, it's time to figure out where you can trim your spending.

If you're spending less than you're bringing home, you have the good fortune of showing a surplus. Note that the "savings" category is in the fixed-expenses column of the ledger. That's because you can develop good habits by thinking of saving as a fixed payment to yourself. If you have a surplus, you might consider giving yourself a raise.

Calculating your net worth. An annual checkup on this key household figure is also good for your financial health. The measure is a valuable baseline to see if you're achieving your financial goals—saving for college tuition or for retirement, for example—or if you're falling behind. If you find you're slipping, your options are to cut spending, take on more work, or go back and reassess your dreams.

To calculate how much you're worth, you can turn to personal finance software, internet calculators and tried-but-true financial tomes. But you will still have to dig into your store of financial files to plug in your figures. Once you've gathered up the documents and the data you will need to fill out the chart on the next page, it's a simple calculation—assets minus liabilities—to arrive at your net worth.

FIGURING YOUR BUDGET

INCOME

Salaries (after taxes)	$
Part-time work	$
Child support/alimony	$
Investment interest, dividends, real estate income	$
Other	$
Adjusted net income	$

EXPENSES

Fixed expenses

Savings	$
Taxes (federal, state and local)	$
Rent or mortgage payments	$
Utilities (gas, electric, water, telephone)	$
Insurance (health, life, disability, house, car)	$
Food	$
Education	$
Personal fixed expenses (i.e., hair care)	$
Transportation	
Total Fixed Expenses	$

Variable expenses

Credit card bills	$
Loans	$
Clothing	$
Gas	
Car maintenance	$
Home improvements	$
Parking, tolls	$
Restaurant meals	$
Entertainment	$
Charitable contributions	$
Gifts	$
Vacations	$
Miscellaneous	$
Total variable expenses:	$
Total fixed and variable expenses:	$

TOTAL NET INCOME - TOTAL EXPENSES= SURPLUS OR SHORTAGE

CALCULATING YOUR NET WORTH

ASSETS

Cash and investments

Cash on hand	$
Savings and checking accounts	$
Certificates of deposit	$
Money market funds	$
Common and preferred stock	$
Mutual funds	$
Bonds	$
Brokerage funds	$
Cash value of life insurance	$
Equity in profit-sharing plans	$
Equity in pension plans (401K's)	$
Individual Retirement Accounts (I.R.A.'s)	$
Business and real estate investments	$
Loans owed to you	$
Other	$

Personal Assets (est. market value)

Home or homes and furnishings	$
Cars	$
Boats and other recreational vehicles	$
Furs and jewelry	$
Art, antiques and collectibles	$
Other assets	$
Total assets	$

LIABILITIES

Balance owed on mortgage	$
Outstanding loans:	$
Auto, bank, student or others	$
Home equity credit line	$
Other credit lines	$
Bills due	$
Credit card bills due	$
Outstanding taxes due	$
Other bills	$
Total liabilities	$

TOTAL ASSETS – TOTAL LIABILITIES = NET WORTH

Steps Toward a Balanced Budget
And a few systems to keep it from imploding

The road to a balanced personal budget is strewn with good intentions—and often failed attempts. Drawing up and sticking to a budget takes discipline, flexibility, and an unfailing focus on the numbers. But it's not impossible to do. Here's the best advice out there on making sure your budget adds up.

Set a goal. What are you saving for? A vacation, a house, college tuition, retirement? Or, a little pocket money for the occasional dinner out? Once you identify your goal, large or small, determine how much it will take you to reach it. Establishing a fixed target makes it easy to measure your progress along the way.

Track your expenses. Before you can draw up a realistic budget, track where your money is going. Record your expenditures methodically for at least two weeks. Not just the easy to identify mortgage payments and credit card bills, but periodic expenses like medical co-payments and new car tires. This step is especially important when you are starting out so that you become fully conscious of every dollar that leaves your wallet.

Pick a budgeting system. You have a choice of a few popular budgeting systems: the envelope system and the 60% solution. Which one you pick is a matter of personal preference. Both require some advance number-crunching. Based on your records of expenditures for categories such as food, transportation, clothing, savings, etc., determine how much to allot to each item. Pick a budgeting cycle, perhaps to coincide with your weekly or bi-monthly pay schedule.

In the envelope system, you allot predetermined amounts to each category and limit spending to those amounts. Leftover funds for food, for example, can be transferred to clothing or preferably stashed into the savings envelope.

The 60% Solution allocates 60 percent of your gross income to fixed expenses like taxes, insurance, recurring bills and house payments. The other 40 percent is divided equally among retirement, savings, unexpected expenses and spending money. In this method, 10 percent of your gross income is set aside as savings each pay period.

Be flexible. Setting too rigid a budget is self-defeating. Like an overly-restrictive diet, you won't stick to it. But slow and steady gains can be made by setting realistic goals and leaving yourself some wiggle room as you periodically reassess your target goals.

Finance 101 for the Married
A little fiscal discipline can do wonders for your romance

When it comes to finances, your marriage is likely to be your most valuable asset—or your largest liability. Here's how a couple can increase compatibility and, ultimately, financial prosperity:

Run your home like a business. Set up a weekly meeting with your spouse to discuss finances and set goals. Make a budget and keep track of earnings, expenses and debts. Structure your partnership: share responsibilities and rotate tasks such as investing and bill paying.

Enjoy, but within reason. Create a cash cushion, and live a lifestyle you can sustain.

Be supportive of careers. A supportive partner helps you professionally, which should bolster mutual bottom line.

Use a mediator. Are you are a saver while your

☑ **TIMELY TIPS**

Personal Finance Sites Worth a Click

These personal finance sites help you pull together your financial data and create a budget. Some also offer a community where you can discuss finances with others.

✔ **Cake Financial:** Cake aggregates all your brokerage accounts and makes recommendations based on high-performing portfolios on the site. People can talk about questions like, "Are we all better off in cash right now?" Unlike other stock message boards, Cake shows whether people own the stocks they are talking about and how their portfolios have performed. The Investor Quick Check benchmarks your portfolio against the market and other investors. *www.cakefinancial.com*

✔ **Credit Karma:** Unlike other credit score sites that charge for or limit the number of times a year you can check your credit score, Credit Karma lets you check your scores as much as

you want, free. Users can track their scores over time and talk with others about how to improve them. *www.creditkarma.com*

✔ **Mint:** Give Mint the log-in information for your bank, credit card and brokerage accounts, and each night it pulls in your data and arranges it in charts to show you how much you are worth and where you spend your money. Text "Balance" to MYMINT to get your account balances on your cellphone. Mint does not have a social networking component, believing that you can get bad personal finance advice from amateurs. *www.mint.com*

✔ **PearBudget:** This simple tool guides you through a budgeting spreadsheet. It does not pull your account balances in from the Web—you have to enter them. There is a small monthly charge for using the site; in exchange it doesn't show ads. *www.pearbudget.com*

✔ **Quicken Online:** Originally bookkeeping software available on disc, Quicken now offers a Web-based version. It also offers mobile applications, like

Quicken Beam, which allows you to view your last five transactions from your phone. *www.quicken.intuit.com*

✔ **SmartyPig:** At this virtual piggy bank, you set savings goals, and the site withdraws money from your checking accounts each month and holds it an interest-bearing account. Users share their accounts with family and friends, to solicit donations or moral support, and add widgets to their social network profiles or blogs. When it's time to cash in, you have the option of getting retailer gift cards worth a few percentage points more than you saved. *www.smartypig.com*

✔ **Wesabe:** Like Mint, Wesabe aggregates your financial accounts and enlightens you about your spending patterns. But it also offers a social network, where you can chat with others online, anonymously, about how much you lost in your retirement accounts or how to cut spending, for example. *www.wesabe.com*

—Claire Cain Miller

spouse prefers to splurge? An independent third party, such as a financial planner or a therapist, can help you find a middle ground.

Maintain some independence. Carve out some money for each of you to spend on things that make you happy. And when paring back, each of you must make sacrifices.

Invest in your partnership. Spend time and money together, even when you're short on both. Think of it as the marital version of dollar-cost averaging your marriage—making small investments over time. Waiting until retirement could be too late.

—Tara Siegel Bernard

How to Bank Safely Online

It's easy to put your bills on autopilot, but beware of the downsides

Millions of consumers swear by the simplicity of online banking—and the money they save by not using stamps. But paying bills online is not risk free. One potential pitfall is that online bill payment is not synonymous with instantaneous payment. You still have to plan your payments well in advance or risk late fees.

And while electronic bill payment reduces desk clutter, it also means that when a mistake is made there is less of a paper trail. Even though federal laws provide the same protections for electronic facsimiles as they do for paper checks, tax experts say hard copies might also be helpful if you ever have a run-in with I.R.S auditors.

Before you make the leap to online banking, be sure to follow these safety guidelines.

When using your bank's Web site:

- Choose a unique password, preferably with at least eight keystrokes combining lower- and upper-case letters as well as numbers and symbols. Do not use your e-mail address, phone number or mother's maiden name.

- Don't trust e-mail purporting to be from your bank, especially messages asking you to update your passwords or accounts. Get in touch with your bank to verify data.

- Bookmark the bank's address in your browser rather than typing in the address each time you want to visit. Slight mistakes in entering the address may take you to a "spoofer" site set up by criminals to trick you into entering your account number and password, giving them access to your account.

When paying bills online:

- Plan your payments well in advance. Funds are withdrawn from your account on the day the bill payment is due to be sent. Update your checkbook register to reflect any scheduled payments so that you do not overdraw your account.

- Recurring bills of the same amount can be scheduled to be paid automatically. For cellphone or electric bills that vary from month to month, it is possible to set up parameters so that all bills under a certain amount are paid automatically while larger sums require your approval.

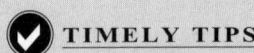 **TIMELY TIPS**

Safe Deposit Box: Dos and Don'ts

✔ Some insurance companies offer lower premiums on valuables kept in a safe deposit box.

✔ Bank fees for safe deposit boxes range from $10-$40 a year for a 3" by 21" box that is 5" deep, to $100 or more for a 10" by 21" box that is 10" deep.

✔ A strong-box safe for use at home runs from around $40 to several hundred dollars at office supply stores or online.

✔ Here's what to store at the bank:
  - valuable jewelry and collectibles such as coins, stamps or medals
  - birth, marriage and death certificates and other family records
  - home, auto and other insurance policies; deeds, mortgage contracts and titles

✔ Keep originals of your will or life insurance policies in a deposit box at home. That way your survivors won't need court permission to get the documents from the bank safe.

- Not all companies can accept electronic payments. Your bank must send those businesses a check. This can take up to 10 days. Most sites will advise you of this lag time in advance.

- Never conduct online banking from a public computer or from your own in an airport, hotel or other public place. And don't bank online when your computer is very slow or has many pop-ups, a sign of a potential virus. Report suspicious activity to your bank.

—Eric Dash

TIMELY TIPS

Cutting the Cost of Checks

✔ **Buy checks from a mail order company, not your bank.** Banks charge around $25 per box. Mail order discounters charge as little as $5 a box.
   Sources of low-cost checks:

Checks in the Mail
www.citm.com   877-397-1541

Checks Unlimited
www.checksunlimited.com   800-426-0822

Opening a Swiss Bank Account

Looking for a safe haven for your money?
Here's one time-tested option

The allure of a Swiss bank account derives from the country's code of confidentiality (as well as its generally stable currency). By law, Swiss bankers and their staff are not allowed to divulge information about your account, not even to lawyers or investigators digging up data for divorce or bankruptcy proceedings. The few exceptions that require Swiss bankers to "open" your account for scrutiny would be in cases of suspected criminal activity, such as drug trafficking, money laundering and, increasingly, tax evasion.

But behind its James Bond–like mystique, Swiss banking is really quite mundane. With a little effort and fewer funds than you might think, you, too, can open a Swiss bank account.

There are several types of Swiss bank accounts, from those that accept initial deposits of at least one million Swiss francs (around $900,000) to smaller retail accounts that require as little as $250 in deposits.

The first step toward obtaining a Swiss bank account is, not surprisingly, to locate a bank in Switzerland. You can find bank names and contact information from the Swiss Bankers Association online at swissbanking.org/en/home.htm.

Once you've picked a bank, you can apply for an account by mail or fax. To expedite the process, you may want to make the trip directly to the bank's headquarters in Switzerland. In either case, you will have to go through a fairly rigorous screening process in compliance with the country's strict "know your customer" laws, aimed at preventing money laundering and other abuses.

Application forms vary among banks. For a mail application, you will generally need to send a signature certification form and several authenticated copies of your passport. Whether you apply by mail or in person, you will most likely have to verify your address (by showing a copy of a utility bill, for example). If you are charging your deposit, you will have to present a recent credit card statement. In addition, you may be asked for documents to verify your annual income and to prove the "economic origin" of the funds for deposit. In other words, you will need to show how you arrived at the money by providing a copy of your employment contract, a bill of sale or similar documents.

What happens if your Swiss banking expe-

MONEY

rience turns sour? You have three recourses. First, contact the bank's legal department and file a complaint. If your claim is denied, contact a mediator at bankingombudsman.ch/english. If you still get no satisfaction and want to sue, you'll need a Swiss lawyer. Search for one online at www.swisslawyers.com or email:

info@swisslawyers.com.

As for that much-vaunted Swiss bank secrecy, some countries, including the United States, are trying to chip away at the system, insisting on closer scrutiny of Swiss bank accounts as a way of regaining lost tax revenues. Switzerland is resisting demands that threaten confidentiality.

How to Make Saving a Habit

For starters, set up a a rainy day fund for emergencies

Saving money is not the sexiest financial move, but it's probably the most important. So start squirreling. Even if it's the change from your pocket, it's never too early to start incubating a nest egg, which is not just for retirement. A cash account may be used for a flatter television set, a vacation, new clothes, a period of unemployment, a down payment on a house, car repairs or whatever treat you can dream up. Here are some saving strategies and tips to get you started.

- An initial goal of $2,000 in a savings account would cover the average amount of unexpected expenses in a year. That starter emergency fund should be used as needed and replenished.

- It's better to borrow from yourself than to rely on a credit card and feel as if you can never get ahead. Additional savings can be set aside for other short-term and mid-term goals, assuming that you are also putting a percentage of your

---

ⓘ INSIDE INFO

Who's on the Face of a $50 Bill?

○ For several years now, the Bureau of Engraving and Printing has been pumping out more colorful currency designed to thwart counterfeiters. The bills have shades of red, yellow and orange added to the traditional green. A transformed $5 bill made its debut in 2008. A new $100 bill is in the works.

○ Benjamin Franklin still graces the $100 bill, the largest denomination currently issued. Here's the pecking order:

	FRONT	BACK
$1	George Washington	U.S. Seal
$2	Thomas Jefferson	Signers of Declaration
$5	Abraham Lincoln	Lincoln Memorial
$10	Alexander Hamilton	U.S. Treasury
$20	Andrew Jackson	White House
$50	Ulysses Grant	U.S. Capitol
$100	Benjamin Franklin	Independence Hall

○ Martha Washington, the only woman pictured on a U.S. currency note, appeared on the face of the $1 Silver Certificate of 1886 and 1891 and on the back of the $1 Silver Certificate of 1896.

○ The average life span of a $1 bill is about 22 months. A $10 bill survives for about three years.

SOURCE: U.S. Bureau of Printing and Engraving

---

income toward retirement.

- Play with online calculators to see the impact of saving money. The Internet is full of free strategies and motivational stories from fellow savers at sites like www.betterbudgeting.com and www. americasaves.org (where you can register your savings goal).

- For hard-copy tips on how to wring extra expenses out of your budget, take a look at Mary M. Hunt's book *Live Your Life for Half the Price* or *Pay It Down* by Jean Chatzky.

• Include the children in the process. A common lament from adults in financial trouble is that they were never taught about money.

The key is to reverse the habit of spending first and paying later, with interest. The old-fashioned way—saving the money, then spending it—costs less, and causes less stress and anxiety, than using debt or going without.

—Shira Boss

What It Costs to Raise a Child
A lot, but the rewards can be great, too

Child-rearing is expensive: an average of more than $217,000 from birth until age 18, according to the U.S. Department of Agriculture. Depending on family income, it costs a two-parent family with two children somewhere between $148,320 and $298,680 to raise each child. Raising a single child brings up the cost by a factor of 1.24. It really does get cheaper by the dozen: the expenditure per child drops by .77 in a family with three or more children.

Those lofty sums are mostly for basics like food, clothing, housing and medical care. But as many parents know, raising a child doesn't stop after 18 years. To send a kid to college, parents will have to add to that sum about $25,000 a year by 2008-2009 estimates, in tuition for a four-year private college and $6,600 for an in-state public school.

That particular investment holds a big promise of future rewards, however: over a 40-year career, a college grad is likely to earn about 60 percent more than a high school graduate, according to the College Board.

Can I Have an Allowance?
An expert answers that vexing question

Child psychologists believe that a child learns the concept of trading money for goods as early as age 3 or 4. In that case, it would seem that it's almost never too early to teach your child the value of money and how to manage it. Here, Janet Bodnar, an editor at *Kiplinger's Personal Finance* magazine and author of a syndicated column called "Money-Smart Kids," gives her expert advice on the prickly question of allowances.

Q When should you start giving allowances?

It is appropriate to start an allowance around the age of 6 or so, when the child is in the first grade. Age 3 or 4 is a little too early. Children that young think in very concrete terms about money

MONEY

CHILD-REARING EXPENSES FROM BIRTH TO 18*

For a customized estimate of raising your child, plug your own figures into the calculator provided by the U.S.D.A. at www.cnpp.usda.gov.

Family income:	Less than $45,800	$45,800–$77,100	More than $77,100
Housing	$49,320	$68,160	$110,700
Food	$28,890	$34,650	$43,140
Transportation	$21,120	$29,400	$39,450
Clothing	$ 8,370	$9,840	$12,630
Health care	$12,060	$15,630	$18,000
Child care/education	$14,430	$25,230	$40,440
Miscellaneous**	$14,130	$21,150	$34,320
Total:	**$148,320**	**$204,060**	**$298,680**

* Calculated on before-tax income; each child in a two-parent family
** Includes personal care items, entertainment and reading materials
SOURCE: U.S. Department of Agriculture

and can't appreciate the abstract idea of managing an allowance. But in first grade children start to learn about money in school, so they know that one dollar equals four quarters or ten dimes and they have an idea how much that will buy.

How much should you give?

Start with a weekly base allowance that is equal to one-half the child's age. Most parents I talk to feel comfortable with that figure. And you can adjust it up or down based on the cost of living in your area and what you expect children to pay for with their allowance.

At what point during the week should you give your kids their allowance?

Get into the habit of paying them on a regular schedule, preferably a quiet weekday—maybe even on your own payday—instead of during the hectic weekend. You might also consider Sunday night, so the kids aren't tempted to blow the money over the weekend.

What should kids be required to pay for with their allowance?

Start small. Put young children in charge of the one thing they most like to spend money on, whether it's stickers, crayons or mini racing cars. Once they're accustomed to making their own purchases, you can expand the allowance as they get older to cover snacks after school, entertainment and clothing.

Should you pay kids for chores?

I don't recommend that the basic allowance be tied to chores. Children shouldn't be paid to do things that they should do as part of the family, such as washing dishes, cleaning up their room, taking out the trash or setting the table. Instead, the basic allowance should be tied to spending responsibilities. You might require kids to pay for their own collectibles, video games and CD's, movie tickets and mall excursions with their friends.

To teach them the value of working for pay, have them earn extra cash for jobs such as raking leaves, washing the car or cleaning out the garage. Agree on a wage ahead of time, then pay when you're satisfied with their work. This is also a good way to supplement a basic allowance.

What about babysitting for siblings or family members?

It depends on the circumstance. If it's Saturday night and your child could get another babysitting job—you should pay, just as you would a babysitter. It is O.K. to pay less than the going rate as long as you don't take advantage.

Rules for Boomerang Kids

What parents should do when 20-somethings move back in

Young offspring who return to the nest generally do so for economic reasons. In some cases, the offspring, sometimes called boomerangers, may be

Teaching Kids to Use Plastic

✔ **Be a role model.** Use your credit cards the way you want your children to use theirs. Let children see you paying bills and hear discussions of how you spend your money. Be honest about spending mistakes of the past.

✔ **Help children learn the limits of their card.** Go through monthly statements. Teach children about interest rates and how they can raise debt.

✔ **If your children receive an allowance, encourage them to budget,** save and spend their money wisely, showing how interest charges, annual fees and bank charges work.

✔ **Set up long-term financial goals.** Guide them to identify how they are spending their money and whether purchases are wise.

✔ **Teach children what to do if a card is lost or stolen.** Remind your children to keep the 800 number to report lost or stolen cards in a safe place. Urge them to memorize their PINs and tell them not to lend cards.

✔ **Be aware of warning signs of identity theft,** such as preapproved credit card offers arriving in your child's name.

✔ **Check your child's credit report annually** for any unauthorized accounts and requests for credit.

—Jennifer Alsever

struggling to pay off college loans or having trouble finding jobs that can cover housing costs. And their parents are often at the peak of their own earning power and can afford to take them back in.

The best of these parent-child relationships are built on some financial rules, or at least expectations, that encourage responsibility, such as: A child who is unemployed must try to find work. One who has college debts must strive to pay them off. A graduate student has to hit the books hard. Gainfully employed children should pay rent—or some amount that parents will set aside for them—or invest for their own future.

If you are a parent sharing the nest with a 20-something child, here is some financial advice to consider.

Health insurance: Many policies cut off dependents if they have graduated from college or are over 25. If your child has a job that offers no insurance, decide who will pay for it—or run the risk that he or she will be uninsured in the event of illness.

Auto insurance: Multicar discounts usually make it cheaper for a child to stay on his parents' policy, but consider having him pay his share.

Financial expectations: If you require your child to pay rent, you may want to set a lower amount at first, then raise it gradually. If your child is looking for a job, don't let the search become an open-ended excuse for staying in your home.

Nest eggs: Don't assume that by using your own savings to support your adult children, you are guaranteeing that they will support you in the future.

—Dale Buss

Credit vs. Debit Cards

The pros and the cons of each

Credit cards have been around since the 1950s; their plastic cousins, debit cards, were introduced in the mid-1970s. Though the two may be used interchangeably, there are notable differences.

MONEY

Debit cards. These are linked to your bank account so the money you spend is automatically deducted from your account. Since your bank balance decreases with each debit card transaction, you're less likely to overspend. To protect against spending more than is in your account, you can get "overdraft protection" from your bank allowing you to exceed your balance. You may end up paying interest, and maybe extra fees, on the money you tap from your overdraft account.

Credit cards. Basically, they allow you to use someone else's money (the card issuer's) to make a purchase while you repay the money later. Pay back the balance in full within the billing period—generally 15 to 45 days—and you avoid interest payments. Carry over a balance, and interest charges quickly add up. If you drag out paying a $500 balance over two years, for example, at an 18 percent rate, you pay nearly $100 more in interest.

Protections. Credit cards provide more protection if your card or bank information is stolen. If there is a fraudulent charge on your credit card account, you let the card issuer know and the amount is generally removed. In the case of a stolen debit card, it could take weeks for the bank to investigate your claim and replace your lost funds.

Resolving disputes. If you charge an item or service on your credit card and aren't satisfied with the purchase, your card issuer can legally withhold payment from the retailer until the dispute is resolved. You will not be charged.

Debit card disputes are more difficult to resolve

Debt isn't a problem for everyone. Just over half of Americans either don't use plastic or pay off their balances each month.

• • •

and more prolonged. After all, the retailer already has your money, giving you less leverage. There's no guarantee you'll get that money back.

Picking the right card. Which credit card is best? If you plan to pay your credit card bill in full each month, the interest rate on outstanding balances won't matter, so choose a card with no annual fee and with the rewards you really want—be it cash back, frequent flier miles or points redeemable for gifts, for example. Check out Bankrate.com and Creditcards.com for comparisons of reward cards.

Generally, if you make significant purchases, cash-back programs offer the most immediate gratification. You can get money rewards credited to your account or a refund by check. Many large banks also offer debit cards with rewards, so shop around at sites like Creditcards.com and others, which compare various prepaid and debit cards, based on annual fees, related services and credit requirements.

Compare rates. If you know you will carryover a balance from month to month, go with a plain-vanilla credit card with no annual fee and the lowest annual interest rate available. Otherwise, the interest you pay on a carry-over balance could more than offset the perks of a rewards card. Here, too, updated interest rate information can be found for dozens of cards at Creditcards.com and Bankrate.com.

Check monthly statements. Card issuers can legally raise your credit card interest rate, so check your monthly statements. If your rate goes up, call the card issuer and try to negotiate a lower rate. Or, consider transferring your balance to a card with a lower rate. In mid-2010, if not sooner, rules will go into effect limiting the card issuers' ability to raise your rate, unless a payment is overdue.

Shop around. On Billshrink.com, you can determine what you would be saving, or earning in rewards, if you switched to another credit card, based on your credit score and your annual purchases.

—Jennifer Barrett

Improving Your Credit Score
And what lenders are really looking for

Credit matters if you need a new mortgage. It matters for many of the loans you may use to send a child to college. And it matters if you need to use credit cards for a time because your income has fallen or disappeared and there is no other option.

Luckily, your credit score is something that you have a fair bit of control over. But since you don't always know ahead of time when your creditworthiness will be a factor, it's a good idea to focus on it beforehand.

A company called Fair Isaac supplies the formula that generates a FICO (Fair Isaac Corp.) score. If you want to see the credit history that serves as data for the score, you can get three free copies of your credit report each year, once from each of the bureaus, at annualcreditreport.com. (See box on right.)

If you want to see the FICO scores themselves, you can pay about $50 for the three of them at myfico.com. Click "products," then select the "FICO Credit Complete" package. The median FICO score was recently roughly 720, according to Fair Isaac—a good SAT math score, but one that could cause some problems with strict lenders.

Here's how to improve your score.

 **TIMELY TIPS**

Checking Up on Your Credit Rating

Even if you are not planning to take out a loan, it's wise to check your credit report. That way, if something is amiss you can work to fix the damage. By law you are entitled to one free credit report a year. Lots of Web sites and television commercials promise to provide a free credit report, but those offers are mostly come-ons to try to get you to purchase other products.

✔ The only legally authorized online source for obtaining your free credit report is **www.annualcreditreport.com.** That is the central Web site for the country's three major credit reporting companies , which you can also contact directly:

Equifax www.equifax.com; 800-685-1111
Experian www.experian.com; 888-397-3742
TransUnion www.transunion.com; 800-916-8800

✔ To get your free annual credit report, go to
www.annualcreditreport.com
or call 1-877-322-8228.

Or, mail a completed form (available online or by calling) to:

Annual Credit Report Request Services
P.O. Box 105281
Atlanta, Ga., 30348-5281

Check for errors. Examine your credit report for accounts you don't recognize. If you find any, it may be a simple error, but it could be a sign that a thief is opening new accounts in your name.

If you find errors, report them to the credit bureau, since the mistakes are probably hurting your credit score. The bureaus are supposed to respond within 30 days.

MONEY

Pay on time. Obvious, but crucial, because payment history accounts for about 35 percent of the FICO calculation for the general population (it could be more, or less, for certain individuals). Only 60 or 65 percent of credit reports show no late payments, which means a lot of other people aren't helping themselves. Don't think that a mortgage company won't report you.

Redefine your debt. About 30 percent of your score reflects the amount of money you owe. If you pay your credit card bills off each month, you may think that you're home free on this front and that your debt is zero.

But that may not be the case. The credit report data used by the FICO system show your credit limit and your end-of-month balance, before you pay the bill. If you have just one credit card with a credit limit of $5,000 and you're spending $4,000 each month, that can rough up your score, even if you're paying it off in full every month.

One option is to lower your spending so that your monthly bills are no more than 10 percent of the available credit on all your cards. It also may be worth asking for a higher limit on a card or two, just to improve this ratio.

Beware of retail cards. Stay away from those deals offering 10 percent off when you open up a store credit card account. They can hurt your credit score if you open too many in a short time, and their credit limits tend to be lower than standard credit cards. So use an existing credit card, or pay cash.

What lenders are looking for.

Credit cards. If you're looking to get the best interest rate or some of the richest reward offerings, representatives from card shopping sites like cardratings.com and creditcards.com figure you will need a score in the 720 to 750 range.

Auto loans. The minimum credit score required for the very best rate was recently around 786, although experts add that there is no magic number for good rates. Much depends on car type, cost and loan length.

Mortgages. Different entities (lenders, mortgage insurers, Fannie Mae and Freddie Mac) can add fees or dictate terms, so a bottom line number is hard to come by. Generally, the bigger the down payment, the better your chance of getting the best available rate, as long as you have a credit score of at least 740 or so.

—Ron Lieber

How to Get Out of Debt
Tough-as-nails ways to pay off those credit card balances

Credit card companies can be vicious, but consumers who are stuck in the debt maze need to get medieval. Rather than following the old half measures, do what it takes to be debt-free in today's world.

Know thy debt. Read (yes, read) your statements.

Create an aggressive payback strategy. Use online calculators to determine an affordable monthly payment that will get you out of debt fast. Then set up an automatic monthly transfer so you can't talk yourself into smaller payments.

Adjust your cost of living. Debt is code for living beyond your means. Figure out what's causing you to be overextended.

Quit using plastic for a while. This is boot camp. By switching to cash for at least a month, you'll know how much money you can truly afford to spend.

Generate more income. Sorry. Did you think you were going to pull bigger payments out from under the bed? Get another job, a raise, a roommate—then sell anything that you can live without and put the profits toward debt. (Finally, a sane use for eBay.)

Save. The only way to get on top of debt is to live on 80 percent of what you earn. At first, the remaining 20 percent will help you climb out of debt—a savings in itself, if your balances carry interest. From then on it becomes pure savings—and can keep you from ever falling into that hole again.

—M. P. Dunleavey

When Bankruptcy Is Your Best Option

Filing sooner rather than later may protect more of your assets

The idea of declaring bankruptcy may be unpleasant, even abhorrent, but for many people it could be the best option. The question is: How do you make that choice? How bad do things need to get before you throw in the towel and petition the courts for a fresh start?

Beware of Debt Settlement Companies

When belt-tightening doesn't do the trick, what can borrowers do to extricate themselves from overwhelming debt loads?

One option, of course, is a Chapter 7 personal bankruptcy filing that wipes out most credit card debt. Many consumers, however, are loath to file for bankruptcy protection, and many others may find that they cannot qualify for bankruptcy.

Debt settlement is another possibility. With this option, a debtor and creditor agree that payment of a negotiated, reduced balance will be payment in full. Debt settlement generally works best when consumers can offer a lump sum. Consumers may face taxes on the amount the creditor has forgiven.

Consumers can arrange debt settlement themselves, and many Web sites offer advice. Consumers can also hire a lawyer or use debt settlement companies, many of which advertise online and on television. The experts agree, however, that "buyer beware" is the best advice when considering debt settlement companies.

About a thousand such companies exist nationwide, but not all are reputable. In some cases, these companies tell consumers to stop paying monthly minimums, explaining that they will negotiate a settlement and that creditors generally do not negotiate reduced balances with consumers who are still making payments. Meanwhile, these companies take hefty monthly fees directly from clients' bank accounts.

Experts advise consumers to avoid companies that charge large fees upfront or through payments. Rather they should look for services that charge after settlement. The fee is typically about 20 percent of the amount of the negotiated reduction in balance.

Generally experts say that deals may be struck with many original creditors for 50 to 80 cents on the dollar. —Jane Birnbaum

The sting of failure and the dread of ruined credit are, understandably, deterrents to a bankruptcy filing. But those fears can prevent people from taking advantage of the financial protection offered by bankruptcy, which may allow you to erase most of your consumer debt while preserving assets like your retirement accounts and sometimes even your home and car.

Instead, many people delay filing until they are truly desperate. According to a survey by the Consumer Bankruptcy Project, a continuing study of consumer bankruptcy filings, more than 40 percent of people said they struggled financially for over two years before filing for bankruptcy. Their delay may have cost them their retirement accounts or cars, for example.

Because bankruptcy is so complex, and because bankruptcy laws underwent a major overhaul in 2005, many people are not only wary of filing,

Getting money is like digging with a needle. Spending it is like water soaking into sand.

Japanese proverb

but also confused about their options and possible outcomes. The changes included the addition of a lengthy means test to determine a debtor's ability to pay back what is owed. Filers are also required to complete a credit counseling course—at their own expense—before bankruptcy is granted.

One common misconception is that declaring bankruptcy will ruin your credit. If you're at the point of even considering bankruptcy, it's likely that your credit is in tatters anyway and you may not end up much worse off. In some cases, your credit could emerge in better shape once you've dealt with your debts.

Another myth is that you must be at the frayed end of your financial rope before you file. The fact is, you won't lose everything in a bankruptcy because some assets are protected, and you will need those to move forward. Waiting until your resources are entirely depleted defeats an important purpose of bankruptcy, which is to help people start over on a sound footing.

Filing for bankruptcy isn't cheap, and fees vary. But don't skimp on legal advice, especially if your situation is complicated—for example, if you're married but want to file a solo bankruptcy, or if your personal debts are mingled with small-business debts. Avoid cut-rate bankruptcy mills that may make your situation even worse.

Most bankruptcy lawyers offer a free initial consultation. The National Association of Consumer Bankruptcy Attorneys has a Web site (www.nacba.com) where you can search for a lawyer by location. The American Bankruptcy Institute (www.abiworld.org) and your local bar association can also make referrals.

—M. P. Dunleavey

 INSIDE INFO

Filing for Bankruptcy

○ Bankruptcy proceedings are started by filing a petition at a district bankruptcy court. If you are not using a lawyer, you can get the required forms online at www.uscourts.gov/bkforms/index.html.

○ You must provide a list of creditors, data about your assets and liabilities and a long list of other documents.

○ Filing fees vary depending on the type of bankruptcy case, but the most common type filed by individuals, under Chapter 7 of the bankruptcy code, costs about $300 to file.

Investing

Investing in Turbulent Times

Stay disciplined—even when Wall St. panics

One of ace investor Warren Buffett's favorite bits of wisdom about buying and selling stocks goes like this: "When people are greedy, be fearful, and when others are fearful, be greedy." That, of course, is easier said than done, especially during times of panic in the markets. But here are some principles to remember when times are rocky.

Do not try to time the market. Most people earn their fortunes by trusting their own instincts. But as investors, the same people may find that those instincts are often wrong. The problem is worse in volatile markets. "For the average investor, timing markets is a disaster," says Jeremy J. Siegel, a finance professor at the Wharton School of the University of Pennsylvania.

Instead of seeking to trade at the exact top or bottom of a market, evaluate whether you are getting a reasonable return.

Focus on an investment's fundamentals and push your feelings aside. Don't put money out only because it has worked in the past, nor should you sell simply because you are fearful.

In fact, many advisers recommend doing the reverse: buy more of your losers and sell some of your winners. Investments that have performed

MONEY

TAKING THE LONG VIEW ON STOCKS

Forget the daily gyrations of the market. In the past 80-plus years—the history of the Standard & Poor's 500—the stock market has been through a Great Depression and numerous recessions. It has experienced bubbles and busts, bull markets and bear markets.

Many things influence the stock market, of course, making it almost impossible to predict market movements. But long-term investors can take some comfort from the fact that, historically, bad decades are often followed by 10-year periods that are better than the long-term average, which shows a gain of 6.2 percent a year.

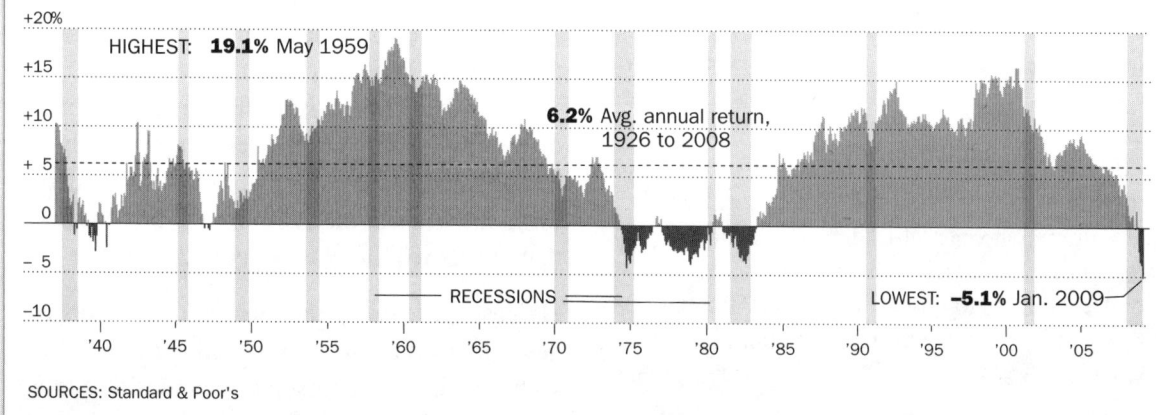

HIGHEST: **19.1%** May 1959

6.2% Avg. annual return, 1926 to 2008

RECESSIONS

LOWEST: **−5.1%** Jan. 2009

'40 '45 '50 '55 '60 '65 '70 '75 '80 '85 '90 '95 '00 '05

SOURCES: Standard & Poor's

Lessons from the Crash of 2008

After the market debacle of 2008, a year when the Standard & Poor's 500-stock index suffered its worst calendar loss since the Great Depression, investors began to rethink some basic assumptions. Here's what they learned the hard way about investing.

✔ **Losses can be long term.** Stocks can lose money, even for a decade or more. Looking ahead, investors nearing retirement don't have that much time to recover from market losses and should think twice before putting all or virtually all of their portfolios into stocks.

✔ **Stocks aren't the only game.** Diversification means owning different assets, not just different stocks. When virtually every type of equity is climbing, investors are generally willing to "diversify" their stock portfolios—but not through different investments like bonds. Rather, they buy different types of stocks, investing in emerging markets, for example, if that's what is soaring.

But the reality is that other types of stocks can't shield a portfolio from losses if the broad market starts to fall. Only bonds can do that, and in the past only ultra-safe Treasury bonds have best accomplished that feat.

✔ **Long live Treasuries.** There's an argument for owning Treasuries at all times, although some investors argue that even during downturns they can find far more attractive yields through other investments.

But only those who own Treasuries for current income need to worry if their government bonds are offering the market-leading yields. For long-term growth-oriented investors, the primary role of Treasuries is to provide ballast and protection to a portfolio—not capital appreciation. That's what stocks are for. —Paul J. Lim

poorly will typically do better; those that have done well will fall to their longer-term historical rates.

Rebalance your portfolio. Many investors wait until the end of the year to do their financial housekeeping. That may be convenient, but in volatile markets it may not suffice. The time to rebalance is when your allocation strays too far from your long-term targets, experts say.

If it fluctuates only a few percentage points, it's probably not worth incurring the trading costs or taxes that would result from tweaking your portfolio. But taking action could make a big difference when there are big market swings.

Communicate with your financial adviser. Financial advisers earn their keep in turbulent times. A good one should be able to walk clients through the holdings in their portfolios and explain the clients' investment strategies and how much they could lose. Then, at least once a week, the adviser should follow up by phone.

But clients have responsibilities, too. Not only should they scrutinize their portfolios, but they should also ask about the overall strategy: what economic conditions are going to affect my portfolio the most? How am I protected from or exposed to a more severe real estate or dollar decline?

For those invested in nontraditional areas like hedge funds, selecting a fund manager is even more critical. And clients should also be sure to ask how their adviser is being paid.

Some financial advisory firms receive a portion of fees for steering their clients to certain money management funds. So if those funds underperform, there is less incentive for the firm to suggest that clients withdraw their money.

Harvest tax losses. High net worth investors have generally used up their tax exemptions. So for some such investors, selling some securities at a loss to offset other investment gains might be sensible. But they must be mindful when selling to avoid replacing those securities with identical investments.

The so-called wash sale provision of the tax code disallows losses from the sale of stock within 30 days of the sale if you acquire shares or options of the same or an identical security. That means that if those shares rebounded, an investor would have to wait 31 days before going back into the market—or forfeit any benefit.

—Eric Dash

The Secret of Value Investing

An argument that the price-earnings ratio is key

More than 70 years ago, Benjamin Graham and David L. Dodd, two Columbia professors, came up with a simple investing idea. After the 1929 stock market crash, they urged investors to focus on hard facts—like a company's past earnings and the value of its assets—rather than trying to guess what the future would bring. A company with strong profits and a relatively low stock price was probably undervalued, they said.

Their classic 1934 textbook, *Security Analysis,* became the bible for what is known as value investing. Warren Buffett took Graham's course at Columbia Business School in the 1950s and later set out to put the theories into practice. Buffett's billions are just one part of the professors' giant legacy.

One of their biggest ideas was about analyzing stock prices—that investors must focus on long-term trends and not get caught up in the moment.

The standard measure for assessing the market is the price-to-earnings ratio. (See Inside Info on right.) In its most common form, the ratio is equal to a company's stock price divided by its earnings per share over the last 12 months. You can skip the math, though, and simply remember that a P/E

ⓘ INSIDE INFO

What Is the P/E Ratio?

○ **THE PRICE-EARNINGS RATIO** is the traditional measure of how expensive stocks are. It divides the current value of a stock (or a stock index like the Standard & Poor's 500) by the annual earnings of the issuing company (or the companies in the index). There are several versions of the ratio, depending on how you measure earnings.

○ **AN ESTIMATE OF FUTURE EARNINGS.** The main problem with this approach is that Wall Street's forecasts of future earnings are often unreliable.

○ **EARNINGS OVER THE PREVIOUS 12 MONTHS.** Here the problem is that in a given year earnings can soar or plunge; stocks, which bet on companies' long-term futures, should be less volatile than earnings. Purists argue that investors should look at earnings over not less than 5 years, preferably 7 or 10 years.

—David Leonhardt

MONEY

HOW TO TELL IF STOCKS ARE CHEAP

A historic look at the price-earnings ratio, 1937-2008.

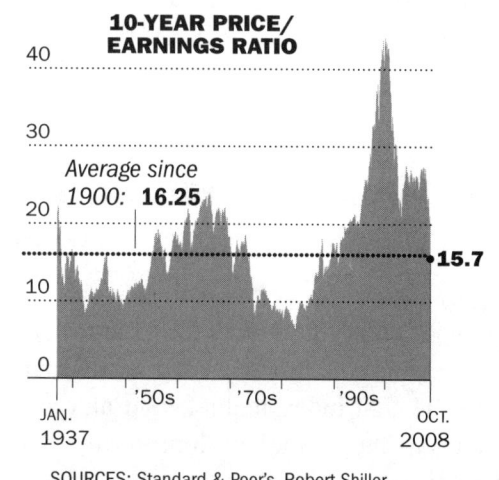

SOURCES: Standard & Poor's, Robert Shiller

ratio tells you how much a stock costs relative to a company's performance. The higher the ratio, the more expensive the stock and the stronger the argument that it won't do very well going forward.

Since World War II, the average P/E ratio has been 16.1. During the bubbles of the 1920s and the 1990s, on the other hand, the ratio shot above 40.

The P/E ratio was a crucial measure to Graham and Dodd, but they cautioned against putting too much emphasis on the recent past, arguing that a few months, or even a year, of financial information could be misleading. A short time frame could say more about what the economy was doing than about a company's long-term prospects. The time frame, they believed, should be "not less than five years, preferably seven or ten years."

For years, at least two economists, John Y. Campbell and Robert J. Shiller have been calculating long-term P/E ratios. They used P/E ratios to argue in 1996 that stocks were badly overvalued. A few years later, of course, the market began its real swoon, turning into a three-year bear market.

Similarly, just before the recession that started in December 2007, the Graham-Dodd approach showed a sobering picture. Based on average profits over the previous 10 years, the P/E ratio hovered around 27, higher than at any other point over 130 years, save the great bubbles of the 1920s and the 1990s.

—David Leonhardt

The Virtues of Diversifying
Hold bonds, don't check your portfolio daily

The search for wisdom in personal finance will take you sooner or later to John C. Bogle, who founded the Vanguard Group, created the first index mutual fund and who still preaches the gospel of long-term, low-cost, diversified investing.

Bogle is armed with statistics showing that a vast majority of investors—including most professional investment managers—should not even bother trying to pick individual stocks. They are just not very good at it, he says. Better to invest in the broad market through index funds with low costs, allowing the shareholders, and not the investment managers, to profit when times are good. (See "Why You Can't Beat the Market" on page 210.)

As for trying to time the ups and downs of the market, Bogle contends that the chances of being right over any extended period are so negligible that it's a fool's errand to try.

For simple, straightforward reasons, when stock prices look attractive, it is a very good time to put money into stocks—not for short-term trades, mind you, but as part of a diversified portfolio that you hold for many years.

There is one big exception: "If you cannot afford to lose another penny, then you simply have no recourse but to get out of the stock market," Bogle says.

Stocks can always fall, and if you aren't in a position to absorb losses, you must protect yourself. And retirees should hold a big dollop of bonds, which generate income and provide ballast in a shaky market. But long-term investors who can afford to wait a decade or more before cashing out generally have good outcomes.

Of course, that doesn't mean you should put all of your holdings into stocks—"unless you're just starting out in investing and you're very young, and you have very little to lose, and an awful lot to gain," Bogle says. Everyone needs to examine their particular situations and tailor an individual strategy, of course. But there are some rules of thumb to "keep you out of trouble," as Bogle puts it. Following is his advice on diversifying and allocating your assets.

● **TIMELY TIPS**

How to Invest—in Just 7 Words

✔ Investing is simple. It can be boiled down to this seven-word mantra:
- **Index—mostly.**
- **Save a ton.**
- **Reallocate infrequently.**

✔ For most of us, the hardest part of the mantra to accept is investing in index mutual funds and similar vehicles and sticking with them. There are about 7,500 stocks on the three major exchanges in the United States and roughly 8,000 mutual funds. It would seem that with such an array of choices, we should be able to create portfolios that can outperform the market averages.

The fact is, besting the overall market in most investment classes is nearly impossible over long periods of time. Sure, it may be fun to try. But if you enjoy that sort of thing, do it with a tiny piece of your portfolio. And remember to call it what it actually is: gambling.

✔ Most of us should save as much as we can in a collection of low-cost index funds. Divide the money among stocks, bonds and other investments according to your time horizon and risk tolerance. Then adjust that allocation only occasionally. Opinions vary on the frequency, but most experts agree that adjusting the mix more often than every 6 to 12 months is unnecessary and possibly costly.

—Ron Lieber

Hold bonds—preferably in a truly diversified, low-cost index fund, and in an allocation roughly equal, in percentage terms, to your age. If you're 50, for example, consider holding 50 percent bonds and 50 percent stocks. This is simplistic, and of course you need to look at your own situation, he says, adjusting the bond proportion up or down depending on your needs and level of risk-aversion.

Once you've set up a conservative, balanced, broadly diversified portfolio, put in place a way to add to it regularly. Then, let it be. Don't check your returns daily. Unless you're a market pro and maybe even if you are, daily market averages are mainly distractions without much meaning or use, says Bogle.

The ideal investor, Bogle says, would methodically put money into, for instance, a 401(k) invested in index funds that track the overall bond and stock markets at minimal cost, adjusting appropriately over time but otherwise forgetting about it.

If long-term investors stick to the basics, "put blinders on" and try to have "strong stomachs," says Bogle, they can ride out any rough patches and ultimately prosper.

—Jeff Sommert

Advice from Omaha's Oracle

A guru on stocks, librarians and other secrets

Warren Buffett, chairman of the Omaha-based holding company Berkshire Hathaway, Inc., is famous both for his spectacular investment acumen and his folksy, commonsense approach to choosing stocks. He is also the richest person in the nation, worth $62 billion in 2009, according to *Forbes* magazine. With an initial investment of $100,000 at the age of 25, Buffett built a business empire that includes financial companies, insurance giant GEICO and a stable of 60 other brands.

Here are some gems of investment wisdom gleaned from published interviews and Buffett's letters to shareholders in Berkshire Hathaway annual reports.

Pick businesses you understand. That means simple, stable companies. No one can predict future cash flows of complex, quickly changing businesses. "What counts for most people in investing is not how much they know, but rather how realistically they define what they don't know. An investor needs to do very few things right as long as he or she avoids big mistakes."

Hang on tight. Hold on to a security as long as "the prospective return on equity capital of the underlying business is satisfactory, management is competent and honest and the market does not overvalue the business."

Be skeptical of past performance. "If history books were the key to riches, the Forbes 400 would consist of librarians."

Pessimism can be a good thing. It produces low stock prices. "It's optimism that is the enemy of the rational buyer."

Beware of pumped-up, short-term earnings. And of managers who don't deliver for long periods and blame it on their long-term view. "Even Alice, after listening to the queen lecture her about 'jam tomorrow,' finally insisted, 'It must come sometimes to jam today.'"

When index funds make sense. By periodically investing in an index fund, "the know-nothing investor can actually outperform most investment professionals. Paradoxically, when 'dumb' money acknowledges its limitations, it ceases to be dumb."

When diversification makes no sense. An investor who understands the economics of, say, five or ten reasonably priced companies is better off putting more money into "the businesses he understands best and that present the least risk, along with the greatest profit potential," rather than diversifying.

Going for the Dividends

The case for investing in companies that pay out dividends

Companies that can increase their payouts even during a tough economy may be a good target for a time-tested conservative investment strategy: buying shares of solid dividend-payers.

Over the long run, this approach has outperformed the stock market. Since the end of 1979, investing in dividend-paying stocks in the S.&P. 500 would have earned you 11.6 percent a year, on average, on a total return basis, versus 10.5 percent for the overall index. And the ability to sustain dividends is often regarded as a sign of a solid company, with strong management.

Dividend increases usually outnumber cuts in the S.&P. 500, partly because under normal economic conditions, only a handful of companies have to resort to pulling the plug on their payouts. In 2007, for example, there were only 12 decreases to 298 increases. Even in 2008, a terrible one for the financial sector, which once supplied a huge percentage of corporate dividends, there were 62 cuts to 241 increases.

But predicting the outlook for dividends is tricky. That's why market strategists suggest spreading one's dividend bets across the broad market, rather than concentrating on just a handful of sectors.

In addition to seeking greater diversification, investors might look to stocks that have consistently managed to raise their dividends over several years, rather than just gravitating toward stocks with the biggest cash payments. That's partly because companies that have the financial wherewithal to consistently raise dividends are likely to have strong cash flows and balance sheets.

—Paul J. Lim

INSIDE INFO

The Bull That Follows the Bear

Assume you are fully invested in stocks, a bear market has just ended and stocks are on the verge of a multiyear rally. What kind of ride are you in for?

○ **Historically, the first year** of a new bull market comes with a surge—a 38 percent climb in the S.&P. on average since World War II.

○ **In the second year** of a bull market, stocks tend to rise by around 11 percent.

○ **In year 3,** prices historically rise 4 percent. So, a $60,000 investment in the first year of a bull market could turn into $100,000 by the fourth year.

—Paul J. Lim

Pick the Stock or the Moment?

Timing the market is everything. Or is it?

Fortunes are made on foreseeing swings in the stock market. But a knack for picking the right stocks and holding on through thick and thin has also proved valuable. So does it make sense for ordinary investors to try to predict a market top or bottom?

Opponents of timing point to studies that show how much worse returns would have been, compared to returns from buying and holding, if investors had been out of stocks on certain important dates. Say you invested $1,000 in the S.&P. 500 at the end of September 1988 and stayed invested for 20 years. Your compounded return would come to $6,573. If you had missed the top 10 days, your return would have shrunken to $3,300, according to Ned Davis Research.

Of course, the reverse is true also. If you had hit the best 10 days your returns would have soared, but what are the chances of any investor having

such exquisite timing? Not great. In general, says Catherine D. Gordon, head of the investment policy group at the Vanguard fund management firm, market timing is a bad idea because "you have to be right on both sides of the decision, when to move in and when to move out," and picking those right moments is difficult.

There are other difficulties, too, such as the drag on timers' returns in the way of fees and commissions. While you may possibly limit commissions and other charges by using index funds, capital gains on fund sales are taxable. Timers argue that if they have capital gains tax to pay, it means that they are achieving capital gains. And while knowing the exact moment to trade would be ideal, they say, just getting close should be good enough to beat a buy-and-hold strategy, and with less risk.

Some experts suggest a middle approach, not quite timing, or buying and holding, but rather allocating assets. A reasonable asset allocation, many advisers say, is 60 percent to stocks and 40 percent to bonds. A number of mutual funds use a similar strategy, providing ways to allocate reasonably and doing it in a disciplined way. That can come in handy, given that markets don't always follow expectations.

—Conrad de Aenlle

As January, So Goes the Year

Why investing clichés are often right

Wall Street is paved with truisms. One favorite is that January is a barometer of the year's market health: if the S.&P. 500 index is up in January, the market average for the year will also rise, and vice versa. Since 1950, according to the Hirsch Organization (www.stocktradersalmanac. com), a publisher of financial newsletters and the annual investing calendar *Stock Trader's Almanac,* the indicator has predicted the annual course of the market with 91.4 percent accuracy, missing only five times in nearly 60 years.

There's no great mystery about why January is such an accurate barometer: it is the beginning of the year, when people set their forecasts for the months ahead; it's also the month in which the government budget is announced and when the president delivers his State of the Union message, laying out the year's national goals. Switch these events to any other month, and chances are the January barometer would switch, too.

Another old chestnut, "sell in May and go away," is also backed by investing data. Research finds remarkable average market gains for each month from November to April, going back to 1950. Hirsh's "best six months" strategy, for example, shows that over a half-century, the Dow gained 9,222 points during these six consecutive months, compared to 1,299 points during the May through October months. The market's sluggish performance through the summer months is generally credited to investors taking vacation, which dampens their interest in investing.

Also rooted in statistical reality is the so-called "Santa Claus rally," in which stocks tend to rise during the week after Christmas. Since 1950, this seven-day period has shown an average growth at least 1.4 percent greater than the S.&P. 500, Hirsch data show. One factor is investor psychology, reflecting the optimism typical of the holiday season.

How to Read a Balance Sheet

A short course by a noted investment authority

John Train is well known as the author of a bounty of business books, including *Money Masters of Our Time,* and is chairman of Montrose Advisors in New York City. In the following explanation,

which originally appeared in *Harvard* magazine, Train takes you on a guided tour of a corporate financial statement:

The most important single truth to grasp about investing is that when you buy a share of stock you become a partner in a business. The essence of investing is thus understanding businesses, companies.

Company events are reported in dollar terms. To invest sensibly you therefore need to understand what the company is trying to tell you in its financial statement, which is published in a conveniently stylized form, like a sonnet. Though the elements are fairly simple, I observe that many of my clients have trouble reading one. So here is a simple guide to help get started. A company's financial statement comes in four parts: the balance sheet, the income statement, the cash flow statement and the statement of shareholders' equity.

The balance sheet is in essence a financial snapshot of the company at one moment in time, the end of its fiscal year. It is generally brought up to date each quarter thereafter.

The income (or profit and loss) statement shows how the business did during the preceding period; that is, sales minus costs.

The cash flow statement shows where cash came from and what it was used for. The amounts don't quite match those on the income statement, which includes, for example, purchases or sales on credit, where cash has not yet changed hands.

The statement of shareholders' equity tells how much the company's book value rose or fell during the period, whether because it made or lost money or took in new capital by selling stock. If the company made money, this statement will show how much of the profit was put back into the business and how much was paid out to shareholders.

A company's financial statement ordinarily includes an auditor's opinion. A "qualified" opinion often indicates trouble.

The balance sheet is called that because it is set up to balance, like an equation: there's an implied equal sign between the two parts. On the left (or "asset") side you show all the assets in the company at that moment—what it owns—and on the right (or "liability") side you show all the company's debt—what it owes—plus the money that has been put up by the owners and kept in the business: the "shareholders' equity." If you think about it, the money you have invested in a house—your equity—plus the mortgage—a debt—perforce corresponds to the physical structure: the asset.

Here is an example. Let's suppose the shareholders of a company put up $1 million, which goes to buy $1 million worth of gold. A simplified balance sheet would look like this:

ASSETS

GOLD	$1,000,000

LIABILITIES + SHAREHOLDERS' EQUITY

SHAREHOLDERS' EQUITY:	$1,000,000

Suppose we now borrow $1 million from the bank and buy an additional $1 million worth of gold. Our simplified balance sheet would then look like this:

ASSETS

GOLD	$2,000,000
	$2,000,000

LIABILITIES + SHAREHOLDERS' EQUITY

BANK DEBT	$1,000,000
SHAREHOLDERS' EQUITY	$1,000,000
	$2,000,000

In other words, the two sides of the equation still balance.

Good. Now suppose that during our first year of business the price of gold doubles, and we happily sell half our hoard for the original cost of the entire amount. Our simplified income statement now looks like this:

REVENUES	$2,000,000
LESS: COSTS OF GOODS SOLD*	$1,000,000
PROFIT BEFORE TAX	$1,000,000
LESS: PROVISION FOR TAXES	$250,000
NET INCOME	**$750,000**

* Sales are ordinarily shown on an accrual basis—that is, what you are committed to—rather than a cash basis (when you actually take in the money).

We can use this $750,000 of free cash to pay down the bank loan, pay ourselves a dividend, build up our shareholders' equity or buy back our own stock. Let's look at the first case. After paying taxes, we pay down the bank loan:

ASSETS

CASH	$1,000,000
GOLD (AT COST)*	$1,000,000
	$2,000,000

LIABILITIES + SHAREHOLDERS' EQUITY

BANK DEBT	250,000
SHAREHOLDERS' EQUITY	
COMMON STOCK	$1,000,000
RETAINED EARNINGS	$750,000

* At market: $2,000,000. Accounting principles require that you show the lower of cost or market value.

"Retained earnings" on the balance sheet is where you put money the company has earned and left in the business, not paid out in dividends.

Footnotes to the financial statements may

include information that does not show up in any of the numerical tables, such as pending litigation, company restructuring or prospective mergers. So always read the footnotes.

Perhaps the biggest difference between the way business professionals and nonprofessionals examine financial statements is that if you have actually been in business, you tend to look at the cash and equivalents, and at the cash flow section of the report. If a business is doing well, cash will be building up and can be put to work in useful ways: paying off debt, adding to plant, buying back the company's own shares in the market. If things are going badly, the company will be short of cash, bank and other debt will be rising and management will be run ragged coping with creditors instead of improving its products. (A hot growth company may also want cash because it has so many opportunities, but that's a more agreeable problem.)

After you have worked with financial statements for a while, you get in the habit of calculating the return on equity, how fast the inventory turns over, the operating profit margin and a hundred other things. The whole thing is a lot more fun than you might think. And consider this: even if you've only got this far, you're already well ahead of the mass of investors!

How Amateurs May Beat Pros

An investment club might outperform the market

Afraid to dip into the stock market alone? Then, an investment club, a group of like-minded people who pool their time, skills and money to research and invest in stocks, might be an option. There are nearly 10,000 clubs in the country, with 100,000 members holding an estimated $1.4 billion in investments. The average club portfolio is $132,000, with some $5 million in new money invested monthly by club members.

On average, investment clubs have generally outperformed market averages, according to the National Association of Investors Corporation (www.betterinvesting.org), the nonprofit group that provides support to investment clubs. During the decade ending 2007, the average club return was 13 percent (compared to 8.1 percent for the Standard & Poor's index). The stock-picking credo of investment clubs that are members of BetterInvesting is simple.

1. Invest a set amount regularly, once a month, for example, regardless of whether it's a bull or bear market.

2. Reinvest dividends and capital gains for compound growth. Don't sell unless the company really sours. One or two down quarters isn't enough to trigger a sell. As long as the company's underlying financials are healthy, it may still be a good time to buy.

3. Look for quality growth stocks, companies with sales and earning that are growing at a faster rate than the industry as a whole.

4. Diversify your portfolio to spread the risk. A balanced portfolio includes companies of various sizes from different industries and mutual funds from various categories.

To start your own investment club, find 10 to 15 members who can handle investigating and analyzing securities and making periodic reports. At the first meeting, set a monthly figure, say $10 to $100 per person, that each will invest. Choose an investment strategy; for instance, will the club buy stock for long-term gain or current income? Research and pick a broker or a discount brokerage firm. In many cases, you can buy stock directly from companies through dividend reinvestment plans, sidestepping commissions and management fees.

The National Association of Investors Corporation offers the clubs investment help, some of it free, in the form of financial materials, guidelines and an investor's manual on stockpicking, keeping tax records, and other basics.

Staying Ahead of the Curve

Where are bonds headed? Consult the yield curve

Should you buy a three-month T-bill, a 30-year bond or something in between? A look at the yield curve, found daily in the *New York Times* business pages, may provide the answer. A yield curve is a line that plots the interest rate paid by similar bonds with different maturities. The X-axis plots the length of time until the bonds mature. The Y-axis plots the yield of each bond. The average spread between the shortest-term and longest-term Treasuries is usually about two percentage points.

Reading the yield curve can be especially useful for long-term investing. If you have a shorter time frame—say, you'll need to cash in your bond in three years for a child's tuition—you should probably buy a bond that matures within that time period. Keep in mind, too, that interest rates and bond prices move in opposite directions: higher rates mean lower bond prices. Rising interest rates can play havoc on the bond market, when even the highest-quality bond

portfolio can lose value as interest rates climb. When rates start heading down, on the other hand, it's usually a good time to buy long-term bonds as a way to lock in current high yields.

A common misconception is that if a bond's yield is going up, the investment is worth more. It's just the opposite: when a bond's yield rises, its price has fallen because the increase in yield comes at the expense of the bond's market value. Conversely, if a bond's yield falls, its market value rises. Another risk: rising inflation, which can cut the worth of a bond's coupon payments and its eventual redemption value.

The yield curve usually slopes upward. That's because longer-term investments carry more risk and pay higher interest rates to compensate. When short- and long-term interest rates are roughly the same, the curve is flat. A thin spread means the market sees little difference between the short-term and long- term risks of inflation, so buying longer-term bonds gives you only a slight premium.

When short-term yields exceed long-term yields, the curve turns downward or inverts. An inverted curve usually means that a recession is coming. An inverted curve has predicted all recessions since 1950.

Some analysts say inverted curves also signal a buying opportunity for long-term bonds. In other words, when the economy softens and interest rates come down, you want to be in long-term bonds because eventually the curve will normalize and the value of long-term bonds will rise.

Ultra-Safe Investments to Consider

If you are about to retire or just risk-averse

If your tolerance for risk is low or you can't afford to gamble with funds you'll soon need for retirement, you may want to consider ultra-safe investments.

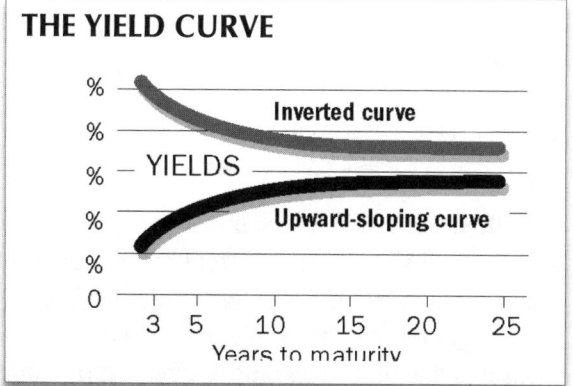

THE YIELD CURVE

Inverted curve

YIELDS

Upward-sloping curve

Years to maturity

MONEY

Certificates of deposit (C.D.'S). They pay a fixed interest rate but lock up money for three months to five years. Callable C.D.'s may offer higher yields, but that's because you are being paid more to take on extra risk: the bank can return your money before the C.D. matures and you may have to reinvest at a potentially lower rate. And keep in mind that C.D.'s will penalize you, sometimes substantially, if you withdraw before maturity. If you stick with C.D.'s be sure to shop around beyond your local bank for the best yields. Bankrate.com is a useful place to start.

F.D.I.C. Bonds. These government-backed bonds come with variable or fixed rates, and they tend to pay more than Treasuries. But before locking into these bonds, check whether there are comparable deals in C.D.'s.

Ginnie Mae. Not to be confused with Fannie or Freddie, Ginnie is owned by the government and issues securities that are backed by federally guaranteed or insured mortgages. Translation: these are safe. Several advisers recommend Ginnie Mae funds—or the actual securities—as a higher-yielding alternative to money-market funds. But there is a big caveat: If interest rates move higher, the value of these securities drops.

Pre-refunded Munis. These municipal bonds are solid options because the payments the bond issuer must make to investors over the life of the bond are held in an escrow fund, usually made up of U.S. government securities. The yields generally pay about two percentage points above Treasuries with a comparable maturity. Just be sure the collateral is Treasuries.

—Tara Siegel Bernard

OLDER BUT NO WISER

A study based on more than 75,000 accounts found that older investors tend to earn lower returns.

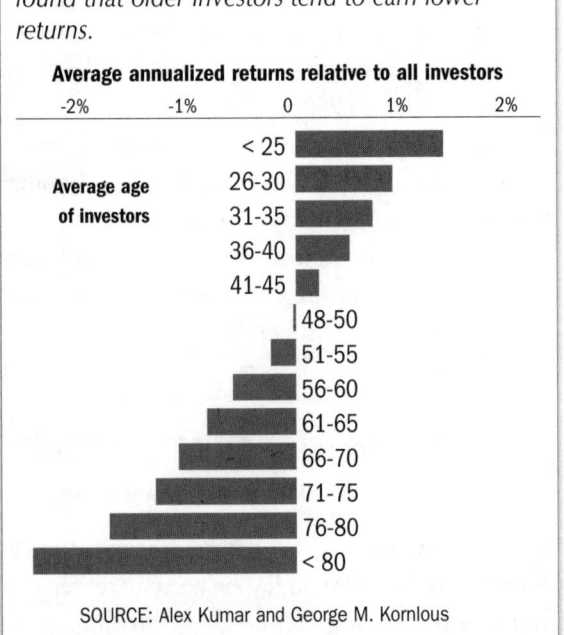

Average annualized returns relative to all investors

SOURCE: Alex Kumar and George M. Kornlous

How to Pick a Mutual Fund
There are lots of choices; here's what to focus on

Mutual fund investors can't make perfect choices every time—too many variables are stacked against them: compiling the ideal portfolio, buying into a fund at precisely the right time and bailing out precisely before the wrong time. But investors can stay a step ahead and avoid serious blunders by knowing the basics of analyzing a mutual fund's performance. There are 8,000-odd mutual funds in the United States, with some $8 trillion in assets. It pays to know what you're getting into. Here are a few basics in evaluating a fund.

RETURN. Many investors obsess over a fund's yield, which tells you the current income distributed annually. But the true test of any fund, even one bought for income, is total return. Total return measures the increases and decreases of your investment over time, assuming the reinvestment of dividends and subtracting the fund's costs. You can find a fund's total return by calling the fund company's toll-free number.

When you compare total returns of several funds, be sure they are from comparable time periods, say January 1 to December 31. Determine, too, whether or not sales charges and other fees have been deducted from total returns. Then, compare the returns annually and, say, over five years or since the fund's inception. If most of the cumulative gains occurred in the most recent years, you're looking at a fund that could burn out.

RISK. It isn't easy to calculate or compare how much risk a mutual fund assumes, but getting an idea of risk is important. A few statistical measures that give an idea of a fund's risk include a fund's alpha, beta and standard deviation. Alpha reports how much the fund's performance deviated from its expected return. A fund with a positive alpha did better than expected. A negative alpha means the fund underperformed.

Beta measures the volatility of a fund's return against an index, such as the S.&P. 500. Aggressive investors prefer funds with a beta above 1.0, which means the fund's returns have moved up and down more than the S.&P. as a whole. A more conservative choice would be a fund with a .75 beta, for example, meaning that the fund is more stable than the market, generally and in the long run.

Academics especially like a risk measure called standard deviation. It gauges how widely a fund's return swings from one time period to another. A fund with volatile returns is supposedly more likely to show a big loss in the future.

INVESTMENT STYLE AND MIX. Two funds can fall under the same general investment category but have different styles that affect their performance. The reason: interpretations of terms such as "aggres-

---

✅ **TIMELY TIPS**

Where to Go for Stock Info

Many firms offer independent stock research, but relatively few focus on individual investors. Here are some that do:

✔ **MORNINGSTAR**   *www.morningstar.com*
Companies covered: 2,000   **Mutual funds:** 2,000
Annual cost: $174
Free info: Stock screens and some stock reports

✔ **NATIONAL ASSOCIATION OF INVESTORS CORPORATION**   *www.betterinvesting.org*
Companies covered: 7,000   **Mutual funds:** 20,000
Annual cost: $79
Free info: Basic corporate information

✔ **STANDARD & POOR'S**
   www.standardandpoors.com
Companies covered: 2,000   **Mutual funds:** 18,000
Annual cost: $199
Free info: Stock snapshots and top recommended buys and sells

✔ **VALUE LINE**   *www.valueline.com*
Companies covered: 8,700   **Mutual funds:** 10,000
Annual cost: $995 for access to entire research center
Free info: Reports on the 30 stocks in the Dow industrials; some investing feature stories

—Donna Rosato

---

sive growth" may vary from fund to fund. The prospectus will give you a precise explanation of a fund's strategy and investment objective. (Funds often change their investment style or management team, making past performance an unreliable measure.) Check out a fund's mix of investments, too. Exposure to a vulnerable industry or to volatile foreign stocks can go a long way toward explaining a fund's performance.

MONEY

LEVERAGE. Many funds hedge against possible changes in interest rates or currency values with strategies that may be risky. Be sure you're comfortable with a fund's hedging strategy. Can the fund invest in risky derivatives, fill up on Latin American stocks, sell short? Often, the techniques help returns, but just as often they can cause deep losses. Scrutinize the prospectus.

TAXES. Don't ignore the tax implications of buying a particular fund, but don't get carried away by potential tax bills, either. No doubt about it, taxes can take the fun out of a mutual fund gain. If you're shopping for a tax-free fund, avoid those that post most of their income in gains. If you're buying stock funds, find out when the fund posts its annual gains, usually at year-end, and wait until after it has done so to buy in.

But don't pick a fund just for its tax advantages. Studies show that there's not much change in equity-fund rankings on an after-tax basis, so, investors should focus on performance first, not taxes. The tax analysis helps if you're deciding between two similar funds with comparable gross returns.

Why You Can't Beat the Market
A market guru makes the case for index funds

Why search for just the right stock fund or manager when you can do better by investing in an unmanaged index fund? That's the question posed by proponents of index funds, which buy the stocks in the Standard & Poor's 500 to get the same performance as the index. Critics of index funds ask,

> A blindfolded chimpanzee throwing darts at the stock market pages could select a portfolio that would do as well as the experts.

Burton Malkiel,
author of *A Random Walk Down Wall Street* and Princeton University professor of economics

● ● ●

"why settle for mediocrity when you could hit a fund that soars?"

Princeton University economist Burton Malkiel, author of the classic investment book *A Random Walk Down Wall Street* (the 9th edition was published in 2007) and a long-time champion of index fund investing, answers those questions. Here are his views on index funds.

Q **Are index funds all they're cracked up to be?**

I have argued for around 35 years that an indexing strategy—simply buying and holding the hundreds of stocks making up the broad stock market averages—is probably the most sensible one for individuals and institutional investors. With index funds, investors can buy different types of stocks and get the benefits of stock and bond investing with no effort, minimal expenses, and big tax savings.

Q **How have index funds performed"**

Over the past 35 years, the Standard & Poor's 500 Index has outperformed about three-quarters of active investment managers and has done well compared to other indexes, too, like the Dow-Wishire 5000 Stock Index.

Q **Which index funds do you like?**

Indexing isn't simply buying the S.&P. 500. I actually prefer funds that match other indexes, such as the broader Dow-Wilshire 5000. Some good values may exist in small-cap stocks, in real estate investment trusts and in foreign equities. Funds that match those indexes have also generally outperformed actively managed funds that invest in similar securities.

Q Do index funds simply guarantee mediocrity, as critics say?

Well, you can't boast about the fantastic gains you've made by picking stock market winners. But index fund investors are likely to get better results than those of the typical fund manager, whose huge fees and large portfolio turnover reduce returns. To many, the guarantee of playing at par with the stock market every time is very attractive.

Mutual Fund Lingo to Master

How to tell one fund from another

Do you know the difference between a "load" and a "no-load" fund? What's a "growth and income fund" or an "aggressive growth" fund? Terms and interpretations vary within the industry and even from firm to firm; the definitions below are from the Investment Company Institute, the trade association for the mutual fund industry. Before you pick a mutual fund, read the prospectus for a precise explanation of the fund's strategy and investment objective. Here are some terms you're likely to stumble across as you pore over the fine print.

Aggressive growth fund. A fund that seeks maximum capital gains. Current income is not a significant factor. Some invest in out-of-the-mainstream businesses, such as fledgling companies, or new or temporarily out-of-favor industries; some invest in techniques such as short-term trading.

Asset allocation fund. A fund that invests in a variety of different asset classes with the goal of providing diversification and consistent returns.

Back-end load. A sales commission charged when you sell your shares in a mutual fund. Usually ranges from 0.5 to 6.0 percent.

Balanced fund. Generally has a three-part investment objective: to conserve investors' initial principal, to pay current income and to promote long-term growth of both principal and income. Balanced funds mix bonds, preferred stocks and common stocks.

Corporate bond fund. Purchases mainly bonds of corporations for the majority of portfolio. The rest may be in U.S. Treasury bonds or bonds issued by a federal agency.

Derivatives. Financial instruments with values linked to some underlying asset, such as a bond, stock or index.

Emerging market fund. Invests primarily in the equity securities of companies in, or doing business in, emerging countries and markets.

Environmental securities fund. Generally invests in environment-related firms. May include companies dealing with hazardous waste treatment, waste recycling and such. Some of the funds may screen companies to determine whether they also meet specific social objectives.

Flexible portfolio fund. A fund that may be 100 percent invested in stocks, bonds or money-market instruments, depending on market conditions. These funds give the money managers the greatest flexibility in anticipating or responding to economic changes.

Front-end load. A sales commission charged when you buy your shares, usually in the range of 1 to 3 percent of your investment.

Ginnie Mae or G.N.M.A. Fund. Invests the majority of its portfolio in mortgage securities backed by the Government National Mortgage Association (G.N.M.A.). To qualify for this category, the majority of the portfolio must always be invested in mortgage-backed securities.

How to Estimate Total Return

Figuring out how much your fund is making

Following your mutual fund's performance in the newspaper alone won't tell you how you're really doing. The quickest and easiest way to learn your fund's total annual return is to call the fund's toll-free number. But, if you'd rather do it yourself, you'll need to know three things to start:

1. The fund's net-asset value per share a year ago.
2. Its NAV now.
3. Distributions per share of dividends and capital gains in the interim.

You should be able to find all this information on your account statement.

Here's how to do the calculation:

Say that your fund's net asset value as of the end of last year was $50 per share. A year later, its NAV was $60. During the year, it distributed $5 per share in income and capital gains. Subtract the starting NAV from the ending NAV and add the distributions to that sum. The result—$15—is the total return in dollars.

Now convert this amount to a percentage by dividing the total return by the starting NAV and multiplying by 100.

Example: $15 divided by $50 X 100 = 30%

Note that this result, while not as precise as one produced by more complicated formulas, is a fairly accurate estimate.

Global equity fund. Invests in securities traded worldwide, including the U.S. Global funds are an easier way to invest abroad than direct investments. Professional money managers handle trading, record-keeping details and differences in currencies, languages, time zones, regulations and business customs. Global funds add another layer of risk—the exchange rate factor.

Growth and income fund. Invests mainly in the common stock of companies that have had increasing share value, as well as a solid record of paying dividends. Attempts to combine long-term capital growth with a steady stream of income.

High-yield bond fund. Maintains at least two-thirds of its portfolio in lower-rated corporate bonds (Baa or lower by Moody's rating service and BBB or lower by Standard and Poor's rating service). In return for generally higher yield, investors bear a greater degree of risk than for higher-rated bonds.

Income-bond fund. Seeks a high level of current income by investing at all times in a mix of corporate and government bonds.

Income-equity fund. Invests primarily in equity securities of companies with good dividend-paying records.

Income-mixed fund. Invests in income-producing securities, including both equities and debt instruments.

Index funds. Construct portfolios to mirror a specific market index. They are expected to provide a rate of return that will approximate or match, but not exceed, that of the market they are mirroring. Index funds offer investment choices that include various stock market indexes or indexes of international or bond portfolios.

Load. A fee or commission imposed by a mutual fund. Some loads are a flat percentage; others are based on the amount you invest or how long you remain in the fund. A load can be as high as 8.5 percent. Low loads run between 1 and 3 percent.

Mutual fund. Pools shareholder cash to invest in a variety of securities, including stocks, bonds and money market instruments.

NAV or net asset value. The market value of one share of a mutual fund, calculated at the close of each business day.

No-load fund. Mutual fund that doesn't charge a fee or commision to buy or sell its shares.

Redemption fee. One to 2 percent charge when you sell your shares. Often waived if you hold shares for a given number of years.

Small company growth fund. Seeks aggressive growth of capital by investing primarily in equity securities of small companies—usually in the developing stages of their life cycle—with rapid-growth potential. Shares of such companies are often thinly traded and may be subject to more abrupt market movements than those of larger firms.

Specific social objectives fund. Screens companies for compliance with certain social or ethical criteria in addition to using traditional measures of financial value when choosing securities for its portfolio.

Taxable money market fund. Invests in the short-term, high-grade securities sold in the money market. Generally the safest, most stable securities available, including Treasury bills, certificates of deposit of large banks and commercial paper (the short-term IOUs of large U.S. corporations).

Tax-exempt money market fund. Invests in municipal securities with relatively short maturities. Investors who use them seek tax-free investments with minimum risk.

U.S. government income fund. Invests in a variety of government securities, including U.S. Treasury bonds, federally guaranteed mortgage-backed securities and other government notes.

Variable annuities. Insurance products, mainly used for retirement income, that offer investors some advantages of mutual funds in addition to tax-deferred earnings.

Just How Safe Are Mutual Funds?

Do mutual fund investors have cause to worry that their nest eggs could disappear? There are no guarantees, of course, but compared with investors in hedge funds or other alternative instruments, mutual fund investors have less cause for concern.

For one thing, mutual funds are pretty well protected from fraud. "There is much greater transparency in reporting and oversight," says Russel Kinnel, director of research at Morningstar. "They don't hold their own securities, and they don't ask you to take it on faith."

That said, a declining market, poor investment decisions and high fees can eviscerate fund performance. As for guarding against huge losses in a declining market, there's little to be done.

The key is to look for good, solid managers. Some experts like exchange-traded funds that passively track the broad market, as trying to beat the market is no easy feat.

Investors can also lose money by paying a lot in expenses. Funds post their expense ratios, which should be compared carefully. In addition, people who buy funds through brokers should take care to note sales fees. Ask your broker whether his or her compensation is from selling you a certain class of shares vs. another class of shares.

Keep an eye on companies that were involved in market-timing scandals earlier this decade. While market timing itself is legal, it is discouraged by most major fund companies because it can involve profit-taking by a few at the expense of a majority of shareholders.

Roy Weitz, who runs Fundalarm.com, a mutual fund watchdog, says he keeps his investment decisions simple by avoiding any funds that have gotten into trouble in a major scandal. Among the fund families he prefers are T. Rowe Price, American Funds and Vanguard.

—Geraldine Fabrikant

MONEY

Beware of Mutual Fund Taxes

Mutual funds seem simple, until it's time to sell

For such a conceptually simple way to invest—people pooling their assets for professionals to manage—mutual funds pose a remarkably complex set of issues for taxpayers. Investors who buy and sell mutual fund shares face an assortment of tax issues. Here are some tax-smart recommendations from financial planners.

- PUT high-tax investments in tax-advantaged accounts. Remember that switching funds, even within the same fund family, can have tax consequences. Such a swap outside an individual retirement account or 401(k) is actually a sale and purchase for tax purposes, though commissions are generally waived.

- AVOID buying shares late in the year, so you are not liable for taxes on gains in which you did not participate; sell before the distribution date. Conversely, sales that are to be minimally taxed should precede this date, which for most funds occurs in the last several weeks of the year.

- CONSIDER taking distributions in cash rather than reinvesting them in new fund shares. That will simplify bookkeeping.

- EVALUATE the various methods of determining the cost basis of shares before making what will be a permanent commitment. One option is to use the average cost of your shares—a method that can be used for mutual fund sales but not for those of individual stocks. Average cost is the most commonly used method, and most fund groups routinely calculate and provide this figure for you. If you are looking to minimize the tax hit of a sale, however, the best method is the most flexible one: the designation of specific shares. Keeping track of specific lots of shares, of course, requires assiduous bookkeeping.

- KEEP IN MIND the rules governing "wash" sales, which can make reinvestments, as well as repurchases, hazardous. These rules deny a deduction if you sell fund shares at a loss and then buy them back within 30 days. You can avoid this problem by reinvesting your money in a different fund, even one that invests in similar kinds of stocks and bonds.

—Robert D. Hershey Jr.

Finding a Broker You Can Trust

Tips for picking a good stock picker

After careful consideration of your financial goals, and the realization that you could use help implementing them, you're ready to pick the broker who will take your money and make it grow. But where do you start?

✓ **TIMELY TIPS**

Is Financial Help Worth the Cost?

✔ Yes, it may well be worth it. Investing is only one part of your financial life. There are also mortgages, taxes, college savings, insurance, debt and more. Perhaps the best thing a versatile professional—whether it is a financial planner, accountant, stockbroker or lawyer—does is provide discipline. It is difficult to get most of this stuff right, and get it done at the right time. Professionals help make sure it all happens on schedule.

✔ True, many financial planners charge 1 percent of a client's assets annually for advice. So if you have $200,000 saved for retirement, that's $2,000 a year. Still, the wisdom and discipline that a professional can provide could boost investment performance at least 1 percent, thus justifying the annual fee.

—Ron Lieber

Consider this advice from Arthur Levitt Jr., a former broker and the longest-serving chairman of the Securities and Exchange Commission.

Ask tough questions. The important thing in picking a broker is to look him or her in the eye and ask some tough questions. What is the broker's philosophy on how best to meet your goals? Has the broker ever been disciplined for wrongdoing? Does the broker seem more interested in selling you a stock than getting to know your financial situation and your future financial needs? Ask questions that will help you determine if the chemistry is right and whether the broker will always put your interests first.

Find out how your broker gets paid. Typically, brokers are paid by commissions that reward them for the quantity of business they do, not for the quality. Ask your broker, "Do you make more if I buy this mutual fund, for example, than if I buy this stock?" Some brokerage firms allow you to pay a flat fee based on the amount of your assets under management. Ask the broker if you would be better off paying a flat fee or a commission.

Determine if your broker is getting you the best price. When your broker quotes you the price at which he'll sell you a stock or bond, ask how much he'd pay to buy it from you. The difference is the spread. You should ask your broker whether you could get a better price for a stock if you place a "limit" order, which specifies a price that falls in the middle of the spread. Also ask your broker if you could get a better price if he routed your order to a particular exchange or another market.

Ask your broker for investment records. Your broker can get key data about the financial health of municipal bond issuers from national or state information centers. For example, your broker can find out if the bond issuer is delinquent on

---

TIMELY TIPS

A Broker by Any Other Name...

✔ Only two types of designations are regulated: broker-dealers (stockbrokers) and registered investment advisers (financial planners). Brokers, who facilitate buying and selling stocks and bonds, report to the Financial Industry Regulatory Authority (FINRA), the industry's self-regulating organization. Financial planners, who provide services such as tax and estate planning and advice on building financial plans, report to the Securities and Exchange Commission.

✔ Watch out for "brokers" with baffling titles like C.S.A. (certified senior advisers). Fancy initials could mean little more than that they attended a one-time seminar. To understand the alphabet soup after a financial adviser's name, check the the FINRA Web site (www.finra.org) for the meanings of professional credentials.

✔ Web sites of organizations, such as the Certified Financial Planner Board of Standards at www.cfp.net, and the National Association of Personal Financial Advisors at www.napfa.org, provide lists of financial planners across the country.

—Coeli Carr

---

principal or interest payments, if its ratings have been downgraded or if it has lost its tax-exempt status. Be sure to ask for this information.

Check out your broker's personal record. Before you hire a broker, check out his record on the FINRA Web site at www.finra.org under "BrokerCheck," or contact your state securities regulator (you can find a link at www.nasaa.org or call: 202-737-0900). Also, scrutinize your account statements for transactions that you didn't authorize, excessive commissions and delays in executing orders. Complain if you suspect wrongdoing.

MONEY

What to do if you run into a bad broker. Most stockbrokers are honest, but if you think you've encountered an unethical one, file a complaint with the S.E.C. online at www.sec.gov (click on "Investor Information"), by fax at 202-772-9295 or mail to S.E.C Complaint Center, 100 F St., N.E., Washington, D.C 20549. The S.E.C. uses "tips" from investors to keep securities markets free from fraud and from bad brokers and financial planners. Report any problems promptly to the branch officer or the firm's compliance officer as well as to FINRA at 866-397-3290.

How to settle a broker dispute. Most investors agree to arbitrate disputes when they sign a customer agreement with a brokerage firm, so arbitration is the main route for settling disputes. You can file for arbitration with FINRA, the New York Stock Exchange (212-656-3000 or www.nyse.com), other exchanges or the American Arbitration Association (www.adr.org/fileacase).

Reducing Your Investment Taxes

Strategies for keeping taxes to a minimum

Asset allocation is one thing: you divide your investments among different kinds of assets—stocks, bonds, real estate, cash—to optimize your returns and minimize your risk. But with asset *location* you determine which securities to keep in your taxable accounts and which should be kept in your sheltered accounts, such as 401(k)'s and individual retirement accounts. The aim is to stop taxes from reducing your returns.

Although creating a strategy for determining the best type of placement for your assets is complex, the idea is intuitive:

- Shelter assets that are taxed at ordinary income rates, like bonds that generate interest income

or actively managed stock mutual funds that produce short-term capital gains, so you get the benefit of the entire return from these investments, which compound tax-deferred until you begin withdrawals.

- Individual stocks that you plan to hold, stocks that produce dividend income, index and exchange-traded funds that generate long-term capital gains and tax-free municipal bonds belong in taxable accounts.

Do it right and your long-term performance will benefit. According to Vanguard, the mutual fund company, after 10 years an investor who started with $1 million split evenly between taxable bonds in the sheltered accounts and index equity funds in the taxable accounts would have had $1,694,671. An investor who did just the opposite would have had $1,531,413—or 9.6 percent less.

Sounds pretty simple, but in practice most people discover that their assets are in the wrong accounts. The most common mistake is to put too many equity investments in sheltered accounts, with the expectation that returns on growth investments will be greater if they increase tax-deferred. But equities produce dividends and long-term capital gains, which are taxed at 15 percent. Put them in the sheltered account, and you'll be paying ordinary income taxes on them when you withdraw the money.

Take a look at your overall portfolio to see where you have placed your high-tax and low-tax investments; that is, what's in the taxable accounts and what's in the sheltered accounts.

Start with the fixed income in your sheltered accounts. Ideally, it would all be in taxable bonds or bond funds where you can benefit from deferring ordinary income taxes on the higher yields. The exception is any short-term debt you might have as a liquidity reserve that would belong in your taxable portfolio for easy access.

If there is space left in your sheltered accounts, you would use it for high-turnover stock mutual funds that throw off short-term capital gains, real estate investment trusts whose dividends are also taxed at ordinary rates and individual stocks you plan to trade a lot.

Now take a look at your taxable accounts. If you were not able or chose not to put your entire fixed income allocation into the sheltered portfolio, you would have added tax-free municipal bonds or bond funds to the taxable one. Along with bonds, there would be individual stocks that you plan to keep, dividend-paying stocks, low-turnover mutual funds and passive investments like index funds or exchange-traded funds.

In reality, because you have been making investments in both of your portfolios for a number of years, they are probably much less tax efficient. So you will need to reposition them. That takes time because you cannot shift assets from one type of account to another, which means you have to buy and sell separately in each portfolio. You can rearrange your sheltered accounts with no tax penalty. But selling individual stocks

in taxable accounts will create capital gains or losses; selling your mutual funds might, too. In taxable and nontaxable accounts, there will be transaction costs.   —Julie Connelly

Planning a Retirement Portfolio
Having enough cash to meet living expenses

Regardless of the vagaries of the economy, a retired investor needs liquidity. Retirees should have enough cash or equivalents like Treasury bills or money-market funds in either regular or retirement accounts to meet basic living expenses for one to three years.

Those age 70½ or older need enough liquidity in their retirement accounts to take required minimum distributions without having to sell securities at an unpropitious time, during a bear market, for example.

Investors with adequate liquid assets and a balanced, diversified portfolio of stocks, Treasury bonds and investment-grade corporate bonds are in a good long-term position, regardless of the market

TIMELY TIPS

Making Your I.R.A. Work for You

✔ Many retirees make the mistake of not contributing to their I.R.A.'s as long as possible.

✔ Retirees in their 60s can contribute to traditional I.R.A.'s as long as they have earned income.

✔ Retirees 70 and older are not allowed to contribute to traditional I.R.A.'s, but they can still contribute to Roth I.R.A.'s if their adjusted gross income falls within the limits for that tax year.

✔ Taxpayers have until April 15 of the tax year to make contributions to a traditional or a Roth I.R.A.
                                        —Alex Tarquinio

outlook. But people whose I.R.A.'s or 403(b) or 401(k) plans are invested entirely in stocks or stock mutual funds may need to make some adjustments during down markets.

Much depends, of course, on whether other sources of retirement income are available. Retirees with Social Security and a defined-benefit pension plan as well as a 401(k) can be more aggressive in their 401(k) selections than people without them.

In structuring a portfolio, retirees shouldn't gamble with what they need for everyday living. They should choose conservative investments to pay for basic living expenses and be a bit more aggressive when saving for discretionary expenditures.

Some target-date mutual funds, those in which you tell the fund manager when you want to retire and the mix of investments is reallocated for you, may be too aggressive an investment to protect funds for basic needs. Instead, a fixed life annuity (a type of insurance that provides an income for a given period of time) if available through an employer plan, could be an appropriate part of a retirement portfolio.

The fixed-income annuity within a retirement plan is for income accumulation. Then when you retire, you can convert it to a lifetime income annuity, which distributes payments regularly to you during the course of your lifetime.

An annuity would be appropriate for 30 to 40 percent of a retirement portfolio, experts say, not for the entire portfolio. The amount of income from a lifetime income annuity depends on the holder's sex, age and various options chosen. A 65-year-old man, for example, can begin a stream of income with a payout rate of more than 8.3 percent guaranteed for life. In other words, for every $100,000 paid as a premium, the annuitant would receive $8,334 a year, or $694.57 a month.

People interested in annuities should check that the insurance company is sound and also be aware that an annuity is a relatively illiquid investment. But it does provide a degree of certainty during times of market instability. —Jan M. Rosen

How Long Will Your Nest Egg Last?
How to calculate your retirement needs

How much can you take out of your retirement nest egg each year without running out of money? Not much, according to the standard, conservative advice of many financial planners. The common maxim is that people who retire at age 65 can safely remove only about 4 percent of their portfolios each year, along with adjustments for inflation. On that basis, the initial withdrawal from a portfolio worth $1 million would be just $40,000.

But some experts suggest that it may make more sense to withdraw bigger amounts in the early years of retirement. They argue that retirees generally spend less as they age, so that it's reasonable for them to spend more when they are in retirement's early stages.

Aside from health care, spending in practically every category, from housing to clothing to entertainment, declines with age, according to the Bureau of Labor Statistics Consumer Expenditure Survey. People over 75 spent 26 percent less, on average, than those in the 65-to-74 age group. And the older the retiree, the greater the difference in spending: those over 75 spent 46 percent less than those aged 55 to 64 and 51 percent less than those aged 45 to 54.

Traditional advice calls for an initial withdrawal of 4 percent. So, someone with a $1 million nest egg could take out $40,000 the first year and $41,200 the next year, for example, at withdrawal rates intended to leave very little

LIVE WELL, DIE POOR

Some financial savings calculators suggest that a couple earning $125,000 a year should have more than $2 million for retirement. Here is an example of how such a couple could save far less and yet maintain their standard of living as they grow old.

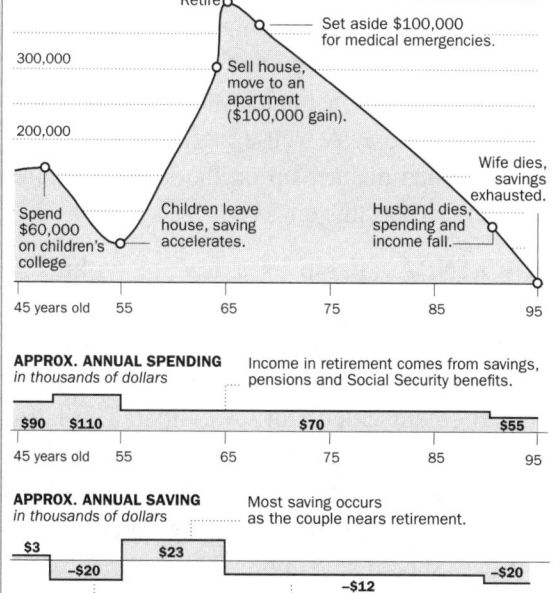

One view of optimal retirement savings

$400,000 saved

Retire

Set aside $100,000 for medical emergencies.

300,000

Sell house, move to an apartment ($100,000 gain).

200,000

Wife dies, savings exhausted.

Spend $60,000 on children's college

Children leave house, saving accelerates.

Husband dies, spending and income fall.

45 years old   55   65   75   85   95

APPROX. ANNUAL SPENDING
in thousands of dollars   Income in retirement comes from savings, pensions and Social Security benefits.

| $90 | $110 | $70 | $55 |

45 years old   55   65   75   85   95

APPROX. ANNUAL SAVING
in thousands of dollars   Most saving occurs as the couple nears retirement.

$3 $23
   –$20   –$12   –$20

Spending from savings occurs during during retirement and when the couple's children are at college.

SOURCE: B. Douglas Bernheim, Lorenzo Forni, Jagadeesh Gokhale and Laurence Kotlikoff, "Setting Retirement Savings Goals"   —*The New York Times*

chance of running out of money.

But in light of retirees' actual spending patterns, some experts argue, a couple in the first year of retirement at age 55, with expenditures of $60,000, might be able to safely withdraw that much from a portfolio worth $1 million—a 6 percent initial withdrawal rate. They would not run out of money as long as they reduced their spending later. Of course, a 6 percent withdrawal rate could vary because of many factors, including a retiree's spending level and the size of the nest egg.

In order to take out more than 4 percent that first year investors need to follow a few rules, according to to some financial planners. To generate income, they must always sell winning stocks before bonds or losing stocks. They cannot add more than 6 percent a year to their withdrawal even if inflation is higher than that. And no increases are permitted immediately after a year of investment losses.

These notions have their critics, of course. Many planners worry that medical costs, including prescription drugs and nursing home costs, may rise so fast that they will undo a well-constructed financial plan. They say people need to save more and withdraw less to hedge against these increases. A more conservative estimate of distribution might be in order. After all, you can't go back and say, "Oops. I shouldn't have taken out so much."

—Ilana Polyak

Are You Saving Too Little?

Online retirement calculators can help you

A bounty of online calculators and software programs can help you calculate your retirement needs.

First, you'll be asked lots of questions about your income, assets and retirement expectations. The two hardest things for most people to figure out on their own is how long they will live in retirement and how much risk they should take in their retirement investments.

The industry's rule of thumb for determining longevity is to add two years to what your parent of the same sex lived, if, of course, that parent died of a natural cause. But that rule needs to be stretched if you are fit and active and dad was not (and not terribly helpful if your parents are still living).

Here are some of the more popular sites and programs and how they can help with your retirement planning.

ESPLANNER. Rather than ask users how much money they want to have in retirement, the program (available at esplanner.com; 2009 price: $149-$199) finds the appropriate spending target for each user. ESPlanner can determine the financial consequences of a number of actions, including moving to a state with lower taxes (the program includes tax data for every state) or taking Social Security before a 401(k). It can determine whether someone is saving too much, resulting in higher-than-necessary taxes.

FIDELITY. The company's free Retirement Income Planner software uses a wide range of financial data to help people determine how much they can spend before the money runs out. Account assets of Fidelity customers are automatically loaded into the program. Sidebar tips help users understand the implications of variables. Users can vary such items as life expectancy and whether they wish to die with or without assets. Fidelity will suggest various mutual funds, including those marketed by other companies and offered through Fidelity's Funds Network program.

FIDELITY.COM has a free, easy online calculator called myPlan Snapshot. It asks five simple questions that require no research or digging up old brokerage statements to answer.

The result is a simple graph showing what you need and how close you are to getting there. Then it offers to take you to a more sophisticated analysis, called Retirement Quick Check, that requires about 30 minutes of effort.

FINANCIALENGINES.COM. Runs what is called a Monte Carlo simulation to give you an idea of what the risks are. You are presented with a series of portfolios containing different kinds of investments and the probability of meeting your retirement goals through each one (2009 price: $150 to use for a full year).

For example, a rich person can afford to take less risk and could be in safe government bonds like Treasury inflation-protected securities, or TIPS. What does it matter if a rich person's money does not double in a decade; she's already rich. But a poor person has to take the higher risk of investing in stocks. He needs the money and actually has less downside risk than he thinks. Why? He didn't have that much to lose. A well-designed program or a well-informed planner up on the latest economic research can sort this out.

QUICKEN. Available as a feature within the Windows-based Quicken Deluxe (2009 price: $59.95), the software can download financial information from 4,300 institutions directly into the retirement calculator. Anticipated inflation rates, age when taking Social Security and tax rates can be changed by the user. Users are advised if they are on their way to having enough assets or if they should save more. The program warns them if their appreciation rate seems higher than normal, or if they forget to enter the value of an obvious asset, like a home.

VANGUARD.COM. The company helps investors determine how much to save for retirement and explains the types of I.R.A.'s, why it pays to start saving early, how investment costs affect savings and when to cash out of an employer's retirement fund. The tools, which can be used at no charge, do not advise people when to start taking Social Security, but they do show the effects of starting it at different ages. Nor are investors advised to switch out of funds if they are not performing well; the company says it does not believe in trying to time the market.

—Damon Darlin, Eric A. Taub

Real Estate

The Long View on Real Estate

What's in store for the housing market?

Yale economist Robert J. Shiller takes a very long view on the housing market. To Shiller, in fact, it's all a question of history.

Most people have never looked at decades and decades of home prices, because such data have been almost impossible to find. Stock charts often go back a century, while housing charts typically start sometime in the not-so-distant 1970s.

When Shiller could not find a long-running index of house prices for the United States, he built one. He combined U.S. government surveys that stretch back decades with for-sale listings that his students found in old newspapers. As the chart below shows, prices have hardly become more stable over the past hundred years; in fact

they have jumped up and down wildly during the past century.

His findings point to an unavoidable truth, Shiller says. Every housing boom of the last few centuries has been followed by decades in which home values fell relative to inflation. Over the long term, the portion of income that families spend on their shelter stays about the same. As the population increases, builders become more efficient and once-sleepy hinterlands become bustling centers to take the pressure off prices elsewhere.

What's in store for the future? Shiller believes, as his research indicates, that lower housing prices in inflation-adjusted terms will be the norm over the next generation. Even armed with formidable data, however, Shiller is a reluctant seer: "I have a lot of humility" about any prediction, he says.

—David Leonhardt

HOW HOME PRICES HAVE FARED

Low interest rates, a growing population and competitive building costs sent home prices soaring in the early 2000s. Economist Robert Shiller believes lower prices are more likely to be the norm during the next generation.

SOURCE: Robert J. Shiller, Yale University

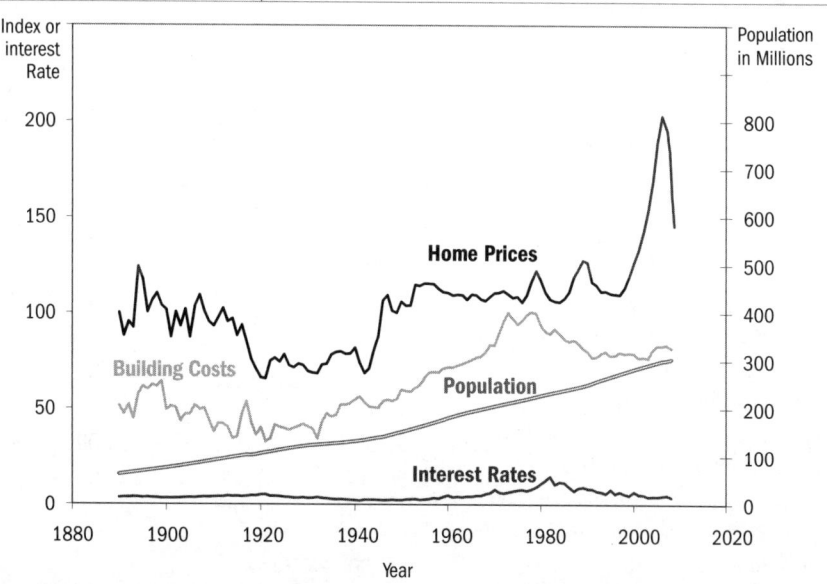

What to Consider Before Buying

Tried and true rules for homebuyers

After the recent housing bust, financial planners and mortgage lenders reconsidered standards on just how much a prospective homebuyer can afford. The consensus is that it may be worthwhile revisiting some of the lessons our parents and grandparents learned long ago.

How much can I afford? Several financial advisers recommend sticking with the old standard rule that households should spend no more than around 25 percent of their gross income on housing costs—including mortgage payments, property taxes and insurance—and less than around 35 percent on all debt. The total includes obligations like car payments, student loans, credit cards and medical debt.

There is some debate about whether you should base your calculations on gross income or take-home pay. While some advisers say using gross income is reasonable enough, more conservative types counsel applying these percentages to net pay.

Your housing budget depends on your situation and priorities. Two-income households with strong earnings potential can probably spend a little bit more than one-income households; as your income rises over the years, your housing costs are likely to become a smaller piece of your expenses. (Of course, that is not necessarily the case if you later buy a bigger house.)

The same goes for individuals who have saved extra money or people who may earn less but who are unlikely to lose their jobs, like teachers. Just be sure you stick with a plain-vanilla 30-year fixed mortgage, because payments will remain steady.

Financial advisers use different methods to ascertain what their clients can comfortably afford. One method is to write down all of your expenses. Then break those down into expenses that are fixed (utilities, groceries, auto expenses, insurance, etc.) and variable (everything else). The idea is that the variable costs could be reallocated toward housing if you are willing to give them up.

Another tack is to start by establishing savings goals and then work backward. Experts recommend setting aside 10 to 15 percent of your salary, preferably in tax-deferred accounts, and then working with what's left over for living expenses and housing costs.

Run the numbers. Before you start hitting open houses, sketch out a rough budget based on the 28 percent rule of thumb, using a simple mortgage calculator. For instance, a family that earns $10,000 a month—or about $7,000 after taxes—should keep their total monthly housing costs, including mortgage,

WHAT YOU CAN AFFORD

Here's the maximum monthly amount you could spend for home payments and total monthly credit obligations at a variety of income levels and meet guidelines required by most lenders. As a rule of thumb, no more than 25 percent of your gross monthly income should be used for your mortgage payment (principal, interest, taxes, insurance, condo fees, owners association fee, mortgage insurance premium), and no more than 35 percent of your gross monthly income should be going toward your mortgage payment plus all other monthly credit obligations.

YOUR GROSS ANNUAL INCOME	MONTHLY MORTGAGE PAYMENTS	MAXIMUM CREDIT OBLIGA-TIONS/MO.
$20,000	$467	$600
$30,000	$700	$900
$40,000	$933	$1,200
$50,000	$1,167	$1,500
$60,000	$1,400	$1,800
$70,000	$1,633	$2,100
$80,000	$1,867	$2,400
$90,000	$2,100	$2,700
$100,000	$2,333	$3,000
$130,000	$3,033	$3,900
$150,000	$3,500	$4,500
$200,000	$4,667	$6,000

SOURCE: Fannie Mae

taxes and insurance, to about $2,800 a month. In one example, the family may be able to spend $440,000 on a home, or about 3.6 times their annual income, as long as they can come up with a 20 percent down payment (and closing costs). If they finance the remaining $352,000 with a 30-year mortgage with a fixed rate of 5.5 percent, that would translate into a monthly payment of about $2,000, leaving $800 to pay real estate taxes and insurance. That leaves $4,200 of their monthly after-tax income to pay for everything else, giving them some breathing room.

Down payment. When the credit market is tight many consumers have no choice but to make a sizable down payment. If you do not, or cannot, it will cost you dearly in the form of a higher interest rate or fees. The ability to put down at least 20 percent is often emblematic of your financial discipline and ability to afford the monthly payment.

Taxes. Consider the tax savings associated with buying a home, but do not use it as an excuse to buy more than you can afford. Property taxes and mortgage interest are generally tax-deductible, but only if you itemize your deductions. Itemizing makes sense when your individual deductions exceed the standard deduction, which is $11,400 for married people filing jointly in 2009. (The standard deduction amount is adjusted annually by the I.R.S.) For many taxpayers in the 28 percent tax bracket who itemize, a $350,000 mortgage may reduce their tax bill by as much as $5,357 in the first year of the mortgage. Since you pay more in interest in the loan's early years, your tax savings will decline over time.

Reserves. Ideally, homeowners should have six months of net pay in the bank. But if you halve that figure and save three months of your take-home pay, that generally translates into eight months of payments. That does not account for food and other necessities, but it does provide some cushion. Two-income households can get away with just a few months of savings put aside, but single-breadwinner households should have at least six months. You also need to account for unforeseen costs.

—Tara Siegel Bernard

Better to Buy or Rent?

Factors to consider when making the big decision

Nearly everyone is faced at some stage in their lives with the conundrum, "should I buy or should I rent?" People looking to buy their first homes typically rent during slow real estate markets in the hopes that purchase prices will drop. And the thought occurs to just about every homeowner during a hot housing market that

FIGURING YOUR MONTHLY PAYMENTS

This chart shows what you pay on every $1,000 you borrow at different rates over the yearly terms. Here's how to figure other amounts. For example, if you take a $120,000 loan for 30 years at 7.5 percent, divide $120,000 by $1,000 = 120. Then multiply 120 x 6.99 (on chart) = $838.88, your payment, including principal and interest. Or, try one of the ubiquitous online mortgage payment calculators, such as the one on www.bankrate.com. Just plug in the numbers to compare different rates and terms.

MONTHLY PAYMENTS FOR $1,000

Rate (%)	30 years	15 years
4.5	$5.07	$7.65
5.0	$5.37	$7.91
5.5	$5.68	$8.17
6.0	$6.00	$8.44
6.5	$6.32	$8.71
7.0	$6.65	$8.99
7.5	$6.99	$9.27
8.0	$7.34	$9.56
8.5	$7.69	$9.85
9.0	$8.05	$10.14
9.5	$8.41	$10.44
10.0	$8.78	$10.75

MONEY

maybe it's time to cash out and rent.

But the buy or rent decision can be highly complex; there are a host of factors to consider, even aside from a quickly changing economic climate. Here are some pros and cons to help smooth the way.

Owning a home often ties up hundreds of thousands of dollars that might be invested more safely and more lucratively elsewhere. And while real estate brokers may hate to acknowledge it, home ownership involves its own versions of throwing money away, like property taxes and the costs of borrowing.

There are obvious benefits to home ownership beyond the financial, like peace of mind and a feeling of stability. Owners cannot have their home yanked away by a landlord who has decided

Just over 69 percent of Americans own their own home. For retirees, the number jumps to nearly 76 percent.

• • •

to move back in. Owners can also change the color of their living room walls or fix a draft seeping through their windows without asking permission. Combine these benefits with the transaction costs of a house sale, and renting probably doesn't make sense for most people who already own their home and feel settled in it.

The economics. But the calculation can look quite different for those who are considering a move anyway or who do not yet own a home. Renters in boom markets, who often lament that they are wasting money, should know that their choice has as powerful an economic rationale as buying does under certain economic conditions. For example, say a typical house in their area sells for $1 million, which is average in some cities. They will spend about $5,000 a month to live there, according to a *New York Times* analysis. The family could rent a similar house for about $2,500 and pay part of that bill with the interest earned by the money that was not used for a down payment.

When the net costs of owning are less than those of renting, of course, the argument for buying becomes overwhelming. And as long as home prices are not falling sharply, home buyers do better than renters. But when owning is more expensive every month, buyers are betting entirely on price appreciation, a calculation that is difficult to predict.

Tax considerations. The single biggest misconception about home ownership, some brokers and economists say, might revolve around tax deductions. Many people seem to believe that buying a home can actually save them money because the interest on their mortgage is tax deductible. But all

 INSIDE INFO

What Buyers Look For

○ A typical buyer checks out nine houses and takes about two months before buying one.

○ More than 70 percent of buyers place energy-efficient features at the top of their home-buying wish list. More than 90 percent would pick an energy-efficient home over one that was 2 percent to 3 percent cheaper, but that was missing energy-saving features.

○ More than one in five home buyers is a single woman. Twice as many more unmarried women as single men buy houses. For more than a decade, single women have outpaced men as home buyers.

SOURCES: National Association of Realtors; National Association of Home Builders; Center for Joint Housing Studies, Harvard University.

that deduction does is reduce the cost of borrowing the money—a cost that would not exist if the family were not buying the home. Families spend about 6 years in a house on average, according to the National Association of Realtors. In that time, the interest on a $600,000 mortgage would add up to about $120,000, even at low rates and even after the tax deduction, according to National City Corporation, a large lender. Don't buy a house just because you think you're saving on the taxes, specialists say. You may save even more by not buying and renting instead.

Many homeowners also do not receive the full deductions from home ownership. Some homeowners must pay the alternative minimum tax, which effectively wipes out part of their property-tax deduction, further cutting into the benefits of home ownership. Other homeowners do not itemize their deductions or, if they do so, end up with total deductions only a little larger than the standard deduction that the government offers to all taxpayers, even renters. Many people overvalue the mortgage deduction because they compare it to no deduction instead of comparing it to the standard deduction.

Emotional issues. But to many people, the psychological benefits of buying are almost impossible to overcome. Owning makes them feel that they have achieved the American Dream, or it gives them the secure sense that, if nothing else, they have a tangible asset where they can sleep at night. Those are nice feelings, indeed. The question is how much they are worth to you.

—David Leonhardt

How to Pick a Mortgage
Rules to follow before entering the market

Rule No. 1 for finding the right mortgage is *never jump into a mortgage deal,* especially not the first product you're offered.

Make a chart of the loan features offered by each potential lender, comparing the term of the loan, the interest rate and adjustable rates, if any; the size of the down payment, whether or not there is a prepayment penalty and the number of points that you will be charged, if any. (Points are upfront fees equal to 1 percent of the total loan amount that are used to lower the interest rate.) But before you even start searching for a home, much less a mortgage, take steps to avoid rushed decisions, dead ends and bad choices that you may have to live with for years.

Determine your credit status. Get your free annual credit report from each of the three major credit bureaus: Equifax, Experian and TransUnion (see "Checking Your Credit Rating" on page 193 for contact details). Not all creditors report your account information to all three bureaus, so it's wise to get

CALCULATING YOUR MORTGAGE PAYMENTS

Conventional wisdom holds that refinancing is attractive when interest rates fall 2 percent. But much depends on how long you intend to live in your home. If you plan to stay for many years, even a 1 percent drop may be worth the refinancing costs.
Here's a picture of payments and savings on a $100,000, 30 year fixed-rate mortgage refinanced to 4.5 percent. Any refinancing costs, typically 1 percent of the total loan, are not included in the payments, nor are property taxes.

Current rate	Current monthly payment	Monthly savings at 4.5%	Annual savings at 4.5%
5.0%	$537	$30	$360
5.5%	$568	$31	$361
6%	$600	$32	$384
6.5%	$632	$64	$768
7%	$665	$97	$1,164
7.5%	$699	$131	$1,572
8.0%	$734	$166	$1,892
8.5%	$769	$201	$2,412
9.0%	$805	$237	$2,844
10.0%	$878	$310	$3,720
10.5%	$915	$347	$4,164

What Lenders Want to Know

Before your loan gets approved

Requirements may differ among lenders, but generally bringing these documents with you on a loan application interview will speed the process.

Purchase agreement/sales contract: A signed copy of the agreement outlining the conditions and terms of the sale, along with any amendments; a copy of the listing form for the property; its legal description; and receipts for or down payment deposits.

Your addresses and personal information: All your addresses for the past 7 years; your Social Security number and date of birth. The names, addresses and telephone numbers of your employers for the past 2 years.

Sources of income: Most recent pay stub that shows year-to-date earnings and your W-2 tax forms (original copies sent to you by the I.R.S.) for the past 2 years.

Current assets: Account numbers and current balances of checking, savings and other investment accounts, including individual retirement accounts (I.R.A.'s), C.D.'s, stocks, bonds, life insurance, cars, etc. Recent statements should suffice.

Current debts: Auto loans, student loans, credit cards and other installment debt—provide name and address of each creditor and the monthly payment and total amount due.

Source of down payment: Can be from savings, stocks, investments, sale of other property or life insurance policies; or from relatives, assuming it doesn't have to be repaid.

If you own a home: The property address, current market value, mortgage lender name, mortgage account number, current monthly mortgage payment and outstanding mortgage balance.

If you're renting: The property address, name and address of the landlord, and current monthly rent. If you've lived at your current address for less than 2 years, bring that information for all previous addresses and landlords.

SOURCE: Fannie Mae

the report from all three and reconcile the information in all of them, ensuring, for example, that your address and employment records are current, that credit accounts you have closed are recorded as closed and that the information is actually yours, especially if you have a common name.

Fix incorrect entries immediately. If an entry is valid but could have an adverse effect on your credit, you can offer an explanation. But avoid credit repair agencies that promise to correct reports for a fee—you can fix errors on your own. Get your credit score, a computer-calculated number from 300 to 850 based on your credit history that lenders use to determine what loan type and interest rate you can get. (Getting your credit score from the three agencies will cost you a small fee.)

What can you afford? Prequalifying for a mortgage helps to determine how much you can afford. Generally, your real estate agent will run your numbers through a basic prequalification calculation to determine which homes to show you. Or, you can use an online calculator to estimate how much you can afford. To get the right loan, consider how long you expect to keep the home and the mortgage; the time periods for the two may not be the same. You will also need to decide how to handle your closing costs. You can pay them at the closing or finance them by taking a larger loan or accepting a higher interest rate.

Finding a loan. Many agencies want your business: banks, credit unions, online lenders, mortgage bankers, mortgage brokers. No one size fits all. Choose one based on the products offered and a reputation for good service. Don't accept loan offers that come to you; rather, seek them out after you have looked at ads and have done an online search to get a sense of prevailing rates and terms. As always be wary of giving out personal information. Among the well-known mortgage comparison sites are www.bankrate.com, www.lendingtree.com and www.eloan.com.

Your first mortgage pitch is likely to come from a mortgage rep in your realtor's office. But be sure to contact other agents as well. First-time buyers should be especially wary of so-called one-stop shops that offer to do it all, from showing you homes to brokering a mortgage to inspecting and appraising the property. Some companies could take advantage of people unfamiliar with the process. Verify that your mortgage broker or lender is licensed by the state banking department and has not been the subject of complaints. Get the product description in writing. Read the documents, understand the terms.

Choose a lender who will establish an escrow account to cover property taxes and homeowner's insurance, adding them onto your monthly mortgage payment. That way, you won't be hit by large tax and insurance bills for which you were not prepared.

Picking a product. For most buyers, the best choice probably remains the traditional fully amortizing loan in which the monthly payment covers both the interest and part of the principal (or face value) of the loan, gradually diminishing the balance. (See "Which Mortgage Is For You?" on page 230.)

Variations on basic products warrant some scrutiny. One risky choice, for example, is a minimum monthly payment based on a very low interest rate that may not even cover all the interest due each month. Over time, that process—called negative amortization—will increase your outstanding loan balance, especially if interest rates rise.

? EXPERT ANSWER

Preventing Mortgage Woes

Q What is your debt-to-income ratio?

Lenders will want to know your debt-to-income ratio, or the percentage of your income that goes toward paying debt, before you get that loan. Mortgage lenders calculate it two ways. There is the front-end ratio, which includes housing costs like the mortgage principal and interest, mortgage insurance premium, if applicable, and property taxes.

The back-end ratio includes any other debts like car or student loans, credit cards and alimony. Mortgage companies once accepted applicants with debt-to-income ratios as high as 55 percent but in recent years the maximum is in the mid-40s. By the way, a borrower's credit card limit counts as actual debt, regardless of whether the card is even used.

Q What happens to your credit score if you are preapproved for a mortgage and then don't buy a house?

Your credit score can be affected anytime you apply for a loan. If you apply and then decide not to buy a house, your score could drop up to five points. When a lender asks for a copy of your credit report during the loan application process, that request is considered a "hard" inquiry.

A "soft" inquiry occurs when you or a creditor checks your report. Hard inquiries stay on your credit report for 2 years and affect your credit score for 1 year. Before you go to a lender, check your score on www.myfico.com.

—Alina Tugend

MONEY

Watch out, too, for so-called interest-only mortgages. Be aware that interest-only really means you pay only interest for a while, typically 5 or 10 years, followed by a sizable jump in monthly payments for the rest of your loan term. Sometimes that jump is into predictable, fully amortizing payments. But, often interest-only loans have adjustable rates that could cause large payment shocks down the road.

Sealing the deal. Don't sign anything you don't understand or anything with a blank space that the broker or lender could fill in later. Don't be afraid to walk away if you're feeling pressured, especially if you are told there are no other options

—Dennis Hevesi

How and When to Refinance

Run the numbers, then run them again

It's always tempting when mortgage rates move tantalizingly lower for homeowners to consider refinancing their loans. But when should you refinance?

If you have top-notch credit and substantial home equity and expect to stay in your home for several years, refinancing may make financial sense. One of the big factors in determining whether refinancing pays is how long you expect to remain in your home. If you expect to stay for less than two years, you're unlikely to recoup your closing costs.

It's probably worth running the numbers if you expect to shave your rate by one percentage point. But, in some cases, that old rule of thumb doesn't necessarily apply: people with larger mortgages can benefit from smaller rate reductions. Smaller reductions may also make sense if you expect to stay in your home for many years.

Of course, you also need to factor in the costs of achieving that rate. Some borrowers pay points,

or a fee, to lower the mortgage rate. Points are expressed as a percentage of the loan amount.

Before you begin tinkering with the many refinancing calculators on the Web, be sure to keep the following in mind.

Consider your reasons. First, think about why you want to refinance. Lowering the overall amount you'll pay over the life of the loan is an obvious one. Home owners may be simply trying to save a couple of hundred dollars a month to improve cash flow (and don't care if refinancing will raise their overall costs in the long run). Others may want to get out of a riskier loan, like an adjustable-rate mortgage.

Or perhaps you want to take cash out of your home, that is, if you have enough equity, to pay off higher-cost debt like credit cards. But be aware that Fannie Mae and Freddie Mac, the two loan guarantors that buy or insure most mortgages, may charge more in fees when you take cash out.

While you're running the refinancing numbers, consider reducing the term of your loan. For instance, if you've been in your home for a decade, consider refinancing from a 30-year fixed mortgage into a 15-year loan. Not only is the rate lower on a 15-year mortgage, but you will be able to pay off your loan earlier and your payment could potentially remain the same. That strategy may work well for people nearing retirement.

Pay attention to rates and points. Since mortgage rates change daily and vary by lender, it pays to do your rate shopping on the same day to perform a valid comparison.

Borrowers with credit scores of about 720 or higher who are borrowing less than 80 percent of their home's value are likely to get the best rates. If your credit score is lower, your rates are higher and may be subject to a fee, typically about 1.75 percent of the loan amount. Pay close attention to points, the fees paid to lower your rate. Historically, paying 1 percent of your loan would lower your mortgage rate by about a quarter of a percentage point. But at some lenders, it can shave half a percentage point off your rate. The longer you expect to stay in your home, the more sense it makes to pay points to lower your mortgage rate rather than tacking them on to the loan amount.

Clearly, it pays to price multiple providers. Start by asking your current lender what they can offer, because sometimes you'll be able to save on closing costs. And if you are having trouble finding financing that suits your needs, check with your credit union and smaller banks and thrifts.

Rate locks. It's important to ask the lender when the loan will close, and what happens to your rate if the loan fails to close before your rate lock expires. Such locks typically guarantee your loan pricing for 30 to 45 days. Get your rate lock in writing. Rising rates diminish the benefits of refinancing, of course. Rate locks can cost money, so factor this into your cost comparisons across lenders.

Consider F.H.A. If you have less than 20 percent in equity in your home you might consider refinancing through the Federal Housing Administration, which insures lenders whose loans meet its guidelines. F.H.A. loans require about 3.5 percent down, though borrowers will pay an upfront mortgage insurance premium of 1.5 to 1.75 percent (usually tacked onto the loan amount) and a slightly higher interest rate.

If you have less than 10 percent in equity, refinancing with the F.H.A. may be your only option. You can get detailed refinancing information at www.fha.org, or consult your mortgage broker about the complexities of qualifying for and getting refinancing through the F.H.A.

TIMELY TIPS

Hard Questions for Your Broker

✔ **It is critical that all aspects of the broker-seller relationship be nailed down from the outset.** After all, as a seller you're hiring someone who's getting a 6 percent or so commission for selling your home, perhaps your most valuable asset. Some questions to ask:

- How exactly will you market my house?
- Are you available for showings all week long, day and night?
- How quickly will the broker return your phone calls?
- What is his or her long-term sales plan?

✔ **Brokerage companies have different policies on marketing budgets.** Ask how much the broker or his company will invest in the process. Then, ask if the marketing budget can be included as part of the contract.

—Hope Reeves

Understand the rules. You will need to document your income fully, and you can expect lenders to check it with the I.R.S. If you're looking to refinance a jumbo loan, you need to have superior credit and a sizable amount of home equity. You have to provide income verification and proof of your financial reserves or liquid assets. That means three to six months of mortgage payments and insurance.

Closing costs. Request closing costs in writing. While lenders are required by law to provide what's known as a good-faith estimate of these costs within three days of receiving an application for a loan, one broker recommends asking for it while shopping. If they aren't willing to tell you their costs, that could be a red flag.

—Tara Siegel Bernard

MONEY

Which Mortgage Is for You?

Brush up on popular options before you make the leap

Online mortgage shopping tools can help. At www.bankrate.com and www.myfico.com, for example, you'll find tutorials and mortgage calculators. But you'll need to know the basic mortgage options first. Here's are some of the most popular.

Adjustable-rate mortgage. *Interest rate changes over the life of the loan, resulting in possible changes in your monthly payments, loan term and/or principal. Some plans have rate or payment caps.*

PROS. Starting interest rate is slightly below the market. Payment caps prevent wide fluctuations in payments. Rate caps limit amount total debt can expand.

CONS. Payments can increase sharply and frequently if index increases. Payment caps can result in negative amortization.

✔ TIP: Remember that if your payment-capped loan results in monthly payments that are lower than your interest rate would require, you still owe the difference.

Balloon mortgage. *Monthly payments based on fixed interest rate; usually short term; payments may cover interest only, with principal due in full at end of term.*

PROS. Low monthly payments.

CONS. Possibly no equity until loan is fully paid. When due, loan must be paid off in full or refinanced. Refinancing poses high risk if rates rise.

✔ TIP: Some lenders guarantee refinancing when the balloon payment is due, although they do not guarantee a certain interest rate. Good for homeowners who anticipate selling or refinancing in a few years.

Buy-down. *Developer (or other party) provides an interest subsidy that lowers monthly payments during the first few years of the loan. Can have fixed or adjustable interest rate.*

PROS. Offers a break from higher payments during the early years. Enables buyer with lower income to qualify.

CONS. As with adjustable-rate mortgage, payments may jump substantially at end of subsidy.

✔ TIP: Consider what your payments will be after the first few years. They could jump considerably. Also see if the subsidy is part of your contract with the lender or the builder. If it's provided separately with the builder, the lender could still hold you liable for the full interest rate amount.

15-year mortgage. *Fixed interest rate. Requires down payment or monthly payments higher than 30-year loan. Loan is fully repaid over 15-year term.*

PROS. Frequently offered at slightly reduced interest rate. Offers faster accumulation of equity than traditional fixed-rate mortgage.

Terms to Learn Before the Closing

How to sound like a real estate pro

Finding your dream house at the right price was the easy part. To help prevent the already-stressful process from turning into a nighmare, here are some basic real estate terms every homebuyer should know.

Amortization. The gradual repayment of the mortgage through periodic installments over the term of the loan. The scheduled payment minus the interest equals amortization.

Assumable mortgage. A mortgage that can be taken over by the buyer from the seller when a home is sold. Note that many mortgages are no longer legally assumable.

CONS. Has higher monthly payments. Involves paying less interest, but this may result in fewer tax deductions.

✔ TIP: If you can afford the higher payments, this plan could save you interest and help you build equity. But consider whether the extra amount you pay is better off invested.

Fixed-rate mortgage. *Fixed interest rate, usually long term; equal monthly payments of principal and interest until debt is paid.*

PROS. Offers stability and long-term tax advantages.

CONS. Interest rates may be higher than other types.

✔ TIP: Can be a good financing method, if you are in a high tax bracket and need the interest deductions.

Graduated-payment mortgage
Lower monthly payments rise gradually (usually up to 10 years), then level off for duration of term. With adjustable interest rates, additional payments chang-

es possible if index changes.

PROS. Easier to qualify for.

CONS. Buyer's income must be able to keep pace with scheduled payment increases. With an adjustable rate, payment increases beyond the graduated payment can result in additional negative amortization.

Growing equity mortgage.
Rapid payoff mortgage. Fixed interest rate but monthly payments may vary according to agreed-upon schedule or index.

PROS. Permits rapid payoff of debt because payment increases reduce principal.

CONS. Buyer's income must keep up with payment increases. Does not offer long-term tax deductions.

Hybrid mortgage. *Fixed interest rate for a set number of years at the beginning of the mortgage, after which they become an annual adjustable-rate. Common fixed-rate periods are 3, 5 and 7 years.*

PROS. More affordable than

fixed-rate mortgages and more stable than A.R.M.'s.

CONS. Do not afford the stability of a fixed rate.

Renegotiable-rate mortgage.
Interest rate and monthly payments are constant for several years; changes possible thereafter. Long-term mortgages.

PROS. Less frequent changes in interest rates offer some stability.

CONS. May have to renegotiate when rates are higher.

Reverse-annuity mortgage.
Equity conversion. Borrower owns mortgage-free property and needs income. Lender makes monthly payments to borrower, using property as collateral.

PROS. Can provide homeowners with needed cash.

CONS. At end of term, borrower must have money to avoid selling property or refinancing.

✔ TIP: You can't obtain a reverse mortgage until you have paid off your original mortgage. (See "Beware of the Reverse Mortgage" on page 232.)

MONEY

Bridge loan. A short-term loan that allows a buyer to use the proceeds to finance closing on a new house before the current one is sold. Also known as a "swing loan." To qualify, the borrower must generally have a contract to sell the current house.

Closing costs (settlement costs). Fees and other costs, including down payment, associated with a mortgage loan, paid generally by the borrower

at the time of settlement. These can include attorney fees, loan origination fee, title insurance and other prepaid items, such as escrow deposits for taxes and insurance.

Equity. The owner's interest in a home. To calculate, take the home's current fair-market value and subtract the outstanding mortgage amount and any existing liens.

Escrow. Money or other valuables deposited with a third party for safekeeping and returned once a condition has been fulfilled. Often used for payment of a specified amount of taxes and insurance along with a mortgage payment. Also used to define the process by which a buyer and seller deliver legal documents to a third party who completes the transaction in accordance with their instructions.

Fannie Mae/Freddie Mac. U.S. government-sponsored entities that ease the flow of credit to the mortgage market by buying mortgages from banks and either holding on to them or selling them to the secondary market.

FICO score. A numerical rating, developed by the Fair Isaac Corp., of the credit history of an individual.

Foreclosure. The legal procedure in which a mortgaged property whose owner defaults on the loan can be sold by the lender to pay the mortgage debt.

Home equity loan. A loan that lets a home owner borrow up to an amount that represents a specified percentage of his or her equity in the property. Also known as a second mortgage.

Loan origination. The process by which a lender makes a loan, possibly including the loan application, processing and underwriting the application, and closing the loan. The buyer generally pays a loan origination fee to the lender.

Lock-in. An agreement in which the lender agrees to honor a quoted interest rate for a specified period of time before the closing date.

Origination fee. An upfront fee paid to a lender to cover the administrative costs of processing a loan application. The fee is typically in the form of points: one point is 1 percent of the mortgage amount.

Pre-approval. A process by which a lender approves a borrower's eligibility to receive a mortgage loan of a certain amount before a specific property is identified. The commitment by the lender comes after reviewing the applicant's credit history.

Refinancing. The process of paying off one loan with the proceeds from a new loan on the same property. This is usually done to take advantage of interest rates that have dropped below the rate of the existing loan.

Seller take-back/owner financing. A transaction in which the seller provides all or part of the financing to the buyer for the home purchase.

Settlement/closing. In the sale of a property, this is the process of completing a loan transaction and transferring the house from the seller to the buyer. Mortgage documents are signed and recorded, funds are disbursed and ownership is transferred. Some jurisdictions call this process escrow. In a refinancing, there is no transfer of ownership; the process simply includes repayment of the former lender.

Title search. A check of the public records to ensure that the seller legally owns the property and to identify any potential liens against the property.

Beware of the Reverse Mortgage
What to ask before you decide to take one

Reverse mortgages are complex loans typically available only to homeowners older than 61. They permit owners to borrow against their houses, but they do not require loan repayment until the borrower moves out of the home or dies. Then the loan is repaid from the proceeds of selling the house.

Here are some questions that financial advisers

and groups say potential borrowers should ask before taking out a reverse mortgage.

1. Is a reverse mortgage the best option? Reverse mortgages can be very expensive compared with other kinds of loans, and the amount owed grows every month. Because of these high costs, someone borrowing only a small amount for a short time is probably better served with another kind of loan, like a home equity line of credit. If borrowers need a large amount, they should consider alternatives to a reverse mortgage. For instance, does it make more sense to sell your house and rent or live off the proceeds after moving to a less-expensive home?

2. How long do you expect to stay in your house? Because the fees associated with a reverse mortgage are high, such loans make sense only for borrowers who expect to live in their home for a number of years. Some financial advisers say anyone who may move in less than 7 years should not take out a reverse mortgage.

3. Do you want to leave your children an inheritance? Because repayment of a reverse mortgage is deferred until the homeowner moves or dies, the amount owed increases over time. If a borrower lives in the home for many years after getting a reverse mortgage, the debt can grow to equal the entire value of the house, meaning heirs will not receive anything.

4. What are you going to do with the proceeds of your reverse mortgage? It is almost always a bad idea to use a reverse mortgage to pay for a vacation or to buy a risky investment, like stocks or deferred annuities.

5. What kind of payout is best? Cash from a reverse mortgage can be paid out in several ways, including a lump sum, a monthly payment, a line of credit or a combination of those. If you do not need money right away, it is usually a bad idea to take all the money up front, since it starts accumulating interest charges immediately.

Because reverse mortgages are complex, homeowners should seek advice from an independent adviser before speaking with a sales agent or mortgage broker. AARP, formerly known as the American Association of Retired Persons, runs a reverse mortgage education program, available at www.arp.org or by calling 800-209-8085.

—Charles Duhigg

Houses on the Cheap

Bargains—and headaches—at foreclosure sales

Buying distressed properties—those that are in foreclosure or have a foreclosure pending—is not easy, and it entails considerable risk. Buyers may find that if they have not done their homework, or lack ready cash and an ability to reason with a distraught homeowner, they don't have a prayer of making a profit and could end up in debt themselves. But the rewards can be great, with the most successful investors getting a good return on their money.

Locating the right place. The first hurdle is finding the right property. Defaulting on a mortgage is a matter of public record, so your local courthouse will have lists including names of people in arrears, their lenders and property addresses. Sometimes that information is available online. Or, for a fee, you could have the list e-mailed to you by outfits like Foreclosures.com, All-foreclosure.com and Foreclosureworld.net.

Announcements of auctions are usually printed in local newspapers; the starting bid is typically only what the lender needs to cover its costs. Depending on competition from other bidders, you can gener-

MONEY

The Risks of Foreclosure Sales

Beware of all the moving parts

You can make money buying properties in foreclosure but there's also money to be lost, if you don't know when and how to jump in:

✔ **Pre-foreclosure:** At this stage, the property owner is in arrears and the lender is threatening foreclosure. For investors, there is medium risk and medium reward. This may be the most difficult time to buy, because a mutually agreeable deal has to be struck with a distraught and often resistant property owner.

✔ **Foreclosure auction:** After a property has been seized by the lender, a public auction is held. Investors often get their best deals at auction, but they are also at highest risk: bidders cannot see the interior of the property before purchase, for example, and the winner must usually pay the full amount in cash or by cashier's check on auction day. There are no warranties or refunds, and the winning bidder may have to evict the person who lost the title.

✔ **Lender listing :** At this stage, the property is known as an R.E.O., for "real estate owned." The lender puts it up for sale usually because it did not receive an acceptable bid at the auction. Investors are at least risk at this point, but they can also expect a smaller discount on the price. Still, they are assured of a clear title and often buy through a real estate agent, so they can tour the property in advance.　　—Kate Murphy

ally buy properties at public auctions at a significant discount, according to real estate experts.

Do your due diligence. The next step is to drive by the property to check on things like structural integrity and whether, for example, there is a toxic waste dump in the area. If the property passes curbside inspection, you will probably want to pay the several hundred dollars it costs to do a full title search to find out if there are additional liens, or financial claims, against the property.

Buying directly from the owner. Many investors prefer to make offers to property owners before foreclosure, though distressed owners don't always open doors. Those who do can often be convinced that they might walk away less scathed if they sell to you than if the bank forecloses on them. One benefit is that you bypass the confusion and competition associated with a public auction—and you can inspect the property.

Buying at auction. Properties bought at auction are proverbial pigs in a poke: there is often no opportunity even to peek inside before buying, much less get an appraisal. And once you buy the property, you're stuck with it. Forget about warranties or refunds. Furthermore, buyers at auction often have to pay immediately, while buying properties facing foreclosure lets you pay owners a mutually agreed upon amount of "walking money," typically a small portion of their equity. The owners sign over the deed, and the buyer can assume their mortgage or refinance the debt.

Buying from the bank. The safest but potentially least profitable way to acquire foreclosed properties is from the lender. Called R.E.O.'s—for real estate owned—these properties usually end up in a bank's possession after they did not fetch desired prices at auction. Buying from the lender ensures that you get clear title, and you do not have to evict anyone. But the discount is generally punier than if you bought before foreclosure or at auction. R.E.O.'s are generally sold through regular real estate agents.

　　—Kate Murphy

Buying a Second Home

Avoiding the pitfalls of that first purchase

A second home—it's a dream come true, right? Unfortunately, some first-time buyers make rookie mistakes that can turn owning a vacation house into a nightmare. Here are a few tips to avoid the pitfalls.

Don't simply buy where you love. You may love spending a week each summer at a particular beach, but when you buy a home and start to spend several months a year in the area, you might realize that traffic is a mess, shopping is limited, and seasonal factors like the influx of tourists change the feel of the area.To avoid that problem, Craig Venezia, author of *Buying a Second Home: Income, Getaway or Retirement,* recommends renting for a few seasons before you buy. "There's no rush to buy a second home, that's the beauty of owning one," he advises. "It's truly a luxury to you, so you can take the time to get to know the area." One thing you should get to know is how long a trip you'll be making. The rule of thumb is that more than a two-hour drive is cumbersome for a weekend.

Know why you're buying. Take a step back and think about why you want to buy this home. Will it be an investment property, a personal getaway or a place you'll ultimately retire to? Those factors cross one another, but if you know the single reason, then that's going to drive where you buy, the type of house you buy and whether you'll rent it out. For example, if you determine that your getaway is going to be your eventual retirement home, you'll want to think about accessibility and the proximity of health care facilities.

Second-home financing is different. For starters getting a loan on a second home is generally more difficult than for a primary residence, and it can carry a higher interest rate. And don't assume your current lender is your best bet for financing; different lenders have different standards for mortgages on second homes.The bottom line is to do your financial research, get help with your potential tax benefits (which can get complicated) and don't stretch yourself too thin, or you will pay for it.

 **TIMELY TIPS**

Your Very Own Private Island

The rich and powerful have been buying their own islands at least since Caesar Augustus acquired Capri. The average tropical island these days seems to go for $2 million to $20 million, although you could land a 6-acre island off Panama for as little as $49,000.

✔ If buying an island fails you, try renting a slice of a private island. Not quite 4 acres, Cayo Espanto in Belize is among the smaller of a number of private island resorts that rent to the public. You can rent a room (about $1,600 a night in 2009) or the entire island for 16 guests (2009 price: $12,000 a night). A butler and three meals are included. A more remote choice is the 16-villa, 735-acre Fregate Island (www.clubairtravel.co.uk) in the Seychelles in the Indian Ocean.

✔ Other rent-an-island options are more like full resorts, such as the 58-villa, 1,000-acre Parrot Cay in Turks and Caicos, which has a gym and a spa. If you like pines instead of palms, you can rent Sleepy Cove Island, Nova Scotia, with its no-frills log house by a lake (2009 price: $165 a day).

✔ For sales or rentals of private islands, check out www.privateislandsonline.com and www. vladi-private-islands.de. For worldwide island rentals, try www.going2travel.com.

—Ray Cormier

Expect hidden costs. "Most people don't factor in the cost of a caretaker when they are putting their numbers together," says Jeff Haden author of *The Second Homeowner's Handbook: A Complete Guide for Vacation, Income, Retirement and Investment.* "They assume they'll love the house so much they'll be there every weekend—and it almost never turns out that way."

Those who plan on renting out their property can be in for some surprises, too. It takes time and money to rent a place out, whether you're doing it on your own or going through a management company, which adds to your fees. Think about how often you will rent it out, and how you will go about doing it.

Plan an exit strategy. Finances aren't the only reason you might need to divest yourself of your vacation spot. You may find, for example, that your company is transferring you. Whether you then decide to rent it or sell it, some forward thinking can help determine where and what kind of property you buy.   —Billie Cohens

Pros and Cons of Retiring Abroad

Here's how to increase your chances for success

As more mobile, active and adventuresome baby boomers hit their retirement years, many are lured overseas by a more affordable cost of living and more temperate weather. Some will want to return to their native countries or to places where they once worked or studied.

Though out-of-country retirement is not the norm, it has become less of an anomaly. Mexico, Costa Rica and Panama are common retirement havens. Nicaragua, Honduras, Ecuador and English-speaking Belize are also attracting retirees. Various countries in Europe are also viable alternatives, though current exchange rates may make them less attractive.

Retiring to an exotic locale sounds like a good plan, but many expatriates return home. They either miss the grandchildren and lifelong friends too much or find that culture shock was a bit, well, shocking. To increase the chances for success, follow this checklist:

First contacts. Verify your prospective country's stance on home purchases, taxes and residency, and the state of its safety and health care. Contact consulates, because information in books and on the internet can be outdated. Remember that real estate agents and developers may have a vested interest in your relocation.

Social compatibility. Be sure that you will be able to find the lifestyle you seek. Do you favor museums or nature walks? Do you crave solitude or a full social life (which could prove difficult where you do not speak the language)? Are you likely to become distressed when the phone service or electricity goes down, or can you handle occasional disruptions?

Online research. Read local newspapers. Links to English-language sites are at www.world-news-papers.com. For advice about living in specific countries go to www.internationalliving.com.

Testing it out. Some specialists suggest living in your desired location temporarily, perhaps for a year, so you can see if you like it year-round. Contact the local expatriate community for answers to nuts-and-bolts questions like availability of domestic help, how to find a contractor, reliability of internet service and the size of the tarantulas. Check on the ease of traveling back to the United States.

Health care. Medicare is not available abroad, so verify that you are eligible for your new country's health care program. Private insurance is available, but it is more expensive than government care.

Government benefits. Have Social Security checks automatically deposited into your bank account.

—Hillary Chura

Foreign Flings: Buying Abroad

Looking for bang for your real estate buck?

The world is dappled with electric and storied cities. And some are even highly affordable. Here's a bargain-hunter's tour of the world real estate market.

Buenos Aires. This sultry, party-until-the-wee-hours city is known as the Paris of South America. The enclave of the moment is San Telmo, a hip, urban, ex-pat-friendly community where the arts thrive. The neighborhood is dotted with fine restaurants, bars, boutiques and colonial houses. Real estate is more costly though still reasonable in Recoleta, an elegant downtown tourist magnet. Check out www.buenosaireshousing.com for listings of apartment rentals.

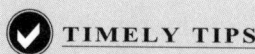 **TIMELY TIPS**

Watch Out for Foreign Laws

✔ Many countries welcome foreign buyers. But that doesn't mean the process is devoid of red tape. You can find information about ownership laws in 30 countries on WorldProperties. com. Click on "Country Info," then "Business Practices." Select a country from the drop-down menu. Where it reads "Select Business Practice," choose "Foreign Ownership." That will note any restrictions. In Mexico, for example, foreigners are prohibited from owning residential real estate within 30 miles of any coastline or 60 miles of either border.

—Stephanie Rosenbloom

Panama City and Ecuador. With its high-rise buildings, restaurants and some 80 banks, Panama City is a first-world town, according to International Living (internationalliving.com). A huge appeal of life as an expat in Ecuador is the cost of living, so inexpensive that a good four-course meal costs less than $2. "A country set back in time with all the comforts of today and the prices and services of the U.S. in the 1950s," says InternationalLiving.com.

Mexico City. Recommended by some property experts, the city makes others cringe with its crowded streets and polluted air. Still, lots of young Americans live and work there. Condesa is a chic area; more reasonable rentals can be found in downtown Mexico City.

Toronto. Toronto is Canada's financial headquarters, and some of its trendiest neighborhoods are among the most affordable. The Beaches neighborhood has a lively beachfront boardwalk yet is close to the city's downtown. Downtown Queen West is known for its galleries, clubs and shopping, and King West Village for its many pubs.

Montreal. The place to be and to be seen is Plateau Mont-Royal, which is popular with young Canadians because of its cafes, restaurants and nightclubs. The Gay Village enclave also draws a number of straight people because of its dynamic night life and affordability.

Quebec City. This Paris of North America is divided into Haute-Ville (the upper town) and Basse-Ville (lower town). Haute-Ville is more expensive than Basse-Ville, which is distinguished by a port (Old Port) along the St. Lawrence River. Warehouses converted into apartments can be had for a fraction of U.S. big-city prices.

Shanghai. Those doing business in China may want to work and buy in Shanghai. Shanghai Properties (www.shanghaiprops.com) suggests looking in People's Square, nestled between two of the city's major commercial and retail streets. One good value, according to Shanghai Properties, is the nearby apartment complex Top of the City.

Eastern Europe. Property experts say the best values may be in Eastern Europe. The streets are often chaotic and the sidewalks crowded, but many expatriates believe Bucharest, Romania's capital, is one of the most rewarding cities in Europe. Bulgaria is another attractive market, with its magnificent beaches and mountains for skiing.

—Stephanie Rosenbloom

Before You Shake on a Land Deal
Neophytes need to consider these factors

By some accounts, acquiring land is the purest form of real estate investing. (As Mark Twain once said, "They've stopped making it, at least around these parts.") Yet buying land (even when prices are depressed) is not nearly as simple as it seems. Real estate experts raise many signals of caution, particularly for the neophyte investor. Here are some factors to consider.

Expenses. For one thing, there are plenty of expenses associated with land ownership. There are property taxes, of course, and there may be liability insurance (in case someone is injured on the property) and maintenance expenses (to cut the grass or provide other upkeep). Plus, there's the expense of getting and paying off a loan to purchase the land.

The Environment. Owners will also need to ensure that the land is environmentally safe. Sometimes toxic trash may be dumped on the property without your knowledge, and you would be responsible for the cleanup.

For that matter, who's to say what might have made its way onto the property before it was sold? Seemingly pristine raw land, for example, could be contaminated with pollutants, which is why real estate experts urge buyers to have an environmental audit done as part of their due diligence. (Also important are engineering reports, to let buyers know if the land is buildable, and surveys, to establish true boundaries.)

Local Politics. Even the most nimble investors cannot control everything, especially when it comes to local politics. A city or town may impose a building moratorium or rezone an area to reduce density. You might buy land that is zoned for 10 houses per acre, for example, and then it goes down to 2 per acre, obliterating 80 percent of your land's value.

Local Economy. There's no guarantee, either, that economic expansion in a community will benefit the land investor. Predicting which way the real estate market will turn is not a science.

Indeed, as many seasoned investors know, waiting for land to appreciate can be, well, like watching grass grow. But the value can also shoot up like a weed almost overnight, providing some hefty returns.

Landing a Property. Investors of all types can find property for sale with the help of brokers as well as through online commercial listing services like LoopNet.com and CoStar.com.

For the less intrepid investor, there are passive investments. Those with larger sums could put their money into private funds offered by companies like Everest Holdings and Timbervest. There are also dividend-paying timber REITs, which hold portfolios of timberland. Their shares are publicly traded.

—Vivian Marino

How to Start a Farm

Why growing veggies is harder than you think

Starting a small farm can pay rich dividends, especially if the farm produces niche foods like artisanal cheeses, natural meats or truffles. But don't quit your day job.

Experts advise a slow and steady approach for first-time farm owners. One bustling business is organic farming, among the fastest-growing segments of U.S. agriculture, according to a Department of Agriculture report. And despite the consolidation of American agriculture, tiny farms are holding their own.

Moreover, as organic farming, farmers' markets, and cooperatives have gained in popularity, and food scares have been the stuff of headlines, many consumers are paying more attention to their food, what is in it and where it's produced.

For entrepreneurs tempted by the rural life, veteran niche farmers proffer this advice.

Create a contingency fund. Wean yourself slowly off outside income.

Do market research. Go to farmers' markets. See what products are common and which ones are missing. Talk to people. Ask if they would buy your product.

Check out the local labor pool to make sure enough workers are available.

Get the advice of an accountant and a lawyer.

Decide early on whether to go into the wholesale or retail market.

Ask yourself whether you will be able to adapt to the lifestyle, notably long hours of hard toil. If you doubt you will enjoy bending over crops under a hot sun, find another line of work.

Do not make the common mistake of growing too big too fast. You will risk discovering you do not have the cash flow to buy the equipment that you need to meet the orders.

Choose a "value added" niche product, like gourmet mushrooms, that is not sold widely in your area.

—Brent Bowers

MONEY

 **TIMELY TIPS**

A Piece of Desert and a Burro, Too

Don't be fooled by newspaper ads touting sales of cheap public land—homesteading laws were repealed in 1976. Occasionally, though, the Department of the Interior's Bureau of Land Management (www.blm.gov) sells off parcels of land considered to be "excess" public acreage, mostly in a handful of western states. You can buy a few acres or a couple hundred.

✔ **Dreaming of digs in the desert?** Sometimes arid or semi-arid land comes up for sale. But to make it habitable you'll have to install an irrigation system ($250,000 or more). Sales are usually held at a site near the property, but you can also submit a sealed bid. After the bid is accepted, it could take a year or more before you get title to your property.

✔ **Want your own wild horse or burro?** Some 8,000 mustangs, mules and burros are put up for "adoption" each year by the BLM under its herd-control program. You can adopt a wild horse or burro for a minimum of $125 or $250 for a mare with an unweaned foal. (Feeding and caring for the animal will run at least $1,000 a year but most likely far more, depending on where you live.) After one year, if you show that you are a responsible caretaker, the BLM will give you title.

✔ **To adopt a mustang or burro,** call 866-4MUS-TANGS or go to www.wildhorseandburro.blm.gov.

Insurance & Taxes

The Lowdown on Life Insurance

Do you have enough? Or are you overinsured?

If you died today, would your family be destitute in a few years, toasting your good planning as they vacationed on the Riviera or merely comfortable? It largely depends, of course, on your investments and how much life insurance you've bought.

The two most basic questions to ask yourself about insurance are: "Do I need it?" and "How much do I need?" If you decide that your investments could not support your family comfortably and that you need life insurance, figuring out how much you need can be difficult. The appropriate amount varies by situation: marital status, number of dependents, earning potential of each spouse and whether both work.

Overinsure, and good money is wasted on the unlikely event of a premature death. Underinsure, and a family may have to lower its lifestyle at an already traumatic time, a house might have to be sold in a bad market or children attending college might have to drop out.

Correct coverage is crucial to a successful financial plan, but before you start comparison shopping, consider these factors.

Figuring how much you need. The amount of life insurance you need roughly correlates with your family's annual living expenses for the number of years you'll need the insurance. Add together all your family's expenses for the years you'll need insurance. You should include future college costs, mortgage payments, costs to settle your estate and an emergency fund (typically, three months' salary). Then subtract all family income other than your salary. Be sure to include Social Security and pension payments as well as any income you may receive from your investments. Adjust both your future expenses and income to account for inflation.

The result of this calculation is how much life insurance you need.

The life insurance industry's rule of thumb is a simpler calculation: multiply your annual salary by 10. But consultants and various online life insurance calculators can provide more specific estimates. The Life and Health Insurance Foundation for Education, a nonprofit group financed by the insurance industry, has a calculator at www.

ⓘ **INSIDE INFO**

Weigh More, Pay More

○ People with medical conditions like high blood pressure and diabetes naturally have a harder time trying to buy life insurance. But overweight people who are otherwise healthy face a similar difficulty.

○ The fact that an obese person can be denied life insurance is not surprising. Obesity poses a range of health problems. But even those whose weight is simply significantly above normal compared to their height can be penalized by higher premiums.

○ A 40-year-old, 6-foot-tall male who weighs 270 pounds will pay 15 to 20 percent more than a person of ideal weight. If the person weighs 300 pounds or more, the amount jumps to 30 to 35 percent, according to a State Farm agent.

SOURCE: Info.insure.com

ⓘ **INSIDE INFO**

Life Expectancy

○ The average American born in 2006 can expect to live more than 31.5 years longer than his ancestor born in 1900.

○ **LIFE EXPECTANCY IN YEARS**

YEAR BORN	MALE	FEMALE
1900	46.3	48.3
1910	48.6	52.0
1920	54.4	55.6
1930	59.7	63.5
1940	62.1	66.6
1950	65.6	71.1
1960	66.6	73.1
1970	67.1	74.7
1980	70.0	77.4
1990	71.8	78.2
2000	74.3	79.7
2001	74.4	79.8
2002	74.5	79.9
2003	74.7	80.0
2004	75.2	80.4
2005	75.2	80.4
2006	76.0	81.0

SOURCE: Department of Health & Human Services

life-line.org. Insurance aggregators, like insweb.com and insure.com, offer calculators to figure life insurance needs as do insurance companies, banks and investment companies.

Varieties of life insurance. There are two basic varieties of life insurance. Term insurance, which covers a set period of time, is cheaper. Permanent insurance, which includes whole life and universal life, does not expire and is often used by wealthier individuals to pay estate taxes.

Many advisers recommend term insurance, often called "pure" insurance because it offers a death benefit without a savings component. Term insurance will pay your survivors a death benefit if you die while the contract is in force. A term life insurance policy can be locked in for 5 to 30 years but coverage is like a lease: it expires when the policy does. It is often the best and cheapest bet for families who want to provide for the future if the breadwinner dies and who want to target the years when their insurance needs will be greatest. But people who are in ill health or are otherwise considered a bad risk may find themselves uninsurable or facing prohibitively higher premiums when their term insurance expires.

Term insurance costs a fraction of permanent insurance like whole life (with a locked-in premium) or universal life (where the premium may vary based on projected interest rates). Whole life insurance premiums are substantially higher at first than the same amount of term insurance, but term premiums can skyrocket as you get older. With whole life you are betting that you'll be around a while, so that the high initial payments will average out the cost over a lifetime.

Whole life policies also offer an investment opportunity. Part of your premium payment is invested into a plan with deferred taxes on earnings, so that the policy builds "cash value" over the years. Permanent insurance should not expire. If policies are surrendered within a short period of time, however, policyholders may receive little of their investment.

One compromise is to convert term insurance to a permanent policy at preset points, allowing coverage to continue but at higher rates.

The goal is for people to withdraw less annually than their investment portfolio returns. This allows for inflation if the money is to support them for long periods. Many advisers recommend an annual withdrawal of 5 percent or less, which would be $50,000 in annual taxable income on $1 million.

MONEY

Remember that not all policies that appear to provide fixed premiums and cash values are guaranteed-permanent insurance. Universal life, for example, is a form of cash-value insurance that combines term insurance with a "side fund" that is credited with earnings. Instead of making fixed premium payments, you have the flexibility of deciding the size and frequency of your payments to the side fund, which accumulates interest on a tax-deferred basis. You get death-benefit protection as long as the amount in the side fund can cover the cost of the insurance. This flexibility means that universal life can function more like a term or guaranteed-permanent insurance, depending on how you fund it.

Variable life insurance products can be even riskier. You choose from among the investment options offered by the insurance company—stocks, bonds, etc. So, you may or may not build up cash value in the policy, depending on how the investments perform. Look carefully at the options the company is offering and be sure they are balanced and let you invest at a level of risk you can tolerate.

Young people in excellent health should not automatically buy extra life insurance through their employers because it can be more expensive than what they could obtain on their own unless they get it at a group discount rate. Conversely, older people, those in poor health or those looking for a convenient way to buy life insurance could benefit from employer plans. —Hillary Chura

A Primer on Health Insurance

The pros and cons of different policy options

With Americans spending an ever increasing amount on medical costs, it's more important than ever to have insurance that fits your health care needs. So when you start shopping for a plan, don't just look for one with the lowest premiums. Consider the services that are most important to you.

The best place to get health insurance, of course, is from your employer. Group plans are typically cheaper, and your employer will probably cover much of the cost.

There are three main types of coverage you can choose from: H.M.O.'s (health maintenance organizations), P.P.O.'s (preferred provider organizations) and the newer option called an H.D.H.P. (high deductible health plan) paired with a savings account. A small number of companies still offer old-fashioned, fee-for-service plans, but their ranks are dwindling. Here's what you need to know about the most common plans:

H.M.O.'s provide comprehensive coverage at a low cost to the consumer. In general, you don't pay any deductibles or co-payments for basic care (and if you do, they will be relatively low). But your choices will be limited. You can generally use only the doctors and hospitals within the H.M.O.'s network, though more plans are easing up on this restriction, and your designated primary-care physician will determine the level of care you require and when you need to see a specialist.

PROS: Low cost. Coordinated care.

CONS: A limited choice of providers. If you go out of network, for example to a specialist, you will probably not be reimbursed.

Preferred Provider Organization and Point of Service plans were created in response to consumer frustrations with the limitations of H.M.O.'s. You can choose to go to network providers and pay a small co-payment, or go out of network and have only a portion, typically around 60 to 70 percent, of your costs reimbursed. The main difference between the two is that a point of service plan requires a referral from your

TIMELY TIPS

Getting Help on Health Coverage

Sites to tap into for more information

✔ **National Association of Health Underwriters** *www.nahu.org.*
Get the lowdown on health insurance topics ranging from high-risk pools to health savings accounts and conduct a search for agents. Or call 703-276-0220 with your questions.

✔ **U.S. Department of Labor** *www.dol.gov/ebsa*
The source for information about Cobra, the federal rule that temporarily extends medical coverage. Or call the Employee Benefits Security Administration hotline: 866-444-3272.

✔ **National Association of State Comprehensive Health Insurance Plans** *www.naschip.org*
For information about states' high-risk insurance pools, which are intended to help provide coverage for the uninsured.

—J. Alex Tarquinio

primary care physician to see a specialist, while the preferred provider plan does not.

PROS: More flexibility than an H.M.O.; lower overall out-of-pocket costs than a fee-for-service plan.

CONS: It's tricky to predict your costs unless you're willing to stay within the network. Getting reimbursed for out-of-network claims can be a hassle.

High Deductible Health Plan. Over the past few years, more employers have begun to offer the option to sign up for a high deductible health plan that is linked to a health savings account or health reimbursement account. Some employers may offer the high deductible health plan on its own and allow the employees to set up a savings account with the bank of their choice.

The plans work like the preferred provider option, but the deductible is much higher: at least $1,150 for coverage of a single person and $2,300 for families. To compensate for the larger deductible, employers typically offer two different savings options:

A health savings account allows you to put away pretax dollars and then withdraw the money to pay your out-of-pocket costs. (Your employer may kick in some money, too.) The money rolls over from year to year, so you can basically store up a medical emergency fund. When you're 65, you can take the remaining money out without paying a penalty, though you'll pay taxes on the withdrawal if you're not using it to pay for medical costs.

A health reimbursement account is financed solely by your employer. Typically, an employer will contribute an amount equal to about half the employee's deductible. The money rolls over from year to year, but you cannot take the money with you when you leave the company.

PROS: Low premiums. Tax-free savings (in the case of the health savings account).

CONS: Potentially high costs, especially if you or a family member becomes chronically ill. Don't choose this option unless you have the money to pay the deductible.

Indemnity or Fee-for-Service Plans are offered by fewer and fewer employers because of their expense. They allow you to go to any doctor, hospital or medical provider you choose. The plan typically reimburses 80 percent of your out-of-pocket costs after you fulfill an annual deductible.

PROS: Flexibility. You can go to any medical provider, anywhere, without seeking plan approval first.

CONS: Your total out-of-pocket costs will probably be higher than in a preferred provider plan or H.M.O. Most fee-for-service plans don't cover preventive care like flu shots or mental health services. To help narrow your choice, take these steps:

1. Ask your favorite doctors which insurance plans they accept. If you find that one or more of your doctors do not accept any insurance plans, then you'll want to select a plan that reimburses you for your costs when you go out of the network.

2. Make a list of all the services you and your family use. Include on the list things like vision care, dental, physical therapy, acupuncture and mental health care. Find out how the plans you like best will cover these services and at what cost.

3. Compare costs. Write down the costs associated with each plan, including premiums, out-of-network costs, and extras like vision or mental health care.

Flexible Spending Accounts. In addition to offering low-cost health insurance, your employer may also offer a health care flexible spending account, which lets you set aside pretax dollars to pay for your out-of-pocket medical costs. (If you have already signed up for a health savings account, you can only use the flexible spending account for dental, vision or post-deductible medical expenses.)

You can deposit up to $5,000 a year in a flexible spending account, depending on the limit set by your employer. The money will be deducted from your paycheck and you can't change the amount midyear. If you have high medical costs, using a flexible spending account can save you hundreds of dollars a year in taxes. But calculate your costs carefully. The money does not roll over to the next year. Any money you don't use will be lost.

Buying an Individual Policy. If you need to buy insurance on your own there are a number of options to consider.

First, if you are about to lose your job at a company with more than 20 employees, you can remain on your employer's plan for up to 18 months under a federal law called Cobra, the Consolidated Omnibus Budget Reconciliation Act. But you will have to pay the full premium plus 2 percent for administrative costs, and the expense is often quite high. This may be a good temporary measure, though, until you can find a more affordable option.

If you're out on your own, try to find a group plan to join since group plans typically cost less and offer more benefits than individual plans. Can you join your spouse's plan? Do you belong to (or can you join) a union, professional organization or alumni group that offers insurance? You may also be able to find a group plan for freelance workers. If you are over age 50, look at the plans offered by the AARP.

If a group plan is not an option for you, you'll have to buy an independent policy. Fortunately, there are numerous plans to consider. The simplest way to compare policies and prices is by going to an online insurance broker like eHealthInsurance.com. At eHealthInsurance, for instance, you simply fill in your gender, ZIP code, date of birth and, if you want, the names of your doctors, and the site comes up with a list of policies for you to consider. You can apply online.

If the prospect of sorting and sifting through dozens of policies seems daunting, consider using an independent insurance agent, who sells many different kinds of health insurance. You can find agents in your area at the Web site for the Independent Insurance Agents & Brokers of America (www.iiaba.net).

Individuals with modest incomes may be eligible for Medicaid. You may be able to get coverage for your children through the State Children's Health Insurance Program, a federal-state partnership, at www.cms.hhs.gov/home/schip.asp.

If you have a serious health problem and are unable to find coverage through a private insurer, find out whether your state has a high-risk pool that you can join. While these plans are not low in cost, they are often the only option for people with pre-existing conditions.

—Lesley Alderman

Coverage for the Self-Employed

The bad news: options are limited, costs are high

If there is one thing that separates the self-employed from those employed by others, it is their preoccupation with health insurance.

Many entrepreneurs seem to find health insurance after doing a lot of research, though they generally pay more than they think they should. Some who are in good health bet on remaining that way and forgo health insurance or get policies with low premiums and high deductibles, choosing to insure themselves for mostly catastrophic illness. Some are lucky enough to have a well-insured partner.

The unluckiest are those with chronic illnesses or the dreaded pre-existing condition that results in a denial of coverage. Many of these people abandon dreams of entrepreneurship altogether because they need jobs that come with a health plan and they cannot find a way to self-insure.

The health care system is a state-by-state patchwork, with options varying based on where you live. One valuable tool, healthinsuranceinfo.net, is maintained by the Georgetown Health Policy Institute. The site shows a map of the country and after clicking on a state, a document is downloaded that covers everything from what kinds of programs are available to small-business owners to whether there is a high-risk pool available

for those who have been rejected by insurance providers. These primers are comprehensive and frequently updated, and they are a great place to start, especially if you have been wondering about the meaning of the jargon that peppers insurance providers' descriptions of their offerings.

Popular sources for buying insurance are local chambers of commerce, the Small Business Service Bureau (sbsb.com), AARP (aarp.org) for those over 50, and industry-specific trade associations like a bar association or the Institute of Electrical and Electronics Engineers. In states that permit it, small-business owners can also start a group with as little as one member. In that case, a good insurance agent comes in handy.

For the reasonably healthy who know what they are looking for, ehealthinsurance.com gets fairly good reviews. The site, which has the feel of an Expedia or Orbitz for purchasing health insurance, allows you to compare a variety of policies offered through about 70 insurance providers. One caveat, is that ehealthinsurance.com does not serve consumers in all states. Rhode Island, Vermont, Massachusetts, Maine and North Dakota are excluded. The company also covers only individuals. So if your company has employees, you will need to explore other options, like starting a group (if your state permits that).

Another possibility for consultants and independent workers is the Freelancers Union, which won consistently good reviews in the reader comments. But the union also has some limitations. It operates in only 30 states, and you have to work in one of the industries or occupations it serves.

While healthy business owners have to incur high costs and navigate a maze of choices, the truly unhealthy face the biggest challenges.

To learn more about options for those whose health is getting in the way of their self-employment, try healthinsuranceinfo.net.

MONEY

Advocacy for Patients With Chronic Illness (advocacyforpatients.org), a nonprofit organization in Farmington, Conn., advises and advocates on behalf of the chronically ill, handling everything from battles to get insurance companies to pay for treatments prescribed by patients' doctors to helping people figure out the best coverage.

Good coverage at a good price is hard to find. Monthly payments of $800 for a chronically ill individual are not unusual.

—Marci Alboher

Do You Need Disability Insurance?

It's expensive but it may be essential

Working people are more likely to become disabled than they are to die prematurely. Yet twice as many people have life insurance as have disability coverage, according to industry statistics.

Disability insurance provides partial income replacement so that if someone becomes disabled, they need not dive into savings, sell a home or radically change how they live. About one-third of 20-year-old workers today will become disabled before they hit retirement age at 67, according to the Social Security Administration. And the primary cause of disability is chronic disease, such as cardiovascular illness, musculoskeletal problems and cancer, rather than work-related mishaps or nonworkplace accidents, according to a recent study for the Life and Health Insurance Foundation for Education, a nonprofit organization that informs the public about insurance needs.

While job-related expenses decrease if someone cannot work, other expenses can soar, especially if homes must be altered to accommodate a disability. Being disabled can quickly push a person into a financial bind. (According to the Department of Housing and Urban Development, illness is a major factor in home foreclosures.) Not only do you have regular living expenses you are unable to meet, but there are also medical bills that health insurance doesn't cover.

There are two major types of disability insurance. Short-term coverage, often offered by employers, covers the first part of a disability and may provide income for a week up to a year or two, depending on the policy. Long-term insurance starts after short-term coverage ends and helps replace income for a predetermined period, usually 2 or 5 years or when the disabled person retires. It can be offered through work—though usually not for free—as well as through private policies.

Even those with a policy through work should consider buying private coverage, as an employer's policy may be bare-bones, could take a while to begin and will not continue when the employee changes jobs. It may also exclude pre-existing health problems.

Specialists agree that if you can afford only one type of disability insurance you should buy long-term coverage, since being without an income for several months would be a burden, but being without an income ever again could be devastating.

Because independent disability insurance tends to be expensive—and becomes more so as people age—specialists urge workers to buy it as soon as they start working so they can lock in lower rates. Besides, young workers often have not yet developed health problems that will hinder coverage later.

Many employers offer disability policies, but some have been shifting costs to employees. At the same time, insurers are changing policies to make benefits less generous. They also are becoming more selective in who is granted a private policy.

The policy should replace at least 60 percent of take-home salary and ideally up to 80 percent, if that

TIMELY TIPS

Disability Policies: Before You Sign

Because disability policies are full of technical language, it pays to ask questions before signing on the dotted line. Some key questions to ask:

✔ How does the insurance company define a disability: inability to do *any* job or any job that you are trained and qualified for?

✔ What is the monthly benefit?

✔ How long will the company pay benefits?

✔ How long should you expect to wait to receive benefits after filing a claim?

✔ What proof of disability is required?

✔ Must you first qualify for state and/or federal benefits?

✔ What weight will the treating doctor's opinion have?

—Michelle Leder

few years, some until Social Security begins.

Premiums vary depending on age, sex, income, health, whether a person smokes, what type of job they have and the exclusions they accept. A 45-year-old man in relatively good health who is paid about $200,000 a year would pay about $2,800 a year for disability insurance that covered 80 percent of his salary and started payments after 90 days.

—Hillary Chura

Betting on Long-Term Care
It's costly, speculative and some won't need it

Most of the nation's 78 million baby boomers are watching their parents grow old, yet not thinking about their own old age or planning how they will pay for nursing homes or home health aides for themselves. With life expectancy steadily rising, odds are they will eventually need some help with basic functions, like dressing or walking, maybe for decades.

After all, Medicare does not cover these ongoing, nonmedical services. Medicaid does, but it has tightened its rules, making it harder for middle-income people to qualify. That leaves essentially two choices: pay cash or buy long-term care insurance.

Long-term care insurance covers services for people who are unable to perform two or more activities of daily living. It can pay for a nursing home, assisted living facility, home health aide, adult day care and family respite (someone to fill in for a family member who is caring for the insured person).

And it is not just for the elderly; young people who are paralyzed by car accidents, for instance, often need home care. The choices among long-term care plans can be mind-boggling. Here are some critical issues to consider.

level of coverage is affordable. Disability insurance will not cover the whole salary for fear that there would be no incentive to work if the entire paycheck could be collected for staying home.

Before purchasing an individual long-term disability policy, it is best to figure out monthly expenses as well as any income from employers, investments or the government. Realize, however, that Social Security payments tend to be minimal, have a five-month waiting period and apply only if someone cannot do any job. Payouts through work policies are subject to taxes, while benefits through independent coverage are tax free.

Disability insurance plans vary. Some pay if someone is unable to work in her own profession; others pay if a person cannot do any job. Some offer a combination. Others provide coverage for only a

Do I need it? Buying insurance is always a bet on probability. For long-term care, there are four basic questions to ask.

1. If I don't buy insurance, how much money can I afford to spend on this care from my own assets and income? AARP reported that the average cost of a nursing home in the United States in 2007 was about $214 a day; a home health aide cost around $19 an hour.

2. Do I have alternatives? Are there friends or relatives who would take care of me without charge?

3. What is the likelihood that I will need this care? (This is, admittedly, an uncomfortable question.) Does my family have a history of debilitating chronic illness, like Alzheimer's disease? Or, on the other hand, do I have a heart problem that makes it unlikely that I will live long enough to use the benefit?

4. Can I afford the annual premiums, which can top $2,000? An individual whose assets or income fall below $40,000 would most likely be better off relying on Medicaid, according to industry experts.

When should I buy it? Experts suggest that people buy policies while in their 40s to mid-50s, mainly because premiums rise with age, roughly doubling every 10 years. For a standard policy at New York Life Insurance Company, for example, the annual rate (priced in 2009) is $1,041 at age 50, $1,941 at age 60 and $3,984 at age 70.

If buying at age 40 is good, why not start at 30? Your first savings should be to take care of income replacement for retirement. Another reason to start younger is that the likelihood of having a claim is fairly remote in the 30s, 40s and 50s.

But an applicant can also be too old. The cutoff at some major insurers is age 79; New York Life will sign new policies for those up to age 85, but with limited benefits.

Where can I get it? Try your employer first. More than one-third of companies now offer long-term care insurance as a benefit, doubling the number from 10 years ago.

Employer-based plans have multiple advantages. Group rates are typically 5 to 15 percent lower than retail, and they often have features and benefits that are more difficult to find in individual plans. Moreover, the employer will have vetted the insurance carrier. One more advantage: policy owners do not need medical screening.

For those who have to buy coverage on their own, how can they be sure the company will still be around when they need the benefits, 20 years from now? One way is to check its standing with a ratings agency like Standard & Poor's or A. M. Best Company.

About two dozen states have extended-coverage "partnerships" that coordinate private insurance with Medicaid. Normally, if people still need help after exhausting their insurance benefits, they must pay out of pocket until nearly all of their assets are gone before Medicaid will step in. With these state programs, however, you can qualify for Medicaid while preserving more assets. (The amount you can preserve depends on the policy you select.)

How much coverage should I get? The typical policy is written as a formula—X dollars per day of Y-type coverage for Z years—although in practice it is more flexible. If a policy covers $200 a day at a nursing home for 5 years and the policyholder ends up in a home that costs only $150, the coverage can continue beyond 5 years until the policy has paid out $365,000 ($200 times 365 times 5). The advantage of this formula is that it helps people calculate how much coverage to buy by breaking the choice into pieces.

How many years of coverage? For nursing homes, 5 years is a common amount, but people can buy anywhere from 2 years to unlimited time. Data show that the average nursing home stay is two and a half years.

And how much money per day? That is fairly easy to calculate, because AARP and many insurance companies track average costs state by state. Consumers can also look up the facilities they are interested in. The catch: think about where you're going to be retired and the average cost of nursing homes there, rather than the cost where you live now. Fees vary dramatically, from $33.50 a day in Louisiana to $237 in Alaska, according to AARP.

Since today's average cost is sure to grow by the time most buyers actually use the benefit, it is important to add inflation protection. A policyholder can increase coverage every few years, with a corresponding rise in the premium, but most experts prefer policies that automatically raise the benefit over time, even though they charge a higher premium from the start.

Should both partners get coverage? Companies often give a 30 or 40 percent spousal discount on both policies, so it can be cost-effective to buy coverage together. But if a couple can afford only one policy, they should focus on the one who's more likely to have the need.

Will I qualify for the coverage? Insurers reject 15 to 20 percent of applicants, mainly those likely to need long-term care soon. The most common red flags are obesity, severe diabetes, cancer within the past 5 years, arthritis, Parkinson's disease and mental cognition problems, along with age limits. The good news is that a family history of these conditions does not count.

—Fran Hawthorne

 **TIMELY TIPS**

Policies You Don't Need

Consumer advocates say these may not be not worth buying

✔ **Air travel insurance:** It costs too much and pays back only about 10 cents for each dollar of premiums. It is not comprehensive, and you are more likely to die from a heart attack than from an airplane crash.

✔ **Identity theft insurance:** It could cost you up to $200 for $25,000 in coverage. It may be better to keep tabs on your accounts and notify issuing companies immediately if you suspect fraud. Law limits your loss to $50 per card. Also check your free credit reports regularly (www.annualcreditreport.com).

✔ **Cancer insurance:** What good is a cancer insurance policy if you have a heart attack? Buying specific illness coverage is like buying toothpaste one squeeze at a time. Plus, your health insurance already covers it.

✔ **Insurance that pays only if you're hurt or killed in a mugging:** A classic example of "junk" insurance. This risk is covered by good life and health policies.

✔ **Life insurance if you're single:** If you have no dependents, there is no economic reason to buy life insurance since there is no economic catastrophe associated with your death.

✔ **Life insurance if you're married with children and your spouse has a good job:** If one of you dies, can the other get along on one income? If so, perhaps no life insurance is necessary beyond that which you have at work.

✔ **Mail-order life insurance:** Stay away unless you compare its price to annual renewable term insurance and find it cheaper.

✔ **Rental car insurance:** Your own auto insurance policy probably covers you if you do damage to a rental car. Also, many credit cards cover this.

Insuring Your Home

How to zero in on what you really need

Whether you are a homeowner, apartment owner or renter, it's important to have the appropriate type and amount of property and casualty insurance coverage. What to look for? Here's a tutorial on policy options, costs and what's covered and what's not.

Do you need an HO-1 or an HO-6? A homeowners policy, a generic term that applies to policies available to owners of single-family homes, condo owners, co-op shareholders and renters, is typically identified by the code "HO" followed by a number.

The most basic policy, the HO-1, provides protection against losses caused by fire, lightning, windstorm, hail, explosion, riot, smoke, vandalism, theft and damage caused by aircraft, vehicles and even volcanic eruptions.

And while that list might appear to be comprehensive, there are other risks that are not covered by such a policy. For example, in addition to insuring perils covered by an HO-1, an HO-2 generally will cover damage caused by other "named perils" like falling objects and the weight of ice, snow or sleet; leaks from plumbing, heating, air-conditioning and fire-sprinkler systems; cracking, bursting, burning or freezing of such systems; and sudden and accidental damage to fixtures or appliances caused by an electrical discharge.

For even more coverage try an "all peril" HO-3 or HO-5 policy. Both cover the structure for all risks except those specifically excluded, with the latter providing broader coverage for contents than the former. Typically, an HO-3 or HO-5 policy excludes coverage for damage caused by flood, earthquake, war, nuclear accident, landslide, mudslide and sinkholes. Some insurers now exclude or limit coverage for mold.

Co-op and condo owners can get coverage similar to homeowners' by purchasing an HO-6 policy, and for renters there is the HO-4 policy.

How much coverage is enough? Homeowners often buy just enough insurance to satisfy the mortgage lender. In many cases, that is the amount of the mortgage itself. If a house is destroyed, however, such coverage might not be enough to rebuild completely. And depending on the type of insurance in effect, coverage for the contents of the home might be much less than what it would cost to replace those items.

There are two basic types of insurance coverage available, actual cash value and replacement cost coverage, but there are also several levels of coverage being offered.

The least expensive, and least desirable, is actual cash value coverage. With such a policy, the home is insured only for the face amount of the policy, no matter how much it might actually cost to rebuild it; the contents are insured for their actual cash value, up to a cap that is typically a percentage of the face value of the policy.

So if a house is insured for $400,000 and contents are covered for 50 percent of the policy limit, contents coverage would be $200,000. While that might seem like a lot of coverage, an actual cash value policy will reimburse a policyholder for only the depreciated value of an item. So, if a $2,000 computer system is worth $500 after depreciation, the insurance will pay only $500, no matter what the limit of coverage is.

Another type of coverage is replacement cost coverage, with different types available. Homeowners typically think a replacement cost policy provides enough coverage to replace the structure and its contents item by item. In practice, most replacement cost policies do not provide that level of protection. For example, most carriers have

TIMELY TIPS

Saving on Policies for Your Home

There are plenty of discounts out there, although they do vary by state and insurance company. Do you live near a firehouse? Do you live in a brick house? Are you a non-smoker? Are you 55 years old and retired? Answer yes to any of those questions and you're likely to get a break on your homeowner's policy. Here are other ways to save, according to the Insurance Information Institute.

✔ **Insure your house, not the land.** Don't include the value of your land in deciding how much insurance you need. After all, the land is rarely at risk, while your home can be harmed by fire, theft, vandalism, storms, etc.

✔ **Raise your deductible.** A deductible is the amount you pay out of pocket toward a loss before your insurance kicks in. Home insurance deductibles usually start at $250. If you raise it to $500, you cut up to 12 percent off your premiums. Raise it to $1,000 and you save 24 percent; $5,000 gets you up to 37 percent.

✔ **Improve security and safety in your home.** A sophisticated home security system could save you 15 to 20 percent. But even items such as deadbolt locks, burglar alarms and smoke detectors give you a little break.

✔ **Stick to an insurer.** If you've had coverage with a company for many years, you could qualify for special loyalty treatment. Some insurers will cut premiums by 5 percent if you stay 3 to 5 years, and as much as 10 percent after 6 years.

✔ **Review your policy annually.** Maybe you sold off a valuable item and no longer need the same amount of personal property coverage. (Or maybe you built a new sun room and need more.)

✔ **Look for group coverage.** Often, insurance companies work out deals with companies, associations, alumni groups and others. Don't simply toss out mail offers you get of this type—check to see if the discount is worth taking them up on.

✔ **Buy your home and auto insurance from the same company.** Many give a multiline discount if you buy both from them.

caps on the maximum reimbursement, with that cap being anywhere from 110 to 150 percent of the face value of the policy.

In addition to providing different levels of maximum coverage on replacement cost policies, insurers often define "replacement" differently. You could have true replacement cost coverage or functional replacement cost coverage; the former would pay to replace an item with its equal, while the latter would replace it with a functional equivalent. So, with true replacement cost coverage, a hand-hewed oak beam would be replaced with a hand-hewed oak beam. With functional coverage, it would be replaced with any beam that would perform the same function.

The very best coverage provides true replacement of the structure regardless of the cost. Such policies generally cost about 25 percent more than less comprehensive policies.

What's insured and what isn't. Studies show that many people believe their homeowners' insurance covers losses that, in fact, are not covered.

Flood damage, for example, is not covered by a typical homeowner's policy. If you buy a house in a flood-prone zone, you will need a separate flood insurance policy. You can get flood insurance information at www.fema.gov, the site for the Federal Emergency Management Agency.

Vehicles stolen from or damaged on your property are often not covered. Nor is damage from a break in the main water line outside your house or from a broken sewer line. Mold damage is typically not covered, nor is damage from termites or other infestations.

Many homeowners do not realize that certain valuables, such as jewelry, antiques and stamp and coin collections, may be significantly underinsured under a standard policy. Most policies provide only limited coverage for such items: a standard policy might limit coverage for such items to just $500.

Homeowners' insurance does not cover personal property and equipment if you are using your

house for business purposes. Further, the liability portion of the policy does not cover injuries if a customer or client gets hurt on the property.

What to do? Check with your insurance agents and buy any additional insurance that may be necessary. (See "Extra Coverage That's Worth It" on facing page.) You should also determine whether endorsements are available to increase coverage for items like jewelry, antiques and valuable collections. If you use part of your home for business buy a separate business policy.

—Jay Romano

✔ TIMELY TIPS

Do You Need Pet Insurance?

Expensive new medical treatments to keep pets living longer have made the question of buying pet insurance more pressing. But before you invest in the coverage consider this:

✔ Pet insurance can cost some $4,000 over a pet's lifetime, and chances are that's far more than you will need for vet expenses.

✔ However, should your dog require a new kidney or radiation therapy (yes, both are performed on pets), it could set you back up to $5,000 or more.

✔ Get quotes for pet insurance from companies like Veterinary Pet Insurance (petinsurance.com, 888-899-4874) or the Hartville Group's Pets Health Care Plan (petshealthplan.com, 800-807-6724). Or ask your employer. More than 1,500 companies, such as Chipotle and Google, offer it as an optional employee benefit.

✔ As always, shop around. Compare monthly and yearly premium costs and find out about co-pays, deductibles and limits. Calculate the final cost over the estimated life of your pet. You may find it makes more sense to funnel premium costs directly into your savings.

What to Look for in Auto Insurance

The protection you need at a cost you can afford

And you thought buying the car was difficult. In most states, drivers are required to have liability insurance for each driver of the car and for the other person's car in case of an accident. Insurance providers are just waiting to insure you and your new automobile, but what protection you need, and how much, may be very different from what they are offering. Here's how to sort through the various aspects of auto insurance and to determine the correct deductibles.

Your options. Most states require bodily injury liability insurance. This way you are covered if you're in an accident and the driver of the other car sues you for his medical bills. Also mandatory in some states is personal injury protection, which covers medical costs for you and your family, even if the other driver caused the accident. Property damage liability insurance kicks in when the car of the other driver in the accident is totaled, for example. Collision insurance covers repairs on or replacement of your car after an accident. Comprehensive insurance kicks in if your car

Extra Coverage That's Worth It

Are your diamonds and pearls insured for their current value? Are you protected from the potential financial ruin of liability suits? The following two types of insurance are worth contemplating.

Insuring Your Valuables

Nearly all home insurance policies come with a provision that pays for stolen jewelry. But that provision is small. Many policies pay up to $2,500 for a stolen item, regardless of how expensive it may be. Some pay as little as $1,000, and a few provide coverage of up to $5,000.

But the cost of that same piece of jewelry rises with inflation, so the value of even a few items could be higher than the minimal coverage. And while your policy may cover the full value of jewelry destroyed in a fire or in the collapse of a house, not much jewelry is lost in those ways. The real problems are crime and just plain losing things. Some 85 percent of insurance company payments related to jewelry are for theft and for what the insurers call "mysterious loss."

All home insurance companies sell extra coverage that will pay to replace prized jewelry or, in some cases, pay the full value of the item in cash. But few people buy additional coverage, which is often referred to as "scheduled personal property" or, in insurance shorthand, as a rider or floater.

Many think they will never need the coverage. And others feel that compiling a list of jewelry—and, often, having to document its value, sometimes with an appraisal—is too much of a bother.

In pure dollar terms, the special coverage often does not seem expensive. Jewelry insurance typically costs $10 to $15 per $1,000 of coverage. At that rate, insurance on $5,000 worth of jewelry can cost as little as $50 a year; for baubles valued at $100,000, the cost, at the lowest rate, would be $1,000. Not a staggering amount, some might say. But you would pay about the same rate for a much broader policy that covered just about everything that could possibly go wrong with a house.

Moreover, the rates are much higher—$25 per $1,000 and more—in places where there are lots of jewels and lots of losses.

The Case for Umbrella Coverage

The kind of accidents that cause elephantine lawsuits are, mercifully, not everyday events. But when they do occur, the results can be devastating. You could lose your savings, your home, even part of your salary for years.

To prevent such a nightmare you could get an extra insurance policy, known as umbrella or excess liability coverage, which takes care of liability for lawsuits, medical bills and such above the $100,000 to $500,000 in liability coverage that comes with a standard homeowners or auto insurance policy. And the cost is usually a fraction of the price of a typical package of home and auto insurance.

Buying such coverage usually does not greatly increase the overall cost of home and auto insurance. For example, insurance on a $1 million home might run $4,500 a year. Two cars could raise the cost of the package to $7,500. And $5 million in umbrella coverage might cost about $600 more, or about 8 percent of the total.

Around the country, at insurance companies dealing with rich clients, the first million in coverage is usually the most expensive, at perhaps $150 to $300 annually. Each additional million in coverage, insurance experts say, could cost around $100 to $125 annually. The situation is often the reverse for the many insurers who specialize in middle- and lower-income clients. Often their rates shoot up after the first million in umbrella coverage because they have only a small group of buyers of umbrella policies larger than $1 million. A smaller pool of customers creates more risk per dollar of premium for an insurer, so the insurer charges more for the coverage.

—Joseph B. Treaster

is stolen or damaged by vandalism or a natural disaster, such as a flood or fire.

Coverage you need. Generally insurance experts counsel that you buy as much liability coverage as you're worth. After all, a lawsuit after an accident could wipe you out.

Collision and comprehensive coverage accounts for 30 to 45 percent of your premium. A higher deductible will mean a lower premium. For example, increasing your deductible from $200 to $500 on collision coverage could reduce your premium

Filing an Auto Insurance Claim

Sooner or later a fender bender is bound to occur. Here's how to file a claim, according to the Insurance Information Institute.

1. Get in touch with your insurer immediately after an accident, regardless of whether you were at fault.

2. Ask your agent what documentation you will need in filing your claim, such as a police report, witness statements, tow-truck receipts, etc. Maintain good records of all conversations, noting times and names.

3. Ask your insurer when a claims adjuster will be assigned to investigate your accident. Keep in regular contact with the insurer and the adjuster to prevent a prolonged process.

4. If your claim is denied and you disagree with the decision, contact your state insurance commission. You can find a directory of state offices at the National Association of Insurance Commissioners website: www.naic.org.

5. Other options for dispute resolutions are to get an arbitrator from the American Arbitration Association (www.adr.org); or, as a final and expensive measure, hire a lawyer to represent your claim.

by as much as 30 percent. If the cost of your collision and comprehensive insurance is more than 10 percent of your car's Blue Book value, you may want to consider dropping it. Remember, though, that if you are in an accident you may find that repairs on your car cost more than your car is worth. In other words, if you drive an old jalopy worth less than $2,000, the premium cost may not be worth what you'd get in case of an accident. The most you might get is the car's Blue Book value—not much if your car is more than 5 years old.

Savings. You may be able to cut your car insurance premiums by maintaining a safe driving record, installing anti-theft devices or simply by driving a low number of miles each year.

Uninsured or underinsured motorist coverage is also available and is probably cheaper if you buy it in your homeowners or life insurance policy. You may also want to consider an umbrella policy (see page 253), which covers a variety of liabilities.

The ABCs of Filing Your Taxes

When paying income taxes, master the basics

Whether you tackle the 1040 on your own or make a mad dash for the nearest H&R Block at 9 p.m. on April 15, there are some fundamentals you need to understand. They could help you save money every step of the way.

How much to withhold. Your employer will typically withhold income taxes from your paycheck. The precise amount withheld for federal income taxes depends on how you fill out your W-4 form, which you complete when you start a new job.

You provide information about your marital status and whether you have children or work more than one job. This information determines how many "personal allowances" you are eligible for.

The more allowances you claim, the less tax will be withheld from your paycheck. You can claim all of the allowances you're eligible for, some of them or none at all.

Just remember that you don't want to have too much withheld, thereby providing the government with an interest-free loan. The I.R.S. (irs.gov) has a calculator that helps you aim for the number of allowances that will come close to matching the amount of tax you'll owe.

Cutting your tax bill. The government allows you to deduct certain items from your gross income (the amount you earn before taxes) thereby shrinking the pool of money you're taxed on. This can be done in several ways:

EXCLUSIONS: These items either help reduce your gross income or they don't add to it. For instance, pretax contributions to your employer-sponsored retirement account or a flexible spending account will reduce your gross income, dollar for dollar. If you collect interest from a municipal bond investment, it won't add to your gross income.

ABOVE-THE-LINE DEDUCTIONS: The next way to whittle down your gross income is through certain deductions available to all taxpayers, known as adjusted gross income, or A.G.I. Once you subtract these—they include items like moving expenses, student loan interest and certain retirement contributions—you arrive at your A.G.I.

These "above the line" deductions are deemed more beneficial than "below the line" deductions, which are often subject to income limits or other restrictions. Meanwhile, your eligibility for other deductions will be based on your A.G.I., so the smaller it is, the better.

BELOW-THE-LINE DEDUCTIONS: Most taxpayers are also eligible for the standard deduction; the amount of this deduction varies depending on your filing status (single, married filing jointly, etc.).

But if your eligible individual deductions exceed the amount of the standard deduction—or you're ineligible for the standard deduction—it makes sense to itemize your deductions.

ITEMIZING: You'll need to list each item on a form called Schedule A, which is part of Form 1040. Some of the most common itemized deductions include mortgage interest, charitable donations, job-related expenses and certain losses arising from casualty and theft.

CREDITS: Some taxpayers are also eligible for tax credits. These are dollar-for-dollar reductions of taxes owed. So, for instance, if you end up owing $2,000 in taxes but are eligible for a $500 tax credit, your tax bill will drop to $1,500. This differs from a $500 tax deduction, which would simply reduce the amount of your income subject to tax by $500. Some of the most commonly used credits include the earned income tax credit, the child and dependent care credit and education credits (all are explained on www.irs.gov).

Dealing with the alternative minimum tax. Some taxpayers might be subject to the alternative minimum tax, which is a parallel tax system set up in 1969 to ensure that the wealthiest taxpayers paid their fair share of taxes. But since the A.M.T. was never indexed for inflation, it now entraps more upper-middle-income taxpayers.

If you expect to be caught by the A.M.T., you should calculate your taxes twice, once under the regular system and again under the A.M.T. rules, which, in part, add back the deductions that are not allowed under its own set of rules and rates.

Filing taxes. Some people prefer to hand over all records, receipts and other paperwork to an accountant. Beyond recommendations from friends and family members, you can find a list of advisers through the National Association of Tax Professionals (natptax.com). Keep in mind

MONEY

Preparing Tax Returns Right the First Time

Avoid these common tax errors before you sign the tax check

- Are your W-2s and 1099s correct? If not, have them corrected so I.R.S. records agree with the amount shown on your return.

- Be sure you claimed all of your dependents, such as elderly parents who may not live with you.

- If you are single and live with a dependent, see if you qualify for the lower tax rates available to a head of household or surviving spouse with a dependent child.

- Recheck your cost basis in the shares you sold this year, particularly shares of a mutual fund. Income and capital gains dividends that were automatically reinvested in the fund over the years increase your basis in the mutual fund and thus reduce a gain or increase a loss that you must report.

- Fill out Form 8606,Nondeductible I.R.A. Contributions, for your deposits to an I.R.A. account if you don't claim any deductions for the contributions.

- If you worked for more than one employer, be sure to claim the credit for any overpaid Social Security taxes withheld.

- Check last year's return to see if there are any items that carry over to this year, such as capital losses or charitable contributions that exceeded the amount you were previously able to deduct.

- Don't report a state tax refund as income if you didn't claim an itemized deduction for the tax when it was originally paid.

- If you adopted a child, check your eligibility for a tax credit for the adoption, subject to certain limitations.

- People 65 and older who don't itemize deductions should claim a special, higher-than-normal standard deduction.

that only certified public accountants, enrolled agents and tax lawyers can represent you before the I.R.S.

If you have a pretty straightforward situation, you may want to do your own return. Here are some options for filing:

I.R.S. FREE FILE. You can file your return online through the I.R.S. Web site (www.irs.gov). But if your income is $56,000 or less, you can use the Free File program, which provides access to free tax software. Remember that while this service is free for federal tax returns, the sites charge different amounts to process your state returns.

If you make more than $56,000, you can still fill out and file your federal forms electronically (free) through the "Free File Fillable Forms" program, but you do not get access to any tax software. Visit your state tax department's Web site to see what options it offers for electronic filing.

TAX SOFTWARE. You can buy and download income tax software online or buy similar packages off the shelf. Prices range from roughly $25 to just under $100. Some of the most widely known programs include TurboTax, H&R Block's TaxCut and TaxAct.

Record keeping. The rule of thumb: keep records supporting your tax return for 7 years. The I.R.S. generally has 3 years to perform an audit. But if the tax man suspects you haven't reported a sizable chunk of income (exceeding 25 percent of the gross income reported on your return), the I.R.S. can try to collect the remainder for up to 6 years.

—Tara Siegel Bernard

25 Easily Overlooked Deductions

Claim any one of these and lower your tax bill

Expenses for everything from contact lenses to dry cleaning could help you lower your tax bill. The tax law allows many personal and business expenses to be deducted from your income before you figure your tax liability. The more you can subtract, the more you reduce the amount of your taxable income. Here's a list from the best-selling *Ernst & Young Tax Guide* of 25 deductions that are easily overlooked.

1. Appraisal fees: When paid to determine the value of a charitable gift or the extent of a casualty loss.

2. Business gifts: No more than $25 to any one person per year.

3. Cellular telephone: When used in your business or required by your employer, the cost of the phone, plus phone calls made, may be deductible.

4. Charitable expenses for volunteer work: Fourteen cents a mile (in 2009) for use of your car, plus out-of-pocket spending for such items as uniforms and supplies.

5. Commissions on sale of assets: Brokerage or other fees to complete a sale are taken into account when you figure your profit or loss (generally added to your cost for the asset).

6. Contact lenses: Also include the cost of eyeglasses or cleaning solution.

7. Contraceptives: Legitimate medical items include birth control pill and legal abortions.

8. Drug and alcohol abuse treatment: Includes meals and lodging when staying at a treatment center. Smoking cessation programs can also be deducted if they are considered medically necessary by your physician to reduce health risks.

9. Educational expenses: To improve or keep up your skills at your current job.

10. Employment agency fees: Whether you get a new job or not; but not if you're looking for your first job or switching occupations. Résumé and travel costs are also deductible.

11. Foreign tax: If you pay tax to another country on income from foreign investments, you can get a deduction or credit for those payments when figuring your U.S. tax.

12. Gambling losses: Only up to the amount of reported winnings.

13. Laundry service on a business trip: You needn't pack for an entire trip.

14. Moving expenses: When changing jobs or starting work for the first time, and only if the new job means a 50-mile-or-longer extra commute if you don't move.

15. Premium on taxable bonds: Investors who buy taxable bonds for more than face value can gradually deduct the excess each year they own the bond.

16. Medical transportation: You can claim 24 cents per mile plus tolls and parking in 2009. The amount can change annually.

17. Orthoepedic shoes: The extra amount over the cost of normal shoes.

18. Penalty for early withdrawal of savings: When a certificate of deposit is cashed in before maturity, a penalty is deductible as an adjustment to income.

19. Points on a home mortgage: Deductible as a lump sum when paid on a loan to buy or remodel a main residence; deductible gradually over the life of the loan when paid to refinance a mortgage.

20. Self-employment tax: Adjustment allows the self-employed to reduce taxable income by half their self-employment Social Security and Medicare tax.

21. Support for special schooling: For the men-

MONEY

tally or physically impaired, when the school is primarily to help them deal with their disability.

22. Support for a visiting student: Up to $50 per month in housing, food and support for live-in exchange student is deductible, only if you're not reimbursed.

23. Tax preparation: Accountant's fees, legal expenses, tax guides and computer programs.

24. Work clothes: When required for work, but not suitable for ordinary wear.

25. Worthless stock: Claimed as a capital loss in the year it first has no value. (Less than one cent per share generally is considered worthless.)

NOTE: Some deductions are limited. For example, only the portion of total medical expenses exceeding 7.5 percent of your adjusted gross income is deductible. "Miscellaneous" deductions, including most employment-related and investment expenses, are deductible only to the extent they exceed 2 percent of adjusted gross income.

SOURCE: Adapted from the *Ernst & Young Tax Guide*

Six Year-End Tax-Saving Tips

As the year closes, consider these strategies

Taxes are among the few obstacles to success that investors can maneuver around. Here are some moves many investors can consider as the year winds down.

Harvest your losers. You cannot will a stock or mutual fund to rise in value as the year comes to a close, but you can extract some benefit from the laggards in your accounts that are not tax-sheltered. When you sell shares of a stock that is trading below your purchase price, those losses can be used to offset capital gains realized elsewhere in your portfolio, thus reducing your tax bill.

Even if you have no gains to offset for the year, you can still realize losses and use them to reduce

ordinary income. Say a stock you bought for $6,000 is now worth half of that. If you took the $3,000 loss, you could reduce your taxable income by $3,000. For investors in the 35 percent bracket, that works out to tax savings of $1,050. So instead of being down $3,000, you're down only $1,950.

What if you book losses of more than $3,000? You can carry forward losses throughout your investing career, which means that today's declines can offset gains in future bull markets.

If you're thinking of dumping shares of a money-losing fund, do so quickly, in case the fund is preparing to present you with a tax bill. Every year, typically near year-end, mutual funds distribute capital gains that they have realized in their portfolios. Even funds that are down at year's end could distribute long-term taxable gains.

Be mindful of the "wash-sale rule." While it makes sense to sell some losers, it's important not to let those losses alter your asset allocation strategy.

One way to avoid this is to get back into the market immediately. But the I.R.S. says the tax-loss benefit is forfeited if you step back into the same or "substantially identical" investment within 30 days of your sale. This is called the wash-sale rule.

If you are selling shares of a particular stock or of an actively managed mutual fund, for example, a simple way around the rule is to buy a low-cost exchange-traded fund—an index fund, of sorts, whose shares trade like stock on an exchange.

Rebalance with taxes in mind. Year-end is a natural time for many investors to adjust their portfolios to keep to their long-term asset allocation goals. But if you plan to do so by trimming your stake in holdings that have appreciated significantly, and if you have both taxable and tax-advantaged accounts, consider selling the appreciated stock in your tax-deferred retirement account. That way you don't create a taxable event.

How to Pick an Accountant

Choosing from the pack of accountants out there is actually fairly straightforward

✔ **First ask for referrals** from friends and associates in similar financial circumstances. Then interview candidates to ensure that they have relevant experience.

✔ **Make sure you understand tax preparers' fee policies,** and don't be afraid to ask how the working relationship will proceed. Some important questions to ask: Who will prepare your return, the accountant you interview or a junior person? Will the return be outsourced to a site in India? What is the firm's policy on returning phone calls?

✔ **Pick your accountant early in the year.** As filing season nears, most accountants have less time to get to know their clients. What's more, many last-minute chances to save on taxes—like making charitable gifts to maximize deductions—disappear at the close of the calendar year.

—Eryn Brown

Give appreciated stock to charity. Year-end is also a good time to consider donating money to a charity, not only for philanthropic purposes, but also for the charitable deduction. But instead of reaching for your checkbook, take a look at your portfolio. By donating appreciated stock, you maximize your gift to the charity while minimizing your taxes. Instead of selling the stock, paying capital gains taxes out of pocket and then sending the cash to the charity, you can donate the appreciated security to the charity, which can then sell the asset on its own without tax consequence. And you can deduct the full market value of the holding at the time of donation.

Give appreciated stock to your children. The same idea for donating appreciated stock works well for paying for a college education. If you're saving money for a child through a custodial account, you can give appreciated shares to the child instead of selling the asset and funding the account with cash. The child can then sell at his or her lower capital gains tax rate, typically 5 percent instead of 15 percent.

Take full advantage of college savings vehicles. Parents who invest in state-sponsored college savings accounts called 529's can rebalance their investments once a year. Moreover, many 529's offer state tax deductions to residents on at least part of the annual contributions, provided that they use the in-state plan. While there are income restrictions and an annual contribution limit on Coverdell education savings accounts (another type of tax-deferred savings plan), there are no such restrictions on 529's. Specific rules vary for each state plan, but contributions into a 529 can be significant.

—Paul J. Lim

What to Show Your Accountant

Leave the shoebox at home, but you'll need brokerage statements and other records

Whether you prepare your own tax return or let an accountant do all the work, the task of gathering up your tax information is unavoidable. In general, you should have documentation that supports all income, deductions and credits that will appear on your return, but supporting documentation can come in many forms, as this listing, adapted from the *Ernst & Young Tax Guide,* shows.

Wages and salaries: W-2 forms, usually provided by your employer.

MONEY

 **TIMELY TIPS**

The Give-and-Take of Charitable Contributions

✔ When you donate goods, always ask for an itemized receipt in case the I.R.S. has any questions later on. You can deduct the fair market price of donations; that is, what they would sell for in a secondhand store. Visit a local thrift or consignment store to get a sense of prices.

✔ **When donating furniture,** support your valuation of how much you originally paid with photographs, receipts or canceled checks.

✔ **When contributing a car,** be aware that if it is worth more than $500, you cannot simply deduct the fair market value of the vehicle for taxes. Instead, your deduction will be determined once your car is sold and the charity sends you a receipt of the sale price.

—Alina Tugend

 **TIMELY TIPS**

Checking Up on Your Charity

✔ **The Internal Revenue Service** at 800-829-1040 or www.irs.gov, for information on a charity's tax exempt status.

✔ **Charity Navigator** at www.charitynavigator. org, for independent evaluations and ratings of charities.

✔ **GuideStar** at www.guidestar.org, for basic information on 1.5 million nonprofit organizations.

✔ **BBB Wise Giving Alliance** at www.give.org, tracks charities and is affiliated with the Council of Better Business Bureaus.

Dividends and interest: Form 1099-DIV and form 1099-INT, usually provided by the bank or company paying the dividend or interest.

Capital gains and losses: Broker's statements for purchase and sale of assets disposed of during the year and form 1099-B, usually provided by the broker who sold the assets.

Business income from sole proprietorships, rents and royalties: Books and records. Form 1099-MISC may also be provided by the payor of the income.

Business income from partnerships, estates, trusts and S corporations: Schedule K-1, usually provided by the partnership, estate, trust or S corporation.

Unemployment compensation: Form 1099-G, usually provided by the governmental agency paying the unemployment compensation.

Social Security benefits: Form SSA-1099, usually provided by the federal government.

State and local income tax refunds: Form 1099-G, usually provided by the state or locality that refunded the taxes.

Original issue discount: Form 1099-OID, usually provided by the issuer of the long-term debt obligation.

All distributions, both total and partial, from pensions, annuities, insurance, contracts, retirement or profit-sharing plans and individual retirement accounts (I.R.A.'s): Form 1099-R, usually provided by the trustee for the plan making the distribution.

Barter income: Form 1099-B, usually provided by the barter exchange through which the property or services were exchanged.

Sale of your home: Form 1099-S should be provided by the person who is responsible for the closing of the real estate transaction.

I.R.A. contributions: Form 5498, provided by the trustee or custodian of the I.R.A.

Moving and employee business expenses: Receipts and canceled checks.

Medical expenses: Receipts and canceled checks.

Mortgage interest and points paid on the purchase of a principal residence: Form 1098 or mortgage company statement, usually provided by the mortgage company.

Business and investment interest: Canceled checks and brokers' statements.

Real estate taxes: Canceled checks and mortgage company statements (if they are applicable).

Other taxes: Receipts and canceled checks.

Contributions: Receipts and canceled checks; written acknowledgment from the charitable organization is generally required for contributions of $250 or more. Form 1098-C if you donated a motor vehicle worth more than $500.

How to Handle an I.R.S. Audit

Chances are you'll end up paying after an audit

A lot of returns do not get audited, but the ones that do must undergo the scrutiny of some annoyingly nosy I.R.S. examiners. Your exam could well go beyond checking the validity of your tax deductions to looking around for income you may have neglected to report.

The I.R.S.'s weapon is what's popularly called a lifestyle audit, in which examiners take a global view of your financial and family affairs to see if your reported income is sufficient to support

INSIDE INFO

Who Gets Audited

O I.R.S. computer programs, using information from forms such as 1099s and W-2s, spew out returns that don't add up.

O The agency follows up on outside leads—from newspapers, public records and even tips from individuals.

O The I.R.S. uses a computer score system to pick audits. After a return is processed, it is assigned a numeric score. The agency says there is a "high potential" that returns with high scores will result in an audit and a higher income tax liability.

SOURCE: Internal Revenue Service

the lifestyle you're enjoying. Besides asking you for receipts for charitable donations, proof of business expenses and details of investment transactions, auditors may ask how you can afford that car and a second home on your income. Questions about the amount of your mortgage payment, whether your children work, what appliances you've recently bought, where you went to college and whether you've been divorced are also fair game.

The I.R.S.'s top audit targets are generally upper-income professionals, self-employed people, investors claiming big losses and people with considerable income from tips—but no group is immune. Most audits end up pulling in extra tax for the I.R.S., so emerging unscathed is a long shot.

Audits come in three flavors. Least intimidating is a correspondence audit—usually a letter asking for documentation to back up a single item. More fearsome are office audits, in which you go to an I.R.S. office for a face-to-face probe that may cover more topics in greater

MONEY

✔ TIMELY TIPS

How to Avoid Tax Problems

Five ways to improve your odds

The tax code is complicated, but that's no excuse for making big mistakes, even though the I.R.S. audits only about 1 percent of all returns (a higher percentage for the wealthy).

✔ **Downsize. Include all compensation.** There are lots of ways to earn taxable income and thus increase the amount we have to pay in taxes. Any time you receive something of value as an employee or consultant, you have to assess it. So ask yourself: What, of any value, did I take in or use last year thanks to someone else, and what might the tax implications be?

✔ **Beware the nanny tax.** If you have a babysitter, home health aide or housekeeper, you're probably responsible for more than just their Social Security and Medicare taxes. There may also be payments related to unemployment or disability insurance or workers' compensation coverage.

If you make mistakes, and the authorities catch up with you, pay the back taxes and fines promptly.

If your accountant expresses any doubt about how to handle all this, look to a specialist like Breedlove & Associates (www.breedlove-online.com), the Nanny Tax Company (www.nannytaxprep.com) or HomeWork Solutions (www.homeworksolutions.net) for help with the blizzard of paperwork that you'll need.

✔ **When not to do your own taxes.** Some people should not do their own taxes. They include: small-business owners; owners of investment properties; second-home owners, particularly those who rent out the property part of the year but also use it themselves; people with large investment losses who wish to reap tax benefits; anyone thinking about selling an asset that will lead to a large capital gain. Good preparers can help find savings, just as they can discover income you haven't reported. Their fees may also be tax-deductible.

✔ **Don't start in March.** Cramming all your thinking about taxes into the few weeks before April 15 is a recipe for errors. Your accountant might miss things, and you could, too. Try having a tax-focused conversation with an experienced accountant during the tax year. Then you'll be more likely to catch the need for quarterly filings or potential nanny tax issues, for example.

✔ **Check your work.** Last year's return is a good reference point, both when you start the filing process each year and again at the end. Double-check the math. The I.R.S. has both addition and subtraction on its list of most common errors. Topic 303 on the I.R.S. Web site (www.irs.gov) ticks off several others.

—Ron Lieber

detail. At the top tier are field audits, which most often involve business-related returns and are conducted by top-trained agents at a taxpayer's home or office. Office audits are most common, partly because budget restraints limit the number of face-to-face encounters the I.R.S. can afford. But exams by mail are also often based on the least solid suspicion of wrongdoing, so they are often the easiest to fight successfully.

When the I.R.S. contacts you, it has usually found at least something suspicious. Generally, it will be up to you to show why any proposed changes are wrong. Mail audits can often be handled on your own, but you may want guidance from an accountant on deeper probes. It's wise not to insist on total victory. Give the auditor a few small wins so the I.R.S. can close your case and move on. And like an elephant, the I.R.S. never forgets: if you have been audited before, the I.R.S. will remember. Don't repeat past mistakes.

SPENDING & SAVING

SPENDING

Consumer Advice

How to Shop Online
Ways to navigate the global flea market

These days shoppers rely on the Internet marketplace as unthinkingly as on a grocery cart in the supermarket. But from its giant worldwide flea markets—from the eBay auction site to specialized search sites like Kelkoo.com that list hundreds of overseas online stores—the Internet still has a way to go in terms of organizing its aisles. Where, then, to start?

For browsing, comparison shopping sites such as Bizrate.com, Shopping.Yahoo.com and Shopping.com, will spit out useful lists of prices and costs of shipping to your ZIP code for millions of items in categories like computers, jewelry and clothing.

Hobbyists and enthusiasts often offer expert advice on a particular category of merchandise. Visit Watchreport.com before buying a wristwatch, for example, Coffeegeek.com before purchasing anything even vaguely related to caffeine and Spongobongo.com before buying an Oriental rug.

If your search is very specific—if you already know the model number or product name—it may

---

 **TIMELY TIPS**

More Sites for Shoppers

✔ **Amazon.com** The online megastore. Books, music, videos, games, electronics, food, sporting goods and more.

✔ **Bankrate.com** and **Eloan.com** For comparing interest rates for mortgage, auto, credit card or other loans.

✔ **Bizrate.com** Lets you see how fellow consumers rate online merchants and compares prices.

✔ **Bizweb.com** Commercial sites on the Internet by category.

✔ **Buy.com** Good prices and service on electronics, books, music and video.

✔ **Buyersindex.com** Searches 20,000 Web sites and catalogs for the product you seek.

✔ **Buysafeshopping.com** Index of retailers pre-screened for safety.

✔ **Consumersearch.com** Reviews of products from a variety of publications.

✔ **Craigslist.org** Online classifieds for your area.

✔ **Deepdiscount.com** Low prices for DVDs, CDs and books.

✔ **eBay.com** The online auction house and storefront.

✔ **Half.com** To buy and sell new and used textbooks at reduced prices.

✔ **Epinions.com** Consumer reviews of many products and price comparisons.

✔ **Glimpse.com** Shop for shoes, clothes, jewelry and more by plugging in your favorite brands.

✔ **Netmarket.com** An electronics superstore.

✔ **Overstock.com** Plenty of bargains from designer pumps to chaise lounges. Check return policies carefully.

✔ **Pricegrabber.com, Pricescan. com** and **Shopping.com** Compare prices for computer hardware and software, electronics, movies, books and other goods.

✔ **Ubid.com** The site for electronics; some may be refurbished. Many items come with a 90-day warranty.

be faster to type in a simple keyword search at Google.com. Follow the resulting links to a store that stocks the merchandise.

Is the store unfamiliar? Before purchasing an item online from a merchant you don't know, conduct due diligence by checking merchant ratings at review sites like Epinions.com, at *Consumer Reports'* Consumerwebwatch.org or at the Better Business Bureau's bbb.org.

Protect yourself further by using a credit (rather than debit) card; federal law limits your liability for unauthorized charges to $50. Or, use the PayPal secure online account service (paypal.com). For more specifics on how to avoid being swindled on the Internet, read about common online cons at the Federal Trade Commission's consumer site at www.ftc.gov.

—Michelle Slatalla

Finding the Best Sales

The best time to buy that computer or refrigerator

There is a rhythm to the introduction of many consumer products, and the year-end holiday buying spree, when about 40 percent of all consumer products are purchased, sets that rhythm. New cars, electronics and most other items have to be in stores and ready to go by September.

A few products don't follow the pattern. The big selling season for large kitchen appliances, for example, is an abbreviated period before what the appliance makers call the cooking season. As you might guess, consumers want new appliances in place and ready to go before the Thanksgiving feast.

Sales of air conditioners are entirely weather related. A mild summer and retailers are stuck with inventory that needs to be cleared out with a big price reduction. Refrigerators tend to break in the heat, so that product has a summer selling season, too.

 **TIMELY TIPS**

How to Barter for Almost Anything

As we all know, exchanging goods and services goes back, well, forever. But a growing community, offline and online, is increasingly embracing bartering, often finding it more palatable to spend time than money. As for taxes, all trades must be treated as ordinary sales—there is neither a tax advantage nor disadvantage.

✔ The ubiquitous **Craigslist** (www.craiglist.org) offers barters for anything (clean my place and I'll give you a free massage, jewelry for high-end catering). But there are many quickly growing sites that are item-specific.

✔ At **Swaptree.com**, you can trade books (including textbooks), video games, CDs and DVDs online, paying only for shipping. Registration is free. Swaptree knows the weight and shipping cost of every item on its site and lets you pay online and print a postage label immediately. The site uses the same trust system as eBay. Traders are rated—the community self-polices.

✔ **Titletrader.com** also helps in exchanges of books, DVDs, CDs and games, using a credit system. You can give away an item and once it is received, you get request credits that you can use to get something else on the site.

✔ **Textswap.com** allows college students to trade textbooks. **Paperbackswap.com** is one of the most popular book-exchange sites.

✔ **Itex.com.** and International Monetary Systems (**ims.com**) are publicly traded and two of the largest bartering sites. Itex, founded in 1982, has 24,000 members. It works on a nonreciprocal trading system, using Itex accounts and Itex checkbooks. Itex dollars are earned by members who sell their products and services online; Itex charges a 5 to 7.5 percent fee for all trades.

—Alina Tugend

SPENDING

✔ TIMELY TIPS

How Much Do I Tip?

Tip jars are everywhere, even in self-serve cafeterias. Drop in a few coins if you wish, but it's no faux pas to pass. Tipping abroad varies by country and culture, so it's best to consult local guide books. Some guidelines for tipping domestically:

✔ AIRPORT

Car shuttle driver	$1-$2 per use
Hotel courtesy van	$1-$2
if driver helps with luggage	+$2
Taxi dispatcher	none
Taxi driver	15-20% of fare
Car service	Gratuity included or 15% of bill
Curbside baggage handler	$1-$2 per bag

✔ HOTEL

Doorman for special services	$1-$2
for help with baggage, depending on number of bags	$1-$2
Bellhop for taking baggage to room	$5-$10
(minimum of $1-$2 per bag)	
for delivering messages or packages	$1-$2 per delivery
Housekeeper	$5-$8 per day
for special service	+$1-$2 per day
Room service waiter	15-20% of bill
(if service is included in the bill)	5% or $1 minimum
Concierge	
for tickets, etc.	$5 to $10

✔ RESTAURANT

Coffee shop server	15-17% of bill
Maitre d'	
to get a good table	$10 for two
for four or more	$20 to $100
(upper amt. for five-star restaurants)	

Waiter/waitress	15-20% of bill

(if gratuities are included, an additional tip is due for special service)

Wine steward	15% of wine bill
Bartender	15% of liquor bill
Hat/coat check	$1-$2 per coat
Door attendant	$1-$2 per cab

✔ OTHER

Apartment doorman (at Christmas)	$20-$100
Barber	15% ($1 minimum)
Hairdresser	15%
Hair washer	$2 minimum
Manicurist	15%
Parking valet	$1-$2 per use
Rail porter	$1-$2 per bag

✔ 15% TIP TABLE:

Check	Tip	Check	Tip
$10	$1.50	$60	$9.00
$20	$3.00	$70	$10.50
$30	$4.50	$80	$12.00
$40	$6.00	$90	$13.50
$50	$7.50	$100	$15.00

It used to be that you'd pick up bargains after Christmas. But that is no longer the case. Merchants, who start putting up Christmas decorations at Halloween, extend the season in the other direction, too, well past New Year's Day. As shoppers use gift cards, the season moves out a few weeks more. It then gets pushed to the Super Bowl, especially for big-screen televisions. The selling season does finally screech to a halt near the end of February.

The big retailers—Wal-Mart, Costco and Best Buy, where Americans buy the bulk of their gear—rarely get stuck with much unwanted merchandise, so there's no need for a big sale. The stock has been carefully tracked with inventory control software, which keeps merchandise tight.

So this software is nothing but bad news for the consumer, right? Actually, it has been good news.

Though there are fewer jaw-dropping bargains, it allows customers to get a good price.

So is there still a way to game the system? Yes, but it takes a little more diligence. You have to avoid impulse buying, but still be ready to pounce quickly.

Know your product. Web sites like Engadget.com and Gizmodo.com are places to gather information on product releases. Twice.com also tracks developments that come out of trade shows like the Consumer Electronics Show in January or the Photo Marketing Association conference in early spring. Google Product Search (at google.com/products) and other price-comparison sites allow you to study which reputable dealer is also aggressive on price.

Monitor the prices. Watch the Sunday circulars or review them at SundaySaver.com. NexTag has a number of useful features to help you track price cuts. It e-mails you when a product finally drops to the price you are willing to pay. The site also lists products that recently had price cuts.

Wait for your price. NexTag also displays price history charts. You can divine a little from those as well. A constantly downward sloping line suggests that the manufacturer has control of inventory and prices are dropping at a natural pace. That means there's not much you can do. When it comes to electronics, anything you buy will be cheaper a month from now.

But a flat line that also shows some abrupt drops, however small, suggests a struggling product. A need to outflank a competitor with price promotions or trim growing inventories can cause that pattern. If the line is flat for a while, hold off buying. It will drop soon enough. It always does.

—Damon Darlin

How to Save on Your Wedding

A planner could actually help you rein in costs

The average American wedding runs nearly $28,000, according to a study by the Condé Nast Bridal Group. Some 36 percent of couples spend more than they had planned; 30 percent of brides' parents pay for the whole event. And more couples want extravagant gestures such as blanketing an entire ballroom with flowers or shooting off fireworks.

Overspending may be out of control for some, but here are a few commonsense approaches for those who want to keep costs down.

A wedding is a business transaction. As such it is also an opportunity to bargain and save hun-

INSIDE INFO

How America Tips

o Americans are giving tips to an "ever-expanding cadre, including fitness trainers, spa attendants, dog walkers, and elder-care workers," according to *Consumer Reports*.

o A survey of more than 1,800 Americans found average tip ranges of $10 to $20 for a newspaper carrier, $10 to $25 for a sanitation or recycling collector, $20 to $50 for a child care provider and $25 to $75 for a housekeeper. When in doubt, *Consumer Reports* advises, a worker who provides a weekly service should be given the equivalent of one week's pay.

o People in the Northeast are likely to tip the most, and people in the South the least, although southerners are more likely to supplement or substitute the tip with a gift.

TIMELY TIPS

Don't Forget to Tip the Hotel Maid

Seasoned business travelers always make sure to have a bunch of singles on hand to take care of the parking valet, the bellhop, the doorman and the cabby. But the hotel maid? Yes, although she may be unseen she shouldn't be overlooked.

✔ Ignore the laughable advice, frequently seen on Internet sites about travel and tipping, stating that $1 a day is standard for the maid. Actually, $5 to $8 a day is more like it.

✔ Keep in mind that hotel maids worry about being accused of stealing loose cash, and sometimes will not pick up a tip if they aren't sure it is a tip. So leave the tip on the pillow with a note that clearly indicates what it is. Write "For the housekeeper," or simply "Thanks."

—Joe Sharkey

SPENDING

✓ TIMELY TIPS

How to Save $100 or More This Year

Forget dumpster diving, recycling tin foil and other tacky tightwad tips. Instead, take a systematic look at your spending habits, then apply these suggestions for saving substantial sums.

✓ **1. Pick a bank wisely.** Look for free checking and no A.T.M. or debit card fees. Some banks will waive fees if you have your paycheck deposited directly.

✓ **2. Take advantage of your utility's "load management"** or "off-hours" programs for cheaper electricity bills. You save by allowing the company to switch off your water heater and air conditioner briefly during times of high demand.

✓ **3. Drop telephone calling plans with monthly fees** or minimum usage if you make few toll or long distance calls. Check your bill to see if you have optional calling services you don't use. Each one you drop could save you $40 or more a year.

✓ **4. Forgo stopping at convenience stores,** which often charge the highest prices around. Go to the nearest discount grocery store or drugstore instead.

✓ **5. Go grocery shopping with a list and stick to it.** Pay attention to the price per pound or other unit; compare among brands and go with the lowest price per unit.

✓ **6. Buy in bulk,** especially goods like paper towels and diapers. For example, babies use about 2,400 diapers their first year. A 5-cent savings in the cost of one diaper adds up to $120 a year.

✓ **7. Don't stick to one drug store.** They charge widely differing prices. Shop around and buy generic drugs, when possible. Order prescriptions by mail or through your health plan.

✓ **8. Keep your car engine tuned** and tires inflated to the proper pressure. Doing so can save you up to $100 a year on gas.

✓ **9. Cut round-trip airfare** by up to two-thirds. Buy in advance and include a Saturday night stayover.

✓ **10. Reconfigure your vacation plans.** Consider alternative travel programs that let you stay free with local families if you host others in your home. (See www.exchangezones.com, for example.)

SOURCES: Consumer Literacy Consortium, Federal Trade Commission

dreds, if not thousands, of dollars, says Shirit Kronzon, a lecturer at the Wharton School of Business of the University of Pennsylvania who wrote *The Bargaining Bride* with Andrew Ward, associate professor of psychology at Swarthmore College. "Most elements of the wedding are negotiable," she says.

You needn't be a pit bull to get a bargain. "You don't have to think of it as a formal, tough, adversarial negotiation," Kronzon says, "You just have to frame it as asking a question: 'What specials or promotions are you currently offering? Can you discount the gown or give me more photos for the same price?'" One potential money trap is an expensive outdoor wedding—with no Plan B for bad weather. A tent for a potential downpour can cost $40,000, depending on the size.

Hiring a wedding planner may help you keep on budget. Carley Roney, co-founder of TheKnot.com, which helps brides-to-be plan their weddings, says she doesn't think wedding planners are an assault on your budget. "You give them a budget, and their job is to make the wedding happen within that budget," she says. By not overspending, they can save you thousands of dollars.

Don't forget to calculate often-overlooked expenses or potential savings as you plan your budget. Consider tipping: 15 percent of a $20,000 catering bill means an additional $3,000. Or, if you're holding your wedding at a popular beach site, a difference of one weekend can bring you from high-season rates to off-season rates.

—Francine Parnes

Lowering Your Medical Bills
When money is tight, everything is negotiable

Doctors, hospitals and medical labs are accustomed to negotiating. After all, they do it all the time with insurers. A hospital may have a dozen or more rates for one procedure, depending on whether Medicare, Medicaid or a private insurer is paying the bill. Your request for a special arrangement will hardly confound their accounting department, and it is usually in everyone's interest to avoid dealing with a bill collector. Here are some bargaining tips to keep in mind.

Dealing with doctors. Don't be shy. Talk directly to your doctor about your financial situation. If that makes you uncomfortable, then go to the billing manager. The office may be able to offer you a discount of 10 to 30 percent depending on the practice (specialists may offer a bigger break), or propose a plan in which you pay your balance in a few installments or on a monthly basis—typically at no interest.

Offer to pay cash up front. Doctors can lose thousands of dollars every year on unpaid bills and spend countless hours haggling with insurers over reimbursements. If you can make their life simpler by offering to pay right away, you're likely to get a small discount—even if you don't have financial hardship.

Be respectful. You're negotiating for your health, not haggling over a used car. So don't take bids and ask your doctor to match it. That could spell the end of the relationship.

Talking to hospitals. Strike a deal, then check in. If you need shoulder surgery, for instance, but don't have insurance—or are facing a high hospital co-payment—call the hospital's billing department and explain that you would like to discuss getting a discount and why. You may want to ask to pay the lowest rate they give an insurance company.

Make a counteroffer. Like doctors, hospitals would rather be paid something than nothing. They would rather set up a payment plan than turn it over to a collections agency and then expect to write it off.

If you end up with a bill you can't pay—or at least can't pay right away—don't panic. Find out what Medicare would pay for your condition or surgery, since that program tends to pay less than private insurers. You can find that figure at the Department of Health and Human Services database, www.hospitalcompare.hhs.gov, by clicking on the button "find and compare hospitals." If your situation is truly dire or your bill very large, you may qualify for charity care. But you'll have to show the hospital proof of your income and your hardship.

Bargaining with labs. Charges for lab work can be exorbitant. But, as with hospital bills, the numbers you see on your statement may not reflect what most insurers actually pay. Negotiate just as you would with your doctor or hospital. Quest Diagnostics, the largest clinical laboratory in the country, for instance, offers a six-month interest-free payment plan, as well as financial assistance for those with real hardship.

—Lesley Alderman

SPENDING

How to Save on Your Eyes

A frugal look at careful vision care

It's easy to spend hundreds, if not thousands, of dollars on your eye care, when you throw in designer frames and prescription lenses with a high-tech coating. As for contact lenses, the daily wear variety can easily run $500 a year. Here's a look at careful vision care.

1. Study your coverage. If you have coverage, call your carrier or visit its Web site to find out what you're entitled to. Ideally, use an eye doctor covered by your plan. Not only will it be less expensive, but a network doctor can help you determine what your coverage entails by tapping into the insurer's database.

2. Go easy on exams. Contrary to what you may have read or heard, if you're under 40 and healthy, you need an eye exam only every 5 to 10 years. If you already wear glasses or have a family history of eye disease, you may need to have your eyes checked more frequently. Once you hit your 40s, you'll need a checkup every 2 to 4 years. For ages 55 and up the recommendation is to get an exam every 1 to 3 years.

3. Know your discounts. If you buy glasses from a retail store, ask about discounts. LensCrafters, for instance, offers a 30 percent discount to members of AAA and AARP.

4. Take your prescription home with you. After your eye exam, ask for a copy of your prescription so you can buy your glasses or contacts lenses from any supplier you choose. An eye examiner is required to give you the prescriptions once an exam (or fitting, in the case of contact lenses) is complete. If the eye shop doesn't offer it, ask. Or call later and request that it be faxed, mailed or e-mailed to you.

5. Comparison-shop for frames. Look at a local retail store for a style you like and then price it at outlets including your doctor's shop, Internet sites, chains like LensCrafters and wholesale clubs like Costco. Online, go to framesdirect. com, where you can upload a picture of yourself and try particular frames on your face.

For reviews of Internet retailers, look at eyeglassretailerreviews.com. For a cheap pair of backup glasses, try zennioptical.com, which sells generic frames, including lenses with anti-scratch coating, at bargain prices.

6. Don't scrimp on your eyeglass lenses. It's hard to cut corners here, especially if you have a complicated prescription. But be sure to ask about the warranty on your lenses and on any additional coatings you've opted for. Scratch-resistant coatings and shatter-resistant polycarbonate lenses, for instance, are typically covered for a year. If your lenses break or get scratched, you'll be able to get them replaced.

7. Do scrimp on your reading glasses. If you use a separate pair of glasses for reading, in most cases those basic magnifying glasses are fine for short-term tasks. But if you have an astigmatism, or your eyes do not have the same prescription, a custom-made pair will be better. Discuss the purchase with your doctor.

8. Shop around for contact lenses and cleaning fluids. Look at sites like 1800contacts.com or drugstore.com and compare. The more your order, of course, the better the deal. Just remember to take shipping into account when you order online. Offline, Costco, Sam's Club and BJ's are also good sources for well-priced lenses and glasses.

9. If your pennies are truly pinched... Look at the list of organizations that provide financial aid for eye care at the National Eye Institute's site. For instance, the American Optometric Association, through its Vision USA program, provides free eye care to families that don't qualify for government aid or private health insurance.

—Lesley Alderman

Are Warranties Worth It?

Consumer advocates are dubious about many

Extended service warranties, or product "accessories," as they are known in the business, are available for everything from $20 DVDs to $9,000 stoves. And they seem like a good idea: products are increasingly complex and expensive, or impossible, to repair. Where once appliance repairs rarely hit $400, today, $1,000 repairs are not uncommon. Yet consumer advocates generally advise against extended warranties.

Extended warranties are a huge business for retailers, who depend on them to lift profits in competitive markets. In electronics, the difference between what a store pays for goods and what it sells them for, is about 25 percent at chains like Best Buy. Extended service contracts, on the other hand, produce an estimated gross margin of 45 percent or more. Hence, the hard sell.

In some cases, they may be worth it. Repairing a ruined laptop screen costs about the same as a new machine, or $1,000 for a top-of-the-line model. So a policy that covers repairs or replacement for any reason, including damage caused by the customer, makes sense.

Cellphone coverage is another matter. Millions of cellphones disappear or are damaged each year, and some kind of coverage sounds practical. Usually offered by service providers for about $5 a month, the plans seem cheap. If you often lose phones, or if yours is stolen within three months, coverage can save money.

But depending on the company and the fine print, there might be a deductible and limitations on how the phone was damaged, for example. If a phone lasts 23 months before it breaks, the cost of coverage could be about $165 ($115 in premiums, $50 for a deductible) on a phone that might sell

 TIMELY TIPS

What to Ask About Warranties

Consumers should consider extended service warranties product by product, knowing that all products carry some risk of malfunction. While you cannot compare prices on warranties as you do on products, you can ask questions—and plenty of them—even at the cash register.

✔ **Is there a copy of the agreement?** Is it for parts and service only or replacement? What kind of replacement?

✔ **Is there a deductible?** How much?

✔ **Who provides service?** What training do they have?

✔ **Does the coverage duplicate the manufacturer's warranty?**

✔ **Does coverage start at the time of purchase or after the manufacturer's warranty expires?** Many products break, if they break, in the first year. What is the risk that the product will break while under extended coverage?

✔ **What is the consumer's obligation if something breaks?** Is the product mailed to the dealer or manufacturer? Is that convenient or practical?

✔ **What is your realistic use of this product going to be?** Do you lose cellphones often? Do you sometimes kick refrigerators? Is your son likely to take his laptop to the beach?

—Susan Ferraro

new for $150 or, with rebates and special offers, might cost nothing.

Consumer Reports generally advises against buying extended service contracts because the cost of repairing could be the same as the warranty cost, so why not keep that money in your pocket. One *Consumer Reports* survey found that 3 years after purchase just 5 to 7 percent of televisions needed repair, and 13 percent of vacuums (not counting belt replacements). But 33 percent of laptops had been sent to the shop or the recycle bin.

The consumer group recommends extended service policies on three items: laptops, treadmills (too cumbersome to take to the shop, and service calls are expensive) and plasma TVs, because of their expense. Some consumers skip extra coverage and choose, when possible, products with long-lasting manufacturer's warranties. It pays, then, to compare not only price but also warranty duration to get the best deal.

—Susan Ferraro

The Deals at Your Post Office
The next best thing to a personal assistant

Sure, the lines are often long and the staff is sometimes surly, but if you go on vacation your local post office will hold your mail for free, and if you move, will forward it to you for one year. Here are eight other ways the post office can save you time and money.

1. Get special rates. Packages that contain books, printed materials, DVDs, CDs and the like get a special "media mail" rate, also known as the book rate. It's cheaper than Parcel Post, though a bit slower. Just keep the package weight below 70 pounds and don't include advertising in it.

2. Send mail fast. Priority mail lets you send your items in envelopes and boxes that are provided for free. They must weigh less than 70 pounds and are delivered within 2 to 3 days. Fastest and most expensive is Express Mail, for packages weighing

---

 TIMELY TIPS

How to Be a Wise Consumer
A lifetime of rules for consuming sensibly

✔ Never pay a real estate agent a 6 percent commission.

✔ Buy used things, except maybe used tires.

✔ Get on the do-not-call list and other do-not-solicit lists so you can't be tempted by marketers.

✔ Watch infomercials for their entertainment value only.

✔ Know what your credit reports say, but don't pay for that knowledge: go to www.annualcreditreport.com to get them.

✔ Consolidate your cable, phone and Internet service to get the best deal.

✔ Resist the lunacy of buying premium products like $2,000-a-pound chocolates or $3,000 handbags.

✔ Lose weight. Carrying extra pounds costs tens of thousands of dollars over a lifetime.

✔ Do not use your home as a piggy bank if home prices are flat or going down or if interest rates are rising.

✔ Enroll in a retirement plan.

✔ Postpone buying high-tech products like PCs, digital cameras and high-definition TVs for as long as possible. And then buy after the selling season or buy older technology just as a new technology comes along.

✔ And, finally, make your own coffee.

—Damon Darlin

less than 50 pounds. Choose overnight or second-day delivery. On-time delivery is guaranteed.

3. Secure your package. For nominal amounts, you can get a slew of safety services: package tracking, confirmation, insurance, etc. Or, get a package of services for about $10 using registered mail.

4. Buy stamps 24/7. For a nominal fee, order stamps for home delivery online at www.usps.com or by phone at 800-STAMP-24. Nearly 45,000 stores, from supermarkets to big-box stores, also sell stamps at face value. To ship a package domestically or overseas, figure how much postage you need at www.usps.com, then charge it and print out a shipping label. For an extra charge, a letter carrier will come to your place to fetch it.

5. Get money orders. For amounts less than $1,000, you can buy a money order, a safe alternative to sending cash through the mail. It can be cashed only by the recipient, and because it is prepaid it can't bounce. If lost or stolen, take your receipt to the Post Office for a replacement. If you receive a money order as payment and want to verify its authenticity, hold it to the light. You should see a watermark of Ben Franklin on the left side and the letters "USPS" from top to bottom.

6. Find ZIP codes. Use the ZIP code locator at www.usps.com or call 800-ASK-USPS for missing ZIP codes.

7. Customize your own stamp. Brides and proud dads everywhere love personalized postage stamps (worth the going postage rate). Photos must meet certain standards—no pornography or images of Hitler, for example. And, no advertising allowed. Go to an approved vendor, such as Endicia.com, Stamps.com or Zazzle.com; order and pay online, and stamps arrive within a week or so.

8. Expand your collection. Start or expand a stamp collection. Most post offices stock new issues and mint sets of commemorative stamps, as well as special stamps, such as the Love and Christmas stamps. Workaday stamps, called definitive stamps, feature contemporary people, places and causes and sell indefinitely.

How to Fight Identity Theft
Tips for protecting your personal data

Some 9 million Americans fall victim to some sort of identity theft each year, says the Federal Trade Commission. In its worst form, a victim's Social Security numbers is stolen and credit card accounts are tapped. The private information is used by thieves to open new accounts, to secure loans and often to lead parallel lives of luxury.

You can take steps to protect yourself from becoming an identity or data theft victim. Here are some tips on what to do to prevent it.

Restrict access to your personal data by signing up for the national do-not-call registry (www.donotcall.gov). Remove your name and address from the phone book and reverse directories. Remove your name from the marketing lists of the credit bureaus to reduce credit card solicitations. Go to www.optoutprescreen.com to start.

Rein in your Social Security number. Remove it from your checks, insurance cards and driver's license. Ask your bank not to use it as your identification number. Refuse to give it to merchants, and be careful even with medical providers. The only time you are required to give it by law is when a company needs it for government purposes, such as for tax matters and Medicare.

SPENDING

How Thieves Take Your Identity

Skilled identity thieves use a variety of methods to get hold of your credit card and Social Security card numbers, as well as other personal data. Here are five ways.

○ **Dumpsterdiving**. Rummaging through trash looking for bills or other paper with your personal data on it.

○ **Skimming.** Stealing credit or debit card numbers by using a special data storage device when processing your card.

○ **Phishing.** Pretending to be financial institutions or companies and sending email spam or pop-up messages to get you to reveal your personal data.

○ **Changingyour address.** Diverting your billing statements to another location by completing a change of address form. They then receive the bills with your data on them.

○ **Old-fashionedstealing.** Stealing wallets and purses, mail, including bank and credit card statements, pre-approved credit offers and new checks or tax data. Stealing personnel records or bribing employees who have access to them.

SOURCE: Federal Trade Commission

Sites for More on Identity Theft

○ FederalTrade Commission: Consumer.gov

○ FreeAnnual Credit Report: Annualcreditreport.com

○ PrivacyRights Clearinghouse: Privacyrights.org

○ IdentityTheft Resource Center: Idtheftcenter.org

○ Internet Crime Complaint Center:Ic3.gov

○ UnitedStates Postal Inspection Service: usps.com

○ IdentityTheft Assistance Center: Identitytheftassistance.org

Avoid linking your checking to savings. Use a credit card for purchases rather than a debit card. While individual liability for fraudulent credit card purchases is only $50, it can be higher for debit cards: up to $500, or even all the money in your account in some cases.

Do not let your credit cards out of your sight. Do not let store clerks take away your card on the pretext that there is a "problem." Shred all unneeded documents that contain personal data.

Protect your home computer with virus software and a firewall, especially if you have a high-speed connection.

Unfortunately, despite all precautions, there are still no guarantees. If you are a victim, here's what to do after an incident.

Review your report. You are entitled to a free copy of your credit report from each of the three credit agencies: Equifax (800-525-6285), Experian (888-397-3742) and Trans Union (800-680-7289). You can also get one free copy of your credit report per year at www.annualcreditreport.com. Once you get the reports, pore over them for any suspicious information and report it. One in four credit reports contains errors—not fraud, just mistakes—so it's worth doing.

Place an extended fraud alert on your credit reports. An alert requires creditors to contact you if anyone wants to open an account in your name. To place an extended alert you will need to provide a copy of an official, valid report filed by you with a federal, state or local law enforcement agency, according to the Federal Trade Commission. So, when reporting data theft, don't just call your bank; contact your local police precinct and file a copy with the F.T.C.'s identity theft hotline: 877-438-4338.

Freeze your report. This step offers the most data protection but is not available in every state. The beauty of freezing your reports is that only you have the ability to thaw them. One downside is that your access to credit can be delayed for a few days. Depending on the state, you may have to pay fees to each credit bureau to freeze your report.

Start fresh? If your identity has been stolen, you might be tempted to consider starting fresh with a new Social Security number. It doesn't pay. Not only is it difficult to obtain, but your new number is forever linked to the old one, creating even more confusion when employers or banks try to verify your personal data. Better to be aggressive about guarding your current number.

Notify the Federal Trade Commission. E-mail consumerline@ftc.gov, or call the F.T.C. hotline at 877-438-4338. The F.T.C. has counselors to help you resolve financial and other problems associated with the crime.

—M. P. Dunleavey

Data You Need for a Quick Getaway

If danger strikes, here's what to grab

Like most people, you probably have documents stashed in various places throughout your home, perhaps some under lock and key. And should danger strike, you might not have the time to retrieve what you need. A bounty of technology makes the task of organizing your records less onerous. You can probably secure your records in one afternoon. Even better, doing so has a beneficial side effect: it makes you smarter about how you spend and save money.

First, compile a list of where everything is, such as account numbers and important documents.

The list will help you locate information for the insurance adjuster, for example. But it's also the list that financial planners recommend you compile for your heirs. Then, follow these steps to protect your records and yourself.

RECORD: Once you have made your basic list, save it on a U.S.B. flash drive, also called a thumb drive, which you can buy for $20 or less. It gives you more than enough space for your list and all the other suggestions mentioned below. Many thumb drives come with encryption software, a good safety measure for your sensitive data. It is also a good idea to copy the contents onto additional drives for backup and for other members of the family.

BONUS: When you are listing the credit cards, also note the credit limits, so you will know how much you could spend in an emergency. If your credit cards are at their limits now, you are not going to have any cushion to fall back on. So, start paying off balances, beginning with the card carrying the highest interest rate.

SCAN: You will want copies of these documents: tax returns for the last 3 years (your 1040 forms are all you will need in an emergency), a recent pay stub, birth certificates, marriage license, the deed to your home and insurance policy pages that list your coverage. If you do not have a scanner, take the documents to a copy center to scan. Record the image files on the U.S.B. drive.

BONUS: Check your insurance coverage for potential disasters, like fire. You may find you need to increase coverage.

SHOOT: Some personal finance advisers suggest making a spreadsheet of all your goods, listing date of purchase and prices paid. But will you ever do it? Instead, creating a detailed inventory is easy with a camcorder or digital camera. Take a picture of each item in each room and store the photos on

SPENDING

In Case You Get Hit By a Bus

Keep this list someplace secure, but where family members can get it quickly. Storing it on an encrypted flash drive is a good idea, as long as family members can recall the password for access.

Here are the account numbers for the . . .

✔ **Credit cards** + toll-free numbers of companies

✔ **Bank accounts** + PIN numbers or passwords, toll-free numbers

✔ **Investment accounts** + online passwords, toll-free numbers

✔ **Insurance policies** +toll-free numbers

✔ **Family Social Security numbers**

Here is where the following are stashed . . .

✔ **Wills**

✔ **Living will**

✔ **Power of attorney**

✔ **Any property deeds**

✔ **Insurance policies**

✔ **Company benefits**

✔ **Safe deposit box key** and location of box

✔ **List (or pictures) of valuables** and their worth

---

a memory card (or transfer them to the same flash drive as your other documents). Describe objects on the camcorder or in the file name of the digital photo. Make an extra copy.

You could also upload the photos of your possessions—as well as beloved family photos—to a free online photo service such as Flickr.com or Snapfish. com. Anyone you choose can access them from any computer. (Make sure you set the privacy options.)

BONUS: You may discover stuff you no longer want. Sell it, or donate it and take a tax deduction. At itsdeductible.com (part of TurboTax) you can estimate the value of your donated items; Bankrate. com and Salvationarmyusa.org also have free valuation guides.

SECURE: Now you can place your health history as well as digitized copies of X-rays, scans and electrocardiograms on the same encrypted flash drive.

Those with serious medical conditions may want to consider a special flash drive called MedicTag from www.my-healthkey.com, which sells for about $35. It stores your medical history to alert emergency room personnel, for instance, about any allergies or your use of a pacemaker. Make sure medical information on the drive is encrypted.

—Damon Darlin

How to Keep Funeral Costs Down
A fond farewell without spending a fortune

Every year, Americans arrange funerals for more than two million deceased at a cost of up to $10,000 or more per funeral, not including cemetery costs. A little research and planning can help keep funeral costs down.

Shop around. Contact at least three funeral homes before choosing one. Funeral directors will try to sell you a package deal, but keep in mind that by law they must show you an itemized price list of their goods and services. You have the right to buy items separately. Nor can they refuse to handle a casket you bought elsewhere or charge you a fee for using it. They can, however, charge you a "basic services fee," which runs about $2,000 and includes use of the facilities and coordinating with the cemetery or crematory.

Check out a range of caskets. Caskets run an average $2,000 for a metal, fiberboard or plastic model. Mahogany, bronze or copper models go for up to $10,000 or more. Get the price list and detailed descriptions before you look at actual models. Ask to see lower-priced models, often made of pine;

chances are they won't be prominently displayed.

Don't believe the sales pitch that metal caskets have special protective features to seal in the remains. Regardless of price and materials, no casket can permanently keep out water or other natural elements. In fact, federal law prohibits claims that a casket can preserve the remains indefinitely.

Clarify plot charges upfront. Cemetery plots run from $500 to several thousand dollars, depending on the area. But that's just the beginning. Removing earth and replacing it after internment costs an average of $900 (often double on weekends and holidays). Cemetery operators require a grave liner or vault (around $1,000) to enclose the casket. A headstone or marker costs from $500 to several thousand dollars, depending on materials and design. Some cemeteries tack on 10 percent or more for maintaining the grave site. For a mausoleum burial you will need to buy a crypt, which costs about the same as a burial plot.

Cremation can be cheaper. Cremation services are available from a crematory or cremation society. The cost of a simple cremation starts at several hundred dollars, not including the urn ($85 to $1,500 and up) or a crypt or memorial site. All told, the average cremation runs about $1,500. A casket is not required for a direct cremation. Undertakers are required to make available a simple wood box or alternative container.

Memorial societies can help. Memorial or funeral societies, nonprofit organizations run mostly by volunteers, can help keep costs down. For a onetime $35 membership fee, your local society can help you plan a funeral with an eye to saving money. Members get reduced prices and rarely spend more than $1,000 for a funeral. To find a memorial society in your area, call the Funeral Consumers Alliance at 800-765-0107 or go to www.funerals.org.

Plan yes, prepay no. Planning and setting aside money for your funeral is wise, but paying for the arrangements in advance, through so-called pre-need plans, is risky. There are too many unknowns: What if the funeral home goes under? Or you decide you'd rather be cremated? Depending on state regulations, the plans may be nonrefundable and sometimes carry hidden fees that your survivors may be liable for.

One way to set aside money for your funeral is to set up a Totten trust fund, or pay-on-death account, with your bank. The trust is portable and accrues interest. You deposit your desired amount and select a beneficiary. On your death, the beneficiary uses it to fulfill your funeral wishes.

The Truth About Embalming

Preparing a body for public viewing nearly always involves embalming and cosmetic restoration, processes that can add $600 or more to a funeral bill. Is embalming otherwise necessary or required? Not really.

• **Embalming generally is not necessary** if the body is buried or cremated within a reasonable time after death.

• **Embalming is not required by law** except in certain cases when a body is transported across state lines.

• **Embalming does not preserve the deceased's body indefinitely;** it merely masks the appearance of death and temporarily postpones decomposition.

• **Embalming chemicals are highly toxic.** Embalmers must wear a respirator and full-body covering while performing the procedure.

• **Refrigeration is an alternative to embalming** for maintaining a body intact while awaiting a funeral service. Although not all funeral homes have refrigeration facilities, most hospitals do.

SOURCE: Funeral Consumers Alliance

SPENDING

Autos

What Car Dealers Won't Tell You

With the right data, the salesman will be at your mercy

Most people approach buying a new car with fear and trepidation. But there's no need to feel you are at the mercy of a car salesman if you've done your homework. Here's how to gain control of your car buying experience and save money in the process.

Research the cars on your list using sites like ConsumerReports.org, Edmunds.com and Kelleybluebook. com. Those sites are storehouses of information about cars: you get reviews, specs, and consumer feedback. Check a car's reliability, safety, and performance. Sometimes you may have to choose between style and reliability. Choosing style alone could mean losing money to depreciation and the repair shop.

Before going to a showroom, solicit bids. Call a number of local dealers. Describe the car you want, with as much detail as possible, and tell them you are shopping for the best offer. Tell each of the competing dealers that if they are interested in selling you a car, they should call you with their best price. Chances are you will get bids from interested dealers within a few days.

Or get your bids online. Start your research at a site like Edmunds.com, which also has an option

> **❝**
> **Seventy-five percent of female car buyers plan to bring a man with them to the dealer to ensure fair treatment.**
>
> **•••**

to have local dealers send you quotes. Check off that option and within 24 hours, you will have several quotes from local dealers. You may want to test drive the car at the dealer closest to you, even if he's not offering the lowest price. If the car is right for you, ask the dealer to meet the lowest price quote you received.

Don't begrudge a dealer a modest profit. Books and online services provide basic car cost numbers. But the amount a dealer pays for a car varies, sometimes from day to day. Some services track dealer costs on a daily basis. One of them, Fighting Chance (800-288-1134; www.fightingchance.com), provides a package of data on a car, including factory incentives and other factors that can change a car's price. The service costs $39.95. Once you've determined an accurate dealer's cost, figure in a reasonable amount for profit.

Consider using an auto-buying service that will do the bidding for you. One example: CarBargains (800-475-7283; www.checkbook.org), operated by the Center for the Study of Services, a nonprofit group in Washington, D.C., solicits bids from at least five dealers in your area. You get the dealer quote sheets as well as information on financing, service contracts and the value of your trade-in car, if any. The $200 fee will spare you the hassle of having to tangle directly with dealers yourself.

CHECKING OUT A USED CAR

You don't have to get yourself covered with grease to tell quickly whether a used car has been well maintained. The following tips for reading a car's history will save you lots of headaches later.

STEERING WHEEL: There should be no play for power steering when the engine is off, and no more than 2 inches for manual steering

INTERIOR: Resale value as well as comfort will be affected by seats and carpets that look shabby or smell musty.

FLUID LEAKS: Checking a car's fluid levels and condition is like taking a person's blood pressure and doing a blood test. They can indicate both present and future problems. Oil spots around the engine or beneath the vehicle are obvious signs that something's leaking.

Other signs are less obvious: transmission fluids should be pink, not dirty.

BODY CONDITION: Rust, especially in the rocker panels under the doors, in the trunk or around the wheels is bad news. Sooner rather than later, your car will fall apart.

TIRES: Original tires should be good for 25,000 miles. Uneven tire tread can mean an alignment problem, which is easily remedied.

SUSPENSION: Does the car look lopsided from the side or rear? Bad springs are probably the culprit. Does the car bounce more than a couple times when you push down hard on a corner? The shocks or struts could need replacing. If a front tire can be noticeably lifted by pulling on the top of the tire with both hands, you may have bad bearings or suspension joints.

BRAKES: Look for wear on the pads or scars on the rotor disk.

Be wary of end of model-year deals. The end-of-the-month rule generally holds. Most car salespeople have monthly quotas to meet and may be willing to give you a bargain simply to make the sale. But buying a year-end model at a discount doesn't make up for the depreciation factor: at that point the car has already lost 12 to 20 percent of its value.

Walking out is still a good negotiating strategy. The best you have. Keep the process with the salesperson impersonal. Submit an offer and say that if he or she turns you down, you will simply take your business to the competitor. The dealer may let you walk away, but chances are he'll come get you in the parking lot. At that point, you have the upper hand. Say that you will not go back in unless they accept your price.

How to Buy a Used Car
The key is knowing more than the seller

Buying a used car is always a perilous endeavor. Almost everyone has heard that a new car loses an average of 12 percent of its value the moment it is driven off the dealer's lot. Economists tell us this happens not because the new car is losing a premium, but rather that the used car carries a "risk discount." That's because it is hard for a buyer of a used car to trust a seller, who could very well be passing off a lemon he just bought new. So used cars are more heavily discounted for the risk.

Getting a good price boils down to whether you have better information than the seller. One way to even the odds is to check a service like Carfax (www.carfax.com) to trace a car's history. Basic used car data is free; more extensive customized reports cost $29.99 for one vehicle history. You'll find more than 4 billion reports on individual car histories in their database.

Other sources for more general information are consumer groups, such as carconsumers.com, which issue warnings, for example, about flood-damaged used cars entering the market after major hurricanes strike. A car damaged by water can never be fully repaired, although unscrupulous sellers can use a number of ways to "wash" a car's history. The

solution? Find someone you can trust.

Buying a "certified" used car is an increasingly popular option. This concept, popularized by BMW and Toyota's Lexus luxury brand, lets you buy a formerly leased or owned car that has been cleaned up, inspected and often sold with a manufacturer's warranty. For those reasons, certified cars command a premium over other used cars. When buying a certified used car, work with a dealer who also sells new cars. He may have more of a reputation to protect.

Also consider that a used luxury car may actually be a better bet than a used economy car. Drivers of luxury cars tend to be a bit more fashion conscious, so they will unload a car for the next new thing long before the car has hit that critical point where things start to go wrong.

—Damon Darlin

TIMELY TIPS

How to Deal with Used Car Dealers

Arm yourself before stepping onto the used car lot

✔ Get pre-approved for a loan before you go car shopping.

✔ Before you go loan shopping, get a copy of your free credit report (www.annualcreditreport.com) and correct any errors that may appear in it.

✔ Before you step into a used car dealership, check to see that it is licensed by your state consumer affairs department.

✔ Don't negotiate a purchase based on what your monthly payment would be. Negotiate on the full price.

✔ Never sign a contract that is blank or incomplete or an agreement that contains terms you don't understand.

✔ Say no to add-ons and extra options.

✔ If your car sale is negotiated in another language (say, Spanish, Mandarin or Korean), the contract must also be written in that language.

✔ Always retain copies of any contract or paperwork you sign.

—Jennifer 8. Lee

Proving a Recalled Car Was Fixed

Before buying a used car, check that repairs were done

One problem with recalls is that owners don't always act on them—and the next owner may suffer if the car is resold. How does a shopper know if the problem has been fixed, or even if there was a recall on the car in the first place?

Finding out is actually easy. Recalls are ordered by the National Highway Traffic Safety Administration, which posts recalls on its Web site, nhtsa.gov. Users can search the database by model. So if a buyer were looking at a 2001 Lincoln Navigator, for example, the agency site would show that the vehicle was recalled not only for a faulty cruise-control switch, but for four other problems as well.

Armed with that information, the buyer can demand proof from the seller that the problems were fixed, or have a mechanic check.

Getting information from the automakers on

whether work was done to a specific vehicle is a mixed bag. On the Ford Web site, for example, users can type in a vehicle identification number to get recall information for a specific vehicle. If the site says there are no recalls, the company said that means either that there have indeed been none or that the repairs have been made. You can also call Ford's Customer Relationship Center at 800-392-3673, where non-owners can get detailed recall information.

General Motors does not offer the information online, but owners can get recall news from the OnStar operator or from customer assistance at 800-231-1841. Non-owners can get details on a specific car only by providing the vehicle identification number to a dealer.

For Toyota cars, non-owners can call the Customer Experience Center at 800-331-4331 to get detailed recall information. The information can also be obtained from a dealer, but at the dealer's discretion.

—James Schembari

✔ **TIMELY TIPS**

Car Sites That Cater to Women

Women buy some 8 million cars and trucks each year and influence more than 85 percent of vehicle purchases. Yet studies show they are often intimidated or ignored by car dealers.

Several online sites give women a place to car shop without being humiliated by insensitive salesmen.

✔ **AskPatty.com** Get mileage and seating capacity, recommended models and a list of "women friendly" car dealers in your area, as well as other advice on car purchases and maintenance.

✔ **Motherproof.com** Eight real life moms offer reviews as they pursue their quest for the "quintessential mom-mobile."

✔ **Roadandtravel.com** Advice and reviews from founder Courtney Caldwell on car buying and safety, as well as on family trips. Sends a free monthly newsletter by e-mail to its readers.

—Mickey Meese

Buying a Car When Credit Is Tight

Strategies for getting a car loan

When loans are hard to come by, how should you go about making your purchasing decision? Should you lease or own? And what should you do about your old vehicle? When credit is tight be sure to consider the following.

Explore your financing options. The contrast between the most creditworthy borrowers and those with black marks is great during times of tight credit. If your credit record is stellar, you can expect a smooth approval process as well as attractive rates. Those with subpar credit records will face big challenges. And what can you expect

if you fall somewhere in between? Ordinary borrowers will still be able to obtain financing but the terms will be more stringent.

Lenders will demand higher down payments, say, 10 to 15 percent of the loan, from weaker borrowers. They will ask for more data to verify your income and may even raise interest rates, depending on your personal credit history.

That makes it important to shop for the car loan before you look for the car. Start by going to an online lender, like Capital One Financial or E-Loan. It will take your application, offer an interest rate, approve you for a specific dollar amount and mail you a bank check the next day. Or head to your local bank or credit union to check its offers. The car dealership

Taking On a Seller's Lease

How to assume someone else's lease

Leaseholders who want to escape their multiyear contracts before they expire have some friends on the Internet: Web sites designed to create a secondary market for car leases. Sellers post descriptions of their cars and the terms of their leases on the Web site. Many also offer to pay some amount of cash to induce a buyer to take on the responsibility of making the rest of the payments.

Here's what it costs to assume or escape a car lease at two prominent online lease marketplaces. These fees are in addition to any charged by finance companies for the legal transfer of the lease, which can run as high as $600.

✔ **LeaseTrader.com** – Buyer's fees: $39.95 for contact information on sellers. Seller's fees: minimum $39.95 to post vehicle, $250 transaction fee.

✔ **SwapLease.com** – Buyer's fees: $50 to $100. Seller's fees: $50 to $150.

—Patrick McGeehan

should be your last stop for a loan. Typically, dealers offer loans from the financing arm of the car's manufacturer, and then mark the rate up for a profit, making them the most expensive option.

Think twice about leasing. For many buyers, it generally is a toss-up whether it's better to lease or own. Not when credit is tight. Leasing may not be available, and if it is, it could end up being more costly.

Keeping your monthly payment low is a two-step process. First negotiate the lowest possible purchase price as if you were buying the car for cash. Then shop around for the highest possible residual price, which is the vehicle's projected value when you turn it back in.

In a lease deal, the vehicle is owned by a bank or finance company, and you effectively rent it, typically for 2 or 3 years. Selling the vehicle at lease-end becomes the leasing company's responsibility, so the higher the residual value, the better your lease deal is likely to be. Different leasing companies may set different residual values.

But when a car's residual value plunges (think of gas-guzzlers when gas prices are high), the economics of leasing are no longer as favorable. On top of that, automakers may not be subsidizing finance charges, making leasing even costlier.

Beware of longer loans. To keep monthly payments lower, car companies push longer loans, sometimes for 6 years or more. If you plan to keep a car that long, the longer payback schedule may not matter much. But for anyone who plans to get a new vehicle in 2 or 3 years, longer loans are not a good deal.

Here's why: if you are spreading payments over 8 years, but the vehicle is going to depreciate greatly over 5 years, you still have to make another 3 years of payments. The potential risk is that when you want to get out of the deal, you may have to dig into your savings to pay off the loan.

Look before you trade in. Buyers have long braced themselves for high prices on their dream cars. But many are even more surprised by how little their vehicles are worth when they sell them.

Because selling your car during tough economic times is like selling stock at the bottom of the market, it may be prudent to keep it.

To get a sense of what your car is worth, consult the Kelley Blue Book or its online edition at KBB.com. But there is no substitute for testing the market yourself. On the flip side, those ending a lease could hit a jackpot. You might be able to negotiate a lower price to buy the car outright instead of turning it back in.

Know when to walk. Buying a car can be stressful. In part, that's because it really means negotiating two deals—and possibly three. Savvy buyers will negotiate the purchase price of their car first, then haggle over the terms of the financing. Finally, they negotiate the value of a trade-in separately. If the dealer refuses to discount the car unless you use the company's financing, that's your cue to leave.

—Eric Dash

Are Extended Warranties Worth It?

You may spend more for the protection than you'd save on repairs

Your car salesman will make a fervent pitch to sell you an extended warranty to cover your new car beyond the manufacturer's regular warranty. And there are people all over the Internet eager to sell something called service contracts, promising even more coverage at lower rates. What's a car owner to do?

Consumer Reports argues that generally extended new-car warranties are poor deals. A survey they conducted in 2008 found that 65 percent of about 8,000 *Consumer Reports* readers said they had spent significantly more for a new-car warranty than they had saved in repair costs. Only about 5 percent said they had a net savings, and about 42 percent of extended warranties were never used.

Extended warranties are a major profit center for dealerships; on average, dealers collect around $800 on each extended warranty sold. In addition, many manufacturers offer volume incentives to dealerships to sell as many of these warranties as possible.

Still, there are consumers who want the assurance that if a serious problem occurs after the original warranty runs out, they will be covered and will not have to scramble to cover major repair bills.

So what's the advice for those people? First of all, wait. There is no reason to buy the extended warranty right away, even though dealers often say it will be cheaper when you are buying your new car because you get a better deal when the car is in good shape.

One reason to wait is that when the warranty is rolled into the purchase price of the car, it is easy for dealers to hide the true cost you're paying. In most cases, you can buy one up until your regular warranty expires. After a year or two of driving your car, you'll know how long you want to keep it and if the car seems to need a lot of repairs.

It is also not true that you need to take the extended warranty to get the low-interest financing, as some people may be told.

If you decide to buy an extended warranty, you still have choices. Whether buying it directly from the dealer who sold you the car or over the Internet, you can buy an extended warranty sold and backed by the vehicle's manufacturer, or you can seek out one from an independent company, also known as an aftermarket or third-party warranty.

Both can offer different levels of coverage. Some may pay only for replacing major mechanical parts. Others sell bumper-to-bumper coverage that can include more than the original warranty. Prices vary according to the type of coverage, the deductible and the length of the policy.

It's important to read the fine print and know what you're getting. Do you, for example, have to

SPENDING

✔ TIMELY TIPS

When You Get a Lemon

✔ At **Consumeraffairs.com** you can get an overview of state laws regarding cars that turn out to be lemons

✔ At **Autopedia.com** you can find lemon-law rights, state laws, attorney links and a free Car-Fax lemon-check link.

first pay for the repair and then be reimbursed? Is the warranty transferable if you sell the car? Do you have to go to the dealership to repair the car?

In general, people tend to be more leery of the aftermarket or third-party warranties, and for good reason. Consumer experts say that holders of some independent extended warranty contracts have complained that they could not get their repairs authorized for payment or were required to jump through hoops to do so. Better to stick with your manufacture: buy a GM warranty for a GM car, for example.

Keep in mind, too, that if your independent warranty company goes broke, you may be stuck with a worthless contract. Laws regulating such companies vary by state. Edmunds.com advises on its Web site that you take a look at how the company's financial strength has been rated by A.M. Best or Standard & Poor's.

You can also buy a manufacturer's warranty from a dealership in another state to cover your car—and it can be hundreds of dollars cheaper. A valid manufacturer's warranty is good in any state, and there's nothing wrong with buying it online.

So, what's the best solution? A simple and wise choice is one suggested by *Consumer Reports:* Put $1,500 to $2,000 in an interest-bearing account when you buy a car. Then you can tap it if you need to pay for repairs. If you never use it, you have a down payment for your next car.

— Alina Tugend

Before You Buy a Motorcycle
Avoid first-time-buyer mistakes

Motorcycle Hall of Fame inductee Ed Youngblood talks about motorcycling as "a spiritual activity, essential for maintaining a healthy mental perspective." The nation's more than 6 million motorcycle enthusiasts no doubt agree

> ⓘ **INSIDE INFO**
>
> ## Profile of a Biker
>
> Think of bikers and images of modern-day desperadoes come to mind. In reality, the 292,000 members of the American Motorcyclist Association are established, well educated and financially successful.
>
> ○ Average age: 40
> ○ Average household income: $91,500
> ○ Post–high school education: 79 percent
> ○ Average number of motorcycles owned: 2.8 per member.
>
> SOURCE: American Motorcyclist Association

with Youngblood, who spent nearly 20 years as president of the American Motorcyclist Association (ama-cycle.org) and has written a handful of books on motorcycle history.

Youngblood's romance with the motorcycle began nearly 50 years ago, when, at age 14, he took $60 in savings and bought his first bike, a 1953 Harley-Davidson 165. For anyone tempted to take a cycle for a spin, Youngblood has this advice.

1. Before you buy a motorcycle, sign up for a motorcycle training course. The Motorcycle Safety Foundation (800-446-9227; msf-usa.org) has a referral service for courses. The course will take you through all aspects of motorcycle operation and maintenance, including an introduction to motorcycle makes and sizes to help pick one that fits your personality and size.

For my first 20 years of riding, no instruction was available and I believed I didn't need any. After participating in my first course, I was horrified to learn of my poor technique and riding habits. I was so taken by the course that I became an instructor and lifelong advocate. If you don't intend to go through a training course, don't ride.

2. Decide on a bike type. Do you want an on-road or off-road motorcycle? Do you plan on riding over dirt trails or on the open highway? For an off-road, you can choose between a total dirt bike and a trail bike made street-legal, which comes with turning signals and other requirements of a highway vehicle.

If you favor the highway, there are essentially three bike types: the sport bike, which is light and quick, best suited for short rides; a cruiser, designed for comfort and local riding, such as commuting or weekend riding; and a touring bike, larger, often with saddlebags for luggage, meant for long-distance traveling.

3. Select a brand. Motorcycle selection is determined by personal taste and style Most A.M.A. members own more than two cycles, and many own more than four. As far as the leading makes available, you have Harley-Davidson, Honda, Kawasaki, Suzuki, Yamaha, BMW and a variety

of smaller manufacturers. All these manufacturers put out high-quality products.

The choice among them usually comes down to brand loyalty. I know people who have driven Harleys for over 20 years and would never try anything else. The same is true for BMW's and most other brands. It's all up to the individual.

4. Avoid first-time buyer mistakes. Often first-time buyers purchase bikes that are too small. Going into the showroom, most first-timers lack confidence, so they choose the smaller bikes, which are easier to handle. After their first month, they're ready for a larger model.

I'm not suggesting every first-time buyer needs a larger bike, but I would recommend some riding experience before going to the dealer.

5. Choose your accessories. If you intend on having a passenger, install a backrest for his or her comfort. A rider taking long trips should consider installing saddlebags. I prefer a windscreen, simply for the comfort. If you like camping, there are specially made motorcycle trailers, which many people use to haul their outdoor gear.

INSIDE INFO

The Case for Motorcycle Helmets

- Motorcycle deaths account for 13 percent of all driving related fatalities, and the number is on the rise. Head injuries are the leading cause of motorcyclists' deaths.

- When gas prices go up, so do motorcycle deaths as more car drivers shift to gas-saving cycles. In 2007, a year of sky-high gas prices, motorcycle deaths rose nearly 7 percent.

- Helmets reduce the likelihood of a fatality by 37 percent. Helmets are 67 percent effective in preventing brain injuries.

- Unhelmeted motorcyclists involved in crashes are three times more likely to suffer brain injuries.

SOURCE: National Highway Traffic Safety Administration

Make Room for Scooters
Wimps no more, anti-hogs get great mileage

Drivers who fear hulking cruisers like Harley-Davidsons, yet want to cut back on gas bills might want to consider a scooter. Just do the math. While the Prius, Toyota's huge-selling hybrid, has a combined city/highway mileage rating of around 45 miles a gallon, some scooters can approach 80 miles a gallon.

A commuter on a motorcycle or scooter faces some hurdles, of course. The first one is safety. Motorcycle deaths have been rising. The second one is climate. Riding to work in the rain or

● TIMELY TIPS

Smart Ways to Save on Gas

Gas is liquid gold; how to get better mileage

For as long as traditional gasoline-powered vehicles are with us, you'll need to fill up that tank. Here are six smart ways to save on gas.

✔ One way to get better mileage is to pick a smaller, four-cylinder engine rather than the more powerful, heavier and thirstier V-6 or V-8 version.

✔ Vehicles with manual transmissions generally get better fuel economy than those with automatic. An aerodynamic design also improves mileage, but that is hard to discern. One of the biggest gains in decreasing drag is if the design has a smooth underside.

✔ Follow the manufacturer's recommendations for replacing spark plugs and air filters. Clogged filters and crusty spark plugs, which prevent gas from burning completely, can reduce mileage by up to 12 percent. Use the recommended grade of motor oil; putting 10W-30 oil into an engine intended for 5W-30, for example, will lower mileage by 1 to 2 percent.

✔ Any vehicle will get better mileage if tires are kept inflated to the manufacturer's specifications. Underinflated tires degrade fuel efficiency by 2 percent for every pound per square inch below specifications. Buy a digital tire gauge, (about $10), and an electric tire pump, (about $50), to keep tires inflated properly.

✔ Lighten the load by getting rid of unnecessary stuff in the trunk. An extra 100 pounds reduces fuel efficiency by up to 2 percent. And avoid attaching anything to your car, like racks for luggage or bikes; they add weight and create aerodynamic drag.

✔ The biggest factor in your car's gas mileage is how you drive. Aggressive driving that causes you to brake and accelerate often can use up to 33 percent more gas than a more staid style. And speeding can make even the most fuel-efficient engine guzzle gas. The Energy Department says every 5 m.p.h. over 60 m.p.h. cuts gas mileage by 6 percent. Putting your car into a higher gear whenever possible, to slow engine speed, saves gas and reduces engine wear. And turn off the engine if the car won't be moving for more than 30 seconds—it's a myth that more gas is needed to restart the engine than to let it idle.

—Kate Murphy

when it's cold can be miserable.

But the upsides are appealing. Along with the incredible gas mileage, you can park them almost anywhere. Scooters have also become less wimpy. Maxi-scooters, with engines of about 250 c.c. and higher, developed for urban commuters, can be purchased for around $6,000. Most have storage (usually under the seat or in a compartment in the front), can carry two passengers and feature twist-and-go automatic transmissions so you don't need to work a clutch. Some are suitable for short highway trips.

—Brian Alexander

How to Make Your RV "Green"

Even motor homes are becoming ecofriendly

Recreational vehicles, which get about 8 miles to the gallon, are often considered the antithesis of low-impact living. But it doesn't have to be that way.

Amid growing interest in alternative-fuel vehicles and environmentally friendly building methods, a handful of designers and do-it-yourselfers are taking on an unlikely challenge: reinventing the motor home, with a goal of transforming the typical wide-body gas guzzler into a model of compact green construction and fuel efficiency. These modern-day RV owners are using their retooled motor homes as vehicles, literally, to promote ecological awareness as they travel.

"If you can make an RV sustainable, you can make any industry sustainable," says Ty Adams, a Portland, Ore., resident who spent a year visiting 25 states and promoting renewable energy in the BioTrekker, an RV powered by biodiesel, a fuel made from refined vegetable oil. Adams paid $108,000 for the RV and $12,000 more for the biodiesel upgrade and campaign.

The trend received a boost when Willie Nelson began powering his tour bus with biodiesel, which he called BioWillie, and later convinced other musicians to do the same. But regular RV owners say that their tours serve another purpose besides sustainable travel, namely to reflect a desire for a simpler, if not entirely bygone, era of road tripping and nature appreciation.

Although hybrid and alternative-fuel RV models have yet to find a mass market, the industry is moving toward fuel-economy prototypes and environmental designs, says a spokesman for the Recreation Vehicle Industry Association, based in Reston, Va. Individual RV owners are leading the way. A recent industry survey found that about 18 percent of RV owners are already using solar panels.

Some of the luxury RV models are replacing ubiquitous vinyl interiors with hardwood, which is considered more environmentally friendly. And some RV owners are taking matters into their own hands, retrofitting their vehicles to include solar-powered water and electrical systems, composting toilets, rainwater harvesting system, recycled denim insulation, LED lighting and bamboo interiors.

—Linda Baker

Trust the Manual or the Mechanic?
When to change the oil, inflate the tires and use low-octane gas

Service practices listed in a car's manual are intended to give cars their best performance and longest life. Yet, take the car to a mechanic, and he's bound to improvise. As a result, many consumers don't know whether to trust the manual or the mechanic.

One problem is that manuals are becoming the size of phone books, as manufacturers try to address every ownership issue to avoid being sued.

While independent mechanics may disagree, manufacturers and industry experts generally think that following the manufacturer's guidelines closely is the best way to maintain a vehicle. But reading the manual is not just reading the chart in the back. The subtleties lie within its pages. Unfortunately, even those who read the manual often run into contradictory or unclear advice. Here are some of the most perplexing maintenance practices and what to do about them.

When to change the oil. Is changing the oil every 3,000 miles, as many quick-lube chains recommend, a waste of money and oil? Can cars that use synthetic oils go much farther without a change? Auto experts recommend a 7,000-mile-change interval with synthetic oil, and a 3,000-to-5,000-mile interval for those who use regular oil. Severe driving, such as driving 10 miles at low speeds and then shutting off the car, requires more frequent changes. An oil change is the one place where you can err on the side of caution.

Proper tire inflation. Few drivers keep their tires inflated to the right pressure, which manufacturers stress is the amount that they have determined based on the tire and the weight of the car. The "maximum tire pressure" embossed on the side-

SPENDING

walls can be more than 20 pounds higher than the pressure that should actually be used.

Proper inflation pressures are listed in the manual as well as on a sticker usually located in one of the door sills. The manual is the only place to find the right tire pressure for driving in an empty vehicle; the door sticker only lists the proper pressure for a full load.

Proper gas grade. With high gas prices, many drivers are tempted to use a lower grade than the manufacturer recommends. In most cases, that is fine. The fuel requirement listed next to the gas cap is the worst-case scenario. Many modern cars have anti-knock sensors, which protect the engine from damage when gas with a lower octane rating is used. General Motors prefers to have customers follow the manual's advice, because many people do not know if their car has anti-knock technology. For cars requiring higher-octane fuel, some mechanics advise staying away from low octane. They agree that an anti-knock sensor could adjust the engine, but the electronics could be affected as the engine tried to compensate.

—Eric A. Taub

How to Drive Defensively

Tips from one of the world's top race drivers

For premier race car driver, John Andretti, stopping on a dime at over 200 m.p.h. or taking razor sharp curves at head-spinning speeds is all in a day's work. The nephew of racing legend Mario Andretti (John's father, Aldo, is Mario's twin), Andretti says he's raced cars "practically since birth."

Along the way, he's driven dragsters, midgets, dirt cars, sprint cars, you name it, winning prestigious races like the 24 Hours of Daytona and

becoming a top Nascar driver. Here are Andretti's tips on driving safely off the race track.

Q What is the best way to handle turns and curves?

Always at a safe speed. When the road is dry and it's clear out, if the speed limit says 35 m.p.h., a corner should be quite easily taken at 35. At the same time, you have to be aware that if there's a car coming from the other direction, that car may not be totally under control—it may be coming toward you at a high speed, and maybe the driver has lost control of the vehicle. If you're not prepared and don't pull off to the side of the road, for example, it could be a deadly situation.

Q What has racing taught you about tailgating and trailing other vehicles?

Appropriate distances between cars vary with the situation. With today's traffic, there are few opportunities to maintain large gaps between cars, so drivers really must pay attention.

My rule is, no matter how fast I'm driving, if someone wants to go faster, they're welcome to pass me. In fact, I try to make it easy for them to get by, which is the opposite of what 90 percent of drivers might do. Most would speed up, or become angry and tailgate. That makes no sense to me. When I'm not on the track, I'm not in a race.

Q What's the best way to change lanes or pass other vehicles?

Many drivers have trouble changing lanes safely. On the highway, for example, you often find the "left-lane hanger," who rides in the left lane no matter what. They make others pass them in the right lane, creating a difficult situation. Often, they speed up as people try to pass, making it worse. There are plenty of open spots in the slow lane. Let others pass you and then get behind them. Most of the time, you don't even have to slow down to allow them to pass.

WHAT IT TAKES TO STOP IN TIME

Tailgaters beware: the stopping distance required for a car going 35 m.p.h. is just over half a football field, even when the road is dry.

At 65 m.p.h. the distance required is equal to the length of one and a third football fields.

SOURCE: National Highway Traffic Safety Administration

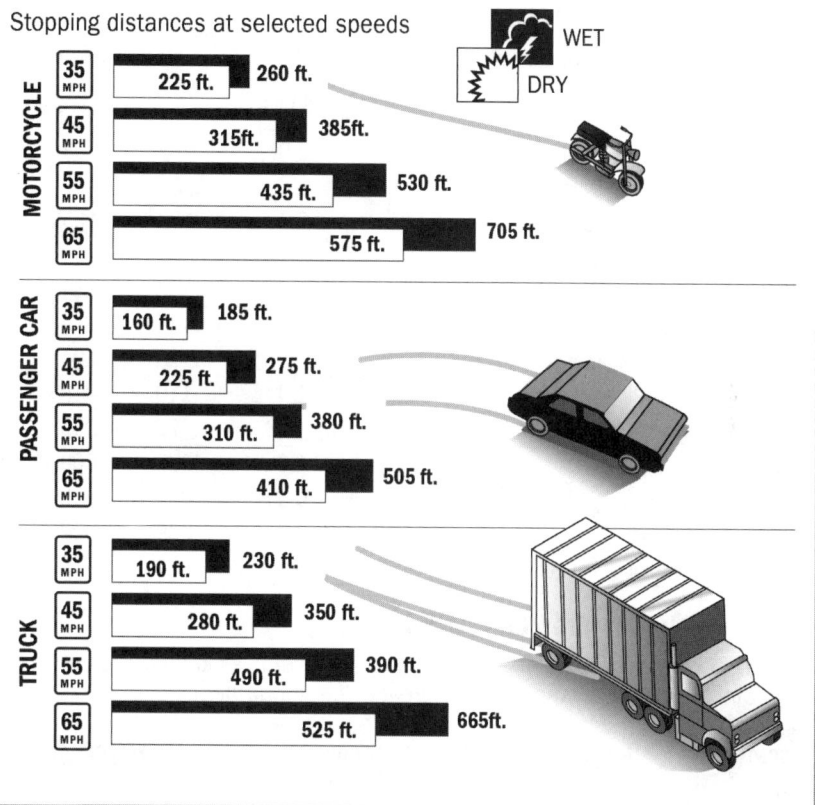

Stopping distances at selected speeds

WET
DRY

MOTORCYCLE
- 35 MPH: 225 ft. / 260 ft.
- 45 MPH: 315ft. / 385ft.
- 55 MPH: 435 ft. / 530 ft.
- 65 MPH: 575 ft. / 705 ft.

PASSENGER CAR
- 35 MPH: 160 ft. / 185 ft.
- 45 MPH: 225 ft. / 275 ft.
- 55 MPH: 310 ft. / 380 ft.
- 65 MPH: 410 ft. / 505 ft.

TRUCK
- 35 MPH: 190 ft. / 230 ft.
- 45 MPH: 280 ft. / 350 ft.
- 55 MPH: 490 ft. / 390 ft.
- 65 MPH: 525 ft. / 665ft.

● Is a stick shift superior to an automatic transmission in terms of safety?

Both are equally safe in dry and sunny conditions. I find that in very snowy and icy conditions, a stick shift provides more control. Often in an automatic, when you approach a stop sign and the road is icy, if you don't put the car in neutral, you're really fighting the vehicle, because it wants to go forward. In a car with a stick-shift transmission, not only can you switch to a higher gear to get going and avoid wheel-spin, but you can also use the neutral position and the rear tire to slow you down a bit, giving you more control.

● How do you alter your driving for various conditions, such as poor visibility, bad weather, etc.?

You should drive within your control. Obviously, that means different things for different people. The conditions I race in are not always ideal. Often I can hardly see ahead of me, and I have to adapt to very difficult situations. On the road, you should drive at whatever speed is necessary for safety.

However, if you feel you must drive at a very slow speed in extreme conditions, it's important to put on your hazard lights so you won't get hit in the back if drivers can't see you. Again, remember that even though you may be in control of your car, that doesn't mean others are, so be constantly aware of other drivers.

● If you are approaching an accident or dangerous situation, what is the best way to proceed?

The whole time I drive, I'm always looking for escape routes from potential problems.

SPENDING

HOLDING YOUR LIQUOR

Approximate percentage of alcohol in the blood one hour after drinking

ALCOHOLIC DRINKS	AMOUNT OF ALCOHOL (OZ.)	BODY WEIGHT (LBS.)					
		100	120	140	160	180	200
Three Dubonnet cocktails	3.0	.252	.208	.176	.152	.134	.119
Four Bloody Marys, Daiquiris, Whiskey Sours	2.8	.234	.193	.163	.141	.124	.110
Three Martinis, Manhattans	2.4	.199	.163	.138	.119	.104	.092
Two Mai Tais, Mint Juleps	2.2	.181	.149	.125	.108	.094	.083
Four Champagne cocktails	2.0	.163	.134	.113	.097	.084	.075
Two Margaritas	1.8	.146	.119	.100	.086	.057	.066
Two Martinis, Manhattans	1.6	.128	.104	.087	.075	.065	.057
Two Highballs, Bloody Marys	1.4	.110	.089	.075	.063	.055	.048
Two 5-oz. glasses table wine	1.1	.075	.063	.054	.047	.042	.038
Two Beers	1.0	.075	.060	.049	.041	.035	.030
One Black Russian	0.8	.057	.045	.037	.030	.025	.021
One Sloe Gin Fizz	0.6	.039	.030	.024	.019	.015	.012
One 1-oz. cordial or liqueur	0.4	.021	.015	.011	.008	.006	.004

KNOWING WHEN YOU ARE TIPSY

Levels above the double line indicate that a driver is legally intoxicated. The darker the levels, the higher the blood alcohol content and the greater the impairment.

BLOOD ALCOHOL CONTENT	EFFECTS ON FEELING AND BEHAVIOR	EFFECTS ON DRIVING ABILITY
.40 **.20** **.19** **.18**	**At this point, most people have passed out.**	**Hopefully, driver passed out before trying to get into vehicle.**
.17 **.16** **.15** **.14** **.13**	**Major impairment of all physical and mental functions. Irresponsible behavior. Euphoria. Some difficulty standing, walking and talking.**	**Distortion of all perception and judgment. Driving erratic. Driver in a daze.**
.12 **.11** **.10**	**Difficulty performing gross motor skills. Uncoordinated behavior. Definite impairment of mental abilities, judgment and memory.**	**Judgment seriously affected. Physical difficulty in driving a vehicle.**
.09 .08 .07	Feeling of relaxation. Mild sedation. Exaggeration of emotions and behavior. Slight impairment of motor skills. Increase in reaction time.	Drivers take too long to decide and act. Motor skills (such as braking) are impaired. Reaction time is increased.
.06 .05 .02	Absence of observable effects. Mild alteration of feelings, slight intensification of existing moods.	Mild changes. Most drivers seem a bit moody. Bad driving habits slightly pronounced.

SOURCES: National Clearinghouse for Alcohol and Drug Information; National Safety Council

That's become natural to me. As you go down the road, always be prepared for anything that might confront you. Be aware of the limitations of your car. Understand your car and how it will respond to situations in order to avoid accidents. You could save a life or serious damage to the car by driving defensively.

Q What other safety advice can you give drivers?

Pay attention. I get more frustrated with drivers who aren't courteous and don't pay attention than with those who drive too fast. I just let the fast drivers pass so that I can see them. Don't get angry at situations that are beyond your control. Cars take more lives every year than guns. A car can be a very deadly weapon and should be treated with respect.

Helping Your Child Drive Safely

Bad things can happen when cars and children come together; here's how parents can help

Of the three major initiatives taking place nationwide in recent years to reduce accidents among teenage drivers, two involve parents. One requires parents to certify that they have spent a certain minimum amount of time practicing driving with their children. The other trend is the use of "contracts" between parents and new drivers outlining the rules of the road.

The third major initiative, which has become law in a majority of states, is graduated licensing, which requires new drivers to pass a probationary driving period before they can acquire an unrestricted license.

Contracts and supervised driving both focus on building better habits from the beginning—an approach that makes sense, experts say, because the first five months of driving have been found to be the most dangerous.

TIMELY TIPS

How Safe Is Your Car?

Find out how your car would fare in a crash

Road fatality rates are down overall but there are still more than 40,000 deaths a year in cars, minivans, S.U.V.'s and pickup trucks, and many more injuries. When considering safety, these sources can help.

✔ **For free information,** go to the National Highway Traffic Safety Administration at www.safercar. gov, for a list of investigations, complaints and recalls, and to the Insurance Institute for Highway Safety, a research group financed by auto insurers, at www.iihs.org for crash test results.

✔ *Consumer Reports* (www.consumerreports.org) compiles testing results from the government and insurers, runs vehicles through dozens of drive and handling tests and evaluates various design attributes, from blind spots to the difficulty of installing child seats. Getting a vehicle report from its Web site costs $14 per car.

✔ **To find out how specific car models fared** on government ratings from front and side crashes to rollover tests, go to www.safercar.gov. Click on the listing for each test to bring up a more detailed explanation of the methodology behind the testing. For example, for rollover testing, the star rating is largely computed from a mathematical formula factoring in a vehicle's dimensions; lesser emphasis is put on tests conducted on a track, because most rollovers do not occur on a uniform surface.

—Danny Hakim

While not regulated by law, contracts are becoming increasingly popular. Some Web sites, like DriveHomeSafe.com, offer detailed advice on setting rules between parents and teenagers. At the American Automobile Association Web site (aaa.publicaffairs.com), you can get a sample copy of a parent/child driving contract.

Contracts cover everything from who is allowed in the car to how late the children can drive and who pays for the gas. They can prevent conflict down the road when teenagers may try to angle for more freedoms.

Some states have also begun requiring parents to spend a certain number of hours teaching their children how to drive, going beyond driver's education programs. In Maryland, for example, parents must certify that they have spent 40 hours in the car with their children.

Statistics show that increasing restrictions on young drivers has reduced accidents—in part because some teenagers are simply waiting to drive until they are 18, when they qualify for an unrestricted license. And if they don't drive, they don't crash.

—Eric Nagourney

ⓘ **INSIDE INFO**

Driving Ages Nationwide

○ In all 50 states, anyone applying for a first driver's license must take tests for vision, knowledge of state driving laws and driving skills.

○ All the states and the District of Columbia require learner's permits before getting a license. In a few states (like Alaska, Iowa, and North and South Dakota), the minimum age for getting a permit is 14. In most other states the age is 15. In a handful of states (such as Connecticut, North Carolina and New Jersey), new drivers must wait until 16.

○ In most states, the minimum age for getting a driver's license is 16. The few exceptions include South Dakota, with the lowest minimum of 14 and a half, and New Jersey, with the highest age of 17.

Choosing a Driving School

How to find a driving school that will train your teen well

For teenagers, getting a driver's license is a rite of passage; for parents, it can be a source of high anxiety. In fact, young drivers ages 16 to 20 make up only 7 percent of licensed drivers but suffer 14 percent of the fatalities and are involved in 20 percent of all reported accidents. Inexperience is the main culprit in teen accidents. With driver-education courses curtailed in many schools, the solution for many parents is to turn to professional driving schools.

Locating a driving school is the easy part. There are hundreds—from one-man shops to nationwide operations. Here's a quick guide to choosing one that's best for your child and your peace of mind.

Finding schools. High schools often provide a list of driving schools. Many local chapters of the Automobile Association of America (aaa.com) also operate driving schools.

Checking references. Confirm a school's accreditation by asking for the phone number of its accrediting organization, as well as information on its standards. Regulations vary from state to state, and a license does not guarantee a good school, but the most prominent seal of approval comes from the Driving School Association of the Americas (thedsaa.org), the international organization of driving schools. Members are provided with up-to-date technology and teaching methods. Reputable schools will also offer names of past customers as references.

Reviewing the school. Finalize your selection only after visiting each school on your short list. Check the following points:

• Classroom lessons should work in tandem with in-car sessions. How much time is spent on classroom lessons and how much behind the wheel? A total of 30 classroom hours is average. Beginners learn best with two 45-minute in-car lessons each week, totaling six hours of behind-the-wheel training in varying circumstances and driving environments.

- For the classroom sessions, check to see if textbooks are current and in good condition. Each student should also receive a copy of the state's driver's handbook.

- Are instructional vehicles late-model cars? Are they in good condition? Some states bar the use of driving-school vehicles that are more than four years old. Check that the cars have dual-control brakes, power steering and power brakes, along with safety belts and air bags, of course.

 INSIDE INFO

Licensing Aging Drivers

○ Rarely is anything more than a vision test required to renew a senior's driver's license, and renewal cycles vary from state to state. While most states require renewals every 4 or 5 years, in seven states it is 8 years, in two states it is 10 years and in one (Arizona) no renewal is required until age 65.

○ Colorado shortens the time between renewals starting at age 61, but Illinois doesn't start until 75. Connecticut doesn't require a vision test at renewal; Illinois and New Hampshire require a road test starting at 75.

—Jane E. Brody

When Older Drivers Must Quit

How to know when it's time to hang up the keys

It's not unusual these days for people in their Medicare years to drive thousands of miles to visit family and friends or escape summer's heat or winter's fury. By 2020, more than 40 million Americans 70 and older will be licensed drivers, and these older drivers are now driving more miles a year, and at older ages, than ever before.

Yet, compared with middle-aged drivers, older drivers are about three times as likely to be involved in a crash per mile driven. They are also more likely than younger drivers to die as a result of a crash of similar severity. Are older drivers putting themselves and others at risk?

AARP, the advocacy group for older Americans, lists 15 warning signs that should alert drivers to the need to limit driving or stop driving entirely. (For more information on driver safety for older motorists, try seniordrivers.org and aarp.org/55alive.)

- Feeling less comfortable and more nervous or fearful while driving.

- Having difficulty staying in your lane.

- Experiencing more close calls behind the wheel.

- Getting more dents or scrapes on your car or on other objects.

- Finding it hard to judge gaps in traffic at intersections and on highway entrance and exit ramps.

- Having other drivers honk at you more often.

- Being told that friends or relatives no longer want to ride with you.

- Getting lost more often.

- Failing to notice vehicles or pedestrians on the sides of the road while looking straight ahead.

- Having trouble paying attention to traffic signals, road signs and pavement markings.

- Responding slowly to unexpected situations.

- Becoming easily distracted or having difficulty concentrating while driving.

- Finding it hard to turn to check over your shoulder when you are backing up or changing lanes.

- Getting more traffic tickets or warnings.

SPENDING

- Experiencing a worsening of medical conditions or the need to take medications that can impair driving safety.

—Jane E. Brody

How to Pick Your Roadside Aid
What to do when you're stranded en route

It used to be that when your car broke down on the road, AAA—a name virtually synonymous with roadside help—was the only game in town. Now, consumers have many options from a variety of sources, including car makers, insurers, and cellphone companies.

Most of the big car manufacturers offer roadside assistance as part of their warranty package for the first 3 to 5 years, or 36,000 to 50,000 miles, depending on your deal. With some brands, such as Mercedes-Benz, you have the assistance as long as you own the car.

Some credit card, insurance and cellphone companies also offer services. For less than $5 a month for single lines, Cingular Wireless and Verizon Wireless send assistance as long as you have your cellphone with you. They supply the usual tire changes, lock-out services, jump starts and fuel delivery if you have run out of gas. Services differ, so check a plan's rules concerning towing distances, number of calls you can make per year and other features. Since the plan is attached to the phone, not the car, these services are particularly appealing for someone who does not own a car but wants coverage when renting one.

One heavily advertised assistance system available in many General Motors vehicles is OnStar, which uses wireless and global positioning system technology and car battery power to provide live voice assistance. The service provides emergency help, contacts you if your airbags deploy, finds a sto-len car and, depending on your plan, can also give you driving directions. Typically, OnStar service is free for the first year; afterward, subscriptions average about $300 a year, depending on the plan.

The old standby, AAA, with more than 60 clubs in North America, is still by far the largest provider of roadside assistance in the country. Depending on the plan, membership costs $65 to $125 a year. Aside from standard roadside assistance, membership entitles you to other AAA offerings, such as travel packages and information, insurance, car rentals and cell phone packages that include roadside assistance and navigation systems. AAA Plus and AAA Premier, the more costly membership options, include extras such as up to 100 miles of free towing, locksmith services and free passport photos.

Other, smaller companies offer similar services, including GM Motor Club, at $99 a year, and Better World Club, "an environmentally friendly auto club" that also offers roadside assistance to bicycle riders for less than $60 a year. If you belong to GM Motor Club, there are no towing mileage limitations, and if your car is disabled more than 100 miles from home, the club will reimburse a portion of the cost of your meals, lodging and transportation.

It's not necessarily a bad idea to have double coverage, for a number of reasons. For one, with a car warranty package, you may be towed to a dealership, where you may not want to go if you just need a new battery or tires. And roadside assistance plans generally limit the number of miles they tow for free, usually a minimum of 3 to a maximum of 10 miles. If you want your car towed farther, you could end up paying out of pocket; insurance may or may not cover the difference.

A word of caution about being pressured into having your car taken somewhere you do not want it to go, especially after an accident, when you may be dazed and vulnerable. Some tow-truck drivers may work with certain garages to bring in cars, particularly those that have been in accidents and could prove to be lucrative to repair. If a tow-truck driver insists on taking your car to a specific garage, call another service, or complain afterward to the agency that provides your assistance.

Finally, if you're stranded and your roadside assistance provider cannot help you, just dial 911.

—Alina Tugend

How to Stop a Car Thief

A few smart ways to thwart theft

The American infatuation with cars seems to be shared by criminals. A car is stolen about every 25 seconds, according to the National Insurance Crime Bureau (nicb.org). Although the overall car theft rate has been falling in recent years, thanks to new safety features and increased vigilance by owners and the police, the rate for older models has stayed constant. Thieves target older cars because they are easier to break into and because of the high demand for stolen car parts.

How can you foil a car rustler? Aside from obvious theft deterrents, such as locking your car, parking in well-lit areas and never leaving your car running as you hop out for a quick errand, the N.I.C.B. suggests taking a layered approach to protecting your car by using a variety of measures.

Scare thieves away. Have and use a visible or audible alarm. Young thieves in particular are scared off by autos emitting a shrill warning. You can get optional sensors to detect tampering, glass breakage, and towing. Attach a decal to your window indicating that the car is protected by an anti-theft device.

Immobilize your car. Invest in low-cost but effective devices, such as a hidden "kill" switch that lets you stop the flow of electricity or gas to a car engine. It goes for $10 to $125. Or buy a locking device. You can choose from an array, such as floorboard locks that disable the brake pedal, gearshift locks to disable shifting of the transmission, steering-wheel or tire locks to prevent the car from moving, and hood locks that stop thieves from getting access to the battery and security system. A steering-wheel lock, for example, costs $100 to $200 installed.

Get smart. Some cars come with "smart keys" containing computer chips or radio frequencies unique to your car. If your car won't start, it won't get stolen.

Partner with the police. On the higher end of high-tech gadgets are tracking devices that can alert you—and law enforcement—the moment an unauthorized user moves your vehicle. LoJack, for example, lets the police use a hidden transmitter to find your car. It comes at a big price: $600 and up.

ⓘ INSIDE INFO

Hot Wheels

Many of these models have appeared on lists of the ten most-stolen cars for several years, proving that thieves prefer car parts to luxury wheels.

- 1995 Honda Civic
- 1991 Honda Accord
- 1994 Acura Legend
- 1994 Nissan Sentra
- 1989 Toyota Camry
- 2007 Toyota Corolla
- 1988 Toyota Pickup
- 2004 Dodge Ram Pickup
- 1997 Ford F-150 Series Pickup
- 1994 Chevrolet 1500 Pickup

SOURCE: National Insurance Crime Bureau

SPENDING

Home Technology

How to Network Your Home

It's easier than you think—and well worth it

Over 22 million American households have networked their computers and other machines, according to recent research, and you have plenty of motivation to do the same.

First, a network can save you money. It allows one cable modem, DSL box or printer to serve all the computers in the house.

Second, a network lets your computers share information. You can copy files from one computer to another. You can sit upstairs at your Windows PC, listening to the iTunes music collection from the Mac in the kitchen.

Finally, there's the convenience factor. A network enables a TiVo to display photographs, or a SliMP3 box to play music files, that actually reside on a computer somewhere else in the house. And you can set up networkable computer games to play with other family members. Plenty of people have set up their own home networks and lived to tell the tale. If you want to join their ranks, here is your complete frequently asked questions sheet for home networking.

Q Which kind of network should I set up: wired or wireless?

In the olden days, people connected their computers using fat wires known as Cat 5 Ethernet cables. This method still has a lot to recommend it. It's supercheap, it moves data superfast and, compared

with wireless networks, it's extremely secure.

All Macs and many Windows computers have built-in Ethernet ports, which look like overweight phone jacks. The idea is to connect all your computers to a small box called a router (each one accommodates as many as four computers). The router lets all of the computers communicate with one another and with your cable modem or DSL. Most routers also act as firewalls to keep out Internet no-goodniks. The disadvantage of Ethernet is that it means trailing cables along your floors or, worse, snaking them through your walls.

> **Microwaving a bag of popcorn can temporarily interfere with your network signal.**

• • •

The most promising alternative is the wireless network, also known as Wi-Fi, 802.11 or AirPort. This system works something like a cordless phone: you buy a central base station (also called an access point) that blankets your house with a network signal. A wireless adapter lets each computer receive the signal. Most laptops have this feature built in; others can be retrofitted with a Wi-Fi card adapter. You can make a desktop computer wireless by adding a U.S.B. Wi-Fi adapter. Now, with very little setup, you've united your computers and cable modem into one unit, without drilling a single hole in the walls.

Q What if I have two desktop computers and two wireless laptops?

In that case, consider buying a combination box called a wireless router. It has jacks for, say, four Ethernet cables, as well as antennas that broadcast a wireless signal to your Wi-Fi laptops.

PROTECTING YOUR NETWORK

A Wi-Fi network can let a household share a high-speed Internet connection wirelessly, as well as linking printers and other devices. But without proper security, it can also enable others with Wi-Fi equipment within range of the signal—typically 200 feet—to share the Internet connection, or even gain access to data on home computers.

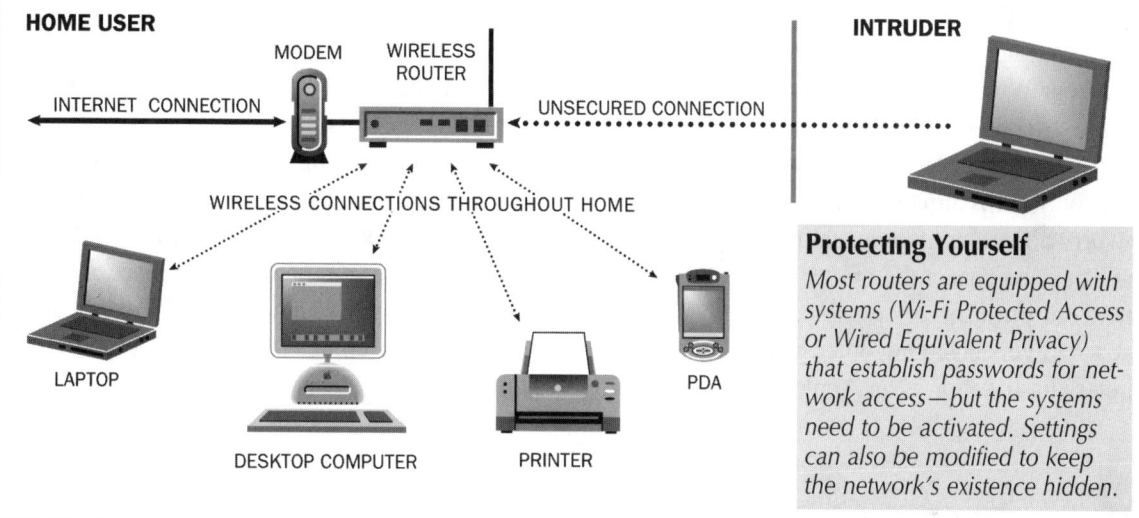

HOME USER

MODEM | WIRELESS ROUTER

INTERNET CONNECTION

UNSECURED CONNECTION

INTRUDER

WIRELESS CONNECTIONS THROUGHOUT HOME

LAPTOP

DESKTOP COMPUTER

PRINTER

PDA

Protecting Yourself

Most routers are equipped with systems (Wi-Fi Protected Access or Wired Equivalent Privacy) that establish passwords for network access—but the systems need to be activated. Settings can also be modified to keep the network's existence hidden.

● **I've heard that if I use a wireless network, snoopers can rifle through my stuff.**

It's theoretically possible for electronic eavesdroppers to intercept text that you send wirelessly, including passwords that you type. On public wireless networks that don't require a password to get online, like the ones in hotel lobbies, there's not much you can do about this risk.

The odds are far smaller that anyone would be interested in spying on you at home. Still, if you're concerned, you can just turn on your base station's optional password feature. Most base stations offer something called W.E.P. encryption (much better than nothing); newer ones offer what's called W.P.A. (much better security, fewer problems). The base station's manual explains how to turn these on.

● **Does that mean I'll have to type in a password every time I want to get online?**

No. Both Mac OS X and Windows XP can memorize the password for you.

● **Which kind of wireless gear should I buy?**

Every couple of years, the computer industry dreams up another, faster wireless standard for wireless networking. They go by annoying names like 802.11a, 802.11b, 802.11g and 802.11n.

The "g" variety is faster and has better coverage than the older "a" or "b," yet is compatible with all three. In general, if you're shopping today, go for the "n." If all of your gear is "n," your network will be four times as fast as "g" gear.

● **I can't wait. My Internet connection is so slow!**

Well, don't spend a lot of money in the expectation that a faster network means faster Internet speed; it doesn't. Even the slowest home network is already much faster than the real bottleneck, your cable modem or DSL box. A faster network transfers files between your own computers faster but generally does nothing for your Web or e-mail activity.

Will I be able to connect my old inkjet printer to my network?

Yes. The free way is to connect the printer to one Mac or PC and then turn on that computer's printer sharing feature. (For instructions, search Mac OS X's or Windows XP's online help for "printer sharing.") The other computers in your house can now send printouts to that printer, as long as the main computer is turned on. If you'd rather not have to worry about the main machine being available, you can also connect the printer to a gadget called a network print server, available in both wireless and wired versions. One other possibility: if your wireless base station is an Apple AirPort Express,

you can plug a printer directly into a U.S.B. jack on the base station. This method saves you both the worry that a certain computer is turned on and the cost of an extra printer-sharing gadget.

It still sounds like I'm in for a headache.

Setting up the network can indeed be a slog; consider inviting a neighborhood teenager over to help. Or, at the very least, visit Google.com and type in "LinkSys wireless Internet sharing" (or whatever problem you're having); the beauty of joining the home-network revolution now is that several million people have been this way before. But look at the bright side: once your network is in place, it's yours for life. There's no monthly fee, no further learning involved, and no annual upgrades to buy and install. In the world of computers and technology, that makes a home network a valuable investment indeed.

—David Pogue

TIMELY TIPS

A Primer on Networking
A checklist for installing a wireless home network

✔ Get wireless adapters for all the computers and peripherals you want to include in your network, as well as a base station to transmit your Internet feed.

✔ Make sure that all your equipment operates according to the same 802.11 standard.

✔ Place your equipment for maximum range and clarity. Higher, more central locations are best. Avoid areas with many obstructions or nearby radio-wave devices like cordless phones and baby monitors.

✔ Consider installing access points in your home to act as signal boosters.

✔ Change channel settings to avoid potential interference from other wireless networks or devices.

✔ Activate the equipment's security features.

—Kate Murphy

Untangling the World of Cables
They're critical but they need not be expensive

Even after researching which TV or Blu-ray player to buy, you still have to deal with the conundrum of the cables. Other format wars get resolved fairly quickly and definitively (Blu-ray over HD-DVD, VHS over Beta), but cable formats last, it would seem, forever. Cables are important, but they should not be expensive. To help untangle some of the confusion, here is a simple, somewhat opinionated taxonomy of most of the cables that we deal with in our lives.

Coaxial. Invented in the 1920s and in commercial use since the 1940s, this is the granddaddy of cables. Medium-thick and either white or black, it has a little screw connector at the end.

BEST FOR: Connecting your cable box to your TV or your cable modem to the wall outlet. Some people use it for digital audio connections as well. **Price:** Your cable company will string your house with as much coax as you need, and it won't cost you a thing. Replacement cable can cost anywhere from 75 cents to $16 a foot. Get the cheap stuff.

 **Composite**. One rung up from coaxial in terms of signal quality, composite cables look like a three-headed hydra of sorts. The red and white strands carry stereo audio while the (non-high-definition) video signal rides the yellow line.

Best for: Connecting DVD players and other video equipment to older analog TV sets.

Price: Unless you're crossing long distances (50 feet and up) with composite, you can go for low-price cables, sold by online retailers such as Monop-rice.com for less than $1 a foot. And even if you are crossing long distances, do you really want to spend a lot on a cable standard that is already dead?

 **S-Video**. S-Video (the "s" is for "separate") is considered better than composite but not as good as component cable. S-Video cables do not carry audio and do not support high-definition video. S-Video has been superseded by component connections for home video, but you still may find it on PCs.

Best for: Linking DVD players, game consoles, computers and older video equipment to the television set when component connections are not available. **Price:** S-Video cable is cheap. Prices should be measured in cents per foot, not dollars.

 **Component.** Another three-headed cable with a name that is frustratingly similar to composite, but there are big differences. Component cables support HDTV signals. Component cables divide video data into three separate signals for a better quality image, but they do not carry an audio

signal. The ends are red, blue and green.

Best for: Connecting DVD players and other video equipment to newer HDTV sets. Component cable was the video cable champ until HDMI came around and is still in wide use.

Price: Avoid the flashily packaged, insanely marked-up cables sold as high-end from big-box electronics retailers that routinely cost into the three figures. You are paying for nothing more than a fat marketing budget at those prices. Monoprice.com sells component cable starting at around 50 cents a foot.

 **HDMI (High-Definition Multimedia Interface).** The current standard for high-end AV equipment. HDMI is an all-digital connection that carries both audio and video over one fairly thin cable.

Best for: Connecting HDTV sets to Blu-ray or DVD players and other home entertainment gear.

Price: Generally, for the average home user all digital cables (meaning HDMI) are more or less the same, because a digital signal is not affected by the things that can muck up an analog signal (such as interference). So buy the most affordable cable out there ($3 a foot or less).

 **VGA (Video Graphics Array).** VGA has been around for 20 years and is considered the lowest-common denominator for video output on many PC systems. Some game consoles and video projectors connect by way of VGA as well. Advanced variations of the technology include Super VGA and XGA (Extended Graphics Array).

Best for: Connecting PCs to external analog monitors. **Price:** Cables can be found for around $10.

 **DVI (Digital Visual Interface).** DVI and HDMI are similar in that they both handle an all-digital signal, but DVI cables are video only.

To confuse you, there are different kinds of DVI cables (some are analog only, some are digital); DVI-I cables can handle both analog and digital signals. Image quality can degrade if the DVI cable is too long, but the technical standard states that DVI cables must maintain the signal up to 16 feet.

BEST FOR: Connecting computers to LCD monitors and digital projectors.

PRICE: Prices have fallen in recent years, from $50 down to around $15 for a standard 6-foot cable.

 **Ethernet (aka Cat-5 or Cat-6).** Ethernet cable looks a lot like telephone cable, but the connectors are a little bit wider than the cords that go into your phone. Ethernet jacks are now standard on desktops and laptops and can also connect game consoles and TiVos to home networks.

BEST FOR: Connecting computers and workgroup printers to high-speed computer networks.

PRICE: Prices vary by length, but cable can be found for as low as $3 for a 10-foot length.

 **U.S.B. (Universal Serial Bus).** U.S.B. is the most common way to attach devices to your computer. It can also provide power to those devices. One end of a U.S.B. cable may look different from the other (printer USB cables usually have a boxier plug at one end), but the flat part always goes into the computer. The latest standard is U.S.B. 2.0.

BEST FOR: Connecting just about any type of computer peripheral (hard drives, MP3 players, printers, etc.) to the computer.

PRICE: Prices for cables can start at less than a dollar for a 3-foot cable (consider eBay) depending on what connector type is needed on the other end.

 **Mini- and Micro-U.S.B.** Mini-U.S.B. and the newer micro-U.S.B. ports are found on the sides of cameras and other devices with limited space for cable jacks. The small end of the cable goes into the device and the large end into the computer's standard U.S.B. port.

BEST FOR: Connecting smaller devices like digital cameras and some smartphones to the computer.

PRICE: Assuming one came with your camera or smartphone, nothing. A replacement cable can cost around $10.

—J.D. Biersdorfer

Which Computer Is for You?
Desktop or laptop? More speed or more memory?

All PCs let you surf the Web, check for e-mail messages, download MP3 players and edit photos. That's why manufacturers may pitch other factors, such as powerful machines for three-dimensional video games, or they may promote

 TIMELY TIPS

Looking for a Cheaper Mac?
Apple itself may give you a discount

Being a student or a teacher has its privileges in the Mac world. The Apple Store for Education (www.apple.com/education) sells products up to $300 less than their Apple Store prices. Since Apple controls how much its authorized resellers charge, these discounts are precious indeed.

To qualify, you identify your school (kindergarten through high school or college) from a menu and agree that you will buy only a total of three computers and one monitor in an academic year.

Once you're in, there may be a bonus: a mail-in rebate or a coupon for a free iPod.

—Wilson Rothman

protection plans and tech support. Fortunately, computer vendors are hungry for your business, and if you know what you want in a computer system, you can strike a bargain. Here's how to decide on just what you want and need.

Laptop or desktop? One big quandary is whether to buy a laptop or a desktop computer. The arguments for buying a laptop are overwhelmingly persuasive. There are plenty to choose from that are under $1,000. Laptops let you gain access to wireless networks found on campuses and other school grounds and at hangouts like coffee shops. For college and boarding school students, they are much easier to manage on move-in day. On trips they double as portable DVD players.

But there are many reasons you may not want your children to have access to a portable computer. If your teenager cannot move the family PC around, the chances of its being stolen, smashed or otherwise damaged are greatly reduced. An economic argument for desktop PCs is also worthwhile. Although the prices of laptops have dropped precipitously, desktop prices have also continued to fall.

How much computer do you need? The longer you plan to keep your PC, the bigger your budget must be. If you buy a computer system with more RAM or a bigger hard drive than you had initially planned, you can avoid having to install RAM or add an external hard drive.

Video games may seem like a frivolous reason to buy a more powerful computer. But a student going to design school or to an audio-visual program, say, may need that processing power and graphics acceleration. And you should always check what system your school recommends or requires. From $300 to $3,000, a PC's basic components vary slightly. Everything still revolves around the processor, the amount of RAM and the size of the hard drive.

Do You Need a Netbook?

It's bigger than a BlackBerry and smaller than a laptop

The netbook—also known as a mini-notebook, a mobile Internet device or, as someone put it recently, a "laptot"—is a "lifestyle" companion that provides portable on-the-go communications and limited computing functionality for $500 or less. A basic laptop starts at about that price, and some models can cost thousands.

Netbooks fit into the technology spectrum between pocket-sized devices like the iPhone and BlackBerry and full-size laptops or notebooks with their larger screens, more powerful processors and other features. They lack the electronic chops of their bigger siblings: forget Photoshop, gameplay or any serious video editing on a netbook. Web browsing and e-mail are their strengths, at least in these early stages.

Hewlett-Packard, Lenovo, Dell, Asus, MSI, Samsung, Sylvania and Acer all have netbook models. Virtually all netbooks are built around Intel's Atom processor, a 1.6-gigahertz chip, and use one gigabyte of RAM, or memory. Nearly all have built-in U.S.B. ports, a Webcam and integrated speakers, and some can connect to a Wi-Fi network. None of the models have CD or DVD drives.

But there are differences. Some netbooks use a hard disk for storage; others use flash memory. Some support 802.11n, the latest version of Wi-Fi, while others rely on older versions of the network format. Screen size varies in these clamshell models, generally from 8.9 inches diagonal to 10 inches. And battery life differs, as do weight and other factors. Because the devices are easy to carry and cheap, people who just use their computer for e-mail, for instance, may find a netbook an attractive alternative.

—Stephen Williams

A word about warranties. There are warranties and there are warranties. Dell typically includes 1 year of limited coverage and technical support for desktop systems. Its extended warranties are among the most affordable: $90 for 2 years of coverage.

Hewlett-Packard also provides a limited 1-year warranty on every system. Its 2-year extended plan costs $170 but covers a far wider range of services. Apple computers come with a 1-year hardware and software warranty but only 90 days of free technical support. Since laptops can be laid low by water, hot tea and wine, Apple's extended protection may be worthwhile. It can cost $150 to $400, but that often includes an underlying warranty of 2 or 3 years.

—Wilson Rothman

Protecting Data on Your Laptop

Back up your files and keep your computer secure

It's hard not to experience anxiety when you're traveling with a laptop—it can fall accidentally during security screenings, it might be stolen from a hotel room or forgotten in a taxi or restaurant or it could fail from too many jolts.

Perhaps the most important safety measure is to protect the information on your computer so that if it is damaged, lost or stolen, the data remains safe. Travelers have many backup devices to choose from. Particularly convenient are flash drives: small plastic devices the size of a key chain that weigh only an ounce or so and plug into a computer's U.S.B. port (the port typically used for connecting printers and other peripherals). You can copy your e-mail files, documents, pictures or data files to a flash drive and can keep the drive with you or in the hotel safe.

Lexar makes JumpDrive U.S.B. memory devices with up to 32 gigabytes of storage, large enough for lots of documents, photos and e-mail (available

---

? EXPERT ANSWER

Do You Need Those Downloads?

● Is it necessary to heed the messages that tell you to download a newer version of something like Acrobat Reader or RealPlayer if you already have a version that works?

Updating this sort of software usually isn't mandatory right away, but it can eventually become necessary when a company makes adjustments to its file formats or adds features that require updated software to function. If you have an outdated version of a media-player program, for example, you may not be able to see or hear a streaming video file that has been created with a new version of the software.

—J. D. Biersdorfer

---

at Amazon.com). The devices include software that allows users with a password to download data.

For additional security, there are flash drives with biometric capabilities, like a fingerprint reader that allows access only with a matching fingerprint. Or, you might consider storing or backing up your data files on the memory cards that slip into comparably equipped digital cameras or cellphones. This solution is good for travelers who simply want backup.

Of course, you want to protect the laptop itself, too. There is your hotel, for instance. Before booking a room, security-conscious laptop owners should ask what size room-safe the hotel offers, or if the front desk is willing to store a laptop in the office safe.

You can also insure your notebook by adding it on to your homeowners or renter's policy. In some cases your existing homeowners insurance policy will cover theft of a laptop, with your standard deductible, if it's not being used for business

TIMELY TIPS

Moving Data to a New Computer

Moving all your stuff out of an old hard drive and into a new one is a rite of passage when buying a replacement computer, and how you go about it may depend on both the hardware involved and your patience.

There are various ways to move your files and settings, but moving programs can be tricky. If possible, track down the original installation discs (if the software is compatible with your new computer) and have them ready for your new laptop.

✔ One way to move files is to copy to a thumb drive or other external hard drive the files you want to move, or burn them to discs, and then transfer the files from the drive or discs onto the new laptop. Thumb drives have emerged as the medium of choice because of their low price, high speed and high capacity.

✔ It may be possible to link the machines with a network cable (or a FireWire cable, if you are moving between Macs) to create a mini-network that lets you copy files from the old computer to the new one.

✔ Several programs are made to transfer data. Microsoft includes a Files and Settings Transfer Wizard in Windows XP that guides you through moving your files and system settings from an older Windows computer. Many Apple computers also come with a program that helps you move files and settings from older Mac systems.

✔ Third-party software like IntelliMover from Detto Technologies (www.detto.com) also can transfer files from old to new PCs. Detto also has a program called Move2Mac that can move files from an old PC to a new Macintosh.

—J. D. Biersdorfer

purposes. Safeware (www.safeware.com) offers insurance for notebook computers and includes coverage for accidental damage, theft, vandalism and other problems.

If you don't want to travel with a computer but need access to data, files or e-mail while on the road and have the use of a hotel business center or other Internet source, you can arrange to have your computer at home run a remote access program that's included in Windows XP, or through a service like GoToMyPC (www.gotomypc.com) that enables users to gain access remotely to their PCs from any Internet-connected computer. To use a service like GoToMyPC, you register the computer you want to make available on the site, download the remote access host software and install it. To access that computer remotely, you then use a Web-enabled PC to log in to your home PC. You are now able to work as if you were at home.

—David A. Kelly

When Your Computer Crashes
If all else fails and you have to recover your data

The data recovery industry would barely exist if all computer users backed up their hard drives. But the routine, like flossing teeth, is practiced regularly by few. And as hard drive capacity explodes, the consequences of catastrophic failure mushroom.

Not every hard drive's files can be recovered, but rates are improving. Where once only half of data could be restored, now nearly all of it can be salvaged from up to 90 percent of drives.

The cost can run to several thousand dollars— the bigger the rush, the higher the price. When nothing can be recovered—typically when drives cannot spin or data has been overwritten—data recovery companies often charge an inspection fee of a couple of hundred dollars.

Once a drive arrives at a data recovery company, it is typically inspected in a "clean room" to prevent dust contamination. If it got wet, it is submerged in a solvent to remove residue. Because data can be retrieved only from operating drives, many companies will try to get the mechanism running temporarily—often by using components from an inventory of different models.

A copy of the drive's contents is then recorded on a server for protection, and another copy is transferred to a functioning hard drive. Using commercial and proprietary software tools, data recovery companies extract the data from that copy. Retrieved files are sent to the customer using DVDs, a new hard drive or Internet file transfer. Generally, companies keep all files confidential and erase them from their servers shortly after delivery to the customer.

—Eric A. Taub

How to Fix Your Own Computer
Patience and a screwdriver can do the job

While personal computers rival the brain's neural complexity, you do not need to be a neurosurgeon to fix one. Many parts can be easily replaced at home for a fraction of what a professional would charge.

You should not bother fixing a PC when the cost equals about half the price of a new machine, according to *Consumer Reports*. And that number is easy to reach. Having a shop replace a laptop's L.C.D. screen, for example, can easily run up to $600. Doing it yourself might cost $200 and a few hours of research and labor.

From adding memory to replacing a motherboard, repair tasks often require little more than patience, organization and a couple of small screwdrivers. There is a downside to doing it yourself. If you guess wrong and replace a part that is not causing the problem, you will have wasted time

and perhaps money. But many hardware problems are fairly easy to diagnose. If you have no idea where to start, the Web has many sites and discussion boards where others with similar problems are eager to analyze, discuss and instruct you.

Most fix-it-yourself sites concentrate on laptop problems for an obvious reason: given that laptops are thrown around in airports and backpacks, they are much more likely to break. And fixing a laptop is more challenging than repairing a desktop. Not only are parts packed in more tightly, but each manufacturer has its own design.

One good strategy for any repair: take digital photographs of all the disassembly steps to try to ensure that you won't have any stray pieces left after you put the laptop back together.

Keeping track of the screws is especially important. Use one that's too small and parts will not hold. Use one that is too big and you could easily short out the new logic board that you just installed. One way to account for all the screws is to tape and label each one on a piece of paper on which you have outlined the computer's shape.

Some items are very easy to replace. Manufacturers have long allowed consumers to replace their own RAM chips without voiding the warranty. And changing out a malfunctioning or too-small hard drive for a new one often requires little more than unplugging a cable and unscrewing the drive from the computer's chassis.

L.C.D. screens are one of the more difficult components to replace. Some are glued to bezels and contain a number of screws and screw covers. To the novice, it may not always be clear whether it's the L.C.D. that is causing the problem. However, if an external monitor works when plugged into the laptop, then the screen is most likely at fault.

Once you have decided to take the self-repair route, illustrated guides are a must. Fortunately, they are readily available on the Web. One site,

Foner Books (fonerbooks.com) offers several flow charts that help isolate the likely problem and take-apart guides for popular laptop models.

Online discussion groups are another good source for diagrams. For Macintosh computers, iFixit.com and PowerbookMedic.com offer extensive free repair guides for a host of problems, with detailed photographs showing how to perform the work.

—Eric A. Taub

Calling in the Geeks
Computer doctors at the local shopping mall

When something goes really wrong with your computer—like an operating system stymied by spyware or a DVD drive that won't play your movies—you may have to call in the experts. Many major chains have their own computer repair departments and in some cases will pay house calls.

Staples, the office-supply chain has a nationwide squad of service techs. These technicians, who have industry certifications for servicing Windows-based computers, provide technical support and hardware repairs in Staples stores or at customers' homes. (866-4EZ-TECS; www.staples.com/sbd/cre/marketing/easytech/)

Macintosh users can take their misbehaving machines to Apple's retail stores around the country. Each Apple store has a Genius Bar, where employees diagnose, advise and repair ailing Macs and other Apple products. A list of Apple stores, each with its own Web page and Genius Bar appointment reservation form, is at www.apple.com/retail. In some places, however, appointments may be hard to come by, unless you're willing to go at odd hours.

TIMELY TIPS

Online Help for Your Computer

Computer geeks love to help others. Check the online forums at computer manufacturers' sites for user support groups. YouTube has a number of how-to videos that take viewers through the assembly and replacement of various parts. Here are more online resources to guide you through the process of repairing your own computer.

PCs
✔ **The Laptop Repair Workbook** offers flow charts and specific information on how to repair various components. *www.fonerbooks.com/workbook.htm*

✔ **Laptop Repair Help** offers free illustrated instructions on how to repair a variety of problems, including broken L.C.D.'s. The site also links to some official repair manuals. *www.laptoprepair101.com*

✔ **AGParts** is a large supplier of disk drives, screens, motherboards and other components for Acer, Apple, Dell, Hewlett-Packard, Toshiba and other machines. *www.agpartsworldwide.com*

MACs
✔ **PowerbookMedic.com** and **iFixit** both sell new and used parts. Both also offer free how-to diagrams and guides for taking apart laptops, iPhones and iPods. *www.ifixit.com*

✔ **MacFixIt** visitors can read a free daily compendium of Macintosh problems and solutions. For $25 a year, they can search the site's extensive archives on hardware and software repair. *www.macfixit.com*

PRINTERS
✔ At **fixyourownprinter.com**, customer help forums and repair parts are available to solve problems with printers from Epson, Hewlett-Packard, Lexmark and several others. —J. D. Biersdorfer

SPENDING

Best Buy's Geek Squad has thousands of "agents" who make emergency visits in Volkswagen Beetles to technology-addled homes nationwide, 24 hours a day. Among other things, Geek Squad (800-433-5778; www.geeksquad.com) offers specialized missions like setting up online gaming consoles, connecting and configuring a new computer and linking home-theater components to a network. The technicians also handle more mundane jobs like software glitches and other annoyances that make computing more difficult than it should be.

—J. D. Biersdorfer

How to Speed Up Your Internet

Update your computer and tweak your browser

In the beginning, the Internet was fast enough for most. Checking e-mail and reading a Web site did not require scads of bandwidth and any broadband connection was more than enough.

But a funny thing happened—many people became power users. They started buying albums from iTunes and watching endless videos on YouTube. All this added activity calls for a faster Internet.

When that day comes, there will be much rejoicing. But until then, there are things users can do to make sure their connections are as fast as possible. Here are a few.

Get the right connection. Consumer broadband is split between two competing technologies: digital subscriber line, or DSL, and high-speed cable. Depending on how many providers are in your area, you may have a choice. Generally speaking, cable is faster, although cable speeds can be affected by how many people are online at once and even by how close your connection is to your local broadband source.

A third option in some areas is Verizon's fiber optic service, called FiOS, which is faster than

---

 **TIMELY TIPS**

Why You Need a Firewall

Firewalls—named after the flame-blocking structures designed to keep fires from spreading—are programmed to analyze the network traffic flowing between your computer and the Internet. The firewall compares the information it monitors with a set of rules in its database. If it sees something not allowed—say, another computer trying to connect to one of the machines on your network—the firewall can block and prevent the action.

✔ Most firewall programs let you adjust the rules to allow certain types of data to flow freely back and forth without interference, in cases where you want to do things like stream music or share files with another computer on your network.

✔ Both Windows XP and Mac OS X include basic firewall programs as part of the operating system, and you can find more complex third-party firewall programs from software retailers. Makers of anti-virus software often have a combination package that includes a firewall program and other security software as

well, which can protect your computer from a variety of threats.

✔ Firewall programs are especially important if you have a high-speed Internet service through a cable modem or DSL, because your computer is typically connected to the Internet for longer periods of time, increasing the exposure to malicious people or programs looking to infect and infiltrate unprotected systems.

And it doesn't take long. A study by a security company found that an unprotected Windows computer was infected within 12 minutes of connecting to the Internet. —J. D. Biersdorfer

DSL. It rivals, and may exceed, cable's fastest speeds. (For a listing of where FiOS is available, go to verizon.com/fios.)

Even with cable and DSL, there are choices of speeds. Most service providers offer more than one tier of Internet access. Pay a higher monthly fee and you will have faster maximum download and upload speeds.

There is a catch. What is advertised as a maximum may rarely be reached. Many Internet service providers do not configure their services to the maximum speed because they are configuring them for shared networks. Their aim is to make sure most users are satisfied, not to cater to the small group that wants the fastest possible speeds.

For example, even raising your maximum download threshold from 1.5 megabits per second to 10 megabits per second, which are the tiers offered by Time Warner Cable, should have a positive effect over all on your browsing and downloading.

Update your computer. Web sites today demand more from your PC than they did even a few years ago, so some upgrades may be in order.

The single most effective thing for improving your computer's performance is to add more random access memory, or RAM. If your machine has fewer than 2 GB of RAM, you should add more. Fortunately, adding RAM is not terribly expensive (an additional gigabyte costs around $40) and is fairly easy to do (you might need a small screwdriver and, at most, 5 minutes). For an instructional video of how to install RAM, go to cnettv.cnet.com and search for "adding RAM." The first search result will show you how. Aside from hardware upgrades, some other tweaks can eke out some extra speed from your PC.

The more programs you leave open and running, the more your computer has to keep track of, so close applications you are not using. If you're

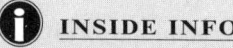

INSIDE INFO

Who Are the Microbloggers?

○ The Internet is rich with ways to broadcast one-sentence updates about yourself to your friends. The best known of these microblogging engines is Twitter. Facebook also contains a similar feature called the "status update," and a program called Yammer lets office workers post short updates about their activities.

○ Who are the users of social networking services? They tend to cluster at around age 25. But microblogging services have plenty of users up to about age 35, according to the Pew Internet and American Life Project, which has surveyed microblogging.

○ The survey also finds that microbloggers are more likely to live in cities than the average Internet user, and far less likely to live in rural areas: 9 percent live in rural areas, as compared to 17 percent of all Internet users.

—Alex Mindlin

connecting to the Internet through a wireless connection, limiting the number of users who share the wireless signal can help.

It also just may be a good time to invest in a new computer. If your PC's central processing unit is running at anything less than 1.5 gigahertz, you will have a tough time keeping up with graphics-heavy Web sites.

For Windows users, viruses can also be a major bottleneck for online connections. If you don't have it already (and you really should have it already), antivirus software from companies like McAfee or Symantec will keep your PC clear of unwanted programs.

Tweak your browser. Another player involved in Internet speed is the browser you use to navigate

SPENDING

the Web. Choosing the right browser has become pretty simple: most experts recommend Firefox, which you can download free from mozilla.com/firefox.

Firefox's open-source architecture means it has been tested and tweaked by far more people than proprietary browsers like Microsoft's Internet

---

● **TIMELY TIPS**

Where to Find a Podcast
Look here for digital audio files

Podcasts are simply digital audio files, usually created in a common file format like MP3 that just about any digital audio player can handle. Podcasts range from professionally produced radio shows to exuberant homemade rants on a theme that anyone with a computer, a microphone and the right software can create.

✔ Most podcasts are free. Once you find and download a show you would like to hear, you just transfer the podcast file from your computer to your portable music player, as you would a music file.

✔ News organizations often have podcasts posted on their pages. National Public Radio makes many programs available to download in podcast form at www.npr.org/podcasts/. You can find several programs from the British Broadcasting Corporation at www.bbc.co.uk/radio/downloadtrial.

✔ Searching site by site can be time consuming, but you have plenty of options if you want to browse a lot of podcast offerings at once. Resources like PodCast.com and PodCastAlley.com serve as online directories of podcasts and podcasting information. With Apple's iTunes you can browse lists of podcasts in the iTunes Music Store and "subscribe" to shows that you would like to download regularly as new installments appear.

—J. D. Biersdorfer

Explorer. Firefox also uses less of your computer's memory, freeing it up to handle other tasks.

But Firefox's real advantage is its collection of user-generated add-ons. These are small, free modifications to the Firefox browser that can do many things (like change the browser's appearance, help manage content and integrate third-party search features).

If you've ever noticed that a site is slow to load because of graphics-heavy ads, you can install the Adblock plug-in, which eliminates ads from your browser (blocking ads has benefits beyond improving speed—cleanliness and tranquility are two that come to mind).

Sites that use a lot of animation (known as Flash animation) can also be slow; Firefox has another plug-in, called Flashblock, that allows you turn the Flash portions of a site on or off. For these reasons, Macintosh users may also want to download Firefox. While Apple's Safari browser is quick (and far less susceptible to viruses), it does not work with any of these add-ons.

Another simple thing to do is to periodically clear your browser's cache (what Microsoft calls Temporary Internet Files). Frequently visited pages are stored there for quick access, but things can also get bogged down.

More advanced users may want to adjust some of the more esoteric settings of their browsers. To simplify the process, the Web site Broadband Reports has a "tweak tester" that will suggest settings to modify (dslreports.com/tweaks).

Speedguide.net offers a similar tweaker, called TCP Optimizer, as a download for Windows 2000 or XP users (speedguide.net/downloads.php).

Extending beyond browser settings, Google has a free application in beta, or test mode, for Windows users called Google Web Accelerator, available at webaccelerator.google.com. The application aims to speed up the way pages load by employing a variety of strategies (compressing data, storing frequently visited pages and others). Using Web Accelerator means that all your surfing is routed through Google's computers, but if you're comfortable with that (all of your surfing already goes through your I.S.P., remember), the application should improve your site browsing (it will not, however, improve download speeds).

All these applications cost nothing and are based on proven methods. Enough free downloads are available that anyone charging for a miracle remedy should be looked at askance.

—Azadeh Ensha

Making Calls Over the Internet

The pros and cons of the many alternatives

If you're under 30 or so, you probably know all about Skype. It's a free program (Mac, Windows or Linux) that connects you to other people who have Skype. You can type instant messages back and forth, make crystal-clear audio calls and even make video calls, provided your computers have webcams or built-in cameras—all without paying a penny.

Plenty of other programs do similar things: iChat, Google Talk, MSN Messenger, AIM, Yahoo Messenger, SightSpeed and Oovoo. But because of its simplicity, its quality and its early start, Skype is the one whose name has become a verb.

For those who need to get over the unfamiliarity hump of the technology, here is the lowdown on Internet phoning options.

Your VoIP BOX. VoIP is the name for voice calls carried over the Internet's wiring. (VoIP stands for voice-over-Internet protocol.) For example, companies like Vonage offer cheap long-distance rates and features not found with conventional

TIMELY TIPS

Online Help for Your Smartphone

✔ **Crackberry.com**'s forums break down problems by model, including Apple's iPhone. It also has a section for older BlackBerrys (forums.crackberry.com/f29/), which is helpful because not everyone switches models every year. You can also search by carrier. *forums.crackberry.com/*

✔ **Users of the iPhone** can turn to the iPhone Blog, which is helpful because it uses screen images and other visual aids instead of dizzying amounts of text. Even better are video tutorials. Instead of wasting time trying to locate your SIM card tray, just mimic the video's step-by step instructions and pause and replay as needed. *www.theiphoneblog.com/ iphone-help-and-how-to-guides/*

✔ **CNet's video tutorials** are organized and presented by the site's editors, who should be qualified to solve your problems. The site's Quick Tips section is good to browse if you're looking to better navigate your gadget. In one video, a CNet editor gives BlackBerry navigation tips—far more colorful than reading your phone's instruction manual. *cnettv.cnet.com/2001-1_53-28619.html*

✔ And if you insist on speaking to a human being, go to gethuman.com first. It will tell you the fastest, most direct number to use to reach a living, breathing technician on the line. *www.gethuman.com/*

—Azadeh Ensha

phone services. To make these services work, you plug your existing home telephone handset into an adapter box (usually free with a subscription). You plug this adapter into your Internet connection rather than a phone line. You can place and receive calls normally, but the Internet, not the phone company, is carrying the calls.

Travelers who sign up for a VoIP service take the adapter box with them. They can land in any country, plug their adapter into the hotel room phone and a wired high-speed Internet connection, and place calls back home. When someone calls their home number, the adapter box rings, no matter where it is. It comes with a few drawbacks: you need a telephone handset, and it's not wireless.

V-Phone. Vonage offers the same service, for the same rates, in a tiny box that looks like a standard flash drive—also known as a U.S.B. drive, memory drive or keychain drive.

When you insert it into a Windows XP computer (not Vista, Macintosh or Linux) a simulated dialing keypad and phone book list pop up on the screen. You can dial any number and, through an included stereo earbud microphone that plugs straight into the flash drive, have clear phone chats with anyone in the world. It also works with computers at an Internet cafe or an airport terminal.

But even if you're already a Vonage subscriber, the V-Phone means having a second phone number and paying an added monthly fee. And there's not much point to the V-Phone if you bring your own laptop anyway (see V-Access, next).

Vonage V-Access. This service lets anyone, even nonsubscribers, make free overseas calls to Vonage subscribers from the United States, Canada, Mexico and a number of European countries.

You need no equipment whatsoever. You just dial a local access number in whatever country you're in. (The list of local numbers appears at vonage.com.) At the tone, dial your Vonage pal's phone number—and you're connected, gratis. But, remember, you can make free calls only to Vonage subscribers and 800 numbers.

Vonage Softphone. Another option for Vonage subscribers is the SoftPhone software for Mac or Windows. You pay a slight monthly fee for unlimited service, and you don't need an adapter box. (The software uses a second phone number—not the same one as your primary Vonage account.)

A few drawbacks are that you have to wear a headset, and when your laptop battery dies, you can't make calls.

Skype. If you travel with a laptop, you get the same features—unlimited, flat-fee, Internet-based computer dialing—using free software (skype.com).

Calls made using Skype and its rivals (Google Talk, AIM, iChat and more) are absolutely free, as long as you're having computer-to-computer chats, where you and the person on the other end are both wearing headsets. Here, again, you have to lug your laptop and wear a headset.

A Skype Phone. A few companies have scrapped some required ingredients for Internet phone calling—microphone, speaker, computer, Internet connection and software. The result is self-contained Skype hot-spot phones.

Phones by Netgear and the Belkin Wi-Fi Phone for Skype, for example, look and work like cellphones, complete with vibrate mode, headphone jack and removable battery. But they don't connect to cellular networks; they connect to wireless Internet hot spots and make calls using Skype.

Sound quality is good, operation is simple—your existing Skype buddy list appears on the phone—and the economy is unbeatable, especially when you're making calls from abroad.

The downside is again that you can talk only to Skype buddies. But if you sign onto the SkypeOut service, you can use the Wi-Fi phone's keypad to dial out to traditional phone numbers (that is, non-Skype members).

Google Voice. An expanded version of a service previously known as GrandCentral, Google

Voice lets you make calls through the Internet for free domestically and for a small fee internationally.

Calls work differently on Google Voice than on Skype. Rather than starting a call from a computer, a specialized phone or an application on a mobile device, Google Voice lets you call into its voice mail service from any phone. Once there, you can push a button to get a dial tone and call a different number.

For international calls to landlines in a handful of major countries, Google Voice is marginally cheaper than Skype, while Google Voice calls to international mobile phones are as much as a third cheaper than Skype's.

A drawback: The service is not set up to handle video calls, although Google offers simple video-chatting capabilities through Google Talk, its instant-messaging service.

—David Pogue

Picking the Right TV

Plasma or L.C.D.? It's not an easy choice

Walk into any electronics retailer and you not only face a wall of screens, you face a barrage of jargon, conflicting standards and an alphabet soup of terminology. How do you cut through the clutter?

There is no easy answer because selecting the right television depends as much on your personal circumstances as on the choice of a plasma, liquid-crystal-display (L.C.D.) or digital-light-processing (D.L.P.) screen. Your finances, the size of your room, the position of the furniture in it and whether the room is wired for cable determine the size and the kind of TV that's best for you.

You can compute the size value by using a tool of the TV marketers: price per diagonal inch.

TIMELY TIPS

Is a Flat Screen a Mantel Piece?

Before you start drilling into the wall above your hearth to hang your pricey L.C.D. or plasma set, consider this: running either of those TVs above the recommended ambient temperature (between 90 and 100 degrees Fahrenheit) can prematurely damage the electronic components inside.

✔ Most L.C.D.'s and plasmas are built to operate within a temperature range of 32 to 100 degrees Fahrenheit. You can find out where your set lies by checking the tech specs in your instruction manual.

✔ Practical Home Theater Guide suggests you tape a thermometer up where you plan to mount your flat panel, build a fire, grab a book and let it roar for a few hours. Once your room's temperature has stabilized check the thermometer. If it's near or above 90 degrees Fahrenheit it's time to find a new place for your TV.
www.practical-home-theater-guide.com/

—Sonia Zjawinski

(Digital TVs, like analog models, are measured by the screen diagonal.) Or compute the value more accurately by determining the price per square inch. Either way, you'll see that larger models are generally a better value than small ones. But before you get hung up on what technology is best, let's figure out what you really need by answering a series of questions.

How much can I afford? Come up with an affordable number, perhaps budgeting more if the set is going into a room where it will be watched by many people. Consider also that the one you buy will most likely last 15 to 20 years. That means you should ignore any unit that says EDTV, standard definition or flat-tube TV. It's old technology.

How much space do I have? The new digitals come in a 16:9 "aspect ratio," much like the dimensions of a theater screen. So if your old 32-inch tube set, which has a 4:3 ratio, fits into the living room armoire, a 32-inch HDTV will be about a half foot too wide. (Refresh your knowledge of the Pythagorean theorem to make the measurements, or go to www.1728.com/pythgorn.htm for a calculator.) You might have to go with a 26-inch screen, but account for big frames or speakers that stick out from the sides when you shop. In general, don't obsess about size. It's high-definition television, after all, which means the picture looks sharper even if the screen isn't as tall.

How far will I sit from the screen? You probably aren't going to be moving your couch, your bed or the kitchen prep island to accommodate the new set. So choose a TV size to fit your viewing habits.

The industry rule for most of the current HDTVs on the market is to multiply the diagonal by 2.5 to get the distance at which a person with perfect vision can see pixels in the image. The more expensive sets deliver a screen resolution with 2 million pixels, or twice the resolution of the standard digital TV. That allows you to comfortably sit much closer, about 6 feet for a 50-inch set. But those models, known as 1080p, cost about twice as much.

Will I hang the TV on the wall? Manufacturers say that the desire to hang the set on the wall like a painting is the leading reason people want a new digital TV. But only about 18 percent of consumers actually do it. The reason? Cords and peripherals. It doesn't look as pretty as a picture when a tangle of cords dangles from the set and a stack of devices—including a cable box, a DVR, an amplifier and maybe a PC or a TiVo-like device—sit beneath that handsome new screen.

Should you still want to hang it on the wall, buy an L.C.D. or plasma screen. Even the very thinnest D.L.P. TVs, at about 9 inches in depth, are too thick for a wall mounting.

Where and how will I watch it? There are some minor differences in screens. In a sunlit room,

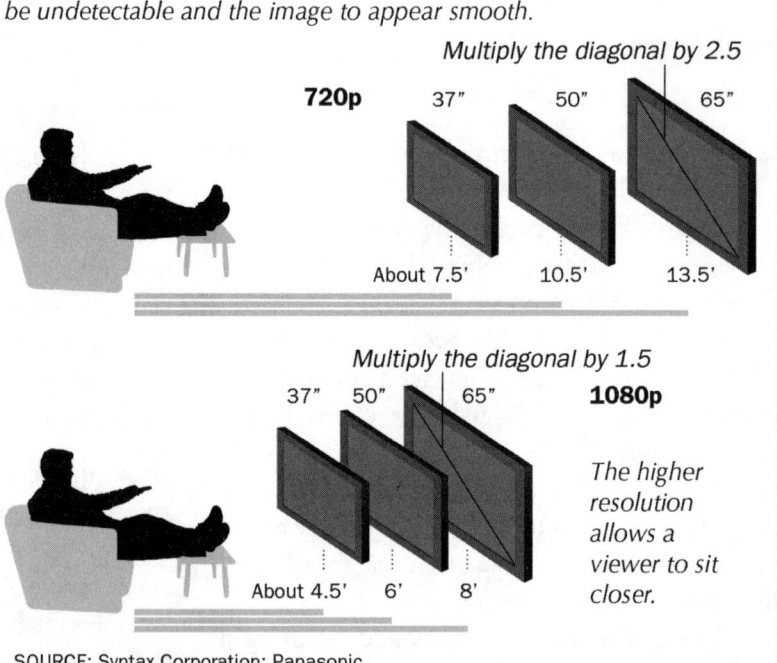

THE DISTANCE BETWEEN YOU AND YOUR TV

Consumers thinking of buying a high-definition television should consider how much space will be between them and the TV. A standard formula in the industry allows enough distance for pixels to be undetectable and the image to appear smooth.

Multiply the diagonal by 2.5

720p 37" 50" 65"

About 7.5' 10.5' 13.5'

Multiply the diagonal by 1.5

37" 50" 65" **1080p**

About 4.5' 6' 8'

The higher resolution allows a viewer to sit closer.

SOURCE: Syntax Corporation; Panasonic

L.C.D. has the edge. In a room with less light, plasma wins. If you are watching from a wide angle or from the floor looking up, D.L.P. isn't as good as the other two technologies. For sports or other fast-action viewing, plasma and D.L.P. generally trump L.C.D.

Which screen looks better? In the end, it's a personal preference. Ignore such specifications as contrast ratios and response time if the sales representative starts lobbing those terms at you. Just remember, you stand about 4 feet away from a TV in a store, while most people at home view a TV from about 9 feet. So bring your tape measure along with your wallet.

—Damon Darlin

Adults are exposed to screens–TVs, cellphones, even G.P.S. devices–for about 8.5 hours on any given day.

● ● ●

download a book in less than a minute. Set up your account and you can buy your reading material directly from Amazon.com. Kindle's sharp screen produces easy-to-read, crisp text. But the joystick that you use to maneuver through menus is somewhat clumsy.

Sony. As with the Kindle, you can make notes, and Sony's reader remembers where you left off in a book. Unlike the Kindle, this reader displays page numbers, should you lose your spot.

But in order to download books on the Sony, you have to connect it to a PC (it's not for Mac users). Sony's book collection is smaller than Amazon's, but the reader supports a universal e-book format, which allows you to download books from other Web sites, and even libraries that offer digital collections.

iPhone applications. A handful of applications let you read books on devices that you may already own, like an iPhone or BlackBerry. Two applications on the iPhone, Stanza and Shortcovers, are better used for short reads.

Stanza can be downloaded free from the iTunes App Store. You can buy books from a variety of e-book retailers directly from the phone. Using the virtual keyboard, you can download a free book from Feedbooks in less than a minute.

Shortcovers, a new online community from the Canadian book retailer Indigo, is available for the Apple iPhone, BlackBerry smartphones and other devices. On the Web site or through the application on a mobile device, you can sample books and articles, with the option to download or buy hard copies of books in its catalog.

Shortcovers includes the ability to share chapters with your friends, offer commentary, Twitter

Buying an E-book Reader
Readers can save you money—and back pain

Proponents of electronic book readers, such as the Kindle by Amazon and the Sony Reader, celebrate their ability to store thousands of titles on a single lightweight device; the access to newspapers, magazines and blogs while on the go; and the ability, at the click of a button, to own one of hundreds of thousands of titles in seconds. Here are some features of the most popular e-book readers.

Kindle. It gives you access to hundreds of thousands of books in electronic form, and dozens of digital subscriptions to newspapers, magazines and blogs. Most book downloads cost less than the price of paperback.

Amazon's Whispernet wireless service lets you

about something you're reading or rate a book. Writers can also upload their books to the site for consumption.

—Danielle Belopotosky

How to Use a Digital Camera

Tips to enhance your point-and-shoot pictures

If you point your point-and-shoot digital camera at something and push the big button on top of the case, you will take a picture. That doesn't mean, necessarily, that you will have taken a good one. The not-so-dirty, not-so-little secret about even the simplest point-and-shoot cameras is that they work best if you know just a tiny bit about what's going on when you snap a picture. Otherwise, even scads of megapixels, image stabilization and other ballyhooed features can't save you from overexposed images and washed-out colors.

Below are some basic tips and tricks. They apply to most of the cameras on the market today, even if the manufacturers have different names for their various features and settings (word to the wise: don't throw away the owner's manual). Putting this advice into action won't make you a great photographer, but it will elevate you to the glorified realm of the "not bad."

SETTING UP YOUR SHOT. *Photography is, at its core, about making the most of light. All cameras include a fully automatic mode that sets optimal exposures based on lighting conditions, but most also give the user some degree of manual control to adjust settings.*

Scene modes. The entry-level, basic snap-shooters may offer little to no manual control, but all cameras include scene modes. These are presets that adjust the camera to perform best in a given situation. Typical scene modes include party, night, portrait, snow, beach, sunset, fireworks, sports and kids and pets. In

sports mode, for instance, the camera will automatically set a fast shutter speed to freeze the action.

Scene settings are a great place to start experimenting because they help you capture the best shots in specific shooting conditions, and you don't have to know a thing about exposure.

ISO. One of the most basic ways to control the light is to adjust the ISO. Doing so will make your camera more or less sensitive to light. Cameras use lower ISO settings of 80 or 100 for photographing in bright conditions like sunny days. Higher ISO settings—400 and up—enable the camera to capture the details of subjects in lower light. Today's cameras may include ISO settings of 3200 or higher, but use them judiciously—you'll start to see "noise," or multicolored specks in images, starting at ISO 400.

Exposure compensation. This feature can save the day in difficult lighting conditions, such as bright sunlight and strongly backlit scenes. For instance, if you photograph a friend with very bright lighting behind her, the details of her face will probably be in shadow. Set the exposure compensation to a positive value to capture more details of the foreground and her face.

White balance. Another useful setting that is available on most cameras is white balance, which ensures that the light source—fluorescent or tungsten lamps, for instance—does not apply an artificial color cast to your image. For instance, white objects snapped under fluorescent lighting often exhibit a greenish tint. To correct white balance, simply select the correct light source from a list that typically includes tungsten, fluorescent, shade or sunlight.

Flash modes. Most people set their flash to Auto and don't think about it again. But auto flash isn't always the best flash, which is why cameras typically offer a couple of flash settings that can greatly enhance photos. For instance, if you're taking an outdoor photo of someone whose face is in shadow, using force flash (or flash on) will coax your subject's face out of the shadows. Many cameras also enable you to adjust the brightness of the flash, which is useful when snapping shots of subjects in close range. You'll want to decrease the brightness of the flash so that the image isn't washed out.

Another useful flash setting is slow synchro (also called nighttime mode), which slows the shutter speed in combination with the flash. With slow synchro, you can get more background detail in dimly lighted scenes, such as portraits shot outdoors at twilight or indoor shots where you want the right amount of flash for your subject but don't want to wash out the whole room with a bright flash.

SNAPPING THE SHOT. *Now that you understand the adjustments to make in order to capture the right exposure, you're ready to shoot.*

Auto-focus. Auto-focus is a two-step process. First depress the shutter button halfway to focus on your subject and set the correct exposure. You'll hear a beep to indicate that the lens has focused and that the automatic exposure is locked. Then depress the button all the way to snap the shot.

Optical zoom. Most basic point-and-shoot cameras have an optical zoom range of 3X to 5X, which enables you to zoom in (or out) on your subject. Many models also include a digital zoom.

You can tell the difference when zooming in because you can feel and hear optical zoom—the lens is actually moving. If you zoom in after that, it will be silent, because digital zoom is happening deep inside a microchip in the camera. It's best to ignore digital zoom because it simply enlarges the pixels and results in inferior images. Also, zoomed-in shots are more prone to the blurring caused by shaky hands. So if you are in close, make sure that your camera's image stabilization is turned on.

Macro mode. Macro enables you to move in as tight as an inch to take extreme close-ups of objects. You'll need to enable macro mode to ensure the proper focus.

Burst mode. Most digital cameras have a burst mode that snaps off a series of photos in quick succession. It's a useful feature for capturing a soccer goal or Junior's quick smile. A caveat is that many cameras will save burst-mode shots in a lower resolution. Also, continuous shooting will not work with flash, because the electronic flash cannot recycle that quickly.

Movie mode. Just about any point-and-shoot camera will record a movie with sound (digital S.L.R.'s traditionally have not offered video, although some high-end models add movie capabilities). Increasingly, newer cameras let you capture video in high definition.

Movie mode is typically selected on a top-level dial. To use movie mode, depress the button halfway to focus and set the exposure, then fully depress to start recording. To stop, fully depress the button again. Note that most cameras do not allow you to use the zoom while you're recording a movie, so you'll need to decide on focal length before you begin.

Another thing you can and should do: take a lot of pictures. A whole lot. Play with the settings and see what kind of pictures you get. After all, you're not going to have to shell out for extra film.

—Rik Fairlie

Easy Fixes for High-Tech Problems
What to do when your gadgets malfunction

Americans, it seems, are finding their own tips and tricks for fixing misbehaving gadgets by using supplies as simple as paper and adhesive tape. How well some of the following tips work is open to argument. But wacky as they may sound, many home solutions can be explained by a little science.

Cellphone losing charge. If your cellphone loses its battery charge too quickly while idle in your pocket, part of the problem may be that your pocket is too warm. Cellphone batteries do indeed last a bit longer if kept cool. The 98.6-degree body heat of a human, transmitted through a cloth pocket to a cellphone inside, is enough to speed up chemical processes inside the phone's battery. That makes it run down faster.

Carry your cell in your purse or on your belt to keep it cooler. This same method can help preserve your battery, too, if you are traveling and don't have your charger. Turn off the phone and put it in the hotel refrigerator overnight to slow the battery's natural tendency to lose its charge.

Remote car key. Suppose your remote car door opener does not have the range to reach your car across the parking lot. Hold the metal key part of your key fob against your chin, then push the unlock button. The trick turns your head into an antenna, says one Silicon Valley radio engineer. With all the fluids in your head, it ends up being a conductor. Using your head can extend the key's wireless range by a few car lengths.

 INSIDE INFO

Coming Soon: A New Phone Charger

○ If you've ever shaken your fist at the cellphone gods for not making all phone chargers alike, help is on the way. Manufacturers will adopt a single charger interface, more specifically, a micro-U.S.B. plug, for all its phones. The industry has until January 1, 2012, to comply.

—Alex Mindlin

Dry ink cartridge. If your printer's ink cartridge runs dry near the end of an important print job, remove the cartridge and run a hair dryer on it for 2 to 3 minutes. Then place the cartridge back into the printer and try again. The heat from the hair dryer heats the thick ink and helps it to flow through the tiny nozzles in the cartridge. You could squeeze a few more pages out of the cartridge.

Cellphone in the toilet. It happens a lot: you dropped your cellphone in the toilet. Take the battery out immediately to prevent electrical short circuits from frying your phone's fragile internals. Then wipe the phone gently with a towel and shove it into a jar full of uncooked rice.

The molecules in the rice have a nearly magnetic attraction for water molecules, which will be soaked up rather than beading up inside the phone.

Longer Wi-Fi reach. If your home Wi-Fi router doesn't reach the other end of the house, don't rush out to buy more wireless gear to stretch your network. Instead, build a 6-inch-high passive radio wave reflector from kitchen items, for instance, an aluminum cookie sheet.

Follow the instructions at freeantennas.com/projects/template. Place the completed reflector—a small, curved piece of metal that reflects radio waves just like a satellite TV dish—behind your Wi-Fi router. It focuses the router's energy in one direction, toward the other end of the house, rather than letting it dissipate its strength in a full circle. No cables, no batteries, no technical knowledge required. Yet it can double the range of your network.

Dirty discs. If your skipping DVD or CD needs cleaning but you don't have any cleaning solution, soak a washcloth with vodka or mouthwash. Alcohol is a powerful solvent that will dissolve fingerprints and grime on the surface of a disc.

Too much flash. If your cellphone's built-in camera flash is much too bright, washing out photos, tape a small piece of paper over the flash. Experiment with different colors and thicknesses of paper to tone down the flash from superbright white to a more pleasing glow for evening photos.

Crashed hard drive. If your PC's hard drive crashes and can't be read, don't be too quick to throw it out. Stick it in the freezer overnight.

Many hard drive failures are caused by worn parts that no longer align properly, making it impossible to read data from the drive. Lowering the drive's temperature causes its metal and plastic internals to contract ever so slightly. Taking the drive out of the freezer and returning it to room temperature can cause those parts to expand again. That may help free up binding parts or at least let a failing electrical component remain within specs long enough for you to recover your essential data.

These tricks may or may not work, but then again, what have you got to lose?

—Paul Boutin

Home Tech Energy-Saving Tips

Machines are sucking energy—even if they're off

Most people assume that when they turn off the television set it stops drawing power. But that's not how most TVs (and VCR's and other electronic devices) work. They remain ever in standby mode, silently sipping energy to the tune of 1,000 kilowatt hours a year per household, drawing more than enough current in the typical house to light a 100-watt light bulb 24/7.

These silent energy users include the chargers for devices that run on batteries, like cellphones, iPods and personal digital assistants, and all the devices around the house that have adapters because they run on direct current, like answering machines. Some have both batteries and steady power use, like cordless phones. Experts call all those adapters "wall warts." Many deliver in direct current only half as much energy as they suck out of the wall; the rest is wasted.

DSL, or cable modems, are also increasingly likely to be left on around the clock. A computer left on continuously can draw nearly as much power as an efficient refrigerator—70 to 250 watts, depending on the model and how it is used.

Among the worst energy vampires are big-screen televisions, mainly because of satellite and cable boxes, which can draw up to 30 watts when turned off, experts say. The answer to the question of whether to shut down your computer at the end of the day or leave it up and running is this: although it does take an extra bit of electricity when the computer pops on after being shut down, the amount of power is less than what would be consumed if the machine was left on continuously.

Leaving the computer on—and linked to the Internet with a high-speed connection—all the time can also make it more vulnerable to infection and invasion by intruders. Even if the machine is turned off every night, though, security programs like firewall, anti-virus and anti-spyware software should be installed and updated regularly to help keep the computer safe when on and online.

You obviously save electricity when you shut down the computer after you have finished using it. Turning your machine off at night also clears up items in the computer's memory and gives it a fresh start in the morning, which may make it appear less sluggish if you generally have a lot of programs running over the course of the day.

If you are torn between on and off, consider

the third option: setting the machine to hibernate or sleep for the night. The computer uses minimal power in this state but starts much faster than if it was started up cold in the morning.

—Matthew L. Wald

Cutting Your High-Tech Budget
You could save big by considering these tips

You might think of high-tech gadgetry as something that drains your bank account—but it can save you money, too. A lot of it. Herewith, a few suggestions for using tech to save money. Savings may vary depending on your current technology and service plans.

Cut the TV cord. Cancel cable or satellite TV service and watch TV over the Internet. At the major network and various cable networks' Web sites, you can watch many regular, up-to-date TV shows on demand, completely free, with excellent video quality and only a couple of 15-second ads an episode. Or visit Hulu.com, where thousands more episodes are gathered into a simple, easy-to-use virtual TV.

The sacrifice: Watching TV on your computer screen (unless you hook your PC up to your TV, which is not simple). Some shows still aren't available legally. And, of course, you need high-speed Internet.

The savings: $500 to $1,200 a year.

Get a hi-def antenna. TV over the Internet generally looks great, but isn't in high definition. So why not get a hi-def antenna for your roof or bookshelf and enjoy free over-the-air hi-def TV.

The sacrifice: Some technical setup. Fewer channels.

The savings: $500 to $1,200 a year.

Cancel your movie channels. Can't bear to cut all your cable service? An HBO/Showtime package is probably adding about $20 a month to your cable bill. If you're in it just for the movies, you can do much better. Netflix has irresistible deals that let you take in unlimited on-demand movies, brought to you by the Internet, from a library of 12,000-plus films.

The sacrifice: You lose the non-movie programming on HBO, for one; then again, why not get those on Netflix DVDs?

The savings: $130 a year.

Eliminate your cell phone contract. The average American's cellphone bill is about $73 a month. Over the life of your 2-year contract, that's about $1,750. If you talk more than your allotted minutes in a month, punitive per-minute overage fees apply; if you talk less, you're not getting your money's worth. Why not sign up for a prepaid cellphone instead?

These phones and plans (TracFone, AT&T GoPhone, Verizon InPulse and T-Mobile Prepaid), let you pay for cellphone service by the minute, not by the month. There's no contract, no commitment, no penalties and no chance of "going over."

You can buy minutes, usually in $25 to $100 chunks, by calling a toll-free number with a credit card or by buying a refill card at a phone center or convenience store and plugging its code into your phone. Or pay a flat per-minute fee plus a small amount for each day that you use the phone.

The sacrifice: If your cellphone is your primary phone and you use it extensively, traditional plans may be more cost-effective.

The savings: $900 to $1,500 a year.

Eliminate your home phone. More consumers are using cellphones exclusively. And to call overseas, there is free computer-to-computer "telephone" software like Skype, iChat and Google Talk, programs that are easy to use and have excellent sound quality.

Recycling Gadgets After They Quit

Americans discard 2.25 million tons of computers, cellphones and other electronics in a typical year; about 82 percent ends up in landfills.

Here are some gadget recycling tips from Jason Linnell, executive director of the National Center for Electronics Recycling.

Most household electronics can be recycled because they have metal and other materials of value to recyclers. But the longer you hold on to a device, the higher the chances it cannot be reused.

Some places sponsor drop-off centers or periodic collection events. You can find out when and where they are at electronicsrecycling.org, MyGreenElectronics.org and Earth911.com.

Some big chain stores, like Best Buy and Staples, let you drop off most small electronics for recycling. And some makers, like Apple, Dell and Sony, offer free recycling through mail-in programs or at drop-off sites found on their Web sites. Most services are free. But certain components, like cathode ray tubes, are difficult and costly to recycle, so you could pay $5 to $20 to recycle an old TV or monitor. Try Earth911.com to find a place that will take them.

Dumping household electronics in the regular trash is legal in most states, even though TVs and computer monitors are hazardous. Cathode ray tubes contain lead, which can leach, and the heavy metals in batteries are also bad for the earth. Sears, Staples, Target, Lowe's and other big chains participate in a national recycling program for rechargeable batteries.

Web sites like Techforward.com, Gazelle. com and MyBoneyard.com might pay you for old gadgets. Name the product and its condition, and they will make an offer. And, of course, there are eBay and Craig's List.

Other ways to keep gizmos out of landfills: repair them and resist the urge to constantly upgrade.

—Julie Scelfo

If that route doesn't appeal, sign up for T-Mobile's HotSpot@Home Talk Forever plan. It's intended for people who don't want to lose a home phone line altogether.

The deal: unlimited nationwide calling from your home phone for about $10 a month. (Your calls are carried over the Internet, but you won't notice any difference; you keep your existing phone and phone number.)

The sacrifice: This service is available only if you also have a T-Mobile cellphone. (If you have T-Mobile coverage in your area, it might be worth investigating; T-Mobile cell service is generally less expensive.)

The savings: About $250 a year.

Buy refurbished computers. You can find refurbished computers and other electronic gear advertised on the makers' Web sites, offered at hundreds of dollars below retail price. Who wants a used computer, you say?

"Refurbished" doesn't mean used; it usually means "returned, sometimes without even having been opened." People change their minds, get the same product as a gift, whatever. In any case, a refurbished machine has been brought up to brand-new standards by the manufacturer, and is inspected and tested more than a brand-new item. Aficionados consider refurbished gear one of the great secrets of the tech world.

The sacrifice: Some companies, like Hewlett-Packard, issue a shorter warranty on them (90 days instead of a year).

The savings: On a computer, from $300 to $2,000.

—David Pogue

Collecting

Starting an Art Collection

How to handle intimidating dealers and more

The art world can be a confusing place for even the most experienced of art buyers. Squishy factors such as "historical interest" or "artistic integrity" will determine whether your purchase is the bargain of a lifetime or just expensive wallpaper. And if you're just starting out, you're at the mercy of often-intimidating dealers.

To even the odds, we asked Alan Bamberger, an art consultant (Artbusiness.com) and author of three art books, including *The Art of Buying Art*, to advise the beginning art collector.

First of all, be sure that what you want is there to collect. Once you decide, collect the best in the field. Obviously, if you want to collect works by Vincent Van Gogh, you'll have to have a lot of money; otherwise, you'll get the worst of the worst of his work because that's what's most likely to be on the market. To research what's available, talk to dealers

and ask them to direct you to other dealers in the same field, read art magazines that focus on the art that interests you, do a thorough online search and turn to international directories of dealers.

Start by collecting an artist's typical works. It's a question of salability down the road—if you want things that will be liquid, you'd be well advised to go with the mainstream. First, find out what the artist is most famous for. Or if you like landscapes of Cape Cod, say, find out what people who collect them like to have in them and, if it also appeals to you, look for that in your pictures.

Don't confuse the work with the environment. Properly lit and displayed, even a sack of trash can look great. You can take anything—a tape measure, a can of soup—put it up on a pedestal, give it good lighting, put it in a gallery and you'll have people walk by and say, "Wow, that's fantastic." But when you get it home, all it is is a can of soup. Take the piece out of the gallery environment, take it home on approval for a week. Usually you can just leave a deposit, with no commitment to buy.

At the same time, unless you're really experienced, it can be hard to see how beautiful something is. At a garage sale, for example, it may look like a piece of junk, but a collector who knows what he's doing will clean it up and display it properly and it'll look like a million dollars.

Establish as wide a net of resources as possible. Not only will you see and learn more, but you'll also be able to play the market for the best price and make intelligent price comparisons. But don't purposely play dealers off one another. Just ask intelligent questions. It's a little like comparing cars at auto dealerships. You should ask dealers to explain why you saw something similar somewhere else for a different price.

Don't take bullying. If an art dealer is giving you a hard time, leave. When you hear comments like "The artist is almost dead" or "This will be your last chance to buy at this price," it's best to exit. If you feel pressure in any way, that's a warning sign that you're in the wrong place.

Work with experts. Avoid galleries with no direction or focus. Such galleries tend to be repositories for miscellaneous pieces that locals happen to find at flea markets and estate sales. Their main focus is often on selling whatever they can to make money, not on quality. Those galleries have their place, and if you have experience, you can find bargains there. But beginners are better off going with more professional dealers.

Don't ask, don't tell. Forgeries are a touchy area. You don't want to ask one dealer to comment on the authenticity of a painting another dealer is selling. For one thing, you may not get a straight answer, since the second dealer would rather sell you one of his paintings. Rather, educate yourself. As you spend more time collecting, try to meet people—museum curators, scholarly types or true collectors who are not overly concerned about the money and who will give you the straight dope. If you suspect a forgery, you may be better off not pointing it out. You might be wrong, you could get entangled in legal problems and you certainly will make enemies fast.

Don't let investment factors weigh too heavily. Art is immediately liquid only if you want to take a severe hit. If you buy and sell stocks and bonds and the like, you normally pay a small percentage in commission; in the art world, you pay a 20 percent commission to buy a work of art and then pay a 20

TIMELY TIPS

Brushing Up on Art

Check these sites before starting your collection

✔ **Artnet.com** – The magazine's site, with everything you need to know about the fine arts market. Research a piece's history by tapping into nearly 4 million auction sales records from more than 500 international houses.

✔ **ArtQuest.com** – This listing service connects collectors and sellers by e-mail, eliminating dealer fees and commissions. The site charges sellers $10 for a six-month listing. To check out available art, click on "Search for Art" and then "Just Browsing."

✔ **BoundlessGallery.com** – More than 25,000 pieces of art for sale by 2,000 artists and dealers from 100 nations.

✔ **Eyestorm.com** – Online retailer of limited edition contemporary art; focus on emerging artists and photographers.

✔ **GalleryGuide.com** – The online version of *Gallery Guide* magazine. A comprehensive and easy to use source of art gallery and museum exhibits.

✔ **iCollector.com** – One of the oldest traders of fine art, antiques and collectibles on the Internet. Your portal to the world of live auctions.

✔ **PaintingsDirect.com** – A huge offering of original artworks, representing more than 500 artists from 40 countries; the site boasts 10,000 paintings, photographs and limited edition prints.

✔ **Picassomio.com** – You'll find curated modern and contemporary art. The pieces are mostly American and Spanish and were jury-selected.

SPENDING

percent commission when you sell it—and those are very modest commissions in the business. The art has to increase in value 40 percent before you see your first penny of profit.

Don't try to chisel on prices unless you have a really good argument. Don't worry about letting on that you really like a painting. A poker face won't work anyway. If dealers suspect that you're the type of person who expects to get a deal, they'll bump their price up a bit when they see you coming and then drop it to the price they wanted in the first place. Or, worse, they will sell you medium-quality art that they would rather have out the door anyway. Sure, they'll flex on

What to Look for in a Painting

Roosters sell, sheep and pigs don't

Nearly every dealer knows what sells and what doesn't, or they quickly learn before bankruptcy sets in. Some artistic compositions will never grace the white walls of their galleries: a vertical painting of rough waters, for example, or a dark, church-side cemetery. Here are other well-known secrets of what's taboo in the art world.

WHAT SELLS	WHAT DOESN'T
Horizontal landscapes	Vertical landscapes
Paintings with roosters	Sheep, cows, pigs
Young women, children	Old folks, particularly men
Brightly colored paintings	Dark scenes
Calm waters	Rough seas
Grouse and pheasant	Crows and mallards
Floral still life	Fruits and vegetables
Roses	Chrysanthemums
Setters, spaniels, terriers	Mongrels, dachshunds
Lions, leopards, elephants	Wolves, wild boars

SOURCE: Chicago Appraisers Association

the price a little bit, but you're not going to get the good stuff. You have to work for that—you have to fight the competition.

The Dos and Don'ts of Buying Art
Five steps toward your new art collection

It sometimes feels as if there is a black hole between the college-student-poster stage of wall decorating and the multimillionaires who can afford to buy originals of well-known artists. It's a big step a lot of people are afraid to take. Looking online can feel overwhelming. Going into those small chic galleries can feel intimidating. But it's time to get over it.

There is no mystique about buying art. Barbara Guggenheim, an art consultant and author who has built up the art collections of numerous celebrities and major corporations, says, "There's no difference between an art dealer and a used-car dealer—they both want to sell you something."

It might be nice if the used-car world adopted some of the common practices of many galleries: they often will allow prospective buyers to take a piece of work home "on approval" for a short time to see how it looks in situ.

Prospective purchasers should remember that gallery owners don't just want one-time buyers, they want to develop collectors. So don't be afraid to ask questions.

Take your time. When starting out, don't grab the first piece in your price range. Browse for a few months, because as you look, your eye will develop and change. Most galleries rotate exhibits fairly often, so if you discover one whose work you like, drop by frequently.

But beware of second-guessing yourself so much that you become paralyzed. It's a balance:

if you hesitate too much, you might miss out on something you really want.

Don't buy on vacation. One place, however, where you might want to hold yourself in check is while on vacation. You may be taken in by the atmosphere and then regret your decision when you return home. Galleries in tourist towns, shopping malls and airports should be avoided. If you want to bring back some art from your holiday, you're better off with ethnic crafts or pottery.

Where to look for art. Traditional galleries aren't the only place to find art. Many schools of art and design have student exhibits—often called senior thesis shows—where work is exhibited and sold.

The Pratt Institute, for example, has exhibits of the works of its Masters of Fine Arts students throughout the year at its Manhattan and Brooklyn galleries. The Rhode Island School of Design also holds alumni and student shows and sales several times a year, and carries many of its items online (risd.edu).

There's a big online world of art Web sites out there (see "Brushing Up on Art" on page 321). While these are good places to go for research and perhaps eventually to buy, you should try to see the actual artwork before buying.

Art fairs are often another good and less-expensive option; what many people like about buying directly from artists is that they know that 100 percent of the price is going to the artist. Galleries often take up to a 50 percent commission on every work they sell.

Art for art's sake or as an investment? The two don't have to be mutually exclusive; the first rule of thumb is buy what you like, but if you're interested in collecting up-and-coming artists whose work might appreciate, check out their résumés. If the work is in a gallery, the résumé should always be available; otherwise look online.

See if the artist has been in a steady progression of shows and won any awards or grants; also inquire if she has been included in any group shows in museums or is represented in any particular collections.

Don't avoid prints. Prints shouldn't be avoided, although buyers should understand what the numbers in the corner mean. The larger number indicates the total number of prints made, while the smaller is where the piece falls in the series. However, No. 3 out of 200 is not necessarily more valuable than No. 150, because there is no guarantee that No. 1 was actually the first off the press.

More important is to look at the total number of works printed; those of more than 200 are often considered commercial rather than fine art. But ultimately it comes down to what you like, which is sometimes hard to know.

—Alina Tugend

How to Spot a Real Antique
Examine finish, hardware and feet—then smell it

How can a casual buyer tell if that attractive antique chest is genuine, a reproduction, a mongrel or a fake? Antique experts say that when you're trying to determine whether an antique is authentic, you should examine several things: finish, backboard, drawers, hardware and feet. Sometimes, even smell will help. You shouldn't detect any oil or paint-type odor, which suggests the piece has been recently worked on.

Good, early, untouched furniture gives off a nutty smell from inside the drawers. Once you smell it, experts say, you never forget it. Here are more tips on sizing up an antique chest, bed, mirror and chair from the 18th to early 19th century.

CHEST OF DRAWERS

In American chests, backboards generally tell you a lot. Look at the back carefully. It's usually made of pine and should be well darkened with age and exposure to air and dirt.

The older or earlier the finish, the better. A piece should not be refinished or painted. It should have a uniform patina and age to it.

Pull out the drawers. Dovetails—a special type of tongue-in-groove joint—on drawers are important. They should be hand-done. Often cabinetmakers would number the drawers in pencil and the numbers are sometimes still visible. There should be no shellac or finish on the inside of the drawers. Glue or black gunk is a sign of repair.

The color of the wood inside the drawers should vary. The bottom drawer should be darker in the front and lighter to the rear. The bottom of the bottom drawer should be darkest of all—it gets more exposure. The middle drawers, which get less exposure to light, shouldn't show as much darkness as the bottom drawer.

Look at the hardware. Is there an extra set of holes? Then the original hardware has probably been replaced. Check out the feet, too. Do they look as old as the chest? If the feet have been replaced, the price of the piece goes way down.

ANTIQUE BED

As tastes in beds have changed over the years, many antique beds have been altered to suit successive generations. As a result, beds don't usually bring in a lot of money.

There were no king-size beds 100 years ago, of course, so if the bed's been used, the rails will probably have been lengthened. Another compromise you may have to accept is the addition of box spring holders.

Look at the legs. Most early beds were too high for modern tastes and people have cut off the legs. Beds should be made of all hard woods, such as mahogany, maple, cherry, walnut or birch. The main things to look for in the wood are signs of smeared stain or wood that doesn't match, which suggests that the bed has been altered in some way.

Antique beds should have hand-fashioned bed-bolts holding them together. If it's a tall poster bed, look for the original tester (pronounced "teester"), the framework that holds the cloth canopy over the bed. If there is carving on the bed, be sure it is consistent with the bed's style and period.

ANTIQUE MIRROR

If the mirror was made before 1830, the back shouldn't have circular saw marks on it. It should have plane marks instead.

Look for major replacements. Curlicues or ears on a mirror often break and get replaced. A number of those round mirrors have eagles or gilded work on them—it's hard to tell if they were made in 1820 or 1920—but you want to look for obvious changes in the finish or breaks in the design. The early ones were made of gesso, plaster with gold leaf rubbed on it.

The nicest thing to find in a mirror is a label. Labeled furniture is rare, but you find more labels on mirrors than on any other antique. It's nice to know who made the piece, and it helps date it.

An early mirror will have wavy glass. You'll see some breaks in the reflectivity. Look for original glass, if possible.

ANTIQUE CHAIR

A really early chair may have sat in a cellar or on a dirt floor, and part of its feet may have

HOW TO RECOGNIZE FAMOUS-NAME ANTIQUES

English designers Thomas Chippendale, George Hepplewhite and Thomas Sheraton helped make the 18th century the golden age of furniture.

CHIPPENDALE
1750-1785

CHAIR. *S-shaped curved legs and ball-and-claw feet. Back is fiddle-shaped with decorative carvings.*

CHEST. *Rococo carving often used. Big brass pulls on drawers. Legs curved, ball-and-claw feet common.*

MIRROR. *Frames made of thinly cut mahogany and often feature elaborate, pierced-scroll fretwork.*

HEPPLEWHITE
1785-1810

CHAIR. *Distinctive shield-shaped chair backs. Legs are usually tapered, with spade-like feet.*

CHEST. *Usually made of fancy woods, often with inlays. Feet curve outward. Oval brass drawer pulls.*

MIRROR. *Frames are elaborate and heavily gilt. Typical design features a floral urn atop an oval inlay.*

SHERATON
1790-1830

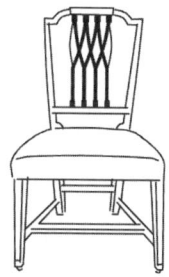

CHAIR. *Thin, tapered legs. Brass casters under feet. Chair backs usually square or rectangular.*

TABLE. *Typically drum-shaped. Curved and fluted legs. Top often covered with leather.*

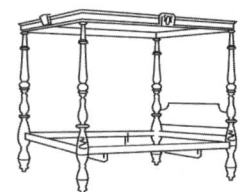

TESTER CANOPY BED. *Foot and head posts usually lightly tapered. Edge of headboard arched or flat.*

SPENDING

rotted away. Look for replacement of the bottom 3 or 4 inches of the legs, which seriously lessens its value.

If the chair is reupholstered, try to see the frame under the upholstery. See if it's the original frame and that no one has put in a bigger wing than was there, for example. Be very careful if it's the original upholstery; that makes the chair worth a lot more. You don't see much original upholstery anymore.

Beware of a chair that has screws in it. The chair will be unstable because screws don't hold well in wood under the stress of a chair.

A Windsor chair with its original paint is more valuable than if it's been stripped down. In a Windsor chair, the legs are generally made of maple or birch, the seat is usually pine, the spindles and back are hickory or ash and the arms might be oak. So to get a uniform color, Windsor chairs were painted. Collectors are really after a Windsor with the original paint.

The Fine Art of Antique Buying
Finding the good stuff at an auction or shop

Many new collectors are faced with a series of questions: Where to start? How focused should their collection be? Should they shop at one or two major auction houses or include country auctions, too? Should they hire an expert to help them vet the objects or rely solely on their own instincts?

Whether collecting pocket watches, rosewood divans or Sèvres porcelain, seasoned collectors and auctioneers alike say the most important requirement is to find something you love.

The experts' best suggestion: buy things that stir you, that talk to you, and avoid them if the only reason to buy them is because they're a bargain.

To Leslie Keno, who directs American furniture and decorative arts at Sotheby's, the first step in becoming a collector is to find a good bookstore. "Find out what appeals to you, whether French, English or American," he says. "Then pick the period, say, midcentury modern. Narrow your

---

 **TIMELY TIPS**

How to Spot a Fake

David H. Wilson, an antiques restorer in New Jersey who consults for Christie's, offered these tips for spotting fakes.

✔ A 200-year-old antique should show its age: wood shrinks with the grain, separating joints, so crisp joints are suspect.

✔ Marks from a circular saw, a product of the Industrial Revolution, indicate that the piece was produced since then.

✔ If the wood grain is undetectable or looks muddy, someone might be trying to hide something.

✔ Examine the inside, the underside and the back of an antique for color consistency; variations indicate that it might have been altered.

✔ Be wary of very thin veneers; those made before about 1850 were cut by hand and are usually at least 1/16-inch thick.

✔ Pairs of mirrors, commodes and side tables are more desirable, but make sure surfaces and undersides match; if they don't, one piece may be a copy.

✔ Check for signs of surface distress that seem implausible. Dents at the top, rather than the bottom, of a chair leg, for example, indicate reused wood.

✔ When in doubt, consult an expert. Expect to pay $200 to $300 an hour, or for each item appraised.

—Christopher Mason

focus, because it's easier to know more about a specific area in terms of pricing, quality, aesthetics. Forming your own reference library is key."

Read everything you can on your chosen area—or on the areas you are considering. But books, even those published recently, won't say which categories are undervalued right now, and they can't advise you whether to buy a specific piece at a specific auction. Herewith some tips.

What's hot and what's not. For those who are undecided—or who love a variety of things—a good first step is to study the terrain and learn which categories are more or less languishing in the marketplace and which are selling for record prices.

Auctioneers agree that fine 18th-century furniture, like Chippendale, might not be the place to jump in if you're on a budget. But if you like American Classical furniture—pier tables, sideboards and sofa tables that date from 1810 to 1840—that might be a good place to begin, mainly because prices have dropped dramatically in the last couple of decades. These days, Oriental rugs and early European porcelain, like Meissen and Sèvres, are also selling at bargain prices.

Talking with auctioneers. For advice on what to collect, which specific pieces to go after and how much to pay, go to auction exhibitions, even if you do not intend to buy.

Many would-be collectors don't realize that if they spot something they like, they can ask to see an in-house expert, a staff curator. Question the provenance of a piece. Try to ascertain, for example, if a piece is fresh to the market, perhaps from an estate, or whether it's consigned by a dealer, which could mean it's something that, for whatever reason, didn't sell in the shop.

Many auction houses welcome "privates," that is, people who are not dealers, and are happy to entertain questions. People new to the world of auctions may not know to ask for a condition report, a document that is often much more detailed than the catalog description. While the catalog might only note "repairs," the condition report would

SPENDING

TIMELY TIPS

A Lesson in Haggling

Whether you're at a flea market, thrift shop or the local furniture store, negotiating a good price requires a few bargaining strategies.

✔ **Ask about the basics.** Is there any room in the price? Is there a discount for a floor model?

✔ **Identify the deal maker.** Salesclerks are sometimes allowed to negotiate, but often only the manager or owner can. Save the real haggling for the one with the power to make a deal.

✔ **Don't fixate** (or don't let on if you do). If you're clearly determined to have a particular item, you won't have much leverage.

✔ **Think big.** Deep discounts are much likelier on expensive items and multiple-item purchases.

✔ **Don't lowball.** Offering $500 for a $3,000 item will insult the store. Base your desired price on comparable but less expensive items elsewhere.

✔ **Ask about sales.** Is there one coming up? If so, will the store hold an item until then or sell it to you now for the sale price?

✔ **Think beyond dollars.** Focus negotiations not just on price but also on other important issues, like warranty and delivery terms.

✔ **Offer to close the deal.** Can you get a break if you buy the piece now and take it with you?

✔ **Be prepared to walk away.** But leave your number, in case the store has a change of heart.

—Marianne Rohrlich

elaborate. Likewise, a condition report should detail the nature of restoration to a piece of pottery or porcelain or to a teddy bear's ear.

These condition reports are sometimes available on the Web, so read the small print; sometimes one click can take you to them. Or customers can call the auction house and ask to be sent a report. Meanwhile, online catalogs are usually available at least 2 weeks before a sale.

Working with a dealer. Aspiring collectors may prefer to work with a dealer, who will accompany them to an exhibition (or go alone, if the buyer wants to keep a low profile) and may or may not bid on their behalf. Some wealthy collectors like to hire the most prestigious dealers. Fees vary widely from dealer to dealer but usually start at 10 percent of the hammer price. One sees these celebrity dealers strolling around auction houses Sotheby's and Christie's, turning over candle stands and pointing out the nail holes (bad) or pegged joinery (good) to appreciative onlookers.

But it may be even smarter to use a trusted dealer or expert at a country auction, where things can sometimes go quite high and where there is often no in-house expert on hand—and sometimes no catalog at all. (The idea of getting a steal at a country auction is not entirely without merit, but it is rare.)

At the auction house. Auctions offer the thrill of the hunt and the ability to find things that are fresh out of somebody's attic, but before bidding, it's best to figure out a strategy. Some prefer to signal discreetly to the auctioneer when a desired object is brought forward (by "runners" at a smaller auction; increasingly on an overhead screen at the larger ones). Then, after the auctioneer's attention is secured, a simple nod will do the trick until the limit is surpassed. Then a negative head shake suffices.

Others advertise the fact that they are retail shoppers. They raise their hand deliberately to call atten-

First Dibs on Your Next Antique
Forget antiquing and auctions, just go online

Every Wednesday, seconds before 11 a.m. Eastern time, furniture fans are stationed at their computers, poised to point and click. It's the countdown to the weekly posting of new items at 1stdibs.com, an online decorative arts marketplace with dealers from the United States and Paris.

The site, which represents nearly 400 dealers, is a favorite among professional interior designers and do-it-yourself decorators. It is not only a primary resource for locating and acquiring new pieces but also a way to discern the latest design trends.

Buyers can choose to pay 1stdibs.com a 20 percent commission to submit their asking price, haggle with vendors and arrange delivery. But you can also negotiate price and shipping directly with dealers, since their contact information is visible even if you don't register with the site.

Dealers pay a monthly fee plus additional fees per item posted. Fees range from about $400 to $700 per month, plus $10 to $20 per posted item.

The site lists more than 700 pieces from the 18th to 20th centuries, sold by dealers from Los Angeles to Paris. Prices range from less than $1,000 to more than $200,000.

—Kate Murphy

tion to themselves and act as if they were prepared to keep bidding no matter what. (All the time, of course, keeping to their preset limit.) The purpose is to drive away the dealers who have to get it at a wholesale price in order to make a profit when they resell.

If you made a mistake. Another common fear of the beginning bidder is: what happens if you learn you have bought a fake?

If it's an out-and-out fake—say, a chair offered as from the 18th century that turns out to be a so-called "centennial" copy made around 1875—chances are good that you will get your money back, even at a small country auction. Even so, you may be in for a prolonged wrangle, especially if there is a disagreement among experts. Ideally, if there's a problem, it's best to bring it up within a month of the purchase because the consignor—the seller—is paid by the auction house in the first 35 days. But even if it's later, the sale can be canceled.

The major auction houses hold to what they call the "bold-faced description," in other words, the heading that defines each piece. "If the catalog says 'no major alterations' and there's a leg replaced, then that's pretty serious and the sale will probably be canceled," says Keno. If it's a 2-inch patch, he added, that might be arguable.

All in all, though, it's better to make sure you're buying what you want before you bid. Come prepared. Do your research. Bring your tape measure to make sure the treasure you seek will fit the space you want it for. Bring your reading glasses, to double-check that there are no catalog changes, and your distance glasses, for seeing the auctioneer.

Finally, don't leave the room for any reason—any reason at all—when your item's number is about to be called. Auctioneers dine out on tales of tearful buyers who missed that one perfect item because they snuck out ... just for one minute.

—Tracie Rozhon

Strategies for a Charity Auction
Going, going, gone—for a song?

Charities are increasingly turning to black-tie benefit auctions, using donated items as the fund-raising tool of choice. As benefit auctions proliferate, and as their offerings turn more elaborate to entice buyers, more bidders are getting a shot at luxury at bargain prices.

For all the glitz and glamour, there is a science and even a formula to charity auctions, according to organizers, auctioneers and veteran bidders. The same types of offerings generally soar: a private dinner prepared by a superstar chef, the coveted bottle of Champagne or—a blockbuster of school auctions—the chance for a child to be principal for a day.

But most items, like a trip to a popular resort, end up selling for about 15 percent off their retail price or fair market value. And in silent auctions, in which bidders place bids on sign-up sheets, the deals can be greater, with luxury listings like Coach bags or skybox sports tickets selling for as much as 35 percent off.

A quick look at an event's format can provide clues to the likelihood of bargains. People seated at dinner tables for an auction almost always bid more aggressively than those sitting in rows. That results not only from the availability of liquor but also from peer pressure from tablemates.

Bargains aren't always just about price. Some charity art auctions give buyers the rare opportunity to get works by hot artists who have waiting lists of collectors. One tip when buying art at a charity auction: check to see if it has been donated by an artist or by a dealer. Artists tend to donate high-quality works but also tend to overstate their fair market value. Indeed, a buyer should research the price of any big purchase at auction, since a donor may have a tax incentive to inflate value.

Bargain hunters do better at larger sales, say, of 20 or more items, where interest may flag. Single-theme food or travel auctions of trips with stiff timing restrictions, for example, reduce the number of potential bidders and up the chances of bargains.

Items at private secondary school auctions, where parents do most of the bidding, don't tend to sell at low prices. You do better at auctions for churches and colleges, auctioneers say. And best of all, at least from the perspective of bargain hunt-

SPENDING

✔ TIMELY TIPS

Spotting Knockoffs on eBay

How not to get taken online

Counterfeit goods are rampant on the Internet, and buyers using online auction sites like eBay are especially vulnerable. Artwork, jewelry, designer accessories, autographed sports memorabilia and other collectibles are popular among counterfeiters. How can you prevent being taken? A few basics:

✔ **Know your merchandise.** If you learn, for instance, that a certain cookie jar from the 1930s is a rare collectible and you see someone selling dozens of them at low prices, consider yourself warned that it is probably counterfeit.

✔ **Look at the starting bid price.** If it is low, be suspicious. Prices that seem too enticing are a reason for wariness, according to an eBay spokesman.

✔ **Look for a certificate of authenticity** from a reputable appraiser that has been scanned into the listing.

✔ **Know your seller.** Take the time to look at the details of a seller's feedback. A good sign is a comment from a satisfied buyer who took the extra step to have an item appraised and then reported back on its authenticity.

✔ **If there is any negative feedback on the site, scrutinize it carefully.** To report suspicious listings, hit the "Report This Item" button on each listing.

✔ **If you buy an item that you believe is counterfeit using PayPal,** you are likely to have recourse under the PayPal buyer protection system (pages.ebay.com/paypal/buyer/protection.html).

—Katie Hafner

ers, are auctions that are scheduled to start only after a series of speeches, or after a dinner, when people start streaming out. Bidders who tough it out do well.

For some buyers, the biggest discounts may come in the days after the auction. As many as 10 percent of the buyers at any sale wind up not paying, organizers say. So an item may become available again, this time at a bargain price.

—Alexandra Peers

Buying from Uncle Sam

You may score at an auction, but there are risks

Some bargain hunters see government auctions as a way to save a bundle on cars, furniture, diamonds and flat-screen televisions. For informed buyers, bidding may yield good investments. But the bang of the gavel can hold risk for novices.

Sponsored by federal, state and local agencies selling seized property, hundreds of auctions are held around the country each year. Depending on the sale, bidding may be done online, by phone or in person.

The merchandise is an eclectic mix—from big-ticket items like homes, cars and trucks to products like Rolex watches and Bose speakers. There may also be cartons of air conditioners, pottery, clothing and shampoo—and even slabs of granite and machine parts.

Many buyers are merchants who conduct business at a low and steady hum, eager to make an eventual profit, but others are individuals looking for that unbelievable bargain. For those interested in shopping at a government auction, specialists offer these pointers.

• Look for auction announcements on Web sites like firstgov.gov/shopping/shopping (for federal sales) and gsaauctions.gov (for sales of "surplus federal property").

- Attend several auctions, without bidding, to get an idea of fair prices.

- When you are ready to buy, go to an auction preview and determine your top potential bids. Consider retail prices and past winning bids.

- If you are buying a car, check the blue book value and get a Carfax report (carfax.com). At the preview, ask if you may start the car.

- Be sure you have everything you need to register to bid, such as a photo ID.

- Understand the payment requirements. Some auctions require up to $5,000 on the spot, often by cashier's check or cash.

- Establish a pickup time for the property you purchased.

- Auction items are sold as is, come with no guarantees from the government and cannot be returned or exhaustively checked out ahead of time. Ask manufacturers whether they will honor warranties.

—Hillary Chura

❓ EXPERT ANSWER

What's Hot on eBay

Q. **What do eBay buyers covet most?**

Americana, cross-stitch samplers featuring fairies, Budweiser tap handles, Mrs. Beasley dolls, pre-1980 trombones and cornets, fluorescent mineral samples, scratch-and-sniff stickers, Dakota china, postcards from Eastern Europe with views of towns, Disney timepieces, reindeer figurines and vintage Pioneer reel-to-reel tape recorders.

—Virginia Heffernan

Picking the Perfect Diamond
Tips for finding the ideal engagement ring

To the Greeks, diamonds were tears of the gods. To the Romans, they were splinters from falling stars. Today, the glittery chunks of crystallized carbon signify "Forever," as the marketing slogan for the diamond company the De Beers Group puts it. That hopeful sentiment no doubt drives the fact that three-fourths of first-time brides are proposed to with diamond engagement rings, according to industry figures.

Picking a diamond is fraught with peril, especially for novice buyers, who will have to determine the value of a particular diamond. Fortunately, the Gemological Institute of America (GIA) developed a standard for grading diamonds, referred to as the four C's: the stone's carat weight, its degree of clarity, its color and the skill with which it was cut. Here's what's behind the four C's.

CARAT WEIGHT. Gemstone weight was traditionally measured with carob seeds, which weigh about one-fifth of a gram. Today's standard measure, the carat, sprouted from the carob seed—one carat equals 200 milligrams, or one-fifth of a gram.

CLARITY. Nothing is perfect, but the closer to flawless a stone is, the more valuable. In this case, a flaw refers either to tiny mineral deposits, which are called inclusions, or to fractures in the stone, which are called cleavages. Internal imperfections are graded starting from F for Flawless or IF for Internally Flawless; then VVS 1 or VVS 2, meaning Very, Very Slightly Included; VS 1 or VS 2, Very Slightly Included; SI 1 or SI 2, Slightly Included; and I 1, I 2, or I 3, Included.

COLOR. Color quality is determined by the stone's actual color (hue), how rich the color is (saturation) and how light or dark it is (tone). This is by far the most important factor affecting price. Slight differences in color may mean great differences in price. Unfortunately for the beginner, judging color is a highly subjective process and one that requires a practiced eye. Color is graded starting with D as the best. D to F are colorless; G to J are nearly colorless; K to M are tinted yellow or brown.

CUT. This factor is the only one determined by the cutter, not by nature. A gemstone is like a tiny prism—the slightest change in the angle of a cut will affect how it refracts light—thus the "fire" in a stone can only be released by a skilled cutter. A well-polished gem will be far more radiant and therefore more valuable. The GIA ratings for cut are: Excellent, Very Good, Good, Fair and Poor.

Pricing Diamonds *Cost of a round-cut diamond, based on a standard of Very Good (from GemGuide)*

ROUND	G/VS1	H/VS2	I/SI1	J/SI2
½ carat	$3,300	$2,400	$1,900	$1,600
1 carat	$12,800	$9,600	$7,880	$6,500

Remember that although stores like Tiffany & Co. and Harry Winston carry a certain cachet, they don't have a monopoly on fine diamonds. Just be sure to shop at a trustworthy jeweler who will be around if there's a problem. If it's an investment-quality diamond you're after, however, stones from the upscale shops tend to be high in quality and classic in design, and therefore retain their value best.

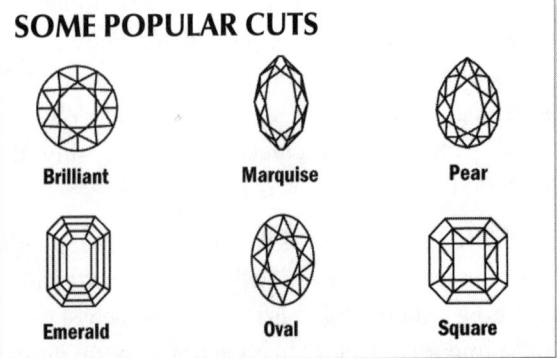

SOME POPULAR CUTS

Brilliant   Marquise   Pear

Emerald   Oval   Square

Finding the Perfect Pearl
How to tell a real one from a phony

There are two types of pearls these days, the experts say: real ones and fakes. Real pearls come in two varieties: natural and cultured. Natural pearls, which are increasingly rare, are made of layers of nacre, the material that coats an oyster's shell. Cultured pearls are made by introducing a piece of shell into an oyster, which it then combines with tissue to produce the pearl.

Most "natural" pearls found in jewelry stores today are actually cultured pearls. They range in price from the least expensive, freshwater, to the Japanese akoya, the traditional white variety, to the large and often colored pearls of the South Seas.

The Price of Pearls *Cost of a Japanese akoya cultured pearl necklace, 16-inch length (from GemGuide)*

SIZE	COMMERCIAL	GOOD	FINE	EXTRA FINE
4½ to 5 mm	$285	$485	$750	$1,000
5½ to 6 mm	$450	$825	$1,275	$1,950

Fake pearls are made of coated beads, plastic, resin or other artificial material. Sometimes, even jewelers can't tell the real from the fake, so if you suspect granny's inherited strand is made of museum-quality natural pearls, it's best to have it appraised by a certified professional. Otherwise, here's the reliability of some common tests to separate the real and the cultured from the faux.

The tooth test. Gently rub the pearl against the edge of your front teeth. Do not scrape the pearl, simply test to see if it feels rough and sandy. Real pearls have a grainy feel as a result of the natural buildup of nacre, or layers of crystal. Imitation pearls feel hard and uniformly smooth. This test is more reliable in distinguishing truly natural pearls from imitations, less so in picking phonies from cultured pearls, which have fewer bumps and ridges and therefore feel smoother.

The clasp test. A fabulously expensive strand of pearls will have an equally exceptional clasp. It will have a secure closure made of gold, silver or platinum. You can inspect the clasp under a magnifying glass for manufacturer markings. An engraved "M," for example, means the pearls were made by Mikimoto, a high-quality Japanese producer. Good-quality pearl jewelry is generally strung with silk threads and with knots between each pearl.

The eye test. Real pearls are not as uniformly perfect in appearance. Like anything made naturally, they vary in size and shape. A series of perfectly round, perfectly white beads is suspect. Look at the drill holes in the pearls. Genuine pearls have tiny holes, drilled from both sides of the pearl. The holes on imitation pearls are generally larger and may even show some flaking of the lacquer or the bead inside.

The X-ray test. This is the only definitive analysis. The lab X-ray shows whether the core of the pearl is naturally produced or is a cheap lacquered bead.

Valuing Your Jewels

Beware: gemstone prices are highly volatile

Gemstone prices rise and fall due to factors such as supply, demand, and changes in treatment and production technology. Prices in these charts were compiled by Richard Drucker, publisher of *GemGuide* (gemguide. com), an industry pricing standard. They are average retail prices prices per carat, not per stone unless otherwise stated, and are accurate as of spring 2009. Remember that these are benchmark prices; you may find prices above or below these at your jeweler.

WEIGHT	COMMERCIAL	GOOD	FINE	EXTRA FINE
Amethyst				
1 carat	$ 6	$ 15	$ 35	$ 60
3 carat	$ 25	$ 60	$ 130	$ 225
Aquamarine				
1 carat	$ 35	$ 110	$ 380	$ 850
3 carat	$ 150	$ 525	$ 1,375	$ 2,775
Citrine				
1 carat	$ 4	$ 10	$ 27	$ 45
3 carats	$ 15	$ 35	$ 100	$ 165
Emerald				
½ carat	$ 105	$ 700	$ 2,000	5,000
1 carat	$ 160	$ 1,100	$ 4,800	$10,000
Garnet (Rhodolite)				
1 carat	$ 15	$ 30	$ 60	$ 100
3 carats	$ 65	$ 160	$ 285	$ 390
Opal (white with play of color)				
1 carat	$ 10	$ 40	$ 135	$ 480
3 carats	$ 30	$ 120	$ 405	$ 1,440
Peridot				
1 carat	$ 20	$ 50	$ 105	$ 195
3 carats	$ 60	$ 150	$ 315	$ 585
Ruby				
½ carat	$ 55	$ 550	$ 1,320	$ 2.200
1 carat	$ 290	$ 1,300	$ 3,700	$ 7,200
Sapphire				
½ carat	$ 35	$ 155	$ 475	$ 775
1 carat	$ 145	$ 650	$ 1,650	$ 4,100
Tanzanite				
½ carat	$ 75	$ 150	$ 265	$ 375
1 carats	$ 215	$ 450	$ 775	$ 1,025
Turquoise				
8 x 6 mm	$ 4	$ 10	$ 20	$ 40
10 x 8 mm	$ 6	$ 16	$ 30	$ 60

SOURCE: Richard Drucker, Publisher, *GemGuide*

SPENDING

The Silent Secrets of Silver

Before buying, check the markings on the back

Since silver can be easily altered or imprinted with a phony hallmark, it pays to look carefully before you buy. Sterling silverware is made by mixing pure silver with copper or some other alloy to make it harder and more durable. Three grades of silver are commonly used: sterling, which is 925 parts per 1,000 pure silver; English, at 975; and European Continental, at 800. To identify silver flatware, turn the piece over: you may need a magnifying glass to decipher the markings on the back.

Before 1860, American silversmiths marked their wares on the back with their initials or full name. Silver made in America after 1860 is marked with the word "sterling." Sometimes there may also be initials or a silver maker's identification. For example, the markings for American Gorham are a lion, an anchor, a "g" and the word "sterling."

British silver has a complete set of hallmarks, including when and where it was made. Look for a king's or queen's head, a lion or a leopard, among assorted other markings. A lion signifies that the piece is sterling silver. A leopard's head means it was made in London. A king's or queen's head indicates that the piece was made during the reign of the monarch depicted.

There are often other marks as well, which can be identified by referring to one of the many tomes on silver markings, such as *The Book of Old Silver* (Crown Publishers, 1937; available in

libraries) by Seymour B. Wyler, the definitive source for silver marks.

The marking on European Continental silver is "800," the designation for Continental-grade silver. Russian pieces are engraved with an "840." Pieces with no markings are either silver plate or some other alloy. Silver plating, which began on a large scale in the 19th century, consists of a metal base with a thin silver coating, usually applied by electroplating. Silver-plated ware sells for about one-third the price of sterling.

> **It's always best to buy silver on the secondary market, because older silver is heavier and much better crafted than today's silver.**
>
> *Silver* magazine

● ● ●

Virtual Stamp Collecting

Philatelists find it all online

Like other collectors, stamp lovers have a ready-made marketplace on the Internet. But the Web offers philatelists especially significant resources and risks.

Help identifying lineage. One great challenge for collectors is to identify the lineage of a stamp. Which historical painting was it based on? When was it released, and in what quantity? What variations of the stamp exist, either in denomination or in size? This arduous research is far more manageable online, where you can post images of your stamps and ask others for help identifying them.

Newsgroups are one way to gather this information. Galleries created by individual collectors to help document and preserve the images and history of stamps are also good sources. There are hundreds of exhibits broken down by themes, like stamps of birds, or by region or period.

Many philatelists say they would never see such collections were they not displayed on the

Profiting from Botched-Up Stamps

A printer's mishap can bring big rewards

Botched-up stamps are a rarity, but collectors lucky enough to own one stand to win big. The aristocrat of all botched-up stamps is the invert, or stamp on which the design is mistakenly printed upside down.

The most famous invert is the Jenny, a 1918 stamp featuring the Curtiss JN-4 biplane in the design. It was the first American issue for air postage; its value was set at 24 cents. But of the roughly two million printed, 100 bore the topsy-turvy center plane and quickly became the stuff of philatelic legend.

A block of four Jennys set a world record for a stamp item in 2005, when they sold for $2.97 million. Several factors contributed to the stamps' value, such as their status as a unique block of a famous error and their excellent condition.

The record price for a single stamp belongs to a Swedish stamp, the 3-skilling yellow error of 1857, which sold for $2.2 million in 1996. The most expensive single American stamp is the 1-cent stamp of 1868 with a rare so-called Z-grill, an experimental security waffle pressed into the paper; it sold for $935,000 in 1998.

—Matthew Healey

Internet. Stamp dealers also digitize their collections and post the images online, or provide catalogs on CDs.

Collectors can search databases that include the inventory of numerous participating dealers. Such portals include ZillionsofStamps.com, PostBeeld.com and StampFinder.com.

Buying and selling online. While many sites specialize in collectibles, eBay is by far the largest source for stamps. At any given time, there are 40,000 to 50,000 lots of stamps on eBay alone, collectors estimate. Stamps for sale range from garden varieties to rarities in the $6,000 range; auction watchers note seeing some for up to $35,000. But buying stamps online—especially through auction sites—can be risky.

Beware of stamp fraud. Consumer advocates warn that with stamps, unlike with other valuables, fraud artists need few special tools or skills. Counterfeiting a valuable coin takes special tools and dies; reproducing a painting requires a skilled artist. With stamps, a common ruse is to clean up a used stamp and make it appear new, a step that may drastically increase its value.

Stamp fraud predates the Internet, of course. The main difference now is how quickly con artists can move a large volume of altered stamps online. Connoisseurs can also pull a fast one on neophytes who sell stamps without realizing their value. People troll for such bargains on the Internet.

—Sandeep Junnarkar

ⓘ **INSIDE INFO**

What Are Your Coins Worth?

○ A rare coin collection, including an 1872 Amazonian gold set, sold for more than $30 million in 2007, setting a record for the largest private coin collection sale in numismatic history. Buyer and seller remain anonymous.

○ Previous records include the $15 million sale of the Trompeter gold coin collection in 1998, and the 2005 sale of a world-famous coin set, called the King of Siam, for $8.5 million. President Andrew Jackson presented it in 1836 to the King of Siam, whose son was immortalized in *The King and I.*

SPENDING

How to Pick an Oriental Rug

Learn how to assess quality first

Oriental rugs have long been valued for their artistry and durability, not to mention their association with taste and gentility. But these days you don't need to be a Brahmin to buy one. The glut of Oriental rugs on the market in recent years has made them quite affordable.

Discerning quality can be tricky, due to subtleties in materials, design and craftsmanship, but with a few basic guidelines you can find a rug that not only suits your style but is also a sound investment.

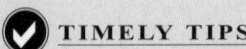

TIMELY TIPS

Sites for Collectors

With these sites, collectors can spare themselves hunting trips to shows and shops.

✔ **Cocacolaclub.org** For kicking off a lifetime of coin collecting.

✔ **Coin-newbies.com** If prices are low, be suspicious. Too-enticing prices are a reason for wariness.

✔ **CollectorsQuest.com** and **CollectZing.com** Offer social networking and gadgets for categorizing collections.

✔ **ComicConnect.com** Auction site for comics.

✔ **ComiXology.com** Lets you value your comic book collection or acquire someone else's.

✔ **Mycoincollecting.com** To keep numismatists collecting.

✔ **Replacements.com** A huge online warehouse for china and other table settings.

✔ **Stamps.org** The site for philatelists.

✔ **1stdibs.com** A decorative arts marketplace for antique dealers from the U.S. and Paris.

—Virginia Heffernan

Where do you want to put the rug? If it is destined for the dining room, you'll want it to be bigger than the table, and you may want a dark color that camouflages spills. And just so you don't come across as a rug rube, call the rug a "carpet" only if it is more than six feet long.

Do you want a modern or antique rug? Your next decision is whether to buy a modern or antique rug. Though there are exceptions, the best-quality rugs are either very old or very new but made in the old tradition, most dealers and collectors say. That's because in recent years there has been a move to make rugs the way they were made a century ago, before the widespread use of chemically treated wool, synthetic dyes and mass production techniques discouraged weavers' creativity.

Historically, the great carpet-making areas have been Iran, Turkey, Turkestan and the Caucasus. But you can also add Afghanistan, Pakistan, Nepal, India and China to the list.

How much do you want to spend? Prices vary according to design, provenance and condition; you can get comparable antique and new room-size Oriental rugs for $1,000 to $10,000 or more. Rare collectors' rugs, like a 12-by-14-foot Sultanabad circa 1870, may go for $100,000 to $200,000. New rugs have the advantage of no wear, but an antique rug that is well made and well maintained will outlast your grandchildren—and hold its value or even appreciate.

How to assess quality. When evaluating a rug, look for warm colors that change hue when viewed from different angles. Avoid rugs with brash, one-note colors, like taxicab yellow or mailbox blue, as those can indicate synthetic chemical dyes rather than natural dyes derived from plants and insects. And natural dyes do not run the way some synthetic ones do. Dampen a white handkerchief and

EXPERT ANSWER

Collecting Wine

Q **Is wine collecting a good investment?**

From an investment perspective, wine and some fragile collectibles, like old manuscripts, can be especially risky. A wine collection can occupy a lot of space, and that space has to be temperature- and humidity-controlled.

Besides, even the most cellar-worthy bottle has a finite life. Eventually, it has to be drunk. And when you pull the cork, the asset's gone. Then again, wine does have a benefit that stocks and bonds lack. When stocks go sour you have nothing to show for it. If the wine market takes a downturn, you still have the wine to drink.

SOURCE: Stuart H. Brager, a Baltimore physician and wine collector

rub it over the pile to check for colorfastness.

Next, turn the rug over. Don't worry about counting knots per square inch, because the weave's tightness does not always indicate value. More important is that the weave has some irregularity in the knotting. If it's flawless, it may not be handmade; machine-made rugs are anathema to collectors.

Check its condition. Look at the back of the rug to check for repairs—and to see if the rug may have been cut down from a larger size. Tip-offs are lines that look like seams running through the design, or obvious overstitching. Such modifications can reduce the value. Check whether the colors on the back match those on the front. If not, it may have been chemically "aged" to appear antique. You can also check for such aging by separating the pile and looking for dark roots.

The most durable and valuable rugs are usually made of wool and should feel soft, springy

and lustrous. If a rug is frizzy or coarse, the wool has probably been scalded and mechanically spun, which strips away its protective fibers and lanolin.

Rugs as investments. Dealers and appraisers say well-made Oriental rugs increase or at least hold their value over time, and collectors say that some rugs are worth 10 times what they were 20 years ago. But nothing is certain. More important than the potential return on investment, experts agree, is knowing that you enjoy the rug.

—Kate Murphy

Telling One Barbie from Another

Collectors crave the pale, stiff Barbie of 1959

Barbie's inventor, Ruth Handler, a founder of the doll's maker, Mattel, based the Barbie's hourglass figure on Bild Lilli, a German doll that in turn was based on a foul-mouthed, promiscuous newspaper cartoon character.

Since the original pale, stiff Barbie—a version collectors call "#1 Ponytail"—appeared at the International Toy and Trade Fair in New York in March 1959, the doll has taken on a variety of other racial identities, not to mention more than 100 professions. But her nose has remained pert, and her gaze vacant, while her plastic skin formula has grown dewier, her hair-plugs have multiplied, her forehead proportions have shrunk and her joint movement has been upgraded.

Yet it's "#1 Ponytail" that collectors crave. "The '59 is absolutely the holy grail and almost impossible to find in great shape," says Sharon Korbeck Verbeten, author of *The Best of Barbie: Four Decades of America's Favorite Doll.* The record for a Barbie sold at auction is $27,450, reached in May 2006 at Sandi Holder's Doll Attic in Union City, Calif., for a never-removed-from-box blond dressed

SPENDING

Culling the Junk from the Collectibles

When it's time to unload

Downsizing isn't easy. The first inclination may be to bring in a garbage bin and move on, or maybe hold a yard sale. That could be a costly mistake.

✔ **Hire an appraiser.** Not every dingy piece of furniture is a prized collectible, of course, but one way to know for sure, short of poring through scores of research books, is to hire an appraiser, who can pinpoint items that could be valuable. Appraisal fees run between $60 and $300 an hour. You can find a database of accredited members of the Appraisers Association of America on www.appraisersassoc.org.

✔ **Auction houses** also provide appraisals for varying fees, although they typically do them free if you also allow them to sell the items, as will professional home- or estate-sale organizers. Both work on commissions ranging from 15 to 40 percent and may charge additional fees for services like advertising, cleanup or insurance.

✔ **In an estate or home sale,** usually held on the premises, merchandise is tagged and buyers are expected to pay that price or close to it. (They can leave bids for more expensive pieces.) In an auction, everything is sold to the highest bidders, although you can set a "reserve," or price beneath which you won't sell an item.

✔ **Selling to a dealer** is another option, but here again, it's crucial to do some research beforehand. "If you don't know what you have, you've got no bargaining hand," says David Rago, an appraiser on the *Antiques Roadshow*. It's important, too, to understand that tastes and interests constantly change. The big sellers of three years ago may be less in demand today.

✔ **You may find that using a variety of selling methods works best.** Maybe a house sale for furnishings and auction or private sales for expensive things like the Navajo rugs. Another option is to donate, for example, a sculpture to the local high school, and get a tax deduction.   —Vivian Marino

for a barbecue. No fading or chips mar her pale blue eyelids or red lips and matching nail polish, and her ears do not suffer from a common Barbie skin malady called "green ear," caused by deteriorating metal earrings. The corrosion gets into the pores in the vinyl and cannot be cured. It can even occur to a doll that hasn't been played with.

Prices for undamaged Barbies have held steady in recent years. In addition to die-hard buyers, part of the market also taps into the popularity of midcentury furniture. Vintage Barbie, dealers say, goes with the aesthetic of stylish 1950s objects like Eames chairs or George Nelson clocks. One dealer has charged up to $15,000 for a 1959 blond in "Christmas-morning-new" condition. Such flawless pieces keep turning up, dealers say, found slumbering in storage.

Why the fascination with Barbies? Christopher Varaste, author of *Face of the American Dream: Barbie Doll 1959-1971*, says that the "heart of collecting these is that every one is individual; they're not as standardized as you'd think." The early ones were hand-painted in Japan; you can see the styles of different artists in the eyebrows and eyes. And there've been endless variations over the years to the faces and bodies and fabrics, as the Mattel designers have stayed on top of every trend in popular culture.

In honor of Barbie's 50th birthday in 2009, Mattel rereleased half a dozen retired models, including a 1971 Malibu in gauzy bell-bottoms, a 1977 SuperStar in feather boas and a 1986 Rocker in a spiky pink wig. The replicas, however, do not seem to dampen the prices for vintage stock. Rather they serve to increase interest and often ramp up prices.

—Eve M. Kahn

EDUCATION

EDUCATION

Pre-K through 12

What's the Right Age for Reading?

Pushing it too early is a big mistake

Learning to read early has become one of those indicators—in parents' minds, at least—that their child is smart. In fact, reading early has very little to do with whether a child is successful academically. Research over the past few decades has shown that difficulty with reading is often due not to inferior intelligence but to differences in the developmental wiring of each individual child. In some cases, there are neurological problems and developmental lags, many of which, if identified early enough and properly remediated, can be overcome.

If children with a language disability can be screened and diagnosed as early as kindergarten or first grade, they can benefit from phonological training at the outset and will have fewer problems in learning to read at grade level than they might if they are not identified until third grade or later.

Before her death, the late Harvard School of Education professor Jean Chall, author of *Learning to Read: The Great Debate* and other seminal books in the education field, shared her perspective on teaching reading.

Q At what age should a child learn to read?

Traditionally American schools teach children at age 6, but many schools begin teaching informally in kindergarten and prekindergarten. If parents start too early to encourage reading, and a child does not immediately succeed, the parent has a hard time relaxing and letting the child go at his or her own pace.

Q Which teaching method works best?

Over the years, research has proved that the use of both the "whole language" method and the "phonic" method is the best way for a child to master reading. While the whole language approach, which includes reading to children and getting them interested in both the activity of reading and the story they are reading, is helpful, phonics must be taught. Children must be taught that one of the squiggles they see on a page is a "p" and another a "b" and that those two letters sound different and are written differently. Getting the print off the page requires a different ability than being able to understand the meaning of what is written. It is very important for normal progress, and especially for children at risk, that both methods be taught.

✔ TIMELY TIPS

Reading Sites for Young Learners

✔ One More Story. For an elegant and serious early-reading experience, try www.onemorestory.com, the subscription-only online library. For $44 a year, you get a sparkling-clean interface, acclaimed tried-and-true picture books, lovely narration and a glitch-free player.

✔ Starfall. In early childhood education, nothing is underthought. Except, refreshingly, Starfall (www.starfall.com). The eccentric, cheerful learn-to-read site is loaded with scattershot activities. Some of them are great, while some miss the mark. All told, though, the site is fun, free and effective.   —Virginia Heffernan

Q How do you lay the groundwork for reading in a young child?

You can start developing the skills needed in reading at a very young age without putting any pressure on children. Besides reading to them, parents can start "ear training" their child by playing rhyme games. This develops the child's ability to discern different sounds and to realize that certain words begin to look and sound the same. In reading to children, parents also can point to words as they go, teaching the child that the funny lines on the page are the words you are saying. All of this "early teaching" should not be a serious thing. It should be a fun activity. There is plenty of time for serious learning later.

Q When should you "get serious"?

Once a child is in school, learning to read is inevitably more serious. If children do not already know how to identify and write letters, and to recognize words, they start to learn it in a systematic way. I am reluctant to tell parents when to teach reading to their children, as they often embark on too serious a task too early for the child.

Q How many children suffer from learning disabilities?

Most schools cite a 10 to 15 percent learning disability rate among their student body; some as high as 20 percent. Many children have some kind of reading difficulty.

Q What if your child is having difficulty with reading?

You must get a professional diagnosis. While the teacher might say the child is merely disinterested but will get over it, disinterest or poor performance in reading can stem from a number of things, some being very specific learning disabilities that can be identified and worked on.

Correcting these early can circumvent a lot of potential problems for the child later in school. Learning disabilities have now been shown to be neurological problems that can be corrected with the proper training. It is very tricky for parents to deal with their own child's learning disabilities, and I most certainly do not recommend it.

How to Pick a Kindergarten
Research shows that play, not academic work, is vital for future success

Instead of digging in sandboxes, many of today's kindergartners prepare for a life of multiple-choice boxes by plowing through standardized tests with cuddly names like Dibels (pronounced "dibbles"), a series of early-literacy measures administered to millions of kids. Or, they toil over reading curricula like Open Court, which features assessments every 6 weeks.

But according to *Crisis in the Kindergarten,* a report recently released by the Alliance for Childhood, a nonprofit research and advocacy group, all that testing is wasted: it neither predicts nor improves young children's educational outcomes. In addition, along with other academic demands, like assigning homework to 5-year-olds, it is crowding out the one thing that truly is vital to their future success: play.

A survey of 254 teachers in New York and Los Angeles the group commissioned found that kindergartners spent two to three hours a day being instructed and tested in reading and math. They spent less than 30 minutes playing. "Play at age 5 is of great importance not just to intellectual but emotional, psychological, social and spiritual

66

Sixty percent of kids ages 2 to 5 do not have daily access to outdoor play.

● ● ●

EDUCATION

development," says Edward Miller, the report's co-author. Play, especially the let's-pretend, dramatic sort, is how kids develop higher-level thinking, hone their language and social skills and cultivate empathy. It also reduces stress, a word that should not figure in the life of a kindergartner in the first place.

Accelerating kindergarten is unnecessary, says Miller, since any early advantage fades by fourth grade. "It makes a parent proud to see a child learn to read at age 4, but in terms of what's really best for the kid, it makes no difference."

For at-risk kids, pushing too soon may backfire. The longitudinal High/Scope Preschool Curriculum Comparison Study followed 68 such children, who were divided between instruction- and play-based classrooms. While everyone's I.Q. scores initially rose, by age 15, the former group's academic achievement plummeted. They were more likely to exhibit emotional problems and spent more time in special education.

—Peggy Orenstein

Identifying a Gifted Child
Their high intelligence is often mistaken for a disorder

Discerning gifted children, long an imperfect science, is even tougher in today's label-prone culture. James T. Webb, a clinical psychologist and author of *Misdiagnosis and Dual Diagnosis of Gifted Children and Adults*, explains what can go wrong.

Q Parents throw the word "gifted" around. What does it mean, really?

❝

"Intellectually gifted" may have a variety of definitions. Assuming that people scoring in the top 10 percent of intelligence tests meet the criteria, the country has millions of gifted children.

Julie Bick

● ● ●

"Gifted" comes in different forms and degrees. Gifted children excel in such areas as general intellectual ability and in specific aptitudes like math, creative thinking and visual or performing arts. Most have I.Q. scores between 130 and 155. Above that range are the profoundly gifted—a tiny fraction of the group. Over all, the gifted represent about 3 percent of our population.

Q Why would gifted children be tagged as having psychological disorders?

Behaviors of many gifted children can resemble those of, say, attention deficit/hyperactivity disorder. Most teachers, pediatricians and psychologists aren't trained to distinguish between the two. Most gifted kids are very intense, pursuing interests excessively. This often leads to power struggles, perfectionism, impatience, fierce emotions and trouble with peers. Many gifted kids have varied interests, skipping from one to the other—a trait often misinterpreted as A.D.H.D.

Q You write that these misdiagnoses are common.

About a quarter of gifted children have their giftedness misinterpreted as a disorder and aren't recognized as gifted. Even when flagged as gifted, another 20 percent are misdiagnosed. Among children referred to me with a bipolar diagnosis, almost 100 percent have been misdiagnosed, as are 70 percent of those with obsessive-compulsive diagnoses and 55 percent of those with A.D.H.D.

Q What's a parent to do?

Parents should educate themselves about the characteristics of gifted children: intense curiosity, unusually good memory, a remarkable sense of humor, exquisite sensitivity to others and extensive vocabularies. And identify them early. Children's attitudes toward learning get set before age 10.

Preschool and the early grades generally turn off gifted kids: they are told to stop asking so many questions and wait their turn. They need an appropriate learning environment. If not, seeds for underachievement are sown.

—Abigail Sullivan Moore

When to Learn a Second Language
If you wait until adolescence, it's too late

English has always been the "American language," but because of the global economy, foreign language ability is increasingly important for Americans. Starting when a child is young is critical, argues Nancy Rhodes, director of the foreign language education division at the Center for Applied Linguistics in Washington, D.C. Rhodes offers this advice on training children to speak foreign tongues.

Start foreign language training early. After 12 or 13, it is very difficult to learn a language and be able to speak it like a native speaker. Young kids like playing with language and are not embarrassed by making strange sounds, so it's ideal for them to learn a foreign language. If you wait until kids are in adolescence, they are very inhibited and worried about how they appear to their peers.

Don't worry that studying a foreign language will harm a child's native language ability. All of the research shows that studying another language actually enhances your native language abilities. By the time children in foreign language immersion programs get to fifth or sixth grade, they score as well or better in English than their peers who have been studying only in English.

If you have a choice, select a program that integrates foreign language instruction into the rest of the curriculum. About a fifth of the elementary schools in the U.S. teach some type of foreign language. It could be just an introduction, or it could be an immersion experience in which the foreign language is the medium of instruction, so that the students are learning language as well as their content areas through the foreign language. The successful programs are integrated into the school day so that everybody sees foreign language as part of the curriculum.

When a family is multilingual, be as consistent as possible about who speaks what. Children can learn five or six different languages. The important thing is to separate the languages. If the mother speaks English, for example, and the father speaks Spanish, they should try to keep those roles the same. Do not be surprised or alarmed, however, if a young child mixes the languages he or she hears. This is normal and a phase. Do not react with impatience. Remember that by teaching a foreign language early, you are imparting a great gift.

Does Music Make You Smarter?
Research suggests it helps develop spatial reasoning

When champions of the liberal arts argue that there's more to education than just reading, writing and arithmetic, music and arts are often cited for their value in stimulating students' creativity and expanding their cultural horizons. Now there is evidence that students who receive formal musical training may enjoy higher standardized test scores and demonstrate greater powers of spatial reasoning than students who do not get this experience.

Two studies by researchers at the Center for the Neurobiology of Learning and Memory at the University of California at Irvine have suggested that there may indeed be a causal link between music and spatial intelligence. Spatial intelligence is the ability to perceive the visual world accurately, to form mental pictures of physical objects and to recognize when objects differ physically. Having well-developed powers of spatial reasoning is considered crucial for excelling at complex mathematics and playing chess, among other things.

In one of the two studies, the U.C. Irvine team led by a psychologist and a neuroscientist compared the spatial reasoning abilities of 19 preschool children who took music lessons for eight months with the performance of a demographically comparable group of 15 pre-

school children who received no music training. The researchers found the first group's spatial reasoning dramatically better. The team also reported that the ability of the music students to do a puzzle designed to measure their spatial reasoning powers rose significantly during the experiment.

A second study, which replicated and expanded on results of an earlier study in the journal *Nature*, found that when college students listened to 10 minutes of Mozart's piano sonata K.448, their spatial I.Q. scores rose more than when they spent the same amount of time sitting in silence or performing relaxation exercises. Curiously, the researchers observed no improvement in the students' spatial skills after 10 minutes of listening to the avant-garde composer Philip Glass or to a highly rhythmic dance piece, suggesting that hypnotic musical structures do nothing to improve spatial skills.

ⓘ INSIDE INFO

The Classroom of the Future

○ Online courses were once viewed as a poor substitute for in-class learning or a temporary solution for child actors and others who had to miss classes regularly. But in the past decade, virtual courses have cropped up nationwide as public schools have rushed to reconfigure traditional courses, from creative writing to calculus, for the Internet age.

○ More than 70 percent of the nearly 15,000 school districts nationwide offer at least one online course, enrolling more than a million students, according to the International Association for K-12 Online Learning. The group estimates that online enrollment has increased about 30 percent annually since 1997, growing faster than any other innovation in K-12 education.   —Winnie Wu

---

How to Succeed in Science
It helps to have an adult mentor to make it to the top

Ward Melville, a suburban Long Island public school, had 10 semifinalist winners out of 300 nationally in the prestigious Intel Science Talent Search in 2009. The year before it had 13, the highest number among the high schools represented. The public school even beat out so-called magnet schools, such as Montgomery Blair High in Silver Spring, Md., Stuyvesant in New York City and Thomas Jefferson in Alexandria, Va., which require an admissions exam.

How does a regular public school do it? Partly it's because Ward Melville is a well-to-do district with lots of parents who are doctors and other scientists. But there's more to it than that. They've

The Secret Powers of Chess

It's a good educational tool

Once a week second- and third-grade teachers in Idaho unpack chessboards and pieces and spend an hour teaching students how to play the game. That's not because all the teachers are passionate about chess but because they are part of a pilot program that offers chess to all second and third graders, making Idaho the first state to offer a statewide chess curriculum.

There are no studies showing that teaching chess has benefits for children, but anecdotal evidence suggests that chess is a productive educational tool. Proponents say it improves problem-solving skills, discipline, memory and mathematical skills.

Idaho and many other school systems across the country are using a curriculum called First Move, which was developed by America's Foundation for Chess, a nonprofit organization that promotes teaching chess in school.

First Move uses an interactive DVD and a series of exercises to introduce children to the game. In addition to focusing on rules and basic strategy, the program weaves in math exercises. (For more information on First Move and other chess resources, go to America's Foundation for Chess website at af4c.org.)

For some students, the benefits of learning chess can also include helping to pay for college. The U.S. Chess Federation (uschess.org) lists a number of colleges offering scholarships focused on chess players and those who excel in tournaments.

—Dylan Loeb McClain

---

also made scientific research a top priority, naming a former university professor to run the school's science program. The school provides technical support as well, subscribing to an online service that gives students unlimited access to the latest research papers. The program has a state-of-the-art printer that can produce an entire science fair poster board in a single 42-inch-wide sheet and a large budget to pay travel expenses to nine science fairs a year.

Dr. George Baldo, who runs the school's program, called InSTAR, has a large enough staff to ensure that the massive Intel International Science and Engineering Fair applications get filled out correctly by the students.

But none of these is the main reason Ward Melville excels. High school students cannot do research at this level without adult mentors—often a university professor plus a team of grad students—to help pick a topic that will break new ground, yet be manageable, and to supervise them at every step.

Ward Melville is close to the State University at Stony Brook, so students can bike to the labs daily. All told, the program makes available nearly 50 mentors from the college, New York University and other nearby research labs. For big-time science fairs, the single most important research students do is to find a willing mentor to oversee their work.

—Michael Winerip

Why Recess Is Crucial

Downtime and nature walks mean better behavior and maybe better grades

The best way to improve children's performance in the classroom may be to take them out of it. Recent research suggests that play and down time may be as important to a child's academic experience as reading, science, and math, and that regular

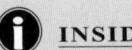 **INSIDE INFO**

How Children Really Learn

○ From John Dewey to Jean Piaget, educators have generally agreed that while didactic teaching has its place, small children learn mainly from interacting and not passive listening, understanding and not memorizing, reading for fun and not simply decoding.

○ The good news, say educators, is that children can be taught basic academic skills—fundamentals of reading, writing and mathematics—in a way that uses, rather than destroys, their natural desire to learn. Vocabulary can be taught by conversation, awareness of print developed through reading and talking about books and mathematics learned with games like a pretend restaurant.

—David L. Kirp

recess, fitness or nature time can influence behavior, concentration and even grades.

A study published recently in the journal *Pediatrics* studied the links between recess and classroom behavior among about 11,000 children age 8 and 9. Those who had more than 15 minutes of recess a day showed better behavior in class than those who had little or none. Although disadvantaged children were more likely to be denied recess, the association between better behavior and recess time held up even after researchers controlled for a number of variables, including sex, ethnicity, public or private school and class size.

The findings are important because many schools did not view recess as essential to education. But kids need that break because the brain needs that break. And many children are not getting it. In the *Pediatrics* study, 30 percent were found to have little or no daily recess. Another report, from a children's advocacy group, found

that 40 percent of schools surveyed had cut back at least one daily recess period.

Also, teachers often punish children by taking away recess privileges. But psychologists say that just as you don't punish children by having them miss math class, they shouldn't be denied recess in punishment, either.

In another study Harvard researchers reported that the more physical fitness tests children passed, the better they did on academic tests. The study, of 1,800 middle school students, suggests that children can benefit academically from physical activity during gym class and recess.

A small study of children with attention deficit hyperactivity disorder last year found that walks outdoors appeared to improve scores on tests of attention and concentration. Notably, children who took walks in natural settings did better than those who walked in urban areas, according to a report, published online in *The Journal of Attention Disorders*. The researchers found that a dose of nature worked as well as a dose of medication to improve concentration, or even better.

Other research suggests that all children, not just those with attention problems, can benefit from spending time in nature during the school day. In another study of children who live in public housing, girls who had access to green courtyards scored better on concentration tests than those who did not.

The reason may be that the brain uses two forms of attention. "Directed" attention allows us to concentrate on work, reading and tests, while "involuntary" attention takes over when we're distracted by things like running water, crying babies, a beautiful view or a pet that crawls onto our lap.

Directed attention is a limited resource. Long hours in front of a computer or studying for a test can leave us feeling fatigued. But spending time in natural settings appears to activate involuntary attention, giving the brain's directed attention time to rest. Playtime and nature time are important not only for learning but also for health and development.

Young rats denied opportunities for rough-and-tumble play develop numerous social problems in adulthood. They fail to recognize social cues and the nuances of rat hierarchy; they aren't able to mate. By the same token, people who play as children learn to handle life in a much more resilient and vital way, says Dr. Stuart Brown, a psychiatrist and author of *Play: How It Shapes the Brain, Opens the Imagination and Invigorates the Soul.*

Play is "a fundamental biological process," says Brown. "Teachers feel like they're under huge pressures to get academic excellence to the exclusion of having much fun in the classroom," says Brown, "but playful learning leads to better academic success than the skills-and-drills approach."

—Tara Parker-Pope

The New New Thing in Phys Ed
Competitive sports are out; aerobics are in

While traditional video games are often criticized for contributing to the expanding waistlines of the nation's children, hundreds of schools in more than a dozen states are using Dance Dance Revolution, or DDR (www.ddrgrame.com), as a regular part of their physical education curriculum.

 **TIMES TIPS**

Cures for Test Anxiety
If you can keep your wits about you, chances are you'll pass

Test anxiety can mean disaster for a student. Instead of feeling challenged by the prospect of success, they become afraid of failure. This makes them anxious about tests and their own abilities.

Ultimately they become so worked up that they feel incompetent about the subject matter or the test. It does not help to tell the child to relax, to think about something else or to stop worrying. But there are ways to reduce test anxiety. Some suggestions from your government:

✔ **Space studying over days or weeks.** Real learning occurs through studying that takes place over a period of time. Understand the information and relate it to what is already known. Review it more than once.

✔ **Don't "cram" the night before**—cramming increases anxiety, which interferes with clear thinking. Get a good night's sleep.

✔ **Read the directions carefully** when the teacher hands out the test. If you don't understand them, ask the teacher to explain.

✔ **Look quickly at the entire examination** to see what types of questions are included (multiple choice, matching, true/false, essay) and, if possible, the number of points for each. This will help you pace yourself.

✔ **If you don't know the answer to a question, skip it and go on**. Don't waste time worrying about it. Mark it so you can identify it as unanswered. If you have time at the end of the exam, return to the unanswered question(s).

SOURCE: U.S. Department of Education, Office of Educational Research and Improvement www.ed.gov/pubs/parents/TestTaking/index.html

MORE HELP FOR ANXIOUS STUDENTS:

✔ The Institute of HeartMath, a nonprofit research group, sells an interactive CD called TestEdge, which has strategies for controlling test anxiety for students in grades 7 to 12. The group also offers materials geared to help kids in grades 3 to 8 "neutralize" strong emotions. (www.heartmath.org)

EDUCATION

The blood-pumping video game, which requires players to dance in ever more complicated and strenuous patterns in time with electronic dance music, is the latest weapon in the nation's battle against the epidemic of childhood obesity.

Born a decade ago in the arcades of Japan, DDR has taken hold among a generation of young Americans who appear less enamored of traditional team sports than their parents were and more amenable to the personal pursuits enabled by modern technology.

As a song plays, arrows pointing in one of four directions—forward, back, left, right—scroll up the screen in various sequences and combinations, requiring the player to step on corresponding arrows on a mat on the floor. Players can dance by themselves, with a partner or in competition. (Though the game, which is made by Konami of Japan, began in arcades, it is now most commonly played on Sony's PlayStation 2 and Microsoft's Xbox game consoles.) More than 1,500 schools are expected to be using the game by the end of the decade. Incorporating DDR into gym class reflects a general shift in physical education, with school districts de-emphasizing traditional sports in favor of less competitive activities.

West Virginia, which ranks among the nation's leaders in obesity, diabetes and hypertension, has committed to installing the game in all its public schools. A recent multiyear study in the state found significant health benefits for overweight children who played the game regularly, including improved blood pressure, overall fitness scores and endothelial function, which reflects the arteries' ability to deliver oxygen. —Seth Schiesel

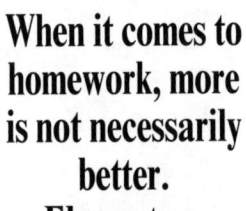

When it comes to homework, more is not necessarily better. Elementary schoolchildren probably spend too much time on homework, and a lot of what they do is busywork.

• • •

Does Your Child Do Too Much?

The more kids take on, the less enriched their educations are

Every parent knows the exasperation that comes from having a child who "acts up"—whether it be the 5-year-old who is terrorizing other children at nursery school, the 7-year-old who throws a fit every morning before leaving the house, or the 10-year-old who refuses to do her homework. What can a parent do in such cases?

Dr. David Elkind, a leading child development expert and author of *The Hurried Child,* shares his views about how to evaluate and cope with your child's behavior.

❓ How can you tell the difference between a child who is acting up because of stress, and one who is precocious and simply wants more stimulation?

Parents experience very different demands from children depending on what that child is experiencing. For example, a gifted child might demand constant stimulation to try to satisfy his or her voracious appetite for information—a chorus of whys ringing in your ears all day. That's very different from a child who battles for attention and presents parents with strain and power struggles. You need to look at how many demands there are on a child. Does he have to adapt to too many places and people each day (e.g., school, daycare, babysitters)? The more changes a child experiences in a day, the more stress he feels. Also, if you are troubled or there is distress in the family, your child's behavior will often mirror it.

❓ What can be done to relieve stress at school?

Increasingly, with so many early education programs, educators are assuming that children know their numbers and letters at a younger and younger age. This might not be the case, and it is no reflection on the child's intelligence—different children have different rates of development. If your child has a September or October birthday, especially for boys, you may want to wait a year before enrolling him. This is much preferred to starting your child and then having him repeat a year.

There is such a stigma for kids who are held back that if you are considering holding your child back a year, I recommend allowing him to continue to the next grade and providing additional tutoring.

◉ How many activities can a child manage adequately?

There is no need for a child to have any organized activity like sports or music before the age of 5 or 6. For school-age children, a sport, a musical instrument and maybe a "peer activity" like scouts

Homework is certainly a good idea in high schools, but a lot of thought has to go into making it worthwhile.

Helen Featherstone, editor of the *Harvard Education Letter*

● ● ●

is plenty. These should not take more than a few hours a week. It is very important for a child not to have all his time programmed. Children must learn to manage their own time. I see a lot of new college students who simply do not know how to manage their time because they have had such "planned" lives.

◉ How do you allow a child to manage his or her own time yet limit television or video games?

You can lay down some ground rules. For instance, you allow your child a certain number of hours of video games per week, and the rest must be spent doing other things. You are not saying that he or she can't do something, but you are setting limits on it.

◉ What's the best way to help a child deal with a stress that won't go away, like a death, a divorce or a move?

The most important thing is to talk to your child and help him or her deal with his or her feelings. If someone has died, it's very important for the child

Should You Help with Your Kid's Homework?

Lending a hand in after-school work

For parents eager to help their children's learning, getting involved with homework is one of the best methods. Yet all too often, homework becomes a battleground for wars of words between parent and child.

"The relationship [of parent helping the child] is supposed to go on for years," says Dr. Joyce Epstein, who studied homework issues extensively as director of the Johns Hopkins Center on School, Family, and Community Partnerships. "You

have to be careful that one night of confrontation doesn't ruin you for 12 years of school."

To develop good family communications, says Epstein, it's important how a parent talks to a child about school. "Many parents are told or advised to ask their child, 'How was school today?' as a way of interacting," says Epstein.

"Better to ask, 'Show me something you learned in math today,' because that makes the youngster demonstrate and re-create, rather than comment on nothing." From there, she says, parents can build the kind of interaction that will not only help the child's work but will improve the way the parent and child communicate.

Keeping the Same Teacher

The pros and cons of having a teacher who gets promoted with the class

Having a tteacher stay with a class for more than a year—or "looping," as it is known—is on the rise, according to many experts. "As schools try to improve their standardized test scores, this appears to be catching on," says Arthur E. Levine, the former longtime president of Teachers College at Columbia University.

Looping is most common in elementary schools, though some middle schools do it, too. The roots of looping trace back to the one room rural schoolhouse and to educational innovations in Europe in the early 20th century.

As educational innovations go, it is remarkably simple. So are its benefits, proponents say. Teachers get to know their students, and the students' parents, extremely well. They know each child's strengths and weaknesses, and the children know the teachers' expectations and methods. This familiarity can save a lot of time at the beginning of the school year. Many educators think both lower-income and middle-class children benefit from a more prolonged relationship with teachers.

The potential disadvantages of looping are also clear-cut. If parents think a teacher is inadequate, they would surely oppose having their child spend an additional year in his or her class. Advocates of looping say options need to be built into any program, so that parents and teachers can decide to place a child in a different class if remaining with a teacher would be detrimental.

Research into looping suggests that it can pay substantial dividends. A school district in East Cleveland, Ohio, experimented with looping in the 1990s. A class in each of four elementary schools stayed with their teachers for 3 years, generally from kindergarten through second grade. The teachers worked extensively with parents to reinforce lessons in school, and the classes also met for 5 weeks each summer. After 3 years, students in the looped classes scored an average of 25 percentage points higher on standardized tests in reading, language arts and math than other students in the school district, says Frederick M. Hampton, an associate professor of education at Cleveland State University who oversaw the research project.

—Alan Finder

to talk about that person and to articulate how he or she feels. Similarly, if a child sees something frightening on TV, the child needs to talk about it and be allowed to work through his or her emotions.

Q When is professional help advisable?

While there are cases where a child needs therapy, a parent must be very careful. Being sent to see someone can label the child as abnormal and become yet another form of stress. When there is a problem for which a parent wants to seek professional counseling, this should be done as a family. A child does not become emotionally distressed overnight, but in response to the cumulative effect of family behavior patterns. Even when a child is experiencing a physiological problem, such as attention deficit disorder, the parents need counseling as well.

Q What is the biggest mistake parents make in helping children deal with life's stresses?

One of the biggest mistakes is to think that bad experiences prepare children for other bad experiences. I believe that the more good experiences parents can give their children—doing things with their children, giving them loving and successful experiences—the better they feel about themselves, the better the relationships they have with their parents, the better they are able to cope when something difficult does happen.

The Case for Single-Sex Education

Teaching boys and girls separately in the middle school years can be a good idea

The most challenging time for educators to engage children in learning is generally held to be the middle school years. Hormones are raging, and girls, in particular, are jockeying for position in the social pecking order. Being in a coed environment is confusing and distracting for most preadolescents, leaving them little time to focus on their studies and leaving them, often, with very poor self-esteem. For that reason, many schools all over the country are opting for a separate-but-equal educational experience for the middle school years.

This island of sex segregation between the ages of 11 and 16 takes into account the different learning styles of boys and girls; the uneven pace of their physical, emotional and cognitive development; the hormonal assault at puberty, when the part of the brain that governs judgment is still forming; and the effect of a sexualized culture that has made 13 the new 17. It also assumes that if girls gained confidence learning in single-sex math and science classes, popular for the last decade, boys might get a comparable boost in the humanities.

"This is the single most critical time in a child's life, and we are asking them to grow up way too fast," says Dr. Everett J. Wilson, head of the middle school at the Masters School. "This way, the girls get the opportunity to find their voice, and the boys get the opportunity to find their voice in an appropriate way. The conventional wisdom is that girls benefit and for boys it's a wash. But we don't buy that here."

Michael Thompson, co-author of *Raising Cain,* says that boys become angry and resentful and "fight back" in middle school because they feel "defective" when compared to girls, who are "lit-erally out-thinking them." Thompson endorses the separate-but-equal model as a "fascinating, interesting, wonderful experiment" that potentially has more to offer boys than girls.

Carol Gilligan, author of *In a Different Voice,* says she is certain that girls who are "confident at 11 and confused at 16" will more likely be creative thinkers and risk-takers as adults if educated apart from boys in middle school. "It is the most effective moment to stop something from happening that has both personal and cultural costs," she says, referring to the loss of confidence.

—Jane Gross

TIMELY TIPS

Calling in the Online Tutors

An army of tutors is available online to help your student with homework problems. Here are sites for students from kindergarten to grade 12.

✔ **Brainfuse.com** works primarily through libraries and schools. Students can log on to the site from a home computer by using a library card number as a password. The student selects a grade and subject and connects with a tutor to ask a specific question.

✔ **Tutor.com** also works with libraries to connect students to tutors day or night for help with core subjects, from world history to English to physics. Customized tutoring packages are available for individuals; they typically go for around $30 for one hour, although students generally use 15 minutes here and there a few times a week.

✔ **TutorVista.com** offers unlimited online tutoring in as many subjects as you like for $99 a month. Get immediate online help or schedule a session with a preferred tutor.

EDUCATION

The Best Books for Kids 2004-2008

Some great choices for children of all ages

Each year, the editors of the *New York Times Book Review* select the most notable children's books of the year. Here are the editors' picks for the last 5 years. (Reviews of most of the titles can be found online at www.nytimes.com.)

2008

WABI SABI. *By Mark Reibstein. Illustrated by Ed Young.* $16.99. (Ages 3 to 6) Ingeniously layered text, both narrative and haiku, and gorgeous collage art. A cat named Wabi Sabi sets out to discover the meaning of her name.

THE KINGDOM ON THE WAVES: The Astonishing Life of Octavian Nothing, Traitor to the Nation, Volume 2. *By M. T. Anderson.* $22.99. (Ages 14 and up) This sequel completes the story of race and revolution told in *The Pox Party,* encompassing the comedy and tragedy of Octavian Nothing's ambition.

SUNRISE OVER FALLUJAH. *By Walter Dean Myers.* $17.99. (Ages 12 and up) An idealistic young soldier lands in Iraq's deadly hall of mirrors, in a kind of sequel to Myers's 1988 Vietnam novel, *Fallen Angels.*

THE HUNGER GAMES. *By Suzanne Collins.* $17.99. (Ages 12 and up) A brilliantly plotted tale that begins after North American society has been decimated by climate change and war.

LITTLE BROTHER. *By Cory Doctorow.* $17.95. (Ages 13 and up) A near-future terrorist attack hits San Francisco, and Marcus Yallow, 17, playing hooky from high school, is detained in the crackdown that follows.

ABC3D. *By Marion Bataille.* $19.95. (Ages 5 and up) A simple but sophisticated idea animates this small, chunky pop-up book, which does wonders with the letters A through Z.

TEN LITTLE FINGERS AND TEN LITTLE TOES. *By Mem Fox. Illustrated by Helen Oxenbury.* $16. (Ages 3 to 5) A witty and winsome look at babies around

❝

When you're driving over the summer to different places, listening to some really good children's books on tape is a great way for the family to share that experience.

•••

the world that has a toe-tapping refrain: the words sound easy and familiar, as though they have been handed down to children forever.

THE DISREPUTABLE HISTORY OF FRANKIE LANDAU-BANKS. *By E. Lockhart.* $16.99. (Ages 12 and up) In this homage to girl power, "a nice girl" remakes herself as a "near-criminal mastermind," with pranks that upend her school's oppressive power structure (created by and for boys).

2007

GLASS SLIPPER, GOLD SANDAL: A Worldwide Cinderella. *By Paul Fleischman. Illustrated by Julie Paschkis.* $16.95. (Ages 5 and up) Multicultural versions of Cinderella aren't new, but Fleischman's text, woven together from some of the 1,000 sources of the Cinderella story, has to be one of the most artful.

HARRY POTTER AND THE DEATHLY HALLOWS. *By J. K. Rowling. Illustrated by Mary GrandPré.* $34.99. The last of the best-selling 10-year series exceptional for its appeal to fans from 7 to 70. In this final volume, Harry faces his last battle with Voldemort and solves the mystery behind his enigmatic elders.

EXTRAS. *By Scott Westerfeld.* $16.99. (Ages 12 and up) The finale to Westerfeld's thought-provoking Uglies series, set in a postindustrial dystopia, continues its dissection of a culture transfixed by beauty and celebrity.

THE ABSOLUTELY TRUE DIARY OF A PART-TIME INDIAN. *By Sherman Alexie. Illustrated by Ellen Forney.* $16.99.(Ages 12 and up) This young adult novel overflows with truth, pain and black comedy amid lacerating memories of life on the reservation.

HOW TO BE A BABY ... BY ME, THE BIG SISTER. *By Sally Lloyd-Jones. Illustrated by Sue Heap.* $15.99. (Ages 4 to 8) An ultracharming picture book presented as a kind of comic how-to manual to a baby brother, full of love, self-importance and well-meaning scorn.

THE ARRIVAL. *By Shaun Tan.* $19.99. (Ages 10 and up) This graphic novel portraying a stranger's arrival in a strange land draws on landscapes from Australia to America and dreamlike imagery.

2006

THE END. A Series of Unfortunate Events: Book the Thirteenth. *By Lemony Snicket. Illustrated by Brett Helquist.* $12.99. (Ages 10 and up) A chronicle of unending misfortune comes to an end, as three unlucky but resourceful orphans appear to escape their enemies.

OWEN & MZEE: The True Story of a Remarkable Friendship. *By Isabella Hatkoff, Craig Hatkoff and Dr. Paula Kahumbu. Photographs by Peter Greste.* $16.99. (Ages 4 to 8) It sounds like a folk tale, but the story of the abandoned baby hippo who found unexpected companionship with a 130-year-old giant male tortoise is all true. Should prove irresistible to animal lovers.

THE MIRACULOUS JOURNEY OF EDWARD TULANE. *By Kate DiCamillo. Illustrated by Bagram Ibatoulline.* $18.99. (Ages 7 and up) A vain china rabbit takes a perilous journey when he is separated from his owner. Edward Tulane's unsettling journey is matched by the haunting illustrations.

GOOD BOY, FERGUS! *Written and illustrated by David Shannon.* $15.99. (Ages 3 to 6) The author's own West Highland terrier inspired the delightful vignettes that firmly contradict the title of this book.

RASH. *By Pete Hautman.* $15.95. (Ages 12 and up) With inventiveness and wit, Hautman imagines life for a 16-year-old who doesn't fit in to an un-brave new world of the late 21st century and has to find his own way out.

JOHN, PAUL, GEORGE & BEN. *Written and illustrated by Lane Smith.* $16.99. (Ages 5 and up) Refreshingly different and

gorgeously designed introduction to ye olde founding fathers: John Hancock, Paul Revere, George Washington and Ben Franklin.

THE POX PARTY: The Astonishing Life Of Octavian Nothing, Traitor to the Nation. Volume I. *By M. T. Anderson.* $17.99. (Ages 14 and up) A brilliant satire set in 1760s Boston about an African-American boy who gradually learns he is both a slave and subject of an experiment.

2005

ENCYCLOPEDIA PREHISTORICA: DINOSAURS. *Written and illustrated by Robert Sabuda and Matthew Reinhart.* $26.99. (Ages 5 and up) Brilliantly designed and executed pop-ups.

HARRY POTTER AND THE HALF-BLOOD PRINCE. *By J. K. Rowling. Illustrated by Mary GrandPré.* $29.99. (Ages 8 and up) This installment, though darker, has humor, romance and snappy dialogue.

TERRIFIC. *Written and illustrated by Jon Agee.* $15.95. (All ages) Eugene Mudge mutters a sarcastic "Terrific" to everything that befalls him, from winning a free ocean cruise to meeting a talking parrot.

TRACTION MAN IS HERE! *Written and illustrated by Mini Grey.* $15.95. (Ages 4 to 8) The best toys have powerful secret lives,

EDUCATION

and Traction Man, described as a "generic action figure with dazzle-painted battle pants" on the box he arrives in, is a fine example.

THE OLD COUNTRY. *By Mordicai Gerstein.* $14.95. (Ages 10 and up) The story of a girl who saves her family by becoming the thieving fox she sets out to kill. A reminder that tales of wonder are sometimes history, too.

THE GAME OF SILENCE. *By Louise Erdrich. Illustrated by the author.* $15.99. (Ages 8 to 12) The sequel to *The Birchbark House* picks up the story of Omakayas, a girl growing up in a small Ojibwa community in Minnesota in the mid-19th century.

FLUSH. *By Carl Hiaasen.* $16.95. (Ages 10 and up) The plot involves real threats to Florida's ecosystem, slapstick villains and a boy hiding in the ladies' room.

THE BABY ON THE WAY. *By Karen English. Illustrated by Sean Qualls.* $16. (Ages 3 to 6) In this exquisitely illustrated and beautifully written story, Jamal wonders if his grandmother was ever a baby.

THE LIGHTNING THIEF. *By Rick Riordan.* $17.95. (Ages 12 and up) Percy Jackson's senses are better than a mortal's because he is part Greek god. Not bad for a boy who was told he had A.D.H.D.

2004

DREAM OF FREEDOM: The Civil Rights Movement From 1954 to 1968. *By Diane McWhorter.* $19.95. (Ages 12 and up) A young people's history of "America's second Civil War."

THE PEOPLE COULD FLY: The Picture Book. *By Virginia Hamilton. Illustrated by Leo Dillon and Diane Dillon.* $16.95. (Ages 4 and up) The old story of a magical African people who escape plantation hardships by flying away, now beautifully illustrated.

MISS BRIDIE CHOSE A SHOVEL. *By Leslie Connor. Illustrated by Mary Azarian.* $16. (Ages 4 to 8) Miss Bridie travels on a boat to New York, finds a job, rents a room, starts a garden, meets a man, marries him and buys a farm . . . for starters.

CHASING VERMEER. *By Blue Balliett. Illustrated by Brett Helquist.* $16.95. (Ages 10 and up) A first novel about a stolen Vermeer painting set at the Uni-

versity of Chicago's Laboratory Schools.

POLAR BEAR NIGHT. *By Lauren Thompson. Illustrated by Stephen Savage.* $15.95. (Ages 3 to 5) A comforting bedtime story to teach children that darkness can be a friend.

MADAM PRESIDENT. *By Catherine Thimmesh. Illustrated by Douglas B. Jones.* $17. (Ages 10 and up) The story of a pigtailed girl who wants to be president introduces first ladies, suffragists, congresswomen and foreign leaders.

KITTEN'S FIRST FULL MOON. *Written and illustrated by Kevin Henkes.* $15.99. (Ages 2 to 5) A large-format book about the moon, which doubles as a bowl of milk, and Kitten.

THE BARTIMAEUS TRILOGY, BOOK TWO: The Golem's Eye. *By Jonathan Stroud.* $17.95. (Ages 10 and up) The top of the class of the currently popular fantasy series, set in a London governed by magicians.

A CHILD'S CHRISTMAS IN WALES. *By Dylan Thomas. Illustrated by Chris Raschka.* $17.99. (All ages) An artist-musician offers a contemporary take on a Christmas classic.

College & Beyond

The ACT vs. the SAT

Which test will help you put your best foot forward?

A generation ago, taking a standardized test was a no-brainer: it was mainly a matter of geography. In the Midwest, students took the ACT. If you lived on the coasts, or were applying to a highly selective college or university there, you took the SAT.

Now, with some Ivy League schools rejecting 9 of 10 qualified candidates, applicants are looking for any edge to improve their chances. Many, particularly those in traditional SAT territory, are taking both tests and submitting the higher score or both scores. In recent years, the number of ACT takers on the East Coast has risen 66 percent, and on the West Coast 46 percent, according to ACT Inc.

But not everybody has the time or money to prepare for both tests. And the truth is, most probably don't need to. While the tests have distinct personalities—the ACT is curriculum-based, while the SAT is aimed more at general reasoning and problem-solving skills—spokesmen for both say their formats favor only one type of student: the one with a good grasp of material taught in rigorous high school courses.

While many colleges swear they don't prefer one over the other, some college counselors believe otherwise. In the absence of quantitative studies, they suggest asking yourself a few questions.

> ❝
> **More than 800 colleges do not require applicants to submit ACT or SAT scores, according to FairTest.org.**
>
> • • •

Which format feels right?

You can take predictive tests (the PSAT and PLAN) sophomore year and extrapolate scores you're likely to get on the SAT and ACT. The practice tests cover much the same material as their respective cousins, which they imitate in style and content.

Experts recommend that if your school gives both, take both. If not, test prep companies offer free full-length practice tests for the ACT and SAT online (at Princetonreview.com, Petersons.com and Ivybound.net).

Take each test in as realistic conditions as possible, with no distractions. Time yourself. Your score is a benchmark, but also think about how you felt while taking each test. Did you understand the format? Did one experience cause you more stress than the other?

How long can you sit without fidgeting?

If you have a short attention span and difficulty maintaining focus, the ACT may be better for you. The ACT lasts 2 hours, 55 minutes (plus 30 minutes with the optional writing test). The SAT lasts 3 hours, 45 minutes.

Similarly, counselors say that students with learning disabilities that make it difficult to process information may do better on the ACT. That may be because the ACT questions are more knowledge-based and straightforward, while the SAT is more nuanced and trickier.

Both cover English and math, but there are

EDUCATION

notable variations in content. For instance, in measuring verbal skills, the SAT focuses on vocabulary whereas the ACT concentrates on grammar, punctuation and syntax. And if you want to avoid science and trigonometry, stick with the SAT, which has neither.

Overachiever or underachiever?

College counselors say they see two groups of students, with distinctly different approaches to learning, who may score markedly higher on one test or the other. Bright underachievers who are bored and get through school using one quarter of their brains may do better on the SAT, because it requires good reasoning skills.

Overachievers, those who get the highest grades in the toughest classes because they work really hard, may do better on the ACT. A cluster in the middle—the average to above-average subgroup who work hard but are not intellectually flashy—may also do better on the ACT, which is more like a school test than the SAT.

But differences in scores, counselors say, are not significant for students at either end of the test-taking spectrum.

Girl or boy?

The observation has been made that boys surpass girls on standardized tests. But the ACT gender gap has narrowed. Recent data shows that boys scored 21.2 on average, with girls just behind at 21 (the equivalent of 1500 on the SAT, according to the Princeton Review formula).

But boys as a group do better on the SAT, according to data published by both testing companies: 1037, compared with 1001 for girls. That doesn't mean that every boy should take the SAT and every girl the

Apples to Apples

Below, Princeton Review estimates of SAT-ACT score equivalents, based on data from freshmen enrolled in 2006-7.

ACT	SAT
36	2400
35	2340
34	2260
33	2190
32	2130
31	2040
30	1980
29	1920
28	1860
27	1820
26	1760
25	1700
24	1650
23	1590
22	1530
21	1500
20	1410
19	1350
18	1290
17	1210
16	1140
15	1060
14	1000
13	900
12	780
11	750

The Mix

Below, percentage of 2006-7 freshmen submitting each score.

CORNELL
ACT 20%
SAT 98%

HARVARD
ACT 18%
SAT 99%

POMONA
ACT 29%
SAT 94%

STANFORD
ACT 25%
SAT 96%

ACT. But, says John Katzman, chief executive of the Princeton Review, "Girls tend to fit pretty well into the group of high achievers, who get good grades and do well in school, who also do well on the ACT."

The test makers' statistics also indicate that members of minority groups score better across the board on the SAT than on the ACT. But that can be explained: top students in all ethnic groups tend to take the SAT, while some Midwestern states require all juniors to take the ACT, thus lowering the mean.

Which do you think you'll do better on?

You'll probably live up to those expectations, especially if you are a girl or a member of a minority group. The reason is a phenomenon called "stereotype threat," identified more than a decade ago by behavioral scientists Claude M. Steele and Joshua Aronson after they discovered that individual test scores changed with the test taker's sense of confidence.

"Women and minorities feel stereotypes in our society, that they don't have the same innate academic abilities as men and Caucasians," says Steele, director of the Center for Advanced Study in the Behavioral Sciences at Stanford University. "So if they are taking a test that they have been told is difficult and then they experience frustration in the middle of it, that makes the stereotype relevant to them and they perform dramatically worse." But, he says, if you believe you will do well on a particular test, your performance is less likely to be impaired by difficult problems.

—Michelle Slatalla

Does Prepping for the SAT Help?

Possibly, but much depends on a student's effort

Armed with sharpened number-two pencils, nearly 1.5 million students each year take the College Board's SAT, a lengthy multihour assessment, revised in 2005 to produce critical reading, math and writing subscores. As many as 10 percent will have bolstered their test-taking skills with short-term coaching courses. And at least half will have spent hours poring over study manuals or clicking their way through test preparation software programs.

Should every student facing the SAT do some prepping? If so, is a course a better route to honing SAT skills than a guidebook or a software program? Many students require little or no SAT preparation, according to officials at the National Center for Fair & Open Testing (FairTest) in Cambridge, Mass. Others who do not test well should consider taking the other national college admissions test, the ACT, or applying to the more than 800 bachelor-degree granting schools that do not require test scores before making admissions decisions (lists at www.fairtest.org/optinit.htm).

A student's first step toward gauging how much help may be needed is to take an SAT practice test, available for free from the school guidance office or from the test-maker online at www.collegeboard. com. If your score is within the average range at the schools you would like to attend, experts advise passing up any prep tools. But if your scores are well below par, it's time to explore alternatives.

The range of SAT help tools includes software programs, guidebooks, classroom courses and private tutors. Students who are comfortable on the computer would do well to invest in a software or online program designed for SAT

The Truth About College Rankings

Are they useful or useless?

Ever since *U.S. News & World Report* started its extensive rankings of colleges—and subsequently graduate schools and hospitals—in the late 1980s, the lists have been the source of endless discussion and controversy. The rankings are partially available online for free at www. usnews.com. You can also buy the latest annual data on the site.

To compile its ratings, *U.S. News* groups thousands of colleges, universities and graduate schools into categories of size, geographic location and educational orientation. It then surveys thousands of college presidents, deans and admissions directors around the country for their assessment of the quality of peer institutions and combines that reputational data with objective information about an institution's selectivity in admissions, faculty resources, graduation rates and alumni satisfaction, among other factors, to rank schools in the different categories.

Users of the list should keep a few caveats in mind. No ranking system can produce a totally accurate measure of a school's quality, and a college that is appropriate for one student may be a poor match for another, despite the school's ranking.

So how useful are the lists? That depends. They make accessible lots of data that are unavailable collectively. A student lucky enough to be admitted to Harvard, Princeton, Yale and MIT—perennially the top-ranked national universities—might well make a decision based on a subtle parsing of all the data and factors presented.

Are the rankings deceptive or misleading? It's hard to argue that miniscule differences can make one school No.1 and another No.2. But the purpose of the rankings goes beyond which school is first or second. The goal is also to provide useful information for potential college students, and, by that measure, the rankings do succeed.

EDUCATION

preparation. The self-motivated can probably benefit from using one of the hundreds of SAT guides available in bookstores. Students requiring a more disciplined approach may want to try after-school courses or personalized tutoring.

When it comes to test prep books, some of the best-known publishers are Kaplan, the Princeton Review and the College Board itself. All their guides are hefty and sell for between $20 and $30. The best way to find one that's right for you is to browse through a few at a library or bookstore. As you do, keep in mind the following questions: Does the book include practice tests that mimic the SAT's format and length? Does it offer explanations or simply provide answers to questions? And does it explain the exam's structure and offer test-taking strategies?

For students searching for a solid SAT preparation course, the leaders in the field are also Kaplan (800-KAP-TEST; www.kaplan.com) and the Princeton Review (800-2-REVIEW; www.review.com). Classroom programs typically run six weeks and cost around $1,000. Both companies offer financial aid to some needy students.

Many good and less expensive local programs can be found, but because the quality of instruction varies, experts advise researching them carefully. Prep sessions with private tutors are vastly more expensive, ranging from around $100 an hour to more than $600 an hour (for the top tutors in New York City).

Does prepping pay off in the end? The answer is mixed. Prep tutors say it could raise a student's combined SAT scores by an average 150 points on the three-part exam. But a recent study by the National Association for College Admission Counseling disputes that claim. The study found that coaching yields relatively small average gains of about 30 points overall. Of course, how well the preparation works depends on a student's effort.

Whether you prepare or not is your choice, but at the very least, it is wise to read the SAT registration booklet carefully—it contains vital instructions for the exam along with sample items and test-taking hints. Anyone who waits to read the directions during the test is wasting time.

How Important Are A.P. Courses?
Most colleges count them in your favor

The Advanced Placement program, administered by the College Board, began more than 50 years ago as a way to give a select few high school students a jump-start on college work. But in recent decades, it has morphed into a mass program that reaches more than a million students each year and is used almost as much to impress college admissions officers and raise a school's reputation as to get college credit.

As the admissions race has hit warp speed, Advanced Placement has taken on new importance. More than 60 percent of American high schools participate in the program, which offers courses in 37 subjects, from macroeconomics to music theory. The number of students taking A.P. courses has increased tenfold since the early 1980s; students took more than 2 million A.P. exams in 2008.

Some students use the A.P. program tactically, knowing that their senior-year A.P. course listings will appear on their transcripts, and be counted in admissions decisions, long before they take the A.P. exam in May, if they ever do. (Students can also take the exams, which run 3 hours, without taking the courses.)

Part of the pressure to take A.P. classes also springs from the fact that most schools weigh A.P. grades more heavily than others—an A in A.P. is often worth five points, while a regular A is worth four—so savvy students know that A.P.

courses can raise their G.P.A.'s, one of the most important elements in college admissions.

So, how important are A.P. courses in college admissions? That depends. Certainly, most schools count them in an applicant's favor. Some admissions officers tally the number of foreign language, math and science courses an applicant has taken, along with the number of A.P. or other advanced courses. Other admissions officers look at the grade-point average and SAT scores, circle the number of A.P. and honors courses, consider what coursework was available at the high school and make a nonnumeric judgment.

At the most elite colleges, admissions officers say they want students who have taken the most rigorous program their school offers. While they acknowledge that taking the most difficult A.P. courses, like Calculus BC, indicates a strong academic background, they take pains to say that there is no magic, no numeric formula—and no penalty for students from schools that do not have an A.P. program.   —Tamar Lewin

Getting Credits Before You Go

How to take half your college courses while you are still in high school

Earning college credit in high school is becoming increasingly popular, with half of all juniors and seniors taking a college-level course, according to Jobs for the Future, a nonprofit organization that promotes school reform. Some students do it to distinguish themselves at college admissions time; others to opt out of introductory freshman classes, allowing them to save on tuition by compressing the time spent in college or to dive quickly and more deeply into an intended major; still others simply seek a more challenging curriculum.

The granddaddy of programs, of course, is Advanced Placement (see previous story), which offers 37 college-level courses taken, on average, by one in four students. But there are other ways to earn credit before getting to campus, meant not

---

 **TIMELY TIPS**

How to Save on College Tours

Students apply to so many colleges these days that some families visit a dozen or more campuses, many of them far afield geographically (read: airfare). All those hotels, rental cars, trains, cabs, meals and gas can add up. Here are some money-saving suggestions from college-tour veterans.

✔ **Schedule information sessions in the morning and early afternoon.** Most schools give at least one and sometimes more lunch passes to the dining hall—a good way to sample food choices and get a free lunch.

✔ **Travel with a cooler** of sandwiches, snacks and drinks and stay in discount hotel chains with microwaves in the room.

✔ **Put off tours until the end of junior year,** when you know which college is appropriate. Advanced Placement classes can lower a grade point average, or SAT scores may be substantially higher than expected.

✔ **Make contact from home.** Admissions officers try to be sensitive to students' economic circumstances, and applicants can signal their interest in a school by communicating by e-mail or telephone and meeting with admissions staff who visit high schools.

✔ **Take a reality check:** More than 50 percent of freshman attend college within 100 miles of home, more than 85 percent within 500 miles, according to a survey by the Higher Education Research Institute. It only takes a tank or less of gas to visit a range of colleges in your own backyard. And, you don't even have to stay overnight. —Tanya Mohn

only for the high achiever but also for those not traditionally tagged for college.

International Baccalaureate. Taken over the last 2 years of high school, the I.B. curriculum (www.ibo.org) is intended to provide a classic education and mimics the intensity of the final year of secondary school in much of Europe. Students may take individual I.B. courses, which are more challenging than traditional high school courses, or work toward an I.B. diploma with a package of six courses a year in literature, foreign language, social science, experimental science, math and arts. Many colleges and universities award credit or preferential admissions treatment to students in the program.

Nearly 700 secondary schools in the United States, 90 percent of them public, offer the diploma. I.B. administrators stress that the program is for motivated rather than gifted students, but each school sets its own standards for enrollment, be they academic cutoff, lottery or student interest.

Concurrent enrollment. High school students take a partner college's courses, taught by approved high school teachers, in the comfort of their own classrooms. Students pay reduced tuition or an administrative fee. Generally, courses count toward grade-point average but don't fulfill a graduation requirement. One major drawback: while many colleges accept credits for these courses, the most selective ones do not.

Concurrent enrollment, for example, is not to be confused with programs in which students travel to a campus or college faculty members travel to the high school. Such high school–college partnerships are offered in nearly every state, with more than one million students taking part. Such programs give students who would not otherwise consider college a taste of postsecondary education; they also lower costs by reducing the time spent in college.

Early college high schools. In a relatively new initiative, Jobs for the Future (www.earlycolleges.org or www.jff.org) has partnered with universities and other organizations to establish small schools where students earn both a high school degree and 2 years of college credit, either an associate's degree or enough credits to enter a 4-year college as a junior.

The initiative's hope is to help students who might not otherwise complete—or begin—college, such as "first-generation, low-income, English-language learners, and students of color," according to its Web site. There are now 200 early college high schools in 25 states. The first, Bard High School Early College in New York City, is a success story of a different nature: with its stringent entrance requirements, it is one of the city's more selective public schools.

—Cecilia Capuzzi Simon

How Colleges Decide
Who gets in—and who doesn't?

On what basis do admissions committees anoint the chosen? The question has preoccupied generations of applicants. There is no magic formula, admissions officers say. Nonetheless, the College Board's survey of colleges and universities asks them to rank admissions criteria. No surprise: high school academic record is consistently rated "very important," as are standardized test scores (Harvard contends they're only "important").

But what about all that other stuff? Institutions listed here admit the country's best students: 25 percent of incoming freshman typically score 700 or more on the math or verbal SATs and place in the top 10 percent of their high school graduating classes. But academics alone won't get you in.

The charts, facing, show what else matters.

RELATIVE IMPORTANCE OF THESE FACTORS IN ADMISSIONS DECISIONS:

KEY

1 Very important
2 Important
3 Considered
4 Not considered

College	Interview	Extracurriculars	Recommendations	Essay	Talent / Ability	Alumni Relations	Minority Status
Amherst (Mass.)	4	1	1	1	1	2	3
Bard (N.Y.)	3	1	1	1	1	3	3
Barnard (N.Y.)	3	2	1	1	2	3	3
Bates (Me.)	1	1	1	1	1	3	3
Beloit (Wis.)	2	3	1	1	3	3	4
Bethel (Kan.)	3	4	3	3	3	3	4
Boston College (Mass.)	4	2	2	2	2	2	3
Boston U. (Mass.)	4	3	2	2	1	3	4
Bowdoin (Me.)	3	1	1	1	1	2	2
Brandeis (Mass.)	3	2	2	2	2	3	3
Brown (R.I.)	3	2	2	2	1	3	3
Bryn Mawr (Pa.)	3	2	1	1	3	4	4
Bucknell (Pa.)	3	2	1	3	1	3	2
Calif. Inst. of Tech.	4	3	1	1	3	4	3
Carleton, (Minn.)	3	2	2	2	2	3	2
Carnegie Mellon (Pa.)	3	2	2	3	2	2	3
Case Western (Pa.)	2	1	2	2	1	2	2
Claremont McKenna (Calif.)	2	2	2	2	4	3	3
Colby (Me.)	2	2	2	2	2	3	2
Colgate (N.Y.)	4	2	1	2	2	3	3
Columbia (N.Y.)	3	2	1	1	2	3	3
Connecticut College	3	1	1	1	2	2	1
Cooper Union (N.Y.)	4	3	3	3	1	4	3
Cornell (N.Y.)	3	1	1	1	1	3	3
Dartmouth (N.H.)	3	1	1	1	2	3	3
Davidson (N.C.)	4	2	1	2	2	4	3
Duke (N.C.)	3	1	1	1	1	3	3
Emory (Ga.)	4	1	1	1	2	2	3
Franklin W. Olin Col. of Engineering (Mass.)	2	1	1	1	1	4	3
Georgetown (D.C.)	2	2	1	1	1	3	3
Georgia Tech.	4	2	4	2	2	4	4
Grinnell (Iowa)	2	1	1	1	1	3	2
Hamilton (N.Y.)	2	2	1	2	3	3	2
Hampshire (Mass.)	3	2	1	1	2	3	3
Harvard (Mass.)	2	1	2	1	1	3	3
Harvey Mudd (Calif.)	2	2	1	1	2	2	2
Haverford (Pa.)	3	2	1	2	3	3	3
Hendrix (Ark.)	2	2	2	1	3	4	3
Hillsdale (Mich.)	2	2	2	2	3	3	4
Illinois Inst. of Tech.	3	3	2	2	4	3	4
Johns Hopkins (Md.)	3	2	1	1	2	3	3
Kalamazoo (Mich.)	3	1	2	2	1	3	3
Kenyon (Ohio)	2	2	1	1	2	3	3
Knox (Ill.)	3	3	2	2	3	3	3
Lehigh (Pa.)	4	2	1	2	2	3	3
Macalester (Minn.)	3	2	2	2	3	3	3
M.I.T. (Mass.)	2	2	2	3	2	3	3
Middlebury (Vt.)	4	1	2	2	1	3	2
Mt. Holyoke College (Mass.)	2	2	1	1	2	3	3
New College of Florida	3	3	2	1	3	3	4
N.M. Inst. Of Mining &Tech.	3	3	4	4	3	4	4
N.Y.U.	4	2	2	2	2	3	3
Northwestern (Ill.)	3	2	2	1	2	3	3
Notre Dame (Ind.)	4	1	1	1	1	3	3
Oberlin (Ohio)	3	2	2	2	2	1	3
Pomona (Calif.)	1	1	1	1	1	3	3
Princeton (N.J.)	3	1	1	1	1	3	3
Reed (Ore.)	2	3	2	1	3	3	3
Rensselaer Poly (N.Y.)	4	2	3	3	3	3	3
Rice (Texas)	3	1	1	1	1	3	3
Rose-Hulman Inst. of Tech. (Ind.)	3	3	2	4	3	3	2
Sarah Lawrence (N.Y.)	3	2	1	1	2	3	3
Scripps (Calif.)	1	1	1	1	1	1	1
Smith (Mass.)	2	2	1	2	2	3	3
St. John's College (Md.)	1	3	2	1	3	3	3
St. John's College (N.M.)	1	3	2	1	3	3	3
St. Olaf (Minn.)	3	2	2	1	2	3	3
Stanford (Calif.)	4	2	1	1	2	3	3
Stevens Inst. of Tech. (N.J.)	1	2	1	1	2	3	4
Swarthmore (Pa.)	3	2	1	1	3	3	3
Trinity (Conn.)	2	2	2	2	2	3	2

KEY

1 Very important
2 Important
3 Considered
4 Not considered

Interview, Extracurriculars, Recommendations, Essay, Talent / Ability, Alumni Relations, Minority Status

EDUCATION

RELATIVE IMPORTANCE OF THESE FACTORS IN ADMISSIONS DECISIONS:

KEY

| 1 Very important |
| 2 Important |
| 3 Considered |
| 4 Not considered |

	Interview	Extracurriculars	Recommendations	Essay	Talent / Ability	Alumni Relations	Minority Status
Tufts (Mass.)	3	2	2	2	2	3	3
Thomas Aquinas (Calif.)	3	3	1	1	3	4	4
Tulane (La.)	4	3	2	2	3	3	3
U.S. Air Force Acad. (Col.)	1	1	3	1	1	3	3
U.S. Naval Academy (Md.)	1	1	1	1	2	3	3
U. of Calif., Berkeley	4	2	4	1	2	4	4
U.C.L.A.	4	2	4	1	1	4	4
U. of Calif., San Diego	4	2	4	1	1	4	4
U. of Chicago	3	2	1	1	1	3	3
U. of Illinois, Urbana	3	2	3	1	2	3	3
U. of Md., College Park	4	3	2	2	2	3	3
U. of Mich., Ann Arbor	4	3	2	2	2	3	2
U. of Mo., Kansas City	3	3	3	3	3	4	4
U. of N.C. Chapel Hill	4	1	1	1	1	2	2
U. of Pennsylvania	3	2	1	1	3	3	3
U. of Richmond	4	3	3	2	2	3	3
U. of Rochester	1	3	2	2	2	3	2
U. of Southern Calif.	3	2	1	1	2	3	3
U. of Virginia	4	2	1	2	2	1	3
U. of Wisconsin	3	3	2	3	2	3	3
Vanderbilt (Tenn.)	4	1	1	1	1	3	3
Vassar (N.Y.)	4	3	2	2	3	3	3
Wake Forest (N.C.)	4	2	2	2	2	2	2
Washington & Lee (Va.)	4	1	2	3	3	3	3
Washington U. St Louis	3	1	1	1	1	3	3
Webb Inst. (N.Y.)	1	3	2	4	3	4	3
Wellesley (Mass.)	3	2	1	1	3	3	3
Wesleyan (Conn.)	3	2	2	2	2	2	2
Wheaton (Ill.)	3	3	1	1	2	2	2
Whitman (Wash.)	3	2	2	1	2	3	2
William & Mary (Va.)	4	3	3	2	3	3	3
William Jewell (Mo.)	2	2	2	2	2	3	3
Williams (Mass.)	4	2	1	1	3	3	3
Worcester Poly (Mass.)	3	3	1	2	3	3	3
Yale (Conn.)	3	1	1	1	1	3	3

SOURCE: College Board (based on 2004 data; updated study due in late 2009 from the College Board)

How To Pick an Art School

Should serious artists choose an art academy or a university?

For any college-bound student, many factors weigh in the decision of which school to select—cost, distance from home, courses. But art students have an additional criterion: should they enroll in an art academy or university? In some ways, the experience is identical. Students at both take a mix of studio and academic courses from professional artists and scholars. But subtle and not-so-subtle differences can be found.

Art schools are for the artsy only. Art schools tend to be small, with fewer than 1,000 students and a student-faculty ratio of nine to one. On the other hand, art departments of many universities are larger than entire art schools and can still be the smallest department on campus.

Syracuse University, for example, has 12,000 undergraduates, with around 1,100 in its School of Art and Design. Its studio classes have up to 18 students. And all those liberal arts and science majors—students who are just fulfilling a distribution requirement—can slow down a class.

But there's an upside to a large student population. Heterogeneity can expand a studio artist's thinking, and it is the mix of people and ideas that make up what we think of as the university experience. Students with broader interests may find the environment of an academy limiting.

Everyone is a star—in high school. Only about half of the freshmen entering an art academy finish within 6 years, according to surveys by the art college association. There are many reasons students drop out or transfer from any program, but art tends to attract students who are not sure what they want to study.

At a university, students can switch majors,

Preparing Your Portfolio

Tips on what to include—and what to exclude

Admissions to visual arts programs are based heavily on a student's portfolio of work. That's true whether the interest is fine arts, fashion, interior or graphic design, architecture or illustration.

Yet few students have any idea what their portfolio should contain. Here's some practical advice:

Less animé, more range. An acceptable portfolio generally contains 15 to 20 drawings, paintings, collages, small three-dimensional works or photographs of these (digital images on CDs are increasingly being submitted, too). The idea is to present a selection of drawings and other media, like watercolor, oil and pastels that show the depth and range of your talents.

One portfolio might fit all fields. Most students enter a Bachelor of Fine Arts program with limited exposure to fields like architecture, graphic design and interior design. And they usually don't make career choices until sophomore year. So, for some schools, such as the School of the Art Institute of Chicago, the same portfolio applies for graphic design, architecture, and fine art.

To the extent that a portfolio might differ from one institution to another, it's more a matter of adapting it to a teaching philosophy than to a field of interest. At the Pennsylvania Academy of the Fine Arts, drawings that reveal good technical skills are favored over abstraction or art installations. The School of the Art Institute of Chicago, on the other hand, puts greater emphasis on concepts and theory.

A few places, such as the San Francisco Art Institute, want specialized portfolios. It asks design and technology majors to provide digital work along with observational drawings and samples in other mediums.

Students at the Fashion Institute of Technology in New York declare their majors when they apply, and portfolio requirements vary by area of study. For fashion design, for example, portfolios must include 6 to 10 fashion sketches (plus an at-home project given to all applicants).

Polishing your portfolio. The National Portfolio Day Association, a nonprofit organization of more than 100 degree-granting institutions, runs roughly 35 one-day events at campuses around the country from September through January; anywhere from 15 to 50 institutions participate at any given location. The most important business of the day: evaluating portfolios brought in by students.

Admissions officers comment and take notes on each portfolio; the notes become part of an applicant's materials and are factored into the school's decision. No student, however talented, is admitted on the spot, though top-notch candidates may be strongly encouraged.

Take prep classes, for a leg up. Portfolio preparation classes can cost thousands of dollars, and the more professional-looking a portfolio, the more likely the student is to receive a scholarship.

Unlike an SAT class, which strives not to teach literature or math but to make students better test-takers, a portfolio prep class is much like a real art class, with a specific product in mind. Classes are usually offered via continuing education departments.

—Daniel Grant

while unhappy students at an art school must apply all over again somewhere else. A student on the fence about the future may find that a university means fewer complications if things don't work out.

Making art will be a job. In decades past, institutions like the Yale University School of Art had a reputation for giving their M.F.A. graduates a head start because of faculty members' gallery contacts. But the field has leveled out consider-

Waltzing into a Dance Program

Choreographer Mark Morris believes dancers should be practicing, not studying

Mark Morris possesses a handful of honorary doctorates. But the acclaimed dancer, choreographer and director did not spend a day in college, rather training for a dance career in what he calls "L'École of Hard Knocks." This consisted of heading to Europe after high school to practice folk dancing in Macedonia, and Spanish dancing in Madrid, while cooking chickens and hanging out at weddings.

No surprise, then, that he dismisses what is almost de rigueur for modern dancers: a college-level education. "Most of it in my opinion is just a big bag of wind," says Morris, founder of the Mark Morris Dance Group. Conservatory training fares little better in his view. "I mostly think it ruins people," he says.

Nevertheless, college-level dance programs are proliferating. *Dance Magazine*'s 2009 College Guide lists more than 600 such programs, up from 131 in 1966. But stable, paying jobs in the field are hard to find. And the utility of a college degree in dancing is a matter of endless debate.

Not going to college at all gives young dancers a head start on what in many cases is a short career, and it remains the norm for professional ballet dancers. Modern dance is physically more permissive, but still mainly a young person's pursuit.

Much of the training of modern dancers still takes place in independent dance studios, not colleges, universities or conservatories. Indeed, conservatories like the Juilliard School and the dance program at New York University's Tisch School of the Arts admit students only by audition, which means most people have some kind of training before they even apply.

Those who rise through the ranks outside academia may be at a disadvantage when it comes to finding teaching jobs after they retire from the stage. "In this climate, if you want to teach, you have to have a master's," says Maile Okamura, who joined the Morris company after a career in ballet, and is one of Morris's few dancers who lack a college degree.

The dance department at Juilliard, which admits only the very best, estimates that in the last few years some 60 to 70 percent of students have found work as dancers after graduating. Tisch does not maintain graduate employment statistics, but a spokesperson in the dance department does acknowledge the awkwardness of preprofessional training for a profession with few paid jobs. Nonetheless, around 500 applicants typically apply each year to the Tisch dance program, which has around 30 slots.

Ultimately, Morris says he does not care what kind of degrees, if any, his dancers have; he cares only that they can dance. His advice to aspiring dancers: "Dance," he says. "Read. Learn music. Look around. Participate in the world."

—Erika Kinetz

ably. Successful artists have emerged from large and small art academies as well as university art programs. Institutions of each type make a point of highlighting the exhibition records of their faculty, and they bring in visiting artists with ties to the contemporary art scene to bolster networking opportunities.

Some universities like the University of Texas, Austin, and the University of Illinois, Urbana, have career offices for the fine arts, but most university career offices focus on general résumé writing and interviewing. The likelihood that a staff member has specific help to offer a B.F.A. student is remote.

The career services office of an art school, however, is tailored more to helping the artist. It may offer courses on topics like finding representation at an art gallery and preparing a portfolio. The School of Visual Arts in Manhattan invites recruiters from design firms to review students' portfolios. The career center at the Moore College of Art and Design in Philadelphia holds seminars on how to price work and install it.

You'll still be writing term papers. The artist Jackson Pollock followed the traditional European model of training: learning how to think about painting and how to paint. Some students think they will never have to read a textbook again.

But to earn a baccalaureate, art students take a third to half their classes in academic subjects. The whole idea of the B.F.A. is to combine professional training and a liberal education.

At universities, applicants are first accepted into the institution and then the art department, meaning academics matter more than artistic ability. At art academies, admissions officials and art faculty look over applications together, and some don't even require SATs. But there is a move to focus more on academic history.

"Students who have done well in high school, even if they haven't had as much art training as other students, are more likely to do well here than students who haven't demonstrated high achievement in high school," says Judith Aaron, dean of admissions at the Pratt Institute in Brooklyn. The typical Pratt student, she adds, had a high school grade-point average of at least 3.2.

But providing a variety of liberal arts courses is a challenge, even at large schools like the Rhode Island School of Design, which has a full academic faculty. Some academies have tried to solve the problem by establishing a relationship with an institution nearby. Beginning in their sophomore year, students at the Rhode Island School of Design may cross-register at Brown. Students

at the Pennsylvania Academy of Fine Arts can take classes toward a B.F.A. at the University of Pennsylvania's continuing-education arm; and those at the School of the Museum of Fine Arts in Boston can earn B.F.A.'s from Tufts.

Other considerations abound: most full-time faculty members at universities have doctorates; at art schools they have master's degrees. Art schools, many of which don't offer tenure, might have trouble attracting strong general education teachers but don't pass off instruction on graduate students. And academic expectations do tend to be lower.

—Daniel Grant,
author of *The Business of Being An Artist.*

How to Save for College
You have 18 years to plan; here's how

Want to pick up the tab at Harvard for a child born today? It will probably cost about half a million dollars come 2027. Still, if you can break the process of saving for college into smaller pieces, it starts to seem more manageable. Start by reminding yourself that almost nobody can save enough to pay for four years of private education, let alone for more than one child. That's not the goal here.

But when planning ahead, some financial advisors suggest, use a "20-20-20" approach. Take the current average cost of attending 4 years at a public university: roughly $60,000. Save $20,000 before your child begins college by putting aside $50 a month starting at birth and assuming a 6 percent annual return. Then pay $20,000 out of current income while the student is in college. Finally, have your child take out $20,000 in federal student loans over 4 years. The $200 monthly payments afterward are not a horrible burden for people in their 20s to bear, and they'll be debt-free once the 10-year payback period is over.

EDUCATION

You can aim higher, or lower, but the longer you wait to start, the more money you'll probably need to borrow later. Better, then, to start at the birth of your first child and follow as many of the steps below as you can.

Newborns and toddlers. For most people, the best way to save for a child's college education is still through a 529 savings plan. With 529s, you deposit after-tax money, but any earnings are free of taxes as long as you spend them on tuition, room, board and other postsecondary educational expenses.

You can look up your state's plan at www.savingforcollege.com, a directory of college saving plans and advice. Most states have their own accounts, and many have two different kinds: investment accounts and prepaid accounts.

Investment accounts are a bit like 401(k)s in that you can usually choose from a handful of mutual funds and other investments, including one that gets less aggressive as your child's date of college matriculation nears. (Just be sure that the fund manager's definition of "aggressive" is similar to yours; some 529 investors have been surprised at the extent of their losses.)

Credit cards can help feed your savings. Some will reward you with refunds into a 529 account based on how much you spend. Card earnings alone can easily add up to five figures after 20 years, depending on how much you put on the plastic annually. A few caveats, though. If you carry a balance or pay bills late, the interest and fees will more than wipe out the rewards.

Credit card companies also often reduce rewards over time. And to maximize earnings, you'll have to give up using your other credit cards to collect frequent-flier miles.

The preschool years. Once the grandparents tire of buying baby gear and cute outfits, you might sit them down for a conversation about how they can make a more lasting cash contribution to your toddler's future. If you're a grandparent and your financial plan for retirement is secure, putting aside just one Social Security check a year for 18 years could pay for a good chunk of a child's college education.

The question, however, is where to park that money during the intervening years. Grandparents can set up their own 529 accounts, which come with a few advantages. If something happens and they need the money, they can take it back out of the 529 and pay taxes and penalties. And if there's a falling out with the kids or the grandkids, they can change the beneficiary and bestow their largesse on a more favored family member.

Keep in mind, too, that a growing number of

DON'T FORGET PERSONAL EXPENSES

Some colleges provide a projection of students' expenses (one place to look is the College Board Web site, www.collegeboard.com). Yale estimates $5,050 a year with books. New York University suggests $1,000 for spending money alone.

Average undergraduate expenses, not including tuition, room and board, 2008-2009

	BOOKS AND SUPPLIES	TRANS-PORTATION	OTHER EXPENSES	TOTAL
4-YEAR PUBLIC				
Resident/out of state:	$1,077	$1,010	$1,906	**$3,993**
Commuter:	$1,077	$1,401	$2,197	**$4,675**
4-YEAR PRIVATE				
Resident:	$1,054	$807	$1,397	**$3,258**
Commuter:	$1,054	$1,241	$1,784	**$4,079**

SOURCE: College Board

colleges are asking whether grandparents or others have set up 529 accounts for a student and taking it into account when awarding their own grants.

Some financial advisors suggest that grandparents simply give money to the parents, who can then deposit it in their own 529. Many accounts will accept gifts from grandparents.

One other big financial decision looms during the preschool years: when (or if) to have another child. Many space their children out when they imagine two future tuitions at the same time. But, if you have two children in college at the same time, your eligibility for financial aid actually grows significantly.

Grades 1 to 9. One decision you'll eventually face is whether to put some (or all) of your savings into a prepaid 529 plan. Not every state offers one, and some states' plans are closed to new investments. The rest, however, let you essentially pay today for tuition and fees in the future.

There are a number of catches here, depending on the state. You can usually participate only in your own state's plan, and it often covers only tuition and fees. (Another plan, called the Independent 529, allows you to pay for member private colleges and universities around the country.)

There are also a number of ways states calculate the current "price." While the idea of locking in a price may sound tempting, it's crucial to understand exactly what $1,000 today will buy you when your child finally goes to college. What sort of discount do you get for prepaying part of the tuition each year? And what happens if you're in a state plan and your child decides to attend an out-of-state university? How much of a return will your money have earned in that case? In the Independent 529 plan, for instance, your money won't have earned more than 2 percent annually (nor can it lose more than 2 percent a year).

> **ⓘ INSIDE INFO**
>
> ## Students in the Red
>
> ○ Two-thirds of college students graduate with some debt.
>
> ○ The average debt for a graduating senior in 2007 was $22,700, according to the College Board.
>
> ○ A newly minted M.D. owed an average $139,517, according to the Association of American Medical Colleges.

By the time middle school draws to a close, you should have a fairly clear sense of your financial picture and whether you might qualify for financial aid. The government's expected family contribution calculator at www.fafsa4caster.ed.gov can help on this front.

Now you have to decide what to tell your child about the money situation and when. By early in high school, colleges are already marketing to potential students, and if there are financial constraints, it's important for the child to understand that.

Freshman year in high school is also a good time to ratchet back investments in stocks, if you've had an aggressive asset allocation in your 529 funds so far. If you're in a target-date mutual fund, with the date of your child's matriculation in its name, check to see what percentage of the fund is in stocks and then reallocate your savings to something safer if you feel the need.

10th and 11th grades. This is the moment to consider whether to hire an adviser who will examine your income and assets to better position your aid application. This can easily cost $1,000 in fees, but it may pay for itself if you receive more grants or qualify for better loans because of it.

Whether you hire an adviser or try to sort out the financial aid applications on your own, remember

EDUCATION

✔ TIMELY TIPS

Priming Your Athlete for College

The straightest line for some is through the locker room

So you think your child has talent? Might even have the fire to play college lacrosse or some other sport? Dave Prossner, a former defenseman for the University of Pennsylvania lacrosse team, a youth coach, certified referee and author of *High School Athlete Recruiting Guide*, a booklet for lacrosse parents, offers tips on how to leverage that ability.

✔ **Be realistic.** As early as middle school, children with ability begin to shine. But have them play other sports both to develop skills and "to keep it fun," says Prossner, who coached two sons to Division I play and two to Division III. One good indicator is being picked for end-of-season or all-star teams. (Parents, beware: politics may play a part in that selection process.) In high school, ask the coach for an honest assessment.

✔ **Attend camps.** Freshman and sophomore years, seek out skills camps run or frequented by coaches from your favored college campuses. Exposure is invaluable, Prossner says, and the competition will raise your athlete's level of play. After junior year, focus on summer recruiting camps scouted by college coaches.

✔ **Make contact.** Sophomore year, compile a list of 20 colleges and send each coach a one-page sports résumé with a personal letter expressing interest in the athletic program. As seasons and academics change, update and resend it. Junior year, edit the list to eight schools and initiate unofficial visits to coaches and admissions officers. A brief video of best plays on the field should be sent only to coaches who express an interest (say, by writing back).

✔ **Encourage academics.** Coaches always ask about grades. Aim for the university that's going to meet your educational needs. A sport may help get you into college, but your brain is going to get you through life.

—Abigail Sullivan Moore

that colleges and universities currently consider the year from January 1 of junior year to December 31 of senior year as the "base" year for figuring out what the family can afford to pay for the first year of college.

That means that if you're going to make any big changes to qualify for more aid, you need to do it between January 1 of sophomore year and December 31 of junior year—and start planning those moves even sooner. What sort of moves might you make? Since financial aid offices will tap some of your assets in calculating what you can afford to pay, there's no shame in spending them down a bit sooner than you might have. If you need a new roof or new car, spend the money before the base year arrives. And pay down credit card debt. A big balance doesn't win you a break when applying for aid, but colleges could tap your cash.

Since colleges generally take more from your income than they do from your assets, the base year or right before is a great time to start your own business (assuming your income will fall for a while in the start-up years). And to lower the income number that the financial system uses, front-load individual retirement account contributions before the base year.

By now you may be wondering about the ethics of all of this money moving. Do not lie on financial aid forms, but aid planning, like tax planning, is perfectly legal and appropriate.

Senior year. Just as students should apply to at least one college where they know they will be accepted and happy, add at least one school your family is

Decoding Financial Aid Offers

Colleges don't make it easy to compare offers. Each one looks different. Often, they use different terms for the same thing. Here are a few sites to help you decode college aid offers.

✔ **FinAid.org** has a calculator (www.finaid.org/calculators/awardletter.phtml) that allows you to compare three schools. It does take time to look up and fill in the information.

✔ **FinancialAidLetter.com** has a glossary of all the terms colleges use in the award letters. The Letter Decoder page includes actual aid offer letters with helpful translations.

✔ **Sallie Mae,** which is in the business of selling loans to students, also has a calculator, www.collegeanswer.com/deciding/award-comparison/ac_index.jsp. It requires registration and can be cumbersome to use.

certain you can afford. If you're going to get need-based aid, then you have to target the colleges that have enough money to give it.

The student also has to fit the college personally before you worry about money. If not, they may drop out, transfer or do poorly, all of which could make college last longer, and therefore cost more.

Then, finally, comes application time, a process you'll repeat at least three more times because you have to refile each year. The Free Application for Federal Student Aid and other forms you may encounter are intimidating. Fill them out anyway, even if you don't think you'll win grants from your chosen college, because you never know where you might end up or how your financial circumstances may change. If grandparents wish to step in at this late stage, be aware that giving money

to parents or making tuition payments directly to the college can have a big impact on aid eligibility. Consider paying off the child's loans (or the parents') after college graduation.

A final word about financial aid officers. They can and will do what they want to sweeten packages for more desirable students. While many a parent tries to play one offer off another, the decisions of the financial aid officer are final and cannot be appealed to the government.

All the more reason, then, to start early.

—Ron Lieber

Shopping for College Loans

Exhaust government loan options first

The best way to finance college is clear: a federally guaranteed loan. Stafford and Perkins loans go directly to students, and PLUS loans are for parents or graduate students. Students can take out such loans from banks, other private lenders or state agencies. The federal government guarantees the lender against default and caps the interest rate, although lenders can offer a lower rate. At some colleges, students may also borrow directly from the government.

But federal loans have a yearly and lifetime cap; for example, undergraduates with parental assistance have a lifetime maximum of $23,000 in Stafford loans. And so students and their families increasingly turn to private loans, which are also offered by banks, other private lenders or state agencies. Yet not only do private loans tend to have less favorable terms, but they can be the hardest to shop for. Like car loans, rates turn on individual credit history, and are not capped, so to learn how much a loan will cost, a student must apply for it. A less-than-stellar credit rating and origination fees can raise the rate to as much as 18 percent for some, says Mark

EDUCATION

College Loans from Uncle Sam

Federal loans come in three types: Perkins, Stafford and PLUS. The loans are explained here, in order of most desirable to least:

✔ **Perkins loans.** For students with exceptional need. The Perkins, has a fixed 5 percent interest rate. Total borrowing maxes out at $27,500 over an undergraduate's entire college career. For graduate students the limit is $60,000, including undergraduate studies.

✔ **Stafford loans.** With some $50 billion to lend, Staffords are the largest loan program. The loans come in two varieties: subsidized, meaning that for those with financial need the government pays the interest until the student is out of college; and unsubsidized, available to everyone, but interest is charged right away.

Below-market rates make Staffords appealing. Most students are limited to $31,000 in total Stafford money. The cap increases to $138,500 for graduate students. While the Stafford is federal, only about 25 percent of this money represents direct lending from the government. Most colleges provide Staffords through banks or other private lenders and send students lists of preferred ones. But borrowers are free to hunt around. Many lenders give discounts for prompt repayment or when payments are debited directly from bank accounts.

✔ **PLUS.** Parents can borrow up to the total cost of undergraduate education (minus other aid) under this program. PLUS loans were extended to graduate students beginning in 2006. Interest rates are fixed at 8.5 percent, plus a loan fee of 4 percent, which is deducted from each disbursement check.

—Sandra Salmans

Kantrowitz, who runs the comprehensive college financing site finaid.org and is co-author of *FastWeb College Gold,* a guide to paying for college.

For years, students seeking private loans, or any advice on financing their education, have turned to university aid offices, which maintain lists of "preferred lenders" or recommended commercial banks and loan companies. These days, students may be wary of relying on the lists after revelations a few years back that some lenders won places on the lists after giving gifts to financial aid officers and making payments to universities.

Still, whether you are looking for a federal or private loan, the financial aid office is a good place to start. Students should ask officials up front whether they have any financial arrangements with any of the lenders they recommend.

Then you should keep researching, going beyond the university's list, to compare rates and benefits available from different lenders.

For both federal and private loans, students should check with the bank that holds the family's home mortgage, or with state nonprofit agencies that offer student loans. For example, the Missouri Higher Education Loan Authority, known as Mohela, accepts applications from students nationwide for both federal and private loans. Mohela is one of 30 such state agencies, some of which deal only with residents. Their umbrella group is the Education Finance Council, which offers a Borrower Benefits Book, Outreach Book and Financial Aid Guides, at www.efc.org/cs/root/resources/resources.

The federal Department of Education also offers a guide to student loans, *Funding Education Beyond High School,* which is available at www.studentaid.ed.gov/students/publications/student_guide/2006-2007/english/index.htm.

Be warned that too much shopping around could hurt your credit score, as lenders may get the impression that you are desperate for funding. A lower credit score could mean higher interest rates on the potential loan. Kantrowitz suggests shopping one bank and one finance company that specializes in student loans and then looking for nonprofit loan agencies that work with people in the state where you live or the state where you attend college. You can find such a list on Kantrowitz's website, finaid. org, or you can ask the financial aid office whether a nonprofit lender serves the college.

When comparing lenders, also look for differ-

ent "borrower benefits" that they offer, such as interest rate reductions after on-time payments or as a reward for using direct debit from a bank. But keep in mind that one late or missed payment could cancel the discount.

The bottom line is to seek private loans that mirror federal loans as much as possible, including allowing an extended repayment if the borrower becomes unemployed or returns to school. Commercial online sites like SimpleTuition.com and eStudentLoan.com allow you to compare loan options for both federal and private loans.

—Elizabeth Olson

 **TIMELY TIPS**

Grants You Don't Have to Repay

From a few hundred dollars to a free ride

✔ **National Merit Scholarships.** The National Merit Scholarship Committee gives out 8,200 one-time scholarship awards worth $2,500 each to National Merit finalists based on their PSAT scores, their school record and their abilities, skills and accomplishments. In addition, some corporations and colleges agree to sponsor one or more scholarships for National Merit award winners; these can vary in size from a few hundred dollars to a full ride through college.

✔ **Pell Grants.** A federal Pell Grant, unlike a loan, does not have to be repaid and is meant to help lower-income families. Generally, Pell Grants are awarded almost exclusively to undergraduate students who have not earned a bachelor's or professional degree. Pell Grants are usually a component of financial aid to which aid from other federal and nonfederal sources might be added. The maximum Pell grant for 2009-2010 was $4,860. The amount is set to increase to $5,400 by 2012.

✔ For a quick summary of student aid programs available from the U.S. government, go to studentaid.ed.gov.

Health Insurance for College Kids

How to make sure you're covered while you're a full-time student

Most group health plans have traditionally allowed dependent children to stay on a parent's policy until the age of 23 or, in some cases, 25, if the child is a full-time student. Although that's still typically the case, many insurers are scaling back. And 20 percent of traditional-age college students don't have health insurance at all, according to the Government Accountability Office.

With the maze of options on health insurance for college students, what's a parent to do? The primary goal of parents should be to make sure their students are protected before they head off for school. Here are some tips for doing so.

Recheck benefits. If you're lucky enough to have employer-sponsored insurance, your first step is to make sure you can keep a full-time student on your policy. Even some people who could do so until recently may no longer be able to.

Verify coverage. If you are covered under a network-style plan like a health maintenance organization or

EDUCATION

Making Work-Study Programs Work for You

Work-study, a federally-subsidized program, lies somewhere between a grant and a loan in the college-aid universe. The school promises to make a job available at a rate of pay that is at or slightly above minimum wage.

There is a cap on pay, depending on other ingredients of your financial aid package. The government pays 75 percent, the school chips in 25 percent. You don't get the money unless you put in the hours. Students typically have to apply for jobs, a process that is more challenging during a poor economy when demand for the jobs increases.

We asked Rick Kincaid, coordinator of student employment at the College at Brockport, State University of New York, and a past president of the National Student Employment Association, for tips on getting the most out of work-study programs.

✔ **Apply early, for aid and jobs.** When a campus uses up its allotted funds, no more students are deemed eligible. And not everyone deemed eligible can participate, either. Most departments hire in the summer for the fall, but some jobs are posted the previous spring.

✔ **Look off-campus, too.** Many schools make arrangements with nonprofit groups, public agencies and even businesses, though the job must relate to your field of study. (Caveat: income from a regular job may diminish your aid.)

✔ **Apply like a professional.** Jobs are generally low level, but a résumé and cover letter can help eliminate competition.

✔ **Make yourself promotable.** Even campus jobs have a career ladder, and you could end up supervising other student workers. Real-world employers are also impressed by evidence of work ethic and time-management skills

—Lisa Belkin

preferred provider organization, and if your child is attending school away from home, you'll need to ask some questions. This applies whether you have employer insurance or an individual policy.

Call the insurer to learn whether there are network-affiliated doctors and other health care providers close to your child's school. If not, ask whether out-of-network providers are at least partly covered by your plan and what percentage of their fees you'll be expected to pay. Finally, if your child needs specialized care while away, will he or she need to get a referral from a hometown physician, or can the student receive a referral from a physician near campus?

Because most plans cover out-of-network care in full in emergencies, parents can usually work out these details, especially because most colleges offer student health services that can help take

care of routine medical needs. For students with a chronic illness, though, attending a college beyond the network coverage area may pose challenges.

Defining "full-time." Group health care policies that cover full-time students often come with a loophole: how to define full-time. If an injury or illness forces the student to take a leave from school or cut back on classes, is that student still "full-time?" Under "Michelle's Law," all group insurance plans must cover students on medical leave for up to one year. (The law is named for Michelle Morse, a student in New Hampshire who died of colon cancer. She had continued her full college course load throughout her treatment so she could keep her health insurance.)

Despite that layer of protection, you may still want to ask exactly how your insurer defines

TIMELY TIPS

Coping with A.D.H.D in College

The transition from high school to college can be tough enough for most students. But for those with attention deficit hyperactivity disorder, university life can pose even greater academic, medical and personal challenges.

Some colleges have specialized services for students with A.D.H.D., dyslexia and other learning disabilities. Here are some guidebooks that list campuses with special programs.

✔ *The K&W Guide to Colleges for Students With Learning Disabilities or Attention Deficit Disorder* (Princeton Review)

✔ *Survival Guide for College Students With ADHD or LD* (American Psychological Association)   —Tara Parker-Pope

"full-time student." You don't want your child to lose coverage because he or she happens to take a light load one term.

Shopping for an individual policy. If you don't have a group insurance option, you'll need to shop for an individual policy for your child. Because college students are usually young and healthy, premiums for fairly comprehensive coverage are relatively low.

And this is one actuarial category in which plans with high annual deductibles are not significantly cheaper than traditional coverage. But there is at least one situation in which a high-deductible plan may be a good option for a student: if the family is already covered under a high-deductible policy that is linked to a tax-advantaged health savings account to pay out-of-pocket health expenses. The I.R.S. allows parents to use such accounts

for a dependent full-time student. The extra tax break can make insuring your child under a high-deductible plan worthwhile. One place to look for such an individual policy is a Web site like eHealthInsurance.com.

Checking out college plans. More than half of all colleges offer their own health policies for students. But the provisions vary widely from state to state and college to college, so be cautious. Some limit the number of doctor visits, prescription drug coverage and length of hospital stays. The maximum benefits on these plans can also be extremely low, like $2,500 per condition per year to $1 million per lifetime.

Finally, be sure to ask college administrators if they accept the health insurance your family has. If the answer is no, ask why not. If enough parents ask, experts say, it might pressure universities to consider doing so, making health care one less thing for parents to worry about.   —Walecia Konrad

The 2-Year Degree Option
Community colleges offer lots of choices

Community colleges have been traditionally known as stepping stones: students with dubious academic records, shaky finances or no family tradition of higher education often spend 2 years at a community college gaining confidence before transferring to a more glamorous 4-year campus. But a lesser-known pool of students head the other way: they start their postsecondary education at a 4-year college and switch to a community college.

Some "reverse transfers," as they are known, discover belatedly that 4 years of semiotics and sociology are not for them and seek practical expertise that can translate into secure jobs; others are foundering academically or socially at a traditional university. For still others, the abrupt

EDUCATION

transition from the comfort of high school to large survey classes can be daunting.

"Often they get to campus and find they're just not ready," says Barbara K. Townsend, author of *Understanding the Impact of Reverse Transfer Students on Community Colleges* and a professor of educational leadership and policy analysis. Community colleges usually limit classes to fewer than 30 students—not the 500 that are packed into large lecture courses at state universities. Besides, community colleges cannot relegate teaching to graduate students because there are none, though they often rely on adjuncts.

Some students intend to advance no further than the associate degree awarded by 2-year colleges; but many expect to return to a 4-year institution once they have found their footing in a less pressurized environment.

The rapid rise in university tuition is also pushing students—or parents who pay the bills—to consider a respite at a community college. An analysis by the American Association of Community Colleges using data from the National Postsecondary Student Aid Study, a survey sponsored by the National Center for Education Statistics, found that 32 percent of community college students had previously attended a 4-year college. Some say the number is most likely even higher.

Credits are still a tricky issue when transferring between 2- and 4-year colleges, though. Community colleges honor coursework from an accredited college or university, and public universities consider that a student with an associate degree is halfway toward a bachelor's degree. But the attitudes of private colleges vary widely. Some grant a limited number of credits for an associate degree while others scoff at community college credits altogether.

Evan S. Dobelle, who has seen both sides as president of the 4-year Trinity College in Hartford and the University of Hawaii and community colleges in Massachusetts and California, says the line is blurring between the two types of institutions. Many community colleges now collaborate with 4-year universities to act as satellite campuses or to offer distance-learning programs for universities.

—David L. Marcus

... Or a Degree in 3 Years

One way of cutting college costs: get a degree in 3 years instead of 4

At Hartwick College, a small liberal arts college in Oneonta, N.Y., students have the option of graduating in 3 years, at a savings of more than $40,000. In the college's 3-year degree program, students complete the standard 120 credits, taking 18 credits in the fall, 4 in a January term and 18 in the spring. Students are still able to keep their summers free for internships or jobs.

Although most American students now take longer than 4 years to complete their degrees, the idea of 3-year degrees has been gaining favor in some circles, with several colleges talking about or experimenting with such programs, often involving online courses or summer school.

Some schools that consider the 3-year approach encounter strong resistance from faculty—or little interest from students. Three-year undergraduate degrees, however, are the norm in Europe, but for the most part, students there have an extra year of schooling before going to a university, apply to a particular department and do not take general-education courses.

Although a growing number of American students arrive in college with several Advanced Placement credits, the College Board presents that program not as a route to early graduation but rather as a tool to promote on-time graduation.

—Tamar Lewin

Enrolling for an Online Degree

First consider the cost, value and downsides

Online degree programs can be a boon to your career and your life, particularly if you are a full-time professional who can't afford the time to follow a traditional program. But first understand the commitment that will be involved.

Time considerations. Be prepared to spend at least 10 to 20 hours a week, for at least 1 or 2 years, on your online learning, and possibly more, depending on the degree. And be aware that this type of education requires much more self-direction and self-discipline than traditional classes do.

The online education process entails a lot of time in front of the computer. In most cases, educators record lectures off-line and upload them to a password-protected Web site for students to view when time permits. Independent of these sessions, students are required to read supplemental texts, many of which are also available in electronic form and downloadable from the class site.

Most online degree programs also involve discussion groups in which students post comments and feedback to a Web-based discussion board. Many of these sessions occur in real time, in chat rooms where students can interact with one another and, sometimes, with their professor.

The costs. Price varies, but in many cases tuition fees are comparable to those at brick-and-mortar schools, minus the expenses of things like room and board, and travel costs. In online programs affiliated with state universities, fees can be less expensive for in-state residents.

Many employers cover online education as part of existing tuition reimbursement programs, provided that employees prove that the online degree pertains to their current job. Once employees complete their degrees, experts report, many

are rewarded with additional compensation for advancing their education.

How employers view such degrees varies, of course, but experts say that most treat online degrees as equivalent to degrees obtained from traditional institutions.

Online degrees are also becoming more accepted by hiring officers. Generally, when employers are evaluating prospective employees, most don't ask applicants to specify how they obtained their degrees, just where they obtained them. "It's not as if you have to put on your résumé that you got your master's online," says one work-development director. "All that matters is that you have a degree."

Downsides. Your time-management skills will be put to the test; it won't always be easy to concentrate on your schoolwork after a long day at the office. By opting for an online degree you also miss out on impromptu lunches, barroom debates and other learning experiences that can occur on a college campus. And making lasting

---

 **TIMELY TIPS**

How to Succeed at College

✔ **Don't take on too much.** You have less time than you think, especially if you are involved in athletics or you have a job. The rule of thumb is three hours of studying for every hour of class, meaning a course that meets three hours a week is actually a 12-hour course.

✔ **But be sure to sign up for enough,** educators say. If you can handle four courses, you may lose momentum if you take only three. "Students that get in trouble are students that seem to have lots of time and just don't know how to allocate it," says Alexander M. Thompson III, former long-time dean of studies at Vassar.

—Samantha Stainburn

personal and professional connections becomes more difficult.

But perhaps the biggest risk associated with online degree programs is that not all the programs are created equal. John Bear, co-author of *Bear's Guide to Earning Degrees by Distance Learning,* says prospective students should apply only to accredited institutions, and should first contact the Council for Higher Education Accreditation (www.chea.org) to be sure that the accreditations are legitimate.   —Matt Villano

Getting a College Degree Abroad

Even with airfare, it's a whole lot cheaper

Trinity College, in the heart of Dublin, is Ireland's oldest institution of higher learning, chartered by Queen Elizabeth and home to the illuminated *Book of Kells,* from the year 800. Oscar Wilde studied here; so did Oliver Goldsmith and Jonathan Swift. Trinity is considered the Harvard of Ireland, but at $28,000 in tuition and living expenses it costs far less than a similarly top-ranked institution in the United States.

The price tag may be too steep for families with state-university budgets, but a high-end foreign university will most likely cost the same or less than its American counterpart. Students attending college overseas are eligible for the same federal student loans that are available here, though not Pell grants and National Merit Scholarships.

As domestic tuitions rise and the world grows smaller by the minute, going to an English-language college abroad is an increasingly popular option for superior students. You won't bump into many fellow countrymen at Oxford, where Americans make up just 1 percent of the student body. But that's not the case at the University of St. Andrews, on Scotland's east coast, where Americans account for 20 percent of all students.

While requirements vary among departments, St. Andrews generally wants SATs of 1950 (out of a possible 2400) and a 3.3 grade-point average. The University of Edinburgh looks for a 3.0 grade-point average and balanced SATs of 1800 as well as two Advanced Placement scores of 4 or 5, or scores of 600 or more on two subject tests.

American students who have applied say they like how the admissions process in Europe (and elsewhere) focuses on academic promise rather than considering the other factors that are important in the United States: extracurricular activities, athletic ability, ethnicity, geography or personal connections.

At foreign universities, what matters are grades, test scores and class rankings. Most foreign universities are public—even elite ones like Cambridge and Oxford—and are heavily subsidized by their governments. Homegrown undergraduates pay a small fraction of the true cost of their education, if anything at all. In Ireland, for example, citizens pay a one-time registration fee of about $2,000 and otherwise attend college free. In Australia and Scotland, tuition for citizens is not only low, but payment is deferred until graduates start earning money. Students from other countries pay full tuition.

How to apply. While it may sound intimidating, applying to an English-language college overseas is fairly straightforward. While you can apply directly to the college of your choice in Britain or Ireland, you can also apply to more than one college or program on a single form from the national offices: the Universities and Colleges Admissions Service in Britain, at ucas.com, or the Central Applications Office in the Republic of Ireland, at www.cao.ie. But you can't apply to both Cambridge and Oxford in the same year.

 **TIMELY TIPS**

Study Abroad Programs On the Cheap

While tuition for foreign universities is cheap by U.S. standards, study abroad programs organized by American schools often cost the equivalent of attending Harvard, Princeton or another big-ticket school for a year.

Organizers of study abroad programs are quick to tick off support services that make up a big part of the cost difference: cultural outings, security briefings, orientation programs, on-site staff to help get credits transferred and sort out visa problems. Will someone translate at the doctor's office? Is there a driver? How much hand-holding and service students want is an individual matter. If you don't need much, can study abroad be done for less? Absolutely. Here's how.

✔ **One way to save: seat for seat.** Exchange agreements, which allow students at an American university and a foreign university to literally trade places, tend to be cheaper, because colleges aren't sacrificing a tuition-paying student for the semester. The International Student Exchange Program, a group of 275 colleges in 39 countries, lets students pay room and board at home and essentially switch with students abroad. Some 2,500 students a year take part in the program.

✔ **Find out about course credits.** Colleges don't like to give credit for programs that compete with

their own—about 36 percent never do, and 39 percent only sometimes do. When going outside a college's offerings, get an O.K. in advance. Otherwise, you may not get credit from your school. At the very least, be sure to keep the syllabus and academic work you've done abroad to show your college officials. Getting credit toward general education requirements is easier than getting credits in advanced courses toward a major, even in college-approved programs. The takeaway message is to plan early, at least a year in advance and maybe more, depending on your major.

✔ **Do it yourself.** How to tell a well-thought-out program from one with a well-designed Web presence but little substance? The Forum on Education Abroad recently articulated some standards of good practice on matters from safety to help for students in transferring credits.

Generations of students have bypassed prepackaged programs to enroll in foreign ones on their own. Some colleges allow a leave of absence and accept the transfer of some credits. At New York University, about 70 of the 2,000 students who go abroad on semester programs do it that way.

The risk of going it alone, of course, is the possibility of forfeiting financial aid and course credit. Further, you have to get your own visa, register for courses (and know which ones to take) and get foreign universities, some of them notoriously lax, to send back the transcripts. Since academic calendars don't necessarily align, you could even miss the start of your next semester.

—Lisa Belkin

EDUCATION

Most foreign universities ask for a personal statement—usually an essay on why you want to attend the college or pursue a certain field—and an interview, either over the phone or someplace close to home. They accept the same forms of measurement—SAT, ACT and Advanced Placement—common in the United States.

Clear directions are on university Web sites: Trinity (www.tcd.ie), Utrecht (www.uu.nl), St. Andrews (www.st-andrews.ac.uk), Cambridge (www.cam.ac.uk) and Oxford (www.ox.ac.uk). Information about colleges in Australia can be found at studyinaustralia.gov.au.

—Leslie Berger

Transferring to Another College

It's getting tougher, but here's what admissions officers look for

When Harvard announced it would not accept transfer students for the 2008-09 school year, later extending the policy indefinitely, it closed a side door to the world's most selective college. Harvard joined fellow Ivy Princeton, which closed its doors to transfers in 1990. O.K., Harvard and Princeton are out. What about the rest?

The reality. It has long been assumed that it's easier to be accepted as a transfer. That still holds true for most campuses. But at the Ivies and highly competitive campuses like Stanford and Amherst, transfer rates have dropped by roughly 50 percent since 2000.

Stanford admits a mere 1 to 2 percent of transfer applicants a year. At the University of Pennsylvania, 2,000 students from other colleges competed for 175 slots in 2008. Yale and Dartmouth admitted 4 percent and 7 percent respectively, half the percentage of freshmen admitted. Yale fills fewer than two dozen places a year.

The reasons: increased pressure to attend a top school, more rejected quality applicants who want a second chance, and higher retention rates.

Better shots. Transfer applicants typically get their verdict in May, after a bed count of sorts. But don't expect an economic mass exodus that will open up spots; wealthier colleges provide enough aid to cover the cost of going there.

Of course, space does open up at competitive colleges. Transfer hopefuls in 2008 did better than freshmen applicants at Cornell, M.I.T., Georgetown and Notre Dame, but by only a few percentage points. Vanderbilt, by design, it says, admitted 55 percent of transfer applicants compared to 25 percent of the freshman pool.

One new route into top schools leads straight from community colleges. At Amherst, 12 of the 21 transfers admitted recently came from community colleges. (Transfer admit rate: 5 percent.) With a grant from the Jack Kent Cooke Foundation, Amherst and seven other elite institutions are actively seeking high-achieving transfers from 2-year colleges.

ⓘ INSIDE INFO

How Students Spend Their Time

Unlike working stiffs, college students usually only have to be in class 4 days a week. So how do they fill their time? To find out, the National Survey of Student Engagement recently polled more than 48,000 seniors. Here are the percentages of seniors who reported spending their time in the following ways.

○ **Studyingand preparing for class**

1-5 hours per week	20%
6-10 hours per week	25%
11 or more hours	55%

○ **Workingfor pay**

0 hours per week	56%
1-5 hours per week	6%
6-10 hours per week	9%
11 or more hours	29%

○ **Organizations,publications, student government, sports**

0 hours per week	43%
1-5 hours per week	30%
6-10 hours per week	12%
11 or more hours	15%

○ **Relaxingand socializing**

0 hours per week	2%
1-5 hours per week	33%
6-10 hours per week	29%
11 or more hours	35%

SOURCE: Center for Postsecondary Research, Indiana University, Bloomington

What they want. In transfer candidates, colleges look for qualities that can enrich classes composed largely of students straight from high school, like experience, maturity and diversity.

Deans say the constant at the transfer level is academic success. "To be even in the game, you've got to have a 3.5," says Tom Parker, dean of admissions at Amherst. "And the essay on why you want to transfer is absolutely critical. It's not your freshman essay."

—Tom Connor

Harvard at a Bargain Price

For those who will accept nothing less

Students who find rejection letters from Harvard in their mailboxes have another shot at attending the prestigious university. They can enroll in a bachelor's degree program at Harvard University Extension School—for a fraction of the admissions requirements and a fraction of the cost.

Harvard Extension School, with its mission of making a part of Harvard broadly accessible (it has graduated more than 10,000 over the years), is unusually inexpensive, charging between $800 and $2,000 for undergrad and graduate courses, compared to about $7,000 per course at Harvard College.

Students have access to Harvard faculty, even Nobel laureates like Roy J. Glauber, a physicist who has taught extension classes. At least 52 of the 128 credits required for the extension bachelor's degree must come from courses taught by Harvard instructors. And some courses are virtually identical to those at Harvard College, professors say.

There are no requirements to take extension courses; getting into the bachelor's degree program is permitted if students get at least a B minus in three extension courses, including expository writing. What extension students do not get is the experience of living in college dorms, socializing routinely with others their age and having access to all libraries, dining halls and other facilities. They also do not get as much faculty advising.

At Harvard, although extension students must maintain a C average and fulfill language, science and math requirements, they may deal with the perception that they are not full-fledged Harvard citizens. Social life can be challenging because most classmates are older and return home to families.

But some students like the mix of ages, and that the evening classes allow daytime pursuits. And there is the diploma, a bachelor of liberal arts in extension from Harvard University (that other diploma says bachelor of arts from Harvard

 INSIDE INFO

How Hard Are They Working?

A recent poll of nearly 380,000 randomly selected freshmen and seniors at 722 4-year institutions found that:

O About one in five frequently came to class without completing readings or assignments.

O Freshmen wrote an average 92 pages and seniors wrote 146 pages during the academic year. Seniors majoring in the social sciences and arts and humanities wrote considerably more than those studying the physical and biological sciences.

O Students spend about half as much time preparing for class as faculty expect.

O Seniors who entered as transfers lag behind their peers, talked less frequently with faculty about future plans, and were less likely than their peers to work with their classmates on assignments outside of class.

Source: The National Survey of Student Engagement

EDUCATION

College). As one Harvard professor put it, students getting bachelor degrees from the extension school are "brilliantly milking the cow of Harvard University."   —Pam Belluck

How to Win a Rhodes

A postgraduate degree from Oxford for free

A lot has changed since William Jefferson Clinton won his Rhodes from Arkansas in 1968. While the Ivy League schools, elite private colleges and military academies have long dominated, in recent years aggressive state universities have begun to make some inroads, and the competition is more intense than ever.

At 100-plus years, the Rhodes, the granddaddy of all fellowships, is the most prestigious and the most arduous. To become one of the lucky 32 scholars selected nationwide each December, candidates must be nominated by their university, be approved by their state Rhodes committee, pass muster at a cocktail party, interview at the state level and, finally, survive a second cocktail party and interview at the regional level. In sparsely populated states such as Arkansas, maybe one applicant wins

---

● **TIMELY TIPS**

Stay-at-Home Exchange Programs

Students are increasingly seeking out exchange programs within the U.S.

The idea of spending a junior year—or some other period—abroad is well known and increasingly popular. But many campuses now sponsor domestic exchange programs that tap into the country's diversity. Students can have a variety of academic, cultural and personal experiences without leaving the United States.

Some students might be chasing an appealing academic opportunity. Fashion design and technology majors at Buffalo State College can study the textile industry at North Carolina State University, or a marine biology student at the University of Rhode Island can experience the Pacific Ocean at the Hatfield Marine Science Center of Oregon State University, for example.

Sometimes students hope one day to work in the exchange city or to do graduate study at the exchange campus. Here's how domestic exchanges typically work.

✔ **Who goes.** Mostly juniors, though some domestic exchange programs accept sophomores and seniors.

✔ **Credits.** Coursework usually transfers back to the home school for full credit. Before signing up, work with an academic adviser to determine which courses will fit into your degree program. Many exchange programs require students to get a written agreement.

✔ **Costs.** Students usually pay their travel expenses and room and board to the host campus. And because tuition at private universities is higher than at public ones, more often than not domestic exchange students at private colleges go to other private colleges, and students enrolled in public universities go to other public universities. Participants in the mostly public National Student Exchange pay tuition either at their home campus or the host campus at state residency rates. Students usually get to choose where to pay tuition. (The exchange's Web site, www.nse.org, provides details about programs and majors offered by the 200 colleges and universities that participate.)

✔ **Financial aid.** Federal aid tends to travel with the student, but policies concerning other loans and scholarships vary. Check with your financial aid office to see if you can use them at another college.

—Mary C. Bounds

a Rhodes. Some years, none does. Here is an idea of what it takes to win the coveted scholarship.

- Maintain as close to a perfect grade-point average as you can.

- Have some extraordinary talents and accomplishments, or extracurricular activities, or leadership roles. One recent winner had a perfect G.P.A. Another researched female factory workers in Latin America and China and is organizing a national network of student-run tutoring programs for prisoners. She also pursued bachelor's and master's degrees concurrently in anthropology. Another had already had his poetry published in the *New York Times.*

- Get eight recommendations from professors who know you well.

- Travel abroad, not just as a tourist, but in some meaningful endeavor. One candidate traveled extensively in Jordan, worked at an orphanage in Honduras and spent her junior year at Cambridge University in England.

- Meet for three hours every Sunday afternoon during senior year fall semester with your fellowship adviser for coaching on interviews.

- Read daily e-mail messages from advisers crammed with suggested articles to read from *The Economist, The New Yorker, Foreign Affairs,* the *New York Times* and the *Society for Medical Anthropology,* as well as books, poems and the odd tidbit about Cecil Rhodes, the scholarship's founder.

- Undergo numerous mock interviews with faculty members in varied campus settings.

- Write and rewrite your essays.

- Practice answers to questions such as "You have one minute to tell the prime minister of India how to end religious violence. What do you say?"

 INSIDE INFO

Grade Inflation

○ One third of students surveyed by researchers at the University of California, Irvine, said they expected a B just for attending lectures; 40 percent said they deserved a B for completing the required reading.

- Practice your skills at a mock cocktail party to simulate the one with the Rhodes committee.

In their book *The Founder: Cecil Rhodes and the Pursuit of Power*, authors Miles F. Shore and Robert I. Rotberg point out that Rhodes himself was every bit as odd and eccentric as Rhodes the fellowship. His scholarship to his alma mater, Oxford University, was not to be for bookworms (no "Latin and Greek swots") but instead for, well, young men like Rhodes: outgoing fellows of action.

The original formula counted academics four-tenths, athletics two-tenths, character two-tenths and manhood two-tenths. Over time, the formula has been modified (for one thing, women became eligible for the scholarship in 1977), and today, athletics is interpreted to mean personal vigor.

—Michael Winerip

Other Scholarships to Snag
The Rhodes is just one of many options

The Rhodes is just one of a number of international fellowships coveted for their prestige and opportunity. The programs, which pay tuition and a stipend, seek postgraduates who have demonstrated academic excellence and leadership potential in their fields.

EDUCATION

Marshall Scholarship. The British government established the Marshall as a gesture of thanks to the United States and General George C. Marshall, who oversaw the economic recovery program to rebuild Europe after World War II. Inaugurated in 1954, the scholarship was conceived as a coeducational alternative to the Rhodes, which until 1977 excluded women and requires study at Oxford University.

The Marshall, on the other hand, allows 2 years of study at any British university. There is no age restriction, but applicants must have earned a bachelor's degree within the previous 2 years. The program, which covers the entire cost of study abroad, is highly competitive. Generally, at least 40 winners are selected from a nominated pool of more than a thousand applicants. Many applicants have grade-point averages of 4.0.

Past winners include Ray Dolby, inventor of the eponymous noise reduction system, and Justice Stephen G. Breyer of the Supreme Court. www.marshallscholarship.org

George J. Mitchell Scholarship. George Mitchell, a former senator from Maine, mediated the Northern Ireland peace process in the late 1990s. The scholarship, administered by the United States-Ireland Alliance, was established in 1998 to promote exchanges between the two Irelands and the United States. Students spend a year at any institution in Ireland or Northern Ireland and typically earn a master's, but some apply their year toward a degree they have already started, like an M.D. Each class is limited to 12 scholars, who must be no older than 30.

The Mitchell, which awards a $12,000 stipend,

> 66
> **The principle of study-abroad programs is that young Americans be introduced to the idea that other people have important things to contribute to societies.**
>
> Sanford J Ungar, President of Goucher College
>
> ● ● ●

is financed by the Northern Ireland executive and the Irish and British governments. Because the Mitchell seeks to introduce future American leaders to Ireland, applicants without a connection to Ireland may have an edge. But being of Irish descent has no bearing on the selection process. www.us-irelandalliance.org/scholarships

J. W. Fulbright Student Program. This flagship program of the American government was inaugurated in 1946 by Senator Fulbright (himself a Rhodes scholar) to promote international understanding after World War II.

Each year, over 1,000 American students—seniors or graduate students—are given full income support for a year to study in foreign countries, many of them uncommon destinations for scholars. In fact, applicants whose proposals entail research in less-sought-after nations (and veterans) may have an advantage in the selection process. On the flip side, 1,300 foreign students study in the United States under the program. Recipients design their own course of inquiry and need not be pursuing a degree.

Past recipients include Joseph E. Stiglitz, who shared the 2001 Nobel Memorial Prize in economics; Ruth J. Simmons, president of Brown University; the actor John Lithgow; and the soprano Renée Fleming. www.iie.org

Harry S. Truman Scholarship. Recipients are expected to pursue careers in the public sector, including uniformed service, and must have demonstrated such a commitment during college. To prove the point, applicants submit a one-page statement tackling a public policy issue and offering a solution.

Truman Scholars are nominated by their university while in their junior year, and get a tenth of their $30,000 stipend in their senior year, the balance during graduate work. Scholars may study at any university or professional school in the United States or abroad, though they typically stay here. Congress established the scholarship in 1975 as the federal memorial to the 33rd president, who had dabbled unsuccessfully in haberdashery, oil wildcatting and banking before entering public service. An endowment for the government-financed program is held in trust at the Treasury.

Past winners include political analyst George Stephanopoulos (who went on to win a Rhodes) and Janet Napolitano, secretary of homeland security and former Arizona governor. www.truman.gov

Gates Cambridge Scholarship. In 2001, Cambridge University welcomed its first group of 153 Gates recipients, who can work toward a second bachelor's degree on up to a doctorate.

Applications are accepted from any country but Britain, with about a third from the United States.

In what was then the biggest single gift to European higher education, the Bill and Melinda Gates Foundation granted $210 million to Cambridge to endow the scholarship, which awards a $15,000 annual stipend.

The university had approached Gates, who had shown interest in the city of Cambridge's ambitions to become Britain's Silicon Valley, with its research institutions and start-up technology companies. www.gates.scholarships.cam.ac.uk

—Sara Ivry

Law School Not Required
You can become a lawyer without setting foot in a law school

For some, there is a much cheaper way of becoming a lawyer. A few aspiring lawyers are getting their legal educations in programs that require no law school whatsoever. California, Vermont, Virginia and Washington allow law readers to take bar

The Best Guide to Law Schools
The American Bar Association fills in some holes

Prospective law students looking to compare particular law schools may be best served by going to the source—the American Bar Association. Each year, together with the Law School Admissions Council, the association publishes a portion of the information collected for its annual questionnaire in the *Official Guide to A.B.A.-Approved Law Schools.* (You can search the guide for free at officialguide.lsac.org.)

The *Official Guide* does not rank law schools but fills in many of the holes in the *U.S. News & World Report* rankings (usnews.com, click on "rankings"). After reviewing *U.S. News,* for example, an applicant might consider the University of California, Los Angeles, for its 96.5 percent

employment rate within nine months of graduation. But as part of its computation, *U.S. News* removes graduates not seeking employment—39 in the case of U.C.L.A. The bar association guide showed that these 39 students made up 12 percent of the graduation class—one of the largest proportions in the country—and that the employment rate was actually closer to 85 percent.

The bar association and the admissions council also offer an interactive Web site (officialguide.lsac.org/docs/cgi-bin/home.asp) that helps students sort and evaluate different law schools, using criteria like employment rates after graduation, bar passage rate, size of faculty, student body breakdown and tuition. The site includes descriptions, photographs and admissions profiles for all A.B.A.-approved law schools.

—Alex Wellen

EDUCATION

examinations after 3 or 4 years in apprenticeships registered with the state. Three other states—New York, Maine and Wyoming—let those who have not graduated from law schools take bar examinations if they have a combination of office study and law school experience.

By comparison, more than 140,000 students attend law schools approved by the American Bar Association, and thousands more attend schools not approved by the association.

Despite some challenges, law readers can rise high in the profession. Marilyn Skoglund, for instance, sits on the Vermont Supreme Court, and Gary Blasi is a professor at the University of California, Los Angeles. "I'm really sort of a bizarre case," says Blasi, who has an M.A. from Harvard. "The first time I was ever in a law classroom, I was teaching law."

The practice was once far more common. For example, Abraham Lincoln and Thomas Jefferson both read law. But it isn't easy. In a typical year, only one law reader passes the Virginia bar, for

example, out of nine or so taking the exam. The big benefit to law reading is that students get one-on-one instruction from someone who cares about them. Indeed, the supervising lawyers cannot take money for the substantial time they put into training their apprentices.

A downside to skipping law school is that a degree can be a job requirement, though in some cases it is possible to get a waiver. Although the bar association maintains rigorous standards for approved law schools, it does not advise against law reading. Some groups see it as a state's right to allow an alternative to law school.

Choosing the Right B-School
First decide on your ultimate goals

Learn through case studies or hands-on experience? Generalize or drill down? Stay home or go abroad? These are just a few of the choices facing students who are contemplating a master's in business administration.

How does a student find the right educational fit? Of course, time and money often make the choice for you; faced with the cost of tuition and the need to work, nearly 80 percent of M.B.A. candidates attend part time, often subsidized by their employers. Grade-point averages and admissions test scores may also limit your options. But all else being equal—which it rarely is—here are some questions to consider, depending on what you want to do and who you are.

Are you a specialist or a generalist? Most newly minted business school graduates begin their careers in a department like product management or finance. But if your goal is to move into general management in 5 to 10 years and ultimately lead an organization, it makes sense to get a strong foundation.

ⓘ INSIDE INFO

Is There a Doctor in the House?

○ The number of medical school graduates has remained constant at about 16,000 a year since the 1980s. But the number of new doctors has fallen as a percentage of a rising population.

○ In response, medical schools have stepped up annual admissions to 18,036 in 2008 from 16,170 in 1998, according to the Association of American Medical Colleges.

○ The gap between supply and demand for doctors could be 125,000 to 159,000 by 2025, reports the Association of American Medical Colleges, if the training of doctors fails to keep pace with population growth and a rising need for specialists catering to the aging demographic.

Most of the perennially top-ranked graduate business schools—Stanford, Harvard, Columbia, Kellogg at Northwestern, Wharton at the University of Pennsylvania—still adhere largely to the traditional core curriculum, which is meant to provide an overview of the entire corporation. Students get little or no choice of courses in the first year, typically taking multiple classes in each of some half-dozen categories—strategy, operations, finance, accounting, marketing, leadership and organizational behavior. In the second year, the universe widens to include electives.

There's an additional advantage to mastering business basics: trendy concentrations can be a blot on one's résumé when a hot market cools. Stanford's M.B.A. program was criticized for not focusing on Internet-related business during the dot-com bubble. But the school believed strongly in sticking to fundamentals.

Do you have a particular passion? Many business schools are adding "tracks" to their curriculum that play to their particular strengths and, they hope, to a marketplace that wants M.B.A.'s prepared to hit the ground running. If you already know that you want to work in a specific field, this could be a good fit.

The specialized curriculum that the Tepper School of Business at Carnegie Mellon rolled out a few years back, for example, includes tracks in biotechnology, computational marketing, technology leadership, operations strategy and management, management of innovation and product development, and management of wealth and assets. The idea is to build not scientists and engineers but the people who can manage them.

Are you still looking for a field of interest? While all graduate business schools have greatly expanded their lists of electives, some M.B.A. programs make a point of giving students free rein, not only in the business school but in other

TIMELY TIPS

Finding the Right Med School

✔ **Consider attending a public medical school in your own state.** Just about half of the best medical schools in the country are public. Some state medical schools give in-state applicants preference and lower tuition as well.

Resources for medical school applicants include the following:

✔ **Medical Students' Resource Guide** (studentdoc.com) provides information and strategic advice on a number of topics related to medical school applications.

✔ **Princeton Review** (princetonreview.com) has a medical school search tool that allows you to see how your academic record and MCAT scores stack up in comparison to others who have been admitted to particular schools.

✔ *U.S. News & World Report* (usnews.com, click on "rankings") has a comprehensive set of rankings for medical schools around the country as well as information on the sorts of candidates are admitted to each medical school.

schools within the university.

The University of Chicago, that champion of free-market economics, boasts on its Web site that "we offer the most flexible curriculum of any top business school in the world," with "very few required courses."

In recent sweeping changes at the Massachusetts Institute of Technology, the Sloan School of Management halved the number of required courses to a half dozen. What's more, M.I.T. added a number of six-week courses and divided the traditional 13-week semester into two sessions, with an "innovation" week in between when professors present their research. This schedule

EDUCATION

allows students to sample a greater variety of subjects. Compared with the track approach, the M.I.T. program gives students more opportunity to explore, and customize their own curriculum.

Do you want to create a business of your own?
If you were the kind of child who couldn't wait to set up a lemonade stand each summer—and maybe took over the neighbor's stand as well—then you may be interested in one of the growing number of hands-on programs for entrepreneurs.

The Henry W. Bloch School of Business and Public Administration at the University of Missouri, Kansas City, which has a strong emphasis on entre-preneurship, offers a program in which student teams create and run their own companies for six months.

At the F.W. Olin School of Business at Babson College, entrepreneurship is embedded in the core curriculum, with yearlong consulting projects for local companies. While only 20 percent of Babson graduates start their own businesses, the rest tend to go into new business development in established concerns.

Are your sights set on the global marketplace?
These days, it's the rare M.B.A. program that doesn't include an opportunity to study abroad. An M.B.A. candidate at one of two dozen Jesuit

universities participating in a consortium, includ-ing Fordham, Boston College and Loyola Univer-sity Chicago, can take up to 12 credits at Beijing University.

The University of Chicago has a campus in Sin-gapore. The Stern School of Business at New York University lets you spend a couple of weeks in Chile or Denmark. To intensify their international per-spective, an increasing number of students are leav-ing the country altogether to get their M.B.A.'s—in Canada or Britain or elsewhere in Europe.

Studying with students and faculty represent-ing dozens of nationalities helps prepare M.B.A.'s for doing business internationally, even if based in the United States. If English is your only lan-guage, not to worry: generally M.B.A. classes are taught in English, even in France and Spain.

—Sandra Salmans

Is B-School Worth the Money?

The degree may not justify the investment

Students at second- or third-tier schools can certainly build successful careers. But given the degree's hefty price tag, deans and corporate recruiters warn that a master's degree in business administration does not necessarily translate into a high-salary job. And the path to a leading investment bank or consulting company runs almost exclusively through a narrow band of elite business schools.

"The elite jobs that everybody seems to want—you're not even going to get an interview unless you go to one of the elite schools," says Robert H. Frank, a Cornell University management professor and co-author of *The Winner-Take-All Society*.

"Core schools" are those where companies recruit in person year after year. Many have only five or so core schools, some as few as two. At big-time companies, only a few business schools turn up

---

ⓘ INSIDE INFO

Diploma Hogs

○ For a number of years, women have surpassed men in gaining associate and bachelor's degrees, a trend that continues.

○ But women now surpass men in gaining every major degree category: associate, bachelor's, master's, professional and doctorate, accord-ing to 2008 data from the Department of Education.　　　　—Catherine Rampell

on list after list: Harvard, Northwestern, Stanford, Chicago, University of Pennsylvania, Massachusetts Institute of Technology, Columbia.

What do these gold-plated programs bring to the table? Jeffrey Pfeffer, a professor at Stanford's business school, published a study a few years back based on decades of data to determine what the M.B.A. degree actually did for students. Internal studies by leading consulting firms and investment banks of their M.B.A. and non-M.B.A. employees showed that the degree had no impact beyond helping them get the job. The conclusion: there is little evidence that mastery of the knowledge acquired in business schools enhances people's careers, or even that attaining the M.B.A. credential itself has much effect on graduates' salaries or career attainment.

But even critics say that top business schools do something of value: sort students. People who invest in an M.B.A. are often bright in the first place, and those with the most potential attend business schools from which they can land jobs with important futures.

Roger L. Martin, a former recruiter for Monitor, a top consulting company based in Cambridge, Mass., says he recruited almost entirely from the Harvard Business School (of which he is a graduate). But, says Martin, who went on to become dean of the business school at the University of Toronto, "If you gave me a choice of recruiting with the admissions list or the graduating list—I'd go with the admissions list. If people were smart, they would apply to Harvard, get in and then send their admissions letters out and use that to get jobs."

Harvard, he adds, "is a magnificent vehicle for extracting out of the global economy those people who are destined to be great business leaders and motivated and smart." But beyond that, he believes, Harvard adds nothing.

—Scott Jaschik

What Happens to B-School Grads?

Here's a look at how graduates of full-time, 2-year M.B.A. programs fare. The figures below are a snapshot of job prospects for the Class of 2008, before the depths of the Great Recession were reached the following year. Nevertheless, by comparing the total degree cost of a particular school with the median base salary that graduates of the school were offered, you can get a rough idea of the value of a degree from that school.

CLASS OF 2008	Job Offer at Graduation	Median Base Salary	Base Salary Range	Median Signing Bonus	Total Degree Cost
	%	$ K	$ K-$ K	$ K	$ K
Arizona State	80	85	50-125	10	33
Babson (Mass.); Olin	61	91	15-250	15	66
Baruch (N.Y.); Zicklin	47	80	15-125	10	22
Boston College; Carroll	83	85	50-160	15	62
Carnegie Mellon (Pa); Tepper	96	100	47-150	20	88
Case Western (Ohio); Weatherhead	60	76	50-160	10	86
Claremont (Calif.); Drucker	76	80	31-125	3	83
Clark (Mass.)	45	45	30-130	4	52
Columbia (N.Y.)	87	100	16-250	30	82
Cornell (N.Y.); Johnson	84	95	40-185	25	80
Dartmouth (N.H.); Fuqua	92	95	22-145	20	84
Fordham (N.Y.)	N.A.	90	60-125	10	68
George Washington (D.C.)	68	79	44-200	5	69
Georgetown (D.C.); McDunough	91	95	35-170	20	78
Georgia Tech	98	93	59-125	15	18
Harvard (Mass.)	95	120	50-500	20	90
Hofstra (N.Y.); Zarb	84	65	47-135	3	44
Indiana U; Kelley	87	92	35-125	20	31
M.I.T. (Mass.); Sloan	91	113	35-162	20	138
Michigan State; Broad	87	92	60-115	15	37
N.Y.U; Stern	82	95	55-185	35	82
Northwestern (Ill.); Kellogg	95	105	N.A.	20	85
Notre Dame (Ind.); Mendoza	80	91	40-155	15	70
Ohio State; Fisher	72	90	48-160	15	42
Penn State; Smeal	91	90	52-110	13	36
Purdue (Ind.); Krannert	83	85	33-140	15	38

What Happens to B-School Grads? (Cont'd.)

CLASS OF 2008	Job Offer at Graduation %	Median Base Salary $ K	Base Salary Range $ K-$ K	Median Signing Bonus $ K	Total Degree Cost $ K
Rice (Tex.); Jones	81	92	26-130	15	70
So. Methodist (Tex.); Cox	80	85	46-177	15	76
Stanford (Calif.)	94	120	30-250	20	87
Texas A&M; Mays	91	88	58-125	10	20
Thunderbird (Ariz.)	73	85	24-135	12	76
U. of Buffalo (N.Y.)	53	55	35-95	3	17
U. of Calif.-Berkeley; Haas	90	110	60-167	20	52
U. of Calif.-Davis	79	87	66-115	10	48
U. of Calif.-Irvine; Merage	62	85	31-120	8	51
U.C.L.A.; Anderson	74	96	17-175	20	67
U. of Chicago; Booth	92	100	45-250	25	85
U. of Florida; Hough	85	50	43-100	10	14
U. of Georgia; Terry	58	75	20-105	10	18
U. of Illinois-Urbana	75	90	60-160	11	40
U. of Iowa; Tippie	86	84	57-127	12	29
U. of Maryland; Smith	81	88	30-125	15	61
U. of Minnesota; Carlson	91	88	35-125	17	68
U. of N.C.; Kenan-Flagler	82	95	37-130	20	42
U. of Pennsylvania; Wharton	89	110	30-300	25	92
U. of Rochester (N.Y.); Simon	80	88	35-130	17	76
U. of Southern Calif.; Marshall	85	92	30-160	18	78
U. of Texas; McCombs	88	95	6-140	20	40
U. of Virginia; Darden	92	100	32-175	20	73
U. of Washington; Foster	84	87	47-160	15	42
U. of Wisconsin-Madison	84	90	53-125	15	22
Vanderbilt (Tenn.); Owen	83	90	50-160	15	81
Washington U., St. Louis; Olin	81	90	60-125	20	76
Yale (Conn.)	89	95	49-160	20	85

ℹ INSIDE INFO

Graduate Cheating

O A recent study of cheating among graduate students, published in a *journal of the Academy of Management,* found that 56 percent of all M.B.A. students cheated regularly—more than in any other discipline.

What Happens to Law School Grads?

How law school graduates fared in 2008

CLASS OF 2008	MEDIAN SALARY Private Sector $ K	MEDIAN SALARY Public Sector $ K	SALARY RANGE Private Sector $ K-$ K	SALARY RANGE Public Sector $ K-$ K	Total Degree Cost $ K
Brooklyn Law School	145	55	70-160	50-58	111
Columbia (N.Y.)	160	54	95-168	20-75	124
Duke (N.C.)	160	54	55-250	40-76	116
Emory (Ga.)	145	53	50-165	37-65	110
Fordham (N.Y.)	160	53	150-160	37-57	112
George Washington (D.C.)	160	56	29-185	36-108	125
Georgetown (D.C.)	160	58	80-235	36-85	112
Harvard (Mass.)	160	55	30-250	22-90	116
Hofstra (N.Y.)	75	52	30-160	41-73	118
Indiana U.-Bloomington	100	60	38-165	52-60	48
N.Y.U.	160	55	60-275	30-100	121
Northwestern (Ill.)	160	55	110-160	36-60	121
Ohio State	100	43	31-170	29-60	121
Rutgers-Newark (N.J.)	120	41	25-195	38-102	59
Seton Hall (N.J.)	120	39	45-495	39-68	106
Stanford (Calif.)	160	56	80-200	46-58	114
U. of Alabama	90	44	20-160	26-78	30
U. of Buffalo (N.Y.)	75	48	35-165	22-67	42
U.C.L.A	160	60	40-170	32-70	77
U. of Chicago	160	59	30-165	12-61	114
U. of Colorado-Boulder	98	52	35-160	43-103	49
U. of Georgia	130	55	40-250	30-90	32
U. of Michigan	160	56	75-190	30-61	107
U. of Pennsylvania	160	46	50-170	34-49	126
U. of Southern Calif.	160	57	60-165	40-62	121
U. of Texas	160	50	38-165	32-70	56
Vanderbilt (Tenn.)	145	50	52-165	45-70	109
William & Mary (Va.)	140	54	50-225	34-75	50
Yale (Conn.)	160	60	55-200	30-150	123
Yeshiva (N.Y.)	143	53	35-175	40-85	111

CAREERS

Getting Hired

Which Job Is Right for You?

The clueless might get some clues from a psychological profile

Whatever your age, whatever your career accomplishments, it seems that the nagging question remains: is this what I am best fit to do? One popular way to try to discern where your strengths lie is to take a personality test. The testing business is huge: there are 2,500 profiling "instruments," as those in the testing business call the tests.

Personality tests were once thought to be helpful only for those wanting to change careers in mid-stream. And, indeed, they remain most popular in the workplace, where companies rely on them increasingly when deciding to hire or promote. A recent

---

ℹ INSIDE INFO

What Hiring Managers Look At

O The top keywords they search for when screening résumés:

Problem-solving/decision-making	56%
Leadership	44%
Oral/written communications	40%
Team-building	33%
Performance and productivity improvement	31%

O And what annoys them most—the top five worst mistakes on résumés:

Spelling errors	63%
Résumé not tailored to the job	30%
Mistruths	23%
Too much detail about job duties	21%
Résumés longer than two pages	21%

SOURCE: CareerBuilder.com (multiple answers were allowed)

---

survey showed that 65 percent of the companies polled reported using them, according to *Staffing Industry Report*, a human resources newsletter.

But the tests are now administered to people of all ages. Some high schools give them to students to help them with college choices and long-term goals. Some college career centers administer them to seniors before they head into the "real" world. You can take them on the cheap by using the modified versions found in books in the careers section of your local library or bookstore or on numerous career Web sites (search: "career tests"). But the full-dress instruments, administered by career counselors, psychologists or psychiatrists, can cost hundreds of dollars.

Here's an assessment of the two most common tests, the Myers-Briggs Type Indicator and the Strong Interest Inventory. Both involve completing a lengthy questionnaire that attempts to gauge an individual's interests and temperament. They are best administered and interpreted by professional counselors. But before you spend hundreds, check with the career office at a local university; many allow students or alumni to take the tests for free.

Myers-Briggs Type Indicator. Nearly 90 percent of Fortune 100 companies, including AT&T, Exxon and General Electric, use Myers-Briggs to identify job applicants whose skills match those of their top performers. This test categorizes people based on four scales of personal preferences: extroverted or introverted, sensing or intuiting, thinking or feeling and judging or perceiving. The answers place individuals in one of 16 personality groups (see box on next page). Once M.B.T.I. identifies your type, a counselor provides you with a list of

What's Your Personality Type?

After you take the Myers-Briggs, you are given a score in the form of four letters. These are your personality preferences. They indicate into which four of the 16 possible categories you fall. For example, ENTP means you are an extroverted, intuiting, thinking, perceiving personality. Here are some characteristics of the different personality types.

• How you deal with others

E= EXTROVERTED Energized by interacting with others. Act first, think and reflect later. Studies show that about 75 percent of people are extroverted.

I = INTROVERTED Motivated internally. Prefer quiet reflection. Think first, then act. Only 25 percent of people are introverted.

• How you process data

S= SENSING Practical, orderly, use common sense. Good ability to recall details and facts. About 75 percent of people indicate this preference.

N= INTUITING Creative, imaginative, theoretical. Memory emphasizes hazier connections. Only 25 percent indicate this approach.

• How you make decisions

T= THINKING Objective, critical, analytic, logical. About 60 percent of men show this preference.

F= FEELING Use personal feelings to make decisions. Seek consensus. About 60 percent of women indicate this preference.

• How you approach life

J= JUDGING Planned, structured, focus on completing tasks on time. More than half of people have this approach.

P= PERCEIVING Spontaneous, flexible, value freedom. About 45 percent show this preference.

job fields best suited for you. One drawback is that it's a personality, not a skills, test. Another, say critics, is that it is an unreliable monitor, in that a person can be "introverted" one morning and "extroverted" in the afternoon. Others question its core assumptions, that is, whether the four basic scales actually exist.

Strong Interest Inventory. Many counselors recommend taking this test in conjunction with Myers-Briggs. The test collects information about an individual's interests and recommends potential occupations based on work activities involved, the traits of the working environment and personality characteristics that can affect work. Individuals are categorized by one of the six occupational types (realistic, investigative, artistic, social, enterprising and conventional) that correspond with a list of career options. This test works best for college students or individuals with a college degree.

A word of advice when testing: there is no point in trying to outsmart the questioners, for example by projecting what you think they want to hear about a skill. The tests ask the same questions repeatedly in different ways, and you could lose track of insincere answers. It's best to tell the truth.

Landing Your First Job
How new grads can approach the search

Most job hunters scour major online job boards for work. But there are less-trafficked ways for you to approach your first job search, especially during a sour economy. Here are ten steps for landing your first job.

1. Use the big job boards to figure out which industries and jobs you should be focusing on. But smaller, specialized job boards for a geographic area or occupational field are more likely to yield useful leads. One example is CollegeRecruiter.

CAREERS

☑ **TIMELY TIPS**

Best Web Sites for Job Seekers

Relying on the Internet alone won't land you a job. You'll need to take some warm and fuzzy steps, too, like networking and making personal contact with prospective employers. But the Internet can be valuable for identifying openings, getting career advice and researching companies. No single site will do it all, however, so look around.

✔ **AfterCollege.com** Jobs, internships and career information for students and recent graduates.

✔ **America's Career InfoNet** Educational, licensing and certification requirements for different jobs by state. Wages and cost of living; employment trends. Helps identify skills. www.acinet.org

America's Service Locator Locate local employment offices and career centers by plugging in your ZIP code. Free service helps you determine if you are "job ready" or require counseling and testing services. www.servicelocator.org

✔ **CareerBuilder.com** Vast network of more than 9,000 web sites, including those of 140 newspapers and online portals. Access to more than one million job listings.

✔ **CareerOneStop.org** A huge database of jobs, résumés, and career resource tools.

✔ **CollegeRecruiter.com** Specializes in jobs for college students and recent grads.

✔ **CraigsList.org** In all major cities yet retains the feel of a community bulletin board. Jobs are easily searched by titles.

✔ **Jobs.com** A Monster.com company. Easy to access domestic and international listings.

✔ **Monster.com** Veteran job seeker site. Covers all aspects of career help, from finding educational programs to a résumé service ($140 and up) that promises to create your document and email it to you overnight.

✔ **Theladders.com** A site for finding jobs that pay more than $100,000.

✔ **USAJOBS.gov** Search the maze of federal government jobs and then apply directly.

Résumé Resources

✔ **CareerLab.com** Struggle no more with job search letters. Peruse samples for good ideas. Free access.

✔ **CollegeGrad.com** Résumé advice customized for the new graduate with little job experience.

✔ **JobSearch.About.com** Tips from Alison Doyle, author of *Internet Your Way to a New Job*. Loads of sample letters: cover letters, interview thank you's, even resignation letters.

✔ **SusanIreland.com** 90+ sample résumés from the author of *The Complete Idiot's Guide to the Perfect Resume* and other books.

✔ **The Résumé Place** Experts on writing résumés for federal jobs. Services start at $125. www.resume-place.com

---

com, a career Web site for college students and recent graduates. And don't forget to visit corporate Web sites for lists of job openings.

2. Look at companies that aren't in your chosen field but that may be hiring. You don't have to be an accountant to work in an accounting firm or an engineer to work in an engineering firm; there are often many disciplines, such as marketing, human resources and facilities maintenance, within those companies.

3. Don't overlook jobs in the federal government, which often hires on a large scale, even in downturns. And you don't need to move to Washington, D.C. The federal government has offices in virtually every city in the country. Check out the government job site, usajobs.gov. Some agencies, such as the Federal Bureau of Prisons (bop.gov/jobs/3steps), provide advice and steps to take when applying for a federal job.

4. Don't forget a resource in your own backyard: your college's career services office. Not only can career counselors help with résumés, but they can also determine what industries and employers you should focus on, assist with researching jobs and connect you with alumni working in your field.

5. Consider doing unpaid work if you can't find a paying job. Many companies and nonprofit organizations advertise paid and unpaid internships, but you can also create your own. Contact companies, especially small ones, in your field and ask if they would allow you to do unpaid, entry-level work in exchange for the experience and industry connections.

Volunteer at a nonprofit organization in an area relevant to your career, like accounting, marketing or education. You can stay involved in the work force, and develop marketable skills for when the market turns around.

6. Do use Facebook to network, but first clean up your page and delete any controversial content or photographs. Use the status update tool on the site to ask your friends for help. Write, "I'm looking for a job in D.C. in public policy. Anyone got any ideas? Leads? Advice?" You are sure to get feedback and help.

7. Search Twitter to find employees' thoughts about their jobs. They may mention job openings that have not been posted or reveal information about a company that you wouldn't find elsewhere.

8. Create a profile on LinkedIn.com and urge your parents to sign up as well, so you can have access to their contacts. After all, you'll need to tap anyone and everyone who can help you.

9. Once you find people who might be able to help, ask if you can meet with them briefly to talk about the career. Don't ask about job openings at their company. Your approach is that you want information.

10. While searching for a job, you still have to pay your bills. Doing something not related to your chosen profession—like making lattes for a year—could actually make you a more valuable candidate in the future. You'll be able to tell employers how you made the best of a difficult situation, and few recruiters would hold that against you.

—Eilene Zimmerman

Smart Strategies for Job Hunting

How to make a personal connection, project self-confidence and other practical advice

No matter what the state of the economy, job hunting is never simple. Making matters tougher still, plenty of today's job hunters might have problematic résumés, because they have been unemployed, underemployed or employed in positions where they have languished.

What is the most effective way to pursue a job hunt? Stephanie L. Marks, president of Human Resources on Call (www.hr-oncall), which provides executive recruiting and career coaching for job hunters, discusses strategies that work.

Q How can an applicant stand out from the pack?

No matter what the state of the job market or your résumé, some truths are timeless. Job candidates stand out when they make the extra effort to establish a relationship with the person who's doing the hiring.

People who make the biggest impressions on me are those who follow up by phone or e-mail to thank me and to reiterate their strong interest in the job and the company.

It's particularly effective when people manage, in a 20- or 30-second message, to make a connection between something specific in their work experience and key details relating to the job opening. I'm impressed by people who make an effort to stay in touch, even if the original job they applied for wasn't right for them.

Q Don't such people run the risk of seeming annoyingly persistent or even desperate?

I don't think so. I respect it when a job hunter asks me to keep him or her on my radar screen and works to make that happen. It's a matter of behaving professionally. If someone sends me an e-mail every couple of weeks or telephones me once a month to stay in touch, it's a sign of real interest.

Q So many job searches take place on the Internet. How can an applicant make that personal connection?

For one thing, you can't just sit at your computer, look for online job postings, e-mail your résumé and wait for something great to happen.

Most e-mail résumés just disappear into a black hole. Sometimes a job hunter will tell me, "I e-mailed 30 résumés today." My response is, "To whom? What do you know about the company? What's your strategy going to be for following up in a meaningful way?" Job hunting through the Internet can be a waste of time, unless you do it the right way.

Q What is the right way to job hunt?

If I'm handling a job search for, say, a marketing position, I might list it on the Internet and receive 300 or more résumés. Who am I going to remember? The person who picks up the phone and calls me to leave a quick voice mail message: "Hi. I'm John Smith. I saw your ad online, and I'm extremely interested. I've just e-mailed you my résumé." Hopefully, John will end with a quick sentence or two about how he believes he can make an impact on the company.

True, I can't call back, at least not at that stage. But I've heard his name, and I can tell

---

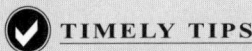 **TIMELY TIPS**

Want a Job? Get an Internship First

Employers are relying more and more heavily on interns to fill their entry-level ranks. "In an uneven job market, an internship is, or can be, the deal closer for permanent employment. If you don't have one, you're at a competitive disadvantage," says one career counselor.

✔ About 80 percent of graduating college seniors complete an internship, either for pay or school credit, according to a Vault.com survey. "They've moved from résumé enhancer to résumé necessity, and this is reflected in today's frenetic process," says Mark Oldman, a co-author of *The Vault Guide to Internships*.

✔ The Web makes it easy to go online and zap out résumés, but students shouldn't overlook the importance of personalization. "It's too easy to blast a résumé to 60 places, and the results you often get are proportionate to the work you've put in," says Oldman. "If you cut the number of companies in half and craft those approaches, it really pays off."

✔ A recruitment officer for General Electric, where 1,800 students annually are offered internships from a pool of more than 15,000 candidates, offers similar advice. "It is always beneficial to demonstrate that you know something about the company that you are applying to. It could be the one thing that distinguishes you from the pack," he says. And while referrals or connections might help they would not guarantee selection. Each candidate stands on their own merit.

—Marc B. Zawel

you that I'm going to make a point of looking for his résumé.

● What about all those job postings that do not list anyone's name? Aren't they really encouraging job hunters to keep their distance?

You've got to work harder in those cases to make that personal connection, but it's every bit as important. The person who stands out will be the one who spends the time to do some due diligence, to research the company and try to find out who in human resources might be involved with the search. Maybe this will take some phone calls or a visit to the corporate Web site.

I encourage job hunters to send e-mails to any Internet user groups or other networks they belong to—maybe someone out there will be able to come up with a contact name or other useful advice about a particular company.

● What about the fear factor associated with personal contacts, especially when job hunters feel less than confident about their prospects?

I'm the first to admit that job hunting can be frightening. But you've got to take risks. As a coach, I try to help people see this as a time of change and of growth. If you don't go out of your comfort zone, you're probably not going to be able to make something good happen.

● What's the worst mistake a job hunter can make, besides hiding behind the computer?

Lack of preparation. I warn people, every time you answer the phone, you've got to be ready—it could be a hiring manager on the other end. You've got to be prepared to communicate effectively, every minute of the day. One good technique is to keep index cards, alphabetically organized, about each job you've applied for. Keep notes on everything connected with your application, as well as what you've learned about the company.

Write down a phrase describing how you could make an impact. That way, you'll be ready to make your best case, any time you get the chance.

● The big risk, of course, is sounding glib rather than persuasive.

That's why people need to develop what I call a communication strategy for every job application. After all, every job and company is different. This becomes easier after you perform some due diligence. Let's say you read in a recent article or the latest annual report that the company is diversifying into a certain geographic region or new client base. You might want to prepare a sentence or two that reiterates your expertise in this area.

● Any words of advice for those who have been either unemployed or underemployed for a long stretch?

It's important for them to take a step back and assess their past job searches. Have they been aggressively networking or just relying on a click-and-send approach? Are their résumés up to speed? Have they been looking for jobs at the wrong level? To some extent, people need to rely on their instincts. The problem may be something permanent within their industry. Or maybe something needs to be changed about the way that they're presenting themselves.

● Any interview tips you can offer?

I often conduct mock interviews with my clients. When people get nervous, irritating habits might surface. I've seen people who slouch when they're asked questions. One of my clients kept clicking a pen. Another was a foot-tapper. You can change those habits, if you really work at it. It's a question of learning how to project self-confidence and enthusiasm.

● What other advice can you give job hunters?

Consider whether you need to take some classes to refresh and upgrade your job skills. Maybe you

CAREERS

need to work with a career coach to learn some more effective communication techniques. Or maybe you'll figure out that you need to reinvent yourself by finding ways to transfer your skills and interests into a more robust industry or job category.

● That sounds intimidating.

On the contrary, it's often invigorating and exciting for people to get to the point where they feel they have a positive plan for moving forward. What's frustrating is going around in circles, when all your job searches end in rejection and you don't know how to break the pattern.

—Jill Andresky Fraser

A Year Abroad as a Career Move
Banking your future on working abroad

Armed with a bachelor's degree and not quite ready for the briefcase or the Brooks Brothers look, an increasing number of college graduates are heading abroad. With an estimated 35,000 young Americans working abroad—teaching, bartending, taking care of children, typing or picking grapes—the trend has moved well beyond just trust-fund types.

They are finding that far from being career suicide, it can actually provide a professional boost. Once back in the States, they find their updated résumés more enticing to recruiters, who say that foreign experience demonstrates entrepreneurship, resourcefulness and independence.

Graduates unencumbered by technicalities—like working legally—often branch off on their own with little more than a debit card and confidence. Many depart not knowing how they will earn a living once they hit the ground. With hustle, they often find employment before the jet lag wanes (to

---

✔ TIMELY TIPS

What to Know Before You Go

Those who need help finding work overseas should know that some groups charge hefty placement fees. Determine whether the groups are covering room and board or are charging you just for the paperwork, and which programs require applications a year ahead of time or accept only recent graduates. Here are some Web sites for job and volunteer opportunities and general information.

✔ **Bunac** provides work permits, though not employment, and volunteer opportunities. www.bunac.org

✔ **Dave's ESL Cafe** lists teaching jobs. www.eslcafe.com/jobs

✔ **GoAbroad.com** lists foreign jobs, courses and more.

✔ **Japan Exchange and Teaching Program** offers college grads jobs in education and local government. www.mofa.go.jp/j—info/visit/jet

✔ **The National Consortium for Study in Africa** at Michigan State University lists opportunities. www.isp.msu.edu/ncsa

✔ **Princeton in Asia** places business, media and nongovernmental fellows in countries like East Timor, Kazakhstan and Hong Kong. piaweb. princeton.edu

✔ **Transitions Abroad** is a portal for information about working abroad. www.transitionsabroad. com/listings/work

✔ **WorldTeach** dispatches volunteers to developing countries like Costa Rica, China and Poland. Volunteers need not be aspiring teachers. www. worldteach.org

—Hillary Chura

the relief of worried parents), according to some who have taken the plunge. Many aspiring expatriates first live at home and work a few months to save money before they leave.

Those working legally tend to earn more, but their stays have a set duration—generally 4 months to 3 years, depending on the country or program. People working illegally may earn less, but can slip under the radar and stay in a country longer. A word of warning: that can result in deportation in extreme circumstances.

Years ago, recent graduates headed for Britain and other parts of Europe. That has changed. "Most students and young people have been to Europe on vacation and are thinking much further afield," according to Bunac USA, a group that facilitates the process. Australia and New Zealand are now popular.

—Hillary Chura

Four Steps to a Perfect Résumé

Writing a killer résumé means putting yourself in the employer's shoes

For many job hunters, especially entrepreneurial types, the day is almost here when traditional résumés alone will not suffice. Instead, they will rely on narrative bios, personal Web sites, or preformatted résumés posted on social networking sites like LinkedIn. But until that time, it's wise to have a traditional résumé handy.

Susan Strayer, a private career coach and author of *The Right Job, Right Now*, says there are two major areas you can focus on to ready your résumé for a company or recruiter's eyes: format and content. Format is easy to fix. (See "Preparing an Online Résumé" on page 399.) You want your résumé to be simple and easy to read once it is scanned. Since most organizations use applicant tracking systems

---

✔ **TIMELY TIPS**

20 Terms to Avoid on a Résumé

The words below may sound positive, but they will ring hollow unless you back them up with hard facts.

Aggressive	Ambitious
Attention to detail	Capable
Consistent	Effective
Entry-level	Hard worker
Knowledgeable	Mature
Original	People person
Qualified	Responsible
Significant	Self-motivated
Special	Stable
Team player	Well-rounded

✔ Rather than stating "effective," indicate your sales growth rate above the previous year, or the number of published articles you've written in a six-month period.

✔ New college grads: refrain from listing "entry-level" job as your objective. Why cut your chances of attaining something better?

(online recruiting tools), your résumé is scanned regardless of how, and to whom, you submit it.

On the content side, you're a product competing in a busy field of similar products. You have to write your résumé so that it is easy for anyone who reads it to see whether you are a fit for the job.

Here are Strayer's simple steps and tests.

Profile and title. Your résumé should have a title at the top. Not your current title necessarily, but the type of professional you'd call yourself if someone asked. "I'm an experienced marketing manager." That title should be followed by a profile, which should be customized for every job to which you apply. The profile should tell the recruiter or reader, who you are, what you bring to the table and what you are looking for in a job.

TEST: Have someone read your résumé for 10 seconds. If they can't tell you the specific type of job the résumé is intended to attract, how can a recruiter?

Professional and Personal Development. Recruiters and hiring managers first want to know your professional strengths in addition to work experi-ence and formal education. So before you get to your personal accomplishments, focus on things that have helped you develop professionally, and make those easy to find.

Create a professional development section, and if there is room, add one or two more lines where you can include anything personal that both differentiates you and demonstrates the strengths you'd bring to the job. Running a 5k? Not superlative. Training for your third full tri-athlon? That's impressive.

TEST: If your supplemental skills are all over your résumé—languages, technology skills, post-graduate certifications—organize them in one place and limit the personal details to one or two exceptional successes.

Positions Broken Out. If you've been promoted, show it. Progression is important—it shows commitment to a job, to a company and to success. Don't hide behind strange titles. Try to simplify your titles in a professional and honest way so the reader gets it. Junior L-Accountant II should just be Accountant.

TEST: If your title changed and your responsibilities increased, make sure it is obvious from your résumé.

Overall Differentiation. A position opens up for a marketing manager. The recruiter gets 100 résumés for the position. The 20 that the recruiter is even considering all generally have the same skills. If you list only your basic responsibilities, you will just be one of the 20. Stand out: don't just include what you did, but how you did it, and for whom. This doesn't mean you should dump a list of key words into your résumé either. That might get you a glance from a company, but a résumé with purposely placed key words sticks out like a sore thumb. Instead, focus on applying for jobs that you are fit for and then carefully craft your content to be persuasive. Think like the best product brands

---

TIMELY TIPS

How to Pick the Ideal Reference

At some point you'll be asked to provide references. So what qualities should you look for when choosing a reference? Here's how to find the perfect one.

✔ You must be certain that they think highly of you, will take the request seriously and be prepared and thoughtful in their answers, even if you don't have time to brief them beforehand (though building in time for a thorough briefing is a wise idea).

✔ They must understand the context in which the reference is being given (for a job in marketing, for example).

✔ They will know, intuitively, how to present any of your potential weaknesses as strengths.

✔ They know how to express themselves well, either verbally or in writing, depending on which type of reference they will be giving.

✔ A final consideration: a fancy title or prestigious organization is a great quality in a reference, but don't choose those things unless all the other qualities are also present. The worst possible reference you can get is someone with a great reputation or affiliation who is not able to convey high praise for you and your abilities.

— Marci Alboher

you know—how do they stand out?

TEST: If your résumé reads like a job description, then you need to make the content stronger to show what you have accomplished.

—Marci Alboher

Preparing an Online Résumé

And strategies for making good use of it

Updating the content of your résumé is only half the battle. How you wield it determines how effective it can be. Below are some ways to make sure you're well positioned in case using your résumé becomes a necessity.

Keep your résumé at the ready. Ideally you should keep an electronic version of your C.V. fully updated and accessible from any computer, ready to be sent out at a moment's notice. E-mailing a version to yourself is a simple way to do this (saving it to a dedicated inbox folder ensures you can find it when needed) and minimizes the risk of missed opportunities that can occur if people are kept waiting while you're frantically finding, revising or, worst of all, piecing together a new résumé from memory.

Don't waste your formatting. Your up-to-date and available résumé should also be saved as a PDF document. This way your format remains intact regardless of whether someone uses an older version of Microsoft Word or a different document software altogether. And since PDF documents are read-only, you eliminate the possibility of accidental changes that can happen when a file is opened and forwarded by multiple people. You also come across as having more technical expertise.

Make an initial public offering. If you're not content to wait for a request, you can make your work

TIMELY TIPS

What *Not* to Do at the Interview

You left the interview believing you'd aced it. But the interviewer never called again. Sure, there are mercurial managers, but maybe you're unknowingly committing some interviewing gaffes. Here are some don'ts from career-consulting professionals.

✔ **Don't let your eyes wander** to the floor, ceiling or walls of the interviewer's office. As basic a tip as it may be, maintaining eye contact with the interviewer is essential.

✔ **Don't forget to research the company.** Know its hot issues before going into an interview. Read the papers and business magazines, and check the Internet for the most up-to-date information about company performance and any breaking news.

✔ **Don't interrupt or answer too quickly.** Listen carefully to questions, and answer each one before elaborating on other points. Be specific and give examples.

✔ **Don't fudge.** Specifically, don't misrepresent salary or benefits. A potential employer may ask you to produce a pay stub or a tax form that shows your former salary. If it shows that you have exaggerated, you will be eliminated immediately.

✔ **Don't forget to maintain your professionalism,** including your in e-mail address and home answering machine message. More than one prospective employer has been turned off by a wacky voice mail message.

✔ **Don't forget to say thank you.** Most employers expect a thank-you letter after an interview. Nearly 15 percent of 650 hiring managers surveyed by CareerBuilder.com say they would not hire a candidate who failed to send a follow-up note.

CAREERS

experience public via professional networking sites like LinkedIn, Plaxo and Xing. While you can't upload your résumé directly, the benefit to using these sites' online formats, which require you to create an individual listing for each job, is that they find and suggest as contacts other members whose education, work or even club and organization affiliations overlap your own. Once you're connected to former colleagues or others, you share their address book and they yours, exponentially increasing your exposure (in theory, at least).

Show your e-mail skills. Sending an e-mail message and a C.V. as an attachment is simple enough, but what do you do when you're sending additional materials, like large image files or other supersize attachments? The old method was to attach the jumbo file, cross your fingers and hope for the best. A small evolution of that method was to break the delivery into chunks the recipient's e-mail system could properly digest. (This was often accompanied by an apologetic "Sorry for the seven e-mails. This is the last one!" message.) There is, however, a more elegant solution. For very large media files that surpass an e-mail system's size limit, simply create links to files hosted on sites like drop.io and filedropper. com, which allow uploads of up to 100 megabytes (for drop.io's free version) or much higher. Filedropper is a pay service, with plans ranging from 99 cents a month for 5 gigabytes to $10 a month for 250 gigs.

Think beyond the résumé. With a little creativity, people in almost any profession can make online applications or a personal Web site work for them. Samples of your marketing materials or corporate presentations can be posted onto online photo-sharing and slideshow resources like Flickr and Picasa. Simple introductory videos can be posted to a video-sharing site like Vimeo or YouTube.

You can gather these elements together and build a personal Web site. Anyone with a Google account, for example, can design a personal Google Site (sites.google.com) at no cost using a simple, intuitive interface. You can create multiple pages, easily upload image, audio and video files up to 10 megabytes each (with a total storage cap of 100 megabytes), and ensure straightforward site navigation via customizable sidebars.

Tumblr is another free option. Technically a blog platform, the site offers various layouts that allow it to function more like a landing page (the "Silo" and "Museum" themes are especially nice), with different posts spread across the page rather than stacked vertically on top of one another as in a traditional blog format. Tumblr is also endlessly customizable and lets users upload or embed media files up to 50 megabytes.

Regardless of where you create your site, adding a link in the signature of your outgoing e-mail messages under a header like "professional site" is a great way to pique interest and point prospective employers in the right direction.

Think before you post. When it comes to putting work you've done professionally in a public space like the Internet, use caution. Even if you've created a product, be it a video, presentation or packaging copy, from beginning to end, it's still the intellectual property of the company for which it was produced. It could be problematic if you share it without permission. (This is a bit of a gray area, but it's much more black-and-white if what you did involved a nondisclosure agreement or other sort of privacy contract.)

Intuition is a good rule of thumb: if you don't think a current or previous employer would want you posting examples of your work for them online, then you probably shouldn't.

Search yourself online first. Pointing a company to your LinkedIn profile or professional site doesn't mean that's the only part of your online world they'll see; if a potential boss or human resources assistant finds an unflattering photograph or blog post from you—and there's a definite possibility someone will do a search—it's fair game for them to consider that material reflective of you as a potential employee, even if, to you, it's part of your "private" life. Keep all settings for your social networks as private as possible, and do the same on photo-sharing sites like the ones mentioned above. For better or worse, every public aspect of your online life is now part of your résumé.

—Joshua Condon

Don't Forget the Cover Letter

It can give you a serious edge, if it's done right

You are getting ready to apply for a job electronically, and your résumé is ready to go. But you wonder whether a cover letter is necessary in this day and age. Yes, cover letters are necessary, even in this more casual electronic age. In a competitive market they can give you a serious edge if they are written and presented effectively.

Cover letters are a graceful way to introduce yourself, to convey your personality and to impress a hiring manager with your experience and your writing skills. You can also tailor them to a specific company in ways that you cannot with a résumé.

First, do your best to find the decision maker's name, and use it in the salutation. If you are applying to a blind ad, say "Dear Sir or Madam" or "To the Hiring Manager." Leading off with "Hey there" is not a strong start. If you want to be on the safe side, use a colon after the salutation, although some people now feel it is permissible to use a comma in an e-mail message.

Your cover letter should be short—generally no longer than three or four paragraphs. In your first paragraph, explain why you are writing—it may be that you are answering an ad, that you were referred to the company through networking or that you learned that the company is expanding.

In the middle paragraphs, explain why you are a good candidate and show that you are knowledgeable about the company. Then convey a clear story about your career and highlight specific past achievements. This can either be done as a narrative or in bullet points. You can also highlight qualities you possess that may not fit into the confines of a résumé.

Finish your letter by indicating that you will follow up in the near future (and make good on that promise). Sign off with a "Sincerely," "Cordially," "Thank you for your consideration" or similar closer, followed by your name and, if you like, your e-mail address.

Include your letter in the actual text of your e-mail message or place it above your résumé in an attachment. If you put it in a separate attachment from your résumé, you run the risk that a harried hiring manager will not click on it at all. If you place it in the text of your e-mail message, it should generally be shorter than if you use an attachment.

Then, if you really want to make an impression, make a hard copy of your cover letter and résumé and send it to the hiring manager by regular mail. Attach a handwritten note that says, "Second submission; I'm very interested."

But avoid some common mistakes. A cover letter with typos, misspellings and poor sentence structure may take you out of the running for a job. If you cannot afford to pay someone to review your cover letter and résumé, enlist a friend or a

THE 30 FASTEST GROWING PROFESSIONS

The best job opportunities often are not where the most jobs are, but instead where the most job growth lies. Explosive growth in a relatively small pool indicates an industry in need of a rapid infusion of labor. The following industries are expected to grow at a pace far above average. Three of the occupations— personal and home care aides, home health aides and computer software application engineers—are especially hot: they will also have the largest total number of new jobs.

	Jobs, 2006	Anticipated no of new jobs by 2016	Anticipated % change	Education or training[1]
Network systems and data communications	262,000	140,000	53.4	Bachelor's
Personal and home care aides	767,000	389,000	50.6	On-the-job
Home health aides	787,000	384,000	48.7	On-the-job
Computer software application engineer	507,000	226,000	44.6	Bachelor's
Veterinary technologists and technicians	71,000	29,000	41.0	Associate
Personal financial advisors	176,000	72,000	41.0	Bachelor's
Makeup artists, theatrical and performance	2,000	1,000	39.8	Vocational
Medical assistants	417,000	148,000	35.4	On-the-job
Veterinarians	62,000	22,000	35.0	Professional
Substance abuse and behavioral disorder counselors	83,000	29,000	34.3	Bachelor's
Skin care specialists	38,000	13,000	34.3	Vocational
Financial analysts	221,000	75,000	33.8	Bachelor's
Social and human service assistants	339,000	114,000	33.6	On-the-job
Gaming surveillance officers and gaming investigators	9,000	3,000	33.6	On-the-job
Physical therapist assistants	60,000	20,000	32.4	Associate
Pharmacy technicians	285,000	91,000	32.0	On-the-job
Forensic science technicians	13,000	4,000	30.7	Bachelor's
Dental hygienists	167,000	50,000	30.1	Associate
Mental health counselors	100,000	30,000	30.0	Master's
Mental health and substance abuse social workers	122,000	37,000	29.9	Master's
Marriage and family therapists	25,000	7,000	29.8	Master's
Dental assistants	280,000	82,000	29.2	On-the-job
Computer systems analysts	504,000	146,000	29.0	Bachelor's
Database administrators	119,000	34,000	28.6	Bachelor's
Computer software systems engineers	350,000	99,000	28.2	Bachelor's
Gaming and sports-book writers	18,000	5,000	280	On-the-job
Environmental science, health and protection technicians	36,000	10,000	28.0	Associate
Manicurists and pedicurists	78,000	22,000	27.6	Vocational
Physical therapists	173,000	47,000	27.1	Master's
Physician assistants	66,000	18,000	27.0	Master's

1 Education or training needed by most workers to become fully qualified in that occupation.   SOURCE: Bureau of Labor Statistics

family member with good language skills to do it instead.

Another danger is including too much information, for example, very specific salary or geographic requirements. Nor should you point out that you do not meet all the criteria in the job description. Save that for the interview.

— Phyllis Korkki

Where the Best Jobs Will Be

Service industry jobs will continue to lead

Ask a career counselor what you should do for a living, and more likely than not you'll be told to follow your passion. That's not bad advice, of course. But economists, labor analysts and management consultants who study broad trends shaping the economy and the labor market, will undoubtedly offer a different perspective.

The prism through which they see the world shows an economy that continues its decades-long transformation away from manufacturing and toward service positions. Over the coming decade, demand in services will continue to rise as the population grows and as Americans age in larger numbers. So if your passion leads you toward the high-demand, high-growth service industry, then you are way ahead of the game.

Employment growth is determined by a number of factors, such as aging baby boomers, changes in demand for goods and services, worker productivity and foreign competition. The government's Bureau of Labor Statistics projects that the total number of jobs in the country will rise 15.6 million, or 10.8 percent, between 2006 and 2016 (somewhat below the 14 percent the BLS expected during the 2004-2012 period). The BLS job projections include new jobs created through corporate ingenuity, as well as those required to replace an

BEST JOBS FOR COLLEGE GRADS

These jobs, which require advanced degrees, are expected to have the most job openings by 2016. But that doesn't mean every qualified job seeker will be guaranteed a position. The relatively high salaries they command also make them popular job choices, so competition could be tough.

JOB	NEW JOB OPENINGS	MEDIAN SALARY*
Registered nurses	1,000,000	$65,130
Postsecondary teachers**	662,000	$73,890
Teachers K-12	545,000	$52,240
Sales representatives***	476,000	$66,676
Accountants & auditors	450,000	$65,840
Secondary school teachers**	368,000	$54,390
Computer software engineers	300,000	$87,900
Computer systems analysts	280,000	$78,830
Management analysts	265,000	$82,920
Lawyers	228,000	$124,750

*In 2008   **Except special education teachers
***Except technical and scientific products

BEST JOBS FOR HIGH SCHOOL GRADS

Most jobs for workers without a degree beyond high school are concentrated in the food and transportation industries, which typically employ half of all U.S. workers. Below are jobs that will have the most openings by 2016. Even so, the average growth rate projected for high school-level jobs is lower than the average for all occupations.

JOB	PROJECTED JOB OPENINGS	MEDIAN SALARY*
Cashiers**	1,664,000	$18,880
Wait staff	1,537,000	$19,580
Food prep & serving***	927,000	$17,400
Laborers, stock movers	823,000	$24,690
Janitors	802,000	$23,500
Personal & home care aids	519,000	$19,690
Truck drivers	523,000	$34,490
Maids, housekeepers	463,000	$20,290
Home health aids	454,000	$21,440
Food prep workers	451,000	$19,850

*In 2008   **Except gaming   ***Includes fast food
SOURCE: Bureau of Labor Statistics

CAREERS

WHAT 100 JOBS PAY

Below are the salaries of 100 occupations, according to the Bureau of Labor Statistics. In real life, of course, salaries can vary considerably by region, level of experience and other factors. Another consideration is that federal government employees generally earn less than workers in the private sector. However, the list provides a good comparison of average annual earnings among the different professions.

TITLE	NO. OF JOBS	AVERAGE EARNINGS*
Executive, administrative and managerial occupations		
ACCOUNTANTS & AUDITORS	1,133,580	$65,840
ADVERTISING, MARKETING MGRS.	202,890	$106,440
CHIEF EXECUTIVE OFFICERS	301,930	$160,440
EDUCATION ADMINISTRATORS	394,230	$75,645
FUNERAL DIRECTORS	25,680	$58,810
HUMAN RESOURCE MANAGERS	129,140	$97,053
SALES MANAGERS	333,910	$110,390
Professional specialty occupations		
ACTUARIES	18,220	$95,980
ARCHITECTS	110,990	$76,750
ARCHIVISTS	5,330	$48,220
ASTRONOMERS	1,280	$99,730
BIOLOGICAL SCIENTISTS	28,290	$68,030
CHEMISTS	83,080	$57,820
DANCERS	11,370	$14.50/hr
DENTISTS	85,910	$154,270
DIETITIANS	53,630	$51,470
ECONOMISTS	12,600	$90,830
ENGINEERS	169,240	$89,080
FASHION MODELS	1,660	$30,160
FINANCIAL ANALYSTS & ADVISORS	383,410	$88,875
LAWYERS	553,690	$124,750
LIBRARIANS	151,170	$54,700
MATHEMATICIANS	2,770	$94,960
OCCUPATIONAL THERAPISTS	94,800	$67,920
PHARMACISTS	266,410	$104,260
PHOTOGRAPHERS	61,670	$35,640
PHYSICIAN ASSISTANTS	71,950	$81,610
PHYSICIANS & SURGEONS	262,850	$165,000
PHYSICAL THERAPISTS	167,300	$74,410
PODIATRISTS	9,670	$125,760
PSYCHOLOGISTS	63,430	$101,356
REGISTERED NURSES	2,500,000	$65,130
SCHOOL TEACHERS (K-12)	1,471,290	$53,315
SOCIAL WORKERS	185,380	$54,175
SPEECH-LANGUAGE PATHOLOGISTS	107,340	$66,130
STATISTICIANS	20,680	$74,790
SYSTEMS ANALYSTS	489,890	$78,830
UNIVERSITY PROFESSORS	168,000	$73,890
VETERINARIANS	53,110	$64,560
WRITERS & AUTHORS	44,170	$64,560
Technician and related support occupations		
AIRCRAFT PILOTS	77,090	$119,750
AIR TRAFFIC CONTROLLERS	24,260	$108,090
COMPUTER PROGRAMMERS	394,230	$73,470
EMERGENCY MEDICAL TECHNICIANS	207,160	$31,980
ENGINEERING TECHNICIANS	73,870	$56,560
MEDICAL & CLINICAL TECHNICIANS	149,670	$37,150
NUCLEAR MEDICINE TECHNICIANS	21,200	$67,480
PARALEGALS	253,040	$48,790

aging workforce. In fact, more jobs are expected to arise due to replacement needs than as a result of the forces of economic growth.

But even within an industry, jobs may grow at different rates, depending on factors such as technological strides and changes in production methods, for example. Replacement jobs also vary by industry. For example, industries with high concentrations of professional and technical positions that require advanced education generally have a lower turnover. More replacement openings occur in fields with greater numbers of lower-paying service and labor jobs. Which industries will drive job creation, that is, generate

Marketing and sales occupations

CASHIERS	3,545,000	$18,880
COUNTER AND RENTAL CLERKS	448,480	$24,430
INSURANCE AGENTS	327,780	$60,440
REAL ESTATE AGENTS & BROKERS	215,470	$65,875
RETAIL SALESPEOPLE	4,426,280	$25,050
SALES REPRESENTATIVES	2,484,000	$66,676
TRAVEL AGENTS	86,420	$32,470

Administrative support occupations

BANK TELLERS	600,380	$24,250
COMPUTER OPERATORS	109,450	$37,070
COURT REPORTERS	17,930	$51,960
DATA ENTRY KEYERS	272,810	$27,110
GENERAL OFFICE CLERKS	2,906,600	$26,830
MAIL CARRIERS	354,570	$46,970
MEDICAL TRANSCRIPTIONISTS	86,200	$32,960
SECRETARIES**	1,872,070	$29,990
TEACHER AIDES	1,266,900	$23,560
TELEPHONE OPERATORS	22,820	$33,800

Service occupations

BARTENDERS	503,420	$20,460
CHEFS & HEAD COOKS	98,040	$42,410
CORRECTIONAL OFFICERS	428,040	$41,340
COSMETOLOGISTS & HAIRDRESSERS	355,990	$21,113
DENTAL ASSISTANTS	293,090	$33,170
FIREFIGHTERS	298,900	$45,700
FLIGHT ATTENDANTS	99,480	$39,840
HOME HEALTH AIDES	892,410	$21,440
HOME APPLIANCE REPAIR	37,300	$35,690
JANITORS	2,145,320	$23,500
MAIDS & HOUSEKEEPERS	917,120	$20,290

MEDICAL ASSISTANTS	475,950	$29,060
OCCUPATIONAL THERAPY ASSISTANTS	25,610	$48,440
PHYSICAL THERAPY ASSISTANTS	61,820	$46,300
POLICE OFFICERS	633,710	$52,810
PRESCHOOL TEACHERS	392,170	$26,610
SHORT-ORDER COOKS	168,770	$20,230
TREE TRIMMERS	35,420	$31,450
WAITERS/WAITRESSES	2,371,750	$19,580

Mechanics, installers and repairers

AIRCRAFT MECHANICS	116,310	$51,650
AUTOMOTIVE BODY REPAIRERS	147,200	$39,950
ELEVATOR INSTALLERS	25,070	$67,750

Construction trades occupations

CARPENTERS	899,000	$42,940
CARPET INSTALLERS	34,390	$41,330
ELECTRICIANS	633,010	$49,890
PAINTERS	250,310	$36,510
PLUMBERS & PIPEFITTERS	437,540	$49,200

Production occupations

BUS DRIVERS	644,260	$31,380
BUTCHERS	128,210	$29,700
JEWELERS	24,780	$35,360
MACHINISTS	419,070	$37,490
POWER PLANT OPERATORS	34,700	$58,340
PRINTING PRESS OPERATORS	193,510	$34,150
TOOL & DIE MAKERS	85,610	$48,180
TRUCK DRIVERS	2,481,540	$34,490

NOTES: * Annual salaries, except as indicated.
Salaries are as of May 2008.
**Excludes legal, medical and executive secretaries

SOURCE: Bureau of Labor Statistics, 2008

greater than average job openings in the coming decade? Here's a snapshot of selected industries and their anticipated job outlook, based on data compiled by the BLS.

Health care. Fueled by population growth and longer life spans as well as medical advances that increase the numbers of treatable diseases, the health care sector is expected to create the greatest number of new jobs—almost 3 million by 2016. Hospitals, both public and private, will account for 691,000 of the new jobs.

The high levels of education and skill needed in many health care jobs are generally rewarded by higher than average salaries.

CAREERS

Educational services. This sector is expected to grow by nearly 11 percent, adding about 1.4 million jobs. Teachers will be needed at all levels, but especially at the post-high school level, as children of baby boomers continue to reach college age, and as more adults turn to continuing education to enhance or update skills. Demand for elementary and high school teachers is also expected to increase, but job growth will be tempered by the decrease in the number of younger children starting school.

Management, scientific and technical consulting. This fast-growing sector is expected to add more than 700,000 jobs by 2016. The growth is due to the continuing complexity of doing business in technical fields and the need for specialists to help provide planning and operations advice.

Food and drink industry. Behind the continued job growth in these establishments are dual-income families, a growing population and increased dining sophistication. Growth will be pronounced in establishments that offer a wide variety of ethnic foods.

State and local governments. Nearly 617,000 jobs are expected in state and local governments (except in education and health care), as the population grows and states take on greater responsibility in running federally funded programs.

Wholesale trade. An anticipated rise in trade will mean more jobs—428,000 by 2016—especially for sales representatives at the wholesale and production level. Tempering the jobs growth rate in this field, however, is an ongoing consolidation among companies in the industry and the increasing use of the Internet to conduct business.

THE BEST AND WORST INDUSTRIES FOR JOBS

Are you in a growing or declining occupation? If you're in one of these top 10 industries with a higher than average anticipated growth in the number of jobs, prospects look good. On the losing end are industries, such as textiles and apparel, which will continue to face inroads from foreign imports. The following numbers are for jobs expected to be created or lost between 2006 and 2016.

THE TOP 10 INDUSTRIES FOR JOBS

Industry	Jobs created
1. Health care	2,954,000
2 . Leisure and hospitality	1,873,000
3. Education services	1,412,0004
4. Food and drink services	1,024,000
5. Social assistance (except child care)	823,000
6. Construction	781,000
7. Management and technical consulting	718,000
8. Employment services	692,000
9. Government and advocacy	685,000
10. Natural resources (construction and utilities)	634,000

THE 10 WORST INDUSTRIES FOR JOBS

Industry	Jobs lost
1. Textiles and apparel	-211,000
2. Computer and electronic manufacturing	-157,000
3. Motor vehicle and parts manufacturing	-153,000
4. Machinery manufacturing	-146,000
5. Printing	-138,000
6. Agriculture, forestry and fishing	-105,000
7. Chemical manufacturing (except drugs)	-90,000
8. Publishing, except software	-49,000
9. Steel manufacturing	-39,000
10. Utilities	-31,000

SOURCE: Bureau of Labor Statistics

On the Job

Once You Have a Real Job

A primer on taxes and benefits for new members of the workforce

Employee manuals that detail all your fabulous benefits are boring and confusing, and they start in the middle instead of defining things from the beginning. Benefits administrators are trying to help improve the situation, but most employers still have a long way to go. So to make things easier, here's a proper primer on health insurance, taxes and retirement plans for employees starting their very first jobs.

Health insurance. Priority No. 1 is to protect yourself from some huge expense that you cannot possibly afford. That is what insurance, in any form, is supposed to do. As for health insurance, most of you probably won't run up big bills anytime soon. But some of you will get appendicitis or crash your cars and end up in a hospital for a stretch. And if any of those things happen, insurance should pay for a big chunk of the treatment.

Health insurance is expensive. Employers generally pay for some or most of it, but usually not all. You'll probably pay your share of the cost in at least two ways. First, your employer will probably take some money out of your paycheck regularly. This is called the premium. Then, there's something called a deductible, where each year you have to pay at least the first couple of hundred dollars toward many kinds of medical expenses, like prescription drugs, doctor fees or payments to mental health practitioners. Finally,

there's the co-payment, a $15 (or $50 or $100) fee you pay for every doctor visit or prescription.

You may be able to choose from a few different types of insurance plans. If you are, you will almost certainly be confused by the options. Most employers have a human resources or benefits staff member who can help. Don't be shy. The only stupid question is the one you don't ask. Ignorance can easily cost you hundreds of dollars.

For some more background, you might also check out allaboutthebenefits.com, a Web site created by the health insurance giant Aetna and the Financial Planning Association.

 INSIDE INFO

Best and Worst Jobs

○ JobsRated.com evaluated 200 jobs taking into account factors like income, stress, environment and stamina needed to perform the work. These jobs surfaced as the best and worst jobs in America.

	BEST	WORST
1	Mathematician	Lumberjack
2	Actuary	Dairy farmer
3	Statistician	Taxi driver
4	Biologist	Seaman (boat, barge operator)
5	Software engineer	Emergency medical technician
6	Systems analyst	Roofer
7	Historian	Trash collector
8	Sociologist	Welder
9	Industrial designer	Roustabout (oil rig worker)
10	Accountant	Ironworker

CAREERS

Books for Budding Managers

What literary classics can teach you about being a leader

John K. Clemens, a professor of management at Hartwick College in Oneonta, N.Y., and author (with Scott Dalrymple) of *Time Mastery: How Temporal Intelligence Will Make You a Stronger, More Effective Leader,* uses literature, including Shakespeare, to teach managerial skills to business students. Here are Clemens's picks of literary classics for managers and aspiring leaders in search of a good read and a few leadership pointers.

✔ *Billy Budd* **by Herman Melville.** The plot is perfect for exploring problems that arise when company decisions are based on rules, not circumstances, and for discussing ensuing decisions on doing the right thing. And, nearly everyone can relate to the book's primary conflict: the effects of one co-worker's dislike of another.

✔ **Chief Joseph.** In his writings, Native American leader Chief Joseph offers an in-depth look at three styles of leadership, the types of organizations they are associated with (bureaucratic, entrepreneurial and integrative) and the problems and benefits unique to each of them.

✔ *Glengarry Glen Ross* **by David Mamet.** This dark play presents a leader most readers will not admire. Yet by analyzing him and other characters, readers can evaluate management strategies and decide what, if anything, they have to do with the organization's fate.

✔ *Henry IV* and *Henry V.* **by Shakespeare.** A study of these two kings (and their differing leadership styles) offers lessons on personal and political traits of leaders and on what works and what doesn't.

✔ *The Iliad* **by Homer.** The major figures in this epic poem are driven by compelling needs and forces not immediately apparent. Once discovered, however, they help to reveal the inner workings of leadership in any setting.

✔ *Letter from a Birmingham Jail* **by Martin Luther King.** This offers a classic lesson in how language is a leader's most effective tool. King also reveals in great clarity his four steps for organizational change. This "recipe" can be used in any social setting, including modern corporations.

✔ *The Bird of Dawning* **by John Masefield.** The most important lessons here concern recognizing how to transform vision into reality, and the critical but often unappreciated importance of challenging employees or co-workers to do more than even they thought possible.

Many employers offer a new kind of insurance that pairs high deductibles (often more than $1,000) with some sort of savings account that you can use to pay for health expenses before your insurance starts contributing. These plans may not be ideal if you have a chronic condition, like asthma or diabetes, or see a chiropractor or psychologist regularly. If you do, add up the cost of your office visits and make a list of the prescription drugs you take. Then, see what your plans will cover and what kind of deductibles and co-payments are involved. Also, be sure to check if there is any kind of annual or lifetime limit on what the insurance will cover.

Taxes. Sadly, a $36,000 annual salary won't turn out to be anything close to $3,000 a month. One big reason is that your employer takes money out to send directly to the government for taxes.

When you start work, you'll need to fill out a form called the W-4. This tells your employer how much money to take out of your check to pay federal income taxes. (Companies also usually hold back money for Social Security and Medicare taxes and state and local income taxes where they exist.)

If you're young, single and don't have any student loan debt, the W-4 is fairly straightforward as tax forms go, but it contains at least one line that may be confusing. Line A instructs you to enter a "1" if no one else can claim you as a dependent. Ask your parents whether they intend to do so this year.

If you do have student loan debt and plan to deduct the interest you're paying, it gets a bit more complicated. There's a good worksheet at paycheckcity.com that will take you through some questions and then fill out the W-4 for you. From the home page, look under "basic" and click "Form W4 Assistant." To complete the worksheet, you'll need to know how much interest you'll be paying this year. Your student loan provider should be able to tell you what part of your monthly payment is interest.

Retirement. Depending on how high your student loan bill is, putting something away for retirement may seem impossible. Vanguard, a mutual fund company that also administers 401(k) plans for employers, ran a survey that suggested that credit card debt was an even bigger impediment for those under 35. High rent can make saving seem daunting as well.

You may be facing down all three of these bills. Your student loans might average 6 or 8 percent interest, while your credit cards might run at 18 percent. Always make at least the minimum payment on time, since that will make it easier to get other loans later.

But if your employer offers a 401(k) or other similar retirement plan where it matches your contribution, pay careful attention. With these plans, you tell your employer to set aside a small portion of your paycheck before payroll takes out

federal and other taxes (you don't have to pay any taxes on these savings until much later).

Your employer may contribute one dollar for every dollar you put in, up to 3 percent of your salary. Or maybe it chips in 50 cents for every dollar you save up to 6 percent of your salary. The amount varies by employer, but this match is, in effect, an instant 50 or 100 percent "return" on your savings.

Consider this an optional raise. Turning it down would be a real shame. Nor will it cost you as much as you think. Saving 3 percent out of an annual salary of $36,000 amounts to roughly $20 a week. If you want to run your own numbers and test the impact of different amounts of savings, try the Salary Paycheck Calculator at paycheckcity. com, under "basic."

Once you decide how much to save, you'll have to figure out where to invest the money. Fidelity, another big 401(k) plan administrator, notes that in recent years the company worried about bombarding people with too much investment information.

The fact is, however, that the majority of Fidelity's 401(k) customers don't adjust their investments for years at a time once they put money in. If you think you may leave yours alone too,

---

ℹ **INSIDE INFO**

Testosterone and Money

○ On Wall Street, one of the most male-dominated bastions in the business world, it seems that some men are biologically programmed to perform better than others. A recent British study, published in the *Proceedings of the National Academy of Sciences,* found that a trader's testosterone level in the morning, predicted his day's profitability. Higher testosterone meant more risk-taking and, usually, more money.

CAREERS

consider investing in something called a lifecycle or target-date fund, which is fast becoming a standard offering in retirement plans. These funds will have names like the 2050 fund, which correspond to the year when you'll probably be thinking about retiring. Managers allocate the money (mostly in stock mutual funds now, though the investments get more conservative over time), and all you have to do is shovel more in.

–Ron Lieber

What Not to Wear at Work

It never hurts to dress conservatively

Despite the casual trend in work environments, some fashion rules still apply. Here's how the experts answer questions about building a work wardrobe.

● You're a recent college graduate getting ready for the working world. Can your college wardrobe make the transition with you?

If you dressed casually throughout college, you may need to rethink your approach and invest in some new clothes. But it will be worth it. In interviews and in the office, dressing appropriately may be a simple way to gain an edge.

Some young people aren't aware of the importance of work clothing, says Barbara Pachter, an author and business etiquette lecturer. Unlike more experienced workers, they may not have enough work history to realize that they need to follow new rules, or they think the rules don't apply to them, she says.

Fairly or not, you are judged to some extent on the visual impression you make. Managers are more likely to hire and promote people who dress in a neat, professional way that shows they fit in with the organization.

● You have an interview coming up. What should you wear?

For an interview, it rarely hurts to err on the side of conservatism. When in doubt, wear a suit. In some cases, business casual can work, but don't assume that. Ask your recruiter, a department manager or a college career adviser for guidance.

For a man, this could mean a suit and tie and leather shoes with dressy socks; for a woman it could be a blazer and a blouse with a skirt or slacks, along with low heels and hosiery, among several possibilities.

Many young women today have never worn pantyhose in their lives, but the consensus among human resources managers is that you should wear hosiery to an interview. (Once you have the job, you may be able to go back to bare legs, depending on the office.)

● Should you get dressed up for a career fair?

Wearing a business suit, or at least a business casual outfit (like a polo shirt and khakis or a blouse and skirt), is an excellent way to make a good impression at a career fair. One human resources manager related that she would not have hired anyone at a recent career fair because of how casually they were dressed.

● How should you dress once you get a job?

You have more leeway once you are hired, but tread carefully at first. Ask if the company has a dress code, but don't stop there. Observe the people around you before you decide whether it's O.K. to wear, say, jeans or casual shoes.

● What are some clothing pitfalls to avoid?

Be careful about revealing too much. Underdressing will get you noticed in the work world, but for the wrong reason. Cleavage is not a corporate look. The same goes for very short skirts and extremely high heels.

Q You can't afford to buy a whole new wardrobe. What should you do?

A few basic pieces in a few matching and muted colors, perhaps bought at a discount, can go a long way and last a long time. A classic interview suit that will last for years is a better investment than the latest trendy attire that will only last a season.

Q But, shouldn't you have some freedom to express yourself through your clothing?

Once you get the job, there's nothing wrong with showing some individual style. A 23-year-old certainly doesn't have to dress like someone in his or her 40s. You may even reach a point where you feel you can break some of the rules, but first you need to know what they are.

—Phyllis Korkki

 INSIDE INFO

Women in the Workplace

○ Women put a premium on autonomy, flexibility, proximity to home, fulfillment and safety. Nearly 76 percent of men say money is the primary motive for working, according to a Rochester Institute of Technology survey.

○ There are 80 jobs in which women earn more than men, among them financial analyst, speech-language pathologist, radiation therapist, library worker, biological technician and motion picture projectionist.

○ Women who have never been married and are childless earn 17 percent more than their childless male counterparts.

○ Female sales engineers make 43 percent more than their male counterparts; female statisticians earn 35 percent more than men make at the same job, according to Warren Farrell, author of *Why Men Make More: The Startling Truth Behind the Pay Gap.*

Handling an Office Mistake
How to rectify that blunder you made

You realize that you made a terrible mistake at work. Your first instinct is to deny that it happened or to cover it up. Then you feel angry and defensive, and want to blame other people. Then you want to hide. Are these reactions normal?.

It is only human for people who have made a mistake to have any or all of these initial reactions. A mistake can contradict your view of yourself as an effective worker, creating cognitive dissonance, says Carol Tavris, a social psychologist and co-author of *Mistakes Were Made (but Not by Me)*. You think, "I pride myself on my abilities, how could I have messed up?"

To reconcile these opposing views, the mind tries self-justification, says Tavris. It's "the protective process by which we get to keep seeing ourselves as ethical, smart and competent, and reject, ignore, dismiss or minimize the evidence that we were wrong," she says.

That's when the lies, the blame and the defensiveness erupt. But these self-protective responses don't help you or your organization because they block any understanding of what went wrong. Not only that, but covering up one error can lead to more, and bigger, mistakes, until you are entangled in a mess you never intended, Tavris says.

One key to handling errors effectively is to recognize that they aren't necessarily a reflection of your native abilities and intelligence. Once you have separated the action from yourself as a person, you can work quickly to correct the error and move on.

Still, you can't help thinking, "How could I have let such a stupid thing happen?" Mistakes will happen; that's a given, especially in complex work environments, says Amy C. Edmondson, Novartis professor of leadership and management at the Harvard Business School. In any job that requires continuing thought and judgment, we need to be "aware of the huge potential of things to go wrong," Edmondson says, because "we all can handle only so much cognitively at a time."

How do you start dealing with your mistake? First, go to the people affected by it and apologize, Edmondson says. Then work with them to correct the situation and come up with changes you can make so the error won't happen again. The sooner you come clean, the better, both for your peace of mind and the good of the organization.

Acknowledging a mistake is hard because of the fear of being perceived as stupid or incompetent, but keeping it inside can be an enormous psychological burden. "People are often surprised to learn that when they admit the mistake, not only do they feel better, but the response is often much better than they expected," she says.

Your manager can affect the way you deal with your mistake, of course. If your manager is the type who will become angry at you for a mistake, you will be less likely to disclose it, which wastes valuable time. The best companies make it a policy to show gratitude and reward employees for revealing their mistakes. Workers and managers need to view a mistake "as an inevitable human step on the path to improvement," Tavris says.

Sometimes, a mistake might be a sign of a larger problem in your organization. You may view your error in very personal terms, but it may reflect a fundamental flaw in a company, a system or a product. It might, for example, be a result of a breakdown in communication among departments, a fear among subordinates to question higher-ups or a failure to incorporate crosschecks, the way airline workers do for safety reasons, or checklists. The lesson, then, is to see a mistake as an opportunity for the system to learn and change.

—Phyllis Korkki

How to Make Meetings Work

Rules for setting limits and reining in the blatherers

You're expected to attend many meetings at your company, and most of them are a waste of time. The same people hog the floor with pointless, redundant comments, while others say nothing. The discussion inevitably goes off topic, and you start to feel trapped. It's excruciating. So can anything be done?

Yes, if the meeting leaders make a commitment to set ground rules and take an active role in guiding the discussion. But before a meeting is even scheduled, it's important to know whether it should be held at all.

In general, companies probably hold about twice as many meetings as are necessary, says John E. Tropman, a professor of nonprofit management at the University of Michigan who has done research on meetings. Less is better than more because of "the ineptitude of this social form," he says.

Too often managers hold meetings in the vague, wishful hope that something will happen; they may even use them as a way to avoid work. A result is a meeting that yields no decisions, which, in turn, leads to yet another useless meeting. Here's some expert advice on how to hold meetings that don't drive people crazy.

❓ How can a manager tell if a meeting is necessary?

Hold a meeting "when you have a task that requires group effort," says Steve Kaye, president of One Great Meeting in Placentia, Calif. Make sure you can write out specific goals or outcomes for your meeting, for example, "Find ways to reduce the budget by 5 percent," he says.

❓ Once you've decided that a meeting is necessary, how can you make sure it is successful?

Two main ingredients are needed. First, the

How to Shush the Office Big Mouth

Telling a co-worker to shut up may not be the best strategy

One of your co-workers loves to chat and regularly barges into your work space to shoot the breeze. As tempted as you may be to tell him to scram, it's best to approach the situation with tact, says Gini Graham Scott, president of Changemakers, a consulting firm in Oakland, Calif. "Be as diplomatic as possible," says Scott. "But if the person doesn't get the hint, then you have to be firm." Here are some options.

Give nonverbal clues. For example, continue staring at the computer screen in front of you and refuse to make eye contact. Another approach is to check your watch repeatedly. Cal LeMon, president of Executive Enrichment, a management consulting firm in Springfield, Mo., says more overt gestures include packing your briefcase and putting your hand up, like a policeman stopping traffic. "Open-palmed gestures say to the person that you're trying to wrap things up," LeMon says.

Use technology. Alisa Cohn, president of AC & Associates, an executive coaching company, says she once advised a client to set her Microsoft Outlook calendar program to chime every 10 minutes. When the office chatterbox heard the chime, he assumed that Cohn's client had an appointment.

Confront the chatterbox. If your colleague will not take a hint, then it's time to be more direct. Start with the facts: tally the number of times this person interrupts you throughout the day, note the length of each visit, and then use these statistics in a confrontation about the behavior. Simply outlining the problem may not solve it. Larina Kase, president of the Philadelphia firm Performance and Success Coaching, says it's important to have a plan for further action. Ask the talker if you can catch up over lunch. Let him know how to tell whether you have time to talk (for example, if your door is open—if you're lucky enough to have a door).

Keep it civil. Generally, lashing out or yelling in the office is not a great idea. You never know who else may be listening. And shouting is likely to make an unpleasant situation worse. Furthermore, says Don Gabor, president of Conversation Arts Media in Brooklyn, "The chatterbox is annoying, but he might be someone who can help you down the road."   —Matt Villano

leader needs to cultivate "a safe environment, so that people feel creative and candid enough to express useful ideas," says Kaye. Second, there must be methodical progress that leads to results. Set an agenda with time limits (for example, 2:10 to 2:15) for each item, and make sure to follow it, Tropman says. He developed a concept known as the "agenda bell," a curve that reflects the idea that energy is lower at the beginning of the meeting, rises at the center and declines at the end. The best meetings, he has found, tend to have announcements at the beginning, followed by action items that lead to decisions.

But even though decisions are the goal, they can disrupt group cohesion because they tend to produce winners and losers. That's why the end of the meeting should be spent brainstorming for the future, as a way to repair any rifts that have developed in the group, he says.

❓ One or two blatherers always end up monopolizing the discussion at meetings, and running everything off the rails. How do you get them to stop?

Monopolizers need to be reined in because they rarely have the self-awareness to stop talking themselves, says Glenn Parker, a team-building

CAREERS

consultant and co-author of *Meeting Excellence.*

It's O.K. to interrupt a monopolizer, says Parker. But be polite about it, perhaps by validating what the person has said. You might say something like this: "I think you're making a good point. Let's see how the rest of the team feels about that." Then turn away from the talker, preferably to another part of the room, and ask someone else his or her opinion on the topic.

Similarly, he says, if a monopolizer or anyone else goes off on a tangent, you can say something like: "I may be wrong here, but I thought we were supposed to be dealing with customer complaints. If you all agree, let's get back to the agenda."

● What about the people who never say anything. Why don't they participate?

"The tendency of people to withhold work-relevant information is probably greater than you think," says Amy C. Edmondson, Novartis professor of leadership and management at Harvard Business School.

People stay silent to avoid conflict and to protect their careers, she says. They fear the consequences if someone with more power—like a manager leading a meeting—hates their ideas. Nonparticipants overestimate the risk and underestimate the reward of expressing themselves, she says.

To make sure everyone participates, the meeting leader must communicate a sense of "psychological safety," says Edmondson. At the same time, there are ways to lower the psychological cost of speaking up and to raise the cost of silence.

Asking questions can be a way to accomplish that, and it is not done often enough, she says. Research shows that in corporate meetings, a very low number of comments are questions; people are mostly telling and not asking.

Doing something as simple as turning to a non-participant and saying, "What's on your mind?" can help redress the communication imbalance, says Edmondson.

● How can you tell if a meeting has been effective?

For one thing, it ends on time or even early. (Anything longer than an hour tests human endurance.) More important, a problem gets solved, a decision gets made, a plan gets developed, a query gets answered. And people leave the meeting thinking, "We made good use of our time."

—Phyllis Korkki

When Your Boss Is a Bully
Here's how to escape his or her clutches

The American workplace can be a brutal place. On any given day, according to Columbia University psychologist Harvey Hornstein, one in five people is abused by a boss. Using questionnaires filled out by nearly 1,000 men and women over an 8-year period, Hornstein estimates that over 90 percent of U.S. workers experience some form of abusive behavior during their working life.

In his study of managerial abuse, *Brutal Bosses and Their Prey*, Hornstein discusses what separates "bully bosses" from those who are merely "tough, but fair" managers. Here he describes brutal bosses and how to deal with them.

● Are there any places where bully bosses tend to exist more than others?

No, and that's the scary part. By the end of our research, almost all industries were equally represented. Gender was equally represented. Blue-collar workers and white-collar executives were all represented. In some cases, the abuse may have taken different forms—usually verbal or physical—but I don't know that the pain was any less in each case. Abuse occurs in the boardroom as well as on the shop floor. There really are no differences. Some abuse literally occurred in manholes where utility workers were working, as well as on the 68th floor.

A Spotter's Guide to Brutal Bosses

In his book, Harvey Hornstein identifies six different types of brutal bosses. Here are his descriptions of each.

CONQUERORS. Concerned with power and making sure it's not undermined in any way, they use words to bludgeon you. They want to make you feel small. They are the classic schoolyard bullies.

PERFORMERS. These types are threatened by anyone who challenges their competence, or whom they perceive as outperforming them. Rather than take a subordinate's performance as a plus for their camp, they see it as a minus for themselves. Their favorite weapon is to belittle. They are known to put comments in your personnel file without telling you and criticize your work without giving you a chance to explain or respond. They are also the type to ask for positive comments to affirm their own self-worth. You end up not giving honest feedback, but rather absolute approval.

MANIPULATORS. Concerned with how they are being valued; whether people like them and care about them is what's important. They will attack you personally. Their weapon is to smear your reputation. They take credit for your successes but will attribute their own failures to you, or anyone else who is around. You can't win with these folks.

DEHUMANIZERS. They turn people into numbers. They look at you as simply cogs. They have a machine-like view of human beings and the social world, and that permits them to abuse. It's much easier to abuse someone when the target of your abuse is seen as a "thing," rather than a person.

BLAMERS. They write off their harm by saying that you and the others "deserved it." This is the blame-the-victim attitude. They will say, "I didn't do a bad thing. They deserved what happened to them."

RATIONALIZERS. These brutal bosses don't blame the victim of abuse; they use abuse to justify a greater cause. Rationalizing brutal bosses say things such as, "Just helping out the organization" or "Well, someone had to do it." They use these self-justifying terms to cover up their own feelings about the abuse they have inflicted.

Q **Which kind of bully bosses are people likely to encounter?**

Our evidence suggests that conquerors, performers and manipulators (see box above for descriptions) are the most common. Power organizations focus you on power. That's the name of the game, that's what the trade is about. Turf and power are the issues. It's what's traded. And the subordinates are the ones made to suffer.

However, I have found dehumanizers, blamers and rationalizers most frequently arise in organizations facing issues such as downsizing, or other measures that are taken in the face of difficult times. Whenever companies are making a transition, these three seem to pop up.

Q **What is the most effective way to deal with a bully boss?**

From an individual perspective, what works well is to try to find protection within the organization. This can usually be found through an ombudsperson, a grievance committee, or even by pursuing legal options. Options do exist, but not always.

One of the reasons I wrote the book was to enable workers to learn the patterns of the predator. What triggers them? What kinds of issues are their major concerns? And how do workers try to

CAREERS

avoid them? In many cases, it was quite literally physically avoiding bosses at times when they are at their most volatile. That's how a lot of folks survive working for these kinds of people.

● What if you can't avoid them?

When you are attacked, it's important to make a good-faith response. Focus on the content of what's being said, not on the curses. Focus on the meaning of the message, not the malevolence. Otherwise, you just inflame them.

● What about confronting bully bosses when they are being abusive?

That may be the noble thing to do, but it is often the costly thing to do—very costly. Most of the time you pay the price. If you don't lose your job, you certainly get labeled as someone who is a troublemaker. You get pushed into positions that are undesirable. That's the potential downside of taking legal action or invoking other forms of protection. And that's why people are afraid to do it.

The shortcoming of these solutions is that they really don't solve the problem from an organizational perspective. The brutal characters are still there. And even if you get out of their way, and mitigate the harm that's coming your way, they are still free to roam the corridors and beat up on someone else. So the organization hasn't solved the problem.

● Does senior management need to step in and address the bully boss problem?

Yes, exactly. Ways to do that include introducing progressive management tools such as 360-degree feedback, which gives employees a greater voice and makes them more equal. It gives them access to senior-level management and puts bosses at all levels on notice that their misbehavior will be part of the record and will not go unnoticed.

Disagreeing with the Boss
It's always tricky—especially with a new boss

After a management change, your new boss reverses some popular policies of your previous boss. What should you do?

If you feel that the new boss is being unfair, it's important to express your frustrations, consultants say, provided you can convey your message in ways that don't make the new manager defensive. Set a tone of honesty early on.

Although it's hard to know which changes are worth disputing and which are not, experts advise that in the first few weeks of a new regime, employees should be selective about the causes they champion. If the incoming manager eliminates casual Fridays, for example, it is not a good idea to complain loudly. But if the new boss puts an end to something more substantive—tuition reimbursement, for instance, or a policy that damages the fabric of a workplace environment—employees might want to speak up.

Whether to talk about your misgivings with co-workers is a touchy issue. The best advice is to talk to colleagues you trust, but do it quietly, in ways that the boss cannot construe as gossiping or backbiting. Employees may even want to appoint one of their own to act as a moderator for such discussions. Constructive conversations could end up convincing employees that a new policy is palatable.

But, if that's not the case, consultants say that you may want to wait a few weeks to observe the new rules in action before expressing your concerns to the new supervisor. Just as employees are sizing up the new boss, the boss is evaluating them, noting who embraces change and who resists it.

Still, patience should have a limit. If you are still dissatisfied after a few weeks, you might request a meeting with your boss. If and when you do air your frustrations, you don't want to sound like a complainer. You should be concise, respectful and positive. Focus on how policy changes would affect the company as a whole. Andrew J. DuBrin, author of *Essentials of Management,* says employees should approach this meeting as if they were presenting a report, providing statistics, facts and figures that support a return to the way things were. "Instead of giving the impression that you're emotionally committed to something," DuBrin says, "present information that makes an objective case for what you want."

—Matt Villano

Ways to Beat Burnout

Smart strategies to deal with that sinking, can't-take-it- anymore feeling

Millions of Americans report that they are burned out, job-weary, bored, frustrated, overworked or just plain stressed out. Relax, help is just ahead. Cynthia Scott is a clinical psychologist, the author of 10 books on achieving optimal happiness and performance in the workplace, and founder of the consulting firm Changeworks Global. Here's her advice.

Know the burnout signs. The best indication of burnout is your day-to-day relationship with your immediate supervisor. Supervisors who communicate, share information, collaborate and allow some control over how work is done produce less burnout in their co-workers. Research suggests burnout is less related to how much pressure people feel than to how meaningful they find their work. People who work hard but love what they do don't get burned out—unless they're working around abusive people or doing a job without a clear goal related to it.

Seek balance. If you don't have a lot of control in the workplace, you may need to take on more control at home. Vacuum the rug, clean the house, plant a garden, take up a sport—anything that moves your body, lets the tension out and gives you control. If your work involves long assignments, go home and do things with a quick finishing point. If you're working on real choppy, quick stuff, do something at home that has some longevity, like building a ship in a bottle. If you're isolated all day, go home and talk all night. If you talk to people all day, spend a quiet night reading. Whatever you do, don't get into numbing yourself; that can lead to alcohol and drug abuse, and isn't a real release.

Step back. If things at work are really getting to you, take a day off and get some distance. Ask yourself, "Is the problem short-term stress that will be over soon?" If I'm overloaded with

CAREERS

a short-term stressor, I might just go off for an hour and do something nice for myself. If it's a long-term pressure that doesn't stop—like a long commute you have every day—taking an hour off won't do anything. For a chronic pressure like this, you need to ask yourself, "Is it going to get better?" Then see what options might work.

Consult family and friends. I call it bringing together your "board of directors"—the people who know you from different stages of your life. Have a pizza party, bring everyone together, and get their opinions, just as you would in a business meeting. The perspective of others is important, because each has a different view of you and a different time frame. They can often help you deal with some things you thought you could do nothing about.

Learn the truth about your job status. It's better to get laid off than to worry about it. Our worst anxieties come from lack of information. If you know that you will lose your job in three months or three weeks, you can learn coping strategies. If you hear a bunch of "wells" and "maybes," you remain in a perpetual state of anxiety. Approach your boss and ask what's going on; this will release you to take other action. If your boss is not specific, ask for further clarification. The more you know, the better.

Air your work concerns. I'm a fan of not choking on it—of trying to communicate how you feel. Women often have a higher emotional literacy, so they can express their concerns—and don't mind doing so to another person. Try saying to your boss, "Your last comment made me feel devalued. I'm not sure what role I have in this project now. Could we try and work it out?" If a problem is really stressful, and you don't want to deal with it, do something to get yourself centered again. Try deep breathing or taking a walk—just get out of the stressful situation.

Use mental imagery and calming techniques. If you're doing a stressful task, you should envision a place that gives you a sense of ease. People choose lots of different things, such as lying on the couch, going to the beach or sitting in a bathtub.

I encourage people to have one image ready. If you practice this kind of self-care strategy, you can meditate and go to your safe place mentally whenever you want—even as you're being screamed at by your boss. You can have your eyes open and be attempting to listen, but the rest of you is thinking your way into your place of ease.

Sometimes you need time to unwind to alleviate stress. If you've just left an awful meeting with your boss, take the stairs instead of the elevator. Ease the butterflies in your stomach by breathing in as you take each step to let out tension and get oxygen to your brain.

Judge the stress level of your job. Jobs that are high demand but have low control are the most stressful. It's more about position than occupation. For instance, a nurse working in a clinic has high demand and low control, with no way of knowing how many patients will be coming in each shift.

Curing E-mail Anxiety

Make an empty inbox your daily goal

What is it about e-mail that consumes us and makes us wish for extra hours in the day to deal with the deluge? More importantly, how can we overcome the anxiety brought on by a disorganized inbox and responses sent way too late?

Here is a simple plan, based partly on a system devised by productivity guru David Allen, author of *Getting Things Done.*

Limit your time with it. Turn off all auto-notifications that alert you to incoming mail, and if you must check mail, keep it to a minimum. One good guideline: don't dip into your inbox more than three times an hour. It's unlikely that any message is so urgent that it can't wait 20 minutes for your response, and, if it were, the sender would call, send an instant message or find some other way to reach you.

Clear out your inbox. Set aside an hour or two to respond to every important message that has dogged you in the last couple months (anything older than that is too ancient to bother with). Next, move everything else into a new folder called Archive, which will be your storehouse of old mail.

Your inbox should now be empty. Your goal, from now on, will be to keep this space as pristine as possible. To realize that goal, live by this precept: whenever you receive a new message, do something with it. Don't read your e-mail and then just let it sit there; that's a recipe for chaos.

This isn't always so easy. A day's worth of mail demands a variety of complex actions, and figuring out how to respond to each message is probably what made your inbox untidy in the first place. That's where the next steps come in, an algorithm for dealing with incoming e-mail messages. For each new one you receive, take one of the following actions:

Archive it. Most e-mail messages require no action or response on your part, among them messages from Facebook letting you know that an old college pal has commented on your wall, for instance. Skim through these (or leave them unread), then shoot them into your archive and forget them.

Respond to it. If the e-mail message calls for an easy answer, send it. Say a colleague wants to know if you're up for dinner at his place on Saturday, or your boss wants to praise you for a job well done. Shoot back a quick response—"Yes!" or "Thanks!"—and then push the original message into your archive. Allen's rule of thumb is: if responding is going to take two minutes or less, you're better off doing it now than procrastinating.

Forward it. If the message is better handled by someone else, send it off to that person, then archive it.

Hold it for later. Some e-mail messages demand complicated answers. Others simply require information not yet available. You can leave these messages in your in-box with a promise to come back to them soon. Depending on the mail program you use, you might want to set a reminder or a flag to make it stand out.

But don't let too many of these pile up. Carve out perhaps 15 to 30 minutes at the end of the day to respond to all flagged e-mail. Remember, your goal is to keep your in-box empty. Each message sitting there should serve as a stark, visible reminder of your undisciplined ways.

—Farhad Manjoo

Help for Perfectionists
How to relieve the stress of getting everything just right

All employees want to make the boss happy. Which means that when given an assignment, you want to do your best. But at what cost?

Is it better to focus your attention on that one assignment, ignore all your other responsibilities, and turn in a perfect product? Or would your boss prefer that you balance the demands of your job, do your best given your time limits, and hand in something that is pretty darn good? The only person who can answer this question is your boss, but what happens if you're incapable of handing in anything that is less than perfect?

The answer is: you focus so intensively on each project that you take too long, and you hand things in late. Many bosses would prefer that an employee hand in a pretty good assignment on time, rather than something polished to perfection but past the deadline.

It can be just as destructive to be a perfectionist boss. Not only do you demand too much of yourself, but you also subject employees to your attention to detail. You also may find it hard to delegate because, after all, no one can do things as well as you.

How do you know if you have perfectionist work tendencies? Here are some examples of the way you might think. See if you recognize any.

- "The only way to get the job done right is my way."

- "I shouldn't make mistakes."

- "I must get perfect reviews."

- "I am surrounded by idiots."

- "If I ask for clarification from my boss, he/she will think I am incompetent."

- "I need to be at work before anyone else."

- "If I leave work before anyone else, my job will be in jeopardy."

Luckily, there are numerous ways to relieve some of this self-induced pressure. After all, you don't want to be miserable 5 days a week, 50 weeks a year.

Cultivate calm. Arrange your schedule so the start of the day can be spent planning, and the end of the day on loose ends.

Reward good behavior. Break assignments up into smaller tasks, then reward yourself for meeting each mini-goal. For every page reviewed, you are allowed to read an e-mail joke, for example.

Watch your co-workers. Are they always at work on time? Is every report perfect? Have they ever taken a long lunch and not been fired? Comparing yourself with others might help acquaint you with reality.

Stop trying to impress. Pleasing others can take a lot of time. Express your needs clearly and learn to say no when appropriate.

Prioritize. Assign each incoming task to a category: must get done today, would be nice if it were done today, and must get done eventually.

Finally, try letting go a little at a time. Remember: practice makes perfect.

—Alice D. Domar, author of
Be Happy Without Being Perfect.

How to Get Your Next Raise
Timing, common sense and a lot of self-confidence will help

The last thing anyone wants to do is alienate the boss by asking for a raise, regardless of the economic climate. While it's impossible to predict exactly how your boss will react, your chances for a favorable outcome increase by avoiding a few pitfalls. Here's a roundup of the best advice career counselors have to offer on when to strike, what to say and what to avoid saying.

Time it right. A little common sense helps. If your company has just lost a major contract, released poor earning or is downsizing, hold off. Similarly, if your job performance has slipped lately, it's no time to call attention to yourself.

When is a good time? If you work for a large organization with a formal human resources policy, the best time is during your performance review. If you work for a small company with no structured policy, approach your boss just after you've made a big sale, brought in a new client, implemented a new computer system or written a blockbuster story, for example.

Another timing tip: Don't hit your boss with it unexpectedly. Make an appointment for an appropriate time, say, after the day's big meetings end.

Research comparable salaries. Be armed with data on comparable salaries in your industry. Such information is readily available. Professional associations publish salary surveys, for example, and state employment services also put out statistics. Check online job postings for work similar to yours to get an idea of salary ranges. Go to the Bureau of Labor Statistics site at www.bls.gov for average pay scales for different jobs (see also page 404), to America's Career Infonet (www.acinet.org) or to salary comparison calculators at www.salary.com and www.hotjobs.com, among others. At Glassdoor.com you will find anonymously posted salary information. The site is one of a growing number of Web sites that list salaries by specific company rather than by general job description.

But keep in mind that salaries for the same position can vary by location. So the more localized the information, the better. Remember, too, that salaries will also differ depending on specific responsibilities, years worked and level of expertise.

Do not try to find out how much your co-workers are being paid. Many companies are highly secretive about this information, and some prohibit the practice.

Accentuate the positive. Don't assume that you deserve a raise just because of seniority or because your colleague got one. You will have to sell yourself. A PowerPoint presentation may be over the

---

? EXPERT ANSWER

How Much Is He Making?

💡 If you know how much your colleagues make, should you ever reveal it to your boss?

Just because Marvin Gaye crooned about what he heard through the grapevine doesn't mean you should, too. Human resources managers say employees should stick to generalities when referring to the salaries of co-workers, because many companies have policies that prohibit employees from discussing salary issues with each other. Mentioning specifics about others' raises may identify you (and your co-workers) as violators of company policy.

Those who openly discuss the salaries of co-workers run another risk: alienating the boss. Typically, a general manager of an independent film company says he never responds in a positive way to this tactic. "My response to the old 'I know I'm not making as much as so-and-so' complaint is, 'What someone else at this company earns is none of your business,'" he says. "I don't care what industry you're in, it's a terrible negotiating strategy, and it gets you nowhere." —Matt Villano

---

top, but you will need to prove specific contributions. Point out the sales growth in your portfolio over the previous year, for example, or itemize changes you made in your department and the resulting savings to the company. Use the industry salary data to prove that you are working for less but producing more.

When you enumerate reasons why you deserve a raise, be sure to focus on your successes, not on sacrifices you may have made.

Ultimatums rarely work. Be assertive and self-confident but not aggressive. Clearly state what you want and why you deserve it. Ask for an amount that's a bit higher—say, a few percentage points—than what you're willing to accept. You may end up with close to what you want. Or, consider accepting certain perks or increased vacation time instead of a flat raise.

If you use an ultimatum as part of your raise negotiations, be prepared to follow through. Don't threaten to quit unless you are willing to walk out the door. Remember, too, that even if your boss gives in, your reputation may suffer in the end. No one likes to be coerced.

Take the high road. At the end of your pitch, your boss may agree that you deserve a raise, or a few more weeks of vacation, or a more flexible schedule.

But what if your boss turns down your request? Whatever you do, say career counselors, don't lose your cool. Hold in your anger. Focus, instead, on asking about areas that you can improve, then make an appointment to discuss your progress within a few months. Don't forget to keep detailed documentation on your performance until then.

When You Get a Better Offer

If you're lucky enough to be approached by another firm, here's what to do

Out of the blue, a competitor offers you a job for more money than you're earning now. Should you try to use the offer to get a raise from your current employer?

Any attempt to parlay a competitor's interest into more money from your boss is likely to be fraught with peril. Mark Oldman, a founder of the recruitment firm Vault.com, says that while employees may see this as an opportunity to leverage a raise, employers could view it as a reason to question your commitment to the company.

"Playing a game of offer-counteroffer immediately calls your loyalty into question," Oldman says. "There are ways to do this successfully, but to get what you want without alienating the boss requires you to proceed with caution." Here is some further advice on how to proceed.

Q What should you do first?

Review the offer thoroughly and be sure you are willing to take it, because if your salary gambit fails, you may have to. Most surprise offers come by telephone, but it's important to meet with the competitor after hours or on a lunch break to discuss the offer. This meeting is also a good opportunity to get information about the job, your prospective colleagues and the corporate culture you might join. Ideally, by the time you're ready to make up your mind, you will have met 10 or 12 people and will have a solid understanding of what the job will be like.

But avoid planning these meetings over company e-mail or your work phone. Also, if you signed a noncompete agreement when you took your current job, any form of employment with a competitor could be prohibited. Check with an attorney before making a mistake that could cost you everything.

Q At what point should you inform your boss of the offer?

While it may be tempting to get excited about an offer as it develops, Anthony Townsend, associate professor at Iowa State University, says employees should not consider any overtures official until they have received at least a letter outlining specifics like salary, benefits and general responsibilities. Once they are willing to put it in writing, then you can treat it more like a contract.

Q How do you conduct negotiations with your current boss?

Explain how the offer came in, outline what

aspects of it appeal to you, and enumerate what components of your current job make you want to stay. Another strategy is to couch the issue as a collaborative problem-solving discussion, seeking input from your boss rather than demanding answers. Enlisting your boss in the solution shows that you are not just engaged in an offer-counteroffer game, but that you're interested in getting past it together.

● How much should you reveal about the offer?

It's not necessary to say how much money the competitor is willing to pay you, says Jim Camp, president of Coach 2100, a negotiation training firm in Vero Beach, Fla., but you should outline what kind of salary increase you require to stay. Camp warns that revealing details of a competing offer might put your boss on the defensive.

Don't exaggerate the terms of the offer in an effort to get more out of your current employer. Most senior executives have a solid understanding of the employment market and will know when you're embellishing the truth.

● If your boss counteroffers with a competitive salary, is it time to celebrate?

Not necessarily. A counteroffer could begin a journey to the unemployment line. Katherine E. Simmons, chief executive of NetShare, an online job board, says she once capitulated after an employee used an offer from a competitor to leverage a heftier salary. Looking back, Simmons says she felt as if she had a "gun to her head" to increase the employee's pay, but did so because she needed the help. After that, her relationship with the employee fell apart, and the employee resigned four months later. "Once an employee violates the boss's trust, both parties will want to end the relationship quickly," Simmons says.

—Matt Villano

How to Fire Someone

It's a nasty job, but there are ways to make "parting company" less odious

For every person who is fired, there is someone whose job it is to fire them, and those who have dismissed colleagues say it is something they dread. And it is a job made more complicated by the fact that most people who fire others are figuring it out as they go along. Not that such knowledge makes it easier if you are the one being let go.

If you find yourself being fired, the most important thing to remember is that you'll be in shock, and you won't be thinking straight, so don't feel the need to ask every question then and there. You should make sure to leave the room knowing how to contact someone who can answer your questions later on, when you have a chance to calm down. Try not to become defensive or argumentative; if there are issues to be disputed, you can do that later.

The same general advice applies to those charged with doing the firings, namely, keep things short and calm. "The goal is to do it in a way that you don't feel awful about yourself, that you treated someone with respect," says Donna Flagg, president of the Krysalis Group, a business and management consulting firm, who has fired more than two dozen people during her decade in retail sales. "I don't think anyone is actually good at it," she says.

When those with experience were asked for the dos and don'ts of how to fire an employee, they all agreed on one thing: don't ever use the word "fire." "It's time for us to part company," is Flagg's preferred phrasing. Others opt for the phrase "let you go." Or, as one manager says when breaking dismissal news, "It's time to help you succeed elsewhere."

There are two kinds of exit conversations, those that are personal (an employee has done something to warrant dismissal) and those that are not (the company is foundering or merging and someone

CAREERS

Pregnant and Laid Off?

What to do when the stork carries a pink slip

It may not sound fair, but it is entirely legal to lay off a pregnant woman or a woman on maternity leave, as long as the employer can make the case that she is being let go for a reason unrelated to her pregnancy.

It is, of course, illegal to dismiss someone or refuse to hire her specifically because she is pregnant, according to Title VII of the Civil Rights Act of 1964. But few employers are foolish enough to cite pregnancy as the reason for firing or not hiring someone.

Aside from such blatant discrimination, pregnant women have no special protection under federal employment law, says Elizabeth Grossman, a lawyer for the New York district office of the Equal Employment Opportunity Commission.

How should a woman proceed if she has a complaint? Expectant or new mothers who suspect employer discrimination should talk first to the company's human resources department, experts say. If the company is unresponsive, call an employment lawyer (some give free consultations), or phone or e-mail the WorkLife Law hot line (800-981-9495; hotline@worklifelaw. org). If you are being terminated, do not sign anything until you have spoken with a lawyer.

If you decide to file a discrimination charge with the federal Equal Employment Opportunity Commission (800-669-4000; www.eeoc. gov/charge/overview_charge_filing.html), do it sooner rather than later. The deadlines can come quickly, depending on the state in which you work. But be warned: the agency's process can take months, and only 30 percent of charges end with a benefit for the employee.

To learn more about your rights, go to these E.E.O.C. Web pages: www.eeoc.gov/types/ pregnancy.html and www.eeoc.gov/policy/ docs/caregiving.html.   —Lesley Alderman

has to go). Of the two, the first is far more complicated. The dismissal is in fact a direct attack on a worker's worth. There is no ego-shielding veil, like a poor economy, to hide behind.

The goal for those handling a difficult employee firing is to treat the worker like a person, not like an item you delete from your screen. That advice also happens to make good business sense. Every dismissal has an audience, veterans say, consisting of employees who remain. If you march a staff member out of the office sobbing, people watch. The best of your staff can always get good jobs elsewhere, even in the worst economy, and they will, if word is that you mistreat others.

Another rule on the list of don'ts is never to fire people online. Radio Shack made headlines when it did that a few years back, sending an e-mail message to 400 employees that read, "The work-force reduction notification is currently in progress. Unfortunately your position is one that has been eliminated." Large-scale layoffs are less of an ego blow because a company is flailing. But they are stressful, and the end result is the same: you are out of a job.

—Lisa Belkin

What to Do If You Lose Your Job

Smart career moves for a poor economy

You've been laid off and are having trouble finding another job. Should you consider applying to graduate school? That depends on several things, including your industry, your long-term career goals and your financial situation.

If a graduate degree makes sense generally for your career, this period of unemployment could be seen as a window of opportunity, says Jeffrey A. Heath, a managing director of the Landstone Group in Manhattan, an affiliate of the recruitment firm MRINetwork.

"Let's say you've spent 10 years in finance and you want to stay in this career," he says, "In a couple of years the market will be healthier, and you will have your master's degree."

Being unemployed for a prolonged period can take a psychological toll. "People begin questioning their value, often for the first time in their lives. Knowing you're working toward something will make you feel better."

Graduate school can also be a way to reinvent yourself. If you have previously thought of going in another direction, now may be the time to do so. You will need contacts in any new profession, and graduate programs can help connect you with alumni working in that field, says Eileen Kohan, executive director of the career planning and placement center at the University of Southern California.

Regardless of your motivation, carefully consider your personal financial situation before making a decision. Graduate school isn't cheap. If your portfolio is down and cash reserves are short, it may not be a wise choice right now. Many students pay for their tuition with federal and private loans. Individual schools and certain organizations—such as local bar associations, fraternities and sororities, social clubs and veterans groups—may offer scholarships and grants based on merit, financial need or both.

Ask yourself how much more marketable you will be after getting the degree. What do jobs in this industry pay for those with a master's degree? And is the industry growing or shrinking? What will the return be on your investment?

If you want to move into a new field, how do you decide what to study? You may want to explore the "road not taken," a career that previously appealed to you but that you never had a chance to pursue. Still, be realistic. Take a hard look at which areas in the economy are hiring and where the need for workers is growing, like science, health care and accounting. Join professional associations and do some research on their Web sites to learn about hiring trends and industry leaders. After all, you don't want to go into another industry that is about to go belly up.

One factor that may affect your decision to return to school is that competition for admission could be stiff because others who are unemployed are also heading back to school. All recessions since 1980 have corresponded with an upswing in the number of Graduate Management Admissions Tests taken. Sheer volume will make it tougher to get into grad school.

Another decision is whether to attend school full time or on nights and weekends. Much depends on how you can manage without a paycheck for 2 years. Attending part time takes longer but gives you the flexibility to look for work during the day and take a new job, even a part-time one.

For many graduate degrees, attending full time or part time doesn't affect how employers perceive the degree. But some full-time programs, such as an M.B.A. or a law degree from a top school, have a pedigree that is more attractive to employers. And daytime programs are where a school's career resource efforts and recruiting programs are focused.

—Eilene Zimmerman

When to Jump Ship
Steps to take when the job isn't as promised

You've been on the job a month, and your responsibilities aren't what the boss said they would be. You may be overwhelmed with unexpected tasks, like overseeing an intern program in addition to performing day-to-day duties. Or you may find yourself outside the circle of power—left out of important meetings and limited in the num-

CAREERS

ber of colleagues with whom you are allowed to consult. What should you do?

By all means, speak up, says Francie Dalton, president of Dalton Alliances, a Columbia, Md., consulting firm. "If you don't say anything about your frustration with the situation, you're simply implying your consent," she says. Express your concern to the boss in the context of the business. Marky Stein, author of *Fearless Interviewing*, suggests that logging daily work activities for at least two weeks to create a pie chart or bar chart that shows how your time is spent. Stein says the chart should provide detailed proof of how and where your job differs from what was promised.

"You could call this a type of 'time motion' study with the subject as yourself," she says. "Bosses love visuals, and if you are very detailed about your study, the evidence will be hard to challenge." Such a chart could also help employees ensure they haven't confused their own fantasies with what the boss told them to expect—a common problem that comes with excitement about a new job opportunity.

So, how much time should you give a disappointing job before complaining? Even in the most disappointing jobs, patience can be a virtue. Experts say 90 days is a fair amount of time to assess a new job. Many employers use the first 6 weeks for training new hires, making that period an unreliable representation of how a job will play out.

Once you've made your position known, there should be some give and take. If your employer shows no interest in improving your situation, it may be time to start circulating your résumé again.

There are ways to prevent this problem from happening in the first place, however. Before you take the job, find out what the new workplace is really like. Some employers offer "realistic job

---

☑ **TIMELY TIPS**

If Your Company Is Sold

Should you sit tight or head for the exits?

Your company's been acquired, and you're waiting for the ax to fall. When do you pursue a new job?

✔ **It's never too early to line up an exit strategy.** Charlie Fleetham, president of Project Innovations, a consulting firm, says employees should send out résumés immediately upon news of an acquisition. If you interview at other companies, it's acceptable to tell them that the acquisition inspired you to look around. But, don't dwell on it.

"Go in and talk about how you're worried you're going to lose your job and you'll end up with nothing at all," he says. "Instead, mention the transition, but focus on your strengths and talents and how they will fit the new position."

✔ **If you choose to leave, make sure you are not walking away with money on the table.** Career coach Marc Karasu says many stock options vest immediately in an acquisition, so it pays to check what you have earned. Many companies also offer bonuses for staying through a transition, and these financial incentives can be lucrative if you are willing to endure the uncertainties.

—Matt Villano

---

previews"—opportunities to spend some time on the job with current employees, for example, or videos that demonstrate typical workdays. Prospective employees can also ask on their own to spend some time in the office to experience the culture.

More fundamentally, before accepting a new job, ask for a written description of the position, spelling out the specific responsibilities. That could save you grief down the road.   —Matt Villano

How to Get Your Head Hunted

A top headhunter on what it takes to get on a "most wanted" list

Headhunters prowl the corporate jungle, trying to lure the best and brightest managers and executives from one company to another. So why hasn't your phone rung with a juicy job offer? One of the nation's leading headhunters, Gerard Roche, spent a 50-year career at the executive search firm Heidrick & Struggles, Inc., in New York. His clients have included Disney, Coca-Cola, Office Depot, Starwood Hotels and Resorts and Home Depot. Here's his advice.

Q How do you get a headhunter's attention?

Do an extraordinary job at the job you're in, and set a track record where you get recognition. The thing that will get our attention is your current job reputation. Nothing else is nearly as important. If you succeed to a high extent, we'll smoke you out.

One way to get noticed is to be active in your industry—attend association meetings, give a speech, write an article or get a top newsmagazine to quote you. Do whatever you can to be unique and let people know you're a leader. A strong reputation and résumé are mostly gained through individual effort, not public relations departments.

Q Say you're ready to move on. Is it wise to approach a headhunter yourself?

This is a networking game. I get hundreds of résumés a week, so just sending a résumé isn't the best move. If you want to approach a top headhunter, try to get someone who knows them to recommend that they pay special attention to you.

Q If a headhunter calls, how forthcoming should you be?

It's strictly a matter of whether you're the one pursuing a job, or the one being pursued. If you're secure in a position with an established reputation and not looking for a job—which is the type of people we normally go after—listen, see what the person has to offer, then respond as you see fit and feel comfortable doing.

If you're looking for a job, never take a headhunter's call raw. Ask if you can call back; this gives you a chance to find out exactly who is calling. Call back when it's convenient for you to talk privately. How forthcoming you are depends on how much you're interested in a new job. Even if you're looking, you should still have a certain amount of detached interest.

Q Sure, headhunters are hired to search for C.E.O.'s. What if you're a smaller fish in the corporate pond?

It's simple—just do your job. If you excel, we'll pick you up on our radar. If you spend most of your time trying to get our attention, you're probably not going to get it.

Re-entering the Workplace

When jumping back in, prepare for resistance and a long hunt

It happens. You launch a career, then take time off to tend to a growing family and later try to jump back in. Legions of men and women leave the work force to take a break. Sylvia Ann Hewlett, founding president of the Center for Work-Life Policy, has described this type of career detour, which is more common for women than for men, as "off-ramping." Typically it occurs when the balancing act of parenting and work becomes too arduous.

A study by the center found that more than 90 percent of women who off-ramp want to on-ramp back into the work force eventually. But making the transition back to work is rarely easy, and it is even harder during times of layoffs and hiring freezes.

CAREERS

Generally, say those who have made a successful re-launch, the time it takes to find a position is more prolonged and more involved than just mining postings on the Internet. Networking like crazy and hiring a career coach to ensure that your re-entrance looks more like a pirouette than a clumsy stumble can help.

Emma Gilbey Keller, who wrote *The Comeback: Seven Stories of Women Who Went From Career to Family and Back Again,* says that one of the most efficient ways to return to the work force is to look for project-based employment and temporary work. "Short-term work is going to be easier to come by than landing the managing editor position or a getting on the partner track at a law firm," she says.

According to one school of thought, women looking to make a comeback might even have an advantage in a down economy, especially if they are looking for part-time or consultant positions that do not offer benefits. And a majority of on-rampers are women with extensive résumés that could give them an edge over less-experienced competition.

Regardless of the job sought, though, experts and those in the trenches warn to be prepared for resistance. "You have to anticipate questions about whether you are really ready to get back into the work force and why now," says Sarah Grayson, a partner at On-Ramps, a recruiting and consulting firm specializing in workplace innovation. "Some employers have been burned by on-rampers" who have changed their minds, she says.

Even if many on the hiring side are empathetic, coming up with a language to talk about a career detour is crucial. For one thing, you cannot be defensive about why you off-ramped. One response might be, "Yes, I have been out of the work force, but here is where I can make significant contributions." —Hannah Seligson

---

ⓘ **INSIDE INFO**

Making a Comeback

○ For all the comeback success stories (consider the tumultuous careers of Donald Trump and Martha Stewart), corporate comebacks are by no means easy. A study by two professors at Yale and the University of Georgia, found that of the chief executives at the 1,000 largest American companies who were dismissed for negative reasons, only half had returned to leadership roles.

○ Those who do succeed do so by dint of their own optimism, experts say; others use the skills that got them to the top in the first place. A few use connections they made over the years. Often they attain their goals simply because they refuse to give up.

—Geraldine Fabrikant

When It's Time to Switch Careers

A guidance guru's secrets for making a successful switch

The typical American worker can expect to have two or three different careers during his professional life. So, what's the best way to make a smooth transition to a new career? Here's some advice from Richard Bolles, author of the perennially popular *What Color Is Your Parachute?,* a useful guide for first-time job seekers and seasoned career switchers.

Q How do I know when I'm ready for a career change, and not just bored in my current job?

Ask yourself these questions:

1. Do I like my present boss or bosses, and do I enjoy working for them?

2. Do I like my co-workers and enjoy working with them?

3. Do I like what I do—the tools I work with, the product I produce, the information I disseminate, or the people I am trying to help?

4. Am I using the skills I most love to use?

5. Do I really like the field I am in?

If your answer to either of the first two is no, you should consider changing your job, though not necessarily your career. But if your answer to any of the last three questions is no, you probably need to think about changing careers.

Q **Let's say I know I want to make a career change but don't know what I want to do.**

There are two ways to solve this common puzzle. First, think about all the people you know or see in a given week. Ask yourself if any of them has a job you would really like to have. If so, what is that job? Second, identify your favorite skills and fields of interest. Your skills are verbs ending in "ing," such as "designing," "writing," "researching," "sewing" and the like. They are transferable from one field to another. Fields of interest are nouns, like "stamps," "computers," "gardens," "design" and "insurance." Your favorite transferable skills, plus your favorite fields of interest will define a new career.

Q **Once I've decided what I'd like to do, how do I find a job that matches my skills and interests?**

If you know the skills you'd like to use, and the field you'd like to be in, but are not clear as to which career it all points to, there's an easy way to find out. Talk to people in the field. Make use of the Internet and the Yellow Pages to contact them. Ask what kinds of careers in that field require the skills you have identified as your favorites. Keep going, until you find some answers you like.

Q **If I want to break into an entirely new field, where and how do I start a job search?**

Once you have identified the career, talk to at least five people who are doing that work. Locate associations of companies in that field. Find out everything you can about that career. When talking to people in your targeted career, ask these questions: How did you get your job? What do you like most about it? What do you like least? Who else would you recommend I talk to? Since you're talking to workers, not employers, and you're asking them how they found their job, you'll get plenty of ideas about finding work in the field. If your sources live nearby and the career still interests you, ask them if you can observe them at work for a day to see what the job involves in detail.

Q **What is the most challenging aspect of changing careers?**

Most challenging is taking the time to identify your favorite skills and fields of interest. The process, if done right, takes a full weekend. Next comes taking the time to interview workers in your new career before going job hunting. Most people want to leap over these two essential preliminary steps. Consequently, their career change is often an "out of the frying pan, into the fire" experience.

Q **If I'm changing careers at midlife, how do I compete with younger candidates?**

Know your skills better, know the field better and be a harder worker. Come in earlier, stay later, miss fewer days. Finally, you have to be able to tell an employer why you can do the work better than other candidates, whether they're younger or older.

Q **Should I work with a career counselor? If so, what should I expect?**

The rule is "Don't rely just on the advice of well-meaning friends." Instead, master the process of changing careers through your own self-study course. Less than $20 for a helpful book may be all you need to spend. But if that doesn't work,

How to Take a Sabbatical

Plan carefully before you present your case

In academia, professors routinely take sabbaticals in order to recharge. Could that be an option for you in the corporate world? Yes. In fact, 16 percent of American companies have formal unpaid sabbatical programs, and 5 percent offer paid sabbaticals, according to the Society for Human Resource Management.

Corporate sabbaticals are usually shorter than academic ones. One reason, experts say, is that the longer you're out of touch, the higher the risk that you will seem less important in your job than you are. Experts generally suggest taking no more than three months off.

But don't even consider asking for a sabbatical unless you are a high-performing employee who has been at the company for several years. If you are an average or marginal performer, you risk being perceived as someone who isn't serious about his or her career.

Before you present your case to your manager, decide exactly why you want to take the sabbatical and how you want to spend it. The best case you can make to your manager is a business case, not a personal one. Being burned out is a reason for a vacation, not a sabbatical. Write a proposal outlining how both you and the company will benefit from your time away, what you intend to do and what you hope to achieve, consultants say.

If you want to take a continuing education class, for example, or volunteer to work in Africa on a project to fight AIDS, describe how your efforts will relate to your professional development goals. You might mention how it will make you a better employee and that you will come back refreshed and more creative.

You will also need a plan for covering your responsibilities, one that shows how your work will be seamlessly handled by others while you are away, so that neither clients nor co-workers suffer.

Make structured plans, also, for how you will use your time. Otherwise, you may be apt to waste it. Set out your goals—to take a class, to read several business books, to spend some time with family—and block out time daily for each activity.

Once you return, your work colleagues will be curious and perhaps a bit resentful, thinking that you have been idle. The best way to handle a transition back to the office is to talk to them as soon as possible. Have a lunch and discuss what you learned and how it will let you contribute more to the team. Engender camaraderie rather than resentment. Just don't gush about the singing lessons you took or how you learned to play the guitar. —Eilene Zimmerman

look for other low-cost resources—seminars, testing, counseling—available through a community college, library or chamber of commerce.

Only when you have exhausted these resources should you turn to a paid career counselor. When you do, find one who charges by the hour. (Fees are generally the same as those of a competent therapist.) You should not have to sign anything before you begin counseling, and you should be able to end the hourly meetings at any time. The counselor's stated goal should be to teach you how to change careers yourself, rather than trying to do it all for you. Visit at least three counselors before choosing the one you feel is most competent.

● What about using a headhunter?

Headhunters generally work for employers, who have hired them. They typically look for candidates who already work for organizations or companies and are tops in their field. A career-changer's chances of being of interest to a headhunter are slim. Still, it can't hurt to send your résumé to a headhunter, as long as it doesn't take too much of your time.

● What if I identify a dream career but can't find a job in that field?

Your backup is to pick up your list of favorite skills and fields of interest, each ranked in order of preference. Show this list to everyone you know and ask them which careers or jobs the list might suggest to them. Then interview workers in the careers that interest you. Your dream may have more than one form, but you should never give up on that dream.

Hot Jobs for Career Switchers
Three popular choices for those who move on

Restlessness, corporate burnout, the desire for autonomy, the need for flexibility: these are some of the motives driving people toward a career change. And thanks to longer life spans and shifting cultural norms, midcareer transitions are increasingly common.

Here are three of the most popular fields for people making a change—and the educational skills you'll need to make the transition—according to career consultants and those who track employment trends. But use the list cautiously. Consider first your personal interests, talents, life goals and whether the career makes sense for you. Can you handle the considerable workload demanded for a master's degree, or just juggle a few skill-building courses? Are you willing to take a pay cut? Be low man on the totem pole? As Helen Harkness, author of *Don't Stop the Career Clock*, says, "Look inward first, and then outward to see if there is a marketplace fit."

Nonprofits. Employment in nonprofit organizations has grown by more than 30 percent in the last decade, according to the Independent Sector

in Washington, an industry coalition. Midcareer changers who choose nonprofit work are typically burned out by the business world, yet still game for professional challenge, despite salaries that are 20 to 50 percent lower than in business or government.

SKILLS: Follow the money. That means learning grant proposal writing, fund-raising, and nonprofit operations and management. The Nonprofit Academic Centers Council (www.naccouncil.org) can connect you to schools that offer degree programs and certification courses.

For example, the Association of Fundraising Professionals (www.afpnet.org) offers certification programs in fund-raising techniques and other essentials. The Foundation Center (www.fdncenter.org), offers online tutorials and classes in grant writing, fund-raising and management at centers across the country. The Grantsmanship Center (www.tgci.com) holds hundreds of workshops a year around the country. Its basic programs teach researching and writing grant proposals and negotiating with financing sources.

Nursing. The demand for registered nurses is greater than ever, as is the shortage: more than a million additional nurses will be needed by 2016, according to government figures. Compensation matches the demand: with salaries of $40 to $50 an hour plus overtime, nurses can earn more than $100,000 a year. This would seem to make nursing a good bet for midcareer changers, and in fact, a third of students enrolled in training are 31 to 50 years old, according to the National League for Nursing.

SKILLS: The most efficient way in for an adult is through an accelerated bachelor's of science in nursing degree—concentrated, rigorous training for those who already hold a bachelor's in another area and want a quick transition into nursing. More than 160 universities around the country offer accelerated, 11-to-18-month degrees. Lists of programs

CAREERS

can be found on the Web site of the American Association of Colleges of Nursing (www.aacn. nche.edu) and at the online guide All Nursing Schools (www.allnursingschools.com).

Teaching. Hundreds of thousands of teachers are set to retire, and schools are counting on older workers entering the profession to help fill the gap. The biggest needs are in the West and Northeast, and in urban schools. Career changers are hearing the call: some 70,000 have turned to teaching in the past few years.

SKILLS: Many career changers, unwilling or unable to invest the time or money needed for a traditional university education degree, take advantage of fast-track training and job placement programs leading to certification. Virtually every state has alternative

routes into teaching, some accelerated.

Two ways to find them are through Recruiting New Teachers (www.rnt.org) and the National Center for Alternative Certification (www.teach-now. org). Education departments at local colleges and universities can also provide information on available programs and state licensing requirements.

—Cecilia Capuzzi Simon

Over 55 and Job Hunting?

How to approach the search—and answer touchy questions

You are over 55 and job hunting for the first time in many years. Will potential employers be leery of hiring you because of your age?

Possibly. Although it is illegal to exclude an older candidate based on age, there is still plenty of age discrimination in the job market, according to labor practice lawyers. Most hiring managers know enough not to ask about age, but their concerns about energy level, technological ability and retirement still exist.

Older workers can take a proactive approach to overcoming those concerns in their résumés and in interview conversations by staying focused on long-term objectives.

Your age and your résumé. You should never lie about your age. At the same time, you can take steps to minimize attention to it. Your goal is to use your résumé to get an interview, because that's where you will have an opportunity to show that your age is not an issue.

Revise descriptions of your previous jobs to ensure that the terms being used are current. For example, if 15 years ago you were head of the personnel office, that should be changed to human resources. Do not list the years when you graduated from college or

---

ⓘ INSIDE INFO

Where Career Switchers Go

○ Nearly 60 percent of workers have changed careers—not just jobs—and more than half of those have done so more than once, according to a recent survey by the University of Phoenix, whose emphasis is adult education programs.

○ "Recareerists"—as they are called—are transforming education, leading to all manner of continuing education classes, online universities, certificates and graduate degrees designed to qualify workers to do something completely new. Adults age 25 and older account for more than a third of those enrolled at degree-granting institutions, according to the National Center for Education Statistics. Enrollment is projected to increase 13 percent among 25- to 29-year-olds and 23 percent among 30- to 34-year-olds by 2014.

○ Most workers who set out to change their lives wind up in positions related to the ones they left, according to Right Management Consultants.   —Lisa Belkin

graduate school. The omission may or may not raise a red flag, but when a résumé is screened, recruiters are looking for specific degrees and minimum experience requirements, not specific dates.

Show your level of energy by adding a section on your activities or hobbies. If you are an avid runner or recreational cyclist, say so. To illustrate your ability to work with people of all ages, include any mentoring you have done, either at previous jobs or in your community through volunteer work.

Keeping up with technology. Many employers worry that older workers can't keep up with changing technology. To reassure potential employers, it is crucial to show them that you are comfortable with technology and can adapt easily. Join social networks like LinkedIn and Facebook and include your address on the site on your résumé.

Create a Web site, or have one professionally done, with a résumé and samples of your work, and include that Web site link on your résumé also. Take classes to familiarize yourself with new software programs in your industry and add those courses to your résumé.

Handling the interview. If you get an interview, how do you handle issues, like your health, energy level or when you plan to retire? You won't be asked about them directly, but if you sense that there is concern about any of these issues, ask about them directly. If you plan to keep working for a long time, you can say something like, "Do you have concerns I might retire soon? I have had a strong career in marketing and am still very creative. I love the work, and as I get older I find I don't want to move from company to company. I want to stay here for the next decade."

Be sure to mention any recent courses you have taken that relate to your field, like an updated management or accounting practices class. This will show that you are still learning and intend to

be working in your industry for a long time. And if you enjoy taking bike rides on the weekends, playing tennis and doing volunteer work, slip in a comment about them, too.

Capitalizing on your age. Many companies welcome older workers because of the breadth of their experience and knowledge. Rather than combing the large job boards for openings, you might start with job boards that cater to older workers, like retireeworkforce.com, primecb.com and retirementjobs.com.

Research companies before you apply, looking for those with a diversity of age and experience in their work force. Take the same approach when you work with staffing agencies and recruiters. That way, you will stop seeing your age as a liability and will be in a position to confidently convey the major professional advantages that your age, and the experience that goes with it, has conferred on you.

Your legal rights. If you feel you have been discriminated against because of your age, contact a lawyer who specializes in employment law, but keep in mind that age discrimination is very hard to prove unless the interviewer has made a statement directly related to your age.   –Eilene Zimmerman

CAREERS

Being Your Own Boss

Thinking about self-employment? Consider these factors first

In a society that reveres rugged individualism, self-employment has always had a certain allure. In fact, each month from 2002 through 2007, just under 300 of every 100,000 adults in the United States started a business, according to the Kauffman Index of Entrepreneurial Activity.

When the economy is strong, people may try self-employment because the opportunities seem plentiful and financing is easy to get. And in harder times, it can seem a tempting option for people who have just been laid off or are watching as colleagues all around them lose their jobs.

But mystique aside, is self-employment always an attractive option? Working for yourself offers distinct advantages. You can say goodbye to that pointless 10 a.m. sales meeting, for example. Your schedule is often your own. If a one-person business succeeds, well, owner takes all. And when opportunities surface, there is no bureaucracy to slow response time.

Many find, however, that being their own boss is harder than they expected. Isolation and loneliness are possibilities, and the risk of failure is high. Fewer than half of all start-ups survive 5 years, and only 25 percent last 10 years, according to Ari Ginsberg, professor of management and organizations at the Stern School of Business at New York University. Moreover, a failed stint in self-employment is not exactly a plus for a résumé.

What helps, several experts say, is thinking of self-employment as a business problem and adjusting corporate management skills to a one-person operation.

Consider performance measurement. An independent marketing consultant needs a set of business goals just as much as a midlevel corporate marketer needs performance objectives. "Self-employed people need to create a structure for themselves, and a schedule," says Howard Seidel, a partner at Essex Partners, an outplacement and career counseling firm specializing in senior executives. "They need to create measurements for themselves. If you have a business plan to map against, you can look at what you're doing."

Then there is administration. A corporate manager relies on others to handle filing, purchasing and the like, but that infrastructure disappears in a one-person shop. There is no lawyer on staff, and no one to order Post-it notes. Self-employed people who learn to manage behind-the-scenes functions efficiently have more time for their core business.

They also need to focus on selling, and, although not everyone has a sales personality, you have to

---

✓ **TIMELY TIPS**

A Chair Fit for a Chairman

Chances are you haven't given a lot of thought to what you sit on at the office. But ergonomics experts have. Here are some tips.

✔ **Fit comes first.** Find a chair that fits your body.

✔ **Beware cushy seats.** You don't want too much weight concentrated on your seat bones.

✔ **Avoid long cushions.** If you can't get against the backrest, you can't get a comfortable, healthy posture.

✔ **Keep moving.** The best way to stay pain-free is to avoid spending hours on end at your desk. Take a break every hour to walk around.

✔ **Backrests and armrests.** A chair with good back support gets the spine back into the natural "S curve" equilibrium.

SOURCE: Richard Holbrook, Pasadena, Calif.

accept that you are a salesperson, and build that into your infrastructure.

The self-employed also need certain skills, including attitude skills, which they may not have developed in corporate life, says Ginsberg. "You have to have the stomach for setbacks, great tenacity and commitment and passion. Those are things that you can't take for granted that someone necessarily possesses as a career manager."

—Kelley Holland

Launching Your Own Business

Here's how to minimize the risks

Before you join the ranks of the self-employed, think through the financial and emotional ramifications, says Jane Applegate, author of *201 Great Ideas for Your Small Business.* Applegate offers the following advice on launching your own business.

● How do I decide which business to go into?

Base the decision on skills you already have. It doesn't make sense to change careers completely, unless you plan to go to school or take special training classes. Figure out if the work you are doing for your current employer is salable and if you can promote those services or goods to former clients and customers after you leave your job. One way to test the market is to conduct your own short survey asking people if they would buy the goods or services you have to offer.

● What research should I do before starting a business?

Before you sink your savings into a business, sign up for classes, attend seminars and consider volunteering in a business similar to the one you have in mind. Meet with other small-business owners—they'll probably tell you more than you ever wanted to know. You can also get free counseling

through your local Small Business Development Center. Another program, sponsored by the Small Business Administration, is called SCORE, for the Service Corps of Retired Executives.

● How much of my own money should I invest?

That depends on the business you're setting up. If you plan to open a retail store, you will need money to buy merchandise, and pay rent and the staff—all before you make your first sale. A service business usually needs less capital to get started. No matter what sort of business you start, as a general rule, set aside twice as much as you think you'll need. And sock away at least six months' worth of living expenses—it always takes longer to get off the ground than you expect.

● How do I attract business investors?

You need more than a dream to share with investors—you need a well-written business plan that will serve as a personal and professional road map. Most major accounting firms offer free business-planning guides, and there are many good planning resources on the market and the Internet.

● What are the best sources of financing?

Friends, family, shirttail relatives and colleagues are best. Many entrepreneurs think venture capitalists fund most new businesses, but in reality, they reject about 99 percent of the deals they consider. On the other hand, so-called angel investors—typically professionals looking to invest in a nearby business—put up about $6 out of every $10 invested in very small firms.

● What about bank loans?

Many banks shun high-risk start-ups, but if you have a substantial net worth or other investments, you can probably get a bank loan for your new business. If you don't qualify, try to get a loan guarantee from the Small Business Administration, which guarantees up to 90 per-

CAREERS

✔ **TIMELY TIPS**

Curing Home Office Chaos

Lisa Whited, an interior designer who specializes in adapting work spaces to her clients' particular needs and habits, offers the following tips for organizing your work space.

✔ The cardinal rule is to clear out the clutter. Get rid of broken things that you won't ever get around to fixing. A helpful guide is Karen Kingston's book *Clear Your Clutter With Feng Shui.*

✔ Color can help make a small or confined space feel more livable, and paint is the cheapest way to get it. Lighting is important: beyond a room's general illumination, which could be overhead lighting, you will need task lighting to work at your desk and accent lighting, like a hanging light, to create an inviting space.

✔ Organize your supplies in containers that are an appropriate size to hold what you're putting in them. They don't need to be fancy, but if they are going to be visible, they should at least look similar, so the space looks more pulled together.

✔ Get the best chair you can afford. It's like your bed: you spend a lot of time in it, and it has to provide you hours of support.

✔ Stockpile extra supplies like printer cartridges, reams of paper, staples, tape, etc. That way you won't waste time with frequent runs to the supply store.

✔ Don't dismiss the importance of candles, flowers, a great piece of art—whatever inspires you. It all helps.   —Sara Rimer

---

cent of the loan value. Small Business Investment Companies (www.nasbic.org), a group of private companies, offers government-backed loans and equity investments.

❓ When can I expect a profit?

If you are selling a product, you can potentially make money from day one. Other businesses, such as manufacturing or exporting, can take years to pay off. Service businesses may also take longer to build a clientele.

❓ How can I compete with a giant in my industry?

Entrepreneurs competing with a Goliath say the only way to succeed is to figure out a unique way of selling your products. You can't outspend a big corporation, so outsmart it: provide better and faster service, more personal attention, more intelligent sales people or a unique approach.

❓ How much should I pay myself?

There is no magic formula—just be sure that you are able to take something home. Calculate your total living expenses for a few months, and put that in the bank before you open the business. You don't want to sacrifice your family and your home for the business venture.

❓ What sacrifices will I need to make?

Be prepared to give up a steady paycheck, a worry-free life, and time for fun and family. You could be sacrificing your company's pension or 401(k) plan, so try to set up an I.R.A. or a small business pension plan to protect yourself when you retire.

❓ What are some benefits?

You'll enjoy a roller-coaster ride full of adrenaline and the potential to make more money than you ever dreamed of. You can also expect enormous flexibility, a sense of accomplishment and a realization that though you work hard, all the money will come straight back to you and your family.

HOUSE & GARDEN

HOUSE

Around the House

How to Pick a Contractor

It may be the most important decision you make in building your dream house

Whatever the economic climate, it seems that Americans revel in renovating their homes. Yet in making the most important decision in a major renovation—selecting the contractor who will be charged with turning a drawing into a dream house—many people rely on thirdhand hearsay, personal vibes and a big dose of optimism. Here is some advice on how to renovate successfully.

 INSIDE INFO

Smaller Families = Bigger Houses?

○ The size of the average new house built in the United States increased more than 50 percent since 1970, even as the size of the average family grew smaller.

○ Eighty-four percent of all new homes built in 2005 had two- or three-car garages, double the number in 1970, according to the National Association of Homebuilders.

○ Nearly a quarter of all spending on home improvement is being done by "zoomers" and "single empty nesters," according to NPD, a market research group, referring to couples and single parents 50 to 64 who have no children under 18 at home.

○ Projects people undertake: Enlarged, updated kitchens; bathroom complexes with ensuite dressing rooms; deluxe home offices.

—Jane Margolies

Before you start. Most experts suggest that you start planning what you want and how to finance it a year or more before you hire a contractor.

Your research should include visiting showrooms and decorator house shows to get ideas, developing a clipping file of things you like and surfing the Web—some helpful sites include www.thisoldhouse.com, www.hgtv.com and www.improvenet.com. You also need to learn the contracting lingo.

Unless you are an organizational whiz and know how to obtain permits and variances and schedule workers, you really do need a contractor on most jobs. If you are moving or removing walls or are redesigning a kitchen, you may also need an architect or a professional designer.

If you are planning just one change, like painting a room or redoing a bathroom, you may want to work directly with one reputable contractor in that trade instead of going through a general contractor.

In choosing the contractor, references alone mean next to nothing. It's how you check them that counts. Check not only for raves but also for the presence of repeat customers. Look for gaps. Ask clients not just whether they were happy but, more important, whether the job was done on time and on budget. How did the contractor handle unexpected glitches and changes?

Beyond solid references, look for a contractor who is a good communicator and a good executor. This person should tell you what is going to happen, when it will be messy, how long you will be without lights or water—then draw up a realistic schedule and stick to it.

Competitive bidding will not always result in the best deal. Architectural drawings almost always leave contractors room for interpretation. A good paint job, for instance, is typically described as "patching, priming and two coats of Benjamin Moore or equivalent." But how much sanding is enough: a couple of days or a couple of weeks? How smooth does smooth have to be? In a large home, the difference could amount to tens of thousands of dollars and weeks of work.

Contractors will bid on the scope of the work, which should be very specific, including model numbers of window and appliance choices, if possible. The more you can tell a contractor about your project, using blueprints or drawings, specifications, paint chips and hardware preferences, the better.

Beware of low-ballers. If one contractor bids more than 20 percent below the others, you have reason to be suspicious. Has the low bidder really taken a good look at the drawings, or is he just winging it? Is he so desperate for the work that he may not have enough money to carry it out? Some low bidders may count on compensating themselves for lost profits by charging unusually high prices for the inevitable changes. When a hidden pipe turns up in a wall you want to knock down, it's going to cost you.

A bid that goes into great detail is a good sign. Proposals that include quantities and unit prices are better than those that just say "Plumbing: $10,000." An attentive contractor will also ask probing questions and may well suggest ways to save money before the contract has been signed. He may want a small fee for fine-tuning such suggestions. That's O.K. Spending a little extra money and time here can save a lot of both later on.

Once you have checked out the company, do the same for the team assigned to your job. You

Should You Take a Low-Ball Bid?

Advice from three New York City contractors on how to handle home construction bids

Douglas Reetz: The issue is the spread. If you have bids within at most 15 percent of each other, there's probably no reason not to go with the lowest bid. On the other hand, if one bid is 25 percent lower than the rest, there is a problem. It should set off alarms.

Bill Paster: Generally, the low bid will come from someone who hasn't thought through the job properly, or doesn't have enough experience to understand what the job entails, or might be looking to get the job and make up some money with add-ons once you get started, or is looking to cut corners on materials and insurance and things you don't want him to cut corners on.

Stephen Fanuka: I won't tell you never to accept the lowest bid. You might get lucky and find a contractor who is really good but desperately needs a job to fill in a space in his calendar and keep his guys working. Ask for at least three references. Check to see there are no complaints against him and that he's fully licensed and insured.

—Edward Lewine

are well advised to ask for references on the two key figures on your contracting team: the project manager, who is responsible for your job, and the construction supervisor, who is the day-to-day representative (the one who will be sitting in your kitchen with your keys in his pocket). If you are audacious, you might also ask for the names of dissatisfied customers, to see if the problem was shoddy work or just poor chemistry.

Visits to work sites are of limited use to amateurs. Sure, a neat and organized site is a plus. On the other hand, construction is supposed to be messy.

Just in Case Things Go Wrong

Most contractors are reliable and hardworking, insists Thomas Kraeutler, host of the nationally syndicated radio show *The Money Pit.* But to guard against the few who aren't, here he suggests ways to forestall a home improvement disaster.

✔ **Pay the bill in installments.**
A common complaint is that the job takes longer to complete than a contractor estimated. To avoid this, include a "time of essence" clause, which charges the contractor penalties if the work takes too long. The contractor should also set forth a payment schedule. As a general rule, put up a small down payment and space out the remainder. Reserve at least 25 percent of the total amount for a final payment and release it only when you're completely satisfied with the work.

✔ **Check insurance.**
When checking insurance, make sure the contractor provides a "certificate of insurance" which names you as an "additional insured." This guarantees that the contractor's insurance company will attempt to notify you if the policy is canceled for any reason. Also, be sure to check the policy limit of the general comprehensive coverage. A basic policy offers a limit of $50,000. This isn't very much coverage in today's litigious world. For peace of mind, insist on at least $300,000 coverage. In New York City, the average is $1,000,000.

✔ **Keep a written record.**
Good documentation of the job is crucial if something goes wrong later or if disputes arise. Keep written notes of starting and stopping times, how many people are working and what's getting (or not getting) done. This is especially important if you are paying for the job by the hour. Also, for bigger jobs, keep notes of conversations you've had with contractors about problems, changes, etc.

✔ **Get an outside review.**
If any question arises about the quality of the job, have the work inspected by an independent professional, such as a home inspector. To find a good one in your area, go to the Web site of the American Society of Home Inspectors at www.ashi.org. With all contracts, be sure to have them reviewed by your attorney before signing. The expense of such a review can be well worth it in the event of future problems.

It would be more helpful to have your contractor arrange visits to several projects, each of them at least a couple of years old, to see how they are holding up. (Or better yet, arrange your own visits through references or friends, since the contractor is likely to send you to only his best work.) Are bathroom tiles loose? Are the moldings cracking? How about the paint job? Any sign of leaks?

A big name does not guarantee good service, especially with interest rates so low that work is plentiful. "All you get with a big company," says one New York architect, "is a guy in a suit."

The firm should be experienced in your type of renovation, the size of your project and budget, and your kind of apartment building or house.

The company should also be well versed in the permit process, which paralyzes many jobs. A crew of 30 skilled workers can't do much if they are locked out by the super. Nor will it help for the work to be completed on time if the contractor has neglected to arrange for the proper inspections.

Establishing that a contractor has basic competence is easy. Look for a licensed contractor,

The Renovation Roller Coaster

Anyone who has ever renovated a house knows about the highs and the lows, from the first thrilling moment when the old walls come down to the dark days when the plumber disappears and the carpenter changes his home phone number. But a mood indicator plotted on a timeline? Even a serial renovator might be surprised to learn that for some contractors, monitoring the client's emotional life is just part of the job.

David Lupberger, a contractor who serves as a kind of coach for others in the business, lays it out in a book, *Managing the Emotional Homeowner*.

The graphic below, based on the one in Lupberger's book, suggests that the typical construction project takes nine months. Any longer, and emotions no doubt run off the charts.

—Marco Pasanella

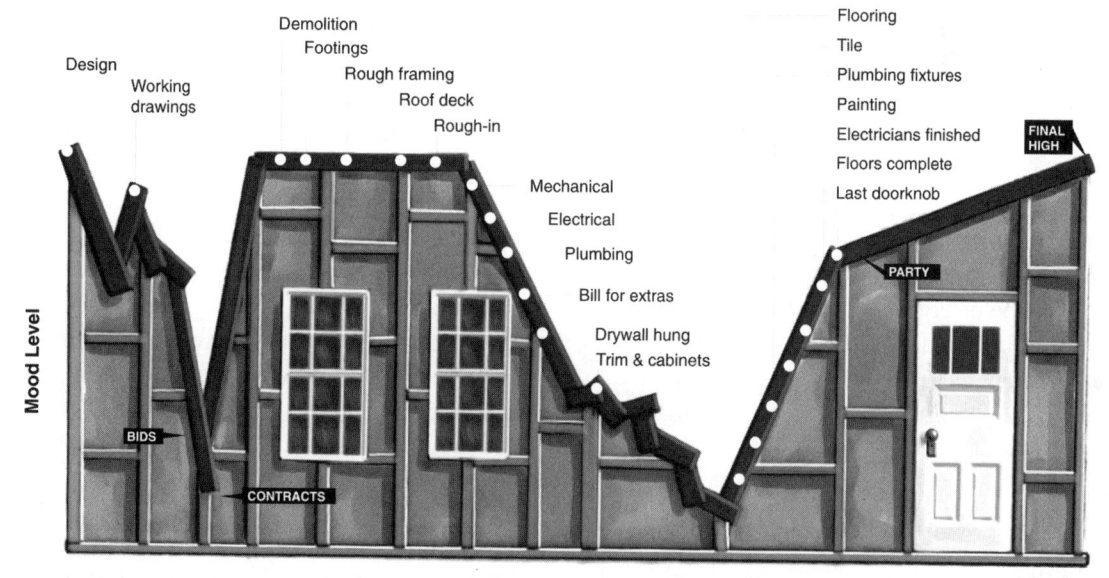

but realize that passing the license exam is just the first of many requirements he must meet. You can eliminate deadbeats and fly-by-nights by checking with the Better Business Bureau, www.bbb.org.

And then, the contract. Once you get to the contract stage, have a lawyer ensure that the contract is comprehensive, including a start and finish date (with a penalty for not meeting the deadline), a payment schedule and required starting fee, how changes and problems will be handled and a request that the contractor let you

know if he changes his insurance, bonding or workers' compensation. The contract should also include a retaining fee—for example, about 10 percent of the total budget—until all the work is finished.

You will need to decide between a fixed-price and cost-plus contract. If you know exactly what you want, a fixed-price contract may be your best bet. But be aware that a contractor will pad a fixed-price contract slightly to cover complications. With cost-plus, you pay as you go without a total estimate. You can put a cap on

A New Look for an Aging Deck

A once-a-year cleaning with detergent and sealer can make a huge difference

Whether your deck or terrace is made of ordinary treated wood, exotic hardwood, cedar, redwood or one of the new composite materials, it will look better and last longer with regular maintenance.

As a rule, every deck needs to be cleaned at least once a year. Start with a deck detergent, available at home centers and hardware stores, mix it according to the instructions and apply it with a garden-style sprayer. Saturate the entire deck, let it sit for 10 or 15 minutes to loosen up the dirt, and then use a stiff brush or pressure washer to clean off all the dirt and grime. Be careful with a pressure washer because using too much pressure or holding the tip too close can gouge the wood.

Once the detergent has been thoroughly rinsed away, allow the deck to dry for 2 or 3 days before applying a stain or sealer. If you want to change the color of the deck, a semi-transparent stain should go on next.

The sealer, which waterproofs the wood and protects it from sun damage, can be applied after the stain dries. "I recommend putting a clear sealer on it," says Danny Lipford, host of the nationally syndicated home improvement show, *Today's Homeowner.* "That will darken the wood just slightly." And apply two coats, one on one day, and the other on the next.

Consumer Reports recommends a few deck sealers as being effective: Flood Solid Color Deck & Siding Stain, Sikkens Cetol SRD, McCloskey Storm Coat Deck, Fence & Siding Stains, Thompson's WaterSeal Deck & House and True Value Woodsman Deck & Siding Stain. To clean decks or terraces made of exotic woods like ipe, mahogany, teak or ironwood, Al Ismaili, the owner of All Pro Painting and Deck Restoration in San Francisco, recommends a mop and a solution of water and mild soap, like dish detergent.

If cleaners fail to bring a deck back to life, it may be time for more drastic steps, such as resanding, but that work is much more expensive.

—Jay Romano

the amount or work out an incentive for meeting a certain price.

Contracts, including the array available from the American Institute of Architects, offer substantial protection. But they cannot guarantee a good working relationship any more than a prenuptial agreement ensures a happy marriage. Instead of trying to nail down every contingency at the outset, which tends to set up an adversarial relationship, pick someone you trust and can comfortably talk through the rough spots. Performance clauses may sound appealing, but they are hard to enforce and rarely have the desired effect, partly because they can cause contention in the working relationship.

—Marco Pasanella and Anne Krueger

Do-It-Yourself Remodeling

The pros and cons of doing your own renovation

Steve Thomas, former host of the acclaimed television series *This Old House,* and author of *This Old House Kitchens* and *This Old House Baths,* two very successful books, undertook his first home renovation project in 1974. He has renovated his own 1836 Colonial Revival and 1846 Greek Revival homes, among numerous others. Now pursuing his own projects, he offers us some sage advice on tackling remodeling jobs in any home, no matter how humble.

Q **Which remodeling jobs can a homeowner take on without too much difficulty?**

It really depends on your skill level. If you're willing to put in the time to do a quality job, just about anyone can improve the cosmetic appearance of their home with some fresh paint and new wallpaper, for example. Another type of remodeling job that can be accomplished with few skills but a substantial amount of sweat equity is landscaping. Though many homeowners overlook its importance, landscaping is one of the few renovations that can dramatically increase the value of your home. You should treat landscaping as another renovation project that needs to be well planned and budgeted.

Which jobs are better left to the experts?

Any job that is potentially dangerous or involves meeting building codes should be done by a licensed expert. That would include electrical, plumbing, heating and roofing work. In addition, any job that has to do with critical structural elements, such as load-bearing walls, should be done by a pro.

What's a good starting point for a novice to gain more expertise?

One of the best ways to enhance your level of experience is to specialize in an area of renovation, such as painting or carpentry. Focusing on one aspect will allow you to build upon your experience and over time to acquire more skills and better tools. You should start with a simple project. Building a deck, for example, requires relatively average carpentry skills, but you can learn a tremendous amount about renovation by going through the process. It's a good starting point—from getting the proper permit to creating a good set of plans and buying the right tools.

What are some of the common mistakes that do-it-yourself remodelers make?

For one thing, they generally underestimate the time it's going to take to complete the project. When budgeting, they fail to allow for a contingency of at least 25 percent to cope with unforeseen problems. Difficulties can arise and you may well need to allow time and money to resolve them.

Often they underestimate the importance of the design process. It's crucial to work with a design professional who not only can help you create the home you want but also has the foresight to articulate the details of the process, from the structural to the ornamental.

ⓘ INSIDE INFO

How Long Things Last

○ *Nothing really lasts forever, of course, but some materials do have greater durability. If you're undecided about whether to put down vinyl or ceramic tiles in your new kitchen, for example, this life-expectancy list can help.*

	YEARS
Slate roof	50 to 100
Wood shingle roof	25
Asphalt shingle roof	15 to 30
Chimney, fireplace, and brick	100
Drywall and plaster	up to 70
Paint	5 to 10
Wallpaper	7
Ceramic tiles	100 or more
Oak or pine floors	100
Carpeting	11
Wood siding	10 to 100
Vinyl siding	50
Aluminum siding	20 to 50
Brick or concrete patio	24
Wood deck	15
Asphalt driveway	10
Swimming Pool	18

SOURCE: *Residential Inspection Guide*, U.S. Dept. of Housing and Urban Development.

Q **How can pitfalls be avoided?**

Having a great set of detailed plans will ensure that the work is done in the correct sequence and that the job goes smoothly for all involved. Homeowners who invest a substantial amount of time in the planning phase can potentially save between 20 and 30 percent in the overall cost of their renovation.

When working with a contractor, there is a tendency to take the lowest bid, which may end up costing a homeowner more in the end. It's wise to solicit bids from a number of contractors and compare them carefully. For a successful bid competition, you'll need to provide complete and detailed specifications to ensure that everybody is bidding on exactly the same project. The more decisions you can make about materials, finishes and detailing before asking for bids, the easier it will be to select a contractor, and the fewer problems you will have once he begins the job.

Decorators' Tricks You Can Use

Whether your home is a loft or a mansion

Large houses (those bigger than 4,500 square feet), a product of the Great Housing Boom, can now be found all across America. The result is an epidemic of vast living areas that often look as cavernous and appealing as airport lounges. It's enough to make a housewife desperate.

Taming the jumbo room is mostly about restoring human scale. Here are a few ways to do it.

Use furniture to define "rooms" within the overall space. For example, if you have a space 20 feet by 60 feet, divide it into three areas: eating, talking and playing games by the fire. Sideboards can be used to separate the dining table from the seating area and the conversation area from the fireside furniture. Rugs are used to further reinforce the groupings.

Don't fill an oversize room with oversize furniture. It only pushes people farther apart and inhibits conversation. Even if you have a living area the size of a basketball court, massive chairs are not going to make it more comfortable. Your legs and arms are the same length no matter how large your home.

Color can help to tame the scale. Light floors and dark ceilings will bring an intimidating height down to size. A taupe ceiling, for example, will make a study feel cozy. Another way to break down a larger space is to highlight moldings. Paint a picture molding blue-gray to encircle the room. Or highlight window or door openings with other strong (but not too strong) shades. In a more standard space, 9 feet by 12 feet, you may want to pick just one element, a crown molding for example, and highlight it more gently with a softer tint.

Don't be afraid to consider patterns. A pattern on the walls also helps to break down a jumbo expanse into more pleasing sizes.

You can shrink a room with lamps, making even a cavern seem snug. An impressive chandelier on the ceiling can provide decorative sheen, but the real light, the one by which you read the paper, must come from some nearby source. The best of the great rooms have pools of light clustered on furniture groupings and accented by some pretty fixture overhead. Many soft lamps (not brighter than 40 watts) at eye height will bathe guests in a flattering glow.

For small places. In more modest-scale rooms, by contrast, the challenge tends to be squeezing in everything you want to do. To live large in tight spaces, try these tricks.

• Use furniture that has more than one function, like a coffee table that can be raised for eating.

Or use the same spot for different tasks at varying times of day. A studio apartment in New York has a bookcase that runs from one end to the next. At night, portions of it swing out on hinges to create a bedroom; by day, they reconfigure to form a designer's workspace.

• Paint the rooms in warm, but not dark colors to create a cozy feel for small rooms.

• Mirror the walls to create an illusion of depth where there is none.　　　　—Marco Pasanella

Choosing a Paint Color
An artist's advice on how to make your home beautiful with paint

Donald Kaufman, a well-known color field painter, author and architectural color guru, has worked with architects and designers such as I. M. Pei and Philippe Starck. The Donald Kaufman Color Collection (www.donaldkaufmancolor.com), his line of paint colors, remains a perennial favorite. Here are his practical tips for choosing paint for the home.

Start by noticing which colors are already in and around your home. An old rug, a painting, a stone terrace outside the house or even a favorite pair of pants may provide the perfect inspiration. Computers can help turn these colors into paint, but they have limited formulas. Getting a painter to mix the paint often results in more complex colors.

Understand the psychological effects of color. People have different reactions to cool and warm colors. Cool colors—especially blues and violets—tend to create a sense of darkness and depression. They are the most difficult to use successfully because of these unsettling effects. Warm colors—reds, oranges and yellows—are generally more pleasing and fulfill the basic human need for light. For this reason, they account for nearly 90 percent of the paints on store shelves. Warm colors

---

 **TIMELY TIPS**

How to Stencil a Floor
You can find great patterns online

Stenciling a wood floor can be a challenge for novices, as well as time-consuming, so as a beginner, you might want to start with a basic project such as a repeating design as a border along the walls. Greek key patterns and other geometrics are simple to plan, as long as you measure carefully so that the patterns line up and meet correctly. Use masking tape to get the lines straight.

✔ Many stencil patterns are downloadable online for free. Simply transfer the design to thin Mylar and cut it out with an X-Acto knife. If you prefer to buy stencils, check out a craft store or .www.stencilwerks. com, which offers more than 3,000 patterns.

✔ To do a proper job, you need to sand the floor and apply a single sealer coat of polyurethane, well-dried and lightly sanded. Then tape your stencil in place, dabbing on or spraying paint or stain and allowing it to dry thoroughly.

Now peel up the stencil and repeat. When the entire stencil design is in place, apply several coats of clear polyurethane. Water-based polyurethane is recommended because oil-based varieties tend to yellow.

✔ If you like the look of the grain of your floor, consider using a thin single coat of artist acrylics to let it show through. Or if you prefer pure color, build up several applications of paint. If you want a truly opaque design, start with a white primer.
　　　　—Stephen Treffinger

Not All Paints Are Created Equal

Latex paints are getting better, and they are safer than oil-based

In the past, smooth, hard finishes were the decided advantage of oil-based paints. Advances in paint chemistry, however, have improved the performance of latex paints, and they are now preferable for a number of reasons.

Latex paints are water based and therefore easy to work with, since they can be thinned with water, and paint splatters can be wiped away with a damp sponge before they dry. Latex dries quickly, does not yellow and has less odor. At one time latex paints were more likely to show brush strokes and less able to cover stains, and they were less durable than oil paints as well. Manufacturers point to improvements on all three counts.

All of which is a good thing, because oil-based paints are coming under increasing scrutiny from the Environmental Protection Agency (epa.gov/iaq/voc.html) and others. A variety of health problems, including rising asthma rates in cities like New York and Los Angeles, have been linked to the presence of volatile organic compounds (V.O.C.'s) in oil-based paints. V.O.C.'s have also been identified as significant contributors to smog. Though nearly all latex paints emit some V.O.C.'s, they do so at relatively low levels, and there are now several low-V.O.C. latex paints, including Eco Spec by Benjamin Moore (benjaminmoore.com) and Lifemaster 2000, from a company called ICI (icipaintstores.com).

In choosing your paint finish, remember that glossier finishes are harder and more durable. Use them in high-wear or high-humidity areas, such as on woodwork or in kitchens and bathrooms. Low-luster finishes generally have greater hiding power. Use them on walls and ceilings.

—Stephen Treffinger and Danny Hakim

are a safe choice for the dining room and kitchen because they improve the look of food. They also flatter the skin color of guests surrounding the table. If a cool color is a must, use green or a blue that has some yellow in it.

Take the time to test samples. A major complaint about final paint jobs is that they are too bright. Colors on a paint swatch appear twice as bright and twice as light when applied to a wall. Therefore, an adequate mock-up is essential. Paint a 5-foot-wide sample swath from floor to ceiling. Block out existing colors with your hand and see how the new colors interact with the room and especially with the color of the floor. Look at the test area at different times of the day to see how it reacts to fluctuations in natural light and to artificial light at night. People who want to paint a brightly colored room a neutral color should prime the entire room before trying samples. Reflected light from strong colors will alter the perceived color of the mock-up.

Brighten rooms. The common solution to a dark room is throwing white paint on the walls to reflect more light. But the lack of light generally makes the white room look washed-out and gray. A better solution is to use a warmer and deeper color, which often can provide the luminosity that is missing from the room. Yellows are particularly effective, because the color value can be kept light enough while still adding warmth.

Enlarge living spaces. If you have light-colored floors, choose a deeper wall color and a light ceiling color to reflect the floor. Walls will appear to recede above the floor. If you have dark floors, keep walls and ceiling light and the same color. Eyes are attracted to contrast, and high contrast between walls and ceiling closes spaces. Some people think they can lift a ceiling by painting it white. That is often the case, because a white ceiling reflects more light. But if there's already plenty of light, similarly colored walls and ceiling can make a room appear more open and atmospheric.

Use the same trim color throughout a number of rooms. The wall color in each room will make the trim appear different. Keep the trim lighter than the walls. Using darker trim colors can be beautiful, but it is much more difficult to pull off.

Think about how the colors of adjoining rooms interact. Colors in abutting rooms tend to reinforce each other—which can have dramatic or unpleasant results. A subtle beige room can appear much stronger if viewed from a subtle blue room, and vice versa. Also, thinking about rooms as a series of colors can make cramped quarters seem roomier. For a three-room apartment, if the kitchen and living room have light, warm colors, a bedroom with stronger and deeper colors can provide a perfect escape.

Address the architecture. Architectural details can be divided into two categories—structural and decorative. Neutral colors work better with structural details such as columns or door frames. Something that looks like it provides support is not the place for a pale peach color. Decorative colors would be more appropriate with friezes and other ornate moldings.

Use top-of-the-line paint from any of the major manufacturers. It lasts the longest and provides the best coverage. Don't overlook regional paint companies. Their top paints are just as good and sometimes better. But preparation is all-important. Clean, smooth surfaces lead to the best results.

And remember, there are no bad colors. Colors change and create different perceptions depending on where and how they are used. A very bright, garish green might seem a bad color for a dining room, but it could be absolutely beautiful as a thin stripe underneath crown molding in a beige living room.

How to Light Up a Room
The right lighting can fill a room with warmth

For years lighting design has been nearly an afterthought for many residential architects and general contractors. The attitude was "what more could there be than a ceiling-mounted fixture in the center of the room or a homeowner's table lamps?" But such light fixtures often tend to call attention to themselves and cast shadows in unflattering ways. Here, lighting designer Randall Whitehead, author of *Residential Light-*

 **TIMELY TIP**

The Right Shade for the Right Lamp

In any given room, shades should be in the same simple style, either white or cream and made of fabric or paper. Simple in style means less visual confusion, and the white or cream color ensures an inviting atmospheric glow.

Trimmings, known as *passementerie* in France, are the most effective way to customize plain shades and the easiest to manage—if you can wield a glue gun. They can be gimp, braid or fringe. If you are unsure about the effect, fix them in place with straight pins, allowing easy substitutions if you want a new look.

The important thing is to keep them simple; avoid trimmings with the kind of operatic effusiveness that might look dated in a few years. As decorator Mark Hampton once noted, nothing ages a room more than a fussy lampshade.

—Mitchell Owens

ing: A Practical Guide and *Lighting Design Sourcebook: 600 Solutions for Residential and Commercial Spaces,* tours the home and offers some advice on lighting.

The entry. The entrance sets the mood and tone for the rest of the house. In the entryway, lighting can be used to open up the space and provide a welcoming environment for guests. Make sure lights create a warm glow. Avoid harsh shadows by using uplighting instead of recessed downlights.

The living room. The goal here is to create a soft island of illumination that invites people in to relax and converse. Layering the light creates an environment that is humanizing and dramatic. Wall sconces and torchères can generally provide ambient illumination, which softens shadows on people's faces and fills the room with a soft glow. Recessed adjustable fixtures or track lighting can be utilized to provide the necessary accent light for artwork, plants or tabletops. But be sure not to let accent lighting overpower you or your company.

The dining room. This is where dramatic lighting can come into play. Wall sconces are a good source of ambient lighting in this room. A chandelier should only give the illusion of providing the lighting in the room, as otherwise it will be too bright or distracting. Using recessed, adjustable fixtures on either side of the chandelier will produce the necessary focal point lighting for the table, without eclipsing the decorative fixture.

The kitchen. With today's open floor plan designs, the kitchen should be as inviting as the rest of the house. Mount fluorescent lights above cabinets, so light is bounced off the walls and ceilings, providing ambient lighting. Lights under cabinets provide good, unobstructed task light for the counters. Pendant-hung fixtures can be used for task light where cabinets are not present.

Skylights can provide a cheery feeling during the day and, through the use of fluorescent fixtures mounted in them, can avoid becoming "black holes" at night. A pot rack over a center island may appear to be a perfect idea, but how do you light work surfaces without creating shadows by trying to light through pots and pans? If you have sloped ceilings, special care must be taken to select fixtures that don't glare into people's eyes. Also, remember that an all-white kitchen is going to require dramatically less light than a kitchen with dark wood cabinets.

HOUSE

Bathrooms. Lighting at the mirror is most important. Vertically mounted strip fixtures generally provide the best task light. Wall sconces or fluorescent strip fixtures mounted above cabinets, ledges or beams provide the necessary ambient illumination.

Bedrooms. It is important that there is good color-corrected light, especially in closets, to aid in the selection of properly color-matched clothes. Aside from the usual ambient light concerns, easily adjustable reading lamps at the bed are a must. A "panic switch" for outside lighting is often a desirable feature.

How to Organize Your Closets

These companies can help you sort your socks

Closets, along with kitchens and bathrooms, now form part of a holy trinity of domestic obsession. Americans spend more than $2 billion a year on closet renovations, according to *Closets*, a magazine devoted to home organization.

A closet by one of the cost-conscious renovation companies can come in at under $1,000, including a free initial consultation. By contrast, a dressing area designed by an architect can easily set you back tens of thousands of dollars (if you spring for fancy hardware, lots of drawers and a few dozen bubinga wood hangers).

There are definite cost benefits to using some of the cheaper companies; the trade-off is that you may need time and skill to install the closet components yourself. Although the details of their offerings are prone to change, here are some of the more well-known closet companies.

- California Closets (800-336-9178; www. calclosets.com) helps the client envision the finished product, by means of a highly detailed sketch and gives a price and estimated installation date. Their price included installation.

- Clos-ette (212-337-9771; www.clos-ette.com) offered a free consultation, but after that it charged a small fee for the design. Its typical custom closet ran from $15,000 to $20,000, installed.

- EasyClosets.com (800-910-0129) offers an online design tool that allows you to plan the closet yourself.

- The Container Store (888-266-8246; www. containerstore.com) closet, uninstalled, can be as low as $500. Customers generally meet with a designer at one of its stores.

Installation is as important as design in determining which supplier works best for you. Some companies have their own crews; others require you to install products or will refer you to installation services.

—Marco Pasanella

 **TIMELY TIPS**

Decorating Behind Closed Doors

✔ Since your closet is an extension of your bedroom, why not make a virtue of it? Use a dramatic color to brighten it, such as Exotic Red by Benjamin Moore. This fire-engine color is pretty cheering at any time of day.

✔ The small size of most closets means you can often afford to line them with expensive hand-blocked wallpapers. Especially appealing are the 18th- and 19th-century reproduction papers from Adelphi Paper Hangings, (518-284-9066; www. adelphipaperhangings.com) a small company with headquarters in The Plains, Va., whose reproduction papers hang in the Lincoln Room at the White House and at Colonial Williamsburg.

—Mitchell Owens

Shelves That Last a Lifetime

Why bother with built-ins when you can get these off-the-shelf?

Along with built-ins, which can be expensive, there are many great shelving systems that vary widely in the way they are configured, what the shelves (and tracks) are made of and how they go up. Check your walls (and your lease) before shopping: some systems require strong wallboard and studs while others are free-standing.

The Container Store sells a simple, easy-to-install shelving system called Elfa. Its shelves come in two lengths and four depths, allowing one or more to hold a laptop or an in-basket while the others hold books. Shelf choices include white melamine, beech and walnut veneer. The top track and the hanging standards can be ordered in three lengths or custom cut. (800-733-3532; www.containerstore.com)

For something with a bit more style, BoConcept, the Danish contemporary furnishings chain, makes shelving that seems to float. Installation involves screwing brackets into wall studs. The solid-looking shelves are 2-inch-thick particle board with a white laminate or a wood veneer (wenge, cherry, walnut or maple). They can hold up to 33 pounds. The shelves are 8¾ inches deep and come in two widths, 30¾ inches and 59 inches. Brackets, free with the shelves, come in sets of two or three.

You can install one set or many and arrange the shelves however you like: staggered, unevenly spaced, random or one over the other. (888-616-3620; www.boconcept.com)

Moss, the trendy New York City design store, sells a high-end system of shelving by Vitsoe, a British company. Called the 606 Universal Shelving System, it was designed in 1960 by Dieter Rams and has been produced ever since with

Getting Rid of Household Junk

If spring cleaning has left you with piles of unwanted stuff, here's how to unload it

First, many towns have "heavy-trash nights" during which homeowners can put their items on the curb. Check with your town to determine if, and when, it allows residents to discard their detritus in this way.

There are circumstances, though, when a homeowner is not allowed to leave a washing machine, dryer, freezer, air conditioner or refrigerator on the curb, or is not able to get it out there. In these cases, professional help may be available.

For example, a junk-removal company, 1-800-GotJunk, based in Vancouver, British Columbia, has franchises all over the United States. Price is determined by the space the debris takes up in the truck, which measures 10 feet long, 8 feet wide and 5 feet high. In New York City, for example, half a truckload would cost $568, while a full load would cost $898.

Another option for homeowners is to have a Dumpster-style bin delivered to their property. These bins can be 10, 20 or 30 cubic yards. Preferably, the bin is put in a driveway and can stay for about 5 to 7 days. The price is determined both by the size of the container and the weight of the debris put in it. Items like refrigerators and air conditioners must have the Freon removed before they are picked up.

Another solution is to give unwanted items to charity. If you want to donate things to the Salvation Army, for example, you can drop them off at a thrift center or call 800-728-7825 to arrange a pickup. Tax deductions can range from $1 to $12 for a hat to $250 to $1,000 for a bedroom set. (For more on disposing of unwanted items, see "Culling the Junk from the Collectibles" on page 322.)

—Jay Romano

only slight changes along the way (806-888-6677; mossonline.com). Materials are basic: anodized aluminum and steel shelves and poles, and lacquered beech or laminated cabinets and shelves. Some of the cabinets have fold-down doors, and others have doors that slide inside. The system starts with vertical posts. They can be free-standing, or wall-supported for heavy loads. They can also be compressed, fitting between ceiling and floor. An "E track" is mounted to the posts or to the wall to give support.

There are no brackets: the shelves sit on the E track with the help of small pins. Components are sold individually and include such options as cabinets, drawers, sloping shelves for magazines or a dictionary and even a workspace.

The system has a look of permanence, yet it is easy to take down and pack up. And it is so clean-lined it can fit in almost any interior. Because of the components' variety, you can always modify or expand the configuration.

—Stephen Treffinger

Searching for Vintage Hardware?
Where you can find an old door and more

Hardware can be the great finishing touch in a renovation project, and for homeowners who are restoring an old house or apartment, the right touch is often a period knob, hinge or door knocker. But a house does not have to be old to be flattered by a period piece. Vintage hardware can also enrich a modern white box.

Charles Lockwood, author of *Bricks and Brownstone,* and a specialist in restoration, points out that "19th-century New Yorkers were very proud of their hardware"—as were other well-to-do homeowners nationwide—so there is a rich trove of salvaged fine period hardware or reproductions of it to be found all across the country in specialty hardware houses. Here are a few examples.

- Crown City Hardware in Pasadena, Calif. Victorian-style interior doorknobs and plates, as well as reproductions of 19th-century hinges. (800-950-1047; www.crowncityhardware.com)

- Historic Houseparts in Rochester, N.Y. Bathroom hardware. (888-558-2329; www.historichouseparts.com)

- House of Antique Hardware in Portland, Ore. Has original hardware and also does custom reproductions. (888-223-2545; www. houseofantiquehardware.com)

- Liz's Antique Hardware in Los Angeles, Calif. Sells doorhandles cast in bronze and based on a 19th-century design as well as vintage iron doorknobs and plates dating from the early 20th century. (323-939-4403; www. lahardware.com)

- Van Dyke's Restorers in Woonsocket, S.D. Antique door hardware. (800-558-1234; www.vandykes.com)

—Marianne Rohrlich

Beds You Won't Lose Sleep On
Almost a third of life is spent sleeping, so take your mattress seriously

Your mattress sags, creaks and wobbles. It's probably time to toss this relic and invest in a new one. Is there any purchase that's more personal? The next time you go mattress shopping, keep these tips from the Better Sleep Council in mind:

Support. Wear comfortable clothes to your local mattress retailer so you can lie down on a number

Put Some Spring in Your Sofa

If you're in the market for a new sofa, you're probably wondering what makes a hand-made $8,000 sofa any different from one that you can buy for $600 at IKEA. The difference lies in the frame, padding, cushions, springs, fabric and finish.

PADDING: Sofas often wear at the arms because the maker has scrimped on padding. The better sofas have a layer of cotton or polyfiber over a layer of foam. Cheaper sofas have fabric right on top of the foam.

FABRIC: The grade of a fabric determines the price, but is not a measure of the fabric's durability. Grades are based largely on fiber content and on how much waste results from matching the pattern. For durability, consider spending the extra money to treat the sofa with fabric protection.

SPRINGS: Eight-way hand-tied springs used to be a sign of a top-notch sofa. No more. Many less expensive sofas also have them, although they are of inferior quality. A better question: how many rows of springs are used in the seat? The best use four rows.

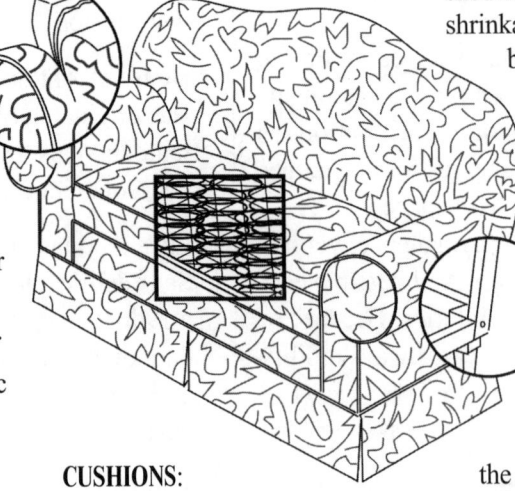

CUSHIONS: Top-quality foam cushions are made from virgin foam with a density of 2.2 pounds per cubic foot. Accept no less than 1.8. Lower-density foam deteriorates more

quickly. If you're looking for a soft down cushion, be sure the cushion has at least 30 percent down feathers in it. Otherwise, you'll be paying for down and getting far less.

FRAME: Maple and other hardwoods that grip nails well make the best frames. The wood should be kiln-dried to prevent shrinkage and warping. The best frames are $1\frac{1}{2}$ inches thick. (Experts refer to it as a $^6/_4$ frame.) To keep a sofa from sagging, joints and legs must be firmly attached to the frame. The best joints are double- or triple-doweled at the top corners and firmly attached with reinforcing blocks where the arms meet the seat.

FINISH: Attention to detail makes a difference. In a high-quality sofa, seams are straight, pleats lie flat, corners fill out and cushions have metal zippers.

of mattresses. The best ones support your body at all points. Pay attention to your shoulders, hips and lower back. Too little support can result in back pain; too much can lead to uncomfortable pressure.

Space. Sleepers toss and turn 40 to 60 times a night. If you are constantly fighting your partner for space, it may be time to upgrade to a queen- or king-size bed. Both are several inches longer and wider than the standard double bed.

Coil count. The common innerspring mattress gets its support from tempered steel coils. A full-size version should have more than 300 coils, a queen-size more than 375 and a king-size more than 450.

Wire guage. The lower the number, the thicker, stronger and more durable the wire. Stronger coils generally provide better support. Many manufacturers are introducing wire-engineered innersprings that employ lighter wire. They claim these systems make less noise and offer more support. Lie down and shift positions—it's the best way to test these claims and to see which mattress lends your body's curves the most support.

Cover. Look for superior stitching, quality seams and an extra-soft surface. Don't buy a bed based solely on a pretty treatment.

Padding. Layers of upholstery insulate and cushion the body from the innersprings. Once you've purchased a mattress that meets your comfort needs, remember to flip it regularly from head to toe. This extends mattress life and helps prevent the creation of an uncomfortable impression in the padding.

Foundation. Don't blame a bad night's sleep on the mattress alone. The foundation, or box spring, may also be showing some signs of wear and tear. A mattress and its companion foundation are designed to work as a system. Putting a new mattress on an old foundation can reduce the life and comfort of a mattress.

Warranties. Top brands generally come with 15 years' protection against product defects, but don't let the salesperson sell you a mattress based solely on the warranty. Let comfort and support guide your decision.

Foam mattresses. Made of a solid core or different types of foam laminated together, these mattresses should come with a minimum density of 2.5 pounds per cubic foot. High-resilience polyurethane and the more traditional latex, or synthetic rubber, mattresses provide the best performance. Memory foam—developed by NASA to cushion astronauts' bodies during space travel—is another popular (and expensive) component, which molds the mattress to the body's curves.

Waterbeds. Whether you are choosing full motion or waveless, with or without additional lumbar support and memory foam, dual or single mattress systems, make sure the mattress vinyl is a minimum of 20 mm thick and pay close attention to seam durability.

A Thing or Two About Linens
Or why thread count doesn't matter

When it comes to bed linens, Julian Tomchin is a debunker of myths, like the one that says a 1,000-thread-count sheet must be of superior quality (not necessarily, he says) or the one that claims a pure cotton sheet can be wrinkle-free (don't get him started).

Tomchin has been involved with linens since 1979, first at Bloomingdale's, next at Fieldcrest and then at Macy's West. And he has strong opinions about thread counts. The Martha Stewart Everyday sheet (available at K-Mart), a 300-count solid-color cotton set, suits him just fine. So do Ralph Lauren's Cole Brook, a handsome 350-count cotton with green and cream stripes (he liked the woven look), and Calvin Klein's Bamboo Flowers, a 220-count cotton in pale blue or hyacinth ("Lovely, lovely soft blue"), both available at Macy's.

It may sound like a relatively low count, but Tomchin prefers it. In fact, he advises, "Once you get beyond 400 threads per square inch, be suspicious." The standard for counting is to add each warp (vertical) and filling (horizontal) thread per square inch. The most that normally fits, he said, is 400, after which the threads are thinner and weaker. Some companies use two- or three-ply threads and multiply the count. "An 800-thread-count sheet made of two-ply yarn should legitimately be relabeled as 400," he says. "That's how you get 1,000 threads per square inch: creative counting."

A Little Pillow Talk
You will sleep better with the proper headrest

Even if you aren't the Princess and the Pea, you will sleep better with a proper headrest. "Somewhere near 50 percent of the country is sleep deprived," says Dr. James Maas, a professor and sleep researcher at Cornell University, and pillow issues are definitely part of the problem.

The main difference in pillows comes down to down versus synthetic fill, but a good pillow of either stuff should last up to 10 years. You can test your pillow to find out if it's past its prime. You take your pillow and fold it in half. If it doesn't spring forward and open instantly by itself, you've got a dead pillow. Replace it.

Maas says he likes the quality of pillows manufactured by United Feather and Down, an Illinois company whose products, both down and synthetic, sell under various private labels. For instance, United Feather and Down's Insuloft down and PrimaLoft synthetic-fill pillows are for sale online at thecompanystore.com, Landsend.com, Potterybarn.com and llbean.com.

No matter where you shop, expect to pay $30 or more for a good synthetic pillow and upwards of $60 for a goose down pillow with a minimum of 550 fill power. Fill power is a measurement of how lofty an ounce of down is and how high it comes up on a beaker after it's compressed.   —Michelle Slatalla

One type of sheet gaining popularity these days is bamboo, which Tomchin praises for its softness. (He found a set at Bed Bath & Beyond.) Still, to Tomchin, nothing beats pure cotton. Once a bed is cloaked in it, he says, "I defy anybody to turn out the light and say one sheet is more comfortable than the other."

—Elaine Louie

Making a Home Energy Efficient
When to replace your furnace, install new windows and more

The frugal American now faces a tough call: the most effective way to cut heating expenses may be to spend thousands of dollars to replace an inefficient furnace.

That one device uses nearly half of the energy piped into your home. Sure, you can save money by tackling the less expensive projects like turning down thermostats, caulking windows and adding insulation. But cost-effective as that is, it has its limits. Most new homes are built to be snug, using 22 percent less gas than they did 20 years ago. That leaves you staring at the furnace, which stands between you and several hundred dollars of additional disposable income.

Furnace makers like Carrier or Trane will tell you that you can save as much as 35 percent of your heating bill with a new one. But replacing your old one could cost from $2,000 to more than $7,000 depending on size, type and energy efficiency, as well as local labor rates and the amount of ducting and retrofitting that must be done.

There is no pat answer for this question, but if prices stay high or go even higher, a new furnace could be one of the best investments you will ever make. The problem is that no one can predict the short-term price of natural gas or heating oil, let alone its price in 5 years. You could stop right here and hope fuel prices drop, but it might be worth running some calculations to see if you would benefit.

Pull out your utility bills to determine how much you've spent on heating your home. That is simple with oil because it is used only for heating. With natural gas, take the bills from last winter and subtract what you normally spend in a month like September or May, when you are not running the furnace.

The chart opposite shows you how to calculate

WEIGHING POTENTIAL SAVINGS FROM A NEW FURNACE

I. FIRST COLLECT THE FOLLOWING INFORMATION:

- ANNUAL HEATING COST—Total winter heating bills, subtracting nonheating energy use, using a bill from May or September as a base.

- EFFICIENCY RATING OF CURRENT FURNACE—Furnaces bought after 1992 should have an annual fuel utilization efficiency (A.F.U.E.) rating. Assume anything older than 15 years is around 65 percent.

- NEW FURNACE AND INSTALLATION COST—Get several estimates for the total cost of installation. Local labor costs, house size and insulation, and extent of new ductwork needed will factor into total cost.

SOURCES: Department of Energy; American Council for an Energy-Efficient Economy

SAVINGS TABLE

EXISTING FURNACE	NEW FURNACE EFFICIENCY RATING (AFUE)								
	55%	60%	65%	70%	75%	80%	85%	90%	95%
50%	$9.09	$16.76	$23.07	$28.57	$33.33	$37.50	$41.24	$44.24	$47.36
55		8.33	15.38	21.42	26.66	31.20	35.29	38.88	42.10
60			7.69	14.28	20.00	25.00	29.41	33.33	37.80
65				7.14	13.33	18.75	23.52	27.77	31.57
70					6.66	12.50	17.64	22.22	26.32
75						6.50	11.76	16.66	21.10
80							5.88	11.11	15.80
85								5.55	10.50
90									5.30

Estimated savings for every $100 currently spent. With fuel costs rising, savings will be greater. Assumes new furnace has the same heat output.

II. THEN ESTIMATE YOUR TOTAL SAVINGS

- YOUR ANNUAL SAVINGS—If your old furnace is A.F.U.E.-rated at 65 percent, your savings per $100 dollars would be $31.57 if you installed a furnace with a 95 percent rating. If your annual fuel bill is $1,500, your annual savings would be 31.57 times 15 or $473.55.

- TIME UNTIL PAYOFF—Divide the investment—say, $4,000—by your annual savings. In this case, it would take more than eight years to break even.

- RETURN ON INVESTMENT—Divide the annual savings by the cost of the installation and multiply that by 100. If the new furnace will cost $4,000, your first year return on investment would be 11.8 percent.

your annual savings. The table determines the difference in operating costs between old models and new, fuel-efficient ones. A new furnace can save money because it does not waste as much fuel.

The federal government began requiring in 1992 that furnaces have an annual fuel utilization efficiency, or A.F.U.E., rating of at least 78. With electronic ignitions instead of pilot lights and quiet variable-speed motors, some heaters have ratings as high as 95 percent. You will find, for example, that your new furnace does not need to be as

powerful as your old one, because of its greater efficiency. Installing a furnace that is bigger than necessary is a common and costly mistake.

Any good furnace dealer—obtain estimates from several before signing a contract—will help you through these calculations. You may discover, for instance, that you will save as much as $500 a year. If the installation costs $2,000, that means you will recoup your investment in 4 years.

If you plan to sell your house long before that, you may want to skip this project. Many real estate agents and the furnace dealers themselves say a new furnace does not add much to the resale value of a home. If you plan to keep the house, however, you should look at the expenditure in other ways as well. The American Council for an Energy-Efficient Economy, a Washington advocacy group, suggests consumers use a measure of return on investment. Dividing the annual savings by the cost of the project gives a yield, not unlike a real investment. Using the same numbers as in the example above, you would have an impressive return of 25 percent. It is enough to make you want to start spending money to make money.

Figures provided by the federally financed Weatherization Assistance Program Technical Assistance Center suggest that if you can achieve fuel savings of $500 a year over the life of the furnace, an installation cost of up to $5,800 would be cost-effective. Were the annual savings only $250, you might want to draw the line at any project costing more than $3,000. If the numbers are not convincing or if your furnace is fine, there are other things you can look into.

Installing new windows usually makes little economic sense. But if you are considering replacing windows for aesthetic reasons, the high cost of fuel will get you a payoff sooner.

Replacing a refrigerator, which typically is responsible for about 6 percent of a home's energy bill, is a consideration. But finding an energy-efficient clothes washer that uses less water might be even smarter, because you get to save twice—on the washer's power and on the power used to heat the water.

An old water heater, which accounts for 11 percent of the home energy bill, frequently gets singled out as another money waster. You can start by insulating the tank and the pipes leading from the tank.

Some people are buying tankless water heaters that heat the water only as you need it.

Thermostats that can be programmed to lower the temperature when no one is home can cost less than $100. For every degree you reduce the temperature, you can save 3 percent on heating costs.

As you cost out these projects, do not forget to check the rebates your local utility will offer for these improvements. —Damon Darlin

Making Your Home Toasty Warm
Radiant heating is comforting and economical

One way to guarantee that your home is warm and comfortable on a winter evening is with radiant heating—"one of the most efficient ways of delivering heat in a home," says an editor of This Old House magazine. With radiant heat, homeowners typically save about 30 percent on annual home fuel costs per room no matter what kind of fuel they are using. And because less fuel is used, it is considered more ecologically sound than traditional home-heating methods.

There are two types of radiant heating: hydronic systems, which distribute heated water through tubing beneath the floor, and systems that use electricity as the heat source underfoot.

Because electricity is more expensive, the latter systems are usually limited to one or two small rooms, like a bathroom or kitchen. That makes the hydronic method the system of choice.

A professional can do the installation for about $12 to $15 a square foot, including the cost of installing a water heater and a set of controls linking it to the hydronic flooring. But homeowners who leave only the water heater and valves to the pros and put the flooring system in themselves can save about $4 a square foot.

The Best Ways to Heat Your Home

Advice from three contractors on heating your home without unsightly radiators

Diane Slovak, Innovative Concepts, Weston, Ct.: There are essentially two ways to do it. Radiant heat works through plastic tubing or electric coils placed under the flooring. When hot water is passed through the tubes or electricity heats the coils, the warmth rises into the room. In a forced-hot-air system, the air is heated by the boiler and delivered through ducts in the floor or ceiling like central air-conditioning. Hydro air is a type of forced-air system, but the air is heated by water-filled coils.

Gerry Holbrook, Taconic Builders, New York City: Hydro air is better than forced air because the hot-water coils only heat the air to about 180 degrees. In forced air, the boiler gets the air much hotter, and that bakes the moisture from the air. You'll need a humidifier.

John Teschky, Northbrook, Ill.: Radiant heat is great. The heat is uniform, and it makes the floor quite comfortable. The problem is the heat only goes so far up, so it is less effective in rooms with tall ceilings and in old houses that leak cold air.

—Edward Lewine

The best time to install a system is while a house is being built. Older houses can be retrofitted, but it's not always simple: if the underside of the floor can't be reached through a basement or crawl space, the floor has to be torn out and replaced, adding to the cost. Even so, many homeowners consider the net savings in fuel worth it, especially if they plan to keep the home awhile.

For houses with cellars or crawl spaces, the typical way to install a hydronic system is to attach PEX tubing (made of flexible petroleum-based polyethylene) to the floor's underside. This is done by stapling two parallel lines of tubing in the spaces between joists. One line doesn't make enough heat to evenly heat the space between the joists. Then the tubing is covered with aluminum to direct heat up to the subfloor.

Not all floors sit over basements or crawl spaces, especially in multistory buildings. So the floor is usually torn up to expose the subfloor. Aluminum-backed panels, 7 inches wide by 48 inches long with a groove cut lengthwise down the center, are attached to the subfloor to accommodate the PEX. Silicone is squirted into the grooves, and the PEX is tapped in with a rubber mallet.

In either case, once a hydronic system is installed, a plumber is called in to attach the tubing to a pump, heater and manifold (a set of controls screwed together and connected to a hot-water source). Each valve corresponds to a specific part of the house and is controlled by its own thermostat. The water can be heated by a separate hot-water heater, a furnace or a household hot-water supply. (To warm the house, the water must be between 85 and 105 degrees Fahrenheit, depending on how cold it is outside.)

How does this make a home warm and toasty? "The floor now functions like a huge radiator," says one expert builder.

City dwellers who want hydronic radiant heating in their living room or bedroom may be out of luck. Most buildings in New York City, for example, limit hydronic systems to bathrooms or kitchens, because that is where the plumbing is. But electric heating mats are an option. Some mats can be installed under an area rug, wall-to-wall carpet or tile and are hard-wired into the electrical system or plugged into an outlet. The total cost of a system for a bathroom would typically be between $400 and $800.

—Jay Romano

WHEN TO FIX IT, WHEN TO JUNK IT

To help you decide whether to repair or replace an appliance, consult the chart below, devised by Tom Kraeutler, host of the radio show The Money Pit. *In one typical scenario, you're stuck with an air conditioner that dies because the compressor is 7 years old. An entirely new system would cost $3,500, but the compressor repair alone would be $950.*

According to the chart, a 7-year-old central air conditioner has a low risk of repetitive failure, so it's okay to spend up to 50 percent of the replacement cost on repair. Since the $950 repair cost is 50 percent of the replacement value, go ahead and call for service.

APPLIANCE:	ESTIMATED REPLACEMENT COST[3]	AGE RANGE[1] : % REPAIR COST LIMIT[2]		
		Low Risk of Failure	Medium Risk	High Risk
FURNACE	$1,500–$3,500	up to 12 years: 30%	12–24 years: 20%	25 years & up: 10%
WATER HEATER	$500–$900	up to 7 years : 30%	7–14 years: 20%	15 years & up: 10%
CENTRAL A/C	$1,800–$4,000	up to 8 years: 50%	8–15 years: 30%	16 years & up: 10%
REFRIGERATOR	$500–$2,200	up to 8 years: 40%	8–15 years: 30%	16 years & up: 20%
KITCHEN RANGE	$500–$1,700	up to 15 years: 30%	15–25 years: 20%	26 years & up: 10%
DISHWASHER	$450–$1,250	up to 10 years: 40%	10–15 years: 30%	16 years & up: 20%
WASHER	$450–$1,500	up to 10 years: 40%	10–15 years: 30%	16 years & up: 20%
DRYER	$450–$1,000	up to 10 years: 50%	10–20 years: 40%	21 years & up: 10%
BUILT-IN MICROWAVE	$350–$1,500	up to 4 years: 20%	4–10 years: 15%	11 years & up: 10%
GARBAGE DISPOSER	$150–$350	Repair only if under manufacturer's warranty; otherwise, always replace		—

NOTES: 1. Risk of failure or breakdown increases with age.
   2. Percentage indicates minimum cost of repair limit. If cost of repair is greater than percentage of replacement cost shown, then replacement is recommended. If cost of repair is less than percentage of replacement cost show, then repair is likely to be cost-effective.
   3. Assumes replacement with like kind and quality as original appliance.

© 1995-2005 Squeaky Door Productions, Inc.

How to Keep Appliances from Getting Zapped

Voltage surge suppressors are key

Fluctuations in electrical service, whether because appliances cycle on and off or because of a lightning strike or damage to power lines, can lead to power surges that can damage sophisticated electronics in home appliances.

A power surge is a sudden increase in voltage that can burn out electronic circuits and the computer chips used in many newer appliances. A power surge can occur when lightning strikes a utility line feeding the home or a transformer on that line, or when power is restored after a failure. Or a surge can enter the home over telephone lines or coaxial cable.

The most common way to safeguard electronic equipment is the use of surge suppressors, which protect individual devices. A suppressor, which plugs into an electrical outlet and contains a number of outlets for audio and video systems and appliances that rely on computer chips, contains circuitry that absorbs electrical spikes before they can damage equipment.

But the suppressors can overheat if the surge is too great. Then the unit will not only fail to suppress a surge, but can become a hazard itself.

An overheated surge suppressor can cause burns if touched, can damage carpeting and draperies, and can even cause a fire.

That is why consumers should choose high-quality and appropriate-size suppressors. Information on the suppressor's package will show whether it has been approved by an independent testing laboratory, like Underwriters Laboratories.

While some suppressors resemble multiple-outlet power strips, not all power strips are capable of suppressing surges. Consumers should be sure that the product is labeled as a U.L.-listed transient voltage surge suppressor.

Most suppressors contain a metal oxide varistor that absorbs the surge. Its ability to block a surge is rated in terms of joules; the higher the rating, the more it can handle.

"Look for suppressors that have joule ratings of 1,900 or more," says Tim Carter, founder of askthebuilder.com, a home improvement Web site. Buyers also need to be aware of the suppressor's clamping voltage, the amount of voltage it will admit before it begins to suppress a surge. High quality suppressors will have clamping voltages of 330 volts or less.

Another way to protect a home against electrical surges is to install a whole-house surge suppressor at the electrical panel.

Such devices generally cost between $250 and $500, and installation can be another couple of hundred dollars, depending on where you live.

Surge protection at the panel should be installed by a licensed electrician in accordance with local electrical codes. —Jay Romano

When You Fire the Handyman

Determined to do it yourself, but still need a little help? Try these books on the art of repair and home construction:

HELP, IT'S BROKEN! A Fix-It Bible for the Repair-Impaired.
Arianne Cohen. Three Rivers Press.
Arianne Cohen tackles household fix-it crises with lucid, easy-to-follow instructions to stop the most ham-handed handyman from hyperventilating.

READYMADE: How to Make (Almost) Everything: A Do-It-Yourself Primer.
Shoshana Berger and Grace Hawthorne. Crown.
The editor and publisher of the magazine *ReadyMade* offer a collection of suggestions for turning detritus into home furnishings, using Marcel Duchamp as their muse.
—Liesl Schillinger

How to Fix It Yourself

From stuck windows to trickling toilets

The roof leaks, the basement is damp, and the toilet won't stop running. This scenario represents a homeowner's worst nightmare. But who can afford to call a plumber at the first sign of a leak? Tom Kraeutler, host of radio's *The Money Pit*, and George Pettie, president of the home inspection firm HomeChek Service, have developed the following repair and maintenance guide that will help you protect your number-one investment.

Wet basement. A homeowner once attempted to fix a leaky basement by calling a waterproofing contractor. Quotes ranged from $7,500 to $20,000. Yet he was eventually able to correct his outside drainage and easily fix the problem for under $500. In fact, good gutters and properly sloping soil on a home's exterior can fix 99 percent of wet basement problems.

HOUSE

Start by cleaning out gutters, downspouts and underground drain pipes. A water hose is very useful for flushing out debris. When the accumulated mess in downspouts and drain pipes proves stubborn, rent a power auger to clear a passageway. If the gutter system doesn't empty into underground pipes, be sure to install downspout extensions that carry water 4 to 6 feet from the foundation. Also, inspect gutters for leaks and sags. Aluminum gutters can be sealed with poly-urethane or butyl caulk. Repair sags by removing the spikes that hold the gutter in place, raising the gutter so that it slopes evenly to downspouts, and nailing the gutter back in place.

To keep rainfall from collecting near foundation walls, soil should slope downward 6 inches over the first 4 feet from the foundation wall. Thereafter, it can be graded more gradually. Use clean fill dirt (not topsoil). Tamp the fill dirt down to the correct slope and finish with a layer of topsoil and grass seed, mulch or stone.

Leaky roof. Watch out for unscrupulous contractors who try to sell you a new roof that you don't need. Most roof leaks can be remedied with minor flashing repair. Look for loose or deteriorated flashing around chimneys and vent pipes. Fill any gaps with a good asphalt roof cement. A neatly applied bead of sealant from a caulking gun is better than a thick, troweled-on application.

Loose flashing should be tightened up with masonry nails before resealing. Expect to seal flashing every 2 years. If sealing doesn't fix the problem, the roof

shingles may be in fact worn out. To check your roof for signs of wear and tear, look for cracked, curled or broken shingles. If the worn area is small, it can be repaired by replacing the old shingles or patching with asphalt roof cement. If the entire roof looks this way, replacement is best. Shingles that are allowed to deteriorate can cause major leaks leading to expensive repairs.

Exterior joints and gaps. Open joints and gaps in the outside envelope of a house waste energy and provide easy entry for insects and vermin. Gaps often exist where siding meets trim, where electric cables or pipes enter the building, or where the sill of the house meets the foundation. For cracks from $1/4$ to $5/16$ inches, a smooth, even bead of caulk applied with a caulking gun is best. For wider openings, use an aerosol spray foam insulation. Let the foam expand to fill cracks, and slice away the excess after a day's drying time.

Stuck windows. Stuck windows are an inconvenience as well as a potential hazard, because they can impede escaping from fire. Most stuck windows are painted shut on the inside, outside or both. With double-hung windows, place the heels of your hands on either end of the sash's top rail and rap sharply upward. Start with light impacts

---

WHAT TO LOOK FOR ON A LEAKY ROOF

The source of a leak may not be where you see the leak, so inspect the entire roof. Flashing is material— usually rustproof metal or plastic— used at joints (see right) to keep water from getting into the house. Check for looseness, gaps and holes. Check shingles for rips, curled edges and missing sections.

Vent flashing

Valley flashing

Curled shingle

Chimney flashing

and don't get violent. If the sash doesn't move, cut the painted joint between the sash and the window stop or weatherstripping. Repeat the process on the outside. If cutting sash joints fails, work a putty knife deep into the joint between stop and sash. If it still won't budge, you may have to remove the stop. Removing the stop will chip paint and requires careful carpentry skills.

Trickling toilets. Toilets are one of the most used, yet least understood home appliances. They have two basic moving parts: the flush valve, which lets water out of the tank and down the drain; and the fill valve, which lets the toilet fill up after the flush cycle is complete. Small leaks in either of these valves can waste thousands of gallons of water in the course of a year. Here's how to tell if your valves are leaking:

To test the flush valve, open the top of the tank and pour a small amount of food coloring into the water. After an hour, if there is any colored water in the bowl, the flush valve is leaking and should be replaced.

To test the fill valve, open the top of the tank and find the hollow plastic pipe that sticks up from the bottom of the tank. The water level should be about an inch below the top of the pipe. If the water level is even with the top, the fill valve may be leaking or improperly adjusted and should be repaired or replaced. Next, flush the toilet and watch the top of the valve. If any water squirts up, you may have a leaky seal, which also means you need a new fill valve. Both of these parts are easy to replace and cost less than $20. Fluidmaster makes good replacement valves with clear instructions that teach you how to do the job. You can find them at any home center.

Bathroom caulking and grouting. Neglecting to replace old grout and tired caulking in the bathroom is one of the most common home maintenance

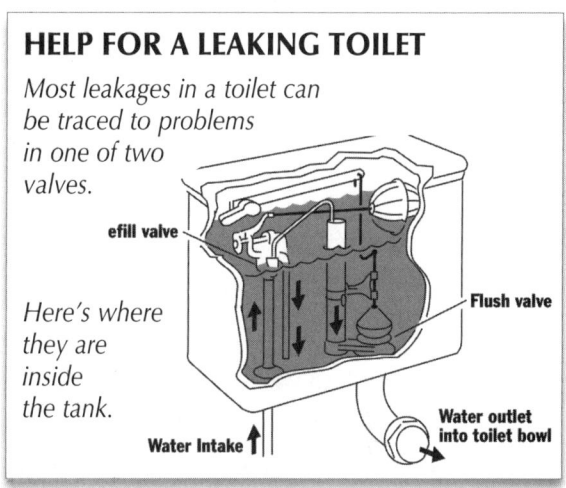

HELP FOR A LEAKING TOILET

Most leakages in a toilet can be traced to problems in one of two valves.

efill valve

Flush valve

Here's where they are inside the tank.

Water Intake ↑

Water outlet into toilet bowl

HOUSE

failures. It may not seem to be a big problem, but over time, the ceramic tiles loosen, allowing moisture to damage underlying wall materials. To prevent headaches later on, old grout, especially at horizontal tile joints where water penetration is greatest, should be scraped out. Before replacing grout, thoroughly wash tiles and joints with a tub and tile cleaner and then rinse.

Faucet, control and spout joints in the shower or tub also should be well sealed. If they are not, remove the faucet escutcheon plates. Many of these plates have small set screws that must be loosened first. Some plates can be unscrewed after you've removed the faucet handles. Using a putty knife or blade scraper, remove all old caulking, dirt, mildew and soap residue. Finish cleaning with a tub and tile cleaner and then rinse thoroughly. Next, seal all faucet penetrations with a good adhesive caulk. Before reinstalling the escutcheon plates, run a bead of caulk around the plates' mating edges. Tighten the plates against the wall and run another bead of caulk around the outside, where the plates meet the wall.

Don't neglect replacing the worn-out caulk between the tub and the wall tile. Dig out the old caulk to full depth with an old screwdriver or

Getting Spots Out Fast

How to remove some stubborn stains

Consumer Reports says that these home-made brews will remove stains. For all, blot the spill, then place dry paper towels on the spot. Stand on them a minute, then apply the appropriate series of potions, blotting after each application. End with a cold water rinse and final blotting.

✔ **Pasta sauce or salad dressing.** Mix one teaspoon of a clear (not colored) hand dish-washing liquid per one cup of lukewarm water. Hand dishwashing liquid residues can cause rapid resoiling, so rinse thoroughly after using. Note: never use laundry detergents on uphol-stery or carpets; they contain optical brighten-ers that may discolor the fibers or affect light and white colors.

✔ **Wine.** Sprinkle fresh stains with club soda. For red wine spills, it might be beneficial to blot; sprinkle on white wine, and blot again. For washable clothing, pouring boiling water through the fabric from a height of 12 inches may help.

✔ **Coffee and tea.** Try detergent mixture (see pasta sauce, above). Then try a mix of $1/3$ cup of white household vinegar with $2/3$ cup of water. Consumer Union testers also found that Spray 'n Wash stick laundry booster helped remove tea stains.

✔ **Soda, fruits and juices, beer, Kool-Aid, chocolate, animal stains.** Try the detergent mixture, above. Then try a mix of one table-spoon of household ammonia with $1/2$ cup of water.

SOURCE: *How to Clean Practically Anything*, Consumer Reports Books

sharp utility knife. Squirt tub and tile cleaner in the joint. Remove all residual caulk, grout, dirt and mildew by working a rag or paper towel with a putty knife into the gap. Keep working until the towel comes out clean and dry. To seal the gap, run a bead of caulk into the joint. Placing a strip of masking tape along the tile just above the tub results in a neat, crisp edge. The caulk should fill the joint $1/4$- to $3/8$-inch deep. Smooth in the caulk with your finger, wipe away excess from the tub and tile, and then let dry for several hours.

If Your House Is a Hot Zone

What to do about environmental hazards

Environmental pollution can be a serious prob-lem even in one's own home. To advise poten-tial homeowners of the environmental hazards that may be present in a house's walls, plumb-ing and foundations, a group of government agencies and private organizations, including the Environmental Protection Agency (E.P.A.), the Department of Housing and Urban Development and the National Association of Realtors, have joined forces to develop a primer for consumers. Highlights follow.

RADON is a colorless, odorless, tasteless gas that occurs worldwide in the environment as a byprod-uct of the natural decay of uranium present in the earth. Over time, it breaks down into radioactive particles (called decay products) that remain in the air. Outdoors, this is not a problem, because the gas diffuses in the atmosphere.

THE PROBLEM: When radon gas and its decay prod-ucts enter your home, they remain in circulation in the enclosed air. As you breath these particles, they can become trapped in your lungs. As these particles continue to break down, they release bursts of energy (radiation) that can damage lung tissue. This damage can cause lung cancer.

THE SOLUTION: Preliminary screening test kits can be bought over the counter in many hardware, grocery and convenience stores. Tests that measure the amount of radon in water normally require you to send a sample of tap water to a laboratory for analysis. Most homes contain from one to two picocuries of radon per liter of air. If preliminary tests indicate radon levels greater than four picocuries per liter of air in livable areas of the home, the E.P.A. recommends that a follow-up test be conducted. The E.P.A. estimates that the risk of an annual radon level of four picocuries is equivalent to the risk from smoking ten cigarettes a day or having 200 chest X-rays a year.

In some cases, homeowners may be able to treat the problem themselves However, radon source diagnosis and mitigation normally require skills, experience and tools not available to the average homeowner.

Installing radon reduction equipment may cost from several hundred dollars to several thousand dollars. If the system chosen involves fans, pumps or other appliances, operating costs for these devices may cause increases in monthly utility bills. When seeking a contractor to assist with a radon problem, ask local, county or state government agencies for a recommendation.

LEAD is a metallic element found worldwide in rocks and soils. Its toxic effects have been known since ancient times. Recent research has shown that lead represents a greater hazard at lower levels of concentration than had been thought. Airborne lead enters the body when an individual breathes lead particles or swallows lead dust. Lead can be present in drinking water, in interior or exterior paint, in the dust within a house and in soil outside.

THE PROBLEM: When ingested, lead accumulates in the blood, bones and soft tissue of the body.

✔ **TIMELY TIPS**

Homemade Cleaning Products
How to whip up a batch of furniture polish

Following are recipes for household cleaning products that use substances people tend to have around the house. The first one, for window cleaner, is from *Consumer Reports*. The others are distributed by Women's Voices for the Earth at parties it holds to encourage the use of homemade cleaners.

✔ **Window cleaner.** Combine half a cup of sudsy ammonia, a pint of rubbing alcohol, a teaspoon of dish detergent and a gallon of water. If you wish, add blue food coloring. Put in a spray bottle, spray on windows and wipe.

✔ **Creamy soft scrub.** Combine 2 cups baking soda, half a cup liquid Castile soap, 4 teaspoons vegetable glycerin, and, if you wish, five or more drops of an essential oil like tea tree, rosemary or lavender. Store in a sealed jar; it should last for 2 years. Use on stoves, counters and sinks.

✔ **Drain opener.** Pour half a cup of baking soda into the drain and then pour in half a cup of vinegar. Let stand 30 minutes, then flush with boiling water.

✔ **Furniture polish.** Combine a quarter cup of olive oil with a quarter cup of white distilled vinegar. If you want to scent it, use 20 to 30 drops of lemon essential oil or two teaspoons of lemon juice. Apply to furniture, then rub off.

✔ **Toilet bowl cleaner.** Sprinkle the bowl of the toilet with baking soda, then drizzle in some white vinegar. Wait 30 minutes, then scrub. Or, another way: Sprinkle in a quarter cup of borax and then a few drops of pine oil. Wait 30 minutes, then scrub. —Donald G. McNeil, Jr.

High concentrations of lead in the body can cause death or permanent damage to the central nervous system, the brain, the kidneys and red blood cells. Even low levels of lead may increase high blood pressure in adults.

Infants, children, pregnant women and fetuses are more vulnerable to lead exposure than others, because the metal is more easily absorbed into growing bodies. Because of a child's smaller body weight, an equal concentration of lead is more damaging to a child than it would be to an adult.

THE SOLUTION: The only way to determine lead levels in water is to test a sample of the water. Should you suspect that lead is present in drinking water, or if you wish to have water tested, contact local, county or state health or environmental departments for information about qualified testing laboratories.

It is best to leave lead-based paint undisturbed if it is in good condition and there is little possibility that it will be eaten by children. Other procedures include covering the paint with wallpaper or some other building material or completely replacing the painted surface.

Pregnant women and women who plan to become pregnant should not do this work. Professional paint removal is costly and time-consuming and requires everyone not involved in the procedure to leave the premises during removal and cleanup.

ASBESTOS is a fibrous mineral found in rocks and soil throughout the world. It has been used in construction because it is strong, durable, fire retardant and a good insulator.

THE PROBLEM: When ingested, asbestos fibers lodge in the lungs, where they remain in tissue and concentrate as repeated exposures occur. Prolonged work-related exposure can cause cancer of the lungs and other diseases. The health effects of lower exposures in the home are less certain; however, experts are unable to provide assurance that any level of exposure to asbestos fibers is completely safe.

THE SOLUTION: Asbestos is sometimes found around pipes and furnaces in older homes as insulating jackets and sheathing; in some vinyl flooring materials; in ceiling tiles; in exterior roofing, shingles and siding; in some wallboards; mixed with other materials and troweled or sprayed around pipes, ducts and beams; in patching compounds or textured paints; and in door gaskets on stoves, furnaces and ovens.

Generally, if the material is in good condition and is in an area where it is not likely to be disturbed, leave the asbestos-containing material in place. Extreme care should be used in handling, cleaning or working with material suspected of containing asbestos. If it is likely to be banged, rubbed, handled or taken apart—especially during remodeling—you should hire asbestos removal workers who are protected under federal regulations that specify special training, protective clothing and special respirators, and reduce your exposure as much as possible. (For more tips on dealing with asbestos, see box on facing page.)

FORMALDEHYDE is a colorless, gaseous chemical compound that is generally present at low, variable concentrations in both indoor and outdoor air. It is emitted by many construction materials and consumer products that contain formaldehyde-based glues, resins, preservatives and bonding agents. Formaldehyde also is an ingredient in foam that was used for home insulating until the early 1980s. In homes, the most significant sources of formaldehyde are likely to be the adhesives used to bond pressed-wood building materials and in plywood used for construction.

THE PROBLEM: Formaldehyde has been shown to cause cancer in animals and may cause cancer in humans. Higher-than-normal levels of formaldehyde in the home can trigger asthma attacks in

TIMELY TIPS

Dealing with Asbestos

Trying to remove it may be your worst option

Asbestos is classified by the federal government as a carcinogen. It was used in flooring and building products for decades. Many such floors are still in place, covered by newer floors or by carpeting.

Asbestos can be found in shingles (beneath aluminum siding), on ceilings (in popcorn paint or acoustic tiles) or in insulation (as loose-fill between attic-floor joists or wrapped around heating pipes in the cellar).

"The first thing to do is to avoid disturbing it," says a spokesman for the federal Environmental Protection Agency. Since it is dangerous when airborne, it is usually best to leave the material alone if it is not flaking or crumbling. (Information about asbestos is at epa. gov/iaq/asbestos.html.)

✔ The best way to deal with an asbestos-tile floor is to lay another floor or carpet over it. A sealant is usually not needed.

✔ A ceiling coated with popcorn paint can be repainted, which should seal the material in place. If the ceiling must be scraped, the paint should be tested to see if it contains asbestos (not all popcorn ceilings do). If asbestos is found it should be removed by a certified remediation company.

✔ In most cases, asbestos siding should be removed because nailing new siding on top of it could crack the shingles and release fibers. Insulated heating pipes can be encapsulated by a professional with a special sealant, and loose-fill can be left in place if not disturbed.

✔ Any time there is any question about whether a crumbling or flaking material contains asbestos, it should be tested. The easiest way to test is to wet a small section (so fibers don't become airborne) and break or cut off a piece about the size of a nickel (gloves are not needed). The sample can then be sent to a testing lab. The cost can be $100 or more. A list of federally accredited labs is at ts.nist.gov/standards/ accreditation/index.cfm.

✔ If contaminated material is to be removed, it typically must be done by a licensed asbestos remediation company, although the rule varies by state. Most asbestos-removal jobs for a homeowner run $5,000 to $10,000.

—Jay Romano

those who have this condition. Other symptoms may include skin rashes; watery eyes; burning sensations in the eyes, throat and nasal passages; and breathing difficulties.

Materials containing formaldehyde were used extensively in the construction of certain prefabricated and manufactured homes. Although the federal government has curtailed the use of materials containing formaldehyde since 1985, formaldehyde compounds are still widespread in the manufacture of furniture, cabinets and other building materials.

THE SOLUTION: In the case of a new home, you should consult with the builder before you purchase the house if you suspect the presence of materials that emit high levels of formaldehyde. Most builders will be able to tell you if construction materials contain formaldehyde, or they may direct you to manufacturers who can provide information about specific products.

In older homes, formaldehyde- emitting materials may not be apparent, and the current owners may not have specific product information. Consider hiring a qualified building inspector to examine the home. Home monitoring kits are also available. If subflooring, walls or foam insulation is the problem's source and increased ventilation is inadequate, removal of the material may be necessary. Such procedures will be costly, time-consuming and temporarily disruptive.

SOURCE: Adapted from *A Home Buyer's Guide to Environmental Hazards*

Your Home's Carbon Footprint
How to reduce your impact on the environment

The term "carbon footprint" is used to describe the amount of greenhouse gases that are emitted into the atmosphere each year by a person, household, building, organization or company. And one of the main sources of greenhouse gases is the home. For individuals, about 40 percent of our carbon emissions come from our homes.

Activities outside the home, like driving or flying, are part of the problem, too. But what happens in the kitchen, living room, bedroom, bathroom and yard is important, from heating to cooking to using products whose manufacture produces emissions that can be harmful.

According to the E.P.A., the average carbon footprint for a two-person household in the United States is 41,500 pounds a year. That's far from the ideal: environmentalists hope that all households, no matter the number of people living there, will reduce their levels by as much as 50 to 80 percent in the next 40 years. So, what to do now?

Among the appliances that add to the overall number are stoves, barbecues, refrigerators, fans, microwave ovens, televisions, radios, air conditioners, lights, computers, you name it—virtually any device the average person uses in a day. Even simple tasks like mowing the grass can add to the problem if the device uses gas or electricity. Lighting a gas or electric fireplace raises the number, while using a wood-burning fireplace does not.

Breaking old habits is not easy, but experts say the rewards are worth it, not only for the environment but also for the pocketbook. Those who reduce their carbon footprint by decreasing their energy use, usually reduce their energy costs as well.

Replacing an inefficient hot-water heater with an energy-efficient model can reduce annual carbon dioxide emissions by as much as 3,285 pounds and energy costs by $263, *Consumer Reports* says. Lowering a house's temperature by 5 degrees for 8 hours while people sleep and 10 degrees while they are at work can save 3,150 pounds in emissions and $252 in annual energy expenses. (Other suggestions are at greenerchoices.org.) Experts say that upgrading inefficient systems could save 30 percent in heating costs.

To reduce energy expenses and carbon levels, buy appliances with the E.P.A.'s Energy Star label. Energy Star clothes washers are at least 25 percent more efficient than the standard product and meet water efficiency requirements, which also helps save energy. Most of these machines cost more than traditional ones, but energy costs are less. (A product list is at energystar.gov.)

Many Web sites offer calculators to help figure out carbon footprints, factoring in data like a house's age, its insulation and the types of fuel, electricity and bulbs used. (Though the E.P.A. gives an average for a two-person home, the calculators give figures for all household sizes.) Among those recommended by experts are the Cool Climate Carbon Footprint calculator (coolclimate.berkeley.edu); the Low Impact Living calculator (lowimpactliving.com); the World Resources Institute's calculator (safeclimate. net); TerraPass (terrapass.com); and one on the E.P.A.'s site (epa.gov/climatechange/emissions/individual.html).

—Jay Romano

ONE MAN'S ENERGY DIET *How to drop 1,700 pounds of carbon dioxide emissions*

ACTIVITY	INCONVENIENCE FACTOR	ANNOYANCE FACTOR	TIME REQUIRED	COST	SAVED CO$_2$ *
Turn the thermostat down 1 degree at night in the winter	Reprogram thermostat	None expected	30 seconds	None	79
Don't leave the bathroom while the shower heats up	None	None	None	None	342
Wash whites with a warm/cold cycle	None	None	None	None	62
Cancel delivery of print catalogs	8 phone calls, 2 e-mails	None	22 minutes	None	154
Buy and put in 2 cool white compact fluorescent bulbs in non-annoying places	Install bulbs (but won't have to install again for about 80 years)	Light less warm, but in unobtrusive places	20 minutes	$4 more than for 2 regular bulbs, but they last longer	300
Buy 2 power strips with surge protectors, turn them off at night	Trip to hardware store, plug in	Turn off at night and on in morning	25 minutes, plus 10 seconds per day	$33	315
Hand-wash any dishes made dirty after dinner	None	Extra time for dishwashing, but I enjoy the reverie	5-10 minutes some nights	None	200
Set computer to "sleep" sooner	Modify "System Preferences"	A few extra seconds to get going after a lull	20 seconds	None	250

* Reduction in CO$_2$ emissions (lbs. per year)   —Andrew Postman

How to Make Your Home Green

And save on your taxes, too

Greening your home means you can get more greenbacks in return. The stimulus plan of 2009 offered tax credits for making your home more energy efficient. Here's some advice from Kateri Callahan, president of the Alliance to Save Energy, a nonprofit group.

● What credits are available for making our homes greener?

Uncle Sam offers up to $1,500 in tax credit for energy-efficiency upgrades like new insulation and windows. The credits are worth 30 percent of the total cost for the upgrades. For example, if you spent $3,000 on eligible windows, you can get back $900.

● What exactly is covered? Can I get money back for weather stripping?

Yes. There are four types of upgrades that are covered. The first batch are home-shell improvements like insulation, windows and sealing. These are designed to make the home tighter and close up leaks. The next batch are home heating, ventilating and air-conditioning, or HVAC. This includes efficient air conditioners and furnaces. A third batch is renewable energy technology like geothermal heat pumps, solar water heating, small wind generators and photovoltaic systems. The last batch—and perhaps the most popular—are hybrid and diesel cars.

● For what period of time are the credits available?

The credits for the home shell and HVAC are available if you make these investments anytime before Dec. 31, 2010. Investments in renewable energy systems are eligible for credit until December 31, 2016.

❓ What's the best way to use these tax credits?

As a general rule of thumb, the first thing is to seal and insulate your house, which can reduce your heating and cooling bill by about 20 percent. But what will make the biggest impact is specific to each home, so get an energy audit. Check the Web site of your local utility or state energy office, which sometimes offer an audit for free or for a nominal fee.

❓ How about solar cells and wind generators?

The 2009 law authorized an additional $2,000 for installing these renewable energy systems. A lot of people think that it only makes sense to install renewable energy technology if you've already made the home very energy efficient. If you live in a leaky home that wastes a lot of energy, installing solar energy panels doesn't make sense. Also, solar panels cost a lot more than storm windows.

❓ Where can people go for more information?

Products need to meet certain criteria to qualify, so it's a good idea to do some research. Ask your retailer, check product packaging or try manufacturers' Web sites. The Alliance to save Energy's Web site, ase.org, and the Tax Incentives Assistance Project Web sites, energytaxincentives. org, have information and links to I.R.S. forms. Energy Star (energystar.gov) also provides details on qualifying products and estimated savings.

❓ What about a less obvious move, like buying a new wood-burning stove?

The law does cover any stove with a thermal efficiency of 75 percent or more that uses a "biomass fuel," which means anything from crops to wood. So, yes, a very efficient wood stove is covered. But the most important thing still is to make sure your house is insulated and sealed. It may not be sexy, but at the end of the day, it's what puts more money in your pocketbook.

—Julie Scelfo

How to Keep the Mice Away

Simple precautions to keep mice and other pests from invading your home

The primary line of defense against mice and other vermin is to prevent them from entering in the first place. You want to seal up every entry point you can find, experts advise. The first thing to do is check for spaces under doors, even in apartment buildings. In larger buildings, mice can get into upper hallways by climbing up dumbwaiter or elevator shafts or along pipes in walls. Because they can squeeze through spaces as small as a quarter inch, gaps under or around doors should be sealed with weatherstripping and with coarse steel wool around pipes.

Mice can be deterred from entering a building by cleaning out debris in basement window wells and keeping wood piles two feet from the house.

Owners of all buildings—including apartment buildings—should make sure there are no cracks or other openings in the exterior that can provide entry. If windows are open in your basement, you should make sure there are screens on them. There also should be no shrubbery against the house, and no excessive amount of mulch, which rodents can easily burrow into.

Mice typically mount a ground assault on a house, but squirrels usually attack at the roofline. Squirrels can be a particular problem because they gnaw incessantly on anything they can sink their teeth into, including electrical wiring. Tree limbs should be cut back a sufficient distance—at

Ghosts in the House?

Help for de-spooking your home

A recent Google search for getting rid of ghosts yielded nearly two million hits. In a recent Harris poll of 2,000 adults, 41 percent said that they believed in ghosts.

Before attempting to cleanse a household of ghostlike sounds and scents, the homeowner must first determine whether such sounds and scents are actually of the other world. Happily, there is no shortage of instruction manuals. One, an e-book called *Is My House Haunted? A Practical Guide,* was written by Bonnie Vent, the medium who founded the San Diego Paranormal Research Project. Those who dismiss the paranormal may wish to check out her Web site, sdparanormal.com.

Vent's guide contains a paranormal activity log in which to record such things as electrical devices going on and off, unexplained noises and cold and hot spots. It lists common misconceptions, including the notion that "paying someone to spread lotions and potion all over the house" will make the spirits go away.

"What does work? Communication!!!" writes Vent, whose cleansing services cost $125 an hour. "This does not necessarily mean that they will leave, but you should be able to work out a livable situation."

She also offers a word of warning: "There are people who will take advantage of others by using holy water, burning sage and spreading salt around the perimeter of the house. Spirit people are people—these things have no effect in the long term. You really have to get to the root cause."

Many hauntings are so slight that the hom-eowners may feel equipped to handle the problem themselves. Guy Clark, for example, an interior desginer who owns an old stone house in Bullville, N.Y., says spirits do not trouble him. Clark says he was lying in bed shortly after he took possession of his house and had a vision.

"I opened my eyes for a second, and someone passed over my head through the window in a blue cabana suit, blue shorts and a shirt, like what people wore in the '60s," Clark says. How did Clark deal with the spirit? "I said, 'O.K., this is my house. If you need anything, I'm here, but you don't live here anymore, move on.' " However contradictory the message, the ghost apparently understood, for Clark never again had a problem.

Other times, ghost hunters call in others to rid a home of ghosts: so-called house cleaners or, in some cases, demonologists. Patty A. Wilson, the author with Mark Nesbitt of *The Big Book of Pennsylvania Ghost Stories* and a founder of the Ghost Research Foundation, says the time for homeowners to call for professional intervention is when they feel frightened or threatened.

Concerned homeowners by now understand that how best to rid the home of spirits is debatable. Megan Hoolihan, manager of Marie Laveau's House of Voodoo, has studied the occult for 18 years and seems to take her calling seriously. Contrary to Vent's beliefs, Hoolihan says many people in the South believe sage has cleansing properties. "I recommend making a mixture of powdered sage, holy water and cedar oil, some water from a church or that has been blessed by someone. You can also use lavender oil or violet oil. The smells are soothing; it's a comfort."

—Joyce Wadler

least 6 feet from the house—so they can't go airborne to the roof, where they can chew their way in through soft wood or crawl through spaces between flue pipes or chimneys.

Wasps are another common pest. Wasps can make nests in the overhang of a roof or behind aluminum siding, and they get into attics and roof areas through vents or around pipes and windows.

Wasps typically hibernate over the winter, but can be trouble come spring. Once they're inside the attic or the walls and it starts to warm up, the wasps start looking for light. If the first light they find is indoors, they will end up inside. One solution is for a professional to spray areas where wasps enter to prevent them from making nests behind siding (generally $120 to $150 a treatment). Another is to install screens on attic vents.

Spiders, cluster flies, ladybugs and beetles typically invade houses when winter approaches. While the latter three are little more than a nuisance, spiders bite, and some people are allergic to the venom. So any spider webs outside or inside should be removed. Using a vacuum cleaner is a good solution.

—Jay Romano

Closing Up a House for Winter
Most important is protecting your plumbing

Whether your vacation home is in the Florida Keys or on the Maine coast, there are things that must be done when you're closing it for the season. A house-closing to-do list starts with protecting the plumbing.

Turn the heat down but not off. You don't want your pipes to freeze; also, older houses may have plaster that's vulnerable to freeze-and-thaw cracking. Set your thermostat between 45 and 55 degrees. If the furnace relies on fuel oil, be sure that your oil supplier will keep oil in the tank.

Turn off the water at the inside shut-off valve or at the main valve outside. If your house is supplied by a well, cut off its power. If there are hoses supplying a washing machine or an ice maker, look for valves where the hoses come out of the wall or floor and turn them off. If a pipe or hose freezes and breaks, the damage will be minimal if there's no water pressure.

If the house is in an area with very cold winters and you do not leave any heat on, you should drain the system by shutting off the supply and opening the lowest tap or faucet in the house until the water stops flowing. Empty toilet tanks and bowls, the water heater and anything else in the house that holds water. Pour an antifreeze solution into drain traps.

Unplug TVs, cable or satellite boxes and most kitchen appliances to protect them in case of a power surge or a lightning strike.

Take out trash, especially food waste. If you're in an area with raccoons or bears, do not leave food waste anywhere on the property. If you have a compost bin, cover it securely. Empty, clean and store bird feeders. Check your foundation and eaves for openings that might be used by mice, squirrels or raccoons. Close your fireplace damper.

Give your phone number to a year-round neighbor who can call you if anything seems amiss. Perhaps she will also pick up any circulars tossed in your driveway.

Be sure that your insurance policy covers your house even if it's empty over the winter. Read it carefully for clauses that could be invoked to deny coverage.

—Steve Bailey

In the Garden

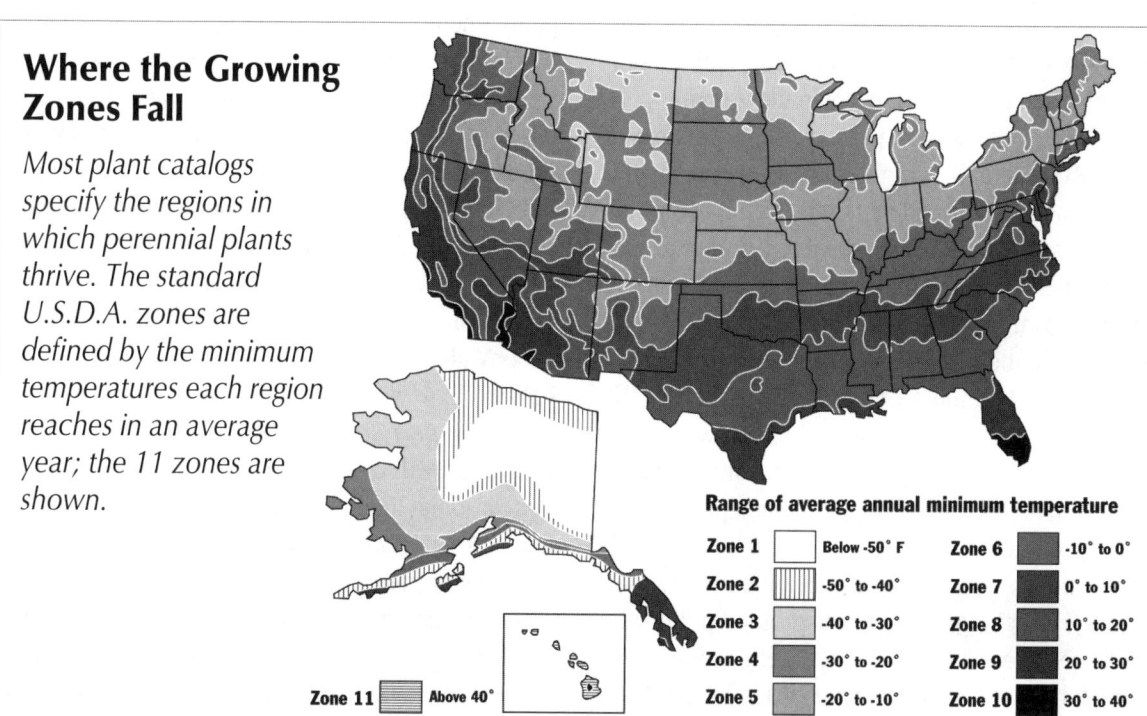

Where the Growing Zones Fall

Most plant catalogs specify the regions in which perennial plants thrive. The standard U.S.D.A. zones are defined by the minimum temperatures each region reaches in an average year; the 11 zones are shown.

Range of average annual minimum temperature

Zone 1	Below -50° F	Zone 6	-10° to 0°
Zone 2	-50° to -40°	Zone 7	0° to 10°
Zone 3	-40° to -30°	Zone 8	10° to 20°
Zone 4	-30° to -20°	Zone 9	20° to 30°
Zone 5	-20° to -10°	Zone 10	30° to 40°

Zone 11   Above 40°

Starting a Garden

A master gardener reveals her springtime rituals

Anne Raver is the *New York Times* gardening columnist and the author of *Deep in the Green: An Exploration of Country Pleasures* and other books. Here she shares some of the secrets of her rites of spring.

March is the time to plant my kitchen garden, putting seeds of leeks, broccoli rabe, the tiny specks of alpine strawberries in sterile potting soil. They incubate in trays under plastic lids on my concrete floor, which is warmed by water pipes that keep them a cozy 68 degrees.

Many gardeners don't have time to start their own plants. But some mail-order companies will ship interesting, well-grown varieties. Burpee, for instance, offers Fairy Tale eggplants, tender little purple and white 6-inchers that can be grown in a pot (see contact information on page 472). Seed Savers Exchange grows rare heirlooms like red milkweed, a prairie flower crucial to monarch butterflies (563-382-5990; www.seedsavers.org). Seeds of Change sells all kinds of peppers, like Corno di Toro, which is delicious roasted (888-762-7333; www.seedsofchange.com).

Check out local farmers' markets, herb festivals and botanical gardens to discover new plants that you won't have to start from seed. I found some yellow Brandywine tomato plants at Maryland's famous Sheep and Wool Festival (www.sheepandwool.org) among some of the most beautifully grown organic seedlings I'd ever seen.

Meanwhile, see if your soil is ready for potatoes and peas. If you pick up a handful of soil and squeeze, and it wads into a sticky ball or glistens with water, it's too wet. If it crumbles like damp, rather cool, chocolate cake, get those taters in the ground.

All Blue potatoes are perfect for purple French fries; Red Gold is a highly disease-resistant red potato with yellow flesh; and Yellow Finn is buttery and sweet. I presprouted some of my spuds one spring after reading how to do it in the catalog from Ronniger's, a potato farm in Moyie Springs, Idaho (208-267-7938; www.ronnigers. com). I just laid them out on a newspaper on the floor in indirect light about a week or two before planting, and stubby sprouts grew from the buds. The plants from these sprouted spuds popped out of the ground quickly, grew into bushy plants with dark green leaves and bore more plentifully than plants that developed from unsprouted potatoes.

As for peas, I like a French petit pois variety from John Scheepers Kitchen Garden Seeds (860-567-6086; www.kitchengardenseeds.com). I'll plant sugar snaps along the fence and flowering sweet peas to ramble up bamboo tripods set about the garden. Cupani, a fragrant purple-blue bicolor sweet pea, and Captain of the Blues, a fragrant deep mauve, are only two of the many offered by Select Seeds (800-684-0395; www.selectseeds.com).

I love to plant nasturtiums like deep red Empress of India on the ends of my raised beds, to spill into the paths, and borage, which has a gray leaf and a gray-blue flower, among blue-green broccoli and kale.

For flowers, zinnias are a must, among them *Z. angustifolia,* the little white daisylike flower with a gold center, and double hybrid forms of *Z. elegans* like Scarlet Splendor and Envy, a chartreuse. I also put a bevy of tall sunflowers outside the kitchen garden fence. Cook's Garden has a knockout deep red sunflower called Moulin Rouge as well as Moonwalker, a pale yellow with a dark center (800-457-9703; www.cooksgarden.com). The cup plant, *Silphium perfoliatum,* looks wonderful against that outer wall of tall annuals. Its delicate, canary-yellow, daisylike blossoms rise above broad green leaves that form little cups where they meet the square stem and capture rainwater.

All the greens thrive in cool weather. I can never grow enough mesclun or arugula, especially the wild self-seeding sylvetta, *Diplotaxis muralis,* which has narrow leaves and a sharper flavor than the regular roquette type, *Eruca vesicaria* var. *sativa.* Tatsoi, kyona mizuna and Osaka purple, a tangy mustard green with a sturdy purple-green leaf, are a few of the many Asian greens on offer.

Where Green Thumbs Shop

Sources for seeds and plants

W. Atlee Burpee & Co. Seeds, bulbs, shrubs and gardening supplies. 800-888-1447; www.burpee.com

Park Seed Co. Seeds, plants and gardening supplies. 800-213-0076; www.parkseed.com

Jackson & Perkins. Wide selection of roses and perennials, also garden accessories. 877-322-2300; www.jacksonandperkins.com

Thompson & Morgan. English catalog with over 2,500 varieties of flower and vegetable seeds. 800-274-7333; www.thompson-morgan.com

Wayside Gardens. Large selection of perennials, trees and shrubs. 800-213-0379; www.waysidegardens.com

White Flower Farm. Perennials, bulbs, trees, shrubs. Excellent catalog with detailed plant and growing instructions. 800-503-9624; www.whiteflowerfarm.com

TIMELY TIPS

A Picture-Perfect Garden

✔ On my list of most useful garden tools, some people might be surprised to find a camera. A camera won't prune a rosebush or dig a hole, but for design help it can be essential. Through its single eye I discover things that are not visible when I walk through my garden: things that can be improved, moved or removed. I can also snap records of successful experiments and other plantings to remember and repeat. And photographs, with dates and notes scribbled on the backs, slip nicely into my garden journal.

—Ken Druse

Unlike a lot of red lettuces, which tend to be bland and soft, Hyper Red Rumple Waved has a savoy-type leaf and plenty of flavor. The seeds come from Fedco Seeds (207-873-7333; www. fedcoseeds.com). Red Rumple looks gorgeous with Australian Yellowleaf, a lime-green lettuce from Seed Savers Exchange. A fellow gardener also talked me into Red Iceberg, another Seed Savers gem.

Purple Dragon, a reddish-purple heirloom carrot with a yellow-orange core, is available through Seed Savers Exchange and Bountiful Gardens (707-459-6410; www.bountifulgardens.org). Cosmic Purple, a newer hybrid with a plumper, more consistent shape, and Kinbi, a golden yellow, are both offered by Johnny's Selected Seeds (207-861-3900; www.johnnyseeds.com).

On the tomato front, my favorite is still Brandywine, and Yellow Brandywine, too. I've always sneered at yellow tomatoes as tasteless, bland things, but these have a more tangy, if slightly sweeter, taste than the regular reddish-pink ver-

sion. And people like my mother, who have trouble digesting the more acidic types, can eat these with impunity. I found Yellow Brandywine seeds in the Heirloom Seeds catalog (412-384-0852; www.heirloomseeds.com).

HOUSE

A Sower's Guide to Soil
Germination goes better when the soil is better

Soil pH is just one of several factors that can determine whether a seed develops into a thriving plant or fails to grow at all. Maureen Heffernan, author of *Burpee Seed Starter: A Guide to Growing Flower, Vegetable, and Herb Seeds Indoors and Outdoors,* explains here how a savvy gardener can give seeds a healthy start in life.

Q When should I start seed?

Most seed packages come with full instructions of when to start the seed. As a rule of thumb, however, most annual vegetable and flower seeds should be started indoors about 6 to 8 weeks before the average last frost date in your area. (See the table on page 488 for details.)

Q What is the best soil medium?

Always use a germination mixture that's been

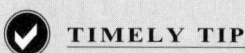

TIMELY TIPS

Cleaning Your Dirt

✔ **Make sure your dirt is clean.** To sterilize a seed medium in an oven or microwave, you can use a medium-size potato as your "sterility gauge." Place the soil in a tray at the same depth as you would need to fill a seed flat. Put the potato on the soil and place in the oven. When the potato is done enough to eat, the soil should be clean enough for your seeds.

specially formulated for starting seeds. Home-made soil mixtures are easy to make and cheaper than buying premade ones, especially if you start large quantities of seed. One of the best recipes is Cornell Peat-Lite, developed by agronomists at Cornell University. Its ingredients include one bushel of shredded sphagnum peat moss; one bushel of horticultural vermiculite (No. 4-fine); four level tbsp. of ammonium nitrate (a nitrogen source); two level tbsp. of powdered superphosphate (20 percent); and ten level tbsp of finely ground dolomitic limestone.

Never use as your germination medium soil from the yard or garden because it is often too "heavy" and can cause disease problems since it is not sterile. Homemade or bought, seed starting mixture should be light and almost fluffy even after it is watered.

Q What is the right temperature for planting?

✔ TIMELY TIP

A Gourmet Meal for Your Garden

✔ **Compost is the all-purpose answer to everything.** If you have enough of it you won't need much of anything else. Though different crops have different needs, they will be able to serve themselves from the smorgasbord provided by healthy soil with plenty of compost in it. Once you start adding specific fertilizers, you start having to pay close attention to each individual diet. In practice, though, it can be hard to create soil so fertile that no amendment is necessary, especially when growing vegetables in a small space. But before you break out the fertilizer cookbook and start concocting special meals for all the crops you want to grow, make sure the soil is "in good tilth"—well drained and well aerated—and that the pH is between six and seven (the best range for most vegetables).

—Leslie Land

Most seedlings do best with "warm feet and cool heads." Make sure soil temperatures are at least 70 and no more than 80 degrees Fahrenheit. Air temperature can be about ten degrees cooler at night. Heat cables or heat mats, placed under germination containers, are the best way to insure evenly warm soil temperatures. They are inexpensive and can be found in many gardeners' supply catalogs and most garden centers.

Q How much watering is necessary?

Water immediately after sowing seeds. Use a spritzer bottle to evenly moisten the surface. The most common mistake is applying too much or too little water. Just keep seeds and seedlings evenly moist and never allow seeds to dry out, even temporarily. A good tip is to premoisten the soil mixture before sowing seeds. This ensures that soil has been thoroughly moistened from top to bottom. It also prevents seeds being displaced when trying to get the soil thoroughly watered after sowing seeds.

Q How much light do seeds need?

Some seeds need light to germinate, some need darkness. Check the light requirements on the seed packet. Once germinated, however, all seeds need bright light to develop. Light can come from a sunny window—south is best—or fluorescent lighting. Most seedlings need at least 12 to 16 hours of direct light each day.

If you're using fluorescent light, seedlings need about 15 to 20 watts per square foot of growing area. A double row of fluorescent tubes is enough for a flat up to 16 inches wide. Place the light tubes about 3 to 4 inches above the plants. Be sure to raise light tubes as plants grow.

Q When should seedlings be thinned out or transplanted?

After seedlings have germinated and developed at least two leaves, thin out seedlings by gently

TIPPING THE pH SCALES

Soil pH measures the relative acidity of the earth; here's how to find the right balance:

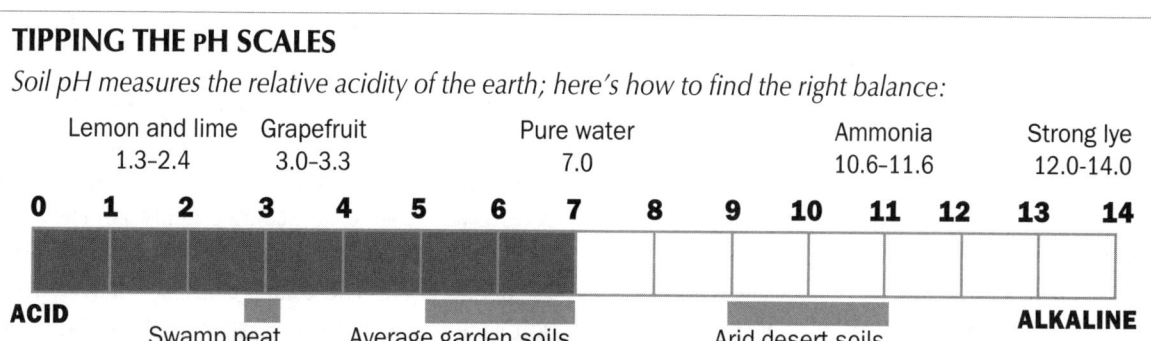

Lemon and lime
1.3–2.4

Grapefruit
3.0–3.3

Pure water
7.0

Ammonia
10.6–11.6

Strong lye
12.0–14.0

0 1 2 3 4 5 6 7 8 9 10 11 12 13 14

ACID

Swamp peat
(sphagnum
moss)

Average garden soils

Arid desert soils

ALKALINE

BEST
for most plants

TO RAISE pH VALUE ONE UNIT:

CONDITION	ADD (lbs./100 sq. ft.)		
	Ground limestone, marl or oyster shells	Burnt lime	Hydrated lime
Light, sandy soil	3	2	2.5
Sandy loams	4.5	2.5	3.3
Loams	6.75	3.75	6
Silt loams and clay loams	8	4.5	6

TO LOWER pH VALUE ONE UNIT:

CONDITION	ADD (lbs./100 sq. ft.)		
	Sulphur	Aluminum sulphate	Iron sulphate
Light, sandy soil	3	2	2.5
Silt loams and clay loams	8	4.5	6

NOTE: To raise pH in soils lacking in organic matter, reduce table amounts by 25 percent; for soils with high organic content, double the measurement.

pulling them up, being careful not to disturb the root systems of seedlings that will grow on. You can also thin them by cutting them at soil level with scissors so remaining seedlings are one inch apart. If seedlings aren't thinned out, they will get crowded and become thin, weak and disease-prone.

Transplant seedlings to wider and deeper containers after they have developed at least two to four leaves. Transplanting allows seedlings to develop a stronger root system before being planted outdoors.

● What kind of soil do seedlings need when they are moved outside?

Good growing soils are fertile, well drained and well aerated. When you pick up a handful of earth, it should have a crumbly texture and, ideally, be filled with organic matter, worms and other enriching organisms. To prepare outside plots for planting, add at least 3 to 4 inches of organic matter to your garden beds every spring or fall. Work in the organic matter to a depth of at least 12 inches. If you are working with soil that has a lot of heavy clay or sand, add more organic matter and work it in several inches deeper in both the spring and fall. If your soil is poorly drained, you may need to add sand, build raised beds and/or install drainage pipes.

● Is soil pH an important factor?

A soil's pH number indicates the soil's level of acidity (sourness) and alkalinity (sweetness). Numbers below seven indicate more acidic levels, and numbers over seven indicate alkaline conditions. The scale is logorhythmic, meaning that a soil pH of five is 10 times more acidic than four. The majority of garden plants prefer a slightly acidic soil (i.e., pH 6.2 to 6.5).

TIMELY TIP

Persuading Bulbs to Bloom

From the fridge to a sunny room

✔ If you are chilling bulbs in the refrigerator or some other cold place that hovers around 40 degrees and forcing them in soil, use any pot that appeals to you as long as it is at least 2 inches deeper than the bulbs and has drainage holes. Regular potting soil will do fine. One intrepid bulb forcer plants the bulbs close together, nose up, and covers them with a bit of soil. You don't need to fertilize.

✔ If you use clay pots, the clay and the soil can increase moisture in the refrigerator. Try putting a piece of aluminum foil over the top of the pot to cut down on evaporation, taking care not to fasten it too tightly, because bulbs need air. You should take the bulbs out every couple of weeks to see if they need a drink, and when the shoots begin to grow, put the bulbs in a sunny room.

✔ If you are confused about how long to chill your bulbs, check out the timing chart under "spring bulbs" on the public part of bulb. com, the Netherlands Flower Bulb Information Center's Web site. My favorite sources for bulbs are Brent and Becky's Bulbs, in Gloucester, Va., which sells precooled bulbs (877-661-2852; brentandbeckysbulbs.com); John Scheepers, in Bantam, Conn. (860-567-0838; johnscheepers. com); and Old House Gardens in Ann Arbor, Mich. (734-995-1486; oldhousegardens.com).

Q **How do I know what my soil pH is?**

As a general rule, if you live in an area with little rainfall and high temperatures, like the Southwest, you probably have alkaline soil. If you live in a region with high rainfalls and temperate climate, like the Northeast, the soil is probably acidic. To get an exact soil pH reading, you will need to get your soil tested, however.

Most county extension agencies will do such analyses if you bring or mail a sample to them. Be sure to follow the lab's soil-collecting directions carefully to ensure an accurate analysis. They are listed in the blue government services pages of the telephone book. These labs can also analyze your soil's nutrient and organic matter levels and advise if nutrients or other soil amendments need adding.

Q **How reliable are pH home test kits?**

While not as accurate as soil-testing labs, they will give a fairly general pH measurement. You can buy such do-it-yourself soil-testing kits from garden catalogs and centers. Just be sure to carefully follow all directions.

Q **If my soil's pH level is off, what should I do about it?**

Soil pH can be lowered (made more acidic) by adding a combination of ground sulfur, aluminum sulphate, iron sulphate and garden gypsum. In addition, pine needles, pine bark and peat moss will slowly bring about slight drops in pH naturally. To raise pH, add agricultural or dolomitic limestone to your soil. See the charts on the previous page for more precise instructions.

What to Do Before You Plant

Start with a soil test and add a little nutrition

Soil is the foundation for any garden. The effort given to its preparation will largely determine the success of your garden. Soil quality varies widely depending on location, and your local agricultural extension service is likely to be the best information source about the soil in your region. Horticulturalist Chris Curless offers some tips for getting your garden ready for planting.

A BULB LOVER'S FAVORITE CHOICES

They can come back to the same spot for decades, or you can dig them up and move them

	Height (in.)	Planting depth (in.)	Planting time	Blooming time
SPRING-FLOWERING BULBS				
CROCUS *Crocus* species	3-5	3-4	EARLY FALL	EARLY SPRING
CROWN IMPERIAL *Fritillaria imperialis*	30-48	5	EARLY FALL	MIDSPRING
DAFFODIL *Narcissus* species	12	6	EARLY FALL	MIDSPRING
DUTCH IRIS *Iris xiphium*	24	4	EARLY FALL	LATE SPRING
FLOWERING ONION *Allium giganteum*	48	10	EARLY FALL	LATE SPRING
GRAPE HYACINTH *Muscari botryoides*	6-10	3	EARLY FALL	EARLY SPRING
HYACINTH *Hyacinthus orientalis*	12	6	EARLY FALL	EARLY SPRING
SNOWDROP *Galanthus nivalis*	4-6	4	EARLY FALL	EARLY SPRING
TULIP (early) *Tulipa* species	10-13	6	EARLY FALL	EARLY SPRING
TULIP (Darwin hybrid) *Tulipa* species	28	6	EARLY FALL	MIDSPRING
TULIP (late) *Tulipa* species	36	6	EARLY FALL	LATE SPRING
WINDFLOWER *Anemone blanda*	5	2	EARLY FALL	EARLY SPRING
SUMMER-FLOWERING BULBS				
ANEMONE *Anemone* species	18	2	N: EARLY SPRING S: LATE FALL	LATE SUMMER
BUTTERCUP *Ranunculus*	12	2	SOUTH: LATE FALL	MIDSUMMER
CROCOSMIA *Crocosmia* species	24	4	APRIL-MAY	MID- TO LATE SUMMER
DAHLIA (dwarf varieties) *Dahlia* species	12	4	AFTER LAST FROST	LATE SUMMER
DAHLIA (large varieties) *Dahlia* species	48	4	AFTER LAST FROST	LATE SUMMER
GALTONIA *Galtonia candicans*	40	5	APRIL-MAY	MID- TO LATE SUMMER
GLADIOLUS (large flower) *Gladiolus* species	60	3-4	APRIL-JUNE	MIDSUMMER
GLADIOLUS (small flower) *Gladiolus* species	30	3-4	APRIL-JUNE	MIDSUMMER
LILY *Lilium* species	36-84	8	FALL OR EARLY SPRING	ALL SUMMER
TIGER FLOWER *Tigridia paronia*	16	3	EARLY SPRING	MID- TO LATE SUMMER

HEIGHT AND DEPTH

A bulb that is planted deep will not necessarily grow tall.

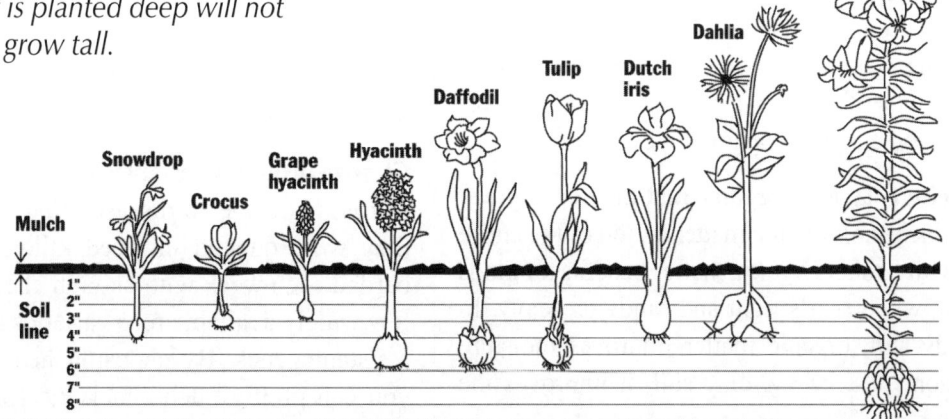

Test your soil to find out how well it will support plant growth and what you might have to do to improve it. A soil test will show your soil pH and how to adjust it if needed, as well as the levels of specific nutrients to determine fertilizer needs. Agricultural extension services can perform these lab tests on your soil and give you a detailed profile of what you've got in your yard. Most plants prefer a slightly-acidic-to-neutral soil. Your soil test will indicate how much lime or sulfur needs adding if adjustment is required. It will also recommend what other nutrients may be needed as supplements.

Mark the area for your garden before you dig. If it's a simple shape like a rectangle or square, stakes and string are an easy way to do this. For a curved bed, a garden hose will allow you to make smooth bends. Mark the edge of the bed with white spray paint or powdered lime so you know exactly where you want to dig. It's easy to think you know and still get lost in the middle of your digging.

Remove existing grass to get to the soil. If you are going to put a border into a lawn, you want to get rid of the turf. If it's a large, relatively flat area, consider renting a sod cutter—a heavy, gas-powered machine. It's not great at corners and awful on a hillside because it weighs about 300 pounds, but for flat areas it is very fast. Smaller mechanical gadgets are also available to cut turf. But the tried-and-true method is to use a sharpened spade to undercut the turf. Since you're removing the top inch or so of soil and a lot of green material, put it in the compost pile so you can use it again in the future.

Add a hefty layer of organic matter. Next, spread 3 to 3 inches of organic matter on top of the entire area with a rake. Organic matter benefits all kinds of soil, whether it's light and sandy or heavy. In a sandy soil, organic matter improves moisture retention; in a heavy, clay soil, it improves the drainage. Remember, if you're planting woody stock or perennials, you have only one chance to work the soil like this, so take advantage of the opportunity. Some good types of organic matter include aged manure, peat moss or leaf mold. In some areas of the South, ground-up pine bark is recommended because it lasts longer in warm, moist soil. If you need to add soil amendments, spread them evenly on top of the organic matter.

Thoroughly mix the organic matter and other additions into the soil. The next step is digging. I think turning the soil to the depth of a shovel is enough. Many books recommend double-digging—which means digging twice as deep—but for most people, that's just way too much work.

Start at one corner and work your way backward, so you don't compact the area you have turned. Break up big clods as you go. Digging and incorporating the organic matter and fertilizer creates air spaces in the soil, making it easier for the roots of your plants to get around. The goal of all this is to make it easier for plants to grow.

A Perfect Rose Garden

Without a ton of chemicals and constant worry

The rose's reputation as an aristocrat is well deserved—it is a regal flower that requires the attention usually reserved for royalty. But rose lovers need not quit their day jobs to grow perfect roses. Here's how.

Choose disease-resistant varieties. Most varieties of roses become so diseased that they look like they were dunked in weed killer unless bombarded each week with enough chemicals. But a few widely available rose varieties have disease-resistant genes. By choosing healthy varieties, you can pretty much chuck the sprayer. If you

HOUSE

 TIMELY TIPS

Out, Out, Black Spot

Black spot is a nasty fungus *(Diplocarpon rosae)* that attacks roses, causing circular black spots with fringed margins to form on the foliage. Infected leaves eventually turn yellow and drop, leaving the plants severely damaged and nearly nude. Because the spores are spread by splashing water, the fungus is worse in periods of rain or high humidity. Preventive sprays like the one below, made from nontoxic ingredients, can help quite a bit. You can also try to control the fungus by keeping the foliage dry between rains (water only at the base of the plant), pruning off infected canes and removing all diseased leaves from the soil. Leaf cleanup is especially important in autumn, since the fungus spends the winter on infected leaves and canes, only to rear its ugly head once again in the spring.

HOMEMADE FUNGUS PREVENTION SPRAY:

- 1 gallon unchlorinated water
- 1 tbsp baking soda
- 1 tbsp summerweight horticultural oil (optional)
- 1 tbsp detergent (dishwashing liquid works fine)

✔ **This concoction, with an alkaline base of baking soda,** prevents the acid conditions necessary for diseases such as black spot and powdery mildew to thrive. Baking soda, being alkaline, neutralizes leaf surfaces and keeps the fungus spores from taking hold.

✔ **Adding a spoonful of detergent helps the soda cling to the leaves.** Adding summerweight horticultural oil increases the fungus-preventive punch while also helping the spray to stick. It's important to have the spray come out as a fine mist, so use a garden sprayer, not an ordinary squeeze bottle.

✔ **Make a fresh batch each time you spray.** Be sure you get the whole plant, including the undersides of the leaves. Spray in the early morning; horticultural oil applied when temperatures are high can damage sensitive plants, and wetting leaves in the evening is counterproductive when you are dealing with black spot.

✔ **Finally, spray often.** The mixture does not last long and its effects are entirely preventive. This isn't a cure, so if you wait until you have problems, you will have waited too long.

—Leslie Land

look closely, you might notice an insect or two or a nibbled leaf or bloom, but you don't need to get compulsive about your rosebushes.

Use organic fertilizers for the most part, and boost only when necessary with a chemical fertilizer. Organic fertilizers are generally better than chemical ones, because they are gentler to the plant, contain many important trace nutrients and contribute to soil health. Nonetheless, an occasional booster of balanced rose food is often helpful, with most experts favoring a balance of heavy nitrogen, light phosphorus and medium potassium (18-6-12 and 15-5-13 are typical formulations).

When to feed and how much varies with the quality of the soil and the type of rose, since fast-draining soils need supplementation more often than rich, moisture-retentive loams. If a rose is a repeat bloomer, each bloom cycle should be supported with another meal. In practice, this means one feeding in the early spring for everybody, then follow-up feedings at 6-week intervals for heavy bloomers only. It is easiest to start out with dry fertilizer and then follow up (if necessary) with foliar feeding. Many rose growers also give their plants a good shower of seaweed extract in early midseason, and others give their roses vitamin supplements.

TIMELY TIPS

How to Train a Rose

✔ Training a rose is not hard. It just takes time and patience. The main thing is this: a rose cane that grows straight up will most likely flower at its tip; if forced into a lateral position, it will bloom all along the stem.

✔ Any canes that start growing into the path or start taking over some other plant's space should be trimmed back to 3 or 4 inches. The buds on these shortened stems will produce flowers.

✔ To train roses up a stone wall, you could drill into the mortar and insert iron anchors, or use mortar screws. But don't use wire, which cuts into the canes. If you wish to have individual supports for each climbing rose, you can use cedar posts sunk 2 feet into the ground as vertical supports and plant a climbing rose at the base of each post. Or a simple tripod can be made with bamboo canes.

—Anne Raver

Don't forget to water your roses—but don't overwater. Roses do best when they grow in soil that is consistently moist—but not wet—for most of the root zone. In nature, the standard moisture requirement for roses is 1 inch of rainfall a week, but this ignores important differences between soils. A rose growing in sandy ground that's low in humus might need twice as much water as one growing in rich loam over clay.

To figure out how much your roses need, turn on the watering system you plan to use (drip, sprinkler or hose) and let it run for 10 minutes, then turn it off and do something else for a half hour or so. When the half hour is up, dig a test hole next to the rose, right outside the root zone, and see how far down the water has penetrated. Adjust the watering

time as necessary to get moisture all through the root zone, then wait 3 or 4 days.

Dig again. The top inch or two of soil may be dry, but things should still be damp farther down. If you are looking at soil that is dry at 3, 4, or 5 inches underneath the surface, get ready for watering twice a week (and get some more organic matter into the soil before you plant any more roses).

10 (Comparatively) Easy Roses

Keep it simple: concentrate on hardiness

Species roses are tougher than hybrids, and roses on their own roots are more likely to thrive than those that have been grafted. Once-blooming shrub and climbing roses are almost always easier than rebloomers, and everything else in the world of roses is easier than hybrid teas. For maximum grief avoidance, gardeners in zone 5 and further north should concentrate on hardiness; those in zone 6 and further south should bank on disease resistance.

Autumn Sunset (Climber). Very cold-hardy and disease resistant. Semidouble, fragrant flowers in apricot-gold or very pale orange.

Betty Prior (Floribunda). The plant is short and the fragrance delicate, but the single, true pink flowers are abundant and charming and well set off by the darker pink of the buds.

Bonica (Shrub). Good foliage and repeated flushes of double pink flowers on a bush that may reach 4 by 5 feet. Lots of small orange hips. Functionally fragrance-free.

Carefree Beauty (Shrub). Large, loosely double pink flowers opening from narrow buds. Moderate fragrance and good cutting stems on a bush large enough to have presence without overwhelming.

Knock Out (Shrub). Phenomenal disease resistance, near constant flowering and plenty of medium-green foliage on a well-rounded 3-foot bush. Not fragrant, not easy to integrate with other colors; masses of single flowers are a screaming scarlet-magenta euphemized as cherry red.

Rosa rugosa alba (Species). Hardy and disease resistant, with deeply wrinkled foliage and high pink-tinged buds that open to very fragrant single white flowers. Huge orange hips, and frequently good foliage color in autumn.

Scarlet Meidiland (Shrub). More like a ground cover than an upright bush. Low and wide, and well covered with loosely doubled, clear red flowers borne in large sprays. Small, rather shiny medium-green leaves. Negligible fragrance.

The Fairy (Shrub). Very nearly unkillable. The 2½- to 3-foot bushes are covered from early summer to mid-fall with large clusters of small, very double, light pink roses that have only a slight fragrance and tend to fade in the sun.

Thérèse Bugnet (Hybrid Rugosa). Huge bush, as

much as 6 by 6 feet. Very cold hardy and strongly fragrant. Though described as blooming continuously, the very double, medium-pink flowers often take breaks between flushes.

William Baffin (Climber). The hardiest repeat-blooming climber, according to most; it's rated to do well without protection as far north as zone 3. The deep pink, semidouble flowers are not fragrant, but you can't have everything.

—Leslie Land

HOUSE

The Scent of a Garden
Ah, the sweet smell of fragrant flowers

Smell is returning to garden fashion. Ken Druse, author of the "Cuttings" column for the *New York Times,* discusses how to make your garden not only look great but smell great, too.

More nursery catalogs have begun to include lists of fragrant plants on equal footing with categories like hardy vines and ground covers, and breeders are starting to take notice. Still, many fragrant flowers are still not promoted, and many old or overlooked varieties have yet to make a well-deserved comeback, including native azaleas, bearded iris and clethra. Roses, such as Sombreuil, a white climber from the late 19th century, are enjoying a resurgence. Another shrub, the old-fashioned mock orange, smells like orange blossoms. My favorite is the double-flowered *Philadelphus x virginalis* variety. It fills the air with perfume and lasts nearly two weeks as a cut flower.

Scent is invisible, but its placement is crucial. I wouldn't make a planting themed on fragrance, for example, as I would for spring color or dwarf evergreens. I prefer to sprinkle the smells like punctuation. The lily is an exclamation point; the

---

ⓘ **INSIDE INFO**

Flower Talk

○ The term **remontant** was brought into the English-speaking rose world from the French in the late 19th century. It refers specifically to roses that bloom at least twice, with distinct rest periods between flowerings.

○ The term **recurrent** can also be used for those same roses, but it is more commonly applied to roses that bloom in overlapping flushes, with no clearly discernible hiatus between blooming times.　　—Leslie Land

scent of Carolina sweetshrub floats on the evening air like a question mark: "What's that smell?"

I plant fragrant flowers under windows and by doors, places where people are most likely to walk or sit. A *Wisteria venusta* climbs a trellis beside the porch door where its early-spring fragrance of honey is intoxicating. I planted tall lilies next to a garden path so beautiful flowers on tall arching stalks would grab passers-by. Immersed in the deep perfume of those lilies, I am reminded of burnt sugar and clove. The yellow primrose hints of linen drying on the clothesline, with jasmine and a top note of sweet butter.

One of my favorite scents is *Daphne caucasica*; its nearly insignificant flowers remind me of the scent of lily with a trace of honey and a smoky undertone that smells the way a camping lodge does on a rainy day, when memories of crackling fires creep back into the atmosphere.

When the Carolina sweetshrub is in bloom, from May to July, visitors to my garden often debate what the small red-brown flowers smell like. One will say bubble gum, others will say raisins, cider vinegar, pineapple or crushed strawberries.

I love the fragrance of lilacs. The wonderfully fragrant President Lincoln, a variety with about the bluest of lilac flowers, is as lanky as its namesake (great planted under a second-story window). Lilacs come in many colors: one has double snow-white flowers; another's blossoms are cream. There is a double mauve shrub, and one with deep wine-red blossoms. The range of the flower colors is easier to describe than their similarly varied scents.

Free-range flowers worth seeking out include pinks, or dianthus. They have the aroma of clove. The August lily, *Hosta plantaginea*, has giant trumpets that smell like honeysuckle. Heliotrope is one of many plants in which some scent was lost in breeding, but old-fashioned ones can still be found that smell like baby powder haunted by black cherry. *Clematis montana* is an early spring blooming vine that smells like vanilla trailing off to birthday cake.

Perfect Plants for Tough Places
Solutions for problem areas in your garden

Nearly every garden has a tough spot, where the sun doesn't shine, or shines too much, or the drainage is poor, or the kids have made it a place to play ball. Instead of altering the nature of those problem spots, it's often easier to find plants that are suitable for the particular conditions. Here are some solutions for problem areas in your garden.

For damp, shady or wooded areas. Moist ground at the edge of the woods is an ideal environment for many plants that do not flourish in the bright heat of a conventional flower garden. Among them are the low growers such as ajuga, creeping blue phlox, moneywort, bunchberry, epimedium, sweet woodruff *(Galium odoratum),* foamflower *(Tiarella cordifolia),* Virginia bluebells *(Mertensia virginica),* lily-of-the-valley *(Convallaria majalis),*

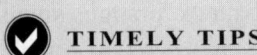

TIMELY TIPS

How to Delay Blooming

✔ If you prune the buds on *Chrysopsis villosa,* coneflowers, garden phlox, helliopsis and helianthus, among others, they will hold off blooming for a few weeks. This will allow you to plan a vacation or special event around the prime blooming time of your plants.   —Suzy Bales

❓ EXPERT ANSWER

When to Tidy Up the Garden

Q. **Is it better to cut back perennials in the fall, or should I wait until spring?**

As is so often the case, the best answer lies in between. The first rule: don't cut back at all until several hard frosts have occurred and the leaves and stalks are brown, indicating that the plants are truly dormant. Pruning too early can signal a plant to send out new stalks and leaves, which is a waste of its energy at the end of the season.

—Stephen Orr

Canada mayflower *(Maianthemum canadense)* and Jack-in-the-pulpit *(Arisaema triphyllum).*

Taller, showier plants include bleeding heart, columbine, hellebore, celandine poppy *(Stylophorum diphyllum),* Solomon's seal, hardy begonia and astilbe, as well as blue lobelia *(Lobelia siphilitica)* and cardinal flower *(Lobelia cardinalis),* astilbe, turtlehead *(Chelone glabra)* and black snakeroot *(Cimicifuga racemosa).* You can also go to town with hostas, which have lovely midsummer flowers, or ferns and moss, which should be very happy in these conditions.

In a really wet spot, you have to make a virtue of it and plant a bog garden, using plants that like their roots in downright wet conditions. Among those are marsh mallow *(Althaea officinalis),* goatsbeard *(Aruncus dioicus),* queen-of-the-meadow *(Filipendula ulmaria),* marsh marigold *(Caltha palustris),* cattail, Louisiana iris, spider lilies, Japanese iris and yellowflag iris *(Iris ensata* and *Iris pseudocorus),* bronze-leaf rodgersia *(Rodgersia podophylla),* meadow rue *(Thalictrum* spp.), and globeflower *(Trollius europaeus).*

For dry areas. For very dry and sunny places, you may want to try plants that tolerate drought, and have leaves that are narrow, hairy or silvery (or all three)—strategies to keep evaporation to a minimum. Or they may have the alternative: very thick, succulent leaves that act as waterstorage devices. Choices include *Achillea* spp. (yarrow); *Armeria* spp. (thrift, sea pink); *Artemisia* spp. *Aurinia saxatilis* (basket-of-gold); *Catanache caerulea* (Cupid's dart); *Centaurea* (perennial cornflower); *Cerastium tomentosum* (snow-in-summer); *Coreopsis* spp. (tickseed); *Eryngium maritimum* (blue sea holly); *Gaillardia* spp. (blanketflower); *Nepeta* spp. (catmint); *Papaver orientale* (oriental poppy); *Portulaca* spp.; *Santolina chamaecyparissus* (lavender cotton); *Stachys byzantina* (lambs' ears) or *Yucca* spp.

For sunny corners. For very sunny places, perennials such as the purple coneflower, rudbeckia, daylily and peonies do very well. Lavender, chrysanthemums, geraniums, zinnias and cosmos like the sun, too.

For high-traffic lawns. Plants other than grass can be used as lawns—chamomile, for example, and dichondra, which is used mainly in California—but none of them is entirely trouble-free, and all of them, including those just mentioned, aren't a perfect solution for the rough-and-tumble play of energetic children, for example.

For really tough areas that defy the possibility of grass, bark mulch works very well, or a rubberized surface, both of which have the added advantage of providing a cushion for falls. Gravel is also an alternative in those absolutely, positively impossible areas where the grass won't grow.

But before you abandon grass altogether, you might first try a tougher variety that is recommended for your part of the country and specifically for playing fields and high-traffic areas. And once it grows, don't be too fussy about it; the children will be perfectly content if you grow what's called a yachtsman's lawn: "He mows what grows." Just rake off the leaves in the fall or, even better, mow them with a mulching mower.

In early spring, before the lawn greens up, broadcast a generous sprinkling each of compost and corn gluten (a natural fertilizer that suppresses the sprouting of annual weeds). Repeat the gluten every 6 weeks or so, stopping at the first sign of frost.

Keep your mower sharp, and don't use it too much. Longer grass, a good 3 inches tall, will cut down on weeds, providing more shade and keeping the grassroots cool and healthy while making it harder for weed seeds to sprout and find the light. And if the grass becomes too compacted because of high-traffic use, you may need to call in the pros to aerate the lawn or buy a machine and do it yourself. (For more tips about grass, see "The Perfect Lawn" on page 502.)

Sloped areas around the house. If an incline is too steep for mowing a lawn safely, plant a low-upkeep groundcover like pachysandra, myrtle or ajuga, along with shrubs and understory trees. If the slope is extremely steep, install retaining walls in a series of terraces, and then plant whatever you wish.

For clay soil. This is a common problem in much of the country. Sometimes the answer is to install raised planting beds and fill them with well-prepared planting soil. If you are planting directly in clay soil, you should incorporate lots of well-rotted compost. Dig the clay soil 8 inches deep and add at least 4 inches of compost. You can fork or rototill the compost in. You can also treat soil that is too sandy the same way—add lots of well-rotted compost.

Near a stream bank favored by deer. You are describing an ideal spot for drooping leucothoe (*Leucothoe fontanesiana*), a deer-resistant broad-leafed evergreen with shiny foliage and graceful arches of white flowers. The species form can

 TIMELY TIPS

Weekenders' Advice

Gardens can handle being on autopilot for much of the summer if their owners take a few crucial steps.

✔ **Install automatic irrigation.** Watering by hand is a time-consuming chore and uses much more water than a drip system.

✔ **Learn to love perennials and shrubs.** Plants that return year after year will establish deep roots that require less water.

✔ **Avoid lanky varieties that need support.** Shop for sturdy species that don't require staking.

✔ **Shop for natives and wildflowers.** Be sure to look around to see what is already growing in your area. These varieties are sure to thrive.

✔ **Pay attention to the locals.** Look at your neighbors' plants to see which types can handle neglect. Some specimens will have been growing successfully for generations. Ask at the local nursery for recommendations.

✔ **Use wildlife barriers.** The animals will soon discover that you've left them an unguarded feast. Fence for deer and use 1-inch-by-1-inch wire netting against rabbits and woodchucks.

✔ **Avoid container plantings during the height of summer.** Potted plants may need water every day during the hot months.

✔ **Don't be a control freak.** Mother Nature is running this show. Just relax and enjoy the process of gardening. Nothing will ever go just as you planned.

—Steve Orr

grow to 7 feet, but there are smaller varieties. Nana, the best-known dwarf form, stops around 2 feet. Rainbow, named for the red and cream streaks on its young leaves, grows to 3 or 4 feet. Leucothoes are useful as well as lovely, forming dense thickets that hold the soil on slopes and give the plant its common names of doghobble and fetterbush. And planting them at a distance is wise; the flowers have a strong fragrance that many find unpleasant. —Leslie Land

The 60-Second Gardener

Some time-saving techniques to keep your garden in shape

As in all areas life, time pressures are transforming the way many backyard gardeners are pursuing their avocation. Shortcuts are in much demand today, giving rise to what one gardening writer recently called "quick-thumb gardening." The object of these new techniques is to keep maintenance low, yet still get beautiful results.

The first principle of quick-thumb gardening is to start out small. Work up to larger gardens and beds once smaller ones are self-sustaining. Careful plant selection also is crucial. Go with plants that are drought tolerant, disease resistant and suited to your climate. More and more gardeners are turning to native plants because they are likely to thrive in their climate and region without chemical fertilizers and sprays. Your local public garden, agricultural extension agent or state native plant society can tell you which plants are native to your area.

Hurried gardeners should avoid high-maintenance plants such as hybrid roses or fruit trees that require lots of fertilizer, water and spraying to keep them healthy. Plants that need staking and continual deadheading like dahlias, hollyhock and delphinium also are impractical. Select trees and shrubs that don't have fruits or nuts to rake up. If you must grow high-maintenance plants, group them together so that they can be cared for in a single place.

If you don't want to spend time planting and pulling out annuals every spring and fall, hardy perennial flowers are a natural alternative. Although they will need to be divided every 3 years or so, they still save time and money in the long run.

Probably the most tedious of all gardening jobs is weeding, so all garden beds and pathways should be mulched once or twice a year to keep down weeds and keep soil moist, which also saves time on watering. In addition to organic mulches like compost, pine bark and pine needles, there are new products that can virtually eliminate weeding without harmful chemicals. These synthetic landscape fabrics are spread out in garden beds and completely block weed growth. Unlike regular plastic mulches, they have microscopic holes that permit air and moisture exchange, keeping plants and soil healthy.

To cut down on lawn-maintenance time, replace traditional grass lawns with low-maintenance plantings such as native trees, shrub borders, hardy ground cover and native perennials and brick, stone or concrete patios.

Watering chores can be reduced by using drip irrigation or soaker hoses instead of watering by hand or relying on overhead sprinklers. Soaker hoses are set down at soil level near plant roots. They save on water because water is emitted directly where it is needed and not lost to evaporation. You can cut down on regular fertilizer feedings of plants by using slow release pellets that last throughout the growing season.

For people with limited space and time, raised bed gardens and container plantings are popular. They are easily planted and watered and stay virtually weed-free. If you have a sunny back door area, plants in containers right outside the door can be easy to water or harvest.

HOUSE

Look for tools and equipment that can save time, too. For example, a mulching lawn mower will save raking lawn clippings, and some new mowers allow you to lime and fertilize as you mow.

For the truly hurried person, there's a gardening trend called "ungardening," which promotes the idea that weeds, faded flower heads and unpruned shrubs enhance a garden's charm. Nature isn't perfect, so why should your garden be?

Late-Season Vegetables

It's almost never too late to start planting

Early August is the perfect time for planting a fall vegetable garden. Anne Raver, the *New York Times* gardening columnist, tells us how to extend the summer pleasures of stepping outside to harvest herbs for dinner well into October.

There is nothing better than September lettuce: Forellenschluss, an heirloom romaine from Austria whose name means "speckled like a trout's back"

(888-762-7333; seedsofchange.com), and lolla rossa, a frilled, magenta loose-leaf lettuce that matures in 55 days if you don't eat all the baby leaves much sooner (563-382-5990; seedsavers. org).

Unprotected, these lettuces will not last all winter, but they will thrive with cooler weather, through August and September. To determine if a particular lettuce, or any other crop, is a good candidate for fall planting, look at the number of days to maturation listed under the variety in the catalog and count backward from your first hard frost date. For instance, many spinach varieties, which love cool weather, take only 40 days or so.

Springer spinach is getting a lot of attention lately because it doesn't bolt or go to seed or develop brown soft spots in hot weather. It has a very mild, almost buttery, but still tangy taste. It's available from John Scheepers Kitchen Garden Seeds (860-567-6086; kitchengardenseeds.com).

Melody hybrid spinach has a dark green, slightly crinkled leaf with loads of flavor. And Tetona, a

What Makes Them Heirlooms?

Planting the seeds of yesteryear

For years, the only way to grow the vegetables popular in your great-grandmother's day was to get heirloom or open-pollinated vegetable seeds through specialty catalogs devoted to saving a bit of horticultural history. Unlike hybrids, heirlooms can be saved year after year, and passed down to future generations.

More and more gardeners are recognizing the appeal of these antique varieties. Heirlooms offer great flavor and enable gardeners to grow new plants from their seeds. But they offer a lot more than just freedom from the need to buy seed each year. Heirlooms are the special province of individuals and small, regional seed companies who tend to be better attuned to specific local

conditions (drought in the Southwest, humidity in the Southeast, cold in the North) than "one size fits all" hybrids.

Unlike hybrids, each heirloom plant is individual, subtly different from every other. Heirlooms grow and ripen unevenly, so you get a longer harvest period. Also unlike hybrids, which are both identically disease-resistant and identically vulnerable to disease, heirlooms react individually to disease. Heirlooms give gardeners a chance to do their part for the preservation of genetic diversity.

The Garden Seed Inventory, available from Seed Savers Exchange (563-382-5990; www. seedsavers.org), explains why heirlooms are important and lists nearly all the open-pollinated (nonhybrid) vegetable seeds available commercially in the United States, along with the names and addresses of the companies that supply them.

smooth-leafed variety from Thompson & Morgan (800-274-7333; thompson-morgan.com), is touted as a good fall producer.

With protection (under a floating row cover like Reemay, a light fabric made of spun polyester) planted in a cold frame or covered by a simple Hoop House, these leafy crops will produce long after frost. Such crop extenders, as they are called, are widely available from mail-order companies, including the Gardener's Supply Company (888-833-1412; gardeners.com) and Johnny's Selected Seeds (800-879-2258; johnnyseeds.com).

If space is a problem, you can plant a fall salad garden in a whiskey half-barrel or two, so long as you don't let the soil dry out.

My favorite greens for fall include sylvetta arugula, which has a sharp, peppery taste and easily self-seeds; claytonia, or miner's lettuce, which tolerates frost and will grow all winter in a cold frame; and minutina, another cold-hardy green with a crunchy texture. These three greens alone could get more than a greens-deprived miner through winter.

You might also take a look on the Internet at the long list to choose from, including all the upland cresses, which have the pepper flavor of watercress but thrive on land; and mâche, or corn salad, famous for growing year-round.

As for beets, try Bull's Blood and Chioggia, an old-time variety with red and white rings, and De Milan Rouge, a quick-growing turnip with pink shoulders and white bottoms, best eaten between 2 and 3 inches.

Baby turnips are delicious raw, in salads or mashed with potatoes. And I love them in pot roast, with onions and carrots. Hakurei, a white, flat, round turnip, ready in 38 days, is another good one for salads, or lightly cooked (800-213-0076; www.parkseed.com). And don't forget the radishes: Miyashige, a white Daikon, is ready in

TIMELY TIPS

Feeding Your Plants

Here's when and how to side-dress your vegetable plants

How should you nurture your vegetables to ensure a bountiful harvest? The best way is to give them a fertilizer boost. Most commercial fertilizers contain three major plant nutrients: nitrogen is essential for leafy growth, phosphorus promotes root and fruit development and potassium encourages vigor. On the package labels you'll find a set of numbers that refers to the percentage of each of the three ingredients in the product. The ingredients are always listed in the same order. For example, a fertilizer labeled 10-15-10 contains 10 percent nitrogen, 15 percent phosphorus, and 10 percent potassium. Here are guidelines for choosing the right fertilizer for your garden.

✔ Granular fertilizers are standard for long-term release of nutrients. Incorporate them into soil before planting. Use liquid fertilizers to give plants a quick boost during the growing season.

✔ Most vegetables benefit from another application of granular fertilizer after they have begun to flower and set fruit. This midseason boost is called side-dressing. Sprinkle the fertilizer along each row of plants and mix it into the soil. Water well.

✔ For leafy crops, such as spinach and lettuce, use a fertilizer that has a higher ratio of nitrogen. For other vegetables, use a higher ratio of phosphorus.

✔ Chemical fertilizers can't improve soil. To improve the soil, use organic materials, such as leaf mold, peat moss and manure, which provide many nutrients to the soil but perhaps not enough for optimum plant growth.

HOUSE

A VEGETABLE FOR EVERY POT

Most vegetables are easily grown from seed. For plants that require a long growing season, you can start the seeds growing indoors during winter months, then transplant the seedlings into your garden after the last frost. Your local agricultural extension service or plant nursery can tell you the best time to plant in your area. As a general rule, plant at a depth four times the seed's diameter.

VEGETABLE *When to sow**	Days to germinate	Light	Space between		Days to harvest
			plants (in.)	rows	
ARTICHOKE	7–14	Full sun	36	3 ft.	**90–100 after transplanting**
Start indoors 8 to 10 weeks before last frost, then transplant outdoors					
ARUGULA	7–14	Full sun to partial shade	8–12	18–24 in.	**35–45**
Early spring, as soon as soil can be worked					
ASPARAGUS		Full sun to partial shade	15	3 ft.	**First harvest in second** **or third year**
Best to start with year-old roots. Plant in spring; comes back every year.					
BEANS, bush*	7–14	Full sun	4	2 ft.	**45–60**
BEANS, lima*	7–12	Full sun	6–8	18 in.	**55–75**
BEANS, pole*	7–14	Full sun	36	4 ft.	**45–65**
BEANS, pole lima*	7–12	Full sun	6–8	18 in.	**88–92**
BEETS*	7–14	Full sun	3	15 in.	**49–60**
BROCCOLI	5–10	Full sun	24	30 in.	**50–65**
Start indoors 5 to 7 weeks before last frost, then transplant outdoors					
BRUSSELS SPROUTS	5–10	Full sun	18	2 ft.	**78–100**
Start indoors 5 to 7 weeks before last frost, then transplant outdoors					
CABBAGE, Chinese*	4–10	Full sun to partial shade	12	18 in.	**43–55**
CABBAGE, head	4–10	Full sun to partial shade	18	2 ft.	**50–95 after transplanting**
Start indoors 5 weeks before soil can be worked in spring, then transplant outdoors					
CARROTS	12–17	Full sun	3	14 in.	**60–75**
As soon as soil can be worked in spring					
CAULIFLOWER	5–10	Full sun	18	2 ft.	**45–75 after transplanting**
Start indoors 5 to 7 weeks before soil can be worked in spring, then transplant outdoors					
CELERY	21–28	Full sun	6	2 ft.	**98–105 after transplanting**
Start indoors 10 to 12 weeks before last frost, then transplant outdoors					
CORN, sweet*	7–10	Full sun	10	3 ft.	**66–92**
CUCUMBER	7–10	Full sun	48	6 ft.	**55–62**
After last frost and soil has warmed					
EGGPLANT	7–10	Full sun to partial shade	24	3 ft.	**50–70 after transplanting**
Start indoors 8 to 10 weeks before last frost, then transplant when soil has warmed					
KALE	5–10	Full sun	12–15	2 ft.	**55–65**
As soon as soil can be worked in spring; also in early fall for winter crop					
LEEK	7–12	Full sun	2	1 ft.	**110–145 from planting seed**
Start indoors 6 to 10 weeks before last frost, then transplant outdoors; or sow outdoors 3 weeks before last frost					
LETTUCE, butterhead **and romaine (Cos)**	7–10	Full sun to partial shade	6	14 in.	**60–75**
As soon as soil can be worked in spring; resow every 2 weeks into fall for continuous harvest					
LETTUCE, crisphead	7–10	Full sun to partial shade	10	14 in.	**56–84**
As soon as soil can be worked in spring; resow every 2 weeks into fall for continuous harvest					

VEGETABLE *When to sow**	Days to germinate	Light	Space between		Days to harvest
			plants (in.)	rows	
LETTUCE, leaf	7–10	Full sun to partial shade	6	14 in.	45–50
As soon as soil can be worked in spring; resow every 2 weeks into fall for continuous harvest					
MELONS	5–10	Full sun	36	6 ft.	68–88 from planting seed
(cantaloupe/muskmelon, honeydew)					
After last frost and the soil has warmed; or, for earlier harvest, start indoors 4-6 weeks before last frost, then transplant outdoors after soil has warmed					
OKRA	7–14	Full sun	10	2–4 ft.	50–60
After last frost and soil has warmed					
ONIONS	10–14	Full sun	2	15 in.	85–120 after transplanting
Start seeds 12 weeks before last frost, then transplant outdoors; or grow from sets instead of seed and plant sets after last frost					
PARSNIPS*	21–28	Full sun	3	18 in.	100–120
PEANUTS*	7–10	Full sun	12	30 in.	120–135
PEAS	7–14	Full sun	8	2 ft.	62–72
As soon as the soil can be worked in spring					
PEPPERS	10–20	Full sun	24	2 ft.	65–75 after transplanting
Start indoors 8 to 10 weeks before last frost, transplant outdoors after soil has warmed					
POTATOES	From tubers	Full sun	12	3 ft.	60–80
As soon as soil can be worked in spring					
PUMPKIN*	7–10	Full sun	60	12 ft.	80–120
RADISH	5–10	Full sun to partial shade	2	14 in.	22–28
As soon as soil can be worked in spring					
SPINACH	7–14	Full sun to partial shade	3	14 in.	39–45
As soon as soil can be worked in spring					
SQUASH, summer	7–14	Full sun	48	3 ft.	45–52
After last frost and soil has warmed					
SQUASH, winter	7–14	Full sun	60	6 ft.	75–110
After last frost and soil has warmed					
SWEET POTATOES	From plants	Full sun	12	3 ft.	90–120
After last frost and soil has warmed					
SWISS CHARD*	7–10	Full sun to partial shade	9	18 in.	60–63
TOMATOES	7–14	Full sun	36	3 ft.	55–85 after transplanting
Start indoors 6 to 8 weeks before last frost; transplant outdoors after soil has warmed					
TURNIPS*	7–14	Full sun	3	15 in.	35–60
WATERMELON	7–14	Full sun	96	8 ft.	65–100
After last frost and soil has warmed					

* Direct sowing in garden after last frost.

40 days (714-637-5769; www.evergreenseeds.com); White Icicle, a slender heirloom also known as Lady Fingers, is ready in 30 days (Scheepers and other suppliers).

A member of the cabbage family that deserves more attention is kohlrabi, whose leafy, bulbous stem is as crisp as an apple and more tender than a turnip. Scheepers suggests interplanting Kongo kohlrabi, which is pale green with creamy white flesh, with Kolibri, which is purple on the outside and white on the inside.

Asian greens are another great fall crop. My favorites include Osaka Purple mustard greens, whose rumpled green leaves are tinged with purple, and tatsoi, which forms rosettes of spoon-shaped leaves with a mild but still peppery flavor. A good source for Asian vegetables is www.evergreenseeds.com.

Kale also thrives in the fall. Red Russian is a more tender variety. Its gray-green, purple-veined leaves are delicious, if picked young, in salads. It keels over with the freeze, however. So I plant curly kale and one of the heirloom Italian Lacinato types, whose narrow, tough, savoyed leaves—best sautéed or simmered in a hearty soup—sweeten after a hard frost or a light snow.

The same is true of carrots, say Barbara Damrosch and Eliot Coleman, who have made an art of growing winter crops under protection at their Four Season Farm in Harborside, Maine. They say the best carrot varieties for winter are Napoli and Adelaide. (Napoli is available at 800-363-7333; www.veseys.com; Adelaide at Scheepers.) They start them in late August or early September and harvest carrots until mid-February. They plant the seeds in a cold frame and mulch the young plants with straw. "That's all the covering we need to harvest all winter," Damrosch says.

And if you plant them in late July or early August, the Burpee company (800-888-1447; www.burpee.com) promises that its hybrid Sunflower Del Sol, a 5-footer with long-stemmed flowers with bright yellow petals and deep brown centers, is ready for cutting within 50 days of sowing.

Growing Blueberries
Your own berries make the best pies

Blueberries are incredibly tough, versatile plants. The low-bush, sun-loving native *Vaccinium angustifolium* grows wild from just south of the Arctic tundra clear down to Georgia. The high-bush native *V. corymbosum*, which frequents bogs and lightly shaded woodlands, rambles all through the East and over to Michigan and Oregon. The Southern rabbit-eye blueberry, *V. ashei,* a high-bush type, is native to Florida and grows up to North Carolina and west to Mississippi. Other native species thrive in the Northwest.

Thanks to hybridizers, cultivated blueberries can be grown just about anywhere as long as you get the soil right and don't let the plants dry out. No matter where you are, the trick is acid soil—with a pH between 4.5 and 5.0—with plenty of drainage. And don't overfertilize.

Jim Plyler of Natural Landscapes Nursery (www.naturallandscapesnursery.com), in West Grove, Pa. is partial to the high-bush blueberry, *Vaccinium corymbosum.* "It's a four-season plant," he says. "Why not grow the biggest, sweetest berries?" adds Plyler, who also likes *V. corymbosum*'s many cultivars, known for their large fruit. Blueberry plants will bear more profusely if you grow two or more cultivars to increase cross-pollination. It's nice to plant them in groups of three or five, and if you have the space, 25 to 50 plants, spaced 4 to 5 feet apart, will allow for serious eating. Deer and birds like to share, so some people cover their plants with netting.

But if you don't have much space, blueberries will flourish in pots, the larger and deeper the better. Try some of the low-growing varieties, like Top Hat, Northcountry and Northsky, or shorter forms notable for their fall color, like Burgundy, Claret and Jonesboro. A mix of potting soil, peat or fir bark and enough sulfur to achieve the right acidity should get them off to a good start. Don't overwater, and don't let them dry out. With proper pruning, high-bush cultivars do well in pots too.

But if you have a yard, there isn't anything better to do with it than plant blueberries. The first step is to kill the grass. Otherwise, the tough rhizomes will just send more grass up into your blueberry beds. Gardeners not averse to herbicides could use Roundup (glyphosate), one of the most benign herbicides, which breaks down quickly in the soil. Wait a few weeks, then dig or till plenty of peat moss or composted pine bark into the soil to improve drainage and help acidify it. Adding elemental sulfur will also make an alkaline soil more acidic.

Organic gardeners can kill the grass by covering it with layers of newspaper and then mulching with acidic materials like pine needles, composted oak leaves or shredded pine bark. But that takes months, so don't plan on planting blueberries until the fall.

Plyler plants his high-bush shrubs in raised beds, at least a foot deep, which ensures good drainage. The fluffy soil also encourages the plants, which are relatively shallow-rooted, to reach deep into the soil for nutrients.

Online sources for blueberry plants include Wayside Gardens (800-213-0379; www.waysidegardens.com), which sells Darrow, a prolific high-bush type, and Sunshine Blue Dwarf, especially suited to containers; and Edible Landscaping (800-524-4156; www.ediblelandscaping.com) and Forestfarm (541-846-7269; www.forestfarm.com), both of which carry about a dozen different cultivars.

—Anne Raver

The Essential Herb Garden

Fragrant, tasty and beautiful—outdoors or in

Patches of garden that seem to sprout nothing but weeds should not be written off. "If you can't grow anything else," says gardening and food writer Sally Freeman, "herbs are the answer." Herbs have a long, noble history. They've been used to flavor food, prepare medicinal brews and beautify gardens from at least as far back as, well, the beginning of recorded history.

Growing herbs isn't difficult, as Freeman, author of *Herbs for All Seasons* and *Every Woman's Guide to Natural Home Remedies*, explains.

Essentials for an herb garden. Ideally, there are three essentials for an herb garden: good drainage, plenty of sunlight and light soil enriched with compost. Try to keep your garden away from trees; the roots rob soil of moisture and nutrients.

But many herbs will do well without all three. Rosemary doesn't mind some shade. Basil, fennel, dill, Italian parsley and chives do well in soil suitable for growing vegetables. Peppermint doesn't mind wet conditions. Thyme tolerates acid soil, while lavender requires more alkalinity than most herbs.

Indoor herb gardens. If your windows face south, you should have adequate light for even sun-loving herbs such as dill, coriander, oregano, thyme and marjoram. If your windows face in other directions, you should be able to grow rosemary, sweet woodruff or bay laurel in natural light. You may have to augment natural light with special lighting.

Be sure to place herb containers as far as possible from radiators and other heating appliances, in a room that is cool, moist and well ventilated. On very cold winter days they should be placed away from windows.

Growing from seed. Most herbs will grow easily from seed, germinating in 5 to 7 days. There are exceptions. Lavender can take up to a month to germinate. Rosemary is best propagated by cuttings, and French tarragon, which is more flavorful than the Russian variety and preferable for cooking, must be propagated by root division. Parsley can be very difficult to germinate. Italian parsley is easier to grow than regular parsley and, to my mind, tastes better.

Fertilizer of choice. Compost is best because it won't burn the tender roots. Enrich your compost pile by including some weeds, especially dande-

A Recipe for Growing Lavender

Tina Marie Wilcox, who runs the Heritage Herb Gardens at the Ozark Folk Center, in Mountain View, Ark., and Susan Belsinger, a Maryland-based herbalist and writer, share their recipe for growing lavenders and other herbs in pots or in the ground. This aggregate mix combines materials rich in calcium, potash and lime, while ensuring good drainage and the slow release of nutrients.

✔ Combine 1 gallon each of the following four ingredients in a 5-gallon bucket:

- Oyster shells or the poultry feed known as chicken scratch (both have 35 to 55 percent calcium, with trace elements, including aluminum, copper, iron, magnesium, manganese and phosphate). If soil is alkaline, omit this ingredient.

- Activated charcoal (the porous carbon, potassium and other minerals improve drainage).

- Greensand or glauconite (it has potash, silica, iron oxide, magnesium and other trace elements).

- Granite meal, or finely ground granite, another good source of potassium; available at nurseries or on the Web.

✔ Use from 1 to 4 gallons per 100 square feet, mixing in; for pots, use 10 percent aggregate to 90 percent compost-rich soil.   —Anne Raver

lion, whose long roots bring up minerals from deep in the soil. A layer of mulch conserves moisture and suppresses weeds in the summer.

Watering herbs. Water herbs as soon as the soil feels dry. Rosemary, especially, should never be allowed to dry out. You may need to water every day. Your herbs will also appreciate a daily misting.

Doing Battle with Blight
Stressed-out plants are the most vulnerable

Diseases and pests know easy marks when they see them. Fallen fruit and leaves left too long on garden beds, plants placed too close together and diseased vegetation are all danger signs. The first principle of preventive maintenance, says plant pathologist Neil Pelletier, is to keep plants adequately watered, weeded, pruned and fertilized. Plants that are well maintained and healthy will resist most attacks.

Diversifying what you plant and where you plant it is helpful. By planting a variety of flowers and vegetables, you help ensure that even if one plant species is destroyed by disease or pests, there will still be an abundance of other plants. By rotating vegetable crops to different locations within the garden bed each year, you reduce the risk of infestation.

If you're worried about a particular pest, find out from your local county extension office when that pest will be at its most destructive stage and plant before or after that time.

You can also use nature to repel nature. For example, many insect pests are repelled by strong-smelling plants such as marigolds, mint, basil, garlic, onions, chives, nasturtiums and savory. Plant these in and around your vegetables and ornamental plants and they'll keep uninvited guests away.

If all this fails to stop incursions, construct barriers around plants to prevent pests from laying eggs nearby or crawling up plant stems. The barriers may include plant collars made of plastic, metal or sticky tape. Why should you provide summer lodging for bad houseguests?

Here's a natural arsenal, the best organic disease-fighters to defend your turf.

HOMEMADE CURES FOR PESTS AND DISEASES

Organic gardening specialists recommend these do-it-yourself recipes for ridding your garden of unwanted visitors.

Cooking oil solution: Effective against eggs and immature insects.

> **1 cup cooking oil**
> **1 tbsp liquid dish soap**

Mix oil and soap. Use 2¹/₂ tsps per 1 cup of water. Pour into a spray bottle and spray surface and undersides of leaves. Apply once every 2 to 3 weeks until pest is gone.

Potassium bicarbonate solution: Effective as an anti-fungal agent, especially against black spot, powdery mildew and brown patch.

> **4 tsp potassium bicarbonate**
> **1 gallon water**

Combine ingredients. Spray on top and undersides of foliage.

Neem oil solution: Interferes with the reproductive cycle of insects.

> **4 tsp neem oil**
> **1 tsp mild dishwashing detergent**
> **1 gallon water**

Combine ingredients. Cover plants with a fine spray. Neem oil is used widely as an organic pesticide in India. It is extracted from neem tree seeds and contains azadirachtin, an effective pest control agent.

Garlic-pepper solution: Effective against a wide range of chewing insects and animals.

> **2 cloves garlic**
> **1 tsp liquid detergent**
> **2 tsps cooking oil**
> **1 tbsp cayenne pepper**
> **2 cups water**

Put all the ingredients in a blender and mix until the garlic is thoroughly pureed. Spray solution on affected plants. Reapply as needed.

Bordeaux mixture: Effective against common fungal disease. Often used on small fruits.

> **2 heaping tbsps. fresh hydrated spray lime**
> **2 level tsps copper sulfate crystals**
> **3 gallons water**

Dissolve lime in 2 gallons of water. In a separate container, dissolve the copper sulfate in 1 gallon of water. Add the copper sulfate solution to the lime solution. Strain the solution through a cheesecloth directly into a sprayer. Spray to cover foliage. When dry, it forms an insoluble copper precipitate that prevents fungal spores from entering and infecting plants. Begin applications in spring; repeat once every 7 to 14 days through early fall. Don't apply during cool and wet weather.

Bacillus thuringiensis: a natural biological control that is sprayed on plants and soil to control caterpillar pests. Available at most garden centers. Follow package directions.

Bordeaux mixture: a classic organic spray used for decades in France's wine-growing region. It is effective for preventing most foliage fungal problems on fruits, vegetables, flowers, trees and shrubs (see recipe above).

Liquid copper: a copper salt mixture used for controlling powdery mildew, bacterial blights and anthracnose problems on vegetables, fruits and ornamental plants.

Diacide: a mixture of diatomaceous earth and Pyrethrum. It will destroy aphids, beetles, leafhoppers, worms, caterpillars and ants.

Diatomaceous earth: a naturally occurring material with sharp, jagged edges. It is sprinkled around the base of plants to act as a barrier against soft-skinned pests like slugs.

Dormant oil: a petroleum-based substance which is applied in the fall to smother over-wintering insects. It is very effective against spider mites, scale and aphids. Often used on fruit trees.

Pyrethrum: a dust or spray made from a chrysanthemum species. It kills a wide variety of insects from aphids to caterpillars.

Rotenone and Sabadilla: two botanical insecticides (made from plants) that are used to kill aphids, worms, beetles, borers, thrips and other hard-to-kill insect pests.

Biodegradable soaps: composed of nonphosphate liquid soaps. Mixed with water and sprayed on plants, they control a range of insects, including aphids and mealy bugs. Sometimes referred to as insecticidal soap, examples include Safer and Reuter.

Lime sulphur: useful in preventing fungal outbreaks on fruits, nuts, berries and ornamental plants.

Wettable dusting sulphur: a finely ground sulphur; effective against many foliage diseases.

Here are some natural predators to fight pests: friendly enforcers, what they can help control and some places to get them:

Assassin bug: Aphids, caterpillars, leafhoppers and a variety of beetles.

Ladybugs: Aphids, chinch bugs, rootworms, scale, spider mites, weevils, whiteflies.

Praying Mantis: Aphids, beetles, caterpillars, flies, leafhoppers.

Robber, Syrphid and Tachinid flies: Aphids, Japanese beetles, leafhoppers, mealybugs, scale, caterpillars.

Top suppliers of predatory insects are Planet Natural (800-289-6656; www.planetnatural. com); Gempler's (800-382-8473; www.gemplers.com); and Peaceful Valley (888-784-1722; www.groworganic.com).

How to Attract Butterflies
Create a garden that entices them

Everyone loves butterflies, and attracting them to your own garden is a fairly easy undertaking. Plant what butterflies like to eat, drink and use for resting and laying eggs, and they will likely pay a visit. Here are some essentials for enticing butterflies to your garden.

Where to plant the garden. Most butterflies are sun lovers. Pick a spot that gets at least five to six hours of full sun. Sheltering the garden from the wind with a hedge or vine-covered lattice increases chances that butterflies will settle long enough to lay eggs. You can also attract butterflies to your windowsill, balcony or rooftop by planting some of the flowers recommended below in large containers or window boxes.

What to plant. Groupings of flowers that create large splashes of color are more effective than single plants. Butterflies like brightly colored blossoms with short flower tubes that let them reach the nectar with their proboscoes. Some butterfly preferences include milkweed, dogbane, Joe-Pye weed, purple coneflower, thistle, aster, goldenrod, lilac, zinnia, cosmos, strawflower, marigold, verbena and tickseed sunflower.

Some common plants that serve as hosts for caterpillars are Queen Anne's lace, which provides food for the larva of the eastern black swallowtails; milkweed, which feeds monarchs; dill and parsley for various swallowtails; and thistle and hollyhock for painted ladies.

Other lures. Butterflies take in salt and minerals by sipping from mud puddles. Create a shallow puddle in your garden to serve as a drinking hole. Place some flat stones in the garden, which butterflies can use as resting spots. Also try scattering pieces of rotting peaches or plums and putting out small, flat containers filled with sugar water.

Pest control. Never use pesticides in or near a butterfly garden. To control pests, try using predatory insects or insecticidal soaps. A healthy butterfly garden will usually attract beneficial insects, such as lady beetles, praying mantis and lacewings, which help the garden care for itself.

Choosing a Bird Feeder
Get a bird's-eye view of your avian neighbors

The easiest way to attract birds to your yard is to put up a bird feeder. There are many different ones on the market today. Most are made for seeds, but there are also specialty feeders for certain foods, such as sugar solution for hummingbirds, suet or peanuts. Which should you choose? The answer depends on the kinds of birds you want to attract.

The ideal bird feeder is sturdy enough to withstand winter weather, tight enough to keep seeds dry, large enough to avoid constant refilling and easy to assemble and clean. Plastic or metal feeders usually beat wooden ones in meeting all these requirements.

If you want to attract the greatest variety of birds to your yard, you'll want to use several different feeder types offering a variety of foods. Alternatively, you may want to attract certain bird species but dissuade others. The following information will help you make the correct feeder choice.

Tray or platform feeder: *Any flat, raised surface onto which bird food is spread.*

Trays attract most species of feeder birds, but they offer no protection against squirrels, chipmunks, rain or snow. Plus the seed can quickly become soiled by droppings because birds stand right on top of it.

Tray feeders placed near the ground are most

 TIMELY TIPS

To Lure a Hummingbird

If hummingbirds live in your area you can attract them to your garden. The frenetic little bird—the smallest species is the size of a bumblebee—is fascinating to watch. It hovers like a helicopter, moving forward, sideways or backward at speeds of up to 200 wingbeats per second.

✔ Hummers are attracted to red, tubular flowers. The National Wildlife Federation suggests planting, among others, trumpet honeysuckle, trumpet creeper, cardinal flower, scarlet penstemon, scarlet morning glory, cypress vine, scarlet paintbrush, scarlet salvia, bee balm, fire pink, scarlet petunia, red buckeye, geiger tree, scarletbrush and coral bells.

✔ You can attract hummers by hanging a red feeder outdoors in the shade, not too close to a window. Fill it with a solution of four parts water to one part sugar. Clean the feeder every 3 days using a brush and mild soap. Rinse well.

likely to attract ground-feeding birds such as juncos, doves, jays, blackbirds and sparrows. Tray feeders work well mounted on deck railings, posts or stumps, and also can be suspended. Some models have a roof to provide some protection from the weather. Be sure your tray feeders have plenty of drainage holes.

Hopper or house feeder: *Platform with walls and a roof, forming an enclosed "hopper."*

This type protects seeds fairly well against the weather but less well against squirrels. It also keeps seed cleaner. Hopper feeders are attractive to most feeder birds, including finches, jays, cardinals, buntings, grosbeaks , sparrows, chickadees and titmice. Most hoppers hold a good quantity of seed. Few are weatherproof, however, so the food may get wet and

TIMELY TIPS

This Recipe Is for the Birds

✔ Although sunflower seeds are the all-round favorite, particularly for tree-dwelling birds, some birds prefer different foods. Blackbirds relish corn, for instance, whereas doves, like many ground-feeding birds, prefer white millet or red milo. Certain species may even have different food preferences in different parts of their range.

WILD BIRD FOOD RECIPE:

Pour about 25 pounds of black-oil sunflower seed, 10 pounds of white proso millet, and 10 pounds of cracked corn into a clean trash can. Then use a broom handle to mix it up.

SOURCE: Cornell Lab of Ornithology

moldy if it sits for a few days. Hopper feeders can be mounted on a pole or suspended.

Window feeder: *Usually made of clear plastic and suction-cupped to a window.*

This type of feeder attracts finches, sparrows, chickadees and titmice, allowing close-up views of the birds as they come to feed. Be aware, though, that the birds feed while standing on a pile of seeds inside the feeder, so the food risks becoming soiled.

Tube feeder: *Hollow cylinder, usually of clear plastic, with multiple feeding ports and perches.*

Tube feeders keep seed fairly clean and dry, and if they have metal feeding ports they are somewhat squirrel-resistant. The birds attracted depend on the size of the perches under the feeding ports: short perches accomodate small birds such as sparrows, grosbeaks, chickadees, titmice and finches (such as the familiar house finch) but exclude larger birds such as grackles and jays. Styles with perches

above the feeding ports are designed for seed-eating birds that like to feed hanging upside down, such as goldfinches, while dissuading others.

Thistle feeder: *Special tube feeder designed with extra-small openings to dispense tiny thistle seeds.*

These feeders attract a variety of small songbirds, especially finches and redpolls. Thistle "socks"—fine-mesh bags to which birds cling to extract the seeds—are also available.

Suet feeder: *Wire-mesh cage or plastic-mesh bag, such as an onion bag, which holds suet or suet mixture.*

This type of feeder can be nailed or tied to a tree trunk. It can also be suspended. Suet can also be smeared into knotholes.

Suet feeders attract a variety of woodpeckers and nuthatches as well as chickadees, titmice, jays and starlings. Suet cages that are open only at the bottom are starling-proof; they force birds to hang upside down while feeding, something starlings find difficult.

SOURCE: Cornell Lab of Ornithology

Getting Rid of Geese
Solutions for getting them to fly away

The average Canada goose can produce 1 to 2 pounds of droppings every day, so experts have devised a variety of ways to make them go away: offend their palate; give them indigestion; block them; make them insomniacs; and scare them.

Thomas G. Barnes, an extension professor at the University of Kentucky in Lexington, says products that contain the chemical methyl anthranilate can be applied to grass to make it taste awful. Another chemical gives them indigestion. Arkion Life Sciences (arkionls.com) in New Castle, Del., says its product, Flight Control, is mixed with water and sprayed on a lawn. Once applied, it changes the way that ultraviolet light is reflected, making the lawn appear unappetizing to geese.

If that doesn't deter them and they land and eat anyway, they'll soon regret it. "It tastes O.K. and doesn't harm them, but it causes intestinal irritation," says a company spokesperson. After 2 or 3 days, geese get the message and forage elsewhere. One gallon costs about $220, covers an acre and lasts through about two mowings. (Different states have different rules about where the chemical can be used. Check with authorities in your area for local rules.)

Since geese tend to dine on grass around their watering hole before looking elsewhere, another way to annoy them away is to set up a barrier at the water's edge. The Goose Grid (aquaticbiolists.com) is a black nonreflective plastic line that is installed around a pond. Typically, three lines are installed: one at 6 inches, another at 12, and another at 18. While the geese can fly over the line to get into the pond, they quickly tire of running into a virtually invisible barrier as they waddle out for lunch. Goose Grid costs around $40 a pound; there are 780 feet of line to the pound.

AwayWithGeese.com offers another goose deterrent. Since geese like to sleep on water to stay safe from predators, this product makes it impossible for the geese to get a good night's sleep. It consists of a light attached to a flotation device. The light flashes every 2 seconds and keeps the geese awake. After 3 or 4 sleepless nights, they look for a better spot. One light—which uses solar power to charge a battery—covers about 3.5 acres and costs $335.

Fair Game Goose Control has another way to discourage geese (fairgamegoosecontrol.com). It patrols its clients' properties with border collies. The dogs, according to a spokesperson, scare the geese, using a "stalking predatory crouch" and "an intense predatory gaze." The cost runs a couple of hundred dollars a week and up.   —Jay Romano

How to Plant a Tree
Picking the right tree is the key decision

A well-chosen tree on the right site can transform even the plainest house into a home with visual appeal. Here are some arborists' responses to FAQs about trees.

◉ What factors go into selecting a tree for a landscape?

First of all, you look at ultimate size. You don't want to plant a tree that's going to get too big growing too close to your house. Consider then what type of tree you want—evergreen or deciduous, flowering or something that may have other attractions, like colored leaves in the autumn, or colored leaves all season. Finding trees that have practically no disease or insect problem is also important.

ⓘ INSIDE INFO

Trees You Can Adopt

○ Free Trees and Plants in Lincoln, Neb., salvages unsold saplings, shrubs and bulbs from nurseries and garden centers, selling them by Internet or phone order for about $7 for packages of two or more plants to cover shipping and processing. A white pine sapling from Free Trees, 10 to 20 inches tall, could someday grow to 70 feet or higher; shrubs may include lilacs, forsythia or rose of Sharon. The inventory changes regularly. Find listings of available plants at www.freetreesandplants.com. Order online or at 402-475-5631.

HOUSE

Q What should you look for at the nursery when buying a tree?

Most of the trees at nurseries are sold in containers. Look for a tree that has a large enough container so that a pretty decent portion of the root system will be intact. It's very difficult to make any judgments when you are viewing a plant at a nursery because even a plant with a really tacky root system can look good if it's kept watered. You can't pop it out of the container to see the roots. So you've got to go on the general reputation of the nursery.

Q How about mail-order trees?

Stay away from them. There are some firms with a pretty decent reputation, but there are many horror stories—poor quality, small plants. Specialty items can be an exception, but go to your local nursery first and ask if they can get it for you. They should know where to get the best-quality material.

Q When is the best time for planting?

That depends on where you live. In New England, for example, plant in the spring because fall comes a little fast. Ideally, spring planting is done before growth begins, though with container-grown plants, you can plant a little later. In most of the United States, fall planting is also good. When you plant in the fall, wait until after the buds have set on the tree and growth has ceased, and do not fertilize afterward, which could promote new growth on the tree that sets it up for a killing frost.

Q How should a new tree be planted?

One of the myths people believe is that they must fill a planting hole with manure and peat moss to make a nice home for the tree. If the tree is going to survive, the roots have to get out of that hole. In most areas, your home soil is worthless. Generally, you should dig a hole twice the size of the container. When you take the tree out of the container, cut down the roots to promote their growth outward. Make enough room in the hole so the roots can escape that bound mess. Otherwise, they will continue to circle. When you backfill the hole, use what you have taken out of the hole—beat it up and put it back. If you have to amend the soil, use some loam or sandy loam. Do not plant the tree too low.

Q How deep should the hole be?

If the plant comes in a container, look where the soil level is and plant it just a tad high in the ground. It's going to settle in.

Q Should the burlap be removed if the roots are covered with it?

If there are any ties, burlap, plastic wrap or anything, remove it. In the days when burlap was burlap, it might have rotted, but now, with the

---

TIMELY TIPS

Fruit Trees for Every Yard

Fruit can be grown almost anywhere, but that said, fruit is picky. Particular varieties prefer particular regions.

✔ According to Terry Freed, a pomologist and an owner of Garden of Eden Orchards, a commercial grower in Salisbury, Md., most citrus trees can be grown in Florida and in the Southwest.

✔ The Macintosh apple does well in the Northeast, while the Fuji apple grows better in the mid-Atlantic states.

✔ The Red Haven peach can be grown on the East Coast, from Georgia to New England, and in California.

✔ The tart cherry does well in Michigan. The Bartlett pear can be grown on the East Coast and in the Pacific Northwest. The sweet cherry does well in eastern Washington. Figs can be grown in mid-Atlantic and Southern states.

—Steven Kurutz

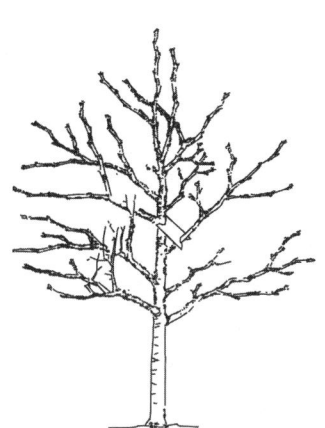

PRUNING TREES

Once a tree is established, it will need periodic pruning. The best time to prune deciduous trees is in winter, when trees are dormant—it's also easier to see the problem branches and the general shape of the tree without the leaves. If you're pruning an evergreen tree, wait until spring. Remember to prune with a light hand; over-pruning can destroy your tree's look—and your investment.

WHAT TO PRUNE

Crossing branches: When branches rub against each other, they may damage the bark and make the tree susceptible to disease and insects.

Dead, diseased or broken branches: Cut back to a healthy branch.

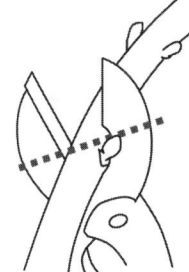

Crowded branches: Thinning weak branches improves the tree's shape and allows better air circulation and light penetration.

HOW TO PRUNE

When pruning a tree, be sure that you cut just above a branch's slightly swollen base at the point where that branch meets another branch. This base consists of plant tissues that help the cut to heal. Leaving too much of a stub creates a conduit for diseases to attack the tree.

If you want to shorten a branch that's too long, make a cut on the branch just above a bud at a 45-degree angle. Pick a bud facing the direction that you want a new branch to grow.

---

synthetic things being used, it's just a tragedy to leave them. The roots can't get out. More trees die because of a lack of planting care than any other factor, although they don't die immediately. At least unwrap the burlap to let those roots get out.

● What should you do once a tree has been planted?

Mulch. It keeps the soil relatively warm; if you are planting in the fall, it might allow more root growth before the cold weather sets in. It also keeps the lawn mower and weeding equipment away from the tree. A 2-inch layer of mulch is recommended.

● How about watering?

Absolutely the first thing you have to do is water, and make sure the plant is well seated.

Keep the tree watered in times of stress without overwatering.

● Should new trees be staked?

The average homeowner is dealing with a tree that has a trunk with a 2- to 2½-inch maximum caliper. If it's well planted, well watered-in originally and well sited, it's not going to blow over. Just tamp it down.

● Should you fertilize your tree?

Most trees do not need fertilization, but if your tree is in your lawn and you fertilize your lawn, don't worry about it. If you do fertilize, use a slow-release fertilizer. A common mistake is when people use lawn fertilizers with weedkillers. This material leaches into the ground and is taken up by the roots. Eventually it's going to get your tree.

Q   **Should a newly planted tree be pruned?**

Tree growth promotes root growth. The only pruning that should be done on a newly planted tree is if there is a broken branch.

When Plants Need a Clipping

How to give new life to a disheveled garden

Tracy DiSabato-Aust is an expert pruner with bachelor's and master's degrees in horticulture. After 2 years interning at botanical gardens in Europe, "Tracy Scissorhands" returned to tend her clients in the Midwest. She is the author of *The Well-Tended Perennial Garden.* Here are her tips.

The lure of pruning is working like a sculptor to form and shape plants. It is a nurturing, gratifying, almost religious experience, bringing me closer to my plants. Sometimes the plants send signals: leggy old growth and fresh new growth at the base of a plant are both red flags. Any outer stems at ground level or panicles at the top are candidates for removal because they tend to shadow their neighbors.

In late spring, try pre-emptive pruning, cutting a tall clump of summer or fall bloomers like bee balm into a slope so that one bloom won't hide another. Crop the plants at the front by half, the middle by a third and the back not at all. The uncut portion blooms on schedule while the pruned parts are delayed a week or two, extending the overall bloom time.

Pruning can also eliminate the need to stake plants and will yield a more compact plant. Generally, perennials that bloom in summer and fall, with multiple flowers on a single stem, can be halved

---

☑ **TIMELY TIPS**

Where to Find Organic Christmas Trees

Several online sites can help you locate a Christmas tree that has been certified as organic or chemical-free.

✔ **Agricultural extension offices** often keep lists of local growers; consult the Department of Agriculture's Web site, csrees.usda.gov/Extension.

✔ **Beyond Pesticides,** a nonprofit group, provides sources for organic and naturally grown trees, as well as up-to-date information on pesticides. 202-543-5450; beyondpesticides.org

✔ **Green Promise** provides information about sustainable products and lists sources for organic trees around the country on its Web site, greenpromise.com.

✔ **Local Harvest,** a national network of local products, lists sources for Christmas trees and wreaths, both organic and conventionally grown. 831-475-8150; localharvest.org   —Anne Raver

---

in late spring when they reach 16 to 24 inches. Candidates include nepeta, asters, garden phlox, balloon flowers, goldenrod and toad lilies. The result is a tidier plant with more (albeit slightly smaller) flowers. (There are exceptions, of course: day lilies refuse to flower the summer they are pruned.)

A clip in time will do wonders for plants like *Eupatorium maculatum,* a Southern favorite that often shoots up to 15 feet. When cut down to a foot or so in early June, it holds its flowering later to a 3-foot stem. And if you pinch back the outer stems of a shorter plant, Gateway, you will have a rounded dome and four or more smaller flowers instead of one big one on each stem. But every gardener develops a personal pruning philosophy, and every garden is different: if a 15-foot-tall Eupatorium is your garden's exclamation point, let it be.

Often, spring-blooming perennials look tattered by midsummer, flopping and parting down the middle. You can shorten and shape *Baptisia australis* after flowering to give them structure and substance. Maiden pinks get a crew cut with hedge sheers, and once ribbon grass sports brown tips, cut it to the ground.

By cutting hollyhocks back after blooming, and despite their biennial classification, they return year after year, and their life span increases because they have not been allowed to seed. This sort of pruning can save foxgloves and other biennials as well.

Haircuts are followed by watering and a top dressing of compost to hold moisture and quicken growth. Within two weeks, most perennials will look reborn. There are some renegades, though: asters and mums will refuse to rebud.

—Suzy Bales

Pruners and Spades to Die For

Wooden handles cause fewer blisters

The gardening rage has brought forth an abundance of top-quality tools, many of them fashioned after classic English tools. But at current prices, equipping yourself fully can be quite an investment, so you must choose wisely.

Materials are important. Metal tools should be made from tempered, heat-treated or forged metal. Stainless steel tools are most expensive, but they are also the strongest and should last you a lifetime.

Choose wooden-handled tools over metal ones whenever possible because they are less likely to cause blisters. Hickory and ash wood make the best handles. Handles made from Douglas fir will be weak and should be avoided. And make sure that there are no cracks or flaws of any kind in the wood before buying. Here is some advice on what to look for in garden tools.

Pitchforks: Look for pitchforks with springy stainless steel tines.

Hoses: Those made from rubber or Flexogen last longer than plastic ones.

Pruners: Hand pruners that work like scissors make the sharpest cuts.

Trowels: A narrow-bladed trowel, sometimes known as a rock-garden or transplanting trowel, will also work well for planting bulbs.

Shovels: The best shovels and spades have a Y-brace handle to add strength by increasing leverage.

Rakes: Bamboo lawn rakes are the lightest and easiest to handle. They're usually the best for raking leaves. But for raking leaves within flower beds, use a rake that is rubber-tipped. It won't damage the plants.

Rototillers: Unless you have a large garden, you should probably just rent a rototiller once a year. Look for models that you can easily handle and don't allow you to step on the area just tilled as you move it along the bed. Rear-tined (where the wheels are in front) are best for compacted or rocky soils.

Tool Sources

Where to get a great rake or the best English trowel and other tools that get the job done.

Ames Truetemper Inc.
800-393-1846; www.ames-truetemper.com

Griffin Greenhouse and Nursery Supplies
800-443-4437; www.griffins.com

Smith & Hawken
800-776-3336; www.smithandhawken.com

HOUSE

The Perfect Lawn

Hold the chemicals and follow these 12 steps

The most ubiquitous feature of the American landscape is the lawn of closely mown turf-grass, currently covering more land area than any agricultural crop. Lawns cover upward of 50,000 square miles, more than 80 percent of which is residential land. Clearly, the American lawn is an icon that has more than functional value to the average homeowner—it is an emblem of pride of ownership—and it is unlikely that any alternative treatment for the residential landscape, no matter how attractive or environmentally preferable, will be easily embraced by Americans. Here's how to cultivate a lawn you can be proud of.

Prepare the soil. Though they are seldom thought of that way, expanses of mown grass are actually very intensive gardens. Loose, fertile soil of the right pH is even more important for good lawns than it is for tasty tomatoes or lavishly blooming shrubs.

Invest in the best seed, use enough of it and plant at the right time. The first defense against weeds is a turf that is thick enough to prevent them from getting the light they need to sprout and grow. The grass won't be thick if you're stingy with either quality or quantity, and it won't fill in properly unless you give it a proper start.

Think long term. Be sure the seed mixture comprises grasses that will be long lived, such as red fescues and blue grasses. There should be only a very small amount of rye grass, if there is any at all.

Rye grasses grow quickly, helping the lawn to look good fast and preventing the growth of some weeds. But because they are up so quickly, they steal nutrients, water and light from slower-growing but more durable types. As a result, newly established turf has a lot of rye in it. This is fine for a short while. But even perennial rye dies out within a few years, and when it does, it leaves a whole lot of room for weeds to move in.

A sprinkling of rye can be used if you are the impatient type. But you'll have better long-term weed control if you go for the slow stuff and hand-weed for the first year or so while the good grasses are settling in.

Adjust the mower to the season. No matter what height you like your lawn, let it get a bit shaggy in summer. Longer grass, a good 3 inches tall, will cut down on weeds, providing more shade and keeping the grassroots cool and healthy while making it harder for weed seeds to sprout and find the light.

Water during the day. After a lawn is established, mow and water it once or twice a week. Watering at night during the summer can invite fungal problems caused by standing water and high humidity. It's better to water during the day.It takes heat stress off the grass and keeps the roots from coming up to the top.

Don't water if there's a drought. This may seem counterintuitive, but if you do not have an endless supply of water during a drought and cannot water the lawn thoroughly, you are much better off letting the lawn go dormant than trying to give it just enough to stay alive. Grasses naturally lie low and turn brown during droughts. They aren't dead—they're just sleeping. A small amount of water won't be enough to keep the grasses green, but it will keep the lawn green because the watered weeds will thrive.

Don't throw away the leaves; mulch them. Don't just rake the leaves off your lawn in fall; mow them with a mulching mower. According to studies done at Michigan State University, the nutritive value of mulching and leaving grass clippings

How to Build a Labyrinth

The ancient garden paths can be relaxing and fun

The design of a labyrinth echos spirals in nature, from a snail's shell to the inner ear to the winding of a bean vine as it springs from the earth. Evidence of labyrinths has been found in Minoan Crete as well as Europe, India and the American Southwest, according to Hermann Kern's *Through the Labyrinth: Designs and Meanings Over 5,000 Years,* translated by Abigail Clay and edited by Robert Ferré, a labyrinth builder and teacher in St. Louis, and Jeff Saward, a British authority on labyrinths. Kern, a German historian who died in 1985, was probably the world's foremost scholar on labyrinths.

Unlike a maze, which can have more than one entrance and many paths, a labyrinth is unicursal: one path to the center and one path out.

The two most familiar labyrinth types are the classical, or Cretan, form, which has seven concentric paths around the center, and the medieval form, which has 11 circuits around the center, like the one at the Chartres cathedral in France.

The simpler Cretan form recalls the Greek legend of the Minotaur; when Theseus, the son of Aegeus, the king of Athens, killed the Minotaur, he found his way out by following a ball of thread that he had unwound along the twisting path.

Labyrinths are easy to draw, find and reproduce, as shown on the Labyrinth Society's Web site labyrinthsociety.org, a good source of information, both historical and practical. Click the link to the labyrinth locator on the Web site.

—Anne Raver

saves 20 to 25 percent of the fertilizer one would ordinarily use.

If you have to fertilize, try corn gluten. In early spring, before the lawn greens up, broadcast a generous sprinkling each of compost and corn gluten (a natural fertilizer that suppresses the sprouting of annual weeds). Repeat the gluten every 6 weeks or so, stopping at the first sign of frost. Keep your mower sharp and don't use it too much.

Aerate your lawn. Lawns should be aerated yearly, and twice yearly is a good idea where the lawn is green year-round. You can do it at any time. There is no rule about the season and no need to do it all at once. Handheld spiking tools for aeration work fine on small areas. If the lawn is large, a power-driven aerator will make the task easier.

Get rid of dead grass at the end of summer. In late August or early September the first year, and every 4 or 5 years after that, rent a thatching machine to remove the lower layer of thatch—the dead, dying and decaying organic matter, mostly old turf stems, that accumulates just above the soil. Then put down some more seed. That should get you ready for winter and a healthy lawn for next spring.

Keep your lawn moist after seeding. If you have to reseed a part of the lawn or overseed it, it's very important to keep the seed wet until germination. This takes about 2 weeks. When the grass is about 3 inches tall, cut it to 2 inches. After that, start mowing it to about 3 inches.

Mow with sharp blades and avoid mowing when the grass is wet with dew or rain. Cutting the living tissue of a grass blade reduces the area of leaf surface, reducing photosynthesis and the ability to take up water. These stresses make the plant weaker and less able to fight off diseases, and slow down root growth. When the cut is ragged or torn, the increased surface area open to the air means a 10 to 15 percent additional water loss through evaporation, and a longer time to heal. Diseases find it easier to enter a host with weakened defenses. It is also important to avoid mowing when the grass is wet with dew or rain. Not only are fungal populations higher when it is damp or humid, but the water on the grass impedes the lawn mower blade, leading to a poorer quality cut.

The Best Grass Seed for a Lawn

Consider microclimate and foot traffic

To pick the best grass seed for your lawn, take into account the growing region (defined by humidity level and mean temperature), microclimate (how much sun the lawn gets throughout the day), maintenance time and expected foot traffic.

BAHIAGRASS *Paspalum*　　GULF COAST
This wide, coarse-bladed grass is not particularly attractive, but its ruggedness and deep root system make it good for erosion control.

MICROCLIMATE	FOOT TRAFFIC	MAINTENANCE
Sunny to partly shady	High	Low

BENTGRASS *Agrostis*　　NORTHERN
Often used on putting greens, this high-maintenance grass should be used only on low-traffic areas or where soft-soled shoes are worn.

MICROCLIMATE	FOOT TRAFFIC	MAINTENANCE
Sunny to partly shady	Low	High

BERMUDAGRASS *Cynodon*　　SOUTHERN
Fast-growing, this wide-bladed grass requires frequent edge-trimming, but will tolerate high traffic. Popular in the South for its vigor and density.

MICROCLIMATE	FOOT TRAFFIC	MAINTENANCE
Sunny	High	Medium to high

BUFFALOGRASS *Buchloe*　　WEST CENTRAL
Like wheatgrass, a native turf that is thick and rugged; requires low maintenance and will not grow over 4 or 5 inches if left unmowed. It is very tolerant of drought.

MICROCLIMATE	FOOT TRAFFIC	MAINTENANCE
Sunny	Medium	Low

CARPETGRASS *Axonopus*　　SOUTHERN
Coarse but sensitive to wear, this grass is used primarily on hard-to-mow places because of its low maintenance and slow growth rate.

MICROCLIMATE	FOOT TRAFFIC	MAINTENANCE
Sunny	Low	Low

CENTIPEDEGRASS *Eremochloa*　　SOUTHERN
A good "middle-of-the-road" grass—easy to care for, will tolerate some shade and is vigorous and attractive. It requires two seasons to grow.

MICROCLIMATE	FOOT TRAFFIC	MAINTENANCE
Sunny to partly shady	Low	Low

KENTUCKY BLUEGRASS *Poa*　　NORTHERN
The most popular of cool-season grasses for its beauty, ruggedness and flexibility. It will excel with minimum maintenance almost anywhere.

MICROCLIMATE	FOOT TRAFFIC	MAINTENANCE
Sunny to partly shady	Medium to heavy	Low to high

PERENNIAL RYEGRASS *Festuca*　　NORTHERN
This quick-growing and reasonably hardy grass is used in seed mixes to provide cover and erosion control while the other seeds take root.

MICROCLIMATE	FOOT TRAFFIC	MAINTENANCE
Sunny to partly shady	Medium	Medium to high

ST. AUGUSTINE   SOUTH ATLANTIC
GRASS *Stenotaphrum*

Dense and spongy, this low-growing, coarse-textured grass is prized for its high shade tolerance. Not available in seed form but usually sold as fairly inexpensive sod.

MICROCLIMATE	FOOT TRAFFIC	MAINTENANCE
Sunny to shady	Medium	Medium to high

TALL FESCUES *Festuca*   NORTHERN

Though it is a cool-season grass, this tough, wide-bladed turf has good heat tolerance and grows well in areas with a steep range of weather. Often used on playgrounds because of its ruggedness.

MICROCLIMATE	FOOT TRAFFIC	MAINTENANCE
Sunny to partly shady	Heavy	Medium

WHEATGRASS *Agropyron*   HIGH PLAINS

Thick and tough, this grass is native to the high plains of the Northwest. It withstands weather extremes and heavy traffic and needs mowing about once a month.

MICROCLIMATE	FOOT TRAFFIC	MAINTENANCE
Sunny	High	Low

ZOYSIA *Zoysia*   SOUTHERN

Takes root very quickly and crowds out other grasses and weeds. It turns a not entirely unattractive straw yellow in cold weather and requires little maintenance in general. Heat- and drought-tolerant.

MICROCLIMATE	FOOT TRAFFIC	MAINTENANCE
Sunny to partly shady	High	Low to medium

SOURCE: Dr. H. A. Turgeon, Pennsylvania State University

Shedding Light on Houseplants

Fluorescent bulbs are best; they don't throw off a lot of heat

Unless you have a sunroom or greenhouse, the biggest dilemma of having plants indoors is providing them with enough light. Even if you have windows, they may be less than ideal if they're facing in a direction that gets little sun or if they're shaded by a tree or porch overhang. Plants suffering from light deprivation are often lanky, with pale or yellowed leaves. Luckily, you can lend a helping hand with artificial lighting.

The best type of artificial light is fluorescent. Incandescent light doesn't provide the right kind of light for optimal growth, and it produces heat, which can burn plants. Fluorescent lights come in several varieties: the standard ones, which you can find at any hardware store or home improvement center, are fine for growing small plants such as African violets, but for larger plants, go for higher-output fluorescents, which emit much more light and can be found at most well-equipped garden centers or through mail-order gardening supply catalogs. Bear in mind, too:

- When growing plants under artificial light, choose those that prefer low to medium sunlight.

- Keep your plants very close to the light source— no more than 6 to 12 inches away. The intensity of light diminishes drastically the farther away you move from it. To increase intensity, add more fluorescent tubes, grouped together.

- Rearrange your plants regularly around their light source to ensure that they all receive equal exposure. The greatest amount of light is emitted from the center of a fluorescent tube.

- Leave the lights on 14 to 16 hours a day. A couple of hours daily won't suffice. But don't leave them on all the time; plants need darkness to rest.

LOCATION, LOCATION, LOCATION

How to match up a plant's light, temperature and humidity needs to the best window in your house.

NORTH WINDOWS: Receive no direct sun—but, if unobstructed, they do receive good, bright light. Plants grown in a shaded north window during the winter months would appreciate extra light. When choosing plants for a dark window, remember that plants with variegated leaves require more light than ones with strictly green leaves. Consult the key below.

PLANT	WATER	TEMPERATURE	HUMIDITY	FERTILIZER
CAST-IRON PLANT *Aspidistra eliator*	WET / DRY	INTERMEDIATE	MEDIUM	INTERMEDIATE
FERN, BIRD'S NEST *Asplenium nidus*	MOIST	INTERMEDIATE	HIGH	LOW
FIG *Ficus pumila*	MOIST	INTERMEDIATE	HIGH	LOW
PHILODENDRON, VELVET LEAF *Philodendron hederaceum* var. *hederaceum*	WET	INTERMEDIATE	HIGH	LOW
PRAYER PLANT *Maranta leuconeura*	MOIST	WARM	MEDIUM	INTERMEDIATE
SPATHE FLOWER *Spathiphyllum*	MOIST	WARM	MEDIUM	INTERMEDIATE
WANDERING JEW *Zebrina pendula*	MOIST	INT./ WARM	MEDIUM	INTERMEDIATE

EAST AND WEST WINDOWS: Both are excellent for growing houseplants. East windows tend to be cooler than west. If you can't grow the following plants in east or west windows, they should do fine in a south window—but add some shading during the day in the summer, especially for ferns.

PLANT	WATER	TEMPERATURE	HUMIDITY	FERTILIZER
BROMELIAD *Bromeliacea*	WET	INTERMEDIATE	MEDIUM	LOW
CAPE PRIMROSE *Streptocarpus*	MOIST	INTERMEDIATE	HIGH	HIGH
FERN, BOSTON *Nephrolepsis exaltata*	MOIST	INTERMEDIATE	HIGH	LOW
IVY, GRAPE *Cissus rhombifolia*	MOIST	INTERMEDIATE	MEDIUM	INTERMEDIATE
LILY, AMAZON *Eucharis grandiflora*	MOIST	INT./ WARM	MEDIUM	HIGH
LILY, BUSH *Clivia miniata*	MOIST	INTERMEDIATE	MEDIUM	INTERMEDIATE
LADY PALM *Rhapsis excelsa`*	WET / MOIST	INTERMEDIATE	HIGH	INTERMEDIATE
NORFOLK ISLAND PINE *Araucaria heterophylla*	MOIST	COOL	MEDIUM	LOW
PAINTED BEGONIA *Begonia rex*	MOIST	INTERMEDIATE	HIGH	HIGH
ROSARY VINE *Ceropegia woodii*	MOIST/DRY	INTERMEDIATE	LOW	INTERMEDIATE
RUBBER PLANT *Ficus elastica*	MOIST	WARM	MEDIUM	LOW
SHAMROCK PLANT *Oxalis*	MOIST	INTERMEDIATE	MEDIUM	LOW
FIG, WEEPING *Ficus benjamina*	MOIST	WARM	MEDIUM	LOW
VIOLET, AFRICAN *Saintpaulia*	MOIST	INT./ WARM	MEDIUM	HIGH

SOUTH WINDOWS: South windows receive the most light. During the summer months they even can be too bright for many kinds of houseplants—you may need to shade them a bit. All of these plants, while preferring south windows, can also be grown in east or west exposures.

PLANT	WATER	TEMPERATURE	HUMIDITY	FERTILIZER
ALOE *Aloe vera*	WET / DRY	INTERMEDIATE	LOW	LOW
BEGONIA, TRAILING *Cissus discolor*	MOIST	INTERMEDIATE	MEDIUM	INTERMEDIATE
CACTUS *Cactaceae*	WET / DRY	INT-WARM	LOW	LOW
GERANIUM *Pelargonium*	MOIST	INTERMEDIATE	MEDIUM	LOW
GERANIUM, STRAWBERRY *Saxifraga stolonifera*	WET	INTERMEDIATE	MEDIUM	LOW
IVY *Hedera helix*	MOIST	INTERMEDIATE	MEDIUM	INTERMEDIATE
IVY, GERMAN OR PARLOR *Senecio mikanioides*	WET / DRY	INTERMEDIATE	LOW	INTERMEDIATE
JADE PLANT *Crassula argentea*	WET	INTERMEDIATE	LOW	LOW
PASSION FLOWER *Passiflora*	MOIST	INTERMEDIATE	MEDIUM	INTERMEDIATE
POMEGRANATE, DWARF *Punica granatum 'Nana'*	MOIST	INTERMEDIATE	MEDIUM	INTERMEDIATE
SHEFFLERA, HAWAIIAN *Erassaia arboricola*	WET	INTERMEDIATE	LOW	INTERMEDIATE

KEY

WATER

WET/DRY	Water thoroughly, let dry fully before rewatering.
WET	Water thoroughly but don't let it totally dry out before rewatering.
MOIST	Keep soil evenly moist, but don't let it stand in water. Top inch of soil should always feel moist.

TEMPERATURE

COOL	45° nights, 55° to 60° days.
INTERMEDIATE	50° to 55° nights, 65° to 70° days.
WARM	60° nights, 75° to 80° days.

HUMIDITY

LOW	20 to 40 percent.
MEDIUM	40 to 50 percent.
HIGH	50 to 80 percent.

FERTILIZER

HEAVY	Use balanced fertilizer recommended for frequent feeding, feed each watering.
INTERMEDIATE	Feed every other week with a balanced fertilizer.
LOW	Feed about once per month with a balanced fertilizer.

Gardening from A to Z
Two unbeatable gardening guides

American Horticultural Society
A to Z Encyclopedia of Garden Plants
Christopher Brickell, H. Mark Cathey, ed., 2004
Comprehensive guide to 15,000 plants grown in American gardens.

The All New Illustrated Guide to Gardening
Trevor Cole, Fern Marshall Bradley
Reader's Digest, 2009
You could develop terrific skills with this book alone. More than 2,500 stunning photos, a directory of 700-plus plants and all the eco-friendly gardening tips you need.

10 Terrific Public Gardens

Gardeners looking for inspiration may well find it here

The American landscape is scattered with thousands of spectacular public gardens. Here are ten considered to be among the best in the country.

ATLANTA BOTANICAL GARDEN, *Atlanta, Ga.* Beautiful display of rare and endangered plants; also a gorgeous conservatory.
404-876-5859; www.atlantabotanicalgarden.org

BROOKLYN BOTANIC GARDEN, *Brooklyn, N.Y.* Famous for its systematic collection of plants in a beautifully designed garden setting.
718-622-7200; www.bbg.org

CHICAGO BOTANIC GARDEN, *Glencoe, Ill.* Its walled perennial garden is one of the best in the country. Outstanding educational programs.
847-835-5440; www.chicagobotanic.org

HOLDEN ARBORETUM, *Kirtland, Ohio.* Famous for its woody (trees and shrubs) plant collection.
440-946-4400; www.holdenarb.org

HUNTINGTON BOTANICAL GARDENS, *San Marino, Calif.* World-class bonsai, succulent and rose gardens.
626-405-2100; www.huntington.org

LONGWOOD GARDENS, *Kennett Square, Pa.* Perhaps the most outstanding display garden in the world. Included are 20 theme gardens.
610-388-1000; www.longwoodgardens.org

MISSOURI BOTANICAL GARDEN, *St. Louis, Mo.* A geodesic dome houses a full-fledged tropical rain forest.
314-577-5100; www.mobot.org

NEW YORK BOTANICAL GARDEN, *Bronx, N.Y.* Outstanding herb and rose gardens and a wonderful conservatory.
718-817-8700; www.nybg.org

 TIMELY TIPS

Beautiful Gardens That Gather Moss

It's not a cinch to grow, but worth the effort

Growing moss can be tricky, unless you are lucky enough to have the right conditions: a shady, moist spot under trees, for example, or a wet spot in the lawn. Moss spreads by spores, not seeds, and thrives on compacted acidic soil or moist bricks and stone.

✔ You can encourage moss that is already growing in your garden by digging up surrounding grass, weeds and woody seedlings, then planting more moss, from other places.

✔ Transplanting chunks of moss and pressing them into bare spots can fail, because birds turn them over, looking for grubs. A better strategy is to make a slurry of moss particles mixed with a solution of seaweed fertilizer, and spread it over the bare spots.

✔ Moss Acres (866-438-6677; www.mossacres. com), in Honesdale, Pa., ships moss, ferns, soil amendments, misting devices and netting to protect newly planted moss from birds. It also offers a pamphlet, *Gardening With Moss: The Lawn of the Future* by David E. Benner.

—Anne Raver

SAN FRANCISCO BOTANICAL GARDEN AT STRYBING ARBORETUM , *San Francisco, Calif.* A collection of mediterranean, mild temperate and tropical cloud-forest plants displayed in designed gardens and habitats.
415-564-3239; www.sfbotanicalgarden.org

UNITED STATES NATIONAL ARBORETUM, *Washington, D.C.* Spectacular display of azaleas and a nearly 3-acre herb garden.
202-245-2726; www.usna.usda.gov

Pets

Picking a Canine Companion

A dog's breed is no guarantee of good behavior

Every dog has its own personality. But some breeds are better suited to being jostled by children than others, while the circumstances of other pet lovers may require quite different choices. Here, veterinarian Sheldon L. Gerstenfeld suggests which dogs make good pets for families with children, owners with active lifestyles and people who are older and looking for easy pet companionship. Gerstenfeld is the author of numerous books about pet care, including the *ASPCA Complete Guide to Dogs.*

DOGS FOR CHILDREN

Collie. They're gentle and predictable and won't bite around your kids. They're easy to train and really want to please. Adult collies weigh about 50 pounds, and their long hair requires grooming. Lassie was a rough-coated collie. The smooth-coated collie is somewhat less popular.

Golden Retriever. Easygoing, active and alert, golden retrievers have the best temperaments. They love to interact with kids and to play ball. The adult female weighs 50 to 60 pounds; the adult male 70 to 90 pounds. They need to be groomed and fed, and that teaches kids about being responsible.

Labrador Retriever. Black, yellow and chocolate Labs are known for being even-tempered and friendly. They are always ready to play, and kids can just lie on them. Adult dogs weigh 60 to 70 pounds. They need grooming, so they also teach kids to be responsible. Avoid the Chesapeake Bay retriever, which has a curlier coat. It can be a little nasty and unpredictable and will bite more readily than the others. Labrador retrievers are the most popular American Kennel Club (A.K.C.) breed.

Newfoundland. The Newfoundland is a sweet-tempered and devoted companion for children. They love to be included in children's activities and are strong enough to handle rough and tumble play since they weigh 100-150 pounds and were developed on the island of Newfoundland in the 18th century to haul fishing nets and to pull carts. It is important to obtain a Newfoundland from a reputable breeder and from a stock whose hips have been certified by the Orthopedic Foundation for Animals or PennHip.

 INSIDE INFO

Dog Years vs. People Years

A popular myth says that household pets—specifically dogs and cats—age 7 years for each human year. Technically, there is no direct correspondence between how dogs (or cats) and humans age, but here's a rough guideline.

○ A 1-year-old dog or cat has generally reached its full growth, although, like a 14- to -15-year-old human, it still might be lanky and need to fill out.

○ After the second year, a dog or cat has gained the equivalent of another 7-8 years in terms of physical and mental maturity.

○ After that, each year is equivalent to only about 4 human years, but the rate of aging varies tremendously from breed to breed.

TIMELY TIPS

Adopting from an Animal Shelter

You can take home a homeless pet at a fraction of the cost

✔ About four million dogs enter shelters nationwide each year. Some two million of them end up being euthanized, about 5,000 dogs each day, one every 16 seconds. According to nationwide surveys, as many as 25 percent of the dogs who end up in shelters are purebreds: Boston terriers, border collies, Pomeranians, standard poodles and so on, the sorts of dogs that people pay thousands of dollars to obtain.

✔ The leading cause of dog abandonment is behavioral problems, such as biting, chewing furniture and the like. But many shelters are putting problem dogs through behavior training to address individual issues. As a result, the number of dogs returned to the shelter for behavior problems appears to be on the decline.

✔ For more information on how to adopt either a mongrel or a purebred shelter dog or cat, go to www.aspca.org and click on "Adopt." For purebreds specifically, go to www.akc.org/breeds/rescue.cfm. Be wary of any shelter that asks for a large fee for adoption; it should be a mere fraction of what one would pay for a new purebred puppy.   —Charles Siebert

DOGS FOR THE ACTIVE PERSON

Beagle. A small, very friendly dog that loves everyone and is always ready for a busy day's activities. Like many dogs for active people, beagles need training at an early age so that behavioral problems such as barking, howling or digging holes in the back yard don't occur. Beagles adapt to city living as well as suburbs or the country.

Boxer. Animated, with outgoing personalities, boxers respond readily to playfulness. They are the sixth most popular A.K.C. breed. Prospective owners looking for a dignified dog, however, should be wary of the boxer: They tend to drool and snore.

Bull Terrier. Terriers start out their morning as if they have had eight cups of coffee, so they are good for an active person. One recommendation is the bull terrier, which was bred for pit fighting. They are always ready to frolic and so need firm training, but they are also known for their sweet personalities. The adult bull terrier weighs in at about 50 pounds.

Greyhound. They are a little aloof, but also very gentle. Most are adopted from the racetrack. Greyhounds have a regal personality and don't slobber with affection like a retriever. They're also very athletic, so they're good for active people. Adult greyhounds weigh 70 to 80 pounds. One caution: they are high-strung and easily upset by sudden movements at times.

DOGS FOR OLDER PEOPLE

Chihuahua. If they are from a good breeder, they will have a good personality. Because chihuahuas have short hair, they don't need a lot of grooming and so are a good choice for an older person living alone. An adult Chihuahua weighs about 3 pounds and is the smallest of all the breeds. They can be yappy and clannish at times.

Miniature Poodle. These poodles are intelligent, and they're good for older people because they're small and don't shed a lot. They love attention. The poodle is a popular A.K.C. breed (ninth on the 2008 list), so owners have to make sure the dog is not inbred. All poodles are fast learners; generally the smaller they are the faster they learn. The adult miniature poodle weighs in at about 15 pounds.

Pug. A small dog, weighing about 15 pounds, the pug is happy to see everyone, especially the grandchildren. This delightful dog doesn't need a lot of exercise. A leisurely walk around the block three or four times a day is fine for the pug and good for an older person, too.

Yorkshire Terrier. These dogs are small and easy to care for, and can be picked up. They weigh about 7 pounds and have silky, long, draping hair. Their coats require grooming, however, which may not be good for an elderly person who doesn't have the energy or who has arthritis. The Yorkshire terrier is the second most popular A.K.C. breed.

For more information about various breeds, see the American Kennel Club's website at akc. org.

Buying a Pedigree Pup Online

Check both the dog and the breeder

Hundreds of thousands of people buy puppies online each year. But not all Internet purchases have a happy ending. There have been numerous cases of charges filed by consumers who received sick puppies or who paid more than $1,000 for a dog that was never delivered. The American Kennel Club—the largest registry of purebred dogs—says that more people are reporting health problems in dogs bought online.

To help buyers find the right breed and to choose responsible sellers, the A.K.C. has introduced a Web-based service called "Breeder Classifieds," at www.akc.org. Only breeders in good standing can advertise. The site includes a list of questions to ask of breeders. Some people mistakenly think that A.K.C. papers alone guarantee that a puppy is healthy and of good quality. They prove only that a puppy is the offspring of a known sire and dam.

Prices for pedigree puppies vary by region, depending on the type of dog, its health-screening tests and whether the parents are champions. In general, buyers can usually expect to pay $500 to $2,500 for a pet-quality pedigree puppy—one that the breeder believes won't be able to compete successfully in dog shows. Pedigree show dogs fetch a much higher price. Fans of purebreds say you can tell you are working with good breeders if you can confirm the following:

- They are not in the business solely to make money. For many, it is a hobby, with the goal of improving the breed.

- They often specialize in one breed.

- They raise puppies in a loving home environment, not in a kennel, since socialization to humans occurs between 1 and 18 weeks.

- They sell only healthy animals and guarantee them for reasonable periods. They have tested a puppy's parents for hereditary diseases, and the puppy's vaccinations should be up to date.

✓ **TIMELY TIPS**

Let the (Dog) Buyer Beware

If you bought a puppy online and can't pick it up yourself, here are some expert recommendations.

✔ **GET** the seller's phone number and mailing address. Call the number to verify it.

✔ **CHECK** with people who have bought puppies from the seller, and check the Better Business Bureau in the seller's area and the Internet to see if any complaints have been lodged.

✔ **HOLD** funds in escrow until the puppy arrives and is checked out by a veterinarian. There are escrow sites available online.

ℹ INSIDE INFO

Congenital Defects in Dogs

Before selecting a dog, first check out the list of the most common potential problems in the type of dog you are choosing. Here are a few of the breed-specific diseases.

○ **COCKER SPANIEL:** Cataracts, kidney disease, hemophilia, spinal deformities, behavior abnormalities

○ **COLLIE:** Deafness, epilepsy, hemophilia, hernia

○ **GERMAN SHEPHERD:** Cataracts, epilepsy, kidney disease, bladder stones, hemophilia, cleft lips and palate, behavior abnormalities

○ **GOLDEN RETRIEVER:** Hip and elbow dysplasia, cataracts, bone degeneration, allergies, cardiomyopathy, blindness

○ **LABRADOR RETRIEVER:** Cataracts, bladder stones, hemophilia

○ **TOY POODLE:** Epilepsy, nervous system, defects, collapsed trachea, diabetes, spinal deformities, limbs too short, skin allergies, behavior abnormalities

They are willing to put you in contact with the veterinarian who has cared for the puppy.

- Their contracts stipulate that if the buyer does not meet specified conditions of care, or becomes unable to keep the puppy, they will take it back. (Most contracts for pet-quality dogs also have a clause that requires spaying or neutering the dog.)

- They are willing to let you meet at least one of the puppy's parents; the appearance and temperament of the parent can provide an idea of how the pup may turn out.

- They have a good reputation at the local breed club. —Maryann Mott

Choosing a Cat
From pharaohs' favorites to loving tabbies

Celebrated for their highly independent nature, cats have been everything from lap companion to religious idol in the pages of human history. Today, an estimated 88.3 million cats reside in American homes, making them even more popular than dogs as household pets. Here's a list of the best, brightest, most elegant and cuddly cats from Sheldon L. Gerstenfeld, veterinarian and author of *The Cat Care Book.*

Abyssinian. One of the oldest known breeds, their slender, elegant, muscular bodies were often featured in paintings and sculptures in ancient Egyptian art. Abyssinians have arched necks, large ears, almond-shaped eyes, and long, tapered tails. The Abyssinian's soft and silky medium-length coat is one of its most unusual features. Each hair has two or three distinct bands of black or dark brown, giving the breed a subtle overall coat color and lustrous sheen. Abyssinians also can have a rich copper-red coat. They are particularly loyal and make good companions.

American Curl. The name comes from the breed's unique curled ears, which curl away from the head to make it look as if this cat is always alert. The American curl is moderately large, with walnut-shaped eyes. Its ears are straight at birth and curl within 2 to 10 days. A relatively rare breed, the American curl usually weighs 5 to 10 pounds. Curls are short-haired, and their coats come in all colors possible. Even-tempered and intelligent with a playful disposition, American curls adore their owners and display affection in a quiet way. They adapt to almost any home, live well with other animals and are very healthy.

American Shorthair. The descendants of house cats and farm cats, American shorthairs are easy to care for and resistant to disease. They have big bones and are docile and even-tempered. The breed is strongly built, with an agile, medium to large body. They have a short, thick coat that ranges in colors from black to white to red to tabby.

American Wirehair. Uniquely American, the breed began as a spontaneous mutation in a litter on a farm in New York in 1966. Its dense, coarse coat is hard to touch and sets these cats apart from any other breed. Some also have curly whiskers. The breed is active and agile and has a keen interest in its surroundings. Although it is quiet and reserved, owners find the breed easy to care for.

Balinese. Related to the Siamese, it has a long silky coat, but unlike most long-haired cats, its coat doesn't mat. Endowed with a long, muscular body, the Balinese can come in several colors, including seal point, blue point and chocolate point. Intelligent, curious and alert, the Balinese is as affectionate and demonstrative as the Siamese, but it isn't as talkative and has a softer voice.

British Shorthair. Perhaps the oldest natural English breed, the British shorthair is enjoying new popularity. These cats tend to be reserved, devoted and good companions. Because of their dense coats, they also are easy to groom.

Burmese. Known as the clown of the cat kingdom, the Burmese thrives on attention and is very gregarious. It has a compact body and a glossy coat. Burmese live well with children and dogs. They are smart, loyal and devoted. Despite their hefty appetites, they seldom are fat. They are very expensive, though.

Cornish Rex. The Rex has the body of a greyhound, huge ears set high on its head and large eyes. These cats fastidiously groom themselves—and their human companions. If that's not to your liking,

choose another cat, since the problem may be impossible to eliminate. The Cornish Rex are excellent choices for people who love cats but dislike cat hair, because they have an undercoat but no outer coat.

Exotic Shorthair. Sometimes called the "Teddy Bear" cat, exotic shorthairs have a medium-to-long coat that does not mat. They will jump in your lap to take a nap, but generally prefer cooler places to sleep. They are very quiet but tireless—they will retrieve a toy until you get tired of throwing it.

Japanese Bobtail. The Japanese consider bobtails a symbol of good luck. They are medium-size and muscular with a short tail that resembles a rabbit's. They have high cheekbones, a long nose and large ears. Active, intelligent and talkative, their soft voices have a whole scale of tones. They almost always speak when spoken to. Japanese bobtails are good travelers and good with dogs and children.

Maine Coon Cat. The Maine coon cat was chosen as best cat at the first cat show ever held in America. It is a native American long-hair. Originally a working cat, it is a very good mouser. The Maine coon cat is solid and rugged. It has a smooth, shaggy coat and is known for its loving nature and great intelligence. The breed is especially good with children and dogs.

 TIMELY TIPS

Finding a Boarding Kennel for Fluffy or Fido

Need to go out of town? You wouldn't stay in a hotel that has fleas, nor should you expect your pet to. One way to check out a prospective kennel is to find out if it is accredited by the Pet Care Services Association (877-570-7788; www.petcareservices.org), which inspects kennels before it offers accreditation.

How to Give a Dog a Bath

Being washed isn't any easier for the dog

When it comes to baths, almost all dogs second the notion attributed to Elizabeth I: once a month would be just fine, whether she needs it or not. And most dog owners would subscribe to that view, too, given the fuss their charges make, if it weren't for their habit of lolling in mud puddles and rolling ecstatically over dead fish on the beach.

Slowly, basic dog shampoo is being replaced by a bewildering array of "pet spa" products, with names like Earthbath Mediterranean Magic, and Salon Details Tropical Twist. Are all these exotic-sounding products really any better than a basic dog shampoo?

"That depends," says Dr. Heather Peikes, a veterinary dermatologist. A dog with dry skin can benefit from shampoos made with extra fatty acids or oatmeal (which has anti-itch properties and helps moisturize). But pet owners should pay attention to ingredient lists.

"There are products out there that claim to prevent itching, and if you read the label, you'll find they contain steroids," Peikes says. "That's not something we recommend."

In general, because dogs' skin has a pH level different from human skin, it's wise to use a shampoo especially formulated for them. Some human shampoos may dry out their coats. However, says Peikes, "To be honest, a lot of dogs do just fine with Johnson's Baby Shampoo."

—Peter Jaret

Oriental Shorthair. The extremely long Oriental shorthair is medium-size and can be a choosy eater at times. They are easy to care for and make a practical pet. The Cat Fanciers' Association says, "Their innate sensibility verges on psychic. Once communication is established, you'll never need an alarm clock or wonder where the cat is when you arrive home from work."

Persian. The most popular breed, Persians have long, flowing coats that require an indoor, protected environment and regular combing and bathing. They have a massive head and a very round face, as well as short, thick necks and legs and broad, short bodies. Persians have gentle personalities that fare best in serene households.

Russian Blue. Fine-boned with short hair and a regal appearance, Russian blues are clean, quiet cats that don't shed a lot. They are very intelligent and are well attuned to the moods of their owners. They generally do well in a house full of kids and dogs.

Siamese. Like dogs, Siamese cats will fetch and do tricks, talk a lot and follow their owners around the house. They have blue eyes and a dark, raccoon-like "mask" around them. They have long, svelte bodies and short, finely textured coats. Siamese cats have distinctive voices and are intelligent, dependent and affectionate. But because they have been highly inbred, they can be extremely timid, unpredictable or aggressive.

Putting Your Pet on a Diet

Fitness and diet hold the key to a healthy pet

More and more dogs and cats are adopting the habits of their human companions, and like them, they are increasingly overweight. Between 25 and 40 percent of America's pets are obese, according to expert estimates.

There are two basic reasons pets are getting rounder. One is too little exercise. The second is too many treats, especially people food. Pets are suffering the same consequences as overweight people, including joint problems and diabetes.

TIMELY TIPS

How to De-Skunk Your Pet

This skunk smell remedy is reputed to have been concocted by Paul Krebaum, a chemist and inventor, and has become a widely used remedy.

> **1 quart 3 percent hydrogen peroxide**
> **¹/₄ cup baking soda**
> **2 tbsp dishwashing detergent**

✔ Mix the ingredients together. The concoction will foam as the mixture of hydrogen peroxide and baking soda creates a lot of oxygen. It is important that, once it is mixed, you cover your dog, cat or family member with it as soon as possible, as the oxygen will dissipate almost immediately.

✔ Work the mixture in well to the skin or coat. Krebaum claims that the thiols in the skunk oil which cause the odor are neutralized when they interact with the oxygen. The dish detergent breaks up the oil and makes it easier for it to be rinsed off with water. Rinse thoroughly with warm water. Keep the solution away from the face and eyes.

Too many treats may even shorten their lives.

Pet supply companies have begun marketing weight loss supplements, including products like Canine Slim Results and Vetri-Lean. But these don't work any better for pets than they do for people, veterinarians say.

Dozens of companies sell low-fat or low-calorie pet foods. Researchers in France and Belgium who evaluated an Atkins-like high-protein, low-carbohydrate diet for obese dogs found that it worked, but not much better than diets that merely cut back on calories. Many veterinary experts say giving smaller portions of a balanced pet food is a healthier choice for weight loss.

The best—and simplest—approach is to buy pet food from a reputable manufacturer and follow the directions. "Feeding instructions are very reliable," says George Fahey, a professor of nutrition at the Univeristy of Illinois Animal Sciences department. "If the package says your dog should be eating a cup a day, that's what they should get. A little less if your pet needs to lose weight." Treats should be reserved for special occasions. Your dog may not like that idea. But the second part of Fahey's prescription—more exercise—should get tails wagging.

—Peter Jaret

When Your Pet Gets Sick

Some common diseases and their symptoms

Once your pet is weaned, the natural protection it garners from its mother's milk eventually wears off, leaving it prey to a host of opportunistic viruses. As with humans, pets' diseases often are highly contagious and, in cases such as rabies, pose a serious threat to humans as well.

The diseases listed below are those that most commonly affect pets. Vaccines are available for all of these diseases, but not necessarily recommended for all pets. (See page 517 for recommended vaccinations.)

Rabies (canine and feline). Rabies is a viral disease that can attack the central nervous system of all warm-blooded animals, including humans. It is fatal if not treated. Most states require dog and cat owners to vaccinate their pets against rabies. The disease is transmitted by saliva, which is usually transferred by a bite from an infected animal and is frequently found in wild animals, such as skunks, raccoons and bats.

There are two types of rabies—"dumb" and "furious." Both cause a departure from normal behavior. Animals with furious rabies will have a period immediately prior to death in which they appear to be "mad," frothing at the mouth and biting anything that gets in their way. Dumb rabies differs in that there is no "mad" period. Instead, paralysis, usually of the lower jaw, is the first sign. The paralysis spreads to limbs and vital organs, and death quickly follows. Wild animals that are unusually friendly and appear to have no fear of man or domestic animals should be avoided and reported immediately to the police or animal control authorities.

Rabies is almost totally preventable by vaccination. Dogs and cats should receive an initial rabies vaccination by the age of 3 to 4 months. Protection lasts from 1 to 3 years. Regular boosters are required.

Canine and feline bordetellosis. Caused by bacteria in the respiratory tracts of many animals, it is the primary cause of kennel cough. Besides the cough, some animals suffer from a purulent nasal discharge. Transmission usually occurs through contact with other animals' nasal secretions. Vaccination is generally administered by nasal spray.

Canine distemper virus (CDV). A highly contagious viral disease, canine distemper is transmitted by direct or indirect contact with the discharges from an infected dog's eyes and nose. Early signs are similar to those of a severe cold and often go unrecognized by the pet owner. The respiratory problems may be accompanied by vomiting and diarrhea. A nervous system disorder may also develop. The death rate from canine distemper is greater than 50 percent in adult dogs and even higher in puppies. Even if the dog survives, distemper can cause permanent damage to a dog's nervous system, sense of smell, hearing and sight. Partial or total paralysis is not uncommon.

Canine leptospirosis. A bacterial disease that harms the kidneys and can result in kidney failure. Vomiting, impaired vision and convulsions are all tip-offs. Transmission results from contact with the urine of infected animals, or contact with something tainted by the urine of an infected animal.

Canine parainfluenza. A viral infection of the respiratory tract, it is frequently accompanied by other respiratory viruses and is usually spread through contact with the nasal secretions of other dogs.

Canine parvovirus (CPV). A serious problem because the virus withstands extreme temperature changes and even exposure to most disinfectants. The source of infection is usually dog feces, which can contaminate cages and shoes and can be carried on the feet and hair of infected animals.

CPV attacks the intestinal tract, white blood cells and heart. Symptoms include vomiting, severe diarrhea, a loss of appetite, depression and high fever. Most deaths occur within 48 to 72 hours after the onset of clinical signs. Infected pups may act depressed or collapse, gasping for breath. Death may follow immediately. Pups that survive are likely to have permanently damaged hearts.

Infectious canine hepatitis. Caused by a virus that can infect many tissues, the disease usually attacks the liver, causing hepatitis. In some instances a whiteness or cloudiness of the eye may accompany the disease. Another strain of the same virus can cause respiratory tract infections. These viruses are transmitted by contact with objects that have been contaminated with the urine from infected dogs. Infectious canine hepatitis is different from human hepatitis.

Feline panleukopenia. Also known as feline distemper, the disease comes from a virus so resistant that it may remain infectious for over a year at room temperature on inanimate objects. Spread through blood, urine, feces, nasal secretions and fleas from infected cats, the virus causes high fever, dehydration, vomiting and lethargy and destroys a cat's white blood cells. It is 50 to 70 percent fatal, but immunity can be developed by vaccinating kittens and giving booster shots.

Feline leukemia virus. A disease of the immune system that is usually fatal, its symptoms include weight loss, lethargy, recurring or chronic sickness, diarrhea, unusual breathing and yellow coloration around the mouth and the whites of the eyes. Confirmation of the virus requires a blood test. There is a vaccine that provides protection.

Feline viral rhinotracheitis, feline calicivirus and feline pneumonitis. All three are highly infectious viruses of the respiratory tract for which vaccinations are available.

Boosting Your Pet's Well-Being

Vaccines your pet needs—and some it doesn't

With an increased awareness of the dangers of overvaccinating, many professionals recognize the difference between the universally necessary, or "core" vaccines, and "noncore" vaccines, those which should be administered only if it seems indicated because of risk of exposure.

The American Animal Hospital Association and others recommend that after your puppy or kitten receives the initial series of vaccinations and the appropriate booster, she or he may only need vaccinations in some cases every 3 years and may not need to be vaccinated against noncore diseases at all, unless the animal is at risk of exposure.

Following are the suggested guidelines for canine and feline vaccines, listed according to those that are essential (core) or optional (non-core). All others are not recommended. Consult with your veterinarian regarding appropriate vaccines and schedules for your pet.

CORE VACCINES FOR ALL PUPPIES

Rabies. *There are two vaccines for rabies, Rabies 1-year (killed) and Rabies 3-year (killed). Both are approved for use, though a statute may dictate which one must be used in each state.*

PROTOCOL: *RABIES 1-YEAR (KILLED).* Should be given initially at 12 to 16 weeks, with a booster at 1 year and revaccinations every year. Dogs older than 16 weeks should receive a single dose and the booster shot every year thereafter.

RABIES 3-YEAR (KILLED). Initial dose as early as 3 months of age. Where authorized by local/state statutes, a 3-year rabies vaccine may be substituted for initial and subsequent doses. A second vaccination is recommended 1 year following the initial dose regardless of the animal's age at the time the first dose was administered. Booster vaccines should be given every 3 years thereafter.

Canine distemper virus. *There are two types of vaccine recommended: modified live virus (CDV) (MLV), or recombinant (rCDV), which may be used interchangeably. The recombinant version is more likely to immunize puppies against the distemper virus, even in the face of passively acquired maternal antibody.*

Canine parvovirus. *(CPV-2) (MLV)*

Canine adenovirus. *(CAV-2) (MLV parenteral)*

PROTOCOL FOR THE ABOVE: All puppies should be given a minimum of three doses, with the first dose at 6 to 8 weeks and then one every 3 to 4 weeks until, but no later than, 16 weeks of age. Boosters are given 1 year after the completion of the initial puppy series and then every 3 years or longer thereafter. Dogs older than 16 weeks should receive 2 doses, 3 to 4 weeks apart, and the booster shots.

NONCORE VACCINES FOR DOGS

Bordetella. *(all types)*
Parainfluenza. *(CPIV) (MLV-parenteral)*
Lyme vaccine. *(all types)*
Distemper-measles. *(combined vaccine)*
Leptospirosis. *(all types)*

PROTOCOL: Noncore vaccines for the above diseases are available and should be administered at the discretion of the veterinarian.

SOURCE: 2006 American Animal Hospital Association Guidelines

CORE VACCINES FOR ALL KITTENS

Rabies. *Three types of vaccine are recommended, Recombinant or 1-year or 3-year killed.*

PROTOCOL: For both *RABIES 1-YEAR (KILLED)* and *3-YEAR (KILLED),* one dose should be given initially at 12 to 16 weeks, with a booster 1 year after the initial dose and revaccinations every 3 years thereafter unless otherwise required by state or local statutes. Cats older than 16 weeks should receive a single dose, a booster a year later, and then an approved vaccine booster every 3 years after that.

RABIES RECOMBINANT VACCINE should be given initially at 12 to 16 weeks, with a second dose 1 year later and a booster every year thereafter. Cats older than 16 weeks should receive a single dose with a booster shot a year later and every year after that.

Feline herpes virus-1. *MLV (FHV-1)*
Feline calcivirus. *MLV (FCV)*
Feline panleukopenia virus. *MLV (FPV)*

PROTOCOL: These are administered in combination. Three doses should be given, with the first at 6 to 8 weeks, and then every 3 to 4 weeks thereafter until 16 weeks of age. Boosters are given at 1 year after the first dose, and then every 3 years thereafter. For cats older than 16 weeks of age, two doses of vaccine are recommended. After a booster at 1 year, revaccination is suggested every 3 years thereafter for cats at low risk of exposure.

NONCORE VACCINES FOR CATS

Feline leukemia virus. *(FELV)*
Feline immunodeficieny virus. *(FIV)*

A Dr. Spock for Pet Owners

Why does your gerbil seem depressed? Why is its coat rough, its appetite flagging, its posture hunched?

The Merck/Merial Manual for Pet Health: Home Edition (Merck & Company, $22.95), an exhaustive guide to the illnesses and care of many pet species, aims to help you find the answer.

In the pet bible's 1,345 pages, written by 200 veterinarians, readers can find, among other things, the anatomy of a turtle; six signs of hyperparathyroidism in a dog; a list of 27 houseplants poisonous to pets; a description of lockjaw (an infection that leads baby birds to starve to death); instructions for what to do if your pet is shot with an arrow (don't pull it out); seven causes of liver injuries in horses; the necessary components of a pet travel kit; 161 diseases that can be passed to humans from animals; and yes, a proper diagnosis for a sick gerbil.

The bulk of the manual, a popular translation of the handbook for veterinarians published by Merck since 1955, is devoted to the three most common household animals: dogs, cats and horses. But the guide also includes chapters on birds and so-called exotic pets, like fish, reptiles, amphibians, chinchillas, ferrets, gerbils, guinea pigs, hamsters, mice, rats, rabbits, prairie dogs, pot-bellied pigs and sugar gliders, as well as sections on emergency care, poisoning, cancer and other subjects and useful descriptions of a variety of medical tests and treatments.

—Erica Goode

Feline Chlamydophila felis
Feline Bordetella bronchiseptica

PROTOCOL: Noncore vaccines are administered at the discretion of the veterinarian.

SOURCE: AAHA Feline vaccine guidelines (2006-2009)

New-Age Care for Your Pet
High-tech advances are helping vets help pets

These days, pet owners are demanding the same kind of care for their pets as they can get for themselves and their families. The pet care business is responding with medical and technological advances that are helping pets live longer and healthier lives. Because many of these procedures are costly, it may be worth the money to invest in pet insurance.

Farewell to fleas. Not long ago, pet owners had few choices: use flea powders and collars on their pets and spray the yard with chemicals.

Today, options include pills and topical spot-on solutions. The pills prevent flea eggs from hatching, and the skin treatments kill fleas on contact for 30 days. Both are available at your vet's office. Advances in outdoor flea control are available that contain nematodes, live organisms that feed on flea larvae. These products reduce harm to the environment, as well as to humans, animals and insects.

Computer ID. One way to identify your pet if it strays from home involves implanting a tiny microchip—about $1/4$ to $1/3$ inch long—under the skin of just about any animal. The result is a lifetime ID that can't be lost or removed. The information can be read by scanners now used by animal control centers and humane societies. So if your dog strays and ends up at one of these centers, the scanner reads the identification number that traces the pet back to you. The chip is injected by a vet with a device that looks like a syringe and needle.

Patching up pain. The patch technology used for humans is also used on animals. If an animal is in pain after an accident or is having a major dental procedure, a time-release patch can steadily relieve the pain, rather than the pet's having to wait until he or she needs another dose of pain killer. Time-release patches are expensive, but they last several days. At the vet's office, an owner can choose between the patch technology and standard medication. Most owners pick patches because they don't have to get up in the middle of the night or come home from work to redose their pets.

Modifying your pet's behavior. Shelters and humane groups destroy millions of dogs and cats each year because of the animals' behavior problems. That's more than the number killed each year by any disease. But behavior problems like aggression, digging, barking, biting and house-soiling can now be resolved through behavior-counseling programs. The earlier in a puppy or kitten's life that behavior problems are picked up, the greater the success in resolving them. Pets can get behavior counseling at special clinics or

---

ⓘ INSIDE INFO

A Dog's Best Friend Is...

A dog may be man's best friend, but for help in coping with stress, a dog's best friend may be another dog, according to a recent study.

○ One finding: an owner's efforts to calm a dog had no effect, either positive or negative, on the animal's stress levels during a thunderstorm.

○ Dogs that lived in households with other dogs recovered faster from such stressful situations.

SOURCE: Nancy A. Dreschel and Douglas A. Granger, Pennsylvania State University

through veterinarians or specialists that your vet can recommend. Many counselors will even come to your home.

A pet's behavior can also be modified with drugs. Until a few years ago, information on treating animals with drugs was limited, but now disorders such as car sickness, aggression and separation anxiety can be treated with a combination of behavior training and drug treatments.

Diagnosis and surgery. Ultrasound and endoscopy for pets are becoming more routinely used to diagnose and treat health problems. They have revolutionized exploratory surgery. If an animal has a serious heart problem or cancer, for example, it can be diagnosed without having to make any incisions. The result is lower costs and less stress for owners.

Pet surgery has also come a long way. Dogs no longer need to go blind from cataracts. Cataracts can be removed surgically, and artificial lenses can be implanted. And pets that suffer from chronic hip or knee deformities can have their joints replaced surgically, just like humans.

Small Pets for Small Kids

Guidelines for picking a healthy, sturdy first pet

While cats and dogs pose certain health issues for humans, most are well known and well mitigated by veterinarians and doctors—unlike the risks posed by certain other pets.

Salmonella, for example, can be carried by a wide variety of animals, not just the cute little turtles under 4 inches long that are officially banned but available nonetheless. The list includes gerbils, hamsters and other rodents, reptiles, and chicks.

The Centers for Disease Control and Prevention recommends keeping these and other nontraditional pets out of homes with children under age 5. In addition, children and adults alike should avoid kissing animals and take care to wash hands after handling; cage-cleaning duties should be assigned to adults or responsible older children.

To further minimize the risk of acquiring a diseased pet, use only highly reputable breeders, shelters or pet stores. "Extreme stress and crowding raise the risk factor for stress-induced bacterial shedding," says Dr. Nina Marano, branch chief of the C.D.C.'s geographic medicine and health promotion branch.

Animals brought from other parts of the world can also bring along diseases that pediatricians and veterinarians are unaccustomed to seeing. For example, wild chinchillas in South America have been associated with hemorrhagic fevers. Using a domestic breeder can cut down on these types of risks, says Dr. Marano.

Experts suggest some good choices for children. Guinea pigs are a good first pet for children

---

ⓘ **INSIDE INFO**

The Life Span of Songbirds

○ Several criteria go into choosing a pet bird. Is it sociable, or does it have a sweet voice? Can it talk? Is it noisy? The answer is that like dogs and cats, each bird species has its own unique personality. To give you an idea, however, of what kinds of birds have the most universal appeal, here is a listing of the five most popular birds—and their life expectancy.

1.	Parakeet (Budgerigar)	12-14 yrs.
2.	Cockatiel	15-20 yrs.
3.	Finches and Canaries	15 yrs.
4.	Lovebird	20 yrs.
5.	Parrot (African Gray)	50-60 yrs.

SOURCES: American Pet Products Association National
Pet Owners Survey; About.com

because they don't bite, are relatively sturdy and don't run very fast, says Stephen Zawistowski, an animal behaviorist with the American Society for the Prevention of Cruelty to Animals. "And they're interactive and don't need a huge cage," he says.

He also recommends "fancy" mice (mice selectively bred as pets or show mice) and domesticated rats, which resemble lab rats, not the ones outside ransacking your garbage. "They are very hardy and intelligent," he says, "and if you're looking for something to cuddle, they'll sit on your shoulder."

In the reptile family, he suggests chameleons for children around age 10 or older who know how to hold rather than squeeze. "The big ones only grow to about 6 inches, and they can run up and down your arm."

Rabbits, too, make good mobile pets for children of parents who don't mind putting their furniture, baseboards and electrical cords at some peril. (Tip: Male rabbits tend to "spray" outside the litter box, though neutering may limit this behavior.)

Finally, don't overlook fish. They will require some maintenance, says Zawistowski, but new equipment available for filtration helps minimize it.

—Teri Karush Rogers

Thinking of Getting a Gerbil?

Some facts to gnaw on

Mongolian gerbils are the species most commonly kept as household pets. They make efficient use of food and water, and have little body waste; consequently, their cages do not need to be cleaned as frequently as those of other rodents. (Be sure to buy your gerbil from a clean and reputable source to prevent getting a diseased animal.)

But gerbils are gnawing and scratching animals, so their cages must be made of gnaw-proof mate-

TIMELY TIPS

The Price of Your Pet

The American Pet Products Manufacturers Association asked 580 dog owners and 402 cat owners to record the amount they spent during a 1-year period on specific pet-related items.

✔ The dog owners spent almost $2,000; cat owners about $1,200. Small animals came in at just under $300.

✔ Spending can run even higher in the first year, when dogs need training; private trainers can cost over $800 for a package of lessons, while an obedience school is about $400.

✔ Spaying and neutering is another big expense. But there are cheaper options than paying a vet $550 or more for the procedure. The ASPCA (aspca.org) and the nonprofit groups Happy Tails (happytails.org) or Friends of Animals (friendsofanimals.org) offer information about how to obtain low-cost spaying and neutering in your area. —Alina Tugend

A NOAH'S ARK OF HOUSEHOLD PETS

What kinds of pets do Americans own, and how many? Here are the results of a recent survey of pet owners in the U.S. (in millions of pets):

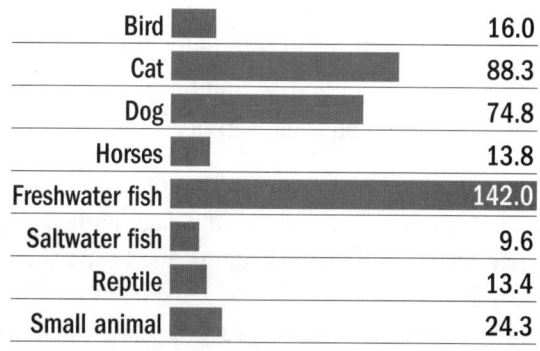

Bird	16.0
Cat	88.3
Dog	74.8
Horses	13.8
Freshwater fish	142.0
Saltwater fish	9.6
Reptile	13.4
Small animal	24.3

SOURCE: American Pet Products Manufacturers' Association 2007/2008 National Pet Owners Survey

rial. Gerbils are social. In their ancestral desert habitats, they lived in colonies, and therefore feel most comfortable living with others. So buy a pair, preferably of the same sex (unless you want to breed them) and from the same litter, if possible.

Gerbils can be territorial, so it is important to introduce a newcomer slowly, preferably by dividing the cage in two at first with glass or wire, to get them used to each other. If there is evidence of injury, remove the gerbil who is least injured, as that is certainly the one who is causing the trouble.

What a gerbil's residence will need. Bedding should be spread thickly over the bottom of a cage or large glass aquarium. The best materials for this are Aspen wood chips or corncob bedding.

- A nesting box made out of wood serves as the bedroom area of the cage. Torn strips of tissue make the optimum nesting material.

- Gerbils need a source of fresh water, which can be supplied by a self-feeding bottle attached to the side of the cage.

- Food may be placed in a gnaw-proof dish or scattered around the cage. As gerbils are foragers, this act of hunting for food provides stimulation, and is recommended. You can find premixed gerbil food at most pet stores. It must have protein, minerals, vitamins and bulk, but not too many sunflower seeds, which are fattening.

- A running wheel is also highly recommended, as gerbils need physical activity.

Home maintenance. Clean food dish and water bottle regularly. Wash down the cage with warm water and soap. Replace bedding and tissue about every 2 weeks.

SOURCES: The American Gerbil Society (www.agsgerbils.org)

Providing for Your Pet
Care for your animals when you no longer can

Unlike in ancient Egypt, when a diseased pharoah's pets were buried along with him, pets live on today, sometimes long after their owners die. Yet in many cases, there is no one to properly care for them. Laws in at least 39 states—including Arizona, Colorado, Florida, New Jersey and New York—allow owners to establish trusts for pets.

Leaving money to a pet became legal in 1990. A trustee and caregiver are named; the trustee is in charge of the money and pays the caregiver a set amount each month for expenses, like food, grooming and veterinary care.

Creating a trust can cost as little as $100, if you draw up a will for yourself at the same time, or up to a few thousand dollars. If money is no object, a trust can act like an endowment, experts say, with the interest generated covering expenses. Then, when the pet dies, the remaining balance can go to a charity or family member.

The best way to prevent fraud, trust experts suggest, is to get a DNA sample from the animal. Then, if the trustee becomes suspicious, a comparison can be made.

Instead of a trust, owners can include a provision for pet care in their will. But there are some drawbacks to that approach. A will takes effect only upon your death, not if you become ill or incapacitated. And it must go through probate, which can temporarily freeze funds for your pet's care and delay determining the rightful new owner. For more information go to the Human Society Web site: humanesociety.org/petsinwills.

—Maryann Mott

CHAPTER **8**

TRAVEL

Getting There

Planning Your Next Trip

Eight easy steps for preparing a smooth and inexpensive trip

As a travel reporter for the *New York Times,* Matt Gross is on the road up to six months out of the year. All that wandering takes not just stamina but organization as well, he says, from researching destinations to booking flights and hotels to figuring out what to do when he arrives. Here he shares his tried-and-true process for researching what's new, interesting and inexpensive.

1. After deciding on a destination, I head straight for Google; mastering its nooks and crannies is a skill all travelers should develop. One of the first searches I perform is for my destination plus the words "frugal" and "affordable." Seriously, I have found steals in America's most expensive vacation spots this way. But Google lets me do much more: with Google Maps, I can familiarize myself with a

city's layout and neighborhoods, and I can search for user-created maps of worthy landmarks. I also set up daily Google News alerts to get a regular feed of articles about various destinations sent directly to my e-mail inbox. With Google Blog Search, I hunt for food blogs everywhere from Istanbul to Seoul.

2. I don't just surf the Web, however—print still has its uses. My go-to guidebook is the Luxe series. The chic hotels, restaurants and boutiques that these lightweight, accordion-style booklets cheekily review are rarely frugal, but I don't care. When I travel for work, I want to know what to aspire to, and what's happening right now, and since Luxe guides are updated at least once a year, the intelligence they provide is always fresh. And occasionally, I even find bargains.

In an attempt to get the flavors of a culture, I often turn to novels, like *In the Skin of a Lion* by Michael Ondaatje, which framed how I saw Toronto, or *The Long Day Wanes: A Malayan Trilogy* by Anthony Burgess, which informed my sense of Malaysia's multicultural mix. Visit your local independent bookstore—or public libraries. And if there's really nothing in your area, log on to LongitudeBooks.com.

3. When it's time to book a flight, it's back online I go. Kayak.com, which searches virtually every other booking site, is my first stop. Its flexibility, range, speed and ability to filter your results in specific ways are almost unmatched. But I also use ITAsoftware.com's QPX system, which was developed for the airline industry. It's not exactly user-friendly, but it finds some surprising routes that don't always show up on Kayak.

✔ TIMELY TIPS

Find Cheaper Fares Midweek

✔ In general, you can often find lower fares by traveling on Tuesday or Wednesday, when planes are less crowded and cheap seats are more likely to be available.

✔ When airlines announce sales, the prices are sometimes valid only for travel on certain days—often Tuesday or Wednesday—so you can increase your chances of catching a sale by researching midweek prices.

Online Travel Sites Worth a Visit

These travel sites are worth checking out whether you are looking for a cheap flight or are just an armchair traveler.

Airfarewatchdog.com, Cheapflights.com, Farecast.com, Farecompare.com, SmarterTravel. com, Travelzoo.com and **Yapta. com** are airfare tracking sites that compare deals.

Avis.com, Budget.com, Hertz. com, and **Nationalcar.com** will rent you a car.

Betterbidding.com helps you understand what kind of hotel bids succeed on Priceline and Hotwire.

CheapTickets.com, Expedia. com, and **Travelocity.com** have airline tickets, car rentals, hotel reservations, travel information.

Concierge.com From the publisher of *Condé Nast Traveller.*

Flightstats.com compares timeliness record for particular flights.

Fodor's (fodors.com) Online home of the classic travel books.

Forbes.com (forbes.com/lifestyle/travel) The business magazine's travel pages include an archive of useful city guides.

Frommers.com Online home of the well-known travel books.

Gorp (gorp.away.com) Guide to adventure travel and outdoor recreation.

Hotels.com Hotels, vacation rentals, packages.

Hotwire.com can help you find travel bargains if you're flexible.

InsideTrip.com Data from public and private sources on mishandled luggage, security checkpoint wait times, etc.

InfoHub.com Travel guide organized by specialties.

ITASoftware.com Clear, well-organized listings of flights and fares, domestic and international, with booking codes.

Kayak.com, Mobissimo.com and **Sidestep.com** To search for travel fares and prices across multiple sites.

LonelyPlanet.com Home of the well-known travel books.

LuxeCityGuides.com Pocket guides for the sophisticated traveler.

National Geographic Travel (nationalgeographic.com/travel) and *Traveler* magazine.

PlanetRider.com collects and rates more travel sites than we could list here.

Priceline.com lets you name your own price for travel and more

and see if anyone bites.

Quikbook.com Bargain hotel rates for mostly domestic destinations.

Rough Guides Travel (travel. roughguides.com) Online version of the travel guides.

Transportation Security Administration (tsa.gov) For security checkpoint wait times.

Travel+Leisure (travelandleisure.com) From the American Express magazine.

Travelers' Health (cdc. gov/travel) Health information for worldwide destinations from the Centers for Disease Control.

Travelzoo.com collects special travel packages from many sites.

TripAdvisor.com Well-organized site, particularly strong for traveler feedback and multisite hotel rate searching.

US.lastminute.com Big discounts on last-minute travel.

U.S. State Department (state. gov/travelandbusiness) For country background papers, passport and visa information, travel warnings and advice.

ViaMichelin.com Travel guides, hotel and restaurant ratings and directions from the venerable Michelin.

—Richard J. Meislin

TRAVEL

When I'm ready to make a purchase, I go to the airline's own Web site to simplify the reservation, avoid third-party booking fees and ensure I have the lowest fare. Then I check SeatGuru.com, which has seat maps of most major airlines' planes, to find the best, most comfortable spot available.

4. As often as possible, I try to book hotels through their own Web sites—to avoid extra charges and to create a direct relationship between myself and the hotel—but I always check Kayak, Hotels.com and DealBase.com to make sure I'm getting a

---

TIMELY TIPS

Stacking Up Frequent Flier Miles

How to chose the right credit card

For millions of travelers, credit card reward programs are the best way to score free airline tickets and hotel rooms. But with credit card issuers and travel companies ratcheting up the competition for customers, how do you know which card in your wallet is worth reaching for?

✔ Experts on loyalty programs say that all card offers should be weighed carefully. Too often, consumers sign up for cards that are aligned with a particular travel company only to find that the marriage doesn't work.

✔ Generally, travelers should consider a card that is affiliated with an airline that serves their favorite foreign destinations and offers them the particular advantages that suit their traveling style. Some cards do not impose blackout dates; others offer double points for many purchases.

✔ FrequentFlier.com has charts that allow visitors to compare offers on airline- and hotel-related cards, and it provides details about bank-specific cards that yield travel rewards

—Bob Tedeschi

---

good rate. Despite its popularity, I don't often use TripAdvisor.com—it's centered on user reviews, which are based on specific personal experiences (too personal for my taste), and generally, if it's on Trip Advisor, it has already been "discovered." But when I do find myself there, I skip over its hotel listings and change "Property Type" to "Other Lodging," which turns up pensions, campgrounds, hostels and other accommodations that I often find more intriguing (and usually less expensive) than hotels.

5. If I want to rent an apartment, I check out Craigslist first. The listings there offer a good overall picture of what's available but can also provide clues to finding less-touristic apartment-rental sites, like PAP.fr in France.

6. Once I have all my confirmation e-mails, I forward them over to TripIt.com, which automatically turns them into an easy-to-edit itinerary. It's a free service, and it helps me keep my plans in some kind of order with—and this is the important part—minimal effort on my part. Plus, I can access the data via TripIt's iPhone application and share the details with my family and friends.

7. Speaking of friends, they're key to setting up a successfully frugal journey. Once I know where I'm heading, I update my Facebook status with that information and with a request: "Know anyone there?" Usually the names and introductions start flowing in—and with them, up-to-date insider info about the destination—but if they don't, I turn to CouchSurfing.com. Famous for helping travelers score free, comfortable places to sleep, it's just as good, if not better, for simply making connections between like-minded people. Even if none of my friends know anyone in, say, Bucharest, it's a good bet CouchSurfing will find me a pal there.

8. Having exhausted the resources of my friends, bookstores and the Internet, I'm pretty much ready to travel. Before I leave, I check the latest exchange rates on Oanda. com, tell my credit card provider where I plan to use my no-foreign-exchange-fee Visa card, cruise the Flight 001 travel store in search of sale items, check my flight status with that TripIt app and figure out the fastest, cheapest public transit route to the airport. If I've done everything right, I'll arrive at my destination—whether it's Punta del Este or Palm Beach—already knowing my way around, with semi-familiar people to meet, blogger-approved restaurants to try and high-end boutiques for some window-shopping.

> **The world is a book, and those who do not travel, read only a page.**
>
> St. Augustine

• • •

ment. One trend that's catching on are mini-guides designed for short trips to a single city. The British publisher Dorling Kindersley has its "Top 10" series, shorter versions of its DK Eyewitness Guides, known for glossy pages and color photographs. The Top 10 books choose 10 attractions as the best to see or do and give additional lists, like the top 10 Belgian beers in the Brussels book. Fodor's has a similar "See It" series. The See It guides are nearly 400 pages, but Fodor's also sells a smaller City Pack guide to a city's top 25 sights, including a foldout map. Both series feature lots of color and pictures. A chapter at the beginning of most Frommer's guidebooks showcases the "best of" a destination. The Frommer's Portable Guides are among the most compact available.

Lonely Planet has a shorter "Best of" series of city pocket guides and another series, called "Road Trip" and focused on weekend road trips, which complement its core lineup of country and regional guides. Its "On a Shoestring" series is still popular with the backpacker set. Rough Guides publishes a new Directions pocket series, with more color and photos than its other guidebooks. It, too, is designed for shorter trips.

Seasoned travelers will appreciate the stylized, sophisticated advice of the Luxe guides (luxecityguides.com). Be advised, however, that while their recommendations are up-to-date and quality-conscious, they can be expensive.

So which guidebook should you choose? Paper quality, the book's weight, the writing style, the size of the type, the number of photos, the quality of the maps and even page layout are all personal preferences—which often vary depending on the trip's length, the destination and who else is traveling. Don't forget to check the copyright

Picking a Travel Guide

It can be more difficult than picking a place to go

Planning a trip involves many difficult decisions, but one of the toughest may be choosing from a daunting lineup of guidebooks.

The choice was once simple. Backpackers and budget travelers hit the road with *Let's Go, Rough Guides* or *Lonely Planet.* Retirees packed Fodor's or Frommer's, less adventurous but good for nuts and bolts like museum hours and restaurant addresses. Art and culture connoisseurs carried a *Blue Guide,* and high fliers relied on Michelin guides to steer them to Europe's notable hotels and chefs.

To some degree, those characterizations still hold true. But mainstream guides have become more hip of late and increasingly geared to a wider range of travelers taking different types of trips. Hence the titles for hikers, bikers, women, families, gay travelers, people traveling with pets and more.

With all these choices, it may be time to branch out from a favorite series and experi-

date on any book you're considering; newer is definitely better.

There are dozens of other series. Get Lost Travel Books (getlostbooks.com) has helpful descriptions of more than 25 series. No doubt there will be even more options to consider by the time you read this.   —Susan Stellin

Taking the Fear Out of Flying
Advice to help get you off the ground

Aviophobia, the fear of flying, is common. Some 64 percent of women and 36 percent of men have it. If you are one of those people, here are a few words of advice.

Get to the airport early. Rushing causes anxiety that won't vanish once you're on board. Plan to arrive at least one hour beforehand for domestic flights and two hours for international flights, giving you enough time to go through security, settle down and walk on board in a relaxed state.

Eat something nutritious. Cut back on caffeine and sugar the day before your flight. Protein and unrefined carbohydrates fortify you best. Have a snack or meal at least every three and a half hours while you are flying.

Try to relax. You can help control your anxiety with relaxation techniques. Try deep-breathing exercises, and listen to the relaxation tapes often available on the airline's audio channels. Or imagine a relaxing scene, such as lying on a beach watching the waves rush in and out. Focus solely on that scene.

Pick the right seat. Many fearful flyers become claustrophobic. Breathing deeply from the diaphragm can help. So can your choice of seats. Choose a forward aisle seat on a wide-body plane, allowing you to move around more freely.

✔ TIMELY TIPS
If You Are Bumped from a Flight

It's bumpy out there—and we haven't even left the ground. Each year, almost million people are bumped from a flight. Considering the total number of air travelers, it's a small number (considerably less than 1 percent), but that's not much comfort to those who involuntarily lose their seats. Most bumped passengers, in fact, volunteer to give up their seats in return for some form of compensation, like a voucher for a free flight. But the payoff can be even greater for people who know how to bargain.

✔ **The best-informed travelers reject vouchers** that are good for a free ticket anywhere the airline flies, because often the seats are as difficult to book as frequent-flier seats. Instead, they hold out for denied-boarding certificates with a cash value.

✔ **If there are no volunteers,** an airline will sweeten the offer, adding upgrades or increasing the value of the certificate. Then, if there are still no takers, it starts turning away passengers, which in airline-speak is called "involuntary denied boarding." That is when passengers strike gold: under an airline contract, the holdouts get not only a seat on the next flight but also cash compensation.   —Christopher Elliott

Don't hide your anxiety. Flight attendants will generally go out of their way to help you. Asking the crew for a tour of the cockpit can also help put you at ease.

Resources.
ONLINE: GuidetoPsychology.com is a comprehensive site with information on the causes of the fear of flying, explanations of the mechanics of flying and links to treatment resources.

BOOKS: *The Fearless Flier's Handbook: Learning to Beat the Fear of Flying With the Experts From the Qantas Clinic* by Debbie Seaman (Ten Speed Press).

COURSES: Some airlines and airports offer courses on how to overcome aviophobia. One such course is a 4-day program offered by the Fear of Flying Clinic at San Francisco International Airport, 650-341-1595; www.fofc.com. Of course, sufferers of aviophobia could find it difficult to travel to a workshop. SOAR, or Seminars on Aeroanxiety Relief (800-332-7359; www.fearofflying.com), is a video program developed by a therapist and retired airline pilot for home use.

MEDICATION: You might want to talk to your doctor about an anti-anxiety medication for a flight. "For a short-term solution, we will sometimes recommend an anxiolytic medication such as Klonopin, which is short-acting, or Xanax, which is a bit longer-acting for longer flights," says Dr. Bradley A. Connor, medical director of the New York Center for Travel and Tropical Medicine. —Marjorie Connelly

How to Choose the Safest Flight

By picking the safest plane, airport and seat

Statistics on airline safety can be elucidating—and sometimes misleading. One airline carrier may have a better safety record than another because its routes are in an area of the country that has generally good weather, while another carrier may fly more frequently in an area where poor weather conditions make flying more dangerous.

Pick the safest airplanes. The picture is less cloudy when it comes to budget and commuter carriers, whose safety records are generally poorer than those of the majors. "If you have a choice between a small regional airline and a large jet, take the jet," says one air safety analyst. Safety is directly related to the amount of material and space under your seat to absorb the energy of the impact, so you have a better chance of surviving a crash if you're on one of the bigger planes, such as the Boeing 767s, 777s and 787s. Newer planes are preferable to older ones, which may suffer from corrosion, wear and stress fractures.

Pick the safest airports. Not all airports are created equal, either. Pilots note that Washington's Reagan airport, New York's LaGuardia airport

TIMELY TIPS

Making the Best of a Long Layover

If you are faced with a 6-hour layover at, say, the airport in Narita, Japan, there are several things you can do: practice Zen meditation, read *War and Peace* or make a brief escape out into the real world.

✔ Airwise.com and WorldAirportGuide.com provide news, driving directions, contact information and the Web address for each airport. They list the nearest city to each airport and provide brief directions to and from it. For those trying to get into the city and back during a layover, WorldAirportGuide.com's public transport section offers advice on the various options available and how long each will take.

✔ The airports themselves now offer increasingly better information on their own Web sites. BAA.com, the British Airport authority site, for instance, has comprehensive information on what to expect at its airports.

✔ To learn how long it takes to clear airport security at American airports, go to the Transportation Security Administration site, waittime.tsa.dhs.gov, which lists wait times at hundreds of American airports. —Bob Tedeschi

and the San Diego airport are surrounded by city neighborhoods and have intersecting runways. Boston's Logan airport is plagued by adverse weather conditions and other runway hazards. Idaho's Sun Valley airport is situated so that a landing plane barely clears a mountain range. Similarly, Alaska's Juneau airport is surrounded by glaciers and mountain peaks.

Pick the safest seat. Knowing where to sit could save your life. Since in most accidents an aircraft travels with its nose down, bumping along the ground for a bit after impact, it stands to reason that sitting in one of the front rows won't increase your chances of survival. But are some seats on a plane really safer than others? Experts usually duck the question since there are so many possible crash scenarios, but here are some precautions you can take when reserving a seat.

- Seats that face the bulkheads and interior dividers provide more legroom, but they can also be more hazardous. Serious head injuries resulting when passengers hit their heads on the walls and bulkhead during air turbulence and landings top the list of noncrash injury concerns. The F.A.A., airlines and safety researchers are continuing to look into ways to lessen the danger, such as shoulder belts and airbags. Until an appropriate solution is designed for all aircraft, airline crash injury specialists at the National Institute for Aviation Research advise passengers who are taller than average not to sit in the bulkhead row.

- Request a wingside seat. Seats close to the aircraft wings are structurally more sound and have better support.

- Look for an exit row. The emergency exit row provides more legroom and allows easier escape from fire and smoke. Wherever you sit, count the number of rows you are from an exit. Then, if the lights go out, you can still find your way out.

Learn before you fly. To learn more, check out AirSafe.com (www.airsafe.com) or the site of the National Transportation Safety Board (www.ntsb.gov) and the F.A.A.'s Web site (www.faa.gov). All the latest incidents are posted, ranging from crashes to turbulence resulting in injury, as well as the types of planes that each airline flies. If you're traveling abroad, call the F.A.A. (800-FAA-SURE) or go online at www.faa.gov to determine if your destination has been cited for failing to meet international safety standards.

How to Get Your Choice of Seat
Window or aisle? Increase your odds

It's getting harder to score a good seat in the air because fliers are increasingly selecting seats as soon as they book their flight. But some airlines have changed the rules of the game by adding new seat selection options.

In general, there are no hard and fast rules for landing a good seat. Because each airline has its own seating configurations and policies, a strategy that may work on one airline may not make a difference on another. For example, JetBlue makes most exit-row seats on its A320 aircraft available to passengers just after purchase. Other airlines tend to hold on to those seats for their top-tier frequent fliers or release them just before boarding. That said, there are a few basic guidelines that travelers should consider when trying to get the seat of their choice.

Most major airlines let passengers select seats when booking. Look at diagrams on the airline's homepage to see which spots are open. Then cross-reference your findings with Web sites like SeatGuru.com or SeatExpert.com, which rank seat quality and offer insider information like which exit-row seats won't recline.

Orbitz, Travelocity and Expedia also let passen-

INSIDE INFO

The Scourge of the Middle Seat

○ Seatguru.com, which offers detailed charts on the best and worst airplane seats, recently conducted an online survey of 1,600 fliers. When it comes to seat comfort, the study found, 42 percent of fliers said they would pay more—up to 10 percent of the cost of the ticket—in exchange for 5 additional inches of legroom.

○ The middle seat remains a scourge to avoid: when asked if they would consider squeezing into the middle if they could cozy up to star couples like Brad and Angelina or Ashton and Demi, more than half of fliers (56 percent) said they would decline.

○ Perhaps most disturbing, 13 percent of fliers said they had knowingly transported banned items through security, though the survey didn't delve into exactly which prohibited items were sneaked onboard.

—Michelle Higgins

gers view seating maps early in the booking process. The earlier you do choose your seat, online or through an agent, the better. When a flight is nearly full, airlines sometimes deny advanced seat selections, forcing latecomers to get their assignment at the airport. That's because airlines hold back some spots for flexibility in seating families or passengers with disabilities and only release those seats at the gate.

Just because you selected your seat in advance doesn't mean you'll actually get it. Planes are sometimes switched because of maintenance or schedule changes. With passengers able to change spots online, seats are often in flux until the aircraft doors are shut, so it can pay to check back to see if any better seats have opened up.

Another reason to keep checking is that some airlines allow elite frequent fliers or full-fare coach passengers to upgrade to first or business class starting 5 days before departure, depending on status. When they do, they often leave behind prize coach seats that you might nab. Knowing when those upgrades take place can be a key advantage in scoring a good spot. Northwest, for example, confirms platinum elite member upgrades 5 days before departure; gold elite, 3 days before departure; and silver, 24 hours before the flight.

Become an elite flier. Airlines save their best seats for their best customers. United, for example, lets elite frequent fliers sit in the "economy plus section" of the aircraft, or the front part of coach, which has up to 5 more inches of legroom than standard economy. Non-elite customers must pay extra for such seats.

Northwest and Continental save the first few rows in coach for elite members. US Airways lets elite fliers secure seats in exit rows through Web check-in 24 hours before departure. Non-elite fliers must wait until they get to the airport to select those seats.

Another tip: Airlines sometimes rotate jumbo jets used on long-haul flights through their domestic routes. When this happens, business class seats are classified as part of the coach cabin, and high-ranking frequent fliers can nab one by selecting a seat in the first few rows of coach.

Know when to ask for an upgrade. You can still ask for a new seat just before boarding. That's when airlines tend to release empty seats, often those toward the front of the plane, that they had been holding for families or disabled passengers. American and JetBlue release those seats up to 4 hours before boarding. At least one airline, Northwest, releases exit-row seats 24 hours before departure, precisely when Web check-in is available to customers. Travelers can sign up at nwa.com to receive an e-mail reminder to check in 24 hours before their flight.

—Michelle Higgins

TRAVEL

A Cure for Jet Lag?

The jury is still out on whether melatonin works

Some bleary-eyed travelers swear by melatonin as a way to beat jet lag. But experts say research on the hormone's effectiveness is far from clear-cut.

Over the years, more than a dozen studies have tried to determine whether melatonin can ease symptoms of jet lag by adjusting the body's internal clock to new time zones. Some have shown that it helps in small doses; others have found that it is no better than a placebo.

Dr. Michael Terman, director of the Center for Light Treatment and Biological Rhythms at New York-Presbyterian Hospital, who published a study on melatonin and jet lag in 1999, says the split stems from confusion over how jet lag is defined. While taking melatonin has been shown to help reset body rhythms, he says, there is little evidence that it can alleviate symptoms of jet lag that result from the stress of traveling itself—running through busy airports, an altered diet, sudden weather changes or the prospect of meeting new business clients. All of these contribute to exhaustion and sleep disturbances.

"We cannot say that all of the symptoms of jet lag are unequivocally due to circadian rhythm shifting," Terman says. "We see, for example, that some people traveling long distances barely complain

---

ⓘ INSIDE INFO

Some Tested Jet Lag Remedies

- ○ Begin observing mealtimes of your destination as soon as possible on your day of travel.
- ○ Avoid alcohol while traveling.
- ○ Avoid caffeine while traveling.
- ○ Drink a pint of liquids during flight.
- ○ Sleep according to the schedule of your destination.

---

of jet lag, even though their internal clocks are undergoing marked change. Overall, the evidence for using melatonin is not strong," he adds.

—Anahad O'Connor

The Baffling World of Visas

When getting there may be easier than getting in

Obtaining entry to foreign countries can be complex and confusing for many travelers. Depending on the country, travelers may be turned away based on nationality, profession or the stamps in their passports from countries they visited in the past. And policies can and often do shift based on diplomatic relations, making who is or is not let in seem somewhat random to those applying for entry.

Anyone with a criminal record, including a drunken driving conviction, may be turned away at the Canadian border. Several countries ban HIV-positive visitors, including Brunei, China and the United States, though exceptions may be granted in certain circumstances for visitors to the States. And some places in the Middle East, including Syria, Lebanon and Libya, rigidly enforce restrictions on prior travel to Israel and do not allow people with passports bearing an Israeli visa or entry and exit stamps to enter.

Religion and sexual preferences, too, are sometimes cited as reasons for tourists to be denied entry to one country or another. According to the State Department, United States citizens whose stated purpose of travel was tourism but who engaged in religious proselytizing have been expelled from Vietnam, which requires foreigners to undertake only the activities for which their visas were issued. And gay and lesbian tour groups have encountered issues visiting certain destinations.

With careful planning, it's possible for many tourists to overcome some entry obstacles, even

TIMELY TIPS

Getting an 11th-Hour Passport

Give yourself ample time for a child's passport

If you're leaving on a foreign trip and discover your passport has expired or that you don't have one, you can get one quickly at one of the 13 passport agencies in the United States. Generally, the agencies serve only travelers who are departing within 2 weeks and accept applications only by appointment. Addresses and phone numbers can be found at travel.state.gov/passport/about/agencies.html. The necessary forms can also be downloaded from the site. Applicants can also call the National Passport Information Center at 877-487-2778. The agencies are located in: Boston, Chicago, Honolulu, Houston, Los Angeles, Miami, New Orleans, New York, Norwalk (Connecticut), Philadelphia, San Francisco, Seattle and Washington.

✔ If you can't go to a passport agency yourself, try a private expediter. There are about 100 expediters operating in the U.S., many of whom are members of the National Association of Passport and Visa Services, an industry group. Members are listed online at www.napvs.org. Even if you apply in person, the U.S. Passport Agency charges a $75 application fee in addition to a $25 facility fee for expedited services. Private expediters often charge an additional $60 to $200.

✔ Most people who are applying for a child's passport will find that the process is more complicated than ever. In 2004, the government started requiring that children appear in person when they apply for a passport and that the consent of both parents be documented. There are also additional costs and rules that may mean you'll have to make several trips to apply. The State Department's easy-to-navigate travel site, www.travel.state.gov (click on "Passports" and then on the page titled "Minors Under Age 14"), will give you a good start, but the bottom line is this: give yourself plenty of time so you can avoid last-minute panic or expediting fees.

✔ If both parents don't appear with the child at one of the 6,000 "passport acceptance facilities" (go to www.iafdb.travel.state.gov to find the one nearest you), written permission from an absent parent or another documented explanation, like proof of sole custody of a child, an adoption decree or the death certificate of a deceased parent, must be supplied. A sample form letter stating consent is available on the State Department Web site, and it must be notarized. If the form isn't available, a letter with the same information will do. For a regular application, the passport will be issued in 6 weeks.   —Barry Estabrook and Jeanne B. Pinder

to countries with rigid restrictions. For example, anyone with a criminal record, including a drunken driving conviction, should contact a Canadian consulate or embassy before traveling to Canada. Waivers of exclusion may be obtained, though the process can take several weeks.

Travelers who plan to visit Israel and other Middle East countries on the same trip are advised to ask immigration officials not to stamp their passport in Israel but rather to stamp a separate piece of paper, like a landing card, instead.

Another solution: apply for a second United States passport, which is good for 2 years and costs $75. Travelers must submit a detailed written statement explaining why the second passport is needed—as, for example, when a foreign country would deny a visa or entry to an individual whose passport showed travel to a particular country.

For travelers looking for information on passports, visas and health advice, a good resource is www.iatatravelcentre.com, developed by the International Air Transport Association. A traveler can

INSIDE INFO

Travelers' Illnesses

O   About 8 percent of travelers to developing countries require medical care during or after travel, according to a study of more than 17,000 people who became ill while traveling from 1996 to 2004.

O   Overall, the most common ailment was acute diarrhea, but among travelers to Africa, it was malaria.

O   Respiratory illness is second only to gastrointestinal illness as a cause of illness in travelers.

SOURCE: GeoSentinel Clinics

TIMELY TIPS

Drawing Up a Safety Plan

What to do when traveling to high-risk zones

The likelihood of a hotel guest being a victim of a terrorist attack is minimal: about one in a million, experts say, compared to a one in 8,000 chance of dying in an auto accident at home. But if you are traveling to an area where your safety might be compromised, here are a few tips.

✔ Put together a kit with four essential items, the Association of Corporate Travel Executives recommends: a flashlight with an LED bulb for illumination or to signal for help; a handheld water purifier in case the water isn't potable; a portable radio; and a cellphone or a BlackBerry with international service.

✔ Get a hotel room above the second floor and below the seventh floor, security experts say. Criminals can easily access most ground-floor rooms, and many fire department ladders won't extend beyond the seventh floor.

—Michelle Higgins

use the country information tool to plug in her itinerary, passport details and countries visited in the last six months, and the site spits back information on the relevant travel documents, vaccinations or other requirements needed for that specific trip. Perhaps even more useful, it flags any restrictions that a traveler may encounter.

The State Department's Web site also lists entry and exit requirements to foreign countries at travel.state.gov. For information on countries that ban HIV-positive visitors, go to www.hivtravel.org.

—Michelle Higgins

The Case for Trip Insurance

Most health insurance doesn't cover you abroad

Travelers wondering whether it's worthwhile to purchase trip insurance might want to consider these facts.

• Medical care—even in an emergency—is not covered by Medicare or many private health insurance plans when Americans travel overseas.

• Some Medicare supplemental plans include foreign travel emergency coverage, as do some private plans, but they often require notification to qualify for reimbursement of medical expenses (and, often, insurance cards include only toll-free numbers that don't work all over the world).

To get medical insurance coverage when venturing abroad, travelers have several options:

• Package travel policies that also cover things like trip cancellation and lost baggage

• Medical-only policies, which can be bought for a single trip or multiple trips within a year

• Medical transport policies, which primarily cover emergency evacuation (often with exceptions for risky activities like rock climbing)

The price of travel insurance is typically based on the traveler's age, the amount of coverage desired and the cost or length of the trip.

A general guideline is that package travel policies cost 4 to 7 percent of the trip's price (about $200 to $350 to insure a $5,000 trip), while a travel medical policy for a single trip costs roughly $20 to $50 for $50,000 to $100,000 worth of coverage. Both types of policies generally cover medical evacuation, up to a limit specified in the policy, but you can also buy just a medical evacuation policy for less than $50 a trip.

Most package travel policies also include trip interruption benefits that cover expenses like additional hotel nights or airline ticket change fees and offer reimbursement for the missed portion of a trip.

In general, buying travel insurance doesn't mean you can cancel a trip for any reason and get your money back; policies stipulate acceptable reasons for a cancellation, and there are exclusions for things like existing medical conditions, acts of war and in some cases acts of terrorism. So it's important to read the fine print on a policy to understand what it covers and what's excluded.

Unlike some other types of insurance, travel insurance usually does cover natural disasters—like tsunamis. Another benefit typically provided by travel insurance involves the worst-case scenario—repatriation of remains—but again, each policy defines specific benefits and limits.

—Susan Stellin

When Talk Is Anything but Cheap
Tips for using a cellphone abroad

While Americans have embraced the convenience of using cellphones, trying to dial from overseas often brings surprises. Even if the phone works, voice mail may not. Depending on the handset, coverage can be spotty. Make the wrong choices, and you may find a huge bill. The right tactics to avoid those headaches depend on which carrier you use, the length of your trip and your destination.

A majority of the world's cellphone subscribers use the GSM technology standard. In the United States, the major carriers use two systems. Cingular (now AT&T) and T-Mobile use GSM, while Sprint, Nextel and Verizon use CDMA, an incompatible technology, on most of their phones.

CDMA technology is found in North America, as well as some Asian countries, but it is basically nonexistent in Europe. So while AT&T and T-Mobile customers can potentially use their phones in more than a hundred countries, in many places abroad most Sprint and Verizon customers won't be able to get a dial tone.

 **TIMELY TIPS**

Finding a Travel Policy

✔ Insurance can be bought through insurance or travel agents and tour operators. You can research and purchase insurance online at sites like Insuremytrip.com, Squaremouth.com and Totaltravelinsurance.com, which offer side-by-side comparisons, including prices; agents can answer questions on the phone.

✔ Medex Global Group (www.medexassist.com) sells medical travel insurance. Another option is a prepaid air medical transport program, which allows its members to choose a hospital. MedjetAssist (www.medjetassist.com), for example, will transport a member hospitalized more than 150 miles from home to another hospital of his choice. —Mary Billard

Call Home for Less

Mom is just 37 (or so) digits away

Whether you prefer high-tech options or more conventional landlines, there are affordable ways to call home from abroad even if you don't carry an internationally-capable cellphone.

✔ **PREPAID CALLING CARDS.** Calling cards provide the ultimate in flexibility: they can be used from most locations, including pay phones, cellphones and landlines. But not all calling cards are equal, especially overseas. Compare the rate options associated with different cards, whether you buy them before you travel or on the road. Some charge a per-connection fee as well as a per-minute fee, for example. **Who should use them:** Travelers who don't carry computers; technophobes.

✔ **CALLBACK SERVICES.** As the name suggests, these services call you back and then place your call at cheaper rates. You initiate the call by dialing a "trigger" number—a connection to the callback service's computers. Let the call ring once and then hang up. The computer calls you back from the United States using lower international rates and makes the connection after verifying your account number. Often cheaper than direct-dial calls and even some prepaid calling cards, but the services may not work at hotels, where staff may not accept the return calls. **Who should use them:** Those traveling for long periods who plan to make lots of international calls.

✔ **VOICE OVER INTERNET PROTOCOL (VoIP).** VoIP works by digitizing your voice and sending it via the Internet to the person you're calling, who hears it on his PC speakers, or by routing it through regular telephone lines to anyone's standard phone line. VoIP services generally work best with a broadband or wireless Internet connection and can be used from hotel rooms, Internet cafés or wireless hot spots if you have a notebook computer. Since most calls use the Internet and connections into and out of the Internet are typically local calls, the rates are astonishing low. **Who should use it:** Travelers who have access to broadband or wireless Internet.

—David A. Kelly

While most of their phones use CDMA technology, Sprint, Nextel and Verizon do offer several GSM models for rent or purchase that are geared to the international traveler. Cingular and T-Mobile customers have more options—if their existing phones can pick up multiple frequencies.

To use an American GSM cellphone in a foreign country, the handset you own must be tri-band or quad-band and able to operate on one or both of the frequencies used outside the United States. The Cingular and T-Mobile Web sites, as well as Telestial's and others, list the predominant frequencies used in each country and show if your phone can operate on one or both overseas bands.

To protect against fraud, American cellphones are typically blocked from making calls when used abroad. Before traveling, call your provider and ask to have that restriction removed.

GSM phones use SIM cards (subscriber identity modules), tiny electronic chips that hold a cellphone's "brains," including the subscriber's contact numbers and phone number. (CDMA phones store such information directly in the hardware.)

GSM customers can avoid sky-high roaming charges by replacing their American SIM cards with ones from other countries. For example, travelers to Britain can pick up a SIM card from the British carrier Vodafone; once inserted, it gives the phone a temporary British phone number. Calls within Britain and to the United States would be much cheaper. Another benefit when using overseas SIM cards is that incoming calls are typically free in most countries.

Overseas SIM cards can be purchased before you travel from companies like Cellular Abroad (www. cellularabroad.com) and Telestial (www.telestial. com) or at local shops in foreign countries.

Even if you have a GSM phone that operates on both overseas frequencies, domestic cellphone providers do not want you to use your phone with another company's SIM card because they do not make any money when you do. To prevent your doing so, cellphones bought through Cingular and T-Mobile are electronically locked—they accept only their own company's SIM cards.

Before you throw your phone off the Eiffel Tower in frustration, know that there are several ways to unlock your phone and avoid those high overseas roaming rates. Cingular and T-Mobile will unlock their customers' phones under certain conditions. If you do not meet your provider's requirements, you can still get your phone unlocked from a private company. For a few dollars, the Travel Insider (www.thetravelinsider.com) and UnlockTelecom (www.unlocktelecom.com) will provide your phone's specific unlocking code.

Other GSM Phones. Cellphone customers with dual-band GSM phones that cannot be used overseas can always purchase unlocked quad-band phones from third-party providers such as www. cellular-blowout.com. Cellular Abroad and Telestial also sell unlocked phones. However, because these unlocked phones are not subsidized by a carrier the price is generally higher. These phones can be used solely when traveling outside the United States. Since they are unlocked, they can also be used instead of your current phone on your American network.　　　　　—Eric A. Taub

TIMELY TIPS

More Tips on Cellphones Abroad

✔ When entering numbers in your cellphone, always add the plus (+) sign and the country code; that way, the number can be dialed automatically no matter from what country you are calling.

✔ Store your GSM phone's numbers in the phone itself rather than the SIM card. Then the numbers will still be available to you when you use an overseas SIM card. To transfer them to a new phone easily, store them on a device like Backup-Pal (www.backup-pal.com), an external U.S.B. memory unit.

✔ While you will not pay any charges for incoming calls when you use a foreign SIM card, tell your American callers to get an overseas calling plan from their phone company before you ask them to ring you. If they do not, they could be paying the same sky-high rates that you just avoided.

✔ And if you take your American phone overseas, make sure that its battery charger is dual voltage; without one, all the effort to get your phone to work in other countries may go up in smoke the first time you plug it in.　　　—Eric A. Taub

Stowing Away on a Freighter
If you like staring at saltwater, this trip's for you

Freighter travel is still available to the general public today (see "Cruising the World" on page 538), but it isn't for everyone. Christopher Buckley, author of *Steaming to Bamboola,* a first-person account of his trip from South Carolina to the North Sea on a tramp freighter, offers some firsthand counsel.

Those who like shuffleboard, mints on their pillow at night and driving golf balls off the afterdeck, read no further. Freighter travel is not for you. It's also not for people with medical conditions, because

see "Cruising the World" on page 538

TRAVEL

DECK BY DECK

Your cabin's location can have a profound effect on your enjoyment of a cruise.

The first important choice is either an inside or outside cabin. Inside cabins are cheaper, usually quieter and good for sleeping. Outside cabins often have deck access, light and a view. Cruise ships are now bigger and more stabilized, but positioning at the center of the ship still helps prevent seasickness. Cabins should be at least 170 sq. ft. for two people.

AFT: The aft (back end) of a boat pitches less than the bow in high seas, but there can be engine noise.

LOWER: Smaller, cheaper cabins nearer the engine. Some drawbacks: engine vibration, noise and crew traffic.

BRIDGE: Expensive, spacious cabins with more amenities (e.g., whirlpools) and verandas; some rolling and pitching.

UPPER DECKS: Often offer the best value for relative cost if there are no lifeboats blocking the view.

PROMENADE: The most public deck. Can be noisy, and the exterior views are mostly of people passing by.

MAIN: The noisiest deck and usually the one with most traffic. Pick a cabin insulated by cabins on as many sides as possible, and do not take a cabin that connects to another cabin, unless it is filled with your relatives.

SOURCES: www.sealetter.com; www.cruisevacations.guide.com; *Frommer's Cruises & Ports of Call*

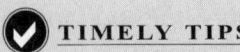 **TIMELY TIPS**

Cruising the World

To find out who's sailing where, when and on what kind of ship, from deluxe to bare-bones, check out these Web sites.

✔ **CruiseCritic.com.** Online cruise magazine; reviews, ship ratings, exclusive deals, huge cruise forum.

✔ **EasyCruise.com.** Less expensive, more youth-oriented than your parents' cruise line.

✔ **FreighterCruises.com.** Maris Freighter Cruises arranges bookings on freighters and other types of specialty ships, including container ships.

✔ **FreighterWorld.com.** Freighter World Cruises Inc. offers information on freighters and conventional and expedition cruises.

✔ **IndependentTraveler.com.** Offers a calculator that figures in all costs you're likely to face on a cruise.

✔ **Search2cruise.com.** Comprehensive information about cruises and cruise lines. You can search the site by destination, cruise line or specific ship.

there's usually no doctor on board. That's why only 12 people are allowed on board at once. But for those who enjoy reading the classics and long, long hours of boring, endless, blue saltwater, this is your trip. It's a reader's vacation—or a writer's vacation. Nelson Algren reread all of Hemingway's works while on a freighter from San Francisco to Yokohama and then wrote about the experience in his book, *Notes from a Sea Diary: Hemingway All the Way.*

A generation ago, you could go down to the dock, talk to a freighter captain and get a job and berth on board. I arranged to work with the crew to pay my way on a freighter; you can't do that today. But a freighter is still a lot less expensive than traveling on a cruise ship.

My first freighter trip came when I was 17 and about to start college; I saw a bit of the world at a young age and developed a real relationship with the men on board. I only made $20 a week but felt rich because I could buy cigarettes for $1 a carton and beer for $3 a case at the ship store.

It's like apples and oranges between the way I traveled and a freighter trip today. I doubt someone traveling now would be able to really get to know the crew or share in their misadventures in quite the same way.

The World's Best Train Trips

Riding the rails—some itineraries that beckon

With every uptick in gas prices and every degree rise in global warming, trains become more and more sensible. And trains have never failed to inspire wanderlust. Around the world, several trains run on particularly scenic routes, across continents or on small slices of inviting terrain.

The Cardinal and the Zephyr. An Amtrak cross-country trip from New York to San Francisco can begin with the Cardinal, which runs 3 days a week from New York's Pennsylvania Station to Chicago, heading south before turning west. From Chicago, the California Zephyr runs daily to Emeryville, Calif. (buses take riders into San Francisco), using double-decker trains with wraparound windows in an observation car.

The full trip, which can take less than 4 days, is a journey through American history and geography: the industrial Northeast, Washington, Civil War Virginia, Chicago, coal towns and cornfields, Rocky Mountain meadows and red rock canyons, the stark Nevada desert, the Sierra Nevada and San Francisco Bay. (800-872-7245; www.amtrak.com)

The Blue Train, South Africa. This five-star hotel on wheels—a consistent winner of the "World's Leading Luxury Train" award—runs between Pretoria and Cape Town. Suites are equipped with marble baths; butlers serve a glass of port or after-dinner cigar. You never have to leave the comfort of your private lounge: a large video screen magnifies real-time views of grasslands, giraffes and elephants, forests, gorges, cliffs, citrus orchards and snow-capped mountain peaks. (086-000-888; www.bluetrainsouthafrica.com)

The Canadian, Canada. The Canadian, VIA Rail's cross-country service, traverses the lakelands of northern Ontario, the Saskatchewan and Manitoba prairies and the soaring Canadian Rockies on a spectacular 3-day, 4-night journey from Toronto to Vancouver. The refurbished 1950s Art Deco trains have two classes: Comfort, with reclining seats, a domed viewing car and a coffee shop (drinks and meals are extra); and Silver & Blue, which includes sleeping accommodations, meals, a plush bar/lounge and a private sightseeing car. With 48 hours' notice, passengers can request unscheduled stops on some segments. (888-842-7245; www.viarail.ca)

TRAVEL

540

MILEAGE · TRAVEL

DISTANCES BETWEEN SOME MAJOR U.S. CITIES

MILES ☐ / ☐ KILOMETERS	Atlanta, GA	Boston, MA	Chicago, IL	Denver, CO	Houston, TX	Kansas City, KS	Los Angeles, CA	Minneapolis, MN	Miami, FL	New York, NY	San Francisco, CA	Seattle, WA	Washington, D.C.
Atlanta, GA		1110	715	1405	800	805	2185	1135	665	865	2495	2785	620
Boston, MA	1790		1000	2000	1830	1440	3020	1390	1520	210	3130	3020	450
Chicago, IL	1150	1613		1000	1085	525	2020	410	1380	795	2135	2070	710
Denver, CO	2260	3226	1615		1120	600	1025	915	2065	1780	1270	1335	1620
Houston, TX	1285	2951	1750	1805		795	1550	1230	1190	1635	1930	2450	1370
Kansas City, MO	1295	2302	850	965	1280		1625	440	1470	1195	1865	1900	1040
Los Angeles, CA	3515	4871	3250	1650	2495	2610		1935	2740	2800	385	1140	2650
Minneapolis, MN	1825	2242	665	1470	1980	680	3110		1795	1200	2010	2015	1090
Miami, FL	1070	2451	2220	3320	1915	2365	4405	2885		1280	3115	3365	1060
New York, NY	1390	338	1275	2865	2630	1925	4505	1935	2060		3055	2860	240
San Francisco, CA	4015	5048	3435	2040	3105	3000	615	3240	5015	4915		810	2840
Seattle, WA	4485	4871	3330	2140	3940	3060	1835	2675	5415	4600	1305		2720
Washington, D.C.	1000	725	1145	2613	2209	1677	4274	1753	1709	387	4580	4387	

The Overlander, New Zealand. The Overlander's 423-mile, 12-hour journey from Auckland to Wellington, down the lush spine of New Zealand's North Island, passes farming hamlets, snow-capped volcanoes and steep river gorges. The train runs on a line built in 1908 with engineering features like the Raurimu Spiral, with two tunnels, three horseshoe curves and a complete circle. The train runs daily from December through April and on weekends from May through November. (64-4-495-0775; www.tranzscenic.co.nz)

Glacier Express, Switzerland. This breathtaking, seven-and-a-half-hour journey from St.-Moritz or Davos to Zermatt through a Swiss alpine wonderland rollercoasters across 291 bridges, through 91 tunnels and over the Rhone and Rhine Rivers and the 6,670-foot-high Oberal Pass. The postcard views include the Matterhorn. (41-27-927-7777; www.glacierexpress.ch; but for fewer than 10 tickets, passengers must go to a travel agency or a main railway station; www.raileurope.com)

The Bergen Railway, Norway. From Oslo, this scenic seven-hour journey ascends to the mountain resort towns of Geilo, Gol and Nesbyen and across the vast Hardanger plateau on the way to the charming port city of Bergen. (47-23-15-15-15; www.nsb.no)

El Chepe, Mexico. The 408-mile, 14-hour Chihuahua al Pacifico Railway, or El Chepe, links the Pacific coast in Sinaloa with the Chihuahua desert on a spectacularly rugged route though the Copper Canyon. Between Los Mochis and Chihuahua, it climbs 8,000 feet on 37 bridges and through 86 tunnels. It runs daily. (888-484-1623; www.chepe.com.mx)   —Andy Isaacson, with additional reporting

How to Get the Best Hotel Deal

Finding bargains through online booking sites

With Priceline.com, a traveler can choose trip dates, a preferred neighborhood to stay in and hotel star rating. Then you take take a deep breath and make an offer, without knowing what price the site will actually accept.

With Hotwire.com and Lastminutetravel.com, travelers don't bid at all. Rather, they are given the prices but don't learn the name of the hotel until they've paid.

But you don't have to enter into the world of opaque travel booking alone. There are some lesser-known sites, like Biddingfortravel.com and Betterbidding.com, designed to help travelers navigate it. They provide strategic advice and offer tips from other travelers on how to game the system. Here's a practical guide to finding a hotel deal through opaque booking sites.

Figure out the going rate. After determining where you want to go, check other mainstream hotel booking sites, like Travelocity.com or Hotels. com, to get an idea of what hotels are charging for the dates you want to travel.

The star ratings on Priceline, Hotwire or Lastminutetravel may not coincide with those on the more transparent sites, however. For more insight, check Betterbidding, which offers a running commentary by purchasers of the hotel deals they received on Hotwire or Priceline—"4-star Philadelphia (downtown) Loews, $70," for example. This can also help you get an idea of the hotels probably being offered through the opaque sites.

Another option: Biddingfortravel, which is geared specifically to Priceline users, offers a list of Web sites it recommends for checking hotels' standard rates and displays winning bids posted by users.

Bid or no bid? Next, decide if you want to avoid Priceline's bidding model entirely. Some travelers prefer Hotwire and Lastminutetravel because they don't require users to make an offer, eliminating any haggling. They also may allow a traveler to make a more specific room choice—a suite, for example—or to pinpoint neighborhoods more closely.

Know the bidding rules. Priceline requires that travelers wait 24 hours before placing the same bid a second time. But you can get around this by changing something in the initial bid, like dates, neighborhood or star rating—a move Priceline aficionados call a "free rebid."

Bidontravel.com, another bidding advice site, urges users to start bidding at the highest star rating that interests them so that they can make immediate subsequent bids using lower stars if the first bid is rejected. If you are interested in more than one neighborhood, the site says, hold back your second or third choice in case you have to bid again.

Make an offer. Bidontravel has typically recommended bidding about 30 percent lower on Priceline than the asking prices you found on other sites and about 15 percent less than those on Hotwire. But you could try going much lower, unless you're going at a really peak time.

You can compare rates at Lastminutetravel as well. If your Priceline bids are not successful, you can go back to whichever of the other two sites had the best rate and still get a bargain.

Celebrate or rebid. If Priceline accepts the bid, it makes the booking, charges your credit card and tells you what hotel you won. If it rejects the bid, you can make a new one, raising the price by a few dollars, or adding a neighborhood or a different star rating.

—Michelle Higgins

The World's Most Charming Inns

Hard-to-find gems in America and Europe

Small hotels with charm and character can be difficult to find through tourist agencies and guides. But Karen Brown has made that her specialty. She has spent the past three decades evaluating small inns, hotels and bed and breakfasts and publishing discerning guidebooks of her discoveries. See www.karenbrown.com for titles.

Here are some of Brown's personal choices of the best country inns in the U.S. and Europe. While not necessarily the most luxurious or the best bargains, the hotels are chosen for their charm; most also offer excellent value.

Pacific Northwest

Just Inn Bed & Breakfast, *Paso Robles, California.* A glorious setting on the grounds of the Justin Winery, 16 miles west of Paso Robles. The inn has four suites that combine the luxury and amenities of a five-star hotel with the friendliness of a family-run inn. There is also an excellent six-table restaurant. 805-238-6932; www.justinwine.com

Run of the River, *Leavenworth, Washington.* A few miles beyond the charming Bavarian village is an even more fairy-tale place: a log cabin nestled amid pine and aspen trees against a rugged backdrop of mountains. 800-288-6491; www.runoftheriver.com; info@runoftheriver.com

Springbrook Hazelnut Farm, *Newberg, Oregon.* Situated on 70 acres, this enchanting hazelnut farm property is only 20 minutes from Portland, but you'll swear that you are in the Italian countryside. 800-793-8528; www.nutfarm.com

Mid-Atlantic

Goodstone Inn & Estate, *Middleburg, Virginia.* Located on a 265-acre spread in Virginia horse country. A former carriage house on the grounds hosts a traditional afternoon tea. The most popular accommodations are in the former horse stables. 877-219-4663; www.goodstone.com.

Inn at Warner Hall, *Gloucester, Virginia.* Warner Hall dates back to 1642, and the owners have taken this plantation house and re-created a home and a style that will delight the traveler. 804-695-9565; www.warnerhall.com

Morrison House, *Alexandria, Virginia.* An 18th-century Federal manor in the heart of old-town Alexandria with a staff that provides a level of service that's European in style. The ideal place to stay in the Washington, D.C. area. 703-838-8000; www.morrisonhouse.com

New England

Homestead Inn, *Greenwich, Connecticut.* Only a few inns anywhere in the world can begin to approach the level of accommodation here. 203-869-7500; www.homesteadinn.com

Maple Leaf Inn, *Barnard (near Woodstock), Vermont.* Although newly built, this beautiful three-story, gray-and-white inn with wraparound porch has a traditional feel. 800-51-MAPLE; www.mapleleafinn.com

The Wauwinet Inn, *Nantucket, Massachusetts.* Located on a spit of land jutting into the sea, a 10-minute drive from the town of Nantucket; a wildlife refuge north of the inn offers many more miles of wonderfully wild isolation. All rooms are individually decorated with original country antiques. 800-426-8718; www.wauwinet.com

ENGLAND (COUNTRY CODE 44)

The Soho Hotel, *London.* Central to the attractions of Covent Garden, the British Museum and the National Gallery, the Soho is located on a quiet cul-de-sac. Rooms are sleekly modern and

TIMELY TIPS

Taking in the Big Apple

Affordable Manhattan hotels

There are two rules to finding an affordable hotel room in Manhattan: do your research and book early. Rates vary wildly, depending on the season and availability. Prices tend to be highest in the fall, when conventioneers converge on the city, and again in December, when holiday shoppers swarm Fifth Avenue. The hotels below are generally considered moderately priced; rates are quotes for winter 2009, for the least expensive room, single or double.

Affinia Dumont. *From $269.* A business and pet-friendly spot with gym and spa. 150 East 34th Street. 212-481-7600; www.affinia.com

Chelsea Hotel. *From $159.* The storied bohemian landmark. 222 West 23rd Street. 212-243-3700; www.hotelchelsea.com

Doubletree Metropolitan. *From $159.* A recently renovated landmark. 569 Lexington Avenue. 800-836-6471; www.metropolitanhotelnyc.com.

Excelsior Hotel. *From $224.* Cozy Upper West Side elegance, steps from Central Park. 45 West 81st Street. 212-362-9200; www.excelsiorhotelny.com

Gershwin Hotel. *From $45.* Hotel-cum-hostel popular with young Europeans. 7 East 27th Street. 212-545-8000; www.gershwinhotel.com

Hotel Grace. *From $189.* A cheap, chic hotel. 125 West 45th Street. 212-354-2323; www.hotelqt.com

Hotel Stanford. *From $109.* The staff at this Koreatown hotel speaks Korean, English and Spanish. 43 West 32nd Street. 800-365-1114; www.hotelstanford.com

Hudson Hotel. *From $159.* A former Y.W.C.A. redesigned and updated. 356 West 58th Street. 212-554-6000; www.hudsonhotel.com

Off SoHo Suites Hotel. *Rooms from $199* (sharing kitchen and bath); *suites from $189.* Euro-style suites between SoHo and the Lower East Side. 11 Rivington Street. 800-633-7646; www.offsoho.com

The Time. *From $152.* Another hip, high-concept hotel in Times Square. 224 West 49th Street. 877-846-3692; www.thetimeny.com

—Denny Lee

appointed for the sophisticated traveler. 4 Richmond Mews London W1D 3DH, England. 20-7559-3000; www.sohohotel.com

Chewton Glen, *New Milton, Hampshire.* With 58 bedrooms, world-class leisure and sporting facilities, an award winning spa and a Michelin-star restaurant, the hotel has been voted the "Best Small Hotel under 100 Rooms in the World" for 2 years running. 800-344-5087 or 1-425-275341; www.chewtonglen.com

Bolhays, Salisbury, *Wiltshire.* An 1899 Victorian townhouse built on church land; it is a 10-minute walk from a magnificent cathedral. 01722-320603; www.bolhays.com

FRANCE (COUNTRY CODE 33)

Manoir d'Hautegente, *Coly.* Down a private drive, the manoir sits idyllically beneath shady trees in a garden. The bedrooms vary greatly in size, but all enjoy river views. 05.53.51.68.03; www.manoir-hautegente.com

Château de Garrevaques, *Garrevaques.* The château is lovingly decorated with heirlooms and beautiful antiques. Dinner is a gala event and great fun. 05.63.75.04.54; www.garrevaques.com

Château-Hôtel André Ziltener, *Chambolle-Musigny.* In a delightful village nestled among the vineyards in the heart of Burgundy, this is

TRAVEL

✔ TIMELY TIPS

Hush-Hush Hotels

Tiny hotels, and oh-so-private

Ring the unmarked doorbell at 5, rue de Moussy, a small street in the chic Marais district of Paris, and you'll encounter an unaccustomed breed of luxury accommodation.

Found in some of Europe's most fashionable neighborhoods, these hotels are marked by several key characteristics: a striking (often eccentric) style, fewer than eight bedrooms, rarely any signs, nothing that resembles a reception area, a fan base built only by word of mouth and usually owners with a strong, and sometimes famous, personality.

Chic Retreats is a London-based agency with the motto "Small Is Beautiful" representing privately owned luxury hotels with fewer than 30 rooms. You can find more than a few of the properties on the agency's Web site (www.chicretreats.com) that fit within the haute B&B trend. The trend is moving to the States, too. Miami Beach has the five-suite Casa Tua, whose fitting motto is "Privacy Is So Precious."

Antwerp: Miauw Suites Antwerp, Marnixplaats 14. 32 (0)3 2484 707; www.analik.com/miauwantwerp.html

Madrid: Casa de Madrid, Arrieta, 2. (34-91) 5595791; www.casademadrid.com

Miami Beach: Casa Tua, 1700 James Avenue. 305-673-0973; www.casatualifestyle.com

Milan: 3Rooms 10 Corso Como, 10 Corso Como. (39-02) 626163 www.3rooms-10corsocomo.com

Ouderkerk aan de Amstel, the Netherlands: Lute Suites, 54-58 Amsteldijk Zuid. 31-20-4722462; www.lutesuites.com

Paris: 3Rooms 5 Rue de Moussy, 5, rue de Moussy. (33-1) 44.78.92.00 or email info@3rooms-5ruedemoussy.com

Rome: Residenza Napoleone III; Largo Goldoni, 56. 39-347-7337098; www.residenzanapoleone.com

Venice: Charming House DD.724, Dorsoduro 724. (39-041) 2770262; www.thecharminghouse.com

—Gisela Williams

one of the region's most elegant properties. 03.80.62.41.62; www.chateau-ziltener.com

La Bastide de Moustiers, *Moustiers St. Marie.* A 17th-century inn in the pilgrimage city of Moustiers. Its grounds feature a pool and a pasture of grazing horses. It has 12 rooms, some in cottages. The restaurant is a maze of cozy rooms. 04.92.70.47.47; www.bastide-moustiers.com

IRELAND (COUNTRY CODE 353)

Ballaghtobin, *Callan, County Kilkenny.* The town is an excellent location for exploring the counties of Waterford and Kilkenny. Bedrooms are absolutely gorgeous. Breakfast is the only meal served. 056-7725227; www.ballaghtobin.com

Coopershill, *Riverstown, County Sligo.* Built in 1774, the house offers the best of both worlds—the luxury of a country house hotel and the warmth of a home. 071-91-65108; www.coopershill.com

Rathsallagh House, *Dunlavin.* On 530 acres of farmland, it boasts stables and its own golf club. Hotel managers manage to retain the bonhomie of a friendly, relaxed country house, complete with touches like turf and log fires. 45-403112; www.rathsallaghhousehotel.com

Shelburne Lodge, *Kenmare, County Kerry.* A Georgian farmhouse with attractive grounds, but it is the interior that is outstanding. Scrumptious breakfasts. 064-41013; shelburne@kenmare.com

ITALY (COUNTRY CODE 39)

Albergo Villa Belvedere, *Argegno.* An enticing 18th-century villa. Only a private terrace separates it from Lake Como. This intimate inn is an incredible value, but the furnishings are simple. 031-82-11-16; www.villabelvedere-argegno.it

Hotel Flora, *Venice.* Located down a tiny lane, just off one of the main walkways to St. Mark's Square. Although it is a fairly simple hotel, it is a rare find for those who want a relatively inexpensive place to stay in the heart of Venice. 041-52-05 844; www.hotelflora.it

MEXICO

Dolphin Cove Inn, *Manzanillo, Colima.* A well-priced, charmingly decorated place to stay, with breathtaking views that can't be surpassed anywhere in Mexico, not at any price. Toll-free from U.S.: 866-360-9062; toll-free in Mexico: 800-713-3250; www.dolphincoveinn.com

La Casona, *Mexico City.* A beautifully managed small hotel nestled in a lovely residential area. 800-522-7662; www.hotellacasona.com

Hacienda de los Santos, *Alamos, Sonora.* If you are anywhere near the colonial village of Alamos, a wonderful old mining town, this hotel is a must. 647-428-0222 or 428-0217; www.haciendadelossantos.com

Finding a Vacation Villa

Rental agencies can do the legwork for you

The best way to save money on a vacation rental home is to bypass the middleman. You can save 20 to 30 percent by renting directly through the owner. A couple of ways to do so are to contact local tourist boards or to check the classified ads in college alumni magazines.

Rental agencies, on the other hand, offer the convenience of an experienced pro minding the details. If you use a rental agency, try to choose one with a local agent based near the town in which you intend to rent. That way, you'll have someone to contact in case anything goes wrong. Following are some resources.

MULTINATIONAL AGENCIES

At Home Abroad. Established in 1960, it has years of experience in catering to an upscale market. Villas, castles and apartments in the Caribbean, Europe and Mexico. 212-421-9165; www.athomeabroadinc.com

Barclay International. Specializes in upscale apartment and villa rentals in most major cities in Europe, plus cottage rentals in the U.K. Properties include flats in some luxury hotels. Stay as little as one night or by the week or month. 800-845-6636; www.barclayweb.com

British Travel International. Properties in France, England, Spain, Portugal, Ireland, Wales, Scotland and Italy, including over 9,000 country cottages. Linked up with Cottages4you. Also offers advice on hotels throughout Europe. 800-327-6097; www.britishtravel.com

Creative Leisure International. Private homes and resorts in Hawaii, the Caribbean, Mexico and Tahiti. Will arrange everything from airfare to activities. 800-413-1000; www.creativeleisure.com

Homes Away. Rentals in the south of France, in Umbria and Tuscany in Italy and in Andalucia and Catalonia in Spain. 800-374-6637; www.homesaway.com

Interhome. One of the oldest and largest home rental agencies in the world, with over 20,000 listings of apartments, houses and villas in Europe and the U.S. 800-882-6864; www.interhome.us

✔ TIMELY TIPS

Swapping Homes

How to save by trading places

A beach house in Carmel, a condo in Captiva, an apartment on the Champs Elysées—imagine vacationing at each and paying little more than the airfare. For the thousands of Americans who swap their homes with like-minded travelers, it's no daydream. House swapping is not a difficult undertaking. To get started, list your home with a home exchange agency such as Intervac or HomeLink. It is not expensive to list a home, but you must take care of setting up an exchange with the homeowner in your chosen destination.

The first step is to pick a few preferred destinations, and decide how long you want to visit (the average exchange is 2 to 3 weeks). Start planning 9 to 12 months before you intend to travel. When listing with an agency, describe your home in great detail, including amenities and access to tourist attractions as well as any pets, and include a picture of your home. About 75 percent of home swappers also exchange the use of their cars.

Once your home has been listed, you will be contacted by interested parties, who will provide information about themselves and their properties. You can also contact people whose properties interest you.

Home Exchange. Usually there is a listing fee. Arrangements are left to the homeowners. 800-877-8723; www.homeexchange.com

HomeLink International. Extensive listings worldwide and in the continental U.S. and Hawaii. Provide use of a database to members for a fee. Members make their own arrangements. 800-638-3841; www.homelink-usa.org

Intervac. Thousands of international and domestic listings for home exchanges. 800-756-4663; www.intervacusa.com

FRANCE

Fédération Nationale des Gîtes Ruraux de France. An organization that preserves old country houses and promotes rural tourism. The network consists of over 50,000 houses and modest apartments, or *gîtes*. 33-1-49-70-75-75; www.gites-de-france.fr

The French Experience. Has short-term rental apartments. It also handles reservations at small hotels, chateaux, bus/boat tours and various other excursions, with links to Web sites for Italy and the UK. 800-283-7262; www.frenchexperience.com

ITALY

Villa Vacations. Rents villas throughout Italy (also France and Spain) with or without house staff. Prices depend on the size and level of comfort of the home. The focus is on the higher end of the rental market. 800-261-4460; www.villavacations.com

SCANDINAVIA

Scanam World Tours. Rents private homes and offers tours throughout Scandinavia. 800-545-2204; www.scandinaviantravel.com

These tourist boards also have listings for vacation rentals:
www.visitdenmark.com
www.visitfinland.com
www.icelandtouristboard.com
www.visitnorway.com
www.visitsweden.com

SCOTLAND

National Trust Scotland. This is the Scottish equivalent of the National Trust in England (see

Dos and Don'ts of Private Rentals

How to avoid the pitfalls of renting long distance

The Internet has made it ever easier for travelers to search for vacation rentals across the globe, but at the same time it has also made it possible for just about anyone with a spare room to post a listing. So how do you avoid the pitfalls? First decide if you want to rent directly from an owner or from a property management company.

Professionally managed rentals, like most of the properties featured on Zonder.com, forGetaway.com and PickPackGo.com, promise a certain level of quality control since the homeowner pays the management company to inspect the home, clean it and handle any issues that arise— if a pipe bursts, for example, or the air conditioner suddenly gives out. And most accept credit card payments, which affords an added layer of protection in case the transaction goes sour. But the extra security tends to come at a higher cost.

Property managers charge homeowners anywhere from 10 to 45 percent of the rental revenue for services and commission, and some of that cost gets passed on to consumers. "There's a middleman there, with property managers," says Steve Hassett, who heads up for Getaway.com. "They have to make money off it. Some of that comes from the owner of the property and some from the renter, but both sides feel like it offers a lot of value."

No such quality control exists with owner-rented properties, found on sites like Homeaway.

com and Vrbo.com, but what you gain is cost savings. Both parties must work out the details of the rental agreement themselves, from the price to where to pick up the keys.

No matter who you rent from, it's a good idea to seek out recommendations from fellow renters. Vacation rental sites are increasingly offering customer reviews, making it easier to evaluate whether a property lives up to its description.

But how those reviews are handled varies quite a bit. For example, Cyberrentals.com, which is owned by Homeaway, notifies owners of user reviews before they are posted. This gives homeowners the opportunity to respond to unfair criticisms or to dispute false reviews posted by someone who did not stay there, the company says. Still, some users say that negative reviews have been censored. FlipKey.com, a vacation rental site, restricts reviews to past customers. To access the feedback page, users must receive an e-mail invitation.

After narrowing your search, don't be shy about asking for more photos. If the listing says the home has three bathrooms, but only pictures two, ask to see the third. Some sites like PickPackGo.com and Zonder.com show where each property is on a digital map, so users can see how far the property is from the ocean or other attractions. Once you have the address, you can also scope out the property on Google Earth, the satellite mapping service, or Zillow.com, which lists home valuations and amenities based on public records.

—Michelle Higgins

below). 28 Charlotte Square, Edinburgh, Scotland EH24ET. 844 493 2100, or from the U.S. toll-free: 1866 211 7573; www.nts.org.uk or www.nts.org.uk

UNITED KINGDOM

National Trust Holiday Booking. Travelers can find real bargains at this branch of the National Trust (a private charitable organization preserv-

ing national landmarks and gardens) in England. Through the trust they have access to 300 magnificent historic properties and cottages throughout England, Wales and Northern Ireland. The National Trust. P.O. Box 39, Warrington WA5 7WD. 0844 800 1895; www.nationaltrust.org.uk Click on the "Visits and Holidays" section for more information on rental properties.

UNITED STATES

Landmark Trust. A charitable trust that rescues and preserves historic landmarks from abandonment and neglect. The trust offers the restored properties as vacation rentals. All featured properties are quaint, rural and private. 707 Kipling Rd., Dummerston, Vt. 05301 802-257-7783; www.landmarktrustusa.org

Finding Room at a Monastery

Here are 11 heavenly places for resting body and soul

Christian monasteries have opened their doors to strangers in search of rest and reflection since the sixth century, when St. Benedict, founder of Western monasticism, made it a tenet that guests be received "as Christ himself." Robert Regalbuto, author of *A Guide to Monastic Guest Houses,* has been visiting monasteries and convents across the nation and in Canada since he was in prep school, decades ago. In his book he lists locations from midtown Manhattan to the Hawaiian rain forest.

The monasteries and convents span a spectrum of Christian traditions yet are open to visitors of all faiths. Generally they impose periods of quiet, and often some of the services and parts of the compounds are off-limits to visitors.

The rooms are typically spare, but the monastery and its surroundings can be splendid. A day's room and board may cost around $40 to $50 a person at most of these monasteries and convents to defray expenses, but in some cases, there is no fee required. Guest facilities are limited at most of these retreat houses, so make reservations well in advance. Here are some of Regalbuto's favorites.

Abbaye Cistercienne D'Oka *Roman Catholic,* Oka, Quebec J0N 1E0, Canada 450-479-8361; www.abbayeoka.com

Bay View Villa Guest and Retreat House *Roman Catholic,* Saco, Me. 04072 207-286-8762; scimsisters.org

Monastery of Society of John the Evangelist *Episcopal,* Cambridge, Mass. 02138 617-876-3037; www.ssje.org

New Camaldoli Hermitage *Roman Catholic,* Big Sur, Calif. 93920 408-667-2456; www.contemplation.com

Pecos Benedictine Monastery *Roman Catholic,* Pecos, N.M. 87510 505-757-6415, ext. 254; www.pecosabbey.org

St. Anselm's Abbey *Roman Catholic,* Washington, D.C. 20017 202-269-2300; www.stanselms.org; abbeyandguests@stanslems.org

St. Augustine's House *Lutheran,* Oxford, Mich. 48371 248-628-2604; www.staugustineshouse.org

St. John's Convent *Anglican,* Willowdale, Ontario M2N 2J5, Canada 416-226-2201 ext. 305; www.ssjd.ca/guesthouse

St. Leo Abbey *Roman Catholic,* Saint Leo, Fla. 33574, 352-588-8182; www.saintleoabbey.org/retreat

Skete of the Resurrection of Christ *Synod of Bishops of the Russian Orthodox Church in Exile,* Fridley, Minn. 55432 763-574-1001; www.skete.info

Weston Priory *Roman Catholic,* Weston, Vt. 05161 802-824-5409; www.westonpriory.org

How to Blog While on the Road
Start a travel blog and share your adventures

Reading an online travel blog may never have the romance of receiving a dog-eared postcard in the mail, but travelers armed with their digital cameras are finding that blogging on the road can be a good way to keep in touch with friends and family. To start your own blog, you can join one of a number of travel blog sites. Of course, anything you post online can be found by a Web-surfing stranger, so for privacy choose a site that offers password protection. Here are some travel blog site options.

BootsnAll (blogs.bootsnall.com) is free, but your membership must be approved, which can take 24 hours. The site hosts numerous travel blogs and offers a wide array of travel features, making it a good choice if you are also looking for inspiration for a trip.

Blogger.com, owned by Google, is not designed specifically for travelers, but unlike some travel sites, it allows you more freedom in posting pictures and designing your site. Choose from a variety of design templates and post your pictures through Flickr.com, the large photo site, by simply clicking on an icon. Since the site is not exclusively for travel bloggers, however, you won't find travel forums or easy ways to see other travelers' blogs. Both Blogger and Flickr are free.

IgoUgo.com is affiliated with Travelocity. It has thousands of members who regularly post detailed journals and photos. Each member fills out a personal profile that can be accessed by a journal reader. Four editors regularly read IgoUgo reviews and journals, and work with writers to sharpen them. Each journal is then rated by the editor, and subsequently by readers, on writing quality,

accuracy and usefulness—a great place to hone travel writing skills.

MyTripJournal.com features a convenient itinerary function that is linked to a map showing the route you are taking. MyTripJournal offers a free 45-day trial period, after which you pay a yearly fee. The fee includes storage of up to 60 photos a month.

TravelPod.com, one of the original sites, is simple to join and easy to use. It's free, unless you prefer to pay a fee and eliminate advertising banners from your page. It offers password protection. Features include a map of your destinations, with routes highlighted.

TravelBlog.org is free and very easy to navigate, making it a good site for first-time users. Its main page offers a world map that lets you read other people's journals by clicking on a particular location. A photo gallery lets you view the 30 top-rated travel pictures; the images change every 10 minutes.

—Fred Bierman and Joe Sharkey

More Sites for Travel Bloggers
Travel reporter Joe Sharkey's list of somewhat specialized blog sites for travelers

Airlinemeals.net
Flyertalk.com
Gadling.com
Joesentme.com
Johnnyjet.com
Lonelyplanet.com/travel.blog/community
Offbeattravel.com
Onlinetravelreview.com
Realtravel.com
Topsites.blogflux.com/travel
Travelbuddy.com
Travelpost.com Tripadvisor.com
Womenstravelclub.com.

Great Destinations

Asia's Next New Meccas

Four exotic spots for cultural exploration or simple relaxation

Asia has emerged as one of the fastest growing tourist markets in the world, both for the hard-core adventurer and the upscale vacationer just looking for a nice place to relax. According to the World Tourism Organization, India and Southeast Asian countries like Vietnam, Cambodia and Indonesia have had double-digit increases in international tourists in recent years. For those who want to stay ahead of the crowds, here are a few emerging destinations with the makings of the next Asian hot spots.

Laos. Waves of travelers are being lured to Laos by the promise of extreme luxury and the Southeast Asian government's embrace of eco-tourism. The picturesque town of Luang Prabang, named a Unesco World Heritage Site for its unique blend of Laotian and European architecture, has some upscale offerings: Villa Maly, with 33 rooms and a central building that was once the residence of a Laotian prince and princess, and Amanresorts, by the luxury hotelier.

Elsewhere in the country, eco-tourism is gaining ground. The Laotian government is developing eco-tourism projects in Luang Namtha, Luang Prabang, Khammouane and Champassak provinces, according to Ecotourismlaos.com, an official site of the Lao National Tourism Administration.

Tour companies currently offer tours of the Plain of Jars, an area in northern Laos known for its ancient stone urns. For people excited by archaeology and unsolved mysteries, the site is a perfect match. There are also many hill tribes in the area, allowing for more cultural exploration.

Vietnam. For some time now, Vietnam has been popular with budget travelers for its cheap eats, low-priced lodging and shops that count on travelers to bargain for souvenirs. But that isn't stopping luxury hotels like the Four Seasons and Banyan Tree from trying to turn Vietnam into a posh getaway. After all, the country offers beautiful beaches, exotic cuisine and a burgeoning art scene. It also has Unesco World Heritage Sites like the ancient town of Hoi An, a well-preserved example of a traditional Southeast Asian trading port, and Ha Long Bay in the Gulf of Tonkin, with some 1,600 limestone islands and islets jutting out of the water. (For traveling to Vietnam with kids, see page 571.)

Some upscale hotel chains, like Park Hyatt, can be found in Ho Chi Minh City, the country's largest city. But if you are seeking out lesser known regions, Six Senses, based in Bangkok, has a high-end resort on the remote island of Con Dao in southeast Vietnam. The resort has 51 villas with private infinity pools (some villas have two) and a private plane to shuttle guests from Ho Chi Minh City, 45 minutes away. Six Senses resorts are found also in Nha Trang, on the south central coast, and Dalat, in the central highlands.

Banyan Tree is developing a complex with hotels, spas and an 18-hole golf course along a pristine stretch of the famed China Beach on the south central coast. And in the works is a 75-room Four Seasons resort on Charn Island, a 15-minute boat ride from historic Hoi An.

Cambodia's Magnificent Ruins

Seeing Angkor Wat and staying next door

Angkor, Cambodia, was once the most magnificent city in Indochina. At its height, the Khmer empire extended from the coasts of Vietnam to the borders of Burma. Angkor Wat, the most famous of the country's ancient ruins, as well as one of the better preserved, was built in the 12th century. The walls of Angkor Thom, one of the ancient capitals, enclose a space larger than that of any medieval European city.

Khmer cities were allegorical representations of the heavens, built around temples constructed atop natural or man-made hills. Most of the architecture combines Hindu and Buddhist symbolism. Angkor Wat boasts the longest bas-relief in existence, extending over 12,000 feet.

The town next door: Siem Reap, the town that lodges and feeds Angkor's million annual visitors, is a chic haven of rest and relaxation. An international group of chefs has set up the country's finest tables there, and bartenders in the vibrant nightlife are versed in sophisticated cocktails.Contemporary art galleries seem intent on nurturing local artists. It's as though Siem Reap is picking up where the Angkorian kings left off some 600 years ago, resurrecting itself as the center of Khmer taste and culture.

Cambodian cooking doesn't get the attention it deserves, especially compared with the fare of its food-trendy neighbors, Thailand and Vietnam. Though the basic ingredients are similar—lemongrass, garlic, ginger, fish sauce—Khmer cooking is subtler and lighter, employing less chili, pungent herbs and coconut

milk. For an innovative lesson on local flavors, sample the seven-course Khmer tasting menu at Méric, a dimly lighted Art Deco-themed restaurant, also at the Hôtel de la Paix (note: dollars are widely accepted in Siem Reap).

Getting around: If the lure of limos, plunge pools and glamorized peasant food leads you to Siem Reap, here's what you'll need to know.

The tuk-tuk, or motorized rickshaw, is the most common means of transport, since Siem Reap has no formal taxi service. Most rides around town cost less than $2.

Renting a car is more relaxing. Your hotel can arrange anything from a four-wheel drive to a vintage limo.

To see the temples by helicopter, contact Angkor Scenic Flights, (855-12-814-500; www.helicopterscambodia.com). It'll cost you.

Where to stay: More than 100 hotels now serve tourists of all budgets.

Raffles Grand Hotel d'Angkor (855-63-963-888; www.raffles.com). The past is on display here: a white gravel driveway, iron-cage elevator, colonial-style bathroom fixtures and ceiling fans.

Hôtel de la Paix (855-63-966-000; www.hoteldelapaix angkor.com) is relatively new, though its roots run back a half-century to an Art Deco hotel that stood on the same spot.

La Résidence d'Angkor (855-63-963-390; www.residence dangkor.com). Its Khmer chic rooms have hardwood floors, silk and bamboo accents and giant whirlpool tubs. Rooms start at $175.

—Matt Gross and Naomi Lindt

Times Picks: 43 Must-See Destinations

From the Aegean Sea to Zambia, these compelling places were recently selected by New York Times *contributing travel writers Seth Sherwood and Gisela Williams as not-to-be-missed destinations. The sites are awash in sublime landscapes, cutting-edge art, gala music festivals, and stylish new resorts.*

Beirut, Lebanon	**Seychelles**
Washington, D.C.	**Florianópolis, Brazil**
Galapagos	**Copenhagen, Denmark**
Berlin, Germany	**Boracay, Philippines**
Las Vegas, Nevada	**Monument Valley**
Fjalinas, Sweden	**Star Island, Bahamas**
Hawaii	**Castles in Britain**
Vienna, Austria	**Cologne, Germany**
Doha, Qatar	**Reykjavik, Iceland**
Dakar, Senegal	**Red Sea, Egypt**
Maremma, Italy	**Deauville, France**
Phuket, Thailand	**South Africa**
Marrakesh, Morocco	**India**
Chicago, Illinois	**Kazakhstan**
Aegean Sea	**Madagascar**
Monterrey, Mexico	**Metz, France**
Dallas, Texas	**Tasmania**
Bhutan	**Stockholm, Sweden**
Florida Keys	**Alaska**
Rome, Italy	**Lancaster, Pa.**
Cuba	**Zambia**
Penang, Malaysia	

Hainan Island, China. Floating off the southern tip of China, the tropical island of Hainan has drawn vacationers from mainland China for years with palm-fringed beaches and warm temperatures year round.

Major resorts along its shores include Starwood's Le Méridien, the Fairmont and the Four Seasons. Most of the high-end developments are clustered in Sanya, on the island's southern coast. A 450-room Ritz-Carlton has 33 pool villas, each with a private butler. The Banyan Tree, with 61 villas in nearby Luhuitou Bay, and the Mandarin Oriental, with more than 290 rooms, are two other luxury resorts.

Concierge.com, the travel Web site of *Condé Nast Traveller,* has put Hainan Island on its "It" list, naming it one of the 10 must-see destinations and even comparing it to Hawaii, without the Honolulu high-rises and crowds.

Kerala, India. Goa, the former hippie enclave on India's west coast, is often cited as the hot spot for travelers seeking spiritual enlightenment and all-night beach parties.

Kerala, about 400 miles south of Goa along India's southwestern tip, is emerging as a quieter alternative with its long shorelines, sprawling plantations and soothing spas that specialize in the healing practice of ayurveda, the traditional Hindu medicine of India.

There are dozens of ayurvedic spas and health centers to choose from. One of the newest is at the Leela Kempinski Kovalam Beach hotel, which has an 8,000-square-foot spa ayurvedic wellness center called Divya with 18 therapists, four physicians trained in ayurvedic medicine and an open-air meditation hall.

So far, foreigners make up a small fraction of the visitors to Kerala. For example, 515,808 foreign tourists visited Kerala in 2007, compared with about 6.64 million domestic tourists. But the number of foreign visitors is growing fast, according to Keralatourism.org, the official Web site of the Kerala Department of Tourism.

Indeed, Western tour companies have started adding Kerala to their standard India itineraries. "Kerala is an up-and-coming destination but still relatively unknown," says Manuela Khoury, director of hotel relations for Butterfield & Robinson, a biking and walking tour company. The company has added Kerala to its repertory of active travel trips. (For more hot spots in India, see facing page.)

—Michelle Higgins

Beyond the Taj Mahal
There's more to India than a Mughal mausoleum

Not so long ago, India, a country of one billion people and more than 100 languages, seemed to have just three tourist destinations: Delhi, Mumbai and the Rajasthan-Taj Mahal circuit. But, thanks to an aviation agreement between India and the United States, it should become easier to reach far-flung parts of the subcontinent, like the east coast cities of Pondicherry and Chennai.

Pondicherry was France's only possession in India, and it retains some of that Gallic flair (policemen in képis, colonial architecture) with the laid-back air of a university town, albeit one with gorgeous golden beaches. One place to stay is the moderately-priced Hôtel de l'Orient, a converted 18th-century mansion (17, rue Romain Rolland,

(91-413) 234-3067; www.neemranahotels.com/pondi).

Eighty miles up the coast, Chennai (formerly Madras, the first big British settlement in India), has millennium-old temples and a thriving technology industry, zoos and markets where whole streets are devoted to selling single products (from lentils to gray-market digital cameras), cricket grounds and one of the longest beaches in the world. You'll find three high-end properties there, the most opulent and modern of which is the Taj Coromandel (37 Mahatma Gandhi Road, (91-044) 6600-2827; www.tajhotels.com).

You won't necessarily find the newest boutique hotels at these places—yet. But they are major cities with their own distinctive scenes and cuisines, and they are far more exciting than the overly documented, postcard-perfect sights and monuments elsewhere in India.

—Matt Gross

✔ TIMELY TIPS

Moonlight on the Taj

Visitors can see the Taj Mahal by moonlight, thanks to a 2005 ruling by India's Supreme Court. The white marble mausoleum, in the northern city of Agra, had been closed at night over fears of Sikh separatist attacks.

✔ You can see the Taj Mahal from 8:30 p.m. to 12:30 a.m. from a platform about 350 yards away, on five nights a month—when the moon is full, as well as the two nights before and after.

✔ Only 50 people at a time are allowed, for 30 minutes. You must buy tickets at least 24 hours in advance, at the entrance ticket office or from tour operators in India.

✔ Contact the Government of India Tourist Office, 212-586-4901; incredibleindia.org.

—Marjorie Connelly

High Living in the Persian Gulf
Dubai gushes with lots more than oil

Described as both the city of the future and the city that hype built, Dubai, one of the seven United Arab Emirates, is what happens when unimaginable wealth meets unlimited ambition. You name it, Dubai has it. Or if it doesn't have it, it's building it. Or if it's not building it, it's dredging up an island to put it on. Dubai is growing so fast that its newest developments can only be measured in hummingbird flaps. Blink and you'll miss the latest superlative. This way to the world's tallest building. That way to the world's largest aluminum plant. Over here to the world's biggest mall.

What to do.

• Seawings seaplane company (971-4-883-3532; www.seawings.ae) provides a 30-minute tour of the city from 1,500 feet overhead: the iconic sail profile of the Burj Al Arab, the impossibly high Burj Dubai building and the artificial archipelagoes fashioned in the shapes of palm trees and continents.

- The Els Club is what you get when you cross 7,500 yards of soft green sod, an opinionated champion golfer and possibly the world's largest sand trap. The 18-hole course (www.elsclubdubai.com) was designed by Ernie Els as a compendium of his favorite links from around the world. The club is in the middle of Dubai Sports City (971-4-425-1111; www.dubaisportscity.ae).

- One of the grandest spas is at the InterContinental Dubai Festival City (Festival City; 971-4-701-1111; www.intercontinental.com/dubai). The spa evokes another world, with flowing strands of neon that resemble seaweed dangling from the ceiling.

- Champagne Bar (971-4-324-8888; www.dubai.raffles.com). Ensconced within the glass apex of the Raffles Hotel, it is one of the hottest—and highest—bars in Dubai. But what makes it really memorable is not the giant pharaoh head guarding the stairway, or the high-priced Veuve Clicquot. It's the view: 360 degrees of twinkling sprawl stretching out to the Arabian Desert.

Where to eat.

- The Fire & Ice Restaurant at the Raffles Hotel (971-4-324-8888; www.dubai.raffles.com) can only be described as warm and inviting: exposed brick walls, leather chairs and flattering lighting. But it's not without its gimmicks. The open-air kitchen is ringed by fire, and the "ice tartar" dishes are injected with liquid nitrogen so they emit a milky white vapor. The menu, billed as "trans-ethnic," is vast.

- Special Ostadi Restaurant (Al Mussalla Road, Bur Dubai; 971-4-397-1469) has only a handful of tables, all covered in a half-century of memorabilia and all packed with local businessmen wearing traditional kaffiyehs or shiny Italian suits. The natives come for one thing: grilled lamb kebabs doused in a tangy yogurt sauce and served with pita, onions, cucumbers, arugula, tomatoes and a fat wedge of lime. Order a dish of sweet dates and a cup of mint tea to wash it all down.

- Thiptara Royal Thai at the Palace, a Sofitel hotel (Old Town; 971-4-428-7888; www.sofitel.com) is as remarkable for its spicy Thai food as its vantage point—steps from the world's tallest building, the Burj Dubai. The restaurant features rich wooden fixtures, lakefront views and terrific dishes like spicy green papaya salad and the chicken stir-fry with cashews, mushrooms and pineapple.

Where to stay.

- Park Hyatt Dubai (Dubai Creek Golf and Yacht Club; 971-4-602-1234; www.dubai.park.hyatt.com) is in the quieter area of Deira and affords great city views. It has a wonderful in-house spa, and a relaxing outdoor bar overlooking the harbor.

- Raffles, Sheikh Rashid Road, Wafi City (971-4-324-8888; www.dubai.raffles.com) is close to the action. The common areas are vast and daunting, but the rooms are spacious and comfortable.

- XVA Gallery in the arty Bastakiya neighborhood (971-4-353-5383; www.xvagallery.com) has only eight rooms and feels like a North African souk.

—Danielle Pergament and Warren Singh-Bartlett

INSIDE INFO

In the Islands

○ The Caribbean islands and the Bahamas together form the West Indies. The islands between the Atlantic and the Caribbean Sea are called the Antilles.

○ Cuba, Jamaica, Haiti and Puerto Rico comprise the Greater Antilles.

○ The Lesser Antilles are divided into the Leeward Islands (north of Dominica) and the Windward Islands (all those from Dominica to Trinidad and Tobago).

○ For more information go to the Caribbean Tourism Organization: www.oneCaribbean.org.

TRAVEL

The Caribbean on the Cheap

Where to find paradise at bargain prices

The Caribbean islands have long been America's tourist playground. Perennially popular islands, such as Puerto Rico, the American Virgin Islands and even once-deserted St. Bart's pack in the crowds. Some travelers find all the activity appealing. But those who dream of basking on their own solitary beach can take comfort: there are many islands yet to be discovered in the more than 2,700 scattered within a 2,500-mile-long arc stretching from just south of Florida to the coast of Venezuela. If sun-drenched, bustle-free, natural paradises are your goal, here are some great choices: six off-the-beaten-path affordable Caribbean islands. Don't worry about being too far from civilization, though—the larger islands are just a short plane or boat ride away.

Antigua. Antigua has long been synonymous with tucked-away upscale resorts like Jumby Bay and the newer Hermitage Bay, where rates can run $500

to $1,000 a night. But the island's vibe is actually more natural than showy, and there is a variety of more affordable lodging options, from budget guesthouses to small inns, including in the popular Dickenson Bay and English Harbour areas.

The island's big yachting scene is centered on Antigua's south shore, along English Harbour and the adjoining Falmouth Harbour, and there is no better place to feel a part of it than at Admiral's Inn (English Harbour; 268-460-1027; www.admiralsantigua. com). The inn is part of Nelson's Dockyard National Park, a historic restoration of the naval base that the future Admiral Horatio Nelson commanded. The main building dates from 1788, and while its rooms are simple (no TV or radio, some without air conditioning), the waterfront setting is truly charming, and the service is gracious. It also has a delightful restaurant with an inviting terrace and reasonable room prices, even in high season.

For a different view of English Harbour, the Ocean Inn (268-463-7950; www.theoceaninn. com) is a B&B perched on a steep hill with mod-

Underwater Treasures
Best off-shore diving spots

Experienced divers exploring popular Caribbean spots such as Little Cayman's Bloody Bay Wall or the Wreck of the Rhone in the British Virgin Islands know well the telltale sign of underwater traffic jams: circles of dive boats moored at the busiest destinations. Avoiding underwater crowds may require an extra plane connection, but there is a reward: more tranquil wonders above and below water. Here are four lesser-known destinations that should guarantee more fish life than fellow divers.

SABA. Five-square mile Saba (pronounced SAH-buh) in the Netherlands Antilles is a rain-forest-covered peak of an island with nary a beach. Underwater, the slope continues, notably in the form of coral- and sponge-encrusted volcanic pinnacles 70 feet and more below the surface. Within the protected Saba Marine Park (www.sabapark.

org), the gorgonian and orange elephant ear sponges are vividly healthy, and the marine life gets big: reef sharks, hawksbill turtles and massive tiger groupers.

TOBAGO. The chance to swim with manta rays lures divers to Tobago, Trinidad's smaller, less-developed neighbor. The Orinoco River's nutrient-rich runoff makes Tobago's reef and marine life prolific. The mantas prowl year round, and great hammerheads school in winter. Coral heads grow to super size, including a brain coral that is 16 feet across and growing. Sluicing the underwater scene are gonzo currents, which often run three or four knots, making this a destination for experienced divers.

DOMINICA. Don't go for powdery beaches or fancy resorts: there aren't any. Divers make the trip to aim their lenses at rare small stuff, like sea horses and frog fish. It's also one of the Caribbean's best spots to see

dolphins and whales, especially from December through March. Day-Glo reefs bristle with netted barrel sponges and green finger sponges. There's underwater volcanic drama as well, with steep 600-foot walls, gaping craters, tunnel-like swim-throughs and geothermal vents that force up warm freshwater bubbles at the Champagne dive site.

GLOVERS REEF ATOLL, BELIZE. It's tough to go far wrong diving the atolls beyond the world's second-largest barrier reef, off the coast of Belize. Eons of coral growth along giant geological fault lines have produced sheer, 2,000-foot dropoffs. Belize's two major atolls, Turneffe Islands and Lighthouse Reef, have renowned dive sites, among them the 412-foot-deep Blue Hole. But farther south, Glovers is out of reach for daytrippers and, therefore, often all yours to explore. You can stay on 13-acre Long Caye.

—Susan Enfield Esrey

erately-priced rooms and thousand-dollar views year round.

In Antigua's northwest, somewhat isolated at the south end of Dickenson Bay, is the Marina Bay Beach Resort (Corbisons Point; 268-462-3254; www.marinabayag.com), a nicely landscaped condo complex that offers studios and spacious one-bedroom units for rent. Each is different, but all have air-conditioning, kitchens and balconies with water views. It is about 50 yards to the least-

crowded section of the white-sand beach and a brief walk to Sandals and other major resorts.

A little inland from Dickenson Bay is the Anchorage Inn (Anchorage Road, St. John's; 268-462-4065; www.antiguaanchorageinn.com), a colorful small hotel with a pretty courtyard and pool.

—Ray Cormier

Aruba. This Dutch territory just off the coast of Venezuela can feel vaguely like Atlantic City.

Fancy resorts line the touristy zone of Palm Beach. Sun-kissed visitors in baseball caps flock to its shiny casinos. But if you are willing to venture off the beaten path, you can discover a more authentic Aruba, and still have enough money to gamble away at the casinos.

Million-dollar mansions in vibrant colors dot Malmok, a seaside community just north of Palm Beach. A cheaper slice of this picturesque shore can be found at **Ocean 105** (L. G. Smith Boulevard 105; 297-592-0287; www.arubaoceanfront. com), a moderately priced boutique hotel nestled on a coral ledge overlooking the Caribbean. Steps away is Boca Catalina beach, known for spectacular snorkeling.

It's also possible to enjoy Palm Beach on the cheap, as long as you're willing to give up amenities like high-thread-count sheets and ocean views. The bohemian-style Arubiana Inn (Bubali 74; 297-587-7700; www.arubianainn. com) is about a mile from beaches, casinos and shopping. Comfortable rooms start at under $100 a night during high season.

A stay at the no-frills Talk of The Town Hotel and Beach Club (L. G. Smith Boulevard 2; 297-582-3380; www.tottaruba.com) lands you across the street from Surfside Beach and a short walk to the shopping district in Oranjestad, the island's frilly Dutch capital. —Jonathan Vigliotti

Cayman Islands. Signs of wealth and extravagance on Grand Cayman are difficult to miss. From the mansions along the southern shore to a Ritz-Carlton resort so large it straddles the island's major thoroughfare, travelers know they have arrived in the Caribbean's kingdom of offshore finance. But if dropping thousands of dollars a night on a suite at the Ritz is not in your budget, you'll be relieved to learn that economizing on Grand Cayman can be done.

Instead of a full-service resort on the beach, book one of the less fancy hotels just off the water's edge. The Sunshine Suites Resort (1465 Esterley Tibbetts Highway; 877-786-1110; www. sunshinesuites.com) is a surprising bargain on an oasis of palms and manicured Bermuda grass opposite Seven Mile Beach, where most of the island's hotels are clustered. Before booking a room online, call first to inquire about specials.

The Comfort Suites (Seven Mile Beach, West Bay Road; 800-517-4000; www.caymancomfort.com) at the southern end of Seven Mile Beach is a bit more

TIMELY TIPS

The Pearl of the Atlantic Regains Its Luster

For decades, Punta del Este, a resort town in the southeast corner of Uruguay, was the Hamptons of Latin America, a watering hole for 1960s film icons like Gina Lollabrigida and Yul Brynner. But the "Pearl of the Atlantic" fell out of favor in the '90s with the development of one too many high-rises and the economic breakdown of nearby Argentina. In recent years, however, Americans have rediscovered Punta, a town with miles of beaches and a bohemian mix of people, from New York socialites to musicians to Brazilian models.

✔ About 25 miles north of Punta is José Ignacio, the secret epicenter of its bohemian jet set.

✔ For dinner, try La Huella (598-486-2279; www.paradorlahuella.com), a rustic beachside spot in José Ignacio that serves grilled fish and sushi.

✔ But the ultimate insider spot is Marismo, a restaurant in José Ignacio that supposedly only people with good directions know how to find. O.K., here's the phone number: 598-486-2273.
—Gisela Williams

commercial, but also offers modern, moderately priced accommodations.   —Jeremy W. Peters

Eleuthera, Bahamas. Lovers of casinos and glitzy boutiques can cross Eleuthera off their lists. But if you value glorious uncrowded beaches, open countryside, and kind and friendly local people, this could be the island for you. A narrow 110-mile-long strip of land 70 miles east of Nassau, Eleuthera is little more than an hour by plane from Florida but embodies the Bahamas Out Island experience: rural, unspoiled and easygoing.

Harbour Island, a three-mile-long cay just off the main island that has drawn celebrities and jet setters to its gorgeous pink sands, is generally expensive but has some affordable options in Dunmore Town, Eleuthera's oldest and liveliest settlement.

Tingum Village International Hotel (Colebrook Street, Dunmore Town; 242-333-2161; www.tingumvillagehotel.com) anchors a small island empire owned by the enterprising Percentie family. The six garden-shaded rooms at the Bahama House Inn (Dunmore and Hill Streets, Dunmore Town; 242-333-2201; www.bahamahouseinn.com) are slightly more pricey, but breakfast is included.

On Eleuthera's main island, near its middle, is the Tropical Dreams Motel Resort (North Palmetto Point; 242-332-1632; www.eleu.net/tropicaldreams.html), a modest, two-story motel that offers clean, simple rooms with kitchens.

Turks and Caicos. Once a haven for divers, the island of Providenciales in the Turks and Caicos chain is now one of the Caribbean's fanciest. Luxury resorts with security gates, high-end condos and designer golf courses now dot the sun-soaked island, leaving fewer choices for the budget traveler. But if you're willing to forgo infinity pools and mud wraps at the flashy megaresorts, you can still have a rich experience on this little island, affectionately nicknamed Provo.

Budget options on this pricey island are almost nonexistent. Sibonné Beach Hotel (Grace Bay Beach; 649-946-5547; www.sibonne.com) may be the best and only bargain on Grace Bay Beach, the island's famed 12 miles of shimmering white sands and sparkling blue waters. This charming two-story hotel has 28 rooms decorated in an island motif. Snag one of its two "value" rooms, located on the first floor, for a bit of a break on prices; these rooms can be booked only by phone. It also has a terrific beachfront restaurant, Bay Bistro (649-946-5396), which serves modern Caribbean dishes.

If you don't mind walking 5 minutes to get your beach fix, check into Grace Bay Suites (Grace Bay Road; 649-941-7447; www.gracebaysuites.com). This new three-story hotel features bright and spacious studios furnished with cushy king-size beds, kitchenettes and glass walk-in showers. All 24 rooms have private patios or balconies.
                                                            —Miki Meek

Cuba: So Near and Yet So Far

Access to the island is easing

With its magnificent, unspoiled beauty and beautiful beaches, Cuba seduces in many ways. To American tourists, it represents the taste of a forbidden fruit—a land that has been off-limits since 1961. But one day soon, and even sooner if you have a reason, you'll be able to go to Cuba.

With a few exceptions, the United States government does not allow Americans to travel to Cuba, just 90 miles from Key West. Among those permitted to travel under a General License (no application necessary) are accredited journalists, research professionals and government officials.

 **TIMELY TIPS**

For Singles Only

✔ **Connecting: Solo Travel Network.** It provides practical information for people traveling by themselves, as part of a tour group or independently, and supplies members with lists of singles-friendly cruise and tour companies to help avoid single supplements. There is a one-time $25 registration fee. The site includes a calendar of singles-only tours and cruises and a bimonthly newsletter. 800-557-1757; www.cstn.org

✔ **Meet Market Adventures.** Specializes in weekend getaways, cruises, international tours and local day trips for single men and women, most of whom are in their 30s and 40s. Clients are matched with a roommate to avoid paying the single supplement. 800-239-0542; www.meetmarketadventures.com

✔ **Singles Travel International.** Organizes activities from weekend getaways to full-length tours to appeal to a wide age range, but it typically provides for clients over 35 and unmarried. The company guarantees a roommate if requested 60 days before departure. 877-765-6874; www.singlestravelintl.com

(For more on singles travel, see page 597.)

Everyone else must get a permit known as a Specific License, issued by the Foreign Assets Control office in the Department of the Treasury. That includes people traveling for educational or religious activities, or to visit immediate relatives.

Though some Americans travel to Cuba from a third country like Mexico or Canada, they risk substantial fines. For more information and travel arrangements, contact Marazul Charters, 4100 Park Avenue, Weehawken, N.J. 07086 (800-223-5334, 201-319-1054; www.marazul.com).

All licensed travelers must also get a visa from the Cuban government. Visas can be obtained through the Cuban Interests Section, 2630 16th Street N.W., Washington, D.C. 20009 (202-797-8518). Foreign currency must be changed to Cuban convertible pesos; for the best exchange rate, take euros or Canadian dollars.

The best hotel in Havana is Hotel Nacional, Calle O at 21, Vedado, (53-7-873-3564; www.hotelnacionaldecuba.com). In the '30s, Hemingway stayed at the Hotel Ambos Mundos, Calle Obispo 153, Old Havana (53-7-860-9529; www.hotelambosmundos-cuba.com), which has undergone a restoration.

There's really only one main attraction in the capital: Old Havana, with museums, cathedrals, plazas, hotels, restaurants and bars. But other areas of Havana—mainly Vedado, Miramar and Siboney—are worth a car tour to get a better view of how the elite live. Outside Havana, the scenic Pinar del Río Province (southwest of Havana) is 3-hour drive on bus tours that leave daily from major Havana hotels. —Luisita Lopez Torregrosa

Costa Rica's Many Charms
For beach lovers, nature geeks and thrill seekers

Costa Rica is tiny, smaller than West Virginia, but huge in versatility, with coasts on two oceans, coral-lined beaches and active volcanoes, luxury resorts and surf camps, roaring streams and rich biodiversity. Twenty-seven percent of Costa Rica's land area is devoted to national parks and reserves, one of the highest percentages for any country.

Monteverde, which is the primary place marketed to eco-tourists, is between two reserves—Monteverde and Santa Elena—deep in the Costa Rican highlands. With its verdant cloud forest and 1,000 endemic plant species, Monteverde offers the pilgrimage to nature that many seek from the tropics It is also well developed, with hotels, several restaurants, shops and art galleries.

Costa Rica is known as one of the best and closest foreign adventure tourism destinations for the United States. The surfing, particularly on the Nicoya Peninsula, is first class. The volcano hiking and Caribbean scuba diving are not far behind. Rafting near Turrialba offers some of the most scenic whitewater an amateur can access—and some of the most challenging.

Manuel Antonio. Several of the country's best beaches are preserved in Manuel Antonio, Costa Rica's smallest and most popular national park, with about 4,000 acres and 150,000 annual visitors. Twenty-five years ago the area nearby held no more than a few cheap cabanas. Now a luxury infrastructure has grown up, but compared with Mexican resort towns like Cancún or Cabo San Lucas, the area still doesn't feel overdeveloped.

To reach the town if you don't like buses, fly to Quepos from San José on Sansa (www.flysansa. com). Manuel Antonio National Park is open 7 a.m. to 4 p.m. daily except Mondays.

The Parador (506-2777-1414; www.hotelparador. com) is the best bet for standard resort-spa luxury.

Makanda by the Sea (506-2777-0442; www. makanda.com) rents moderately priced villas.

Monteverde. The Hotel Belmar has dark-paneled rooms near the jungle and overlooking gardens. (506-2645-5201; www.hotelbelmar.net)

The Monteverde Lodge & Gardens (www. costaricaexpeditions.com) offers all-inclusive stays, including meals and activities.

Turrialba. If you need creature comforts (like air-conditioning) between days of adrenaline, Hotel Wagelia (506-2556-1566; www.hotelwageliaturrialba. com) is the place to go.

Hotel Interamericano (506-2556-0142; www.hotelinter americano.com) offers Spartan accomodations at rock-bottom prices.

Run the Pacuare River with Rio Locos Tropical Tours (506-2556-6035; www.whiteh2o.com) or Rainforest World (506-2556-0014; www.rforestw.com).

—Ethan Todras-Whitehill

Next Stop: Panama

This eco-tourist spot holds plenty of adventure and a mild climate

Tucked in the highlands near the Barú volcano, in the western Chiriquí region of Panama, Boquete is emerging as one of Central America's latest eco-tourism destinations. Surrounded by green mountains topped by misty, craggy peaks, Boquete offers plenty of outdoors adventure, like hiking, climbing, bird-watching and white-water rafting. And thanks to a 3,000-foot elevation, the area's microclimate deducts 10 crucial degrees from the incessant lowland heat.

But unlike most eco-tourist hot spots, Boquete draws people not just to its natural beauty, however lush it may be, but also to its snowbird enclave. Attracted first by the Napa-like weather and low cost of living, and then by the lax real estate laws, not to mention potable tap water, several thousand foreign families own homes in Boquete, according to a local developer.

And while Boquete's real estate market was once dominated by porch-swinging retirees, the latest wave of arrivals tends to be younger couples in their 40s and 50s. Many are opening so-called hobby businesses, restaurants, touring companies, bed-and-breakfasts and wellness spas, all geared for tourists.

Tourism is still light, at least compared to Costa Rica next door, but that is changing. Young tourists, armed with Lonely Planet guides and digital cameras, are increasingly visiting. As one local puts is, Boquete is like Costa Rica was 15 years ago. The comparison is apt but not entirely accurate. Like the popular mountain towns Monteverde and La Fortuna in Costa Rica, Boquete is capitalizing on its forests, rivers and abundant wildlife. But development in Panama is following a more upscale track.

Tourists arrive in rented S.U.V.'s from David, Panama's fourth-largest city, and stay in the high-end hotels hidden off the main road and perched up in the hills. One that is popular with honeymooners is the Panamonte Inn and Spa (Avenida April 11; 507-720-1324; panamonteinnandspa.com), which offers first-name service, candlelit dinners and spa wraps and massages.

Another upscale hotel, La Montaña y el Valle Coffee Estate Inn (Jaramillo Arriba Road; 507-720-2211; coffeeestateinn.com), has three secluded bungalows set among jade green coffee trees and exotic flower gardens.

Boquete's reputation is as a counterpart to Bocas del Toro, Panama's epicenter for Caribbean-style carousal. Whereas the coast is ideal for the partying singles set, there's nary a nightclub pushing beats into Boquete's fresh night air. After sunset, when most of the tourists have retreated to their luxurious hotels and hillside B&Bs, the town square is as quiet as a church.

Morning is when Boquete springs to life. Most days, a steady stream of blue rafts can be spotted bobbing down the Chiriquí Viejo, Gariche and Dolega rivers. One of the region's oldest outfits, Chiriquí River Rafting (Avenida Central; 507-720-1505; panama-rafting.com) runs daily trips, from beginners' to Class IV rapids.

For those who want to remain dry, Coffee Adventures (507-720-3852; coffeeadventures.net) offers tours of the Kotowa coffee plantation, which claims Panama's oldest coffee mill. Visitors hike through rows of coffee trees, meet the pickers and, of course, sample fresh brews in the mill's cupping room.

Panama also offers magnificent bird-watching. The forests in and around Boquete are home to a dazzling array of quetzals, toucans and parrots. But for adventure-seekers, there's only one way to appreciate Boquete's natural beauty: "tree trekking," or zip-lining. Boquete Tree Trek (Avenida Central; 507-720-1635; aventurist.com) offers half-day trips. After a bumpy uphill ride in the back of a pickup truck, nervous tourists are strapped into harnesses and sent on free-falls through the dense jungle canopy.

—Jeff Koyen

Beyond Hawaii's Big Island
These three are beautiful and less traveled

Of the eight Hawaiian islands, it's possible to visit only six: Kahoolawe is uninhabited, and Niihau is privately owned. The popular islands, Oahu, Maui and Hawaii (known as the Big Island), are still a visitor's paradise but one that must be shared with hordes of other tourists, increasingly marred by gridlock and relentless resort development. Fortunately, there are three other Hawaiian options—paradises that are less-trod and perhaps more inviting. Here's a guide.

Kauai

Kauai *533 sq. mi.* Of all the islands, Kauai has the most beautiful natural scenery, thanks partly to its abundant rainfall. The top of Mt. Waialeale (5,238 ft.) is the rainiest place on earth, and the island's interior is virtually impenetrable

The ancient Hawaiians had two ways to get around the tortuously steep mountains that rise along the Na Pali Coast of Kauai. They either canoed, or they walked, gradually carving out an astonishing 11-mile-long ribbon of red dirt called the Kalalau Trail. The centerpiece of Na Pali Coast State Park, the rocky trail snakes its way through spectacular coastal scenery before ending at the broad strand of Kalalau Beach.

There are two ways to hike the Kalalau Trail: get a hike-camp permit from Hawaii State Parks and continue west past Hanakapi'ai, completing the grueling and occasionally dangerous 11 miles to Kalalau Beach; or complete the nonpermit portion in a day. The Sierra Club rates the full Kalalau Trail a 9 for difficulty on a scale of 10. The guidebook *Kauai Revealed* by Andrew Doughty is a must for any serious visitor.

For water sports, head for Nukolii Beach Park or Mahaulepu Beach, with its reef-protected shoreline, pocket beaches and 100-foot sand dunes. Horseback riding is big, especially in Waimea Canyon. Two great golf courses are the Princeville Makai and the Kiele. The village of Hanalei, the setting for the movie *South Pacific*, is worth a visit.

WHERE TO STAY:
- Princeville Resort is the retreat of choice of the wealthy. 808-826-3040; www.princeville.com
- Waimea Plantation, set in a coconut grove, offers cottage-style living. 877-997-6667; waimea-plantation.com
- The Rosewood B&B offers rooms and apartments in private homes and cottage rentals. 808-822-5216; www.rosewoodkauai.com
- Keapana Center is a hilltop B&B with nearby hiking and beach opportunities. 800-822-7968

—Chris Dixon

Molokai

Molokai *263 sq. mi.* Molokai is an island of splendid isolation, offering a nearly complete retreat from tourism and crowds. Its interior is largely privately owned and has vast stretches of dense wilderness. Kamakou, the tallest mountain at 4,970 ft., is surrounded by jungles and pools.

Hiking trails and rutted dirt roads lead through forests, around volcanic mountains and along a coastline with cliffs soaring thousands of feet out of the ocean. The western end of the island is dry, and the south is flat, with offshore coral reefs. Many beaches are for viewing, not for swimming.

There are no traffic lights on Molokai, no buildings higher than two stories, no Starbucks, just a couple of hotels and a few gas stations. Nor is there is jet service to the island. The only way to get there is by prop plane or ferry.

The island's most famous institution is a leper colony created in 1865 and still active today. About 30 people, who call themselves residents rather than lepers, live there. To go—and it's definitely a journey worth taking—you must make a reservation. Only a limited number of visitors are allowed to enter each day. Contact

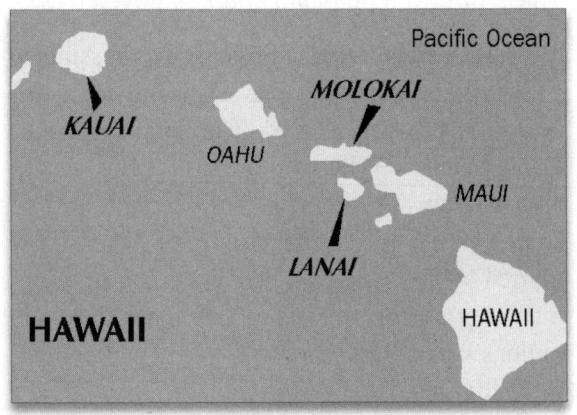

the Molokai Mule Ride (808-567-6088; www. muleride.com) or Damien Tours (808-567-6171; damientours@aol.com).

Getting to the colony is an adventure in itself. You can take a short flight from the other side of Molokai to a landing strip just outside the colony or ride in a procession of mules that winds its way down the cliff to the shore. Another option is to hike the trail. It is a mule trail that involves navigating a steep decline through 26 switchbacks, slippery with dirt and mule dung. Along the way, you encounter breaks in the foliage that permit views of some of the most inaccessible coastline in the world.

WHERE TO STAY: Hotel Molokai, on Kamehameha V Highway (Mile Marker 2) (808-553-5347; www.hotelmolokai.com), is funky if serviceable, though it has seen better days. Ask for a room by the ocean; it's worth the extra cost.

—Adam Nagourney

Lanai *140 sq. mi.* This 140-square-mile island welcomes visitors in a laid-back style all its own. Axis deer roam free in the hills, and on a day hike, you're more likely to run into chattering wild turkeys and quail than people. As you cruise around Lanai's southeastern edge on the 45-minute ferry ride from Maui, a series of strikingly high volcanic cliffs rise before you.

One of Lanai's top off-road attractions is the 8-mile Munro Trail, named for George Munro, the New Zealand naturalist who imported the Cook Island pines. He planted them to attract rain and hold the soil, and made them Lanai's signature plant. You can hike or four-wheel-drive the trail as it climbs through heavily forested slopes and gullies to the 3,370-foot Lanai Hale, the island's single volcano and its highest point.

Northwest of Lanai City is the Garden of the Gods, a bizarre area where rocks and boulders are thrown across a Mars-red landscape. Next to it lies the Kanepuu Preserve, a rare dryland forest that has almost 50 native species, including the endangered Hawaiian gardenia and the sandalwood tree.

The island's most accessible and best swimming and snorkeling spot is Hulopoe Beach. The bay is a protected marine preserve frequented by spinner dolphins and humpback whales. At low tide, shallow lava tide pools along the bay's south shore fill with marine life. Snorkelers in the bay can see vividly blue-green parrotfish, yellow tangs and green sea turtles. A remote beach great for walking is Lopa, near Keomuku Village.

WHERE TO STAY:

• The FourSeasons Resort Lanai at Manele Bay, 1 Manele Bay Road (808-565-2000; www.fourseasons.com/manelebay) and the Lodge at Koele, 1 Keomoku Highway (808-565-4000; www.fourseasons.com/koele) offer high-end accommodations as well as visually stunning, high-level golf courses.

• The Hotel Lanai, 828 Lanai Avenue (808-565-7211; www.hotellanai.com) at a fraction of the price, remains the island's first and only regular hotel. The main house has a large, airy veranda and a popular Cajun-accented restaurant.

—Bonnie Tsui

Finding the Perfect Greek Island
These five are a ferry ride from Athens

The lures of the Greek Islands are many: comparatively inexpensive fares and hotel rates, even during the peak summer months—not to mention near-perfect weather and the warm waters of the Aegean Sea. But travelers are confronted with so many options: 220 islands in the Cyclades, a group of islands off the coast of Athens, and 163 islands in the Dodecanese (although only 26 of them are currently inhabited) off the southwest coast of Turkey. Don't know where to start? Here are five places the Greeks like.

Serifos *Cyclades*
Population: 1,200; area: 70 km

In a testament to the ancient Greeks' sense of irony, the hideous monster Medusa allegedly lived on this stunning island. The approach to Serifos' wide harbor is one of the most beautiful (though least acknowledged) vistas in the archipelago. High above the port, Serifos' main town, Chora, rests on its mountaintop like a crown of white blossoms. The town is a beguiling network of whitewashed houses, bright shutters, clotheslines and steep stone pathways. In summer, Serifos attracts trendy Athenian artists and professionals.

WHAT TO SEE: Rugged rock formations that may or may not be the petrified victims of the Gorgon Medusa. Visit Psili Ammo, the wide beach named for its especially fine sands, or Vaya, a dramatic pebble cove with caves and a deep, cool sea. Climb to the top of Chora and visit the 15th-century Venetian castro. Have a drink at the Yacht Club in Livadi, the definitive "Serifioti" establishment.

WHERE TO STAY: As the island is largely undeveloped, the most comfortable way to experience

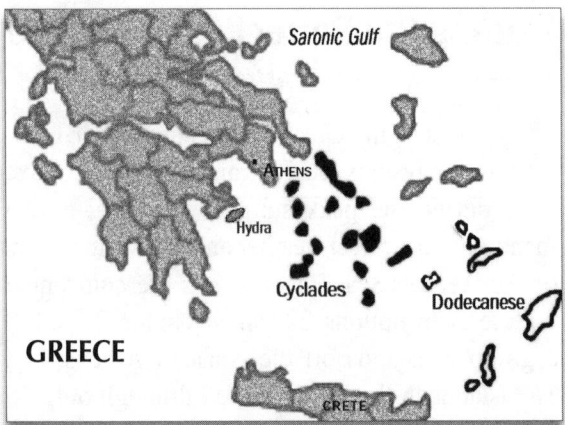

GREECE

Serifos is from a private boat or rented house. Otherwise, the Asteri Hotel (30-22810-51891 / 51191; www.asteri.gr) in Livadi offers clean, air-conditioned rooms.

GETTING THERE: Regular ferries from Piraeus (the port in Athens) and other western Cyclades; 4½ hours from Athens.

Hydra *Saronic Gulf*
Population: 2,800; area: 52 km

Hydra's beauty served as a backdrop for the 1957 film *Boy on a Dolphin*, featuring Sophia Loren. The sophisticated jewel of the Saronic Gulf islands, Hydra has a high concentration of elegant neoclassical mansions and the artsy cognoscenti (Greek and foreign) who inhabit them. Cars, mopeds and even bicycles are forbidden on the island's cobbled streets.

WHAT TO SEE: Hike 1½ hours up to the pretty monastery of the prophet Ilia. Be prepared to spend some time in a water taxi headed to more remote beaches if you want to enjoy Hydra's beauty in peace; more readily accessible shores are crowded and unspectacular.

WHERE TO STAY: A converted sponge factory with pleasing nautical décor, Hotel Bratsera (30-22980-53971; www.bratserahotel.com) has trellised courtyards and the only swimming pool on the island. The Hotel Miranda (30 210 32 25 891), somewhat cheaper, has nice bay views.

GETTING THERE: Twelve ferries leave from Piraeus daily; 1½ hours.

Folegandros *Cyclades*
Population: 600; area: 32 km

People have been hiding in Folegandros for centuries, formerly from pillaging pirates, now from tourists who have trampled many of the larger Cycladic islands. The only tumultuous thing on

Folegandros is the wind, which sweeps across the stone terraces that border its steep hills and into the walls of Chora, the elevated, breathtaking town that gazes upon a cobalt horizon. High, cragged cliffs and an inaccessible port make it one of the most innocent destinations in Greece. The few initiated are Greeks and Italians.

WHAT TO SEE: In addition to outstanding beaches (Aghios Giorgios and Livadaki), Folegandros's main town, Chora, is a gem, retaining vestiges of a dramatic past, during which nearly 200 families lived in a single cliff-top enclosure called Kastro, built during the Venetian rule after the 13th-century Crusades. The church of Panagia above it on Paleo-kastro hill is an excellent place to watch the sunset. Get a local fisherman to take you to Chryssospilia, a stalactite cave with traces of ancient occupation.

WHERE TO STAY: Anemomilos Apartments (30-22860-41309 in season; during winter: 30-210-6827777). Hotel Castro (30-22860-41230; ddcastro@otenet.gr)

GETTING THERE: A ferry from Piraeus departs three times a week; 10-hour trip. Also accessible by hydrofoil from other islands.

Naxos *Cyclades*
Population: 17,000; area: 428 km

Rich in mythological lore, Naxos is the island on which Theseus abandoned his wife, Ariadne. She later took her life on the island's rocky shore. The largest of the Cycladic islands still retains its ancient grace, especially in its quiet mountainous interior. Agriculturally rich, Naxos remains relatively independent of the tourist industry, a stark contrast to the more popular Mykonos and Santorini.

WHAT TO SEE: Apeiranthos, a whitewashed village in central Naxos feels like Greece a century ago. Lord Byron once said he wished to die here. A

winding drive has airplane-like views of the Aegean.

WHERE TO STAY: Chateau Zevgoli (Chateau-Zevgoli@forthnet.gr)

GETTING THERE: High-speed hydrofoil from Athens (3½ hours); ferries from other western Cyclades.

Patmos *Dodecanese*
Population: 2,500; area: 34.6 km

It is said that St. John wrote the Bible's Book of Revelations on leaving this island after a 7-year stint. Patmos is considered the most beautiful island in the Dodecanese archipelago and possibly all of Greece. Called the "Jerusalem of the Aegean," it remains an important site for Christian pilgrimages. More recently, Patmos attracts well-heeled Greek and French vacationers who enjoy the island's stark, volcanic beauty.

WHAT TO SEE: The monastery of St. John, built in 1088. The impressive fortification, with its frescoes and libraries of rare codices, is open to the (respectfully clothed) public. From the mountain town of Chora, walk the short distance to the Monastery of the Apocalypse, near the grotto where St. John purportedly saw his revelation. Some popular beaches: Psili Ammos for seclusion

ⓘ **INSIDE INFO**

Tours for Every Persuasion

○ According to the International Gay and Lesbian Travel Association, a trade group based in Fort Lauderdale, Fla., gay and lesbian travel amounts to a $56-billion-a-year market.

○ Not surprisingly, an increasing number of travel agencies and tour operators are offering specialized trips that cater to single-sex couples and others.

TRAVEL

and sand; Agriolivadi for a rocky cove; and Grikou for a more happening beach scene.

WHERE TO STAY: Galini Hotel (www.galinipatmos. gr); Porto Scoutari (30 6940 827927; www. portoscoutari.com).

GETTING THERE: Daily ferries from Athens (10 to 12 hours) or Piraeus (6 ½ hours).

—Alexa and James Hirschfeld

Perfect Places for Family Travel

Venture beyond Disney World to these real-life theme parks

The humorist Robert Benchley once famously quipped that the two worst ways to travel were "third-class in Bulgaria" and "with children." But that was a long time ago. These days travel conditions in Bulgaria are better, and, while children may or may not be better behaved, family travel has become a mini-industry. Some suggestions for some popular destinations.

LONDON: *Buskers, bunkers, free museums and a cool maze*

If you can close your eyes to the considerable expense—a decent restaurant meal for a family of four can easily exceed $200—London is the perfect place to take children, combining the unknown and the familiar, the thrills of travel with the comforts of home.

Even the native language is exotically skewed enough to provoke endless familial discussions. While there is weird food—spotted dick, fish and chips—there are also options to satisfy the most ethnocentric American palate. The most cost-efficient way to get around is by subway, a.k.a. the tube. One-day family tickets allow unlimited rides on tubes and buses throughout much of London and are a bargain. www.tfl.gov.uk.

Culture and a bit of history. Children tend to be unreconstructed monarchists. Hampton Court Palace, once the home of Henry VIII, is about 30 minutes by train from Waterloo station. The palace is full of jolly touches—cooks in period costumes, for instance—but the best part is the renovated outdoor maze, half a mile of paths enclosed by 7-foot-tall yew hedges (www.hrp.org.uk).

Historically-minded children will love the Churchill Museum and Cabinet War Rooms, on King Charles Street, a thrillingly claustrophobic labyrinth of tiny offices, bedrooms, telephone rooms, broadcasting studios and kitchens constructed under Whitehall during World War II (cwr.iwm.org.uk).

For an excursion that combines history, architecture, exercise, art and food, start at St. Paul's Cathedral near the City (children love the circular Whispering Gallery, where a quirk in the construction allows murmured remarks at one end to be heard on the opposite side). Then walk across the no longer wobbly Millennium Bridge to the spectacular Tate Modern with its cathedral-like Turbine Hall. The museum, like most in London, is free (www.tate.org.uk/modern).

Downtime. Kew Gardens, just southwest of London but easily reachable by subway or train, comprises 300 acres of picnicable land and houses the world's largest plant collection (www.rbgkew. org.uk).

The British Library, at 96 Euston Road, has a collection with much to appeal to both kids and their parents. Here you can look at the original manuscript of Lewis Carroll's *Alice's Adventures Under Ground*, the precursor to *Alice in Wonderland*, electronically turn the pages of a notebook by Leonardo and listen to stirring recordings of Florence Nightingale addressing the old soldiers of Balaclava during the Crimean War (www.bl.uk).

TIMELY TIPS

Chowing Down in London

English food served the old-fashioned way

Butlers Wharf Chop House, 36e Shad Thames, 44-20-7403-3403.

Goring Hotel, 15 Beeston Place, 44-20-7396-9000.

The Ivy, 1 West Street, Covent Garden, 44-20-7836-4751.

Kensington Place, 201-209 Kensington Church Street, Notting Hill Gate, 44-20-7727-3184.

J. Sheekey, 28-32 St. Martins Court, Covent Garden, 44-20-7240-2565.

St. John, 26 St. John Street, 44-20-3328-537.

Sweetings, 39 Queen Victoria Street, 44-20-7248-3062.

Wiltons, 55 Jermyn Street, 44-20-7629-9955.

...And in Paris

At some, you get three-star chefs at one-star prices

Benoît, 20, rue Saint-Martin, (33-1) 42.72.25.76. Run by Alain Ducassse, the superchef who has many Michelin stars.

Gaya, 44, rue du Bac, (33-1) 45.44.73.73. Owned and at least partly run by Pierre Gagnaire, the former enfant terrible whose three-star restaurant of the same name is in the Hotel Balzac.

Le Comptoir, Hôtel Relais St.-Germain, 9, carrefour de l'Odéon, (33-1) 44.27.07.97. Prix fixe. One of the toughest reservations in town. Unless you get lucky or are willing to sit outside in chilly weather, you may have to wait three months for a table.

Mon Vieil Ami, 69, rue St.-Louis-en-l'Île, (33-1) 40.46.01.35. A lovely and unusual bistro.

Outdoors. Covent Garden market is a perfect place to take energetic children. Here there are stores, snack bars, restaurants and buskers, who provide vaudeville-like combinations of magic and music (www.coventgarden.uk.com). —Sarah Lyall

PARIS: *The City of Light for the Babar bunch*

Art and culture come to life for children in Paris, and not just because it is the storybook setting for such favorite characters as Madeline and Babar. Artists paint on the banks of the Seine, and jugglers perform to great crowds in Montmartre. Children are welcome everywhere in Paris—be it a fashionable restaurant on the Champs Elysées or a hushed chapel in Sacré-Coeur.

Culture. With so many museums in Paris, a one-, three- or five-day museum pass is the ideal option for families. It allows parents to skip the ticket line (children under 18 are free at most museums) and saves money at the nearly 70 participating museums and monuments. Museum Day Passes, available at www.parismuseumpass.fr, are for one, three or five days respectively; they must be used on consecutive days.

Young imaginations love the Musée d'Orsay (62, rue de Lille, www.musee-orsay.fr), a former railway station completed in 1900 for the World's Fair, which presents works of art (photography, design, sculpture and painting) from 1848 to 1914. The original archway of the Gare d'Orsay can still be seen, as well as many paintings featuring trains, such as Monet's *La Gare Saint-Lazare.* Young dancers will gravitate to the Degas paintings and sculptures on the upper level.

The outdoor sculpture garden at the Rodin Museum, with more than two dozen famous Rodin sculptures, including *The Thinker* and *The Gates of Hell,* is fairly G-rated and a sanctuary for the restless. A "garden only" ticket costs just

Family-Friendly Fun in the Keys

In recent years, the Florida Keys has seen its "Margaritaville"-minded hedonistic image give way to something more kid-friendly. Families now constitute approximately 25 percent of Keys visitors during the busy winter tourist season, compared with approximately 12 percent 5 years ago. Much of that has been driven by hoteliers. Take Hawks Cay (www.hawkscay.com), which recently underwent a major renovation. The 40-acre property, situated on Duck Key in the middle of the island chain, features 111 two-story villas with the kinds of features—full kitchens, multiple bedrooms—prized by families. So do many other recently renovated and historic Keys properties, including Casa Marina Resort & Beach Club (www.casamarinaresort.com) in Key West, which also features its own slate of children's programs and facilities (they go so far as to pass out free popsicles to the kids at the pool).

Even the newer resorts appear to be sensing the shift and upping the family-friendly ante. At Tranquility Bay Beach House Resort in Marathon (www.tranquilitybay.com), a recent addition to guest activities includes a program that teaches youngsters to scuba dive.

But what if families want to venture beyond the resort? In the Keys, a day can begin with a morning spent spotting the Key deer—a species unique to the region—in Big Pine Key, continue with an afternoon of fishing off any of dozens of bridges and conclude with a glass-bottom boat tour that allows you to see life on a coral reef up close.

Another factor behind the family boom: the relative ease and affordability of a Keys vacation. True, some of these resorts can easily command prices of $500-plus a night for a two-bedroom suite in the prime winter season. But accommodations in the Caribbean and Bahamas can often be more expensive, without factoring in higher airfares. And without the sense of being nickel-and-dimed at every turn, as is often the case at isolated Caribbean and Bahamas properties.

Make no mistake: margaritas are still being poured in "Margaritaville." But at Hawks Cay, they've seemingly found a way to make the happy-hour experience a more family-friendly one. At the resort's main restaurant, a full selection of tequilas and rum drinks are available. But kids can order a nonalcoholic cocktail—say, a "nojito" instead of a mojito.   —Charles Passy

one euro; two sandboxes are hidden in the back behind the circular pool.

Even with a museum pass, entering the Louvre via the glass pyramid can take time because of the crowds. A less dramatic but faster way into the museum is via the Galerie du Carrousel, an indoor shopping mall and food court. Teenagers may beg to be left here, but urge them to venture into the labyrinth of galleries that once housed four centuries of French kings and emperors. For an efficient and educational experience, buy an English-language copy of *Destination Louvre*, available in the children's museum shop.

For families who like to climb, Paris is more challenging than most mountain ranges. There are roughly 300 steps up to the Sacré-Coeur in Montmartre; 704 steps to level two of the Eiffel Tower; 284 steps to the top of the Arc de Triomphe; and 385 steps up to the famous gargoyles at Notre-Dame. Luckily, there is an elevator to all levels of the Eiffel Tower, and a funicular goes up to Montmartre, but the other two are stairs-only.

Downtime. The city's parks have pony rides, carousels, bumper cars and buvettes—fast-food kiosks that sell croque-monsieur sandwiches, hot dogs and cotton candy—and the Tuileries and Luxembourg Gardens often have toy schooners that children can sail across ponds with the push of a stick.

Both the Luxembourg Gardens and the Champ de Mars have big playgrounds and marionette theaters. Though the puppeteers perform entirely in French, children should have little problem following the plots. (Marionnettes du Champs-de-Mars, (33-1) 48.56.01.44; Marionnettes du Luxembourg, guignolduluxembourg.monsite.orange.fr).

On the northwest side of the Tuileries garden, bordering the rue de Rivoli, are trampolines with long benches on either side. Parents can take in the view of the obelisk towering over the Place de la Concorde while their children jump for joy.

To really see the City of Light, take a bateau-mouche tour on the Seine in the early evening. Children love going beneath the many bridges, and the architecture is even more dramatic at night from the water. Aim to depart at the top of the hour, when hundreds of thousands of small lights flicker on the nearby Eiffel Tower.

Shopping. Rue Vavin is a shopping mecca for stylish mothers. This narrow, quarter-mile-long street near the Luxembourg Gardens has more than a dozen children's clothing boutiques.

Shopping for food on Rue Cler, a cobbled street in the seventh arrondissement packed with all the necessary small shops for the perfect picnic, is truly a sensory experience. Children will be drawn to the colorful macaroons in the windows of Le Nôtre (www.lenotre.fr) as well as the sweet-smelling crêpe stand.

—Jennifer Conlin

WASHINGTON, D.C. *First take in the museums, then enjoy the city*

Like many major tourist destinations, the nation's capital has two faces: there's Washington, place of public lives and public monuments, which is where most visitors venture, and there's D.C. (as residents refer to it), the private city where inhabitants live and work. The ideal Washington weekend borrows a bit from each world.

Culture. The Mall is packed with museums, and they're free, but Washingtonians know that the Mall can be an extremely tiring place and have devised ways to concentrate their visits so that everyone is enriched without being exhausted. The Air and Space Museum may be a perennial must-do for many kids, but the National Gallery (Constitution Avenue between Third and Ninth Streets N.W.; nga.gov) makes for an adult-pleasing alternative, and its children's programs are innovative and well thought out (go to nga.gov/kids to find out about drop-in workshops, story hours and films).

The Sculpture Garden, at the National Gallery's northern end, offers ice skating in winter and jazz concerts in summer, and the outsize Oldenburg eraser and Scott Burton chairs present great juvenile art history talking points. Try to visit around lunchtime, as the cafeteria's food is above what you'll find at most of the other Mall museums.

Another great lunchtime museum stop is the National Museum of the American Indian (Fourth Street and Independence Avenue S.W., next to the Air and Space Museum; nasi.si.edu/visit), whose collection aims to present objects like cooking baskets and baby bonnets in context rather than as isolated art objects. The restaurant serves Indian foods from all over the Americas.

A secret to making sense of the abundance of riches on the Mall is to edit well. At the National Museum of Natural History (10th Street and Constitution Avenue N.W.; mnh.si.edu/visit), head upstairs to the O. Orkin Insect Zoo to hold live insects in your hand or to see tarantulas being fed. At the National Museum of American History (14th Street and Constitution Avenue N.W.;

TRAVEL

americanhistory.si.edu), a sure-fire winner is the transportation exhibition, where kids can see vintage subway and street cars.

For further forays into transportation, consider a visit to the Air and Space Museum's Steven F. Udvar-Hazy Center (14390 Air and Space Museum Parkway, Chantilly, Va.; www.nasm. si.edu/UdvarHazy) near Dulles Airport. It's centered on a palatial airplane hangar and covers in three-dimensional form the history of aviation from the Wright Brothers era to the space shuttle *Enterprise*.

Outdoors. A bike ride along the placid C&O Canal's towpath will take you far from the bustle of official Washington. The National Park Service offers guided bike rides there as well as hour-long mule-pulled boat rides (Georgetown Visitor Center, 202-653-5190; www.nps.gov/choh/ planyourvisit/georgetownvisitorcenter.htm).

For a truly surprising adventure, drive about 15 miles up the Potomac to Great Falls, which can be viewed from either the Virginia or the Maryland side of the river. On the Maryland side, a sturdy wooden walkway takes you out over the water to Olmsted Island, a naturalist's delight. Teenagers with bravado might want to attempt the aptly named Billy Goat Trail nearby.　—Anne Glusker

SAN FRANCISCO: *A mostly adult town with kid appeal*

San Francisco already invites sneaker-footed adult tourists to act childlike: Ride a cable car! Gorge on Ghirardelli chocolate! Walk the "crookedest" street in the world! And it is the city's unique low-tech thrills—monstrous hills, cable cars and historic streetcars (free for kids under 5)--that the family will chat about on the ride home.

Culture. A visit to the airy, modern Asian Art Museum (200 Larkin Street; www.asianart.org),

doesn't mean tiptoeing past Ming vases. In the AsiaAlive room, visitors can start a self-guided tour on video touch screens or participate in a Buddhist ceremony hosted by monks from Bhutan. Closed on Mondays.

The cellhouse audio tour at Alcatraz (www. nps.gov/alcatraz), featuring the gravelly-voiced ex-cons' recollections about life on the Rock, are likely to encourage at least an afternoon's worth of good behavior. Cels of another kind—individual celluloid frames of cartoons—are on view at the Cartoon Art Museum (655 Mission Street; www. cartoonart.org). The collection includes characters like Bugs Bunny and Mickey Mouse.

Kids hunt for Dory and Nemo in the California Academy of Arts and Sciences building (55 Music Concourse Drive in Golden Gate Park, 415-379-8000; www.calacademy.org/aquarium). The building, designed by Renzo Piano, includes several restaurants, a 3D theater, an aviary and a four-story rainforest that is home to thousands of plants and animals.

Pier 39 (www.pier39.com) offers a natural attraction: resident sea lions on sun-bleached piers. Kids can learn more at the Gulf of the Farallones National Marine Sanctuary Visitor Center (415-561-6622; www.gfnms.nos.noaa.gov), on the photogenic west end of Crissy Field.

Outside. Just walking the hills and taking in views will provide plenty of fresh air, but it's worth the 12-mile drive north over the Golden Gate Bridge to stroll beneath the giant redwoods in Muir Woods National Monument (415-388-2596; www.nps. gov/muwo). Spur hikes branch off the flat paved loop trail. Rain means banana slugs! Open 8 a.m. to sunset.

Downtime. Vendors charm kids with granola and jam samples at the Ferry Plaza Farmers Market on Tuesdays and Saturdays at the foot of Market

Street (415-291-3276; ferrybuildingmarketplace. com/farmers_market.php). Following the trail south along the water leads to the SBC Ballpark, home of the Giants, and a playground behind the left-field bleachers that includes a miniature replica of the stadium. This Coca-Cola Fan Lot is closed on game days.

—Debra Klein

Exotic Sites for Kids of All Ages

More great family trips—from caves to the Casbah

For a family vacation with even more adventurous turns, try these three far-flung alternatives.

Croatia, in southeastern Europe, offers not only the historic cities of Dubrovnik, Split and its capital, Zagreb, but also the "Dalmatian Riviera." There, active families can take part in sailing, kayaking and even mountain biking trips around the various Croatian islands. This region has some of Europe's best seafood, though the kids might prefer bureks (pies filled with beef or cheese).

Marrakesh. Rock the casbah in Morocco by first visiting Marrakesh, where the main square is like a circus for kids, with snake charmers, jugglers, acrobats and food stalls (lots of child-friendly chicken and couscous here). Then head across the Atlas Mountains and stay in a real 17th-century casbah in the desert. With souks, Berber villages, Roman ruins and even camel trekking, Morocco has something for every age.

Vietnam has historic cities (the picturesque French colonial outpost Hanoi; Hue, a Buddhist center and former imperial capital; and the bustling, urban Ho Chi Minh City) as well as beaches,

✓ **TIMELY TIPS**

Bringing Baby Along

Traveling with an infant age 3 to 6 months can be a pleasure and a good way to bond. But any younger than that would be exhausting, and over 6 months can be trying as well.

✔ An excellent source of advice about traveling with infants is Babycenter.com, which provides health and safety advice and a handy packing list.

✔ *The New Father: A Dad's Guide to the First Year* by Armin A. Brott has a section on infant travel, with good tips like packing all baby essentials in your carry-on in case your luggage is lost.

✔ Another piece of advice: pack a portable crib (first check for product recalls at the Consumer Product Safety Commission's Web site, cpsc.gov). The crib creates a comfortable, consistent resting place for the baby and thus helps maintain nap and bed routines. And, experienced travelers say, a baby stroller and car-seat combination is ideal for planes, trains and taxis.

✔ Talking to your baby's pediatrician ahead of time and preparing contact information for hospitals in the cities you visit also help curb anxieties about traveling with an infant.

—David G. Allan

caves, parks, pagodas and museums. Children should love being pedaled around on a cyclo, shopping at the markets and even eating the food (kid-friendly noodle soups are a Vietnamese specialty). And parents need not worry about finding suitable accommodations—nearly every major hotel chain has an outlet in Vietnam. (For more on traveling to Vietnam see page 550.)

—Jennifer Conlin

Natural Treasures

America's Most Popular Parks

Folks flock to the big 10 for a reason

Italy has Venice. China, the Great Wall. The United States' most remarkable asset is its breathtakingly beautiful national parks, which altogether account for the largest protected wildernesses in the world. While there are 58 national parks, the 10 most popular account for over half the annual visitors. It is not uncommon, for instance, to find yourself bumper-to-bumper or without a parking spot in Yellowstone National Park in its most popular venues.

With a little foresight, you can steer clear of the crowds and parking problems. If you're planning to visit one of the 10 most popular parks during the summer, try to make reservations far in advance. While some campsites are on a first-come, first-served basis, many can be reserved through the National Recreation Reservation Service (877-444-6777; www.recreation.gov).

Following are the 10 most popular national parks, ranked by largest numbers of visitors, and a description of the most interesting tracks they have to offer—beaten or otherwise.

1. Great Smoky Mountains National Park

Over 9.1 million visitors per year
• *Largest national park east of the Rockies*

A world unto itself, Great Smoky Mountains National Park, located in western North Carolina and eastern Tennessee, has over 1,500 species of flowering plants, 10 percent of which are considered rare, 100 native species of trees and over 100 native species of shrubs—more than in all of Europe. In addition, there are 200 species of birds, about 50 native species of fish, 80 species of reptiles and amphibians, and 66 species of mammals, including wild hogs and black bears.

A hike or drive from mountain base to peak is equivalent to the entire length of the Appalachian Trail from Georgia to Maine in terms of the number of species of trees and plants—every 250 feet of elevation is roughly equivalent to 1,000 miles of distance on the trail. A quarter of the park is virgin forest, the largest one east of the Mississippi.

In addition to its natural attributes, Great Smoky Mountains has farms, churches, cabins and gristmills left by the mountain people who moved away when the park was created in 1934. The park has been designated a United Nations International Biosphere Reserve as well as a World Historical Site.

Gatlinburg, Tenn. 37738
865-436-1200; www.nps.gov/grsm

PEAK SEASON TIPS: During the summer, in the lower elevations, expect haze, humidity and afternoon temperatures in the 90s—and terrible traffic jams. Cades Cove is generally less crowded.

CAMPING: During summer and fall, sites at Elkmont, Smokemont, Cades Cove and Cosby may be reserved online or by phone at 877-444-6777. Reservations are accepted only for the May to October period. All other campgrounds are first-come, first-served. Two of the campgrounds, Cades Cove and Smokemont, are open year round.

There is one camping facility, LeConte Lodge, located on the park's third-highest peak, Mt. LeConte (elevation 6,593 feet), a six-hour hike from the main

INSIDE INFO

The Biggest Parks

O   The largest parks cover more ground than some of our smallest states.

Rank	National park or state	Acres
1.	Wrangell–St. Elias, Alaska	13,200,000
2.	Gates of the Arctic, Alaska	8,400,000
	MASSACHUSSETTS	6,755,200
3.	Denali, Alaska	6,028,203
4.	Katmai, Alaska	3,674,530
5.	Death Valley, Calif.	3,367,627
6.	Glacier Bay, Alaska	3,225,284
	CONNECTICUT	3,118,080
7.	Lake Clark, Alaska	2,619,722
8.	Yellowstone, Wyo.	2,219,789
9.	Kobuk Valley, Alaska	1,750,737
10.	Everglades, Fla.	1,399,078
11.	Grand Canyon, Ariz.	1,218,376
12.	Glacier, Mont.	1,400,000
13.	Olympic, Wash.	922,000
14.	Big Bend, Tex.	801,163
15.	Joshua Tree, Calif.	794,000
	RHODE ISLAND	675,200

road. Cabins do not have electricity or running water but do include beds and hot meals. LeConte Lodge is open from April to mid-November, and reservations must often be booked as far as a year in advance. For information and reservations, call 865–429–5704 or e-mail reservations@leconte-lodge.com.

BEST ONE-DAY TRIP: Entering the park from Gatlinburg, continue on U.S. 441 and stop at the Newfoundland Gap, where there are spectacular views of the mountains. From there, turn onto Clingmans Dome Road (closed in the winter), which ends at a parking lot where there is a strenuous half-mile hike to a lookout tower atop 6,643-foot Clingmans Dome—the highest peak in the park. Back on U.S.

441, continue to the Smokemont Campground, where the easy, 2-mile Chasten Creek Falls Trail meanders along a stream through a hardwood forest ending at one of the park's many waterfalls.

BEST EXPERIENCE: The Great Smokies is one of the premier places in the East to enjoy magnificent fall foliage. The season lasts from September through October. Peak time: October 15 to October 31.

2. Grand Canyon National Park

Over 4.4 million visitors per year • The 277-mile canyon is nearly a mile deep in places

A Grand Canyon sunset is glorious, but even during the day the canyon walls' many layers of stone refract hues of red, yellow and green light. On a good day you can see 200 miles across vast mesas, forests and the Colorado River.

The park consists of three areas: the North Rim, the South Rim and the Inner Canyon, which is accessible only by foot, boat or mule. The North Rim and the South Rim are only 9 miles apart as the eagle flies, but 214 miles by road, taking hikers an average of 3 days to travel one way.

The rims are located in different temperate climate zones. The North Rim, on average, is 1,000 feet higher and is heavily forested with blue spruce and alpine vegetation. It is open only from May to late October. The more popular South Rim is closer to population centers and has the juniper bushes and Gambel oak typical of the arid Southwest. The Inner Canyon is desertlike; temperatures there often exceed 110 degrees in the summer.

Grand Canyon, Ariz. 86023
928-638-7888; www.nps.gov/grca

PEAK SEASON TIPS: The South Rim is crowded all year. To escape the masses, take one of the many trails off East Rim Drive to a private spot overlooking the canyon, or try the North Rim.

TRAVEL

CAMPING: For lodging information in the North and South Rims, including Phantom Ranch: 303-297-2757, 888-297-275; www.grandcanyonlodges.com.

BEST ONE-DAY TRIP: The West Rim Drive offers wonderful views of the main canyon. In the summer, it is open only to buses, which can be taken from the visitor center. A paved trail runs along the South Rim. All hikes into the canyon are strenuous.

BEST EXPERIENCE: A raft ride down the Colorado River is a great way to enjoy the splendor of the canyon. Motorboat trips take 7 to 10 days, raft trips take 10 to 12 days and trips on wooden dories usually last 18 days, though 3- to 8-day partial trips can be arranged. Call the park for a list of outfitters licensed by the National Park Service.

3. Yosemite National Park

Over 3.4 million visitors per year
• *Home of the giant sequoia*

Yosemite's majestic granite peaks, groves of ancient giant sequoia trees and waterfalls (including Yosemite Falls, which at 2,425 feet is the nation's highest) inspired some of the earliest attempts at conservation in the United States. In 1864, Congress enacted laws protecting the valley. The journalist Horace Greeley noted that he knew of "no single wonder of Nature on earth which can claim a superiority over the Yosemite." And the naturalist John Muir, whose efforts led to the park's formation, said of the valley, "No temple made with hands can compare with Yosemite."

The enormous park occupies an area comparable to Rhode Island, with elevations of up to 13,114 feet.

Yosemite National Park, Calif. 95389
209-372-0200; www.nps.gov/yose

PEAK SEASON TIPS: During the busy summer months, avoid the 7-mile Yosemite Valley, which attracts the hordes.

CAMPING: Of the 18 campgrounds in Yosemite, the 5 main ones in the valley offer "refugee-style camping"—over 800 campsites crammed into a half-mile of space. For more room and better views, try one of the eight Tioga Road campgrounds. There also are five tent camps on the High Sierra Loop Trail. Campers can obtain meals, showers and cots there. Reservations are advised.

Reservations are required year-round in Yosemite Valley's auto campground and for Hodgdon Meadow, Crane Flat and Tuolumne Meadows campgrounds. Other campgrounds are operated on a first-come, first-served basis. Reservations may be made up to, but no earlier than, 8 weeks. Reservable campsites fill up quickly from mid-May to mid-September. Your best bet for snagging a spot is to start calling the National Recreation Reservation Service, 877-444-6777, at 7 a.m. Pacific Standard Time months in advance of the date you want to camp.

BEST ONE-DAY TRIP: Avoid the congested route to Yosemite Valley, grab a tour bus and get off at either shuttle stop 7, for an easy half-mile, 20-minute hike to Lower Yosemite Falls, or shuttle bus stop 8, for a strenuous one- to three-hour round-trip hike to Upper Yosemite Falls. Other sites include the Native American Yosemite Village and El Capitan, a 3,000-foot face that is popular with rock climbers.

4. Olympic National Park

Over 3 million visitors per year
• *The best example of virgin temperate rain forest in the country*

On a relatively isolated peninsula with no roads traversing it, Olympic is one of the most pristine of the nation's parks. It has been referred to as the "last frontier." It divides into three distinct environments: rugged coastline, virgin temperate rain forest and mountains, at the foot of which is the largest intact strand of coniferous forest in the lower 48 states. The park also has 60 named glaciers.

Port Angeles, Wash. 98362
360-452-4501; www.nps.gov/olym

PEAK SEASON TIPS: Though three-quarters of the precipitation falls between October and March, Olympic still receives more rain than any other area in the United States. Always bring rain gear.

CAMPING: The main coastal campgrounds of Kalaloch and Mora provide privacy and a sense of wilderness. For an even greater sense of solitude, try one of the two smaller campgrounds, Ozette Lake or Ericson's Bay. (The latter is accessible only by canoe.) All of the wilderness campgrounds are available on a first-come, first-served basis.

The Hoh campground is the largest in the rain forest. The smaller campgrounds in that area of the park have more privacy and better wildlife-watching. On the mountain, the Deer Park campground (elevation 5,400 feet) makes an excellent base from which to explore.

Most of the 16 campgrounds in the park are available on a first-come, first-served basis, but in the summer reservations at Kalaloch can be made by calling the reservations number at 888-896-3826.

BEST ONE-DAY TRIP: On a drive up Route 101, you can take in the park's harbor seals, gigantic driftwood and tide pools teeming with activity along the coast. On the right, you'll pass a sign for the world's largest cedar tree. Get off onto the spur road to the Hoh Rainforest visitor center. There is a 3/4-mile round-trip hike that winds through the dense rain forest at the end of the road. Back in your car, turn onto the road to the Mora campground, where there are several short scenic trails along the beach.

 **TIMELY TIPS**

Sure Ways to Beat the Crowds
Travel in the off-season has its own rewards

Traffic on the main roads slows to a crawl, people are everywhere. Morning drive time in New York City? No, it's the summer rush to the nation's most popular national parks. Traffic has gotten so bad at some parks that tourists can spot wildlife simply by looking where other cars have pulled over to the side of the road to gawk.

The surest way to beat the crowds is to visit in the off-season. From June through October, Great Smoky Mountains National Park typically gets well over 1 million visitors a month, but roughly half that number visit in the months between November and April, when temperatures in the lower elevations average about 50 degrees and occasionally reach into the 70's—perfect hiking weather, in other words.

There are other off-season rewards, too. At Rocky Mountain National Park, the bighorn sheep come down from higher elevations in May to feed on the mud deposits, and wildflowers there are spectacular in the spring. Yosemite National Park's waterfalls rush from the melting winter snows. In the fall, the foliage in many parks is absolutely superb. September is the sunniest month at Rocky Mountain National Park. Grand Teton National Park is open all winter, allowing access to excellent cross-country skiing.

Of course, seasonal difficulties abound. There are, for instance, sudden snowstorms at Yellowstone National Park as early as September. And spring weather at Zion National Park is unpredictable; flash floods are not uncommon.

If such perils are too daunting for you, it is possible to avoid the masses in the summer simply by venturing into the backcountry. Most visitors don't wander very far from their cars.

TRAVEL

5. Yellowstone National Park

Over 3 million visitors per year
• The largest concentration of geysers and hot springs in the world

The center of what is now Yellowstone Park erupted 600,000 years ago. The explosion left behind a 28-by-47-mile crater that contained the world's greatest concentration of geothermal phenomena, including hot springs, fumaroles, steam vents, mud pots and over 300 geysers. Among the geysers is Steam Boat, which shoots columns of water a record 350 feet high.

Yellowstone is the second-largest park in the lower 48 states, encompassing an area larger than the states of Delaware and Rhode Island combined. It is also the oldest park in the country, established in 1872. It has the largest mountain lake (Yellowstone Lake, with 110 miles of shoreline); the biggest elk population in America (30,000 strong); and is the last place in the country where there is a free-ranging herd of bison (3,500 of the woolly beasts).

Yellowstone National Park, Wyo. 82190
307-344-2002; www.nps.gov/yell

PEAK SEASON TIPS: This is one of the coldest parks in the continental United States. Be prepared for winter weather at all times. The park receives half its nearly three million visitors in July and August. To avoid the crowds, head for the backcountry.

CAMPING: The 12 campgrounds at Yellowstone are available on a first-come, first-served basis except for Bridge Bay, Fishing Bridge, Madison, Grant Village and Canyon Village. Winter camping is available only at Mammoth campground.

BEST ONE-DAY TRIP: From the west entrance, drive along Grand Loop Road to the mile-long Upper Geyser Basin, where boardwalks and trails run among the most outstanding geothermal phenomena in the world. Continue on to Yellowstone Lake.

6. Cuyahoga Valley National Park

Over 2.5 million visitors per year • Located along the banks of the winding Cuyahoga River, with 22 miles of steep valley walls

The valley itself is the product of two unique geographic landscapes—the Appalachian Plateau and the Central Lowlands—giving the park many different habitats. The park's diverse array of wetland and dry environments offer a wide range of plant and animal life, including 943 species of plants and 194 species of birds as well as 43 different types of fish, 32 species of mammals, 22 amphibians and 20 types of reptiles. The most commonly spotted animals are white-tailed deer, coyotes and great blue herons.

Located in northeastern Ohio, near Akron and Cleveland, the park has four distinct seasons. Winter brings frequent snowfall, spring is the rainy season and summers are hot and muggy with thunderstorms. Fall is the most popular season to visit. The park is open all year round. But visitors should be prepared for all conditions, as the weather is often unpredictable.

Brecksville, Ohio 44141   216-524-1497
www.nps.gov/cuva/home

 **TIMELY TIPS**

Where to Climb Rocks...

✔ Yosemite's dramatic domes and soaring pinnacles make it one of the best places in the world for rock climbing.

✔ The Yosemite Mountaineering School and Guide Service offers beginning through advanced classes from April to mid-October. For information: 209-372-8344; www. yosemitepark.com.

PEAK SEASON TIPS: Although there has been much improvement in the water quality of the park's rivers and streams over the past couple of years, the Cuyahoga River remains unsafe for recreational activities.

LODGING: Cuyahoga Valley National Park does not allow camping. However, there are hostels and hotels within the park's perimeters that are open year round. Cuyahoga Valley lodging is available either at the HI-Stanford Hostel (330-467-8711; www.stanfordhostel.com) or at the Inn at Brandywine Falls (330-467-1812; www.innatbrandywinefalls.com).

BEST ONE-DAY TRIP: The Cuyahoga Valley Scenic Railroad gives visitors the opportunity to tour the park by train. Excursions vary from 1 3/4 hour round-trip rides to all-day expeditions (800-468 4070; www.cvsr.com).

7. Rocky Mountain National Park

Over 2.7 million visitors per year
• One of the highest regions in the country: 114 mountains above 10,000 feet

On both sides of Rocky Mountain National Park's 44-mile Trail Ridge Road, the highest paved road in America, are craggy snow-capped mountain peaks shrouded in clouds, alpine fields ablaze with wildflowers and crystal-clear mountain lakes. Elk, deer, moose, coyotes, marmots, ptarmigan and bighorn sheep—the symbol of the park—can often be seen.

　　Estes Park, Colo. 80517

　　970-586-1206; www.nps.gov/romo

PEAK SEASON TIPS: The road to Bear Lake is jammed in the summer. Consider spending most of your time on the park's west side; it's less spectacular but also less crowded, and there are better chances to see wildlife.

CAMPING: There are five campgrounds in the park, each with a 7-day camping limit. For reservations to Moraine Park and Glacier Basin campgrounds, call the Park reservation service. The other three are available on a first-come, first-served basis. In the summer, Timber Creek, on the west side of the park, is recommended—it typically doesn't fill up until early afternoon. Aspenglen and Longs Peak, where one begins the ascent to the summit, are often full by 8 a.m. Privately owned campgrounds also are available.

BEST ONE-DAY TRIP: For a sampling of the varied topography, take Old Fall River Road to the Alpine visitors center at Fall River Pass, 11,796 feet above sea level. Drive back along Trail Ridge Road. If time permits, turn off Trail Ridge Road onto Bear Lake Road, which winds past lakes and streams to Bear Lake, where there is an easy 2/3-mile nature walk around the lake and a 1.1-mile hike to Dream Lake. A less crowded trail nearby is the Glacier Gorge Junction Trail to Alberta Falls. Those who are in peak physical condition may want to try Longs Peak Trail, a strenuous 8-mile hike at 14,000 feet.

BEST EXPERIENCE: Eighty percent of the park's trails can be ridden on horseback, and there are two historic ranches at the center of the park. Horses can be rented in Glacier Basin and Moraine Park.

　TIMELY TIPS

...Or Glide on Snow

✔ Yellowstone permits the use of snowmobiles (December to mid-March).

　In addition, snow coaches—buses on skis—are a unique way to travel around the park in the winter.

　Call Xanterra Parks and Resorts for reservations and rentals: 866-439-7375; www.travelyellowstone.com.

TRAVEL

8. Zion National Park

Over 2.6 million visitors per year
• The 319-foot Kolob Arch is the world's
largest sandstone formation

Nineteenth-century Mormons named the main canyon in this park Zion after the Heavenly City and gave religious names to many of the brilliantly colored rock formations. The park's outstanding features include massive stone arches, such as the Kolob Arch, hanging flower gardens, forested canyons and isolated mesas.

The varied topography and plant life of the canyon have been caused by differences in the amount of water that reaches the various parts of the park. The microenvironments shelter a wide variety of animals, from black bears to lizards.

Springdale, Utah 84767

435-772-3256; www.nps.gov.zion

Peak season tips: Expect traffic jams on summer weekends, when hordes of people visit the park. The west side is less crowded.

Camping: Two campgrounds are open year-round on a first-come, first-served basis. There are picnic areas with fire pits and flush toilets. Campers should arrive early in the day for the best chance at getting a spot.

Best one-day trip: A spectacular stretch of Utah Route 9 descends 2,000 feet in 11 miles into the park. As you enter the half-mile-wide canyon, the road turns into Zion Canyon Scenic Drive and runs north to the Temple of Sinawava. Riverside Walk, an easy 2-mile round-trip and the most popular trail in the park, begins here.

9. Grand Teton National Park

Over 2.4 million visitors per year
• Best part of the beautiful Teton range

There are not many places in the world where you can literally stand next to a mountain. Imagine then Grand Teton, where the mountains rise out of the relatively flat Jackson Hole Valley like granite skyscrapers.

Another geological oddity formed during the Ice Age, Jackson Hole Valley looks as if some gargantuan infant sculpted it out of Play-Doh. When the valley formed, little driblets from the glaciers formed rocky deposits, called moraines, around the six sparkling mountain lakes that were incongruously punctured into the landscape.

Winding gently through this strange valley is the Snake River, along the banks of which grow willows, cottonwoods and the blue spruces in which bald eagles prefer to nest. Beavers have built dams up and down the river, forming wetlands with a dense concentration of wildlife, including bears, elk, moose, trumpeter swans, sandhill cranes and Canada geese.

Moose, Wyo. 83012

307-739-3300; www.nps.gov/grte

Peak season tips: From June through August, the crowds are near Jenny Lake, which has sand beaches and sometimes is warm enough for a quick swim.

Camping: Campgrounds are generally open from late May to October. In summer, Jenny Lake tent campground fills the fastest and has a 7-day camping limit; the other five parks have 2-week limits. Camping at all five campgrounds is on a first-come, first-served basis, and there are also limited reservations available through the Grand Teton Lodge Company (307-543-2811; www.gtlc.com).

Best one-day trip: Beginning at the south entrance on Route 191, stop at Mentor's Ferry and the Chapel of the Transfiguration for a look at the dwellings of some of the area's first pioneers. Then drive north along Teton Park Road to Lupine Meadow and take the spur road to the trailhead, where, if you're in good physical shape, you can try a difficult hike to Amphitheater Lake near the timberline. Head back up Teton Road for a stop at South Jenny Lake,

TIMELY TIPS

The Best Park Guides

The National Park Service offers a wealth of information on specific parks and publishes a series of helpful guides with photos and maps. Here's how to tap into national park resources.

✔ **National Park Service Home Page.** Data about the parks and links to the homepages of major parks. www.nps.gov

✔ **National Parks Electronic Bookstore.** On this page you can order specialized publications, such as park guides and books about regional flora, fauna and history. www.eparks.com/store

✔ **National Parks And Conservation Association.** A nonprofit citizen group dedicated to preserving the Appalachian Trail and the national parks. The site provides information on various activities and provides a link to the latest issue of *National Parks* magazine. www.npca.org

OTHER RESOURCES

✔ **GORP (Great Outdoors Recreation Pages).** A vast array of offerings, including detailed reports on national parks, forests, wildlife refuges, etc. You'll also find information on hiking, biking, fishing, skiing, caving, etc., as well as tours of wilderness areas. www.gorp.com

✔ *National Geographic Guide to the National Parks of the United States,* Sixth Edition, revised and updated. National Geographic Society. Perfect for the windshield tourist, this book is packed with itineraries, quick hikes and beautiful pictures.

TRAVEL

located at the bottom of the tallest Teton peak. An easy 6-mile hike there circles the lake and affords spectacular views. Finally, stop at Colter Bay for a 1-mile hike that loops around the wetlands.

BEST EXPERIENCE: In winter, horse-drawn sleighs take visitors to see the herd of 7,500 elk that live in the valley.

10. Acadia National Park

Over 2 million visitors per year.
• *Highest coastal mountains on the East Coast*

The park is made of two islands and a peninsula: Mount Desert Island (accessible by a land bridge), Isle au Haut and Schoodic Peninsula.

Artists and writers flocked to Mount Desert Island in the 1850's, attracted by its natural beauty. In the 1890's, wealthy vacationers, inspired by the paintings, came and built opulent "cottages," many of which were destroyed by fire in 1947.

The park's proximity to the ocean gives it a milder climate than that of the mainland, which helps it to sustain more than 500 varieties of wild-

flowers and makes it one of the best places on the eastern seaboard to take in fall foliage. The park also is known as the Warbler Capital of the United States. Over 275 species of birds, including 26 varieties of warblers and the endangered peregrine falcon, inhabit the park's birch and pine forests.

Bar Harbor, Me. 04609
207-288-3338; www.nps.gov/acad

PEAK SEASON TIPS: Expect bumper-to-bumper traffic on the Park Loop Road on the east side of Mount Desert Island in the summer. To avoid crowds, try the island's much less crowded western side or take a ferry trip either to Baker Island or to Isle au Haut. June is the best month to see forest birds; August is the best month for sea birds.

CAMPING: The landscaped Blackwoods campground on the east side of Mount Desert Island has 310 campsites. It is open all year. Reservations are advised. On the less crowded west side is the 200-site Seawell campground, which is open only during the summer. You have to hike in from a parking lot to reach it, but it's worth the effort. Sites are available on a first-come, first-served basis only. Particularly remote are Isle au Haut's five small lean-to shelters. Here you can escape the cars and crowds without sacrificing convenience. The ferry there lands at a nearby hamlet where you can get provisions.

BEST ONE-DAY TRIP: From the visitor center, take Park Loop Road to the 3.5-mile road that leads to Cadillac Mountain, where a short, paved trail winds around the 1,530-foot mountain, the highest coastal mountain in the United States. Back on Park Loop Road, turn around and continue down the East Coast. Stop at Sand Beach for a dip and the 1.4-mile Great Head Trail for a hike around a rocky, forested peninsula. Continue on Park Loop Road to Route 3 and turn onto Route 198. Look for Hadlock Pond Carriage Road Trail, where there is a 4-mile loop across three granite bridges. This trail goes past the highest waterfall in the park and is one of the best places to enjoy the color of flowering plants in the spring.

BEST EXPERIENCE: From mid-June to mid-October, you can take the charming carriage ride through the park that is offered by the Wild Wood Stables (207-276-3622; www.acadiamagic.com/wildwood-stables.html).

This also is one of the few national parks where snowmobiles are allowed. The network of carriage roads provides excellent terrain.

 TIMELY TIPS

Shh! Don't Tell Anyone

✔ The National Park Service has an excellent online guide to the less-well-known, but in many cases no less spectacular, parks called *National Parks: Lesser-Known Areas*. To peruse the site, go to nps.gov/pub_aff/lesser.htm

---

Little-Known Parks Worth a Visit
Less crowded, yet as beautiful as Yellowstone

While most people go for the blockbusters such as Yellowstone and Grand Canyon, there are parks just as magnificent and just as resource-rich with significantly fewer visitors.

Perhaps these undervisited reserves are the way national parks are meant to be. Without the car horns and camera-toting tourists, they better preserve that sense of yesteryear—and besides, you just might be able to grab a campsite at the last minute, instead of having to reserve a year in advance.

Before his death in 2003, Robin Winks was an irrepressible Yale history professor and the first person to visit all the hundreds of units of the National Parks system. He devoted much of his career to the study and protection of the world's natural resources and wrote *The Rise of the National Park Ethic,* a history of the National Park System. Here is a list of what were his favorite lesser-known national parks.

Cumberland Island National Seashore
Approx. 83,000 visitors per year • 36,415 acres • Accessible via the National Park Service ferry, from St. Mary's, Ga., 95 miles from Savannah

Cumberland Island, the largest of Georgia's Atlantic barrier islands, is also the most unspoiled. The southernmost of Georgia's Golden Isles, it has magnificent beaches, dunes, maritime forests, salt marshes and a number of old estates as well as armadillos, wild horses, wild turkeys and loggerhead turtles.

The island can be reached only by ferry. Accommodations are available in five campsites on the island.

St. Mary's, Ga. 31558
912-882-4336 ext. 254; www.nps.gov/cuis

Voyageurs National Park

Approx. 222,000 visitors per year • 218,054 acres • Nearest big town: Duluth, 280 miles

Much of the park is accessible only by boat (free canoes are available from the Park Service). There is, in fact, only one road. This wilderness is composed of 70,000 acres of dense forest, 30 lakes and 900 islands teeming with wildlife, including a pack of timber wolves. The area has remained relatively unchanged from the days of trappers and explorers.

International Falls, Minn. 56649
218-283-6600; www.nps.gov/voya

Grant–Kohrs Ranch National Historic Site

Approx. 17,000 visitors per year • 1,500 acres • Nearest big town: Butte, 45 miles

This was one of the largest and best-known ranches in the country at the end of the 19th century. Today, the ranch is almost unchanged: cowboys still gallop by, herds of cattle bellow, and the smells of a working ranch waft through the place. In addition, the site preserves the original log buildings, the main Victorian-style ranch house and an impressive collection of saddles, wagons and other artifacts.

Deer Lodge, Mont. 59722
406-846-2070; www.nps.gov/grko

Great Basin National Park

Approx. 70,000 visitors per year • 77,180 acres • Nearest big town: Salt Lake City, 230 miles

Situated in one of the most rugged and remote parts of the country, this park is reminiscent of the wide open Old West. It has vast stretches of desert-like open country and dramatic tall mountains, including the 13,063-foot Wheeler Peak, which descends to the Great Basin, one of the lowest points in the state. Among the park's attractions

 **TIMELY TIPS**

Into the Wilderness

✔ Wilderness areas—more than 106 million acres of them—are the most strictly protected lands in the country. "Carry out what you carry in" policies are enforced so that, in the words of the 1964 Wilderness Act, "the imprint of man's works" remains "substantially unnoticeable." For a complete list of wilderness areas, go to www.wilderness.net.

are ancient bristlecone pines, which, at 4,000 years old, are among the oldest living things in the world; Lehman Cave, one of the largest limestone caves in the country; and remnants of Pleistocene lakes.

Baker, Nev. 89311
775-234-7331; www.nps.gov/grba

North Cascades National Park

Approx. 373,656 visitors per year • 504,780 acres • Nearest big town: Seattle, 115 miles

This is one of those hike-all-day-and-not-see-anyone-else parks, largely because Washington's other, better-known park, Olympic, is more accessible. Northern Cascades is sometimes called the American Alps because of its numerous immense jagged glaciers—318 in all. This enormous wilderness boasts 248 lakes, 1,700 species of plants, 207 species of birds and 85 species of mammals, including grizzly bears and cougars.

Sedro Woolley, Wash. 98284
360-854-7200; www.nps.gov/noca

Channel Islands National Park

Approx. 332,000 visitors per year • 249,354 acres • Nearest big town: Ventura, on the coast, is about 14 miles away by boat or plane

Because of the abundant wildlife here, which includes the world's largest creature, the blue whale,

TRAVEL

biologists often refer to these five tiny islands off the California coast as North America's Galápagos. Among the other animals that can be seen are sea lions, sea otters, pelicans and cormorants. Remains of Spanish farms offer examples of how some of the earliest settlers in California lived.

Ventura, Calif. 93001

805-658-5730 ; www.nps.gov/chis

Lassen Volcanic National Park

Approx: 377,000 visitors per year • 106,372 acres • Nearest big town: Chester, 35 miles

Before Mount St. Helens erupted in 1980, Lassen Peak was considered the most active volcano in the lower 48 states. The park provides a great vantage point from which to observe volcanic action—fumaroles, bubbling mud pots and hissing hot springs dot the landscape. There are also 150 miles of hiking trails through densely forested areas.

Mineral, Calif. 96063

530-595-4480; www.nps.gov/lavo

Aniakchak National Monument

Approx: 360 visitors per year • 117,176 acres in the monument and 465,603 acres in the preserve • Nearest big town: Anchorage, 400 miles

This wilderness is the most remote and difficult to visit in the National Park System. The quickest way to get to the focal point of Aniakchak, which is a giant crater, one of the largest in the world, is to fly into it. However, be forewarned if you're contemplating this feat: For every 10 attempts, only one is successful, because winds are constantly closing the only gap a plane can enter. Inside the crater, Surprise Lake's waters course through the wall of the crater to form the Aniakchak River.

King Salmon, Alaska 99613

907-246-3305; www.nps.gov/ania

The National Parks' Great Lodges

Rustic hotels in the middle of the wilderness

America's national parks contain some of the best-preserved rustic hotels in the United States. These capacious lodges, often built with stones and trees hewn directly from the stunning landscapes they occupy, attempt to re-create the great outdoors indoors. Rates range from under $100 a night per person to five-star hotel prices. Here are some of the best places to stay in the national parks.

Ahwahnee Hotel, *Yosmite National Park, California.*
Dating from 1925, this hotel's assymmetrical rock columns and varied levels convey the impression of a mountain range. The floor-to-ceiling stained-glass windows offer splendid views of the soaring walls of Yosemite Valley. Open year round. 866-875-8456; www.nationalparkreservations.com/ahwahnee

Bryce Canyon Lodge, *Bryce Canyon National Park, Utah.*
Atop a mesa overlooking the colorfully hued stone walls of Bryce Canyon, the lodge and adjacent cabins are classic examples of rustic architecture. Open April to November. 888-297-2757; www.brycecanyonlodge.com

El Tovar Lodge, *Grand Canyon National Park, Ariz.*
Only 50 feet from the South Rim of the Grand Canyon, it is one of the most luxurious, with first-rate gourmet meals. Open year round. 888-297-2757; www.grandcanyonlodges.com/El-Tovar-409.htm

Lake McDonald Lodge, *Glacier National Park, Mont.*
The hotel faces out across Lake McDonald, the largest lake in the park, with views of the magnificent snow-capped mountain. Open May to October. 866-875-8456; www.nationalparkreservations.com/glacier.htm

North Rim Lodge, *Grand Canyon National Park, Ariz.*

Lying on the edge of the North Rim, the lodge offers an inexpensive alternative to El Tovar. Open mid-May to mid-October. 888–297–2757; www.nps.gov/grca/grandcanyon/north-rim/lodging.htm

Old Faithful Inn, *Yellowstone National Park, Wyo.*

Built in 1904, many rooms have views of the world-famous Old Faithful geyser nearby. Open early May to mid-October. 307–344–7311; www.travelyellowstone.com

Oregon Caves Chateau, *Oregon Caves National Monument.*

This hotel actually spans a small gorge. A stream runs through the dining room. Open May through October—part of the year at "bed and breakfast" rates; the rest of the year as a full-service hotel. Contact the Chateau for a schedule. 503–592–3400; www.oregoncavesoutfitters.com/home.asp

Paradise Inn, *Mount Rainier National Park, Wash.*

One of the earliest ski resorts in the country, the inn lies at an elevation of 5,400 feet. Open mid-May to October. 360–569–2275 or rainier.guestservices.com/html/accomodations.html

Wawona Hotel, *Yosemite National Park, Calif.*

The largest existing Victorian hotel complex within a national park. Open April to November continuously, and intermittently throughout the year. 559-253-5635; www.yosemitepark.com

Ross Lake Resort, *Ross Lake National Recreation Area, Wash.*

Twelve rustic cabins and three bunkhouses on log rafts along the steep shoreline of the lake. Hike two miles to the resort or go by boat. Open mid-June to the end of October. Book at least a year in advance. 206–386–4437; www.rosslakeresort.com

Hideaways Worth the Hike
Some getaways are more hidden than others

The Lost Trail Lodge, nestled in the Sierra Nevada in California near Donner Memorial State Park, is meant for people who like to work for their rewards—it can be reached only on foot or with cross-country skis or snowshoes.

The lodge has four private cabins connected to a cozy common room, and a shared kitchen outfitted with a full set of antique cast-iron cookware and a six-burner gas stove. It has private Jacuzzis, and wooden lofts where the kids can sleep. It has large windows looking out on snow-covered trees, and a stone hearth that continuously glows with a fire.

But it is missing other amenities, like land-line phones, an Internet connection or direct road access for most of the year. And you have to hike, snowshoe or use cross-country skis (half a mile in the summer and four miles in the winter). The isolation is particularly striking since, technically, the Lost Trail Lodge is only four and a half miles away from Interstate 80 and Truckee, Calif.

The Lost Trail Lodge and its brethren—similarly isolated hotels scattered across the United States and Canada—manage to make deprivation appealing. These are places that really force you to get away from it all. They allow no calls to the office or dashes to the computer "just to check in." The only blackberries are the ones on the bushes.

Another off-grid vacation spot is in Branff National Park in Alberta. Brewster's Shadow Lake Lodge is nine miles by foot, cross-country ski or snowshoe from the trailhead. Once there, guests stay in one of 12 private cabins and share a central washroom that has hot showers and pit toilets. Rates include three meals a day (including packable lunches for day hikes to nearby lakes and passes) and afternoon tea with homemade treats.

TRAVEL

How to Find the Hidden Hideaways

Brooks Lodge: *Katmailand Inc., 4125 Aircraft Drive, Anchorage, 800-544-0551; www.katmailand. com.* Very pricey, but reduced rates are available in package deals with air transportation.

Lost Trail Lodge: *Tahoe West Company, 8600 Coldstream Trail, Truckee, Calif, 530-320-9268; www.losttraillodge.com.* Reasonable rates. Two-night minimum. The Web site has listings for places to rent equipment.

Shadow Lake Lodge: *Box 2606, Banff, Alberta, 403- 762-0115; www.shadowlakelodge.com.* For reservations or to check availability, visit the Web site. Prices vary by season and include private log-cabin accommodation and three meals a day.

Southwest Nordic Center: *Southwest Nordic Center, P.O. Box 3212, Taos, N.M., 505-758-4761; www.southwestnordiccenter.com.* Yurt rates are $65 to $125 a night for a group, depending on which night and which yurt you choose. The trails to the yurts are marked well, but those unfamiliar with finding routes might want to choose a guided trip, which includes the yurt rental, a professional guide and meals. Prices vary; call for details. Yurts are open only for the winter. —Catherine Price

Originally built in 1930 as a rest house by the Canadian Pacific Railway, the Shadow Lake Lodge won the Heritage Tourism Award for Best Environmental Practice a few years back. Supplies for the lodge arrive twice a week by horseback in the summer and by snow vehicles in the winter, and to minimize environmental impact, the lodge treats and reuses the water used for dishes and showers for irrigation. The lodge is propane-heated and solar-lighted.

For an off-the-grid experience without too much physical exertion, there are also fly-in options—Brooks Lodge in Katmai National Park in Alaska is accessible only by float plane.

Brooks's sister lodges—Kulik Lodge and the intimate, six-guest Grosvenor Lodge—are mainly oriented to fishing, but there's more at Brooks than abundant supplies of rainbow trout and arctic grayling. Once at Brooks, you can take a day trip to the nearby Valley of Ten Thousand Smokes, created when a powerful 1912 eruption of the Novarupta Volcano left a 40-square-mile area covered in volcanic ash, where countless wisps of steam still seep out through holes and fissures from the heated ground below. Or you can replace the healthy flush of exercise with the adrenaline rush that comes from close-up viewing of one of the world's largest populations of grizzly bears, which like to fish for salmon in the nearby Brooks River. (Elevated walkways and platforms prevent the bears from fishing for tourists.)

But for a truly bare-bones, off-grid experience, sign up for one of the Southwest Nordic Center's yurts, round, tentlike structures designed, in this case, specifically for winter use. The Southwest Nordic Center offers several options: four yurts in southern Colorado and one larger "luxury" yurt above Taos Ski Valley in northern New Mexico that can accommodate 6 to 10 guests.

The main activities at the yurts—which are open only in the winter—are snow-shoeing and cross-country skiing. The yurts in Colorado have a good mix of downhill and flat terrain that can accommodate groups with uneven skill levels; the New Mexican yurt, on steeper terrain, caters mostly to snowshoers and experienced skiers.

The yurts aren't as isolated as the other lodges (Southwest Nordic Center's are two to four and a half miles from the road), but once you're there, no homemade breakfast awaits. You have to carry in all your food yourself. Each yurt sits on a raised wooden platform and has a wood-burning stove, lanterns, mattresses without linens and a propane stove for cooking. There's no electricity or running water, but cookware and board games are provided. As a touch of comfort, the outhouse's toilet seat hangs on a hook by the stove to keep it warm.

Most Americans don't think of outhouses as a vacation perk, but there's a certain appeal in having to work for your vacation. A little bit of struggle, it seems, can make the escape more fun.

—Catherine Price

America's Greatest Trails

Some no wider than a fat man, all scenic or historic

While they may not have hiked it top to bottom, most Americans have heard of the Appalachian Trail. Many are unaware, though, that the Appalachian belongs to a much larger system of trails. In 1968, Congress passed the National Trails Assistance Act to establish a national trail system.

The trails fall into two categories: national scenic trails, which are protected scenic corridors for outdoor recreation, and national historic trails, which recognize prominent past routes of exploration, migration and military action and may consist of no more than a series of roadside markers.

The entire system includes 19 trails and covers most of the country. Here are eight of the loveliest hikes in America, whatever your stamina.

Appalachian National Scenic Trail.

Length: 2,174 miles

Beginning in Georgia and ending in Maine, the trail hugs the crest of the Appalachian Mountains and is open only to hikers. Appalachian Trail Conservancy, Harpers Ferry, W.V. 25425. 304-535-6278; www.appalachiantrail.org

Continental Divide National Scenic Trail.

3,100 miles

The trail provides spectacular backcountry travel through the Rocky Mountains from Mexico to Canada. The trail is open to hikers, pack and saddle animals and, in some places, off-road motorized vehicles. Continental Divide Trail Alliance, Baltimore, Md. 21218. 303-838-3760; www.cdtrail.org/page.php

TRAVEL

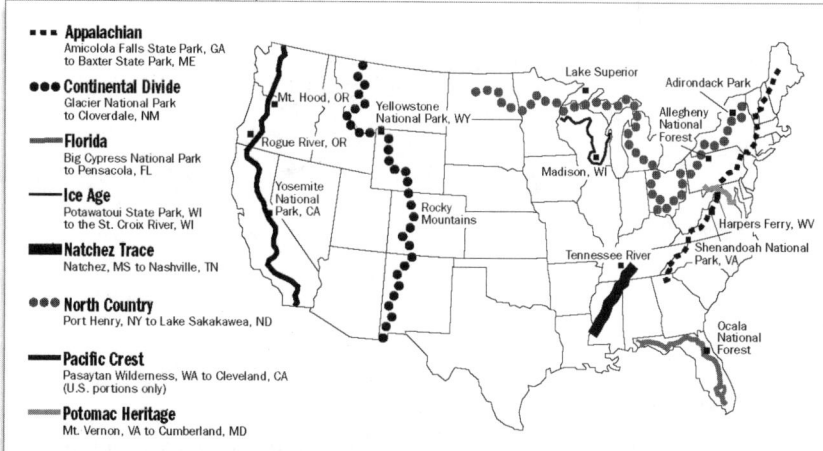

Appalachian
Amicolola Falls State Park, GA to Baxter State Park, ME

Continental Divide
Glacier National Park to Cloverdale, NM

Florida
Big Cypress National Park to Pensacola, FL

Ice Age
Potawatoui State Park, WI to the St. Croix River, WI

Natchez Trace
Natchez, MS to Nashville, TN

North Country
Port Henry, NY to Lake Sakakawea, ND

Pacific Crest
Pasaytan Wilderness, WA to Cleveland, CA (U.S. portions only)

Potomac Heritage
Mt. Vernon, VA to Cumberland, MD

NATIONAL SCENIC TRAILS

Benton MacKaye, the man who created the Appalachian Trail, thought it should be no wider than the space required by the average fat man. The majority of the trails are open to hikers only, although some allow mountain bikes and horses. Many are works in progress and have large sections closed to the public. Call ahead to inquire about available sections, allowable modes of transportation and camping permits.

Florida National Scenic Trail. *1,300 miles*

The Florida Trail extends from Big Cypress National Preserve in south Florida to just west of Pensacola in the northern part of the Florida Panhandle. The trail passes through America's only subtropical landscape, making it popular in winter. Florida Trail Association, Gainesville, Fla. 32064. 352-378-8823; www.florida-trail. org

Ice Age National Scenic Trail. *1,200 miles*

The trail follows a chain of moraine hills zig-zaging across Wisconsin from Lake Michigan to the St. Croix River. Almost half the trail is open to the public, and certain sections are sometimes even used for marathons, ski races and ultrama-rathons. National Park Service, Madison, Wis. 53711. 608-441-5610; www.nps.gov/iat

Natchez Trace National Scenic Trail. *110 miles*

The trail lies within the boundairies the Natchez Trace Parkway, which extends from Natchez, Miss., to Nashville, Tenn., and com-memorates an ancient path that began as a series of animal tracks and trails used by Native Amer-icans. Natchez Trace Parkway, Tupelo, Miss. 38801. 800-305-7417; www.nps.gov/natt

North Country National Scenic Trail. *4,000 miles*

Conceived in the mid-1960s, this trail links the Adirondack Mountains with the Missouri River in North Dakota. National Park Service, Madison, Wis. 53711. 608-441-5610; www. nps.gov/noco

Pacific Crest National Scenic Trail. *2,650 miles*

Running along the spectacular shoulders of the Cascade and Sierra Nevada mountain ranges from Canada to Mexico, the trail is the West Coast coun-terpart to the Appalachian Trail. U.S.D.A. Forest Ser-vice, Portland, Ore. 97204. 707-562-8881; www.fs.fed. us/pct

Potomac Heritage National Scenic Trail. *770 miles*

Commemorates the unique mix of history and recreation along the Potomac River. The last 20 or so miles of the trail along the Chesapeake and Ohio Canal provide a wonder-ful bicycle ride that ends in the heart of Washington, D.C. National Park Service National Capital FDO, Washington, D.C. 20242. 304-535-4014; www.nps.gov/pohe

— **California**
Independence, MO to Sacramento, CA

‧‧‧‧ **Iditarod**
Seward, AK to Nome, AK

●●● **Juan Bautista de Anza**
Nogales, AZ to San Francisco, CA

●●● **Lewis and Clark**
St. Louis, MO to Astoria, OR

▬ **Mormon Pioneer**
Nauvoo, IL to Salt Lake City, UT

— **Nez Perce (Nee-Me-Poo)**
Wallowa Lake, OR to Chinook, MT

— **Oregon**
Independence, MO to Oregon City, OR

▬ **Overmountain Victory**
Abington, VA to Kings Mountain National Military Park, SC

‧‧‧‧‧ **Pony Express**
St. Joseph, MO to Sacramento, CA

▬ ▬ **Santa Fe**
Santa Fe, NM to Boonville, MO

▬ **Trail of Tears**
Charleston, TN to Tahlequah, OK (northern)
Chattanooga, TN to Tahlequah, OK (southern)

NATIONAL HISTORIC TRAILS

National historic trails are somewhat more conceptual than national sce-nic trails. Their objective is to preserve any historic remnants of the trail rather than provide a continuous footpath across its entire length. They are often are no more than a series of roadside signs that direct travelers to historic sites or markers, though foot trails do appear from time to time at the roadside stops. The GORP website has detailed informa-tion on each National Historic Trail at gorp.away.com/gorp/resource/ us_trail/historic.htm.

The Top 10 Parks Around the World

Spectacular scenery on every continent

When wanderlust sets in, you might just pack your backpack and head for one of these national parks around the world. The list was compiled by the Coalition of National Park Service Retirees (CNPSR), a 700-member group of former U.S. national park workers.

1. Tongariro National Park, *New Zealand*
This is one of the North Island's three World Heritage Sites. It features volcanic peaks (one of which is active) and is still home to many Maoris, who donated the park to New Zealand in 1887, when it became the world's fourth national park.

2. Kakadu National Park, *Australia*
This World Heritage Site has magnificent vistas, great waterfalls and stunning displays of Aboriginal rock art, and is habitat to an awesome predator, the estuarine (saltwater) crocodile.

3. Snowdonia NationalPark, *Wales, Great Britain*
Snowdonia is a lovely mountain park, with Mount Snowdon, which is comprised of slate, rising to 3,560 feet. While this park is not particularly geologically or scenically spectacular, its appeals in part due to its peaceful nature.

4. Kruger National Park, *South Africa*
Millions of acres of habitat and little development give visitors an opportunity to see many large African mammals and magnificent birds. It is one of the few places where wildlife is in charge—it wanders free and the visitors are controlled.

5. Tikal National Park, *Guatemala*
This World Heritage Site contains the spectacular ruins of a Maya settlement from around 250–900 A.D. rising from the jungle that surrounds them. Tour the site with a Mayan guide for a thrilling visit. (See "The Pyramids Next Door" on page 593.)

6. Iguazu National Park, *Argentina*
Iguazu Falls are 70 meters high, but even more impressive is their width: the river at the falls is 1500 meters wide. A thrilling experience is the short boat ride and walk along the catwalks to the most striking of the hundreds of falls, Garganta del Diablo, the Devil's Throat.

7. Sagarmantha National Park, *Nepal*
The park includes Mount Everest, among other peaks. It has distinctive wildlife and small picturesque Sherpa villages with their gumpas (monasteries).

8. Madain Saley National Historic Park, *Saudi Arabia*
Between 500 B.C. and 100 A.D., the Nabatean people created 125 monumental cut-rock tombs and facades, edifices up to 130 feet tall, that are still standing today, remarkably well preserved.

9. Plitvice Lakes National Park, *Croatia*
Located inland, about halfway between Zagreb and Split, the park features small lakes, streams, beautiful waterfalls and moderately mountainous terrain. Travertine gives the water a distinctive blue-green color. Quiet, non-polluting electric ferries connect some of the trails by way of the lakes. The fall "color season" is especially spectacular.

10. Hortobagy National Park, *Hungary*
Located on great Hungarian plains, this park is a World Heritage Site. It is a refuge for the Przewalski horse and migratory waterfowl. Culturally, it preserves and interprets traditional Hungarian folkways, such as the country's nomadic herding culture.

TRAVEL

Catching a Glimpse of a Bighorn

The best places to see magnificent animals

It seems to be an inexorable law that as the human population expands wild animal species decline. Viewing large numbers of wild animals in a relatively pristine habitat is increasingly a rare experience. But it's still possible—even in America.

Bighorn Sheep

Georgetown Viewing Site, Georgetown, Colorado

Located along Interstate 70, about halfway between Denver and Vail, the Georgetown Viewing Site is probably the most accessible place for viewing Rocky Mountain bighorn sheep. Between 175 and 200 bighorns occupy the rocky cliffs along the north side of Clear Creek Canyon. Fall and winter are the best times to look for them. (There's a lookout tower shaped like a ram's horns.) An exhibit includes interpretative displays and mounted viewing scopes.

303-569-2555; wildlife.state.co.us/Viewing/WheretoGo/AccessibleViewingSites/

Manatees

Crystal River National Wildlife Refuge, Florida

Crystal River N.W.R. is made up of nine small islands totaling little more than 40 acres, but their location in Kings Bay is critical. The headwaters of the Crystal River, Kings Bay is fed by fresh water springs at a consistent 72 degrees year round. It is this warm water that attracts the large manatees during cooler weather when temperatures in open water fall. The refuge is critical habitat for 15 to 20 percent of the U.S. manatee population, and is one of six places in Florida with climates unaffected by outside changes.

352-563-2088; www.fws.gov/crystalriver

Rocky Mountain Elk

Horseshoe Park, Rocky Mountain National Park, Colorado

During September and October, bull elk bugle as a means to intimidate rival males and as a physical release for the tensions of the mating season.. Bugling usually begins an hour before sunset and starts off as a buildup of deep, resonant tones rising quickly to a high-pitched squeal before dropping to a series of grunts. It is this call, or bugle, that gives rise to the term *rut* for mating season.

970-586-1399; www.nps.gov/romo/resources/plantsandanimals/featuredpanda/elk.html

Wintering Elk

National Elk Refuge, Jackson Hole, Wyoming

When snow comes to the high country in the Grand Tetons, elk migrate from their high-elevation summer range to a winter range in the valley. Almost 7,500 elk inhabit the area. Elk arrive in early November and return to the high country in early May. In the winter, visitors can view elk from a horse-drawn sleigh. Sleighs run from late December to March, 10 a.m. to 4 p.m. daily. Tours operate from the National Museum of Wildlife Art, 3 miles north of Jackson on U.S. Highway 26/191.

307-733-9212; www.fws.gov/nationalelkrefuge

Sandhill Cranes

Platte River, Nebraska

For about 5 weeks in early spring (usually starting in March), more than three-quarters of the world's population of sandhill cranes gathers along the Platte River in central Nebraska. More than 500,000 of these stately birds rest and fatten up here on their way back to breeding grounds in the Arctic. A website has information on viewing areas, crane migration, and nearby lodging. There is also a live webcam so people can watch the migration from their computer screens: nebraskaflyway.com

For more information, contact the U.S. Fish and Wildlife Service's Nongame Migratory Bird Coordinator (303-236-4409 or 308–382–6468; www.fws.gov/mountain-prairie/migbird).

Gray Whales
Point Reyes National Seashore, California

Gray whales engage in the longest migration of any mammal in the world, swimming 6,000 miles from feeding grounds in the icy waters north of Alaska to warm breeding lagoons off Baja California, Mexico, and 6,000 back.

Every autumn, the entire gray whale population of more than 18,000 heads south at about the same time. That means that as many as 30 whales an hour may be moving in "pulses" past a particular point during peak weeks. Though other California counties boast worthwhile whale-watching venues, it is the Point Reyes Peninsula that has geography working heavily in its favor.

415-464-5100; www.nps.gov/pore

California and Steller's Sea Lions
Sea Lion Caves, Oregon

After descending more than 200 feet in an elevator to Sea Lion Caves on the coast of Oregon, you will find dim light, the hollow sound of waves crashing against cliffs and the echoed barks of hundreds of Steller's sea lions (present year round) and California sea lions (present from September to April). Sea lions swim and loaf below a cliff-top observation deck.

541-547-3111; www.sealioncaves.com

TRAVEL

Where Else to Watch the Whales Around the World

Thar she blows! According to the World Wildlife Fund these are the spots where whales are most likely to spout off around the world.

WHERE, Country	*Access*	**Whales**	Peak season
S. OCEAN WHALE SANCTUARY, Antarctica	*Boat access only*	**Humpback, southern right, minke whales**	Summer
SAMANA BAY, Dominican Republic	*Boat and shoreline access*	**Humpback, pilot, Bryde's whales**	January–March
CAMPBELL RIVER, British Columbia	*Shoreline, sailboat access*	**Minke and orcas (killer whales)**	June–September
CAPE COD, Massachusetts	*Boat access only*	**Humpback, fin, northern right, minke, pilot whales**	April–October
BAJA CALIFORNIA, Mexico	*Shoreline and boat access*	**Gray, blue and humpbacks**	Almost all year round
LOFOTEN ISLANDS, Norway	*Boat access only*	**Sperm, minkes and orcas**	Summer
KAIKKOURA, New Zealand	*Boat, shoreline access*	**Sperm whale, orcas, also Hector's & dusky dolphins**	Year round
WHALE ROUTE, South Africa	*Shoreline access*	**Southern right, humpback, Bryde's whales, orca**	August–November
PATAGONIA, Argentina	*Boat and shoreline access*	**Southern right whale and orcas**	June–December
SHIKOKU, Japan	*Boat access only*	**Bryde's whales**	Year round

Mexican Free-tailed Bats

Carlsbad Caverns National Park, New Mexico

On warm summer evenings in the Chihuahuan Desert, thousands of Mexican free-tailed bats exit in a whirling, smokelike column from the natural mouth of Carlsbad Caverns. Research indicates that Mexican free-tailed bats have inhabited the Carlsbad taverns for over 5,000 years, with an estimated 300,000 bats in the caverns.

They emerge at dusk to feed on moths; other flights occur in late August and September, when young bats born in June join the evening ritual. Flight Amphitheater, which is located at the mouth of the cavern, seats up to 1,000 people. Park rangers offer programs about the bats from Memorial Day to Labor Day prior to the evening flights. But don't expect to see bats if you visit during the winter—they will have migrated to Mexico (505-785-2232; www.nps.gov/cave).

Bald Eagles

Skagit River, Mount Baker–Snoqualmie National Forest, Washington

One of the largest concentrations of wintering bald eagles in the lower 48 states occurs at the Skagit River Bald Eagle Natural Area in northern Washington State. More than 300 bald eagles gather along the river's gravel bars between 7 a.m. and 11 a.m. to feed on spawned-out salmon. The eagles feast here between November and early March, with peak numbers occurring in mid-January.

For more information: The Nature Conservancy, Washington Field Office (206-343-4344, www.nature.org/wherewework/northamerica/states/washington) or Mount Baker Ranger District, Sedro Woolley, Washington (206-470-4060; www.fs.fed.us/r6/mbs/contact).

The Galápagos Unbound

Free as a breeze with the blue-footed boobies

It can be tough deciding which wildlife encounters are worthy of pause after only a few days in the Galápagos, those South American islands of evolution cauterized by sun and magma. Nearly any tour that cruises this isolated yet popular chain, 600 miles west of Ecuador, comes packaged with extreme closeups of washer-size tortoises, swimming lizards and crabs the color of rainbows.

Trips to the Galápagos archipelago—nearly all of which is a national park—typically unfold aboard the commercial yachts that ply the waters here. From 4 to 100 passengers at a time are whisked around on tightly choreographed schedules between islands. While convenient and comfortable, wildlife encounters are often limited, since passengers must sleep on the boats and disembark only at strictly controlled wildlife viewing sites for short periods.

But now, for the adventurous there's another option: sea kayaking. Unlike yacht-based trips that may offer some kayaking, these excursions are all about melding into the sea and letting the landscape slide by under blue-footed-booby skies. Come evening, paddlers run the kayaks into the sand, pitch tents on the beach and wait for birds to scream in the dawn. The combination is spectacular. Not only do paddlers have the thrill of being among the first tourists to camp in these locations, but along the way, they also nuzzle bow to beak with so much kooky wildlife that stumbling upon sea turtles in the act becomes, well, normal.

An 8-day itinerary offered through ROW International, a division of River Odysseys West (800-451-6034; www.rowinternational.com), samples six of the chain's 18 or so islands and islets and includes a mix of hiking, snorkeling and well-earned rests at an inn.

Though the campsites are spectacular, as a whole the Galápagos are not particularly beautiful, at least not in the way tropical islands often are. There are few palms among uninterrupted stands of haggard salt scrub plants. Some beaches have azure waters and baby-powder sand, but most shorelines are rocky and lapped by dark waves cold enough to warrant a wet suit. "We fancied even that the bushes smelt unpleasantly," Charles Darwin wrote during the voyage of the Beagle, the trip in 1835 that sparked his theory on evolution.

It is the diversity of animals—penguins and flamingos, for example—and their bizarre mutations that bring people here today. After countless generations of not needing to fly, some cormorants can't; the four-eyed blenny fish can crawl on land; iguanas sneeze salt. Most creatures are freakishly unafraid of people. The interaction with wildlife is extraordinary. Sea lions nibble on flippers while others play tug-of-war with a small section of cord. Frigate birds, iguanas, giant tortoises and even a short-eared owl all sit patiently for their portraits.

But it is the slow pace of gliding inches over the water in a kayak that makes this Galápagos experience special. While kayakers can't disembark anywhere they please, the boats are maneuverable enough to ride tidal surges through caves and to cruise rocky shorelines that motorized craft cannot. —Tim Neville

Wet and Wild Rain Forests
South America's top tropical forests

Tropical rain forests occupy only 7 percent of the earth's land surface, yet they contain over half its living organisms. What makes all that life possible is warm weather—averaging 80 degrees—and, of course, rain—lots of it. Tropical rain forests average 100 to 400 inches of rainfall a year, whereas

---

TRAVEL

ⓘ **INSIDE INFO**

Where to Catch a Butterfly

○ From mid-September through early November, about 300 million monarch butterflies flit and flutter from Canada and the northern United States to their winter homes in California and Mexico. Accordingly, the annual spectacle of southbound swarms of orange-and-black-speckled monarchs inspires festivals and butterfly-tagging events across the continent.

○ The tagging is coordinated by Monarch Watch, a research program based at the University of Kansas. Researchers there supply the numbered tags, which look like the stickers used to mark produce at the grocery store. Volunteers at various tagging sites demonstrate how to capture butterflies and affix the stickers to their wings. Then, anyone can track tagged butterflies' progress by checking for sightings on the Monarch Watch Web site (www.monarchwatch.org).

New York City receives 43 inches a year and San Francisco only about 20 inches a year.

In contrast to other places on earth, most of the plant life in rain forests is in the treetops. Below this primary canopy is a secondary one where shrubs and smaller trees grow. Plant life on the forest floor is limited because of the lack of light.

Where should one go to witness the glories of wet and wild habitats up close? Thomas Lovejoy, former president of the H. John Heinz III Center for Science, Economics and the Environment, and conservation pioneer Russell Mittermeier suggest these South American spots.

COSTA RICA: *Costa Rican rain forests do not have the staggering variety of species or sheer density of plant and animal life of the most* *significant rain forests in the world, such as those along the eastern Andes. However, they contain about 5 percent of the world's plants and animals.*

Parque Nacional Corcovado. *On the Peninsula de Osa, about 115 miles southeast of San José*

The largest primary lowland rain forest in Costa Rica. Over 400 species of birds live here, including scarlet macaws. The park is also home to pumas, ocelots, tapirs and jaguars, as well as numerous rare butterflies and the almost extinct Harpy eagle.

Monteverde Cloud Forest Reserve. *A 4-hour drive north of San José*

Situated on a mountain 4,600 feet above sea level, the reserve is a tropical cloud forest where constant low clouds hover in the treetops, creating a highly humid environment. The park contains over 2,000 species of wildlife, including mantled howler monkeys. Also, one of the last remaining nesting sites of the quetzal, reputedly the most beautiful bird in the world.

EASTERN SLOPE OF THE ANDES: *This area extends from the southern part of the Colombian*

Guides for a Rainy Stay

The following groups organize eco-sensitive expeditions to many of the rain forests discussed here.

- FIELD GUIDES. Austin, Tex.
  800-728-4953; www.fieldguides.com

- INTERNATIONAL EXPEDITIONS. Helena, Ala.
  800-633-4734; www.ietravel.com

- MOUNTAIN TRAVEL/SOBEK EXPEDITIONS. Emeryville, Calif. 888-831-7526; www.mtsobek.com

- VICTOR EMANUEL NATURE TOURS. Austin, Tex.
  800-328-8368; www.ventbird.com

Amazon through Ecuador and Peru. Norman Myers, a leading expert on biodiversity, says these rain forests constitute the richest biotic zone on earth.

Yasuni National Park. *Oriente region of Ecuador*

The lakes in Yasuni National Park are home to piranhas and caimans (relatives of the crocodile). A number of Indian tribes also live here, including the Waorani, who until recently have avoided contact with outsiders.

Tambopata-Caudano Reserve and National Park. *About 40 miles south of Puerto Maldonado in the Madre de Dios region of Peru*

This park is contiguous with the Madidi National Park in Peru, and together the two form the largest uninterrupted rain forest on earth. Tambopata-Caudano is also the best place to see butterflies—over 1,100 species live here. In addition, this park has the largest known macaw lick in South America.

Manu National Park. *About 75 miles northeast of Cuzco in Peru*

This rain forest is the largest biosphere reserve zone in South America. It has the highest documented diversity of life in the world, containing an estimated 8,000 plant species, 200 animal species and over 900 species of birds.

RAIN FOREST, BRAZIL: *This belt of rain forest once extended along the coast of South America; today, only a small portion remains. Up to half of the plant species found here are not found anywhere else. The forest contains the largest variety of primates in South America—over 24 different species.*

Itatiaia National Park. *Located between Rio de Janeiro and São Paulo near Itatiaia, Brazil*

This park, with its numerous hiking trails, is

very accessible. Over 100 plants found here are endemic to the Atlantic rain forest. Itatiaia National Park is also home to the three-toed sloth and the red-breasted toucan.

The Pyramids Next Door

Mayan ruins are magnificent—and much closer

Scattered throughout Central America are more ancient cities and ruins than are found in all of Egypt. They are from the Mayan civilization, the most advanced and longest-lived in ancient America. Starting in 300 B.C., the Mayans built metropolises that rivaled those of Rome and Greece—complete with large pyramids, ornate palaces and temples. Mayan civilization was highly developed. But, even before the conquistadores arrived, Mayan civilization began to decline because of war, it is surmised, and diminishing natural resources.

La Ruta Maya, also known as Mundo Maya, is a 1,500-mile route that runs through the lands of the Maya—western Honduras, northern Belize, Guatemala, El Salvador and the Mexican states of Yucatán, Quintana Roo, Tabasco, Campeche and Chiapas. Mostly paved, the route is a modern creation, dedicated to the preservation of Mayan heritage and wildlife habitats. Below is a list of some of the most significant Mayan cities, compiled with the help of Gordon Willey, a former professor of archaeology at Harvard, and Joyce Kelley, author of *An Archaeological Guide to Northern Central America: Belize, Guatemala, Honduras, and El Salvador*.

Calakmul. *Campeche, Mexico.* Calakmul was one of the largest Mayan cities. It is estimated that over 60,000 people lived here at one time. One of the oldest Mayan sites, it was established around 1500 B.C. So far, 6,500 structures have been mapped at Calakmul, including a 175-foot-high, 500-square-

foot pyramid. From the top of it one can see the Danta Pyramid at El Mirador, another preclassic Mayan city over 20 miles away. Until recently, Calakmul, located in a large jungle reserve, was reachable only by an overgrown jeep path. However, a road has been built into the site, and travel time from the main road is only several hours. (For more on traveling to Mexico, see "Off the Beaten Track Mexico" on page 608.)

Chichén Itzá. *Yucatán, Mexico.* Over three million people visit Chichén Itzá each year; it is the most well-known and most extensively excavated Mayan city. Built around A.D. 500, it was the most important city in the late classic period. Between the 11th and 13th centuries, this was where some of the last great Mayan buildings were constructed. Of all the Mayan cities, Chichén Itzá has the most varied architecture and sculpture, due in part to the influence of the Toltec Indian civilization of central Mexico.

LA RUTA MAYA
A modern-day creation, La Ruta Maya takes visitors through parts of Central America where ancient Mayan civilization once flourished.

CHICHÉN ITZÁ ■
COBA ■
UXMAL ■
CALAKMUL ■
PALENQUE ■
TIKAL ■
Mexico
Belize
Guatemala
COPÁN ■
Honduras
El Salvador

0   50   100
Miles

TRAVEL

Uxmal, *Yucatán, Mexico.* Uxmal has some of the finest of the restored ruins and is considered by many to be the most beautiful of the Mayan cities. Many important satellite sites such as Kabah, Sayil and Labnó are nearby.

Uxmal is where Mayan civilization reached its apogee between A.D. 800 and 1000. The Governor's Palace is testimony to the Mayan's knowledge of astronomy. The central doorway of this 24-room building is aligned with the path of the planet Venus. At the bright planet's southern solstice, the doorway is suffused with light illuminating the throne in the courtyard, as well as a temple on a hilltop 10 kilometers away.

Several hours' drive away is Mérida. Built by the Spanish in the 16th century, Mérida has fine examples of Spanish colonial architecture, excellent cuisine and a vibrant nightlife and is a good departure point for many day trips to the Gulf Coast.

Coba, *Quintana Roo, Mexico.* Located in a jungle, the mainly unexcavated ruins of Coba, connected by Mayan limestone causeways, cover an area of 20 square miles. From the 140-foot-high Nohoch Mul pyramid, the views across the jungle and of the other ruins are magnificent. Nearby is Tulum, a Mayan site by the sea, south of which are pristine beaches bordered by verdant jungles.

Palenque, *Chiapas, Mexico.* In 1952, an excavation uncovered the intact tomb of Lord Pacal, one of the greatest Mayan kings, who ruled the city in the seventh century. At winter solstice, the sun enters a doorway, hits the back wall and appears to descend the stairway into a tomb.

Tikal National Park, *Guatemala.* Tikal was a great commercial and political power from 100 B.C. to A.D. 900. Plaza Mayor features well-restored buildings dating from 200 B.C. The 212-foot-tall temple is the second-tallest pyramid built by the Mayans. The area known as the Petén is one of the most remote on the Ruta Maya. Eighteen miles from Tikal is Flores, the regional capital of the Petén.

Copán, *Honduras.* The southernmost Mayan city, Copán lies in one of the most remote parts of Honduras. For more than 1,000 years, Copán was a center of culture and learning. The Hieroglyphic Stairway is composed of 2,500 blocks of stone and records the history of 17 rulers of a single royal dynasty. Fine pottery, jewelry and jade carvings are on display at the Museo Regional de Arqueológica near the site.

Copán Ruinas, one of a number of interesting Spanish colonial villages in the area, is situated a few miles from the ruins. There are some small hotels here that offer simple but comfortable lodgings. About 10 miles from Copán is Agua Caliente, where one can swim in hot springs.

The Best African Safaris
Try these great spots for viewing game

For years, if you were heading out on a safari, you headed for the game parks of Kenya and Tanzania in East Africa—most notably Serengeti National Park, the Ngorongoro Conservation Area and Masai Mara Natural Reserve—where huge herds of animals still wander across the plains. Nowhere else in Africa could you see such a vast collection of wildlife in its natural habitat.

But other less frequently visited parts of Africa also beckon. Notably, southern Africa (Namibia, Zimbabwe and Botswana) is increasingly popular. Instead of the endless savannahs of eastern Africa, immense swamps and forests predominate in southern Africa. In general, safaris to the southern part of the continent offer more options for the active tourist—from walking safaris to expeditions on elephant and horseback. Also, night drives are

WHERE THE WILD THINGS ARE
Africa's best game-watching parks

KENYA: **1.** *Sibiloi NP* **2.** *Samburu-Isiolo and Shaba NR* **3.** *Nakuru* **4.** *Meru* **5.** *Masai Mara NR* **6.** *Nairobi NP* **7.** *Tsavo NP* **8.** *Amboseli NP*

TANZANIA: **9.** *Serengeti NP* **10.** *Ngorongoro Cons. Area* **11.** *Tarangire NP* **12.** *Gombe NP* **13.** *Mahale Mts. NP*

UGANDA: **14.** *Kibale FR*

ZAIRE: **15.** *Virunga NP* **16.** *Kahuzi Biega NP*

ZIMBABWE: **17.** *Mana Pools NP* **18.** *Hwange NP* **19.** *Gonarezhou NP*

BOTSWANA: **20.** *Chobe NP*

SOUTH AFRICA: **21.** *Kruger NP* **22.** *Hluhluwe and Umfosoli GR*

NAMIBIA: **23.** *Etosha NP*

NOTE: NR = Nature reserve; NP = National park; GR = Game reserve; FR = Forest reserve.

SOURCE: *The Safari Companion, A Guide to Watching African Mammals* by Richard Estes (Chelsea Green Publishing)

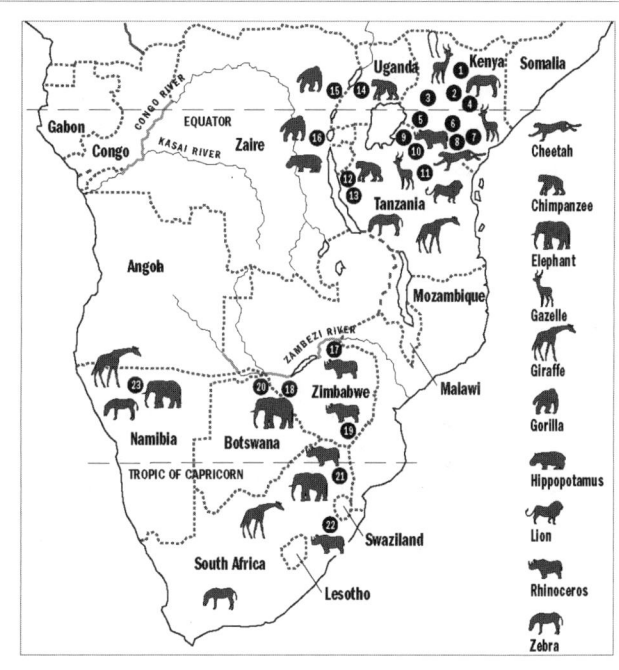

TRAVEL

much more common, an activity prohibited in national parks in eastern Africa. Such forays afford a different perspective on the wild kingdom, since some animals, like leopards, are nocturnal.

Below are some of the game-viewing spots that are not to be missed in Africa. Note: For a successful safari, timing is everything. At certain times of the year, the animals you wish to see may be away on migration or dispersed amid thick vegetation (during the rainy season), so plan ahead.

Kenya *(East Africa)* has the highest concentrations of animals and tourists. Its biggest draw is the greatest game migration on the planet, which moves from the Serengeti in Tanzania up to the Masai Mara every year. Over a million wildebeests and hundreds of thousands of zebra can be found here from mid-July to mid-September. The best places to see game are in central Kenya at the national parks—Tsavo, Samburu, Amboseli and Masai Mara (which boasts the largest lion population in Africa).

Kenya is also one of the best places in the world to see birds; over 1,000 species of birds live here in a variety of different habitats. In addition, Kenya has some of the most varied and distinctive tribal cultures in Africa, including the Masai, who still maintain their traditional nomadic life.

Tanzania *(East Africa)* has Kenya's game without the crowds. The Serengeti and the Ngorongoro Crater (the largest caldera in the world and the best place to see black rhino in Africa) abound with large herds of zebra and wildebeest. As in Kenya, tourists are restricted to safari vehicles in the national parks.

For walking or canoe safaris, head south to the Selous Game Reserve, the largest wildlife preserve in Africa, uninhabited except for a half dozen small tourist camps.

Uganda *(East Africa).* This landlocked country is mostly forested and mountainous, with a terrain reminiscent of Asia—very green, with terraced farming. Uganda is the best place in Africa to see primates and a safe place (safe from warring humans, that is) where one can comfortably see gorillas. Visitors to the primate forests—the most notable of which is the Bwini or Impenetrable Forest—must be ready for hard hikes and prepared for occasional deluges of rain.

Botswana *(Southern Africa).* The wildlife is abundant, the lodges are comfortable and the transportation is good. Botswana has more intimate camps and lodges, which makes it a more expensive place to visit than other African countries. While much of the country is arid and desertlike, the Okavango delta, in the northern part of the country, is like a primordial oasis. The only inland delta in the world, the Okavango is a lush swamp whose numerous rivulets and waterways empty directly into the Kalahari desert; the best way to explore it is by canoe. In addition, this wilderness contains more plant species than all the rain forests of West and Central Africa combined.

Adjoining the Okavango, the Moremi Reserve and Chobe National Park have a high and varied concentration of wildlife (including some of the largest elephant herds) in Africa. Botswana, together with Namibia, is home to the majority of the 60,000 Bushmen in Africa.

Zimbabwe *(Southern Africa).* Zimbabwe has traditionally had a good tourist infrastructure, excellent conservation programs and perhaps the widest variety of safari options, including walking, kayaking, houseboat safaris and some of the best white-water rafting in the world. Seven percent of the country is protected, and the national parks, especially Mana Pools, located on the Zambezi river gorge, offer opportunities to see one of the greatest concentrations of wildlife during the dry season. However, check first with the State Department (www.travel.state.gov) about the safety of traveling to the country.

Zambia *(Southern Africa).* While it is more of a challenge to get to and travel through Zambia than other African countries, it rewards the intrepid traveler. The Luangwa Valley is one of the most beautiful places in Africa. Crisscrossed by numerous rivers, the valley is home to many birds, African buffalo, hippos, crocodiles, zebras and elephants. Walking and night safaris are readily available.

Malawi *(Southern Africa).* There is not much tourism in Malawi, although there are numerous game-watching opportunities. Lake Malawi, which takes up a fifth of the country, contains over 300 varieties of fish, the greatest diversity of tropical freshwater fish of any lake in the world; it's also an excellent snorkeling spot. Zomba plateau, an enormous 8,000-foot plateau that topographically looks like Switzerland—except for the plethora of brilliantly colored orchids and the leopards and antelope roaming about—can be explored on horseback.

Safari Travel Agents

These agents book lodges, safaris and tented camps throughout Africa.

ABERCROMBIE & KENT, INC. 1411 Opus Pl., Downers Grove, Ill, 60515 (800-554-7016; www.abercrombiekent.com)

AFRICAN TRAVEL 1000 East Broadway, Glendale, Calif. 91205 (800–421–8907; www.africantravelinc.com)

UNCHARTED OUTPOSTS INC. 9 Village Lane, Santa Fe, N.M. 87505 (888-995-0909; www.unchartedoutposts.com)

MICATO SAFARIS. 15 West 26th Street, New York, N.Y. 10010 (212 545-7111; www.micato.com)

OVERSEAS ADVENTURE TRAVEL 124 Mount Auburn St., Cambridge, Mass. 02138 (800-493-6824; www.oattravel.com0

Adventures

The World's Best Treks

From Katmandu to Peru, classic trails not to be missed

Today, trekking has gone mainstream. Companies with glossy brochures offer deluxe trips to every imaginable corner of the globe. You can take your pick from a classic trek in Nepal to a pure wilderness experience in New Zealand. And you can pay Ritz-Carlton prices to sleep in tents under the stars.

The immense popularity of trekking is sparking environmental concerns. Once-pristine environments have become less so as trekkers have passed through. Cultures once isolated from outside influences now experience them with fair regularity.

We asked veteran trekker Robert Strauss, who has hiked on six continents and written numerous books on the subject, including *Adventure Trekking: A Handbook for Independent Travelers*, to pick what he considers the world's classic, still relatively pristine treks. Here are his some of his choices.

ALASKA. Three-quarters of Alaska is protected wilderness. Backcountry trekking through Denali National Park is regulated through zoning and permit quotas. Free permits are issued a day in advance by the Visitor Access Center. Once you have your permit, a shuttle bus will drop you off at your assigned zone. The park has no marked trails; hikers find their way with topographical maps. Denali, which is dominated by Mount McKinley, America's highest mountain at 20,320 feet, is accessible from Anchorage by car, bus and rail.

GREENLAND. A demanding terrain, lack of trails (for navigation at these latitudes you'll need to adjust your compass) and fickle weather make this destination at the Arctic Circle a challenge even for experienced trekkers. The 5- to 6-day trek between Qaqortoq, the major town in southern Greenland, and

TRAVEL

Igaliku offers the scenic variety of icebergs, bays, waterfalls and boulder fields. There are also Norse church ruins dating back to medieval times.

NEPAL. The main gateway for the Annapurna region is the town of Pokhara. The Annapurna Conservation Area Project, based in Pokhara, provides regional support for minimizing impact on the environment. The Annapurna Circuit is a trekking tour de force: it passes through alpine forests to arid semidesert characteristic of Tibet; crosses over the Thorong La pass with dazzling views at 17,650 feet; and drops into the Kali Gandaki gorge, the world's deepest. The full circuit takes around 18 days for seasoned trekkers putting in some seven hours of hiking each day. Be prepared for the effects of high altitude and a possible wait to cross the pass if it's snowbound. The trail has plenty of teahouses and lodges en route.

NEW ZEALAND. Tramping (the New Zealand term for hiking/trekking) has become a passion for the locals. At the southern end of the South Island lie Mt. Aspiring National Park and Fiordland National Park, which are straddled by the Routeburn Track. This very popular 3-day tramp has great alpine scenery and passes through valleys covered by rain forest. There is a booking system for huts and campsites on the Routeburn. (Less crowded tracks in the same area are the Greenstone and the Caples.) Information is available from the Department of Conservation in Queenstown (www.doc.govt.nz), which provides a transport base to access the northern end of the trail; Te Anau is the nearest town at the southern end.

PAKISTAN. The northernmost region of Pakistan, where four mountain ranges (Himalaya, Hindu Kush, Pamirs and Karakorum) meet, boasts the largest number of high peaks in the world. The Concordia trek, which passes through this area, is rated as one of the world's best. Because of the travel restrictions here, your best bet is to go on a trip organized through a tour operator. From the trailhead in Askole, the trek takes 2 weeks or longer, crossing awesome wilderness and glaciers into a natural amphitheater where colossal mountains (K2, Gasherbrum, Chogolisa, Broad Peak and others) soar above you.

PERU. The Inca Trail, a once-secret passage between Cuzco and Machu Picchu, the legendary lost city of the Incas, was rediscovered in 1911. The 3-day trek features high passes, forests and ancient ruins. It is strenuous in parts and often crowded, since it is easily the most well-known trekking destination in South America. The best time to go is in September.

You can combine this with a second 6-day trek, a stremuous circuit of Ausangate, the highest peak in the Vilcanota range, which threads its way through high passes with spectacular views and remote llama and alpaca pastures and finishes with a camp near relaxing, natural hot springs.

VENEZUELA. In the southeast of the country is La Gran Sabana, a region renowned for its many *tepui*, or tablelike mountains of sandstone. The Roraima tepui rises 9,216 feet and is accessible via the village of San Francisco de Yuruaní. The trek itself takes about 6 days. The trail starts in flat savannah and rises through rain forest, passing waterfalls and streams before the final steep ascent to the stepped plateau. It is strenuous in parts; take warm gear for the cold nights, rain gear and insect repellent. Hiring local guides is advisable. Overnighting en route consists of sleeping under rock overhangs or in caves.

TASMANIA. The delightful island state of Tasmania is a bushwalking magnet. Weather can change with amazing speed, so be prepared with cold-weather and wet-weather gear. In the center of the island, the popular 50-mile-long Overland Track in the Cradle Mountain-Lake St. Clair National Park can be covered in a week or less. The trailheads at Cynthia Bay and Waldheim, at the southern and northern ends of the park respectively, are served by a shuttle bus during the prime summer season. Permits are issued by park offices at both points.

Bhutan: A Trekker's Paradise

Hiking through mountain passes, forests and jungle

To Western eyes Bhutan can seem like a precious relic from a lost century. Slightly bigger than Switzerland but more rugged, it is significantly less populated—some estimates are as low as 700,000 people—and heavily forested. Most Bhutanese own and work small farms. Automobiles are rare; much of the country is connected only by walking trails. There are only two major roads, and they were built in the last 25 years. Journeys by foot of three hours or more between villages are common.

One popular route is the 350-mile trek from the eastern town of Tashigang to the Bhutanese capital, Thimphu, along a track over mountain passes more than 13,000 feet high (see map, right). The trek takes about 15 days, with 8 to 10 hours' walking every day, and has no signposts. The majority of it is through the jungle, the habitat of leopards, wild boars, tigers, yeti, bears and snakes, and flora and fauna unrivaled in the Himalayas. (Bhutan's forests, which cover 72 percent of its land, are in fact increasing.)

As in medieval Europe, religion permeates Bhutan, the last remaining independent Buddhist kingdom in the Himalayas. Twelve-foot-tall prayer flags flutter on lonely ridges. Small temples called *chortens* squat beside trails and settlements. Aus-

tere *dzongs*, fortress-monasteries, preside over deep valleys.

This pristine country is attracting those in search of a spiritual journey or a hiking adventure. Until 1972, outsiders weren't even allowed into the hermetic kingdom. But the country is changing fast: Bhutan became a democracy in 2008, and the number of visitors is increasing.

Unlike, say, Nepal, however, Bhutan has taken a cautious approach to tourism. From the start, travelers have been required to get visas and book with an authorized tour operator (independent travel in Bhutan is not permitted), and visitors have to pay a hefty per-day fee.

Bhutanese guest houses, though they might offer the charm of stenciled walls and handpainted furniture, have been notoriously lacking in hotel amenities (and even, at times, adequate heating). But resorts in the settlement of Paro are upping the ante: one, the Amankora Paro, is the first of six spa-equipped lodges being built in Bhutan by the Singapore-based Aman Resorts chain.

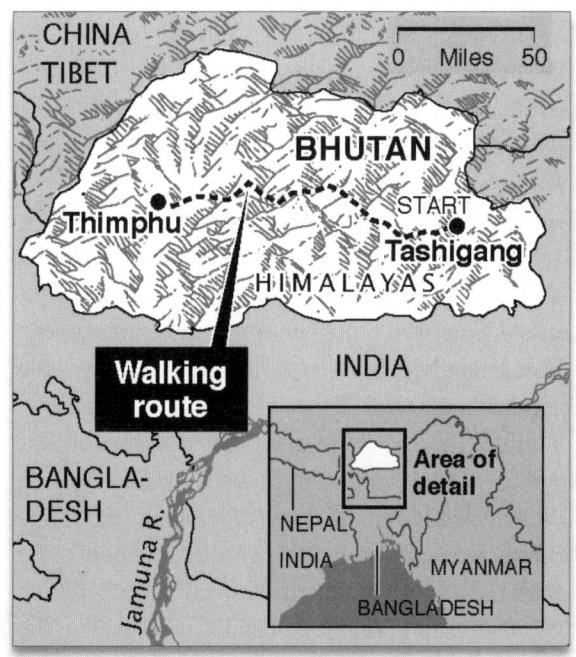

TRAVEL

A Perfect Spot for Yak Butter Tea

The Taktsang monastery, perched inside a recess on the face of a dark cliff in the Paro Valley, is at once Bhutan's most imposingly dramatic and holy site. According to myth, Guru Rimpoche, the eighth-century founder of Tibetan Buddhism, transformed his favorite consort into a tiger and flew on her back to this site. Guru Rimpoche meditated in a cave on the same rock face for three months, and when he had finished, he descended into the Paro Valley to bring Buddhism to Bhutan. Six centuries later, the first temple was built on the site of the current monastery, which, despite its traditional elegance, has been variously destroyed and rebuilt over the centuries.

✔ Though the ascent to Taktsang Lhakang (the Tiger's Lair) is a strenuous hike at an elevation of 3,000 meters, aesthetic and spiritual rewards abound. Stop at the charming teahouse on the way up for a wonderful view of the monastery and a cup of yak butter tea.

✔ **Geographic Expeditions,** San Francisco, Calif., (800-777-8183 or 415-922-0448; www.geoex.com) offers a variety of trips to Bhutan.

—James Hirschfeld

At peace with itself and its neighbors, Bhutan isn't marred by political conflict or extreme poverty. There are no beggars or crime, and one can have friendly contact with the Bhutanese people (their schools teach English). Although they allow satellite TV and cellphones, the government has mandated that women wear the traditional *kira*, a Bhutanese kimono, and men the *gho*, a smocklike wrapper that comes to the knees, in schools and public offices. Bhutan's traditional culture, which revolves around Buddhism and is preserved in the life of its pastoral hamlets, remains largely intact. This is in large measure due to its revered king, who has instituted a policy of "gross national happiness" as a way to measure progress in his land.

—Jane Margolies, Barbara Crossette and Mary Tannen

Exploring Europe on Foot
Hike all day, a shower and a good meal at night

With all due respect to campfires, cowboy coffee and "roughing it," it's hard to beat ending a good day of hiking with a glass of beer, a comfortable bed and a dinner whose preparation doesn't include the direction "just add boiling water." For those who lean toward a little nurture with their nature, Europe is the answer to a hiker's prayers. In almost every old-world country there are civilized multiday hikes sprinkled with lodges, inns or mountain refuges: treks through France's Alps, walks along Hadrian's Wall in England, trips across glaciers in Switzerland—you name it. Here are a few options—classics as well as new destinations—for the traveler who wants to explore Europe on foot.

Hadrian's Wall Path, Britain. In A.D. 122, the Emperor Hadrian ordered a 73-mile-long wall to be built near what is now the border with Scotland to separate northernmost Roman Britain from the "barbarians" beyond. Those walls and turrets today are a World Heritage Site, a lichen-speckled vestige of Roman domination reaching from Wallsend in the east to Bowness-on-Solway in the west. In 2003, Hadrian's Wall was given another designation, as an 84-mile national trail. Although many people walk the route west, as many guidebooks are written going in that direction, there are decided advantages to walking to the east to keep the prevailing winds (and occasional lashing rains) at your back.

A 6-day self-guided hike begins among the salt marshes and peat bogs of the Solway Firth estuary and soon crosses the pastures and villages of Cumbria. The trip's highlight is a section through Northumberland National Park between Banks and Housesteads, where hikers ramble through rough grazing uplands and rolling moors that are home to some of some of the best preserved sections of the wall. Each day, outfitters move your luggage to your next bed and breakfast destination. Eventually, the trail drops into lowlands again, and hikers walk beside the River Tyne and through the industrial city of Newcastle, finally ending in Wallsend, where Hadrian's legacy disappears under the accretion of centuries of change.

GRUNT FACTOR: Stages are 12 to 15 miles daily for a total of 84 miles, across mostly flat ground,

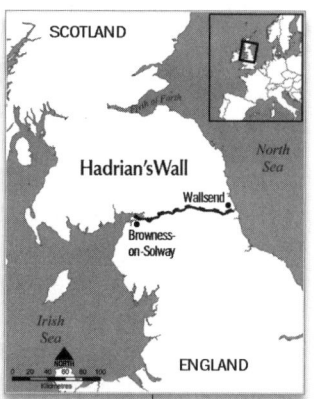

but with some short, steep pitches and steps.

Gran Paradiso National Park, Italy. Originally a royal hunting reserve, Gran Paradiso became Italy's first national park in 1922. Now this sanctuary of 13,000-foot peaks, plunging valleys, larch forests, ibex herds and wildflower meadows near the French border is the happy hunting ground of waffle-tread-wearing hikers. One recommended itinerary traverses a corner of this 173,000-acre park, from Valgrisenche to Cogne.

Starting at the park's westernmost valley, groups can spend a week crossing high passes and traipsing through alpine meadows of nodding edelweiss and mountain lilies, where golden eagles waver in the thermals overhead. Each afternoon, you arrive either at a rustic, high-mountain hut—usually

TRAVEL

● **TIMELY TIPS**

Booking an Alpine Hut

Hut-to-hut or inn-to-inn hiking can include guided or self-guided hikes organized by companies that arrange for such lodging, or you can hike on your own where there is a system of huts or inns in place. In the Alps, dormitory-style huts are generally owned by Alpine clubs and leased to individuals who run them, providing blankets and simple meals; snacks and drinks are often sold.

If you prefer to hike on your own, a good source of informa-

tion on hut systems and trails around the world is the Lonely Planet Walking Guides series, with 13 guides to hiking from the Andes to Australia; they may be ordered at www.lonelyplanet. com. Or you can request information from local tourist offices.

✔ **The Austrian National Tourist Office** provides a free guide for hiking in the Austrian Alps. One of their listings, Wanderweg Holidays (800-270-2577; www. wanderwegholidays.com), has four types of programs, including self-guided "hiking without luggage" tours. Hikes are designed for all ages (212-944-6880; www.austria.info).

✔ **Distant Journeys** has been offering guided and self-guided hikes for two decades in Europe. Self-guided, hut-to-hut hikes described as strenuous include the Mont Blanc Massif (5 to 12 days) and the Dolomites (6 to 9 days). (888-845-5781; www.distantjourneys. com)

✔ **Mountain Sobek** offers a strenuous 10-day guided hut-to-hut hike of the classic Haute Route (Chamonix to Zermatt) in the Alps, in addition to treks in many other countries (510-594-6000 or 888-831-7526; www.mtsobek.com).

—Florence Stickney

The Many Virtues of a G.P.S.

With this device, it's hard to get lost

As Yogi Berra once famously said, "If you don't know where you're going, you're likely to end up somewhere else." That, of course, can often be the case when you are hiking.

Global Positioning System hand-held devices make finding your way effortless. G.P.S. devices use timing signals from a network of 24 satellites to calculate latitude, longitude and altitude and to provide information on how to get to where you want to be. Within the past few years, the accuracy of consumer models has improved from 330 feet to within 15 feet under the best operating conditions.

Navigation companies are now tailoring lightweight hand-held devices to the growing outdoor recreational market. The devices on the market are designed for a range of outdoor activities including hiking, camping, biking and mountaineering. Models loaded with marine navigation aids can also be used for fishing and boating.

Most top-end G.P.S. hand-held devices have mapping, which allows you to view road and topographical maps while navigating. Using an on-screen map, for example, you can locate your position and follow your progress by marking waypoints. Such a mapping unit will not only guide you during the hike but also give you driving directions to the trailhead from your front door.

You can get more map data by hooking the G.P.S. device up to a PC and downloading more content. Because road maps lack the detail necessary for outdoor use, hikers will probably want the MapSource U.S. TOPO map, which is similar to United States Geological Survey topographic paper maps and shows detailed geographic features like elevation contours as well as hiking trails and campgrounds.

Of course, for many hikers there is no substitute for a good topographical map and an old-fashioned magnetic compass. Experts advise, in fact, that you always bring maps and a compass along, because they never run out of power. But as long as you keep a spare set of batteries in your pack, a hand-held G.P.S. unit will make it hard to get lost.

—Bonnie Tsui

above tree line—that's run by the Italian Alpine Club, or, at midweek, the Albergo Savoia, which is in a valley low enough to offer luxuries like showers—and plenty of good Italian wine and polenta. Those who sign on for a longer journey can pick up crampons and an ice ax near trip's end and climb the 13,323-foot Gran Paradiso; though it is the highest peak in the park, the ascent isn't especially steep (no previous mountaineering experience required) until the last 100 feet. Trips end at the village of Cogne, with a visit to a nearby Alpine botanical garden.

GRUNT FACTOR: Four to seven hours of moderately difficult hiking daily, with 1,500 to 3,000 feet of daily elevation gain.

Corsica. Though it is hardly news to Europeans, Americans have only recently awakened to the hiking opportunity on the rugged Mediterranean island of Corsica, France's "mountain in the sea." Those who don't want to commit to the GR20—the spectacular and arduous 130-mile route that many claim is Europe's best backpacking trail—aren't out of luck. Some outfitters offer self-guided trips that give hikers tastes of the GR20 and other trails and also let them experience the comforts of rural village life.

A good starting point is Calacuccia, a lakeside town of homes with thick stone walls. Each morning you walk out of your inn (several former Franciscan monasteries and former convents that now take guest are along the route) and right into the piney woods, passing through golden countryside with braying donkeys, remote mountain villages and high country where some shepherds still take their flocks to forage during the hot Mediterranean summers. At the end, you can drop down to the seaside villages of Porto or Piana, where hikers can snorkel in blue waters.

GRUNT FACTOR: Mellow to moderate, ranging from 4 miles of hilly hiking a day to 8 miles of flat walking.

Bernese Oberland, Switzerland. Only in Europe, with its grand hotel tradition, could a hiker who's meandering down a glacier so big it would be at home in Alaska encounter a "hut" that sleeps 100, serves hot meals and cold beer and has a sundeck crowded with card-playing Germans. More than two dozen huts large and small pepper the Bernese Oberland area of Switzerland's Alps, and they're not just for hard-core mountaineers.

One possible itinerary starts from the cog train station at the Jungfraujoch at 11,333 feet. You step out onto the glaciers and then spend a good chunk of the next few days "on the rocks," wending your way around the crevasses of huge, nearly flat glaciers like the 14-mile-long Great Aletsch Glacier, the longest in the Alps. Hot meals await each night at different huts, like the Finsteraarhorn Hut, on the flanks of the 14,022-foot Finsteraarhorn, the highest peak in the Bernese Oberland. No previous climbing experience is needed.

GRUNT FACTOR: Four to six hours of mellow walking per day, though at altitudes of 9,000 to 12,000 feet, and sleeping at high elevation can be fitful.

Julian Alps, Slovenia. Lovers of the great outdoors are starting to discover the natural beauty that was obscured for decades behind the Iron Curtain. Some trips to Slovenia explore the limestone massif of the Julian Alps, which straddle that country and northern Italy.

While the Alps here are not so high as in the west, they're perhaps more conducive to high-ridge rambling. From near the lakeside town of Bled, you can ascend into Triglav National Park and spend the next few days traversing a 6,000-foot ridgeline, with views down into green valleys that are rioting with wildflowers. Hikers scramble up rocks and occasionally cross short but sheer portions of the route using via ferrata (iron way), a popular European form of hiking in which walkers put on harnesses and attach themselves to fixed cables.

At one point, the trail drops into a high, hidden valley of seven lakes, each a different-colored gem in a stark setting, before arriving at the Prehodavci Hut (6,790 feet), one of the wooden, dorm-style mountain huts where most of the trek's nights are spent. The trip reaches its crescendo when hikers awaken early at the Kredarica Hut to climb Mount Triglav, at 9,390 feet the highest peak in Slovenia.

GRUNT FACTOR: Four to 8 miles of hiking per day, with moderate elevation gains. Hikers should be comfortable with a little bit of scrambling and some exposure to heights.

—Christopher Solomon

Your Personal Tour de France
Bike tours with less haute cuisine, more muscle

Bike tours through Europe used to connote days of gentle exercise followed by nights of gut-busting culinary display at luxury hotels. But say farewell to the foie gras. These days, bicycle tour companies are pushing longer and more difficult trips that follow the great cycling races of Europe.

In the wake of Lance Armstrong's Tour de France wins, cycling as a sport is growing more and more popular; and bike tour companies like Butterfield & Robinson, Trek Travel and Back-

TOUR DE FRANCE
2009 ROUTE

ing. Similarly, meals that used to require their own kind of endurance have been replaced by lighter fare.

- Backroads, 800-GO-ACTIVE; www.backroads. com
- Butterfield & Robinson, 866-551-9090; www. butterfield.com
- Trektravel, 866 464 8735; www.trektravel.com

—Janelle Brown

roads are finding that customers are increasingly interested in following in the treads of the greats, especially people in their 30s, 40s and 50s.

Cyclists who wish to fantasize can do a Tour de France trip in July, which follows the route that the pros will take, albeit at a more leisurely pace. But with the Tour de France route already saturated, companies are expanding their offerings to include other famous (and scenic) European races.

Trek Travel, already the most physically challenging of the bike tour companies, has also added routes that follow the popular European races Giro d'Italia in May and Vuelta a España in September; as well as a route in Girona, Spain, where tour cyclists go to practice in the off-season.

Even nonprofessional routes are becoming more difficult, thanks to the optional challenge days many bike tour companies are adding to their regular trips. To complement the more challenging terrain, tour companies are simultaneously reducing their five-star hotel offerings and replacing them instead with hotels that are slightly more modest but more conveniently located for bik-

Slow Boats through Europe
Moving at a snail's pace, you won't miss a thing

In ancient times, before roads, canals and rivers were the major thoroughfares of Europe. Almost all the major cities of Europe were built on the banks of a river. Canals are hardly the avenues of commerce they once were, but they haven't fallen into total disuse. Pleasure boats and refitted barges laden with tourists now ply the waterways. At 8 to 12 m.p.h., the scenery hardly goes whizzing by—and that's the beauty and charm of this antiquated mode of travel.

The canals pass through some of the oldest and most picturesque parts of many European towns. It's possible for passengers to disembark for a leisurely walk or bicycle ride. The quarters on board have been modernized. Depending on the barge, the food can be of gourmet standard.

There are several barge options: Hotel barges are the most leisurely way to go; you don't have to maneuver boats into locks, and meals, cocktails and excursions are included. Less pricey are self-driven barges, which accommodate 4 to 10 people. Many of these are converted commercial vessels and can be steered by a beginner, after a minimal amount of instruction. Hugh McKnight is a pioneers in the self-driven barge vacation and the author of many books on barges, including *Cruising French Waterways* and *Slow Boat Through Germany*. Here he recommends the continent's best barge trips.

ENGLAND

Leeds and Liverpool Canal. This early-19th-century waterway in the north of England connects the east and west coasts via the rugged moorland scenery of Yorkshire and Lancashire. The canal features stone-built locks, many manually operated swing bridges and appealing small mill towns.

River Thames. A historic and beautiful river with locks and weirs, crossing southern England from London to Gloucestershire and the Cotswolds. Famous towns and cities include Windsor (an 11th-century royal castle), Henley (Europe's premier rowing regatta) and the university center of Oxford.

SCOTLAND

Caledonian Canal. This early-19th-century engineering feat provides a coast-to-coast navigation through the Scottish Highlands from Fort William to Inverness. Spectacular "staircase" (multiple-chambered) locks and lengths of artificial canal link a series of natural lakes, including Loch Ness, renowned for its elusive monster.

IRELAND

River Shannon. The longest waterway in the British Isles, navigable from the south coast and via lakes large and small to the border of Northern Ireland. A 19th-century canal has been restored to provide a link with the huge island-studded Lough Erne.

FRANCE

Canal du Midi Route. Together with the Canal lateral à la Garonne, the largely 17th-century Canal du Midi provides a navigable link through southern France from the Mediterranean to the Atlantic. Locks, buildings and aqueducts are all over 300 years old.

River Meuse. From its upper reaches near the city of Nancy, this canalized river is one of the most beautiful in all Europe, especially as it passes through the Ardennes forests near the border with Belgium.

Waterways of Alsace. The Canal de la Marne au Rhin and associated waterways in the northeastern part of the country have a Germanic character. Radar-operated locks are totally automatic as the route passes through pine forests in the valley of the Zorn River.

GERMANY

River Rhine. The Rhine runs for 640 miles through Europe. The uppermost reaches (Strasbourg to Switzerland) are canalized with giant ship locks. Elsewhere, it flows unimpeded, especially through the castle-filled Rhine Gorge (Bingen to Koblenz). Many large cruise ships ply the river, taking 4 to 5 days to cover the best parts.

River Lahn. The Lahn is a Rhine tributary, branching off near Koblenz and terminating in the cathedral city of Limburg. Although the river is only 40 miles long, a return journey can easily fill a week,

Where to Rent a Barge

A sampling of outfitters who offer barge trips in Europe. Search the Internet for others.

Crown Blue Line Ltd. Britain, France, Netherlands, Germany, Ireland, Italy.
44 8 444 632 389; www.crownblueline.com

Emerald Star Line. Irish waterways.
980 Awald Road, Suite 302,
Annapolis, Md. 21403
353 71 962 7633; www.emeraldstar.ie

Hoseasons Holidays. Britain and France.
Sunway House, Lowestoft, Suffolk, NR32 3LT, Great Britain
44 1 502 502 588; www.hoseasons.co.uk

for every one of the towns and villages en route is well worth exploring.

Mecklenburg Lakes. This is a complicated network of interconnected lakes north of Berlin in former East Germany. The area has been practically untouched by development since the 1930s, though that may be changing.

White-Water Rafting, Family-Style
10 thrilling river trips safe enough for kids

White-water rafting isn't for the faint of heart, but it isn't just for daredevils, either. Outfitters all across the country now offer trips for families. Children generally need to be 11 and up, as well as reasonably good swimmers. But those are the only requirements, plus perhaps an ample supply of adrenaline. Jeff Bennett, author of *The Complete Whitewater Rafter*, recommends these 10 white-water rafting trips for families.

South Fork of the American River
California • 21 miles • Class III

This stretch of California river has dozens of Class II and III rapids, rich gold-era history and easy access to big cities. Its sunshine and scenic rolling hills make for the perfect family trip. The big thrills happen at the river's two Class III rapids, Troublemaker and Satan's Cesspool.

- Beyond Limits Adventures 800-234-7238; www.rivertrip.com
- Tributary Whitewater Tours 916-346-6812; www.whitewatertours.com
- Whitewater Voyages 800-488-7238; whitewatervoyages.com

Deschutes River
Oregon • 13 to 98 miles • Class III

Running through the heart of Oregon's high-desert country, the Deschutes River provides a bouncy 1-day jaunt down the crowded Maupin section or a 2- to 5-day canoeing trip down its more remote corridors. Stair-stepped basalt cliffs, grassy meadows and world-class fishing holes add to the experience.

- Sage Canyon River & Ewing's Whitewater 800-538-7238; www.sagecanyonriverco.com
- High Desert River Outfitters 800-461-5823; www.highdesertriver.com

Salmon River, Upper Main
Idaho • up to 35 miles • Classes II to III +

Just 90 minutes north of Sun Valley, the headwaters of the Salmon River cut a path through the Sawtooth National Recreation Area. The Salmon's emerald currents slip past smooth granite boulders and towering pines, occasionally erupting into a series of big roller-coaster waves.

- The River Company 800-398-0346; www.therivercompany.com
- White Otter Outdoor Adventures 208-726-4331; www.whiteotter.com

Snake River (Grand Teton),
Wyoming • 30 miles • Classes I to II

One of the best ways to soak in the breathtaking beauty of Grand Teton National Park is to float the Snake River downstream from Jackson Lake. You can gaze at distant spires or search the banks for moose, bears, otters and a variety of waterfowl.

- Barker-Ewing Float Trips 800-365-1800; barkerewing.com
- Fort Jackson Float Trips 800-735-8430

Colorado River, Glenwood Canyon
Colorado • 10 to 15 miles • Classes II to III

Just three hours from downtown Denver, the Glenwood Canyon section of the Upper Colorado River carves a narrow, cliff-lined gorge alongside Interstate 70. Layers of sandstone, limestone, and

INSIDE INFO

A Guide to White-Water Rapids

River conditions can vary widely and unpredictably. The following ratings were developed to give those unfamiliar with a river a feel for what they are getting into—before they get into it.

○ **CLASS I:** Flat water, some current.

○ **CLASS II:** Small waves.

○ **CLASS III:** Big waves, requires maneuvering through "hydraulic holes" in which the water breaks back on itself over a rock.

○ **CLASS IV:** Big waves, many rocks, and very fast, powerful water. Requires precise maneuverability. Not fun to swim in if you make a mistake.

○ **CLASS V:** Pushing the limits of navigability, should be done only by experts. Extremely steep gradient of river: 30- to 40-foot drops. Mistakes or capsizing will result in injury or possibly death.

○ **CLASS VI:** Pushing the absurd. Paddlers on the West Coast define it as not runnable. Those on the East Coast recommend it only for experts, lunatics, or both. Injury or death is a distinct possibility.

granite rise from the riverbed while cavalcades of big waves accent the toughest rapids.

• Blue Sky Adventures 970-945-6605; www. blueskyadventure.com

• Timberline Tours 800-831-1414; www.timberlinetours.com

Rio Grande, State Park & Racecourse Sections

New Mexico • 6.5 to 10.8 miles • Classes II to III+

The Rio Grande River rises along the eastern flanks of the southern Colorado Rockies, then flows 1,887 miles south to the Gulf of Mexico. Near Taos, N.M., it enters a spectacular and challenging gorge known as the Taos Box. To catch a taste of the Box, but without the hazards of big rapids, families and the less adventuresome can paddle the Rio Grande's state park and racecourse sections near the quaint town of Pilar.

• Far Flung Adventures 800-359-2627; www. farflung.com

• New Wave Rafting Company 505-984-1444; www.newwaverafting.com

Kennebec River, *Maine*

6 to 12 miles • Classes III to IV+

Controlled releases from the Central Maine Power Company's Harris Station Dam guarantee reliable summertime flows, while memorable rapids like Magic Falls ensure tons of excitement. For a more sedentary experience through the Kennebec wilderness, run the Carry Brook section.

• New England Outdoor Center 800-766-7238; www.neoc.com

• North Country Rivers 800-348-8871; www.ncrivers.com

Youghiogheny River

Pennsylvania • 7.5 miles • Classes II to IV

The lower Youghiogheny traces a serpentine path through the Laurel Mountains near Ohiopyle State Park. It alternates between challenging rapids and calm pools. Although scheduled launch times help keep the river traffic in check, plan your trip ahead of time; over 100,000 people run it every year.

• Mountain Streams & Trails 800-723-8669; www.mtstreams.com

• White Water Adventures 800-992-7238; www.wwaraft.com

• Wilderness Voyageurs 800-272-4141; www. wilderness-voyageurs.com

Ocoee River

Tennessee • 4.5 miles • Class III to IV

The Ocoee has long been a favorite among southeastern rafters. A healthy gradient and an end-

TRAVEL

The Ultimate River-Rafting Trip

Down the Colorado through the Grand Canyon

A rafting trip through the Grand Canyon, along 226 or 277 (depending on where you get off) unspoiled miles of the Colorado River, is the longest and wildest river trip in the lower 48 states.

Nothing matches the magnitude of the Grand Canyon and the stupendous force that created it. Along the edge of the canyon is writ the geologic history of the last 2 billion years—from the relatively recent Jurassic period, 1.2 million years old, to the bottom layer of Vishnu rock, at approximately 2 billion years, some of the oldest rock in the world.

Three-quarters of the trips down the river are via motorized boats, which whisk though the canyon in about 6 days, but the best way to go is on nonmotorized boats, because they don't interfere with the majestic quiet of the canyon. It takes 12 to 18 days to make the trip that way.

The most common type of nonmotorized craft are oar boats, where one or two river guides control the oars while passengers sit back and take in the scenery. For more adventurous types who want an active participatory experience, a few companies run paddle boats where everyone paddles.

Rafting down the canyon may be the experience of a lifetime, but many people have to wait part of a lifetime to do it. The number of people allowed each year is currently limited to around 24,000. Commercial trips are allowed on the river from May 1 to mid-September. For a commercial trip that averages about 28 passengers, you have to plan at least a year in advance. If you are an experienced rafter, you can apply for a permit, but these days, the average wait for private trips is 12 to 15 years. The best times to go are in the spring and the fall, when it's less crowded, and more temperate. Average summer highs are 106 degrees.

FOR MORE INFORMATION: Call Rivers and Oceans (800-473-4576; www.rivers-oceans.com) a central booking agency for rafting outfitters for the Grand Canyon.

---

less assortment of boulders combine to form nearly continuous rapids on the section between the Ocoee Diversion Dam and its powerhouse downstream.

- Nantahala Outdoor Center 800-232-7238; www.noc.com
- Ocoee Outdoors 800-533-7767; www.ocoee-outdoors.com
- Southeastern Expeditions 800-868-7238; www.southeasternexpeditions.com

Nantahala River

North Carolina • 8 miles • Classes II to III

The Nantahala, just east of Great Smoky Mountains National Park, runs along a valley thick with rhododendron, mountain laurel and princess trees. Nantahala Falls (a sharp Class III+) highlights the trip.

- Nantahala Outdoor Center 800-905-7238; www.noc.com

- USA Raft 800-745-9356; www.usaraft.com
- Wildwater Ltd. 800-319-8870; www.wildwaterrafting.com

Off the Beaten Track in Mexico

Amazing adventures just south of the border

B eyond the sunbathers, cervezas and spring break debauchery so conspicuously on display in Cancún and Cozumel, Mexico offers a lesser known adventure experience—the kind that is found deep in the jungle or near small fishing villages and offshore reefs.

The same country that possesses one of the world's most polluted capital cities also ranks as one of the richest in species diversity. Twenty-two biosphere reserves and nearly 50 national parks offer hiking and wildlife-watching opportunities; mountain chains and interior canyons are chockfull of biking trails; fertile warm-water upwellings attract pods of whales and glittering fish. Almost by definition, some of these unexplored gems are in remote areas, so travelers will need to be vigilant about safety. That's where knowledgeable outfitters are key—they can take you to little, touristed places that you might not wish to visit alone. Before you book a trip to Mexico, consult the the U.S. Department of State web site (www. travel.state.gov) for travel advisories.

SURFING: **Sayulita.**

Surfers have been crossing the border to ride waves along Mexico's Pacific coast for decades, and this small coastal fishing village 30 minutes north of Puerto Vallarta has lately achieved the perfect mix of lively beachfront bars, surf camps and terra cotta architectural charm—all, most importantly, with easy access to numerous breaks ideal for beginners and for intermediates looking to sharpen their technique. Advanced riders might head south to the body-wrecking barrels at Puerto Escondido.

ROCK CLIMBING: **El Potrero Chico.**

About an hour northwest of Monterrey, a craggy limestone outcrop named El Potrero Chico has been quietly attracting rock climbers from around the world. What makes the area unusual is the sheer variety of the 600-plus bolted routes—in which permanent artificial anchors are embedded in the rock—all within easy access of a campground and lodge at the base of the rock. El Potrero Chico is just west of the small town of Hidalgo, where the living is simple, with the street markets and hearty food typical of northern Mexico.

DEEP-SEA FISHING: **Cabo San Lucas.**

In 1940, John Steinbeck embarked on an expedition to the Sea of Cortez to catalog marine life along Cabo's rocky, undeveloped coastline and found it "ferocious with life." Though the town of Cabo San Lucas is now known as a luxury golf destination, it first earned its reputation through its prized access to waters teeming with fish. With the Pacific Ocean on one side and the Sea of Cortez on the other, Cabo offers exceptional sport fishing at the confluence of both in the harbor's deep-water canyons. The area hasn't been nicknamed the "marlin capital of the world" for nothing.

Swordfish are most plentiful January through June, as are sailfish, and the best conditions for blue and black marlin are July through November, when big storms put populations on the move. Striped marlin is caught year round.

MOUNTAIN BIKING: **Copper Canyon.**

Barranca del Cobre, or Copper Canyon, is one of the deepest and largest canyon systems in the world. Most visitors show up via train or tour bus, stopping only to take a snapshot or two of the gloriously bizarre rock formations and caves. But the town of Creel in the state of Chihuahua—an eight-hour drive from El Paso, Texas—is the gateway to Mexico's thriving mountain and road biking scene. From this base, at an elevation of 7,600 feet, you'll find that Copper's ins and outs are well suited to two-wheeled exploration. Just about every kind of trail and terrain can be accessed: world-class technical single-track, forest roads, Moab-quality slick rock, rocky desert landscape, challenging long climbs and descents on old mining tracks, and winding back roads.

SNORKELING WITH SHARKS: **Isla Holbox.**

Forty miles northwest of the party port of Cancún is little-known Isla Holbox (pronounced OLE-bosh), a narrow spit of white sand some 25 miles long and no more than two miles wide at its

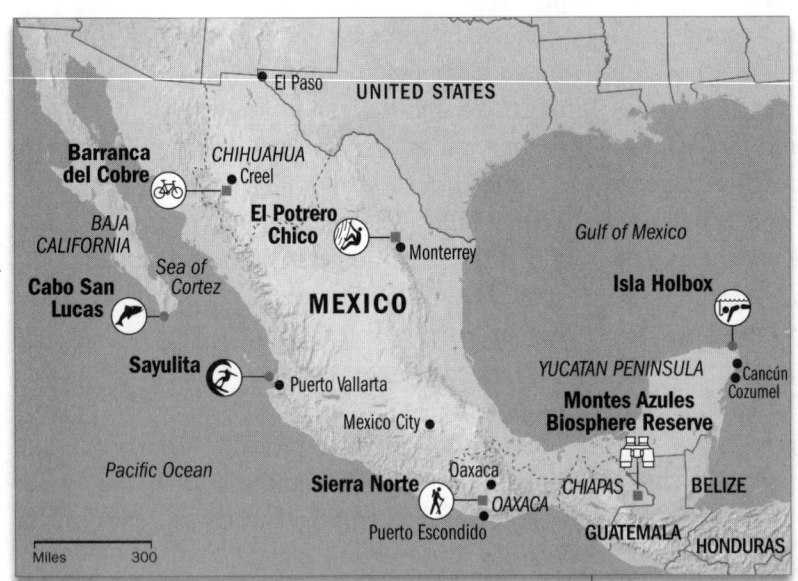

town. Adding to the picture-postcard prettiness are hundreds of flamingos that flock to the island.

BIRD WATCHING: Chiapas.

The southern Mexican state of Chiapas is best known for its incredible biodiversity. In the Lacandón rain forest, the Montes Azules Biosphere Reserve—designated in 1979 as the first biosphere reserve in Mexico—protects more than 1,200 square miles, home to a whopping number of bird species (close to 350, which comprises nearly a third of the country's total).

The reserve is probably the only place where you'll encounter so many rare birds in the wild, including the quetzal—whose feathers were prized by ancient civilizations—and the scarlet macaw, harpy eagle, king vulture and Muscovy duck, all of which are threatened with extinction. The rain forest is also home to endangered jaguars, ocelots and tapirs.

HIKING: The Sierra Norte.

The Sierra Norte is one of the most biologically diverse mountain systems in Mexico, blanketing an area of about 6,500 square miles in the northern part of Oaxaca state. Because of its remoteness, the Sierra Norte is seldom explored beyond the fringes of the city of Oaxaca, and much of it is inhabited by various indigenous communities. But the hiking in the Sierra Norte is stunning. The hiking level throughout is moderate, with most hikes through valley and forest landscapes. (For more on traveling to Mexico, see "The Pyramids Next Door" on page 593.)

widest point, situated in the Gulf of Mexico. From June through September, the island's offshore waters are the site of a large congregation of whale sharks, who come here to feed on seasonal plankton blooms.

The whale shark is the world's biggest fish—it can grow to more than 50 feet in length—and its dark grayish-blue body is dotted with white spots, giving it the local nickname of "domino." Because the whale shark is a vulnerable species, and because coastal mangrove areas are also located here, the Yum Balam Biosphere Reserve was created in 1994 to protect Isla Holbox and its surrounding waters. An active tourism industry has sprung up, providing travelers with the singular experience of snorkeling with whale sharks.

The population of Holbox—which was named for its proximity to a spring (Holbox is Mayan for "black hole")—is less than 2,000. There are no cars; most people get around by bike, golf cart or motor scooter. The local economy is still based heavily on fishing, and there is an abundance of seafood restaurants in the main

—Bonnie Tsui

Sites for the Intrepid Traveler

Evolving destinations—from Andorra to Turkey

As the well-known traveler Richard Bangs wrote, "adventure across the ages—in style, purpose and destination—has rarely suffered stasis. Almost by definition it is in a constant state of evolution, a complex rolling skein of commerce, geopolitics, faddism and shifting belief systems." This has certainly never been truer than it is today. Here are some more evolved ideas for travel, suggested by *New York Times* travel writers.

Albania: *Its capital, Tirana, is full of contradictions*

A majority-Muslim country where the mosques are mute but the miniskirts are loud, where horse carts share highways with Hummers, and where people shake their heads to mean yes—except that sometimes they shake their heads to mean no—Albania can make you shake your own head in confusion. But what can you expect after almost 50 postwar years of hermetic Communism and, more recently, a mania for pyramid schemes that plunged the poor European nation into near-anarchy?

But Tirana, it turns out, is quite lovable. It is distinguished by the amazing graphical flatness of the Italian colonial architecture, the epic ugliness of the Soviet-style architecture and the naïve aspirations of the new glass-and-steel towers. They all have an energy that cannot be dismissed. Many apartment blocks have bright coats of city-subsidized paint, thanks to mayor Edi Rama, an artist and now head of the opposition Socialist Party. Clumps of green and yellow, the boxy buildings look like Tetris blocks that had fallen from the sky.

Apart from the beggars, Tirana feels oddly safe and inviting. It is also extremely affordable. Dinners at the nicest restaurants, like the Sky Club atop one of the "Twin Towers," cost less than $15 a person for dishes like hot yogurt soup and veal medallions, and the Grilled Fish Index rarely exceeded $30.

Albania refuses to resolve into a neat picture. Skyscrapers go up while sidewalks disintegrate; the National Art Gallery displays beautiful artwork,

Following the Silk Road

The former Soviet republics aren't for everyone

If Cambodia and Vietnam are today's pearls of the Orient, then the Central Asian countries of Kazakhstan, Uzbekistan, Turkmenistan, Tajikistan and Kyrgyzstan, commonly called "the Stans," are diamonds in the rough. But what these former Soviet republics lack in polish they make up for in historical riches, rugged beauty and, at least for now, few tourists.

Bisected by the Silk Road, the 2,000- year-old trade route that linked Europe to China, the Stans are dotted with museum-quality ruins and architecture from the Middle Ages. Throw in a countryside of canyons, mountain forests and prehistoric glaciers, and the Stans begin to sparkle beneath their raw edges.

Some of the storybook cities of Uzbekistan, with their ornate mosques and citadel walls, are Unesco World Heritage Sites. Tajikistan's crumbling gems include the eerie lost city of Penjikent. And Kyrgyzstan, perhaps the most welcoming of the Stans, has a stunning terrain that includes the Al-Archa National Park (for bird-watching, trekking and even glacial skiing), and Lake Issyk-Kul, one of the world's largest alpine bodies of water.

The Stans, however, may not be everyone's cup of horse milk. Tourist resources are scarce; rural accommodations may be limited to yurts and tents. But modern-day nomads may find that's reason enough to go.

—Seth Sherwood

Visiting the World's Poorest Slums

"Voyeuristic," say critics, but insightful, too

Slum tourism, or "poorism," as some call it, is catching on. From the favelas of Rio de Janeiro to the townships of Johannesburg to the garbage dumps of Mexico, some tourists are forsaking, at least for a while, beaches and museums for crowded, dirty—and in many ways surprising—slums.

Slum tourism isn't for everyone. Critics charge that ogling the poorest of the poor isn't tourism at all. It's voyeurism. The tours are exploitative, these critics say, and have no place on an ethical traveler's itinerary. Not so fast, proponents of slum tourism say. Ignoring poverty won't make it go away.

Many tour organizers are sensitive to charges of exploitation. Some encourage—and in at least one case require—participants to play an active role in helping residents. A church group in Mazatlán, Mexico, runs tours of the local garbage dump, where scavengers earn a living picking through trash, some of it from nearby luxury resorts. The group doesn't charge anything but asks participants to help make sandwiches and fill bottles with filtered water.

By most accounts, slum tourism began in Brazil when a young man named Marcelo Armstrong took a few tourists into Rocinha, Rio de Janeiro's largest favela, or shantytown. His company, Favela Tour, grew and spawned half a dozen imitators. Today, on any given day in Rio, dozens of tourists hop into minivans, then motorcycles, and venture into places even Brazil's police dare not enter. Organizers insist the tours are safe, though they routinely check security conditions.

RIO DE JANEIRO, BRAZIL: Favela Tour runs daily tours of Vila Canoas and Rocinha, the largest favela in Brazil. Stops include a local handcraft center and a community school, which is financed by the tour. 55-21-3322-2727; 55-21-9989-0074; www.favelatour.com.br

MUMBAI, INDIA: Reality Tours and Travel specializes in tours of Dhavari, Asia's biggest slum, where much of the film *Slumdog Millionaire* was shot. Tour highlights include visits to small-scale slum-based industries such as leather tanning, embroidery and soap manufacturing. 91-9820822253 (24 hr); 91-22 22833872 (office); www.realitytoursandtravel.com.

MAZATLAN, MEXICO: Mazatlan Ministries runs a weekly tour during the tourist high season (approx. October to May) that starts at the Golden Zone church, where visitors prepare sandwiches to hand out to the "scroungers" at the city dump. 521-669-916-5114; www.vineyardmcm.org.   —Eric Weiner

---

but rarely identifies the socialist realist painters and sculptors. A cocktail at Tirana's trendy bar, Flex, could feel like the height of cosmopolitan cool—until you have to contend with adorable but depressing street kids who would kiss your arm in hopes of a 50-lek coin.   —Matt Gross

Andorra: *Foie gras and more skiable terrain than Aspen and Vail combined*

It may not have the glamour of Gstaad or the majesty of Mont Blanc, but little Andorra, once the laughingstock of the Pyrenees, is turning seriously upscale. Two hours north of Barcelona, between Spain and France, this snowball-size nation had been long dismissed as a booze cruise on skis. Lift tickets were cheap, hostels outnumbered five-star hotels (there were none) and the crowd leaned toward beginners, more intent on chugging beers than carving snow.

But over the last several years, some $200 million has been dumped on Andorra, turning it into one of the coolest spots this side of the Alps. There are snazzy new lifts, new hotels with spas and fancy restaurants serving foie gras and baby squid.

More important, the skiing has improved dramatically, with the addition of high-tech grooming and snowmaking (see www.skiandorra.ad).

What was once a hodgepodge of rival resorts has merged into two big "ski stations" linked by a high-speed network of 111 lifts and spanning 7,600 acres of skiable terrain, more than Aspen and Vail combined. Vallnord, in the northwest, is the less challenging of the two, with 66 trails, a halfpipe and well-rated ski schools. Grandvalira, closer to France, has 110 trails (one-fifth of them expert), three terrain parks and a vertical drop of about 3,000 feet—not as lofty as St. Moritz, but still more than Gstaad.   —Denny Lee

Bulgaria: *A rare chance to see Europe as it once was*

Much has changed in Bulgaria since it shook off Soviet domination in 1989. Free elections have been held, and its economic and political capital, Sofia, is thriving. But as it emerges as a tourist destination, mostly in the beach resorts along the Black Sea, Bulgaria is also showing that it is a nation that can celebrate a refreshing lack of progress.

Hidden throughout this big and fertile land, in remote gorges and on craggy hilltops, are dozens of astonishingly intact painted monasteries that are centuries old. They offer visitors a rare chance to see Europe as it once was—before the euro, before World War II, before electricity.

Of the former nations of the Soviet bloc, Bulgaria has been among the slowest to come in from the cold, which means that much of the country remains off the tourist map. But some luxury tour operators have added Bulgaria to their list of tours. There are also some 600 mineral springs in the country, and a few luxury spa resorts are in the works, not to mention nine Unesco World Heritage Sites and rustic camps from which you can hunt for red stags.   —Denny Lee

Ethiopia: *The Land of the Queen of Sheba is rich in archeological treasures.*

Many Americans have associated Ethiopia with images of crushing poverty, and although poverty still remains, the country is finding something of an economic lifeline in cultural tourism. Indeed, the country holds many of sub-Saharan Africa's most astonishing treasures, like the medieval cave churches at Lalibela and the 1,700-year-old stone obelisks in the northern town of Axum.

Ethiopia, which calls itself the Land of the Queen of Sheba, also claims title to the Ark of the Covenant, the box of gold and acacia wood that is believed to have once contained the Ten Commandments. Ethiopian Christians say it is somewhere in the Church of St. Mary of Zion in Axum.

Although the country can't compete with Kenya or South Africa when it comes to big game, Ethiopia does have more than a dozen national parks, which are regarded as among the most beautiful in the sub-Saharan region. The terrain ranges from the plateaus of the Simien highlands to the white-water rapids of the largely uninhabited Omo Valley. There are no luxury tented camps with teak floors and five-course dinners, but several tour operators are offering fly-in safaris into the Rift Valley, Mago National Park and other remote preserves.

Visitors can spend the day spotting leopards and bird-watching before being whisked back to their hotels in Addis Ababa, the bustling capital with its exotic night life, or Gonder, a slower-paced city invariably referred to as Africa's Camelot because of its many castles.   —Denny Lee

Lithuania: *History buffs will be transported to the Stalin era*

Instead of rejecting its Soviet history, the Baltic state of Lithuania is embracing it, in a kind of kitschy salute to its Leninist roots. Gray Soviet-era buildings have been converted into sleek hotels, agitprop statues of Socialist workers have become Kodak moments for amused tourists and trendy restaurants play off the borscht past. NATO, a bar in Vilnius, the capital, for example, was decorated with military hardware, while other bars played old Politburo conferences on their TVs. And in the town of Grutas, there's Grutas Park, better known as Stalin World, styled after a Siberian labor camp, with statues of Marx, Stalin and other Communist icons, a quirky nod to a still-raw chapter—part nostalgia for pre-perestroika innocence, part disaffection with the slow pace of capitalism. —Denny Lee

Montenegro: *The new playground of the glitterati*

Montenegro was once an A-list playground for the likes of Elizabeth Taylor and Richard Burton and was called the St.-Tropez of the Adriatic. That is, until war came to the Balkans in the 1990s, and Montenegro, which allied itself with Serbia, suffered NATO air strikes and trade sanctions, crippling its tourism.

Now this small, craggy republic (it's part of the country of Serbia and Montenegro) with unspoiled beaches, thick pine forests and medieval villages is poised for a comeback.

One of the most distinctive places to stay is the recently restored Hotel Sveti Stefan. The hotel occupies an entire island of cobblestone streets and terra cotta-capped cottages. Hip cafes and boutiques have cropped up, and the glitterati are returning again, like couture-wearing refugees after a war. —Denny Lee

Slovenia: *Tasting its cuisine at the source*

The Karst, a limestone plateau in southwestern Slovenia, is known for its gastronomic heritage, and visitors take away vivid memories of its food: Karst prsut (pronounced per-shoot), prosciutto that is air dried for 14 days in the sharp burja winds; chewy wheat bread smothered with fresh horseradish or zaseka (a spread of cold smoked ground bacon and lard); risotto with just-picked asparagus and nettles; homemade gnocchi with fried pancetta; fish caught off Slovenia's short but idyllic Adriatic coastline.

One way to experience this cuisine, with fresh, seasonal ingredients, is at a kmetija, or tourist farm. Agricultural tourism is not new in Slovenia, which is about the size of New Jersey and just east of Italy and south of Austria. As early as the 19th century, Italian vacationers from Trieste would cross the border to spend summer weekends on farms in the Karst.

Farm holidays have recently taken off, with the number of kmetije doubling to more than 600 in the past decade. The tourist farms offer activities like horseback riding and swimming, and guests who are of a mind to sample the country life in earnest can sometimes pitch in baling hay or picking cherries. Typical rooms recall those in a Swiss hut: spare but immaculate, with lots of unfinished wood. Prices are a fraction of those at a tourist hotel. But the outstanding attraction is the food.

Another attraction of many of Slovenia's tourist farms is their proximity to the country's major tourist sites: the capital, Ljubljana; the dramatic Skocjan Caves, a Unesco World Heritage Site; the Lipica stud farm, where Lipizzaner horses have been bred since 1580; and the tasting rooms of some of Slovenia's best winemakers.

A few hours' drive takes you to Triglav National Park, an unspoiled tract of snow-dusted Alps, forests of larch and spruce, and meadows speckled with gentian and edelweiss. Though development within Triglav is strictly regulated, the park contains dozens of villages where Slovenes live and sell agricultural products like sheep cheese or wool or run restaurants, hotels or tourist farms.

There, you'll find the Pri Plajerju kmetija, an

Camping for the Pampered Set

Where you sleep under the stars in the lap of luxury

If the eco-friendly idea of falling asleep under the stars and roasting marshmallows around a campfire appeals to you, but the reality of pitching a tent and sleeping on bumpy ground does not, glamping, the new term for upscale—or glamorous—camping, could be your ideal green vacation. A relatively new trend in the United States and Europe, glamping sites are popping up everywhere, with prepitched tents, tepees and yurts rising out of the landscape like sailboats on an ocean. Here are some popular glamping sites.

Guests at Cornish Tipi Holidays (www.cornishtipiholidays.co.uk) in England need bring only their food, a towel and bedding, since everything else is provided in their 40 cotton-canvas tepees. The camp has no electricity, no cellphone coverage and no Wi-Fi, but it does have solar panels for hot showers, low-volume lavatories and a wind generator. Tepees come in three sizes, the largest fitting up to eight people.

At Mille Étoiles, a campsite with 14 yurts in the Rhône-Alpes region of France overlooking the dramatic Ardèche River gorge, tents are built on platforms and furnished (four-poster beds, oriental rugs, antiques). At the Canvas Chic (www.canvaschic.com) campsite, paths are lighted with solar-powered lanterns and candles, rainwater is collected and reused, recycling is standard and the food served in the small restaurant is organically grown.

On the California coast an hour south of San Francisco is Costanoa (www.costanoa.com), a lodge and camp surrounded by 30,000 acres of state parks and wildlife preserves; visitors would be hard-pressed to call their 76 tented bungalows "tents." They have canvas walls and ceilings, hardwood floors and made-up beds with heated mattress pads. Campers can cook their own food on grilling stations throughout the campsite or eat meals at the restaurant. There are an outdoor hot tub and a dry sauna and spa.

For the ultimate glamping experience, visit either the Clayoquot Wilderness Resort (www.wildretreat.com) on Vancouver Island in the Clayoquot Sound Biosphere Reserve in British Columbia or the Resort at Paws Up (www.pawsup.com) in Montana. Both have elegantly furnished tents, but the resorts are also dedicated to respecting the environment.

At Clayoquot, which calls itself a Super Natural Adventure, tents are connected by cedar boardwalks and have remote-controlled propane fireplaces, composting toilets, oil lamps and even antique dressers. You will also find tents for games, dining and lounging as well as spa and library tents. At Paws Up, a ranch resort with horseback riding, mountain biking and fly-fishing, among other activities, campers can pass up the cabins and stay in one of the newly built tents at River Camp on the Blackfoot River, complete with king-size beds and art on the walls, a personal butler and private master bath (though it is a short walk away). —Jennifer Conlin

organic farm that sits in the shadows of the Julian Alps, overlooking the iridescent Soca River. Its owners tend a big vegetable garden and raise sheep and goats. Three tourist apartments are in the main house, and two are in Swiss-style huts.

Close to the glassy alpine Lake Bled, Slovenia's most beloved resort, is the Turisticna kmetija Mulej, which offers eight spacious rooms and five two-story apartments. The farm has a herd of grass-fed dairy cows—which means fresh milk, cheese and yogurt at breakfast. Guests can ride the family's two horses and bikes for no extra charge.

Nearby, 10 miles northwest of the town of Bled, which sits on the east side of the lake, is Kmetija Psnak. It has tourist apartments but also welcomes travelers who just want a meal. The rustic fare ranges from pork and handmade sausages to zganci, a thick polenta made of either buckwheat or corn, often served with pork cracklings.

To find more farms that take guests, go to the Slovenia Tourist Board's Web site, www.slovenia.info/touristfarms, and to the Web site of the country's Tourist Farms Association, www.farmtourism.si. —Hannah Wallace

Tunisia: *Where Europe, Africa and the Mideast meet*

Tunis, capital of Tunisia, is known quite well by Europeans—particularly the British and the French, who take cheap flights south so they can be on the nearby Mediterranean beaches in just a few hours. But for most Americans, it is off the beaten path, as Morocco is the much more conventional destination for those who venture to North Africa.

But the Tunis area has an extraordinary amount to offer—and in a way it features more variety and even history, you could argue, than Fez or Marrakesh. The list includes its unrivaled medina, whose alleys and covered passageways go on for miles, filled with markets, mosques and cafes; the nearby ruins of the ancient Phoenician port city of Carthage; the bustling beach town of La Marsa; and the charming hillside village of Sidi Bou Said, where the blue-and-white painted homes have views reaching out for miles over the gentle waters of the Gulf of Tunis.

It has nowhere near the range of luxury accommodations found on the European side of the Mediterranean. But it has an increasing number of upscale places to stay and eat, not only in Tunis's center, but also in the beachside villages and resorts just outside the city.

The highlight of a visit to Tunis is the ancient core of the city itself: the seventh-century medina, which, beyond the most intensely touristy spots surrounding Jemaa Ez Zitouna (the Great Mosque), has a more genuine feeling than its counterparts in Morocco.

It is true that during peak tourist times in the summer, the number of foreigners at the central souks packed into the covered corridors that surround the Great Mosque can easily outnumber the locals. But venture out beyond this area, losing your way through the alternating shadows and sunlight of the twisting streets, and you are overtaken by a sensual assault: the smells of the burning incense and spice stores; the undulating chant of the prayer calls; the blue, beige and orange doors that decorate certain homes; and the local Tunisians, pushing carts or carrying overstuffed bags of goods. —Eric Lipton

Turkey: *For sybarites, Bodrum could be the next St.-Tropez*

With its white-sand beaches and shop-lined streets, the city of Bodrum has long been the favorite seaside retreat in Turkey. But now this ancient fishing village set against the blue waters of the Aegean Sea has crashed the global party circuit. A glance at the megayachts, some of them straight from the ports of Capri or Monaco, hints at its newfound fame. In summer, when the population of 50,000 swells tenfold, Bodrum feels a bit like St.-Tropez, except perhaps for the belly dancers.

What's the draw? Gorgeous scenery for one. Situated on Turkey's southwestern coast, the peninsula is a painterly tableau of white-washed stucco homes, purple bougainvilleas and olive-green hillsides. The city is also awash in historical attractions, including the stumpy foundation of the Mausoleum, one of the seven wonders of the ancient world.

Bodrum's nightlife beckons partiers like a siren's song. Young, well-dressed revelers converge onto Cumhuriyet Caddesi, which visitors call Bar Street, before heading to behemoth discos like Halikarnas, an open-air club that resembles a nearby amphitheater. —Seth Sherwood

SPORTS & GAMES

SPORTS

A Fan's Guide

An Inside Guide to Baseball Parks

Where to sit, where to park and what to eat at major league parks

A sweltering summer afternoon and you're at the game watching your favorite team. Of course, you can get peanuts and popcorn and, if you're old enough, beer. But why not try the ribs or kielbasa or sushi? Here's an insider's guide to America's major league parks, including tips on where to park, sit and eat, as well as stadium stats and the last year your team won World Series and League titles.

AMERICAN LEAGUE EAST

Baltimore Orioles
World Series: 1983. League: 1983.
Oriole Park at Camden Yards: *48,876 capacity; grass surface; built in 1992. Modern amenities with old-time charm. 410-685-9800; orioles.mlb.com*

FAN NOTES: Arrive at least 45 minutes early to get a parking spot. Better yet, take public transportation. Best seats are along first base. On windy days,

avoid top-level seats that have open backs. Former O's first baseman Boog Powell operates a wildly successful barbecue stand in the stadium, near the Eutaw Street entrance.

Boston Red Sox
World Series: 2004, 2007. League: 2004.
Fenway Park: *33,871 capacity; grass surface; built in 1912. A baseball classic. 877-REDSOX9; redsox.mlb.com*

FAN NOTES: Nearly all seats in the grandstand are good. Best bleacher seat: the red one in row 33, where Ted Williams' 502-foot homer landed in 1946. Fenway franks are a legend, but more for tradition than taste.

New York Yankees
World Series: 2000. League: 2003.
Yankee Stadium: *52,325 capacity; grass surface; built in 2009. Replaces the historic "House that Ruth Built," where the Yankees had been playing since 1923. The new $1.6 billion stadium is one of the most expensive ever built. 718-293-4300; newyork.yankees.mlb.com*

FAN NOTES: The stadium has its own subway station, 161st Street—Yankee Stadium. Parking is difficult, but planning is under way for additional garages. Views from about 600 bleacher seats in right and left fields have partially obstructed views, but are available for discounted prices. Reviewers say the food at the park is top-notch.

Tampa Bay Rays
World Series:— League: 2008.
Tropicana Field: *38,400 capacity, artificial turf surface; opened in 1990. The field went from purely*

ⓘ INSIDE INFO

An Olympic Strike Out

○ Although baseball is the American pastime, it wasn't an official Olympic sport until the 1992 Summer Games in Barcelona.

○ Since then, Cuba has taken home three gold medals and the United States one.

○ Both baseball and softball are being dropped from the Olympics, starting in 2012.

SOURCES: BaseballLibrary.com

functional to innovative, after a 1996 renovation. 727-825-3137; tampabay. rays.mlb.com

FAN NOTES: Plenty of amenities, including a cigar bar in the "batter's eye" overlooking center field. Convenient and ample parking, mostly on the park's east side. Seats behind the backstop are as close as they get—only 50 feet from home plate.

Toronto Blue Jays

World Series: 1993. League: 1993.
Rogers Centre *(formerly SkyDome): 50,516 capacity; artificial turf surface; opened in 1989. It boasts the tallest domed roof, when retracted, but some say the park lacks atmosphere. 888-OK-GO-JAY; rogerscentre.com*

FAN NOTES: Parking is ample but expensive; nearby public transportation might be a better bet. The 200-level seats are probably the best. If you're prone to dizziness, avoid seats in the 500 level.

AMERICAN LEAGUE CENTRAL

Chicago White Sox

World Series: 2005. League: 2005.
U.S. Cellular Field: *44,321 capacity; grass surface; built in 1991. Lacks the charm of the original. 312-674-1000; whitesox.mlb.com*

FAN NOTES: Located in a residential neighborhood, so parking is difficult. Wind shifts wreak havoc with the ball, benefiting hitters. Dirt from the original Comiskey field was recycled here.

Cleveland Indians

World Series: 1948. League: 1997.
Progressive Field: *42,400 capacity; grass suface; built in 1994. A cozy, urban ballpark. 216-420-4200*

FAN NOTES: In 2007, Heritage Park, the new home of the Indians Hall of Fame, opened in center

A home run hit 400 feet in Yankee Stadium, which is at sea level, would travel up to 440 feet in Coors Stadium in Denver, the Mile High City

● ● ●

field. The park offers a smorgasbord of foods (which may help explain the wider than normal seats), including deli, baked goods, sushi and a southwestern menu.

Detroit Tigers

World Series: 1984.
League: 1984, 2006.
Comerica Park: *40,000 capacity; grass surface; opened 2000. Built with the hope of revitalizing Detroit's downtown. The Tigers share it with an amusement park and a museum. 313-962-4000; tigers.mlb.com*

FAN NOTES: No upper-deck outfield seats results in a clear view of the downtown skyline. More home runs go to right field. The air-conditioned lounge at section 330 of the upper concourse has a bar, restrooms and a seating area—all open to the public.

Kansas City Royals

World Series: 1985. League: 1985.
Kauffman Stadium: *40,625 capacity; grass surface; opened 1973. A good stadium and seems to get better with age. 816-921-8000; kansascity.royals.mlb.com*

FAN NOTES: More than enough parking. Best visibility for hitters in the majors. Only bad seats in the house: the upper deck, where fans could sit in near darkness. Waterfalls and fountains run for 322 feet on the embankment overlooking right center.

Minnesota Twins

World Series: 1991. League: 1991.
Hubert H. Humphrey Metrodome: *55,883 capacity; artificial surface; opened in 1982. Very loud, but keeps out the cold weather. 612-375-1366; msfc.com*

FAN NOTES: Arrive early and park on the street using 8-hour meters. Power hitters' park. On May 4, 1984, Dave Kingman hit the ball through the

✔ **TIMELY TIPS**

Stadium Eats: Buy Me Some Sushi and Baby Back Ribs

After touring ballparks across the country, a *New York Times* food critic offers his rules on what to eat—and what to pass up—at some of the nation's ballparks.

WHAT TO AVOID:

✔ **Meatless hot dog substitutes,** and most foods bearing the appellation "veggie," may have good intentions but are not good eating.

✔ **Nachos, Chinese food, pizza and pretzels** taste about the same everywhere, except at Dodger Stadium, where the pretzels are particularly greasy. If you must eat them don't expect more than a glimmer of gustatory satisfaction.

✔ **Also, say no to burgers,** which are uniformly desiccated at baseball games. Mustard on greasy napkins would probably be a tastier snack.

✔ **Finally, forget cocktails:** margaritas poured from a beer tap are a travesty, and canned "micheladas" are worse.

BEST DISHES:

✔ **A cedar-planked salmon** in Seattle, a thick pastrami hero at Dodger Stadium, the classic Primanti Brothers sandwich in Pittsburgh.

✔ **AT&T Park in San Francisco** might be the leading example of upscale food. Some of the best food is behind the scoreboard in a terrace overlooking the bay, the Scoreboard Plaza. Try the crab salad sandwich at Crazy Crab'z.

✔ **At Seattle's Safeco Field** you'll find a similarly zealous approach to ballpark dining. The variety of food choices includes pad Thai, chicken teriyaki and strawberries on a stick.

✔ **Miller Park in Milwaukee** prides itself on fare like grilled bratwursts and beer. The brats, from Klement's, have that Germanic sweet spice accent just right and the casings are snappy. Another popular dish is cheese curds, which are crisp, not greasy, and have that unmistakable squeak. And although the stadium's name is owned by the Miller Brewing Company, you'll still find smaller Wisconsin brewers like Lakefront, New Glarus, Stevens Point and Sprecher.

✔ **At Citizens Bank Park,** home of the Philadelphia Phillies, most of the action takes place in Ashburn Alley (named for the Hall of Famer Richie Ashburn), behind center field. Don't miss the hoagies, Chickie & Pete's crab fries (French fries dusted with Old Bay seasoning) and two of the city's respected cheese steak purveyors, Rick's Steaks and Tony Luke's.

✔ **At Dodger Stadium,** try Ruby's Diner, for an excellent pair of sliders with beef jus and horseradish, and Canter's Deli, arguably one of the best Jewish delicatessens in the country. But those spots are only available to holders of expensive field-level tickets.

—Peter Meehan

roof. More home runs tend to be hit when the air-conditioning is turned off.

AMERICAN LEAGUE WEST

Los Angeles Angels of Anaheim
World Series: 2002. League: 2002.
Angel Stadium of Anaheim: *45,050 capacity; grass surface; opened 1966, renovated 1997. Not the prettiest sight in Southern California. 714-940-2000; angels.mlb.com*

FAN NOTES: Parking is ample. The cheapest tickets are in the family zone in left field. Nearby geysers shoot water up 90 feet when the Angels hit homers. A power hitter's park.

Oakland Athletics

World Series: 1989. League: 1990.
McAfee Coliseum *(formerly Oakland-Alameda County Stadium): 48,219 capacity; grass surface; opened in 1966. Neither offensive nor delightful. 510-638-4900; www.coliseum.com*

FAN NOTES: Try to arrive at least a half hour before game time to get a parking spot. Fans can catch home run balls by reaching in front of foul pole screens. Favors pitchers and left-handed batters. Baseball's first appearance of the "wave" took place here in October 1981.

Seattle Mariners

World Series:— League: —
Safeco Field: *47,116 capacity; grass surface; opened in 1999. Can't beat the views of sunsets over Puget Sound. 206-346-4001; mariners.mlb.com*

FAN NOTES: Leave early for a game—traffic is heavy in downtown Seattle around the field. Great sightlines, especially behind centerfield fence. Nearby are local food vendors and an open pit barbecue. Smallish seats. Third-deck seating is very steep.

Texas Rangers

World Series:— League: —
Rangers Ballpark in Arlington: *49,200 capacity; grass surface; opened in 1994. Still a great ballpark. 817-273-5222;*

FAN NOTES: Bullpens are just 5 feet above playing level, so it's easy to identify pitchers as they warm up. With the right-field foul pole only 325 feet from home plate and the fence only 8 feet high, it pays to be a lefty. Parking is easy.

NATIONAL LEAGUE EAST

Atlanta Braves

World Series: 1957 (as Milwaukee Braves). League: 1999.
Turner Field: *50,096 capacity; grass surface; opened*
in 1997. Site of the '96 Olympics, retrofitted for baseball. 404-614-2314; atlanta.braves.mlb.com

FAN NOTES: The parking lot was part of the old Atlanta-Fulton County Stadium; markers show the site of Hank Aaron's record-breaking 715th home run. Air-conditioned concourse. Buy tickets for future games on the suite level.

Florida Marlins

World Series: 2003. League: 2003.
Dolphins Stadium: *36,331 capacity; grass surface; opened in 1987. A quirky park, originally designed for football. 305-623-6100; dolphinstadium.com*

FAN NOTES: Parking is no problem; the lot was built to handle 70,000 football fans. Before some games, a Fiesta Latina takes place, featuring Latin food and live music. Some obstructed views from the lower-level seats near foul poles.

New York Mets

World Series: 1986. League: 2000.
Citi Field: *42,000 capacity; grass surface; opened in 2009. No longer an eyesore, but planes still fly overhead on their way to LaGuardia airport. 718-507-TIXX; newyork.mets.mlb.com*

FAN NOTES: The new stadium, which opened in 2009, replaces Shea Stadium. The new facility offers wider seats, a wider concourse, and a wide assortment of bars and restaurants.

Philadelphia Phillies

World Series: 1980, 2008. League: 1993.
Citizens Bank Park: *43,826 capacity; opened in 2004. One of the more than a dozen spiffy ballparks built since 1991. 215-463-1000; www.citizensbank.com*

FAN NOTES: Ashburn Alley, named for former great Richie Ashburn, opens three hours before weekend games; watch batting practice in a fair atmosphere. Prominent views of the Philly skyline are behind the center-field fence. A 50-foot Liberty Bell chimes after a Phillies homer.

SPORTS

Washington Nationals

World Series: — League:—

Nationals Park: *56,000 capacity; grass surface; opened in 2008. The first green-certified major league baseball stadium. 202-675-NATS; nationals.mlb.com*

FAN NOTES: The new stadium, which opened in 2008, features an innovative design of steel, glass, and pre-cast concrete. There are stunning views from the stadium's circulation ramps of the waterfront and major Washington landmarks.

NATIONAL LEAGUE CENTRAL

Chicago Cubs

World Series: 1908. League: 1945.

Wrigley Field: *39,538 capacity; grass surface; built in 1914. A Chicago landmark. Fans love it. 773-404-CUBS*

FAN NOTES: Parking is almost nonexistent. Bleacher seats are the most popular. After the game a blue flag with a white W or a white flag with a blue L is flown to signify a Cubs win or loss. Strong lake breezes favor pitchers.

Cincinnati Reds

World Series: 1990. League: 1990.

Great American Ball Park: *42,059 capacity; grass surface; opened in 2003. Plain on the outside but good views of the Ohio River from the inside. 513-765-7000; cincinnati.reds.mlb.com*

FAN NOTES: Family-friendly. Clean. A towering smoke stack smokes for home runs and strikeouts. A homey touch, but the stack partially obstructs views from some center-field seats. Red seats are a welcome departure from the ubiquitous green. Parking is ample and efficient.

Houston Astros

World Series: — League: 2005.

Minute Maid Park: *40,950 capacity; grass surface; opened in 2000. Retro look but big on high-tech features. 713-259-8000; houston.astros.mlb.com*

FAN NOTES: The park is wired: 1,400 speaker cabinets get as close to fans as possible, and fans can bring their Wi-Fi compatible devices and surf the Web. Maintains a tradition of $1

Baseball's Winter Games

Who says the season's over in October? Try the Caribbean League

The winter months are dark days for baseball fans, The World Series is a distant memory, and the promise of spring training is still months away. But there's no need to fret: the answer is just a plane ride away. Visit the Caribbean winter leagues, home of 28 teams.

Each winter, from November through January, some of baseball's best players head south to play for teams in the Dominican Republic, Mexico, Puerto Rico and Venezuela. The most established players are generally found in the Puerto Rican league; Mexico features the fewest.

The baseball comes cheap (the best tickets are often around $10) and the sideshows are dis-tinctly Caribbean—salsa music between innings, and piña coladas hawked by vendors. For more information, check out www.latinobaseball.com or contact the leagues directly.

Dominican League   *809-567-6371*
Estadio Quisqueya, Santo Domingo, Dominican Republic

Mexican Pacific League   *555-602-38-21*
                                   or 555-643-38-05
Av. Insurgentes No. 847, Culiacan, Mexico

Puerto Rican Baseball League
                         www.hitboricua.com
Ave. Munoz Rivera 1056, Rio Piedras, Puerto Rico 00919

Venezuelan League   *58-212-761-4817*
Av. Sorbona No. 25, Edif. Marta-2do. Piso Colinas de Bello Monte, Caracas, Venezuela

Following the Boys of Summer in the Spring

For spring training, baseball fans have two choices: the Grapefruit League in Florida or the Cactus League in Arizona. Here are some places to catch a game before the regular season starts.

GRAPEFRUIT LEAGUE—FLORIDA

Team		Stadium	Information
Atlanta Braves	NATIONAL LEAGUE, EAST	Champion Stadium, Kissimmee	407-939-GAME
Baltimore Orioles	AMERICAN LEAGUE, EAST	Ft. Lauderdale Stadium, Ft. Lauderdale	954-776-1921
Boston Red Sox	AMERICAN LEAGUE, EAST	City of Palms Park, Ft. Myers	239-334-4700
Detroit Tigers	AMERICAN LEAGUE, CENTRAL	Joker Marchant Stadium, Lakeland	863-686-8075
Florida Marlins	NATIONAL LEAGUE, EAST	Roger Dean Stadium, Jupiter	561-775-1818
Houston Astros	NATIONAL LEAGUE, CENTRAL	Osceola Stadium, Kissimmee	407-933-5957
Minnesota Twins	AMERICAN LEAGUE, CENTRAL	Hammond Stadium, Ft. Myers	800-33-TWINS
New York Mets	NATIONAL LEAGUE, EAST	Tradition Field, Port St. Lucie	772-871-2115
New York Yankees	AMERICAN LEAGUE, EAST	Steinbrenner Field, Tampa	813-879-2244
Philadelphia Phillies	NATIONAL LEAGUE, EAST	Bright House Networks Field, Clearwater	727-467-4457
Pittsburgh Pirates	NATIONAL LEAGUE, CENTRAL	McKechnie Field, Bradenton	941-748-4610
St. Louis Cardinals	NATIONAL LEAGUE, CENTRAL	Roger Dean Stadium, Jupiter	561-775-1818
Tampa Bay Rays	AMERICAN LEAGUE, EAST	Charlotte Co. Sports Park, St. Petersburg	727-825-3250
Toronto Blue Jays	AMERICAN LEAGUE, EAST	Dunedin Stadium, Dunedin	888-525-JAYS
Washington Nationals	NATIONAL LEAGUE, EAST	Space Coast Stadium, Viera	727-825-3137

CACTUS LEAGUE—ARIZONA

Team		Stadium	Information
Arizona Diamondbacks	NATIONAL LEAGUE, WEST	Tuscon Electric Park, Tuscon	520-434-1000
Chicago Cubs	NATIONAL LEAGUE, CENTRAL	Hohokam Park, Mesa	800-905-3315
Chicago White Sox	AMERICAN LEAGUE, CENTRAL	Camelback Ranch, Glendale	623-877-8585
Cincinnati Reds	NATIONAL LEAGUE, CENTRAL	Goodyear Ballpark, Goodyear	623-882-3120
Cleveland Indians	AMERICAN LEAGUE, CENTRAL	Goodyear Ballpark, Goodyear	623-882-3120
Colorado Rockies	NATIONAL LEAGUE, WEST	Hi Corbett Field Randolph Park, Tuscon	520-327-9467
Kansas City Royals	AMERICAN LEAGUE, CENTRAL	Surprise Stadium, Surprise	623-594-5600
L.A. Angels of Anaheim	AMERICAN LEAGUE, WEST	Tempe Diablo Stadium, Tempe	480-350-5205
Los Angeles Dodgers	NATIONAL LEAGUE, WEST	Camelback Ranch, Glendale	623-877-8585
Milwaukee Brewers	NATIONAL LEAGUE, CENTRAL	Maryvale Baseball Park, Phoenix	602-534-6449
Oakland Athletics	AMERICAN LEAGUE, WEST	Phoenix Municipal Stadium, Phoenix	877-493-BALL
San Diego Padres	NATIONAL LEAGUE, WEST	Peoria Sports Stadium, Peoria	623-773-8720
San Francisco Giants	NATIONAL LEAGUE, WEST	Scottsdale Stadium, Scottsdale	480-990-2977
Seattle Mariners	AMERICAN LEAGUE, WEST	Peoria Sports Stadium, Peoria	623-773-8720
Texas Rangers	AMERICAN LEAGUE, WEST	Surprise Stadium, Surprise	623-222-2222

SPORTS

tickets for kids 14 and under for seats in the outfield deck.

Milwaukee Brewers

World Series: —   League: 1982.
Miller Park: *41,900 capacity; grass surface; opened in 2001. Distinctive fan-shaped roof. 414-902-4400; brewers.mlb.com*

FAN NOTES: Retired numbers of Milwaukee legends like Robin Yount hang above the center-field wall. Tailgate facilities overlook the Menomonee River. Grilled kosher dogs and bratwurst are big here. Parking is tight.

Pittsburgh Pirates

World Series: 1979.   League: 1979.
PNC Park: *38,496 capacity; grass surface; opened in 2001. A classic-style ballpark in the tradition of Forbes Field and Fenway Park. 412-321-2827; pittsburgh.pirates.mlb.com*

FAN NOTES: Easy access across the Roberto Clemente bridge, named for the great Pirates right-fielder. The bridge is pedestrian-only on game days. The park's highest seat is only 88 feet from the field. Former Pirate Manny Sanguillen runs an outfield barbecue.

St. Louis Cardinals

World Series: 1982, 2006.   League: 2004.
Busch Stadium: *50,345 capacity; built in 2005; grass surface. The first season in the new stadium was in 2006. 314- 345-9600; stlouis.cardinals.mlb.com*

FAN NOTES: Dramatic views of Gateway Arch and downtown St. Louis skyline. Nearby are the International Bowling Museum, and the St. Louis Cardinals museum, a shrine to legendary Cardinal, Stan "the Man" Musial. See both museums for the price of one ticket.

NATIONAL LEAGUE WEST

Arizona Diamondbacks

World Series: 2001.   League: 2001.
Chase Field: *49,033 capacity; grass surface; opened in 1998. Comfort and amenities reign. Among the best. 602-462-6500; arizona.diamondbacks.mlb.com*

FAN NOTES: A roof and air-conditioning shelter fans

✔ **TIMELY TIPS**

Snagging a Seat

A scalper's guide to getting a ticket when the game is sold out

Selling tickets at more than face value is illegal in many places. But it is the scalpers who face arrest, not the ticket buyers. Scalping, of course, is somewhat of a covert activity. Reselling tickets at any price on stadium grounds is illegal in some places, so much of the commerce takes place in surrounding areas. Here are a few tips.

✔ **The more scalpers you see, the more patient you should be.** As game time approaches, the prices will drop. If the game is not sold out, or if demand is not high, try to wait until right before the game starts, and you'll discover a buyer's market. Desperate to unload tickets, scalpers will sell them for as little as a third of the price they paid.

✔ **Try to bargain for the best price you can get.** If it's a very big game, the seekers will far outnumber the sellers, and prices may be steep. Scalped tickets at events like the Super Bowl can run $2,000 and up. Most scalpers are trying to do brisk business, so they may take your reasonable offer.

✔ **Before you decide to buy, make sure to get a good look at the tickets.** Fake or expired tickets are often sold and while you may not be able to tell counterfeits, you can at least check the date. Whatever you do, don't buy a press pass; it's probably fake and even if it's not, you're almost sure to get discovered and thrown out.

from sweltering heat and monsoon storms. Good views from most seats. Lots of parking in downtown Phoenix, which is a short walk from the field.

Colorado Rockies

World Series: — League: —

Coors Field: *50,445 capacity; grass surface; built in 1995. An all-round good stadium. 800-388-ROCK; colorado.rockies.mlb.com*

FAN NOTES: Possibly the most spectacular view in baseball; the Rocky Mountains are visible from first base and right field. A hitter's park. Home team has the distinct advantage of being accustomed to Denver's mile-high atmosphere. Limited parking.

Los Angeles Dodgers

World Series: 1988. League: 1988.

Dodger Stadium: *56,000 capacity; grass surface; opened in 1962. Doesn't show its age; meticulously maintained. 213-224-1400; losangeles.dodgers.mlb.com*

FAN NOTES: Parking lots funnel efficiently into nearby freeways. Great views of the San Gabriel mountains, but top-deck seats are too far from the action. Dodger Dogs are required eating. A classic pitcher's park.

San Diego Padres

World Series: — League: 1998.

Petco Park: *42,445 capacity; grass surface; opened in 2004. A spanking new stadium with spectacular views. 619-795-5000; petcoparkevents.com*

FAN NOTES: More than enough parking. Seats have cupholders and lots of legroom. Outstanding sightlines. The Padres are the "Team of the Military;" members of the military often take over sections and outchant each other. Big-time pitcher's park.

San Francisco Giants *World Series: 1954 (as the New York Giants). League: 2002.*

AT&T Park: *41,503 capacity; artificial surface; built in 2000. Urban ballpark with old-time feel.*

 **TIMELY TIPS**

Upping the Odds of Winning the Office Pool

Sports gambling is a losing proposition for all but the savviest—and luckiest—bettors. Russ Culver, former sports book manager at the Mirage hotel in Las Vegas, offers these tips on winning the office pool.

✔ **Look for trends.** Statistics aren't as telling as shifts in a team's fortunes and ability. Knowing that a team goes 8-1 on Thursdays probably isn't important, but knowing that a team hasn't won a road game in 10 years may well be.

✔ **Defy the polls.** Polls of the nation's best college basketball and football teams are like a beauty contest. When you look at the N.C.A.A. tournament bracket in the office pool, bet against the glamour teams when they are playing a strong team that's not as popular.

✔ **Momentum matters.** In baseball, focus on a pitcher's last five starts. In college hoops look at how a team played down the stretch period before the N.C.A.A. tournament. A team that finished third in its league in the regular season but came on strong to win the conference deserves a good look.

✔ **Seedings mean little in the N.C.A.A. tournament.** Seedings are gerrymandered to assure the best matchups for television. The No. 1 and No. 2 ranked teams are accurate, but those ranked No. 4 to about 12 are manipulated for TV.

415-972-2000; sanfrancisco.giants.mlb.com

FAN NOTES: Nine-foot statue of one of the greatest, Willie Mays, greets visitors at the public entrance. Even from the worst seats you get a view of the Bay Bridge and the marina. Public transportation is abundant and easy.

SPORTS

Reading the Football Ref's Arms

Nearly everyone knows that a referee with his arms stretched high above his head means a player has scored a touchdown or field goal. Here's a beginner's guide to other football signals.

First down
Arms pointed toward goal

Invalid fair catch
Hand waving above head

Personal foul
One wrist striking the other above the head

Touchdown, field goal or successful try
Both arms extended in air

Holding
Grasping one wrist with clenched fist

No time-out; with whistle: time-in
Arm makes circular, clocklike motion

Safety
Palms together above head

Unsportsmanlike behavior
Arms outstretched, palms down

Illegal motion at snap
Horizontal arc made with one hand

Offside, encroachment or free-kick violation
Hands on hips

Time-out
Hands crossed above head

Loss of down
Both hands held behind head.

Illegal use of hands
Grasping one wrist with the other hand open and facing forward

Penalty refused, incomplete pass or missed goal
Hands crossing horizontally

Interference with forward pass or fair catch
Hands open and extended forward from shoulders, hands vertical

Illegal forward pass
One hand waved behind back followed by loss of down signal.

SOURCE: www.nfl.com

Getting Ready for the Kickoff

For more information about individual teams, go to www.nfl.com and click on "Teams."

AMERICAN FOOTBALL CONFERENCE

	Team	Last Super Bowl Title	Stadium		Ticket information
NORTH	Baltimore Ravens	2001	M&T Bank Stadium	410-261-7283	www.baltimoreravens.com
	Cincinnati Bengals	—	Paul Brown Stadium	513-621-8383	www.bengals.com
	Cleveland Browns	—	Cleveland Browns Stadium	888-891-1999	www.clevelandbrowns.com
	Pittsburgh Steelers	2009	Heinz Field	412-323-1200	www.steelers.com
SOUTH	Houston Texans	—	Reliant Stadium	713-629-3700	www.houstontexans.com
	Indianapolis Colts	2007	Lucas Oil Stadium	317-297-7000	www.colts.com
	Jacksonville Jaguars	—	Jacksonville Municipal Stadium	904-633-2000	www.jaguars.com
	Tennessee Titans	—	LP Field	615-565-4200	www.titansonline.com
EAST	Buffalo Bills	—	Ralph Wilson	877-BB-TICKS	www.buffalobills.com
	Miami Dolphins	1974	Land Shark Stadium	888-FINS-TIX	www.miamidolphins.com
	New England Patriots	2005	Gillette Stadium	800-543-1776	www.patriots.com
	New York Jets	1969	Giants Stadium	516-560-8192	www.newyorkjets.com
WEST	Denver Broncos	1999	Invesco Field at Mile High	720-258-3333	www.denverbroncos.com
	Kansas City Chiefs	1970	Arrowhead Stadium	816-920-9400	www.kcchiefs.com
	Oakland Raiders	1984	McAfee Coliseum	800-RAIDERS	www.raiders.com
	San Diego Chargers	—	Qualcomm Stadium	877-242-7437	www.chargers.com

NATIONAL FOOTBALL CONFERENCE

	Team	Last Super Bowl Title	Stadium		Ticket information
NORTH	Chicago Bears	1986	Soldier Field	888-79-BEARS	www.chicagobears.com
	Detroit Lions	—	Ford Field	313-262-2003	www.detroitlions.com
	Green Bay Packers	1997	Lambeau Field	920-569-7101	www.packers.com
	Minnesota Vikings	—	H.H. Humphrey Metrodome	651-989-5151	www.vikings.com
SOUTH	Atlanta Falcons	—	Georgia Dome	404-223-8000	www.atlantafalcons.com
	Carolina Panthers	—	Bank of America Stadium	704-358-7800	www.panthers.com
	New Orleans Saints	—	Louisiana Superdome	504-731-1700	www.neworleanssaints.com
	Tampa Bay Buccaneers	2003	Raymond James Stadium	800-282-0683	www.buccaneers.com
EAST	Dallas Cowboys	1996	Cowboys Stadium	817-892-4400	www.dallascowboys.com
	New York Giants	2008	Giants Stadium	201-935-8222	www.giants.com
	Philadelphia Eagles	—	Lincoln Financial Field	888-332-2582	www.philadelphiaeagles.com
	Washington Redskins	1992	FedEx Field	301-276-6050	www.redskins.com
WEST	Arizona Cardinals	—	Cardinals Stadium	602-379-0102	www.azcardinals.com
	St. Louis Rams	2000	Edward Jones Dome	314-425-8830	www.stlouisrams.com
	San Francisco 49ers	1995	Candlestick Park	415-656-4900	www.sf49ers.com
	Seattle Seahawks	—	Qwest Field	888-NFL-HAWK	www.seattleseahawks.com

SPORTS

Scoring Tickets for the Big Events

From the Indy 500 to the World Series, here's how to get a seat

Most couch potatoes' idea of a good seat for the Super Bowl is in front of a wide-screen television. But for real sports fans, nothing beats being there—whether it's the Super Bowl, the World Series, the Masters or whatever. Getting tickets to some of the nation's biggest sporting events—like the Masters, for example—is next to impossible. But you can get in the door to some of the others if you do some advance planning and are prepared for a little hustle. Here's the lowdown on how and where to get tickets to some of the hottest sporting events.

The Super Bowl   www.nfl.com

Super Bowl XLIV - Feb. 7, 2010, Miami, Fla.
Super Bowl XLV - Feb. 6, 2011, Arlington, Tex.
Super Bowl XLVI - Feb. 5, 2012, Indianapolis, Ind.

Football's biggest game is the world's most watched television event each year; but the Super Bowl itself is not all that hard to see in person, if you're willing to pay the hefty ticket prices (about $700 and up). Season-ticket holders of the participating teams have the best shot; the A.F.C. and N.F.C. champs split 35 percent of the Super Bowl ducats, most of which are made available to their faithful fans. The host team gets another 10 percent of the tickets, and every other N.F.L. team gets hundreds of tickets, which they generally sell to their own ticket holders. The league also distributes 500 tickets each year through a lottery it conducts. You can enter by sending a self-addressed stamped envelope between February and June to Super Bowl Random Drawing, P.O. Box 49140, Strongsville, Ohio 44149-0140.

World Series   www.mlb.com

Every October

The participating teams control virtually all the tickets to baseball's Fall Classic, so your best bet is to hold season tickets for your favorite team—and hope they make it all the way.

N.C.A.A. Final Four   www.ncaasports.com

Late March, early April

You practically have to jump through hoops to watch the best college basketball teams fight

---

A Very Short History of B-ball

Basketball rules have changed since a Canadian invented the game more than a century ago

Looking for a vigorous indoor game to keep young men occupied during long New England winters, Dr. James Naismith, a Canadian-born American, invented basketball in December 1891. The first game was played a month later when, as legend has it, he nailed a peach basket to a gym wall. Naismith's original 13 rules have been modified quite a bit over the years, although his basic principles still hold. Some modifications are stylistic maneuvers, like the slam dunk and double pump, which Naismith could hardly have foreseen.

The biggest change came in the mid-1950s with the introduction of the clock rule that gives players 24 seconds to either shoot or lose possession of the ball. The 24-second rule instantly transformed the low-scoring, slow-paced game into an exciting, lightening-quick sport. (At about the same time, the orange ball was introduced to make it more visible to players and spectators.)

The game's organization underwent a major change just after the 1948-49 season when the Basketball Association and the National Basketball League merged and the National Basketball Association was born. But it wasn't until the early '80s that the N.B.A. exploded in popularity. Today it's a multimillion-dollar business with 30 franchises across the country and in Canada.

A Who's Who of Pro Hoop Teams

For more information on individual basketball teams, go to the N.B.A. Web site at www.nba.com and click on the team's name.

EASTERN CONFERENCE

Division	Team	Last League Title	Arena	Ticket information
ATLANTIC	Boston Celtics	2008	TD Banknorth Garden	866-4-CELTIX
	New Jersey Nets	—	Continental Airlines Arena	800-7NJ-NETS
	New York Knicks	1973	Madison Square Garden	212-465-JUMP
	Philadelphia 76ers	1983	Wachovia Complex	215-339-7676
	Toronto Raptors	—	Air Canada Centre	416-872-5000
CENTRAL	Chicago Bulls	1998	United Center	312-455-4000
	Cleveland Cavaliers	—	Quicken Loans Arena	800-820-CAVS
	Detroit Pistons	2004	The Palace of Auburn Hills	248-377-0100
	Indiana Pacers	—	Conseco Fieldhouse	317-917-2500
	Milwaukee Bucks	1971	Bradley Center	800-4NBA-TIX
SOUTHEAST	Atlanta Hawks	1958[1]	Philips Arena	866-715-1500
	Charlotte Bobcats	—	Charlotte Bobcats Arena	704-262-2287
	Miami Heat	2006	American Airlines Arena	786-777-HOOP
	Orlando Magic	—	TD Waterhouse Centre	407-89-MAGIC
	Washington Wizards	1978	Verizon Center	202-661-5050

WESTERN CONFERENCE

Division	Team	Last League Title	Arena	Ticket information
NORTHWEST	Denver Nuggets	—	Pepsi Center	303-405-1111
	Minnesota Timberwolves	—	Target Center	800-4NBA-TIX
	Oklahoma City Thunder	1979[2]	Ford Center	405-208-HOOP
	Portland Trail Blazers	1977	Rose Garden	503-797-9600
	Utah Jazz	—	EnergySolutions Arena	801-355-DUNK
PACIFIC	Golden State Warriors	1975	The Arena in Oakland	800-GSW-HOOP
	Los Angeles Clippers	—	Staples Center	888-895-8662
	Los Angeles Lakers	2009	Staples Center	310-426-6031
	Phoenix Suns	—	America West Arena	602-379-SUNS
	Sacramento Kings	1951	ARCO Arena	916-928-3650
SOUTHWEST	Dallas Mavericks	—	American Airlines Center	214-747-MAVS
	Houston Rockets	1995	Toyota Center	713-627-DUNK
	Memphis Grizzlies	—	FedEx Forum	901-888-HOOP
	New Orleans Hornets	—	New Orleans Arena	504-525-HOOP
	Spurs	2007	SBC Center	210-444-5050

[1] as St. Louis Hawks   [2] as Seattle SuperSonics

SPORTS

for the national championship each year. Chances of getting a Final Four ticket improved when the N.C.A.A. started holding championship games in arenas that seat more than 30,000, but it's still tough. The N.C.A.A. begins taking applications just after the previous year's tournament. A random computerized drawing is held during the summer; winners are notified by mid-August.

The Masters   www.masters.org

Final round is held the second Sunday in April

It's almost as hard to watch golf's big event in person as it is to play a round at Augusta National, the Georgia course on which it is played each year. Only the lucky few on Augusta National's "patron list" are allowed to buy tickets each year. The list is made up primarily of people who had been attending the tournament before 1968 and those who have been added to it off the very long waiting list—which itself was closed to new members shortly after opening in 2000.

Your best bet of seeing top golfers play is to go a few days early to watch a practice round. To try to get those tickets, write the club just after the end of the previous year's tournament. Send your name, address, phone number and the last four digits of your Social Security number to Masters Tournament, Practice Rounds, PO Box 2047, Augusta, Ga. 30903.

Indianapolis 500   www.indy500.com

Memorial Day weekend, Indianapolis Motor Speedway

Hundreds of thousands of people turn out every year for auto racing's big day, which is also one of the world's biggest parties. Despite the huge number of seats, it's still a tough ticket to land. A large percentage of the 300,000 seats are filled through renewals—people who attend the race one year and, within a week, request renewals or upgrades for the next year's 500.

To request tickets for the first time, call 800-822-4639 for information or apply online at www.

The Fastest Game on Ice

Fans watch the fights while hockey players keep their eyes on the prize: the Stanley Cup

As you might expect of a sport as famous for fighting as for skating skill, there's a dispute over whether hockey was first played on a pond in Nova Scotia using cow dung as a puck or whether it began in Montreal, Quebec. But there's no doubt that the sport, which is played almost exclusively in the northern hemisphere, began in Canada.

Fittingly enough, hockey's top prize, the Stanley Cup, was created in 1893 by Lord Stanley, governor-general of Canada. Since then it has not been awarded only twice. Once, in 1919, was when the worldwide Spanish flu epidemic hit Canada and several members of the Montreal

Canadiens team had to be hospitalized. One player died, and the series was called off for the season. The second time was in 2005, when as a result of a labor dispute between the N.H.L. and the players' union, the entire 2004-2005 season was canceled.

The cup is awarded annually to the winner of the National Hockey League playoffs. Each season, N.H.L. teams play 82 games, with the top eight teams in each conference qualifying for the playoffs. Conference winners then vie for the League championship, a best-of-seven series, generally held in the spring.

Over the years, the Montreal Canadiens have won the most Stanley Cups: 24. Though they haven't won one since 1967, the Toronto Maple Leafs come in second with 13 wins. Among the American teams, the Detroit Red Wings have most—11.

Where to Watch the Hockey Puck Fly

Fans can get tickets for favorite teams online at the N.H.L. Web site, www.nhl.com/tickets, through Ticketmaster or by going directly to the arena box office.

EASTERN CONFERENCE

Division	Team	Last Stanley Cup	Arena	Ticket information
ATLANTIC	New Jersey Devils	2003	Prudential Center	800-NJ-DEVILS
	New York Islanders	1983	Nassau Coliseum	800-882-ISLES
	New York Rangers	1994	Madison Square Garden	212-465-6741
	Philadelphia Flyers	1975	Wachovia Center	215-218-7825
	Pittsburgh Penguins	2009	Mellon Arena	800-642-PENS
NORTHEAST	Boston Bruins	1972	TD Banknorth Garden	617-931-2222
	Buffalo Sabres	—	HSBC Arena	888-223-6000
	Montreal Canadiens	1993	Bell Centre	514-790-1245
	Ottawa Senators	1927	Scotiabank Place	613-599-0200
	Toronto Maple Leafs	1967	Air Canada Centre	416-872-5000
SOUTHEAST	Atlanta Thrashers	—	Philips Arena	866-715-1500
	Carolina Hurricanes	2006	RBC Center	919-834-4000
	Florida Panthers	—	BankAtlantic Center	954-835-8499
	Tampa Bay Lightning	2004	St. Pete Times Forum	813-301-2500
	Washington Capitals	—	Verizon Center	202-266-2277

WESTERN CONFERENCE

Division	Team	Last Stanley Cup	Arena	Ticket information
CENTRAL	Chicago Blackhawks	1961	United Center	312-943-7000
	Columbus Blue Jackets	—	Nationwide Arena	614-431-3600
	Detroit Red Wings	2008	Joe Louis Arena	313-396-7575
	Nashville Predators	—	Sommet Center	615-770-7825
	St. Louis Blues	—	Scottrade Center	314-622-5435
NORTHWEST	Calgary Flames	1989	Pengrowth Saddledome	403-777-0000
	Colorado Avalanche	2001	Pepsi Center	303-405-1111
	Edmonton Oilers	1990	Rexall Place	780-414-GOAL
	Minnesota Wild	—	Xcel Energy Center	651-222-WILD
	Vancouver Canucks	—	General Motors Place	604-899-7423
PACIFIC	Anaheim Ducks	2007	Honda Center	877-WILDWING
	Dallas Stars	1999	American Airlines Center	214-GO-STARS
	Los Angeles Kings	—	Staples Center	213-742-7340
	Phoenix Coyotes	—	Jobing.com Arena	480-563-7825
	San Jose Sharks	—	HP Pavilion at San Jose	800-366-4423

indy500.com. Seats available to first-timers are of lesser quality but also cost less, typically under $90. If you really want to see the race, despite poor seat quality, the speedway sells general admission, standing-room-only tickets the day of the race. But this is truly partial-view, last-resort seating.

Kentucky Derby   www.kentuckyderby.com

First Saturday in May, Churchill Downs, Louisville, Kentucky

The infield is the place to be for the Run of the Roses; more than 80,000 people mill around inside the track oval drinking juleps each year, while about 48,000 sit in the cushier boxes.

Only Churchill Downs season ticket holders and sponsors are guaranteed seats. To sign up for the possibility of getting box seats or infield tickets, you have to set up a Twin Spires Club account and then accumulate points by taking part in other Churchill Downs events. You can sign up online; membership is free. Those who show the most "loyalty," as the company puts it, are invited to buy tickets (cost: about $90). It could take years of showing interest in going to the Derby before you're invited to buy tickets. Applicants find out by the end of November if they can purchase tickets for the race the following May. You can buy a general admission ticket (about $40) on race day, but you won't get a view of the racetrack.

A Day at the Race Track

In auto racing, each flag carries a message, but the meaning depends on the track

Auto racing is a high-tech affair, dependent as it is these days on computers, radio communication and spotters who do aerial reconnaissance to ensure the safety of the drivers. But one decidedly low-tech tradition has stuck with the sport since the late 1800s: the use of flags to tell drivers and fans what's happening on the track. Each flag carries a specific message, which may vary from one event to the next or even among tracks.

Following are standard auto-racing flags and their meanings.

 **Solid green:** Signals the start of the race or practice session. Or, when used after a yellow or red flag, means that the track is clear.

 **Solid red :** Tells the driver to stop racing immediately. No passing allowed.

 **Solid black :** Directs a driver to stop at his pit. Usually indicates a penalty on the driver or team for a rule violation.

 Solid yellow: Indicates danger. Drivers should slow down, not pass, and be ready to change direction to avoid a hazard on the track.

 **Solid white:** Signifies that the leader has begun the final lap of the race.

 **White with a red cross in center:** Signals that medical help is on the course or is needed.

 **Black with white cross in center:** Warns a driver that he has been disqualified or accused of unsportsmanlike behavior.

 **Red with yellow "X":** Warns that the pit area is closed.

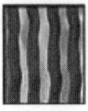 **Red and yellow vertical stripes:** Warns that the track surface is wet or slippery due to oil or water.

 **Light blue with yellow diagonal stripe:** Cautions to yield to a passing car or informs drivers that one lap remains.

 **Black and white checkered:** Signals the end of the race or practice session or that the leader has completed the race.

10 TERMS RACE TRACK TROLLERS SHOULD KNOW

Chassis roll. The choppy movement caused by a race car turning a corner at high speeds.

Drafting. Two or more cars running nose-to-tail, almost touching, while racing.

Groove. The best, most efficient or fastest route around a racetrack. Can change depending on the track and weather conditions.

Happy hour. The last official practice before a race, usually the day before the event.

Marbles. Pieces of rubber, dirt, gravel, etc. on the track, which interfere with driving and sometimes cause drivers to lose control.

Pit Road. The area along the straightaway where pit crews service race cars.

Silly season. The period toward the end of a season during which some teams announce driver, crew or sponsor changes.

Stickers. Race track term for new tires; derived from the stickers that tire makers put on new tires.

Superspeedway. The longest type of oval race track. Short tracks are less than 1 mile long; intermediates are between 1 and 2 miles; and superspeedways are 2 miles or longer.

Victory lane, also called the winner's circle. The place in the track's infield reserved for the winner's car during the victory celebration.

How to Get to the Hall of Fame

To get in, practice, practice, practice; but if you need directions, read this

Pick a sport or pastime and, chances are, there's a hall of fame that honors its legends. Baseball, football and basketball have their well-known and popular halls, of course, but so do bodybuilding, show jumping and drag racing. There's even a dog musher's hall of fame in Knik, Alaska, and a jousting hall in Virginia. Halls of fame are rare elsewhere in the world, but more than 1,000 are spread across America and the vast majority are sports-themed. Here are some worth visiting.

College Football Hall of Fame, *South Bend, Indiana.* Hall of college-football greats, like Jim Thorpe and Knute Rockne. 800-440-3263; www.collegefootball.org

International Bowling Museum and Hall of Fame, *St. Louis, Missouri.* "Tenpin Alley" illustrates the 5,000-year history of bowling. 314-231-6340; www.bowlingmuseum.com

International Boxing Hall of Fame Museum, *Canastota, New York.* Fist castings of boxing legend Jack Demspey. 315-697-7095; www.ibhof.com

International Swimming Hall of Fame, *Fort Lauderdale, Florida.* Exhibit on Johnny Weissmuller, "World's Greatest Swimmer" and star of 16 Tarzan films. 954-462-6536; www.ishof.com

International Tennis Hall of Fame, *Newport, Rhode Island.* Tennis trivia and artifacts galore; spotlights some 200 inductees going back to 1955. 800-457-1144; www.tennisfame.com

Motor Sports Hall of Fame, *Novi, Michigan.* Racers from all over the globe: Indy cars, stock cars, TransAm, dragsters, even snowmobiles. 800-250-7223; www.mshf.com

SPORTS

● **TIMELY TIPS**

Essential Sites for Sports Junkies

✔ **Allsports.com** for news, scores, team odds, audio feeds and more.

✔ **Sportsillustrated.cnn.com** from CNN and *Sports Illustrated*.

✔ **ESPN.com** (**espn.go.com**) for comprehensive sports coverage: news, videos, columns and data galore.

✔ **GolfWeb.com**, **GolfDigest.com** and **PGA.com** have the golf world covered.

✔ **MSN.FoxSports.com** for live scores, videos, rumors, stats, fantasy games and more.

✔ **NBA.com** from the National Basketball Association, with links to individual team Web sites.

✔ **NFL.com** from the National Football League, with links to individual team websites.

✔ **MLB.com** from Major League Baseball for all team news; lets you watch games not broadcast in your local TV market.

✔ **SportsFanLive.com** offers blogs and news on teams and players; lets you connect with fellow fans online or at local sports bars.

✔ **Sportingnews.com** and **Sportsnetwork.com** give up-to-the-minute news and results.

✔ **SportsLine.com** and **www.cbssports.com** for videos, news, fantasy scores and more.

✔ **TennisServer.com** for tennis news, schedules, rules and more.

—Richard J. Meislin

Naismith Memorial Basketball Hall of Fame, *Springfield, Massachusetts.* A big draw is Wilt Chamberlain's uniform from his 100-point game in 1962. 413-781-6500 or 877-4HOOPLA; www.hoophall.com

National Baseball Hall of Fame and Museum, *Cooperstown, New York.* Mother lode of artifacts, including bats and other items used by players who have been linked to steroid use. Organizers say the controversy is also part of baseball history. 607-547-7200; www.baseballhalloffame.org

National Cowboy Hall of Fame, *Oklahoma City, Oklahoma.* Display of more than 100 firearms as "functional sculpture." 405-478-2250; www.nationalcowboymuseum.org

National Fresh Water Fishing Hall of Fame, *Hayward, Wisconsin.* A huge pond surrounds the complex, which is shaped like a giant jumping muskie; its gaping jaw is an observation point that fits 20 people. 715-634-4440; www.freshwater-fishing.org

National Museum of Racing and Hall of Fame, *Sarasota Springs, New York.* Discover the heroes of the racing world—horses, jockeys and trainers. 518-584-0400; www.racingmuseum.org

National Soccer Hall of Fame and Museum, *Oneonta, New York.* More than 100,000 soccer artifacts, photos and memorabilia and thousands of photos going back to the late 1800s. 607-432-3351; www.soccerhall.org

Pro-Football Hall of Fame, *Canton, Ohio.* Impressive enshrinement of 229 members; an entire room is dedicated to Super Bowl fanatics. 330-456-8207; www.profootballhof.com

An Athlete's Guide

Playing Golf from Scratch

These pointers will get you going; the rest is up to you

Golf tournaments haven't quite attained Super Bowl status, but dynamic golfers like Tiger Woods have helped turn a ho-hum sport into one of the coolest games around. If you're contemplating joining the more than 28 million men and women who tee off each year, read this advice from the pros before you hit the green.

● Do I need to join a golf club to play?

No. There are lots of public, daily-fee courses, where you pay per round or for the day. There are about 20,000 golf courses in the country. Only about one-third of them are private courses; others are public, many of them owned by localities.

● How expensive is it to play?

Fees at private clubs vary but are generally fairly expensive. At a daily-fee course, the fees are not insignificant, but it depends on the quality of the course and its location. You can find some good ones in the $30 to $50 range and a lot of good ones in the $100 to $150 range; fees generally go up on weekends.

● What is the best way to learn the game?

Every newcomer should take some lessons very early on. After you've played a round or two of golf, you pretty much have your swing tendencies in place. So be careful at the outset: once you get into a bad habit, it's difficult to break.

The chances of making a hole-in-one with any swing are one in 33,000.

• • •

● How can I locate golf instructors?

Find a teacher at a course, a driving range or an adult education program, or go to a golf school—there are thousands around the country, including ones for kids. Lessons range from a few hundred dollars for a weekend to a few thousand dollars for all-inclusive golf vacations at fancy resorts.

● When should I invest in my own set of clubs?

Not right away. First, figure out your swing, which is apparent only after you've played a few times. Your body shape and size will factor into the size clubs you need. If you are short and round, your clubs will be constructed differently from those that suit a tall, thin person.

Once you've decided to play seriously and invest in clubs, you should have your clubs fitted by a pro, who will watch your swing, take measurements and determine what size clubs you need.

If you're not ready to buy new equipment, you can buy used clubs; many pros and driving ranges often sell used sets. But don't buy any equipment until you've tried it out. At the very least, try hitting with the clubs at a driving range.

● How do I pick golf clubs?

You should like the way the clubs look and you should feel comfortable with the size of the heads. Newcomers and most players who aren't very advanced should buy game-improvement clubs, or "perimeter-weighted" clubs. The weight

SPORTS

of the club is placed around the club head so that even if you don't hit the ball at its "sweet" spot, the clubs will be as forgiving as possible.

● **How much can I expect to spend on golf clubs?**

Very expensive clubs can cost $3,000 and up for a full set. But you can get good sets for a few hundred dollars or less. You can only carry 14 or fewer clubs on the course: 3 woods, a putter, and 10 irons (a 3-iron, a 9-iron and a few wedges). There's no reason why a new golfer shouldn't go to a discount store or local sporting goods chain like Sports Authority and get an adequate set of clubs for less than $250. Some good brands in that price range are Wilson, MacGregor and Dunlop. They are not state-of-the-art clubs, but they are of good game-improvement design. At the high end, the good brands are Callaway, Taylor-Made and Cobra. Callaway makes the famous Big Bertha drivers.

● **Are there any brands to stay away from?**

There really aren't a lot of bad clubs out there. One thing to watch out for is shafts made of cheap graphite. Graphite has replaced steel in making clubs. It's lighter, making the head swing faster, and it absorbs the impact of hitting the ball. But cheap graphite can easily break.

● **How often should a golfer play to see significant improvement?**

Most golfers play once a week, but that's not enough to improve your game. Serious golfers practice every day. To improve, you need to go to a driving range every few days. Shorter, regular practices are better than longer, less frequent sessions. A lot of the game is simply learning and mastering the swing.

● **What can a golfer do to improve his or her swing?**

For 95 percent of golfers the solution is to swing slower and not squeeze the grip so hard. Hold the club just tight enough so that it doesn't fly out of your hands when you swing. When your grip is too tight, your arms and shoulders become tense, making it impossible to swing well. Slow your swing down and then slow it down more. At some

THE TOUGHEST COURSES IN AMERICA

Every golf course receives both a course and slope rating by the United States Golf Association. The course rating is established for the scratch golfer; the slope rating evaluates the relative difficulty of a course for players other than scratch. These courses, which score top USGA ratings in each category, are 10 of America's toughest.

COURSE	LOCATION	COURSE RATING	SLOPE RATING
Castle Pines Golf Club	Castle Rock, Colorado	77.1	155
Hazeltine National Golf Club	Chaska, Minn.	78.0	155
Koolau	Oahu, Hawaii	78.7	155
Ocean Course	Kiawah Island, Kiawah, S.C.	79.6	155
Pikewood National	Morgantown, W.V.	79.3	155
Pines, The International Golf Club	Bolton, Mass.	80.0	154
Rich Harvest Links	Sugar Grove, Il.	79.1	155
The Concessions Golf Club	Bradenton, Fla.	77.6	155
TPC Sawgrass, Stadium Course	Ponte Vedra Beach, Fla.	76.8	155
TPC Treviso Bay	Naples, Fla.	76.2	155

SOURCE: Data from USGA

point you should consult a pro to analyze your swing and to teach you drills.

Q Where's the challenge after you've mastered your swing?

One cliché is that you are not playing your opponents but yourself and the course. Playing the course intelligently becomes the challenge. You are faced with choices: Should I fly it over the stream or lay up short so I have a safer and easier shot? What kind of trouble is over the green? Is there water? Sand? Most novices won't have those experiences for a while, but it all adds to the enjoyment and complexity of the game.

How Handicapping Works
Different strokes for different folks

Golf may be the only sport in which people of differing ability can compete fairly. That's because handicapping allows golfers to shave strokes off their scores depending on the quality of their games and the difficulty of the courses on which they're playing.

In simple terms, your handicap is the number of strokes by which you typically exceed par over 18 holes. But the system used by the U.S. Golf Association for figuring a handicap is far from simple. Each golfer has a USGA handicap index that ranges from +3.4 for outstanding golfers who regularly score under par to 40.4 for players whose scores soar well over 100.

Under USGA regulations, a golf club calculates your handicap index. Each course has its own handicap table, based on the course's difficulty. By checking where your index falls

on the course's handicap table, you can determine how many strokes to subtract from your score in that day's round. The tougher the course, the greater the deduction.

You can estimate your own handicap on sites such as www.usga.org or *Golf* magazine's online handicap estimator at www.golfonline.com. Just plug in the number of rounds you played, your score, the course rating and slope, and you'll see your estimated handicap.

Foul Weather Golf
A good umbrella helps; so does taking fewer practice swings

Playing in the rain used to be truly difficult. But with the right techniques and the right gear putting in a downpour can be fun. Here are six essential pieces of equipment.

- A quality windproof umbrella. Go out and spend a little money. Don't just use the 10-year-old umbrella you found in the corner of the garage.

- Four or five dry towels, stored in the protected pockets of your bag.

- As many golf gloves as you have, and consider keeping a few pairs dry in a small plastic bag. Or invest in rain gloves, which are made with a fabric that grips better when wet.

- A waterproof rain suit made for golf, or at least for athletics, not duck hunting or watching a holiday parade in a mist. This is the biggest expense ($200 to $800), so maybe not everyone needs one. But consider how many days in the

66

Although golf was originally restricted to wealthy, overweight Protestants, today it's open to anybody who owns hideous clothing.

Dave Barry

SPORTS

• • •

next three golf seasons that rain may ruin a round you were looking forward to playing. If it's more than one a year, given the price of greens fees, the suit will probably pay for itself.

- A good hat, not a visor. A bucket hat just for rain may be an even better choice.

- Disposable $2 hand warmers. Ask your skiing friends about them. They'll store well in your bag and will be a welcome relief in your pockets during a wet round.

Playing well in the rain is about technique, too. A rainstorm is no time for a 20-second pre-shot routine. Keeping your grips dry is the chief goal of the day. Choke down on the club and make a smaller swing. The ball usually goes farther when you swing less hard, especially in bad weather. On the tee, tee it lower and use a 3-wood. Near the green, don't be afraid to hit it higher because the ball isn't going to roll, it's going to stop.

Going to the nearest dry point can be a big advantage near the green. You also don't have to putt through puddles. You can move the ball; you might get an easier putt.　　　—Bill Pennington

How to Play Smart Tennis
Five steps –mental and physical– to a better game

As with many sports, first, it's important to be physically fit, of course, and you need to practice, practice, practice. But also as with many sports, there has to be an element of competitiveness. After you get in touch with your inner winner you'll be ready for the following advice from the pros.

Step 1: Assess your opponent. Watch your opponent play or practice before your next match. Study their movements and strokes; figure out where their weaknesses are. Once you've identified those failings, shape your game to determine how you can maneuver your opponent to take advantage of the weaknesses. For example, if the player has a much weaker backhand than forehand, hit to the weaker side. But don't go so far that you change your own game. If you're primarily a baseline player and you're playing a hard-core baseliner, switching to become a serve-and-volleyer won't help. But by hitting a lot of deep balls, balls around the court and in corners, you might force mistakes and put yourself in a position to move in and attack.

✓ **TIMELY TIPS**

A G.P.S. for the Golf Course
How far are you from the center of the green?

The Approach G5 is a waterproof, handheld G.P.S. device that uses the satellite-based G.P.S. network, first developed by the military, for a cause vital to homeland defense: it calculates a golfer's distance to the center of the green or other features of the golf course, so he can select the proper club.

The device, developed by the technology company Garmin (www.buy.garmin.com), is similar to the binocular-like rangefinders popular with some golfers today. But those gadgets use lasers to approximate the distance from the golfer to the target. With the Approach G5, Garmin touts the precision of the G.P.S. network and its touch screen, which lets duffers specify with a few taps on the screen the exact distance to where they want to place the ball.

At $500, the device seems pricey—until you consider what obsessive golfers typically spend on the sport to improve their game by a few points.

The Approach G5 contains detailed layouts of about half the golf courses in the United States pre-loaded in its memory.

—Brad Stone, Matt Richtel

✓ **TIMELY TIPS**

Picking a Tennis Racket

You naturally look for an exact fit in shoes, clothes and everything else you buy. Do the same with rackets, individualized instruments that must be chosen carefully. Any racket can be made more or less powerful by adjusting the three systems—handle size and shape, overall weight and balance, and string type and tension. You should plan to adjust the systems of any racket you buy depending on what you want it to do. Warren Bosworth is a racket consultant to big-name tennis, and chairman of Bosworth Tennis (561-241-9966; www.bosworthtennis.com), a company that builds customized rackets. Here are his suggestions.

✔ **Body.** Wide-body rackets provide power, but at the sacrifice of control. Weight is also a critical factor. Too heavy a racket will strain your wrist, arm, elbow or shoulder, but ultra-lights have also been a principal cause of injury because they are just too light to overcome the impact of the ball.

✔ **String type.** Strings are the most important part of the racket when it comes to storing energy and influencing the spin of the ball. You have two choices: gut and synthetics. Synthetics, which are much cheaper, are thought to last longer, but you really have to take into account climate and humidity (dry weather is better for strings), surface (clay is harder on strings), the type of racket (some have grommets, or stringholds, that are harder on strings than others) and the type of player you are (spin players are harder on strings).

✔ **String gauge.** Gauge, or string thickness, is as critical as string type. Thicker gauges—that is, fatter strings—last longer. Thinner ones provide more feel. Recreational players should expect to get several months out of a set of strings before it loses its flexibility. Tension is another factor. The looser the strings, the more power. Tighter strings may give you more spin control, but also may add shock.

✔ **Cost.** Expect to spend $150 to $250 for a standard retail purchase. Look for the previous year's models, which are often just as good as the new ones.

Step 2: Visualize. Yogi Berra once said that half of baseball is 90 percent mental. Well, you know what he meant, and tennis is, too. Prepare for a match by visualizing your game, playing it out, point by point, in your mind. Close your eyes and picture yourself hitting the strokes exactly the way you want to. Take it to its logical end: make a mental picture of yourself winning.

Step 3: Have a game plan. Say you've developed a good game plan based on your strengths and your opponent's failings. But once the match begins, you fall behind five games to one. Do you dump your plan and try something else? Not at all. Stick with the game plan. That doesn't mean that you don't adapt if you find a bigger hole in your challenger's game than the ones you spotted in practice. But if you were thorough and thoughtful going in, you probably picked the right game plan for you, and dumping it probably won't produce a better one.

Step 4: Hitting winners. A lot of tennis players actively try to hit winners: they rear back and try to rip a hole in the opponent's racket, or try desperately to drop a ball daintily over the net. Bad idea. A better strategy is to fully master the basics of tennis first and then concentrate on making your opponent miss. Practice that until you can place the ball so well that your opponent is out of position. That's how to hit winners.

Step 5: Right mental attitude. Often, players are either over- or underconfident. The overconfident types, believing they are better than they really are, try shots they shouldn't dare try, usually unsuccessfully. The underconfident type of player assumes he'll lose, and the assumption is often self-fulfilling. Both mind-sets are damaging to good, smart tennis. The right approach: don't obsess over your opponent's level—just compete as hard as you can, one point at a time.

Teaching Your Child Baseball
Advice from Hall-of-Famer Cal Ripken

With major-league baseball stars signing multimillion-dollar contracts and basking in the spotlight, it's tempting for parents to look at their little athletes and say, "Hmmm. If I just push him a little harder." Don't do it, says Cal Ripken Jr., who may not be in the spotlight these days (he retired from baseball in 2001) but whose advice is priceless. The former Baltimore Oriole wowed the world with his gritty, gracious pursuit of Lou Gehrig's consecutive-game streak, and as a father of two himself, Ripken says he understands the temptation that parents feel. But he counsels them to let kids develop an appreciation for baseball and other sports at their own pace. Pushing them won't help. "A passion for the game has to be inside of you. And it's only going to develop if a kid comes to it on his or her own and if it's fun," he says.

Although Ripken grew up in a baseball family (his dad, Cal Sr., was a longtime coach for the Orioles), he was not pushed into playing the game. Still, his desire to play in the big leagues burned inside him, and from an early age on the night before his first Little League game each season, he surreptitiously slept in his uniform, his glove by his side. He just wanted to be ready, he said. Here are Ripken's tips for the nearly three million kids who play on Little League teams, and for their parents.

● What's the best way to get kids interested in baseball?

The most important thing is to keep it on a fun level. You've got to gear it to whatever makes kids enjoy playing. The worst thing you can see is to go to a Little League game and have parents yelling at the kids. I understand the competitiveness, but too much emphasis on winning saps a lot of the fun out of it. Kids should be encouraged to play any position they want, and to experiment.

● What's the right age to start?

My first competition was as an 8-year-old, which was the age when kids could really play the whole game—hitting, throwing and running. I think it's great you're now shown parts of the game through T-ball and other games like that. Kids can learn how to slide and run a lot earlier than I did.

● A lot of kids love to play but hate to practice. How do you make practice fun?

To learn baseball, like other things, you have to teach fundamentals, and then give kids ample time to practice them. Repetition is key. But it's got a downside: it's boring. The answer is to try to figure out creative ways to make it fun—to find games within the games. Take a game like pepper, and come up with a system where you get points for catches and good throws and make it a competition. All of a sudden the kids won't even realize they've fielded 100 ground balls.

● Is burnout for young pitchers a real threat?

In order to develop your arm you need to develop arm strength, and the way you do that is by throwing straight. Throwing curves doesn't help build up kids' arms. I don't think that you want to not allow them to throw it, but you should make sure that they throw 70 to 80 percent fastballs. You can always teach a kid who has a good arm to throw breaking balls, but if you don't have arm strength, you can't learn to throw a fastball.

● **Major leaguers aren't always the best role models; some big stars catch with one hand and violate other basic fundamentals. What do you tell a kid who notices that?**

I'll be at a clinic telling kids how important it is to throw overhand, to develop arm strength and accuracy, and a kid will say, "But I saw you on TV and you threw the ball sidearm on a double play." I'll say, "When you get older, you can do some of these things to speed up your throws. But when I was your age, I threw overhand." That's the truth, and it's about all you can say.

Hitting the Softball Every Time

Training, batting practice and strategies at the plate can help get you on base

Professional softball players begin with hours of off-season weightlifting and batting practice, but once they get to the plate they can pursue several different approaches. Here's what the pros do before getting to the on-deck circle and once they're in the batter's box.

Training. Learn to transfer training with weights into hitting with more power. Developing strong leg muscles is important to good hitting, because that's where the spring in your swing comes from. And having a strong lower back is critical to reducing the wear and tear from constant swinging. Work on stomach muscles to keep up with the lower back. For that final burst of power

and for building bat speed, work on strengthening your wrists, forearms and biceps.

Hitting the long ball. Hitting pitches that come into the heart of the plate is easy, but the key to hitting home runs often is knowing how to hit bad pitches hard. Swing to the location of the pitch. If it comes in low, swing with a slight uppercut; for high pitches, swing straight through the ball. The key to hitting any pitch out of the park is to roll the shoulders: turn the hips and transfer weight from the back foot to the front one at the time of contact. Because the pitch floats in slow-pitch softball, the hitter must provide all the momentum.

To get even more power on your swing, use a nontraditional grip. (You can find a list of certified bats and other equipment at the Amateur Softball Association Web site: www.asasoftball.com.) Hold the bat with your left ring finger on the knob, and then overlap your right hand over the left. The extra length gives you more bat whip and thus more power.

Getting a hit every time. You should decide where to hit the ball before you see the pitch. Once you decide where you want to hit the ball, time your swing accordingly. If you want to pull the ball, extend the barrel, the widest part of the bat, in front of your hands at the point of contact. In other words, at the time the bat strikes the ball, the bat barrel is closer to the pitcher than to your hands. If you want to hit the ball up the middle, keep the barrel even with your hands; to hit to the opposite field, point your shoulder in that direction when the bat meets the ball.

Use a level swing no matter where the ball is pitched. Any uppercut can lead to pop outs. The three key factors in hitting are: timing the swing, keeping an eye on the ball and transferring your weight at the right moment.

How to Build a Basketball Hoop

Constructing the court of your dreams

Designing your home court is not easy or inexpensive. But your options are many, ranging widely in quality, durability and price. Mobility is crucial to playing basketball, and it's also a key factor in setting up a home court. For gym rats who want to practice on a regulation hoop, however, the traditional 10-foot mounted backboards and pole-secured backboards are still available.

Portable baskets and baskets with adjustable heights are no longer as flimsy as they once were. Players who compete in leagues or gyms should be especially careful in selecting a rim. A springed rim (which gives a little when the ball hits it) will give the shooter a better bounce, but it can cause frustration when the player returns to a real court where tighter steel rims are the rule. To get the ultimate home court advantage, here are some options.

Mounted backboard. The most common of home court hoops can be attached to the house or garage with a few nuts and bolts. PRICE: around $150.

PROS: Very sturdy because it has to be attached to a wall or the side of a building. CONS: The backboard cannot be moved. The height can't be adjusted, either.

Portable backboard. Wheels on the base of the basket allow you to move it easily by simply tilting the basket forward. The base should be filled with sand or a combination of water and antifreeze to keep the basket from moving. The height can be adjusted from 7 to the regulation 10 feet. Less expensive portable backboards are made of graphite. The more expensive ones have acrylic backboards that shake less and hold up better in inclement weather. PRICE: $200 to $300.

PROS: The basket can be easily moved to other locations, and the height can be adjusted for players of all ages. CONS: Even with the acrylic backboard, the basket will still shake on hard shots. Because the base is portable, it can be wobbly.

In-ground hoop. An acrylic backboard is attached to a steel pole inserted in the ground. The height can be adjusted from 7 to 10 feet. PRICE: around $300.

PROS: With an acrylic backboard and base in the ground, this is the sturdiest option. CONS: It's the most expensive option, and the game cannot be moved.

Should Kids Play Football?

First weigh the risks and benefits, doctors say

Your 8-year-old comes home one day and proudly announces his intention to try out for the local peewee football team. You've just watched another N.F.L. quarterback get carried off the field on a stretcher. It's hard not to picture your son in the same position some day. Do you let him play?

Pediatricians and psychologists see this decision as just one of the many parents confront daily, from what kind of school the kids should attend to whether and when they should drive a car. The first consideration for a child who asks to play football is what are the risks and benefits?

Weighing them depends on the child, especially as he gets older. Participating in a sport like football may be more important for kids who need it for self-esteem, psychologists say, because it makes them stand out in high school, for example, or is their ticket to college. Those psychological factors must be considered against the chances of putting their bodies at risk.

How great is that risk? That, too, varies depending on the level of play In general, football has become much safer in recent years as equipment, especially helmets, has improved and rules have been tightened to prevent certain kinds of tackling and blocking. The number of deaths directly related to football has dropped dramatically since 1968, when 26 high school players died, according to the National Center for Catastrophic Sport Injury. Out of some 1.8 million high school and junior high school teens who played football in 2007, four died from injuries directly related to football (nine died from heatstroke and heart-related pre-existing conditions). Similar declines in the number of permanently disabling head and neck injuries have brought the annual number down to a handful—low numbers but no consolation, of course, if it's your son or daughter.

While catastrophic injuries are relatively rare these days, knee injuries and concussions appear to be on the rise. Knee injuries especially trouble doctors, who point out that once you hurt your knees playing football, they're damaged for your lifetime. Parents should be cautious but not discourage kids totally from playing football, especially at younger ages—when the level of play is less intense and knee injuries are generally less severe.

One step parents can take is to get to know the coach and the program he runs. Find out what emergency equipment he keeps on the sidelines and what measures he takes to prevent players from getting heatstroke. Of course, other sports can be as dangerous as football, if not more so. In fact, per capita, the rates of serious injury are higher in ice hockey, gymnastics and pole vaulting. Some parents might now be asking themselves, "Bowling, anyone?"

ℹ **INSIDE INFO**

The Stats on Football Injuries

○ 28% of kids under 14 who play football are injured each year.

○ Nearly 450,000 injuries occur per year among kids under 14 who play football.

○ 92,000 of these are knee injuries.

SOURCE: American Academy of Pediatrics

Sports for a Summer Day
The long-forgotten rules of badminton, croquet, horseshoes and volleyball

Baffled about how to keep score in badminton? Not sure how to set up the croquet wickets? Unclear on the difference between a leaner and a ringer in horseshoes? Don't know when you've made a point in volleyball? Here are the basic rules and regulations for four popular pastimes. So dig out the equipment stashed away in that musty basement corner and hit the beach or backyard.

Badminton was popular in England in the 1870s, after being imported from India (where it was called *poona*) by British army officers. The eighth duke of Beaufort introduced the game to English society at his estate, called Badminton, in Gloucester.

The game is similar to tennis. The object is to volley, with light rackets, a shuttlecock or bird (a small, hemispheric cork with a tail of 14 to 16 feathers) until it is missed by your opponent or hit out of bounds. The game can be played indoors or outdoors by two or four people.

THE RULES. The initial serve goes from the right half of the court to the half diagonally opposite. The serving team continues to serve until losing a rally or committing a fault. A fault occurs if you serve overhand, touch the net or do not serve diagonally across the court. Points may only be scored by the serving team. In doubles, a player serves until his team commits a fault, at which time the teammate gains the serve. Following each game, the players switch sides. The winning side serves first.

SCORING. All doubles and men's singles games are played to 15 or 21 points; women's singles games go to 11 points. The first player or team to win two games wins the match. If a match goes to three games, the players switch sides when

SPORTS

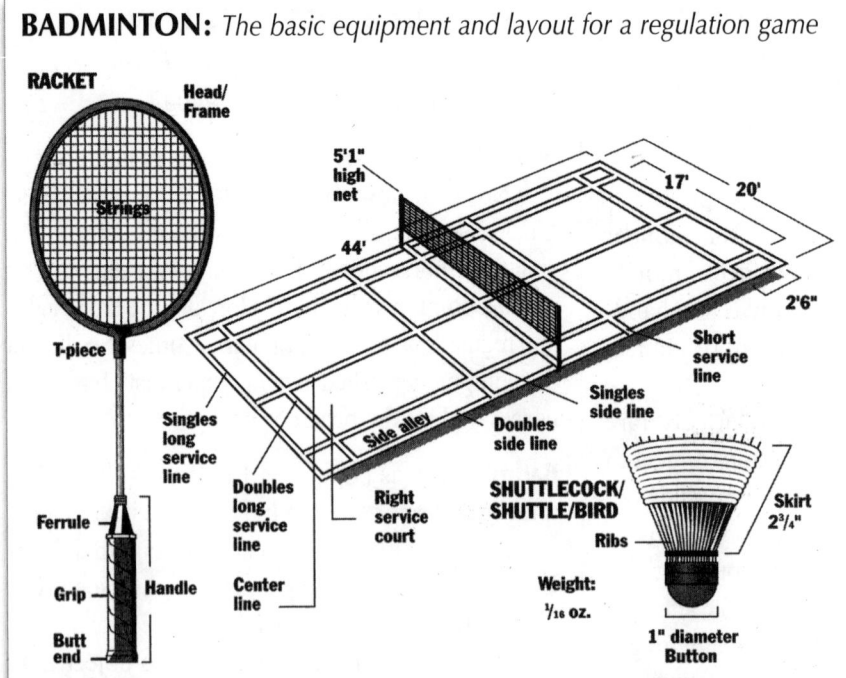

BADMINTON: *The basic equipment and layout for a regulation game*

RACKET

Head/Frame

Strings

T-piece

Ferrule

Grip

Handle

Butt end

Center line

Doubles long service line

Singles long service line

Side alley

5'1" high net

44'

Right service court

Doubles side line

17'   20'

2'6"

Short service line

Singles side line

SHUTTLECOCK/
SHUTTLE/BIRD

Ribs

Weight:
¹/₁₆ OZ.

Skirt
2³/₄"

1" diameter
Button

THE RULES. There are two courses: nine wickets and two stakes or six wickets and one stake. In the American nine-wicket game, the court is fitted to the area available. The English court has definite boundaries and locations for the six wickets and peg (see diagrams on the facing page). A toss determines who gets which color. These colors are usually painted on the stake, or peg, and control the order of play. Players—two to eight people can play at one time—use balls of the color allocated to them. The first striker hits the ball with his mallet at the balkline or home stake, depending on what course you are playing on. Subsequent players do the same. The course leads through the wickets, or hoops.

Strikers alternate turns. Your turn continues as long as you drive the ball through the proper wicket. If you fail to do so or hit another player's ball, you lose your turn. You also lose your turn if your mallet hits the wicket or the ground but not the ball.

A striker makes a roquet by knocking his ball into an opponent's. If you do so you have three options: (1) you may place your ball against your opponent's and, putting your foot on your ball, drive your opponent's ball away; (2) you can drive both balls; or (3) you can simply place your ball ahead of your opponent's and take two strokes. Once you hit an opponent's ball, you cannot hit it again until you go through another wicket.

the score reaches 8 in a 15-point game and 6 in an 11-point game. In a 15-point game, the team to reach 13 first has the option of extending the game to 18 points if the score becomes tied at 13. In 11-point games, the score may be extended to 12 if the game becomes tied at either 9 or 10. In a one-game match to 21 points, the score may be extended to 24 if there is a tie at 19 or extended to 23 if the game is tied at 20.

Croquet. The game probably originated in France in the 17th century. It became popular in England and Ireland during the 19th century and made its way to the United States in about 1870. It was one of the first games in which women and men competed on an even basis. There are three leading modern versions of the game: American lawn croquet, English croquet and roque. Most croquet balls are made of wood, but better balls are made of hard rubber or plastic. The mallet head may be of wood or other material.

CROQUET: *The basic equipment and layout for a regulation game*

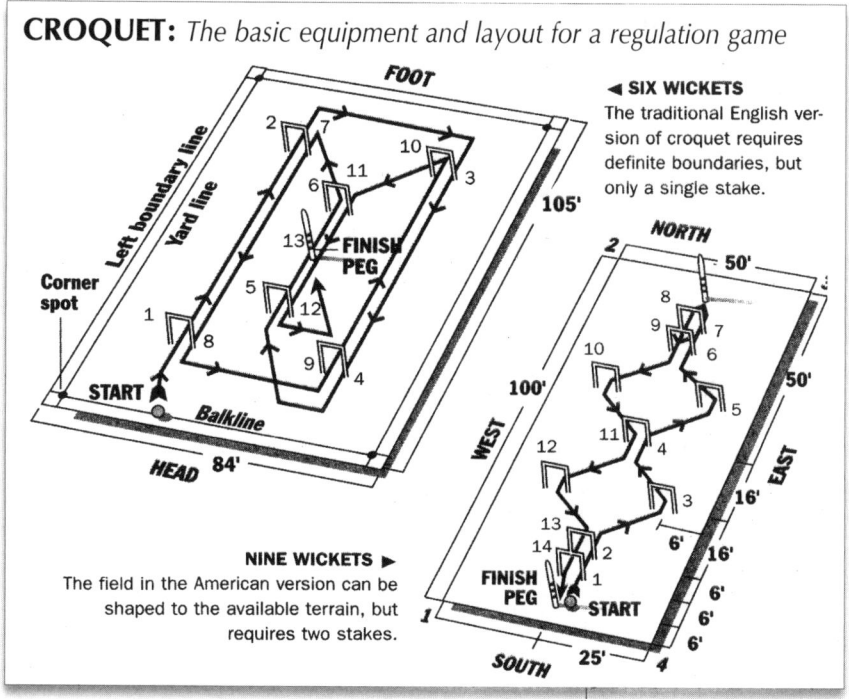

◄ **SIX WICKETS**
The traditional English version of croquet requires definite boundaries, but only a single stake.

NINE WICKETS ►
The field in the American version can be shaped to the available terrain, but requires two stakes.

in tournaments, leagues, parks and backyards across the country and Canada, according to the National Horseshoe Pitchers Association of America (www.horseshoepitching.com).

THE RULES. The object of the game is to toss a shoe so that it rings the metal stake or comes closer to the stake than your opponent's toss. In singles, both contestants throw from the same side of the course. Shoes are tossed underhanded. Each pitcher is allotted two tosses in an inning. The pitcher who scores in an inning leads off the next.

SCORING. A ball put through the proper wicket in the proper direction scores a point. Winners are decided by the total points scored or by the order in which the course is completed.

Horseshoe pitching, by some accounts, originated with Greek and Roman soldiers. The more modern version developed in Europe during the 17th century. Today some 15 million enthusiasts play

SCORING. Each ringer is worth three points. Each shoe closer than an opponent's is worth one point, but shoes only score when landing within 6 inches of the stake. If an opponent's shoe knocks a ringer off, it loses value. Two points are awarded if you land two shoes closer than any of your opponents. Leaners, or hobbers, and shoes that actually touch the stake count only as close shoes. (In informal games,

HORSESHOES: *A regulation course and a look at leaners*

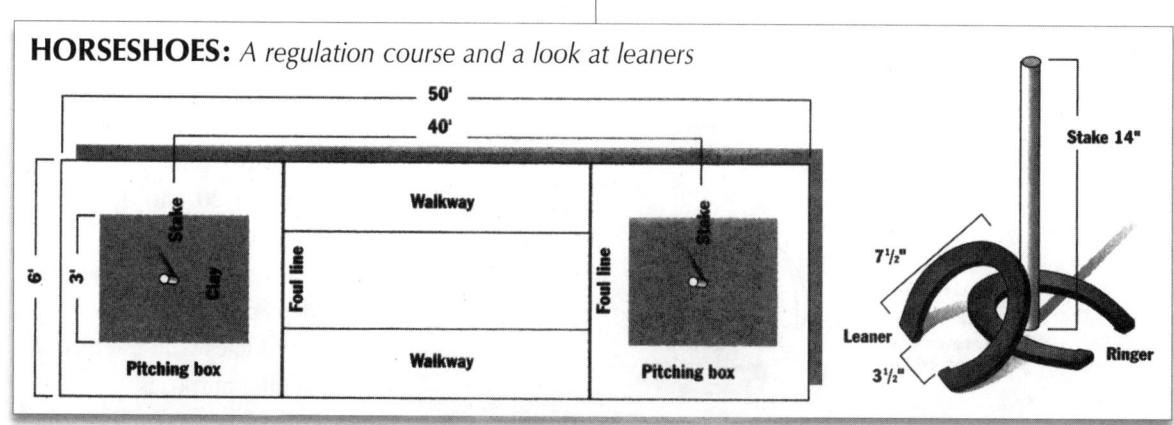

a leaner can count for two points.) Singles matches are usually played to 50 points, doubles to 21.

Volleyball was invented by a Y.M.C.A. director in Holyoke, Massachusetts, in 1895. It's been modified somewhat since and in 1964 was introduced in the Olympics.

THE RULES. There are six people on each team—usually three forward and three back. The height of the net varies: 8 feet high for men, 7½ feet high for women and sometimes lower for kids. The players can hit the ball to each other before hitting it back over the net. However, the ball can only be hit a maximum of three times on one side of the net. A player may not hit the ball twice in a row.

SCORING. Points are scored by hitting the ball into the opposing court in such a way that the competition cannot return it. The team serving gains one point for doing this and continues serving. If the receiving team does it, it wins the right to serve. A game is 15 points, but it must be won by two points; thus a 14-14 tie continues until either team gains a two-point advantage. When the serve changes hands, players rotate clockwise so that each player gets to serve.

Finding the Right Bike
With so many styles, it's hard to chose; here's how

A stroll into today's bike shop is not for the faint of heart. The days of banana seats and coaster brakes are long gone, of course, replaced by the likes of titanium frames and brakes and shock-absorbing suspension forks. Which bike is for you? This guide, compiled from the best advice of biking pros, can help you pick the perfect bike.

Q What types of bikes are there?

There are many types of bikes, among them road bikes, mountain bikes and hybrids. Each is built for a certain type of riding. Here is a breakdown of those popular three.

ROAD BIKES. The lightest and fastest of the three bicycle types, these are primarily for people who want to do distance riding on smooth pavement. The skinny, smooth tires and low handlebars give riders speed and low wind resistance but also make some cyclists feel vulnerable in traffic. Most road bikes weigh between 20 and 30 pounds, but some high-end models can weigh 16 pounds or less. Many people riding road bikes are athletes who use them for training purposes.

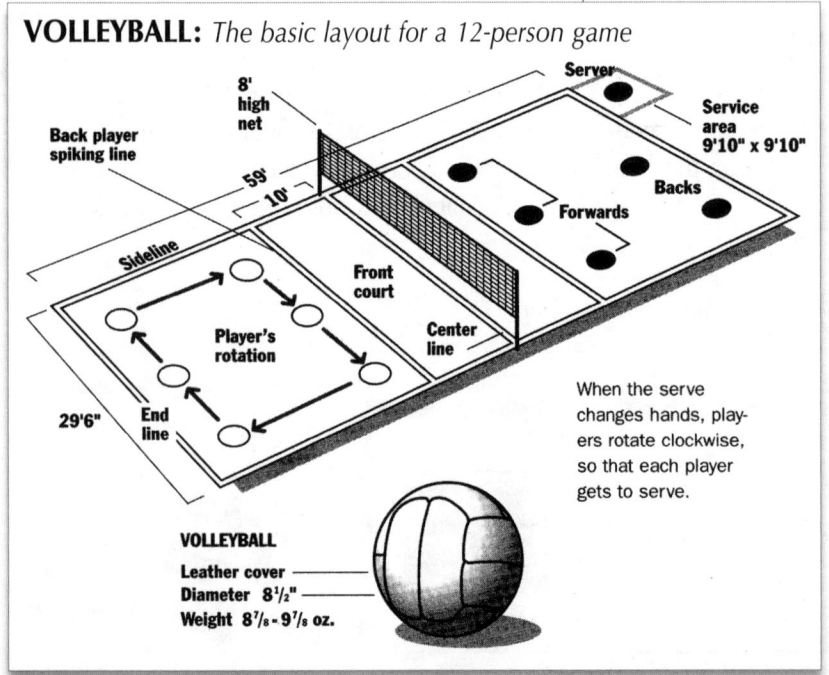

VOLLEYBALL: *The basic layout for a 12-person game*

8' high net

Back player spiking line

Server

Service area 9'10" x 9'10"

Backs

Forwards

59'

10'

Sideline

Front court

Center line

Player's rotation

End line

29'6"

When the serve changes hands, players rotate clockwise, so that each player gets to serve.

VOLLEYBALL
Leather cover
Diameter 8½"
Weight 8⅞ - 9⅞ oz.

Beyond the Basic Bike

Bike shops are dangerous places for those with an itchy wallet finger. There are hundreds of bike accessories you could purchase, but a much smaller number that you actually need. Here are a few of the basics and some exotic innovations.

FRAME: They come in all shapes and sizes, but the lightest and fastest are made of titanium and carbon fiber.

SUSPENSION SYS-TEMS: Similar to shock absorbers on a motorcycle, the pneumatic or hydraulic forks absorb the impact of big bumps and reduce strain on hands and arms. Popular, but not necessary.

TWIST GRIP SHIFTS: Faster and lighter than traditional Rapid Fire gears.

BAR ENDS: They give you extra leverage when you're up and out of the saddle when climbing. Also, when road riding, they allow a more aerodynamic position and a useful alternate hand position.

TIRES: Can be specialized to fit your riding needs. The spacing and pattern of the knobs affect the tire's performance in sand, mud or hard-packed trails.

TOE CLIPS: Road cyclists may want to investigate toe clips that shoes lock into, while mountain bikers should invest in a pair of toe clips that you slide in and out of. Lock clips give better leverage on climbs, but mountain bikers need to easily put their feet down when navigating tricky trail turns.

MOUNTAIN BIKES. Created by outdoors enthusiasts in Northern California, they are among the most popular bikes in the country. The upright seating, knobby tires and easy gearing make these bikes ideal for off-road riding. But even if you live in the heart of the city and only occasionally hit a trail mountain, the bikes offer comfort and stability.

HYBRID BIKES. Hybrids feature the upright seating and shifting of mountain bikes but offer the thin, smooth tires of road bikes for speed. Many bikers like the versatility of a hybrid; you can ride on some less-challenging trails and also make better time than you would on a mountain bike. But don't buy a hybrid if you are a serious cyclist: if you want to ride on challenging trails, the hybrid's frame and thin tires can't handle the

intensity. And if you want to take it on the open road, you'll be battling wind resistance.

Q How much money should I spend on a bike?

Bikes aren't cheap. You can spend anywhere from several hundred to several thousand dollars for a high-end model. It's hard to purchase a bad bike today, though—you can find a decent bike for $500 to $800. But a less-expensive bike won't perform as well or last as long as a high-end model. Your extra money is buying lighter, sturdier frames, and components (like gears and brakes) that can take a beating and last a long time.

Q How do I know if my bike fits me?

One of the most common errors is buying a bike that is too large. The best advice is buy the smallest bike that you can comfortably ride. Test

SPORTS

the bike to determine if the size is right for you. Straddle the bike frame and lift the front tire up by the handlebars. There should be several inches of clearance between your crotch and the bike frame, 1 to 2 inches for a road bike, and at least 3 to 4 inches for a mountain bike.

When riding, you should be able to straighten, but not strain, your leg. Adjusting the seat height can help. Also, especially on road bikes, be sure that you can comfortably reach the handlebars. And on a road bike, make sure your knees are just barely brushing your elbows as you pedal.

Q There are so many frames to choose from. What's best for me?

Frames vary in weight and expense, with the heaviest and least expensive being a steel frame. More expensive and lighter are aluminum, carbon and titanium frames, in that order. One-piece, molded composite frames are lightest of all but they also carry a price tag in the thousands of dollars. If you are planning on racing, a light frame is a necessity. But for weekend riders, it is just a luxury that will make your ride somewhat more enjoyable.

Q Which bike brands should I look at?

The surest way to buy a quality bike is to avoid hot gimmicks and new names and stick with companies that produce consistently high-quality bikes. For mountain and hybrid bikes, try Trek and Cannondale, which are two of the biggest companies. Also try GT, Specialized and Schwinn. For road bikes, Specialized and Trek are reliable. For bikes guaranteed to put a dent in your wallet, look overseas to the Italian-made bikes, such as Pinarello and De Rosa, which some shops carry. They are the most expensive, sometimes as much as $5,000, but not necessarily better than some domestic brands.

Q What are some easy bike repairs I can do myself?

Everyone should know how to fix a flat tire. Always carry a pump, a patch kit and a spare tire tube. If you get a flat on the road or trail, put on a new tube. If you get a second flat, you can find the hole and patch it. Practice patching a hole at home before you go on a trail. You should always carry a mini tool—the Swiss Army knife of the bike world. It's an all-in-one tool that includes an Allen wrench and spoke wrench, and it can be bought at a bike store.

Off-Road Cycle Races

Lots of mud, sweat and gears

Cyclocross, a growing off-road discipline, appears at first to be an amalgam of bike racing and road riding. The sport's short, looped courses include obstacles, ramps, bumps, sand pits, sharp turns and lots of mud—all navigated on a road-bike-like cycle that has drop-bar handles, skinny tires and no suspension.

Cyclocross-specific bikes, unlike mountain bikes, have stiff forks and thin, knobby tires, trading shock absorption and some traction for a cross bike's bigger gears, lighter weight and inherent speed.

The sport was invented nearly 100 years ago in Europe as an off-season training regimen for road-bike racers, and has a storied tradition and a worldwide following. Internationally, professional competition is administered by the Union Cycliste Internationale, the Swiss organization that also oversees the Tour de France.

Cyclocross is a fall sport, with races starting in September and continuing every weekend past Thanksgiving. Hundreds of races are held each year nationwide, many organized into regional series, from Maine to Colorado to California.

For information about cyclocross events and clubs, contact U.S.A. Cycling at 719-434-4200 or visit its Web site at www.usacycling.org.

—Stephen Regenold

People often forget to keep their bike chains clean and lubricated. If you have a grimy chain, first spray the chain and derailleurs with degreaser, then wet a sponge with warm, soapy water and hold it around the chain as you spin the wheels. Continue until the chain is clean, then dry with rags. Or buy a chain-cleaning kit that snaps around the chain and cleans and degreases it. Remember to lubricate your chain regularly. Lubricants made specifically for bikes can be found at all bike shops. If you ride in the rain, be sure to lubricate your chain every time you ride.

How to Swim Like a Fish

Are you an "efficient" swimmer?

Remember those mind-numbing and exhausting laps you were forced to do when you were learning to swim? Unfortunately, many of the swimming techniques you were taught probably won't help you swim better or faster. Terry Laughlin, who runs Total Immersion Swimming in New Paltz, N.Y., is a world-class swimming coach. He has dedicated his career to teaching advanced swimming techniques to people who hit the pool for fun and fitness, not for gold medals.

Laughlin believes you improve your "stroke efficiency" not with endless laps but by making your body more "slippery," so that it glides through the water by offering less resistance. The formula for swimming speed is this: Velocity = Stroke length (how far you travel with each stroke) x Stroke Rate (how fast you take them). Swimmers are naturally inclined to stroke faster, but the potential for improvement there is limited, and the work it takes burns more energy than it's worth.

According to Laughlin, most of the best swimmers in the world actually stroke fewer times than other swimmers: their speed, he argues, comes from

...AND HOW TO BOB LIKE A BOAT

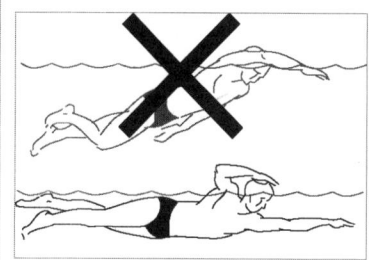

1. *Learn to sink evenly, not like a ship with all its cargo at the stern.*

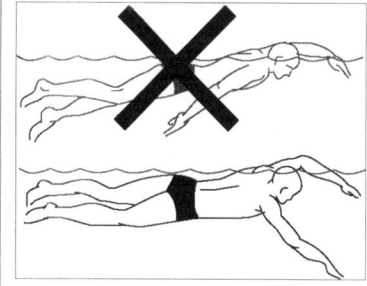

2. *Longer boats go faster. Make yourself "taller" by keeping your arms extended in front as much as possible.*

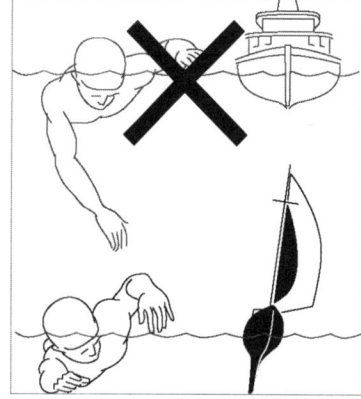

3. *Yachts move more easily through the water than barges, which lie flat in the water. So when you swim, roll from side leaving only a narrow sliver in the water.*

increasing the length they travel on each stroke. Your body's tendency is to do that by stroking and kicking harder, but churning your hands and legs won't help much. A better bet, Laughlin says, is to improve your body position in three ways.

1. Balance your body. Many swimmers find that the lower half of their body—the longer, heavier end—lags beneath the surface when they swim, like a lot of excess baggage in a boat. They kick harder—but it won't help. Laughlin calls the solution "pressing your body": push your chest down into the water as you swim, which has the effect of lifting your hips and hence your legs. It takes practice to master this, but it works.

2. Swim taller. Stretch out your body, which will help you glide through the water. As each hand enters the water, reach forward—not downward—before starting your pull. This will be difficult. Your inclination will be to automatically reach for the bottom as your hand hits the water. To fight the tendency, start each stroke as if you're reaching for the wall at the end of a lap. Leave your hand extended for as long as you can before beginning to stroke. It may seem odd to spend more time than you're accustomed to with both arms stretched in front of you, but it will help you glide.

3. Swim on your side. Yachts move more easily through water than barges do. Yet most of us swim more like barges—which lie flat on the water—than like yachts, which are frequently leaning to the side, leaving only a narrow sliver in the water. So when you swim, roll from side to side as you stroke. It's not natural and your body will fight it because you will feel unbalanced. But master it and you'll swim more fluidly with less effort.

Swimming for Fitness
An Olympian's training techniques

Ryan Lochte was the 2008 Olympic gold medalist in the 200m backstroke and the 4x200m freestyle and the bronze medalist in the 400m and 200m individual medley. Lochte swims 3 to 5 miles most days, sometimes even twice a day. Few non-Olympic-hopefuls could, or would want to, replicate that kind of distance. But other aspects of Lochte's training (such as his use of fins and buoys) and routines (his dry land exercises) can

be adopted by recreational swimmers or athletes, and perhaps even by parent coaches facing a rough patch with their teenage protégés.

Grab the kickboard. One of the most important parts of Lochte's swimming routine is the amount of pure kicking he does, sometimes with fins (his are standard, long fins) or a kickboard, sometimes without. "Kicking stabilizes the body," says Lochte's coach, Gregg Troy. "You achieve correct body position far more with the legs than the arms." Leg muscles require far more oxygen than the arms do, he adds, so the legs "must be fit" or a swimmer risks early exhaustion.

Building muscle. Unlike many young swimmers, Lochte did not work out with weights in high school. His father, a professional swim coach, believed that weight lifting should be done only after a young person's bones are fused and skeletal growth is complete. But now that he's fully grown, Lochte lifts weights for around 2 hours three times a week.Using free weights and machines, he concentrates on his shoulders, legs and back. Before every pool session, Lochte and his swim-mates pass around the medicine ball and do multiple sets of push-ups and 500 abdominal crunches. For mortals, 20 minutes twice a week should be fine.

Bring it on. Even if you're a fitness swimmer, incorporate competition and goal-setting into your routine. You don't necessarily have to sign up for races, but aim to reach the far wall a smidgen faster than you did the day before, or try to break a minute in the 100-meter freestyle, a good benchmark for speed.

Coach's tips. Stronger kicking makes better, faster swimmers. These drills adapted from Lochte's workout should improve any swimmer's speed.

- 100-meter repetitions (or 100 yards in a 25-yard pool). Kick 100 meters at a speed as fast as you can maintain, rest for 20 seconds, then kick for another 100 meters. Try to keep your pace consistent. Do 10 repetitions or work your way up to 10.

- 25-meter sprints (or yards) four times, going faster each time. Rest for 10 seconds. Repeat, increasing your tempo with each repetition. Aim to do the entire drill two to four times.

- Speed work. Kick as hard as possible for 5 minutes, rest for 1 minute; repeat two to four times.

- Continuous kicking. Kick nonstop for 20 minutes, alternating hard 25-meter sprints with slower 50-meter recovery swims. —Gretchen Reynolds

The Best Places to Snorkel
All you need is a mask, fins and a snorkel

Jacques Cousteau was best known for scuba diving, a sport he invented. The films he produced made the ocean come alive, revealing the teeming life and vibrancy of the world's waters. But his own eyes were opened not by scuba diving but by snorkeling, when, in 1936, he first donned a pair of goggles and floated on the surface of the sea. "Sometimes we are lucky enough to know that our lives have been changed, to discard the old, embrace the new and run headlong down an immutable course," he later wrote. "It happened to me on that summer's day, when my eyes were opened to the sea."

Safety for Swimmers, Surfers & Snorkelers

Lifeguards recommend swimming off sheltered beaches

Swimming is easiest out beyond the breakwaters and away from where the biggest sets of waves are breaking. If you are swimming along the shore, first eyeball how long-shore currents are flowing by watching floating debris or swimmers. Then swim with the current to limit fatigue and frustration. Water safety experts offer these additional tips.

Body or board surfers get the longest rides on spilling breakers.

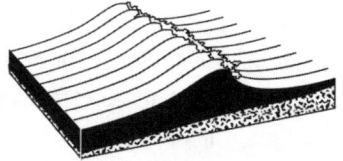

These waves commonly occur on relatively flat beaches and are characterized by foam and bubbles that spill down the front of the wave.

Plunging breakers, which are found on moderately steep beaches, can break with great force directly on top of an

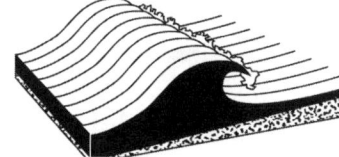

unsuspecting surf swimmer. The crests of these waves curl over a pocket of air and result in splash-up. They are generally short-lived waves and as such not the best for surfing.

Surging breakers slide up and down the beach, creating few challenges for surf swimmers.

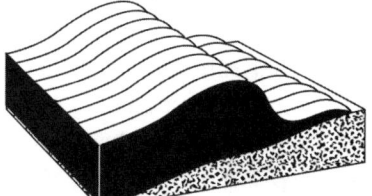

These waves occur on steep beaches and produce few or no bubbles.

Rip currents can endanger even the most experienced swimmer. Remember to swim parallel to the shore to escape the current or to allow it to carry you out to where its strength diminishes.

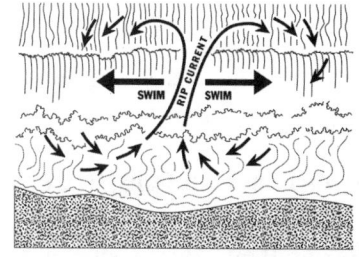

SPORTS

Today scuba diving has largely supplanted snorkeling in the public imagination. But snorkeling still has the power to captivate, and more people snorkel each year than scuba. Partisans say snorkeling offers more freedom than scuba diving, which requires clunky gear and sometimes keeps you tethered to a boat. For snorkeling, all you need are fins, a mask and a snorkel. It's much cheaper, and you don't need the certification that scuba diving requires.

Before you hit the water, you'll need to outfit yourself properly. Most important, pick a mouthpiece and mask that fit comfortably. To test whether a mask fits, hold it to your face, sniff slightly to hold it in place and let go. If the mask stays on and there are no leaks, the fit is sufficient. Try on as many as five masks with different shapes to see which fits best. Buy fins that cover your entire feet instead of the open-heeled fins. And buy your equipment in a dive shop, not a discount store. As for destinations, snorkeling pros say the following are among the best.

Bahamas, Out Islands. You won't find the posh hotels and casinos of Freeport on Abaco, Bimini, Eleuthera and the other small islands in the Bahamas, but snorkeling sites are luxurious. BEST TIME: February-September.

Bonaire Marine Park, Netherlands Antilles. This island off Venezuela's coast, less famous than neighboring Aruba and Curaçao, is a diver's paradise. Snorkeling—from its coral gardens to tube sponges as long as a person—is unmatched. BEST TIME: Year round.

Heron Island, Australia. One of about 900 islands that make up the Great Barrier Reef, Heron sits in a pro-

tected marine sanctuary, so the diversity of fish life is unparalleled. Park rangers are accessible and knowledgeable, so you learn as you dive. BEST TIME: April-July.

Looe Key, Florida. One of dozens of terrific snorkeling spots in the Florida Keys, the most popular diving location in the world. Looe Key features a national marine sanctuary remarkable for fish life and numerous sunken ships that the schoolmasters, snappers and barracuda dart through. BEST TIME: Year round; winds limit visibility in winter.

Flies That Never Fail
How to tell one funny fly name from another

Fly fishermen fish with imitation insects (flies) instead of worms or minnows and pride themselves on the intricacy and variety of their flies. Here is a quick guide to some of the most popular and successful flies, according to fly guru John Bailey, who, from his fly shop in Livingston, Mont., has been supplying fly fishermen with his hand-tied flies for decades. He's also a fly-tier to the stars: he served as a consultant and fly-fishing instructor for the classic Robert Redford movie *A River Runs Through It.*

WOOLLY BUGGER. One of the most universal flies, the woolly bugger works for both trout and bass on eastern and western waters. The woolly bugger is a streamer fly, which means it replicates minnows that swim below the surface.

MUDDLER MINNOW. Like the woolly bugger, the muddler is a streamer for both trout and bass, but it is more effective on streams than it is on lakes.

> ❝
> **God never did make a more calm, quiet, innocent recreation than angling**.
>
> Izaak Walton, from the 1676 edition of his classic, *The Compleat Angler*

● ● ●

TIMELY TIPS

Rare Books for an Angler's Soul

If you'd like to fish in a wiser man's boots or touch the spirit of angling in the past, now or whenever, pick up one of these.

1. Roland Pertwee's *The River God,* in which a great colonel with side whiskers fans the fishing flame in a young man.

2. G.E.M. Skues's *Mr. Theodore Castwell,* the tale of a man who dies, goes to "his own place," asks for and then fishes a lovely stretch of a chalk stream that yields a two-and-a-half-pound trout on every cast, fish after fish.

3. Izaak Walton's *The Compleat Angler* embodies a pastoral tradition; an enduring book that abounds in simple truths.

4. Dame Juliana Berners' *The Treatise of Fishing with an Angle,* written in 1496, gives glimpses into a world that could deepen and enrich the piscatorial experience.

5. Frederic M. Halford, in *Dry-Fly Fishing in Theory and Practice,* depicts the dry-fly revolution of the late 19th century.

6. Henry Van Dyke's *A Creelful of Fishing Stories* is an anthology ranging from Plutarch and Theocritus to John Buchan and Lord Grey of Fallodon. Another, fuller anthology, Charles Goodspeed's *A Treasury of Fishing Stories,* brings us into the beginning of modern-day fishing.

—Nick Lyons

(Essays by Nick Lyons are included in *Upriver and Downstream: The Best Fly-Fishing and Angling Adventures from the* New York Times, published by Harmony Books.)

ADAMS. Good for trout fishing, the Adams is a dry fly, which means it floats on top of the surface like an insect.

ROYAL WULFF. Another dry fly for trout. The white wings on this one allow you to keep an eye on it even in rough or choppy waters.

HARE'S EAR NYMPH, PRINCE NYMPH, BITCH CREEK NYMPH AND DAMSEL. Nymph flies imitate aquatic insects in a particular developmental stage. Although nymphs are primarily for trout, the bitch creek nymph is good for both trout and bass but is rarely used in eastern waters. The damsel is best for catching lake trout.

ELK HAIR CADDIS. Another good dry fly for trout. This one is made out of real elk hair. Because elk hair is hollow, the fly floats well.

DAVE'S HOPPER. This fly, named for fly-fishing expert Dave Whitlock, replicates a grasshopper, floats on the surface and can be used in most places.

The Lure of Night Fishing
When there's a moon out, fly-fishing beckons

Some of the best shore-based fly-fishing for striped bass in the Northeast takes place at sundown and after, and it has its special rewards and challenges.

Stripers do a lot of nocturnal feeding. As darkness falls, stripers often move inshore in quest of forage fish like sand eels, within casting range of the shore-based fly-rod angler. Some fly-rod enthusiasts will not fish at night. For them, it is no fun if they cannot see birds working, baitfish skittering along the surface and bass breaking or slashing at a fly. On some still, foggy evenings without a moon, you're lucky to see just the end of the fly-rod. But on clear, starry nights, you can spot surface-feeding bass out to 50 feet or so. And even when they can't be seen, they can be heard. Night fly-fishing for stripers calls for some special disciplines.

Since you can't see the line as it unfurls fore and aft, you have to rely on rhythm and feel. Some night casters use a heavier line—a 10-weight on a 9-weight rod, for example—to help them feel when the line has straightened out on the back cast. With the heavier line, there is a bit more of a tug. Still others wrap several turns of monofilament 20 or 30 feet from the end of their line, which warns, when it passes through their fingers on the retrieve, that it is time to make another cast.

At night, it sometimes helps to shorten the length of your cast. A shorter line is easier to handle. For instance, if you routinely cast 80 feet without special effort, try cutting back to 60 feet. If you do a lot of after-dark casting, you will sense when you are working the right amount of line. Obviously, a longer cast is sometimes needed to reach the fish, and, if you know that to be so, go ahead and try for more distance.

If you botch your back cast and hit the beach behind you, always inspect the hook. It might have picked up a bit of seaweed or, even worse, gotten its point broken or bent by impact with a stone. It is a good idea to crush the barbs on your hooks with a pair of pliers. That way hooks can readily be removed from bass that you want to release, and if you keep a tight line this won't cause you to lose any fish.

If wind and tide have combined to concentrate a line of weed against the beach, you will have to check your fly often. Fish ignore a fly with weed hanging from it, even if it is just a slender tendril of eel grass an inch or two long. If there is a lot of weed in the water, you will simply have to check your fly frequently. At times the weed is in a band—15 to 30 feet wide—against the beach. You can deal with that situation by casting beyond it and, on your retrieve, picking up your fly before it reaches the weed.

Before setting out for night fishing, stow your gear in your shirt, vest or pack with care. Have a special place for a light—a hat-mounted light is good because it frees your hands to change flies and release fish—knife, pliers, hook sharpener, flies, leader material and close-up glasses (if you need them) for working on leaders and flies. Otherwise, you might wind up kneeling on the beach frantically searching for a key item while stripers are rolling on the surface 50 feet away.

—Nelson Bryant

Hunting: A Beginner's Guide

Choose your prey, dress warmly and head for the woods

Hunting is a sport of precision, skill, challenge and being outdoors. You have actually four sports to choose from: you can hunt waterfowl (ducks and geese), upland birds (quail, dove, grouse and pheasant), deer or elk. Each sport has its own seasons, locations and pros and cons. Dave Petzal, better known as the "Gun Nut" on *Field and Stream's* blog, helped compile this beginner's guide to the basics of hunting.

WATERFOWL are, of course, found near water. Duck hunters spend their time crouched in fields and blinds (structures that hunters erect to conceal them from the ducks) alongside lakes, ponds and marshes. The North American goose population is larger than the duck population. One reason: many geese have adapted to their surroundings and may stay in one spot all year long, rather than migrate. Hunting geese is similar to hunting ducks. The only differences

> 66
> **There is a passion for hunting something deeply implanted in the human breast.**
>
> Ralph Waldo Emerson
>
> ● ● ●

are the seasons and limits. Check with your local fish and wildlife department or a good sporting goods store for local information.

WHERE TO HUNT: There are four principal North American migration routes. So no matter where you live, you're not more than a state or two away from a duck thoroughfare. Much of the best duck hunting land is private. You can to stick to public land or pay a user's fee for the private land.

WHEN TO HUNT: Early in the morning. You can't shoot until the first daylight, but plan on starting your day at about 3 a.m. so you can get set up and ready by sunrise. The best shooting is generally at sunrise and sunset. Duck hunting seasons vary by region but typically run between November and January, depending on how far south you live. Seasons are set each August by the local fish and wildlife department.

ESSENTIAL GEAR: A license and (in many states) proof of a hunting safety course. The limits on ducks are generally small, and some species are limited or restricted. It's essential to have a license and be within local limits. For information on licenses, check with your local sporting goods store.

- 12-gauge shotgun—the accepted gun of choice for all duck hunters. Shotguns actually fire hundreds of tiny pellets, which make them ideal for moving targets, but they don't shoot far, so don't fire at ducks beyond a 40-yard range.

- Camouflage raingear and hip boots. Plan on being cold and wet. The best duck hunting is always in the worst weather.

- A duck call, very important and worth any investment. A good one costs about $50.

- Decoys made of lightweight plastic help lure ducks within range.

- A good retrieving dog is crucial. Labrador retrievers are best, then golden retrievers.

HUNTING TIP: Don't shoot at anything more than 40 yards away. Wait until the ducks are lured into your decoys and then pull the trigger as they're descending. Also, the hunting is best on rainy, overcast days.

UPLAND BIRDS. Upland generally refers to the hunting of inland birds. The most popular targets are dove, followed by quail, grouse and pheasant.

WHERE TO HUNT: Upland hunters generally stand around in fields and prairies, near where birds eat, and wait for the birds to descend and take off. Upland hunting is common in all parts of the country, but find out where the private and public lands are.

WHEN TO HUNT: Upland seasons are generally in the fall and early winter months. The bird populations are more dense than waterfowl populations, so seasons are longer and limits are larger. Inland birds feed at all times of day, so you don't necessarily need to be shooting at sunrise or sunset.

ESSENTIAL GEAR: Proper licenses and safety courses, of course. Unlike waterfowl, no calls or decoys are necessary.

- Any type of shotgun, from a 12-gauge to a .410-gauge, will do.

- Brush pants (heavy canvas pants faced with leather or nylon) for trudging through briers and thickets. A jacket of the same material is also essential.

- A game vest with multiple pockets provides a handy place to store shells and also a place to stuff the game you shoot.

- A good dog, either a pointer (to track down birds), a retriever (to bring back your kill) or a springer (to flush the birds up).

DEER. Two deer species are hunted: the white-tail (the most commonly hunted and found throughout the U.S.) and the mule (only found west of the Mississippi).

SPORTS

WHERE TO HUNT: You can hunt as far south as South Carolina and as far north as Canada. Access to hunting on private land can easily cost several hundred dollars. In some areas, membership in a hunting club grants you access to private areas.

WHEN TO HUNT: Deer hunting seasons tend to be short, simply because the deer can't handle constant hunting pressure. Depending on your latitude, deer season is somewhere between August and January.

ESSENTIAL GEAR: License and proof of hunter-safety course. Safety courses are usually conducted by the local fish and game department at a shooting range.

- Weapon of choice. There are three types of weapons to hunt deer, each having its own season. They are rifle, bow and arrow and muzzle-loading rifle. Proficiency in all three weapons prolongs your hunting season.

- Camouflage gear made of soft fabrics. Your clothes must not rustle when you move or bump into trees. The slightest noise can ruin a day of tracking.

- A bright orange bunting vest is required in most states.

- A telescopic scope on your rifle will help you track your target.

- A good set of binoculars is a must. Using your scope exclusively can lead to misfires.

- Survival kit, including equipment to start a fire. The woods can be cold, and you may end up spending a full day or night outdoors.

- Compass. Don't assume you can find your way back to your car. Trees start to look alike after a while.

HUNTING TIP: Rifles are more precise than shotguns, but you only get one chance. Unlike shotguns, rifles shoot a single, conical-shaped bullet. A careless shot can ruin an entire day of tracking

and scare off all deer within earshot, and deer have great ears.

ELK. Hunting elk is similar to hunting deer, but it's harder, you need to travel farther to do it and you need more expensive stuff.

ESSENTIAL GEAR: Elk are found in the western and Alaskan mountains, so factor in a plane ride if you don't live in the Rocky Mountains or the 49th state.

- A big-game rifle, which can cost about $2,000, is essential.

- An out-of-state elk hunting license, if you don't live in one of the Rocky Mountain states, which runs about $300 to $500.

- An access fee. It's not uncommon to pay $5,000 for prime elk country.

HUNTING TIPS: Hire a guide who knows the area. It's not worth the money to fly out there and spend three days getting the lay of the land.

Top Spots for Rock Climbing
An expert climber picks his five favorite routes

Why do rock climbers risk life and limb to scale craggy heights? Some hope to enjoy what the poet Tennyson called the "joy in steepness overcome...in breathing nearer heaven." Others climb to overcome faintheartedness. But rather than being daredevils, most climbers, in fact, work to reduce the dangers, to have control over their risks.

There are several types of climbing (not counting the ubiquitous wall climbing), each with its own style and risks. Using "top roping," which uses a block and tackle system, a climber can only slip a few inches before the rope stops the fall. Mountaineering, which combines

FIVE BASIC KNOTS FOR ROCK CLIMBING

There are nearly 4,000 possible knots. Although you won't need to know them all to rock climb, these five are essential.

Tape knot/ring bend
This is an overhand knot used to tie tape or ropes into slings. It is used to secure the sling around an anchor.

Clove hitch
An easy, versatile knot often used as an anchor knot. Best used with a carabiner.

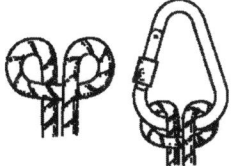

Italian hitch
Technically not a knot, this hitch is used for belaying (securing the rope on a rock or other projection) and abseiling (descending).

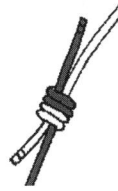 

Double Fisherman
Most often used to construct equipment, but also to join ropes. An alternative to the figure eight.

Figure Eight
Common knot used to attach rope to an anchor and to tie a knot onto a climbing harness, for example.

traditional climbing—in which each climber sets his or her own anchors—and ice climbing on high peaks, can be much more dangerous, mainly because of uncontrollable risks, such as avalanches and blizzards. (For more on ice climbing, see page 668.)

Climbers must always work in pairs, with one "belaying," protecting the other by controlling the rope. And because the belayer literally holds the climber's life in just one hand, it's crucial that climbers have proper training. Rock gyms and many college outdoor clubs offer instruction. The American Mountain Guides Association (303-271-0984; www.amga.com) and the American Alpine Club (303-384-0110; www.americanalpineclub.org), are good places to start for finding guides and programs nationwide and for other resources and guidance.

Rock climbing is not inexpensive. A good-quality equipment package for beginners costs about $400, including about $150 for the rope, $100 for the smooth rubber-sole boots and $150 for a harness, nylon slings and the protection system that helps set the rope, the carabiners, nuts, pitons and camming devices. A daylong private lesson with a guide, well worthwhile, runs about $250.

Across the country, there are plenty of cliffs to climb. Brent Bishop has climbed all over the U.S. and the world, including an ascent of Mt. Everest, also conquered by his late father. Bishop is founder of the Sagarmatha Foundation, which is dedicated to preserving the environment on Mt. Everest. The group has cleaned tons of expedition gear off the mountain. Here are Bishop's favorite climbing spots in the United States.

Yosemite National Park, *California.* A spectacular area with no rival in the U.S. Many climbs demand not only expertise but also spending nights hanging in a bivouac sack, tied to the rock.

CLASSIC ROUTE: Astroman, possibly the best vertical crack climb in the world for its high degree of difficulty It's well over 1,500 feet long.

City of Rocks, *Idaho.* Scores of granite blocks, many 100 to 120 feet high, cater to every ability level and offer awesome traditional crack climbs and hard core sport routes, most of them safe and user-friendly.

CLASSIC ROUTE: Bloody Fingers, a 115-foot-long crack that just fits your fingers.

Devil's Tower, *Wyoming.* Every route up this 365-foot-high core of an ancient volcano requires a sustained crack climb. There's a voluntary hiatus on climbing in June, out of respect for Native Americans who consider this a sacred site.

CLASSIC ROUTE: Durrance. Though the climb is rated as moderate in difficulty, it's still an amazing route every foot of the way up.

Seneca Rocks, *West Virginia.* There are more than 200 routes here, most of them challenging, up this bizarre slab of quartzite, which looks like two gigantic fins cutting through the forest. The summit is only a dozen feet wide. The cliffs have some good sport climbs and also several easy routes for beginners.

CLASSIC ROUTE: Castor and Pollux, two side-by-side cracks, which are steep and scary.

Shawangunk Mountains, *New York.* "The Gunks," as they are better known, are actually four major cliff areas spread over 7 miles and offering more than 1,300 different ways up, each topping out between 30 and 200 feet high. Beginners' routes are often next to ones that can defy the proficient, giving everyone a great chance to mingle.

CLASSIC ROUTE: Foops, one of the best climbs in the country. It's a tough roof problem, meaning that you climb as if you're hanging on a ceiling.

Slopes Every Skier Should Try

A two-time extreme skiing champion's choices for challenging skiing

Skiers are always looking for new terrain and new challenges. We asked Chris Davenport, a two-time extreme skiing world champion and one of America's top skiers, for his choices of the five places every skier should try at least once.

1. Tuckerman's Ravine, *White Mountain National Forest, New Hampshire.* If you're a skier you have to do it before you die. Go spend a sunny, spring day at Tuckerman's with a bunch of friends. That is truly one of the greatest atmospheres and physical locations in the sport of skiing. It's magical up there on the right day. People out West think there's no way that such a place exists in New Hampshire. But it surely exists.

2. Heli-skiing in Alaska. You can go all over Alaska: Girdwood, Haines, Cordova. It's the best snow, and you can ski the steepest stuff more safely than you can in the Canadian Rockies. That stuff is totally bomber. I get goose bumps talking about it. It's for advanced skiers, but anybody who can ski a black diamond run at their local ski area can ski something like this.

3. Whistler/Blackcomb, *British Columbia, Canada.* I like to take the peak chair at Whistler on a powder morning. Anything off that chair is a great run. At Blackcomb, I like climbing up Spanky's Ladder, and that accesses Ruby and Diamond bowls. Those are big, wide open, long and steep powder bowls.

4. Aspen, *Colorado.* Aspen is known as this rich and famous ritzy-ditzy place. In the 1980s, it was totally that: all you saw was people walking around in furs with Gulfstreams at the airport. Aspen reinvented itself in the early 1990s. The

THE BEST OF THE WEST

These resorts have earned their reputation as the top skiing resorts in the country

Resort	Vertical rise (ft.)	Skiable acres		% Runs that are...			Lifts	Snowfall (in./yr.)
				EXP	INT	BEG*		
Alta, Utah	2,020	2,200		35	40	25	12	500
Aspen, Colo.	3,267	6,310		30	35	35	8	300
Crested Butte, Colo.	3,062	1,154		41	44	15	15	300
Deer Valley, Utah	3,000	1,100		35	50	15	21	300
Jackson Hole, Wyo.	4,139	2,500		50	40	10	11	400
Mammoth Mountain, Calif.	3,100	3,500		30	40	30	29	335
Park City, Utah	3,100	2,000		38	44	18	14	350
Snowbird, Utah.	3,240	2,000		37	38	35	9	500
Snowmass, Colo.	4,406	2,962		34	50	6	22	300
Squaw Valley, Calif.	2,850	4,000		30	45	25	34	450
Steamboat, Colo.	3,668	2,965		31	56	13	20	315
Sun Valley, Idaho	3,400	2,067		22	42	36	19	220
Taos, N.M.	2,612	1,094		51	25	24	12	305
Telluride, Colo.	3,530	1,050		38	38	24	16	309
Vail, Colo.	3,450	5,268		40	32	28	34	346

*Expert, intermediate, beginner

... AND THE BEST OF THE EAST

Resort	Vertical drop (feet)	Acres	Trails	Lifts	Contact	
Holiday Valley, N.Y.	1,500	270	53	12	www.holidayvalley.com	716-699-2345
Killington, Vt.	3,050	918	200	33	www.killington.com	800-621-MTNS
Loon, N.H.	2,100	275	45	10	www.loonmtn.com	603-745-8111
Mont Tremblant, Quebec	2,116	625	94	13	www.tremblant.ca	888 738-1777
Mount Snow, Vt.	1,700	750	104	19	www.mountsnow.com	802-464-3333
Okemo, Ludlow, Vt.	2,200	470	115	18	www.okemo.com	802-228-1780
Smuggler's Notch, Vt.	2,610	250	78	8	www.smuggs.com	800-419-4615
Stowe, Vt.	2,360	485	48	12	www.stowe.com	800-253-4754
Stratton, Vt.	2,003	478	93	8	www.stratton.com	800-STRATTON
Sugarbush, Vt.	2,650	500	111	16	www.sugarbush.com	800-53-SUGAR
Sugarloaf, Me.	2,820	1,400	133	15	www.sugarloaf.com	800-THE-LOAF
Sunday River, Me.	2,340	660	128	18	www.sundayriver.com	207-824-3000
Whiteface, Lake Placid, N.Y.	3,430	220	74	10	www.whiteface.com	877-SKI-FACE

For lift ticket prices and other information for all mountains except Alta and Mammoth, call 800-908-5000 or go to www.ski.com. For information on Alta, call 801-359-1078 or go to www.alta.com; for Mammoth Mountain, call 800-MAMMOTH or go to www.mammothmountain.com.

SPORTS

terrain parks are world class, and so is the on-mountain and off-mountain skiing.

5. The Alps. There are more lifts per square mile there than anywhere else in the world. Because it's so big, I'll give you five "must visit spots:"

- CHAMONIX, in France is the birthplace of extreme skiing. It has the longest run in the Alps, 9,000 vertical feet down. Everyone should ride the Aiguille du Midi tram, which goes from the village of Chamonix to this pinnacle of rock, straight up with no lift towers. The ride by itself is a must do. But you have to have a guide—there are big cliffs and glaciers, and you can get into trouble.

- VERBIER, in Switzerland. There's easy access to massive terrain. You can ski a week and never ski the same trail twice. Verbier is very sunny with chalets built on a plateau. Idyllic and scenic.

- ST. ANTON, in Austria. Different from the others because of the Austrian/German influence.

- LA GRAVE, in France. Near the Italian border, this is a whole mountain of off-piste runs. It's a wonderful place. Two big trams and no grooming at all.

TIMELY TIPS

Skiing the Big Resorts for Less

Larger, more expensive resorts don't have to be a washout for those on a budget

✔ Skiers can often find cheaper rates than the standard one-day pass by checking the Web site of their favorite area and buying lift tickets in advance, or by buying a multi-day ticket.

✔ In addition, the Web site Liftopia (www.liftopia.com) sells discounted lift tickets to resorts throughout North America.

—Sarah Tuff

- THE MONTEROSA SKI REGION in northern Italy. It's less well known but it's one of the largest ski resorts in the world. I've spent a lot of time there and have never seen another American. I never wait in line or compete with anyone for powder.   —Bill Pennington

Where Lift Tickets Cost Less

Some lesser-known ski resorts are a bargain

The price of a one-day lift ticket on a weekend at Vail Ski Resort in Colorado is around $100; at Stowe Mountain in Vermont it's close to $90. (And don't even start thinking about the potentially dizzying costs of lodging and travel.) But there are ways around high lift costs. Skiers and riders can head to some of the country's lesser-known ski areas, where rates are often a fraction of those at the bigger resorts. A day on the slopes at dozens of areas can cost less than $50. Here's a nationwide ski sampler.

Snow King Resort, *Jackson Hole, Wy.* A place like Snow King Resort in Wyoming may not boast as much thigh-pounding vertical or skiable terrain as its natty neighbor, Jackson Hole Mountain Resort. But both areas share the same town, and many people find themselves perfectly satisfied with (if not elated by) the under-$50 Snow King experience—leaving you a few extra dollars to spend on Jackson's après-ski scene. www.snowking.com

Camden Snow Bowl, *Camden, Me.* Within a lobster claw's reach of the Atlantic, the 80-acre Camden Snow Bowl gets an annual snowfall of 72 inches and has snowmaking on less than half of the mountain—so it's best to get there right after a storm. The main draws of this municipal facility are its small-town charm and the views of Penobscot Bay. www.camdensnowbowl.com

Sipapu Ski and Summer Resort, *Vadito, N.M.* At this 200-acre ski area in the Carson National Forest, 20 miles southeast of Taos, skiers and riders won't find the knee-knocking steeps of Taos Ski Valley, but they will discover 41 trails of decent length, including seven double-black-diamond slopes. www.sipapunm.com

Ski Cooper, *Leadville, Colo.* At 10,152 feet, Leadville, Colo., claims to be the highest incorporated city in North America; its lofty playground is this 26-run ski area. It sits atop Tennessee Pass, one of the training sites for the 10th Mountain Division for World War II, and if skiers and riders aren't giddy from the altitude, they might be from the 2,400 acres of snowcat-served backcountry skiing on the Continental Divide. www.skicooper.com

Howelsen Hill Ski Area, *Steamboat Springs, Colo.* Receiving the same "champagne powder" as the neighboring Steamboat resort, Howelsen Hill is a town-operated training area that has helped send more than 64 athletes to the Winter Olympics. Howelsen has 15 trails served by four lifts. If the fun runs out on the downhill side, visitors can switch over to cross-country skiing on nearly 13 miles of trails or try out the terrain park. www. steamboatsprings.net

Bridger Bowl, *Bozeman, Mont.* Around Bozeman, the most reliable snow report is found atop the historic Baxter Hotel. If the blue light is flashing, it means that nearby Bridger Bowl has more than 2 inches of fresh snow. And chances are that traveling powder hounds can actually stay right in town and ski 2,000-acre Bridger, thanks to the affordability of the nonprofit community ski area. www.bridgerbowl.com

Badger Pass Ski Area, *Yosemite National Park, Calif.* Long after the summer tourists have retreated from Yosemite National Park, winter storms turn

How Long Should Your Skis Be?

It depends on height, expertise and skiing style

Some skis are too big, some are too small and some are just right. Greenwood's Ski Haus in Boise, Idaho—consistently rated one of the best ski shops in the country by ski magazines—offers these sizing tips.

The first question you need to ask yourself is "What type of skier am I?"

- If you are a beginner to intermediate skier, you should probably buy skis about 4 inches taller than yourself.

- If you are a more accomplished, aggressive skier, you could go 4 to 8 inches over your head.

- If you are very, very aggressive, you could venture up to 12 inches over your head.

- If you are buying hourglass skis, they may be much shorter.

In general, you should buy skis that are on the long side. In the old days, beginners and intermediates were steered toward very short skis. Not anymore.

The longer the ski, the faster the ride. Add 5 cm for fast skiing on groomed slopes. Subtract 5 cm for skiing mostly bumps or if you are a slow, conservative skier.

Intermediate skiers looking for a basic, all-purpose ski should use the chart below as a general guide.

HEIGHT	SKI LENGTH (cm)
5'0"-5'1"	158
5'2"-5'3"	168
5'4"-5'5"	178
5'6"-5'7"	183
5'8"-5'9"	188
5'10"-5'11"	193
6'0"-6'1"	198
6'2"-6'3"	201
6'3"+	201

BEGINNER: 4" longer — EXPERIENCED: 4-8" longer — VERY AGGRESSIVE: 12" longer

SPORTS

Badger Pass into a friendly, low-key ski area. Most of the terrain is beginner or intermediate, and mild temperatures create tolerable learning conditions. www.badgerpass.com

Cochran's Ski Area, *Richmond, Vt.* Blink while driving along I-89 near Burlington, Vt., and you'll miss Cochran's, which has just three lifts and six trails on 350 vertical feet. But since 1961, when it first opened for children and had a single rope tow, this little molehill has churned out a mountain of world-class skiers.

Today, Cochran's is still for kids. But, it's a rambunctious, winter-loving place and can be just as much fun for adults. cochranskiarea.com

—Sarah Tuff

Cross-Country Trails Worth Skiing

Six ways for skiers to escape the local loop

There's a tugging romance to the idea of escaping the orbit of the local cross-country ski loop and heading out on a long-distance ski journey. Unfortunately, Nordic skiers have relatively few options for point-to-point adventures unless they're comfortable carrying an anvil-heavy pack in the backcountry and sleeping in a drippy snow cave. Here, with the help of Ron Bergin, publisher of *Cross Country Skier* magazine, are some alternatives that range from easy to challenging, and the amenities vary from B.Y.O. sleeping bag to feather duvets, post-ski sports massages and tournedos of beef.

10th Mountain Division Hut Association, *Colorado.* The 10th Mountain huts are the closest this continent comes to an extensive mountain hut network like those in the Alps. Most of the 29 huts (the name honors the Army's 10th Mountain Division, whose members trained at Camp Hale in central Colorado during World War II) are at or near timberline, connected to the next by 6 to 8 miles of ungroomed trail.

Almost all the huts along the trail have wood-burning stoves for heating and cooking, propane burners, lighting powered by solar panels, cooking and eating utensils and mattresses and pillows. Skiers must be their own Sherpas for these huts, however, carrying a sleeping bag, food and toiletries between huts, which sleep about 16 people.

Skiers who aren't familiar with navigation, self-rescue techniques, avalanche training and using metal-edged touring skis and climbing skins should polish skills first with a guide. Rates to stay at a hut on your own vary but usually run around $30 per person per night. 970-925-5775; www.huts.org

Catamount Trail, *Vermont.* The longest ski trail in North America is the 300-mile Catamount Trail, which runs from Readsboro, Vt., and snakes through the Green Mountains to North Troy, on Canada's cusp. Though a bit more than half is ungroomed backcountry trail, it links cross-country ski centers as well as inns and lodges like the Trapp Family Lodge in Stowe. Perhaps the best stretch for inn-to-inn skiing lies between Killington and Ripton, about 35 miles in the central part of the state, where at least nine motels, inns and lodges are on or near the trail. Casual skiers can tackle the section in 4 or 5 days, skiing 8 to 11 miles a day, and feel confident that there will be a place to stay whenever they have had enough.

Country Inns Along the Trail (800-838-3301; www.inntoinn.com) creates self-guided ski packages with stays at up to four inns along the route. 802-864-5794; www.catamounttrail.org

The Boundary Waters/Gunflint Trail, *Minnesota.* One hundred and fifty miles north of Duluth (the closest airport) and hard by Lake Superior lies a trail network that resembles a mangled barbell. For

The Dangers of Thin Air

○ **Extreme cold:** Can cause hypothermia, which slows the heart and can lead to death. Wear insulated layers of clothing to minimize exposure.

○ **Oxygen deprivation.** Summit air can contain just one-third of the oxygen at sea level. Some climbers carry extra oxygen.

○ **Impaired judgment:** High altitudes can affect the brain, creating confusion and bad judgment. Climb in teams, so members can help each other in crisis.

○ **Dry air:** The water content in a climber's blood can drop drastically, increasing the chance of frostbite. Drink plenty of water. Bring stoves to melt snow.

SOURCE: *Newsweek*

a four-night trip that covers 28 miles, begin on the right bell, at the Poplar Creek Guest House, and go to the Tall Pines Yurt, a Mongolian-style hut with a wood-fired Finnish sauna, which sleeps six to eight people. Gear and food arrive via snowmobile, so skiers can travel light. The next 2 days skiers traverse the "bar" of the barbell: the Banadad Trail, a narrow, 19-mile, regularly groomed track through the Boundary Waters Canoe Area Wilderness. At the far end of the Banadad lies another skein of 50 miles of groomed tracks and the Gunflint Lodge. 800-322-8327; www.boundarycountry.com

Rendezvous Huts, Methow Valley, *Washington.* In the rain shadow of the Cascade Range, about a four-hour winter drive from Seattle, lies the Methow Valley, a glacier-scooped landscape carpeted with ponderosa pines of such eye-pleasing beauty that Owen Wister called it "the smiling country." The Methow is also home to large networks of groomed Nordic trails—130 miles of rarely crowded classic

and skate-skiing trails. Least visited are the 27 miles of trails in the Rendezvous area, the highest point of which must be reached by kicking and gliding nearly 1,500 feet up the valley's eastern shoulder. Sprinkled along the trails are five basic cabins; picture Grizzly Adams's guesthouse. Most are 2 to 3 miles apart, not far enough to be a genuine hut-to-hut system, but skiers sometimes move between them if they stay several days. 509-996-8100; www. methownet.com/huts/info

Rondane Mountains, *Norway.* Norway has more than 400 alpine cabins that are open to the public. But "hut," a translation of the Norwegian "hytte," doesn't do these places justice. At many of the lodging options skiers may sleep six people to a room. Yet the inns are inviting, wood-paneled Nordic chalets where a tired skier can find a hot shower, a hearty meal (it helps to be fond of reindeer stew) and Scandinavian hospitality. Norwegian Mountain Touring Association: www.turistforeningen.no

The Jura Mountains, *French-Swiss Border.* The mellow, forested Juras lie in the shadow of the Alps literally and figuratively. The mountain chain remains little visited by Americans in winter, despite its wealth of cross-country skiing opportunities: more than 1,800 miles of groomed tracks and ungroomed trails wrapping around 52 villages. The most famous of these trails is the roughly 125-mile Grande Traversée du Jura. The Grand Traversée: www.gtj.asso.fr　　—Christopher Solomon

Snowboarding for Beginners
A head-to-toe guide to catching some air

Once the domain of 16-year-old grunge boarders, snowboarding is no longer limited to youthful thrill seekers. Today the sport attracts everyone from pre-teens to middle-aged men and

BASIC MOVES

*A*ll you do is work just one edge at a time, heel or toe side.

Traversing **(1)** *the board will hold a line like a ski when tilted on edge.*

Release the edge **(2)***: the board will sideslip down the fall line.*

Heel-side turn

Toe-side turn

To make the basic turn, from heel edge to toe edge, say, release the heel edge **(3)**,

pivot the back foot in the direction of the turn **(4)**,

engaging and weighting the toe edge **(5)***. The board's sidecut draws a curve in the snow.*

SOURCE: *Men's Journal*

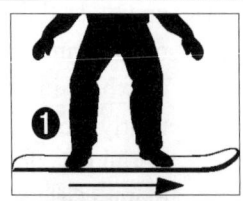

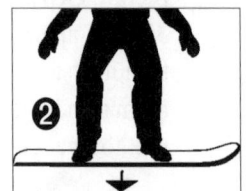

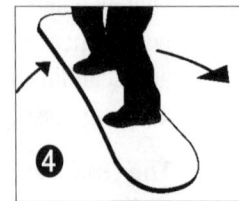

Snowboard Lingo

Air dog. A snowboarder with a preference for aerial tricks.

Bomb. To point the nose of your board straight down the hill to pick up speed.

Butwoker (or Butt rocker). A novice boarder who is on his butt a lot.

Catching air. The time spent in the air after a jump.

Corduroy. Freshly groomed snow.

Crater. To land a bad jump.

Doing hits. Any kind of move on the board.

Fakie. To spin and change the board's direction.

Goofy footed. Riding with the right foot closest to the nose of the snowboard.

Huckfest. A gathering of snowboarders riding hard and wild.

Laying down an arc. Riding at high speed so far over the board's edges that your body is almost parallel to the ground.

Lip. The top of the jump, usually the steepest.

Nose. The front end or tip of the snowboard.

Ollie. Lifting the nose and tail of the board into the air at the same time.

Pipe. Short for halfpipe, the area designated for snowboarders.

---

women enticed by the excellent workout and the time spent outdoors. Snowboarding hit the big time when it became an Olympic sport in 1998. Here's a head-to-toe guide to snowboard gear that will get you up and spinning in no time.

The board: You can plan on spending about $500 for a board with bindings. There are two styles of boards: freestyle and alpine. Freestyle, with its roots in the skateboard culture, is more common here. There is no true front or back of a freestyle

board, as boarders can ride "fakie"—spin and reverse the direction of the board. Alpine, which is popular in Europe, is done on a thinner board designed to carve the snow and work the board's edges more.

Binding and boots: Freestyle boards use boots that are similar to regular snow boots. The binding of the back foot is quickly released, as boarders must skate themselves through the lift line. Boarders either ride regular (left foot forward, right foot skates) or goofy (right foot forward, left foot skates).

Legs and butt: Loose-fitting clothing is a necessity on a snowboard. Snowboard pants come with reinforced knees because you'll spend a lot of time on your knees, either after a fall or simply resting. Some snowboard companies sell extra padding for your butt. But no matter how much you pad, beginners will spend a majority of their time falling on their butt and knees and will feel it afterward.

Torso and arms: Most jackets come with a butt flap that makes sitting on a chilly chairlift more comfortable. Thick gloves with gaiters that come up to the elbows are important, as you will spend much time with your hands on the snow in front of you.

Head: Some snowboarders wear elaborate headgear, including long jester hats. Also popular is the plain wool skull cap, but any snug hat that covers the ears will do. Snowboarders wear sunglasses and goggles under the same conditions that skiers do, but many boarders opt for sunglasses all the time to add to the total look.

Learning How to Figure Skate

A top coach's tips on teaching kids the basics

What are the odds that the hard work of any given child in America interested in a skating career will pay off with fame, riches and a gold medal? Not great, but also not impossible. What it takes to make it in ice-skating are "Talent, motivation and a serious interest in the sport," says Audrey Weisinger, an ice-skating coach, judge and former competitor who has spent nearly her entire life in the rink, earning double gold medals in the United States Figure Skating Association in figures and freestyle.

Here is Weisinger's advice for budding ice-skaters.

How old should a child be to start learning to figure skate?

Anyone can learn to skate and enjoy it as a recreational sport at any age. If you're thinking of a competitive career, though, you have to start young enough to make it feasible—around 6 or 7 for girls, maybe 8 to 10 for boys.

How do you get children interested in the sport?

You can't. If they're not interested in skating on their own, you can't make them interested. You may not want to let your child quit after the first lesson, but be reasonable. If the child has a temper tantrum every day about practicing or going to lessons, it's time to reevaluate continuing.

A parent's role is to be supportive and encouraging—regardless of the skater's ability. Most

SPORTS

✔ TIMELY TIPS

Adventures in Wild Skating

These days, few people skate on nature's ice. Even in the Midwest, where lakes stay hard-frozen for months, estimates are that 90 percent of skaters learn indoors. But a growing number of skaters are heading outside—helped by European skates just finding their way here—for what one enthusiast calls wild skating.

✔ To speed skate on frozen lakes you'll need Nordic skates, a cross between ski boots and kitchen knives. Nordic skate blades with bindings are typically $100 to $250.

✔ Skaters on untested lakes or ponds should be well-versed on ice conditions and carry ice-testing poles, throw ropes and ice claws. For Nordic skating events go to www.nordicskating.com.

—Diane Daniel

Anatomy of an Ice Skate

Keys to putting your best foot forward

BOOTS: Should fit more snugly than street shoes, so should be one size smaller. Toes should be close to the front of the skate. You should be able to wiggle your toes, but neither the ball of your foot nor your heel should move when the boot is laced.

BLADES: Always wear plastic or rubber blade guards when off the ice to protect the blades against scratches and help them remain sharp. But don't store your skates with the guards on—moisture between the guards and blades can cause the blades to rust. Blades should be sharpened whenever they slip sideways or if the edges are rounded or rough.

LACES: Tie them tightest around the ankle, but not too tight at the top hooks; you must be able to bend your ankle. Laces should be tied in a bow, double knotted, and then tucked between the laces and boot tongue. Always carry an extra pair of laces.

TOE PICK: This row of "teeth" at the front of the blade is used for jumping and spinning—not for stopping.

---

skaters don't get to the Olympic or "elite" level of competition, but they can still enjoy the benefits of skating recreationally. Parents should facilitate improvement but not manage it. And they should separate their own goals and desires from their child's. They should provide the opportunities for growth but not demand it. If your child's not enjoying himself, back off.

● When should you invest in good skates?

A basic pair of beginner skates is perfectly fine to start off with. When and if your child shows an interest in learning new skills, begins skating more than once a week and is motivated to practice to improve, then that's the time to invest in a moderately good pair of skates. Good skates have boots and blades that are mounted separately. They cost about $200 to $400.

●How much time should children spend practicing?

That depends on the child's goals. To learn the basics for recreational skating requires about one hour of lessons per week with another two or three spent practicing. But a 10-year-old begin-

ner who has competitive goals in mind should practice at least one hour a day with additional time spent on dance and endurance training.

Skaters at the top competitive level devote the majority of their day to becoming a champion— two or three coaching sessions supplemented by hours of practice and one or two daily lessons in ballet or weight training.

No matter what level of competition they reach, children need to take time off. I would suggest at least one day a week off to relax, pursue other interests and spend time with family and friends.

● How do you find a good coach?

A good coach is one whose primary interest is in the well-being of the child, not winning medals. The coach should be properly trained as a skater—a future can be ruined by starting off with a poor foundation. And a good coach should teach the child according to the child's agenda, not his or her own.

● What expenses can a competitive skater expect?

Serious recreational skaters can expect to pay about $75 for three lessons per week and then

✓ **TIMELY TIPS**

Gear for Toasty Toes and Safe Wrists

There is no more unifying fixation in snow sports than the pursuit of toasty toes. Here are some solutions.

✔ Boots that are too small or too big are always cold boots. For proper fitting boots go to a pro in a good ski shop. Placing specially-insulated insoles in your boots can also help.

✔ Buy a sport-specific sock. For skiers and boarders that usually means a sock that is a thin, light-weight, modern blend of fabrics that will transport moisture away from the foot. Wearing two pairs won't help; consider wearing an ultralight liner sock, usually made of silk.

✔ Buy a pair of heat-inducing toe warmers at the lodge ski shop and take them out of the plastic package at least 5 minutes before placing them in your boots.

✔ For those who can't get their feet warm any other way, battery-heated socks, which cost about $30, are virtually fool-proof. A small battery hooks onto each boot cuff.

✔ The most common serious injury associated with snow-boarding is a broken wrist. A revolutionary glove with a wrist guard built in defuses the impact of the usual bone-jarring fall. The Flexmeter, available at www.snowboarsecrets.com, goes for about $100.   —Bill Pennington

another $10 a day for practice sessions. At the high-est level of competition, though, expenses can reach $50,000 and up a year, including lessons, ice time, costumes, traveling to competitions, etc. The boots alone for custom-made skates can cost $600. For the "elite" class skaters, scholarships and fundrais-ers may offset some of the costs, but until a skater reaches that level, the family foots the bill.

❓ What are the benefits of skating for kids who don't reach elite competition?

After every winter Olympics, we see a surge of kids sign up for lessons, and then quit when they realize how much work it takes. But kids who don't reach a high level still learn invalu-able life skills. I've seen many skaters who persevered, despite not reaching the top, who then went on to become successful doctors, lawyers and bankers, because they can apply the concentration and drive they learned from skating to other areas of life.

❓ What advice would you give parents about intro-ducing their kids to the sport?

Go for it! Encourage them to try to do something a little better, even if it's just for fun. And if your child aspires to climb the competitive ladder, try to find adequate coaching in your own backyard. Keep your family intact and your child in school. If this isn't possible where you live, and if by sixth or seventh grade your child has shown a lot of promise and determination, then maybe you owe your child the chance to pursue his or her dream.

Winter Chills and Thrills

Why not try curling, snowshoeing or polar bear swimming?

Skiing and snowboarding aren't the only cold weather options out there. You may want to try curling, snowshoeing or polar bear swimming. Here's a guide to those activities and others that team up well with ice, snow and chilly weather.

Curling. Curling is a team sport played on ice. Teams of four shove "rocks" down the ice toward a

SPORTS

target. Team members slide along the ice with the rock, steering it by sweeping long-handled brooms in front of it. While curling originated in Scotland in the 1500s, it is found mostly in Canada and in the colder northern tier of the U.S. But there are curling clubs as far west as San Francisco and as far south as Houston. More than 16,000 curling enthusiasts do their stuff all winter long, some of them with dreams of gold: curling debuted as a full-medal sport in the 1998 Olympics.

GEAR: Once you're serious, you'll need Teflon sliders (about $20); a broom and handle ($70 and up); and curling shoes (about $100), although flat-soled athletic shoes will also do. Clubs are also good places to start because many lend equipment to beginners.

TRAINING TIP: Sweeping (the rapid back and forth with the broom in front of the curling rock) is an exhaustive workout for the arms and shoulders. But don't forget about your quads: curling is done primarily in a squat.

KEEP AN EYE ON: The skip (the "captain" of the four-person team) is the strategist and controls the flow of the shots and movement.

CONTACT: U.S. Curling Association (715-344-1199; www.curlingrocks.net) Curling is a club-oriented sport. Your first step is to get in touch with one of the more than 135 area clubs. Most clubs also offer instruction for beginners.

Ice climbing. Ice climbing was invented by restless rock climbers looking for a way to pass the winter months. It is similar to rock climbing, but climbers scale frozen waterfalls instead of sheer cliffs. Climbers can be found in places where the temperature drops. The mecca for ice climbers is the San Juan Range, near Telluride, Colorado, but East Coasters can find excellent ice climbing outside North Conway, N.H., and midwestern diehards have been known to ice down silos for a good climb. The sport's popularity has soared, due mostly to rock climbing's popularity and to advances in safety equipment.

GEAR: To be properly outfitted, you'll need ice-climbing boots, which are plastic versions of stiff hiking boots and run $200 to $250; crampons, the stiff iron spikes you strap to your boots that cost $125 to $150; two hand tools, basically handles with fancy picks on them that cost about $250; and a helmet. Most climbers stick to low climbs, but anything higher requires ropes and harnesses.

TRAINING TIP: Climbing is done with all parts of your body, not just the arms, as many people assume, so general fitness is essential.

 **TIMELY TIPS**

Face-Saving Lessons from the North Pole

In Grise Fiord, Northwest Territories, the sun sets in October and doesn't rise again until February, and the winter temperatures rarely rise above 16 below. How do residents protect their skin from the frigid cold? Ray Richer, general manager of the Grise Fiord Inuit Co-op, says he insulates his skin with Dove body lotion. "It's simple, but it works," he says.

✔ In the old days the Inuit did not take baths because they were afraid of washing off the natural oils that protected their faces from frostbite, says Lonnie Dupre, a polar explorer who lives near the Canadian border. "If you can bring yourself to bathe less often, you can keep the natural protective lanolins on your face."

✔ Lips, too, are vulnerable to dry air. "The wind burns your lips and the sun cooks them," says Dupre. When he's out on expeditions, he coats them liberally with Dermatone, made with beeswax and lanolin. It's sold at sporting goods stores like REI and Eastern Mountain Sports.

—Natasha Singer

How to Build an Igloo

You'll be amazed at how comfy it feels inside

Building an igloo, or snowhouse, is a fairly easy process, but making it safe requires some precautions. Choose an area where temperatures won't rise above 32 degrees and where the snow has been windblown and packs easily. Be sure to follow tips for proper ventilation. Without good ventilation, carbon dioxide levels can build up and cause suffocation. Another precaution: do not use stoves in an igloo; they can trap poisonous carbon monoxide inside.

Once your igloo is built, you'll be amazed at how comfortable and well insulated you feel inside.

1. Find an area with dry, hard-packed snow. Using a snow saw or large knife, carve blocks of snow measuring about 3 feet long, 15 inches high and 8 inches deep.

2. Place the blocks in a circular pattern around the area from which you carved the blocks. This "hole" left in the snow will become the lower half of the igloo. Build up the walls with snow blocks, placing them on top of each other in a spiral formation.

3. Cut a hole under one side of the wall for the entrance and dig a canal for cold air to pass through. (You can also build a roof over the entrance to prevent snow from blowing into the igloo.)

4. From the inside, shape the final block you use to make the igloo roof (this block should be larger than the remaining roof opening) so that it fits tightly between the other blocks. Shape the  entire structure from outside and inside so that it forms a dome.

5. Cut ventilation holes in the walls with an ice ax. Make at least one hole in the roof to ensure there is enough air circulating inside.

KEEP AN EYE ON: Melting ice, and avoid it. A sunny, warm day may tempt you outside, but ice climbing is best—and safest—on chilly, cloudy days.

CONTACT: There are no organized ice climbing organizations, but your local outdoors clubs and retail outlets are good sources. In the west, try Ryder Walker Alpine Adventures in Telluride, Colorado (888-586-8365; www.ryderwalker.com). In New England, International Mountain Equipment in North Conway, New Hampshire (603-356-7013; www.ime-usa.com).

Ice hockey. Want to relive those glory days of peewee hockey? Then strap on your skates and join an amateur hockey league. There are organized hockey leagues all over the country.

GEAR: Hockey requires a fair amount of equipment. You can't play league hockey in your college sweatshirt and a pair of skates; you'll need all the proper body padding (including shoulder pads, shin pads and elbow pads), gloves, a stick and a helmet. Plan on spending anywhere from $400 to $800 or more. You might want to check with used sports stores for good prices on skates and equipment.

TRAINING TIP: Hockey is a grueling cardiovascular workout, so don't hit the ice without doing some conditioning. Also, although most over-35 leagues outlaw checking or blocking an opponent, expect to take some knocks and spills and not complain. Before you even think about joining a team, make sure you're confident on your skates—forward, backward and stopping.

KEEP AN EYE ON: The obvious: the puck, your teammates and the opposing team. If you're playing hockey to relieve a little stress and aggression, you may want to throw the occasional hip check. But if you're playing for pure cardiovascular reasons, watch out so you don't end up with your face plastered against the Plexiglas.

CONTACT: USA Hockey (877-783-GOAL; www.usahockey.com), the national governing body for the sport, can provide information on area leagues. For more information on old-timers' leagues in your areas, try local ice rinks.

Polar bear swimming. Jump into a body of water in the middle of January and you're considered a fool. Do it with a club and you're called a polar bear swimmer. Polar bears have been gathering on frozen U.S. shores for close to 100 years, and today's polar bears claim that the therapeutic benefits of cold-water swimming keep them healthy and happy. It's one of winter's least complicated sports. All you need is a swimsuit, a brisk winter day, a body of water and the determination to walk (or run) into icy cold waves.

GEAR: A swimsuit, goggles, water-proof booties optional, a big warm towel.

TRAINING TIP: Those with heart trouble should check with their physicians before jumping into icy water. The sudden drastic change in temperature could cause problems, but many polar bears are octogenarians who claim the cold water is precisely what keeps them going.

KEEP AN EYE ON: Frolickers. Polar bear swimming is as much about frolicking and splashing in the icy water as it is about exercise. Polar bears swim together because it's fun. If you want a serious, competitive workout, turn down the temperature in the pool and do some laps.

CONTACT: Although you could jump into any old frozen water, it's more fun to do it with members of one the three dozen clubs in the country. The Coney Island Polar Bear Club in New York, N.Y. (founded in 1903), is the nation's oldest club (917-533-3568; www.polarbearclub.org).

Snowmobiling. A snowmobile can take you everywhere that a wimpy pair of cross-country skis can and makes a lot more noise doing it. There are nearly 1.5 million registered snowmobiles in the U.S. Tour operators offer everything from half-day to 3- to 4-day trips.

GEAR: The average snowmobile costs between $5,000 and $10,000, but used ones can be found for about $2,000. Daily rentals can run from about $100 to several hundred dollars, depending on the package. If you don't own them, you'll also need a snowmobile suit, gloves and a helmet.

TRAINING TIP: Always wear a helmet and follow general safety guidelines. There are casualties every year, caused mostly by drunk and reckless driving. Just like cars, snowmobiles must abide by a set of operating laws. Most operators offer a free lesson on mechanics, handling and safety. Physically, riding a snowmobile may not seem taxing, but controlling a large machine for several hours at time can be exhausting. Be sure to head back before you're beat.

KEEP AN EYE ON: Where you are. Snowmobiling on private land without prior consent could land you in jail. There are over 100,000 miles of groomed, marked snowmobile trails in North America. Always be extra cautious about snowmobiling on frozen lakes. And if you're snowmobiling near a road, don't assume the traffic can see you.

CONTACT: The American Council of Snowmobile Associations (517-351-4362; www.snowmobilers.org) is the best place to start. The council can help you organize a trip or direct you to one of 26 state organizations for more region-specific information.

Snowshoeing. Why is snowshoeing one of winter's fastest-growing recreational sports? Because it is, perhaps, the world's simplest sport: if you can walk, you can snowshoe. The Outdoor Industry

Association estimates that of six million snowshoers, about one million are hardcore participants, lured by the woods in winter and the exercise. Many serious athletes now do their winter training on snowshoes, and there are annual snowshoe marathons, but you don't need to be an iron man to snowshoe.

GEAR: The snowshoe is a lightweight (about one pound) platform with crampons on the bottom and a binding system on top that attaches to a shoe or boot, ideally a waterproof hiking boot or a trail-running sneaker. Snowshoes run $150 to $300; poles from $50 to $150. (Many outdoor stores rent them.) A set of poles will give you more balance and stability and also add an upper-body workout. Like cross-country skiers, snowshoers should dress in layers that will keep out the cold but allow you to strip down once you really start sweating—which you will.

TRAINING TIP: Snowshoeing is an excellent cardiovascular workout. In steep terrain, a snowshoer can burn up to 1,000 calories an hour. A simple way to get in shape for snowshoeing is walking up and down hills. When you first start, you'll feel a burn in the tops of the legs at the hip and groin area from lifting a snow-filled shoe.

✔ TIMELY TIPS

Fitting a Snowshoe

✔ The heavier the person and the more powdery the snow, the bigger the ideal snowshoe. But, says Claire Walter, author of *The Snowshoe Experience*, "22 to 25 inches long by 8 or 9 inches wide is the golden mean for size." Women-specific snowshoes are generally narrower.

✔ Beginners may also want to use poles to help with balance.

—Yishane Lee

KEEP AN EYE ON: The scenery; snowshoeing can take you places you couldn't get to on skis or in boots. But if you're in the mountains, be careful in the backcountry—keep an eye out for avalanches.

CONTACT: The U.S. Snowshoe Association (518-654-7648; www.snowshoeracing.com) has information about races, championships, clubs, equipment makers and more.

The Toughest Races in the World
O.K., let's see how tough you really are

Sure, lots of Americans have run a marathon, a 26-mile race. But that's a cakewalk compared to the really tough endurance races out there. Here are seven races that are generally considered the most extreme on the face of the earth, taking into account factors such as toughness of the course, rigor of the action and the small percentage of competitors who actually reach the finish line.

Badwater. *A 135-mile run and walk from Badwater, Calif., the lowest point in the contiguous U.S., to near the top of Mount Whitney, the highest.*

WHERE & WHEN: Death Valley, Calif. July.

HOW TOUGH: Temperatures range from 130 degrees in the desert to 30 degrees on the mountaintop. Runners can face everything from sandstorms to ice storms and take anywhere from 26 to 60 hours to finish the course. www.badwater.com

Iditarod Sled Dog Race. *A 1,100-mile race through Alaskan wilderness that takes the mushers and their dogs 10 to 20 days to finish.*

WHERE & WHEN: Anchorage to Nome, Alaska. March.

HOW TOUGH: Like the Ironman, this race has become an icon. The wintry conditions can be brutal, but the race is even tougher on the dogs when it's overly warm. www.iditarod.com

Training for a Triathlon

The rise of triathlons has occurred along-side the growing interest in cross-train-ing among athletes of all kinds. Alternating between working the upper body and the lower body can be good for overall muscle balance. Getting in shape for a multi-sport race forces you to cross-train, and it also reduces the risk of injury of doing one single sport. The variety also makes triathlons less monotonous than marathons, athletes say.

✔ A triathlete must practice everything from quickly removing a wetsuit to switching from bike shoes to running shoes.

✔ At least a dozen books, like Eric Harr's *Triathlon Training in Four Hours a Week* and Gale Bernhardt's *Triathlon Training Basics,* and Web sites, like www.trinewbies.com, offer training tips for first-timers.

✔ Some triathletes are willing to pay hundreds of dollars for face-to-face attention. At weekend or weeklong training camps, experts analyze partici-pants' swim strokes or assess their bike setups for wind resistance. Camps are often held near a race course so competitors can perform trial runs. For athletes who usually work out alone, the camps offer camaraderie and encouragement.

—Stefani Jackenthal

Ironman Triathlon. *A 2.4-mile ocean swim fol-lowed by 112 miles of cycling and a 26.2-mile marathon.*

WHERE & WHEN: Kailua-Kona, Hawaii. October.

HOW TOUGH: The oldest and probably best-known of the endurance events. Eight to nine hours of grueling competition for some of the world's fittest men and women. www.ironmanlive.com

La Traversée Internationale du Lac Saint-Jean. *A 25-mile swim across a lake in Northern Quebec*

WHERE & WHEN: About 500 miles north of Montreal. July.

HOW TOUGH: Three-to four-foot swells make for a rough ride, and no wetsuits are permitted during the nine-plus-hour swim, even though the water temperatures often fall to the low 60s. www.traversee.qc.ca

Race Across America. *A 3,000-mile bicycle race in 8 to 10 days.*

WHERE & WHEN: California to a preselected point on the East coast, such as Savannah, Ga., or Atlan-tic City, N.J. June.

HOW TOUGH: The winners cycle about 350 miles a day and sleep little more than an hour. About a third of the entrants finish. www.raceacrossamerica.org

Raid Series. *A wilderness endurance race in which five-person teams compete in a long-dis-tance, 5- to 7-day adventure race.*

WHERE & WHEN: The site varies from year to year. Event times vary from year to year.

HOW TOUGH: Races have been held over brutal terrain in Patagonia, Argentina, Costa Rica, Oman and Madagascar. Participants may engage in sea kayaking, mountain biking, white-water canoeing, caving and horseback riding, among other sports. www.theraid.org

Vendée Globe. *A four-month solo sailing race around the world.*

WHERE & WHEN: From France's Les Sables d'Olonne past Western Africa, Antarctica, Cape Horn and back. Every 4 years.

HOW TOUGH: Participants can't go ashore or get assistance, so they're totally on their own for four months. www.vendeeglobe.fr/uk

How to Ride a Bull

Hold on 8 seconds, earn bragging rights for life

By far the rodeo's most popular attraction is the man-versus-beast sport of bull riding. It's one of the most dangerous sports around, yet the rules couldn't be simpler: ride with only one hand on the bull rope and stay on the bucking bull for a full eight seconds. If you let your free hand touch the bull or yourself, or if the bull tosses you off before 8 seconds are up, you are disqualified.

Once the 8-second horn sounds, you must dismount—a process that can be as dangerous as being bucked off. Don't forget, the bulls are bred for their bucking ability and aggressiveness—whether you're on their hump or on the dirt. Stay on for 8 seconds and a set of judges assigns you a score; 100 is a perfect score, which is rarely attained. Only one in ten bull riders stay on for 8 seconds, and those who do usually score between 50 and 80 points.

 INSIDE INFO

Bull Talk: Terms To Learn

○ **Bodacious.** The name of one of the most feared and famous bulls in bull-riding history. Retired in 1995, Bodacious died a natural death 5 years later, when he was 12.

○ **Bull rope (or bell).** A rope wrapped around the bull's chest that a bull rider hangs on to. A bell at the bottom of the rope pulls the rope down once the rider dismounts or is bucked off.

○ **Down in the well.** A dangerous situation in which the bull spins and forcefully pulls the rider down into his swirling movements.

○ **Hooked.** This occurs after a rider is bucked off or dismounts a bull and the animal charges after him, trying to hook him with his horns.

○ **Muley.** A hornless bull.

○ **Rank.** A bull that is difficult to ride.

Getting off isn't easy, either. Not surprising for a sport that involves climbing on the back of a 2,000-pound twisting mass of muscle, injuries are routine. Bull riders suffer injuries mainly to their arms and shoulders. Mercifully, serious chest injuries have dropped considerably since the '90s, when riders started wearing Kevlar vests to protect their chests and internal organs.

Aside from agility, good bull riders need physical and mental strength. Technique is important, too, of course. Professional Bull Riders Inc. offers these pointers for getting off a raging bull:

To dismount, a bull rider reaches down with his free hand, jerks loose his riding hand from his bull rope and flings himself off as the bull is kicking, so that the momentum of the kick will propel the rider as far away from the bull as possible.

When possible, a rider waits until the bull is moving or spinning away from his riding hand, at which time the bull rider dismounts in the direction of his riding hand. For example, a right-handed bull rider waits until the bull spins left, before dismounting from the bull's right side.

Mastering Exotic Martial Arts

Disciplines that take you far beyond judo and tae kwon do

When it comes to the popularity of judo, tae kwon do and other combat disciplines, the math says it all: *Black Belt* magazine counts some 20,000 studios nationwide and estimates that some two million Americans practice Eastern fighting disciplines weekly or more. But a handful of esoteric styles exist that are not nearly so common. While anyone can try them, they seem to attract experienced martial artists seeking higher levels of skill and understanding. These disciplines can tweak conventional notions of athletic prowess. Here are some of the best fighting arts you may never have heard of.

Iaido: Not for the Weak-Kneed

The opponents are imaginary in the samurai martial arts form known as iaido (pronounced ee-eye-doe), an unlikely combination of dancelike movements and a nasty-looking weapon. Iaido can be a "moving meditation," but its operative idea is deadly, explains Noboru Kataoka, one of its leading masters and a martial arts film actor. "The moment you draw the sword, you have to kill your opponent," he says.

Each of its swordsmanship routines, called kata, evokes a specific peril, like fighting in a low-ceilinged tunnel, sparring in the dark or being jumped from two sides. It's not for the weak-kneed—from katas to kowtowing, all the kneeling, squatting and springing could challenge a cheerleader.

Kali, Arnis and Eskrima: A Filipino Solution

The arts of kali, arnis and eskrima, from the Philippines, are vigorous and employ an almost balletic violence. It's no accident that their weapons—rattan sticks, wood daggers and the hard side of one's hand—can be approximated by items you might have on hand, like umbrellas, bottles or even a pen.

Classes consist of sparring and grappling drills called offensiva-defensiva, usually practiced in pairs. But instructors eschew rigid sequences, believing that real attacks are random chaos. "Most people like the Filipino martial arts," or FMA, "because size doesn't really matter," says Steven Dowd of Fallon, Nev., who publishes the online FMA Digest. "No matter how old you are, or how disabled, it can be adapted."

Kyudo: It's Not About the Target

It can be surprising in Japanese archery to see a shooter taking aim a mere bow's length from the target. While that distance can stretch, kyudo is not about the bull's-eye. It is more stillness than action. "It's a standing meditation," says kyodo instructor, Jim Boorstein, an architect who practices kyudo in New York. Kyudo can improve posture and maintain strength, but more important, it helps "heighten your ability to notice, and that's what we're all trying to do in our lives," says Boorstein.

Naginata: The Art of Fighting

Developed a thousand years ago as warrior's pole-arms, or weapons, naginata later passed to samurai wives for defense. In 1912, naginata was introduced in Japanese high schools, where it remains a staple of girls' physical education.

Today's naginata are slender and lightweight, up to seven and a half feet long, with curved tips of wood or bamboo. Their use—to batter, stab or hook an opponent—makes sense for women, as it relies on the centripetal force of rotating hips, swinging arms and the long, rotating weapon rather than on upper-body strength. For more information, go to naginata.org/naginata.html.

Xing Yi: Power From the Body's Core

No photo montage of China is complete without a sunrise shot of elderly people tracing the deliberate gestures of tai chi in a public park. It would be easy to imagine tai chi's sister art, xing yi (pronounced shing-ee), as similarly pacific, but it's not.

More than 1,000 years ago in northern China's hinterlands, there were no police, so xing yi emerged for self-defense. Xing yi relies on power from the body's core, wielded in joint locks, throws and weapons practice, as well as solo and paired open-hand sequences. It builds strong muscular "roots" in the legs, hips and torso, says Mark Li, a sixth-generation instructor and a graduate student at George Mason University in Virginia.

Underlying all is the mind-body concept of chi, a sort of healing internal airflow. Aligning one's chi—as, for example, through breathing exercises—matters as much as the hands, feet and body. "When your chi is able to flow, it improves the function of your whole body," Li says.

—Mandy Katz

Preventing Sports Injuries
Simple precautions can keep you off the list

Overuse injuries happen to the very best of athletes. But for most of us amateurs on the playing fields, walking and running paths, and in swimming pools and weight rooms, overuse injuries are all too often the consequence of poor technique or misalignment of body parts.

To minimize the risk of injuries, learn how to perform your chosen activities correctly from the beginning and have your technique monitored periodically by an expert to be sure you haven't lapsed into body-damaging form. (For more on sports injuries, see page 21.)

Cycling. Most recreational cyclists worry about sore seats. But a more serious problem involves the hands, in particular the ulnar nerve that lies in the outer base of the hand below the pinky finger. This nerve can become irritated when the handlebars are gripped too tightly for too long, resulting in tingling, numbness and weakness that can travel up to the elbow. Wearing padded riding gloves helps but is not always enough. A better approach is frequently changing hand positions on the handlebars, loosening the grip and riding with elbows unlocked.

Golf. In this sport, where strokes involve twisting at the hips, the lower back is most likely to suffer. When driving the ball, lower-back pain is often caused by a side-to-side tilting of the body during the swing. A more upright stance and swing minimizes the twisting motion and resulting "crunch" on the spine. On the other hand, many golfers fail to rotate their hips at all during the backswing and instead generate power by sliding their hips back and then forward. This places the spine in a vulnerable position when the twisting motion occurs later in the swing. Some experts suggest that the risk of injury can be lessened if the hips are rotated instead of sliding them back and forth when transferring body weight during the swing.

SPORTS

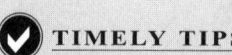

TIMELY TIPS

Waivers: The Fine Print
Trying a new sport? Read this

When faced with a waiver, most people skim the fine print and then sign. But not so fast. Lawyers offer the following suggestions on what to do when confronted with a form.

✔ Read carefully and understand what types of liability you are waiving. A waiver that describes the potential hazards and specifies that the sponsoring company is not liable for injury and property loss may be more likely to be enforced against an adult than one that speaks only in general terms. No matter how well drafted, waivers signed for children may not be enforceable depending on state law.

✔ Ask the proprietor or operator of the company about the maintenance of the equipment.

✔ Ask about recent accidents and your chances of being hurt.

✔ If you are very uncomfortable with the wording of a waiver—if, for example, it appears to exonerate a business for recklessness—do not sign it. Sometimes the employees will permit you to participate without a completed waiver. If not, walk away.

—Ellen Rosen

Running and walking. Many runners and walkers are cursed with a built-in mechanical flaw: too much or too little pronation. In overpronation, the foot rolls inward too far after the heel strikes the ground. In underpronation, the foot doesn't roll over far enough. Thus, only one runner in four has a normal gait. Overpronation is the more serious problem because muscles from the toes to the hips are called upon to stabilize the feet. It can cause excessive torque of the knees and contributes to problems like tendinitis, plantar fasciitis and knee strain.

The usual solution is to use orthotics, shoe inserts that compensate for flat feet and other common causes of overpronation and enable the foot to absorb shock without becoming unstable. It is best to consult a podiatrist or orthopedic surgeon about the best kind of orthotic for your feet. Also, be sure your running and walking shoes have adequate support, reinforced heel counters and motion control features. (For more on exercise shoes, see page 23.)

Swimming. Among swimmers, the shoulders are most likely to take a beating. Many swimmers use strokes that put their shoulders at risk of tendinitis. The usual victims fail to keep their elbows high in relation to their hands and, instead of rotating the shoulder to get "over the stroke," they press downward too soon, which puts excess pressure on the shoulder. In a proper stroke when swimming the crawl, the elbow should be bent 90 degrees as the hand passes the face, and, as if reaching over a barrel, the shoulder remains high while the hand is driven deep into the water.

Tennis. The elbow is the tennis player's Achilles' heel. Tennis elbow, a form of tendinitis, results from repeated vibrations through the playing arm whenever the ball hits the racquet. The usual cause: improper stroking of the backhand—leading with the elbow and using just the upper body to hit the ball. In a proper backhand, the elbow is in line with the racquet hand, and the muscles of the feet, legs, hips, shoulders, arms and hands participate in the stroke and contribute to its power and placement.

Penn State University sports medicine experts cite two ways to fix a backhand. One is to use a grip that permits the inside of the thumb, not its bottom part, to stay in contact with the handle and allow the elbow to drop down and away from the body as you stroke. The second is to use a two-handed backhand, which forces the trunk and arms to move together and involves no movement at the elbows.

Weight training. With this activity, any technique that does not allow the body to move in a biomechanically efficient way is potentially dangerous, doctors say. One example is "cheat curls." Some lifters doing bicep curls with free weights use their back muscles to lift the weight instead of only the muscles of their arms. This causes them to rock or swing the body back when they lift, which can result in lower-back injuries. Done properly, the head is up and facing forward, the torso erect, upper arms still and elbows close to the body.

In doing leg presses, a common error is to quickly extend the legs and lock the knees. With correct technique, the leg is extended slowly and the motion is stopped before the knee is straight.

Keep in mind, of course, that if you haven't done an activity in a while, don't try to resume it immediately at full tilt. Build up gradually. And if you start to feel discomfort associated with an activity, don't ignore it. When an injury is untreated or aggravated by continued misuse, you can end up with a long-lasting problem that may force you to abandon the activity altogether.

—Jane E. Brody

Games & Puzzles

The Best Video Games for Adults

Kids love them and grown-ups do, too

The average gamer is now about 30; the first generation to grow up playing games is now around 40. And your 35-year-old boyfriend is not going to be impressed when you show up with the latest Pokémon or the new "Price Is Right" game. The best work being done in games these days is in interactive narratives for and about adults. Engaging with a current top-end game involves much more cognitive processing (a. k. a. brainpower) than merely watching hour upon hour of prime-time television. So show some respect; your favorite gamer will adore you for it. Here are some of the best games for adults (and some kids) currently available.

Grand Theft Auto IV. *For Xbox 360 and Play-station 3. RATING: M for Mature.*

    IDEAL AUDIENCE: Well-adjusted adults who want

> **INSIDE INFO**
>
> ## Profile of a Gamer
>
> ○ A 2009 survey shows that 68 percent of American households play computer and video games.
>
> ○ The average age of gamers is 35; about 25 percent are over 50.
>
> ○ Women over 18 make up 34 percent of all gamers, compared to 18 percent of boys 17 or younger.
>
> SOURCE: Entertainment Software Association

to explore a rich, intelligent, politically incorrect digital rendition of New York City. As long as you can accept that a great work of modern entertainment can revolve around criminals—something long assumed in television and films—then it is almost impossible to deny that G.T.A. IV is one of the most compelling games in recent years. The driving and shooting is fun, but the real star of the game is the city itself, rendered with a loving sense of decay and populated with perhaps the best cast of dysfunctional characters to grace a pixel.

Sid Meier's Civilization Revolution. *For Xbox 360, PS3 and DS. RATING: E10+ for Everyone 10 and older.*

    IDEAL AUDIENCE: Families interested in global history and strategic thinking; also, commuters looking to upgrade from Tetris. Civilization is the top strategy franchise in the history of video games. With Revolution, the series moves beyond PCs and arrives on consoles and the handheld Nintendo DS. The premise remains the same: guide a historical culture from the dawn of history to the space age. Nothing feels better than dominating Genghis Khan and Napoleon at the same time.

Warhammer Online. *For PC. RATING: T for Teen.*

    IDEAL AUDIENCE: Massively multiplayer online gamers who cannot satisfy their bloodlust in World of Warcraft. Don't get me wrong; like more than 10 million other people, I love World of Warcraft. But great games can stand some competition, and Warhammer Online, the new online version of the decades-old British fantasy universe, provides it. Warhammer's twist: it focuses largely on player-versus-player combat rather than on battling computer-controlled foes.

Wii Fit. *For Wii. RATING: E for Everyone.*

IDEAL AUDIENCE: Couch produce of all ages. One of Nintendo's best games, it is not really a game. It's a light exercise system meant to take just a few calories off. The most surprising thing: it works.

LittleBigPlanet. *For PlayStation 3. RATING: E.*

IDEAL AUDIENCE: Anyone with excellent eye-hand coordination. LittleBigPlanet is in some ways as close to YouTube as games have come. In its essence it is merely a "platformer;" you navigate your little beanbag character mostly by running and jumping. The secret sauce: users can create their own levels and share them with other online players.

Dead Space. *For Xbox 360, PS3 and PC. RATING: M.*

IDEAL AUDIENCE: People who like being scared. Dead Space is a straightforward science fiction survival-horror experience. You, the player, are trapped on a spooky spaceship with a horde of space zombies who want to eat you, or turn you into one of them, or something. You wade through them while engaging in what is charmingly referred to as "strategic dismemberment." Still, Dead Space is conceived and executed at a high level.

Fallout 3. *For Xbox 360, PS3 and PC. RATING: M.*

IDEAL AUDIENCE: Old-school role-playing gamers and anyone who wants to see Washington in ashes. The classic Fallout series is a sprawling re-creation of the Capitol area after a nuclear war. The tone is darker and less slyly humorous than previous Fallout games, but the sheer size and ambition of the game impress.

Professor Layton and the Curious Village. *For Nintendo DS. RATING: E.*

IDEAL AUDIENCE: Puzzle fans. In this sleeper, Professor Layton ties together more than 100 beautifully designed brainteasers with an endearing anime-style story. The puzzles themselves are perfectly intelligible to nongamers, too.

Gears of War 2. *For Xbox 360. RATING: M.*

IDEAL AUDIENCE: Testosterone-fueled core gamers who like chain saws. The stereotypical video game: big guns, voracious alien bad guys, great graphics, huge explosions, cardboard-cutout characters, silly dialogue and cheap thrills all around. Not that there's anything wrong with that.

Fable II. *For Xbox 360. RATING: M.*

IDEAL AUDIENCE: Emotionally mature children and most fans of delicate entertainment design. This game is rated M, not because it is especially violent or profane, but because in between casting spells and swinging swords you can have children, get married (and have affairs if you choose) and buy condoms. For children who are comfortable with the basic facts of life, there is no reason not to share Fable II. It's a wonderful game on its own, and it beats handing a child a virtual machine gun.

—Seth Schiesel

Cues from a Pool Shark

Forget that triple-bank shot until you master these basics

Loree Jon Jones began her pool career at the age of 4, standing on specially-built wooden boxes that enabled her to reach her father's billiard table. She ran her first rack of balls at age 5 and won her first world championship at 15, setting a record for the youngest world title holder. Jones, nicknamed "Queen of the Hill" because

TIMELY TIPS

The Perfect Cue

✔ A top-of-the-line Z Shaft is lighter and more tapered than other shafts—the skinnier halves of cues. It is intended to minimize what modern players call cue ball deflection.

✔ The Z—priced at around $270, more than twice the cost of most conventional shafts, and manufactured by Predator Cues in Jacksonville, Fla.—is so slender at the tip that the weight of the cue ball pushes it aside upon contact. Bigger conventional models, by contrast, slam through the shot, adding unwanted, unpredictable spin. After a few hundred games, Z Shaft users can sense the pleasant vibration that indicates a perfectly struck cue ball, versus the rough twitter that accompanies an uneven stroke.

of her penchant for coming from behind to win the final match, is queen of tournaments. She holds 8 world titles, 3 U.S. Open championships, 3 National championships and 5 Player of the Year awards bestowed on her by *Pool & Billiard Magazine*. In 2002, Jones was inducted into the Billiard Congress of America's Hall of Fame. Here are some pointers from Jones.

Finding the right cue stick. The most important thing in choosing a stick is comfort. A big key is the material it's made of—especially the shaft (or top) part. Men should use a stick weighing between 19 and 21 ounces, women between 18 and 19½. If you're just pulling a stick off the wall to use, make sure it's not too heavy or warped.

Chalking right. This should be done before every shot. Hold the chalk between your thumb, index and middle fingers and stroke downward while turning the middle of the stick. If you hit a ball straight on without chalking, you'll slide off and miscue. Chalk creates friction to prevent this.

Building bridges. The basic or regular bridge is used for average shots where the cue ball rests in the middle of the table. Place your thumb against your middle finger, put the cue stick between them, then wrap your index finger around the cue stick and touch your thumb. Ring finger and pinkie should be spread out for stability. Palm and side of hand need to be on the table, and the three locking fingers can be moved to make the bridge tighter or looser.

- The "rail bridge" is used when the cue ball is frozen against a rail. Place your palm on the table by the rail, hanging it off the edge if necessary. Keep the cue stick level, curl the index finger underneath, then make a "V" with the thumb and lay the stick against it. The key here is to keep the hand flat.

- The "near rail" bridge is used if your cue ball is 1½ to 3 inches off the rail; you need more stability than the rail bridge offers. Put the thumb under the hand, place the cue stick on the side of your thumb and rest the cue stick on the felt of the rail. Bring the index finger over the cue stick so the stick sits between your index finger and thumb. The stick should be touching the felt throughout the shot.

- The "over the ball" bridge is used when you have a ball sitting directly behind the cue ball blocking room for a normal bridge. Get on the tips of your fingers as best you can, place them behind the blocking ball and form a "V" by raising your thumb.

- The "open bridge" is used to stretch way over the table for a shot. Put your hand flat on the table, stretch out your fingers and raise your hand up to the knuckles. Lay the cue stick over the index finger and raise the thumb for support.

How to Play Pool

It helps to know the rules of the game

Pool is one of a number of cue sports—bearing unfortunate names like carom and snooker—within the larger billiards family. The game people commonly refer to as pool, whether played in a dimly lit bar hall or mahogany-paneled parlor, is generally the 8-ball variety. The rules are fairly simple, although variations abound; the challenge is in the execution. Then again, even Minnesota Fats had to start somewhere.

All 15 balls are used for 8-ball. Place the 8-ball in the center of the triangle and the 1-ball in front. Fill the triangle with the remaining balls, alternating the striped and solid colored balls. Flip a coin to determine who will break the ball formation. If the person breaking gets a ball into a pocket and it is a striped ball, for example, he or she must play all the striped balls during the course of the game. The opponent plays the solids.

Players alternate shooting; a player who makes a shot is rewarded with another turn. A player who hits the opponent's ball or who misses a shot, loses a turn. The goal is to shoot all your balls into the table pockets while avoiding the 8-ball—hence the name of the game.

Only after all your balls are in pockets can you sink the 8-ball. If you pocket the 8-ball before your other balls you automatically lose the game. Once you get your chance to shoot the 8-ball, you must announce which pocket you aim to place it in. If you get it in that pocket, you win. If you miss but it doesn't go into any pocket, then your opponent gets a turn. Once he or she misses a shot, you get another turn.

The first to sink all their balls and the 8-ball wins.

If you stroke with your right hand, raise your right leg in the air and stand on your left tiptoe for more stretch.

Developing a strong stance. When you see a great player ready to shoot, everything is lined up. If you're a righty, make a bridge with your left hand. As you stand at the table lining up your shot, your right foot should be under the back of the cue stick and the left foot a little more forward and at a 45-degree angle to the right.

Before shooting, lean down and get as low as you can to the ball. When cue stick meets cue ball, the back elbow should be at a 90-degree angle. It's O.K. to adjust for height, moving your hand forward if shorter or backward if taller.

Learning your shots. Now you're ready to shoot. Not moving the rest of your body, bring the cue stick back with your stroking arm as you begin eyeing the shot. Making sure your bridge is close enough to the cue ball, draw an imaginary line with your eyes or cue stick going directly from the middle of the cue ball through the object ball and into the pocket. Set your aim at the start of that line, moving your eyes back and forth between the cue and the object ball. As you bring your stroking arm forward again, think of your body as a pendulum—nothing else moves besides your lower arm.

FOLLOW SHOT. When you want the cue ball to roll forward after hitting the object ball to set up your next shot, hit the cue ball above its center spot so it spins forward. If you imagine the cue ball as a clock, you should be very high at 12 o'clock. Don't use too much power; it's not power that makes a better roll, it's how high you hit the cue ball.

DRAW SHOT. If you want the cue ball to roll backward after hitting the object ball, strike the cue ball below its center spot at 6 o'clock. To make the shot more effective, snap your stroking wrist back as you make contact with the cue ball.

STOP SHOT. To make the cue ball stop dead after making contact with the object ball, hit the cue ball just a bit lower at 6 o'clock than on the draw shot.

ENGLISH SHOT. This is used to send the cue and object ball to the right or left rather than straight ahead. Try this shot only after you've mastered everything else. If you want the ball to veer to the right, hit it on the right side at 3 o'clock; if you want it to veer to the left, hit it on the left at 9 o'clock. The higher you hit the ball on either side, the less it cuts down an angle shot. The lower you hit it, the wider the angle.

Secrets of a Monopoly Champ

Don't buy Boardwalk, skimp on hotels, gobble up the orange and more

Roger Craig, a commercial tire salesman from Harrisburg, Ill., reigned as champion of the U.S. National Monopoly Game tournament from 1996 until 1999. Astonishingly, during the beginning of the game that placed him on the throne, he opted not to buy Boardwalk, the game's most expensive property and one highly coveted by lesser players. Craig shares here the rationale behind this decision, as well as other secrets of his success.

Craig's strategies are based on the "traditional" game in which each player starts with $1,500 and gives all tax and fine money over to the bank. Nontournament matches often include the "untraditional" $500 bonus pot into which all taxes and fines are placed—a bounty awarded to any player landing directly on Free Parking.

❓ An important tactical question first. Do you prefer a particular token?

I use the iron. It's the smallest piece on the board, and as you're moving it around you can hide it behind hotels and get away without paying rent. It's amazing how much money I've saved over the years using that piece. Once the dice are rolled by two people beyond yourself, you can't be caught for owing money on your last move. In championship finals all moves are announced to the crowd, so I couldn't get away with it.

❓ What is your strategy in acquiring property?

You buy everything you can, until you get around to the three most expensive sets of properties—the yellow ones (Atlantic, Ventnor, Marvin Gardens), green ones (Pacific, North Carolina, Pennsylvania) and the blue ones (Park Place, Boardwalk). They cost too much to buy, get a monopoly on, then have to improve with houses and hotels. If I get one of the green ones or the yellow ones, that's all I'm interested in. It blocks the other monopolies and it gives me something to trade later in the game.

❓ Which properties are the best to acquire?

The orange ones—St. James, Tennessee and New York. The two most common numbers rolled on the dice are six and eight—and rolling them just pops you onto the orange ones. You get those three or the red ones—Kentucky, Indiana and Illinois—and you're going to win 75 percent or more of the time unless you roll very poorly. They don't cost too much to build up and they bring in the best return for what you spend.

Knowing that, if you have one of the yellows and two of the greens—or vice-versa—you can trade them for oranges or reds to people who don't know what it takes to win. They see yellows and greens cost more and they're only thinking about how much they'll get when someone lands there—not how much it will cost to build them up. I figure in how much cash a player can generate. I would never make such a trade if a guy was sitting there with $1,000 in cash.

The Most Landed-on Monopolies

In the 1980s, Parker Brothers, Monopoly's manufacturer, made a list of the most frequently landed-upon monopolies. The list shows the odds of a player landing on one property of a monopoly in one trip around the board.

GO DIRECTLY TO JAIL...

1. **RAILROADS**—B&O, Reading, Short Line, Pennsylvania	64%
2. **ORANGES**—New York, St. James, Tennessee	50%
3. **REDS**—Illinois, Indiana, Kentucky	49%
4. **YELLOWS**—Marvin Gardents, Atlantic, Ventnor	45%
5. **GREENS**—Pacific, Pennsylvania, N. Carolina	44%
6. **LIGHT PURPLES**—St. Charles, States, Virginia	43%
7. **LIGHT BLUES**—Oriental, Connecticut, Vermont	39%
8. **UTILITIES**—Water Works, Electric Co.	32%
9. **DARK BLUES**—Boardwalk, Park Place	27%
10. **DARK PURPLES**—Mediterranean, Baltic	24%

DO NOT PASS GO, DO NOT COLLECT $200...

Using a computer, Irvin Hentzel, a mathematics professor at Iowa State University and a frustrated Monopoly player, calculated the 10 spaces you can count on landing on more than others–see list at right. (The most landed-upon space was Jail, but Hentzel deleted that from his list, since a player in Jail had to remain there for three turns or roll doubles to get out.) Upon making his findings public in 1973, Hentzel promptly quit playing. "It was no fun anymore," he explained. "I had figured it out."

MONOPOLY

1. **Illinois Avenue**
2. **Go**
3. **B&O Railroad**
4. **Free Parking**
5. **Tennessee Avenue**
6. **New York Avenue**
7. **Reading Railroad**
8. **St. James Place**
9. **Water Works**
10. **Pennsylvania Railroad**

Q How does your strategy change once you have a monopoly?

If you can get a monopoly of your own without having to trade for it, you ought to have the game in the hand. Then you can spend the rest of your time blocking everybody else—making a trade that doesn't help any opponent and gets you a piece of property that will block someone else. If you're holding all the single cards to a bunch of monopolies and you've got one monopoly yourself, they can't beat you. The only time I will make a trade that gives someone a monopoly is if I get an outright monopoly itself in exchange.

It usually takes eight or nine times around for everything to be bought up. When all the properties are sold, you start looking around at all the deals you can make. Hardly anybody ever tries to get Boardwalk or Park Place as part of a deal because they cost so much to improve—and at that stage of the game you don't have any money.

Q How much should you build up your properties with houses and hotels?

Everybody wants to build up as many houses as they can—as fast as they can. A good rule is to build up to the three-house level, as quickly as possible. Your return on your money from one house to two houses is almost nothing, but once you make the jump to the third house—that's where your real money is made. The jump from the third to the fourth house and the fourth to a hotel isn't that big. So save your money for something else.

The biggest mistake I saw people make during the championships was that as soon as they got a monopoly, they would spend everything in front of them to build land up—without regard to where they or the other players were on the board. You need to leave yourself enough money to cover yourself. If there are several monopolies out, I'll take whatever money I figure I can spend and put it aside, then see where everyone else is on the board. As soon as they get real close to my property, then I'll build on the property and take a chance they'll land there. I also wait until I pass opposing monopolies before spending cash.

● **What else should players keep in mind?**

Don't always go for cash. Say an opponent lands on your property and they owe you $800. See if they can raise that much cash with what they own and by mortgaging properties. It's not always smart to let them do that because if you leave them with three for four mortgaged properties, the next person who lands there is going to be able to get those properties. So a lot of times, I'll take whatever property they have instead of cash.

A-D-V-I-C-E from a Scrabble Master

Seven things you can do to score big

O nly a handful of top players know *The Offi-cial Scrabble Players Dictionary* by heart. Joe Edley took a job as a night security guard in order to memorize it, and after 2 years of "fanatical study," he won the National Scrabble Championship in 1980. He won again in 1992 and 2000, making

him the only three-time winner ever. Edley is an official with the National Scrabble Association and the author of several books on scrabble, including *The Official Scrabble Puzzle Book* (www.scrabble-assoc.com). The words Edley suggests mastering (below) can be found in *The Official Scrabble Players Dictionary*. The fourth edition contains over 100,000 playable words—4,000 more than the third edition—but without the 100 "offensive" words that were removed from the game in in the early 1990s. Here are seven tips on scoring big.

1. Learn the 94 two-letter words.

2. Learn the 996 three-letter words.

3. Learn the 17 "Q without U" words. Seven of them—Faqir, Qintar, Qanat, Tranq, Qoph, Qaid,

They Are Too Acceptable Words

These two-letter words may not rack up big points, but they will clean up your rack

aa	be	fa	lo	om	ti
ad	bi	go	ma	on	to
ae	bo	ha	me	op	uh
ag	by	he	mi	or	um
ah	da	hi	mm	os	un
ai	de	hm	mo	ow	up
al	do	ho	mu	ox	us
am	ef	id	my	oy	ut
an	eh	if	na	pa	we
ar	el	in	ne	pe	wo
as	em	is	no	pi	xi
at	en	it	nu	re	xu
aw	er	jo	od	sh	ya
ax	es	ka	oe	si	ye
ay	et	la	of	so	
ba	ex	li	oh	ta	

Qat—can also be made plural with the addition of an "S," and "Qindar" (an Albanian monetary unit) can become "Qindarka."

4. Learn the approximately 1,200 four-and five-letter words containing a J, Q, X or Z.

5. Use "vowel dumps"—words containing multiple vowels such as "ourie" (shivering with cold) and "warison" (a battle cry) that get four or more low-scoring vowels out of your rack in one move.

6. "S" and "A" are "hook letters" that can often be used to form two words off of one existing word (e.g., "board" can lead to "aboard").

7. Learn "bingos"—words that use all seven of your tiles, earning a 50-point bonus. Included in the bingo list are about 200 "six to make seven" words that can be built off just three six-letter words (saltine, satire, retain) and one blank tile.

How to Play Mah-jongg

The ancient Chinese game uses tiles instead of cards, and requires practice and patience

Perennially popular in Asia and among women of a certain age in Brooklyn, mah-jongg is seeing a revival, particularly among the young. The ancient Chinese game—a kind of marriage between gin rummy and dominoes—uses tiles instead of cards. Learning the basics of the game won't take long, but mastering its finer points requires practice and patience. One difficulty is figuring out which rules to adhere to—there are at least 25 variations internationally, and even within China there are regional differences.

Rules for the American version—among the more difficult—are determined by the National Mah Jongg League (www.nationalmahjongg league.org) and are available in the League's booklet *Mah Jongg Made Easy*.

New players are better off learning basic mah-jongg rules that cut across many game versions before moving on to more complex variations. The game is played by four players at a square table (or online if you prefer to play alone). The object is to be the first to organize your tiles into a pattern of certain combinations that have the highest point values. It is in the variety of tile combinations and scoring that mah-jongg rules differ most.

The game begins with each player building a wall of tiles on the table using a predetermined number of tiles, usually 34 tiles if four players are in the game. A turn involves a player drawing a tile from the wall and deciding whether to retain it or discard it. Tiles can only be removed from the left to the right edges. A tile that is not on an edge is blocked and cannot be removed. When the player discards a tile, he or she announces the name of the tile discarded. Although tiles are removed clockwise, players take their turns in a counterclockwise direction. A player can take only the most recently discarded tile, and then only if it completes a certain group or hand.

The process of claiming and discarding tiles continues until one player achieves a mah-jongg hand. A complete 14-tile mah-jongg hand, for example,

SAMPLE MAH-JONGG HAND

This sample mah-jongg hand includes four groups and a pair. They are a pung (three dragons), a chow (three of same suit), a pung (three dotted tiles), a chow (three of same suit) and a pair (two of same suit or character)

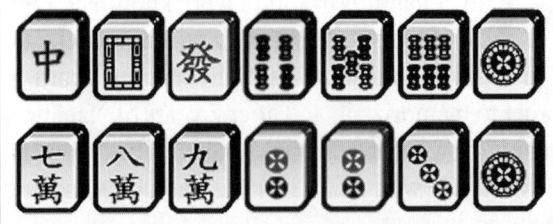

includes four groups (each with three tiles) and a pair. Groups have names like pung, chow and kong, designating whether the tiles are three green dragons, for example, or three of the same suit, such as dotted or lined tiles. A pair must be two identical tiles, of any character or suit. Official scoring rules are complicated in mah-jongg, and often casual players establish in advance their own values of tiles and groups. Strategy is important, but a lot of success in mah-jongg also depends on sheer luck.

Checkers, Chess and More

The rules that rule the pieces in checkers, chess and backgammon

The most exciting board games require a unique mix of brains and imaginative brawn. In the best of matches, the rules metamorphose from simple mathematical variations into the physics of a new world in which pawns become warriors and you are the mastermind behind a war in which everything good and decent is at stake. Here are the rules that govern the battlefield.

HOPSCOTCHING THE CHECKER BOARD

Learning to play checkers is child's play, but devising strategies to triumph over a good player takes skill and lots of practice. The winner, of course, is the first player to capture all of an opponent's men or to block them so that they can't move anywhere on the board. To test your mettle, follow these instructions:

● Opponents face each other across the board, which has eight rows of eight squares each, alternately red and black. One player takes the red pieces, or men, and puts them on the black squares in the three horizontal rows nearest him. The opponent places the black checkers on the black squares in the three rows facing him.

The Ancient Game of Go

The endless possibilities of positions on the board make it more complex than chess

Millions of people play Go in Asia, where the chess-like game dates back more that 2,500 years. In China, Go, or *weiqi,* was condemned as bourgeois during the Cultural Revolution, but today there are roughly 30 million players. Millions more play in Japan, the source of the game's name and much of its terminology, and in South Korea, home of one of the world's top players, Lee Chang Ho.

The game is quickly making inroads in America, thanks partly to its cameo appearances a few years back in the films *Pi* and *A Beautiful Mind.* There are now more than 340 Go clubs across the country; to locate one near you, go to the American Go Association at www.usgo.org.

HOW TO PLAY. Go has simpler rules than chess, but the endless possibilities of positions on the board make it so complex that no one has devised a computer program that can defeat even a talented amateur.

A Go set includes round stones (180 white and 181 black), and a board with a grid pattern of 19 horizontal and 19 vertical lines. The grid contains 361 intersections, on which stones are placed. Players use their stones to gain territory on the board by surrounding and capturing their opponent's stones; the white stones invade black territory and vice versa. It generally takes about 200 moves to complete a game.   —Blake Eskin

● The opponents take turns—black goes first, then red—moving a man forward diagonally toward the opponent's side. Only the black squares are used. With each turn, a player moves one man to an adjacent empty square. When one player's man comes up against an enemy checker and there is an empty space behind it, the player jumps over the enemy, landing

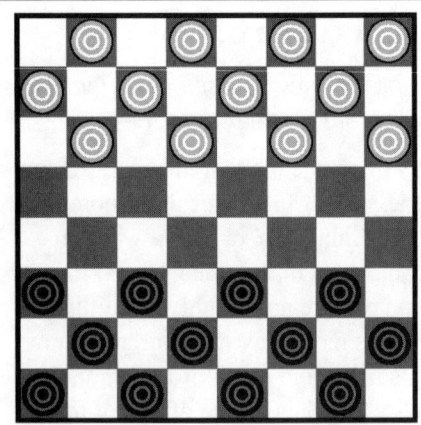

RANK AND FILE: *In both checkers and chess, the rows across are known as ranks; the columns as files. In checkers, only the dark squares are used.*

MANEUVERS: *As shown here, the six chess pieces can move in a variety of ways. The knight, however, is the only one that can move through, or jump over, other pieces. That ability, combined with its unusual L-shaped moving pattern, makes it an end--game linchpin.*

King moves   Queen moves   Bishop moves

Knight moves   Rook moves   Pawn moves

on the unoccupied square. The captured checker is removed from the board.

• One man can jump two or more enemy pieces consecutively, by moving diagonally left or right after the first jump, as long as there are empty spaces to land on between each jump. A checker that makes it to any square in the opponent's first row becomes a king—at which time it gets crowned by a man of the same color that is not in play. The king can now move, and jump, forward and backward.

THE MIND FIELDS OF CHESS

When it comes to drama, intrigue and byzantine rules, few games can match chess, which is thought to date back to sixth-century India or China. Odds

are you won't become the next Bobby Fischer, who at age 15 was the youngest international grand master in history, but here are the rules that will take you to the endgame: capturing the enemy's king.

• Opponents face each other across the board, which has eight rows of eight squares each, alternately white and black. Each player gets 16 pieces of one color, black or white. From least to most important, the pieces are 8 pawns, 2 knights, 2 bishops, 2 rooks (or castles), 1 queen and 1 king.

• Place the board so that each player has a light square at the nearest right-hand corner. In the row closest to you, place in order from left to right: rook, knight, bishop, queen, king, bishop, knight and rook. Line up the pawns next to each other in the row directly in front of these pieces.

• A piece can move only into a square that's not occupied by another piece owned by the same player. If an enemy piece occupies the square, it is captured. You remove the captured piece from the board and put your piece in its place.

• A pawn moves forward one square at a time, except for its first move when it can go one or two squares. A knight makes an L-shaped move, going two squares forward, backward or sideways, then another square at a right angle. It's the only piece that can jump over another piece. A bishop goes diagonally forward or backward but has to stay on the same color. A rook moves forward, backward or sideways, for any distance. The queen is a potent force. She moves forward, backward, sideways and diagonally for any number of squares in one direction. The king's moves are like the queen's except that he moves one square at a time, as long as it's unoccupied or not under attack by an enemy piece.

• When a king is under attack by an enemy piece, the king is in check. The player whose king is in check has several options: to move the king to safety, to capture the attacker or to move another piece to a square between the king and the attacker. If a player can't take any of these moves, the king is captured, or "checkmated," and the game is over.

• Pieces capture an opponent's man by moving as they normally do, except for the pawn. It can capture any of its opponent's pieces that are diagonally next to and ahead of it.

• A pawn can also take an enemy pawn "en passant," or in passing. Say an opponent starts by moving his pawn two squares, instead of one, putting it next to your pawn. You can take that piece by moving diagonally to the square directly behind it. But do it immediately: you can't wait for your next turn.

• Once in each game, in a move called castling, a king gets to move two spaces. Castling is done only if the king is not in check, there are no pieces between the king and a rook and neither piece has yet made a move. The two-part move is done by moving the king two squares toward the rook and then putting the rook on the square passed over by the king. Castling counts as one move.

THE FINER POINTS OF BACKGAMMON

Backgammon is a game played by two players, each with 15 markers or stones—but these days checkers can be used in a pinch. The object is to be the first player to move all his or her markers around the board and then off it.

• To set up, the markers are placed on the board as shown in the diagram below. The board is divided into four "tables" with numbered triangular spaces, or "points." The bar in the middle is also used in the game.

• Each player rolls a die to determine who goes first. The higher one starts. Players then take turns

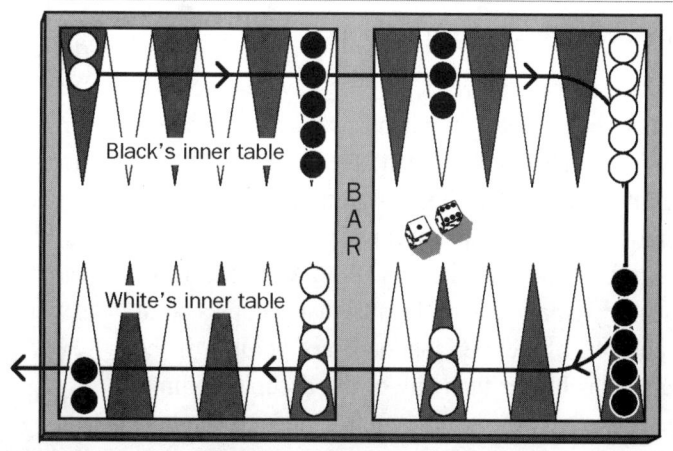

BACKGAMMON: *The board is shown in the starting position. The goal is to move your men from your opponent's inner table to your own inner table on the opposite side of the board. White moves in the direction indicated by the arrows; black moves in the opposite direction. When all of your men reach your inner table, you may begin bearing them off by throwing dice that (hopefully) correspond to the number assigned each point.*

Black's inner table

White's inner table

B A R

rolling two dice to determine how many spaces to move the stones, with black moving around the board in one direction and white moving in the opposite direction. The numbers on each die can be combined so that one piece moves the total amount indicated. Alternatively, each die's value can be applied separately to a single marker.

• Throwing "doubles" (for example, two 4s), allows a player to move twice as many points as shown on the dice—in this case, either four markers can be moved four spaces each, one can be moved four spaces and one 12 spaces, two can be moved 8 spaces each, or one marker can be moved 16 spaces.

• There is no limit to the number of markers of the same color that may stay on one point, but markers of opposite colors may not occupy the same point. If two or more markers are on a point, the point is closed—a marker of the opposite color can't land there. However, a point that is occupied by only one marker is open and is called a "blot." If an opponent lands on a blot, the other player must move his or her man to the bar between the two halves of the board and can play no other man till the one on the bar re-enters. To do so, the player must make a roll of the dice that corresponds to a space on the other player's inner table that is open or blotted.

• Once all of a player's 15 men have entered his or her "inner table" (the opposite side of the board from which the player began), the player may begin bearing them off the board by rolling the dice and removing any men that occupy spaces indicated by the roll. If a player rolls 5 and 4, for example, he or she may remove one of the men that occupies point 5 and one of the men that occupies point 4. If the number is higher than any of the occupied points, the player may remove a man from the next highest

point. Double 6s are an especially good roll at this point. Play continues until one of the players has removed all of his or her men.

Poker: Cut the Deck and Deal
Know when to hold 'em and when to fold 'em

By some estimates, as many as 80 million people in the United States play poker; online poker alone draws several million players per month. Versions of the game abound, with two current favorites—Texas hold'em and Omaha—outshining more traditional stud poker, at least among the young.

Here are basic poker rules, some popular variations—and a few tricks for playing them. There's no guarantee, of course, that you'll draw winning cards, but at least you'll be prepared to call the other guy's bet.

Poker (Five-card draw). Hundreds of card games are based on slight modifications of standard poker, or "five-card draw." Variations include adding wild cards, changing the way players bet and altering the size of each hand. But the goal is always the same: to get a better hand, or selection of cards, than other players.

To play five-card draw, shuffle a regular 52-card deck and deal five cards to each of three to seven players. Typically each player pays a small sum, called an "ante," for the privilege of seeing his or her hand. All bets (and antes) are placed in the pot, a pile of money in the center of the table.

Players bet on their cards in a clockwise fashion, starting at the dealer's left. The first player has several betting options:

• **FOLD:** Throwing in the cards and sitting out the rest of the hand. Any time a player folds at this stage, the ante remains in the pot and goes to the winner.

• **BET:** Placing a wager in the pot.

• **PASS:** Choosing not to make a wager and allowing the next player to go.

If the first player doesn't make a bet, then the next player has the same options. Once a player has made a bet, however, other players may no longer pass and are required to do one of the following:

• **FOLD:** And lose your bets and ante.

• **CALL:** Match the other players' bets by placing an equal wager into the pot.

• **RAISE:** Place a higher wager than others have bet into the pot. All other players will need to match this raised bet in order to stay in the game.

After a round of betting, all remaining players are then allowed to exchange up to three of their cards with those from the top of the remaining deck in the same order that the cards were dealt. At this time, the players have a second round of betting. After this round, all remaining players show their cards to each other. The player with the highest hand wins the pot.

Cards are ranked in the following order, from lowest to highest: 2, 3, 4, 5, 6, 7, 8, 9, 10, Jack, Queen, King, Ace. The box on the next page shows the order of winning hands. Each level of

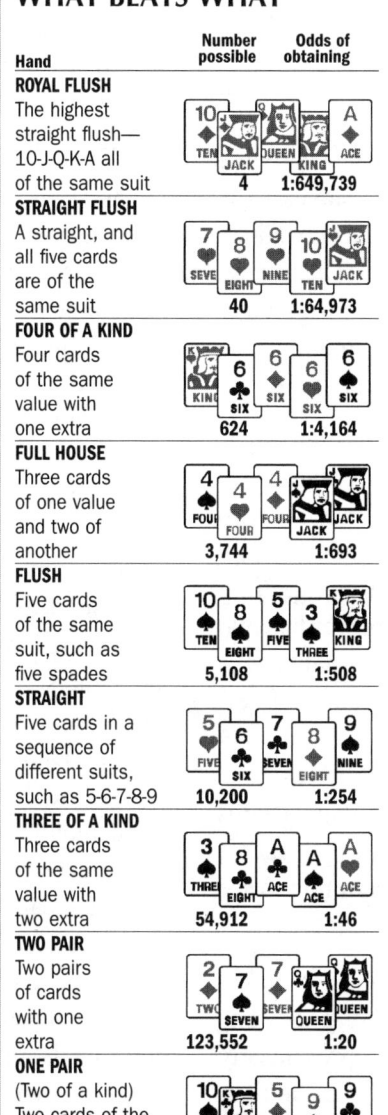

WHAT BEATS WHAT

Hand	Number possible	Odds of obtaining
ROYAL FLUSH The highest straight flush— 10-J-Q-K-A all of the same suit	4	1:649,739
STRAIGHT FLUSH A straight, and all five cards are of the same suit	40	1:64,973
FOUR OF A KIND Four cards of the same value with one extra	624	1:4,164
FULL HOUSE Three cards of one value and two of another	3,744	1:693
FLUSH Five cards of the same suit, such as five spades	5,108	1:508
STRAIGHT Five cards in a sequence of different suits, such as 5-6-7-8-9	10,200	1:254
THREE OF A KIND Three cards of the same value with two extra	54,912	1:46
TWO PAIR Two pairs of cards with one extra	123,552	1:20
ONE PAIR (Two of a kind) Two cards of the same value with three extra	1,098,240	1:1.37
HIGH CARD In a hand with no winning combination of cards, the highest card	1,302,540	1:1

the table beats all hands below it. For example, even the lowest straight (2, 3, 4, 5, 6) will beat the highest three of a kind (Ace, Ace, Ace, King, Queen). In many games, Aces can be both the highest and lowest card, at the player's discretion.

If two players have the same type of hand, the one who has the higher cards wins the hand. For example, a player with a 9, 9, 9, Jack, 2 (three 9s) beats a player with a 6, 6, 6, Ace, Queen (three 6s). Extra cards, such as the Ace, Queen, Jack and 2 in this example, only matter when two players have identical winning combinations. For example, a player with a 9, 9, 5, 5, King (two pair, with a King) would beat a player with a 9, 9, 5, 5, Queen (two pair, with a Queen).

Low-Hand Poker. The rules for this game are identical to poker, except for an interesting 180-degree switch. In low-hand poker, the player with the lowest—not the highest—hand wins. The lowest hand possible is an Ace, 2, 3, 4, 6—known as a "perfect low." The next best low is Ace, 2, 3, 5, 6. In this game, it is common to see players discarding pairs of cards to rid themselves of a beastly hand.

High-Low Poker. Two players split the pot—the one with the highest hand and the one with

SPORTS

the lowest hand. If all but one player folds, then the entire pot goes to the winner.

Five-card Stud. Unlike draw, five-card stud begins by dealing only two cards to each player. One of these cards is placed facedown and one faceup, in plain view of all players. Each player is allowed to look at his or her facedown card, after which a round of betting ensues. Betting starts with the player showing the highest card. After this round, another card is placed faceup for each player. Now each player has two cards showing and one hidden card. Another round of betting follows. This pattern continues until each player has five cards. At any time during the game, a player can fold, and the person with the highest hand at the end wins.

Seven-card Stud. This lively and often high-stakes game is played much like five-card stud. But the game begins by dealing three cards to each player—two are facedown and one is faceup. Rounds of betting are interspersed with getting additional faceup cards until each player has two facedown and four faceup cards. A final card is then dealt facedown, and the final round of betting takes place.

Players can use any of their seven cards to make their best five-card hand. The catch is that the odds are thrown haywire. Having seven cards makes it easier to achieve good hands. It is common to see full houses, straights and flushes.

Baseball. This variation on seven-card stud makes chances of getting a high hand fairly good. The game has wild cards, which can represent any other card in the deck at the player's discretion. All 3s and 9s—the number of strikes and innings in baseball—are wild. But they come with a price: players must either purchase 3s and 9s at a predetermined price if they are dealt them faceup, or they must fold the hand. If a player is

dealt a 4 faceup (the number of balls in baseball), the player is immediately dealt another card facedown.

The wild-card feature in this game and the possibility of having more than seven cards if a 4 is dealt make it common for a player to get the absurd "five of a kind." For example, a hand of 5, 5, 5, 3, 9, would be five 5s. Five of a kind is the highest hand possible, beating a royal flush.

Texas Hold 'em. A popular form of poker these days, also called simply hold 'em, it is played on television tournaments and in card rooms across the country. Players make their best five-card poker hands using seven cards: two cards from the dealer and five "community" cards, which are available to all players.

Betting varies; sometimes antes are used, sometimes not. Most games start with the player (or two players) to the left of the dealer putting a predetermined amount of money into the pot before the cards are dealt. That is called "posting the blinds" and ensures that there is an initial amount to get the game started. Each player is dealt two cards, facedown. These are the "hole" or "pocket" cards. After a round of betting, the dealer discards the top card of the deck, or "burn" card, in case a player accidentally saw it.

The dealer then flips the next three cards faceup. These are called the "flop," community cards that everyone can use in combination with their two hole cards to form their poker hand. At this point, another round of betting starts. During all the betting rounds, players can check, call, raise or fold when it's their turn to bet.

After the betting round, the dealer burns another card and flips one more faceup on the table. This is called the "turn" card. Following this pattern, the dealer will eventually place five community cards on the table. Players can use any of the community cards and their own two hole cards to form their best possible five-card poker hand. After the fourth and final round of betting, the "showdown" occurs when all remaining players reveal their hands. The player with the best hand wins.

Omaha. Similar to Texas hold 'em, except that players are dealt four personal, or hole, cards to start instead of two. Omaha's popularity is partly due to the greater options it gives players. Players form their best possible hands from nine available cards—four hole cards and five flop cards, or community cards. For each five-card hand, a player must use two hole cards and three community cards. Betting is the same as in hold 'em. As in most poker games, at the showdown, remaining players show their hands; the best hand wins the pot. Omaha is often played hi-lo, meaning the player with the highest hand splits the pot with the player holding the lowest hand.

Bridge, Blackjack and More
Rules for playing some classic card games

Poker may be the rage, but some card games call for more than your luck of the draw. Take bridge, for example. "It is an elegant game, full of strategy and tactics. It's part science, part math, part logic, part reason," says Sharon Osberg, a two-time World Champion bridge player. But as a game played with partners, a huge component of bridge is also very human. It's the combination of those elements, she believes, that sets it apart from many board and card games, making bridge cerebral, creative, unpredictable—and hard to master.

If bridge gets the best of you, try pinochle, blackjack, gin rummy, spades or the quintessential time-passer, solitaire. Here are the basic rules for each.

THE BASICS OF BRIDGE

It may lack the flash of poker, but social bridge maintains a loyal and dedicated, if aging, following. The game's origins date back at least to the early 16th century Brits, who played a similar game called whist. But contract bridge, the version commonly played in the U.S. today, was refined and popularized by Ely Culbertson in the 1920s. Bridge is one of the most orderly card games around today, with clubs, tournaments and championships organized all over the globe.

Contract bridge has a number of variations, but the basic type is called rubber bridge and is played by two teams of two players. Chicago bridge, also known as four-deal bridge, has gained in popularity because of its simplicity and greater predictability. Another type, duplicate bridge, is typically played in clubs and tournaments; it requires at least eight players and calls for different sets of players to play the same deals, thereby decreasing the luck factor.

The object of all, however, remains the same: to win as many tricks, or rounds, as possible for the team. The following rules apply to rubber bridge.

Four players sit at a square table. One team member, called North, faces his or her partner, South. Team member East faces partner West. The 52-card deck (minus the jokers) is shuffled, and cards are dealt clockwise and facedown to each player. Cards in each suit rank in descending order from Ace, King, Queen, Jack, 10, 9, 8, etc. to 2, which is the lowest.

Bridge is less about card play, though, and more about bidding, and in the opening part of the game, an auction is held. Each player makes a bid, that is, announces a target number of tricks they expect to win above six. At the same time, the player declares a trump (high-ranking suit) or no trump. For example, "one, spade" is a commitment to take 6+1, or seven tricks, with spades as the trump suit. A player may choose to increase the bid, or to pass, that is, refrain from bidding. The highest bid becomes the "contract." The goal for the opposing team is to prevent the declarer and his partner from fulfilling the contract.

That's done through a series of 13 tricks, begun by the player to the left of the "declarer." All players must follow suit if possible; the highest suit card, or the highest trump card, wins the trick. When all the tricks are taken, team members combine their scores. Scoring is complicated by factors such as whether the contract was made and by how much. There are also ways to score extra points, such as if a doubled bid was made or if a player receives certain high-ranking cards in the deal. The game ends when one team hits 100 points. The team that wins two out of three games wins a rubber, after which players can choose to change teams and start over.

A PRIMER ON PINOCHLE

This card game was developed in the United States in the mid-19th century and shares many similarities with some old European games, such as the French game bezique. Although not as complex, pinochle is similar to contract bridge—they are both trick games and involve bidding, for example. There are many variations of pinochle, played by two to four players, but the most popular form is the four-player double-deck pinochle described here. The basic object of the game: partners compete, two against two; the first team to score 1,000 points, or some other predetermined total, wins.

Double-deck pinochle is played with an 80-card deck (either two pinochle decks or four regular decks) consisting only of Aces, 10s, Kings, Queens and Jacks in all four suits—spades, hearts, clubs and diamonds. The rankings of the cards descend from Ace to Jack, with the 10 ranking just below the Ace and above the King, as in many European games.

A dealer is chosen randomly for the first hand of the game. For successive hands, dealers rotate clockwise. A double-deck pinochle hand is one set of 20 cards for each player. To start off, the player to the left of the dealer places a card faceup on the table. Other players do the same in rotation. At this point, the person to the left of the dealer begins bidding, which starts at 50. The bid indicates the number of points the player intends to get. Bidding progresses in rotation, skipping anyone who passes. If three people pass, the fourth person has won the bid and chooses the trump suit.

Tricks are won by the highest card played and put aside by the winner to be counted later. The winner of the trick picks the suit that others must follow. If a player does not have the suit, then he must play the predetermined trump suit. One rule in trumping is that if you cannot follow suit and hold a trump card, you must play it, even if you know that the card may be overtaken by a higher trump. (Computer pinochle will stop you from holding on to your trump illegally.)

After all the cards have been played, the cards you take in tricks partly determine the score. There are many methods of scoring tricks, but in the traditional method, an Ace counts as 11 points, ten as 10, King 4, Queen 3 and Jack 2 points. The player who wins the last trick gets an extra 10 points. On top of trick points, players can get points from certain combinations of cards, called melds. These include a King and Queen in the same suit, or marriage; the flush, which is an Ace, 10, King, Queen and Jack in the same suit; groups of cards of the same rank, such as four Aces, four Kings, etc.; and the pinochle—Jacks of diamonds and Queens of spades. The player or team to hit the pre-established number of points wins.

HOW TO PLAY BLACKJACK

The roots of this popular casino game go back to the 1700s, when the French began playing a similar card game they called *vingt-et-un*, or twenty one. The British call their blackjack "pontoon." Whatever the name, the object of the game is to have a hand with a point value that is higher than the dealer's. You must do this without going over 21 points, the rule that gives it the alternate name twenty-one. A player or dealer with 22 points or more has busted and automatically loses the hand. All numbered cards are worth their face value. Picture cards—Jacks, Queens, Kings—are worth 10 points each; Aces are worth either 1 or 11—which the player gets to determine. Suits and colors are disregarded in the game.

Before each deal, players make their bets. Two cards are then dealt to everyone including the dealer, who is dealt one card facedown. A player whose first two cards add up to 21, for example, an Ace and a Queen, has a blackjack and is immediately paid 3-2, unless the dealer also has a blackjack. A tie between a dealer and player is know as a "push," and neither one wins the hand.

After the cards have been dealt, players have several options. Your best move depends both on what you have been dealt and on the dealer's exposed card. A player can:

- **HIT:** Take an additional card.
- **STAND:** Take no additional cards.
- **DOUBLE DOWN:** Double the original bet and take only one additional card.
- **SPLIT:** When a player has been dealt two cards of identical value (e.g., two 9s), he can choose to double the original bet and play the two cards as separate hands.
- **CLAIM INSURANCE:** When a dealer is showing an Ace, players are invited to claim insurance that the next dealer's card will be worth 10 (and thus blackjack). Insurance involves risking half the amount of the original bet and pays off at two to one if the dealer has blackjack.
- **SURRENDER:** Forfeit the hand and lose half of the original bet. This may not be an option in many casinos.

Once all the players are either satisfied with their hands or have busted, the dealer proceeds. Unlike the players, who can make choices, the dealer must proceed according to set rules: drawing

 TIMELY TIPS

Hit or Stand?

Knowing when to take a card in blackjack

✔ **Always hit when you have been dealt 8 or less.** You have no chance of busting, and you need to get closer to 21.

✔ **Always stand on hard hands of 17 or more,** regardless of what the dealer is showing. A hard hand is a hand that either has no Aces or has an Ace or Aces that must be worth only one point because to be worth more would mean a bust (e.g., a 6, a Jack and an Ace). If you hit, odds are you will bust.

✔ **Always hit if you have 16 or less and the dealer's card is a 7, 8, 9, 10 or Ace.** These are the best cards, and it is likely that the dealer will beat you. Although you have a good chance of busting, it is worth the risk of getting closer to 21.

✔ **Always stand on hard hands of 12 or more if the dealer's first card is a 2, 3, 4, 5 or 6.** These are the worst cards, and it is likely that the dealer will bust. But you don't win if you bust first!

✔ **Always stand on soft 19s and 20s.** A soft hand is one that has an Ace that can still be valued at either 1 or 11. Don't risk losing the good hand.

on any hand that is less than 17 and standing on anything 17 or higher.

GIN RUMMY FOR FUN OR MONEY

Gin rummy (or simply "gin") may have been introduced to this country by Chinese immigrants. Today's version was created in Brooklyn in 1909 and had its heyday in the '40s, when glamorous film stars turned it into a nationwide fad.

All 52 cards are used to play gin, but suits are not a factor in the game. Face cards are worth 10 points each; numbered cards are worth their face value; Aces are worth one point each. One common variation is to allow Aces to be either high or low. Usually in this case, Aces are worth 15 points instead of one.

The object is to get rid of your cards by creating sets of three or more that can be "melded." Timing is important—the sets are played differently depending on who melds first. The sets can be formed in two ways:

• SERIES: Three or more cards form a series in sequential order, such as a 4-5-6-7 or a 10-Jack-Queen.

• MATCHING SETS: Cards are in groups of the same value, such as an 8-8-8 or an A-A-A-A.

To play, 10 cards are dealt to two players, and the remainder of the deck is placed in a pile between them. The dealer turns over the top card on the pile and places it faceup as a discard pile. The second player then has the option of taking this card and switching it with one of the cards in his hand or passing and giving the dealer the same option. If the dealer also passes, the second player takes the card on the top of the pile so that momentarily there are 11 cards in his hand, until he discards one. The dealer must then either take the card that has been discarded or the next card from the deck. This continues until a player ends the round of play by

melding his or her cards to reveal the hand.

The first player to meld or "knock" must have fewer than 10 points in hand that are not part of sets. For example, after several rounds of drawing cards, a player might knock with the following hand: 5-5-5 (a set), 8-9-10-J (another set) and A, 2, 2, K (not a set). This player can discard the King and then meld with the set of 5s, the 8 through Jack sequence and five points (A+2+2). The second player must meld his or her cards, too. In doing so, the second player has the added advantage of being able to play cards off the first player's hand. For example, the second player might have the following hand: 2-3-4, 9-9-9, 4, 5, 8, Queen. The 2 through 4 sequence and the 9s would be played in their own right. However, the Queen could also be played off the 8 through Jack sequence of the first player, as could the 5 with the three 5s. This would leave the second player with only 12 unused points (4+8). The player who knocked would earn the difference between the two hands, or seven points (12-5).

If a player knocks and then is beaten (or underscored), the second player gets an additional 25 points for the feat. If a player melds an entire hand, with no extra cards, then he is entitled to say "gin" and gets an extra 25 points. The winner of each round deals the next hand. The game continues until one player reaches 100 points (or any score that the players have agreed to before the game).

HOW TO WIN IN SPADES

Once common only in the United States, this card game has taken off internationally over the past decade, thanks to online card rooms. The game can be played by three people, but four is ideal. The goal is to score as many points as possible by collecting tricks.

To begin, deal the 52-card deck evenly to each of the players. If there are four, each player will have 13 cards. The first round is begun by whoever has the 2 of clubs, which is laid in the center of the table. The player to his or her left then lays down any card of the same suit. The next player does likewise, and the next, until each has put down a card. The highest card wins the trick. Aces are played high in spades; 2 is the lowest.

If a player does not have a card in the suit being played, he or she may trump the trick by playing a spade. But if any of the following players in that round also has no cards in the original suit, he or she may "trump the trump" with a higher spade. (No one may open with a spade until spades have been "broken"—that is, played as a trump.) The winner of the book plays the next card, and the round continues until all 13 books have been played.

Each trick is worth 10 points. After a hand is dealt, players must make a bid on how many tricks they expect to get based on the strength of the cards they were dealt. Because each player in a four-person game has 13 cards, there are 13 possible tricks, or 130 points. A player who found among his or her 13 cards a couple of Kings, some Queens and several spades of any value might make a high bid because those cards are all likely to make a trick. The catch: if a player has a strong hand and so bids, say, 6 tricks, that player must make at least those 6. If not, he or she will instead lose 60 points (–10 points for each trick bid).

On the other hand, if the player makes over the amount bid, say, 7 tricks instead of the 6 bid, he or she receives only a single point for each extra trick—in this case 61 points. Another catch: if a player gets more than 10 of those extra single points, he or she loses 100 points. This is called "sandbagging."

A player who is behind by more than 100 points may bid "blind six," a bid of six made before the cards are even dealt. If the six are made, the player gets 100 points; if not, the player loses 100 points.

Players can play as many hands as they like to a preset score. About 500 points is a good goal for a satisfying evening of spades.

WHEN SOLITAIRE'S THE ONLY GAME IN TOWN

Solitaire has hundreds of variations. The most common in the United States is Klondike, also called Patience, Fascination, Canfield, or simply "Solitaire." To play Klondike, deal one card faceup from a standard deck. Then deal six additional cards facedown to form a row to the right of the first card. Next a card is dealt faceup on top of the second card in the row, and five more cards are dealt face down on top of the remaining piles to the right. This pattern continues until 28 cards have been used and there are seven piles or columns of cards, ranging from one card in the left column, to seven cards in the right column. The remainder of the deck is placed facedown on the table.

Cards can be moved onto the next higher card of a different color to form descending sets that alternate by color. In the example shown, the red 8 of hearts can be placed on top of a black 9 of clubs, allowing the card beneath the 8 to be flipped over and brought into play. If a red 10 were to appear, then the 9 and 8 could be moved together on top of the 10, and the player can flip over more cards.

Aces are removed from the layout when they appear and used as starting points to build ascending sets. These sets follow suit rather than the

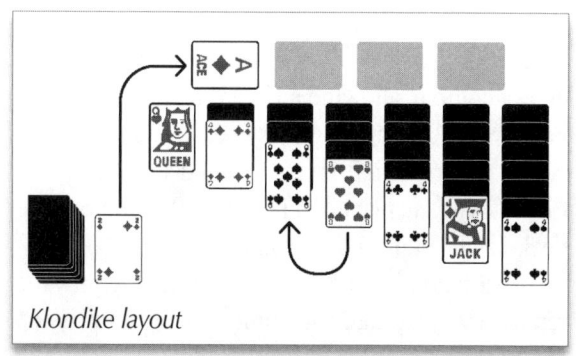

Klondike layout

Seduced By Sudoku

Bet you can't do just one!

As humans we seem to have an innate desire to fill up empty spaces. This might explain part of the appeal of sudoku, the international craze introduced into the U.S. in 2005. The trend started in England in late 2004, when a retired judge from New Zealand persuaded *The Times* of London to print one of the puzzles.

Sudoku is Japanese for "only single numbers allowed." Nearly all sudoku puzzles are computer generated, using programs that understand all the logical solving strategies and so can determine mathematically how hard or easy a puzzle is.

Sudoku's major failing is that if you make a mistake, enter a wrong digit in a square and then base other reasoning on that mistake, it is practically impossible to localize the problem and undo it. You have to erase the entire puzzle and start over.

The number of possible ways to fill a 9-by-9 sudoku grid is calculated at 6,670,903,752,021, 072,936,960—and the number of different ways to give starting digits for solving all these combinations is almost unfathomable. —Will Shortz

Instructions: *Fill the grid with numbers so that every row, every column and every 3-by-3 box contains the digits 1 to 9, without repeating. This puzzle is rated moderate in difficulty. More sudoku puzzles can be found at www.nytimes. com and elsewhere on the Web.*

		1		2		4	8	
			4					
				8			2	3
2	3			7	5	1		
5				8			3	
		2		9			8	7
8	2		6			5		9
	1							4

black-red pattern. In this example, the Ace of diamonds has been set aside. If the two of diamonds appears, it will be placed on top of the Ace, and then the 3 of diamonds, etc. You win if all four Ace piles are built into Ace-through-King sequences.

If one of the seven columns becomes empty because all of its cards have been shifted, any King (and anything stacked on it) can be moved into the empty column, allowing any card under the King to be flipped. After making every possible move on the board, the first card from the remainder of the deck is turned over and played, if possible. When the entire deck has been played, the game is over.

A variation on the game involves flipping the remainder, three cards at a time. If you can play the top card, you can play the next one as well. When you have gone through the pile, turn over the discard pile and go through it again until you call it a loss.

Puzzled by Crosswords?

Help from the puzzlemaster himself

A perfect puzzle may put up lots of resistance. It may, in fact, seem impossible at first. Ideally, though, in the end the solver should triumph and think, "Oh, how clever I am!"

The perfect level of difficulty, of course, differs from person to person. This is why, as editor, I vary the weekday *New York Times* crossword difficulty from easy-medium on Monday, up to what the actor and puzzle aficionado Paul Sorvino calls "the bitch mother of all crosswords" on Saturday. (He said this as a compliment.) The Sunday *Times* puzzle, while larger than its weekday counterpart, averages only Thursday-plus in difficulty.

• Step 1 in solving any crossword is to begin with the answers you're surest of. Fill-in-the-blank clues are easy to spot and often the easiest to solve. Focus on the three-, four- and five-letter words, because the English language has relatively few of these, and they tend to repeat a lot. This is especially so for vowel-heavy words like alee, eel, oreo, etc. Watch for celebrity names (Uma, Erte, Agee) and geographical names (Ada, Ames, Elon).

• Don't be afraid to guess. At the same time, don't be afraid to erase an answer that isn't working out. Don't assume that because you have a few crossing letters that your answer is necessarily correct. And if nothing seems to cross the answer you have filled in, be very wary.

• Let your mind wander. The clue "Present time" might suggest nowadays, but in a different sense it might lead to the answer yuletide. Similarly, "Life sentences" could be obit, "Inside shot" is X-ray and my all-time favorite clue, "It turns into a different story" (15 letters), results in the phrase "spiral stair-case." Be on your toes for multiword answers. One answer that always seems to trip solvers up is r-a-n-d-r, which was clued as "Leave time?"

•A question mark at the end of a clue can mean "This clue is tricky! Be careful!" It can also indicate that the answer only loosely fits the clue. When question marks appear at the ends of the clues for all the long answers, usually the marks are signals for related puns.

• No matter how tricky or misleading the clues, they always follow a fairly strict set of rules. Most important, a clue and its answer are always expressed in the same part of speech and must be interchangeable in a sentence, with the same meaning each way.

• If a crossword answer is not a standard English word, the clue will signal this fact. Thus, a slangy answer will have a slangy clue. The clue for an abbreviated answer will contain the tag "Abbr." or else a word that is not usually abbreviated ("Entrepreneur's deg." = M.B.A.).

• If you get stuck on a puzzle, a time-honored technique is to put it aside and return later. A fresh look at a tough puzzle almost always brings new answers.   —Will Shortz

When You Have a Yen for KenKen

The puzzle game can challenge—and improve—your math skills

KenKen, the numerical logic puzzle from Japan, shares some properties with sudoku. The name means loosely "cleverness squared."

A SAMPLE KEN KEN PUZZLE

KenKen is a registered trademark of Nextoy, LLC. Puzzles © 2009, Gakken Co. Ltd. used under license.

SPORTS

Each is a pure logic challenge in which numbers are filled in on the squares of a grid. Unlike sudoku, though, in which the numbers act solely as symbols (letters or pictures would work as well), KenKen requires arithmetic.

The rules are simple: fill the grid with digits so as not to repeat a digit within any row or column and so the digits within each heavily outlined box (called a cage) go together using the arithmetic operation shown to make the target number indicated.

You can find new KenKen puzzles in the *New York Times* print edition or online at nytimes.com from Monday through Saturday. The first is a four-by-four-square puzzle that increases in difficulty from easy to medium as the week progresses. The second is a six-by-six-square puzzle that goes from medium to hard.

KenKen was invented in 2004 by the Japanese math educator Tetsuya Miyamoto, who founded and teaches at the Miyamoto Math Classroom in Tokyo. Students attend his class on weekends to improve their math and thinking skills. Myamoto says he believes in "the art of teaching without teaching." Given Miyamoto's philosophy of not instructing, one hesitates to offer advice for solving KenKen, but here are some starting tips.

- Fill in any single-square cages immediately.

- Look for cages whose target numbers are unusually high or low for their number of squares. Often these have unique answers. For example, in a six-by-six puzzle, two squares with a sum of 11 must be filled with 5 and 6, in some order. Three squares with a product of 10 must be 1, 2 and 5.

✔ **TIMELY TIPS**

The Thrill of the Cube

✔ **The Rubik's Cube,** the 6-sided cube puzzle, has 43 quintillion possible combinations. Actually, the precise number of cube permutations is 43,252,003,274,489,856,000. That number appears on Rubiks.com, one of several online pit stops for the committed cuber. The cube, once nothing but '80s memorabilia, has found new life on the Internet, in demonstration videos, among online communities of enthusiasts and with commentary on solution methods that have evolved since the cube first appeared stateside in 1980.

✔ **Rubiks.com** is the real one-stop for Rubik's Cube magic. There are other cube sites, but this one has it all: tournament information, videos, a view of the documentary Cubers and an online Rubik's academy. Lively YouTube channels include Michael Gottlieb's Cubing (qqwref2) and Rob's World (RobH0629).

—Virginia Heffernan

- Remember that cages can repeat numbers as long as the numbers do not appear in the same row or column. For example, a three-square L-shaped piece with a sum of 6 could be filled with 1, 2 and 3 or 1, 1 and 4 (with the 4 in the middle square of the L).

- Note that the order of the numbers in cages with subtraction and division doesn't matter.

- Don't forget that each row and column must contain every digit. When you have exhausted arithmetic, use sudoku logic. —Will Shortz

ARTS & ENTERTAINMENT

Movies & TV

The Very Best "Best Movies" List

The finest films of the past 20-plus years, as selected by three eminent authorities

Film fans take endless delight in "Best Picture" lists. To create this one, we relied on the collected wisdom of three respected sources: film critics for the *New York Times*, the Academy of Motion Picture Arts and Sciences, which, of course, presents the annual Academy Awards, and the National Film Registry.

The Registry was established by Congress in 1989 as a way to preserve the best that film has to offer. The Librarian of Congress each year selects up to 25 films for the list, based on nominations from a national panel. Current Congressional librarian James H. Billington says he chooses films that "continue to have historic, cultural, or aesthetic significance." To be eligible for the list, at least 10 years must have passed since the film's theatrical release. As of 2008, 500 films were on the registry; the earliest, *Blacksmith Scene*, dates back to 1893. For a complete list go to the Library of Congress site at www.loc.gov/film.

New York Times critics have generally selected their 10 best films at the end of each year, going back to at least 1931. Full reviews of more than 15,000 films, including those listed here, are at nytimes.com.

Movies are listed under the year when they received the Academy Award or were chosen by the *New York Times*. Registry choices are listed under the year when the film was released. If a film was selected by more than one authority, it is listed under the year of its first award.

THE ULTIMATE BEST MOVIES LIST 1988-2008

KEY

🎞	**National Film Registry selection**
🏆	**Academy Award Best Picture Winner**
𝕿	*NewYork Times* **critics' pick**

NOTES:

1. *Times* critics did not technically designate their choices between 1991 and 1994 as the "10 Best Films of the Year." Rather, during that period they selected films that "impressed" them.

2. From 2003 to 2008, *New York Times* choices reflect the picks of all three of the paper's film critics. Before 2003, the choices were made by the paper's chief movie critic.

3. The National Film Registry selects films only after at least a decade has passed since their release. The Registry typically announces new film choices at the end of December.

1988

- 𝕿 *Au Revoir Les Enfants*
- 🎞 *Drums of Winter*
- 𝕿 *Hotel Terminus: The Life and Times of Klaus Barbie*
- 🏆 1988 *The Last Emperor*
- 𝕿 *Married to the Mob*
- 𝕿 *Mississippi Burning*
- 𝕿 *Patty Hearst*
- 𝕿 *A Taxing Woman*
- 🎞 *The Thin Blue Line*
- 𝕿 *Things Change*
- 🎞 *Tin Toy*
- 𝕿 *Who Framed Roger Rabbit?*
- 𝕿 *Women on the Verge of a Nervous Breakdown*
- 𝕿 *Working Girl*

1989

- 𝕿 *Chocolat*
- 𝕿 *Crimes and Misdemeanors*
- 🎞 𝕿 *Do the Right Thing*
- 𝕿 *Enemies, A Love Story*
- 𝕿 *High Hopes*
- 𝕿 *Little Vera*
- 𝕿 *Mystery Train*
- 🏆 1989 *Rain Man*
- 𝕿 *Roger & Me*
- 🎞 𝕿 *Sex, Lies and Videotape*
- 𝕿 *True Love*
- 🎞 *Water and Power*

1990

- 𝕋 *Akira Kurosawa's Dreams*
- 𝕋 *Alice*
- 𝕋 *Dick Tracy*
- *Driving Miss Daisy*
- 𝕋 *Goodfellas*
- 𝕋 *The Grifters*
- 𝕋 *Metropolitan*
- 𝕋 *Mr. and Mrs. Bridge*
- 𝕋 *My 20th Century*
- 𝕋 *Reversal of Fortune*
- 𝕋 *Sweetie*

1991[1]

- 𝕋 *Barton Fink*
- 𝕋 *Beauty and the Beast*
- *Boyz in the Hood*
- 𝕋 *Cape Fear*
- *Dances with Wolves*
- *Daughters of the Dust*
- 𝕋 *The Fisher King*
- 𝕋 *Life Is Sweet*
- 𝕋 *My Own Private Idaho*
- 𝕋 *Silence of the Lambs*
- 𝕋 *Thelma and Louise*

1992[1]

- 𝕋 *The Crying Game*
- 𝕋 *A Few Good Men*
- 𝕋 *Gas Food Lodging*
- 𝕋 *Howards End*
- 𝕋 *Malcolm X*
- 𝕋 *The Match Factory Girl*
- 𝕋 *One False Move*
- 𝕋 *Reservoir Dogs*
- 𝕋 *Savage Nights*
- *The Silence of the Lambs*
- 𝕋 *The Story of Qiu Ju*
- *Unforgiven*

1993[1]

- 𝕋 *Belle Epoque*
- 𝕋 *Farewell My Concubine*
- *Groundhog Day*
- 𝕋 *The Joy Luck Club*
- 𝕋 *Much Ado About Nothing*
- 𝕋 *The Piano*
- 𝕋 *Remains of the Day*
- 𝕋 *Schindler's List*

1994[1]

- 𝕋 *Crumb*
- 𝕋 *Four Weddings and a Funeral*
- 𝕋 *Hoop Dreams*
- 𝕋 *I Like It Like That*
- 𝕋 *The Madness of King George*
- 𝕋 *Nobody's Fool*
- 𝕋 *Il Postino (The Postman)*
- 𝕋 *Pulp Fiction*
- 𝕋 *Red*
- 𝕋 *Vanya on 42nd Street*

1995[3]

- 𝕋 *Apollo 13*
- 𝕋 *Before the Rain*
- 𝕋 *Dead Man Walking*
- *Forrest Gump*
- 𝕋 *Lamerica*
- 𝕋 *Leaving Las Vegas*
- 𝕋 *Living in Oblivion*
- 𝕋 *Persuasion*
- 𝕋 *To Die For*
- 𝕋 *Toy Story*

1996

- 𝕋 *Breaking the Waves*
- *Braveheart*
- 𝕋 *The Crucible*

- *The English Patient*
- 𝕋 *Fargo*
- 𝕋 *Flirting with Disaster*
- 𝕋 *Jerry Maguire*
- 𝕋 *Lone Star*
- 𝕋 *Looking for Richard*
- 𝕋 *The People vs. Larry Flynt*
- 𝕋 *Secrets and Lies*

1997

- 𝕋 *The Apostle*
- 𝕋 *Boogie Nights*
- 𝕋 *Deconstructing Harry*
- 𝕋 *In the Company of Men*
- 𝕋 *L.A. Confidential*
- 𝕋 *The Pillow Book*
- 𝕋 *Ponette*
- 𝕋 *The Sweet Hereafter*
- 𝕋 *Titanic*
- 𝕋 *Ulee's Gold*

1998

- 𝕋 *The Butcher Boy*
- 𝕋 *The Celebration*
- 𝕋 *The General*
- 𝕋 *Happiness*
- 𝕋 *Henry Fool*
- 𝕋 *Life Is Beautiful*
- 𝕋 *The Opposite of Sex*
- 𝕋 *Saving Private Ryan*
- 𝕋 *Shakespeare in Love*
- 𝕋 *A Simple Plan*
- 𝕋 *The Thin Red Line*

1999

- 𝕋 *All About My Mother*
- 𝕋 *American Movie*
- 𝕋 *Being John Malkovich*

℧ *Boys Don't Cry*

℧ *The Dreamlife of Angels*

℧ *Eyes Wide Shut*

℧ *The Insider*

℧ *The Straight Story*

℧ *The Talented Mr. Ripley*

℧ *Topsy-Turvy*

2000

2000 🏆 *American Beauty*

℧ *Beautiful People*

℧ *Before Night Falls*

℧ *Calle 54*

℧ *Chicken Run*

℧ *The Decalogue 1987*

℧ *Hamlet*

℧ *Traffic*

℧ *Yi Yi: A One and a Two*

℧ *You Can Count on Me*

2001

℧ *A.I.*

℧ *Amores Perros*

2001 🏆 *Gladiator*

℧ *Ghost World*

℧ *The Gleaners and I*

℧ *Gosford Park*

℧ *In the Bedroom*

℧ *The Man Who Wasn't There*

℧ *Monsters, Inc.*

℧ *Sexy Beast*

℧ *Shrek*

2002

℧ *About Schmidt*

℧ *Adaptation*

2002 🏆 *A Beautiful Mind*

℧ *Chicago*

℧ *Far from Heaven*

℧ *The Fast Runner*

℧ *Gangs of New York*

℧ *The Hours*

℧ *The Pianist*

℧ *Spirited Away*

℧ *Talk to Her*

℧ *Y Tu Mamá También*

2003²

℧ *American Splendor*

℧ *Angels in America*

℧ *The Barbarian Invasions*

℧ *Bus 174*

℧ *Capturing the Friedmans*

2003 🏆 *Chicago*

℧ *City of God*

℧ *Elephant*

℧ *Finding Nemo*

℧ *The Fog of War*

℧ *The Good, the Bad, the Ugly*

℧ *House of Sand and Fog*

2004 🏆 ℧ *The Lord of the Rings: The Return of the King*

℧ *Lost in Translation*

℧ *Master and Commander: The Far Side of the World*

℧ *A Mighty Wind*

℧ *Mystic River*

℧ *Pirates of the Caribbean*

℧ *Raising Victor Vargas*

℧ *Spellbound*

℧ *Thirteen*

℧ *The Triplets of Belleville*

℧ *21 Grams*

2004²

℧ *Bad Education*

℧ *Before Sunset*

℧ *The Big Red One: The Restoration*

℧ *Blind Shaft*

℧ *Bright Leaves*

℧ *Collateral*

℧ *The Door in the Floor*

℧ *Eternal Sunshine of the Spotless Mind*

℧ *Fahrenheit 9/11*

℧ *Ghost in the Shell 2: Innocence*

℧ *Goodbye Dragon Inn*

℧ *The Incredibles*

℧ *Kill Bill Vol. 2*

℧ *Kinsey*

℧ *Maria Full of Grace*

2005 🏆 ℧ *Million Dollar Baby*

℧ *Moolaade*

℧ *The Mother*

℧ *Sideways*

℧ *Tarnation*

℧ *Tokyo Godfathers*

℧ *Time of the Wolf*

℧ *Vera Drake*

2005²

℧ *The Aristocrats*

℧ *The Best of Youth*

℧ *Brokeback Mountain*

℧ *Caché*

2006 🏆 *Crash*

℧ *Darwin's Nightmare*

- ℗ *Downfall*
- ℗ *Funny Ha-Ha*
- ℗ *Grizzly Man*
- ℗ *A History of Violence*
- ℗ *The Holy Girl*
- ℗ *Junebug*
- ℗ *Kings and Queens*
- ℗ *Last Days*
- ℗ *Look at Me*
- ℗ *Match Point*
- ℗ *Munich*
- ℗ *Mysterious Skin*
- ℗ *The New World*
- ℗ *Nine Lives*
- ℗ *Princess Raccoon*

- ℗ *Regular Lovers*
- ℗ *Saraband*
- ℗ *The Squid and the Whale*
- ℗ *2046*
- ℗ *Wallace & Gromit: The Curse of the Were-Rabbitt*

2006

- ℗ *Army of Shadows*
- ℗ *Babel*
- ℗ *Borat: The Cultural Learnings of America to Make Benefit for Glorious Nation of Kazakhstan*
- ℗ *Brand Upon the Brain*
- ℗ *Children of Men*

- ℗ *Days of Glory*
- ℗ *The Death of Mr. Lazarescu*
- 2006 ♟ *The Departed*
- ℗ *51 Birch Street*
- ℗ *Heading South*
- ℗ *Inland empire*
- ℗ *L'Enfant*
- ℗ *Letters from Iwo Jima*
- ℗ *Little Children*
- ℗ *Little Miss Sunshine*
- ℗ *Miami Vice*
- ℗ *Our Daily Bread*
- ℗ *Pan's Labyrinth*
- ℗ *A Prairie Home Companion*
- ℗ *The Queen*

● **TIMELY TIPS**

Sites for Movie Fans

✔ **Atom.com** Offers short films, cartoons and animations focused on comedy.

✔ **Hulu.com** A free video service that lets you watch many current TV programs online in an advertiser-friendly atmosphere.

✔ **Internet Movie Database** (us. imdb.com) Bills itself as the earth's biggest movie database. Everything you want to know about films.

✔ **Metacritic.com** Compiles film, music, games and television reviews.

✔ **Moviefone.com, MovieTickets. com, Fandango.com** These three provide movie theater times and advance ticket purchases.

✔ **Moviereviewintelligence.com-** Monitors and scores reviews by critics at over 60 print and broadcast outlets. Charts and graphs track the good, bad and ugly of reviews.

✔ **Movie Review Query Engine** (mrqe.com) Massive online directory of movie reviews; also provides data on current box office hits.

✔ **Reel.com** Stocks more than 85,000 movies for sale and 35,000 for rent. Helps you find movies it thinks you'll like.

✔ **RottenTomatoes.com** Known for its collections of movie reviews, previews and information. Its popular Tomatometer rates movies (from fresh to rotten) based on input from hundreds of critics.

✔ **SundanceChannel.com** Guide for the Sundance TV channel, which shows movies from past festivals and live coverage during the festival.

✔ **Ticketmaster.com** Offers information and tickets for music, theater and sporting events.

✔ **TVGuide.com** Offers a large movie database, celebrity gossip, movie reviews and blogs.

✔ **YouTube.com** Invites you to upload your own videos and share them with family, friends and the world for free.

✔ **Zap2it** (www.tv.zap2it.com) Provides customized TV listings.

ARTS

℡ *Three Times*

℡ *United 93*

℡ *Volver*

2007

℡ *Across the Universe*

℡ *Atonement*

℡ *Away from Her*

℡ *Before the Devil Knows You're Dead*

℡ *The Bourne Ultimatum*

℡ *Colossal Youth*

℡ *The Diving Bell and the Butterfly*

℡ *Don't Want to Sleep Alone*

℡ *Eastern Promises*

℡ *4 Months, 3 Weeks and 2 Days*

℡ *The Host*

℡ *I'm Not There*

℡ *Into Great Silence*

℡ *Into the Wild*

℡ *Joe Strummer: The Future is Unwritten*

℡ *Juno*

℡ *Killer of Sheep*

℡ *The Kingdom*

℡ *Knocked Up*

℡ *Lady Chatterley*

℡ *Live-in Maid*

℡ *The Lives of Others*

℡ *Michael Clayton*

℡ *Monika*

2007 🏆 *No Country for Old Men*

℡ *No End in Sight*

℡ *Paprika*

℡ *Persepolis*

℡ *Ratatouille*

℡ *The Savages*

℡ *Starting Out in the Evening*

℡ *Southland Tales*

℡ *Superbad*

℡ *Sweeney Todd: The Demon Barber of Fleet Street*

℡ *Terror's Advocate*

℡ *There Will Be Blood*

℡ *This is England*

℡ *12:08 East of Bucharest*

℡ *Year of the Dog*

℡ *Zodiac*

2008

℡ *Alexandra*

℡ *Cadillac Records*

℡ *A Christmas Tale*

℡ *The Dark Knight*

℡ *The Edge of Heaven*

℡ *Encounters at the End of the World*

℡ *Flight of the Red Balloon*

℡ *Frozen River*

℡ *Happy-Go-Lucky*

℡ *The Last Mistress*

℡ *Man on Wire*

℡ *Milk*

℡ *Paranoid Park*

℡ *Rachel Getting Married*

℡ *The Secret of the Grain*

℡ *Silent Light*

2009 🏆 *Slumdog Millionaire*

℡ *Still Light*

℡ *Synecdoche, New York*

℡ *Tell No One*

℡ *The Visitor*

℡ *Wall-E*

℡ *Wendy and Lucy*

ℹ **INSIDE INFO**

The True Cost of Entertainment

○ If you accept statistics that the average American's TV is on 8 hours a day, a $100-a-month cable bill is really only a bit more than half a cent for each minute of entertainment.

○ A movie at the local multiplex costs about 7 cents a minute.

○ Live opera works out to about 37 cents a minute for a middling seat in the New York Metropolitan Opera house to hear *Aida*.

○ A big-name rock concert in, again, middling seats is about $1.25 a minute.

—Damon Darlin

The Best Films You Haven't Seen

Four top film buffs pick their favorites

Every year something like 500 new movies make their way to American theaters—sometimes to only a few cities, sometimes only for a short time. Here are some favorites from three *New York Times* critics and from the program director of the Film Society of Lincoln Center in New York City. All these selections are available on DVD.

MANOHLA DARGIS

New York Times co-chief film critic

Army of Shadows. *Jean-Pierre Melville, 1969. 145 MINUTES. FRENCH, WITH ENGLISH SUBTITLES. NO RATING. Lino Ventura, Paul Meurisse, Simone Signoret, Jean-Pierre Cassel.*

A brilliant, soulful moral tale about a handful of men and one tough woman in the French resistance during World War II, from a director who himself fought from the shadows.

Grizzly Man. *Werner Herzog, 2005. 103 MINUTES. R.*

A documentary about the self-styled grizzly expert Timothy Treadwell, who was mauled to death by bears in 2003. A sympathetic if sober exploration of the life and death of a naïf who reinvented himself in the Alaskan wilderness.

Harvard Beats Yale 29-29. *Kevin Rafferty, 2008. 105 MINUTES. NO RATING.*

A documentary about a 1968 tiebreaker between the Harvard and Yale football teams. A preposterously entertaining film, straightforward yet smart.

Inland Empire. *David Lynch, 2006. 179 MINUTES. NO RATING. Laura Dern, Jeremy Irons, Justin Theroux, Grace Zabriskie.*

An alternately hallucinatory, horrifying, hilarious and at times simply inexplicable journey to the dark side from a master surrealist that is as impossible to categorize as it is to shut off.

Killer of Sheep. *Charles Burnett, 1977. 80 MINUTES. NO RATING. Henry Gayle Sanders, Kaycee Moore, Jack Drummond, Angela Burnett.*

A recently restored American masterpiece about a working-class family in a carelessly brutal world, from an under-sung director who locates uncommon beauty and stark poetry amid the ruins.

The New World: The Extended Cut. *Terrence Malick, 2005. 172 MINUTES. PG-13. Colin Farrell, Christopher Plummer, August Schellenberg, Q'orianka Kilcher, Christian Bale.*

This iteration of Terrence Malick's sublimely beautiful tour de force about the founding of Jamestown and the Indian princess called Pocahontas runs 12 blissful minutes longer than the original, theatrical version.

Our Daily Bread. *Nikolaus Geyrhalter, 2006. 92 MINUTES. NO RATING.*

A documentary about industrial food production and its hidden costs. With great formal precision and next to no words, an Austrian director shows everything you always wanted to know (but were too scared to ask) about food production.

Synecdoche, New York. *Charlie Kaufman, 2008. 104 MINUTES. R. Philip Seymour Hoffman, Samantha Morton, Michelle Williams, Catherine Keener, Emily Watson.*

An extravagantly conceptual, morbidly funny story about a playwright who, weighed down by genius, spends decades creating a staged version of his own life, thereby almost missing the real thing.

There Will Be Blood. *Paul Thomas Anderson, 2007. 158 MINUTES. R. Daniel Day-Lewis, Paul Dano, Kevin J. O'Connor, Ciaran Hinds.*

One of the greatest American movies of the past

50 years, with a mesmerizing performance from Daniel Day-Lewis as a petroleum speculator whose soul is swept away by rivers of oil and violence.

Zodiac. *David Fincher, 2007. 158 minutes. R. Jake Gyllenhaal, Mark Ruffalo, Robert Downey Jr., Anthony Edwards.*

A magnificently directed, true-to-life thriller about the cops and journalists who, in the 1960s and '70s, searched for the Zodiac Killer, from a director working at the height of his artistic powers.

A. O. SCOTT

New York Times co-chief film critic

Congorama. *Philippe Falardeau, 2006. 106 minutes. French, with English subtitles. No rating. Olivier Gourmet, Paul Ahmarani, Jean-Pierre Cassel, Claudia Tagbo.*

Never released in American theaters, this madcap postcolonial romp swings from Brussels to Quebec, with Olivier Gourmet, the everyman of

---

 INSIDE INFO

Who Is Oscar, Anyway?

O We've all seen the ebullient Academy Award winners clutching their gold-plated Oscars as they deliver breathless acceptance speeches. But who is Oscar? The still figure of a man holding a sword and standing atop a reel of film was designed by famed production designer Cedric Gibbons (his credits include *A Night at the Opera* and *An American in Paris*). For many years after the 1927 inception of the awards ceremony, the statue was nameless.

O Then, as Hollywood legend goes, a secretary working at the Academy of Motion Picture Arts and Sciences noticed that the statue's face bore a resemblance to her uncle Oscar, and hence the 13 ½-inch–tall figure was christened.

Belgian cinema, as a humble would-be inventor trying to come to terms with an identity crisis as big as the modern world.

Chop Shop. *Ramin Bahrani, 2007. 85 minutes. No rating. Alejandro Polanco, Isamar Gonzales, Carlos Zapata.*

This film takes place in a ragged neighborhood of auto repair shops Queens, in the shadow of Shea Stadium. The story of a brother and sister trying to stick together and find a better life, this tough, artful movie uses nonprofessional actors to service a vision that is unflinchingly realistic and profoundly lyrical.

Darwin's Nightmare. *Hubert Sauper, 2004. 107 minutes. In English, Russian and Swahili, with English subtitles. No rating.*

The feel-bad documentary of the decade. Belgian filmmaker Huber Sauper examines the ecological and human catastrophes unfolding on the shores of Lake Tanzania, where a predatory fish—the Nile Perch—is both a source of income and a metaphor for the ruthlessness of global capitalism.

Funny Ha Ha. *Andrew Bujalski, 2003. 89 minutes. No rating. Kate Dollenmayer, Christian Rudder, Myles Paige, Jennifer L. Schaper.*

A founding film of the low-key, socially networked style of filmmaking known as Mumblecore, this quiet film illuminates the hesitant thought processes of a sweet, uncertain young woman. Not really a romantic comedy, the movie is nonetheless quite funny and, in its unassuming way, genuinely beautiful.

Mysterious Skin. *Gregg Araki, 2004. 99 minutes. No rating. Brady Corbet, Joseph Gordon-Levitt, Michelle Trachtenberg.*

This adaptation of Scott Heim's novel is a bitter, lively, sad and witty coming-of-age story. Two young men grow up in Kansas in the 1980s,

TIMELY TIPS

How to Behave at an Oscar Party

A primer on the tribal customs of Hollywood

Unlike typical cocktail soirees in the rest of America, Oscar parties have rules of behavior that fly in the face of conventional manners. These dos and don'ts are not found in any guidebook to etiquette, but to ignore them is to invite ostracism or at least humiliation.

✔ **If you're someone's date, don't expect to be introduced.** No one cares about spouses, relatives and arm candy at Hollywood parties. You could be a Nobel laureate, but if you're a plus-one during Oscar week, no one will want to meet you. And your significant other probably won't introduce you. Don't take it personally.

✔ **If you haven't worked on one of the nominated films, consider staying home.** Being at an Oscar party without a nomination is like bleeding in an ocean surrounded by sharks. The safest course is to stay out of the water.

✔ **Know when to say when.** Oscar parties are known for their filet mignon and Maine lobster, for rare wines and an endless supply of $100 Champagnes. But don't be fooled. There is little eating at these affairs—how else will you fit into your vintage Jean Dessès gown?—and there is not much drinking. Moderation is the word. Your behavior is always being watched, by the industry and by the press.

✔ **Thou shalt not pitch.** For many, the whole point of attending an Oscar week party is the chance to meet people they can't get on the phone the rest of the year. While subtle pitching is acceptable—as in "Hey, George, can I drop something by next week?"—overt pitching of screenplays and story ideas during an Oscar party is a serious faux pas.

✔ **Give your entourage the night off.** Yes, traveling with an entourage is a standard way of flaunting power in Hollywood. But this is not the weekend to roll up with a dozen friends from your hometown.

✔ **Don't expect to meet your host.** Although everywhere else it is considered good manners to seek out your hosts and thank them, in Hollywood the opposite is true.

✔ **And if you don't get any invitations at all...** For those who live and work in Hollywood and yet for some reason do not show up on any invitation lists, take heart. There is always next year.

—Allison Hope Weiner

ARTS

sharing a terrible childhood experience that shapes their lives in radically different ways.

The Secret of the Grain. *Abdellatif Kechiche, 2007. 151 MINUTES. IN FRENCH AND ARABIC, WITH ENGLISH SUBTITLES. NO RATING. Habib Boufares, Hafsia Herzi, Faridah Benkhetache.*

Filmed in the battered French port of Sete, this film is a warm, noisy family epic; an Algerian patriarch, laid off from the shipyard, decides to revive his fortunes by starting a restaurant. His Quixotic ambition and taciturn demeanor is balanced by the toughness and vivacity of the women in his life, who turn the film from elegy into celebration.

12:08 East of Bucharest. *Corneliu Porumboiu, 2006. 89 MINUTES. IN ROMANIAN, WITH ENGLISH SUBTITLES. NO RATING. Mircea Andreescu, Teo Corban, Ion Sapdaru.*

This deadpan Romanian comedy takes place in a provincial city on the 16th anniversary of the revolution that overthrew the Stalinist dictatorship of Nicolae Ceausescu. A panel of citizens meets to debate whether the revolution really took place or

Where to Watch a Drive-In Movie

As the story goes, the drive-in movie theater was born in 1933 when Richard Hollingshead Jr. experimented with the format by showing movies in his driveway in Riverton, N.J. He hung a bed sheet between two trees and placed a Kodak film projector on the roof of his car.

After a rise in popularity through the 1950s, interest in the drive-in theater steadily waned. But recently a new style of drive-in has cropped up, aided in part by the increased use (and the drop in price) of digital projectors, and it's not too different from Hollingshead's early experiments.

They're called "guerilla drive-ins," or mobile movies, because there is no permanent theater. Organizers screen the movies on warehouse walls and in parking lots. And screenings don't usually take place in the same location twice. Viewers sign up for a service that e-mails them with the time and location a few days ahead of each screening. The movies are generally free, and organizers accept donations to fund the few hundred dollars it takes to secure the location and projector. One web site, MobMov.org, lists more than 240 guerrilla drive-in chapters around the world.

—Richard S. Chang

not; director Porumbiou orchestrates their discussion with sneaky wit and mordant insight.

Tulpan. *Sergey Dvortsevoy, 2008. 100 MINUTES. IN KAZAKH AND RUSSIAN, WITH ENGLISH SUBTITLES. NO RATING. Askhat Kuchinchirekov, Samal Yeslyamova, Ondasyn Besikbasov and Tulepbergen Baisakalov.*

Life on the steppes of Kazakhstan is hard, windswept and short on sensual pleasure, but this Neorealist pocket epic is richly satisfying and full of life. After a stint in the navy, a young man comes to work for his shepherd brother-in-law, who he hopes will help him court the title character, an elusive local beauty.

The World. *Jia Zhangke, 2004. 133 MINUTES. IN MANDARIN, WITH ENGLISH SUBTITLES. NO RATING. Zhao Tao, Chen Taisheng, Jing Jue, Jiang Zhongwei.*

This movie, as encompassing as its title, is also a piercing examination of China in the midst of rapid social and economic change and a poignant urban love story that captures both the heady promise and the desperate loneliness at the heart of China's globalization.

Wristcutters: A Love Story. *Goran Dukic, 2006. 88 MINUTES. R. Patrick Fugit, Shannyn Sossamon, Shea Whigham (Eugene).*

The title may be a little off-putting but this movie shows the kind of irreverent originality that has been all but drained out of more conventional American "independent" movies. In addition to being a love story, it's a road picture, a black comedy, and an allegory whose ultimately hopeful message never feels sentimental or phony.

STEPHEN HOLDEN

New York Times film critic

All About My Mother. *Pedro Almodóvar, 1999. 101 MINUTES. SPANISH, WITH ENGLISH SUBTITLES. NO RATING. Cecilia Roth, Eloy Azorlin, Marisa Paredes.*

The story begins with a mother, Manuela (Roth), who sees her son, Esteban (Azorin), run down by a car on his 17th birthday.

Amores Perros. *Alejandro González Iñárritu, 2000. 153 MINUTES. SPANISH, WITH ENGLISH SUBTITLES. NO RATING. Vanessa Bauche, Gael Garcia Bernal, Humberto Busto.*

A film full of criminal riffraff and violence, it is reminiscent of *Pulp Fiction* in that episodes in separate segments appear out of sequence, only to dovetail at the end.

Beau Travail. *Claire Denis, 1999. 90 MINUTES. FRENCH, WITH ENGLISH SUBTITLES. NO RATING. Grégoire Colin, Denis Lavant, Michel Subor.*

Denis moves Melville's *Billy Budd* to a French Foreign Legion outpost in the East African enclave of Djibouti.

Heading South. *Laurent Cantet. 2005. FRENCH AND ENGLISH, WITH ENGLISH SUBTITLES. 105 MINUTES. No RATING. Charlotte Rampling, Karen Young, Louise Portal, Menothy Cesar, Lys Amroise.*

Feminism, race and the legacy of colonialism converge in the powerful drama of sexual tourism in 1978 Haiti. Rampling plays a vacationing professor at a resort where middle-aged women consort with local beach boys.

L'Humanité. *Bruno Dumont, 1999. 148 MINUTES. FRENCH, WITH ENGLISH SUBTITLES. NO RATING. Emmanuel Schotté, Séverine Caneele, Philippe Tullier.*

Dumont's flawed masterpiece gives the sense that civilization is really a fragile membrane that barely separates us from our most brutal instincts.

Maborosi. *Hirokazu Koreeda, 1995. 118 MINUTES. JAPANESE, WITH ENGLISH SUBTITLES. No RATING. Makiko Esumi, Takashi Naito.*

The meditative film observes the world through the eyes of Yumiko, a young Japanese mother devastated by the possible suicide of her husband. Exquisitely photographed, it distills a mood of profound sadness.

Nine Lives. *Rodrigo Garcia, 2005. 115 MINUTES. R. Glenn Close, Holly Hunter, Sissy Spacek, Robin Wright Penn.*

Set in Los Angeles, these nine interrelated vignettes of women's lives are the cinematic equivalent of a volume of Chekhov short stories.

Close, Hunter, Spacek and Penn contribute indelible performances.

The Sweet Hereafter. *Atom Egoyan, 1997. 112 MINUTES. R. Ian Holm, Sarah Polley, Bruce Greenwood.*

Like Russell Banks' novel, from which it is adapted, Egoyan's film makes a many-faceted moral inquiry into a calamity that has befallen a small Canadian town.

Y Tu Mamá También. *Alfonso Cuarón, 2001. 105 MINUTES. SPANISH, WITH ENGLISH SUBTITLES. No RATING. Maribel Verdú, Gael Garcia Bernal, Diego Luna.*

 INSIDE INFO

Films for a Very Rainy Day
Some of the longest movies ever made

○ **Greed** (1924, approximately 9 hours, 30 minutes) Director Erich von Stroheim's silent masterpiece.

○ **Shoah** (1985, 9 hours, 30 minutes) This may be the greatest film made about the Holocaust.

○ **War and Peace** (1968, 6 hours, 13 minutes) Won the Oscar for Best Foreign Film in 1968.

○ **Little Dorrit** (1988, 6 hours) An overly long film of the Dickens classic.

○ **Sleep** (1963, 6 hours) The film that brought Andy Warhol to prominence.

○ **The Memory of Justice** (1976, 4 hours, 38 minutes) From Marcel Ophuls, an exquisite social commentary about how countries judge their own morality.

○ **The Sorrow and the Pity** (1976, 4 hours, 20 minutes) Ophuls's defining film about the French response during World War II.

○ **Ludwig** (1972, 4 hours, 6 minutes) The film focuses on the Mad King of Bavaria.

ARTS

When her husband is unfaithful, the beautiful, sad-eyed Luisa (Verdú) accepts the invitation of two randy teenagers (Garcia Bernal) and Tenoch (Luna) to accompany them to a Mexican beach.

RICHARD PEÑA

Program director, Film Society of Lincoln Center; director, New York Film Festival

The Chronicle of Anna Magdalena Bach. *Jean-Marie Straub, 1968. 94 MINUTES. GERMAN, WITH ENGLISH SUBTITLES. NO RATING. Gustav Leonhardt, Christiane Lang.*

Straub-Huillet's moving celebration of Bach's music and the ability of art to transform the world.

The Girl with the Suitcase. *Valerio Zurlini, 1961. 111 MINUTES. ITALIAN, WITH ENGLISH SUBTITLES. NO RATING. Claudia Cardinale, Jacques Perrin, Gian Maria Volonté.*

Totally underrated. Zurlini directed Claudia Cardinale to one of her greatest roles, as a young woman who follows her boyfriend to Parma but winds up falling for his younger brother.

The Kingdom. *Lars von Trier and Morton Arnfred, 1994. 260 MINUTES. DANISH, WITH ENGLISH SUBTITLES. NO RATING. Ernst Hugo Jaregard, Ghita Norby, Kristian Rolffes.*

Made for Danish TV, this five-part hospital series is both a hilarious subversion of the TV medical drama and an engaging example of the genre.

Martha. *R.W. Fassbinder, 1974. 116 MINUTES. GERMAN, WITH ENGLISH SUBTITLES. NO RATING. Margit Carstensen, Karlheinz Bohm.*

First screened in the U.S. in 1994, this is perhaps Fassbinder's most outrageous exploration of melodrama, alternately frightening and side-splitting.

The Seventh Victim. *Mark Robson, 1945. 71 MINUTES. NO RATING. Kim Hunter, Tom Conway, Hugh Beaumont.*

The creepiest of the Val Lewton-produced RKO horror films; a grim tale of a woman fallen into the clutches of devil worshippers in Greenwich Village.

Sholay. *Ramesh Sippy, 1975. 204 MINUTES. HINDI, WITH ENGLISH SUBTITLES. NO RATING. Amitabh Bachchan, Dharmendra, Arjun Khan, Jaya Bhaduri.*

If you really want to see Bollywood, you might as well start at the top. A legendary curry western that ran for 5 years in Indian cinemas and made Amitabh Bachchan a megastar.

Starship Troopers. *Paul Verhoeven, 1997. 129 MINUTES. NO RATING. Casper Van Diehn, Denise Richards, Neil Patrick Harris.*

The Dutch-born Verhoeven once mentioned that this is the kind of movie that would have been made had the Nazis won. Probably true, but still an amazing work, exciting and at times terrifying.

The Three Crowns of the Sailor. *Raul Ruiz, 1983. 117 MINUTES. FRENCH, WITH ENGLISH SUBTITLES. NO RATING. Jean-Bernard Guillard, Jean Badin, Lisa Lyon.*

A ragged tale, by Chilean Raul Ruiz, of a sailor wandering the ports of the world in search of getting back to where he started. Pulls out all the visual stops.

When a Woman Ascends the Stairs. *Mikio Naruse, 1960. 111 MINUTES. JAPANESE, WITH ENGLISH SUBTITLES. Hideo Takamine, Tatsuya Nakadai.*

Widely recognized as a master of Japanese film, Naruse gets an exquisite performance from Takamine as a bar hostess who must choose between marriage and owning her own place.

Film Festivals Worth the Journey
Where cinephiles gather around the globe

Not all film festivals are alike, and these days there are more festivals than there are days in the year. Some (like Cannes) are so celebrated that it has become virtually impossible for the public to gain access, and are very much a film professional's festival. Others are far more accessible to the general public and offer just as interesting fare.

Richard Peña is the program director of the Film Society of Lincoln Center and the director of the New York Film Festival (www.filmlinc.com), one of the world's premier events showcasing the newest and most important cinematic works from around the globe. The festival, now over 40 years old, is held every September and October in New York City. Aside from his own festival, we asked Peña to give us his take on the other important and memorable international film festivals worldwide. Here are his picks, and his comments.

Le Festival International du Film *Cannes, France. MAY. www.festival-cannes.fr*

In terms of power and prestige, Cannes is simply in a class of its own. It's actually several simultaneous festivals: the Official Competition, which is the main event; Un Certain Regard, run by the Official Competition for films that for whatever reason weren't invited for the Competition; the Directors' Fortnight, set up after May '68 to feature more "radical" works but now virtually indistinguishable from Un Certain Regard; and the Critics' Week, a small selection of largely first films that often features a few real discoveries.

Venice Film Festival *Venice, Italy. AUGUST/SEPTEMBER. www.labiennale.org*
Berlin International Film Festival
Berlin, Germany. FEBRUARY. www.berlinale.de

The next level down from Cannes would be these two major European competitive festivals. Venice, the world's oldest continuing festival, has in recent years regained some of its lost luster; Berlin, since moving to its new site in the rebuilt Potsdammer Platz, now has excellent screening conditions, but its official competition section is generally a distant third to those of Cannes or Venice. Both Venice and Berlin, like Cannes, have several simultaneous programs going on, and Berlin's International Forum of Young Film, generally known simply as the Forum, always features a remarkable selection of independent, experimental or just offbeat films from all over the world.

Sundance Film Festival *Park City, Utah. JANUARY. www.festival.sundance.org*

Sundance has really become the essential showcase for American independent cinema. Recently, organizers tried to put more emphasis on international films, even creating a competition for their selections, but, in truth, few people go to Sundance to see films from abroad—there are simply far too many new American films to see.

Telluride Film Festival *Telluride, Colorado. LABOR DAY WEEKEND. www.telluridefilmfestival.org*

Held over a long weekend in a former Colorado mining town, the Telluride festival has created in its 30-plus-year history a truly elite reputation. You only discover Telluride's program when you arrive, so people who go there (and it used to be a pretty arduous journey) go on sheer faith that the programmers won't disappoint. They generally don't.

Toronto International Film Festival *Toronto, Canada. SEPTEMBER. www.e.bell.ca/filmfest*

For many people, the most important North American festival is surely Toronto. It is the template for what might be called the "mega-festival": 300 or so films, many of them scooped up from other international festivals, as well as a healthy dose of films having their world premieres. It has a reputation for being impeccably organized and is also one of the few festivals to be both a public and professional event.

Festival Internacional del Nuevo Cine Latinoamericano *Havana, Cuba.* DECEMBER. *www.habanafilmfestival.com*

The Havana Film Festival has survived the demise of the Soviet Union (and the loss of Cuba's annual subsidy) and remains perhaps the key Latin American festival. It's truly an event embraced by the city, and you can see an enormous range of work from all over the Hispanic world.

BAFICI (Festival de Cine Independiente en Buenos Aires) *Argentina.* LATE MARCH-EARLY APRIL. *www.bafici.gov.ar*

Hot on Havana's heels is this excellent festival begun in 1999 that has become the leading showcase for the Argentine New Wave and lots of other fine film movements, Latin American or otherwise. Buenos Aires is an extraordinary film town, and for a 10 a.m. screening you'd better arrive by 9 a.m. Each year brings more foreign guests and a wider range of films.

Pusan International Film Festival
Pusan, South Korea. OCTOBER. *www.piff.org*
Hong Kong International Film Festival
Hong Kong, China. APRIL. *www.hkiff.org.hk*

South Korea's Pusan Film Festival and the Hong Kong International Film Festival are the top Asian festivals. The current explosion in South Korean filmmaking has boosted the importance of Pusan as the place to discover that country's seemingly endless supply of talented new directors. Hong Kong not only offers first-rate Asian and international selections but also each year mounts major retrospectives on Asian cinema each year.

Il Cinema Ritrovato *Bologna, Italy.* JULY. *www.cinetecadibologna.it/en/ritrovato*

Held every July, this wonderful specialized festival brings together many works that have been recently discovered and restored by the world's major film archives. All silent films have first-rate musical accompaniment—ranging from piano to symphony orchestras—but the program can feature everything from Italian '60s experimental films to the comedies of Marion Davies. A film lover's version of paradise.

The Pan-African Film and Television Festival (Fespaco) *Ougadougou, Burkina Faso.* FEBRUARY-MARCH. *www.fespaco.bf*

Held bi-annually in Ouagadougou, Burkina Faso, Fespaco is universally recognized as the main showcase for African film.

The Best 111 Movies for Kids
Guaranteed to last for many a rainy afternoon

Many of these films were made specifically for children, but others reach out to a larger family audience. They were chosen by film critics to give kids up to around age 12 a taste of various eras and genres. Many are better watched with grown-ups on hand to help set the context. For full film reviews, go to nytimes.com or consult *The* New York Times *Essential Library: Children's Movies, A Critic's Guide to the Best Films Available on Video and DVD.* Some additional selections were provided by A.O. Scott, co-chief film critic of the *New York Times.*

- *Abbott and Costello Meet Frankenstein* (1948)
- *The Adventures of Robin Hood* (1938)
- *The African Queen* (1951)
- *Apollo 13* (1995)
- *Babe* (1995)

- *Back to the Future* (1985)
- *The Bad News Bears* (1976)
- *The Bear* (1988)
- *Beauty and the Beast* (1991)
- *Beetlejuice* (1988)
- *Be Kind, Rewind* (2008)
- *Big* (1988)
- *The Black Stallion* (1979)
- *Bound for Glory* (1976)
- *Breaking Away* (1979)
- *Bringing Up Baby* (1938)
- *The Buddy Holly Story* (1978)
- *Butch Cassidy and the Sundance Kid* (1969)
- *Casablanca* (1942)
- *Cat Ballou* (1965)
- *Chariots of Fire* (1981)
- *Chicken Run* (2000)
- *Close Encounters of the Third Kind* (1977)
- *Coraline (2009)*
- *The Day the Earth Stood Still* (1951)
- *Dick Tracy* (1990)
- *Dr. Strangelove* (1964)
- *Duck Soup* (1933)
- *Edward Scissorhands* (1990)
- *Emma* (1996)
- *Enchanted* (2007)
- *E.T. the Extra-Terrestrial* (1982)
- *Fiddler on the Roof* (1971)
- *Field of Dreams* (1989)
- *Fly Away Home* (1996)
- *Gandhi* (1982)
- *The General* (1927)
- *Ghostbusters* (1984)
- *The Gold Rush* (1925)
- *The Great Escape* (1963)
- *Great Expectations* (1946)
- *Groundhog Day* (1993)
- *A Hard Day's Night* (1964)
- *Harry Potter and the Sorcerer's Stone* (2001)
- *High Noon* (1952)
- *Holes (2003)*

- *The Incredibles* (2004)
- *The Iron Giant* (1999)
- *It Happened One Night* (1934)
- *James and the Giant Peach* (1996)
- *Jurassic Park* (1993)
- *Kiki's Delivery Service* (1989)
- *The King and I* (1956)
- *King Kong* (1933)
- *Lawrence of Arabia* (1962)
- *A League of Their Own* (1992)
- *Lilo & Stitch* (2002)
- *The Lion King* (1994)
- *Little Fugitive* (1953)
- *Little Man Tate* (1991)
- *The Little Mermaid* (1989)
- *A Little Princess* (1995)
- *Little Women* (1994)
- *The Longest Day* (1962)
- *The Lord of the Rings: The Fellowship of the Ring* (2001)
- *Lost Horizon* (1937)
- *The Magnificent Seven* (1960)
- *Mary Poppins* (1964)
- *Monsters, Inc.* (2001)
- *Mr. Smith Goes to Washington* (1939)
- *Mrs. Doubtfire* (1993)
- *The Music Man* (1962)
- *My Fair Lady (*1964)
- *My Neighbor Totoro* (1988)
- *National Velvet* (1944)
- *Never Cry Wolf* (1983)
- *North by Northwest* (1959)
- *Peter Pan* (1953)
- *Porco Rosso* (1992)
- *Pinocchio* (1940)
- *The Princess Bride* (1987)
- *Raiders of the Lost Ark* (1981)
- *Rear Window* (1954)
- *The Red Balloon* (1956)
- *Rocky* (1976)
- *The Rookie* (2002)

- *The Secret Garden* (1993)
- *The Secret of Roan Inish* (1994)
- *Shane* (1953)
- *Shrek* (2001)
- *Singin' in the Rain* (1952)
- *Snow White and the Seven Dwarfs* (1937)
- *Some Like It Hot* (1959)
- *The Sound of Music* (1965)
- *Spirited Away* (2001)
- *Star Wars* (1977)
- *Steamboat Bill, Jr.* (1928)
- *Sullivan's Travels* (1941)
- *Superman* (1978)
- *Swiss Family Robinson* (1960)
- *The Three Musketeers* and
  The Four Musketeers (1974 and 1975)
- *To Kill a Mockingbird* (1962)
- *Toy Story* and *Toy Story 2* (1995 and 1999)
- *20,000 Leagues Under the Sea* (1954)
- *Walkabout* (1971)
- *Wall•E* (2008)
- *West Side Story* (1961)
- *Who Framed Roger Rabbit* (1988)
- *The Winslow Boy* (1999)
- *The Wizard of Oz* (1939)
- *Yellow Submarine* (1968)

—Peter M. Nichols

The Movie Mom's Favorite Holiday Movies

Family flicks to feast on for 13 different holidays

Nell Minow, also known as the "Movie Mom," reviews theatrical and DVD releases for Beliefnet.com and radio stations across the country. You can also follow her weekly reviews at www.moviemom.com. Here she selects 13 movies suitable for watching with your kids on 13 holidays.

NEW YEAR'S DAY: **Holiday.** You can't start the year off better than with this gem starring Cary Grant and Katherine Hepburn celebrating New Year's Eve at a party that changes their lives. *(10 to adult)*

MARTIN LUTHER KING DAY: **Boycott.** Jeffrey Wright plays Dr. King in this beautifully told story of the Montgomery bus protest that led to the integration of the city's buses. *(10 to adult)*

VALENTINE'S DAY: **Be My Valentine, Charlie Brown** reminds us that early feelings of love can be difficult but that kindness to everyone is very important. *(8 to adult)*

PRESIDENT'S DAY: **Young Mr. Lincoln.** Henry Fonda plays the young lawyer long before he ran for President, mourning his first love and defending his first clients. *(10 to adult)*

EASTER: **The Gospel of John** is a reverent, dignified, and moving story of the life of Jesus based on the Good News Bible. *(8 to adult)*

PASSOVER: **Moses** (voice of Val Kilmer) is "The Prince of Egypt," who is inspired by God to lead the slaves to freedom. *(All ages)*

MEMORIAL DAY: **Band of Brothers.** This miniseries, based on the best seller by Stephen Ambrose, centers on the World War II experiences of E Company ("Easy Company") and one of its officers, Richard Winters (played by Damian Lewis), from basic training through the end of the war. *(Middle school to adult)*

4TH OF JULY: **1776** is a rousing musical about the Declaration of Independence that makes the Founding Fathers vivid, human and interesting characters; so engrossing you almost forget that you already know how it all turned out. *(All ages)*

LABOR DAY: **The Pajama Game.** In this light-hearted musical, labor and management find a way to resolve their differences. *(10 to adult)*

THANKSGIVING: **What's Cooking?** Four families experience the ups and downs of holiday gatherings and strengthen their connections. *(Mature high school to adult)*

CHRISTMAS: **A Christmas Carol.** An ideal family film in any version; my favorite is the British version starring Alistair Sim. *(All ages)*

HANNUKAH: **The Rugrats Hannukah Special** is a delightful animated story about the holiday and its traditions. *(All ages)*

KWANZAA: **The Black Candle: A Kwanzaa Celebration** is a documentary narrated by Maya Angelou that explores the African-American experience. *(8 to adult)*

The Best TV on DVD

Here's the cream of the crop of thousands

From *I Love Lucy* to *Curb Your Enthusiasm*, thousands of television shows are available on DVD. You can find if your favorite shows are being released on DVD by checking Web sites like tvshowsondvd.com or by searching Amazon.com and other sites. Here are some of the best recent releases, as selected by Ginia Bellafante, television critic for the *New York Times*.

Dr. Katz, Professional Therapist: The Complete Series. Cheeky, quiet, consistently wonderful animated series, which appeared on Comedy Central. Its unstable visual style is called Squigglevision. The voices of Ray Romano and other comedians make up the crazy patient list of a quirky shrink played by comedian Jonathan Katz. *(PARAMOUNT HOME VIDEO, 13 DISCS)*

Fortysomething. Before he starred as a dyspectic genius physician on House, Hugh Laurie starred as a dyspectic physician in the thrall of a midlife crisis in this British comedy. He plays Paul Slippery, a man dealing with his wife's possible wandering eye. At work he is mired in bureaucracy, and at home he is tortured by his three sex-obsessed sons. The series is six episodes long. *(ACORN)*

Foyle's War, Set 5. Three separate but related 100-minute films commissioned by the ITV network and revolving around the assignments that land on the desk of Detective Chief Superintendent Christopher Foyle (played just short of ornery by the talented Michael Kitchen) during World War II. Foyle is riveting at every step of his crime solving. Visually, it is exacting in its period details of wartime English countryside. *(ACORN)*

Freaks and Geeks: The Yearbook Edition. This short-lived dramatic comedy concerns the politics of a suburban Detroit high school in the 1980s. This revamped collection of an earlier version comes with two bonus DVDs, supplemental commentary and interviews and a yearbook, as it were, of essays and memorabilia. Sweet and quietly funny. *(SHOUT! FACTORY)*

Johnny Cash Christmas Specials 1976 and 1977. Ingenious for their guest stars—Roy Orbison, Carl Perkins, Jerry Lee Lewis, Billy Graham—and as historical artifacts, these two specials pay homage to the home and hearth life of Johnny and June Carter Cash. *(SHOUT! FACTORY)*

Mad Men, Season 1. Matthew Weiner's series about consumer glorification and marital malfeasance in the New York of the early 1960s. The first 13 episodes make up a season nearly as perfect as any that have come around. *(LIONSGATE)*

The Mod Squad, Season 1, Volume 1. This youth-generation crime-fighting series from the 1960s came from producers Aaron Spelling and Danny Thomas. These 13 episodes honor a certain kind

ARTS

of high style from which some people have never recovered. *(PARAMOUNT HOME VIDEO)*

Northern Exposure: The Complete Series. The premise of this winsome culture-clash series, which ran from 1990 to 1995, pits a neurotic young New York City internist against the eccentric folkways of a small town in rural Alaska. A comedy, a drama, a love story, the show never got too broad or too bizarre. *(UNIVERSAL STUDIOS)*

Prime Suspect 7: The Final Act. The conclusion of Helen Mirren's exceptional turn as the police detective Jane Tennison has her tracking the killer of a teenage girl and battling the death of her father and her own demon, alcohol. This series is essential to your DVD library. *(ACORN)*

State of Play. This political thriller, produced as a mini-series for British television, won multiple awards in its homeland and features the incomparably sardonic Bill Nighy. Here he plays a newspaper editor overseeing the investigation of two murders: the death of a black teenager at gunpoint and the fall of a research assistant on the tracks of the London Underground. Six sublime hours of diversion. *(BBC VIDEO)*

The Sopranos: The Complete Series. Individual seasons of The Sopranos are available, but this set brings together all 86 episodes on 28 discs. Special features: a photo album, CD soundtracks and a filmed dinner with cast members. One of the greatest series television has ever produced. *(HBO VIDEO)*

 TIMELY TIPS

How to Get on a Reality TV Show

It takes patience, perseverance and a dab of quirkiness

The odds odds are stiff. But, if you have perseverance and plenty of free time on your hands, you too can make it onto a reality TV show. Here are some tips on getting a foot in the door and giving the casting staff exactly what they're after.

✔ **The search.** Publications like *Variety* and *Hollywood Reporter* are a good start for finding casting calls and auditions. For specific reality-show leads check online sites such as reality-tv-auditions.com, castingaudition.com, realityTVcastingcall.com, sirlinksalot.net and realityTVlinks.com. Many sites have e-mail services that notify you if a promising lead comes along. If you have a particular show in mind, check the site of the network that airs the show. Some shows advertise on local radio and papers, too, or even on Craigslist.

✔ **The application.** Each show requires you to fill out an extensive application, which is often available on the network Web site. Some also request a 10-minute video tape stating why you would make a good candidate. If you apply and become a reality show finalist, you'll have to undergo personality testing, a medical exam and reference checks. If selected you will be required to sign massive copies of contracts and other legal documents.

✔ **The audition.** Popular audition spots are Chicago, Dallas, Los Angeles, New York, Orlando and Phoenix. Be prepared for long lines and cutthroat competition, especially for the really hot shows. From among the hordes who show up, a limited, often randomly chosen number will receive a wristband or placard allowing them to prove themselves in an audition. Once you get this far, the best advice is to show your individuality, that is, to unleash the quirkiest aspects of your personality. It doesn't hurt to toss around language that is sure to be bleeped on air.

The best candidates, says one casting director, are "open, enigmatic and unpredictable." In the minds of producers, at least, that makes for good TV.

Music

Musical Picks for a Desert Island

Four New York Times *music critics choose their all-time favorites*

With iPods that can hold thousands of songs, the discerning listener, well, doesn't have to be too discerning in responding to the question "What music would you bring along if you were stranded on a desert island?" "Personally," notes Allan Kozinn, a *Times* music critic since 1977, "I think the iPod makes the whole desert island question obsolete." Kozinn's iPod currently holds nearly 9,000, songs and, he adds, "while some come and go, most are there to stay, to be at hand at all times." Nevertheless, we asked Kozinn and three other *Times* music critics—Anthony Tommasini, Jon Pareles and Ben Ratliff—to name their personal enduring favorites. The critics oblige, below, supplying their expert commentary as well.

ANTHONY TOMMASINI

Times chief classical music critic and author of *Virgil Thomson: Composer on the Aisle*

VERDI: *Otello. Herbert von Karajan (conductor), Vienna Philharmonic; with Mario Del Monaco, Renata Tebaldi, Aldo Protti. (*DECCA, TWO CDS*) Falstaff, Georg Solti (conductor), RCA Italiana Opera Orchestra and Chorus; with Geraint Evans, Mirella Freni, Alfredo Kraus, Robert Merrill. (*DECCA, TWO CDS*)*

I cannot imagine life without Verdi's final two operas. There are half a dozen classic recordings of Verdi's psychologically astute and affectingly tragic Otello, but the one I keep coming back to, from 1961, offers the powerhouse tenor Mario Del Monaco in the title role and the incomparable Renata Tebaldi, my idol as an opera-going teenager, singing Desdemona. At nearly 80, Verdi ended his run of bleak, tragic operas with a humane and hilarious comedy, *Falstaff*. Georg Solti conducts this gossamer-like score with zest, clarity and tenderness on his 1963 recording. The cast, headed by Geraint Evans in the title role, is glorious. The young Mirella Freni and Alfredo Kraus as the sweethearts Nannetta and Fenton have never been topped.

WAGNER: *Die Walküre. Georg Solti (conductor), Vienna Philharmonic; with Hans Hotter, Birgit Nilsson, James King, Régine Crespin. (*DECCA, FOUR CDS*)*

If I could only have one Wagner opera, I'd pick *Die Walküre*. The last 30 minutes, when Wotan, the flawed and self-righteous god, reluctantly punishes his headstrong and devoted daughter, Brünnhilde, is the most movingly sad music ever written. Overall, Solti's recording, with the exciting Birgit Nilsson as Brünnhilde and the noble Hans Hotter as Wotan, is the one to have.

BRITTEN: *Peter Grimes. Colin Davis (conductor), orchestra and chorus of the Royal Opera, Covent Garden; with Jon Vickers, Heather Harper. (*PHILIPS, TWO CDS*)*

So let me sneak Jon Vickers, one of my favorite singers, on to my list by bringing along Sir Colin Davis' recording of Peter Grimes, with Vickers in the title role. Vickers taps into the dangerous and self-destructive emotions simmering below the surface of the character. This is a colossal performance.

Sites for Classical Music Fans

✔ **You want to read about classical music?** There are dozens of sites, from ArtsJournal.com, which links to articles in every area of culture, to NewMusicBox.org, which has demonstrated that a serious online music magazine can indeed endure (with, yes, streaming of concerts).

✔ **You want to listen to classical music?** For opera buffs, Operacast.com has a complete list of broadcasts from around the world that you can hear on your computer.

✔ **Want a reference?** Operabase.com unfailingly tells who is singing what where, and the Metropolitan Opera Archives online database (www.metoperafamily.org) is a treasure trove for fans.

✔ **Want to talk about music?** There are message boards for almost every aspect of music. Then there are blogs. Many music critics keep blogs in addition to their paying work (like Alex Ross of the *New Yorker* at TheRestIsNoise.com).

✔ **And there are more and more places where classical music is sold:** subscription sites like eMusic.com (see facing page), the high-fidelity site MusicGiants.com and Rhapsody.com.

—Anne Midgette

SCHUBERT: *Winterreise*. Peter Pears (tenor), Benjamin Britten (piano). (DECCA)

Britten was arguably the greatest all-around musician of the 20th century, not just a towering composer, but a gifted conductor and a very fine pianist. His pianism is exquisite and musically penetrating on a classic recording of Schubert's autumnal song cycle *Winterreise* with Pears, also Britten's lifelong partner.

BACH: *"Goldberg" Variations*. Glenn Gould (piano). (SONY CLASSICAL, TWO CDS WITH BONUS CD)

With lots of time to kill, I think I'd enjoy hearing a great artist in the throes of an obsession, which describes Glenn Gould playing Bach's "Goldberg" Variations. Gould recorded this work twice: first in 1955, at the beginning of his career, and then in 1981, the year before his death at 50. The early version is impetuous and brilliant; the later version is mellower, yet just as brilliant.

STRAVINSKY: *Symphony in Three Movements, Symphony in C, Symphony of Psalms*. Igor Stravinsky (conductor), Columbia Symphony Orchestra, CBC Symphony Orchestra. (SONY CLASSICAL)

Despite their neo-Classical titles, Igor Stravinsky's "Symphony in C" and "Symphony in Three Movements" are as unconventional as his masterpiece for chorus and orchestra, the "Symphony of Psalms." But I'd rather have the composer's own recordings of these amazing and compact works on my island than a boxed set of the Beethoven symphonies, which I know so well I could run them through in my head.

BERG: *Wozzeck*. Karl Böhm (conductor), Orchestra of the German Opera, Berlin; with Dietrich Fischer-Dieskau, Evelyn Lear. (DEUTSCHE GRAMMOPHON, THREE CDS)

For a break from all the tonal music I've listed so far, my choice would be Berg's searingly beautiful opera *Wozzeck*. On his classic recording, Karl Böhm conducts it like an ingenious extension of the Wagner-Brahms heritage. (The set includes Böhm's recording of Berg's *Lulu*).

BACH: *Mass in B Minor*. Philippe Herreweghe (conductor), Collegium Vocale. (HARMONIA MUNDI, TWO CDS)

I would have to have one of the monumental works by Bach, the father of us all. One could argue that the greatest day in music history was the day Bach passed

Best Music Web Sites

Tunes, news and music blogs are just a click away

✔ **Elbows** (elbo.ws) An aggregator, but with a focus on writing and opinion; blog commentary is posted alongside the MP3 links.

✔ **eMusic.com** The smallest of the major download services, eMusic specializes in independent music. More than 5 million tracks in all genres are available, with varying monthly plans.

✔ **iTunes** (apple.com/itunes) It may be online music's 800-pound gorilla—with an 87 percent market share, it has sold more than 6 billion songs—but Apple's download store is also indispensable. It's "Indie Spotlight" section has exclusives galore.

✔ **KEXP.org** The radio station of the Experience Music Project in Seattle, KEXP is one of the most adventurous and influential noncommercial stations in the country. The Web stream of its signal is a one-click piece of cake, in MP3, Windows Media and Real Audio formats.

✔ **MySpace Music** (music.myspace.com) MySpace has become music's dominant social network. A page packed with multimedia is de rigueur for bands from the garage to the stadium level. Most acts stream full tracks or even albums, and links let you buy MP3s from Amazon.com.

✔ **Other Music** (digital.othermusic.com) Like an iTunes for underground music, this download store is just as eclectic and discriminating as the Manhattan record shop it's named after. Get your ambient noise, 1970s German "krautrock" and

Brooklyn lo-fi here; some of it you can't get anywhere else.

✔ **PureVolume** (purevolume.com) This site's selling point has long been that it is the better MySpace, with a sleek black-and-gray design and higher quality audio. But along the way PureVolume also developed a specialty in emo and punk, and it is now a central resource for all loud music played by musicians with asymmetrical haircuts and skinny jeans.

✔ **The Hype Machine** (hypem.com) This MP3 aggregator scours thousands of blogs and links to the music through an addictively simple interface. The offerings include everything from Cat Power to Chaka Khan but tend toward the indie and trendy; a ticker of the most blogged-about bands refreshes every 30 minutes.

—Ben Sisario

ARTS

out the parts for the Mass in B Minor. There are many fine recordings, but the lucid and stirring account by Philippe Herreweghe, the insightful Belgian conductor and chorus master, is revelatory.

MARIA CALLAS: *Puccini and Bellini arias. Maria Callas (soprano), Tullio Serafin (conductor), mostly the Philharmonia Orchestra. (EMI)*

I could not get by without a Callas recording, and my personal choice would be the collection of arias by Puccini and Bellini released in 1978. Callas's volatile, terrifying and, finally,

heartrending account of Turandot's "In Questa Reggia" always moves me.

Now, if I could fudge things and also bring along just one book, the complete plays of Shakespeare in a single volume, between the Bard and my limited trove of recordings I think I'd be O.K.

ALLAN KOZINN
Times classical music critic

MOZART: *Le Nozze di Figaro. René Jacobs (conductor), Concerto Köln; with Patrizia Ciofi, Lorenzo Regazzo, Angelika Kirchschlager,*

Véronique Gens, Simon Keenlyside. (HARMONIA MUNDI)

Comic and lusty but also a deeply moving study in the power of forgiveness, with magnificently turned arias and fantastic orchestral writing, this is the greatest opera ever written. Among the dozens of fine recordings, this vibrantly played, beautifully sung 2003 period instrument performance gets more directly and vividly to the work's heart than many with starrier casts.

PURCELL: *Dido and Aeneas.* *Emmanuelle Haïm (conductor), Le Concert d'Astrée; with Susan Graham, Ian Bostridge. (EMI/VIRGIN VERITAS)*

Magnificently compact as operas go at just under an hour, this great English work comes to life in Haïm's freewheeling edition, which includes added winds and ample vocal ornamentation, to say nothing of Susan Graham's and Ian Bostridge's deftly drawn and deeply felt characterizations.

MENDELSSOHN: *Symphony No. 4 in A (Op. 90) and Overture and Excerpts from A Midsummer Night's Dream.* *Sir Charles Mackerras (conductor), Orchestra of the Age of Englightenment. (EMI/VIRGIN CLASSICS)*

These youthful, spirited works bristle with joyful energy under just about any circumstances, but the extraordinarily transparent sound Sir Charles Mackerras draws from this period instrument ensemble gives them a truly magical aura.

BEETHOVEN: *Symphony No. 9 in D minor (Op. 125).* *George Szell (conductor), Cleveland Orchestra; with Jane Hobson, Donald Bell, Adele Addison, Richard Lewis; Cleveland Orchestra. (SONY ESSENTIAL CLASSICS)*

Since Szell's entire cycle can be had on an inexpensive 5-CD set, there's no real need to make the difficult choice between the Third, Fifth, Seventh and Ninth Symphonies; but if it's to be just one, the Ninth, with its vigorous Scherzo and fantastic choral finale, has to be it. This remarkably brisk 1961 recording is the one I return to the most.

JOHN WILLIAMS, *guitarist,* ***Virtuoso Variations.*** *(CBS MASTERWORKS)*

An extraordinary collection of variation sets—among them, the Bach Chaconne and Batchelor's "Monsieur's Almaine" and the Paganini Caprice No. 24—played by one of the most eloquent guitarists of our time, this thoroughly satisfying and at times invigorating album has never made the transition from LP to CD. No doubt it will someday, but it's a must-have recording.

DOWLAND: *First Booke of Songes* (1597). *Anthony Rooley (director), The Consort of Musicke. (L'OISEAU-LYRE)*

A perpetual sad sack with a substantial list of grievances, but also a supremely lyrical gift, Dowland pioneered the art of writing angst-inspired music three centuries before Mahler made it his trademark. The songs in this collection are deliciously bittersweet, and the performances by Emma Kirkby and company are irresistible.

BACH: *Brandenburg Concertos.* *Il Giardino Armonico. (TELDEC, TWO CDS)*

Bach made this compilation to demonstrate his compositional fluency with instrumental combinations of all kinds. We take that as a given, but, still, this is a remarkable set of works, and Il Giardino Armonico, a young Italian group, plays the six concertos with an explosive energy.

GLASS: *Koyaanisqatsi.* *Western Wind Vocal Ensemble, Philip Glass Ensemble. (NONESUCH)*

In this film score, which plays continuously through Godfrey Reggio's dialogue-free examination of industrial society, Philip Glass made the transition from minimalism to a quasi-Wagnerian Romanticism still driven by the repeating figures and driving rhythms of the minimalist style. It remains some of his most haunting music.

RICHARD THOMPSON: *Across a Crowded Room.* (POLYDOR)

Recorded soon after Thompson split with his wife and one-time duo partner, Linda Thompson, this 1985 collection raises the breakup song to the level of high art. It also features a good deal of Thompson's brilliant, stinging guitar work, for which he is justifiably revered.

THE BEATLES: *Sgt. Pepper's Lonely Hearts Club Band.* (EMI)

Same problem as the Beethoven symphonies—how can you pick just one? Still, this 1967 classic shows the group at its most brilliantly inventive, with lyrics swathed in colorful imagery and instrumental textures that take in everything from sitars and harpsichords, to full orchestra and tape loops. Get the slipcased British pressing: the artwork is better and more complete.

THE JIMI HENDRIX EXPERIENCE: *Electric Ladyland.* (MCA)

This third and last Experience album, released in 1968, shows Hendrix making his way from being a psychedelic guitar god to—well, unfortunately he didn't live long enough for us to see where he was really headed. But here you have the pure fiery virtuosity of "Come On," "House Burning Down" and "Voodoo Chile (Slight Return)" and brilliantly compact productions like "All Along the Watchtower" side by side with daring electronic experiments like "1983... (A Merman I Should Turn to Be)" and "Moon, Turn the Tides."

ROLLING STONES: *Exile on Main Street.* (VIRGIN)

The last in the great run of middle-period Stones albums that started with *Beggar's Banquet, Exile* has everything the Stones do best, from the undisguisedly nasty, horn-driven "Rocks Off" and the manically punchy "Rip This Joint" to the more soulfully bluesy "Tumbling Dice" and

What Jazzes Wynton Marsalis
The master trumpeter's favorite jazz classics

Jazz, with its mix of bracing intellectuality and moving lyricism, has long been known as America's classical music. Few have done more to foster that reputation than trumpeter Wynton Marsalis, who is renowned both for his classical and his jazz performances. Here, he picks his 10 favorite jazz albums by the greats who inspired him.

LOUIS ARMSTRONG	The Hot Fives (any recording)	Columbia
	The Hot Sevens (any recording)	Columbia
COUNT BASIE	The original American Decca recordings	MCA/Decca
ORNETTE COLEMAN	The Shape of Jazz to Come	Rhino/Atlantic
JOHN COLTRANE	Crescent	Impulse
MILES DAVIS	Kind of Blue	Columbia
DUKE ELLINGTON	The Far East Suite	RCA
THELONIOUS MONK	It's Monk's Time	Columbia
JELLY ROLL MORTON	The Pearls	RCA
CHARLIE PARKER	The complete Dial recordings	Style/Stash

Rock and Roll Royalty
Who's listed in the Hall of Fame

The Rock and Roll Hall of Fame (www.rockhall.com) began its yearly induction ceremony in 1986, and got many of the biggest names out of the way pretty quickly. The first year's haul included Ray Charles, Elvis Presley, Chuck Berry, James Brown, Little Richard, Jerry Lee Lewis and Buddy Holly.

Artists become eligible for induction 25 years after the release of their first record. Aside from recognizing star performers, the Hall of Fame also occasionally inducts artists who had a profound early influence on music and "sidemen" who played significant, albeit supporting, roles. Here's the roster.

1986

Chuck Berry
James Brown
Ray Charles
Sam Cooke
Fats Domino
The Everly Brothers
Buddy Holly
Jerry Lee Lewis
Elvis Presley
Little Richard

EARLY INFLUENCES
Robert Johnson
Jimmie Rodgers
Jimmy Yancey

1987

The Coasters
Eddie Cochran
Bo Diddley
Aretha Franklin
Marvin Gaye
Bill Haley
B. B. King

Clyde McPhatter
Ricky Nelson
Roy Orbison
Carl Perkins
Smokey Robinson
Big Joe Turner
Muddy Waters
Jackie Wilson

EARLY INFLUENCES
Louis Jordan
T-Bone Walker
Hank Williams

1988

The Beach Boys
The Beatles
The Drifters
Bob Dylan
The Supremes

EARLY INFLUENCES
Woody Guthrie
Lead Belly
Les Paul

1989

Dion
Otis Redding
The Rolling Stones
The Temptations
Stevie Wonder

EARLY INFLUENCES
The Inkspots
Bessie Smith
The Soul Stirrers

1990

Hank Ballard
Bobby Darin
The Four Seasons
The Four Tops
The Kinks
The Platters
Simon & Garfunkel
The Who

EARLY INFLUENCES
Louis Armstrong
Charlie Christian
Ma Rainey

1991

LaVern Baker
The Byrds
John Lee Hooker
The Impressions
Wilson Pickett
Jimmy Reed
Ike and Tina Turner

EARLY INFLUENCES
Howlin' Wolf

1992

Bobby "Blue" Bland
Booker T. & the M.G.'s
Johnny Cash
The Isley Brothers
The Jimi Hendrix Experience
Sam and Dave
The Yardbirds

EARLY INFLUENCES
Elmore James
Professor Longhair

1993

Ruth Brown
Cream
Creedence Clearwater Revival
The Doors
Frankie Lymon & the Teenagers
Etta James
Van Morrison
Sly and the Family Stone

EARLY INFLUENCES
Dinah Washington

1994

The Animals
The Band
Duane Eddy
The Grateful Dead
Elton John
John Lennon
Bob Marley
Rod Stewart

"Torn and Frayed" and the country-blues tinged "Sweet Virginia" and "Sweet Black Angel," to say nothing of the great Keith Richard's vocal showcase, "Happy."

JON PARELES
Times chief pop music critic

LOUIS ARMSTRONG: *The Complete Hot Five and Hot Seven Recordings.* (COLUMBIA/LEGACY)

In the late 1920s, leading small groups that always sounded as casual as a house party, Louis Amstrong unleashed huge, audacious ideas: about melody and improvisation, ensemble and anarchy, bravado and finesse, pop songs and the blues, the very particular heritage of New Orleans and the future of popular music worldwide

ROBERT JOHNSON: *The Complete Recordings.* (COLUMBIA)

These archetypal blues present a man, his guitar and his world of trouble, where women leave him lonely and the devil won't leave him alone.

EARLY INFLUENCES
Willie Dixon

1995

The Allman Brothers
  Band
Al Green
Janis Joplin
Led Zeppelin
Martha & the
  Vandellas
Neil Young
Frank Zappa

EARLY INFLUENCES
The Orioles

1996

David Bowie
Gladys Knight & the
  Pips
Jefferson Airplane
Little Willie John
Pink Floyd
The Shirelles
The Velvet
  Underground

EARLY INFLUENCES
Pete Seeger

1997

The (Young) Rascals
The Bee Gees
Buffalo Springfield
Crosby, Stills & Nash
The Jackson Five

Joni Mitchell
Parliament-Funkadelic

EARLY INFLUENCES
Mahalia Jackson
Bill Monroe

1998

The Eagles
Fleetwood Mac
The Mamas & the
  Papas
Lloyd Price
Santana
Gene Vincent

EARLY INFLUENCES
Jelly Roll Morton

1999

Billy Joel
Curtis Mayfield
Paul McCartney
Del Shannon
Dusty Springfield
Bruce Springsteen
The Staple Singers

EARLY INFLUENCES
Bob Wills & His
  Texas Playboys
Charles Brown

2000

Eric Clapton
Earth, Wind & Fire
Lovin' Spoonful

The Moonglows
Bonnie Raitt
James Taylor

EARLY INFLUENCES
Nat "King" Cole
Billie Holiday
Sidemen
Hal Blaine
King Curtis
James Jamerson
Scotty Moore
Earl Palmer

2001

Aerosmith
Solomon Burke
The Flamingos
Michael Jackson
Queen
Paul Simon
Steely Dan
Ritchie Valens

SIDEMEN
James Burton
Johnnie Johnson

2002

Isaac Hayes
Brenda Lee
Tom Petty & the
  Heartbreakers
Gene Pitney
Ramones
Talking Heads

SIDEMEN
Chet Atkins

2003

AC/DC
The Clash
Elvis Costello & the
  Attractions
The Police
Righteous Brothers

SIDEMEN
Benny Benjamin
Floyd Cramer
Steve Douglas

2004

Jackson Browne
The Dells
George Harrison
Prince
Bob Seger
Traffic
ZZ Top

2005

Buddy Guy
The O'Jays
The Pretenders
Percy Sledge
U2

2006

Black Sabbath
Blondie
Miles Davis

Lynyrd Skynyrd
Sex Pistols

2007

Grandmaster Flash and
  the Furious Five
Patti Smith
R.E.M.
The Ronettes
Van Halen

2008

John Mellencamp
Leonard Cohen
Madonna
The Dave Clark Five
The Ventures

SIDEMEN
Little Walter

2009

Jeff Beck
Little Anthony & the
  Imperials
Metallica
Run-D.M.C.
Bobby Womack
Early Influences
Wanda Jackson

SIDEMEN
Bill Black
DJ Fontana
Spooner Oldham
—Kelefa Sanneh

CHUCK BERRY: *Gold.* (UNIVERSAL)

In his pioneering mid-1950s singles, Chuck Berry delivered what his label head, Leonard Chess, summed up as "the big beat, cars and young love." But there was even more to it: a succinctly twangy fusion of blues and country and a wisecracking defiance that uses sheer pleasure to bypass authority.

JAMES BROWN: *Star Time.* (POLYDOR, 4 CDS)

This CD set contains an irresistible overabundance of James Brown: the volcanic R&B belter, the social philosopher, and most of all the genius of funk. The clockwork precision of the grooves is both scientific and sweaty: like a sex machine, absolutely.

BOB DYLAN: *Highway 61 Revisited.* (COLUMBIA)

Electric in more ways than one, Bob Dylan corralled the apocalypse and backed it with blues-rock. The album is a masterpiece of arrogance, sneering and taunting, and cackling with the certainty that anything from gossip to the Bible is entirely his to transfigure.

ARETHA FRANKLIN: *30 Greatest Hits.* (ATLANTIC)

Gospel and jazz taught Aretha Franklin's voice to soar so spectacularly that it would take more than man trouble to bring it down.

THE ROLLING STONES: *Let It Bleed.* (ABKCO)

As 1960s hopes crumbled, the Rolling Stones dug in. They faced up to the lusts and weaknesses of humanity, using fine-tuned irony and chiseled guitar riffs, demanding "Gimme Shelter" because they knew there was none.

STEVE REICH: *Music for 18 Musicians.* (ECM)

The shimmering bell tones echo Indonesian gamelan music, the interlocking xylophones and marimbas suggest West Africa, the orchestral expansiveness hints at Europe and the systematic framework of this symphonic-length piece comes from the classically trained, well-traveled American composer Steve Reich.

BOB MARLEY AND THE WAILERS: *Legend.* (ISLAND)

Reggae's sinuous backbeat became the stoic pulse of righteous resistance once Bob Marley began his ascendance as an icon worldwide. The songs merged protest, spirituality and desire in a ganja haze.

PUBLIC ENEMY: *It Takes a Nation of Millions to Hold Us Back.* (DEF JAM)

Urban density approaches critical mass on this milestone of hip-hop. It's a manifesto punctuated by comedy, a historical montage hurled into the present, an intellectual challenge brandished on the dance floor.

U2: *Achtung, Baby.* (ISLAND)

In a long career of earnest, open-hearted rock anthems, with "Achtung Baby" U2 stirred some fun and electronics into songs that gave the Irish band a rejuvenating remix.

✓ **TIMELY TIPS**

How to Get Backstage at a Concert

One route to the backstage door at a big-name concert is to befriend the opening act—the rising stars who often have few fans and who welcome the attention. First, bone up on their music by visiting their Web site, MySpace page, etc. Next, get to the concert early to catch their act. When their set ends and they head for the concert floor to watch the headliner, advises *Wired* magazine, close in on them—"using flattery, and sometimes tobacco, alcohol," whatever it takes, to make an impression. Finally, when they return backstage, offer to help them pack up. Then, says *Wired*, you're in.

TV ON THE RADIO: *Dear Science.* (INTERSCOPE)

Urban anxieties generate nervous energy, which in turn powers complex structures of organic and computerized sounds, which in turn, through some mysterious alchemy, turns into celebration. The songs are 21st-century doo-wop, earthy art-rock and cerebral funk, with enough layers—musical and verbal—to while away a Long Island exile while dreaming of New York City.

BEN RATLIFF

Times jazz and pop music critic

JOAO GILBERTO: *João Gilberto.* (POLYGRAM).

From 1973, known informally as "the white album," this record presumes that you will have headphones on your desert island: you will want to hear every exhalation, every time a finger hits a string. Gilberto invented bossa nova's guitar rhythm.

DUKE ELLINGTON: *The Okeh Ellington.* (SONY LEGACY)

The best early Ellington reminds you of human possibility: its resourcefulness in melody, harmony and rhythm, arrangement, recording-studio technique, soul and humor.

JOHN COLTRANE: *Live at the Village Vanguard.* (*IMPULSE!*)

I have never been sold on the tracks with Eric Dolphy as an added member to Coltrane's quartet—I sometimes find them enervating. But this, his first live album, made at the beginning point of his great quartet, includes "Chasin' the Trane," a 15-minute blues in F with constant fresh improvising.

SARAH VAUGHAN: *Swingin' Easy.* (*MERCURY*)

I wouldn't call it easy: this is one of the fiercest demonstrations of swing in jazz's entire history. What resonance, what musicality: it was recorded when Vaughan was at her most brilliant.

HECTOR LAVOE: *Hector's Gold.* (*FANIA*)

The great romantic-rhythmic singer of salsa, Lavoe, wasn't just a smooth character: his singing always connoted a slight chaos, intimating that life doesn't always add up. The music, produced by Willie Colon, is brash, brilliant and cinematic at times, amounting to one of the defining sounds of New York City in the last 30 years. It's a best-of collection; if you're allergic to such things, try *La Voz.*

JAMES BROWN: *In the Jungle Groove.* (*POLYDOR/UNIVERSAL*)

In the late '60s and early '70s, James Brown had some of the most advanced bands in the history of pop music, continually alternating between mesmerizing, jolting, minimalism, maximalism. Some of these tracks reach such a high level of funk that you can't quite believe it exists.

TITO PUENTE: *The Essential Tito Puente.* (*RCA/LEGACY*)

Mambo makes you feel good to be alive, and Puente's band was one of the genre's best: the rhythms are giant descriptions of graceful motion, and the rhetoric of the solos is entirely based on cutting through the dense curtain of sound. Every time you hear a singer improvising on this anthology of songs recorded between 1949 and 1962—or a brass player or a percussionist for that matter—they're coming fully prepared.

Cecilia Bartoli's Favorite Operas
The Italian diva's top 10 picks

Cecilia Bartoli is one of the most celebrated classical singers performing today. Highly acclaimed for her concert, opera and recital appearances, she is known to an even wider audience through her immensely popular recordings, which have won numerous awards around the world. Here, the Italian mezzo-soprano known for the warmth and expressiveness of her singing, recommends a list of 10 operas for opera novices and opera lovers alike.

She explains, "In trying to compile a list of 10 operas that are my recommendations for seducing people to become opera lovers, I would like to choose only one opera from each of 10 different composers, although each of them has written many other wonderful stage works. They are mentioned here not necessarily in the recommended order for listening."

Mozart's *Le Nozze di Figaro*. *Le Nozze di Figaro* is a wonderful marriage of perfect music and a perfect story. Some people will chide me for not choosing *Don Giovanni* or *The Magic Flute* as his most perfect opera. I say, start with *Nozze* and then listen to *all* of Mozart's operas.

Rossini's *La Cenerentola*. *La Cenerentola* is Rossini's scintillating setting of the Cinderella fairy tale. It also happens to be one of my favorite roles. And if you like the sparkle of *La Ceneren-*

TIMELY TIPS

How to Get Opera Tickets Anywhere

True opera buffs cannot be denied. And these days, they needn't be. Here's how to get tickets at some of the world's leading opera houses.

✔ **VIENNA.** The Vienna Tourist Board, www.vienna.info, includes a listing of concerts and operas, with links to the Web sites of the **State Opera** and the **Volksoper.** To buy tickets directly for either the State Opera or the Volksoper, call (43-1) 513-1513 or go to www. wiener-staatsoper.at or www. volksoper.at.

✔ **MILAN.** The Web site for the **La Scala** opera house in Milan is www.teatroallascala.org

✔ **PARIS.** To find schedules for both **Palais Garnier** and the **Opéra de la Bastille,** go to www. operadeparis.fr.

✔ **LONDON.** The scrappier younger sibling of the Royal Opera House at Covent Garden is the **English National Opera**, dedicated to presenting opera in English, with an emphasis on innovative productions and nurturing British talent. www.eno. org. Royal Opera House at Covent Garden houses both the **Royal Opera** and the **Royal Ballet** and features more of the traditional repertory. www.royalopera.org.

—Ray Cormier and Alan Riding

---

tola, you will find Champagne in such other works as his *Barbiere di Siviglia* or *L'Italiana in Algeri.* Eventually, you will find your way also to his serious operas.

Puccini's La Bohème. Puccini's *La Bohème* is probably the most directly appealing opera. It's about youth, love, and tragedy in the most realistic terms, set to glorious music. And from *La Bohème* one goes so easily to all the other works of this great composer.

Bizet's Carmen. Many consider the adventures of the Spanish gypsy to be the perfect opera. This is a timeless story set to timeless music. One could say that it is the first really realistic opera—a path to what later became verismo in opera.

Mascagni's Cavalleria Rusticana. This opera is considered the most important step into the verismo era in music. In verismo, best translated as "stark reality," there are no gods, no mythical beings, no royalty, no deus ex machina—just everyday people in some very realistic, and often violent, circumstances. If it were not for its emotionally charged music, it might be a play or a movie.

Verdi's Otello. This is a perfect example of an opera being more powerful than its source. Shakespeare's play is weak in that the jealousy motive built on the missing handkerchief is rather unbelievable. Through Verdi's absolutely glorious music, the story becomes not only completely believable but in the end truly heartrending.

Richard Strauss's Elektra. *Elektra* is probably the prime shocker in music, and there will be eyebrows raised by my including it in a 10-most-accessible-operas list. This searing score is built on the Sophocles tragedy, and it is unsparing in its assault on our senses. But our senses have become accustomed to so much violence in entertainment that *Elektra* may be the very subject matter that has an immediate audience appeal.

Handel's Rinaldo. Written in 1711, *Rinaldo* is based on the text of Torquato Tasso's *Liberation of Jerusalem.* Although it demands female and male singers capable of extraordinary bravura singing, its music has an almost "healing" quality. If one opens one's heart and ears to this music, it can work like a tonic against the burdens of daily life. Let us not forget that because of the *Messiah*, Handel is no stranger to most of us.

Pergolesi's *La Serva Padrona*. *La Serva Padrona* was written in 1733, and its success, in so many countries in addition to its native Italy, established it as groundbreaking in the area of comic opera—or opera buffa. The music is inventive, charming and often witty. It is extremely easy on the ears, which is a quality to be cherished.

Vivaldi's *Orlando Furioso*. *Orlando Furioso*, which premiered in 1727, is based on Ariosto's epic poem, which was also the inspiration for the three Handel operas *Orlando*, *Ariodante* and *Alcina*. Like Handel's *Rinaldo*, this is an opera seria—but listen to the differences in composing styles. To my ears, it takes more liberties within the musical boundaries of that era, just as Vivaldi's *The Four Seasons* is looser in concept than Handel's *Water Music* and *Fireworks Music*.

A Famous Tenor's High Notes

Plácido Domingo's most notable recordings, as picked by a Times *critic*

Plácido Domingo's vast discography of significant opera recordings spans nearly 40 years. Here, *Times* chief classical music critic Anthony Tommasini cites a few notable releases, which he says capture Domingo's "artistry in its glory."

Verdi's *Otello*. *National Philharmonic Orchestra; James Levine; Domingo, Scotto, Milnes. (RCA RED SEAL RCD2-2951; TWO CDs)*

If a tenor who has sung over 130 roles can be said to have a defining role, for Domingo it is probably Verdi's *Otello*. His performance combined urgent lyricism with thrilling power, dramatic volatility with pitiable vulnerability. And his first recording, from 1978, conducted by Levine, with the impassioned Renata Scotto as Desdemona and the great Sherrill Milnes as Iago, is a classic.

Verdi's *Otello*. *Metropolitan Opera Orchestra; James Levine; Domingo, Fleming, Morris. (DEUTSCHE GRAMMOPHON DVD B0002107-09)*

To experience Domingo's mature take on the role, there is the DVD from the Metropolitan Opera's production by Elijah Moshinsky, recorded live in 1995. Renée Fleming sings Desdemona, James Morris is Iago and Levine conducts this dynamic and probing performance. Brian Large, the video director, captures Domingo's magnetic portrayal better, I think, than Franco Zeffirelli does in his film version of *Otello*.

Verdi's *Don Carlos*. *Orchestra of the Royal Opera House, Covent Garden; Carlo Maria Giulini; Domingo, Caballé, Verrett, Milnes, Raimondi. (EMI CLASSICS 7 47701 2; THREE CDs)*

The conductor Carlo Maria Giulini's recording of *Don Carlos,* originally released in 1971, is a landmark of opera discography, and Domingo's performance of the title role is incomparable.

Wagner's *Parsifal*. *Metropolitan Opera Orchestra, James Levine; Domingo, Jessye Norman, James Morris, Kurt Moll. (DEUTSCHE GRAMMOPHON 437 501-2; FOUR CDs)*

Halfway through his career, Domingo took a risk, and won over doubters, by plunging into the Wagner repertory. His performance of the title role in *Parsifal* was among his signature achievements, and this recording, from 1991 and 1992, with Levine conducting the Metropolitan Opera Orchestra, is a hallmark of Domingo's discography. With his slightly Latinate voice, Domingo truly makes Parsifal seem like the outsider of Wagner's creation, a naïve young stranger utterly transformed by his encounter with a band of grail knights.

ARTS

Great Dance Works...and Dance Companies

The New York Times *chief dance critic's top picks*

Alastair Macaulay is the chief dance critic for the *New York Times*. Here he lists and describes five of his favorite dance works, as well as his picks of five great dance companies from around the world.

DANCE WORKS

1. *Giselle* is rightly held up as the greatest ballet from the Romantic era of the early 19th century. But it's too seldom held up as the most enduringly successful of all narrative ballets. What starts out as a simple story of forbidden love between an aristocrat in disguise and a beautiful peasant girl turns into a vortex about dance and death. Giselle, broken-hearted and mad, dies at the end of Act One. The ballet's climax occurs in Act Two, when she rises from the grave as a wili, a female spirit doomed to dance men to death. But she rebels against this wili nature as she tries to save her lover from death, even though he dances ardently in the hope that death will reunite them. The ballet is a masterpiece of suspense.

The original production of *Giselle*, with music by Adolphe Adam, occurred in Paris in 1841; but the version we see now was mainly choreographed in St. Petersburg between the 1860s and 1880s by Marius Petipa, the ballet-master who did most to give classical ballet the character it retains to this day. During the 20th century, this Russian version of *Giselle* gradually became a staple item of repertory for most ballet companies.

2. *Serenade*. Choreographer George Balanchine (1904-83) insisted when he founded New York City Ballet in 1948 that it would not dance *Giselle*. Instead, his company would be principally about the new directions in which he, one of the great modernists and classicists at the same time, was

taking it. And yet the first ballet he made on American soil, *Serenade* (to Tchaikovsky's "Serenade for Strings"), has several passages that refer to *Giselle*. *Serenade* contains the Romanticism and classicism of *Giselle*, but it is also a modernist ballet in that it is simply about dancing itself.

As the ballet proceeds, it has suggestions of narrative, including love, fate, death, transcendence and dancing. Balanchine opened the School of American Ballet in 1934 and soon started to create *Serenade*. Over the years he extended and revised it. Today, it is the most infinitely re-watchable of ballets.

3. *La Fille Mal Gardée*. The first version was made in Bordeaux in 1789, the year of the French Revolution. After an era when most ballets had been about gods and heroes, this ballet's story—about love overcoming parental opposition—concentrates on the lives of farming folk. Several versions have been made over the centuries, but the classic one arrived in 1960, when Frederick Ashton took this French scenario, with an 1828 score by Herold, and found that the sweet ebullience of the music and the impish innocence of the story inspired him to make an irresistible comedy, a work in which love, affection and loyalty are threaded together. Ashton was the chief choreographer of Britain's Royal Ballet, and *La Fille,* with its elements of folk dancing and character acting, was recognized as a masterpiece of the British style.

An immensely sophisticated man, Ashton was at his most extraordinary in re-creating innocence. *La Fille* is an idyll: it starts with dancing chickens in a farmyard, ends with everyone dancing out of the farmhouse door into the countryside in joy and in between makes the poetry of love into something intimate and exceptionally spontaneous. It perpetually creates the wonderland of the happy-ever-after.

4. *Esplanade*. Paul Taylor (b. 1930) was a leading dancer with Merce Cunningham, Martha Graham and George Balanchine in the 1950s. His company, with him as its lead dancer, became celebrated in the 1960s. But with *Esplanade*, which he made in 1975, came three breakthroughs. First, he made his first great work without a role for himself, and, in an era when modern dance companies seemed to hinge on the choreographer as dancing protagonist, he proved that he could excel without himself. Second, using music from two Bach violin concertos, (which had already been definitively choreographed by Balanchine in 1941 as *Concerto Barocco* for the New York City Ballet), he made a no less definitive non-ballet setting of famous classical concert-hall music. Third, he made a dance entirely composed of "natural" movement: walking, running, skipping, swirling, sliding, standing still. *Esplanade* has been a classic since its premiere.

Though it brilliantly demonstrates the design and pattern of choreography, it is also about the spontaneity of living: people caught up in a group, in male-female couples, loners, outsiders. The work contains pain as well as the brightest joy. At every performance, audiences gasp at some of its jumps and catches.

5. *Biped.* Merce Cunningham (1919-2009) was eighty when he made this startling cornucopia, the most sensational dance work of the 1990s. He had always been a radical modernist, and he prepared this work according to his most famous principle: music and dance are composed independently of each other, without the dance responding to the music or being made to fit its workings. It was also prepared to his most recent radical method: he devised its dances initially on his computer and then taught them to his company. Computer-generated dance imagery, much of it projected on an immense scale, also became part of the décor.

Cunningham's choreography showed dancers in constant motion. His "computer" style meant that legs, torso and arms often moved in ways that were not organically connected, and yet the flow of imagery in *Biped* was full of drama, suggesting, among much else, astronauts walking in space, Macbeth meeting the weird sisters, the ephemeral brilliance of dragonflies and multiple aspects of death and transcendence.

DANCE COMPANIES

1. New York City Ballet. Founded in 1948 by George Balanchine and Lincoln Kirstein, it swiftly placed ballet in the forefront of modernism. Pure-dance values dancing to music were foremost. Choreography mattered more than star dancers. (To this day, casting is only announced about 2 weeks beforehand.) Costumes and scenery were often pared away to a minimum. As a result, even though it eschewed much of the traditional pre-Balanchine ballet repertory, the company soon acquired the world's most extraordinary range of ballets. Balanchine's creations remain central to the repertory, and the company also remains the leading proponent of the work of Jerome Robbins. The company has also invested extensively in new choreography, and the ballets made since 2000 by Christopher Wheeldon and Alexei Ratmansky are among the most important classical-ballet novelties of the century.

However, there has been controversy since Balanchine's death about whether his dance values are being adequately honored. Debate is fiercest about a wide range of the company's principal dancers, few if any of whom seriously compare with the finest dancers of Balanchine's lifetime.

2. American Ballet Theater. Since its founding in 1940, it has been a haven for American and foreign dance stars. Likewise, the company's repertory has been a mixture of traditional and new, international and American. In its opening decade, the company was also a haven for

ARTS

the creation of new choreography (by Michel Fokine and Leonide Massine, but more lastingly by Antony Tudor, Agnes de Mille and Jerome Robbins). Since then, it has only sporadically been a place for important premieres, but the brilliant crossover choreographer Twyla Tharp has made some of her most remarkable works for this company since 1976; and in 2008 the Russian choreographer Alexei Ratmansky joined as artist in residence. (Whether he is a major asset remains to be seen.)

The company has had many peaks, notably in the 1970s, when Mikhail Baryshnikov, Gelsey Kirkland and Natalia Makarova were regular performers. Today, its best performances, led regularly by dancers such as Herman Cornejo, David Hallberg, Marcelo Gomes and Paloma Herrera, as well as illustrious guest stars, suggest that it is currently enjoying another.

3. The Royal Ballet. Between 1949 (when it was the Sadler's Wells Ballet) and 1976, the Royal Ballet of London was in constant international demand, the only Western company whose box-office appeal matched that of the foremost Russian ballet companies. Between the late 1970s and late 1990s, it went through doldrums, and even today in some ways its level of style does not match its old form or other world-class ballet companies. None of its current productions of the nineteenth-century classics in which it specializes are first-rate.

And yet the Royal today can still be as fine as any other ballet company in the world. In particular, its best ballerinas—Leanne Benjamin, Alina Cojocaru, Sarah Lamb, Marianela Nunez and the more erratic Tamara Rojo—are superbly individual, mature artists. The company as a whole retains the most multi-layered musicality of any ballet company, and its ballets, from Michel Fokine's *The Firebird* and Bronislava Nijinska's *Les Noces*

through to many ballets by the company's two main choreographers, Frederick Ashton and Kenneth MacMillan, are in exceptionally stylish, vivid shape, engrossing as drama and dance alike.

4. Merce Cunningham Dance Company. The death of choreographer Merce Cunningham in 2009 rendered the future of his company, founded in 1953, uncertain. The company has always showcased Cunningham's own choreography, both avant-garde and classical, pure dance arranged as radical theater, with music, design and dance composed independently of each other and often combined for the first time only on the opening night of each new work. Until his death, many saw him as the greatest living artist since Samuel Beckett. The company has also always contained several of the world's most remarkable dancers.

In Cunningham's dance style, legs, torso and arms are presented in novel combinations: though the feet are bare and the legs are often held parallel to each other, the lower body frequently moves with the detailed articulation and brilliance of ballet, while the torso bends, arches and tips in different directions (sideways, too) with the intense rigor of modern dance. Ordinary movement—walking, lying down, even shaking dice—also occurs naturally as part of the mix.

5. Mark Morris Dance Group. Mark Morris was, and occasionally still is, a star dance soloist capable of astonishing intensity, power and variety. But since his earliest days he has also choreographed group works, most of which have not featured him; many show his complex imagination at its most brilliant, and dancers who maintain superlative standards.

Since the 1990s no company in the world has been more utterly in accord with its choreography and its music, which ranges from Monteverdi, Purcell, Bach and Handel to Stravinsky, Barber and

The Very Best Dance DVDs

Here is a list of the favorite dance DVDs of *New York Times* critics Gia Kourlas and Claudia La Rocco, and of former *Times* critics John Rockwell and Jennifer Dunning.

THE RED SHOES. Written, produced and directed by Michael Powell and Emeric Pressburger. (CRITERION COLLECTION)

MANON. Jennifer Penney and Anthony Dowell, with the Royal Ballet. Choreography by Kenneth MacMillan, with the Royal Ballet. (KULTUR)

SWAN LAKE. Choreography by Marius Petipa and Lev Ivanov, with additional choreography by Frederick Ashton and Rudolf Nureyev. With the Royal Ballet Covent Garden. (KULTUR)

CINDERELLA. Antoinette Sibley, Anthony Dowell and the Royal Ballet. Choreography by Frederick Ashton. (KULTUR)   —Gia Kourlas

BALANCHINE. Directed by Merrill Brockway. (KULTUR)

DRACULA: PAGES FROM A VIRGIN'S DIARY. Directed by Guy Maddin, with members of the Royal Winnipeg Ballet. (ZEITGEIST VIDEO)

THE TALES OF BEATRIX POTTER. With dancers from the Royal Ballet and choreography in a cameo by Frederick Ashton. (ANCHOR BAY ENTERTAINMENT)

ETOILES: DANCERS OF THE PARIS OPERA BALLET. Directed by Nils Tavernier. (FIRST RUN FEATURES)

MAYA PLISETSKAYA: DIVA OF DANCE. Various dancers and ballets. (EUROARTS)

ROMEO AND JULIET. The Royal Ballet with Rudolf Nureyev and Margot Fonteyn. Choreography by Kenneth MacMillan. (KULTUR)
— Claudia La Rocco

GISELLE. Carla Fracci, Erik Bruhn, Bruce Marks, Toni Lander; American Ballet Theater, choreographed by David Blair; Deutsche Oper Berlin Orchestra, conducted by John Lanchbery. (DEUTSCHE GRAMMOPHON)

CHOREOGRAPHY BY BALANCHINE. Suzanne Farrell, Peter Martins, Merrill Ashley, Mikhail Baryshnikov, Patricia McBride; New York City Ballet; conducted by Robert Irving. (NONESUCH, TWO CDs)

SPARTACUS. Vladimir Vasiliev, Natalia Bessmertnova, Maris Liepa, Nina Timofeyeva; Bolshoi Ballet, choreography by Yuri Grigorovich, conducted by Algis Zhuratis. (VIDEO ARTISTS INTERNATIONAL)

BARYSHNIKOV DANCES SINATRA. Mikhail Baryshnikov, Elaine Kudo, Deirdre Carberry, Susan Jaffe; American Ballet Theater, choreography by Twyla Tharp, conducted by Kenneth Schermerhorn. (KULTUR)

CINDERELLA. Françoise Jouillie, Dominique Laine, Jayne Plaisted, Danielle Pater, Patrick Azzopardi, Nathalie Delassis, Bernard Cauchard; Lyon National Opera Ballet, choreographed by Maguy Marin, conducted by Yakov Kreisberg. (KULTUR)   —John Rockwell

STARS OF THE RUSSIAN BALLET, a compilation with Maya Plisetskaya, Galina Ulanova, Vakhtang Chabukiani, Natalya Dudinskaya, Nicholas Sergeyev, and others, and the Bolshoi Ballet. (VIDEO ARTISTS INTERNATIONAL)

THE GLORY OF THE KIROV, film clips from 1920 to 1974, including Mikhail Baryshnikov, Rudolf Nureyev, Natalia Makarova and Natalya Dudinskaya. (KULTUR)

THE GLORY OF THE BOLSHOI, film clips from 1913 to 1984, with Vladimir Vasiliev, Galina Ulanova and Irek Mukhamedov. (KULTUR)
— Jennifer Dunning

ARTS

Bob Wills and His Texas Playboys; no company does better at dancing very precisely set choreography with transfiguring spontaneity.

The dancers tend not to have the hothouse look of many dancers; rather, they look ordinary, unrarefied, moved by the spirit of the moment. In Morris dance classics like *New Love Waltzes, L'Allegro, il Penseroso ed il Moderato, Dido and Aeneas* and *Grand Duo,* generations of performers have come and gone, and though beloved individuals are never forgotten, their successors keep the essence of the choreography fresh to an uncanny degree.

The Best Music Festivals
Where the settings are often as spectacular as the (mostly classical) music

John Rockwell, a former music critic for the *New York Times* and the founding director of the Lincoln Center Festival, has been one of the most respected voices in the performing arts world for many years. Here, he shares some of his favorite music festivals in Europe and the United States.

 **TIMELY TIPS**

How to Find Your Favorite Festival
Online resources for music festivals

✔ **Festivalfinder.com** Details on more than 2,500 music festivals across the country and Canada.

✔ **Festivalnet.com** Provides musicians, agents, bands and music fans an extensive database of musical events.

✔ **Festivals.com** Find musical events from alternative to zydeco.

EUROPE

Aldeburgh Festival. *EARLY TO LATE JUNE.* Founded by Benjamin Britten, it offers a repertory of mostly chamber music. www.aldeburgh.co.uk

Aix-en-Provence Festival. *EARLY TO LATE JULY.* This music festival, the most prominent in France, takes place in the historic center of a lovely town not far from the Mediterranean. www.festival-aix.com

Drottningholm Court Theater. *LATE MAY TO EARLY SEPTEMBER.* This pocket-sized theater, the only fully functioning, unimproved Baroque theater in the world, offers charming performances of 18th-century opera on period instruments. During the intermissions, one can walk on the rolling lawns of Sweden's royal palace. www.dtm.se

Edinburgh Festival. *MID-AUGUST TO EARLY SEPTEMBER.* A sprawling, city-wide festival with a bustling fringe. Edinburgh always has interesting offerings. www.eif.co.uk

Glyndebourne Festival Opera. *LATE MAY TO LATE AUGUST.* Interesting in its repertory and productions. Expect to see England's finest in formal wear, but don't worry about stuffiness—the atmosphere is lightened by picnics among contented cows. www.glyndebourne.com

Lucerne Festival. *AUGUST INTO SEPTEMBER.* A classy panoply of symphonic and chamber music. www.e.lucernefestival.ch

Richard Wagner Festival, Bayreuth. *LATE JULY TO LATE AUGUST.* This festival has not been in the finest artistic fettle under the longtime direction of Wolfgang Wagner, but one hopes things will perk up under the joint leadership of his two daughters (two generations, from two wives), Eva and Katharina. In good years and bad, though, the site and theater and history make this an extraordinary experience for anyone who loves Wagner's operas. www.bayreuther-festspiele.de

Risor Chamber Music Festival. *LATE JUNE AND EARLY JULY.* The pianist Leif Ove Andsnes's lively get-together of first-rate musicians in a small Norwegian town. www.kammermusikkfest.no

Rossini Opera Festival. *MID- TO LATE AUGUST.* A relatively recent addition to the list of major festivals. Pesaro, where the composer was born, offers familiar and exotic Rossini with top-flight singers on Italy's Adriatic coast. www. rossinioperafestival.it

Savonlinna Opera Festival. *EARLY TO LATE JULY.* The festival takes place in a brooding medieval castle in the midst of the Finnish lake district. The operas are always very good and often very innovative. Especially striking is the sunlight, which, due to the far-northern latitude, lasts almost until midnight. www.operafestival. fi/en

Salzburg Festival. *LATE JULY TO LATE AUGUST.* Salzburg, birthplace of Mozart, is spiritually, if not chronologically, the mother of all festivals. www.salzburgfestival.at

Schubertiade. *MID-JUNE; AND LATE AUGUST-MID-SEPTEMBER.* Found in the far-western Austrian town of Schwarzenberg in the Vorarlberg Alps, this festival is devoted mostly to Schubert. Nearly every famous lieder singer imaginable appears here annually, along with fine chamber ensembles and solo instrumentalists. If you want a crème de la crème festival, this is the one. www.schubertiade.at

Verbier Festival and Academy. *JULY-AUGUST.* Top-level conductors and instrumentalists mingle with young artists in a spectacular Alpine setting. www.festwochen.at/wf_servlet/Main

The Battle of the Bands

If you want to be heard, South by Southwest is the place

Why would musicians travel halfway across the world to play a 40-minute set through a mediocre sound system for a few dozen people glancing at their cellphones? Because at the annual music event South by Southwest (www.sxsw.com for dates and details) there's a chance that among those people are the right ones: a booking agent, a manager, a band wanting tourmates, a music supervisor for a video game.

What started in 1987 as a cozy showcase for regional and independent music, with 700 people, has turned into the largest music-business convention in the country. More than 10,000 now attend.

Although it includes a little of everything, SXSW has concentrated on rock. Established musicians play to remind listeners that they're still around, and perhaps to gain a little of the mysterious (and laughable) quality known as "indie cred." Past visitors return for victory laps. Bands from abroad, many subsidized by their governments, arrive to test themselves against American audiences and Texas margaritas. At times, SXSW can be like a musical museum—a good one.

—Jon Pareles

Vienna Festival. *MID-MAY TO MID-JUNE.* The festival concentrates on avant-garde innovations but runs concurrently with the gala performances at the Vienna State Opera. www.festwochen.at/wf_servlet/Main

White Nights Festival. *JUNE TO EARLY JULY.* The venerable St. Petersburg festival of opera and symphonic music, now revitalized by the conductor Valery Gergiev. www.ticketsofrussia.ru/white-nights

ARTS

UNITED STATES

Lincoln Center Festival. SECOND WEEK OF JULY TO END OF JULY. The festival showcases rarely performed or new operas, international dance companies, theatrical extravaganzas and non-Western arts. www.lincolncenter.org

New Orleans Jazz and Heritage Fair. END OF APRIL THROUGH FIRST WEEK IN MAY. A wonderful, vital and diverse jambalaya of folk and commercial popular music, a beacon in a beleaguered city. www.nojazzfest.com

The Most Remote Music Festival

Just a stone's throw from Timbuktu, many arrive on gaily decorated camels

Essakane, an obscure desert oasis a half-day's drive beyond Timbuktu, is the site of what's billed as the "most remote music festival in the world." It's a 3-day Afro-pop powwow held by the Tuareg, the traditionally nomadic "blue people" of the Sahara. The Festival au Désert is open to outsiders, including Westerners as well as other tribes.

A predominantly European crowd shows up, along with approximately 6,000 Malians, most of them Tuareg, who arrive on gaily decorated camels. Tradition still rules during the day, but after the sun goes down, the jamboree transforms into an open-air pop concert, complete with a stage, lights and 20-foot-high speaker stacks.

You can fly to Bamako, Mali's capital, and then drive more than 500 miles over unpaved or barely paved roads to Timbuktu. Allow 6 days for the journey. There is no road between Timbuktu and Essakane, just sand. The Festival au Désert (www.festival-au-desert.org), is usually held in January. Best to check the Web site before setting out. —Adam Fisher

Next Wave Festival. OCTOBER TO MID-DECEMBER. A fall festival concentrating on postmodern performance events of all kinds. Held at the Brooklyn Academy of Music, New York. www.bam.org/events/nextwavefestival.aspx

Ojai Music Festival. EARLY TO MID-JUNE. Wonderful performances of challenging contemporary music in a gorgeous southern California setting. www.ojaifestival.org

Ravinia Festival. JUNE TO AUGUST. The summer home of the Chicago Symphony, along with other kinds of music. www.ravinia.org

Santa Fe Opera. EARLY JUNE TO LATE AUGUST. The most diverse, attractive summer opera festival in the United States, partly for the opera and partly for the location. www.santafeopera.org

Spoleto Festival. END OF MAY TO EARLY JUNE. The charming, historic city of Charleston plays host to a festival with a lively and diverse variety of performing arts. www.spoletousa.org

Tanglewood Festival. EARLY JULY TO MID-AUGUST. Summer performances by the Boston Symphony Orchestra and guest artists in an outdoor theater in western Massachusetts. www.tanglewood.org

How to Buy a Piano

Want to play instead of just listen? Here's what to look for before you enter a piano showroom

Buying a piano is a complicated business for the uninitiated, and it's too expensive a purchase to make a mistake. So here's a basic guide on what to consider before buying a piano.

There are two main kinds of pianos, grands and uprights, and a dizzying array of sizes and styles. Steinway has three brands and 29 models—not counting its custom, art case and limited-edition pianos. Samick, a big South Korean company, offers four brands and 91 models and makes full-size digital pianos. Yamaha offers 34 models of acoustic pianos as well as digital pianos, player pianos and pianos compatible with the MIDI standard (for musical instrument digital interface), meaning that they can connect directly to computers, synthesizers and other instruments. And then there is the influx of pianos made in China.

Grand pianos. Grand pianos produce the best sound and keyboard feel but take up too much room for many homes. A grand can be more than 7 feet long, while even baby grands are nearly 5 feet long. And they are costly, an average of about $11,000.

Uprights. The average sale price of uprights is only $3,100, but parents may be wary of spending even that much only to find that their child shows more interest in a new computer. (Technically these pianos, whose soundboards stand upright, are called "verticals," a category that includes spinets, consoles, studios and uprights, though "uprights" is the familiar term.) A premium upright can cost $10,000.

Digital pianos. Full-sized digital pianos tend to be overlooked, probably because they can't quite recreate the feel of an acoustic piano, especially the action of the pedals. But digital pianos start at about $1,500, making them cheaper than acoustic pianos. And digital pianos are easier to move, require no tuning and don't have as many parts that can wear out. They can also easily connect to PCs or to other devices, and many can be programmed to walk a student through a lesson, for example, or to record what is played and then play it back.

Buying a used piano. With a used piano there is risk that it might deteriorate rapidly. Unlike violins, pianos do not improve over time. The strik-

---

✔ **TIMELY TIPS**

Sites for Piano Hunters

These sites—from piano makers, retailers, technicians and enthusiasts—are priceless resources for piano hunters.

✔ **Bluebookofpianos.com** Compiles new and used piano prices.

✔ **Pianoeducation.org/pnobuyng.html** Provides information about piano types and a buying guide.

✔ **Pianonet.com** The National Piano Foundation offers a guide to playing the piano, finding a teacher and more.

✔ **Ptg.org** The Piano Technicians Guild is a portal to learning everything about pianos and piano playing.

✔ *The Piano Book* by piano technician Larry Fine is an annually updated guide to buying and owning a piano. It can help you decide, for example, whether to buy a new or used piano.

—Michael Fitzgerald

---

ing of keys and action of hammers hitting strings means that over a period of decades, components wear out, and reconditioning an older piano can cost hundreds of dollars.

Buying a used piano involves more risk, of course, than buying a new one, but as with used cars, there are ways to make it work. Know what to look out for—a badly cracked soundboard, for instance, produces a jangly sound, like that of a piano in a honky-tonk saloon.

You should hire a licensed piano technician to check out a used piano before you buy. Some people frequent sales at university music schools, figuring that the pianos have at least been well maintained. And they hope for a little luck.

—Michael Fitzgerald

Museums & Books

The Most Modern Museums
Minimalist, elegant and Zen in character

For aficionados of modernism, sites like the Museum of Modern Art (www.moma.org) in New York, which some days can feel as crowded as a shopping mall, or Frank Gehry's titanium-clad Guggenheim in Bilbao, Spain (www.guggenheim-bilbao.es), are must-see places. But they also enhance the appeal of less trafficked spots, such as these classics.

The Louisiana Museum (www.louisiana.dk) in the remote town of Humblebaek, Denmark, on the rocky North Zealand coast, is a pilgrimage destination with a smart collection and light, airy galleries opening onto sublime views of the sea.

The Menil Collection (www.menil.org), in Houston, Tex., founded by John and Dominique de Menil, mixes Byzantine icons and tribal masks with a refined assortment of French modernist and American postwar art. The collection occupies a wood-and-glass shed designed by Renzo Piano; the building itself is a classic of high modernism.

Kunsthaus Bregenz (www.kunsthaus-bregenz.at), in Bregenz, Austria, designed by the Swiss perfectionist Peter Zumthor, is an immaculate glass, steel and concrete cube it lights up like a lamp at night, the model container for changing installations.

The Chinati Foundation (www.chinati.org), a minimalist museum in the remote, tumbleweed-tossed, west Texas town of Marfa, is the cantankerous sculptor Donald Judd's conversion of a disused army base into a shrine to himself and the few artists he admired. Two barrel-vaulted artillery sheds, their walls removed and turned into windows facing Texas scrub receding to the horizon, make twin cathedrals for 100 of Judd's aluminum boxes.

The Dia Art Foundation (www.diabeacon.org). In the same industrial spirit as Marfa, the Dia Art Foundation, in a former Nabisco factory on the Hudson River in Beacon, N.Y., about an hour's drive north of New York City, is a vast, naturally lighted container for big works by minimalists and post-minimalists like Judd, Walter de Maria, Dan Flavin, Agnes Martin, Michael Heizer, Robert Smithson, Richard Serra and Gerhard Richter.

—Michael Kimmelman, chief art critic
of the *New York Times*

Small European Gems
A connoisseur picks some of his favorite smaller museums

One of the greatest pleasures of Europe is the smaller museums formed by individual collectors rather than the intermediaries of the state. They are often idiosyncratic and contain masterpieces in unusual settings, sometimes of great beauty. James Stourton, the deputy chairman of Sotheby's in Europe and author of *Great Smaller Museums of Europe*, shares some of the best.

Galleria Borghese, *Rome, Italy* (www.galleria borghese.it) Among the prelates in 17th-century

TIMELY TIPS

When You Can't Get to the Louvre

These days, more people visit the world's great museums online than in person. While nothing can replace standing just feet away from a famous artwork, some museum Web sites give art-curious surfers enormous access, from scholarly treatises to shopping in their stores. Here are highlights.

✔ **METROPOLITAN MUSEUM OF ART, New York.** *metmuseum.org*

Fifteen million people a year visit the Web site, more than three times the number who venture inside the museum itself. Learn about the permanent collection, trace a timeline of art history (the site's most popular feature) and log on to activities for children, including learning to draw like Van Gogh.

✔ **TATE, London.** *tate.org.uk*

Online visitors can get lost in the Tate's giant Web site as easily as they can visiting the Tate itself. Explore the collections at the Tate's Britain, Modern, Liverpool and St. Ives galleries through links on the left side of the museum's home page.

✔ **LOUVRE, Paris.** *louvre.fr*

There are many virtual halls to explore. For a remarkable lesson on nearly every element of the Mona Lisa, click on the Eye-Openers tab on the home page, and under that, A Closer Look.

✔ **PRADO, Madrid.** *museoprado.mcu.es*

You can take a virtual tour of the Prado's 15 most relevant works by clicking on the Visits link on the home page.

✔ **MUSEUM OF CONTEMPO-RARY ART, Los Angeles.** *moca.org*

To play around with the museum's fascinating digital artworks, click on the Collections link and then go to Digital Gallery.

✔ **RIJKSMUSEUM, Amsterdam.** *rijksmuseum.nl*

Click on Collections for a look at the museum's masterpieces.

✔ **SAN FRANCISCO MUSEUM OF MODERN ART.** *sfmoma.org*

For an overview of museum's collection, click on Explore Modern Art. A noteworthy online store is also here.

✔ **POMPIDOU CENTER, Paris.** *centrepompidou.fr*

From the home page, click on On-Line Resources. There you will find things like art and biographical videos, access to the Pompidou's collection and a Kandinsky research library. Click on the Webcam linkfor live shots of Paris.

—Lia Miller and Carol Vogel

Other Art Sites Worth a Click

✔ **Art on the Net** *(www.art.net)* 450 artists represented; includes links to other art sites.

✔ **National Endowment for the Arts** *(www.arts.endow.gov)* The government agency that supports artists and the arts.

✔ **The Museum of Online Museums** *(www.coudal.com/moom)* Guides you to some of the Web's best museum sites; offers data on collections and exhibits.

✔ **World Wide Arts Resources** *(www.war.com)* News, links to blogs, galleries and more.

Rome who were busy creating the Baroque, none fulfilled his mission more agreeably than Cardinal Scipione Borghese. He created this pleasure pavilion on the Pincio Hill, from 1612 onward, as a home for his collection of antiquities. Today, it houses the cardinal's matchless collection of sculpture by Bernini and paintings by Caravaggio. Upstairs are paintings by Raphael, including *The Deposition,* and Titian's great *Sacred and Profane Love.* Goethe's father called the villa "the most delicious and remarkable place in the whole of Italy."

ARTS

Gulbenkian Museum, *Lisbon, Portugal* (www.museu.gulbenkian.pt) In no other museum in Europe do Eastern and Western art sit so happily together. The Gulbenkian is a museum where Iznik plates, Persian manuscripts, Mughal carpets and French bookbindings seem to have been born out of the same desire to transmute the designs of nature into art.

Calouste Gulbenkian, known as Mr. Five Per Cent, was the greatest oil tycoon of his era. He acquired his treasures with skill and patience from the Hermitage, carrying off masterpieces by Rembrandt, Rubens and Houdon as well as great 18th-century French furniture and silks.

Kröller-Müller, *Otterlo, The Netherlands* (www.kmm.nl) The first surprise of this museum is its location in the middle of an expansive forest known as the Hoge Veluwe, an hour and a half east of Amsterdam, in which a certain Anton Kröller liked to hunt. You are invited (but not obliged) to leave your car and proceed by bicycle into the forest to discover his wife's great museum.

Helene Kröller-Müller started collecting in 1907 and had an extraordinary knack for picking winners. At the center of her collection is Van Gogh—she managed to acquire 92 of his paintings and 187 of his drawings. Don't miss the first—and still the best—permanent sculpture garden in Europe.

Musée Condé, *Chantilly, France* (www.chateau dechantilly.com) The glory and spirit of France are seen nowhere, except Versailles, to greater advantage than at Chantilly. The surroundings are spacious and noble, the racecourse, the stables—the most splendid ever conceived—and the landscape marvellously tamed. In the middle of it

> **Art is never an empty container. Rather, it is a vessel loaded with meaning. There's no longer a general belief that there exists a single canon for art.**
>
> Stephen F. Eisenman,
> professor of art,
> Northwestern University

• • •

all the château sits magnificently on its lake. Enter and you discover the finest small museum in France. The most spectacular treasure is a book, arguably the most beautiful in the world, the *Très Riches Heures du Duc de Berry*, an extraordinary window into the late Middle Ages. Chantilly is an hour from Paris but worth a day.

Oskar Reinhart Collection, *Winterthur, Switzerland* (www.roemerholz. ch) Winterthur had more collectors than any other small town in Europe. The greatest of them was Oskar Reinhart, who created two museums; one was in his old home, the villa Am Römerholz, for his beloved Impressionist collection. This is one of the most attractive collections of 19th-century painting anywhere, strong on Géricault, Delacroix, Courbet and Daumier and with superbly chosen examples of Manet, Renoir, Van Gogh and Cezanne. Reinhart devoted his life to the collection and enjoyed watching groups of visitors milling around while he pretended to be the butler.

Wallace Collection, *London, England* (www. wallacecollection.org) The Wallace Collection is the supreme example of English francophile taste; it remains the greatest collection of French art outside France. The main collector, the fourth Marquess of Hertford, was a recluse who lived in Paris and instructed his agent to outbid everybody at auction. His taste was mostly for the ancien regime, superb commodes, paintings by Watteau and Fragonard, Sèvres and snuff boxes. The Long Gallery is the best of its kind in the world, stuffed with masterpieces by Poussin, Velazquez, Rembrandt and, most famously, Frans Hals' *Laughing Cavalier*.

Finding Architectural Thrills

For the truly discerning, these architectural masterpieces are worth a detour

A century ago, landmarks like the Pantheon, Chartres Cathedral and Venice's St. Mark's Square were mandatory stops for the educated classes. Today, a similar list might include Frank Gehry's Guggenheim Museum in Bilbao, Spain, and Norman Foster's Gherkin in London. But the most thrilling architectural experiences are apt to occur far from the growing hordes of cultural tourists. Three of them, coincidentally, are in Portugal.

Rem Koolhaas' Porto concert hall is as potent an expression of contemporary architectural ideas as you are likely to find. Located in Porto, an industrial city in northern Portugal, its chiseled concrete exterior has the hard beauty of a cut diamond. Inside, it is packed with urban energy, its foyers spiraling up to a rooftop belvedere, which offers a sweeping view of the old city.

A short drive north in Braga, **Eduardo Souto de Moura**'s soccer stadium is a sensitive union of natural and man-made forms. The stadium's concrete stands embrace two sides of the field like gently cupped hands. At one end, the stadium is embedded into the side of an abandoned quarry; at the other, it opens up to a view of distant hills.

In the village of Marco de Canavezes, also in Portugal, **Alvaro Siza**'s Santa Maria Church is striking in its simplicity: an unadorned, U-shaped white form resting atop a granite base. But beneath that humble appearance is a work of remarkable subtlety. In front, the tall forms of the baptistery and bell tower frame a small entry court. In back, a cloister leads into a mortuary chapel a level below. An exterior stair joins the two. The sense of being deeply connected to the cycles of life and death—and the humility with which it is conveyed—makes this the most exquisite church built in half a century.

Enric Miralles' Igualada cemetery on the outskirts of Barcelona is equally moving. Built in the shadow of a decrepit industrial neighborhood, the cemetery is conceived as a carefully drawn-out procession that winds its way down into the earth. The path is flanked on either side by heavy concrete retaining walls, their forms embedded with rows of tombs. The descent becomes a haunting metaphor for the relentless march toward death.

In London, **Sir John Soane**'s museum is a more personal kind of mausoleum. Overlooking a lovely London square, the 19th-century house is packed with architectural bric-a-brac that the neo-Classical architect collected over the years. The rooms' fragmented pediments and mirrored walls are pictures of architectural eccentricity—the legacy of a fertile creative talent trapped in his own mind.

Finally, two of the most inspiring rooms in America may be the "great work room" in **Frank Lloyd Wright**'s 1936 Johnson Wax building in Racine, Wisconsin, and the interior of **Frank Gehry**'s 2004 Walt Disney Concert Hall in Los Angeles. The slender mushroom-shaped columns, translucent ceiling and vertical bands of glass tubing that envelope Wright's room give it the feel of a gigantic fish tank.

Gehry's hall rivals Borromini's Baroque churches in its wonderful play of concave and convex forms. Some visitors have complained about the lack of legroom, but the compactness of the space is part of what makes this an intense social experience—and one of America's greatest public rooms.

—Nicolai Ouroussoff, chief architecture critic of the *New York Times*

ARTS

The 21st Century's Best Books

The century's young, but there's plenty to read

Each year the editors of the *New York Times* select what they regard as the best books of the year—often 10, but in some years fewer. Here are their selections from 2000 to 2008.

In the accompanying boxes you'll find the 📖 NATIONAL BOOK AWARD and ● PULITZER PRIZE winners for the same period. In nonfiction, the N.B.A. honors one book; the Pulitzers choose three—one in history, one in biography and autobiography and one for general nonfiction. In addition, there is an N.B.A. award for Young People's Literature.

2000 FICTION

BEING DEAD *Jim Crace*

Celice and Joseph, both zoologists, are dead in the first paragraph, murdered naked in the midst of sexual fulfillment on a salt dune by the sea. Crace then weaves together three strands of narrative to create a startlingly beautiful vision of life.

BEOWULF: A New Verse Translation *Seamus Heaney.*

Heaney is a Nobel laureate and the most accomplished poet writing in English. In this edition of the translation, Heaney writes an introduction explaining that he decided to give the poem the voice of Northern Irishmen he'd grown up with.

2000

FICTION

● **Interpreter of Maladies,** *Jhumpa Lahiri*

📖 **In America,** *Susan Sontag*

NONFICTION

● GENERAL NONFICTION
Embracing Defeat: Japan in the Wake of World War II, *John W. Dower*

● HISTORY
Freedom From Fear: The American People in Depression and War, 1929-1945, *David M. Kennedy*

📖 **In the Heart of the Sea: The Tragedy of the Whaleship Essex,** *Nathaniel Philbrick*

● BIOGRAPHY
Vera (Mrs. Vladimir Nabokov), *Stacy Schiff*

POETRY

📖 **Blessing the Boats: New and Selected Poems 1988-2000,** *Lucille Clifton*

● **Repair,** *C. K. Williams*

YOUNG PEOPLE'S LITERATURE

📖 **Homeless Bird,** *Gloria Whelan*

GERTRUDE AND CLAUDIUS *John Updike*

She is too loving and, perhaps more dangerously, too lovable, the young woman in John Updike's novel, whose father offers her, against her wishes, to the older warrior king he admires. But she learns to love her husband, and loves her son too uncritically.

THE HUMAN STAIN *Philip Roth*

Coleman Silk, the central character in Philip Roth's novel, may be the most interesting person Roth has ever invented—a black man of such light hue that he decides simply to pass for white, leave his family behind and go into the world as a Jew.

2000 NONFICTION

GENOME: The Autobiography of a Species in 23 Chapters *Matt Ridley*

Ridley's book is a jargon-free excursion of intellectual discovery that will carry any reader along its tour of exciting stories structured to help us understand in everyday terms the revelations about genetic evolution that have come to light in the last few decades.

A HEARTBREAKING WORK OF STAGGERING GENIUS *Dave Eggers*

When Eggers was 21, both of his parents died within 32 days, leaving him the accidental parent of his 8-year-old brother. He sold the family's suburban Chicago home, and the two set out for San

Francisco for a life that he says was a "campaign of distraction" and "magic tricks."

ONE PALESTINE, COMPLETE: Jews and Arabs Under the British Mandate *Tom Segev*

Probably the best overall history of the period when Britain ruled the Holy Land under the League of Nations mandate.

RIMBAUD *Graham Robb*

Arthur Rimbaud stopped writing verse before he was 20, and published only one volume of his work before he died at 37. Robb has produced the best biography of Rimbaud to date.

WAY OUT THERE IN THE BLUE: Reagan, Star Wars and the End of the Cold War *Frances FitzGerald*

FitzGerald explains Ronald Reagan's Strategic Defense Initiative (Star Wars) better than anyone ever has. One of her points is that no one ever did understand Star Wars—not its scientific champions, not its Congressional promoters and certainly not Reagan.

2001 FICTION

WHITE TEETH *Zadie Smith*

The story is centered on members of two families, one British and one Bengali, all of whom are a bit ridiculous in their own ways, as are all the other characters who pop up in Smith's magnificent first novel.

2001

FICTION

● **The Amazing Adventures of Kavalier & Clay,** *Michael Chabon*

📖 **The Corrections,** *Jonathan Franzen*

NONFICTION

● GENERAL NONFICTION
Hirohito and the Making of Modern Japan, *Herbert P. Bix*

● HISTORY
Founding Brothers: The Revolutionary Generation, *Joseph J. Ellis*

● BIOGRAPHY
W.E.B. Du Bois: The Fight for Equality and the American Century, 1919-1963, *David Levering Lewis*

📖 **The Noonday Demon: An Atlas of Depression,** *Andrew Solomon*

POETRY
📖 **Poems Seven: New and Complete Poetry,** *Alan Dugan*

● **Different Hours,** *Stephen Dunn*

YOUNG PEOPLE'S LITERATURE
📖 **True Believer,** *Virginia Euwer Wolff*

AUSTERLITZ *W. G. Sebald*

Memory is moral treachery in the works of W. G. Sebald, and in none is it more threatening than in this one.

THE CORRECTIONS *Jonathan Franzen*

The important thing to know about Franzen's novel is that you can ignore all the literary fireworks and thoroughly enjoy its people.

HATESHIP, FRIENDSHIP, COURTSHIP, LOVESHIP, MARRIAGE: Stories *Alice Munro*

As Alice Munro gets older, the challenges faced by her characters get darker—in this collection cancer, Alzheimer's disease, suicide to escape debilitation, among others.

JOHN HENRY DAYS *Colson Whitehead*

The ambition of Whitehead's second novel is to define the interior crisis of manhood in terms of the entire pop-mad consumer society—and it succeeds.

TRUE HISTORY OF THE KELLY GANG *Peter Carey*

Carey, widely recognized as one of the most engaging historical novelists alive, surpasses himself in this novel about the Australian version of Jesse James.

2001 NONFICTION

BORROWED FINERY: A Memoir *Paula Fox*

Paula Fox's children's books have been staples

ARTS

for 35 years, and her adult fiction has had a rousing revival recently. But nothing she has done has prepared her readers for this fragmentary memoir.

JOHN ADAMS *David McCullough*

A gentler, quieter John Adams. The story of his devotion to his wife, Abigail, and hers to him, is the affecting centerpiece of McCullough's biography.

THE METAPHYSICAL CLUB *Louis Menand*

The club was a short-lived affair begun in Cambridge, Mass., in 1872, but the ideas espoused by three members and one of their disciples became foundations of American thought in the 20th century.

UNCLE TUNGSTEN: Memories of a Chemical Boyhood *Oliver Sacks*

This account of Sacks' early years not only recreates a very large extended family of highly individual and eccentric adults who fascinated, repelled and inspired him in Britain in the 1930s and '40s, but also focuses on his youthful infatuation with chemistry.

2002 FICTION

ATONEMENT *Ian McEwan*

This novel is shaped as a triptych, each part changing our perspective as it unfolds.

2002

FICTION
📖 **Three Junes,** *Julia Glass*
● **Empire Falls,** *Richard Russo*

NONFICTION
📖 **Master of the Senate: The Years of Lyndon Johnson,** *Robert A. Caro*
● BIOGRAPHY **John Adams,** *David McCullough*
● GENERAL NONFICTION **Carry Me Home: Birmingham, Alabama, the Climactic Battle of the Civil Rights Revolution,** *Diane McWhorter*
● HISTORY **The Metaphysical Club: A Story of Ideas in America,** *Louis Menand*

POETRY
● **Practical Gods,** *Carl Dennis*
📖 **In the Next Galaxy,** *Ruth Stone*

YOUNG PEOPLE'S LITERATURE
📖 **The House of the Scorpion,** *Nancy Farmer*

MIDDLESEX *Jeffrey Eugenides*

This story is epic—in spirit, scope and definitely in organization. Eugenides dares to base the plot on genetic theory, so if Homer is a distant ancestor, Darwin is another.

ROSCOE *William Kennedy*

Is this, the seventh novel in William Kennedy's Albany cycle, a valedictory? It has that feeling. Like Roscoe Conway, its protagonist, it is haunted by history.

2002 NONFICTION

ANTHONY BLUNT: His Lives *Miranda Carter*

Carter's biography of Anthony Blunt is more interesting than the man. For three decades the Richelieu of art history in Britain, maker and breaker of reputations, curator of the queen's pictures and the premier teacher of scholars and gallery directors, Blunt was also, for almost 20 years, a Soviet spy.

BAD BLOOD *Lorna Sage*

Lorna Sage, in 2001, was a literary critic of such quick psychological penetration that one had to wonder where it came from. Now we know. While her father was at war in the 1940's, she and her mother lived with the mother's parents in a Welsh village.

PARIS 1919: Six Months That Changed the World *Margaret MacMillan*

The history of the 1919 Paris peace talks following World War I is a blueprint for the political and social upheavals bedeviling the planet now.

SEEING IN THE DARK: How Backyard Stargazers Are Probing Deep Space and Guarding Earth from Interplanetary Peril *Timothy Ferris*

In his earlier book *The Whole Shebang,* Ferris gave us an account of the entire range of astronomy and astrophysics. *Seeing in the Dark* is as big a book on the same matter, but more delightful because it celebrates the experiences of a growing army of amateurs.

2003 FICTION

BRICK LANE *Monica Ali*

Leaving home is a journey without end in this novel about Bangladeshi immigrants in London's East End.

DROP CITY *T. Coraghessan Boyle*

The debris left scattered up the entire West Coast of North America in this novel is as frightening and spectacular as any Boyle ever dropped on his readers.

THE FORTRESS OF SOLITUDE *Jonathan Lethem*

Everyone seeks his own Garden of Eden, but who would think to find it in a single block of Boerum Hill, Brooklyn, in the 1970s, when New York City was going down the tubes.

THE KNOWN WORLD *Edward P. Jones*

What makes this novel so startling is that the situation Jones imagines was reality in parts of this country in the 1850s: there were more than a few black slave owners, and a few were pretty well heeled.

2003

FICTION
● **Middlesex,** *Jeffrey Eugenides*
📖 **The Great Fire,** *Shirley Hazzard*

NONFICTION
● HISTORY
An Army at Dawn: The War in North Africa, 1942-1943, *Rick Atkinson*
● BIOGRAPHY
Master of the Senate, *Robert A. Caro*
📖 **Waiting for Snow in Havana: Confessions of a Cuban Boy,** *Carlos Eire*
● GENERAL NONFICTION
"A Problem from Hell:" America and the Age of Genocide, *Samantha Power*

POETRY
● **Moy Sand and Gravel,** *Paul Muldoon*
📖 **The Singing,** *C. K. Williams*

YOUNG PEOPLE'S LITERATURE
📖 **The Canning Season,** *Polly Horvath*

2003 NONFICTION

THE BOUNTY: The True Story of the Mutiny on the Bounty *Caroline Alexander*

Alexander's subtitle simply means she sets out to prove that we have never understood the Fletcher Christian who really led a mutiny on the Bounty in 1798, and Captain Bligh and the 18 crewmen who sailed 3,600 miles of the South Pacific after the mutineers tossed them overboard.

KHRUSHCHEV: The Man and His Era *William Taubman*

Taubman presents this sweeping history of the first 47 years of the Communist era and Khrushchev's explosive, vulgar, warm character unobtrusively, but not without measured judgments.

LIVING TO TELL THE TALE *Gabriel García Márquez, translated by Edith Grossman*

This memoir takes the author to his early 20s, before he leaves his country as it sinks into violence.

RANDOM FAMILY: Love, Drugs, Trouble and Coming of Age in the Bronx *Adrian Nicole LeBlanc*

LeBlanc focuses on two Puerto Rican girls: one has a baby by one man and twins by his brother before she's 19 and then hooks up with a heroin kingpin before going to prison; the other has two babies by the first girl's half brother and three more by three other men.

ARTS

SAMUEL PEPYS: The Unequalled Self *Claire Tomalin*

Tomalin rescues Pepys from his own diary, and he becomes a much larger figure outside of it.

2004 FICTION

GILEAD *Marilynne Robinson*

This grave, lucid, luminously spiritual novel about fathers and sons reaches back to the abolitionist movement and forward into the 1950s.

THE MASTER *Colm Toibin*

A novel about Henry James, his life and art—beautifully written, deeply pondered, startlingly un-Jamesian.

THE PLOT AGAINST AMERICA *Philip Roth*

An ingenious "anti-historical" novel set during World War II. Charles Lindbergh is elected president on an isolationist platform, and a Jewish family in Newark suffers the consequences.

RUNAWAY *Alice Munro*

Munro's 11th collection of short stories is about people, often women, living in rural Ontario, whose vivid, unremarkable lives are rendered with almost Tolstoyan resonance.

SNOW *Orhan Pamuk*

The forces of secular and Islamic Turkey collide in this complex and superbly orchestrated novel, begun before 9/11 and completed shortly thereafter.

2004

FICTION
● **The Known World,** *Edward P. Jones*

📖 **The News from Paraguay,** *Lily Tuck*

NONFICTION
● GENERAL NONFICTION
Gulag: A History, *Anne Applebaum*

📖 **Arc of Justice: A Saga of Race, Civil Rights, and Murder in the Jazz Age,** *Kevin Boyle*

🌐 HISTORY
A Nation Under Our Feet: Black Political Struggles in the Rural South from Slavery to the Great Migration, *Steven Hahn*

🌐 BIOGRAPHY
Khrushchev: The Man and His Era, *William Taubman*

POETRY
📖 **Door in the Mountain: New and Collected Poems, 1965-2003,** *Jean Valentine*

● **Walking to Martha's Vineyard,** *Franz Wright*

YOUNG PEOPLE'S LITERATURE
📖 **Godless,** *Pete Hautman*

WAR TRASH *Ha Jin*

A powerfully apposite moral fable whose suffering hero passes from delusion to clarity as a Chinese P.O.W. in Korea.

2004 NONFICTION

ALEXANDER HAMILTON *Ron Chernow*

An exemplary biography—broad in scope, finely detailed—of the founder who gave America capitalism and nationalism.

CHRONICLES: Volume One *Bob Dylan*

A memoir—idiosyncratic and revelatory—by the peerless singer-songwriter who journeyed from the heartland to conquer the Greenwich Village music scene of the 1960s.

WASHINGTON'S CROSSING *David Hackett Fischer*

An impressively researched narrative about the Revolutionary War that highlights the Battle of Trenton.

WILL IN THE WORLD: How Shakespeare Became Shakespeare *Stephen Greenblatt*

Scholarship, speculation and close reading combine in a lively study that gives shape to the life and context to the work.

2005 FICTION

KAFKA ON THE SHORE *Haruki Murakami*

This graceful and dreamily cerebral novel, translated from the Japanese, tells two stories—

that of a boy fleeing an Oedipal prophecy, and that of a witless old man who can talk to cats—and is the work of a powerfully confident writer.

ON BEAUTY *Zadie Smith*

In her vibrant book, a cultural politics novel set in a place like Harvard, the author brings everything to the table: a crisp intellect, a lovely wit and enormous sympathy for the men, women and children who populate her story.

PREP *Curtis Sittenfeld*

This is a calm and memorably incisive first novel about a scholarship girl who heads east to attend an elite prep school and has plenty to say about class, race and character.

SATURDAY *Ian McEwan*

This astringent novel traces a day in the life of an English neurosurgeon who comes face to face with senseless violence. It's as carefully constructed as anything McEwan has written.

VERONICA *Mary Gaitskill*

This mesmerizingly dark novel is narrated by a former Paris model who is now sick and poor; her ruminations on beauty and cruelty have clarity and an uncanny bite.

2005 NONFICTION

THE ASSASSINS' GATE: America in Iraq *George Packer*

A comprehensive look at the largest foreign policy gamble in a generation, by a *New Yorker* reporter

---

2005

FICTION
● **Gilead,** *Marilynne Robinson*

📖 **Europe Central,** *William T. Vollmann*

NONFICTION
● GENERAL NONFICTION
Ghost Wars, *Steve Coll*

📖 **The Year of Magical Thinking,** *Joan Didion*

● HISTORY
Washington's Crossing, *David Hackett Fischer*

● BIOGRAPHY
De Kooning: An American Master, *Mark Stevens and Annalyn Swan*

POETRY
● **Delights & Shadows,** *Ted Kooser*

📖 **Migration: New and Selected Poems,** *W. S. Merwin*

YOUNG PEOPLE'S LITERATURE
📖 **The Penderwicks: A Summer Tale of Four Sisters, Two Rabbits and a Very Interesting Boy,** *Jeanne Birdsall*

---

who traces the full arc of the war, from the pre-invasion debate through the action on the ground.

DE KOONING: An American Master *Mark Stevens and Annalyn Swan*

A sweeping biography, impressively researched and absorbingly written, of the charismatic immigrant who stood at the vortex of mid-20th-century American art.

THE LOST PAINTING *Jonathan Harr*

This gripping narrative, populated with a beguiling cast of scholars, historians, art restorers and aging nobles, records the search for Caravaggio's *Taking of Christ,* painted in 1602 and rediscovered in 1990.

POSTWAR: A History of Europe Since 1945 *Tony Judt*

Judt's massive, learned, brilliantly detailed account of Europe's recovery from the wreckage of World War II.

THE YEAR OF MAGICAL THINKING *Joan Didion*

A prose master's harrowing yet exhilarating memoir of a year riven by sudden death (her husband's) and mortal illness (their only child's).

2006 FICTION

ABSURDISTAN *Gary Shteyngart*

This scruffy, exuberant novel, equal parts Gogol and Borat, is immodest on every level: it's long, crude, manic and has cheap vodka

A R T S

on its breath. It's also smart, funny and, in the end, extraordinarily rich and moving.

THE COLLECTED STORIES OF AMY HEMPEL

A quietly powerful presence in American fiction during the past two decades, Hempel has demonstrated unusual discipline in assembling urbane, pointillistic and wickedly funny short stories.

THE EMPEROR'S CHILDREN
Claire Messud

An intelligent, keenly observed comedy of manners, set amid the glitter of cultural Manhattan in 2001, looks unsparingly, though sympathetically, at a privileged class unwittingly poised, in its insularity, for the catastrophe of 9/11.

THE LAY OF THE LAND *Richard Ford*

The third installment in the serial epic of Frank Bascombe, flawed husband, fuddled dad, writer turned real estate agent and voluble first-person narrator.

SPECIAL TOPICS IN CALAMITY PHYSICS *Marisha Pessl*

The ghost of Nabokov hovers over this literate first novel, a murder mystery narrated by a teenager in thrall to her father, an enigmatic professor, and to the charismatic female teacher whose death is announced on the first page.

2006 NONFICTION

FALLING THROUGH THE EARTH: A Memoir *Danielle Trussoni*

This intense memoir revisits the author's rough-and-tumble Wisconsin girlhood, spent in the company of her father, a Vietnam vet who returned "wild and haunted," unfit for family life and driven to extremes of philandering, alcoholism and violence.

THE LOOMING TOWER: Al-Qaeda and the Road to 9/11.
Lawrence Wright

Wright unmasks the secret world of Osama bin Laden and his collaborators and chronicles the efforts of a few American intelligence officers alert to the approaching danger but frustrated in efforts to stop it.

MAYFLOWER: A Story of Courage, Community, and War.
Nathaniel Philbrick

This absorbing history of the Plymouth Colony is a model of revisionism. Philbrick impressively recreates the pilgrims' dismal 1620 voyage and relates the events of the settlement and its first contacts with the natives of Massachusetts.

THE OMNIVORE'S DILEMMA: A Natural History of Four Meals.
Michael Pollan

"When you can eat just about anything nature has to offer, deciding what you should eat will inevitably stir anxiety," Pollan writes in this supple and probing book. He gracefully navigates within these anxieties as he traces the origins of four meals and makes us see exactly how what we eat affects our bodies and the planet.

2006

FICTION
● **March**, *Geraldine Brooks*

📖 **The Echo Maker**, *Richard Powers*

NONFICTION
● GENERAL NONFICTION
Imperial Reckoning: The Untold Story of Britain's Gulag in Kenya, *Anne Applebaum*

📖 **The Worst Hard Time: The Untold Story of Those Who Survived the Great American Dust Bowl**, *Timothy Egan*

● HISTORY
Polio: An American Story, *David M. Oshinsky*

● BIOGRAPHY
American Prometheus: The Triumph and Tragedy of J. Robert Oppenheimer, *Kai Bird and Martin J. Sherwin*

POETRY
📖 **Late Wife**, *Claudia Emerson*

● **Splay Anthem**, *Nathaniel Mackey*

YOUNG PEOPLE'S LITERATURE
📖 **The Astonishing Life of Octavian Nothing, Traitor to the Nation, Vol. 1: The Pox Party**, *M.T. Anderson*

THE PLACES IN BETWEEN *Rory Stewart*

Stewart, a young Scotsman, was warned by an Afghan official before commencing the journey recounted in this splendid book that "You will die, I can guarantee." Stewart, thankfully, did not die, and his report of walking across Afghanistan in 2002, shortly after the fall of the Taliban, belongs with the masterpieces of the travel genre.

2007 FICTION

MAN GONE DOWN *Michael Thomas*

This first novel explores the fragmented personal histories behind four desperate days in a black writer's life.

OUT STEALING HORSES *Per Petterson, translated by Anne Born*

In this short yet spacious Norwegian novel, an Oslo professional hopes to cure his loneliness with a plunge into solitude.

THE SAVAGE DETECTIVES

Roberto Bolaño, translated by Natasha Wimmer

A crafty, autobiographical novel about a band of literary guerrillas.

THEN WE CAME TO THE END

Joshua Ferris

Layoff notices fly in Ferris's acidly funny first novel, set in a white-collar office in the wake of the dot-com debacle.

2007

FICTION
● **The Road**, *Cormac McCarthy*
📖 **Tree of Smoke**, *Denis Johnson*

NONFICTION
● GENERAL NONFICTION
The Looming Tower: Al-Qaeda and the Road to 9/11, *Lawrence Wright*
📖 **Legacy of Ashes: The History of the CIA**, *Tim Weiner*
● HISTORY
The Race Beat: The Press, the Civil Rights Struggle, and the Awakening of a Nation, *Gene Roberts and Hank Klibanoff*
● BIOGRAPHY
The Most Famous Man in America: The Biography of Henry Ward Beecher, *Debby Applegate*
● POETRY
📖 **Native Guard**, *Natasha Trethewey*
● **Time and Materials**, *Robert Haas*
YOUNG PEOPLE'S LITERATURE
📖 **The Absolutely True Diary of a Part-Time Indian**, *Sherman Alexie*

TREE OF SMOKE *Denis Johnson*

The author of *Jesus' Son* offers a soulful novel about the travails of a large cast of characters during the Vietnam War.

2007 NONFICTION

IMPERIAL LIFE IN THE EMERALD CITY: Inside Iraq's Green Zone *Rajiv Chandrasekaran*

The author, a *Washington Post* journalist, catalogs the arrogance and ineptitude that marked America's governance of Iraq.

LITTLE HEATHENS: Hard Times and High Spirits on an Iowa Farm During the Great Depression *Mildred Armstrong Kalish*

Kalish's soaring love for her childhood memories saturates this memoir, which coaxes the reader into joy, wonder and even envy.

THE NINE: Inside the Secret World of the Supreme Court *Jeffrey Toobin*

An erudite outsider's account of the cloistered court's inner workings.

THE ORDEAL OF ELIZABETH MARSH: A Woman in World History *Linda Colley*

Colley tracks the "compulsively itinerant" Marsh across the 18th century and several continents.

THE REST IS NOISE: Listening to the Twentieth Century *Alex Ross*

In his own feat of orchestration, the *New Yorker*'s

music critic presents a history of the last century as refracted through its classical music.

2008 FICTION

DANGEROUS LAUGHTER: Thirteen Stories *Steven Millhauser*

A master fabulist in the tradition of Poe and Nabokov invents spookily plausible parallel universes in which the deepest human emotions and yearnings are transformed into their monstrous opposites. Millhauser is especially attuned to the purgatory of adolescence.

A MERCY *Toni Morrison*

The fate of a slave child abandoned by her mother animates this allusive novel—part Faulknerian puzzle, part dream-song—about orphaned women who form an eccentric household in late-17th-century America.

NETHERLAND *Joseph O'Neill*

O'Neill's seductive ode to New York—a city that even in bad times stubbornly clings to its belief "in its salvific worth"—is narrated by a Dutch financier whose privileged Manhattan existence is upended by the events of Sept. 11, 2001.

2666 *Roberto Bolaño, translated by Natasha Wimmer.*

Bolaño, the prodigious Chilean writer who died at age 50 in 2003, has posthumously risen, like a figure in one of his own splendid creations, to the summit of modern fiction. This work is a mega- and

meta-detective novel with strong hints of apocalyptic foreboding.

UNACCUSTOMED EARTH *Jhumpa Lahiri*

There is much cultural news in these precisely observed studies of modern-day Bengali-Americans, many of them Ivy-league strivers ensconced in prosperous suburbs who can't quite overcome the tug of traditions nurtured in Calcutta.

2008 NONFICTION

THE DARK SIDE: The Inside Story of How the War on Terror Turned Into a War on American Ideals *Jane Mayer*

Mayer's meticulously reported analysis of President Bush's anti-terrorist policies peels away the layers of legal and bureaucratic maneuvering that gave us Guantánamo Bay, "enhanced" interrogation methods, warrantless domestic surveillance and the rest.

THE FOREVER WAR *Dexter Filkins*

The *New York Times* correspondent, whose tours of duty have taken him from Afghanistan in 1998 to Iraq during the American intervention, captures a decade of armed struggle in harrowingly detailed vignettes.

NOTHING TO BE FRIGHTENED OF *Julian Barnes*

This absorbing memoir traces Barnes's progress from atheism to

---

2008

FICTION

● **The Brief Wondrous Life of Oscar Wao**, *Junot Diaz*

📖 **Shadow Country**, *Peter Matthiessen*

NONFICTION

● GENERAL NONFICTION
The Years of Extermination: Nazi Germany and the Jews, 1939-1945, *Saul Friedländer*

📖 **The Hemingses of Monticello: An American Family**, *Annette Gordon-Reed*

● HISTORY
What Hath God Wrought: The Transformation of America, 1815-1848, *Daniel Walker Howe*

● BIOGRAPHY
Eden's Outcasts: The Story of Louisa May Alcott and Her Father, *William Taubman*

POETRY

📖 **Time and Materials**, *Robert Hass*

📖 **Failure**, *Philip Schultz*

● **Fire to Fire: New and Collected Poems**, *Mark Doty*

YOUNG PEOPLE'S LITERATURE

📖 **What I Saw and How I Lied**, *Judy Blundell*

agnosticism and examines the problem of religion not by rehashing the familiar quarrel between science and mystery but by weighing the timeless questions of mortality and aging.

THIS REPUBLIC OF SUFFERING: Death and the American Civil War *Drew Gilpin Faust*

In this powerful book, Faust, the president of Harvard, explores the legacy of the "harvest of death" sown by the Civil War. Within four years, 620,000 Americans died in uniform, roughly the same number as those lost in all the nation's combined wars from the Revolution through Korea.

THE WORLD IS WHAT IT IS: The Authorized Biography of V. S. Naipaul *Patrick French*

Naipaul, the greatest of all post-colonial authors, cooperated fully on this biography with French, opening up a huge cache of private letters and diaries and supplementing the revelations they disclosed with remarkably candid interviews.

Getting Lost in the Stacks

The favorite libraries of a noted bibliophile

Asking Vartan Gregorian to name his favorite libraries is like asking him to list his favorite colors. "The world is full of a myriad of beautiful hues, and there are hundreds of wonderful libraries," says Gregorian, the president of the Carnegie Corporation of New York and former president of Brown University. The following "is not an objec-

---

2009*

FICTION
● Olive Kitteridge, *Elizabeth Strout*

NONFICTION
● GENERAL NONFICTION
Slavery by Another Name: The Re-Enslavement of Black Americans from the Civil War to World War II, *Douglas A. Blackmon*

● HISTORY
The Hemingses of Monticello: An American Family, *Annette Gordon-Reed*

● BIOGRAPHY
American Lion: Andrew Jackson in the White House, *Jon Meacham*

POETRY
● The Shadow of Sirius, *W.S. Merwin*

* The National Book Awards for 2009 had not yet been announced as this book went to the printer.

---

tive list of great institutions," says Gregorian, who once headed the New York Public Library. "It is more a personal reflection" on some of his favorite libraries. Here are his selections and commentary.

The New York Public Library (www.nypl.org). The N.Y.P.L. is in a class by itself in the sheer size and diversity of its holdings, and because of its writers' room where so many major works of both fiction and nonfiction were written, from Robert Caro's multivolume biography of Lyndon Johnson to Rachel Carson's *Silent Spring*.

The Library of Congress (www.loc.gov). No country in the world boasts a greater national library, and what a glory it is for a nation barely 200 years old that did not have the patronage of an aristocracy to shape its beginnings.

The British Library (www.bl.uk). This was, is and hopefully will remain one of the great libraries of the world.

The Bibliothèque Nationale (www.bnf.fr). Unlike our Library of Congress, the Bibliothèque Nationale in Paris began as a royal collection as early as the 15th century, and one can hardly imagine the depth and variety of its holdings.

The Vatican Library (bav.vatican.va), with its universal holdings on every possible topic, ranks as one of the great libraries in the world.

UNIVERSITY LIBRARIES. The greatest university library in the U.S. is **Harvard's Widener Library** (www.harvard.edu), which, along with its sister libraries

✔ TIMELY TIPS

Great Online Libraries

Here's where to curl up with a good, free e-book

✔ **Bartleby.com** Thousands of free literary classics as well as nonfiction and reference books.

✔ **Bibliomania.com** Hundreds of works of classics, drama and poetry; detailed literature study guides. Large reference book and nonfiction section.

✔ **Classic Book Library** (classicbook.info) Free online library specializing in treasured classics for old and young; genres include children's lit, historical fiction, romance, science fiction and mystery.

✔ **Fiction.us** Public domain novels, short stories, screenplays and English books; books broken down into chapters so you remember where to pick up.

✔ **Fullbooks.com** Thousands of unabridged books, including categories such as business, nations and countries, science and film.

✔ **Internet Public Library** (www.ipl.org) Get answers to your research questions through its ask-a-librarian feature; links to online books, newspapers and magazines.

✔ **The Literature Network** (www.online-literature.com) Literature for students, teachers and book lovers; nearly 2,000 unabridged books, more than 3,000 short stories and poetry; a quotations database has 8,500 quotes.

✔ **The Online Books Page** (onlinebooks.library.upenn.edu) More than 10,000 free online books, offered to the public by the University of Pennsylvania.

✔ **Project Gutenberg** (www. gutenberg.org) This online giant's book catalog features nearly 30,000 free books and thousands more on tap through the site's affiliates.

✔ **ReadBooksOnline.net** One thousand books from hundreds of authors, mainly American, English and Irish; many Nobel and Pulitzer prize winning books.

at Harvard, is a universe apart. Some of the public university libraries are also spectacular, such as the one at the **University of Illinois in Urbana** (www.library.uiuc.edu), which is, with about 10 million books, the sixth largest library in the U.S. after the Library of Congress, Harvard, the N.Y.P.L., Yale and the Queens Borough Public Library. At Oxford is the **Bodleian Library** (www.bodley.ox.ac.uk), and Cambridge has the **King's College Library** (www.kings.cam.ac.uk/library).

Finally, there are our town and small city libraries. Surely it was one of the greatest philanthropic acts of all time that Andrew Carnegie built some 1,600 public libraries in the U.S. The tradition of making reading and research material available easily and freely continues. One can hardly overestimate their value in the success of this country.

❓ EXPERT ANSWER

Beloved American Novels

Q. **What are the best American works of fiction of the last 25 years?**

The *New York Times Book Review* recently asked a few hundred writers, critics and editors to identify the best American works of fiction published in the last 25 years. The results:

THE WINNER: Beloved, *Toni Morrison* (1987)

THE RUNNERS-UP:

Underworld, *Don DeLillo* (1997)

Blood Meridian, *Cormac McCarthy* (1985)

Rabbit, Run (1960) **Rabbit Redux** (1971) **Rabbit Is Rich** (1981) **Rabbit at Rest** (1990), *John Updike*

American Pastoral, *Philip Roth* (1997)

CHAPTER **11**

SCIENCE & SYMBOLS

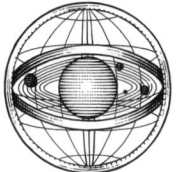
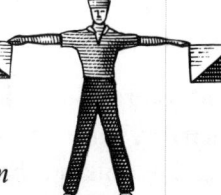

SCIENCE

Weather & Geology

Weather Wisdom You Can Trust

The science behind farmers' and sailors' sayings

Weather folklore has been passed down through the ages by mariners and farmers who relied on their own observations of astronomical events, animal behaviors and atmospheric changes to predict upcoming weather. Today, while the average person's ability to observe the natural world has declined, much of the folklore still exists, partly because of a psychological yearning to keep in touch with a time when humans seemed more in tune with their environment. Here's a look at the hard science behind some of the old weather sayings.

• **Red sky at night, sailors delight. Red sky in the morning, sailors take warning.** Much of the weather folklore based on observations of atmospheric phenomena is a fairly good predictor of short-range weather changes. In the midlatitude regions, the general flow of storm systems follows the jet stream from west to east. The red color at night is due to the reflection of the red colors from the sun as it dips in the western sky. This signals that the jet stream has pushed the storm systems out of your area. If clouds appear red in the morning, this means that the sun is rising in clear skies to the east with clouds approaching from the west, indicating the storm system is to your west and moving your way.

• **Mackerel clouds in the sky, expect more wet than dry.** This is another good example of accurate weather folklore based on atmospheric observations. Mackerel clouds refer to cirrocumulus clouds that appear pearly white with scaly formations akin to the scales on a fish. Ancient mariners knew that these clouds presaged the approach of a warm front that would produce rain or snow within the next 12 to 18 hours.

• **When there is a halo around the moon, the weather will be cold and rough.** The halo is generated by cirrostratus clouds up to 20,000 feet up in the atmosphere. These clouds cover large areas with a uniform thickness of ice crystals, which are responsible for many optical wonders. A halo around the moon generally means stormy weather within the next 24 hours.

• **If bees stay at home, rain will soon come.** This folklore is comparable to stories that associate approaching storms with ants lining up to go back

✔ TIMELY TIPS

When to Believe the Weatherman

✔ **Predicting temperature accurately is more difficult in the cool season than in the summer.** That's because weather systems are stronger and move quickly in the winter, leading to greater temperature variability.

✔ **In predicting precipitation, forecasts generally are less accurate when the weather is warm.** Most precipitation in the warm season comes from showers and thunderstorms, which occur randomly, cover small areas and don't last long. In winter, precipitation usually results from weather systems that cover larger areas and last many hours or days, and thus is easier to predict.

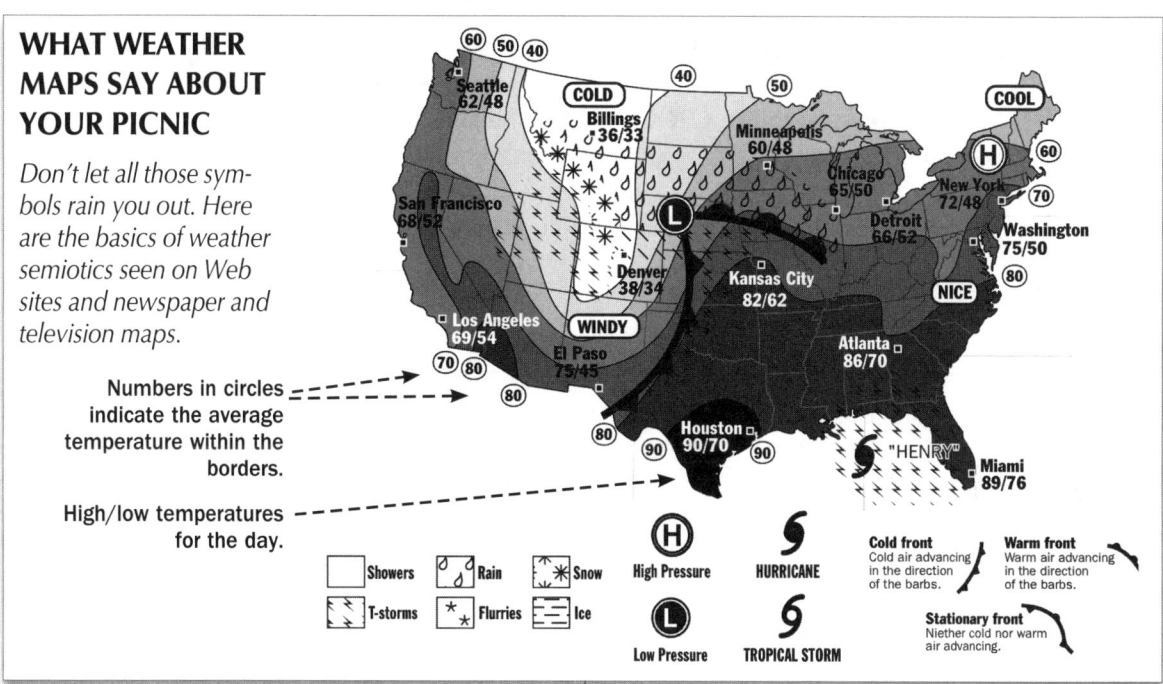

WHAT WEATHER MAPS SAY ABOUT YOUR PICNIC

Don't let all those symbols rain you out. Here are the basics of weather semiotics seen on Web sites and newspaper and television maps.

Numbers in circles indicate the average temperature within the borders.

High/low temperatures for the day.

Showers | Rain | Snow | High Pressure | HURRICANE
T-storms | Flurries | Ice | Low Pressure | TROPICAL STORM

Cold front Cold air advancing in the direction of the barbs.
Warm front Warm air advancing in the direction of the barbs.
Stationary front Niether cold nor warm air advancing.

to their nest, cows lying down in a field and frogs singing more than usual. These examples are difficult to prove or disprove because scientists can't isolate what in the environment would be causing these behaviors. But beekeepers swear by the ability of their bees to predict rain. With cows, the question remains, "If 25 cows are lying down in a field and 25 are standing, does this mean there's a 50 percent chance of rain?"

• **Crickets are a poor man's thermometer.** Counting the chirps of a cricket is an accurate way of determining temperatures above 40 degrees Fahrenheit. Below 40 degrees, a cricket's metabolism is too slow. To get the current air temperature within one degree Fahrenheit, count the number of chirps in a 14-second period and then add 40 to this number.

• **When hornets build their nest close to the ground, expect a hard winter.** Folklore that deals with animals and long-term weather forecasts is generally false. If people observed the hornet's activities over a long period of time, they would find no correlation between the hornet's behavior and seasonal forecasts. The same is true for folklore that links a squirrel's very bushy tail or a large black hand on a wooly-bear caterpillar with an upcoming severe winter.

• **When smoke hangs low, a storm is approaching.** The phenomenon of smoke hanging low is attributable to low-pressure systems that cause the atmosphere to be unstable and can signal the approach of stormy weather. However, sometimes near lakes and in valleys, local air circulation can dominate the larger-scale circulation and can give a false reading.

• **The air smells sweet before a storm.** Science definitely has an explanation for this folklore. Before a storm, lower pressure predominates, which causes plants' stomatic openings to enlarge and emit more gases, including aromatic ones.

INSIDE INFO

WEATHER WATCHING: SUNNY OR COLD? WINDY OR WET?
A breakdown of recent weather patterns in selected major American cities

| City | Average annual sunshine (%) | Mean days below freezing | AVERAGE ANNUAL TEMPERATURE (F) | | Average annual rain (in.) | AVERAGE RELATIVE HUMIDITY (%) | | | | | |
| | | | | | | Annual | | January | | July | |
			High	Low		a.m.	p.m.	a.m.	p.m.	a.m.	p.m.
Albany, N.Y.	52	14.9	58.1	36.6	36.17	79	57	76	63	84	55
Albuquerque, N.M.	76	11.9	70.1	42.2	8.88	60	29	70	40	60	27
Atlanta, Ga.	61	5.3	71.2	51.3	50.77	77	56	74	59	85	60
Atlantic City, N.J.	56	11.0	63.2	42.8	40.29	82	56	76	58	87	57
Baltimore, Md.	57	9.7	65.0	45.2	40.70	75	54	69	57	81	53
Bismarck, N.D.	59	18.6	53.8	29.4	15.47	74	56	75	66	74	46
Boise, Idaho	64	12.4	62.8	39.1	12.11	69	43	81	70	54	21
Boston, Mass.	58	9.8	59.0	43.6	41.51	72	58	65	57	77	56
Buffalo, N.Y.	49	13.2	55.8	39.5	38.58	79	63	77	72	79	55
Burlington, Vt.	49	15.5	54.0	35.2	34.47	77	59	70	63	82	53
Charleston, W.V.	40	10.0	65.8	44.2	42.53	79	56	74	63	90	60
Charlotte, N.C.	63	6.6	70.4	49.7	43.09	76	54	72	56	83	57
Cheyenne, Wyo.	65	17.2	58.0	33.2	14.40	65	44	57	50	70	35
Chicago, Ill.	54	13.3	58.6	39.5	35.82	77	60	75	67	79	56
Cincinnati, Ohio	52	10.8	63.2	43.2	41.33	77	59	75	67	83	57
Cleveland, Ohio	49	12.3	58.7	40.5	36.63	77	62	75	69	81	57
Columbia, S.C.	64	6.0	75.1	50.9	49.91	83	51	78	54	87	54
Columbus, Ohio	49	11.9	61.2	41.6	38.09	77	59	74	67	82	56
Concord, N.H.	54	17.3	57.0	33.1	36.37	82	54	74	58	90	51
Dallas-Fort Worth, Texas	63	4.0	76.3	54.6	33.70	72	56	73	60	67	49
Denver, Colo.	70	15.7	64.2	36.2	15.40	67	40	63	49	68	34
Des Moines, Iowa	59	13.5	59.8	40.0	33.12	75	60	74	67	76	57
Detroit, Mich.	53	13.6	58.1	39.0	32.62	79	60	78	69	81	53
Duluth, Minn.	52	18.5	47.9	29.0	30.0	77	63	74	70	82	59
El Paso, Texas	84	6.5	77.5	49.0	8.81	57	28	66	35	63	30
Great Falls, Mont.	61	15.7	56.4	33.1	15.21	67	45	66	60	66	29
Hartford, Conn.	56	13.5	60.2	39.5	44.14	76	52	69	56	82	51
Honolulu, Hawaii	69	0	84.4	70.0	22.02	76	56	81	61	73	51
Houston, Texas	56	2.1	78.6	57.3	46.07	86	60	82	64	86	58
Indianapolis, Ind.	55	11.8	62.1	42.4	39.94	80	62	78	70	84	59
Jackson, Miss.	60	5.0	76.4	52.0	55.37	87	58	84	65	90	59
Jacksonville, Fla.	63	1.5	78.9	57.1	51.32	86	56	85	57	88	58
Juneau, Alaska	30	14.1	46.9	34.1	54.31	86	73	81	77	87	70
Kansas City, Mo.	62	11.0	63.6	43.7	37.62	74	59	72	63	75	56
Little Rock, Ark.	62	6.0	72.5	51.0	50.86	79	57	76	61	83	56
Los Angeles, Calif.	73	0	70.4	55.5	12.01	79	64	70	59	86	68
Louisville, Ky.	56	8.9	66.0	46.0	44.39	76	58	72	64	81	58
Memphis, Tenn.	64	5.7	72.1	52.4	52.10	76	57	75	63	79	57
Miami, Fla.	72	0	82.8	69.0	55.91	81	61	81	59	82	63
Milwaukee, Wis.	54	14.1	54.3	37.9	32.93	78	64	75	68	80	61
Minn.-St. Paul, Minn.	58	15.6	54.3	35.3	28.32	73	60	72	67	74	54
Mobile, Ala.	59	2.2	77.4	57.4	63.96	83	57	79	61	87	60

City	Average annual sunshine (%)	Mean days below freezing	AVERAGE ANNUAL TEMPERATURE (F)		Average annual rain (in.)	AVERAGE RELATIVE HUMIDITY (%)					
			High	Low		Annual		January		July	
						a.m.	p.m.	a.m.	p.m.	a.m.	p.m.
Nashville, Tenn.	56	7.6	69.8	48.4	47.30	79	57	75	63	85	57
New Orleans, La.	59	1.3	77.6	58.5	61.88	85	63	82	66	89	66
New York, N.Y.	58	7.9	62.3	47.4	47.25	70	56	65	60	74	55
Norfolk, Va.	61	5.4	67.8	50.6	44.64	78	57	72	59	84	59
Oklahoma City, Okla.	68	7.7	71.1	48.8	33.36	72	54	72	59	70	49
Omaha, Neb.	60	14.1	61.5	39.5	29.86	76	59	75	65	78	57
Peoria, Ill.	57	12.9	60.4	41.0	36.25	79	62	78	68	82	59
Philadelphia, Pa.	56	9.7	63.4	45.1	41.41	76	55	71	59	81	54
Phoenix, Ariz.	86	0.8	85.9	59.3	7.66	51	23	66	32	45	20
Pittsburgh, Pa.	46	12.3	59.9	40.7	36.85	75	57	73	65	80	54
Portland, Maine	57	15.7	54.9	35.8	44.34	82	59	74	60	89	59
Portland, Ore.	48	4.3	62.6	44.5	36.30	86	60	86	75	82	45
Providence, R.I.	58	11.8	59.8	41.0	45.53	76	55	69	56	83	56
Raleigh, N.C.	59	7.8	70.1	48.4	41.43	80	54	73	55	88	58
Reno, Nev.	79	17.4	66.8	34.7	7.53	70	31	79	50	63	18
Richmond, Va.	62	8.5	68.8	46.6	43.16	82	53	77	57	88	56
Sacramento, Calif.	78	1.7	73.5	48.1	17.52	82	45	90	70	76	28
Salt Lake City, Utah	66	12.5	63.6	40.3	16.18	67	43	79	69	52	22
San Diego, Calif.	68	0	70.8	57.6	9.90	76	62	70	56	82	66
San Francisco, Calif.	66	0.2	65.2	49.0	19.70	84	62	86	66	86	59
San Juan, P.R.	66	0	86.4	74.0	52.34	83	65	82	64	84	67
Sault Ste. Marie, Mich.	47	18.1	49.6	29.8	34.23	85	67	81	75	90	61
Seattle-Tacoma, Wash.	46	3.1	59.4	44.6	37.19	83	62	81	74	82	49
Sioux Falls, S.D.	63	16.8	56.8	34.2	23.86	76	60	75	68	75	53
St. Louis, Mo.	57	10.0	65.4	46.7	37.51	76	59	77	66	77	56
Washington, D.C.	56	7.0	66.9	49.2	38.63	72	53	67	55	77	53
Wichita, Kan.	65	11.1	67.4	45.0	29.33	73	55	76	63	67	48
Wilmington, Del.	63	10.0	63.6	44.8	40.84	78	55	73	60	83	54

• **When human hair becomes limp, rain is near.** Human hair—especially blond hair—becomes thicker and longer when exposed to increases in humidity, which sometimes means rain is near. In fact, early hygrometers designed to determine the moisture content of the air relied on measuring the changes in the length of human hair.

• **Sinus and joint pain signals stormy weather.** This folklore, at least for arthritis sufferers, has been proved to be true. Pressure changes, which cause joint pain, are brought about by the unstable atmospheric conditions that typically precede a storm.

How to Use a Barometer

Measuring changes in atmospheric pressure

With a simple aneroid barometer, available at a local hardware store or marine supply center, you can make fairly accurate short-range weather predictions for as little as $20. Generally, when the barometer is high and rising, it means high pressure is approaching. High pressure systems typically are associated with fair weather—light and variable winds, dry air and temperatures below seasonal averages. When the barometer is low and falling, it typically means low pressure is on the way. Low-pressure systems tend to bring inclement

SCIENCE

BE YOUR OWN FORECASTER
Basic barometer reading for amateur meteorologists

Barometer reduced to sea level	Wind direction	Character of weather indicated
30.10 to 30.20 and steady	SW→NW	*Fair, slight temperature changes for 1 to 2 days.*
30.10 to 30.20 and rising rapidly	SW→NW	*Fair, followed within 2 days by warmer air and rain.*
30.10 to 30.20 and falling slowly	SW→NW	*Warmer with rain in 24 to 36 hours.*
30.10 to 30.20 and falling rapidly	SW→NW	*Warmer with rain in 18 to 24 hours.*
30.20 and above and stationary	SW→NW	*Continued fair with no decided temperature change.*
30.20 and above and falling slowly	SW→NW	*Slowly rising temperature and fair for 2 days.*
30.10 to 30.20 and falling slowly	S→SE	*Rain within 24 hours.*
30.10 to 30.20 and falling rapidly	S→SE	*Wind increasing in force with rain within 12 to 24 hours.*
30.10 to 30.20 and falling slowly	SE→NE	*Increasing wind with rain within 12 hours.*
30.10 and above and falling slowly	E→NE	*In summer with light winds, rain may not fall for several days. In winter, rain within 24 hours.*
30.10 and above and falling rapidly	E→NE	*In summer, rain probable in 12 to 24 hours. In winter rain or snow, increasing winds will often set in.*
30 or below and falling slowly	SE→NE	*Rain will continue 1 to 2 days.*
30 or below and falling rapidly	SE→NE	*Rain with high wind, followed within 24 hours by clearing and cooler.*
30 or below and rising slowly	S→SW	*Clearing in a few hours, continued fair for some days.*
29.80 or below and falling rapidly	S→E	*Severe storm of wind and rain or snow imminent, followed within 24 hours by clearing and colder.*
29.80 or below and falling rapidly	E→N	*Severe northeast gales and heavy rain or snow, followed in winter by a cold wave.*
29.80 or below and rising rapidly	Going→W	*Clearing and colder.*

WHEN A FINGER TO THE WIND WON'T WORK
The Beaufort Scale of Wind Force can help you estimate wind speed from simple observations.
It also gives the basis for converting the wind descriptions used in weather reports to wind speed
equivalents and vice versa.

Wind speed (m.p.h.)	Beaufort number	Wind effect on land	Official description
Less than 1	0	*Calm; smoke rises vertically.*	LIGHT
1 to 3	1	*Wind direction is seen in direction of smoke but is not revealed by weather vane.*	LIGHT
4 to 7	2	*Wind can be felt on face; leaves rustle; wind vane moves.*	LIGHT
8 to 12	3	*Leaves, small twigs in motion; wind extends light flag.*	GENTLE
13 to 18	4	*Wind raises dust, loose papers. Small branches move.*	MODERATE
19 to 24	5	*Small trees with leaves begin to sway; crested wavelets appear on inland waters.*	FRESH
25 to 31	6	*Large branches move; telegraph wires whistle; umbrellas become difficult to control.*	STRONG
32 to 38	7	*Whole trees sway; walking into the wind becomes difficult.*	STRONG
39 to 46	8	*Twigs break off trees; cars veer in roads.*	STRONG
47 to 54	9	*Slight structural damage occurs; roof slates may blow away.*	STRONG
55 to 63	10	*Trees uprooted; considerable structural damage caused.*	WHOLE GALE
64 to 72	11	*Widespread damage is caused.*	WHOLE GALE
73 or more	12	*Widespread damage is caused.*	HURRICANE

weather—strong winds, high humidity, clouds and storm fronts.

An aneroid barometer has one pointer, similar to the hand on a clock, which measures atmospheric pressure in inches of mercury and another pointer which is used to reference pressure changes. Rising pressure causes the reading pointer to move clockwise, while falling pressure causes it to move counterclockwise.

Once or twice a day, the reference pointer should be placed to correspond with the reading pointer. Over the course of the day, you can track pressure changes by noting how the reading pointer moves in relation to the reference hand.

To ensure accurate readings, aneroid barometers, and even some electronic ones, occasionally need to be recalibrated. Go the National

Barometer, n.: An ingenious instrument which indicates what kind of weather we are having.

Ambrose Bierce
The Devil's Dictionary

● ● ●

Weather Service Web site at nws. noaa.gov to find the pressure in your area adjusted to what it would read at sea level. Adjustments should be made on days with settled winds, which usually indicate the pressure is changing slowly.

A useful forecasting tool for amateur meteorologists is the chart on the facing page, which bases its weather predictions on barometric changes and wind direction. However, meteorologists caution that these are general rules that don't hold true for all locations and situations. For example, west winds off the Great Lakes can bring terrible lake-effect snows even when the barometer is high. Similarly, in the Northeast near the Atlantic Ocean, a sea breeze can bring cooler air, clouds, drizzle and fog when the pressure is high.

 **INSIDE INFO**

How Hurricanes Get Their Names

Meteorologists and others used to identify hurricanes and other storms by latitude and longitude. But experience showed it was quicker and less subject to error to refer to storms by the use of distinctive names. This has proved especially important in exchanging detailed storm information among hundreds of weather stations, coastal bases and ships at sea.

Since 1953, Atlantic tropical storms have been named from lists originated by the National Hurricane Center. They are now maintained and updated by an international committee of the World Meteorological Organization (WMO). The original name lists featured only women's names. In 1979, men's names were introduced and they alternate with the women's names. Six lists are used in rotation. Thus, the 2010 list will be used again in 2016. In the event that more than 21 named tropical cyclones occur in the Atlantic basin in one season, additional storms will take names from the Greek alphabet: Alpha, Beta, Gamma, Delta, and so on. Different lists of names are used for storms in different regions of the world. You can find the list of hurricane names on the internet at www.nhc.noaa.gov.

The only time that there is a change in the list is if a storm is so deadly or costly that the future use of its name on a different storm would be inappropriate for reasons of sensitivity. If that occurs, the offending name is stricken from the list by the WMO, and another name is selected to replace it.

SOURCE: National Hurricane Center (www.nhc.noaa.gov)

SCIENCE

WHAT IT FEELS LIKE OUT THERE

Avoid the gray area of windchill temperatures to prevent frostbite and hypothermia

WIND (m.p.h)	TEMPERATURE (°F)												
	30	25	20	15	10	5	0	-5	-10	-15	-20	-25	-30
5	25	19	13	7	1	-5	-11	-16	-22	-28	-34	-40	-46
10	21	15	9	3	-4	-10	-16	-22	-28	-35	-41	-47	-53
15	19	13	6	0	-7	-13	-19	-26	-32	-39	-45	-51	-58
20	17	11	4	-2	-9	-15	-22	-29	-35	-42	-48	-55	-61
25	16	9	3	-4	-11	-17	-24	-31	-37	-44	-51	-58	-64
30	15	8	1	-5	-12	-19	-26	-33	-39	-46	-53	-60	-67
35	14	7	0	-7	-14	-21	-27	-34	-41	-48	-55	-62	-69
40	13	6	-1	-8	-15	-22	-29	-36	-43	-50	-57	-64	-71
45	12	5	-2	-9	-16	-23	-30	-37	-44	-51	-58	-65	-72
50	12	4	-3	-10	-17	-24	-31	-38	-45	-52	-60	-67	-74
55	11	4	-3	-11	-18	-25	-32	-39	-46	-54	-61	-68	-75
60	10	3	-4	-11	-19	-26	-33	-40	-48	-55	-62	-69	-76

FROSTBITE TIMES: ▨ 30 minutes   ▨ 10 minutes   ☐ 5 minutes

SOURCE: N.O.A.A. National Weather Service

Why Windchill Matters

Your body loses heat faster in cold winds

Whether you're schussing down the slopes, shoveling the drive or simply walking to work, you know that air temperature is one thing and the temperature it "feels like" out there is another. On cold, blustery days, your body may feel far colder than the mercury warrants. That's because body heat loss is directly proportionate to the amount of body surface that you expose to the environment. So as wind increases, your body cools at a faster rate, causing the skin temperature to drop.

The National Weather Service actually calculates windchill temperatures based on the rate of heat loss from exposed skin caused by the effects of wind and cold. When windchill temperatures are potentially hazardous, that is, severe enough to cause frostbite and hypothermia, the agency issues advisories.

Frostbite occurs when unprotected parts of the body such as your face or fingers freeze. When body temperature dips below 90 degrees Fahrenheit, the body's shivering ability ceases, and it cannot warm itself without outside help. Unless you act quickly, hypothermia can set in. When that happens, the heart rate slows, blood pressure falls and a person goes into a semicomatose, then comatose, state.

Shaded areas in the chart above indicate temperatures that can cause frostbite at exposures of 30 minutes or less.

A Cloud-Watcher's Guide

A clear-eyed look at some nebulous situations

No two clouds are alike, as any child gazing up at a billow-filled blue sky knows. Meteorologists identify three basic types: cumulus, stratus and cirrus; but variations on those types can form, depending on the altitude and temperature of moisture-laden air. Below are the types of clouds that can be found at low, middle and high altitudes.

LOW ALTITUDES (below 6,500 ft.)

Cumulus *(from the Latin "heap")*. Large, white, puffy clouds often resembling huge balls of cotton or heads of cauliflower.

These clouds can span all altitudes, with bases from 1,000 to 5,000 feet and tops sometimes reaching 6,000 feet. When they turn dark gray and produce rain or hail, they are called **cumulonimbus** and are often accompanied by lightning and thunder.

Stratus *("stretched out")*. Low layers of clouds that cover the entire sky, like sheets of high fog blotting out the sun. Shapeless, dark and dense, these clouds produce gray, overcast days. Low stratus clouds that produce drizzle, rain or snow but are not accompanied by thunder or lightning are called **nimbostratus**.

Stratocumulus. Dark gray, wavelike formations that contain moisture but don't usually produce rain.

MIDDLE ALTITUDES (6,500 to 20,000 ft.)

Altocumulus. Small, gray, patchy clouds composed of water droplets. These clouds create a scalelike pattern in the sky.

Altostratus. Gray, midlevel, often opaque clouds. They often contain water droplets that may fall but evaporate before reaching the ground.

HIGH ALTITUDES (20,000 to 40,000 ft.)

Cirrus *("curl")*. Wispy, filament-like clouds made of ice crystals.
Cirrostratus. White, thin, translucent clouds that could signal an approaching storm.

Cirrocumulus. Small, loosely connected sheets of white clouds that may contain droplets of water or ice. Vertical air currents cause their patchy, scalelike appearance in the sky, often referred to as a "mackerel sky." They can be a sign of stormy weather ahead.

How to Read Rocks

The earth's history is written in stone

Miners in the Middle Ages were the first to realize the need to understand the geological similarities of rocks. It was during that time that the two basic principles of rock formations evolved: first, that sedimentary—or layered—rocks are laid down horizontally; and second, that younger rocks always rest on top of older rocks. A few centuries later, another concept was introduced, stating that geologic processes take place at a similar frequency and magnitude throughout time. Geology moved along apace with the identification of fossils and the discovery in the 1800s that fossils are found in rocks in a very definite chronological order. That tenet led to the development of the geologic time scale (see page 764), a hierarchical set of time intervals that plot the earth's history.

The earth is made up of rock, from mountain tops to ocean floor, so clues to its history are plentiful. But even though there are thousands of kinds of rocks and minerals, most rocks are formed from just eight elements: aluminum, calcium, iron, magnesium, oxygen, potassium,

SCIENCE

24 COMMON MINERALS AND THEIR USES

The earth is home to about 3,000 minerals. Most minerals are chemical compounds, but a few, like sulfur and gold, are elements. Minerals crystallize in geometric forms, and along with their chemical compositions, their crystalline structure helps determine properties such as color and hardness. Minerals have numerous practical applications, as the table below shows.

MINERAL	SOURCES	USES
Aluminium	*Guinea, Australia, Jamaica*	Packaging, building
Beryllium	*Brazil, South Africa, U.S.*	Nuclear industry, gemstones
Chromite	*South Africa, Zimbabwe*	Chemicals, metallurgy
Cobalt	*Zaire, Zambia, Canada*	Jet engines, chemicals
Copper	*Chile, U.S., Zambia*	Electronics, chemicals, building
Feldspar	*U.S., Brazil*	Glass, ceramics, bonding agent
Fluorite	*Germany, Mexico, U.S.*	Plastics, ceramics, metallurgy
Gold	*South Africa, U.S., Australia*	Dentistry, electronics, jewelry
Gypsum	*Canada, France, U.K., Mexico*	Building materials, agriculture
Halite	*Worldwide*	Food, chemicals (sodium chloride-salt)
Iron Ore	*U.S., Australia, Brazil*	Metallurgy, chemicals, medicine
Lead	*U.S.*	Electronics, construction, ammunition
Lithium	*U.S., Chile*	Electronics, medicine, lubricants
Manganese	*South Africa, Gabon, Australia*	Iron and steel production
Nickel	*Australia, Canada, Norway*	Chemical, aerospace
Platinum	*Canada, South Africa*	Jewelry, automotive, oil refining
Phosphate	*U.S.*	Agriculture, chemicals
Quartz	*Worldwide*	Electronics, instruments, jewelry
Silica	*Worldwide*	Computers, building, chemicals
Silver	*U.S., Canada, Mexico*	Electronics, jewelry, photography
Sulfur	*Worldwide*	Chemicals, petroleum refining, pharmaceuticals
Titanium	*U.S., U.K., China, Japan*	Jet engines, aerospace
Uranium	*Canada, Australia, Africa*	Electricity, nuclear and defense industries
Zinc	*Worldwide*	Chemical, automotive, electrical

SOURCE: Mineral Information Institute

silicon and sodium. The combinations of elements that rocks contain and the wear and tear of wind and water over time account for the huge variety of rocks on earth. However, geologists have identified three basic rock groups: igneous, sedimentary and metamorphic. These groups get their names from the major geological processes that formed them and that make them fairly easy to tell apart.

Pumice

Igneous rocks, or fire rocks, form when magma, or melted rock buried deep within the earth, reacts to heat and pressure. It flows upward or is spewed out by an erupting volcano and then cools and solidifies. Magma, which is called lava when it appears above the ground, is made up of a variety of chemicals and cools at different rates, resulting in different types of igneous rocks. But you can easily identify them as igneous because they are typically crystalline or glassy. Obsidian, a common igneous rock, for example, is actually volcanic glass. Pumice, volcanic froth puffed up by gas bubbles, is also a kind of glass and not a mixture of minerals. Another type of igneous rock is granite, a light, coarse-grained rock formed deep in the earth and then exposed by erosion.

Sandstone

Sedimentary rocks are formed by natural processes, such as weathering and erosion, that occur mainly under water. These rocks consist of layers, or strata, and are also called stratified rocks. The layers are formed by sediments—mineral grains, mud, sand, pebbles, microscopic organisms and even plant material—washed downstream and deposited on top of each other. In time, these layers press down until the bottom layers turn into rock. Sedimentary rocks are rich in geological history, often containing fossils and showing marks left by water currents or cracks formed by mud. Some examples are sandstone, limestone, shale and gypsum, often used in the building industries.

Gneiss

Metamorphic rocks started out as igneous or sedimentary rocks but "morphed" due to changes in temperature, pressure and chemically active liquids. The process transforms them into denser and more compact rocks. Most of the thousands of rare minerals on the earth are found in metamorphic rocks. One type of metamorphic rock, gneiss, may have been granite, an igneous rock, that was changed by tremendous heat and pressure. Look carefully and you'll see mineral layers, or foliation. The mineral grains were flattened and compacted in alternating patterns, giving the rock a striped appearance.

The Ins and Outs of Earthquakes

Shaky about temblors? Here's how to stand on firmer ground

After decades of dissecting seismic fault zones, scientists have gotten good at describing where large quakes are likely to occur. But predicting with precision exactly when and where the next earthquake will strike remains impossible. (For information on what to do if an earthquake hits, see page 113.) Here are some frequently asked questions and answers from the scientists at the U.S. National Geological Survey.

Q Can scientists predict earthquakes?

No. Scientists have never predicted a major earthquake. They do not know how, and they do not expect to know how any time in the foreseeable future. However, based on scientific data, probabilities can be calculated for potential future earthquakes. For example, scientists estimate that over the next 30 years the probability of a major earthquake occurring is 67 percent in the San Francisco Bay area and 60 percent in Southern California.

Q Can animals predict earthquakes?

The earliest reference to unusual animal behavior prior to a significant earthquake is from Greece in 373 B.C. Rats, weasels, snakes and centipedes reportedly left their homes and headed for safety several days before a destructive earthquake. Anecdotal evidence abounds of animals, fish, birds, reptiles and insects exhibiting strange behavior anywhere from weeks to seconds before an earthquake. However, consistent and reliable behavior prior to seismic events, and a mechanism explaining how it could work, still eludes us. Most, but not all, scientists pursuing this mystery are in China or Japan.

Q Is there earthquake weather?

In the 4th century B.C., Aristotle proposed

SCIENCE

that earthquakes were caused by winds trapped in subterranean caves. Small tremors were thought to have been caused by air pushing on the cavern roofs, and large ones by the air breaking the surface. This theory lead to a belief in earthquake weather, the notion that because a large amount of air was trapped underground, the weather would be hot and calm before an earthquake. A later theory stated that earthquakes occurred in calm, cloudy conditions and were usually preceded by strong winds, fireballs and meteors.

However, there is no connection between weather and earthquakes. Earthquakes occur in all types of weather, in all climate zones, in all seasons of the year and at any time of day. They are the result of geologic processes within the earth and originate miles underground. Wind, precipitation, temperature and barometric pressure changes affect only the surface and shallow subsurface of the Earth.

Earthquakes are focused at depths well out of the reach of weather, and the forces that cause earthquakes are much larger than the weather forces.

FREQUENCY OF OCCURRENCE OF EARTHQUAKES

MAGNITUDE	ANNUAL AVERAGE	BASED ON
8 and higher	1	Observations since 1900
7 - 7.9	17	Observations since 1990
6 - 6.9	134	Observations since 1990
5 - 5.9	1319	Observations since 1990
4 - 4.9	13,000	Estimated
3 - 3.9	130,000	Estimated
2 - 2.9	1,300,000	Estimated

Ⓠ Why are we having so many earthquakes? Has earthquake activity been increasing?

Although it may seem that we are having more earthquakes, earthquakes of magnitude 7.0 or greater have remained fairly constant over the last century. According to official records, earthquakes have actually seemed to decrease in recent years. The National Earthquake Information Center now

---

ⓘ INSIDE INFO

Quaking in Our Boots

○ There are 500,000 detectable earthquakes in the world each year; 100,000 can be felt, and 100 cause damage.

○ Depending how big the quake is, aftershocks can last 9 or 10 years.

○ Tsunamis, giant sea waves caused by earthquakes, can travel through the ocean at a speed of 600 m.p.h.

SOURCE: U.S. Geological Survey

---

locates about 12,000 to 14,000 earthquakes each year, or approximately 50 per day. According to long-term records (since about 1900), we expect about 18 major earthquakes (7.0 - 7.9) and one great earthquake (8.0 or above) in any given year.

Ⓠ Where can I get a fault map?

A wide variety of maps are available from the U.S. Geological Survey national mapping program in both paper and digital form. Check the Web site at earthquake.usgs.gov.

Ⓠ How can I find out about earthquakes in my area? Where can I go to see a fault?

Check out the Earthquakes by State section on the US Geological Survey website. The closest fault depends on where you live. Some earthquakes produce spectacular fault scarps, and others are completely buried beneath the surface. Sometimes you may not even know that you are looking at a fault scarp. For more information on faults in your area, go to usgs.gov.

Ⓠ Can I get on a list to receive an e-mail message when there is an earthquake?

Yes, go to Earthquake Notification Services (sslearthquake.usgs.gov/ens) to sign up for free.

● Where can I buy a Richter scale?

The Richter scale is not a physical device, but a mathematical formula. The magnitude of an earthquake is determined from the logarithm of the amplitude of waves recorded on a seismogram at a certain period. (See box at right.)

Earthquake-Prone Zones

Where the earth shakes, rattles and rumbles the most

Earthquakes occur when two tectonic plates, or pieces of the earth's crust under oceans and continents, split, slide or ram into each other. Quakes can happen anywhere on the globe—the earth's surface has seven major tectonic plates and many more minor ones. History shows that countries along these seismic hot spots are especially prone to earthquakes. In the U.S. nearly every state had experienced some earthquake activity between 1975 and 1995, except for Florida, Iowa, North Dakota and Wisconsin. But the areas below are particularly shake-prone.

The circum-Pacific seismic belt. More than 80 percent of the world's largest earthquakes happen along this rim of the Pacific Ocean. Vulnerable areas: the western coast of South America from the tip of Chile northward, Central America, Mexico and northward from California to Alaska. The belt also extends from the Aleutian Islands to Japan, the Philippines, New Guinea, islands in the Southwest Pacific and New Zealand.

The Alpide belt. This zone accounts for about 17 percent of the world's largest earthquakes, including some of the most destructive. It runs from Java to Sumatra through the Himalayas, through the Mediterranean and out into the Altantic Ocean.

Mr. Richter's Shaky Scale
How the Richter scale measures a tremor's intensity

Developed by American physicist Charles Richter in the mid-1930s, the Richter scale uses a logarithmic scale, ranging from 1 to 9 and higher, in which each whole-number increase in magnitude represents a 10-fold increase in terms of the energy released by the tremor, as measured by seismographs.

Shocks that measure 2 or less are called "microearthquakes" and are usually not felt, although they are tracked by local seismographers. Earthquakes with a magnitude of 4.5 and greater occur at the rate of several thousand each year and are powerful enough to be recorded by instruments worldwide. A quake that measures 5.3, such as the one that shook San Francisco in 1957, would be considered moderate, even though its power was comparable to the explosion of 455 metric tons of dynamite. (The 1989 San Francisco earthquake measured 7 on the Richter scale.)

Earthquakes with a magnitude of about 6.3 and above are major events. The largest recorded earthquake in the United States registered 9.2 and occurred in Alaska on Good Friday in 1964. The largest recorded quake in the world took place in Chile in 1960, measuring 9.5. But the record for the most destructive earthquake in history goes to the shock that hit China's Shaanxi province in 1556. It killed more than 830,000 people.

THE TOP 5 EARTHQUAKES OF ALL TIME

Magnitude	Location	Date
9.5	Chile	May 22, 1960
9.2	Prince William Sound, Alaska	March 28, 1964
9.0	Sumatra-Andaman Islands	Dec. 26, 2004
9.0	Kamchatka	Nov. 4, 1952
9.0	Arica, Peru (now Chile)	Aug. 13, 1868

SCIENCE

How to Tell Geologic Time

Geologists use a timeline of the Earth that divides the planet's history into a series of intervals, each defined by significant events that occurred during those divisions. As the geologic time scale below shows, the four eras, the Cenozoic, Mesozoic, Paleozoic and Precambrian, are subdivided into periods. Some of the major events that took place during the different periods, as well as representative animal life, are used to identify them.

AGE (in millions of years before the present)	ERA	PERIOD	ANIMAL AND PLANT LIFE
65 to present	**Cenozoic** *(Age of mammals)*	QUATERNARY	Modern man, modern seed plants.
		TERTIARY	Primitive man, gorillas, elephants, whales, apes, horses, modern birds.
250 to 65	**Mesozoic** *(Age of dinosaurs)**	CRETACEOUS	Birds, snakes, fish. Flowering plants appeared; sequoia trees prominent.
		JURASSIC	Flying reptiles; modern insects. Conifers, ginkos, tree ferns.
		TRIASSIC	Vertebrates, aquatic reptiles such as ichthyosaurs.
550 to 250	**Paleozoic** *(Age of fishes)**	PERMIAN	Small reptiles; ammonites.
		CARBONIFEROUS	Amphibians, large insects. Primitive conifers; first seed plants.
		DEVONIAN	Starfish, primitive land vertebrates. Ferns, mosses, primitive evergreens.
		SILURIAN	Sea scorpions, mollusks, corals.
		ORDOVICIAN	Gastropods, clams, snails; first primitive fishlike. vertebrates.
		CAMBRIAN	Protozoans, first shells. Lichens in some regions.
4,500 to 550	**Precambrian** *The time between the birth of the planet and the appearance of complex life forms*		Jellyfish, amoebas, worms, sponges, algae.

*These designations are popular, but they are somewhat broad. For example, animal life during the Mesozoic era was not limited to dinosaurs; mammals, turtles, crocodiles and many varieties of insects also inhabited the earth.

SOURCE: U.S. Geological Survey

Stars & Tides

Stargazing with the Naked Eye
The beauty and majesty of the night sky

In a world of space stations and orbiting telescopes, stargazing with the naked eye may seem a quaint notion. Hardly. "The beauty and majesty of the night sky can only be appreciated by the naked eye," says astronomer Geoff Chester of the U.S. Naval Observatory in Washington, D.C. Even without binoculars and telescopes, it can be quite easy to enjoy some of nature's most extraordinary spectacles—if you know what to look for.

To familiarize yourself with the stars, constellations and other astronomical phenomena, you'll need a celestial map and a red-filtered flashlight to help you read. You can find such maps online, at planetariums and astronomy clubs and in specialty publications such as *Astronomy* magazine (and in this book beginning below and on pages 766 to 771). Make a filter by covering your flashlight lens with any porous red paper, or buy a red LED (light-emitting diode) at an electronics store. The red filter helps your night vision.

The best locations for viewing the night sky are usually in rural areas, where there is little gazing interference from artificial light and pollution. Begin your celestial search by seeking out the brightest stars. Use the sky's brightest patterns, such as the Summer Triangle (see below), for reference points to the constellations and other celestial objects. The Summer Triangle, found directly overhead in the summer months, is formed by stars in the Vega, Deneb and Altair constellations.

In winter, use the Great Winter Circle, which boasts 9 of the 21 brightest stars in the winter sky. To find it, start with Orion's belt, which lies in the middle of the Circle and points to Sirius. Move clockwise from there to Procyon, Pollux, Castor, Capella, Aldebaran and Rogel.

The Planets. Stars twinkle and planets don't, yet planets, not stars, are generally the brightest objects in the sky. Four planets—Venus, Jupiter, Mars and Saturn—can be seen easily with the naked eye. Venus is the third-brightest object in the sky after the sun and moon and displays a milky white glow. Jupiter, usually the fourth-brightest object,

SCIENCE

TEST PATTERNS IN THE SKY
The Summer Triangle and the Great Winter Circle will help you find your way in the firmament.

The Summer Triangle. Consists of stars Vega, Deneb and Altair (left).

The Great Winter Circle. Use Orion's belt to find Sirius. Then, clockwise, go to Procyon, Pollux, Castor, Capella, Aldeberon and Rigel (right).

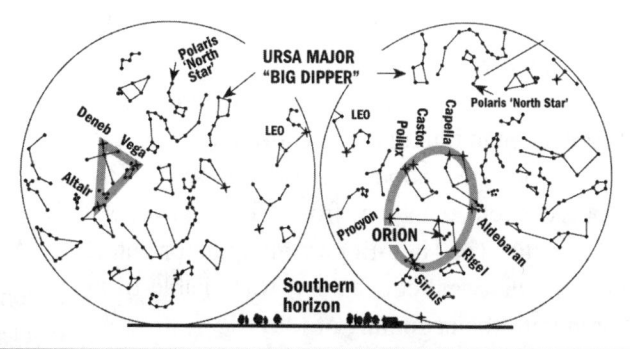

The Night Sky in January

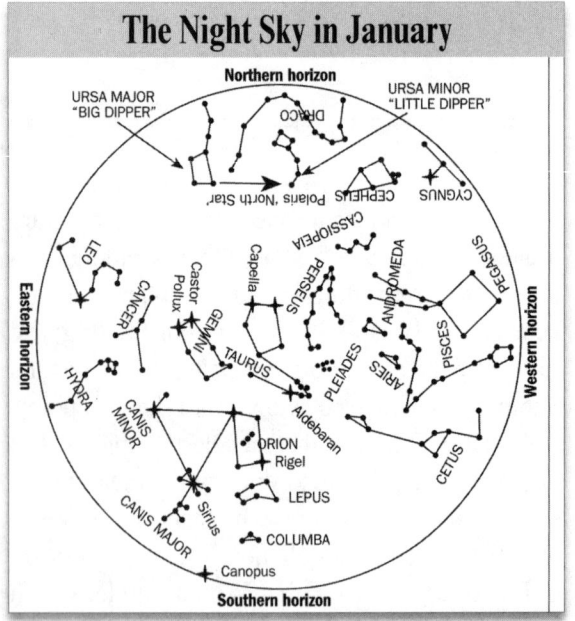

The Night Sky in February

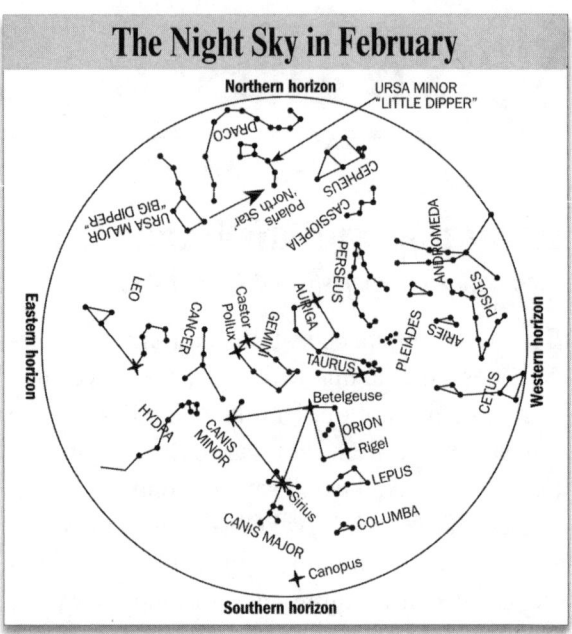

appears creamy or yellow. Mars follows Jupiter in visibility and is the only planet whose color, a pinkish hue, represents its surface color and not its atmosphere. Saturn is the faintest of the naked-eye planets and is yellowish. Mercury can also be seen if you're skilled, but doing so is difficult because of its proximity to the sun. Most astronomers believe Copernicus, the grandfather of modern astronomy, never spotted Mercury.

Shooting Stars and Comets. Ever seen a shooting star? Think of what you viewed as a grain of sand hitting the earth's atmosphere at tremendous speed and bursting into flames. A meteor shower occurs when such debris, usually from a comet, enters the earth's atmosphere. A really bright shooting star is called a fireball. It's not uncommon for such a phenomenon to illuminate an entire state. Comets, like meteors, are random visitors to our world. But comets can remain in view from a few days to several months. The Hale-Bopp comet, the brightest comet in the twentieth century, was visible from March until the beginning of May 1997.

Eclipses. A total solar eclipse is one of the most spectacular sights in the natural world. It owes its occurrence to the fact that the moon is 400 times smaller than the sun, but 400 times closer to earth—hence the moon and the sun appear to have equal diameters. So when the moon comes between the sun and earth, we are left with the awe-inspiring sight of a pearly halo around a black disc.

Total lunar eclipses may not be as impressive, but they more than reward the small effort required to see them. At least once a year the moon passes into the earth's shadow and completely disappears from the night sky. Unlike a solar eclipse, a lunar eclipse can be enjoyed across an entire hemisphere.

Telescopes for Beginners
Computer-assisted devices that will find the stars

These days, even the most casual of backyard stargazers have found their hobby touched by computers. Many of the simplest and least expensive telescopes available for hobbyists contain processors,

The Night Sky in March

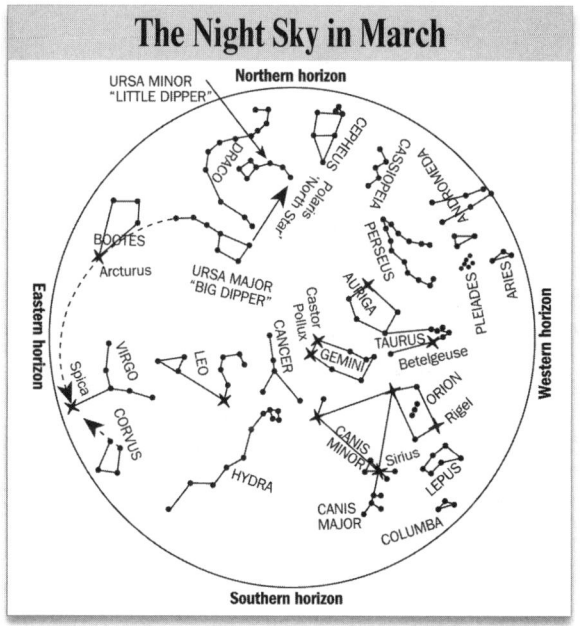

The Night Sky in April

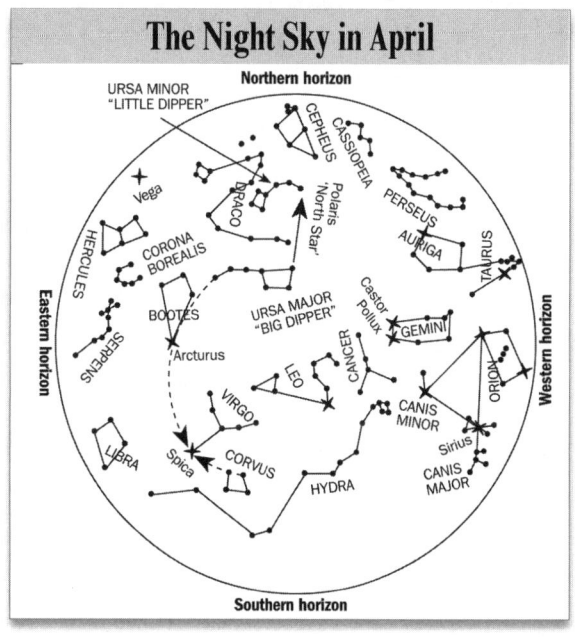

keypads and motors that allow them to be automatically pointed at stars, planets and other objects in the sky just by punching in a number. Since their introduction, prices of these "go to" telescopes, as they are known, have declined, and the technology, at least in its most basic form, is available on scopes costing as little as $250 or less.

A growing number of experienced astronomers are using go-to systems. "If you have a go-to drive on your telescope you don't have to waste an hour hunting for objects," says Bon Gent, president of the Astronomical League, an alliance of amateur astronomers' groups, "you can spend the time observing them." Still, newcomers will find stargazing more fulfilling with some advance study. "Get some beginning astronomy books, subscribe to one or two magazines, learn a little and then get a telescope," Gent counsels.

Besides go-to telescopes, other developments also mean that more amateur astronomers have more sophisticated equipment that they can do a lot more with. Here are some examples.

Software packages for home computers that map thousands of celestial objects and serve as interactive desktop planetariums have replaced printed star charts that filled volumes. Digital cameras now allow amateurs with relatively modest equipment to capture space images easily.

Star charting was one of the first aspects of amateur astronomy to be touched by computers. Today several Internet sites, including one operated by Sky & Telescope (www.skyandtelescope. com), have free online systems that can generate charts for any point on earth at any time over a span of centuries.

Astronomy software packages like Starry Night Pro and Red Shift go even further. Starry Night Pro, for example, has a database of 19 million stars that users can turn into animations showing celestial activity over time. Many astronomy software packages can connect to motorized telescopes. Such connections allow users to select a specific star or planet and then have the computer direct the telescope to the precise location of that object in the sky.   —Ian Austen

The Night Sky in May

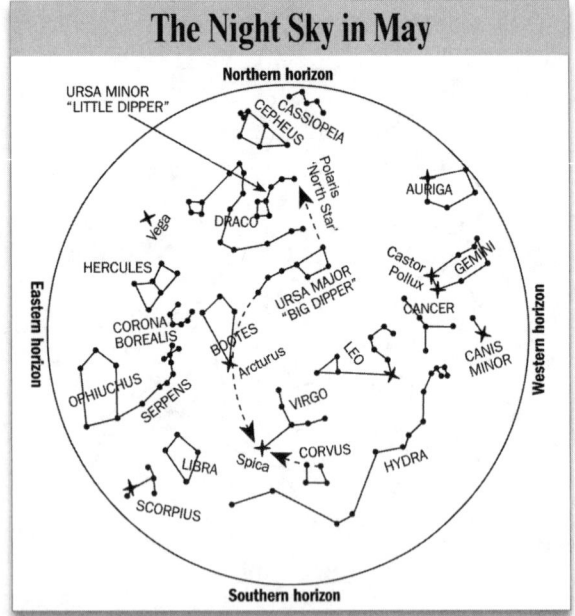

The Night Sky in June

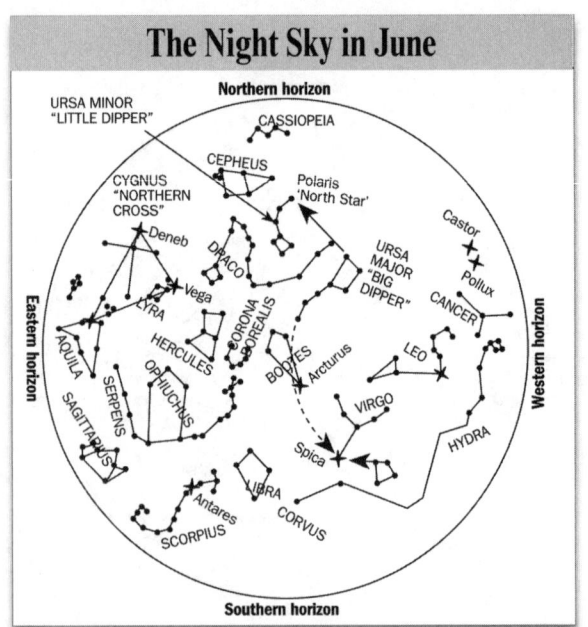

Stars and Constellations

The explosion that created the universe gave birth to trillions of stars

Only about 5,000 stars are visible to the naked eye. Since only half the sky can be seen at any one time, that means only 2,500 stars will be in your field of vision on the next clear night. Constellations are groups of stars whose patterns have reminded stargazers through history of familiar shapes. In 1929, astronomers officially adopted 88 constellations. They are listed here with their names and meanings.

Andromeda	Chained Maiden	**Camelopardalis**	Giraffe	**Cetus**	Whale
Antila	Air Pump	**Cancer**	Crab	**Chamaeleon**	Chameleon
Apus	Bird of Paradise	**Canes Venatici**	Hunting Dogs	**Circinus**	Compasses (art)
Aquarius	Water Bearer	**Canis Major**	Great Dog	**Columba**	Dove
Aquila	Eagle	**Canis Minor**	Little Dog	**Coma Berenices**	Bernice's Hair
Ara	Altar	**Capricornus**	Sea-goat	**Corona Australis**	Southern Crown
Aries	Ram	**Carina**	Keel	**Corona Borealis**	Northern Crown
Auriga	Charioteer	**Cassiopeia**	Queen	**Corvus**	Crow
Bootes	Herdsman	**Centaurus**	Centaur	**Crater**	Cup
Caelum	Chisel	**Cepheus**	King	**Crux**	Cross (southern)
				Cygnus	Swan
				Delphinus	Dolphin
				Dorado	Goldfish
				Draco	Dragon
				Equuleus	Little Horse
				Eridanus	River
				Fomax	Furnace
				Gemini	Twins
				Grus	Crane (bird)
				Hercules	Hercules
				Horologium	Clock
				Hydra	Water Snake (female)

Hydrus	Water Snake (male)
Indus	Indian
Lacerta	Lizard
Leo	Lion
Leo Minor	Little Lion
Lepus	Hare
Libra	Balance
Lupus	Wolf
Lynx	Lynx
Lyra	Lyre
Mensa	Table Mountain
Microscopium	Microscope
Monoceros	Unicorn
Musca	Fly
Norma	Square (rule)
Octans	Octant
Ophiuchus	Serpent Bearer
Orion	Hunter
Pavo	Peacock
Pegasus	Flying Horse
Perseus	Hero
Phoenix	Phoenix
Pictor	Painter
Pisces	Fishes

The Night Sky in July

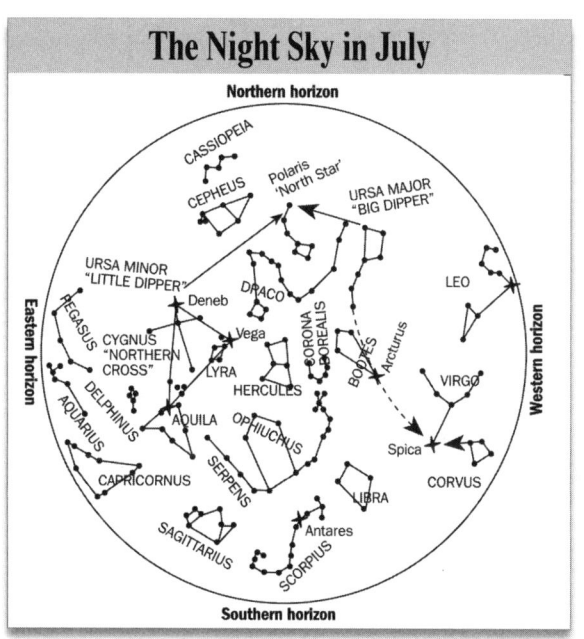

The Night Sky in August

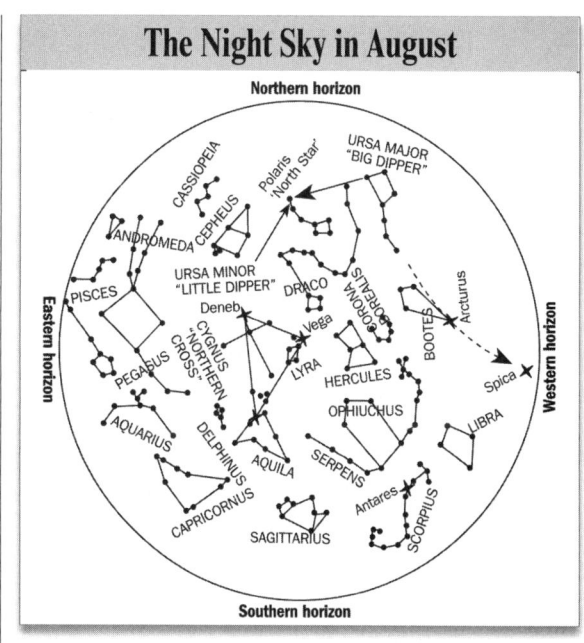

Piscis Austrinius	Southern Fish
Puppis	Stern (deck)
Pyxis	Compass (sea)
Reticulum	Reticle
Sagitta	Arrow
Sagittarius	Archer
Scorpius	Scorpion
Sculptor	Sculptor
Scutum	Shield
Serpens	Serpent
Sextans	Sextant
Taurus	Bull
Telescopium	Telescope
Triangulum	Triangle
Triangulum Australe	Southern Triangle
Tucana	Toucan
Ursa Major	Great Bear
Ursa Minor	Little Bear
Vela	Sail
Virgo	Maiden
Volans	Flying Fish
Vulpecula	Fox

Our 12 Closest Stellar Neighbors

Astronomers are discovering nearby stars at an astonishing rate by using increasingly sensitive detectors. The closest star is the sun, of course; next comes Proxima Centauri, among the dimmest in the firmament. Sirius, also known as the Dog Star, shines brightest after the sun. Another close star, Barnard's, is thought to have planets orbiting around it. Stars are far apart from each other—many light-years separate the stars below. Many stars occur in multiple-star systems, shown here by the suffixes A and B.

NAME	DISTANCE FROM THE SUN (light-years)*	CONSTELLATION
Proxima Centauri	4.3	*Centaurus*
Rigil Kentaurus	4.3	*Centaurus*
Barnard's Star	5.9	*Ophiuchus*
Wolf 359	7.6	*Leo*
Lalande 21185	8.1	*Ursa Major*
Sirius [A & B]	8.6	*Canis Major*
Luyten 726-8[A & B]	8.9	*Cetus*
Ross 154	9.4	*Sagittarius*
Ross 248	10.3	*Andromeda*
Epsilon Eridani	10.7	*Eridanus*
Luyten 789-6	10.8	*Aquarius*
Ross 128	10.8	*Virgo*

*A light-year is the distance light travels in a year, equal to 5.88 trillion miles or 9.46 trillion kilometers.

SCIENCE

The Night Sky in September

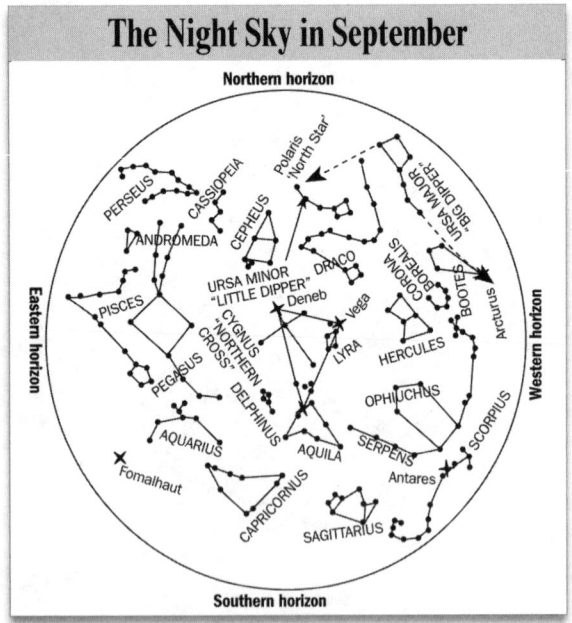

The Night Sky in October

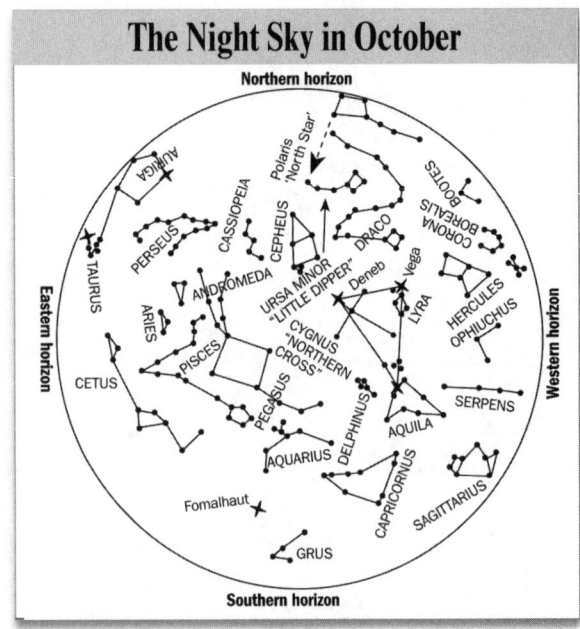

A Portrait of the Planets

Getting to know our neighbors in space

Of the eight planets in the solar system, only four besides the Earth are visible to the naked eye: Venus, Mars, Jupiter and Saturn.

MERCURY. The smallest of the planets is Mercury, with a diameter that is less than half the Earth's. Named for the winged messenger of the gods, it is the planet closest to the sun and has no satellites. It is believed that Mercury always turns the same side toward the sun and that the sunlit part of Mercury has a temperature hotter than 600 degrees Fahrenheit. By contrast, the temperature on the side away from the sun is thought to be –460 degrees Fahrenheit.

VENUS. Named for the goddess of love and beauty, Venus is almost the same size as Earth and is often called Earth's sister planet. The brightest of all the planets in the night sky, Venus is shadowed only by the sun and the moon. It is the first "star" to appear in the evening sky and the

last to disappear in the morning. At its brightest, Venus may even be visible during the day. Many astronomers believe that the core of Venus is largely metallic, mostly iron and nickel. Because of the dense carbon dioxide clouds enveloping the planet, the surface of Venus can't be seen.

EARTH. This is the third-closest planet to the sun—they are only 93 million miles apart. Seen from space, the planet appears as a blue ocean sphere with brown and green areas marking the location of its continents. Its diameter at the equator is 7,900 miles, and its atmosphere contains 78 percent nitrogen and 21 percent oxygen in addition to traces of water in gaseous form, carbon dioxide and other gases. By measuring the radioactive decay of elements in the earth's crust, scientists estimate that the planet is about 4.5 billion years old.

MARS. Like Earth, Mars has four seasons, but its diameter is just about half that of Earth's, and its mass is only about a tenth of ours. Named for

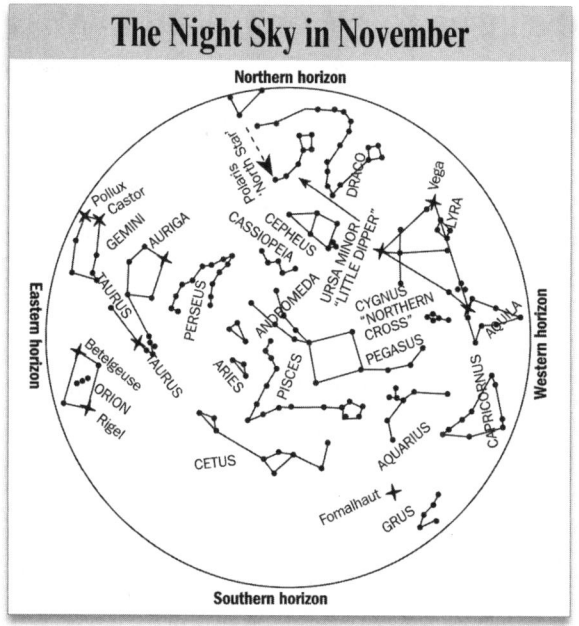

The Night Sky in November

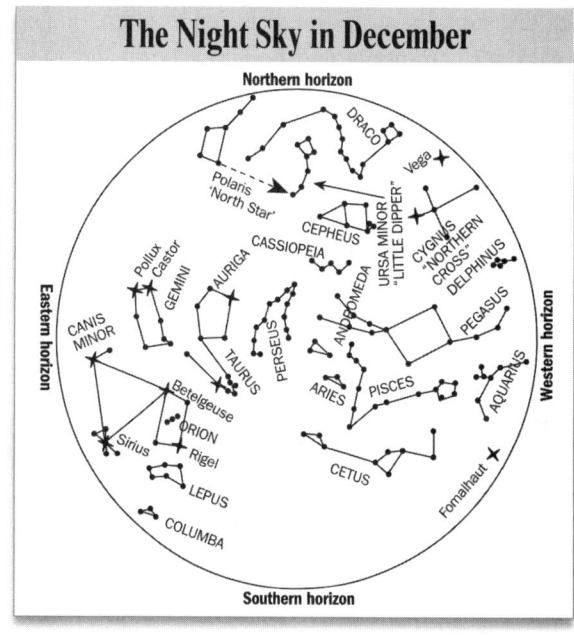

The Night Sky in December

the god of war, Mars takes 687 days to complete one revolution of the sun. About 80 percent of the planet's atmosphere is carbon dioxide. The white caps that cover its poles increase in size during the Martian winter and shrink during the summer. Martian seasons are about twice as long as Earth's.

JUPITER. Next to the sun, Jupiter is the largest and most massive object in the solar system. Named for the leader of the gods, Jupiter has a mass more than twice that of all other planets combined. A body on the surface of Jupiter would weigh 2.64 times its weight on Earth. Jupiter completes a revolution every 10 hours, giving it the shortest day in the solar system. It has 12 satellites, the largest number of any planet in the solar system. It is perhaps most famous for its Great Red Spot, which scientists believe is a storm that has been going on for 300 years.

SATURN. The second-largest planet in the solar system, Saturn is named for Titan, the father of

Jupiter and the god of sowing. It is best known for its system of concentric rings, which are not visible to the naked eye. The rings are probably composed of debris from a shattered satellite. Saturn is the least dense of all the planets but one of the brightest.

URANUS. Visible by the naked eye on a dark, clear night, Uranus is unique because its axis of rotation lies almost in the plane of its orbit. The planet was discovered by the German-English astronomer William Herschel in 1781. Herschel proposed to name the planet Georgium Sidu, in honor of England's King George III. But in keeping with the tradition of naming planets after Greek gods, it was eventually named after the father of Titan and the grandfather of Jupiter. Uranus has five known satellites and a mass over 14 times that of Earth. Its temperature is thought to be below -300 degrees Fahrenheit.

NEPTUNE. Named for the god of the sea, Neptune takes 165 years to complete one revolution

SCIENCE

of the sun. Its atmosphere is made of methane, hydrogen, ammonia and helium, and its mass is about 17 times that of Earth. The planet was discovered as a result of a mathematical prediction. Two mathematicians, John Couch Adams and Urbain Leverrier, calculated that there must be an unknown planet more distant from the sun than Uranus because they could detect the gravitational pull on Uranus.

 INSIDE INFO

Pluto Gets a Demotion

O In 2006, the International Astronomical Union decreed that Pluto was no longer a planet, but a member of a new category known as dwarf planets, bodies that were large enough to be round but which did not gravitationally dominate other celestial objects in their orbital neighborhoods. Then, in 2008, the union announced the creation of the term ''plutoid'' for a dwarf planet, like Pluto, beyond the orbit of Neptune.

O There is only one plutoid other than Pluto: Eris, the sphere of rock and ice formerly nicknamed Xena that is slightly larger than Pluto. (Pluto's diameter is less than one-fifth that of the Earth.)

O There is probably little or no atmosphere on Pluto because of its extreme temperature, which is nearly –400 degrees Fahrenheit. From Pluto the sun would only appear as a bright star.

O Named for the god of the underworld, the dwarf planet's first two letters are also the initials of Percival Lowell, whose research on gravitational forces led him to predict the planet's existence. However, Pluto wasn't discovered until 14 years after Lowell's death in 1916.

—Kenneth Chang

Eclipses You Won't Want to Miss

Catching an eclipse can be a jaw-dropping event

An eclipse occurs when a celestial body, such as the earth or the moon, casts a shadow so that another celestial body seems to disappear.

A solar eclipse takes place when the earth, moon and sun are in alignment. During a total eclipse, all the light of the sun is blocked because of the moon's position. But never stare at the sun with an unprotected eye or you risk serious eye damage. Just a quick glimpse—even when the sun seems dim—is dangerous. Use filtered telescopes or binoculars to protect your eyes.

A lunar eclipse occurs when the sun, earth and moon are aligned so that the moon is in the shadow of the earth.

10 YEARS OF SOLAR ECLIPSES 2010-2020

Date	Time (U.T.)[1]	Type
2010 January 15	7:06	Annular
2010 July 11	19:33	Total
2011 January 4	8:49	Partial
2011 June 1	21:15	Partial
2011 July 1	8:38	Partial
2011 November 25	6:20	Partial
2012 May 20	23:52	Annular
2012 November 13	22:12	Total
2013 May 10	0:24	Annular
2013 November 3	12:46	Partial
2014 April 29	6:02	Annular
2014 October 23	21:44	Partial
2015 Mar 20	9:45	Total
2015 September 13	6:54	Partial
2016 March 9	1:57	Total
2016 September 1	9:07	Annular
2017 February 26	14:52	Annular
2017 August 21	18:24	Total

Date	Time (U.T.)[1]	Type
2018 February 15	20:50	Partial
2018 July 13	3:00	Partial
2018 August 11	9:45	Partial
2019 January 6	1:41	Partial
2019 July 2	19:22	Total
2019 December 26	5:16	Annular
2020 June 21	6:40	Annular
2020 December 14	16:33	Total

UPCOMING TOTAL ECLIPSES

Date	Time (Of greatest eclipse in U.T.)	Duration (Mins. and secs.)
2010 July 11	19:34	5m 20s
2012 November 13	22:12	4m 02s
2015 Mar 20	09:46	2m 47s
2016 March 9	01:57	4m 09s
2017 August 21	18:25	2m 40s
2019 July 2	19:23	4m 33s
2020 December 14	16:13	2m 10s
2021 December 04	07:33	1m 54s
2024 Apr 08	18:17	4m 28s
2026 August 12	17:46	2m 18s
2027 August 2	10:06	6m 23s
2028 July 22	02:55	5m 10s
2030 November 25	06:50	3m 44s
2033 March 30	18:01	2m 37s
2034 March 20	10:17	4m 09s
2035 September 02	01:55	2m 54s
2037 July 13	02:39	3m 58s
2038 December 26	00:58	2m 18s
2039 December 15	16:22	1m 51s
2041 April 30	11:51	1m 51s
2042 April 20	02:16	4m 51s
2043 April 9	18:56	—
2044 August 23	01:15	2m 04s
2045 August 12	17:41	6m 06s
2046 August 02	10:19	4m 51s

Date	Time (Of greatest eclipse in U.T.)	Duration (Mins. and secs.)
2048 December 05	15:34	3m 28s
2052 March 30	18:30	4m 08s
2053 September 12	9:32	3m 04s
2055 July 24	9:56	3m 17s

NOTES:

[1] Universal Time (U.T.) is an astronomical standard that is five hours ahead of Eastern Standard Time.

SOURCE: Eclipse prediction data by Fred Espenak, NASA/GSFC

10 YEARS OF LUNAR ECLIPSES 2010-2020

Date	Time (U.T.)	Type
2010 June 26	11:38	Partial
2010 December 21	8:17	Total
2011 June 15	20:12	Total
2011 December 10	14:32	Total
2012 June 4	11:03	Partial
2012 November 28	14:33	Penumbral
2013 April 25	20:07	Partial
2013 May 25	4:10	Penumbral
2013 October 18	23:50	Penumbral
2014 April 15	7:45	Total
2014 October 8	10:54	Total
2015 April 4	12:00	Total
2015 Sep 28	2:47	Total
2016 March 23	11:47	Penumbral
2016 September 16	18:54	Penumbral
2017 February 11	0:44	Penumbral
2017 August 7	18:20	Partial
2018 January 31	13:30	Total
2018 July 27	20:22	Total
2019 January 21	5:12	Total
2019 July 16	21:31	Partial
2020 January 10	19:10	Penumbral
2020 June 5	19:25	Penumbral
2020 July 5	4:30	Penumbral
2020 November 30	9:43	Penumbral

SOURCE: Eclipse prediction data by Fred Espenak, NASA/GSFC

NEW MOON   WAXING CRESCENT   FIRST QUARTER   WAXING GIBBOUS   FULL MOON   WANING GIBBOUS   LAST QUARTER   WANING CRESCENT

How the Moon Turns
The science behind the lunar calendar

The moon takes slightly longer than 27 days to complete its elliptical orbit around the earth, but because the earth also moves around the sun, it takes 29 days, 12 hours, 44 minutes and 3 seconds to go from one new moon to the next. At the start of each orbit, the moon is directly between the earth and the sun, and thus invisible, because its dark side is toward us. Gradually, a crescent appears and waxes toward the full moon, and then wanes again to invisibility.

The moon has no light of its own; it merely reflects the light of the sun. If the moon did not rotate as it revolves around the earth, we would see all its sides; as it is, we always see the same side.

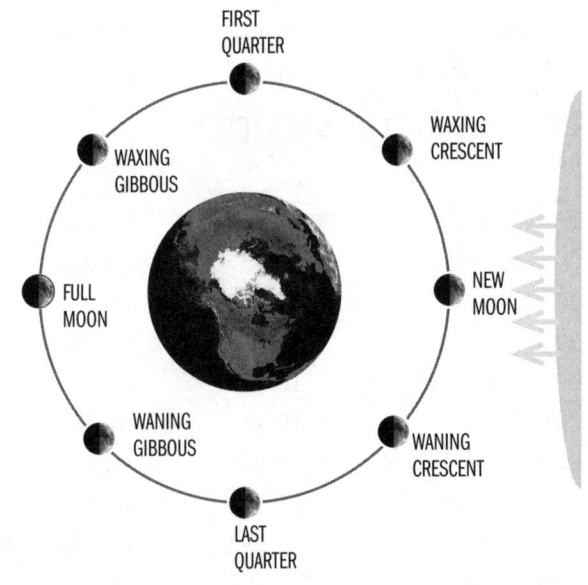

MOONLIGHT SONATA

Here's a month-to-month calendar for the moon's phases from 2010 to 2013. Times are expressed in Universal Time (U.T.), an astronomical standard that is five hours ahead of Eastern Standard Time.

2009-2010	NOV 9 15:56	NOV 16 19:14	NOV 24 21:39	DEC 2 07:30	DEC 9 00:13	DEC 16 12:02	DEC 24 17:36	DEC 31 19:13 P	JAN 7 10:40	JAN 15 07:11 A	JAN 23 10:53	JAN 30 06:18	FEB 5 23:49
	FEB 14 02:51	FEB 22 00:42	FEB 28 16:38	MAR 7 15:42	MAR 15 21:01	MAR 23 11:00	MAR 30 02:25	APR 6 09:37	APR 14 12:29	APR 21 18:20	APR 28 12:18	MAY 6 04:15	MAY 14 01:04
	MAY 20 23:43	MAY 27 23:07	JUN 4 22:13	JUN 12 11:15	JUN 19 04:30	JUN 26 11:30 P	JUL 4 14:35	JUL 11 19:40 T	JUL 18 10:11	JUL 26 01:37	AUG 3 04:59	AUG 108 03:08	AUG 16 18:14
	AUG 24 17:05	SEP 1 17:22	SEP 8 10:30	SEP 15 05:50	SEP 23 09:17	OCT 1 03:52	OCT 7 18:44	OCT 14 21:27	OCT 23 01:36	OCT 30 12:46	NOV 6 04:52	NOV 13 16:39	NOV 21 17:27

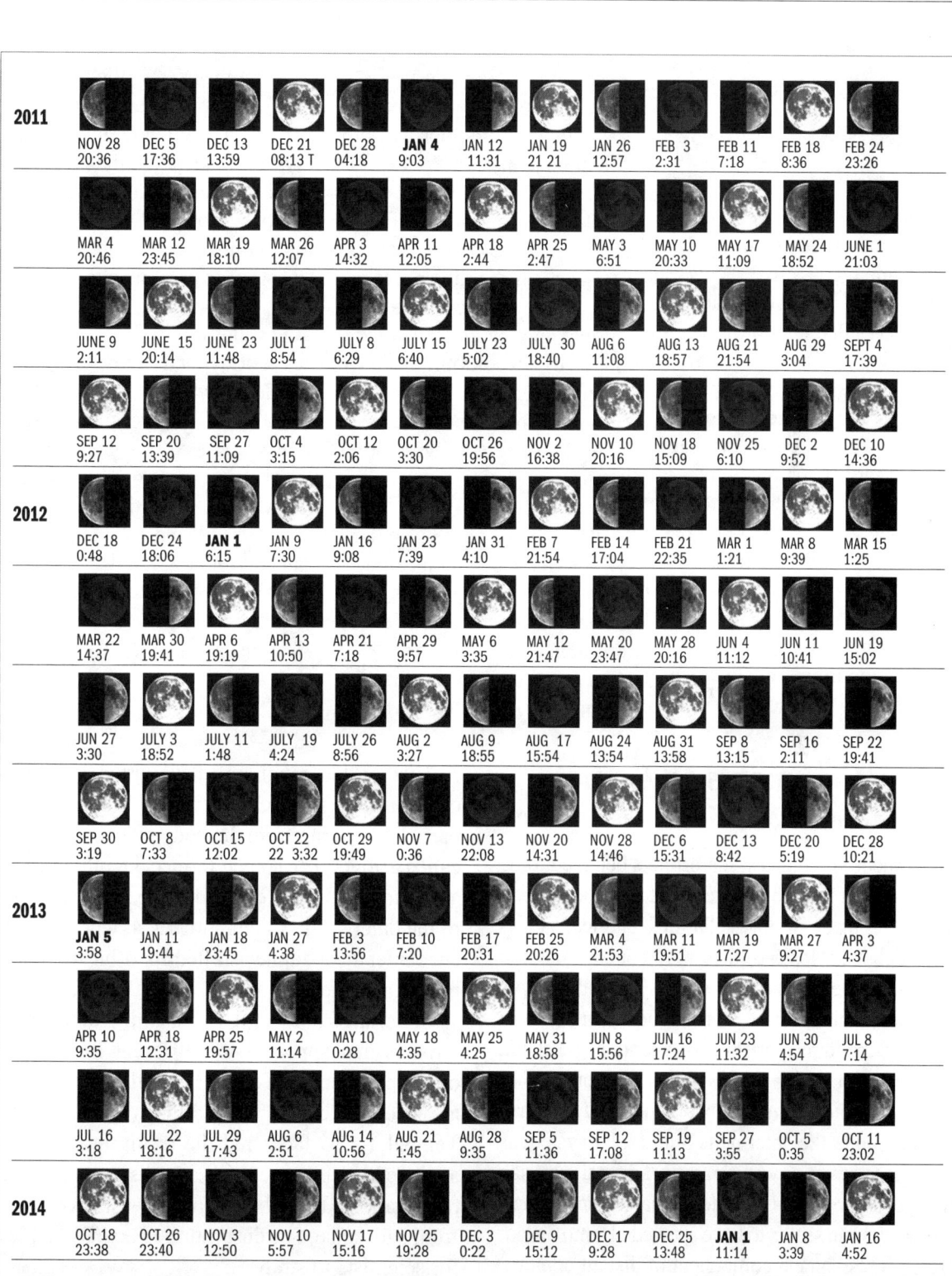

TIMELY TIPS

A Virtual Moon Voyage

Lunar craters are just a click away

Imagine soaring over the surface of the moon, dipping into a crater and seeing rock slides on its slopes and boulders piled up at the bottom. You don't have to wait for a spaceship or even the night sky to get such a close-up view of the moon. You can visit it with a computer and an Internet connection, courtesy of a free public-access program developed by the National Aeronautics and Space Administration's Ames Research Center in California.

The moon views—detailed and three-dimensional—are an extension of NASA's World Wind computer program that has allowed computer users to see almost any place on earth by tapping into databases of satellite information. Using the system's Blue Planet data set, you can see the entire earth down to a resolution of 50 feet and the entire United States to a resolution of about 3 feet. Data for about 30 urban areas lets you see objects one foot wide, good enough resolution to recognize houses and cars.

Programmers expanded this view to the moon by incorporating 1.8 million pictures and other data about its surface acquired by the *Clementine*, which orbited it for two months in the mid-90s. After down-loading the World Wind program, computer users running Microsoft's Windows operating system can tap into the lunar data set. From a vantage point in space, you can see the moon and virtually control its movements. Zoom in and slowly soar over the surface, dip into craters and valleys.

World Wind can be downloaded at www.worldwind.arc. nasa.gov. Some program users have produced a Web site that provides instructions and help, as well as applications that use the World Wind data, such as an add-on program that makes it easier to find spots like the Apollo landing sites. These features and help are online at www.worldwindcentral.com.

—Warren E. Leary

A Few Comments on Comets

They may be more than just dust and particles

Comets, small dusty sun-orbiters believed to be left over from the formation of the solar system, are not all made of interstellar dust and ice, as was once believed. Instead, they may contain material shot from the heart of the solar system during its tumultuous birth. That was the conclusion of scientists after examining pristine particles of a comet that were brought back by the Stardust spacecraft.

The evidence suggests that comets did not form in isolation in the outer parts of the solar system as it coalesced from a swirling mass of primal material. Instead, some of the hot material that formed planets around the sun seems to have spewed off into distant areas and become a component of distant comets.

The Stardust robot craft flew within 150 miles of the nucleus of the comet Wild 2 and trapped particles spewing from the body in a porous foam called aerogel. The comet, formed 4.5 billion years ago, had remained preserved in the frozen reaches of the outer solar system until 1974, when a close encounter with Jupiter shifted its orbit to a path between Jupiter and Mars.

Material from Wild 2 has mineral characteristics that appear to be different from those observed in comet Tempel 1. In that 2005 case, a spacecraft called Deep Impact crashed into Tempel 1's surface, and the resulting dust was analyzed by the spacecraft and distant telescope observations. But while Tempel 1 was examined from a distance, Stardust returned actual samples for scientists to study.

—Warren E. Leary

A Beachgoer's Guide to the Tides

Why the tide comes in and goes out

Some ancient myth-makers held that the earth's pulse or breathing caused the tides. The Greeks began to notice the moon's influence when they started to venture out of the relatively tideless Mediterranean. Our modern understanding of the tides is based on Sir Isaac Newton's equilibrium theory of tides, which described the gravitational attractions of the sun and moon on the earth's waters. Today, tides can be predicted with astronomical precision and need no longer be a mystery. Here's what landlubbers will find when they are at the beach.

If you live on the East Coast, expect the tides to be semidiurnal. That's when high and low tides occur twice per lunar day, and the heights of both the first and second set of tides are roughly the same. A lunar day is 50 minutes longer than a day on earth, which is why in many places high and low tides occur about 50 minutes later than the corresponding tides of the previous day.

If you live on the West Coast, expect mixed tides. The tides on America's left coast rise and fall twice per lunar day, but the heights of the second set of tides differ from the first. The different tides each day are termed high water, lower high water, high-low water and lower low water. The order of occurrence varies over the course of the month and from place to place.

Along the Gulf of Mexico, the tides are diurnal. Here, high and low tides appear only once every day.

About twice a month, near the time of the new and full moon, the tidal range between high and low tides is usually 20 percent above average. These tides, known as spring tides, occur when the sun and moon are in a straight line with the earth. When the sun and moon are at right angles to each other with respect to the earth, tidal ranges between high and low tides are about 20 percent less than average. These tides, known as neap tides, occur around the time of the first and third quarters of the moon.

For another big swing in height between high and low tide, wait until the moon is at perigee. That's when the moon is at its closest point to the earth each month. That's also when the tidal range between high and low tide is greatest. Roughly two weeks later the moon is at apogee, which is its farthest point from the earth for the month. At that point, the moon's influence is at a minimum.

THE MOON AND TIDES

The tide is the rise and fall of water throughout the earth's oceans. Occurring every 12 hours and 26 minutes, tides are created primarily by the moon's pull of gravity on the water.

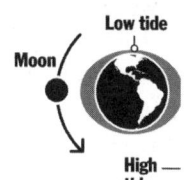

HIGH TIDES are produced when the earth is nearer the moon and water is pulled toward the moon. This happens on the opposite side of the earth at the same time.

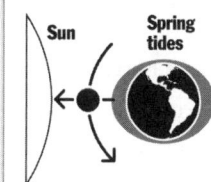

SPRING TIDES occur when the sun and the moon are directly in line. The moon is either in front of or behind the earth. This produces a very high tide twice a month.

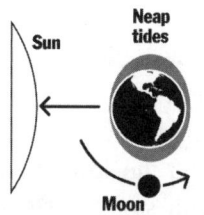

NEAP TIDES do not rise as high as normal because the moon is at right angles to the sun. A neap tide occurs twice a month.

During the course of the month, daily inequities between successive high or low tides also can occur. This happens as the moon moves from about 28 degrees north of the equator to 28 degrees south. When the moon is at one of these extremes, the difference in height between morning and evening tides is greatest. When the moon is at the equator, tides are roughly equal.

The tidal range also increases in January. That's when the earth's elliptical orbit around the sun brings the planet closest to the sun, in what astronomers call the state of perihelion. In July, when the earth is farthest from the sun in what astronomers refer to as the state of aphelion, the tidal range decreases.

The shape and depth of ocean basins change tidal ranges, too. The smallest differences in the heights between high and low tides occur along open coasts. For example, spring tidal ranges (near the time of the new and full moon) vary from about 2 feet on the Gulf Coast to as much as 8 or 9 feet on the California coast. The largest tidal ranges are found in tidal inlets, estuaries and salt marshes. The Bay of Fundy in Canada has the greatest difference in the world between high and low tide. There, the funnel-like opening of the bay concentrates the energy and increases the height of the incoming tide, resulting in average tidal ranges of about 45 feet.

Meteorological conditions can also disrupt normal tide patterns. While the tide tables provide accurate times and heights of high and low tide, strong and persistent winds and the low atmospheric pressure associated with storm systems

❝

Ancient sea-dwellers held that a child could be born only during an incoming tide and a dying person could not expire until the tide went out.

• • •

can alter the time and height of high or low tide. If you are planning to go clamming or to collect seashells at low tide and there is a strong onshore breeze, you may want to delay for as long as an hour after the predicted time of low tide.

Horizontal water movements, known as tidal currents, are generally strongest midway between high and low tide. When the tide rises and water flows in to fill estuaries and inlets, the water is called a flood current. When the tide goes out and water drains from these coastal areas, the flow is called an ebb current. Slack currents are found around the time of both high and low tide.

Surf fishing is best done when tidal currents are strongest. Strong flood currents force bait fish up closer to the beach and cause them to school up tighter and hide behind features such as rocks or jetties. Game fish such as bluefish or striped bass take advantage of these conditions, and so should knowledgeable surf fishermen. Game fish lie in wait for the bait fish to be swept in and out of inlets, estuaries and bays by flood and ebb currents. Slack water is usually the worst time to fish.

Boaters shouldn't rely on the tidal charts in coastal newspapers. While most coastal newspapers list the times and heights of high and low tide, boaters need more tidal information than the papers provide in order to ensure safety over the ocean floor and to know where to anchor. They should consult the tide and tidal current tables published each year by the National Oceanic and Atmospheric Administration, found online at tidesandcurrents.noaa.gov.

Star Talk: Words for Astronomers

Key terms to help you navigate the universe

Do you know the scientific definitions of a "blue moon" and a "white dwarf"? You'll find them here, along with other astronomy terms to master.

Accretion. A process in which matter that revolves around a celestial body is gradually pulled in and added to the body's mass. The process is thought to be responsible for the formation of planets and satellites.

Aphelion. The point in time and distance at which an object orbiting the sun is farthest from the sun.

Asteroid. Rocky object that orbits the sun, mostly in the asteroid belt between Mars and Jupiter. Asteroids are thought to be debris from the formation of the solar system or from collisions between larger planetary bodies. There are an estimated 100,000 asteroids.

Astronomical Unit. An astronomical unit (A.U.) is 93 million miles, or the distance from the earth to the sun.

Big bang theory. The belief that a massive explosion of a dense mass of matter started the universe. After the explosion, the universe was splattered with energy and atomic particles, followed by lower density and lower temperatures. Space itself was thought to expand after the big bang, and continues to expand, according to the theory.

Binary star. A system of two stars revolving around a common center and linked by a mutual gravitational pull.

Blue Moon. The second full moon that occurs within one calendar month.

Black dwarf. A star that has used up its energy sources and can no longer emit light. In theory, the universe is too young to have yet produced a black dwarf.

Black hole. A theoretical region in space thought to contain a body with such a strong gravitational field that no matter or energy can resist the pull. The theory states that even light cannot escape from it, explaining why black holes can never be seen.

Comet. A small object that orbits the sun independently in an elliptical orbit. Astronomers have theorized that comets have three identifying components: the nucleus, made up of rock and ice; the coma, its gaseous atmosphere; and the tail, made up of gases and atomic dust.

Corona. The outer layer and hottest part of the sun's atmosphere. During a solar eclipse, the corona is sometimes visible around the moon's periphery.

Dark matter. Undetected matter in the universe, presumed to exist because of gravitational effects. Astronomers believe it comprises a large part of the universe's mass but have not yet observed it directly.

Equinox. A crossing of the celestial equator by the sun. There are two annual equinoxes—vernal (around March 21) and autumnal (around September 23). On these days, the lengths of day and night are approximately equal everywhere on earth.

Fireball. An exceptionally bright meteor, sometimes visible during the day.

Light-year. The distance light travels in one year, equal to 5.88 trillion miles, 9.46 trillion kilometers or 63,240 astronomical units.

Magnitude. A measure used to describe the brightness of a celestial object. The smaller the number, the brighter the object. The brightest star, Sirius, shines at a magnitude of –1.5. A full moon measures –13, and the sun blazes at almost –26.

SCIENCE

Meteor. Small, rocky, icy particles that produce a streak of light in the sky as they burn up in the earth's atmosphere. Meteors are often called shooting or falling stars because they travel across the sky in short bursts. Meteor showers, it is thought, are produced by debris left by comets as they orbit the sun.

Meterorite. A piece of fallen rock from outer space that has reached the surface of the earth, often creating a crater on impact. The largest meteorite to date weighed 60 tons; it landed in Namibia, Africa, in 1920.

Milky Way. The spiral galaxy to which the earth and its solar system belong. Parts of it appear as a faint band of light in a clear night sky. The Milky Way is made up of billions of stars, is about 12 billion years old and has a diameter of 100,000 light-years.

Nebula. A cloud of interstellar gases and dust in the galaxy that appears as a hazy, fuzzy or dark patch.

Nova. A star that suddenly flares in brightness by more than 10 magnitudes and then slowly fades to its original luminosity. The burst of brightness may be caused by the fusion reaction that occurs when one star mass collides with another. Novas appear every few years; supernovas are a rare.

Penumbra. Faint outer shadow of the moon; partial eclipses are seen from within this shadow.

Perigee. The point in the orbit of a moon or planet in which it comes closest to the body it orbits.

Perihelion. The point in which a celestial body in orbit comes closest to the sun.

Plasma. Hot ionized gas found in the sun and stars, as well as in fusion reactors.

Pulsars. Generally thought to be rapidly rotating neutron stars, pulsars emit brief, intense bursts of radio waves, radiation and X-rays in specific directions. The word comes from a contraction of "pulsating stars."

Quasars. The most distant celestial objects known. These compact objects emit massive amounts of energy, sometimes equal to many times more than the energy output of an entire galaxy. The name is a contraction of "quasi-stellar radio source."

Solstice. The point at which the sun is farthest away from the celestial equator. It signals the beginning of summer in the Northern Hemisphere and the beginning of winter in the Southern Hemisphere.

Supernova. A massive explosion of a large star in the final stages of stellar life that creates a short but intense light that is up to 100 million times the brightness of the sun. The gases produced by the blast spew into space, and the core collapses into a neutron star or perhaps into a black hole.

Syzygy. The straight-line formation or opposition of three celestial bodies. Syzygy takes place during lunar and solar eclipses, for example, when the sun, earth and moon are aligned.

Umbra. Dark inner shadow of the moon; total eclipses are seen from within this shadow.

White dwarf. A dim, dense star that has collapsed on itself and is near the end of its stellar life. A white dwarf is about the size of the earth and has a high surface temperature. An example of a white dwarf is Sirius' companion star in the Canis Major constellation.

Zenith. The point directly overhead in the sky, or 90 degrees above the horizon. The highest point reached by a celestial body.

Zodiacal light. A faint glow of light in the sky visible before sunrise to the east and after sunset to the west. The light is caused by interplanetary dust reflected in the sunlight.

Figures & Formulas

Measure by Measure: A Guide

How to convert miles to kilometers, pounds to kilos and much more

Weights and measures have been a matter for pharaohs, emperors and kings to establish and for practical men and women to follow for thousands of years. The Egyptians based their system of measurement on the human body: the space from the little finger to the thumb tip was considered a span, and two spans were the equivalent of one cubit, which was approximately the distance from a person's fingertips to the elbow. The mile was a Roman unit of measure: it came from the word "mille," which stood for "1,000 paces."

There are several legends to explain where the English unit of measure the yard originated. One is that it was the same length as King Henry I's arm. Another is that it represented the distance from the tip of Henry's nose to the end of his thumb. Yet another version suggests that it was inspired by the length of the arrows used by the king's archers. In any case, the state's role in setting standards has never been in doubt. For many centuries the weights and measures that Americans inherited from Britain were referred to as "the king's standard."

Americans have moved a fair way, however, from both the Queen's English and what has come to be known as the British Imperial System of weights and measures. In the United States today, weights and measures are usually referred to by the name "U.S. Customary System."

Most of the rest of the world, of course, follows the International (or Metric) System, which is a decimal system in which units of measurement increase by multiples of 10. First developed by ancient Hindu mathematicians and then embraced by the Arabs in the 10th century, the Metric System came into gradual use in Europe after 1100 and was officially adopted by the French in the late 1700s, about the time Louis XVI and Marie Antoinette faced the guillotine.

Led by the government agencies and the scientific and engineering communities, metrics are gradually winning wider acceptance in U.S. industry. Still far off, however, is the day when the rulebook states that the proper height of a basketball hoop is 3.048 meters—rather than 10 feet.

 TIMELY TIPS

Making Do Without a Ruler

A little ingenuity can go a long way when you need a quick measurement, albeit an approximate one. Knowing the dimensions of a few common objects can help.

✔ **Need the dimensions of a room?** It helps to know that most floor tile is 9 x 9 or 12 x 12 inches.

✔ **At a flea market with no tape measure?** Use a dollar bill (or any denomination). A bill is 6 $1/18$ inches long.

✔ **For measuring smaller areas, use a coin.** A quarter is approximately 1 inch in diameter; a penny is $3/4$ inches in diameter.

✔ **It pays to know** that a credit card is 3 $3/28$ by 2 $1/8$ inches; a business card is generally 3 $5/8$ x 2 inches.

U.S. Customary Units

LENGTH. *Use to measure lines and distances.*

12 inches =	1 foot
3 feet =	1 yard
1,760 yards =	1 statute mile
5 1/2 yards =	1 rod
40 rods = 1 furlong =	220 yards
8 furlongs = 5,280 feet =	1 statute mile

AREA. *Multiply length by width in units of the same denomination to find surface area.*

144 square inches =	1 square foot
9 square feet =	1 square yard
30 1/4 square yards =	2 square rods
160 square rods =	1 acre
640 acres =	1 square mile

VOLUME. *Multiply length by breadth by thickness to find cubic content or volume.*

1,728 cubic inches =	1 cubic foot
27 cubic feet =	1 cubic yard

LIQUID CAPACITY. *Use to measure a container's capacity to hold liquids.*

1 gill =	4 fluid ounces
4 gills = 2 cups =	1 pint
1 pint =	16 fluid ounces
2 pints =	1 quart
4 quarts =	1 gallon
31 1/2 gallons =	1 barrel
2 barrels =	1 hogshead

DRY CAPACITY. *Use to measure a container's capacity to hold solids such as flour.*

2 pints =	1 quart
4 quarts =	1 gallon
8 quarts =	1 peck
4 pecks =	1 bushel

AVOIRDUPOIS (MASS) WEIGHT. *Use for weighing articles such as grain and groceries.*

27.344 grains =	1 dram
16 drams =	1 ounce
16 ounces =	1 pound
100 pounds =	1 short hundredweight
20 short hundredweight =	1 short ton

HOW FAR IS THAT IN MILES?

Miles to	kilometers	Miles to	kilometers
1.6	1	1	0.6
3.2	2	2	1.2
4.8	3	3	1.9
6.4	4	4	2.5
8.0	5	5	3.1
9.7	6	6	3.7
11.3	7	7	4.3
12.9	8	8	5.6
14.5	9	9	5.6
16.1	10	10	6.2
160.9	100	100	62.1
1,609.3	1,000	1,000	621.4

Metric Units

LENGTH

10 millimeters =	1 centimeter
10 centimeters =	1 decimeter
10 decimeters =	1 meter
10 meters =	1 decameter
10 decameters =	1 hectometer
10 hectometers =	1 kilometer

AREA

100 square millimeters =	1 square centimeter
100 square centimeters =	1 square decimeter
100 square decimeters =	1 square meter
100 square meters =	1 square decameter
=	1 are
100 ares =	1 hectare
100 square decameters =	1 square hectometer
100 square hectometers =	1 square kilometer
100 hectares =	1 square kilometer

VOLUME

1,000 cubic millimeters = 1 cubic centimeter
1,000 cubic centimeters = 1 cubic decimeter
1,000 cubic decimeters = 1 cubic meter

DRY AND LIQUID CAPACITY

10 milliliters = 1 centiliter
10 centiliters = 1 deciliter
10 deciliters = 1 liter
10 liters = 1 decaliter
10 decaliters = 1 hectoliter
10 hectoliters = 1 kiloliter

MASS. *Use to measure weights and both dry and liquid capacities.*

10 milligrams = 1 centigram
10 centigrams = 1 decigram
10 decigrams = 1 gram
10 grams = 1 decagram
10 decagrams = 1 hectogram
10 hectograms = 1 kilogram
100 kilograms = 1 quintal
1,000 kilograms = 1 metric ton
10 quintals = 1 metric ton

Converting U.S. Customary Units to Metric Units

LENGTH

1 inch =	2.54 centimeters
=	0.025 meter
1 foot =	30.48 centimeters
=	0.305 meter
1 yard =	91.44 centimeters
=	0.914 meter
1 statute mile =	1,609.3 meters
=	1.609 kilometers

AREA

1 square inch =	6.452 square centimeters
1 square foot =	929.03 square centimeters
=	0.093 square meter

TEMPERATURE CONVERSIONS

To convert temperatures from Fahrenheit to Celsius, subtract 32 degrees and multiply by 5, then divide by 9. To go from Celsius to Fahrenheit, multiply by 9, divide by 5, then add 32 degrees.

Celsius = Fahrenheit	Fahrenheit = Celsius
450 = 842	450 = 232.2
425 = 797	425 = 218.3
400 = 752	400 = 204.4
375 = 707	375 = 190.6
350 = 662	350 = 176.7
325 = 617	325 = 162.8
300 = 572	300 = 148.9
275 = 527	275 = 135.0
250 = 482	250 = 121.1
225 = 437	225 = 107.2
200 = 392	212 = 100.0
175 = 347	110 = 43.3
150 = 302	105 = 40.6
125 = 257	100 = 37.8
100 = 212	95 = 35.0
95 = 203	90 = 32.2
90 = 194	85 = 29.4
85 = 185	80 = 26.7
80 = 176	75 = 23.9
75 = 167	70 = 21.1
70 = 158	65 = 18.3
65 = 149	60 = 15.6
60 = 140	55 = 12.8
55 = 131	50 = 10.0
50 = 122	45 = 7.2
45 = 113	40 = 4.4
40 = 104	35 = 1.7
35 = 95	**32 = 0.0**
30 = 86	30 = −1.1
25 = 77	25 = −3.9
20 = 68	20 = −6.7
15 = 59	15 = −9.4
10 = 50	10 = −12.2
5 = 41	5 = −15.0
0 = 32	0 = −17.8
−5 = 23	−5 = −20.6
−10 = 14	−10 = −23.3
−15 = 5	−15 = −26.1
−20 = −4	−20 = −28.9
−25 = −8.5	−25 = −31.7
−30 = −13	−30 = −34.4
−35 = −31	−35 = −37.2
−40 = −40	−40 = −40.0
−45 = −49	−45 = −42.8

SCIENCE

1 square yard =	8,361.274 square centimeters
=	0.836 square meter
1 acre =	4,046.856 square meters
=	0.405 square hectometer
1 square mile =	2,589,988.11 square meters
=	258.999 square hectometer
=	2.589 square kilometers

LIQUIDS

1 fluid ounce =	29.574 milliliters
=	0.029 liter
1 cup =	236.588 milliliters
=	0.237 liter
1 pint =	473.176 milliliters
=	0.473 liter
1 quart =	946.353 milliliters
=	0.946 liter

| 1 gallon = | 3,785.41 milliliters |
| = | 3.785 liters |

MASS

1 ounce =	28.349 grams
1 pound =	453.59 grams
=	0.454 kilogram
1 short ton =	907.18 kilograms
=	0.907 metric ton

Converting Metric Units to U.S. Customary Units

LENGTH

1 centimeter =	0.394 inch
1 meter =	3.281 feet = 1.094 yards
1 kilometer =	0.622 mile

AREA

1 square centimeter =	0.155 square inches
1 square meter =	1,550.003 square inches
=	10.764 square feet
=	1.196 square yards
1 hectare =	107,639.1 square feet
=	11,959.90 square yards
=	2.471 acres
=	0.004 square mile
1 square kilometer =	247.105 acres
=	0.386 square mile

LIQUIDS

1 milliliter =	0.034 fluid ounces
1 liter =	33.814 fluid ounces
=	4.227 cups = 2.113 pints
=	1.057 quarts = 0.264 gallons

MASS

1 milligram =	0.000035 ounce
1 gram =	0.03527 ounce
1 kilogram =	35.27 ounces = 2.205 pounds
1 metric ton =	2,204.6 pounds
=	1.102 short tons

The Long and the Short of Clothing Sizes

Here's a look at how European clothing sizes compare with U.S. sizes.

WOMEN

BLOUSES AND SWEATERS

	U.S.	32	34	36	38	40	42	44
	British	34	36	38	40	42	44	46
	Continental	40	42	44	46	48	50	52

COATS AND DRESSES

	U.S.	6	8	10	12	14	16	18
	British	8	10	12	14	16	18	20
	Continental	36	38	40	42	44	46	48

SHOES

	U.S.	5–5½	6–6½	7–7½	8–8½	9
	British	3½–4	4½–5	5½–6	6½–7	7½
	Continental	36	37	38	39	40

MEN

SUITS AND COATS

	U.S. & British	34	36	38	40	42	44	46
	Continental	44	46	48	50	52	54	56

HATS

	U.S.	6⅝	6¾	6⅞	7	7⅛	7¼	7⅜	7½
	British	6½	6⅝	6¾	6⅞	7	7⅛	7¼	7⅜
	Continental	53	54	55	56	57	58	59	60

SHIRTS

	U.S. & British	14	14½	15	15½	16	16½	17
	Continental	36	37	38	39	41	42	43

SHOES

	U.S.	7	7½	8	8½	9	9½	10	10½	11
	British	6½	7	7½	8	8½	9	9½	10	10½
	Continental	39	40	41	42	43	43	44	44	45

SOCKS

	U.S. & British	9½	10	10½	11	11½	12	12½
	Continental	39	40	41	42	43	44	45

CHILDREN

ALL CLOTHING

	U.S.	4	6	8	10	12	14
	British	43	48	55	40	58	60
	Continental (cm)	125	135	150	155	160	165

Special Weights & Measures

ANGLES AND CIRCLES. *Use in surveying, navigating, astronomy, geography, figuring latitude and longitude and computing differences in time.*

60 seconds =	1 minute
60 minutes =	1 degree
30 degrees =	1 sign

45 degrees =	1 octant
60 degrees =	1 sextant
90 degrees =	1 quadrant = 1 right angle
180 degrees =	1 straight angle = 1 semicircle
360 degrees =	1 circle

APOTHECARIES' FLUID MEASURE. *Used in mixing medicines.*

60 minims =	1 fluid dram

8 fluid drams =	1 fluid ounce
16 fluid ounces =	1 pint
2 pints =	1 quart
4 quarts =	1 gallon

APOTHECARIES' WEIGHT. *For weighing medicines for prescriptions.*

20 grains =	1 scruple
3 scruples =	1 dram
8 drams =	1 ounce
12 ounces =	1 pound

MARINERS' MEASURE. *To measure distance, depth or speed at sea.*

6 feet =	1 fathom
1,000 fathoms =	1 nautical mile (approx.)
1 nautical mile =	1.15 statute miles
3 nautical miles =	1 league
60 nautical miles =	1 degree
1 knot =	1 nautical mile per hour

SURVEYORS' MEASURE. *Use to measure the borders and dimensions of a tract of land.*

7.92 inches =	1 link
100 links =	1 chain
1 chain =	4 rods = 66 feet
80 chains =	1 survey mile = 5,280 feet

Measuring Computer Memory

Bits, bytes and beyond

Computer storage capacity is measured in bytes. On the one end is one byte, which holds the smallest unit of data; on the other are petabytes and beyond, which store massive amounts of information. Here's how the units for measuring computer memory break down.

A bit (short for binary digit) is the tiniest unit of information; the number 011, for example, is 3 bits long.

A byte is a very basic computer unit. It takes a collection of 8 bits, or an octet, to make a byte. One byte represents a single character, such as one letter.

A kilobyte, roughly 1,000 bytes, can store about one short e-mail.

A megabyte is about 1 million bytes; a megabyte of storage can hold around one minute of an MP3 music file, for example.

A gigabyte is is about one billion bytes. "Giga" comes from the Greek for giant. Hard drives are typically measured in "gigs," as in, "My computer has 250 gigs of disk space."

A terabyte is about 1,000 gigabytes, one million megabytes or one trillion bytes. "Tera" comes from the Greek for monster. A terabyte hard drive can hold hundreds of hours of video and audio, and massive amounts of word and picture files.

A petabyte is made up of around 1,000 terabytes. Petabytes are typically used to measure the storage capacity of multiple hard drives or other enormous collections of data. Beyond petabytes are exabytes (or about 1,000 petabytes)—a memory capacity so large that all the world's printed matter could be stored in roughly 5 exabytes.

What's a Pixel, Anyway?

A pixel (a contraction of picture and element) is a tiny, basic unit of an image on a display screen, such as a computer monitor or a television.

A megapixel is 1 million pixels. It usually refers to the resolution capability of a digital camera; the more pixels, the more realistic the image.

A computer screen is divided into a matrix of thousands or millions of pixels. You can try to see pixels on your screen by setting your monitor to a low resolution, say, 640 x 480 (that's a matrix of 640 x 480 pixels, or a total of 307,200 pixels). You may be able to see the separate dots, or pixels, that make up the image on your screen.

In color displays, each pixel is made up of red, blue and green subpixels, or rays of light of varying intensity.

SURVEYORS' SQUARE MEASURE. *Multiply length by breadth to find surface area of land.*

272 ¹/₄ square feet =	1 square rod
16 square rods =	1 square chain
160 square rods =	10 square chains
=	1 acre
640 acres =	1 square mile
=	1 section
36 square miles =	36 sections
=	1 township

TROY WEIGHT. *Use in weighing gold, silver and jewels.*

24 grains =	1 pennyweight
20 pennyweights =	1 ounce
12 ounces =	1 pound

WOOD MEASURE. *Use to measure the volume of a pile of wood.*

16 cubic feet =	1 cord foot
	= a wood pile that is 4 feet high by 4 feet wide by 1 foot long
8 cord feet =	1 cord
	= a wood pile 8 feet long by 4 feet wide by 4 feet high

COMMON HOUSEHOLD MEASURES. *Use to measure ingredients for cooking.*

3 teaspoons =	1 tablespoon
1 tablespoon =	¹/₁₆ cup
=	0.5 fluid ounce
4 tablespoons =	¹/₄ cup
5 tablespoons =	¹/₃ cup + 1 teaspoon
6 tablespoons =	³/₈ cup
8 tablespoons =	¹/₂ cup
10 tablespoons =	²/₃ cup + 2 teaspoons
12 tablespoons =	³/₄ cup
16 tablespoons =	1 cup
48 teaspoons =	1 cup
1 cup =	8 fluid ounces
2 cups =	1 pint
4 cups =	1 quart
2 pints =	1 quart
4 quarts =	1 gallon

FORMULAS FOR KEY HOUSEHOLD CONVERSIONS

Ounces x 28.349 =	grams
Grams x 0.032 =	ounces
Pounds x 453.592 =	grams
Pounds x 0.453 =	kilograms
Cups x 0.24 =	liters
Gallons x 3.785 =	liters

The Best Way to Set Your Watch
An atomic clock that lets you always be on time

The oldest clocks date back to the ancient Egyptians and Mesopotamians, who measured time by checking the position of a shadow created by the sun on a sundial. The Greeks, Romans and Chinese used water clocks to calculate the passage of time by observing the level of water flowing from a container. But neither method, although greatly refined over the years, ensured great precision.

The introduction of the pendulum advanced the process significantly. During the mid-1600s, Dutch scientist Christiaan Huygens used a pendulum's motion to turn wheels that controlled the hands of the clock. Pendulum clocks proved accurate to within one minute per day. The next major advance came in the 1927 with the introduction of the quartz crystal, the most commonly used device today. Electricity applied to the crystal causes it to vibrate at a constant rate, making the clock's hands move precisely. But even quartz watches can have their drawbacks. Factors like humidity, for example, can impair their accuracy.

The most precise timepiece around, and the basis of modern timekeeping today, is the atomic clock,

SCIENCE

which was developed in 1949. It uses the vibration of certain atoms to regulate time with great precision; the latest version is accurate to within less than one second in more than one billion years. Not long ago, atomic clocks were large, power-hungry, and expensive to build. But, scientists are

overcoming such problems: miniscule devices, with inner workings about the size of a grain of rice, are being developed by the Commerce Department's National Institute of Standards and Technology (N.I.S.T.). This chip-scale atomic clock opens the door to atomically precise timekeeping in portable, battery-powered clocks for use in cell phones, for example, or in navigation systems.

To set your own clock to a time that's accurate within .3 seconds, go to the agency's site at nist.time.gov and click on Internet Time Service.

Spring Ahead, Fall Back

More daylight for business, and goblins, too

Ben Franklin, as minister to France in the late 1700s, first proposed to the French that shops could save on the cost of lighting by opening and closing earlier. Franklin's idea was taken a step further in the early 1900s by a British builder who pushed for advancing clocks in the spring and turning them back in the fall. The plan took hold during the two World Wars as a fuel-conservation measure. Localities across the United States, however, adopted the practice willy-nilly, wreaking havoc on airline, railroad and broadcasting schedules. President Lyndon Johnson eliminated the chaos in 1966 by creating a uniform time for starting and ending daylight saving time.

Thus began the practice of moving clocks ahead by one hour in the spring and turning them back one hour in the fall, thereby shifting an hour of daylight from the morning to the evening. (Consumer safety advocates advise changing smoke-alarm batteries twice a year, at the

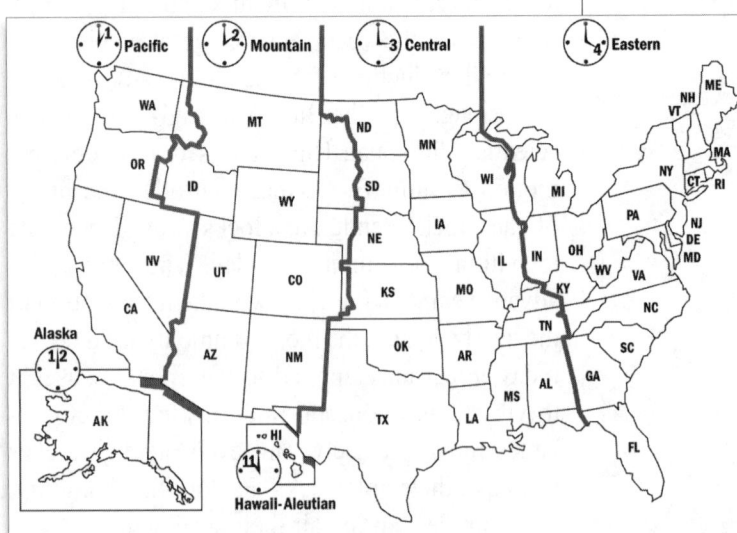

U.S. TIME ZONES AND DAYLIGHT SAVING TIME Note that Arizona and parts of Indiana do not observe daylight saving time.

When It's Lunchtime in New York...

The standard time in 65 major foreign cities, assuming it is noon in the Eastern Standard Time zone.

CITY, COUNTRY	TIME
Addis Ababa, Ethiopia	8 pm
Algiers, Algeria	5 pm
Amman, Jordan	8 pm
Amsterdam, Netherlands*	6 pm
Athens, Greece*	7 pm
Bagdad, Iraq*	8 pm
Bangkok, Thailand	12 midnight
Beijing, China	1am**
Beirut, Lebanon*	7 pm
Berlin, Germany*	6 pm
Bogota, Colombia	12 noon
Brussels, Belgium*	6 pm
Bucharest, Romania*	7 pm
Budapest, Hungary*	6 pm
Buenos Aires, Argentina	2 pm
Cairo, Egypt*	7 pm
Caracas, Venezuela	1 pm
Casablanca, Morocco	5 pm
Copenhagen, Denmark*	6 pm
Dublin, Ireland*	5 pm
Frankfurt, Germany*	6 pm
Geneva, Switzerland*	6 pm
Hanoi, Vietnam	1 am**
Havana, Cuba*	12 noon
Helsinki, Finland*	7 pm
Hong Kong, P.R. of China	1 am**
Istanbul, Turkey*	7 pm
Jakarta, Indonesia	12 midnight
Jerusalem, Israel*	7 pm
Johannesburg, South Africa	7 pm
Kabul, Afghanistan	8:30 pm
Karachi, Pakistan	10 pm
Kuala Lumpur, Malaysia	1 am**
Kuwait City, Kuwait	7 pm
Lagos, Nigeria	6 pm
Lima, Peru	12 noon
Lisbon, Portugal*	6 pm

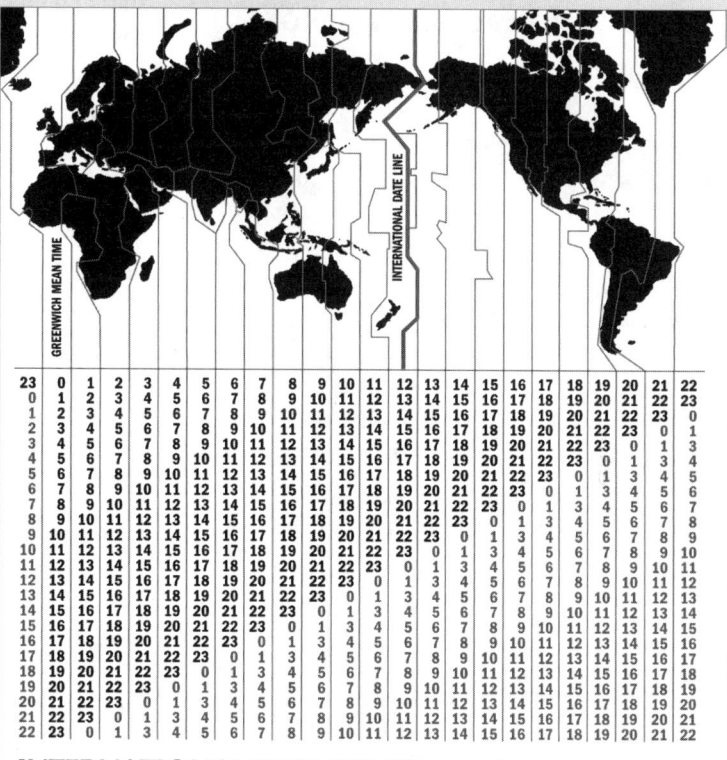

INTERNATIONAL TIME ZONES

The 24 time zones are figured in relation to their distance from the prime meridian, which is the longitudinal position of the Royal Observatory in Greenwich, England. Anyone crossing the International Date Line going west should move the calendar ahead one day; if the line is crossed going east, the date moves back one day.

City	Time	City	Time
London, England*	5 pm	Seoul, Korea	2 am**
Madrid, Spain*	6 pm	Singapore, Singapore	1 am**
Manila, Philippines	1 am**	Stockholm, Sweden*	6 pm
Mexico City, Mexico*	11 am	Sydney, Australia	4 am**
Moscow, Russia*	8 pm	Taipei, Taiwan	1 am**
Nairobi, Kenya	7 pm	Tehran, Iran*	8:30 pm
New Delhi, India	10:30 pm	Tel Aviv, Israel	7 pm
Oslo, Norway*	6 pm	Tokyo, Japan	2 am**
Ottawa, Canada*	12 noon	Toronto, Canada*	12 noon
Paris, France*	6 pm	Vienna, Austria*	6 pm
Prague, Czech Republic*	6 pm	Warsaw, Poland*	6 pm
Rio de Janeiro, Brazil	2 pm	Zagreb, Croatia*	6 pm
Riyadh, Saudi Arabia	8 pm	Zurich, Switzerland*	6 pm
Rome, Italy*	6 pm		
Santiago, Chile	1 pm		

* Cities observe Daylight Saving Time
** The following day

SCIENCE

How to Tell Time Like a Sailor

The age-old practice of sounding the ship's bell on the hour and half- hour lives on in the U.S. Navy, regulating daily routine just as it did centuries ago. Today, mechanical bell clocks do the work on many ships. All ships must comply with maritime law requiring them to carry an efficient bell for emergencies, such as fog. The ship's bell can also be used to ring in the New Year: 16 peals—8 for the old year and 8 for the new. Here's how to decode a ship's bells.

Assume a watch begins at noon:

8 bells	Noon	1 bell	12:30
2 bells	1:00	3 bells	1:30
4 bells	2:00	5 bells	2:30
6 bells	3:00	7 bells	3:30
8 bells	4:00 (The next watch begins.)		
1 bell	4:30 (The pattern starts over.)		

Note that an odd number of bells denotes a half hour and an even number one hour.

Measuring Sound

Noise levels are measured in decibels. A decibel (dB) is a unit for comparing two power levels or measuring the intensity of a sound. The higher the decibel level, the louder the noise. Sound levels greater than 80 decibels are considered potentially hazardous. Here is a range of decibel levels for common noises; the examples are in order of increasing intensity within each range.

Faint to moderate (15-50 dBs): A whisper, quiet library, moderate rainfall.

Very to extremely loud (60-110 dBs): Conversation, vacuum cleaner, lawnmower, shop tools, truck traffic, subway train, snowmobile, chain saw, typical rock concert.

Painful (120-150 dBs): Jet plane takeoff, band practice, jackhammer, shotgun fired at 1 foot, rock music at 50 feet in front of speakers.

start and end of daylight saving time.) Since 2007, daylight saving time has started at 2 a.m. on the second Sunday in March; it extends until 2 a.m. on the first Sunday in November.

Travelers should keep in mind that some states and territories—generally those in warmer climates and those split by time zones—don't observe daylight saving time. These currently include Arizona, Hawaii, Puerto Rico and parts of Indiana. And, in most Western European countries, daylight saving time begins the last Sunday in March and ends on the last Sunday in October.

Practical Math You Can Use

Learning the basics is as simple as 1-2-3

Without numbers it would be impossible to set a clock, keep score or create a symphony. If numbers had not been needed, the civilizations of ancient Mesopotamia, Egypt and China would not have felt it necessary to invent counting systems, which they then applied to their commerce and government. An early appreciation for the principles of geometry helped the Egyptians construct the pyramids and accurately record their boundaries.

By the sixth century B.C., the Greeks took the practical math that they had learned from the Babylonians and Egyptians and ventured into more abstract investigations. The Greek philosopher Pythagoras and his disciples proposed a theorem, for instance, that showed the mathematical relationship among the three sides of a right triangle (see page 793). Another Greek, Euclid, was the first to suggest that geometry possessed a single set of logical rules. Archimedes laid the conceptual groundwork for integral calculus in the third century B.C., and the celebrated astronomer Ptolemy played a leading role in developing trigonometry. The Romans largely contented themselves with the use of math

Roman Numerals for Non-Romans

The Roman system of recording numbers lasted considerably longer than the Roman Empire. As recently as 500 years ago, Roman numerals were still being used for addition and subtraction throughout Europe. But the Roman approach to numbers didn't translate well to higher math, and by the late 1500s Arabic numbers were being adopted in the West.

The Roman system uses only seven symbols, individually or in combination. When more than one symbol is used to form a number, the value of each symbol generally is added together, reading from left to right. To multiply a numeral by 1,000, place a bar over the symbol like a long vowel sound. For instance, X with a bar across its top would stand for 10,000.

1	I	50	L	1000	M
2	II	60	LX	1500	MD
3	III	70	LXX	1900	MCM or
4	IV	80	LXXX		MDCCCC
5	V	90	XC	1910	MCMX
6	VI	100	C	1940	MCMXL
7	VII	150	CL	1950	MCML
8	VIII	200	CC	1960	MCMLX
9	IX	300	CCC	1990	MCMXC
10	X	400	CD	2000	MM
15	XV	500	D	3000	MMM
20	XX	600	DC	5000	$\overline{V}$
25	XXV	700	DCC	10,000	$\overline{X}$
30	XXX	800	DCCC	100,000	$\overline{C}$
40	XL	900	CM	1,000,000	$\overline{M}$

in solving practical problems, but the more ethereal inquiries into the nature of numbers championed by the Greeks were taken up by Islamic thinkers in the 9th and 10th centuries. One of them, an astronomer named Muhammad ibn Musa al-Khwarizmi, laid many of the foundations for algebra.

Beginning in the 11th century, Islamic advances in mathematics gradually made their way to Europe.

But it was not until the Renaissance in the 15th century that Europeans contributed to the breakthroughs, with astronomers such as Nicolaus Copernicus, Galileo Galilei and Johannes Kepler making major contributions. Working independently, Sir Isaac Newton and Baron Gottfried Wilhem von Leibniz invented calculus in the 1680s, effectively ushering in the modern age of mathematics.

Following is a ready reference to many of the most commonly used mathematical concepts and operations.

ALGEBRA

Algebra is based on the five fundamental laws that govern the operations of addition, subtraction, multiplication and division. Each of the laws is expressed in letter variables. Where variables a, b and c are all real numbers, any number can be substituted for a variable without conflicting with the way the rule works.

THE COMMUTATIVE LAW OF ADDITION

$a + b = b + a$

Under this law, the order in which two numbers are added has no bearing on the sum derived. Thus,

$6 + 7 = 7 + 6$, or $(-10)+(-2) = (-2)+(-10)$

THE ASSOCIATIVE LAW OF ADDITION

$a + (b+c) = (a+b) + c$

Under this law, it does not matter which combination of numbers is added first, the sum remains the same. Thus,

$1 + (8+2) = (1+8) + 2$

THE COMMUTATIVE LAW OF MULTIPLICATION

$ab = ba$

Under this law, it does not matter which order numbers are multiplied; the product is the same. Thus, 6 times 7 = 7 times 6

THE ASSOCIATIVE LAW OF MULTIPLICATION

$a\ (bc) + (ab)\ c$

Under this law, numbers can be multiplied in any sequence without affecting the final product. Thus,

$5 \cdot (4 \cdot 3) = (5 \cdot 4) \cdot 3$

THE DISTRIBUTIVE LAW OF MULTIPLICATION OVER ADDITION

$a\ (b+c) = ab + ac$

Under this law, if a number multiplies a sum, the total is the same as the sum of the separate products of the multiplier and each of the addends represented by b and c. Thus,

$3 \cdot (2+9) = 3 \cdot 2 + 3 \cdot 9$

THE QUADRATIC EQUATION

A key algebraic equation is the quadratic equation, in which the highest power to which the unknown quantity is raised is the second. Assuming a, b and c are real numbers, and a does not equal zero, the formula is as follows:

$$\text{If: } ax^2+bx+c = 0$$

$$\text{Then: } x = \frac{-b\pm\sqrt{b^2-4ac}}{2a}$$

Thus, if $a=1$, $b=4$ and $c=3$, and we know that $1x^2+4x+3=0$, then we can find the value of x as follows:

$$x = \frac{-4 \pm \sqrt{4^2-(4\cdot1\cdot3)}}{2\cdot1} = (-1,-3)$$

GEOMETRY

This branch of mathematics deals with points, lines, planes and figures and their properties, measurement and spatial relationships.

ANGLES. *Angles are expressed in degrees, which are fractions of a circle. A circle has 360 degrees.*

An **acute angle** is greater than zero degrees and less than 90.

A **right angle** has 90 degrees. The lines forming the angle run perpendicular to each other.

An **obtuse angle** has more than 90 degrees but less than 180 degrees.

A **straight angle** has 180 degrees and forms a straight line.

Complementary angles exist when two angles total 90 degrees.

Supplementary angles occur when two angles add up to 180 degrees.

Conjugate angles add up to 360 degrees when combined.

THE MEANING OF MATH SIGNS

No science is more elegant at explaining the world around us than mathematics. In examining the properties, relations and measurement of quantities, it relies on a system of mathematical signs, or directions. The most commonly used:

+ plus or positive
− minus or negative
± plus or minus, positive or negative
· multiplied by
÷ or / divided by
= equal to
≠ not equal to
≈ approximately equal to
~ of the order of or similar to
\> greater than
< less than
≥ greater than or equal to

≤ less than or equal to
\>> much greater than
<< much less than
√ square root
∞ infinity
∝ proportional to
∑ sum of
∏ product of
Δ difference
∴ therefore
∠ angle
‖ parallel to
: is to (ratio)

TRIANGLES. *The sum of the internal angles of a triangle is always 180 degrees.*

 An **equilateral triangle** has sides that are of equal length and internal angles that are all 60 degrees.

 An **isosceles triangle** has two sides that are of equal length and two equal angles.

 A **scalene triangle** has no sides and no angles of equal size.

 A **right triangle** has one internal angle of 90 degrees.

 An **obtuse triangle** has one obtuse angle, which is an angle greater than 90 degrees but less than 180 degrees.

 An **acute-angle triangle** has three acute angles, meaning that all are under 90 degrees.

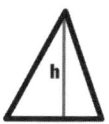 To calculate the area of a triangle, multiply the base by the height by one-half:

$$A = (^1/_2)bh$$

QUADRILATERALS. *A quadrilateral is a four-sided polygon.*

 A **square** has four equal sides and four right angles. To calculate the area of a square, square the length of one side:

$$A = a^2$$

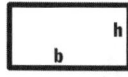 A **rectangle** has equal opposite sides and all right angles. To calculate a rectangle's area, multiply base by height:

$$A = bh$$

The Right Way to View Right Triangles

The relationships between the angles of a right triangle and its sides have been studied by mathematicians for millennia. Among the important trigonometric concepts are:

SINE: In a right triangle, the ratio of the opposite side of a given acute angle to the hypotenuse is known as the sine of that angle.

Sine of angle A = a÷c

COSINE: In a right triangle, the ratio of the adjacent side of an acute angle to the hypotenuse is known as the cosine of that angle.

Cosine of angle A = b÷c

TANGENT: In a right triangle, the ratio of the opposite side to the adjacent side of an acute angle is known as the angle's tangent.

Tangent of A = a÷b

COTANGENT: In a right triangle, the ratio of the adjacent side of an acute angle to the opposite side is known as the angle's cotangent.

Cotangent of angle A = b÷a

THE PYTHAGOREAN THEOREM:

In a right triangle, the square of the hypotenuse is equal to the sum of the squares of the other two sides.

$$c^2 = a^2 + b^2$$

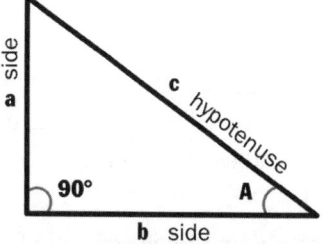

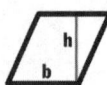

A **rhombus** has equal sides and no right angles. To calculate its area, multiply base by height:

$$A = bh$$

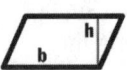

A **parallelogram** has opposite sides that are parallel to each other and are the same length. To calculate the area of a parallelogram, multiply the base by the height:

$$A = bh$$

OTHER POLYGONS

A **pentagon** is a five-sided polygon. To calculate the approximate area of a pentagon, multiply the square of the length of one side by 1.721:

$$A = 1.721a^2$$

A **hexagon** is a six-sided polygon. To calculate the approximate area of a hexagon, multiply the square of the length of one side by 2.598:

$$A = 2.598a^2$$

An **octagon** is an eight-sided polygon. To calculate the approximate area of an equilateral octagon: multiply the square of the length of one side by 4.828:

$$A = 4.828a^2$$

A **circle** is a figure in which every point on its boundary is equidistant from the center. The radius is that distance to the center. The diameter is twice the radius, or the longest distance across the circle. The circumference is the total distance around the boundary of the circle. To calculate the area, multiply the square of the radius by pi (3.1416 …):

$$A = \pi r^2$$

To calculate the circumference of a circle, multiply radius of the circle by 2 and by pi (3.1416 …):

$$C = 2\pi r$$

SOLIDS. *Solids are three-dimensional geometric objects that exist in space.*

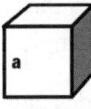

A **cube** is a solid with six equal, square sides. To calculate a cube's surface area, multiply the square of the length of a side by 6:

$$S = 6a^2$$

To calculate the volume of a cube, cube the length of one side:

$$V = a^3$$

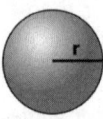

A **sphere** is a body whose surface is equally distant from the center at all points. To calculate the surface area, multiply 4 by pi by the square of the radius:

$$S = 4 \pi r^2$$

To calculate the volume of a sphere, multiply the cube of the radius by pi by 4/3:

$$V = (4/3) \pi r^3$$

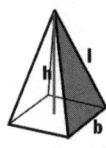

A **pyramid** has a square base and four sloping triangular sides meeting at the top. To calculate the surface area, multiply base by length, and multiply 2 by the base and the height. Add the results:

$$S = bl + 2bh$$

To calculate a pyramid's volume, multiply the base's area by height and by 1/3:

$$V = (1/3)b^2h$$

A **cylinder** is a solid described by a line that always has a point in common with a given closed curve. The surface area of a right, circular cylinder: multiply 2 by pi by radius by height:

$$S = 2\pi rh$$

To calculate a cylinder's volume, multiply the square of the radius of the base by pi by height:

$$V = \pi r^2 h$$

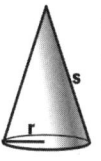

A **cone** is a flat-based, single-pointed solid formed by a rotating straight line that traces out a base from a fixed vertex point. To calculate the surface area of a cone, multiply pi by the radius of the base by the slant height (s):

$$S = \pi rs$$

To calculate the volume of a cube, multiply the square of the radius of the base by pi by height by $1/3$.

$$V = (1/3) \pi r^2 h$$

FRACTIONS AND THEIR DECIMAL EQUIVALENTS

Rounded to the nearest four decimals

$1/2$	.5	$2/11$	.1818	$5/16$	.3125
$1/3$	.3333	$3/4$	.75	$6/7$	.8571
$1/4$	.25	$3/5$	.6	$7/8$	.875
$1/5$	.2	$3/7$	.4286	$7/9$	.7778
$1/6$	.1667	$3/8$	.375	$7/10$	.7
$1/7$	.1429	$3/10$	.3	$7/11$	.6364
$1/8$	.125	$3/11$	.2727	$7/12$	.5833
$1/9$	.1111	$3/16$	.1875	$7/16$	.4375
$1/10$	.1	$4/5$	.8	$8/9$	.8889
$1/11$	.0909	$4/7$	.5714	$8/11$	.7273
$1/12$	.0833	$4/9$	.4444	$9/10$	.9
$1/16$	.0625	$4/11$	.3636	$9/11$	.8182
$1/32$	.0313	$5/6$	.8333	$9/16$	.5625
$1/64$	.0156	$5/7$	.7143	$10/11$	.9091
$2/3$	.6667	$5/8$	.625	$11/12$	.9167
$2/5$	.4	$5/9$	.5556	$11/16$	.6875
$2/7$	.2857	$5/11$	.4545	$13/16$	.8125
$2/9$	.2222	$5/12$	.4167	$15/16$	.9375

A Pocket Guide to Physics

Measuring work, power and energy

Work is done by a force that causes an object to move. Work is equal to the force applied to move an object multiplied by the distance the object travels: Work = Force x Distance.

Work is typically measured in joules or in Newtons, which are the metric units for weight (1 Newton = 0.445 lbs). One joule is equal to the amount of work done by the force of 1 Newton moving an object through a distance of 1 meter. In everyday life, it is about the same weight as a stick of butter. One joule is equal to the energy required to lift a small apple 1 meter straight up.

Power is a measure of how quickly work is done or energy transferred. It is expressed in units of work, or energy, divided by units of time:

POWER = WORK / TIME

Power applies not only to objects moved but also to electric charges moving through a resistor. In electrical terms, power is measured in watts: 1 watt equals the power needed to do 1 joule of work per second.

Energy comes in many forms. In order to do work, we expend energy. Two types of energy are kinetic, or energy of motion, and potential, or stored energy.

Heat energy is measured using the calorie, with 1 calorie equal to about 4,184 joules. Another measure of energy is the British thermal unit, or B.T.U. One B.T.U. is equal to 1,055 joules or 252 calories. One B.T.U. is also the amount of energy needed to raise the temperature of 1 pound of water 1 degree Fahrenheit.

The calorie is familiarly used for measuring the energy content of food: 1 calorie equals 4.187 joules or 0.003969 B.T.U.'s. One calorie also measures the amount of energy needed to raise the temperature of 1 gram of water 1 degree Celsius.

SCIENCE

Chemistry 101

The periodic table of elements includes all the building blocks of matter

The periodic table of the elements was first devised in the 19th century to show the atomic weights of the elements and to group them by similar properties. The discovery of protons and electrons in atoms in the early 20th century gave rise to a new and more accurate arrangement of the elements in a periodic table. This new arrangement is based on the atomic number, which is the number of protons (positively charged particles) present in the atomic nucleus of an element.

The table lists the elements in horizontal rows (or periods), according to their atomic numbers. Each vertical column (except hydrogen in the first column) groups elements that have related proper-

ties and are likely to behave similarly in chemical reactions. Except for hydrogen, the elements on the left side of the table are metals, while those in the last six columns are predominantly nonmetals. In those columns, a heavier, stepped boundary line separates the metals from the nonmetals.

Hydrogen is the lightest and simplest element in the table, but it has many unique properties. For example, in chemical reactions, it can give up or acquire an electron from other elements that are incapable of transferring electrons both ways.

Aside from the atomic number, the periodic table also lists each element's name, chemical symbol and atomic weight (or atomic mass). Atomic weight is the mass of an atom relative to the mass of an atom of carbon-12, which is arbitrarily assigned an atomic weight of 12 by an international convention.

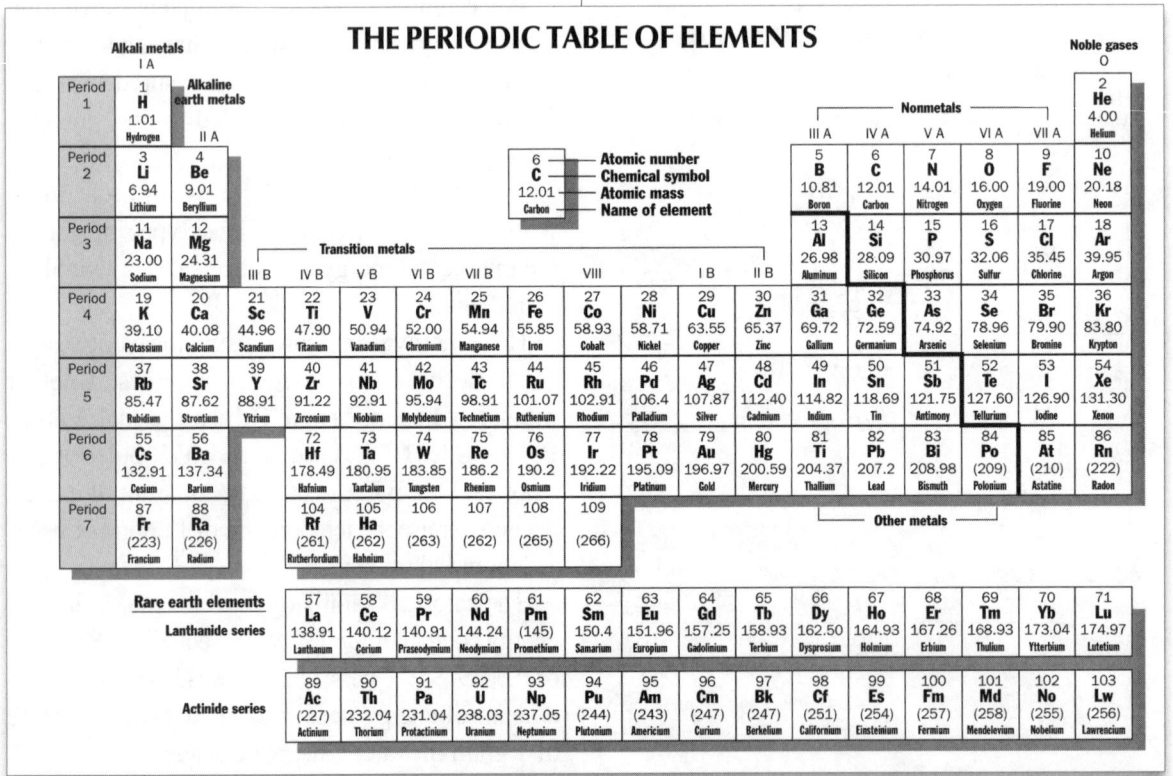

THE PERIODIC TABLE OF ELEMENTS

Signs & Codes

Negotiating Highways & Byways

What you need to know to get from here to there

Whether you're trying to decipher a national, state or local map, the visual vocabulary is fairly standard. Although there are minor stylistic differences among map makers—for example, the use of different colors to differentiate highways and toll roads—the basics generally don't vary. A star signifies a capital, solid lines signify main roads and thinner lines suggest a more scenic route.

There are other similarities nationwide. You can identify an interstate highway—one of the four- to eight-lane roads that link the country—by the sign that has a blue and red shield with the highway number inside. Smaller, older routes known as U.S. Routes (formerly called federal highways because funding used to come from Congress) are two or four lanes wide. In many states, they are often lined with motels, strip malls, amusement parks and other vestiges of Americana. State routes are smaller, slower paced roads, identifiable by a number within a plain white rectangle or circle. These roads less traveled often offer the greatest scenic rewards.

If you're traveling on the autostrada or the autobahn, however, you'll need to learn the language of the international road signs below.

MAP SYMBOLS

BOUNDARIES AND HIGHWAYS

International	State	County	Town	Village

Capital	Urban area	City	Town	Interstate highway	U.S. highway	State highway
✪	◉		○	95	39	1

INTERNATIONAL ROAD SIGNS

Caution, danger	Curve ahead	Intersection	Pedestrian crossing	Road narrows	Road work	Slippery road	Tunnel ahead

No entry	No left turn	No U-turn	No passing	Speed limit	Stop	Yield	Restrictions end
				30	STOP		

SCIENCE

Lost in the Woods?

How to signal your distress

Whether you're lost in the woods or on a tropical island, these ground-to-air communications are a stranded survivor's bible. You can use materials like tree branches, driftwood, large stones or strips of parachute, for example, to cobble together the symbols. Similarly, sticks and stones can be used to form tracking codes if you have lost your way on a hiking trail, for example.

The best-known symbol of distress is the SOS, of course. You can transmit an SOS by forming 3 short, 3 long and 3 short signals, and then repeating the pattern. The signal can be constructed with rocks and logs or by reflecting the sun on a mirror. At night, use a flashlight to send the signal.

The most effective means of signaling for help in the woods is a campfire. During the day, the smoke is visible for long distances, and at night the flames are easily spotted from the air.

The internationally recognized distress signal is to build three fires. You can arrange them in a triangle or in a straight line. Leave about 100 feet (30 meters) between the fires.

SYMBOLS OF DISTRESS

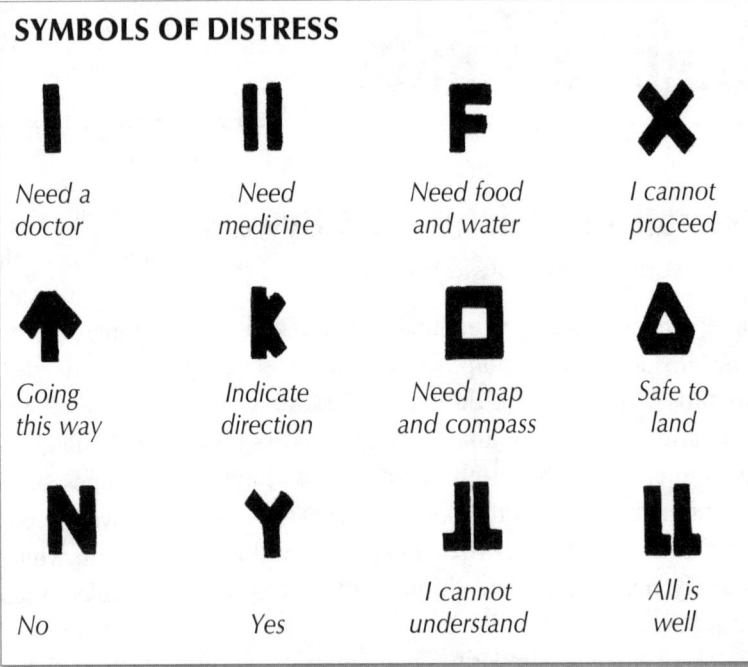

Need a doctor	Need medicine	Need food and water	I cannot proceed
Going this way	Indicate direction	Need map and compass	Safe to land
No	Yes	I cannot understand	All is well

TRACKING CODES

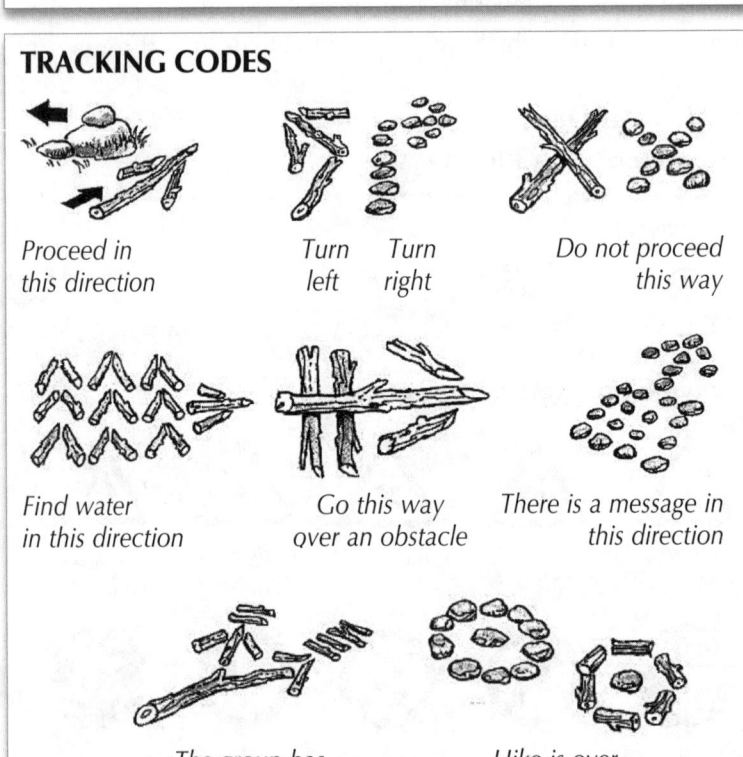

Proceed in this direction

Turn left

Turn right

Do not proceed this way

Find water in this direction

Go this way over an obstacle

There is a message in this direction

The group has divided

Hike is over

Secrets of the Code

These antiquated communication methods are still used by some

The Semaphore Code. This method of sending messages over long distances uses handheld flags that are moved to form letters of the alphabet. The flags are generally square, with red in the top diagonal and yellow in the lower. The system is fast but can be used only during the day and at short distances. It is mostly used to communicate at sea and was established in 1901 as the International Code of Signals, evolving out of an earlier British system. Shown here are the flag positions that form each letter of the alphabet.

The Morse Code. There are many ways to send the Morse code, a standardized worldwide system of dashes and dots that represent letters and numbers (below). A ship's whistle or foghorn can transmit it, as can a signal flag that's raised for a longer interval for dashes than dots.

The Morse code was originally developed for use in the electric telegraph, invented by Samuel Morse, a Yale-educated itinerant artist. The first message transmitted by telegraph asked, "What hath God wrought?" Morse chose the words, which were sent from the U.S. Capitol to the railroad station in Baltimore in 1844.

Modern technologies have made the code nearly obsolete. It is now used mainly by the tens of thousands of amateur radio operators.

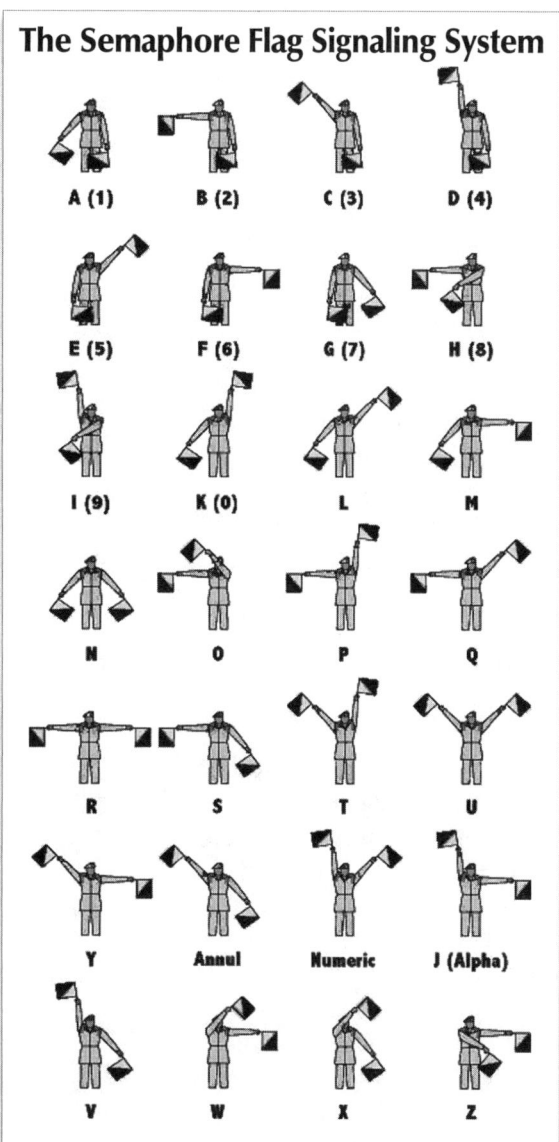

The Semaphore Flag Signaling System

A (1) B (2) C (3) D (4)
E (5) F (6) G (7) H (8)
I (9) K (0) L M
N O P Q
R S T U
Y Annul Numeric J (Alpha)
V W X Z

What the Dots and Dashes Mean									
• —	A	• • — •	F	— •	N	• • • —	V	• • • — —	3
— • • •	B	— — •	G	— — —	O	• — —	W	• • • • —	4
— • — •	C	• • • •	H	• — — •	P	— • • —	X	• • • • •	5
— • •	D	• •	I	— — • —	Q	— • — —	Y	— • • • •	6
•	E	• — — —	J	• — •	R	— — • •	Z	— — • • •	7
		— • —	K	• • •	S			— — — • •	8
		• — • •	L	—	T	• — — — —	1	— — — — •	9
		— —	M	• • —	U	• • — — —	2	— — — — —	0

SCIENCE

For Budding Bachs
Modern musical symbols

The father of our system of musical notation is thought to be the Roman philosopher and statesman Boethius, who lived in the early 6th century. Boethius used letters of the alphabet to signify the notes of the two-octave range that was used at the time. The system of adding the letters A to G in each octave was introduced later, followed by the addition of the five notes of the chromatic scale, or the black keys on the piano.

Guido of Arezzo in the Medieval era is credited with perfecting the staff and developing notations to indicate pitch. A Benedictine monk, he also gets credit for coming up with the familiar "do-re-mi" scale.

Over time, other formulations evolved, such as those to denote pitch and when to rest or repeat. The terminology for musical dynamics, or how softly or loudly a musical piece is played, is said to derive from the Italian Renaissance composer Giovanni Gabrieli. But it wasn't until the late 18th century that use of musical dynamics became popular. Following are essential symbols for learning to read music or play an instrument.

NOTE VALUES OR DURATION

Whole note

Half note

Dotted half note

Quarter note

Eighth note

Sixteenth note

Thirty-second note

Sixty-fourth note

Tie

RESTS

Whole rest

Half rest

Quarter rest

Eighth rest

Sixteenth rest

Thirty-second rest

Sixty-fourth rest

METER

$\mathbf{3_4}$ 3/4 time

$\mathbf{4_4}$ 4/4 time

$\mathbf{2_2}$ 2/2 time

$\mathbf{6_8}$ 6/8 time

PITCH-RELATED

Sharp

Double sharp

Flat

Double flat

Natural

Bass, or F, clef

Treble, or G, clef

STAFF SYMBOLS

Staff

Measure

Final bar

Repeat measure

D.C. (da capo) Repeat from the beginning

DYNAMICS

p   Piano (soft)

mp   Mezzo piano (med. soft)

pp   Pianissimo (very soft)

f   Forte (loud)

mf   Mezzo forte (med. loud)

ff   Fortissimo (very loud)

<   Crescendo

>   Decrescendo

PROOFREADER'S MARKS

These symbols are generally used to correct manuscripts and papers on hard copy. Every symbol used in the text requires a corresponding symbol or notation in the margin of the text.

℘	Delete
◡	Close up (delete space)
℥	Delete and close up
∧	Caret (add material)
#	Add a space
⊙	Add a period
⌃	Add a comma
:/	Add a colon
;/	Add a semicolon
℃ ℣	Add a quotation mark
℣	Add single quotation mark

?	Add a question mark
℣	Add apostrophe
⌊·⌋·⌊·⌋	Add ellipses
|=|	Add hyphen
⊥ᴍ	Add a one-em dash
⊥ɴ	Add a one-en dash
⁽⁾	Add parenthesis
ᴸ/₁	Add square bracket
⅃ #	Add a space between words
stet	Let stand; restore deleted material; use dots to indicate material to be restored
ⓢ℘	Spell out circled text
wf	Wrong font
lc	Lowercase letter

cap	Capitalize letter
s.c.	Set in small caps
rom	Set in roman type
bf	Set in boldface type
ital	Set in italic type
tr	Transpose letters or words
⌋	Move copy right
⌊	Move copy left
⊓	Move up
⊔	Move down
⌋⌊	Center
‖	Align vertically
⁼	Align horizontally
¶	Begin a new paragraph
no ¶	No paragraph here; run sentences together

THE ABCs OF EMOTICONS

An emotional shorthand used to express yourself online:

:)	Smile, happy
: (	Frown, sadness
:-I	Can't decide how to feel; no feelings either way
:-O	Yelling or completely shocked
:-()	Can't (or won't) stop talking
:-&	Tongue-tied
:-X	Lips are sealed
I-O	Yawning or snoring
%-(	Confused, unhappy
:'-(	Crying

:'-)	Crying happy tears
:-} or :-]	Sarcastic smile
:-D	Big, delighted grin
{} or []	Hug
*	Kiss
>3	Love
}:[	Frustration
I-I	Boredom, asleep
:-#	Lips are sealed
:-\	Undecided
;-)	Winking

FREQUENTLY USED ABBREVIATIONS

AFKB	Away from keyboard
BRB	Be right back

BTW	By the way
f2f	Face to face, to refer to meeting an online friend in person
FAQ	Frequently asked questions
IMHO	In my humble opinion
IMNSHO	In my not so humble opinion
IRL	In real life
ITRW	In the real world
LOL	Laughing out loud
MorF?	Male or female? Used when your online name is gender-neutral
OTF	On the floor (laughing)

Learning How to Sign

How to communicate with the deaf

Thomas Gallaudet, a 19th-century educator of the deaf, gets the credit for developing American Sign Language (A.S.L.), which uses hand movements and symbols to express words and ideas. Gallaudet built on the earlier work of the French, who had formulated a sign system for the deaf in the 1700s. A.S.L. is similar to spoken languages in that it has an extensive vocabulary and specific rules of grammar. And like spoken languages, it is subject to regional dialects and the occasional new colloquialism.

Another method of communicating is through the American manual alphabet, used by many deaf people along with A.S.L. and lip reading.

Here are the finger positions that correspond to numbers and alphabet letters, used to spell out words.

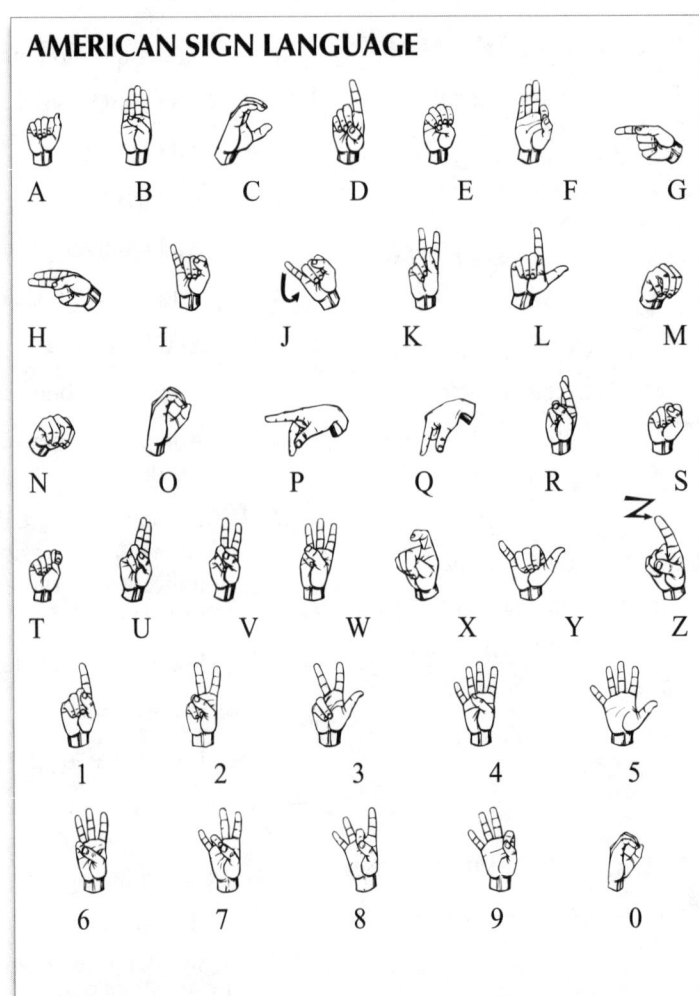

AMERICAN SIGN LANGUAGE

A B C D E F G

H I J K L M

N O P Q R S

T U V W X Y Z

1 2 3 4 5

6 7 8 9 0

The Braille System

Named after its creator, Louis Braille, this system of characters or cells is used by the blind to read and write.

```
1 ● ● 4
2 ● ● 5
3 ● ● 6
```

Each Braille cell has six dot positions (see left, top). Dots are arranged in each cell to make letters and numbers.

```
1   4
2   5
3 ● 6
```

To make a capital letter, a dot in position 6 is placed just before a letter.

Braille is not a language in itself but rather another way to read English or any other language.

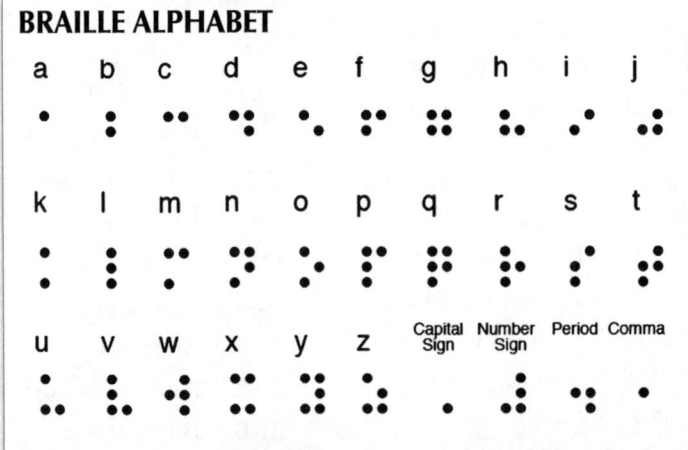

BRAILLE ALPHABET

a b c d e f g h i j

k l m n o p q r s t

u v w x y z | Capital Sign | Number Sign | Period | Comma

MORES & MANNERS

Legal Guide

How to Become a U.S. Citizen

The road to citizenship can be rigorous

What does it take to become American? For many, just a little luck at birth. If your parents are not Americans but you were born on American soil, you can claim citizenship. Even if you were not born on U.S. soil but one of your parents is an American citizen, you are entitled to claim American citizenship. Otherwise, the process of applying for citizenship can be a long and tortuous road. But it's not impossible: in 2008, more than a million immigrants became United States citizens, more than any year since the government began keeping records a hundred years ago.

To become a U.S. citizen an immigrant must meet several criteria: live in the U.S. as a permanent resident for 5 years (3 years for spouses of U.S. citizens), be conversant in English and have a general knowledge of the principles of American government. Application forms are available at local offices of the U.S. Citizenship and Immigration Services (U.S.C.I.S.) or online at uscis.gov. You can also order forms by calling 800-870-3676.

But becoming a permanent resident is not easy. A relative or an employer must sponsor you, or you must be lucky enough to win one of the 50,000 slots in the annual visa lottery. (For more information about the lottery, go to travel.state.gov/visa.) Once you become a permanent resident, you will be issued a "green card," officially known as the Alien Registration Receipt Card. The cards are valid for 10 years. Legal immigrants must present them when applying for jobs or for state and federal entitlements and when they re-enter the U.S. after a trip abroad. Curiously, the color of green cards changed to pink in 1996.

After legal immigrants have lived in the U.S. for a minimum of 5 years (without being jailed for over 180 days or convicted of an aggravated felony or murder), they are eligible to take the citizenship test. People over age 50 who have been permanen U.S. residents for 20 years are exempt from being tested on their English skills. However, everyone must pass the citizenship exam. You can take the test as many times as you need to. The test includes questions on voting requirements, values shared by Americans and the meaning of democracy.

Prep courses for the test are available through public schools and community and private groups. The federal government publishes a citizenship guide containing all the information that appears on the citizenship test. The guide is available for free online at www.uscis.gov/newtest. Hard copies are available for a small fee from the Government Printing Office at 866-512-1800. To order online go to bookstore.gpo.gov.

Once you have passed the citizenship test and interviewed with the U.S.C.I.S. officer, there is a further 30-day wait before you can officially become a citizen. Once your application is approved, you will be invited to participate in one of many annual nationwide ceremonies for new citizens, usually held around the 4th of July. Citizens-to-be take the Oath of Allegiance, agreeing to defend our country in wartime if necessary.

HOW THE ELECTORAL COLLEGE WORKS

To win the presidency, a candidates needs 270 electoral votes, slightly more than a majority

The authors of the Constitution devised the Electoral College to act as a kind of buffer between the masses and the ultimate process of selecting a president. The voters would choose electors for their state on a predetermined election day, and then those individuals, along with electors from other states, would take it upon themselves to choose the president.

Today the Electoral College is a body of 538 people. Each state receives a number of electoral votes equal to the number of senators and representatives in its congressional delegation, and Washington, D.C., which has no Congressional representation, gets three votes. A candidate needs 270 electoral votes, slightly more than a majority, to be elected president. The candidate who wins a majority of a state's popular vote wins all of its electoral votes, except in Maine and Nebraska, which use a different allocation method. As a result, the electoral vote tends to exaggerate the popular support of the winner.

If no candidate receives a majority of the votes of the Electoral College, the election is decided by the House of Representatives. This has only happened once, so far, when, in 1824, Andrew Jackson won the popular vote in a four-way race, but John Quincy Adams was elected president by the House. In 1876, Rutherford B. Hayes lost the popular vote but won the presidency by a single electoral vote.

Electoral college votes, by state

How to Register to Vote

Making your voice heard

Registering to vote couldn't be easier these days, thanks to "get-out-the-vote" groups tripping over themselves to lasso in new voters. The first step is to get a registration form. Check your phone book or online for the number of your local election office; it can usually be found under the county clerk's office or municipal election board.

Or you can use one of several online voting registration tools, such as the ones on the League of Women Voters Web site at www.lwv.org or Rock the Vote at www.rockthevote.com. You can fill out the form online, but in most cases, you'll still need to print it out and mail it to your local election office.

What are the qualifications for registering to vote? You must be a U.S. citizen and at least 18 years old. Some states disqualify anyone who has been convicted of a felony or is mentally incapacitated.

A few weeks after filing the form, you can expect a letter of confirmation, along with the address of where you must go to vote on election day. If you move locally, be sure to update your registration and find out where your new polling place will be. If you move outside your old jurisdiction, you must reregister in your new area. If you change your name, use your state's form to submit the name change, or make the change online at sites such as www.lwv.org.

When you go to the polls, be sure to bring a photo identification that also shows your address, such as a driver's license. If for some reason, your name is not on the registration list, don't panic.

You will generally be permitted to cast a provisional ballot that will be counted after election officials have double-checked your registration. For those who are housebound or will be out of their district on voting day, absentee ballots are available from your local election office.

How to Get a Social Security Card
And how to replace a lost card

The Social Security Administration only came into existence in 1935, in the midst of the Great Depression. But the cards have become indispensable: you need one to open a bank account, get a credit card and apply for most government services for yourself or your child. Legal immigrants are also entitled to Social Security payments and need a number to collect benefits.

 **INSIDE INFO**

What the Numbers Mean

O Does someone else get your Social Security number when you die? No. More than 420 million numbers have been issued so far (around 5½ million each year), but enough new numbers remain to last several generations.

O What do the numbers mean? The first three digits represent the area where you lived when you got the card. People on the East Coast have lower numbers than those on the West Coast. The remaining six digits are issued randomly.

O Members of Congress, the Vice President and the President are covered under Social Security. They have been paying into the Social Security program since 1984.

SOURCE: Social Security Administration

Since 1985, any child you claim as a dependant on your income tax return must have a Social Security number. The easiest way for a child to get a number is at birth. When your hospital asks for the information needed to complete your newborn's birth certificate, ask to have your state's vital statistics office share that information with the Social Security Administration. A Social Security card will be mailed to you directly.

If you decide to wait or your child does not yet have a number, you can get one by contacting the nearest Social Security field office. (You can find it online at www.ssa.gov.) You will be asked to fill out a form SS-5, provide evidence that you are the child's parent or legal guardian and furnish a birth certificate with proof of your child's age, identity and citizenship.

To replace a lost Social Security card, to change the name on your card or to request a new card, call Social Security at 800-772-1213 for an appointment with an agent at your local office. Or start by downloading an application online at www.socialsecurity.gov/online/ss-5.html.

How to Get or Renew a Passport
You can't leave home without it

It is illegal to leave or enter the country without a valid passport, and since it can take weeks, if not months, to obtain one, it's best to apply far in advance of your trip. Keep in mind, also, that some countries require that your passport be valid at least six months beyond the date of your stay. Check with a country's nearest embassy or consulate before you plan your trip.

If you have never had a passport, apply in person at one of 1,000 authorized post offices, or make an appointment before going to one of the 13 passport agencies across the country. Complete the DS-11

Carrying Multiple Passports

Spies do it; so can you if you have dual nationality

Dual passports are no longer the sole province of people who grew up in more than one country. Millions of American citizens potentially qualify for various reasons—ethnic heritage, religion, country of birth or where their spouse was born.

While there are no hard numbers, more Americans seem to be trying to qualify for additional passports. Savvy travelers and business travelers want to make sure they have two passports based on nationality because there are certain advantages. Among those is the ability to work without restriction in various countries, particularly with passports from countries in the European Union. Also, it is a way of hiding where one has been, when traveling among countries with soured relations.

Foreign passport applications can be complicated, particularly in Italy and France, at times requiring a long series of documents to show your genealogy. In addition, anyone considering dual passports should think first of the tax consequences and the potential for military service, though you can get exemptions for such things because you're a U.S. citizen.

Israel allows anyone of Jewish heritage to use what is called aliyah, or the Law of Return, to become a citizen, but the military draft can be an issue. The maximum age for the draft is 28 for men and 22 for women, although married women are exempt at any age. Americans can apply for exemptions. One thing Americans need to bear in mind, however, is that no matter how many passports you have, you must enter and leave with a U.S. passport.   —Michael T. Luongo

application form (but do not sign the form until the passport official asks you to do so) and bring proof of U.S. citizenship, such as a certified copy of your birth certificate or a Certificate of Naturalization, if you are a naturalized citizen. (For information on getting an expedited passport see page 533.)

You must also bring two 2x2-inch color photographs taken within the past six months. The photos must have a plain, white background and show a frontal view of your face. Also bring a picture ID, such as a valid driver's license, government or military ID or previous passport. The current fee for a 10-year passport is $100 (a $75 application fee and $25 execution fee) if you apply in person. Forms of payment vary depending on the individual post office: some accept cash, checks, money orders and credit cards; some take only cash. Be sure to ask in advance.

If you are renewing an expired passport, the process is easier. You may apply by mail if your passport was issued within the past 15 years and you were

at least 16 when you received it. You can get an application form (DS-82) from a post office or online at www.travel.state.gov. Attach your most recent passport, two identical passport photos and a $75 check (payable to the U.S. Department of State) or money order, and mail to National Passport Center, P.O. Box 371971, Pittsburgh, Pa. 15250-7971. The National Passport Information Center at 877-487-2778 can answer all passport-related questions.

How to Register for the Draft

Calling all 18-year-old men

The draft technically ended in 1973, when the country converted to an all-volunteer military, but that doesn't mean young men are totally off the hook. Within 30 days of their 18th birthday, they must register with the Selective Service System. In the event that a national draft returns, a lottery system based on birthdates would go into effect to provide

MORES

Joining the Domestic Peace Corps

You can do good and do well, too

AmeriCorps is a national service organization that lets volunteers earn an array of benefits while doing good in the larger community. Since the program started in 1993, more than 500,000 men and women have helped millions of Americans. In exchange for service, members receive financial support, learn new skills and reap the psychic rewards that volunteering can bring. For more information, log on to www.americorps.org.

Members serve at more than 3,000 nonprofit groups, public agencies and religious and community organizations nationwide, including Habitat for Humanity, the American Red Cross and the New York Police Department. In exchange for a year of service, members receive a modest living allowance, health coverage and free education awards.

Any citizen or permanent resident of the United States who is 17 years (18 for some programs) or older is eligible, regardless of income. Competition is fairly tough. In a recent 5-year period, AmeriCorps received four applications for every available slot. Generally, applicants learn within two months if they have been accepted, rejected or put on a waiting list.

Members who complete a full year of service can get an education award of $4,725. (The amount is prorated for part-time service.) Students can use this amount within 7 years of completing service to help pay for college, graduate school or vocational training, or to repay a prior educational loan. Some members have received college credit for their service, but that decision rests with the individual school.

The application procedures vary with each program, but generally there are two deadline dates: March 15 for the fall cycle, and July 15 for the winter cycle. Selection is continuous, so applicants should file early since a program could fill up even before the deadline date.

Volunteers receive a variety of training, depending on the service project. Members who help build houses, for example, are taught building fundamentals, such as framing a house and putting up sheetrock. Those who work with children in schools will learn tutoring techniques. Members also get CPR/First Aid and Disaster Relief certification from the Red Cross. In addition, training sessions for conflict management, leadership and team and community building are given.

---

the additional soldiers needed to fight wars.

The first to be called would be those whose 20th birthday falls on the date drawn in the lottery. They would be followed by those ages 21 through 25, as needed. Men remain on the list until they turn 26.

Registration forms are available at local post offices and high schools. If you are applying for Federal Student Financial Aid, you can register at the same time by checking "yes" on Box 29 of the form; the Education Department will send the information to the Selective Service System. But the quickest and easiest way to register is online at www.sss.gov.

You should receive acknowledgement of your registration within 90 days. If you don't, it is your responsibility to contact the Selective Service System (847-688-6888). The penalty for not registering is a fine of up to $250,000 or 5 years in jail.

Making a Campaign Contribution

Putting your money where your vote is

Money seems to amplify the voice of the electorate substantially, so you may want to consider supporting the candidate who supports your views. But before you write a check to your favorite candidate or political party, be aware of the federal election laws. Campaign limits change, but for the

2007-2008 election cycle, individuals could give no more than: $2,300 to each candidate or candidate committee in an election (primaries and general elections count separately), $28,500 to a national party committee per calendar year and $5,000 to any other political committee per calendar year.

For more information, contact the Federal Election Commission at 800-424-9530 or go online to www.fec.gov. Foreign nationals are prohibited from donating to campaigns in the United States.

How to Decipher a Poll

A pollster explains the true meaning of polls

Polls putatively take the pulse of public opinion. But do they really tell us what we think? Well, yes and no. How reliable a gauge any poll is often depends on how large the sample size was, how the poll was taken and, of course, precisely how the questions were asked.

Peter D. Hart has been taking and analyzing polls for more than 30 years. He has been a pollster for NBC News and the *Wall St. Journal*, among other organizations, and is a regular commentator on television and radio public-policy programs. Here are his tips for reading a poll.

Take a look at how the poll was conducted. One big problem in the polling business is that the word "survey" refers to any time you to talk to the American people. But questionnaires through the mail or phone-in surveys are self-selecting—anyone who calls a 900-number is a certain kind of person, and it won't make for an evenly distributed survey. Telephone surveys are probably the most accurate, and we do random-digit dialing to make sure we reach people with unlisted numbers, because they make up a segment of the population that has definite opinions about some issues.

Wiring into Washington
How you can speak truth to power

You may sometimes think your elected officials are out of touch, but they are never out of reach. Here's how to find out who they are, what they're up to and how to make your views known. After all, they work for you.

U.S. House of Representatives. Provides access to your individual House members' home pages as well as indexed Congressional Records updates. **www.house.gov**

U.S. Senate. A virtual tour of the Capitol, along with senators' bios and committee listings. **www.senate.gov**

The White House. Features access to all of the Cabinet-level sites and to an archive, updated daily, of more than 4,000 White House speeches, briefs and reports. You can also get information on White House tours and other events at the mansion and send a message to the President. **www.whitehouse.gov**

The Courts. The Federal Judicial Center offers general information about the court system. **www.uscourts.gov** and **www.fjc.gov**

 TIMELY TIPS

Politics on the Web

✔ **Federal Election Commission** (www.fec.gov) provides data on campaign contributions.

✔ **MoneyLine.CQ.com** contains campaign money and lobbying information in a useful format.

✔ **Politico.com** and **RealClearPolitics.com** are daily must-sees for poltical junkies. Contain the latest news, analysis, gossip, opinion and poll results.

✔ **Project Vote Smart** (www.vote-smart.org) is a guide to candidates and issues.

MORES

HOW A BILL BECOMES A LAW

The law of the land and how it comes to pass

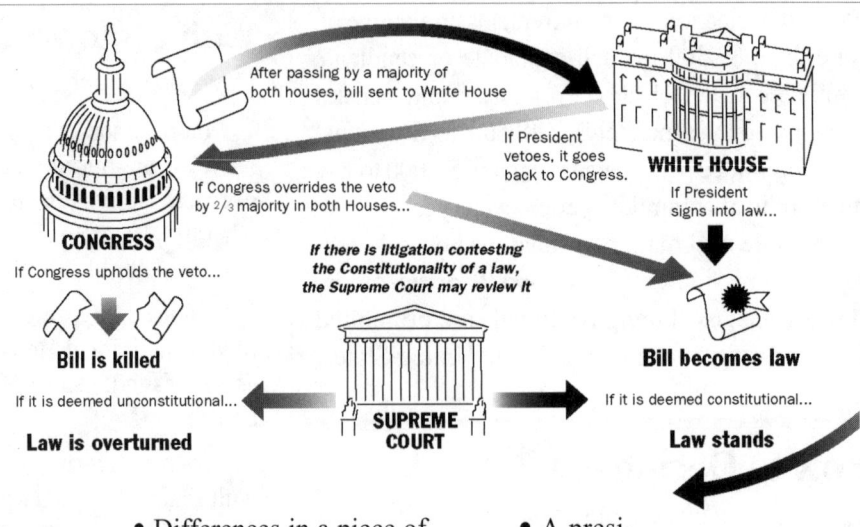

After passing by a majority of both houses, bill sent to White House

If President vetoes, it goes back to Congress.

WHITE HOUSE

If President signs into law...

CONGRESS

If Congress upholds the veto...

If Congress overrides the veto by 2/3 majority in both Houses...

If there is litigation contesting the Constitutionality of a law, the Supreme Court may review it

Bill is killed

Bill becomes law

If it is deemed unconstitutional...

SUPREME COURT

If it is deemed constitutional...

Law is overturned

Law stands

We all learned it in grade school, but for those of us who passed the civics test much too long ago, here's a refresher course on how laws are made.

- The Senate and the House of Representatives have equal voice in making laws, although revenue bills originate in the House.

- Differences in a piece of legislation between the two chanbers are reconciled by a joint committee that includes members of both chambers.

- A presidential veto of congressional legislation can be overriden by a two-thirds vote in each chamber.

Find out the purpose of the poll and who is doing the polling. Is the pollster a news organization, an academic group or a politician? And why are they doing the poll? Do they have an agenda? News organizations are one of the best sources for surveys.

Look for bias in the poll. Look at the choice of answers that respondents were given. Are there four answers in one direction and really only one choice for an answer if you feel differently? Also look at the order of questions. Questions should go from general to specific. The order changes how you think about questions; the previous question always influences the later question.

When you see a person described as a Democratic or Republican pollster, it means that they are specialists. It doesn't mean their polls are going to be biased—because their client wants a very accurate picture of where they stand.

Look at when the poll was done. Maybe a candidate does a burst of media advertising, and I conduct a poll right after that blitz. The poll might show very favorable results that might be a temporary result of the media push. Also, sometimes polls are done before a major event, but not released until afterward. It's important to know when the poll was conducted and to consider what has happened in the interim.

Look at a poll's accuracy rate. A poll with an accuracy of plus or minus 3 percent means that if I tell you 50 percent of people favor welfare reform, that number could be between 53 and 47 percent. The more people you survey, the more accurate the poll. To get an accuracy of plus or minus 1 percent, you have to interview 9,000 people. I tell clients that an accuracy rate of plus or minus 4 percent is fine for most decisions you're going to make.

The size of the sample, not the size of the universe, determines the accuracy of the poll. If you poll 500 people in Nevada and 500 in California, which poll is more accurate? They're both equally accurate. A good analogy is that if you have a 300-pound linebacker and an 80-pound kid and you need blood samples from both, there will be no difference in the sampling.

Jury Duty: The Whole Truth

Revealing the ins and outs of serving on a jury

To meet your civic responsibility when you get a summons for jury duty, work and family schedules often need to be revised. But many say the rewards of serving on jury duty often more than compensate for the inconvenience. What should you expect when you receive a summons? Jury consultant Jo-Ellan Dimitrius, who has advised legal teams on many high-profile trials, including O.J. Simpson's criminal defense team in his murder trial, shares her insights here.

Q What should people know when they show up for jury duty?

Jurors have the right to ask questions: what days will we have off, will I be sequestered, will I remain anonymous? Also, if you anticipate legitimate conflicts, like a long-planned family vacation, the court may be able to work around them.

Q Who makes the best juror for criminal and civil cases?

For a defendant in a criminal trial or a plaintiff in a civil trial, you look for jurors who are liberal. Someone who is a member of the Sierra Club or PETA (People for the Ethical Treatment of Animals), for example, or church members and minorities. For defendants in civil cases, or prosecutors in criminal cases, you look for the more conservative, older jurors, perhaps someone who had been the victim of a crime.

In all cases, you want to have one or two firm, authoritative types who will lead in your direction during the deliberation process. And for the rest, you want followers who will listen.

Q What is the best way to get excused from jury duty?

It raises red flags anytime a juror walks in with sunglasses on, anytime anyone's hiding their eyes. I avoid jurors who give very brief answers on the questionnaire and during the oral questioning. It makes me wonder what they are trying to hide. I look at body language—there have been times when jurors are giving me a positive response, but shaking their heads no. Also, the way they talk about the defendant. For example, a juror was referring to Simpson as "the incarcerated," not a good sign.

Finally, I'll avoid a person who clearly doesn't want to be there. People make up weak excuses, like their dog is sick. When it's clear they don't want to be there, the last thing I want to do is to put that person in the jury box.

ⓘ INSIDE INFO

A Jury of Your Peers

○ Potential jurors are chosen randomly from lists of voters and licensed drivers.

○ People over 70, anyone who served on a jury within the past 2 years and volunteer firefighters and members of a rescue squad or ambulance crew may be excused from serving.

○ Members of the armed forces on active duty, and professional firefighters and police are usually exempt from serving on jury duty.

○ Jurors are paid—usually about $40 a day. (Don't forget to declare it when you file your tax return.) Your employer can choose to continue to pay your salary during all or part of your jury duty but is not required to do so. However, employers cannot legally fire you for the absence.

Having Your Day in Court

When compromise fails, try small claims court

Before filing a suit in small claims court, you need to answer two questions. First: do you have a case? "There is a big difference between having something bad happen to you and actually having grounds for a lawsuit," says Ralph Warner, author of *Everybody's Guide to Small Claims Court.* "You have to know exactly how and why the other party is the author of your misfortune."

The second question: If you win, can you collect? "The biggest mistake people make is suing deadbeats," says Warner. "If they don't have two nickels to their name, don't waste your time."

If you answered yes to both questions, Warner suggests that the next step is to write to the other party. Calmly describe what went wrong and why that party is responsible. Propose a remedy. If the other party is a business, you can contact the Better Business Bureau or local consumer affairs department, which might be able to exert some pressure. If you fail to get satisfaction, it is time to go to court.

The key to victory is doing your homework. States put a cap on the maximum amount you can sue for, so find out your state's limit. The average national cap is about $5,000, but Tennessee has a $25,000 maximum. Most cases boil down to he-said, she-said tussles, but you can gain an edge by gathering corroborating evidence. Log all contacts, keep all receipts and gather every shred of documentation you can. You must file your case at a court near the defendant's home or place of business. You pay a nominal fee and fill out a brief form, stating the claim and providing the defendant's address. A case index number and court date are assigned. If the day is inconvenient, you can ask for an adjournment.

When the day arrives, several things can happen. If the defendant does not show up, you present your case, and your odds of winning are enhanced. If the other party is there, you can make a last attempt to settle: an imminent trial can often make even more unreasonable people reasonable. If you still can't resolve the matter, you go to arbitration, mediation or trial. Most people choose arbitration or mediation, because making an argument and introducing evidence are much more informal than at a trial and resolution is faster.

Even if you opt for a trial and win, your troubles may not be over. Typically, 25 percent of defendants do not pay up. If this happens, you must go back to court to get a default judgment. You can then seek help from the local sheriff's or marshal's office, which can garnish the defendant's wages or put a lien on his bank account.

—J. Peder Zane

The ABCs of Legalese

Arraignment. A court proceeding during which a defendant is formally charged with a crime and asked to plead guilty or not guilty.

Defendant. The person or organization being sued in a civil case; the person accused of a crime in a criminal case.

Grand jury. A panel of citizens who hear evidence of criminal allegations and decide whether there are grounds for a criminal prosecution.

Plaintiff. The person who files the complaint in a civil lawsuit.

Subpoena. A court-ordered command that a person appear at a specified time and place to testify under penalty of law.

Voir dire. French term meaning "to speak the truth;" describes the questioning process used by judges and lawyers to pick a jury from potential jurors.

Where to Go When the Stakes Are Low

Mad as hell at your neighbor who mistakenly cut down one of the trees on your property? Furious at the mechanic who did everything but fix your car? Disputes like these, where the anger quotient is high and the dollar value relatively small, usually end up in small claims court. The filing fee is nominal, often around $25, and most cases are settled within two months. Although you can hire a lawyer to present your case, in most states, representation isn't necessary. Many states send cases to mediators, who help the parties reach a compromise, and arbitrators, whose decisions are binding. These guidelines indicate the maximum dollar amount you can sue for (**$**) and whether your state permits you to have legal representation (**§**).

Alabama. $3,000 §Yes.

Alaska. $10,000 §Yes.

Arizona. $2,500 § No, unless both sides agree in writing.

Arkansas. $5,000 §No.

California. $7,500 *(A plaintiff may not file a claim over $2,500 more than twice a year)* §No.

Colorado. $7,500 §No, allowed only if both sides have representation.

Connecticut. $5,000 §Yes.

Delaware $15,000 §Yes.

District of Columbia. $5,000 §Yes.

Florida. $5,000 §Yes.

Georgia. $15,000 §Yes.

Hawaii. $3,500 *(Counterclaims allowed up to $20,000)* §Yes, except in residential security deposit cases.

Idaho. $4,000 §No.

Illinois. $10,000 §Yes.

Indiana. $6,000 §Yes.

Iowa. $5,000 §Yes.

Kansas. $4,000 §No, but if one party is an attorney, all parties shall have the opportunity to have an attorney.

Kentucky. $1,500 §Yes.

Louisiana. $3,000 §Yes.

Maine. $4,500 §Yes.

Maryland. $5,000 §Yes.

Massachusetts. $2,000 *(No limit for property damage caused by motor vehicles)* §Yes.

Michigan. $3,000 §No.

Minnesota. $7,000 §No, attorneys not allowed unless all sides are represented).

Mississippi. $2,500 §Yes.

Missouri. $3,000 §Yes.

Montana. $3,000 §No, attorneys not allowed unless all sides are represented.

Nebraska. $2,400 *(Adjusted every 5 years by the Consumer Price Index)* §No.

Nevada. $5,000 §Yes.

New Hampshire. $5,000 §Yes.

New Jersey. $5,000 *($5,000 in residential security deposit demand cases)* §Yes.

New Mexico. $10,000 §Yes.

New York. $5,000 §Yes.

North Carolina. $5,000 §Yes.

North Dakota. $5,000 §Yes.

Ohio. $3,000 §Yes.

Oklahoma. $6,000 §Yes, but can't charge more than 10 percent of the judgment in uncontested cases.

Oregon. $7,500 §No, unless court consents.

Pennsylvania. $10,000 *(Philadelphia Municipal Court; $8,000 District or Justice Court)* §Yes.

Rhode Island. $1,500 §Yes.

South Carolina. $7,500 *(None in landlord-tenant cases)* §Yes.

South Dakota. $12,000 §Yes.

Tennessee. $15,000-$25,000 §Yes.

Texas. $5,000 §Yes.

Utah. $5,000 §Yes.

Vermont. $5,000 §Yes.

Virginia. $5,000 §No, unless bringing their own suit.

Washington. $4,000 §No, unless court consents.

West Virginia. $5,000 §Yes.

Wisconsin. $5,000 *(No limit in eviction cases)* §Yes.

Wyoming. $7,000 §Yes.

Source: www.halt.org (see Small Claims Courts)

MORES

Reading Your F.B.I. File

Find out if you're listed as nefarious

Frank Sinatra's racy parties with John F. Kennedy, the Beach Boys' penchant for psychedelic drugs, Liberace's fondness for gambling—all are well-known morsels from F.B.I. files. The bureau won't say how many files it has, but estimates are they number more than six million. Lucille Ball, Marilyn Monroe and even Albert Einstein were checked out by the bureau as potential Communists. Some files are longer than others: Andy Warhol's film company gets 38 pages; Elvis' shenanigans merit 600; and what the government knows about U.F.O.'s fills 1,600 pages.

The F.B.I. maintains that it no longer spies on individuals for political purposes, and hasn't done so since director J. Edgar Hoover's death in 1972. Some civil liberty groups may doubt that assertion, but despite its reputation, the fact is the F.B.I. does not keep a file on every American man, woman and child. However, if you suspect that you have come under the F.B.I. radar—or if you're just curious about a long-dead ancestor—you are entitled to read the file.

Lennon appears to be radically orientated, however he does not give the impression he is a true revolutionist since he is constantly under the influence of narcotics.

From the F.B.I. file on the late former Beatle "John Winston Lennon"

• • •

For access to your personal report, you must file a request under the Privacy Act and the Freedom of Information Act. For information about another individual, an organization or a business, file a request under the Freedom of Information Act alone. For a Privacy Act request, send your complete name, address, date and place of birth, Social Security number and former addresses. If you're asking about a specific incident— F.B.I. agents stormed your house one night, for example—provide as much information as possible about the event. Sign the request and have it notarized.

If your request is for the file of a person who is dead, provide all the pertinent information and send proof that he or she is deceased, such as a published obituary, for example. Mail requests to: Federal Bureau of Investigation, Record Information/ Dissemination Section, 170 Marcel Drive, Winchester, VA 22602-4843. Or file online at foia. fbi.gov.

Even if you don't have an F.B.I. file, chances are that you have a bureau "rap sheet." That's a roster of data on an individual that the F.B.I. gets from fingerprint cards filed by federal government workers, naturalized citizens, members of the military or people who are arrested. You can get a copy of your rap sheet, should you have one, by sending the F.B.I. a letter of request, including proof of your identity and a set of rolled-ink fingerprint impressions, such as those taken at a police station. The fee is $18, payable by certi-

fied check or money order to the Treasury of the United States or by credit card. Send the payment, letter and documents to: F.B.I., CJIS Division, Attention: SCU, Mod. D-2, 1000 Custer Hollow Rd., Clarksburg, West Virginia 26306. If paying by credit card you must include the completed credit card payment form.

As for what fills those 1,600 pages on U.F.O.'s—see for yourself by visiting the F.B.I.'s Electronic Reading Room at foia.fbi.gov.

Divorce on the Cheap

A do-it-yourself divorce may be for you

The statistics are dismally familiar: half of marriages end in divorce. More than a million couples a year call it quits. A full-blown divorce trial can take years of wrangling in court and cost from $60,000 to $100,000 or more, according to HALT, a Washington, D.C. organization that pushes for legal reform. Even an amicable divorce case with no children involved can run about $3,000. By comparison, a do-it-yourself divorce could cost less than $300. The downside: some do-it-yourselfers end up paying for it in legwork and frustration.

You may have no choice but to retain a lawyer if your spouse contests any aspect of the divorce: spousal support, splitting up assets or custody of children, for example. These issues are too contentious and generally require a third party to help resolve. But if you expect a peaceful divorce, have no children and are tenacious, then the cheaper, do-it-yourself route is wide open.

Bookstores and the Internet are rife with divorce software, which costs anywhere from $24.99 for a bare-bones kit to several hundred or more for a package that includes some legal consultation. You get general divorce forms and some specific to your state, but you may not necessarily get all the forms you need for your specific locality. To be safe, contact your circuit clerk's office or family court clerk's office (numbers are found in your phone directory or online) for the list of documents you need. Once you've prepared the documents, file them with the court (filing fees are usually around $250) and ask for a hearing. Once a court date is set, ask the clerk exactly which documents you'll need to bring to the hearing. Then show up on time, with your paperwork in hand.

Don't be surprised if you encounter resistance on the part of clerks and judges during this process. Although attitudes are softening toward those who represent themselves, some courts try to discourage self-helpers, who often come to

---

ⓘ INSIDE INFO

The Great Divide

○ When divvying up a divorcing couple's assets, most states take many factors into account, including length of marriage and a partner's age, marketable skills, lifestyle and needs. In community-property states, however, most assets acquired during a marriage belong to both spouses, while assets brought into the marriage by one spouse remain his or her property.

○ These states split assets equally between spouses.

Alaska*	Arizona	California
Idaho	Louisiana	Nevada
New Mexico	Texas	Washington
	Wisconsin	

*Married couples in Alaska can choose to have assets treated as community property by written agreement.

○ A woman's standard of living drops by as much as 27 percent after a divorce, while for men it rises about 10 percent, according to the Marriage Project at Rutgers University. Single mothers, many of them divorced, suffer some of the highest bankruptcy rates.

MORES

court unprepared, taking up more court time than a lawyer would. But if all goes well, your divorce will be granted, the judge will sign the decree and you will have saved thousands.

When a Child Needs a Guardian

What-if decisions that need to be made

A quick way to cast a pall over a conversation is to ask parents if they've appointed a guardian for their children in the event that, God forbid, both of them should die. It's not at the top of most parents' list, yet the sobering truth is that if parents don't state who they want as guardians in their will, and they both die, a judge will make that decision.

The basic issue parents worry about is finding a relative—and parents overwhelmingly choose a relative—with similar religious and educational backgrounds. Other concerns to resolve before naming a guardian are, for example: Is the person physically up to the job? Does he or she have the time? Does the family have children close to the same age as yours? Would your children have to move? Do you and the potential guardian share the same moral beliefs and parenting style?

A big issue is wealth. Most parents make sure that if they were to die, their children would be taken care of financially, but what if the family the children go to is not as well off? One way to address this discrepancy is to leave money from the estate directly to the guardian, which may help the guardian's children and narrow the gap.

It is important to realize that the person you appoint as guardian does not need to be the same person who controls the finances. It is possible, and some lawyers recommend, naming a guardian, and then naming a separate person as trustee of the financial assets or co-trustee with the guard-

ian. Experts believe naming a different person as a trustee is a good option because it offers a check and balance, and "puts a second head in the process," that is, it doesn't place the entire decision-making burden on one person.

Often trusts are structured so that the child receives the money in stages—one-third at age 25, for example, one-third at 30 and one-third at 35, rather than receiving a lump sum at 18. And make sure you understand where your money is going. You may have your assets, such as proceeds from the sale of your house, for example, going to your children's trust if anything happens to you, but what about your 401(k), your individual retirement account and your life insurance?

Being a guardian is a serious job, a fiduciary responsibility, and you can get sued if you do a poor job. For that reason, think carefully about who you ask to take care of your offspring. The same is true when agreeing to care for someone else's children. Still, as hard as it may be to pick one guardian, many lawyers advise selecting one or even two backups, in case, when the time comes, the chosen person is not in a position to take the children. Also, as families and children evolve, you may want to rethink guardianships down the line and reflect those changes in your will.

You may not need a lawyer to complete the paperwork; companies like Nolo (www.nolo.com) offer books, software and forms for do-it-yourself legal solutions.
—Alina Tugend

Do You Need a Will?

Probably; here's why and what to include

More than half of American adults do not have wills. What are the potential consequences of not planning for the disposition of your estate? Boston attorney Alexander Bove,

Why You Need a Living Will

Living wills give you control and peace of mind

Fewer than 30 percent of Americans have filled out living wills or appointed someone to make medical decisions for them if they become incapacitated.

Living wills describe a person's wishes regarding medical treatment. Another type of document, called a health care power of attorney or health care proxy, names someone else, usually a relative or a friend, to make decisions when a patient can no longer do so. Such written instructions, also called advance directives, can be used in every state. They are backed by either law or precedents set in court cases, and a federal law requires that hospitals and nursing homes inform patients that they have the right to fill out the documents.

Details vary from state to state; in some places no official form is needed, and patients can draw up their own statements. Two witnesses are usually needed. The details should be discussed with family members and doctors, who should also be given copies. A copy should also be included in the medical chart if the person is hospitalized.

Living wills give people a chance to say how far doctors should go in hopeless situations. Patients can specify whether they would want treatments like respirators, feeding tubes, resuscitation, transfusions or kidney dialysis.

The Web site www.medicaldirective.org, a non-profit group, offers documents for $15, along with detailed work sheets describing possible medical situations for patients and families to consider.

But it is nearly impossible to anticipate every situation that will arise during an illness. Therefore, some experts say it is more important to have a proxy than a living will, someone who knows the patient and can make decisions if the unexpected occurs. Picking a backup proxy is also recommended. But patients must discuss their wishes in detail with proxies and make sure that doctors and relatives know who the proxy is.

—Denise Grady

---

a frequent lecturer on estate planning, taxes and trusts, provides the following expert responses to why you (and your heirs) might be better off drawing up a will.

● What happens if I don't have a will?

If you have no will, your estate will end up in probate court and important decisions will be out of your hands. Normally, you name an executor, a trusted friend or family member who is responsible for determining taxes, assets, bills and debts to be paid on your estate. Without a will, the court becomes the executor and your estate is divided under state laws.

● What are the important components of a will?

As a rule, wills are broken up into two parts. Bequests include specified property, such as amounts of money, real estate and stocks that are left to a designated beneficiary. The residue is everything else, or everything not specifically defined, and will normally go to the primary beneficiary of the estate, usually a spouse, children or both. Only property in your name at the time of your death can be passed on to your heirs.

● How often should I update my will?

Whenever there is a major change in the tax laws, or if there is a change in your family or your family's finances, you should reflect that in your will.

● How can I provide for minor children?

If you have minor children, you should be sure to name a trusted relative or friend as the guardian who will be responsible for the "person and property" of the minors.

MORES

Q How are a will and a living trust different?

A living trust is a legal document that you create while you are alive; you can transfer assets to the trust while you are alive, and the trust governs the assets. You may be your own trustee. Whatever is in the trust does not have to pass through probate. Whatever you do not put into the trust goes into a will. A living trust—including a will, durable power of attorney and health care proxy—and a living will are the typical documents in a modern estate plan.

Q What is the difference between a trustee and an executor?

A trustee oversees property that's held in trust and administers it for the benefit of the beneficiaries. An executor carries out the terms of the will—collecting the assets, for example, and investing or selling them. Choose both very carefully.

Q How much should I pay to have a will drawn?

That depends on the complexity of the estate. The process of drawing up a will can cost between $50 and $5,000 or more, depending on how complicated it is. Often the amount of property is not as important a factor as the family circumstances.

How to Change Your Name
You can switch from Mary to Sue if you so desire

"What name to call thee by?" asked the 14th-century poet Petrarch in a poem to his beloved. But the same question can be asked of the more than three million Americans who legally change their names every year. As part of your right to freedom of expression, you can opt for a new name for just about any reason: religious, social, aesthetic or just because you want to—called "desire" in legal lingo. There are limits, however: you can't use a new identity in a fraudulent way, such as to evade debtors, and pornographic or racially insulting names won't pass muster with the court.

Many name changes are simply a result of marriage or divorce. In those cases, changes are made almost automatically. A bride who takes on her husband's name—or, less frequently, a groom who takes his wife's—simply indicates the desired name on the marriage license. A divorced woman who wants to revert to her maiden name can easily make the change in the divorce documents.

But for those who want a fresh persona for other reasons, the process is more complicated. First, you have to figure out what documents your state requires and in which court you need to file the petition. Your county clerk's office (the number can be found in your local phone directory or on your county's Web site) can tell you the requirements and how to get requisite forms. (Some courts will ask you to list your creditors' names and addresses.) You pay a nominal court fee and are given a docket number. A judge reviews your petition and either approves it, or requests a court hearing, which may be routine in some states. The final step, after court approval, is to place an ad in a specified newspaper announcing the name change. The court will then inform you that your new identity is legal.

The process can be done without a lawyer; you can get name change kits online for $20 to $150. A lawyer will do the legwork for $500 to more than $2,000, depending on whether children are also involved. Once you have your new identity, be sure to notify employers, banks, credit card companies, the I.R.S., the motor vehicle department, the Social Security Administration, etc. Remember to revisit your will, retirement plans, contracts and real estate deeds.

Alas, in some cases, your old identity never dies. Your passport, for example, will most likely state your original name with an a.k.a., "also known as," and your new moniker.

Calendars & Customs

Holidays Worth Celebrating

Days to skip work, appreciate moms, presidents and more…

Merchants love holidays, when gift-happy consumers make cash registers ring. The religious faithful take their holy days very seriously; and those who simply need a break cheer at the prospect of a day free of the normal routine.

Whatever your reason to celebrate, here are the dates of major holidays, in the United States and abroad.

MAJOR AMERICAN HOLIDAYS

Dates marked with an asterisk (*) are officially designated national holidays. Federal government offices nationwide and schools, banks and offices in Washington, D.C., are closed.

* New Year's Day, *Jan. 1.* Roman mythology says two-faced Janus, the god of beginnings for whom our first month is named, looked back on the old year and ahead to the new. In the U.S., we ring out the old year at midnight with champagne and a few bars of that cryptic Scottish melody, *Auld Lang Syne* ("The Good Old Days").

* Dr. Martin Luther King Jr. Birthday, *third Monday in Jan.* The civil rights activist, minister and advocate of nonviolent protest was born on January 15, 1929. A bill to make his birthday a federal holiday was first introduced in 1968, the year King was assassinated. President Ronald Reagan signed the bill in 1983.

Groundhog Day, *Feb. 2.* Rumor has it that if a groundhog comes out of his hole on this day and sees his shadow, winter will last for six more weeks. But if the sky is overcast and the groundhog is shadowless, mild weather is on the way. Pennsylvania's Punxsutawney Phil is the country's most famous rodent meteorologist. Since 1887, the Punxsutawney Groundhog Club has gone to Gobbler's Knob to watch successive generations of Phils offer their predictions.

Valentine's Day, *Feb. 14.* The origin of this romantic holiday is uncertain, but it may have been inspired by the martyrdom of St. Valentine in A.D. 270. The first commercial Valentine's Day cards in the U.S. hit the shops in the 1840s; in the early 1900's, when risqué cards were "common," the Chicago postal service refused to deliver 25,000 valentines it deemed unfit to be mailed.

* President's Day, *third Monday in Feb.* Honors two of our most famous presidents, George Washington (born Feb. 22, 1732) and Abraham Lincoln (born Feb. 12, 1809), whose birthdays used to be celebrated separately. These larger-than-life figures stood out in the crowd even by today's standards: Washington was 6 feet tall, and lanky Lincoln was 6 feet 4 inches.

St. Patrick's Day, *March 17.* The patron saint of Ireland was born in England around A.D. 389, and immigrants who came to America from the Emerald Isle brought this holiday with them. So many of George Washington's troops were Irish that the secret password during one Revolutionary War battle was "Saint Patrick."

Vernal Equinox, *around March 21.* Day and night are equally long on this first day of spring.

April Fools' Day, *April 1.* No one is sure when or why the first of April turned into a day for

MORES

A Perpetual Calendar: 1820-2080

Datebooks must reflect changing times

By definition, New Year's Day has always marked the start of a new calendar year, but that calendar year hasn't always been in January. Until the 16th century in Western Europe, New Year's Day was rung in on the vernal equinox, the start of spring in the northern hemisphere. But other, non-Christian cultures have always had festivals to celebrate the birth of the sun around the time of the winter solstice in the dead of December. In 1582, Pope Gregory XIII established the calendar that is now universally used and decreed that the Christian New Year should commence on January 1.

On which day of the week will New Year's fall next year, or in 2020? Or, in case it's slipped your mind, which day of the week were you born? With the perpetual calendar on the following pages, the answers are at your fingertips. The letter shown next to your birth year on the legend below indicates which calendar to use.

THE PERPETUAL CALENDAR LEGEND

Year		Year		Year		Year		Year		Year		Year		Year	
1820	J	1854	K	1888	D	1920	H	1952	F	1984	D	2016	I	2050	C
1821	L	1855	L	1889	M	1921	C	1953	A	1985	M	2017	K	2051	K
1822	M	1856	F	1890	N	1922	K	1954	B	1986	N	2018	L	2052	E
1823	N	1857	A	1891	A	1923	L	1955	C	1987	A	2019	M	2053	N
1824	H	1858	B	1892	I	1924	F	1956	D	1988	I	2020	G	2054	A
1825	C	1859	C	1893	K	1925	A	1957	M	1989	K	2021	B	2055	B
1826	K	1860	D	1894	L	1926	B	1958	N	1990	L	2022	C	2056	J
1827	L	1861	M	1895	M	1927	C	1959	A	1991	M	2023	K	2057	L
1828	F	1862	N	1896	G	1928	D	1960	I	1992	G	2024	E	2058	M
1829	A	1863	A	1897	B	1929	M	1961	K	1993	B	2025	N	2059	N
1830	B	1864	I	1898	C	1930	N	1962	L	1994	C	2026	A	2060	H
1831	C	1865	K	1899	K	1931	A	1963	M	1995	K	2027	B	2061	C
1832	D	1866	L	1900	L	1932	I	1964	G	1996	E	2028	J	2062	K
1833	M	1867	M	1901	M	1933	K	1965	B	1997	N	2029	L	2063	L
1834	N	1868	G	1902	N	1934	L	1966	C	1998	A	2030	M	2064	F
1835	A	1869	B	1903	A	1935	M	1967	K	1999	B	2031	N	2065	A
1836	I	1870	C	1904	I	1936	G	1968	E	2000	J	2032	H	2066	B
1837	K	1871	K	1905	K	1937	B	1969	N	2001	L	2033	C	2067	C
1838	L	1872	E	1906	L	1938	C	1970	A	2002	M	2034	K	2068	D
1839	M	1873	N	1907	M	1939	K	1971	B	2003	N	2035	L	2069	M
1840	G	1874	A	1908	G	1940	E	1972	J	2004	H	2036	F	2070	N
1841	B	1875	B	1909	B	1941	N	1973	L	2005	C	2037	A	2071	A
1842	C	1876	J	1910	C	1942	A	1974	M	2006	K	2038	B	2072	I
1843	K	1877	L	1911	K	1943	B	1975	N	2007	L	2039	C	2073	K
1844	E	1878	M	1912	E	1944	J	1976	H	2008	F	2040	D	2074	L
1845	N	1879	N	1913	N	1945	L	1977	C	2009	A	2041	M	2075	M
1846	A	1880	H	1914	A	1946	M	1978	K	2010	B	2042	N	2076	G
1847	B	1881	C	1915	B	1947	N	1979	L	2011	C	2043	A	2077	B
1848	J	1882	K	1916	J	1948	H	1980	F	2012	D	2044	I	2078	C
1849	L	1883	L	1917	L	1949	C	1981	A	2013	M	2045	K	2079	K
1850	M	1884	F	1918	M	1950	K	1982	B	2014	N	2046	L	2080	E
1851	N	1885	A	1919	N	1951	L	1983	C	2015	A	2047	M		
1852	H	1886	B									2048	G		
1853	C	1887	C									2049	B		

A — 2009, 1998

JANUARY
S	M	T	W	T	F	S
				1	2	3
4	5	6	7	8	9	10
11	12	13	14	15	16	17
18	19	20	21	22	23	24
25	26	27	28	29	30	31

FEBRUARY
S	M	T	W	T	F	S
1	2	3	4	5	6	7
8	9	10	11	12	13	14
15	16	17	18	19	20	21
22	23	24	25	26	27	28

MARCH
S	M	T	W	T	F	S
1	2	3	4	5	6	7
8	9	10	11	12	13	14
15	16	17	18	19	20	21
22	23	24	25	26	27	28
29	30	31				

APRIL
S	M	T	W	T	F	S
			1	2	3	4
5	6	7	8	9	10	11
12	13	14	15	16	17	18
19	20	21	22	23	24	25
26	27	28	29	30		

MAY
S	M	T	W	T	F	S
					1	2
3	4	5	6	7	8	9
10	11	12	13	14	15	16
17	18	19	20	21	22	23
24	25	26	27	28	29	30
31						

JUNE
S	M	T	W	T	F	S
	1	2	3	4	5	6
7	8	9	10	11	12	13
14	15	16	17	18	19	20
21	22	23	24	25	26	27
28	29	30				

JULY
S	M	T	W	T	F	S
			1	2	3	4
5	6	7	8	9	10	11
12	13	14	15	16	17	18
19	20	21	22	23	24	25
26	27	28	29	30	31	

AUGUST
S	M	T	W	T	F	S
						1
2	3	4	5	6	7	8
9	10	11	12	13	14	15
16	17	18	19	20	21	22
23	24	25	26	27	28	29
30	31					

SEPTEMBER
S	M	T	W	T	F	S
		1	2	3	4	5
6	7	8	9	10	11	12
13	14	15	16	17	18	19
20	21	22	23	24	25	26
27	28	29	30			

OCTOBER
S	M	T	W	T	F	S
				1	2	3
4	5	6	7	8	9	10
11	12	13	14	15	16	17
18	19	20	21	22	23	24
25	26	27	28	29	30	31

NOVEMBER
S	M	T	W	T	F	S
1	2	3	4	5	6	7
8	9	10	11	12	13	14
15	16	17	18	19	20	21
22	23	24	25	26	27	28
29	30					

DECEMBER
S	M	T	W	T	F	S
		1	2	3	4	5
6	7	8	9	10	11	12
13	14	15	16	17	18	19
20	21	22	23	24	25	26
27	28	29	30	31		

B — 2010, 1999

JANUARY
S	M	T	W	T	F	S
					1	2
3	4	5	6	7	8	9
10	11	12	13	14	15	16
17	18	19	20	21	22	23
24	25	26	27	28	29	30
31						

FEBRUARY
S	M	T	W	T	F	S
	1	2	3	4	5	6
7	8	9	10	11	12	13
14	15	16	17	18	19	20
21	22	23	24	25	26	27
28						

MARCH
S	M	T	W	T	F	S
	1	2	3	4	5	6
7	8	9	10	11	12	13
14	15	16	17	18	19	20
21	22	23	24	25	26	27
28	29	30	31			

APRIL
S	M	T	W	T	F	S
				1	2	3
4	5	6	7	8	9	10
11	12	13	14	15	16	17
18	19	20	21	22	23	24
25	26	27	28	29	30	

MAY
S	M	T	W	T	F	S
						1
2	3	4	5	6	7	8
9	10	11	12	13	14	15
16	17	18	19	20	21	22
23	24	25	26	27	28	29
30	31					

JUNE
S	M	T	W	T	F	S
		1	2	3	4	5
6	7	8	9	10	11	12
13	14	15	16	17	18	19
20	21	22	23	24	25	26
27	28	29	30			

JULY
S	M	T	W	T	F	S
				1	2	3
4	5	6	7	8	9	10
11	12	13	14	15	16	17
18	19	20	21	22	23	24
25	26	27	28	29	30	31

AUGUST
S	M	T	W	T	F	S
1	2	3	4	5	6	7
8	9	10	11	12	13	14
15	16	17	18	19	20	21
22	23	24	25	26	27	28
29	30	31				

SEPTEMBER
S	M	T	W	T	F	S
			1	2	3	4
5	6	7	8	9	10	11
12	13	14	15	16	17	18
19	20	21	22	23	24	25
26	27	28	29	30		

OCTOBER
S	M	T	W	T	F	S
					1	2
3	4	5	6	7	8	9
10	11	12	13	14	15	16
17	18	19	20	21	22	23
24	25	26	27	28	29	30
31						

NOVEMBER
S	M	T	W	T	F	S
	1	2	3	4	5	6
7	8	9	10	11	12	13
14	15	16	17	18	19	20
21	22	23	24	25	26	27
28	29	30				

DECEMBER
S	M	T	W	T	F	S
			1	2	3	4
5	6	7	8	9	10	11
12	13	14	15	16	17	18
19	20	21	22	23	24	25
26	27	28	29	30	31	

making friends look like fools, but the tradition dates back at least to the early 18th century. April fools are labeled "gowks" (cuckoos) in Scotland, and "gobs" or "noddies" in England; the French call April 1 pranks "poisson d'avril," or April fish.

Earth Day, *April 22.* In 1970, the Environmental Protection Agency first asked us to "Give Earth a Chance." Congress has passed laws that protect our natural resources, and curbside recycling is now common. But the E.P.A. reports that we still produce more solid waste per person every day than any other nation—4.4 pounds.

Mother's Day, *second Sunday in May.* Julia Ward Howe, author of "Battle Hymn of the Republic," first floated the idea of a national holiday to honor mothers in 1872. But Philadelphian Anna Jarvis, whose mother had wanted such a day to comfort families after the Civil War, launched the campaign that made it a reality. President Woodrow Wilson officially established the holiday in 1914.

✳Memorial Day, *last Monday in May.* The government bowed in 1868 to the campaign of a Union veterans group that wanted to honor soldiers who died in the Civil War. The holiday has now become a tribute to all fallen soldiers and deceased loved ones.

MORES

Flag Day, *June 14.* The Second Continental Congress adopted the official flag design on June 14, 1777. Protocol dictates that the American flag may not touch the ground, nor may it be dipped to anyone or anything while being carried in a parade. The star-spangled banner Francis Scott Key saw by the dawn's early light was hit by 11 bullets as it flew above Baltimore's Fort McHenry; it is preserved at the Smithsonian Institution.

Father's Day, *third Sunday in June.* The daughter of a Civil War veteran (whose wife died giving birth to their sixth child) persuaded her church in Spokane, Wash., to conduct a special service in honor of fathers. That was in 1910, and though the idea soon became popular around the nation, it wasn't made an official holiday until 1966.

Summer Solstice, *around June 21.* The first day of summer; the year's longest day.

✱ Independence Day, *July 4.* Fireworks and fanfare generally mark Fourth of July festivities commemorating the 1776 signing of the Declaration of Independence. Two of the signers were loyal to it even in death: On July 4, 1826, John Adams, the second president, died at age 90, and Thomas Jefferson, president number three, died at age 83.

C — 2011, 2005

JANUARY

S	M	T	W	T	F	S
						1
2	3	4	5	6	7	8
9	10	11	12	13	14	15
16	17	18	19	20	21	22
23	24	25	26	27	28	29
30	31					

FEBRUARY

S	M	T	W	T	F	S
		1	2	3	4	5
6	7	8	9	10	11	12
13	14	15	16	17	18	19
20	21	22	23	24	25	26
27	28					

MARCH

S	M	T	W	T	F	S
		1	2	3	4	5
6	7	8	9	10	11	12
13	14	15	16	17	18	19
20	21	22	23	24	25	26
27	28	29	30	31		

APRIL

S	M	T	W	T	F	S
					1	2
3	4	5	6	7	8	9
10	11	12	13	14	15	16
17	18	19	20	21	22	23
24	25	26	27	28	29	30

MAY

S	M	T	W	T	F	S
1	2	3	4	5	6	7
8	9	10	11	12	13	14
15	16	17	18	19	20	21
22	23	24	25	26	27	28
29	30	31				

JUNE

S	M	T	W	T	F	S
			1	2	3	4
5	6	7	8	9	10	11
12	13	14	15	16	17	18
19	20	21	22	23	24	25
26	27	28	29	30		

JULY

S	M	T	W	T	F	S
					1	2
3	4	5	6	7	8	9
10	11	12	13	14	15	16
17	18	19	20	21	22	23
24	25	26	27	28	29	30
31						

AUGUST

S	M	T	W	T	F	S
	1	2	3	4	5	6
7	8	9	10	11	12	13
14	15	16	17	18	19	20
21	22	23	24	25	26	27
28	29	30	31			

SEPTEMBER

S	M	T	W	T	F	S
				1	2	3
4	5	6	7	8	9	10
11	12	13	14	15	16	17
18	19	20	21	22	23	24
25	26	27	28	29	30	

OCTOBER

S	M	T	W	T	F	S
						1
2	3	4	5	6	7	8
9	10	11	12	13	14	15
16	17	18	19	20	21	22
23	24	25	26	27	28	29
30	31					

NOVEMBER

S	M	T	W	T	F	S
		1	2	3	4	5
6	7	8	9	10	11	12
13	14	15	16	17	18	19
20	21	22	23	24	25	26
27	28	29	30			

DECEMBER

S	M	T	W	T	F	S
				1	2	3
4	5	6	7	8	9	10
11	12	13	14	15	16	17
18	19	20	21	22	23	24
25	26	27	28	29	30	31

D — 2012, 1984

JANUARY

S	M	T	W	T	F	S
1	2	3	4	5	6	7
8	9	10	11	12	13	14
15	16	17	18	19	20	21
22	23	24	25	26	27	28
29	30	31				

FEBRUARY

S	M	T	W	T	F	S
			1	2	3	4
5	6	7	8	9	10	11
12	13	14	15	16	17	18
19	20	21	22	23	24	25
26	27	28	29			

MARCH

S	M	T	W	T	F	S
				1	2	3
4	5	6	7	8	9	10
11	12	13	14	15	16	17
18	19	20	21	22	23	24
25	26	27	28	29	30	31

APRIL

S	M	T	W	T	F	S
1	2	3	4	5	6	7
8	9	10	11	12	13	14
15	16	17	18	19	20	21
22	23	24	25	26	27	28
29	30					

MAY

S	M	T	W	T	F	S
		1	2	3	4	5
6	7	8	9	10	11	12
13	14	15	16	17	18	19
20	21	22	23	24	25	26
27	28	29	30	31		

JUNE

S	M	T	W	T	F	S
					1	2
3	4	5	6	7	8	9
10	11	12	13	14	15	16
17	18	19	20	21	22	23
24	25	26	27	28	29	30

JULY

S	M	T	W	T	F	S
1	2	3	4	5	6	7
8	9	10	11	12	13	14
15	16	17	18	19	20	21
22	23	24	25	26	27	28
29	30	31				

AUGUST

S	M	T	W	T	F	S
			1	2	3	4
5	6	7	8	9	10	11
12	13	14	15	16	17	18
19	20	21	22	23	24	25
26	27	28	29	30	31	

SEPTEMBER

S	M	T	W	T	F	S
						1
2	3	4	5	6	7	8
9	10	11	12	13	14	15
16	17	18	19	20	21	22
23	24	25	26	27	28	29
30						

OCTOBER

S	M	T	W	T	F	S
	1	2	3	4	5	6
7	8	9	10	11	12	13
14	15	16	17	18	19	20
21	22	23	24	25	26	27
28	29	30	31			

NOVEMBER

S	M	T	W	T	F	S
				1	2	3
4	5	6	7	8	9	10
11	12	13	14	15	16	17
18	19	20	21	22	23	24
25	26	27	28	29	30	

DECEMBER

S	M	T	W	T	F	S
						1
2	3	4	5	6	7	8
9	10	11	12	13	14	15
16	17	18	19	20	21	22
23	24	25	26	27	28	29
30	31					

```
E                                              2024, 1996

        JANUARY                    MAY                 SEPTEMBER
 S  M  T  W  T  F  S      S  M  T  W  T  F  S      S  M  T  W  T  F  S
    1  2  3  4  5  6                  1  2  3  4      1  2  3  4  5  6  7
 7  8  9 10 11 12 13      5  6  7  8  9 10 11      8  9 10 11 12 13 14
14 15 16 17 18 19 20     12 13 14 15 16 17 18     15 16 17 18 19 20 21
21 22 23 24 25 26 27     19 20 21 22 23 24 25     22 23 24 25 26 27 28
28 29 30 31              26 27 28 29 30 31        29 30

        FEBRUARY                   JUNE                  OCTOBER
 S  M  T  W  T  F  S      S  M  T  W  T  F  S      S  M  T  W  T  F  S
             1  2  3                           1            1  2  3  4  5
 4  5  6  7  8  9 10      2  3  4  5  6  7  8      6  7  8  9 10 11 12
11 12 13 14 15 16 17      9 10 11 12 13 14 15     13 14 15 16 17 18 19
18 19 20 21 22 23 24     16 17 18 19 20 21 22     20 21 22 23 24 25 26
25 26 27 28 29           23 24 25 26 27 28 29     27 28 29 30 31
                         30
        MARCH                      JULY                  NOVEMBER
 S  M  T  W  T  F  S      S  M  T  W  T  F  S      S  M  T  W  T  F  S
                1  2            1  2  3  4  5  6                  1  2
 3  4  5  6  7  8  9      7  8  9 10 11 12 13      3  4  5  6  7  8  9
10 11 12 13 14 15 16     14 15 16 17 18 19 20     10 11 12 13 14 15 16
17 18 19 20 21 22 23     21 22 23 24 25 26 27     17 18 19 20 21 22 23
24 25 26 27 28 29 30     28 29 30 31              24 25 26 27 28 29 30
31
        APRIL                      AUGUST                DECEMBER
 S  M  T  W  T  F  S      S  M  T  W  T  F  S      S  M  T  W  T  F  S
    1  2  3  4  5  6                  1  2  3      1  2  3  4  5  6  7
 7  8  9 10 11 12 13      4  5  6  7  8  9 10      8  9 10 11 12 13 14
14 15 16 17 18 19 20     11 12 13 14 15 16 17     15 16 17 18 19 20 21
21 22 23 24 25 26 27     18 19 20 21 22 23 24     22 23 24 25 26 27 28
28 29 30                 25 26 27 28 29 30 31     29 30 31
```

```
F                                              2008, 1980

        JANUARY                    MAY                 SEPTEMBER
 S  M  T  W  T  F  S      S  M  T  W  T  F  S      S  M  T  W  T  F  S
       1  2  3  4  5                     1  2  3      1  2  3  4  5  6
 6  7  8  9 10 11 12      4  5  6  7  8  9 10      7  8  9 10 11 12 13
13 14 15 16 17 18 19     11 12 13 14 15 16 17     14 15 16 17 18 19 20
20 21 22 23 24 25 26     18 19 20 21 22 23 24     21 22 23 24 25 26 27
27 28 29 30 31          25 26 27 28 29 30 31     28 29 30

        FEBRUARY                   JUNE                  OCTOBER
 S  M  T  W  T  F  S      S  M  T  W  T  F  S      S  M  T  W  T  F  S
                1  2      1  2  3  4  5  6  7                  1  2  3  4
 3  4  5  6  7  8  9      8  9 10 11 12 13 14      5  6  7  8  9 10 11
10 11 12 13 14 15 16     15 16 17 18 19 20 21     12 13 14 15 16 17 18
17 18 19 20 21 22 23     22 23 24 25 26 27 28     19 20 21 22 23 24 25
24 25 26 27 28 29        29 30                    26 27 28 29 30 31

        MARCH                      JULY                  NOVEMBER
 S  M  T  W  T  F  S      S  M  T  W  T  F  S      S  M  T  W  T  F  S
                   1            1  2  3  4  5                        1
 2  3  4  5  6  7  8      6  7  8  9 10 11 12      2  3  4  5  6  7  8
 9 10 11 12 13 14 15     13 14 15 16 17 18 19      9 10 11 12 13 14 15
16 17 18 19 20 21 22     20 21 22 23 24 25 26     16 17 18 19 20 21 22
23 24 25 26 27 28 29     27 28 29 30 31           23 24 25 26 27 28 29
30 31                                             30
        APRIL                      AUGUST                DECEMBER
 S  M  T  W  T  F  S      S  M  T  W  T  F  S      S  M  T  W  T  F  S
    1  2  3  4  5                        1  2      1  2  3  4  5  6
 6  7  8  9 10 11 12      3  4  5  6  7  8  9      7  8  9 10 11 12 13
13 14 15 16 17 18 19     10 11 12 13 14 15 16     14 15 16 17 18 19 20
20 21 22 23 24 25 26     17 18 19 20 21 22 23     21 22 23 24 25 26 27
27 28 29 30             24 25 26 27 28 29 30     28 29 30 31
                        31
```

Women's Equality Day, *Aug. 26.* The 19th Amendment to the Constitution was passed on this day in 1920, giving women the right to vote. In Tennessee's House of Representatives, the last vote needed to ratify the amendment was cast by 24-year-old Harry Burns, who, though his district opposed the measure, had promised his mother he would vote for it to break a tie.

✴ Labor Day, *first Monday in Sept.* During the Industrial Revolution, a bad time for laborers, union leader Peter McGuire drummed up support for a day to pay homage to America's workers. He chose early September for its pleasant weather and because no other legal holiday broke up the stretch between Independence Day and Thanksgiving. It's always been thought of as the end of summer vacation, although many schools now resume in late August.

Autumnal Equinox, around *Sept. 21.* The first day of fall.

✴ Columbus Day, *second Monday in Oct.* Christopher Columbus and his entourage first touched American soil on October 12, 1492, probably on Samana Cay in the Bahamas. At sea, Columbus kept an accurate private log of the miles traveled each day, but subtracted miles for the ship's official log. He did so to avoid mutinies caused by sailors who didn't want to be so far from

MORES

home and to make sure his directions to Asia, which turned out to be wildly inaccurate, wouldn't fall into the wrong hands.

United Nations Day, *Oct. 24.*

When the United Nations was founded in 1945, it had 51 member countries. Now it has more than 190. Its six official languages are Arabic, Chinese, English, French, Russian and Spanish.

Halloween, *Oct. 31.* The

attendant ghouls and goblins stem from the myths of the ancient Celts, who thought witches, ghosts and the souls of the dead wandered about on the last night of their harvest season. The name comes from the Catholic Church, which in the ninth century declared the first of November All Saints' Day and called the previous evening All Hallows Eve. Candy-loving children benefit from the combination of influences, as does UNICEF, which has earned more than $140 million since 1950 from its Halloween fundraising campaign.

*Veterans Day, *Nov. 11.*

Formerly called Armistice Day, it commemorated the end of World War 1 and honored those who had died fighting it. The holiday was renamed in 1954, and its scope widened to include all who have served in the U.S. armed forces. For a short time in the 1970s, the date was changed to the fourth Monday in November to add another 3-day

---

G — 2020, 1992

JANUARY

S	M	T	W	T	F	S
			1	2	3	4
5	6	7	8	9	10	11
12	13	14	15	16	17	18
19	20	21	22	23	24	25
26	27	28	29	30	31	

FEBRUARY

S	M	T	W	T	F	S
						1
2	3	4	5	6	7	8
9	10	11	12	13	14	15
16	17	18	19	20	21	22
23	24	25	26	27	28	29

MARCH

S	M	T	W	T	F	S
1	2	3	4	5	6	7
8	9	10	11	12	13	14
15	16	17	18	19	20	21
22	23	24	25	26	27	28
29	30	31				

APRIL

S	M	T	W	T	F	S
			1	2	3	4
5	6	7	8	9	10	11
12	13	14	15	16	17	18
19	20	21	22	23	24	25
26	27	28	29	30		

MAY

S	M	T	W	T	F	S
					1	2
3	4	5	6	7	8	9
10	11	12	13	14	15	16
17	18	19	20	21	22	23
24	25	26	27	28	29	30
31						

JUNE

S	M	T	W	T	F	S
	1	2	3	4	5	6
7	8	9	10	11	12	13
14	15	16	17	18	19	20
21	22	23	24	25	26	27
28	29	30				

JULY

S	M	T	W	T	F	S
			1	2	3	4
5	6	7	8	9	10	11
12	13	14	15	16	17	18
19	20	21	22	23	24	25
26	27	28	29	30	31	

AUGUST

S	M	T	W	T	F	S
						1
2	3	4	5	6	7	8
9	10	11	12	13	14	15
16	17	18	19	20	21	22
23	24	25	26	27	28	29
30	31					

SEPTEMBER

S	M	T	W	T	F	S
		1	2	3	4	5
6	7	8	9	10	11	12
13	14	15	16	17	18	19
20	21	22	23	24	25	26
27	28	29	30			

OCTOBER

S	M	T	W	T	F	S
				1	2	3
4	5	6	7	8	9	10
11	12	13	14	15	16	17
18	19	20	21	22	23	24
25	26	27	28	29	30	31

NOVEMBER

S	M	T	W	T	F	S
1	2	3	4	5	6	7
8	9	10	11	12	13	14
15	16	17	18	19	20	21
22	23	24	25	26	27	28
29	30					

DECEMBER

S	M	T	W	T	F	S
		1	2	3	4	5
6	7	8	9	10	11	12
13	14	15	16	17	18	19
20	21	22	23	24	25	26
27	28	29	30	31		

H — 2032, 2004

JANUARY

S	M	T	W	T	F	S
				1	2	3
4	5	6	7	8	9	10
11	12	13	14	15	16	17
18	19	20	21	22	23	24
25	26	27	28	29	30	31

FEBRUARY

S	M	T	W	T	F	S
1	2	3	4	5	6	7
8	9	10	11	12	13	14
15	16	17	18	19	20	21
22	23	24	25	26	27	28
29						

MARCH

S	M	T	W	T	F	S
	1	2	3	4	5	6
7	8	9	10	11	12	13
14	15	16	17	18	19	20
21	22	23	24	25	26	27
28	29	30	31			

APRIL

S	M	T	W	T	F	S
				1	2	3
4	5	6	7	8	9	10
11	12	13	14	15	16	17
18	19	20	21	22	23	24
25	26	27	28	29	30	

MAY

S	M	T	W	T	F	S
						1
2	3	4	5	6	7	8
9	10	11	12	13	14	15
16	17	18	19	20	21	22
23	24	25	26	27	28	29
30	31					

JUNE

S	M	T	W	T	F	S
		1	2	3	4	5
6	7	8	9	10	11	12
13	14	15	16	17	18	19
20	21	22	23	24	25	26
27	28	29	30			

JULY

S	M	T	W	T	F	S
				1	2	3
4	5	6	7	8	9	10
11	12	13	14	15	16	17
18	19	20	21	22	23	24
25	26	27	28	29	30	31

AUGUST

S	M	T	W	T	F	S
1	2	3	4	5	6	7
8	9	10	11	12	13	14
15	16	17	18	19	20	21
22	23	24	25	26	27	28
29	30	31				

SEPTEMBER

S	M	T	W	T	F	S
			1	2	3	4
5	6	7	8	9	10	11
12	13	14	15	16	17	18
19	20	21	22	23	24	25
26	27	28	29	30		

OCTOBER

S	M	T	W	T	F	S
					1	2
3	4	5	6	7	8	9
10	11	12	13	14	15	16
17	18	19	20	21	22	23
24	25	26	27	28	29	30
31						

NOVEMBER

S	M	T	W	T	F	S
	1	2	3	4	5	6
7	8	9	10	11	12	13
14	15	16	17	18	19	20
21	22	23	24	25	26	27
28	29	30				

DECEMBER

S	M	T	W	T	F	S
			1	2	3	4
5	6	7	8	9	10	11
12	13	14	15	16	17	18
19	20	21	22	23	24	25
26	27	28	29	30	31	

I   **2016, 1988**

			JANUARY			
S	M	T	W	T	F	S
					1	2
3	4	5	6	7	8	9
10	11	12	13	14	15	16
17	18	19	20	21	22	23
24	25	26	27	28	29	30
31						

			FEBRUARY			
S	M	T	W	T	F	S
	1	2	3	4	5	6
7	8	9	10	11	12	13
14	15	16	17	18	19	20
21	22	23	24	25	26	27
28	29					

			MARCH			
S	M	T	W	T	F	S
		1	2	3	4	5
6	7	8	9	10	11	12
13	14	15	16	17	18	19
20	21	22	23	24	25	26
27	28	29	30	31		

			APRIL			
S	M	T	W	T	F	S
					1	2
3	4	5	6	7	8	9
10	11	12	13	14	15	16
17	18	19	20	21	22	23
24	25	26	27	28	29	30

			MAY			
S	M	T	W	T	F	S
1	2	3	4	5	6	7
8	9	10	11	12	13	14
15	16	17	18	19	20	21
22	23	24	25	26	27	28
29	30	31				

			JUNE			
S	M	T	W	T	F	S
			1	2	3	4
5	66	7	8	9	10	11
12	13	14	15	16	17	18
19	20	21	22	23	24	25
26	27	28	29	30		

			JULY			
S	M	T	W	T	F	S
					1	2
3	4	5	6	7	8	9
10	11	12	13	14	15	16
17	18	19	20	21	22	23
24	25	26	27	28	29	30
31						

			AUGUST			
S	M	T	W	T	F	S
	1	2	3	4	5	6
7	8	9	10	11	12	13
14	15	16	17	18	19	20
21	22	23	24	25	26	27
28	29	30	31			

			SEPTEMBER			
S	M	T	W	T	F	S
				1	2	3
4	5	6	7	8	9	10
11	12	13	14	15	16	17
18	19	20	21	22	23	24
25	26	27	28	29	30	

			OCTOBER			
S	M	T	W	T	F	S
						1
2	3	4	5	6	7	8
9	10	11	12	13	14	15
16	17	18	19	20	21	22
23	24	25	26	27	28	29
30	31					

			NOVEMBER			
S	M	T	W	T	F	S
		1	2	3	4	5
6	7	8	9	10	11	12
13	14	15	16	17	18	19
20	21	22	23	24	25	26
27	28	29	30			

			DECEMBER			
S	M	T	W	T	F	S
				1	2	3
4	5	6	7	8	9	10
11	12	13	14	15	16	17
18	19	20	21	22	23	24
25	26	27	28	29	30	31

J   **2028, 2000**

			JANUARY			
S	M	T	W	T	F	S
						1
2	3	4	5	6	7	8
9	10	11	12	13	14	15
16	17	18	19	20	21	22
23	24	25	26	27	28	29
30	31					

			FEBRUARY			
S	M	T	W	T	F	S
		1	2	3	4	5
6	7	8	9	10	11	12
13	14	15	16	17	18	19
20	21	22	23	24	25	26
27	28	29				

			MARCH			
S	M	T	W	T	F	S
			1	2	3	4
5	6	7	8	9	10	11
12	13	14	15	16	17	18
19	20	21	22	23	24	25
26	27	28	29	30	31	

			APRIL			
S	M	T	W	T	F	S
						1
2	3	4	5	6	7	8
9	10	11	12	13	14	15
16	17	18	19	20	21	22
23	24	25	26	27	28	29
30						

			MAY			
S	M	T	W	T	F	S
	1	2	3	4	5	6
7	8	9	10	11	12	13
14	15	16	17	18	19	20
21	22	23	24	25	26	27
28	29	30	31			

			JUNE			
S	M	T	W	T	F	S
				1	2	3
4	5	6	7	8	9	10
11	12	13	14	15	16	17
18	19	20	21	22	23	24
25	26	27	28	29	30	

			JULY			
S	M	T	W	T	F	S
						1
2	3	4	5	6	7	8
9	10	11	12	13	14	15
16	17	18	19	20	21	22
23	24	25	26	27	28	29
30	31					

			AUGUST			
S	M	T	W	T	F	S
		1	2	3	4	5
6	7	8	9	10	11	12
13	14	15	16	17	18	19
20	21	22	23	24	25	26
27	28	29	30	31		

			SEPTEMBER			
S	M	T	W	T	F	S
					1	2
3	4	5	6	7	8	9
10	11	12	13	14	15	16
17	18	19	20	21	22	23
24	25	26	27	28	29	30

			OCTOBER			
S	M	T	W	T	F	S
1	2	3	4	5	6	7
8	9	10	11	12	13	14
15	16	17	18	19	20	21
22	23	24	25	26	27	28
29	30	31				

			NOVEMBER			
S	M	T	W	T	F	S
			1	2	3	4
5	6	7	8	9	10	11
12	13	14	15	16	17	18
19	20	21	22	23	24	25
26	27	28	29	30		

			DECEMBER			
S	M	T	W	T	F	S
					1	2
3	4	5	6	7	8	9
10	11	12	13	14	15	16
17	18	19	20	21	22	23
24	25	26	27	28	29	30
31						

weekend to the calendar. But many Americans thought making the observance moveable was disrespectful, and the date was changed back in 1978.

✳ Thanksgiving Day, *third Thursday in Nov.* The first Thanksgiving feast was cooked up around 1621 when pilgrims and Native Americans sat down together to enjoy the fruits of harvest. Formerly scheduled for the last Thursday in November (which usually turns out to be the fourth), Thanksgiving was moved up in 1939 by Franklin D. Roosevelt, who wanted to help the economy by extending the Christmas shopping season.

Winter Solstice, *around Dec. 21.* First day of winter; shortest day of the year.

✳ Christmas, *Dec. 25.* Now a widespread secular celebration notable for turkey dinners, holiday cheer and mass gift-exchanges, Christmas has long and complex roots. Biblical historians believe Jesus of Nazareth was born around 6 B.C., but most likely not on December 25. A 6th-century monk suggested that date to commemorate Jesus' birthday, and it stuck through the ages. (See more about Christmas on page 829.)

Kwanzaa, *Dec. 26 to Jan. 1.* The name means "first fruits" in Swahili, and the holiday is based on African harvest festivals.

MORES

Brought to America in the mid-1960s by Maulana Karenga, a civil rights leader who wanted black Americans to learn about their ancestors' cultures, Kwanzaa celebrates the history and culture of African Americans.

SELECTED INTERNATIONAL HOLIDAYS

New Year, China
Second new moon after winter solstice.

Families gather on New Year's Eve for a sumptuous banquet (the fish dish served last is not eaten, symbolizing the hope that there will be food left at the end of the year), and children awaken the next morning to find red envelopes filled with money under their pillows. Chinese tradition says babies are one year old at birth, and everyone's birthday is New Year's Day. So a child born at 11:59 p.m. on New Year's Eve hits the terrible twos in under 3 minutes.

Cinco de Mayo, Mexico
May 5.

Parades, parties, bullfights and beauty pageants commemorate the 1862 Battle of Puebla, when Mexican soldiers beat the odds against the French. France finally conquered Mexico in 1864 but lost the country just 3 years later. A monument of the town of Puebla honors the soldiers of both armies who died there.

K **2017, 2006**

JANUARY

S	M	T	W	T	F	S
1	2	3	4	5	6	7
8	9	10	11	12	13	14
15	16	17	18	19	20	21
22	23	24	25	26	27	28
29	30	31				

FEBRUARY

S	M	T	W	T	F	S
			1	2	3	4
5	6	7	8	9	10	11
12	13	14	15	16	17	18
19	20	21	22	23	24	25
26	27	28				

MARCH

S	M	T	W	T	F	S
			1	2	3	4
5	6	7	8	9	10	11
12	13	14	15	16	17	18
19	20	21	22	23	24	25
26	27	28	29	30	31	

APRIL

S	M	T	W	T	F	S
						1
2	3	4	5	6	7	8
9	10	11	12	13	14	15
16	17	18	19	20	21	22
23	24	25	26	27	28	29
30						

MAY

S	M	T	W	T	F	S
	1	2	3	4	5	6
7	8	9	10	11	12	13
14	15	16	17	18	19	20
21	22	23	24	25	26	27
28	29	30	31			

JUNE

S	M	T	W	T	F	S
				1	2	3
4	5	6	7	8	9	10
11	12	13	14	15	16	17
18	19	20	21	22	23	24
25	26	27	28	29	30	

JULY

S	M	T	W	T	F	S
						1
2	3	4	5	6	7	8
9	10	11	12	13	14	15
16	17	18	19	20	21	22
23	24	25	26	27	28	29
30	31					

AUGUST

S	M	T	W	T	F	S
		1	2	3	4	5
6	7	8	9	10	11	12
13	14	15	16	17	18	19
20	21	22	23	24	25	26
27	28	29	30	31		

SEPTEMBER

S	M	T	W	T	F	S
					1	2
3	4	5	6	7	8	9
10	11	12	13	14	15	16
17	18	19	20	21	22	23
24	25	26	27	28	29	30

OCTOBER

S	M	T	W	T	F	S
1	2	3	4	5	6	7
8	9	10	11	12	13	14
15	16	17	18	19	20	21
22	23	24	25	26	27	28
29	30	31				

NOVEMBER

S	M	T	W	T	F	S
			1	2	3	4
5	6	7	8	9	10	11
12	13	14	15	16	17	18
19	20	21	22	23	24	25
26	27	28	29	30		

DECEMBER

S	M	T	W	T	F	S
					1	2
3	4	5	6	7	8	9
10	11	12	13	14	15	16
17	18	19	20	21	22	23
24	25	26	27	28	29	30
31						

L **2007, 2001**

JANUARY

S	M	T	W	T	F	S
	1	2	3	4	5	6
7	8	9	10	11	12	13
14	15	16	17	18	19	20
21	22	23	24	25	26	27
28	29	30	31			

FEBRUARY

S	M	T	W	T	F	S
				1	2	3
4	5	6	7	8	9	10
11	12	13	14	15	16	17
18	19	20	21	22	23	24
25	26	27	28			

MARCH

S	M	T	W	T	F	S
				1	2	3
4	5	6	7	8	9	10
11	12	13	14	15	16	17
18	19	20	21	22	23	24
25	26	27	28	29	30	31

APRIL

S	M	T	W	T	F	S
1	2	3	4	5	6	7
8	9	10	11	12	13	14
15	16	17	18	19	20	21
22	23	24	25	26	27	28
29	30					

MAY

S	M	T	W	T	F	S
		1	2	3	4	5
6	7	8	9	10	11	12
13	14	15	16	17	18	19
20	21	22	23	24	25	26
27	28	29	30	31		

JUNE

S	M	T	W	T	F	S
					1	2
3	4	5	6	7	8	9
10	11	12	13	14	15	16
17	18	19	20	21	22	23
24	25	26	27	28	29	30

JULY

S	M	T	W	T	F	S
1	2	3	4	5	6	7
8	9	10	11	12	13	14
15	16	17	18	19	20	21
22	23	24	25	26	27	28
29	30	31				

AUGUST

S	M	T	W	T	F	S
			1	2	3	4
5	6	7	8	9	10	11
12	13	14	15	16	17	18
19	20	21	22	23	24	25
26	27	28	20	30	31	

SEPTEMBER

S	M	T	W	T	F	S
						1
2	3	4	5	6	7	8
9	10	11	12	13	14	15
16	17	18	19	20	21	22
23	24	25	26	27	28	29
30						

OCTOBER

S	M	T	W	T	F	S
	1	2	3	4	5	6
7	8	9	10	11	12	13
14	15	16	17	18	19	20
21	22	23	24	25	26	27
28	29	30	31			

NOVEMBER

S	M	T	W	T	F	S
				1	2	3
4	5	6	7	8	9	10
11	12	13	14	15	16	17
18	19	20	21	22	23	24
25	26	27	28	29	30	

DECEMBER

S	M	T	W	T	F	S
						1
2	3	4	5	6	7	8
9	10	11	12	13	14	15
16	17	18	19	20	21	22
23	24	25	26	27	28	29
30	31					

M — 2013, 2002

JANUARY
S	M	T	W	T	F	S
		1	2	3	4	5
6	7	8	9	10	11	12
13	14	15	16	17	18	19
20	21	22	23	24	25	26
27	28	29	30	31		

FEBRUARY
S	M	T	W	T	F	S
					1	2
3	4	5	6	7	8	9
10	11	12	13	14	15	16
17	18	19	20	21	22	23
24	25	26	27	28		

MARCH
S	M	T	W	T	F	S
					1	2
3	4	5	6	7	8	9
10	11	12	13	14	15	16
17	18	19	20	21	22	23
24	25	26	27	28	29	30
31						

APRIL
S	M	T	W	T	F	S
	1	2	3	4	5	6
7	8	9	10	11	12	13
14	15	16	17	18	19	20
21	22	23	24	25	26	27
28	29	30				

MAY
S	M	T	W	T	F	S
			1	2	3	4
5	6	7	8	9	10	11
12	13	14	15	16	17	18
19	20	21	22	23	24	25
26	27	28	29	30	31	

JUNE
S	M	T	W	T	F	S
						1
2	3	4	5	6	7	8
9	10	11	12	13	14	15
16	17	18	19	20	21	22
23	24	25	26	27	28	29
30						

JULY
S	M	T	W	T	F	S
	1	2	3	4	5	6
7	8	9	10	11	12	13
14	15	16	17	18	19	20
21	22	23	24	25	26	27
28	29	30	31			

AUGUST
S	M	T	W	T	F	S
				1	2	3
4	5	6	7	8	9	10
11	12	13	14	15	16	17
18	19	20	21	22	23	24
25	26	27	28	29	30	31

SEPTEMBER
S	M	T	W	T	F	S
1	2	3	4	5	6	7
8	9	10	11	12	13	14
15	16	17	18	19	20	21
22	23	24	25	26	27	28
29	30					

OCTOBER
S	M	T	W	T	F	S
		1	2	3	4	5
6	7	8	9	10	11	12
13	14	15	16	17	18	19
20	21	22	23	24	25	26
27	28	29	30	31		

NOVEMBER
S	M	T	W	T	F	S
					1	2
3	4	5	6	7	8	9
10	11	12	13	14	15	16
17	18	19	20	21	22	23
24	25	26	27	28	29	30

DECEMBER
S	M	T	W	T	F	S
1	2	3	4	5	6	7
8	9	10	11	12	13	14
15	16	17	18	19	20	21
22	23	24	25	26	27	28
29	30	31				

N — 2003, 1997

JANUARY
S	M	T	W	T	F	S
			1	2	3	4
5	6	7	8	9	10	11
12	13	14	15	16	17	18
19	20	21	22	23	24	25
26	27	28	29	30	31	

FEBRUARY
S	M	T	W	T	F	S
						1
2	3	4	5	6	7	8
9	10	11	12	13	14	15
16	17	18	19	20	21	22
23	24	25	26	27	28	

MARCH
S	M	T	W	T	F	S
						1
2	3	4	5	6	7	8
9	10	11	12	13	14	15
16	17	18	19	20	21	22
23	24	25	26	27	28	29
30	31					

APRIL
S	M	T	W	T	F	S
		1	2	3	4	5
6	7	8	9	10	11	12
13	14	15	16	17	18	19
20	21	22	23	24	25	26
27	28	29	30			

MAY
S	M	T	W	T	F	S
				1	2	3
4	5	6	7	8	9	10
11	12	13	14	15	16	17
18	19	20	21	22	23	24
25	26	27	28	29	30	31

JUNE
S	M	T	W	T	F	S
1	2	3	4	5	6	7
8	9	10	11	12	13	14
15	16	17	18	19	20	21
22	23	24	25	26	27	28
29	30					

JULY
S	M	T	W	T	F	S
		1	2	3	4	5
6	7	8	9	10	11	12
13	14	15	16	17	18	19
20	21	22	23	24	25	26
27	28	29	30	31		

AUGUST
S	M	T	W	T	F	S
					1	2
3	4	5	6	7	8	9
10	11	12	13	14	15	16
17	18	19	20	21	22	23
24	25	26	27	28	29	30
31						

SEPTEMBER
S	M	T	W	T	F	S
	1	2	3	4	5	6
7	8	9	10	11	12	13
14	15	16	17	18	19	20
21	22	23	24	25	26	27
28	29	30				

OCTOBER
S	M	T	W	T	F	S
			1	2	3	4
5	6	7	8	9	10	11
12	13	14	15	16	17	18
19	20	21	22	23	24	25
26	27	28	29	30	31	

NOVEMBER
S	M	T	W	T	F	S
						1
2	3	4	5	6	7	8
9	10	11	12	13	14	15
16	17	18	19	20	21	22
23	24	25	26	27	28	29
30						

DECEMBER
S	M	T	W	T	F	S
	1	2	3	4	5	6
7	8	9	10	11	12	13
14	15	16	17	18	19	20
21	22	23	24	25	26	27
28	29	30	31			

Canada Day, Canada
July 1.

In honor of the nation's confederation in 1867, fireworks (heavy on the red and white) light up the skies and "O Canada" echoes through the capital city of Ottawa, which hosts an annual concert on Parliament Hill. Across the country, Canadians trot out their flags and firecrackers.

Obon Festival, Japan
July 13-15 or Aug. 13-15.
(varies by region)

The souls of the dead are said to return for a visit during this festival, so the Japanese go to cemeteries and decorate their ancestors' graves in anticipation. Drummers and kimono-clad folk dancers perform, and lanterns and bonfires are lit to comfort the spiritual guests.

Bastille Day, France
July 14.

A Parisian mob stormed the famous fortress and prison in 1789, not satisfied to eat just cake and hell-bent on releasing the political prisoners they thought were held there. They freed seven inmates, none of whom was actually a political prisoner, but the action marked the lower classes' entry into the French Revolution. Today, the Bastille is gone and Parisians are more restrained: they light firecrackers, decorate their neighborhoods with paper lanterns and waltz in the streets to accordion music.

MORES

Why Are There Leap Years?

We have a pope to thank for fixing the glitch

Our calendar has 365 days, but the earth actually takes 365 days, 5 hours, 48 minutes and 46 seconds to travel around the sun. With an extra quarter-day each year, in 120 years the calendar would be ahead by a month. New Year's Eve would arrive somewhere around Thanksgiving. Luckily, we have a built-in safeguard: the occasional February 29. To avoid the chaos that would ensue should our seasons fall out of sync, every fourth year an extra day is added to keep the calendar consistent with the sun.

Julius Caesar introduced the leap year in 46 B.C., but despite his admirable mathematic and administrative efforts, the calendar was 10 days ahead by 1582. Enter Pope Gregory XIII, creator of the calendar we use today. He got the months back on track by dropping 10 days from October 1582. He also rescheduled leap year to fall every fourth year except in the case of century years that are not evenly divisible by 400. Thus, the year 2000 was a leap year; 2100, 2200, 2300, 2500, 2600, 2700, 2900, and 3000 will not be leap years, but 2400 and 2800 will be.

Most of Europe adopted the Gregorian calendar right away, but England and its American colonies held out until 1752. At that point, they had accumulated 11 extra days. To make up for gained time, September 2, 1752, was followed immediately by September 14.

Sinter Klaas, the Netherlands
Dec. 5.

St. Nicholas is the patron saint of children, so the Dutch celebrate his birthday to please them. Legend says he wears a red cape, rides a white horse and delivers presents via chimneys. Children leave their shoes out overnight (as well as carrots for the horse) and find them filled with trinkets in the morning.

Santa Lucia, Sweden
Dec. 13.

St. Lucia wore a crown of candles to bring light during the darkest day of the bleak Swedish winter. At dawn in homes across the country, one girl dons a wreath topped with burning white candles (electric ones are available for wobbly Lucias) and a long white dress with red sash. She and her white-clad siblings bring coffee and saffron bread to their parents, singing carols as they go.

Boxing Day, United Kingdom
Dec. 26.

Churches used to open their collection boxes the day after Christmas and distribute the contents to the poor. Now Britons use the occasion to give gifts to the people who have helped them throughout the year—such as those who deliver mail and newspapers.

The Ides of March

Thanks to a Shakespearean soothsayer who yelled, "Beware the Ides of March!" to Julius Caesar, warning of his impending assassination, March 15 is jocularly remembered as a good day to watch your back. But who or what are the Ides, anyway?

The ancient Romans used the days called the Nones, the Ides and the Calends to divide the month. These tranches of time can be construed as singular or plural, and it is jarring for us to say either "Today are the Ides" or "the Ides is today." I say in sooth (meaning "truth") to go with the singular, but either way, this is one day to curb your animal spirits.

—William Safire

SELECTED RELIGIOUS HOLIDAYS

Ramadan, Islamic.
Varies. (ninth month of the lunar-based Islamic calendar).

The fourth of the five pillars of Islam is to keep the fast of Ramadan, which celebrates Muhammad's reception of the divine revelations recorded in the Koran. During the month-long fast, Muslims (except soldiers and the sick) may not eat between sunrise and sunset.

Ash Wednesday, CHRISTIAN.
Forty days before Easter.

This day marks the beginning of Lent, a period of fasting that begins 40 days before Easter. The ashes that are smudged on the foreheads of the faithful symbolize penitence and mortality. The Tuesday before Ash Wednesday, or Mardi Gras, which literally means "Fat Tuesday" in French, is typically a day of raucous celebration before the solemn season of Lent begins at midnight.

Passover, JEWISH. *Generally March or April (Hebrew month of Nissan).*

The 8-day holiday reminds Jews that Moses led the Israelites from Egypt, where they had been slaves under the Pharoah. At special dinners called seders, everyone takes part in reading the Israelites' story and tasting foods that symbolize aspects of their journey.

Easter, CHRISTIAN. *Spring (the first Sunday after the first full moon of spring).*

The Christian religion's most important holiday, Easter celebrates the resurrection of Jesus Christ after his death on a cross. It is the last day of Holy Week, which includes Palm Sunday,

Maundy Thursday, and Good Friday, and marks the end of Lent. The traditional Easter eggs represent new life and immortality.

Baisakhi, HINDU.
April 13.

Hindus bathe in the Ganges River or in other holy waters during the celebration of this beginning of the New Year. Charitable acts performed throughout the following month are considered especially good, so people give generously to the poor during this time.

Rosh Hashanah, JEWISH. *Sept./Oct. (Hebrew month of Tishri).*
The start of the Jewish New Year is the first of 10 High Holy Days, during which Jews reflect on their sins of the past year and seek forgiveness for them. A hollowed out ram's horn, called the shofar, is sounded in synagogue to remind people of the trumpets of Judgment Day.

Yom Kippur, JEWISH. *Sept./Oct. (Hebrew month of Tishri).*
This Day of Atonement ends the 10 High Holy Days that begin on Rosh Hashanah and is the most important part of the Jewish year. It is a day of fasting and prayer, repentance and forgiveness.

The first time that the thin, waxing crescent moon is visible after a new moon (low in the evening sky just after sunset) marks the beginning of a month in the Islamic calendar.

● ● ●

Dewali, HINDU.
Late Oct./early Nov.
The 5-day festival of lights celebrates the human desire to move toward truth and light from ignorance and darkness. The streets are strewn with festive lamps, and homes are decorated with flowers and colored paper. Festivities include fireworks, parties and gift-giving.

Hanukkah, JEWISH.
Late Nov./late Dec. (Hebrew month of Kislev).
After a group of Jews recaptured a temple in Jerusalem that had been seized by Syrian-Greeks, they had enough oil to light the temple's lamp for a day. But the lamp burned for 8 days, and Jews celebrate this miracle by lighting candles in the menorah (a special candelabra), adding one each night until all eight candles are lit.

Christmas Day, CHRISTIAN.
Dec. 25.
Christians celebrate the birth of Jesus Christ by attending religious services and displaying "crèches," or nativity scenes depicting Joseph, Mary and Jesus in a manger. The tradition of gift-giving reenacts the story of the Three Kings who brought gifts to the newborn Jesus.

MORES

What the Stars Say About You

Clues to your personality from the heavens

Astrology, the practice of predicting the future based on movements in the cosmos, has deep and tangled roots in astronomy. The two, in fact, were intertwined well into the 1500s, when Copernicus quietly proposed that the earth revolved around the sun rather than vice versa. When Galileo later strongly embraced the theory, the scientific world went into a tailspin, and the two disciplines diverged.

Most horoscope readings today are based on sun sign astrology, which takes into account only one's birth date. Genethliac astrology factors in an array of other information, including a person's time and place of birth, the location of the sun, moon, planets and some asteroids, and the path of the moon's orbit around the earth. What does your sign say about you? Here's a beginner's guide to what astrologers say is written in the heavens.

ARIES

March 21 – April 19; The Ram

Aries, the first sign of the zodiac, represents birth. As such, the ram is like a baby—very self-absorbed. And like a baby, Aries puts his or her needs first. The Ram is fearless, extremely honest and direct, and shows unbridled enthusiasm. Arians often possess a ferocious temper, but after a fight, do not hold grudges. With all the energy they expend, you have to wonder when they relax. But they can be calm, too. They find their soul mates in Sagittarius, Scorpio and Cancer.

TAURUS

April 20 – May 20; The Bull

Taurus is a rocky coast that's been beaten by the elements for centuries. Those born under this sign are strong and stubborn with a quiet demeanor. Taureans are steady, speak sparingly and possess an inner strength, but don't like change. They are outstanding workers who are willing to take orders without resentment. Their hearts and pockets are open to a friend in distress, but they may have trouble expressing their own feelings. Cancer, Leo and Capricorn are most compatible with Taureans.

GEMINI

May 21 – June 20; The Twins

Being born under the sign of the Twins means you never know when you might switch your looks, house, job or spouse on an impulse. Geminis can never get enough money, fame or love. They live by their own rules and do what they want; they have little patience for indecisive people and can be very rude, selfish and immature. The Gemini woman has a hard time committing herself to one man at a time; and the Gemini man may shower a love interest with flowers, but he's unlikely to reveal his innermost core. Still, Gemini will be drawn to Leo, Capricorn and Aquarius.

CANCER

June 21 – July 22; The Crab

The Cancer person is full of laughter and loves a good joke. But at other times Cancer's moods are blacker than the darkest cavern. Yet people from under this sign also are sweet and gentle and will find a way to rise above adversity when the moon changes. Cancerans are sentimental about their roots and their family. They have vulnerable hearts and sensitive feelings. In love, the Cancer person can be so dependent it can border on obsession. Virgo, Leo, and Aquarius are the most compatible.

LEO

July 23 – August 22; The Lion

Leo is the leader of the jungle, a dignified,

stately presence, lying luxuriously in the sun for all to see. Leos have strong personalities and can be vain. But they also are loveable, seldom waste energy on fruitless tasks and are good organizers. The regal ways of the sun sign make them great hosts or hostesses. Leos like royal treatment and spend money freely, but they also give money to just about anyone. They play hard, work hard, rest hard and live hard. Leo will want to meet Pisces, Aries and Gemini.

 ## VIRGO

August 23 – September 22; The Virgin

These perfectionists are dependable, industrious, practical, cool and sincere. They are blessed with great curiosity and are mentally very active, excelling in the written and spoken word. They can endure and thrive on intense work longer than most. But they can also destroy relationships by being too critical, analytic and irritable. If you're in a jam, however, Virgo natives will gladly roll up their sleeves and help. Capricorn, Aries and Pisces are best matches for a Virgo.

 ## LIBRA

September 23 – October 22; The Scales

With the scales as a sign, Libra is a natural balancer. Librans are good listeners but are also inveterate talkers. They are intelligent but naïve at the same time. They love people, but detest crowds. They are gracious, caring and calm, but when the weight of the scales changes they can be stubborn, annoying and depressed. Librans dislike arguments, and, with their desire to please, can make ideal mates. Gemini and Taurus stand the best chance of benefiting from the Libra disposition.

 ## SCORPIO

October 23 – November 21; The Scorpion

The most passionate people in the zodiac, Scorpios are nocturnal creatures. They have hypnotic, intense eyes that make others feel nervous. Scorpios have strong emotions that are deeply hidden. They can be sarcastic, stubborn and even cruel at times to those close to them. They are difficult to get to know and understand and must test a person before showing their true selves. Scorpions are fascinated with death and the spiritual. Scorpio will appreciate Cancer and Aquarius the most.

SAGITTARIUS

November 22 – December 21: The Archer

When you start a new job, the first person to walk up to you with a smile, shake your hand and welcome you aboard will be a Sagittarian. They mean well but often put a foot in their mouth. They make friends easily, are optimists and refuse to take life seriously. But they can show violent tempers, and are unlikely to keep a secret. They have a terrific memory but can't remember where they left their keys. Pisces, Cancer and Leo will be most understanding.

 ## CAPRICORN

December 22 – January 19; The Goat

Like the goat, the Capricorn looks and acts harmless but is tough as nails. Capricorns are steady, serious and sensible and never let obstacles or disappointments block their way to the top of the mountain. They are gentle and persuasive, and though they are sometimes labeled as snobbish, that charge is unfair. The Capricorn person is trustworthy and makes a good provider. Leo, Aries and Virgo are Capricorn's favorites.

AQUARIUS

January 20 – February 18;
The Water Bearer

Freedom-loving Aquarians are unpredictable and secretly delight in shocking others with their erratic behavior. They are natural rebels with a dreamy gleam in their eyes. The Aquarian seeks the security of crowds and then demands to be left alone. When it comes to friends, they seek quantity rather than quality. Trusting people isn't natural for Aquarians, but they love to network. Sagittarius, Taurus and Libra will be most in sync with Aquarius.

PISCES

February 19 – March 20; The Fish

Pisces natives dislike being in the same spot for too long, as their fish sign suggests. They prefer to swim from one spot of light to another. They are the most spiritual of all signs; they are often mystical, impressionable and intuitive. Pisces people are also creative, clever and sarcastic, and never answer a question directly. Yet no sign is more sensitive to human suffering. They are compassionate and love to help. Pisces will find Virgo, Gemini and Scorpio to their liking.

Chinese Zodiac: What Are You?

You may be faithful as a dog, witty as a monkey or wise as a snake

The Chinese zodiac is based on a 12-year cycle, with each year of the cycle represented by a different animal. There is also a cycle of the elements—wood, fire, earth, metal and water—connected with the animal sign of the year you were born. So you

We like to think of ourselves as practicing the second oldest profession.

Richard Brown,
Canadian astrologer

● ● ●

could be an Earth Monkey or a Golden Rat, for example. The ancient Chinese used the signs to match couples, according to the interaction among the five elements and the personality traits of the animals. For example, a Water Dog is compatible with a Wood Pig but dominates a Fire Pig because water helps wood but controls fire.

If the ancient Chinese were right about the traits they ascribed to their calendrical animals, then Leonardo da Vinci, born in the year of the Monkey, was charismatic and witty. Confucius, on the other hand, would have been a pleasing fellow, though perhaps a trifle too sentimental, since his birthdate in 551 B.C. would have made him a Rabbit. Oprah Winfrey, one of the world's richest women, may have achieved her riches from the wisdom, charm and caution with money that come from being a Snake. For clues to understanding Joan of Arc, Picasso, Osama Bin Laden and Madonna, read on.

RAT

● *FIRE: 1936, 1996* ● *EARTH: 1948, 2008*
● *METAL: 1960* ● *WATER: 1972*
● *WOOD: 1984*

Traits: Imaginative, generous, quick-tempered, overly critical, opportunist.
Some Rats: Shakespeare, Truman Capote, Prince Charles, Antonio Banderas, Gwyneth Paltrow.

BUFFALO (OR OX)

● *WOOD: 1925, 1985* ● *FIRE: 1937, 1997*
● *EARTH: 1949, 2009* ● *METAL: 1961*
● *WATER: 1973*

Traits: A born leader, conservative, methodical, chauvinistic and demanding.
Some Buffaloes: Napoleon, Adolf Hitler, Princess Di, B. B. King.

TIGER

- *FIRE: 1926, 1986* • *EARTH: 1938, 1998*
- *METAL: 1950, 2010* • *WATER: 1962*
- *WOOD: 1974*

Traits: Sensitive, emotional, stubborn, rebellious. **Some Tigers:** Marco Polo, Oscar Wilde, Marilyn Monroe, Jay Leno.

RABBIT

- *FIRE: 1927, 1987* • *EARTH: 1939, 1999*
- *METAL: 1951, 2011* • *WATER: 1963*
- *WOOD: 1975*

Traits: Affectionate, obliging, cautious, conservative, overly sentimental.
Some Rabbits: Confucius, Albert Einstein, Fidel Castro, Frank Sinatra, Angelina Jolie.

DRAGON

- *EARTH: 1928, 1988* • *METAL: 1940, 2000*
- *WATER: 1952, 2012* • *WOOD: 1964*
- *FIRE: 1976*

Traits: Enthusiastic, energetic, perfectionist, foolhardy, demanding.
Some Dragons: Joan of Arc, Martin Luther King Jr., John Lennon.

SNAKE

- *EARTH: 1929, 1989* • *METAL: 1941, 2001*
- *WATER: 1953, 2013* • *WOOD: 1965*
- *FIRE: 1977*

Traits: Wise, charming, romantic, intuitive, procrastinator, cautious with money.
Some Snakes: Edgar Allan Poe, James Joyce, Pablo Picasso, Bob Dylan, Oprah Winfrey.

HORSE

- *METAL: 1930, 1990*
- *WATER: 1942, 2002* • *WOOD: 1954, 2014*
- *FIRE: 1966* • *EARTH: 1978*

Traits: Hardworking, independent, intelligent, cunning, egotistical.
Some Horses: Rembrandt, Teddy Roosevelt, Clint Eastwood, Paul McCartney.

GOAT

- *METAL: 1931, 1991*
- *WATER: 1943, 2003* • *WOOD: 1955, 2015*
- *FIRE: 1967* • *EARTH: 1979*

Traits: Charming, elegant, artistic, pessimistic, materialistic. **Some Goats:** Michelangelo, Mark Twain, Mel Gibson, Bill Gates.

MONKEY

- *WATER: 1932, 1992*
- *WOOD: 1944, 2004* • *FIRE: 1956, 2016*
- *EARTH: 1968* • *METAL: 1980*

Traits: Clever wit, well-liked, opportunistic, distrustful. **Some Monkeys:** Julius Caesar, Leonardo da Vinci, Elizabeth Taylor, Pope John Paul II, Tom Hanks.

ROOSTER

- *WATER: 1933, 1993*
- *WOOD: 1945, 2005* • *FIRE: 1957, 2017*
- *EARTH: 1969* • *METAL: 1981*

Traits: Shrewd, straight-talker, boastful, extravagant.
Some Roosters: Rudyard Kipling, Yoko Ono, Osama Bin Laden, Rod Stewart, Britney Spears.

DOG

- *WOOD: 1934, 1994* • *FIRE: 1946, 2006*
- *EARTH: 1958, 2018* • *METAL: 1970*
- *WATER: 1982*

Traits: Loyal, honest, sharp-tongued, fault finder. **Some Dogs:** Socrates, Elvis Presley, Bill Clinton, George W. Bush, Madonna, Donald Trump.

PIG

- *WOOD: 1935, 1995* • *FIRE: 1947, 2007*
- *EARTH: 1959, 2019* • *METAL: 1971*
- *WATER: 1983*

Traits: Good companion, sincere, tolerant, honest, naïve, materialistic.
Some Pigs: Thomas Jefferson, Humphrey Bogart, Ronald Reagan, Elton John.

MORES

Manners & Miscellany

Etiquette for the 21st Century

"Please" and "thank you" are still in favor, but a lot has changed

The day when rules of etiquette were etched in parchment and folks adhered to them blindly is long gone. Etiquette buffs wax nostalgic for those simpler times, when married women took their husband's last name, second marriages were rare and third marriages almost unheard of. The etiquette game is made even murkier these days with high-tech gadgetry and services—cellphones, BlackBerrys, texting and the like—that test the limits of polite interaction with society.

How to navigate this new age of etiquette confusion? For those trying to keep up with changing mores, here's a primer on some of the more contentious issues on the etiquette beat.

High-tech manners

CALL WAITING. The best advice is not to succumb to the rudeness of this service at all. But if you must and your conversation is interrupted by another call on your line, apologize to the person with whom you are talking. Switch to the other caller and tell him or her that you'll call back. Then return to the original conversation and apologize again.

CALLER ID. If you have this service and you know who is calling, do you still answer as if you don't know who is on the line? Yes, say etiquette experts. Avoid greeting callers by using their names. Wait until they say hello and identify themselves.

CELLPHONES, ETC. If you get a call when you are at a dinner party, show or other social event, turn off your cell or BlackBerry immediately and then politely excuse yourself to take the call. When you return you do not need to reveal the nature of the call, unless it is an emergency and you must leave the event immediately. And remember, no cellphone conversation is completely private—your conversation may be picked up on another phone.

UNKNOWN CALLS. A sticky situation arises when a number shows up on your cell that you don't

---

TIMELY TIPS

No Texting at the Dinner Table

It's not O.K. to check for messages during dinner

Husbands, wives, children and dinner guests who would never be so rude as to talk on a phone at the family table seem to think it's perfectly fine to text (or e-mail, or Twitter) while eating.

Texting anarchy is what Emily Post's great-granddaughter, Cindy Post Senning, calls it. "People are texting everywhere," she says. And it is not perfectly fine, she says. In her book *Emily Post's Table Manners for Kids,* written with Peggy Post, she covers it in a blanket ruling: "Do NOT use your cell phone or any other electronic devices at the table."

Be aware, says Post Senning, others can see your thumbs working even when they are in your lap. "If your attention should be focused on others, you should not be texting or e-mailing." —Sara Rimer

recognize. Say you call back and get a strange voice. What do you say without revealing your identity? The proper protocol, according to etiquette experts, is to say, "Hello, this is (your phone number). I noticed you called and wondered if there is anything I can help you with?" It may well have been a wrong number, but you don't want to miss out on opportunities either.

E-MAIL. When you send an e-mail, make the header specific so recipients know immediately whether the message is important. It is acceptable to acknowledge an impromptu missive, such as "Congratulations on your new job," with an e-mail note of thanks, according to manners guru Judith Martin. E-mail is not confidential, however, so

Whenever two people come together, and their behavior affects one another, you have etiquette.

Emily Post

• • •

personal or controversial messages have no place in office e-mail.

FAX MACHINES. Use the fax only for communicating business or nonconfidential information quickly. Never use the fax to send a thank-you note after a job interview.

SPEAKER PHONES. Use speaker phones as infrequently as possible, because they tend to make the person who is not in the room feel uncomfortable. Always apologize for having to use the speaker phone and be sure to end the call with your handset.

VOICE MAIL. Keep your outgoing message clear and brief and update it regularly, especially if you travel frequently. When leaving a message on an

---

 TIMELY TIPS

Minding BlackBerry Manners

It may be O.K. to check for messages in a meeting

As Web-enabled smartphones have become standard on the belts and in the totes of executives, people in meetings are increasingly caving in to the temptation to check e-mail, Facebook, Twitter, even (shhh!) ESPN.com. But a spirited debate about etiquette has broken out. Traditionalists say the use of BlackBerrys and iPhones in meetings is gauche. Techno-evangelists insist that to ignore real-time text messages in a need-it-yesterday world is to invite peril.

In Hollywood, some big-time talent agencies ban BlackBerry use at meetings. Nevertheless, a third of more than 5,300 workers polled by YahooHotJobs, a career research and job listings Web site, said they frequently checked e-mail in meetings. Nearly 20 percent said they had been

castigated for poor manners regarding wireless devices.

Despite resistance, the etiquette debate seems to be tilting in the favor of smartphone use. Very few companies have policies on smartphone use in meetings, which leaves it up to employees to feel their way across uncertain terrain.

To some, different rules apply for in-house meetings (where checking BlackBerrys seems an expression of informal collegiality) and those with clients, where the habit is likely to offend. Beyond practical considerations, there is also the issue of image. In many professional circles, where connections are power, making a show of reaching out to those connections even as co-workers are presenting a spreadsheet presentation seems to have become a kind of workplace boast. It is customary now for professionals to lay BlackBerrys or iPhones on a conference table before a meeting—like gunfighters placing their Colt revolvers on the card tables in a saloon. —Alex Williams

answering machine, follow the same rule: clearly and briefly leave the information requested in the outgoing message. Jot down a few points that you want to make before you call. Try not to hold a prolonged one-way conversation unless you really don't want the person to call you back. Never eat or chew gum while on the phone.

Women's issues

NEVER-MARRIED WOMAN. Steer clear of the antiquated "Miss." Today it's used mainly to address girls younger than 18. Even when addressing formal invitations to adult single women, Miss is no longer used, etiquette experts say. Unmarried adult women, and married or divorced women who prefer not to use their husband's name, are addressed as "Ms."

MARRIED WOMAN. Formally, a woman who takes her husband's name is addressed as *Mrs. Richard Saunders.* Some women prefer to keep their middle name and drop their maiden name: *Ms. Sarah Marie Saunders.*

Although commonly done, a married woman is not addressed as Mrs. with her own first name and married name. Traditionally, that combination is reserved for divorced women.

Mail to the couple is addressed to *Mr. and Mrs. Richard Saunders* or, alternately, to *Mr. Richard Saunders and Ms. Sarah Saunders.* If the woman keeps her maiden name, address correspondence to both *Mr. Richard Saunders and Ms. Sarah Smith,* on the same line.

A woman who uses her maiden name at work and husband's name socially is addressed as Ms. for business and either Ms. or Mrs. socially. For formal correspondence, use *Mr. Richard Saunders and Ms. Sarah Smith*; informally, use the traditional *Mr. and Mrs. Richard Saunders.*

When writing to a woman who uses a hyphenated name, her name goes first: *Sarah Smith-Saunders.* For a couple, both names are used, *Mr. Richard Saunders and Ms. Sarah Smith-Saunders.*

DIVORCED WOMAN. A divorced woman often reverts to her maiden name. But when children are involved, it can get confusing. A divorced woman with children who keeps her married name is addressed as *Mrs. Sarah Saunders,* without her husband's first name. That identifies her as divorced and as the children's parent.

WIDOW. Until she remarries, a widow keeps her husband's name and is addressed the same way as a married woman, *Mrs. Richard Saunders* or *Ms. Sarah Saunders.* If she remarries, she can use either her former husband's last name or her maiden name as a middle name, *Sarah Saunders Franklin* or *Sarah Smith Franklin.*

Relationship rules

LIVING TOGETHER. When addressing mail to an unmarried couple that lives together, each name should be on a separate line; the names should not be joined by the word "and," say the rules of etiquette. When introducing couples who live together, most labels—boyfriend, girlfriend, significant other, date, lover—sound awkward, so it is best to forgo the explanation and simply introduce each person by name.

DIVORCED. A divorced couple does not return wedding gifts. A divorced woman should not wear her engagement ring on her wedding band finger, etiquette authorities hold. Often, the stone is reset into a bracelet or necklace or kept for her children's future use.

Friends of a newly divorced couple should not pry for details of the breakup. A friend's goal should be to help the person get through the difficult time. If children are involved, both sides of the family should respect the other side's efforts to see the children. Also vital: one parent should not criticize the other in front of their children, even if the impulse is nearly irresistible.

Multicultural Manners to Master

How to avoid cultural missteps

The greater frequency of international travel, for business or pleasure, and today's changing demographics at home call for new rules to prevent cross-cultural misunderstandings. As a folklorist, Norine Dresser studies the customs, rituals and beliefs of different cultures. Author of *Multicultural Manners: Essential Rules of Etiquette for the 21st Century,* Dresser offers her dos and don'ts for avoiding cultural faux pas.

Q What are some of the biggest multicultural gaffes Americans make?

Our major problem is that we get too friendly and too informal too fast. Our use of first names when we first meet someone, for example, can be offensive in some other parts of the world. It is interpreted as disrespectful. Americans also have a habit of getting right down to business. In many Asian and Latin American cultures, you don't march in with your product and expect an order after a sales spiel. First you establish rapport by introducing yourself and your company, then you leave a token, such as a company pen or calendar. Finally, you follow up with a phone call later in the week.

Q Can you give us some examples of communications blunders?

Avoid asking questions that require direct yes or no responses. For example, we often say when asking for something, "Please feel free to say no, but would you..." In many cultures, responding "no" directly to a request is unheard of, so the non-American becomes confused. Also, people who

IF THE QUEEN DROPS BY

Bow or curtsey and address her as "Your Majesty" when you run into a queen. Here is the correct form of address for various personages.

PERSON	SPOKEN GREETING
President of the U.S.	*Mr.* OR *Madam President*
Former President	*Mr.* OR *Mrs.* [JONES]
Senator	*Senator* [JONES]
General	*General* [JONES]

FOREIGN HEAD OF STATE

Premier or President of a republic	*Your Excellency*
Prime Minister	*Mr.* OR *Madam Prime Minister*
The Pope	*Your Holiness* OR *Most Holy Father*
Cardinal	*Your Eminence* OR *Cardinal* [JONES]
Priest	*Father* [JONES]
Protestant Clergy	*Reverend* [JONES]
Rabbi	*Rabbi* [JONES]
King or Queen	*Your Majesty* OR *Sir* OR *Madam*
Duke/Duchess	*Your Grace* OR *Duke/Duchess*
Knight	*Sir* [JOHN]
Wife of knight	*Lady* [JONES]

are not fluent in English might be too embarrassed to say they don't understand. Rather than ask, "Do you understand what I mean?" say, "Please tell me what you don't understand."

Q What are some examples of cultural differences?

One example is that yellow flowers in Iran suggest intense dislike for the person receiving

MORES

them. Yellow also has bad connotations for many Peruvians and Mexicans. On the other hand, yellow flowers say "I miss you" in the Armenian culture.

Most Asian cultures respond negatively to white, which has death connotations. Guests to an Indian wedding, for example, should avoid wearing white. It is thought to bring bad luck, even death, to the bride and groom.

Q What are other customs to be aware of?

Removing shoes before you enter the home of a Japanese person is well known. Less known is the fact that you should place your shoes so that the toes face the door. Removing shoes is also a tradition among some Koreans, Filipinos, Thais, Iranians and Indian Buddhists.

Most people know that eating pork is taboo for religious Jews and Muslims, but fewer people are aware that orthodox Jews and Muslims also don't eat shellfish or any fish without fins. Hindus don't eat beef, and Seventh Day Adventists don't eat meat. Muslims, Hindus and Mormons, of course, do not drink alcoholic beverages.

Q What's the best way to approach an unfamiliar multicultural situation?

It helps to be very observant. When in doubt, ask. It's best to ask someone of your own sex, so that it's less awkward for both of you in situations where there are significant male-female differences. Age matters too; young people may feel reluctant to tell older people what to do. It all gets back to the main point: making an effort to understand, and showing others that you're trying to learn from them.

The Art of Greeting with a Kiss

How not to miss the buss

It can happen to anyone. You want to give more than a businesslike handshake as a greeting, and a hug seems disconcertingly personal. You lean in to bestow the compromise—a peck on the cheek—and the person turns her head, and suddenly you're bumping noses or even brushing lips and teeth.

You're not alone—kiss protocol is routinely bungled. And the awkwardness and inevitability of the social kiss has led to strategies to deal with it. If being bussed on the cheek is way too intimate, some advise that sticking your hand out firmly, keeping a straight elbow, is the best way to show yourself willing to shake hands and nothing more.

While the handshake still holds sway in big corporations, the kiss has migrated into areas like sales, where it can denote a warm relationship that encourages buying. Still, figuring out where the limits are can present problems. Etiquette experts advocate steering clear of greeting new business associates with a kiss. Later, kissing as a greeting depends on the relationship.

The double kiss is frequently used in the diplomatic world, but confusion often reigns because there is no set international formula for social kissing. The French, for example, kiss on both cheeks—one kiss each—although in a few regions it is the double-double kiss with two on each cheek. The Belgians, Dutch and Swiss go for the triple kiss. If you can't keep that straight and need a refresher, the lip balm company Blistex has a rundown of European kissing customs on its Web site, www.blistex.com, under the heading Global Lip Customs.

In most countries the social kiss begins with the right cheek, probably because most people are right-handed and, according to a German study, most people tilt their heads to the right when heading for a lip kiss. So it follows that they would lean right for a cheek kiss.   —Elizabeth Olson

A Guide to Gay Manners

For those who are coming out and going out

Steven Petrow, author of *The Essential Book of Gay Manners* and *Etiquette and Gay and Lesbian Manners: Advice for LGBT Folks* (and Their Families and Friends)* (forthcoming from Workman Publishing) and past president of the National Lesbian & Gay Journalists Association, confronts some common dilemmas and offers some tips.

● **Can a gay or lesbian couple kiss in public? On the cheek or on the lips? How about holding hands?**

Yes, yes, and yes—of course depending where you are. The rules about showing affection publicly are the same for gay men and lesbians as they are for straight folks. The acceptable public behaviors we exhibit—regardless of our sexuality—are different, however, whether you're in, say, a nightclub, bar or movie theater versus the church, the classroom or a family dinner. Generally, handholding, eye gazing and light kissing are perfectly fine in public; groping, tongue kissing and touching below the waist are not.

● **What's the right way to address a commited lesbian or gay couple when writing to them?**

Just like any other married couple. So, for example:

> ***"Dr. Susanna Barrows and Mr. Peter Lerner"*** (heterosexual couple)
>
> ***"Ms. Samantha Greene and Ms. Jodie Bonds."*** (lesbian couple)

Once couples are married, partnered or otherwise committed, their names appear on one line with the word "and" placed in between signifying the union.

● **I have a photograph of my boyfriend on my desk at work. What's the right response to curious co-workers, especially since I'm not really out yet?**

Don't let etiquette be marshaled into an argument for keeping you in the closet. Displaying your boyfriend's photo is a good way to come out (at least partially) without shouting, "Hey, I am gay!" Other ways include referring to a girlfriend or a same-sex spouse in casual conversation ("My wife is home with our kids..."), making charitable contributions to an LGBT (Lesbian, Gay, Bisexual, Transgender) rights groups and then asking your company to match or attending the office holiday party with your partner.

Before you come out at work, be sure you understand whether your company has non-discrimination protections based on sexual orientation, gender identity or gender expression as well as checking local or state laws. Most states have no such protections: you certainly don't want to be fired. A good resource is *Your Rights in the Workplace* by Barbara Kate Repa, J.D. (Nolo Press), especially the chapter on illegal discrimination against lesbians and gays in the workplace.

So here's what you can say if a co-worker inquires, "Is that your brother?" "No, that's my boyfriend, Stan. We've been together 5 years."

● **How should you introduce your boyfriend, girlfriend, partner or lover?**

Even Miss Manners punted on this conundrum, referring to it as the "Great Insolvable Etiquette Problem," and she was only thinking about heterosexuals. But for now, here are some practical suggestions:

- Talk to your girl (or guy) about what she would like to be called and tell her how you'd like to be referred to.

- Ask yourself (and her) whether that choice is different in different venues—for instance, out with your friends, at a workplace function or with your parents. Some couples choose to use "boyfriend" or "lover" in a gay environment and "partner" or "friend" in a more mainstream crowd.

- If you have had a civil union, domestic partnership ceremony or a marriage, by all means use the language that the law allows (if this is comfortable for you): domestic partner, spouse or husband/wife.

Finally, don't let this question consume endless hours of your time. Many more important topics exist.

Handling Tricky Predicaments

How to deal with common yet awkward social situations

Who hasn't had an embarrassing moment? Incited an argument at a dinner party. Met someone and then promptly forgotten his or her name. Entered a room and panicked at not recognizing a soul. Agonized over whom to invite with whom, or whether to invite either at all. The list of potentially embarrassing social scenarios is endless. Here are three fairly common yet awkward situations and how to emerge from them graciously.

● What to do when you remember him but he doesn't remember you.

Manner mavens suggest that a quick self-effacing remark like "Oh that's O.K., I forget people all the time" will ease any awkwardness. That's nice advice for the self-effacing, but not for socially obsessed high schoolers, who are a lot more like all of us than we would like to think.

Is it silly to care about any of this? If it's any comfort, some big shots feel just as bad as the rest of us for forgetting faces. Joan Rivers, the comedian, for example, blanks all the time. "I have two ways to deal," she says. "Either I touch the person's chest and look like I'm concentrating and say, 'Yes, I do remember you, but from where?' If that doesn't work, I tell them they look 20 years younger and ask if they've had work done."

Ultimately, not caring who knows you or whom you should know may be the only way to have fun at a party.

● If someone invites you over, do you have to invite them back?

Etiquette suggests that you should reciprocate, of course, but in any way that works for you. If you don't want to make a dinner party for hosts who have entertained you lavishly, taking them out is acceptable, just as it is for houseguests who want to give their hosts a break from cooking.

But what if you can't keep yourself from attending the show-stopping parties of the same great hosts year after year without being able to imagine returning their hospitality? Isn't that completely unacceptable?

Well, maybe reciprocity doesn't have to be the point. There will always be those who want to be more generous than others, whether as philanthropists or hosts. That's all any good host or guest needs to know, along with the simple idea that doing something nice for others doesn't necessarily mean those who have done something nice for you. And without great guests, how could great hosts be great hosts?

● Should you argue about politics, or shut up?

"Fighting about politics is like doing drugs," says author Jay McInerney. "You know you shouldn't get involved, but once you start, you lose all control."

Perhaps that's why etiquette and protocol arbiters have always recommended staying clear of the topic with tactics like changing the subject. Garrison Keillor, the radio host and author, argues, however, that "the hottest place in hell is reserved for those who remain neutral in times of crisis."

How to Give a Toast

Ah, the eloquence of a good toast. Mark Brown, once voted best speaker in the world by Toastmasters International, offers a few tips on how to give terrific toasts anytime.

✔ First of all, a toast and a roast are not to be confused, though they often are. A roast pokes fun. A toast is sweetness and light and never, ever rude.

✔ A good toast should leave a "good feeling," he says. "It leaves a positive taste in the mouth. It should always contain good wishes, warm feelings and convey love and happiness."

✔ Brevity is good. "There is an old adage that says you stand up, you speak up, and then you shut up," says Brown.

✔ Toastmasters International (www.toastmasters.org) offers a few other pointers. Pick a subject that is personal and appropriate. Use humor only if the occasion warrants. Dress your best—if you look good, you'll feel more confident. And practice, practice, practice, using family and friends as sounding boards.

So how do we proceed? "Calm, cool, collected," the late New York socialite Pat Buckley once suggested, adding that she often found her "blood boiling" over what she heard at dinner parties. "I'll listen for a while, then I'll speak up," she said. "But I'll always do it in a civilized way. You don't want to frighten the horses."

Don Gabor, author of *Words That Win: What to Say to Get What You Want,* says, "My advice is, don't even pick up the gauntlet when it's thrown down. Most political arguments don't do any good at all." The only time to get into one, Gabor says, is if you are with someone who hasn't made up his mind. Even then, proceed with caution, and follow some rules: Don't be disagreeable when you disagree. Don't interrupt or argue one point to death. Don't expect someone to agree with you just because you think you're right. And don't assume that you and the other person disagree on all issues.

In such a loudly opinionated, powder-keg culture, maybe the best way to promote peace is by not saying what's on your mind at all. Or as Calvin Coolidge once said, "Nobody ever listened himself out of a job."

—Bob Morris

Rules for Weekend House Parties
Whether you're a host or guest, know what's expected

One of the many pleasures of having a weekend house is being able to entertain. But being able to and actually doing it are two different things. Some people with weekend homes and lots of friends never get around to having everyone up for the weekend, perhaps because they're unsure of their skills as hosts or because they're afraid they won't be able to keep everyone entertained.

Emily Post, who lives eternally online, has wonderfully dated advice on how to host a weekend party. The 25th chapter of her 1922 book, *Etiquette,* is entitled "The Country House and Its Hospitality," and it can be found at www.bartleby.com/95/25.

One bit of advice: "In big houses, breakfast trays for women guests are usually carried to the bedroom floor by the butler (some butlers delegate this service to a footman) and are handed to the lady's maid who takes the tray into the room. In small houses they are carried up by the waitress."

That world is obviously long gone, even if the desire to have a weekend-long party isn't. Without involving any footmen or ladies' maids, you can easily entertain a group for a couple of days at your weekend home. Here are some post-Emily Post

✔ TIMELY TIPS

Entertaining with Children

The proper protocol is ever changing in the world of parties and kids. Here are a few ironclad rules regarding whether to lug the kids along or leave them home with the babysitter.

✔ **If the invitation does not specify that it is a family event or that children are invited,** you should not ask to bring them to a party. Some invitations are quite explicit, with notes such as, "Nobody under 4½ feet tall, even though we love them" or "Book your babysitters early." Do not ignore those messages.

✔ **If both you and the hostess have little kids,** and you assume that she assumes you will bring your kid to her 5 p.m. Sunday event, it is O.K. to call and ask, and you probably should. Anyway, the hostess can always say no.

✔ **If children are invited,** remember it's the host's duty to provide entertainment for the kids. A good hostess also provides kid-friendly food. And if your little guest announces, "I hate chicken fingers," no need to panic. Pasta and butter seems to meet with universal approval. Plus, everything grown-ups liked when they were kids, kids still like. Except peanut butter, which is a big allergy food.   —Joyce Wadler

tips for planning your own weekend-long party.

Invite guests who will most likely enjoy one another's company and who have common interests, even if they haven't yet met. Don't invite people at random, no matter how much you like them individually.

Ask guests who know each other whether they would mind sharing a bed or a room. Let others know in advance that they may be sleeping on an inflatable mattress or a sleeper-sofa.

Plan some activities, but be flexible. Guests will sometimes entertain themselves. One might want to putter in your garden; another might be intent on finishing a book. But you should have something in mind to fill most of the hours on Saturday. If your house is on the water, you might have a kayak rental company deliver enough boats to let everyone have a paddle. If your house is in or near a village center, you can suggest that some guests might want to poke around the shops.

Volleyball and croquet are easy to set up, and almost anyone can play. Croquet has an advantage in that participants can drink while playing. Board games like Scrabble or Cranium might help if the weather turns bad. But whatever you've planned, abandon the plan if guests want to do something else.

Be prepared to cook. Say your guests arrive Friday night; you should have something ready for them to eat upon arrival. Set up a buffet that you can replenish. And your guests will be looking to you for breakfast Saturday and Sunday mornings. There are few things better (or easier) than a spread of bagels, cream cheese, lox, whitefish and onions.

If people decide to explore the village, you can say that they're on their own for Saturday lunch. Most of your culinary efforts should focus on Saturday night's dinner. If you're not a good cook, you can still toss steaks onto the grill and put potatoes in the oven. Even if you are a good cook, you won't want to spend most of the day in the kitchen. Perhaps the main dish can be something made in advance, or at least brought to the weekend house ready to slide into the oven.

Even with sleeping arrangements and meal service that would appall Emily Post, your weekend party can be a success if hosts and guests follow her best advice. The host never appears inconvenienced by a guest, and a guest "shall show neither annoyance nor disappointment—no matter what happens."   —Steve Bailey

Nothing Beats an R.S.V.P.

When a response—even an e-mail—is expected

A new indifference to the old-fashioned protocol of invitations is turning entertaining into a guessing game, say hostesses, party planners and etiquette authorities. Nobody seems to bother to R.S.V.P. anymore. Even requests to attend seemingly monumental events like weddings, 40th-birthday parties and Christmas dinners routinely go unanswered.

Whether it is a result of a more casual attitude toward socializing or an overabundance of non-events that generate a kind of lavish junk mail of their own, hosts—and not guests—are now the ones feeling left out in the cold. Etiquette experts fear the practice is giving so many people heartburn that they aren't entertaining anymore. Proper manners, experts say, call for a response to an invitation within 48 hours.

Etiquette experts say that *répondez s'il vous plaît* became a chic addition to invitations in the late 1800s. At one time, a wedding invitation never asked for a response. Getting an important invitation was the highest honor that could be bestowed, and it was expected that you would respond in the same degree of formality. That meant sitting down and writing a letter.

But in these less formal times some manners experts are reluctantly accepting that there's nothing improper in replying by e-mail to an engraved request for the honor of your company at a black-tie wedding reception. Most important is the response, they say, whether by a handwritten note or a quick e-mail.

Expressing appreciation after a social occasion need not be a chore. The only imperative when it comes to thank-you notes is to send them. Drew Souza, a New York City stationer, suggests you write at least three sentences, avoid clichés—an anecdote specific to the evening or gift is thoughtful—and do it preferably by hand.

For Christmas presents in particular, he advises waiting until January to send holiday-related thanks: "If it arrives on Dec. 22, no one will have time to open it."

—Kimberly Stevens and Mark Ellwood

Looking for Mr. Right

Anyone looking for a mate these days knows that there are scores of online dating services—from Match.com to eHarmony.com to JDate, each with its own distinct personality. One newly single, 40-something user of the services characterizes JDate as "the Jewish equivalent of safe sex, with a platinum card." (Spark Networks, the owner of JDate, runs 32 dating sites, including for Greek singles, Catholics, African-Americans, Asians, and Seventh Day Adventists.)

Nerve.com is "much edgier," and eHarmony, she says, has "a geezer/Republican feel to its marketing," along with a rule disqualifying separated people from using the site. You can go to any search engine, like Google, and find a long list of online dating services and judge for yourself.

Whatever the opportunities, however, Internet dating is not without its issues. Unearthing a potential mate's cheating, thieving and maybe even psychotic ways during the early stages of courtship has always been tricky business. But it is particularly difficult today, when millions are searching for dates online and finding it far easier to lie to a computer than to someone's face.

But the Internet is offering up an antidote, as well. Web sites like DontDateHimGirl.com and TrueDater.com are dedicated to outing bad apples or just identifying people who may not be totally rotten, but whose dating profiles are rife with fiction.

—Lizette Alvarez

MORES

Weddings Ring a New Bell

The bride's family doesn't always foot the bill

Weddings are hard work. Just ask Diane Forden, editor in chief of *Bridal Guide* magazine. "Planning a wedding is probably the best training for marriage," she says. "You have to talk things out, to compromise." For starters, all those rules you learned growing up are now as obsolete as dowries. Here are some examples.

OLD RULE: White gowns are a symbol of purity.

MODERN PRACTICE: Anything goes, including red on a first-time bride or white on a serial spouse. "Queen Victoria got married in an ivory gown; that's the only reason the style took off," Forden says. "Before then, all brides got married in their Sunday best."

✔ TIMELY TIPS

Advice for Grooms

There are few places where men can go for guidance and advice on how and what to contribute to their big day, but here are a few.

✔ *The Guy's Guide to Dating, Getting Hitched and Surviving the First Year of Marriage* by Michael R. Crider.

✔ **GroomGroove.com.** A site for men that tackles such wedding-related topics as knowing if you're ready to get married, how to pop the question, what are the bridegroom's and best man's duties, how to deliver a toast, how to plan a mild bachelor party and how to plan a wild one.

✔ **Mywedding.com.** Founded by four men, the site has, according to one of its founder, roughly 100,000 links to free wedding sites, everything from simple postings to blogging.

—Vincent M. Mallozzi

OLD RULE: The bride's parents pay for the wedding, while the groom's parents pay for the flowers and the music.

MODERN PRACTICE: Nearly half of couples pay for their whole wedding, and the vast majority pick up a large share of the cost. The reason may be that money is control and couples want to call the shots on what kind of wedding they want to have.

OLD RULE: Couples register for china, silver and other household items.

MODERN PRACTICE: Many couples already have well-stocked linen closets and silverware drawers—and little need to discard his and hers in favor of ours. Increasingly, they are registering at sporting goods stores, electronics shops and even travel Web sites. "It's perfectly O.K. to want luggage for the honeymoon, or a monetary contribution to the honeymoon itself," she says. But it is also perfectly fine for a guest to give nothing at all. "The bridal shower is the only time you really have to give a gift," she says. Play it safe and give at least enough to cover the cost of your meal—in many metro areas that's probably upward of $100.

MORE WEDDING PLANNING TIPS

- Don't think that ancillary celebrations are just for first-timers. Second-time brides deserve a shower, and couples who have lived together for years deserve an engagement party, but invitations should probably specify that while presence is requested, presents are not.

- Don't be constrained by gender when assembling your wedding party. There is no reason that brides must be attended by women, grooms by men. These days it's more about whom you want to honor. You can also have more than one maid or man of honor, so you don't have to choose between sister and best friend, or mother and stepmother, or brother and father.

- A pregnant bride can choose a long wedding gown or a maternity dress in white or another light color, depending on how comfortable she is with her condition. Traditionally, a bridal veil is a symbol of virginity, so she may want to opt against it. When announcements are sent by the bride's parents, it shows that they support the couple's decision to marry.

- If your betrothed really wants a big wedding, give in. You can have hundreds of intimate dinners and parties during a marriage, so why deprive someone of a celebration he or she may have been dreaming about since childhood?

- Stand your ground with parents—to a point. "If you want roses, don't get peonies because mom likes them better," Forden says. "But compromise on hot-button issues." For an interfaith marriage, consider having clergy members of both faiths present. Or if parents want a much bigger party than you do, suggest that they have a second reception after your honeymoon.

- Set up a wedding Web site. It's a good place to list details about rehearsal dinners, day-after brunches, hotel rates and your gift registries.

- Find ways to save money without looking chintzy. Buy your own flower vases, and supplement costly flowers with greenery and candles. Ask the guitarist from the wedding band to play at the cocktail reception; it will cost less than hiring a separate pianist. A designer bridesmaid dress in white is a lot cheaper than a wedding dress and often just as elegant. A small ornate wedding cake is symbol enough: while you are cutting that first

> **By the time you swear you're his, shivering and sighing, and he vows his passion is infinite, undying— Lady, make a note of this: One of you is lying.**
>
> Dorothy Parker

● ● ●

slice, the staff can be unobtrusively slicing up a cheaper, unadorned version to feed the guests.

- Use the occasion to reach out to others. Donate centerpieces to a nursing home or hospital; your guests don't really need them. Instead of tossing the bouquet, give it to the grandmother whose marriage has lasted the longest. Some brides donate their dresses to a consignment store.

- Attend your own wedding, for goodness' sake. "So many brides say the wedding went by in a blur," Forden says. "Visit the tables, dance with your siblings, make the guests feel wanted, eat the food you've spent so much on. In the end, the best weddings are the ones where the bride and groom really enjoy themselves."

—Claudia H. Deutsch

 TIMELY TIPS

What to Say if You Get Cold Feet

What does one do when "I do" becomes "Um, maybe not?" The experts say that when time is short, the telephone is the method of choice. Etiquette queen Letitia Baldrige recommends that you "hire a couple of widows who need money and have attractive, educated voices, give them the entire wedding list and have them call everybody and talk to them personally, or leave a message." She adds, "You should give a reason if possible—for instance, if the bride's father has suddenly taken ill. But if it's simply that one person jilted the other, the reason should be that it was by mutual consent."

—Shannon Donnelly

How to Get Your Wedding into the *New York Times*

Who makes the wedding pages and why

In a sense, the weddings and celebrations pages of the *New York Times* have always been a battleground. They are studied as sociological raw material reflecting the rise of new elites and the decline of old, the increasing diversity of the country and the changing roles of women. They are parodied online and in the book *Weddings of the Times*. They are featured in *New Yorker* cartoons (bridesmaid to downcast bride: "So what if he's not the man of your dreams. The *Times* is going to be there.") and dismissed as "wedding porn" by people who find them an irresistible guilty pleasure.

Through it all, some 200 couples a week submit announcements of weddings or commitment ceremonies, competing for no more than 40 or so spots in each Sunday's *Styles* section and one video on the paper's Web site. They must comply with three pages of rules (found on www.nytimes.com/ref/fashion/weddings/howtosubmitwedding.html) and submit to rigorous fact-checking. Everyone involved in a wedding, including the person performing the ceremony, is interviewed, and some are asked for documentary proof of things like degrees and honors.

The editor decides who makes it in. How does he choose? The basic premise is to look for people who have achievements, no matter what field. But the announcements have become more diverse; parents like a union electrician, a retired firefighter and even a courier have popped up beside orthopedic surgeons and authors.

Still, the brides, grooms and same-sex partners in a recent sample were heavily Ivy League, 40 percent, and clustered in prestige occupations. The top three fields for men were finance, media and law. For women, it was media, education and current student. Nearly half had advanced degrees.

—Clark Hoyt

That First Dance

Practice can help relieve the pressure of hitting the dance floor

Bridal couples preparing for the traditional first dance, and anyone who wants to avoid the all-too-familiar "clutch and sway," can now tap online dance masters and learn to dance like stars.

Learntodance.com, for one, walks you through learning the tango, swing, salsa, even ballet. The site, and others like DanceVision.com and Dancetv.com, will also sell you instructional videos for just about any dance imaginable. At Learntodance.com you'll find 30 different ballroom-dance videos alone. And if virtual dance lessons don't appeal, you can also locate a bricks-and-mortar dance studio on the site. Just plug in your ZIP code and nearby options appear.

Whatever method you choose, learning the fundamentals isn't difficult. Several dances have a basic box step as their foundation. Master this dance figure and you're on your way to learning the waltz, fox trot and rumba, at least in their American guises.

The box step is so called because the steps form a box or square, with your feet resting on the corners as you move. Here's how it's done:

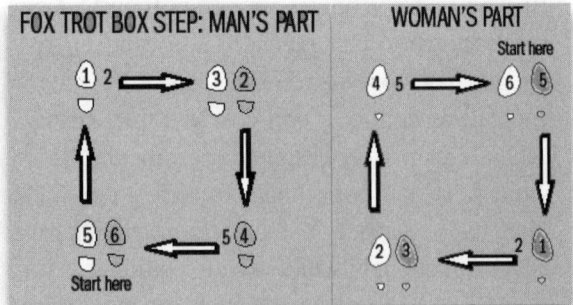

The leader starts by moving his left foot forward, then sliding the right foot up to meet the left. The right foot then moves to the right and the left foot meets it. That's the first half of the box. Now, the right foot steps back and the left foot slides to meet it. The left foot then moves to the left and the right foot slides over to meet it. That completes the box. The steps are repeated, with the pace and rhythm changing—and other flourishes added—depending on the specific dance.

Locating a spry and compatible dance partner is no easy feat, but online sites like DancePartner.com and 1greatdancesite.com can help. Prospective partners post their profiles and hope a suitable match gets in touch.

Wedding Gifts You Can Afford
Matching your gift to the price of your dinner is not a rule

Who says you have to spend a fortune on a wedding present? Etiquette experts and style-makers have helpful tips on how wedding guests can buy impressive, yet affordable, gifts.

Martha Stewart suggests a dozen fluffy white towels tied together with a wide white ribbon for presentation. "There are always white sales for good buys," she says. Consignment shops, she says, also have bargains on silver and china.

Bee Kim, a wedding blogger (weddingbee.com), says the amount to spend depends on your financial situation and how close you are to the couple. "There are no rules," she says. But there are many ways to give a personalized gift on a budget. "You can frame the wedding invitation, or why not give the couple three bottles of wine

> 66
> **Where there is marriage without love, there will be love without marriage.**
>
> Benjamin Franklin
>
> • • •

and tag each bottle." The tags would note the celebration of their first and sixth months of marriage and one-year anniversary.

Roseann Hirsch, a freelance book editor from New York, says she's probably been to 75 or 80 weddings over the years. She suggests a gift certificate to a restaurant, concert tickets or a stack of art books from a museum. "Art books are an interesting gift that has legs in terms of longevity," she says. "They will decorate a coffee table long after they are read." Any of those gifts could be bought for about $100.

Letitia Baldrige, the etiquette expert in Washington, says gift-giving isn't just about emptying the pocketbook. "The whole idea of a present is to please people and make them happy." She goes to small, unknown antiques shop and buys something inexpensive. "I write a lovely note on the card that this item is very old, perhaps 100 years old, and from Vienna. Just that note makes the gift rise in value. It's called a gentle white lie."

Some practical advice comes from www.weddingchannel.com. Its rule of thumb is not to spend more than you can afford. "If money is an issue, try your hardest not to be impulsive when you're out there shopping for just the right present," according to the site.

And what happened to the notion of matching the amount of the present to the price of your dinner at the wedding? In a column posted on the Web site lifestyle.msn.com, Miss Manners answered that question. "That this idea is widespread does not rescue it from being astonishingly vulgar and crass," she wrote. "Etiquette recognizes no such rule, Miss Manners assures you."

—Marianne Rohrlich

MORES

Ways to Remember a Big Day

Easy, meaningful gifts every month of the year

The origins of ancient birthstone designations are lost to history, but how modern birthstones were designated is clear. The inspiration comes not from a poet in love or a qualified stone interpreter, but from a jeweler's association. One consideration that may have entered into the jewelers' decisions was the limited availability of some gems. Florists were no doubt driven by the same motivation in assigning flowers to birth months: the availability of certain blooms during certain seasons.

MONTH	STONE Color	SOURCE	FLOWER
January	**GARNET** *Dark red*	Brazil, India, Sri Lanka	Carnation, snowdrop
February	**AMETHYST** *Purple*	Brazil, Uruguay	Violet, iris
March	**AQUAMARINE** *Pale blue*	Brazil, Nigeria, Zambia	Jonquil, daffodil
April	**DIAMOND** *White*	South Africa, Congo	Sweet Pea, daisy
May	**EMERALD** *Green*	Colombia, Brazil, Pakistan	Lily of the valley
June	**PEARL** *Cream*	Japan, China, Australia	Rose
July	**RUBY** *Red*	Myanmar,* Tanzania, Kenya	Larkspur
August	**PERIDOT** *Pale green*	Myanmar, Pakistan, U.S.	Gladiola
September	**SAPPHIRE** *Pale to dark blue*	Austrialia, Madagascar, SE Asia, U.S.	Aster
October	**OPAL** *Variegated*	Australia, Mexico, U.S.	Calendula
November	**CITRINE** *Yellow*	Brazil, Nigeria	Mum
December	**BLUE TOPAZ** *Sky blue*	Brazil, Sri Lanka, Nigeria	Narcissus

AFTER THE FIRST DIAMOND

Everyone knows it's silver for a 25th anniversary. But for a 9th? Try leather.

YEAR	TRADITIONAL GIFT	MODERN GIFT
1	Paper	Clock
2	Cotton	China
3	Leather	Crystal or glass
4	Fruit or flowers	Appliances
5	Wood	Silverware
6	Candy or ironware	Wood
7	Copper or wool	Pens, desk sets
8	Pottery or bronze	Linens or laces
9	Pottery or willow	Leather
10	Aluminum or tin	Diamond jewelry
11	Steel	Fashion jewelry
12	Silk or linen	Pearls or gems
13	Lace	Textiles
14	Ivory	Gold jewelry
15	Crystal	Watches
16	Silver hollowware	
17	Furniture	
18	Porcelain	
19	Bronze	
20	China	Platinum
25**	Silver	Silver
30	Pearl	Diamond
35	Coral	Jade
40	Ruby	Ruby
45	Sapphire	Sapphire
50**	Gold	Gold
55	Emerald	Emerald
60**	Diamond	Diamond
75**	Diamond	Diamond

*   Formerly called Burma

* * Indicates jubilee anniversary

SOURCES: Jewelers of America; Leading Jewelers Guild, Inc.

The Ins and Outs of Re-Gifting

You shouldn't have; how to get away with it

Will that present you wrapped so beautifully measure up aesthetically, socially, fiscally and—most importantly in family gatherings—be nicer than your brother's? Will it be a genuine hit, or will the recipient, oohing and aaahing with suspiciously loud enthusiasm, really be feigning the ecstasy of giftgasm?

Here's a bit of information to help put you at ease: unless it is cold hard cash, it's going to be re-gifted. The most beautiful glassware, those color-coordinated throw pillows, a Ming Dynasty vase—nobody keeps anything these days, even a crowd-pleaser like a bottle of Champagne. Especially, as it turns out, Champagne. Put a trace tag on a Champagne bottle you give someone, in the manner of the scientists that study the migration patterns of birds, and you're likely to see it make a half-dozen stops before someone finally opens it.

Check out sites like AOL's Regifting Gone Wrong or Regiftable.com, run by Money Management International, a nonprofit organization that helps educate people about their finances, and it's obvious just how widespread re-gifting is. A survey by MMI of 1,049 people found that 58 percent considered the practice acceptable.

Which is not to say re-gifting is without peril. The Web is filled with stories of re-gifters who have fouled up: the crystal vase, that perennial wedding favorite, with a gift card inscribed to somebody else; the fancy food with an expiration tag dating back to the late 1990s; the freshly washed pajamas that might have passed as new if it weren't for the sock and dryer sheet inside the leg. Asked for the worst story she has ever heard, Kim McGrigg, a spokeswoman for Money Management International, pauses. "One woman was given a meat grinder with bits of meat still in it."

The rules of re-gifting are nothing but simple common sense: do not re-gift items that have been opened or used (a family heirloom, presented as such, is the exception); do not re-gift one-of-a-kind items, which will nail you, if the item is spotted, as certainly as a DNA sample; examine any gift carefully for old cards (one may have been tucked into the box); do not re-gift to someone in the same social group in which you received the gift. It is also essential that you keep meticulous records.

Should I lie or confess if I'm found out while re-gifting? There is no consensus on the right thing to do when you're caught. Barbara Bitela, author of *The Art of Re-Gifting: Your ABC's Guide to Re-Gifting; the Do's and Don'ts, Urban Legends and Folklore,* says that "if someone lacks the class to not ask you if something is a re-gift, you have to be prepared with an honest answer. Lying is no good."

But Regiftable.com seems to suggest otherwise: "If you don't plan to announce the gift as a re-gift, ask yourself if you can keep the secret. Never feel guilty about re-gifting once you've done it."

—Joyce Wadler

Tracing Your Family Tree

How to track down your elusive ancestors

Haunted by your past? Curious to learn about your ethnicity? Unearthing your ancestral roots can be a long and arduous process, but there is no lack of resources to help you. Here's how to conduct the search.

1. Interview family members. Scour through memorabilia, keeping detailed notes. Look for these documents: birth, death and marriage certificates: baptism and christening records, family Bibles, diaries, letters, as well as school records, scrapbooks, military discharge papers, naturalization records and passports.

2. With clues in hand, consult libraries and genealogical societies. The huge collection of the Church of Jesus Christ of Latter-day Saints (or the Mormon church) in Salt Lake City, Utah, is open to all. You can also visit them online at Familysearch.org, a free site. To find a genealogical society near you, try the *Directory of Historical Societies and Agencies in the United States and Canada.* At Genealogy.com you can get subscription access to genealogical records.

Check large libraries and the U.S. Census records at the National Archives in Washington, D.C. (866-272-6272; www.archives.gov), which has records from 1790 to 1930. The online site Ancestry.com has two billion records from thousands of sources, including the Census.

3. Search passenger arrival records for immigrant ancestors. The National Archives and some regional libraries have passenger and arrival records dating back to 1817. To find when your ancestor arrived, or the ship's name, try P. William Filby and Mary K. Meyer's *Passenger and Immigration Lists Index.* Ellisisland.org lets you search the records of anyone who entered the country through Ellis Island.

4. Genealogical database programs can help you organize your search. One popular software program is Family Tree Maker ($20 to $100). A free program, Gramps (gramps.sourceforge.net), lets you enter data, store results and produce charts and Web pages. For reviews of genealogy software packages, go to genealogy-software-review.com.

5. To skip the whole time- and labor-intensive process, hire a genealogical sleuth. For a list of certified genealogists in your area, go to the Board for Certification of Genealogists at www.bcgcertification.org.

Finding Grandma, the DNA Way

DNA testing has added a new twist to genealogy: using genetic data to uncover details about your heritage.

More than a dozen companies, like Family Tree DNA in Houston, Relative Genetics in Salt Lake City and African Ancestry in Washington, D.C., sell home DNA tests priced from $100 to $900. Here's how the tests typically work: Order the test online and you get a kit with toothbrush-like scrapers, collection tubes and instructions on how to take a swab from inside the cheek. The samples are mailed to a lab, where scientists analyze DNA markers, or genetic traits. You get test results in 2 to 8 weeks, depending on the type of test and the company.

The broad array of tests and the accompanying jargon may be confusing. Tutorials on company Web sites, online discussion forums and newsletters dedicated to "genetic genealogy" can help. Or hire a genealogy consultant, for about $50 an hour, to muddle through the process for you. 　　　　　—Jennifer Alsever

Grammar in a Jiffy
Common mistakes that can be easily corrected

For many people, knowing that the grammar police may be lurking in their midst is an unsettling situation. If you were absent the day your teacher covered sticky grammar rules in class, here are a few pointers on gaffes to avoid.

• **Nouns following prepositions (even when they are compound) are always objects.**
She gave the message *to me*. 　　　　(not *to I*)
Tim lied *to Jane and me.* 　(not *to Jane and I*)
I gave it *to Sue and them.* (not *to Sue and they*)

- **Any word that is a contraction is actually a shortening of two words, and does NOT imply possession.**
  EXAMPLES:

CONTRACTION	POSSESSIVE ADJECTIVE
IT IS: *It's* a sunny day.	France has *its* wines.
THEY ARE: *They're* here.	*Their* dog barks.
YOU ARE: *You're* right.	I took *your* pen.
WHO IS: *Who's* that?	*Whose* hat is this?

- **Do not confuse the use of simple past verbs with past participles.**

CORRECT		INCORRECT
She *sang* the song.	NOT	She *sung* the song.
She *has sung* the song.		
Tom *spoke* to us.	NOT	Tom *has spoke* to us.
Tom *has spoken* to us.		

- **The subject of a dependent clause stays a subject, even after a preposition.**

That's *for*		That's *for*
whoever needs it.	NOT	*whomever* needs it.

- **Use the subjunctive tense for statements contrary to fact.**

If she *were*	NOT	If she *was*
a rocket scientist...		a rocket scientist...

- **Don't use adjectives to modify a verb.**

She did *really* well.	NOT	She did *real* well.
He sang *beautifully*.	NOT	He sang *beautiful*.

The Demise of the Semicolon

The semicolon is dead; long live the semicolon

In literature and journalism, not to mention in advertising, the semicolon has been largely jettisoned as a pretentious anachronism. Americans, in particular, prefer shorter sentences without, as style books advise that distinct division between statements that are closely related but require a separation more prolonged than a conjunction and more emphatic than a comma. "When Hemingway killed himself he put a period at the end of his life," Kurt Vonnegut once

---

✔ **TIMELY TIPS**

Me, Myself and I

A perspective on the "I" and "me" dilemma

It's a common conundrum for many: when to use "I" or "me." The rule, according to conventional wisdom, is that we use "I" as a subject and "me" as an object, whether the pronoun appears by itself or in a twosome.

But for centuries, it was perfectly acceptable to use either "I" or "me" as the object of a verb or preposition, especially after "and." Literature is full of examples. Here's Shakespeare, in *The Merchant of Venice:* "All debts are cleared between you and I." And here's Lord Byron, complaining about the English town of Southwell, "which, between you and I, I wish was swallowed up by an earthquake."

These days it seems standard practice to bypass "I" and "me" and use "myself" for emphasis or to refer to the speaker ("I'll do it myself"), not merely as a substitute for "me." But some language authorities accept a looser usage, pointing out that "myself" has been regularly used in place of "me" since Anglo-Saxon days.

—Patricia T. O'Conner and Stewart Kellerman, authors of the forthcoming *Origins of the Specious: Myths and Misconceptions of the English Language*

---

said. "Old age is more like a semicolon."

Semicolons are generally introduced into the curriculum in the third grade. But whatever one's personal feelings about semicolons, some people don't use them because they never learned how.

These days they may not need to learn how, with e-mail messages and text-messaging jeopardizing the last vestiges of semicolons. They still live on, though, in emoticons, those graphic emblems of our grins, grimaces and other facial expressions. The semicolon, befittingly, symbolizes a wink.

—Sam Roberts

MORES

Your Reference Desk

For further research on practically anything, try these reputable Web sites.

GENERAL REFERENCE

Answers.com Responses to questions on an infinite number of topics.

Babel Fish (babelfish.yahoo. com) and **SDLFreeTranslation.com** Basic (and sometimes amusing) translations of words or text.

Bankrate.com Cost of living calculator and many other useful financial tools.

BibleGateway.com Research the Bible in a language of your choice.

Biography.com Brief, cross-referenced biographies of thousands of notables.

C.I.A. World Factbook (www.cia. gov/library/publications/the-world-factbook) The state of affairs in every corner of the world.

Encyclopedia Britannica (www. britannica.com). Once the one and only, now with a fee for full articles.

Google Maps (maps.google.com); **mapquest.com** Find a business or destination, view the neighborhood, get directions.

Infoplease.com A comprehensive encyclopedia, almanac, atlas, dictionary and more.

I.R.S. (www.irs.gov) All the tax information, publications and forms you need.

Itools.com An all-in-one reference desk: define and translate words, find directions, maps and more.

LawGuru.com Access to hundreds of legal search engines; free answers to common legal questions.

Lawyers.Findlaw.com Legal resources, lawyer locator and links to other legal sites.

Library of Congress (www.loc. gov) Access to the voluminous resources of the nation's oldest and largest library.

LibrarySpot.com An extensive guide to online reference works.

MayoClinic.com Explore your symptoms and find the most common causes.

Refdesk.com A portal to a world of reference materials.

Roget's Internet Thesaurus (thesaurus.reference.com) Finding a better word for free.

The Internet Drug Index (www. rxlist.com) Extensive information on prescription and over-the-counter drugs.

Social Security death index (ssdi. genealogy.rootsweb.com) A useful tool for filling out the family tree.

Taxsites.com Quick access to federal and state forms; calculators; links to other tax related sites.

The Elements of Style (www.

bartleby.com/141) The 1918 version of the classic handbook for conscientious writers.

The Merck Manual (www.merck. com/pubs) The classic medical reference guide.

The New York Public Library (www.nypl.org) Noted for sheer size and diversity of holdings.

The WWW Virtual Library (vlib. org) Find resource links on topics from agriculture to social behavior.

Travlang.com Translation dictionaries, currency converters and other travel tools.

Wikipedia.org The popular, but not uniformly accurate, user-maintained encyclopedia.

YourDictionary.com and **Onelook. com** Access to hundreds of dictionaries.

Zillow.com Free real estate information, from buying and selling homes to the latest sale prices.

TELEPHONE AND MAIL DIRECTORIES

Anywho.com Find home and business phone numbers from this AT&T service.

Superpages.com and **Switchboard. com** National business yellow pages, residential listings and reverse directory.

ZIP Code and ZIP+4 Finder (usps. gov/zip4) The U.S. Postal Service directory of ZIP codes.

—Richard J. Meislin

INDEX